PATHWAYS TO PSYCHOLOGY

SECOND EDITION

ROBERT J. STERNBERG

Yale University

Harcourt College Publishers

Fort Worth   Philadelphia   San Diego   New York   Orlando   Austin   San Antonio
Toronto   Montreal   London   Sydney   Tokyo

Publisher	Earl McPeek
Executive Editor	Carol Wada
Market Strategist	Kathleen Sharp
Project Editor	Louise Slominsky
Art Director	Carol Kincaid
Production Manager	Angela Williams Urquhart

ISBN: 0-15-508047-4
Library of Congress Catalog Card Number: 99-64294

Address for Domestic Orders
Harcourt, Inc., 6277 Sea Harbor Drive, Orlando, FL 32887-6777
800-782-4479

Address for International Orders
International Customer Service
Harcourt, Inc., 6277 Sea Harbor Drive, Orlando, FL 32887-6777
407-345-3800
(fax) 407-345-4060
(e-mail) hbintl@harcourtbrace.com

Address for Editorial Correspondence
Harcourt College Publishers, 301 Commerce Street, Suite 3700, Fort Worth, TX 76102

Web Site Address
http://www.harcourtcollege.com

Harcourt College Publishers will provide complimentary supplements or supplement packages to those adopters qualified under our adoption policy. Please contact your sales representative to learn how you qualify. If as an adopter or potential user you receive supplements you do not need, please return them to your sales representative or send them to: Attn: Returns Department, Troy Warehouse, 465 South Lincoln Drive, Troy, MO 63379.

Printed in the United States of America

9 0 1 2 3 4 5 6 7 8 032 9 8 7 6 5 4 3 2 1

Harcourt College Publishers

To Alejandra

TO THE INSTRUCTOR

The first edition of *Pathways to Psychology* received broad-based acceptance among teachers of psychology, perhaps because it offered a new alternative for briefer books, one that allowed students with diverse learning styles—memory, analytical, creative, or practical—to benefit maximally from the introductory psychology course. But no first edition is ever perfect, and I received feedback from around the country as to how I could improve *Pathways*. This second edition is my best effort to make the book even better by incorporating the comments I got from you and your peers. I have learned to listen to people, just as I have learned to do better on IQ tests!

As a child, I bombed on IQ tests. By the time I reached college, I was determined to understand why. I decided to major in psychology. However, I received a grade of C in the introductory psychology course. It was looking like the IQ tests might have been right—I did not seem to have the ability to study psychology. Fortunately, I switched to math, did worse in math than I had in psychology, and switched back to psychology, where I have been ever since. I have come to realize that the way my introductory psychology course was taught did not match the way I best learn.

These experiences have helped me to shape this book. In the introductory psychology course, students think to learn, in order to learn to think. I am committed to the view that students learn and think in different ways, and that teaching and testing need to take into account these diverse styles of learning and thinking if they are to recognize and reward students' many different kinds of talents.

Pathways to Learning and Using Psychology

The unifying vision underlying this book is one of multiple pathways to psychology. These pathways include the diverse routes by which students can successfully learn, understand, and use psychology. In this edition, I have focused the theme of pathways on the paths in life we all choose, and how psychological concepts can explain and sometimes provide these paths. You will notice that, at the beginning of each chapter, I have added stories of people who are at a point of making a decision about what path in life to choose. These decision-making situations are not unlike the decisions your students, and you and I, may make in our lives. I challenge the students as they are reading to try to figure out how the concepts in the chapter could help the person decide upon a path to take. May some paths be open or closed to this person based on psychological principles? Will this person be more likely to make a decision because of psychological factors? What do psychological theories have to say about the impact of a decision? At the end of each chapter, I discuss the path that the person could take based on the concepts presented in the chapter. From this, students can see the relevance of psychology to many decisions and outcomes in everyday life.

The book also recognizes the diverse pathways of input as well as output that appeal to different learners. Students are given opportunities to learn both visually and verbally, and to learn by doing, as well as by reading and listening. Thus, this is a book for all students including, but in no way limited to, those who learn best in traditional ways.

Pathways to Linking the Approaches and Methods of Psychology

Just as there are different pathways to learning and using psychology, so are there different pathways to the field of psychology itself. These pathways lead us through different terrains. Psychologists choose different pathways to studying psychology with respect to the approaches they use (e.g., psychodynamic, behavioral, cognitive) and with respect to their methods (e.g., experimental, naturalistic, case study). But these psychologists all seek psychological understanding. Ultimately, however, just as all roads once led to Rome, so do all the pathways presented here lead to psychology. By following and exploring these various pathways, students learn about the different fields of psychology, and from different points of view. The fundamental idea of these pathways is expressed through the discussions, questions, activities, and artwork throughout the book.

The book equally balances the diverse pathways to psychology, with regard not only to approach, but also to content. Such balance is especially important today, when traditional boundaries within the field are breaking down. Thus, this book balances and integrates biological, cognitive, developmental, social, personality, and clinical subject matter. These integrations are illustrated throughout the text.

Pathways to Linking Biology and Behavior

Some psychologists emphasize the biological bases of behavior, and study humans through their biology. These psychologists may study directly the human nervous system or endocrine system. Other psychologists may concentrate on behavior as a focus of their investigations. But because, ultimately, the goal of all psychologists is to link the study of biology with that of behavior, these different pathways may be viewed as ultimately having the same goals or destinations.

Pathways to Linking Basic and Applied Research

Some psychologists do basic research and care little about application. Other psychologists do applied research and are interested in problems only if they lead to practical solutions. But, ultimately, all psychologists hope to see theory linked to practice and basic research lead to applications in the years to come. Once again, then, psychologists follow different pathways to a common ultimate goal.

Pathways to Linking Commonality and Diversity

Some psychologists emphasize commonalities among humans and even across species; others emphasize difference and diversity. Just as there are different pathways to thinking about psychology, so are there different pathways of thinking in the populations studied by psychologists. This book explores multicultural pathways to psychological diversity not because multiculturalism is "in," but because there is no other way to understand psychology fully. I have lived with the richness of multiculturalism in my own experience, and I have embraced it with enthusiasm in research with my colleagues.

For example, Lynn Okagaki and I have found that parents of children of diverse ethnic groups have different conceptions of what it means for their children to be intelligent. In raising their children, parents try to develop the skills that will help the children show the behavior that their groups consider to be adaptively intelligent. How intelligent the children are perceived to be in the school, however, depends largely on the extent to which the parents' beliefs about intelligence match those of the children's teachers. Without understanding the children's strengths, the teachers cannot possibly appreciate the children's full complement of abilities.

Pedagogical Features in *Pathways to Psychology*

Distinctive pedagogical features in every chapter encourage students to develop and apply their own pathways. The following features appear in every chapter:

- New to this edition are chapter-opening vignettes that pose real-life problems for students to consider as they read chapters. Possible solutions to the problems can be found at the end of chapters.

- A chapter outline in question format provides a preview framework for organizing the material.
- Putting It to Use boxes show how psychology can be used outside of the classroom.
- Branching Out boxes show how to extend what is learned in new and interesting directions.
- Finding Your Way demonstrations get students actively involved in the topics they are reading.
- Glossary terms appear in the margins of each chapter when students are likely to need them most. A glossary at the end of the book includes all terms for easy student reference.
- A page-referenced chapter summary appears at the end of each chapter.
- Pathways to Knowledge questions at the end of each chapter test factual comprehension of topics.
- Pathways to Understanding thinking questions at the end of each chapter test creative, practical, and analytical skills.

Changes in the Second Edition

In response to many and diverse helpful evaluations from teachers and students alike, the following key modifications have been made in the second edition of *Pathways to Psychology*.

1. *Updating.* Based on reviewers' input, *Pathways to Psychology* has been extensively updated. These changes should enhance the book's usefulness as a learning resource.
2. *Streamlining.* Material that instructors found to be peripheral has been deleted.
3. *Practical Examples.* Both reviewers and students asked for more examples to enhance chapter concepts and I have tried to include as many as possible throughout.
4. *Chapter Dilemmas and Solutions.* Each chapter begins with a vignette that presents a real-life dilemma that can be solved through a knowledge of introductory psychology. Each chapter ends with a possible solution to the dilemma.
5. *Careers in Psychology Appendix.* Reviewers wanted students to know more about what one can do with a degree in psychology, so a new appendix has been added that describes various careers one can pursue in psychology.
6. *Updated Glossary Terms.* Each glossary term has been reviewed and revised when necessary to provide students with a comprehensive list of terms needed to understand chapter concepts.
7. *Pedagogy and Art Program.* The pedagogy and art program have been enhanced to facilitate learning and better tie in with the pathways theme.
8. *Chapter on Life-Span Development.* At users' request, this chapter has been moved from the previous placement as chapter 3 and is now chapter 9. In addition, the chapter has also been renamed to highlight its life-span approach.

The Ancillary Program: Pathways to Teaching

The *Pathways to Psychology* ancillary program was developed with the help of a faculty panel from diverse colleges and universities.

The Study Guide, by Ellen Pastorino (Valencia Community College) and Susann Doyle (Gainesville College), opens with a description of effective ways of studying, different thinking and learning styles, and test-taking strategies. Each chapter has a variety of types of exercises to help students master the material. The practice tests include a self-assessment scale. An extensive front section of the study guide provides studying and test-taking strategies.

Drs. Pastorino and Doyle have taught introductory psychology for more than 10 years at diverse 2-year and 4-year institutions. They have collaborated on several articles, and on a daily basis, they conquer the challenge of meeting various students' needs when tackling the learning process. They have brought their collective expertise to producing a truly outstanding study guide.

The Instructor's Manual, by Dr. Stephen Chew (Samford University), provides easy-to-find information to help instructors minimize their time and maximize their effectiveness in preparing for lectures. The manual is designed to help instructors develop class presentations consistent with the textbook and to facilitate use and integration of the other ancillary items available to users of *Pathways to Psychology.* An introductory section includes teaching tips and a sample syllabus. Each chapter includes teaching objectives, extensive lecture outlines, handouts, suggestions for incorporating the other items in the package, and forms that assist in coordination of the course. The final section includes a video instructor's manual.

Dr. Chew is an experienced introductory psychology instructor who has led seminars on college teaching. He has given guest lectures at a number of community colleges and state universities, maintaining an emphasis on making students lifelong learners. His experience and dedication to teaching have resulted in a manual that helps instructors to locate and use the information that they need.

The Test Bank, prepared in the first edition by Drs. Doyle and Pastorino and revised in the second edition by Dr. Kevin Larkin of West Virginia University, is coordinated and consistent with the study guide. Each chapter has approximately 125 multiple-choice and essay items, classified by the ways of thinking described and used in the textbook. Each item is also identified by level of difficulty, learning objective, textbook features, and page number. The test bank is available in printed and computerized versions.

Dr. Larkin is a recognized teacher at both the graduate and undergraduate levels at West Virginia University. His involvement in the instruction of introductory psychology courses includes not only classroom instruction but the ongoing supervision and training of graduate student instructors. He has been instrumental in obtaining several course development grants to integrate technology into the instruction of introductory psychology courses, including both creation of multimedia-based course activities and the computerized assessment of student performance. His creative ability to develop test items that measure students' abilities to apply their knowledge of psychological principles in new ways has resulted in an extremely functional test bank.

EXAMaster+™ Computerized Test Banks (IBM, MAC, and WINDOWS versions) offer easy-to-use options for text creation.

- *EasyTest* creates a test from a single screen in just a few easy steps. Instructors choose parameters, then select questions from the database or let *EasyTest* randomly select them.

- *FullTest* offers a range of options that includes selecting, editing, adding, or linking questions or graphics; random selection of questions from a wide range of criteria; creating criteria; blocking questions; and printing up to 99 different versions of the same test and answer sheet.

- *Online Testing* allows instructors to create a test in *EXAMaster+™*, save it to the OLT subdirectory or diskette, and administer the test online. The results of the test can then be imported to *ESAGrade.*

- *ESAGrade* can be used to set up new classes, to record grades from tests or assignments utilizing scantron, and to analyze grades and produce class and individual statistics. *ESAGrade* comes packaged with *EXAMaster+™.*

- *RequesTest* is a service for instructors without access to a computer. A software specialist will compile questions according to the instructor's criteria and mail or fax the test master within 48 hours!
- *The Software Support Hotline* is available to answer questions 24 hours a day, 7 days a week.

(1-800 telephone numbers for these services are provided in the preface to the printed test bank.)

Additional ancillaries available to qualified adopters include:

- **Psychology MediaActive.** A CD-ROM psychology image bank to be used with commercially available presentation packages like PowerPoint and Astound.
- **The Harcourt Psychology and Human Development Multimedia Library.** Consisting of a variety of videos and videodiscs for classroom presentation, this library's selections include materials exclusively created for Harcourt College Publishers as well as videos from *Films for the Humanities and Sciences, Pyramid Films, PBS Video,* and other sources. Please contact your sales representative for adoption requirements and other details.
- **Introductory Psychology Overhead Transparencies.** This set of more than 130 acetates covers the full range of topics typical to an introductory psychology course.
- **The Whole Psychology Catalog: Instructional Resources to Enhance Student Learning, 1997,** by Michael B. Reiner (Kennesaw State College). Instructors can easily supplement course work and assignments with this manual of perforated pages containing experimental exercises, questionnaires, lecture outlines, visual aids, and Internet and World Wide Web guides.
- **Harcourt Psychology Instructor's Resources on the Web.** Come visit us at www.hbcollege.com

Harcourt College Publishers may provide complimentary instructional aids and ancillaries or ancillary packages to those adopters qualified under our adoption policy. Please contact your sales representative for more information. If, as an adopter or potential user, you receive ancillaries that you do not need, please return them to your sales representative or send them to:

Attn: Returns Department
Troy Warehouse
465 South Lincoln Drive
Troy, MO 63379

Acknowledgments

I am grateful to the instructors and colleagues who reviewed the first edition of *Pathways to Psychology* and the second edition manuscript: Christina Adams (West Virginia University); Stephen Chew (Samford University); Thaddeus M. Cowan (Kansas State University); Stephen Donohue (Grand Canyon State University); Robert Fisher (Lee University); Karen Frye (University of Akron); Sam Gaft (Macomb Community College); Stan Gilbert (Community College of Philadelphia); Carol Hayes (Delta State University); Barb Kabat (Sinclair Community College); Kevin Larkin (West Virginia University); Patricia Laser (Bucks County Community College); Ron Mulson (Hudson Valley Community College); Robert J. Pellegrini (San Jose State University); Brady Phelps (South Dakota State University); Marsha Butler Tindel (Roane State Community College); Karen Williams (Illinois State University); Allen Winebarger (Grand Valley State University); and Mary Wood (Grand Valley State University).

I am also indebted to the instructors and colleagues who reviewed the first edition manuscript: Lou Banderet (Quinsigamond Community College); Don Devers (Northern Virginia Community College); Charles Early (Roanoke College); John

Foust (Parkland College); Richard Gist (Johnson Community College); Kathryn Jennings (Salt Lake City Community College); Jane Kelly (Hinds Community College); D. Brett King (University of Colorado); Mike Knight (University of Central Oklahoma); Kris Kumar (Westchester University of Pennsylvania); Kevin Larkin (West Virginia University); Paul Levy (University of Akron); Dan Lipscomb (Collin County Community College); Joan Piroch (Coastal Carolina University); Cary Schawel (Oakton Community College); Peggy Skinner (South Plains Junior College); Lori Temple (University of Nevada at Las Vegas); Harry Tiemann (Mesa State College); Tim Tomczak (Genesee Community College); Jim Turcott (Kalamazoo Valley Community College); and Frank Vattano (Colorado State University).

I am also grateful to colleagues who contributed valuable information concerning multicultural diversity to the following chapters: Toy Caldwell-Colbert (University of Illinois) in "Abnormal Psychology"; Janet Fritz (Colorado State University) in "Thought and Language"; Jules Harell (Howard University) in "Health Psychology"; Yvette Harris (Miami [Ohio] University) in "What Is Psychology?"; Fred Leong (Ohio State University) in "Personality"; Chieh Li (Northeastern University) in "Intelligence and Creativity"; David McPhee (Colorado State University) in "Development"; Joan Miller (Yale University) in "Social Psychology" and "Motivation and Emotion"; and Kumea Shorter-Gooden (California School of Professional Psychology) in "Psychotherapy."

My thanks also go out to the following instructors who helped to review the ancillary program: Bill Bachofner (Victor Valley Community College); Eugene Butler (Quinsigamond Community College); Minor Chamblin (University of North Florida); Dennis Cogan (Texas Tech University); Jorge Conesa (Everett Community College); Linda Noble (Kennesaw State College); William Price (North Country Community College); Nancy Simpson (Trident Technical College); Peggy Skinner (South Plains Junior College); Jim Turcott (Kalamazoo Valley Community College); and Diana Younger (University of Texas-Permian Basin).

I am also grateful to Carol Wada, who served as acquisitions editor, for her support and encouragement of this project; to Laurie Runion, for her superb work in managing the development of this book; to Susan Petty for her work in getting the second edition revision underway; to Louise Slominsky, for her responsibility and exacting standards in seeing the book through the production process; to Andrea Archer and Angela Urquhart, for ensuring that production deadlines were met; to Carol Kincaid, for her creative oversight and development of the design of the book and art program; to Caroline Robbins and Sue Howard, for securing the permissions and an outstanding set of photos; to Kathleen Sharp, marketing manager, for her sensitivity to market demands at all phases of the project; to Earl McPeek, publisher of Harcourt College Publishers, for his support and encouragement of my work on this and other projects; to Sai Durvasula, my administrative associate, for helping at all stages in the coordination with everyone involved in the project; to the Harcourt sales representatives all over the world who have made a concerted effort to make potential adopters aware of what the book has to offer; and most of all, to my wife, Alejandra Campos, and my children, Seth and Sara Sternberg, all of whom have contributed to my ideas about psychology and put up with me while I worked on this book.

Robert J. Sternberg

HOW TO USE THIS TEXTBOOK

When I received a grade of C in my introductory psychology course, I thought I did not have the ability to study psychology. I switched my major to math, but I did even worse in math, and switched back to psychology, where I stayed. Now, after 31 years, I realize that students in introductory courses think and learn in different ways.

I wrote *Pathways to Psychology* to help you succeed in your introductory psychology class. Use this textbook to help you strengthen and improve your learning and thinking skills, as well as to understand the multiple perspectives in psychology.

Please spend a few minutes looking over the following pages. This section will help you take full advantage of some of the unique features of this book.

Bob Sternberg

The theme of this book is "pathways to psychology." The chapters use "pathways" in a variety of ways, to show there are many ways to learn, understand, think about, and use psychology.

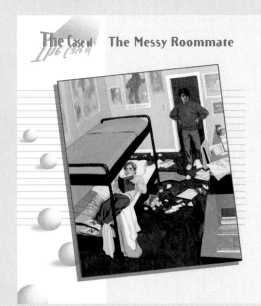

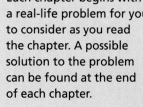

Each chapter begins with a real-life problem for you to consider as you read the chapter. A possible solution to the problem can be found at the end of each chapter.

The Case of the Messy Roommate

Pedro remembers reading about representative samples in experiments while reading chapter 1 of his *Pathways to Psychology* book. Pedro realizes that the solution proposed by Phil represented the wrong path. The reason is that the test of the other roommates' views was poorly conceived. For one thing, they asked only three individuals for their opinion. More importantly, however, the sample asked may not have been *representative*. Phil chose the three roommates and Pedro could not be assured that the roommates in that particular room were truly representative of other first-year students.

After reading the chapter, Pedro decided to check out the room above his room with Phil. Sure enough, it was a mess. Pedro knew from having visited many other rooms that many rooms were quite neat. Whether intentionally or by accident, Phil had chosen a room full of messy roommates. They, of course, represented their own messy point of view.

Pedro insisted that they ask first-year students in some other rooms what they thought, and most of them did indeed end up supporting Pedro. Phil admitted he was wrong but never said how he had chosen the first group of three. Phil reformed at least partially, enough for Pedro to get through the year and find himself another roommate the subsequent year.

1

CHAPTER OUTLINE

WHAT IS PSYCHOLOGY?

Do you ever wonder about what it means to be smart, to love someone, or to be attractive to someone? Do you want to know how salespeople persuade you to buy things you do not want? Do you sometimes wish you could better understand how to get along with other people or how to study and learn more effectively? Do you wonder why people like Phil can be such slobs? These kinds of questions are answered by studying psychology, the scientific study of *mind* (the means by which people and other living organisms perceive, think, and feel), *behavior* (what people and other living organisms do), and the relationship between them.

These are also the kinds of questions that first interested me in psychology. I became interested in psychology when, as an elementary school student, I bombed group IQ tests. As a result of my low scores, my teachers had low expectations for me. I then gave the teachers what they expected and became a mediocre student. It was not until the fourth grade, when I had a teacher who expected more of me, that I started performing at a higher level. Psychology has provided a way for me to study intelligence. At various other times, I have had problems coming up with ideas and problems in my close relationships with other people, and at those times I studied creativity and then love. The wonderful thing about psychology is that one can take issues of importance in one's life and try to understand and even resolve them through scientific study and research.

To study psychology is to try to understand how we think, feel, learn, perceive, act, interact with others, and even understand ourselves. As a student of introductory psychology, you study the mind, behavior, and their interrelation. You and your fellow students (both amateurs and professionals) study various psychological phenomena (processes or events that can be observed, e.g., the process of decision making, the expression of emotions, or the response to a personal crisis). Table 1.1 will give you an idea of the range of the kinds of questions psychologists ask. It shows just a small number of the many kinds of questions asked by psychologists when studying phenomena related to diverse fields of psychology. These diverse fields are studied through a large variety of careers. Appendix B describes some of the careers you can pursue if you choose to specialize in psychology.

Psychology is both a *natural science* and a *social science*. Psychologists study both the laws of nature and how these laws apply to people. Actually, some psychologists and other social scientists also study the minds and behavior of other animals, but generally, they do so in order to gain insights into human beings. Different kinds of scientists have slightly different perspectives. They therefore follow different pathways and have different emphases in their study of people and other organisms.

- *Psychologists* generally focus on the individual person alone or in interaction with others and the environment.
- *Geneticists* study the influence of genes on behavior, as well as the interactions of the effects of genes with the effects of the environment.
- *Physiologists* study physical and biochemical influences on behavior.
- *Neuroscientists* study the brain and nervous system and their relations to behavior.
- *Political scientists* study systems and structures of human power relationships.

TABLE 1.1
What Do Psychologists Do?

Field of psychology	Sample problems and questions
Psychobiology. The biological structures and processes underlying thought, feeling, motivation, and behavior (see chapter 2)	▪ What portion of the brain is active when a person learns the meaning of a new word? ▪ How do various kinds of drugs affect the brain and behavior?
Developmental psychology. How people develop over time (see chapter 9)	▪ How do children form attachments to their parents? ▪ How do people acquire an understanding of what others expect of them in social interactions?
Cognitive psychology. How people perceive, learn, remember, and think about information (see chapters 3, 4, 5, 6, 7, and 8)	▪ Why do people remember some facts but forget others? ▪ How do people think when they play chess or solve everyday problems?
Social psychology. How people interact with each other, both as individuals and in groups (see chapter 10)	▪ Why are people attracted to one another, and why do people like and even love one another? ▪ Why are people sometimes generous and helpful, and why are they sometimes not?
Personality psychology. Personal dispositions that lead people to behave as they do (see chapters 11 and 12)	▪ Why are some people highly sociable, whereas others seem to prefer just the company of very few other people? ▪ What makes some people highly conscientious and others less so?
Clinical psychology. Understanding and treatment of abnormal behavior (see chapters 13 and 14)	▪ What behavior is just a little out of the ordinary, and what behavior is truly abnormal? ▪ What causes people to do things that they themselves consider inappropriate and even abnormal and would like to stop if they could?
Health psychology. The dynamic interaction between the mind and the physical health of the body (see chapter 15)	▪ How does terminal illness (e.g., AIDS) affect how people think or feel about themselves and other people? ▪ How do personality factors contribute to the likelihood that people will become ill with particular diseases (e.g., heart disease or cancer)?

Note: Some other specialties exist, as well. For example:
Educational psychology uses psychology to improve and develop methods of teaching and learning.
Industrial/organizational psychology applies psychology to decision making about employees and hiring in institutional settings, such as workplaces and businesses.
Engineering psychology deals with human–machine systems and how instruments such as computers and automobile dashboards can be made more user-friendly.
Psycholinguistics investigates the ways in which humans learn and use language.

- *Economists* study the various ways in which resources are traded, produced, and used.
- *Sociologists* study groups of individuals, such as groups of people in various kinds of work or having different incomes.
- *Physical anthropologists* study human evolution from simpler animals and even from one-celled creatures.
- *Cultural anthropologists* seek insights into various cultures.

Psychologists also learn from artists, computer scientists, novelists, and many other people who try to understand the human mind and behavior. By learning from diverse sources, psychologists may avoid some of

psychology • the study of the mind and behavior of people and other organisms and of mind–behavior interactions

A chapter outline opens the chapter. Each major section heading poses a question, which alerts you to the key issue that the section will explore.

Three features provide how-to applications to guide you in using psychological principles in your life.

How Do Drugs Induce Alterations in Consciousness? **149**

4.2

IS SOMEONE YOU KNOW AN ALCOHOLIC?

The National Institute on Alcohol Abuse and Alcoholism has developed the following seven questions for you to use to check whether you (or someone you know) may be having problems due to alcoholism. If you answer "yes" to even one question, alcohol may be a problem in your life (or in the life of someone you know). If you answer "yes" to several questions, you (or someone you know) may be an alcoholic. Most of these questions boil down to a central issue: Is the use of alcohol creating problems in one or more areas of your life?

1. Has someone close to you expressed concern about your drinking?
2. When faced with a problem, do you often turn to alcohol for relief?
3. Are you sometimes unable to meet home or work responsibilities because of drinking?
4. Have you ever required medical attention as a result of drinking?
5. Have you ever experienced a blackout, which is a total loss of memory while still awake, when drinking?
6. Have you ever come in conflict with the law in connection with your drinking?
7. Have you often failed to keep the promises you have made to yourself about controlling or cutting out your drinking?

cut short by an average of 10 to 12 years (M. A. Block, 1970; Ciompi & Eisert, 1969). Overuse of alcohol also can lead to many health problems, including increased risk of cancer (Herity, Moriarty, Daly, Dunn, & Bourke, 1982; Heuch, Kvale, Jacobsen, & Bjelke, 1983). To help detect the signs of alcoholism, see Putting It to Use 4.2.

The effects of alcohol depend upon concentrations in the bloodstream. When concentrations are around 0.03% to 0.05%, people often feel relaxed, uninhibited, and have a general sense of well-being. At a blood-alcohol level of 0.10%, sensorimotor functioning is impaired markedly. Many states consider people to be legally drunk at this level. People may exhibit slurred speech and grow angry, sullen, or morose. At a concentration of 0.20%, people show grave dysfunction. With concentrations of 0.40% or more, there is a serious risk of death. College students may underestimate the risks they are taking. Recently, a first-year student at MIT died from alcohol intoxication. Unfortunately, such incidents are not uncommon. Drinking coffee or other stimulants does not cure drunkenness: It creates an awake drunk.

Sedative–Hypnotics

sedative–hypnotics • one of the two primary types of CNS depressants, used to calm anxiety and to relieve insomnia

Sedative–hypnotics are depressant drugs that are used to calm anxiety and to relieve insomnia. The two most widely used sedative–hypnotics

Putting It to Use boxes show examples of how psychology can be used outside the classroom.

82 **Chapter 2** Biological Psychology

et al., 1992; Corina, Vaid, & Bellugi, 1992; Haglund et al., 1993; Poizner, Bellugi, & Klima, 1990). On the other hand, so to speak, gestures that are not specific ASL signs are localized in the right hemispheres of native signers, just as they are in native speakers of English. Similarly, spatial information seems to be localized in the right hemisphere of native ASL signers (Poizner, Kaplan, Bellugi, & Padden, 1984). These findings support the view that language, not just speech, is localized in the left hemisphere. The following Branching Out box shows another way in which understanding of hemispheric specialization is important in the real world.

HEMISPHERIC SPECIALIZATION AND LANGUAGE SYMBOLS

Cross-cultural research offers yet another way of looking at the contrasting localizations of visuospatial and sound-based language symbols. Based on split-brain research, one would expect the visuospatial system to be based in the right hemisphere and sound-based language symbols to be based in the left hemisphere. In school, Japanese children study two forms of written language: *kanji,* which is based on Chinese ideographs and conveys an entire idea within each symbol, and *kana,* which is based on phonetic syllables and can be used for writing foreign words, such as scientific terms. In the 1970s, Japanese researchers started wondering whether the pictorial versus the phonetic forms might be processed differently in the two hemispheres of the brain. Some researchers concluded, in line with prior expectations, that Japanese children and adults process the phonetic-based *kana* entirely in the left hemisphere but the picture-based *kanji* in both the left and right hemispheres (Shibazaki, 1983; Shimada & Otsuka, 1981; Sibitani, 1980; Tsunoda, 1979). Interestingly, then, research on perfectly normal individuals in Japan confirms findings of research on split-brain patients in the United States. When research on such different populations comes to roughly the same conclusions, we can have more confidence in our results. To explore and understand the diverse abilities and functions of the human brain, researchers should study the rich diversity within the human community.

Lobes of the Cerebral Hemispheres and Cerebral Cortex

lobes • each of the four major regions of the cerebral cortex, comprising the frontal lobe (motor, planning), parietal lobe (somatosensory), temporal lobe (auditory), and occipital lobe (visual)

Hemispheric specialization is only one way through which to view the various parts of the cerebral cortex. Another way is to divide the cortex into four **lobes** (rounded sections): frontal, parietal, temporal, and occipital (refer to Figure 2.15). The *frontal lobe* handles planning, reasoning, and other high-level thought processes, as well as motor processing (see Figure 2.16); the *parietal lobe* governs somatosensory processing (sensations of feeling in the skin and in the muscles of the body; see Figure 2.17); the *temporal lobe* handles auditory processing (hearing); and the *occipital lobe* oversees visual processing (seeing). In addition to these localized functions, the lobes also interact constantly, and many functions overlap among the lobes.

Branching Out sections illustrate applications of psychology in real life.

Is Hypnosis an Altered State? **141**

disruptive, as anyone knows who ever has been questioned while daydreaming in class, in cognitive processes requiring focused attention on environmental events. Hyponosis is another state that can be helpful or disruptive.

4.3

This is probably the first time you have seen this instruction in a textbook: Stop reading your textbook and take a few minutes to daydream. When you return to studying, think about both the content and the process of your daydreaming. How does daydreaming seem to differ from what you know about the content and the process of dreams that come to you during your sleep?

IS HYPNOSIS AN ALTERED STATE?

The Phenomenon of Hypnosis: Real or Fake?

An altered state of consciousness that somewhat resembles sleep is **hypnosis.** Historically, the man credited with introducing hypnotism as a psychological phenomenon is Franz Anton Mesmer (1734–1815), who referred to the phenomenon he discovered as *mesmerism.* In his own lifetime, Mesmer came to be considered a fraud, perhaps because he had some strange beliefs, such as that "animal magnetism," a never well-defined construct, could cure illnesses.

A person undergoing hypnosis usually is deeply relaxed and extremely sensitive to suggestion. For example, hypnotized people may imagine that they see or hear things when they are prompted to do so (Bowers, 1976). Hypnotized people also may receive a posthypnotic suggestion. In a **posthypnotic suggestion,** participants are given instructions during hypnosis to carry out after they awake from the hypnotic state. Participants often do not remember receiving the instructions, and many do not even recall having been hypnotized (Ruch, 1975). People differ in their susceptibility to hypnotism, and scales can be used to measure this susceptibility. These scales largely measure the extent to which a person is susceptible to actual suggestions made when the individual is under hypnosis.

Hypnotized research participants also may not sense things that they otherwise would sense. For example, a hypnotized person may not feel pain when dipping an arm into icy cold water. Hypnosis has been particularly effective in relieving pain for which physical causes have not yet been found (e.g., Siegel, 1979).

Some scientists have argued that the very phenomenon of hypnosis is phony (Meeker & Barber, 1971; also described in Barber, 1964a, 1964b). According to this view, hypnotized research participants actually only pretend to be hypnotized. Some people may participate in the hoax even without realizing that they are doing so. These people may believe so strongly in the powers of the hypnotist that they believe that they are hypnotized, even when they are not. Some people in stage demonstrations may only pretend or may believe they are hypnotized when they are not.

hypnosis • an altered state of consciousness that usually involves deep relaxation and extreme sensitivity to suggestion and appears to bear some resemblance to sleep

posthypnotic suggestion • an instruction received during hypnosis, which the individual is to implement after having wakened, often despite having no recollection of having received the instruction

Finding Your Way demonstrations ask you to participate in an exercise that will help you remember the key points you are learning. Active learning is one of the best ways to remember something.

A running glossary allows you to learn and review terms at your own pace.

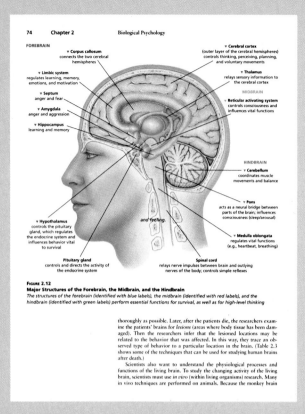

FOREBRAIN

▾ **Corpus callosum**
connects the two cerebral hemispheres

▾ **Cerebral cortex**
(outer layer of the cerebral hemispheres) controls thinking, perceiving, planning, and voluntary movements

▾ **Limbic system**
regulates learning, memory, emotions, and motivation

▾ **Thalamus**
relays sensory information to the cerebral cortex

MIDBRAIN

▾ **Septum**
anger and fear

▾ **Reticular activating system**
controls consciousness and influences vital functions

▾ **Amygdala**
anger and aggression

▾ **Hippocampus**
learning and memory

HINDBRAIN

▾ **Cerebellum**
coordinates muscle movements and balance

and feeling.

▾ **Pons**
acts as a neural bridge between parts of the brain; influences consciousness (sleep/arousal)

▾ **Hypothalamus**
controls the pituitary gland, which regulates the endocrine system and influences behavior vital to survival

▾ **Medulla oblongata**
regulates vital functions (e.g., heartbeat, breathing)

Pituitary gland
controls and directs the activity of the endocrine system

Spinal cord
relays nerve impulses between brain and outlying nerves of the body; controls simple reflexes

FIGURE 2.12
Major Structures of the Forebrain, the Midbrain, and the Hindbrain
The structures of the forebrain (identified with blue labels), the midbrain (identified with red labels), and the hindbrain (identified with green labels) perform essential functions for survival, as well as for high-level thinking

thoroughly as possible. Later, after the patients die, the researchers examine the patients' brains for *lesions* (areas where body tissue has been damaged). Then the researchers infer that the lesioned locations may be related to the behavior that was affected. In this way, they trace an observed type of behavior to a particular location in the brain. (Table 2.3 shows some of the techniques that can be used for studying human brains after death.)

Scientists also want to understand the physiological processes and functions of the living brain. To study the changing activity of the living brain, scientists must use *in vivo* (within living organisms) research. Many in vivo techniques are performed on animals. Because the monkey brain

Informative illustrations showing parts and functions enable you to master anatomical material visually and verbally.

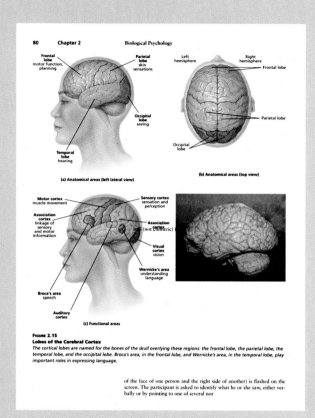

Frontal lobe
motor function, planning

Parietal lobe
skin sensations

Left hemisphere

Right hemisphere

Frontal lobe

Occipital lobe
seeing

Parietal lobe

Temporal lobe
hearing

Occipital lobe

(a) Anatomical areas (left lateral view)

(b) Anatomical areas (top view)

Motor cortex
muscle movement

Sensory cortex
sensation and perception

Association cortex
linkage of sensory and motor information

Association (not chimeric)

Visual cortex
vision

Broca's area
speech

Wernicke's area
understanding language

Auditory cortex

(c) Functional areas

FIGURE 2.15
Lobes of the Cerebral Cortex
The cortical lobes are named for the bones of the skull overlying these regions: the frontal lobe, the parietal lobe, the temporal lobe, and the occipital lobe. Broca's area, in the frontal lobe, and Wernicke's area, in the temporal lobe, play important roles in expressing language.

of the face of one person and the right side of another) is flashed on the screen. The participant is asked to identify what he or she saw, either verbally or by pointing to one of several nor

A page-referenced summary at the end of the chapter reviews point by point the key topics in the chapter.

Summary

1. *Social psychologists* try to understand and to explain how the presence of others (actual, imagined, or implied) affects the thoughts, feelings, and behavior of individuals.

What Is Social Cognition?   340

2. *Social cognition* refers to the ways in which we perceive and interpret information about people, whether the information comes from others or from inside ourselves.
3. An experiment in social psychology established the theory of *cognitive dissonance*, which states that when a person's behavior and cognitions do not go together, discomfort results. To ease this discomfort, the person must justify his or her behavior. The experimental results that led to cognitive-dissonance theory have also been explained in other ways, such as by *self-perception theory*, according to which we form our beliefs about ourselves, based on our actions.
4. *Attribution theory* deals with how we explain the causes of behavior—why we and other people do what we do. In making *attributions*, we look for the cause of the behavior, which can be *personal* or *situational*.
5. Although biases and heuristics help us to make attributions, these mental shortcuts also sometimes lead to mental distortions.

How Do We Form and Change Our Attitudes?   345

6. *Attitudes* are learned (not inborn), stable, relatively lasting evaluations of people, ideas, and things. Attitudes affect our behavior but the links between attitudes and behavior are not always predictable.
7. In studying what influences changes in people's attitudes, psychologists consider characteristics of the recipient of the message, of the message itself, and of the source of the message.

What Are Liking, Loving, and Interpersonal Attraction?   349

8. Social–psychological research asks why we are attracted to some people and not to others. Learning theory answers that we like (or dislike) a person because of the emotional rewards (or punishments) we get in that person's presence. According to *equity theory*, attraction involves a fair balance of give and take. *Cognitive-consistency* theories,

such as *balance theory*, focus on a balance both of give and take and of similar likes and dislikes.
9. The *attachment theory of love* suggests there are three main ways in which people relate to those they love: secure, anxious–ambivalent, and avoidant. The *triangular theory of love* posits that love has three components: intimacy, passion, and commitment.
10. According to the *love-is-a-story theory* of attraction, each of us is drawn to partners who closely match the types of characters in our own personal idealized love stories. Studies show that attraction is based on physical attractiveness, arousal, familiarity, proximity, and similarity.

How Do We Communicate in Our Personal Relationships?   354

11. Successful communication is essential to interpersonal relationships.
12. Men and women appear to communicate differently. Men seem to prefer establishing higher status and preserving their independence; women seem to seek closeness and agreement.

How Do We Interact in Groups?   354

13. Some social psychologists try to understand and explain how groups reach agreement and how individuals perform in a group.
14. In *social facilitation*, the presence of other people improves our performance. In *social interference*, the presence of others hurts our performance.
15. In *social loafing*, individuals show less personal effort as the size of the group increases.
16. Groups often become *polarized*, due both to new information and to shifts toward the group's social *norms*.
17. *Groupthink* occurs when a closely-knit group cares more about agreement than about discussing objective, rational opinions regarding suitable actions. Stress, biased leadership, like-minded group members, and isolation from diverse views make the problems of groupthink worse.

What Are Conformity, Compliance, and Obedience?   358

18. People yield to social pressure by *conforming, complying,* and *obeying.*
19. A member of a group may conform only publicly or may also conform privately as well. People who

458   Chapter 12   Personality

Pathways to Knowledge

Choose the best answer to complete each sentence.

1. Temperament is best described as an individual's
   (a) personality characteristics that begin in adulthood.
   (b) mood, activity level, and disposition, an aspect of personality.
   (c) tendency to get irritable, frustrated, or angry.
   (d) moods that are dependent on situational factors.

2. The order in which Freud's psychosexual stages of development proceed is
   (a) oral, anal, phallic, latency, genital.
   (b) anal, oral, latency, phallic, genital.
   (c) anal, oral, genital, phallic, latency.
   (d) oral, anal, genital, latency, phallic.

3. Psychodynamic determinism refers to
   (a) behavior that is ruled by unconscious forces over which we have no control.
   (b) behavior that is conscious in origin.
   (c) id impulses that forever will remain unfulfilled.
   (d) the delimiting characteristic of the superego.

4. According to Jung, all archetypes are
   (a) held in the collective unconscious.
   (b) dark and forbidden instinctual urges.
   (c) those parts of the unconscious that are unique to each individual.
   (d) the manifest content of dreams.

5. Carl Rogers's self theory assumes that
   (a) humans are isolated individuals in an indifferent world.
   (b) a person's acceptance of her- or himself leads to a selfish view of the world and to egocentric behavior.
   (c) the self is the focal point from which reality is constructed.
   (d) most people see problems and difficulties only in terms of themselves, rather than by showing unconditional positive regard for others.

6. According to Julian Rotter's social-learning theory, a primary factor that differentiates individuals is in how they
   (a) devote the majority of their psychic energy.
   (b) cope with the numerous unconscious forces that act on their lives.
   (c) show their sociability.
   (d) view their locus of control.

7. The "Big Five" theory of personality includes all the following factors *except*
   (a) altruism.
   (b) neuroticism.
   (c) extroversion.
   (d) conscientiousness.

8. Interactionist approaches to personality assume that
   (a) most people tend to show their characteristic traits across various situations, but some people do not.
   (b) neither the situation nor the person's characteristics alone are the sole influence on behavior.
   (c) individuals show consistent behavioral patterns across situations.
   (d) situations ultimately determine how a given individual will act.

9. According to Erik Erikson, all of the following are core issues that must be confronted during the course of personality development *except*
   (a) guilt versus initiative.
   (b) trust versus mistrust.
   (c) happiness versus sadness.
   (d) identity versus role confusion.

10. In psychosexual development, according to Freud, latency refers to
    (a) the period during which the child explores both male and female sex roles.
    (b) a period when psychosexual development is very rapid and intense.
    (c) a period of dormant and repressed sexual desires.
    (d) the brief period before which the child's sexual orientation becomes solidified.

Answer each of the following questions by filling in the blank with an appropriate word or phrase.

11. Researchers who endorse a _____-_____ theory of personality are concerned with the relationships among people's thoughts, their actions, and their personality characteristics.

12. That part of a dream that deals with events in the dream as we experience them is referred to as the _____ content.

13. Psychodynamic theorists view the mind as organized at two basic levels: the _____ and the _____.

Pathways to Understanding   459

14. Personality attributes that are consistent in an individual are referred to as _____.

15. According to psychodynamic theory, the _____ mediates among the id, the superego, and the external world.

16. The defense mechanism of _____ is characterized by various forbidden thoughts and impulses being attributed to another person rather than to the self.

17. Alfred Adler believed that a primary motivator in our lives is our striving for _____.

18. Karen Horney has proposed that people experience _____, a condition of isolation and helplessness brought about by a competitive world.

19. Psychodynamic assessment sometimes involves the use of _____, which are designed to assess individuals' personality characteristics and conflicts via their responses to ambiguous test questions.

20. According to Eysenck's theory of personality, _____ refers to an individual's tendency to be solitary, lacking in feeling, and insensitive.

21. The _____ is an objective test that is frequently used as a diagnostic tool to assess personality characteristics.

Answers

1. b, 2. a, 3. a, 4. a, 5. c, 6. d, 7. a, 8. b, 9. c, 10. c, 11. cognitive-behavioral, 12. manifest, 13. conscious, unconscious, 14. traits, 15. ego, 16. projection, 17. superiority, 18. basic anxiety, 19. projective tests, 20. psychoticism, 21. Minnesota Multiphasic Personality Inventory

Pathways to Understanding

1. Think about the various theories of personality proposed in this chapter. Which theory seems to you to be most reasonable; that is, which theory explains personality most effectively? Describe the strengths and the weaknesses of this theory, as you view them.

2. What steps can you take to ensure that someone you love (hypothetical or real) feels sure of your unconditional positive regard for her or him?

3. What do you consider to be the essential personality characteristics, based on yourself and on the people you know?

Pathways to Knowledge questions test your factual comprehension of those topics.

Pathways to Understanding questions at the end of the chapter enable you to exercise your creative, practical, and analytical thinking skills in mastering the material.

ADDITIONAL STUDY AIDS

The following items are available for student purchase. Ask your college bookstore manager for ordering information.

The **Study Guide** reflects the theme of the textbook and provides study tips, practice exams, and answer guides to the Pathways to Understanding questions.
ISBN: 0-15-508058-X

A CD-ROM for students lets you explore psychology through dozens of interactive, multimedia minilectures and activities. Multiple choice questions let you test your mastery of the material.

CONTENTS IN BRIEF

CONTENTS

CHAPTER 7   Thought and Language   229

CHAPTER 8   Intelligence and Creativity   267

CHAPTER 9   Life-Span Development   303

CHAPTER 10   Social Psychology   339

CHAPTER 11   Motivation and Emotion   381

PATHWAYS TO PSYCHOLOGY

SECOND EDITION

The Case of The Messy Roommate

The Case of

Pedro and Phil are first-year students and roommates at college. Six weeks into the term, they generally have gotten along well and like each other. But one aspect of Phil's behavior is driving Pedro crazy. Pedro thinks Phil is a slob. The room always seems to be a mess, with Phil leaving dirty laundry, leftover candy bar wrappers, and practically any assorted junk you can think of lying around the room. Pedro nicely has asked Phil to clean up after himself, but to no avail. If anything, the room is getting to be a bigger and bigger mess as the term moves along. Finally, in desperation, Pedro confronts Phil and tells Phil that he just can't take it anymore: Pedro says that the mess in the room is interfering with his studying, with his finding things, and with his peace of mind.

Phil seems unperturbed. He says that it is normal for college students to leave things around and that Pedro is too hung up on neatness. But Phil goes even further. He says he will ask the three roommates in the room immediately above them how they feel and even invites Pedro to present his side of the story. Phil assures Pedro that he has not talked to the three roommates about this issue so that they will not have a prior bias about it. Although Pedro does not know the three roommates above them well, he concedes that asking some other first-year students their view seems like a reasonable test. Pedro can't believe that even one of them would side with Phil. So they telephone the roommates on the floor above and ask them to come down for a moment.

Pedro and Phil both present their side of the story and to Pedro's amazement, all three of the roommates side with Phil. All three of them suggest that Pedro indeed is too hung up on neatness. One of them suggests to Pedro that he should chill out and get a life. Pedro feels embarrassed about the whole matter and decides he should let it drop.

Maybe Pedro shouldn't let the matter drop. Think about it while you read chapter 1. Is Phil's test of the rightness of his position valid? Are the people he asked a representative sample of first-year students; or is his pathway to solving the problem the wrong one?

1

WHAT IS PSYCHOLOGY?

Do you ever wonder about what it means to be smart, to love someone, or to be attractive to someone? Do you want to know how salespeople persuade you to buy things you do not want? Do you sometimes wish you could better understand how to get along with other people or how to study and learn more effectively? Do you wonder why people like Phil can be such slobs? These kinds of questions are answered by studying **psychology,** the scientific study of *mind* (the means by which people and other living organisms perceive, think, and feel), *behavior* (what people and other living organisms do), and the relationship between them.

These are also the kinds of questions that first interested me in psychology. I became interested in psychology when, as an elementary school student, I bombed group IQ tests. As a result of my low scores, my teachers had low expectations for me. I then gave the teachers what they expected and became a mediocre student. It was not until the fourth grade, when I had a teacher who expected more of me, that I started performing at a higher level. Psychology has provided a way for me to study intelligence. At various other times, I have had problems coming up with ideas and problems in my close relationships with other people, and at those times I studied creativity and then love. The wonderful thing about psychology is that one can take issues of importance in one's life and try to understand and even resolve them through scientific study and research.

To study psychology is to try to understand how we think, feel, learn, perceive, act, interact with others, and even understand ourselves. As a student of introductory psychology, you study the mind, behavior, and their interrelation. You and your fellow students (both amateurs and professionals) study various psychological phenomena (processes or events that can be observed, e.g., the process of decision making, the expression of emotions, or the response to a personal crisis). Table 1.1 will give you an idea of the range of the kinds of questions psychologists ask. It shows just a small number of the many kinds of questions asked by psychologists when studying phenomena related to diverse fields of psychology. These diverse fields are studied through a large variety of careers. Appendix B describes some of the careers you can pursue if you choose to specialize in psychology.

Psychology is both a *natural science* and a *social science*. Psychologists study both the laws of nature and how these laws apply to people. Actually, some psychologists and other social scientists also study the minds and behavior of other animals, but generally, they do so in order to gain insights into human beings. Different kinds of scientists have slightly different perspectives. They therefore follow different pathways and have different emphases in their study of people and other organisms.

- *Psychologists* generally focus on the individual person alone or in interaction with others and the environment.
- *Geneticists* study the influence of genes on behavior, as well as the interactions of the effects of genes with the effects of the environment.
- *Physiologists* study physical and biochemical influences on behavior.
- *Neuroscientists* study the brain and nervous system and their relations to behavior.
- *Political scientists* study systems and structures of human power relationships.

TABLE 1.1
What Do Psychologists Do?

Field of psychology	Sample problems and questions
Psychobiology. The biological structures and processes underlying thought, feeling, motivation, and behavior (see chapter 2)	■ What portion of the brain is active when a person learns the meaning of a new word? ■ How do various kinds of drugs affect the brain and behavior?
Developmental psychology. How people develop over time (see chapter 9)	■ How do children form attachments to their parents? ■ How do people acquire an understanding of what others expect of them in social interactions?
Cognitive psychology. How people perceive, learn, remember, and think about information (see chapters 3, 4, 5, 6, 7, and 8)	■ Why do people remember some facts but forget others? ■ How do people think when they play chess or solve everyday problems?
Social psychology. How people interact with each other, both as individuals and in groups (see chapter 10)	■ Why are people attracted to one another, and why do people like and even love one another? ■ Why are people sometimes generous and helpful, and why are they sometimes not?
Personality psychology. Personal dispositions that lead people to behave as they do (see chapters 11 and 12)	■ Why are some people highly sociable, whereas others seem to prefer just the company of very few other people? ■ What makes some people highly conscientious and others less so?
Clinical psychology. Understanding and treatment of abnormal behavior (see chapters 13 and 14)	■ What behavior is just a little out of the ordinary, and what behavior is truly abnormal? ■ What causes people to do things that they themselves consider inappropriate and even abnormal and would like to stop if they could?
Health psychology. The dynamic interaction between the mind and the physical health of the body (see chapter 15)	■ How does terminal illness (e.g., AIDS) affect how people think or feel about themselves and other people? ■ How do personality factors contribute to the likelihood that people will become ill with particular diseases (e.g., heart disease or cancer)?

Note: Some other specialties exist, as well. For example:
Educational psychology uses psychology to improve and develop methods of teaching and learning.
Industrial/organizational psychology applies psychology to decision making about employees and hiring in institutional settings, such as workplaces and businesses.
Engineering psychology deals with human–machine systems and how instruments such as computers and automobile dashboards can be made more user-friendly.
Psycholinguistics investigates the ways in which humans learn and use language.

- *Economists* study the various ways in which resources are traded, produced, and used.
- *Sociologists* study groups of individuals, such as groups of people in various kinds of work or having different incomes.
- *Physical anthropologists* study human evolution from simpler animals and even from one-celled creatures.
- *Cultural anthropologists* seek insights into various cultures.

Psychologists also learn from artists, computer scientists, novelists, and many other people who try to understand the human mind and behavior. By learning from diverse sources, psychologists may avoid some of

psychology • the study of the mind and behavior of people and other organisms and of mind–behavior interactions

Psychologists probe the relationship of the brain and the mind, using both case studies and experimental methods, often employing sophisticated technological equipment.

In exploring how people think, cognitive psychologists use various methods, such as controlled experiments, tests, computer simulations, and naturalistic observation.

To study how people change across the life span, developmental psychologists use various methods, including elaborately controlled experiments involving sophisticated equipment, intensive case studies, naturalistic observations, and surveys.

For investigating how people interact, social psychologists use diverse methods ranging from experiments to surveys to naturalistic observations.

the pitfalls of studying the human mind and behavior from only one point of view. Consider the following story (M. M. Hunt, 1959, p. 10):

> Once upon a time, an anthropologist was telling an English folk-fable to a gathering of the Bemba of Rhodesia. She glowingly described "a young prince who climbed glass mountains, crossed chasms, and fought dragons, all to obtain the hand of a maiden he loved." The Bemba were plainly bewildered, but remained silent. Finally an old chief spoke up, voicing the feelings of all present in the simplest of questions: "Why not take another girl?" he asked.

The chief's question illustrates that various cultures may view the link between romantic love and marriage in different ways. Our culture strongly links the two, but not all cultures do. The chief's question also shows that when studying love and marriage as they exist around the world, psychologists must ask various kinds of questions about how people find and pursue love and marriage. By considering multiple points of view (e.g., anthropological studies, as well as European literature), we can avoid making false assumptions about how people think, feel, and act.

Most of us can guess quite a bit about the human mind and behavior just through our own experiences. Why do psychologists go to the trouble

Personality psychologists use various methods, such as tests, to investigate personality.

Clinical psychologists (who have doctorates in psychology) and psychiatrists (who have medical degrees) frequently use case studies, tests, and various other methods for conducting research, as well as for diagnosing and treating patients.

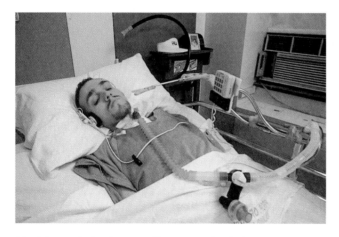

Health psychologists use diverse methods (e.g., surveys, case studies, experiments, naturalistic observation) for studying how the mind interacts with our physical health.

In addition to the main kinds of psychologists described in Table 1.1, there are many other kinds of psychologists. For instance, engineering psychologists deal with how to enable humans (e.g., data analysts) and machines (e.g., computers) to work well together.

of using scientific methods to study human behavior and the human mind? For one thing, psychologists often find out things that surprise them. For example, Bibb Latané and John Darley (1968, 1970) surprised their colleagues when they found that if you need help in an emergency situation you are more likely to be helped if there are fewer, rather than more, people available to help you (see chapter 10). Their research came back to haunt U.S. society in 1998, when numerous people in Denver saw a murder being committed and no one helped or even called the police.

Later in 1998, a college student at the University of California, Berkeley, observed the murder of a young girl by his friend and apparently did absolutely nothing to help the girl. Psychological research helps us understand why people do things that at first seem utterly incomprehensible.

Examples of psychological inquiries that originate from murders or similarly sad events may make the field of psychology seem rather grim. Actually, the opposite is true. Psychologists look at the problems of

Would you climb glass mountains and fight dragons to gain the love of someone you find attractive? How do most people find and attract someone to love?

society, such as murders, to help us understand both why such problems occur and what we can do to correct them.

WHY DO PSYCHOLOGISTS DO WHAT THEY DO?

Does all psychological research lead to surprising discoveries? No, but it does help us to learn more about the human mind and behavior, even when what we discover does not astonish us. We generally distinguish among four main goals for psychological research: description, explanation, prediction, and control. Table 1.2 summarizes these important goals.

Description involves observing and noting what, when, and how people think, feel, or act in various kinds of situations. To create accurate descriptions, psychologists must make observations and gather **data** (observable facts). Take, for example, the observation that about half of all people in the United States who get married end up divorced from their spouses. Before trying to understand why people do or do not stay married, psychologists may describe how people feel, think, and act when they have stayed married up to a certain point, and compare those data to parallel descriptions of people whose marriages have ended in divorce at that point. Once psychologists fully and accurately have described what, when, and how something happens, they can try to explain why it happens.

Explanation addresses why people think, feel, or act as they do. To explain various data, psychologists propose tentative **hypotheses,** which are

data • facts, numbers, and other information

hypothesis • tentative statement of belief regarding expected outcomes

TABLE 1.2
Four Primary Goals of Psychological Research

Goal: How psychologists try to achieve it	Questions in trying to reach this goal
Description. Try to characterize how people (and other living beings) think, feel, or act in various kinds of situations	What happens? When does it happen? How does it happen?
Explanation. Try to understand why people think, feel, or act as they do	Why does it happen?
Prediction. Attempt to anticipate how people will think, feel, or act, based on available information about past performance	What will happen next?
Control. Seek to influence how people think, feel, or act	How can we influence people's thoughts, feelings, or actions?

preliminary guesses about how to interpret and explain what is observed. Psychologists and other scientists use various formal methods for gathering data as the basis for their hypotheses. Informally, we all constantly gather data about what we observe, and we frequently form tentative hypotheses regarding what we have observed. For instance, based on your observations of married people, why do you believe some people stay married, whereas others end up being divorced?

You may very well come up with some accurate hypotheses to explain why some people stay married and others divorce. How do you know which of your hypotheses, or those of anyone else, are correct? You might conduct research that tests the various hypotheses; based on your findings, you then could see which hypothesis does the best job of explaining the phenomenon in question. Often, when psychologists conduct research, they find out some information that supports their own hypotheses and other information that does not support their initial beliefs. As psychologists conduct more research and learn more about the phenomena of interest, they modify their hypotheses or perhaps replace their old hypotheses with new ones that better explain the new information. The important thing is that you not only propose hypotheses, but devise ways of testing them.

For example, suppose that psychologist Kim Yee initially proposed this hypothesis: People who stay married are better listeners and communicators than people who divorce. She might then conduct research to assess the two-way communication skills of people who are about to marry. She could then trace the progress of their marriages and observe any changes in their communication skills. Chances are that some information she gathered would confirm her hypothesis and other information would not. (Even superior communication skills are no guarantee of a long-lasting marriage. For instance, a highly communicative pair of jealous and adulterous ax murderers might have other problems.) Given this new information, Kim would revise her hypothesis, allowing for other factors that may influence whether people stay married. Good communication also is essential in less intimate relationships, as shown at the beginning of the chapter by Pedro's failed attempts to communicate to Phil his distress over the mess Phil has created in the room.

Psychologists, like other people, sometimes make mistakes. Often, their own beliefs (e.g., Kim's belief in the importance of communication

NASA scientists failed to take steps to avoid confirmation bias, and the crew aboard the shuttle Challenger *suffered the tragic consequences of that error.*

skills) can bias their interpretations of data. Hypotheses based on personal beliefs may lead to the trap of *confirmation bias,* the tendency to confirm what is already believed to be true.

How do psychologists and other scientists avoid the trap of confirmation bias? For one thing, they base their research on what others before them have discovered and what others around them are discovering. That is, science is *cumulative,* building up over time. In order to accumulate knowledge, scientists agree to share information—to make it *public.* The main way they do so is by publishing their findings in scientific journals. Examples of journals in psychology are *Psychological Review,* which publishes new theories in psychology; *Psychological Bulletin,* which publishes comprehensive reviews of literature in psychology; and the *Journal of Personality and Social Psychology,* which publishes research studies presenting new findings in the fields of personality and social psychology.

By reading how various findings were obtained, other scientists can see whether they agree with the original interpretations. If these scientists do not agree they then may come up with their own interpretations. If they are surprised by the findings, and they doubt the results, they can even *replicate* the work (i.e., repeat the research procedures that were described in the published report). In that way, scientists can *verify* (confirm the accuracy of) the data.

Often, the beliefs that lead to various research hypotheses come from a **theory,** an organized set of general principles that explain a phenomenon or a set of phenomena. Theories allow us to make predictions, based on those general principles. Informative theory and research enable us not only to describe and explain how people think, feel, and act as they do but also to *predict* how people will think, feel, and so on. *Prediction* can be very important in practice, as well as in theory.

For example, according to one theory in psychology, people tend to engage in behavior that is rewarded and to avoid behavior that is punished (e.g., described in Skinner, 1974). According to this theory, the rewards and punishments people receive affect whether they will continue or will

theory • a statement of general principles explaining one or more phenomena (events or processes)

Although most people who marry expect to have a lasting marriage, about half of all marriages end in divorce. Why do some couples stay married longer than others?

stop behaving in particular ways. A prediction based on this theory may be that people will tend to stay in marriages they find rewarding and will tend to leave marriages they find unpleasant. It turns out that this prediction is partly true. Psychologists have observed that many people who have been unhappily married or who have divorced have reported that their marriages, or their spouses, were not rewarding (Notarius & Markman, 1993; Weiss, 1975; see also R. J. Sternberg & Hojjat, 1997). At the same time, other factors (e.g., communication patterns) seem to influence marital happiness and the likelihood of long-lasting marriage versus speedy divorce (Gottman, 1994; Notarius, 1996; Notarius & Markman, 1993). For some psychological phenomena, once we can predict outcomes (e.g., marital happiness or unhappiness) we can start looking for ways to try to influence or control them.

In psychology, one method of *control* is **psychotherapy,** the use of psychological means to help people to control mental disorders and their related physical problems, as well as to improve or enhance people's adjustment to their life circumstances. Psychotherapy often involves *therapeutic interventions*, which are active attempts to change thoughts, attitudes, or actions that cause problems for the person. Many married people who are experiencing difficulties in their marriage seek help from psychotherapists, to address and possibly to resolve the problems in their marriage.

Although this textbook does not provide psychotherapy, or anything resembling psychotherapy, it may be able to help you with a difficult task you are now facing: studying. The information in Putting It to Use 1.1 describes what psychologists have learned about when, where, and how to study. It will help you to put their knowledge to work in your own life.

In sum, psychologists try to describe, explain, predict, or control the processes and products of the human mind. Often, they can try to meet more than one goal during their work. The goals also often interact, so that achieving one goal helps in achieving another. In order to achieve these goals, psychologists use particular methods of conducting research.

psychotherapy • the use of psychological principles to treat mental disorders or otherwise to improve psychological adjustment and well-being

1.1

WHAT HAVE PSYCHOLOGISTS LEARNED ABOUT WHEN, WHERE, AND HOW TO STUDY?

PUTTING IT TO USE

Here are a few tips for productive studying.

1. Do not try to skimp on the time you spend studying. How much you learn is a function of how much time you devote to learning.

2. Spread out your study sessions. Study a little at a time, rather than bunching your study sessions together or spending long hours studying at one stretch. To avoid having to cram for tests, set small, realistic study goals for yourself, which you can accomplish each day or each week.

3. Do not try to study when you are tired, hungry, or otherwise unable to concentrate on understanding what you are studying. Study when you feel refreshed and ready to learn the material.

4. You should study material in a context that is as close as possible to that in which you will be tested on the material (i.e., in the same type of setting). Ask yourself the characteristics of the setting in which you will be tested (e.g., type of room, noise level, lighting), and try to study in such a setting. In addition, it may help you to study in a variety of contexts with features similar to the testing environment (e.g., a study hall, a library reading room, a dorm study lounge).

ANALYTICAL AND OTHER FORMS OF HIGHER ORDER THINKING IN PSYCHOLOGY

The example of confirmation bias, which was presented earlier in this chapter, points out the importance of analytical (critical) thinking in psychology or in any other field, as well as in daily life. Analytical thinking is important in psychology, as in any field, because each psychologist and student of psychology needs to examine claims on their merits. One cannot assume that what one reads is true, simply because someone states or believes it.

Analytical thinking is employed when one analyzes, evaluates, interprets, criticizes, or judges a claim or a piece of work. Sometimes, these different mental processes are grouped together under the label of "analytical thinking."

Consider some examples (from R. J. Sternberg, 1986a) of *informal fallacies* that can creep into our thinking.

1. *Irrelevant conclusion.* We commit the fallacy of irrelevant conclusion when our conclusion is irrelevant to the line of reasoning that led to it. Can you see how the following example illustrates this fallacy?

   Joni has been observing her boyfriend, Robert, who is paying his way through school. Lately Robert's boss has been asking him to work extra hours, which has led Robert to have less time to spend with Joni. Robert has explained the situation to Joni, but Joni has been skeptical. Joni then comments to her friend, Sarah, "I guess Robert is losing interest in me, because he has not been coming much to see me lately." In fact, Robert has been busy meeting the demands of his boss.

2. *Composition.* We commit the fallacy of composition when we reason that what is true of parts of a whole is necessarily true of the whole itself. In fact, though, elements (such as members of a team) may interact in ways (such as through poor teamwork) that render untrue for the whole what is true of each part. Can you see how the following example illustrates this fallacy?

Alberto is bragging about his favorite team, the Bluehawks. He comments to Nico, "The Bluehawks have the best player in each position, so they have to be the best team." In fact, good individual players do not always work well together as a team.

3. *Personalization.* If you see yourself as the cause of some event for which you were not primarily responsible, you have committed the fallacy of personalization. Taking personally a statement that is not directed toward you is also an inappropriate personalization. Can you see how the following example illustrates this fallacy?

Sharlene has just received a grade of *D* on her English paper. She comments to her friend, Leesa, "Professor Mackey really hates me. Look at the grade she gave me on this paper!" In fact, Sharlene simply wrote a bad paper.

4. *False cause.* The fallacy of false cause is committed when someone concludes from the fact that two events happened in rapid succession, or have tended to happen together, that the first event must have caused the second. Can you see how the following example illustrates this fallacy?

Federico bought a class ring and immediately afterward went to take a history test. He had not expected to do well, but nevertheless received an A−. He decided that the ring had brought him good luck and he decided to make sure he wore it for each and every test he took thereafter. In fact, the ring had nothing to do with Federico's strong performance.

5. *Ad hominem argument.* In this type of argument, one attempts to attack an individual personally in order to undermine the individual's position. Can you see how the following example illustrates this fallacy?

George picked up a new book on the history of the United States. He read in the "About the Author" portion of the book jacket that the author of the book was 22 years old. George put the book down, commenting that "No one who is only 22 years old possibly could write knowledgeably about U.S. history."

Of course, there are other kinds of informal fallacies that can creep into our thinking. The important thing is to be on guard for these fallacies and to catch ourselves when we make them. In this way, we improve both our thinking and the conclusions we draw from it.

Two other kinds of thinking beyond analytical (critical) thinking also are important in psychology. Creative thinking involves generating one's own ideas and products. In creative thinking, one creates, discovers, invents, or imagines. The final important kind of thinking beyond analytical thinking is practical thinking. In practical thinking, one applies, uses, or implements ideas in everyday life.

Analytical, creative, and practical thinking often are used together. For example, consider the question of why people become depressed. You would use analytical thinking to evaluate the quality of a theory of why people become depressed. You would use creative thinking to come up with your own theory of why people become depressed. But because you would draw on other people's thoughts, you would necessarily combine analytical and creative thinking. You would use practical thinking to decide how to help someone who is depressed come out of his or her depression. But in order to help the person, you would need to analyze which theory of depression to use and you would have to formulate your own ideas about how to help the person. So, in thinking as a student of psychology and helping someone, you would combine the three kinds of thinking: analytical, creative, and practical.

HOW DO PSYCHOLOGISTS CONDUCT RESEARCH?

Psychologists can use various methods to study problems that interest them. Each method represents a different pathway toward understanding how people are both similar and different. Some of the main methods include: (a) tests and surveys, (b) case studies, (c) naturalistic observations, and (d) experiments. These research methods are summarized in Table 1.3, which highlights some of the advantages and disadvantages of each method.

TABLE 1.3
Research Methods

Method	Advantages	Disadvantages
Tests and surveys. Tools for obtaining samples of behavior, beliefs, and abilities at a particular time and place	1. Ease of administration 2. Ease of scoring and statistical analysis	1. May not be able to generalize results beyond a specific place, time, and test content 2. May be discrepancies between real-life behavior and test behavior
Case studies. Intensive studies of single individuals, which draw general conclusions about behavior	Highly detailed information, including the context surrounding the person being studied	1. Small samples of people, which reduce the researcher's ability to generalize conclusions 2. Limitations on the reliability of the data
Naturalistic observations. Observations of real-life situations, as in classrooms, work settings, or homes	1. Wide applicability of results 2. Understanding of behavior in natural contexts	1. Loss of experimental control 2. Possibility that the observer's presence may influence the observed behavior
Experiments. Controlled investigations that study cause-and-effect relationships through the manipulation of variables	1. Precise control of independent variables 2. Usually, large numbers of participants that allow results to be generalized	1. Usually, less intensive study of individual participants 2. Limitations on the ability to generalize to real-life behavior

Tests and Surveys

One way to study human behavior is to use tests. **Tests** are procedures for measuring a characteristic or an ability at a particular time and in a particular place. In tests, the responses are scored as being either right or wrong, or at least as being stronger (more accurate, more appropriate, more creative, etc.) or weaker. As an example, the Scholastic Assessment Test and the American College Test are tests used by many colleges and universities for admission purposes. The tests generally are used to predict academic success in undergraduate school. Test scores vary not only with different people, but also for a given person, due to various factors such as ill health or noise in the environment that can affect performance at the time of testing.

Unlike tests, **questionnaires,** used in conducting **surveys,** almost never have right or wrong answers. They typically measure beliefs and opinions rather than abilities or knowledge. For example, you might use a questionnaire for a survey to determine the attitudes or opinions of students regarding the use of alcohol. Surveys easily can be interpreted in many ways. During political campaigns, you probably have heard the exact same survey data interpreted very differently by opposing candidates. Nonetheless, surveys are handy research tools.

Case Studies

Surveys and tests can be used to gather some information about a lot of people. In **case studies,** psychologists gather a lot of information about only a few people. That is, psychologists investigate a few individuals intensively in order to draw general conclusions about how those individuals think or feel, or about how or why they do what they do. The psychologists then may apply these conclusions to the studied individuals and perhaps to others as well. Case studies tend not to lead to firm *causal* conclusions, that is, about what in a person's life caused something else to happen. Rather, case studies tend to be suggestive of possible causal links between life circumstances and behavior.

Psychologists use case studies in various ways. For one thing, many psychologists use case studies when they treat clients in clinical work. *Clinical work* refers to the observation and treatment of patients with physical or psychological problems, as might be done in a psychological or medical clinic. *Clinicians* are psychologists, who usually have PhD (doctor of philosophy) or PsyD (doctor of psychology) degrees; psychiatrists, who typically have MD (doctor of medicine) degrees; and other professionals who provide treatment to clients. For clinicians, case studies are essential for understanding the problems of individual clients, as well as for deepening their insights into psychological problems in general. Note that clinicians are specially licensed psychologists who are trained to evaluate problems of clients and then to administer therapy. Many psychologists are not specially trained in clinical psychology but rather in other branches of psychology.

Researchers also use case studies to gain insights into the human mind and behavior. Some psychologists study many individuals. For example, Robert Weiss drew on many case studies to find some common reasons why marriages fail (Weiss, 1975). Howard Gardner (1993a, 1995) used multiple case studies in investigations of creativity and leadership. Other investigators study just one person in great depth: Howard Gruber (1981)

test • a method for measuring a given ability or attribute in particular individuals at a particular time and in a particular place

questionnaire • a set of questions used for conducting a survey

survey • a method of observing various people's responses to questions regarding their beliefs and opinions

case study • intensive investigation of a single individual or set of individuals

studied Charles Darwin (famous for his theory of evolution; see chapter 2). The case-study method offered Gruber the details he needed in order to understand how creativity changes over a lifetime (described in Gruber, 1995). Gruber concluded that creative insights evolve over many years, rather than appearing suddenly, and that most major creative insights are a combination of many minor insights.

Case studies often are used in conjunction with other kinds of evidence in order to establish a point. For example, David Lykken (1998) draws upon a variety of kinds of evidence in order to make the point that the results of polygraph (lie detector) tests are highly questionable and can have disastrous results for individuals and for society. Lykken presents a number of case studies, such as that of Mack Coker who worked for a company that was experiencing thefts. First, Coker lost his job as a result of a failed polygraph test for which no other evidence was offered to support the results of the test. He then became the object of vicious rumors in the community in which he lived. Lykken points out that Coker eventually got his job back, but that many others are not so lucky.

Naturalistic Observations

In **naturalistic observations,** also known as *field studies,* the researcher leaves the laboratory or the clinic. Out in the community (the field), the naturalistic observer listens, watches, and records what people do and say during their normal activities. For example, Shirley Heath (1983), an anthropologist, found dramatic differences in how parents and children defined intelligence in three communities in North Carolina. These differences included differing emphases given to nonverbal communication skills, verbal skills, memory skills, and academic skills. Parents in one community (Trackton) more strongly emphasized nonverbal communication skills, whereas parents in the other two communities (Roadville and Gateway) more strongly emphasized verbal skills. When the children went to school, verbal skills were emphasized more than were nonverbal ones,

Psychologists often use naturalistic observation to study children at home, in school, at a park, or in other natural settings.

naturalistic observation • a research method in which the researcher observes people engaged in the normal activities of their daily lives

giving children from Roadville and Gateway a competitive edge in the school setting. In a later study, Heath and Millbrae McLaughlin (1993) used similar methods to study the role of after-school organizations in providing youth with a sense of identity.

What is the value of naturalistic observations? For one thing, we learn from Heath's studies that different kinds of parenting styles may lead to differences in how well children are prepared for the school environment. For another thing, we learn that intelligence is multifaceted, involving far more than the intellectual skills that are used in school. A child from Roadville or Gateway placed in Trackton might appear relatively unintelligent by Trackton standards, due to the child's relatively weaker background in developing nonverbal skills. Unfortunately for the children from Trackton, the intellectual abilities valued at home did not closely match what the school valued. However, if schools had valued the nonverbal skills emphasized in Trackton homes, the children from Roadville and Gateway might have had more difficulty performing well in school. A contribution of Heath's research is in helping teachers realize the need to be sensitive, not only to the skills that the school typically values, but to the skills that are valued in the home and community. Children may have well-developed skills that are important to their lives and that could help them learn in school, if only these skills were recognized and appreciated.

Experiments

In the strictest scientific sense, an **experiment** is an investigation that studies cause–effect relationships. It does so by controlling characteristics or quantities that vary and that are known as *variables*. In general, experimenters carefully manipulate one or more particular variables to note their effects on other variables.

A given experiment has two main kinds of variables: independent and dependent. **Independent variables** are carefully manipulated by the experimenter. In this way, some aspects of the investigation are varied, but other aspects are not allowed to vary. The values of **dependent variables** are (usually quantified) outcome responses. These values depend on how one or more independent variables affect the phenomenon being studied in the experiment. For example, one might study the effects of different lighting conditions (the independent variable) on scores on a college admissions test (with the scores serving as values on the dependent variable, the college admissions test).

You probably do not conduct rigorously controlled scientific experiments every day, but you often do manipulate independent variables to observe their effects on dependent variables. For example, in trying to find out why your car will not start, you manipulate various independent variables (e.g., the battery, the fuel supply, the ignition) and observe the effects of your manipulations on the dependent variable (whether the car starts). In trying to find the best recipe for your favorite dish, you manipulate various independent variables (e.g., the ingredients, the sequence of steps, the cooking time or temperature), and you observe their effects on the dependent variable (i.e., how delicious the resulting dish tastes). In a wide variety of situations, you manipulate one or more independent variables and observe their effects on the dependent variables.

Of course, in your everyday experiences, you probably do not exert rigorous control of every variable or conduct sophisticated analyses of your data. In scientific research, the method of experimentation is much

experiment • an investigation of cause–effect relationships done by controlling or carefully manipulating particular variables to note their effects on other variables

independent variable • an attribute that is manipulated by the experimenter, while other attributes are held constant (not varied)

dependent variable • an outcome characteristic that varies as a consequence of variation in one or more independent variables

more tightly controlled. For example, suppose that Juana Perez wants to know whether the use of word processors affects the quality of writing. Juana has half of her participants (sometimes called *subjects)* use word processors to write a brief report. She has the rest of the participants use pen and paper to write the report. Juana then has all the reports typed so that they look similar, and a panel of experts then rates the quality of the writing. In this case, the independent variable is the means of writing the paper—either the word processor or the pen and paper—and the dependent variable is the quality of the writing.

Experiments involve at least two different types of conditions to which participants are exposed. In the first type of condition, the **experimental condition,** participants are exposed to an experimental treatment, which is a carefully prescribed set of circumstances. The experimental condition is also described as the *treatment condition.* In Juana's experiment, the treatment is the use of word processors. In the second type of condition, the **control condition,** the participants do not receive the experimental treatment, although they may receive an alternative treatment. In the control condition, the participants do not have access to word processors. Juana's goal is to see whether the participants who use word processors perform the writing task differently than do the participants who do not use word processors.

Usually, two different groups of participants are used for the experimental condition versus the control condition. When two or more groups of participants are used, the participants who receive the experimental treatment are the *experimental group.* The participants who are used as a comparison group are the *control group,* which may receive some alternative treatment or no treatment at all. Psychologists compare the outcomes for the control group with the outcomes for the experimental group. The use of control groups also allows psychologists to minimize the influence of *confounding variables* (situational or personal characteristics that would make it hard to draw conclusions without being confused). Without a control group, it usually is hard to draw any conclusions at all. In Juana's experiment, the experimental group works with word processors and the control group works with pen and paper. If Juana had all of her participants use word processors, the lack of a comparison group would leave Juana unsure of whether the quality of work in the writing task was higher (or lower) than otherwise as a function of the use of word processors. If the essays were all quite good (or bad), it might be because of the choice of topic, the abilities of the participants, or some other variable. (See Table 1.4 for a summary of the key terms in this section.)

Thus far, we have defined experiment in the strictest sense. In addition, however, people sometimes broaden the use of the term *experiment.* More loosely speaking, an experiment studies the effect or effects of some variables on other variables. The key benefit of using experiments is the ability to draw conclusions regarding causality.

By using a variety of research methods, psychologists have been able to study many aspects of how people think, feel, and act. Much of the work of psychologists is intended as **basic research,** which involves a search for fundamental relationships and principles of the human mind and behavior. In addition to basic research, psychologists often conduct **applied research,** which is a search for ways in which to put psychological discoveries to practical use. Among the many outcomes of applied research is information that directly relates to your own experiences: how to study so that you remember the information you are learning. For example, research has shown that you will learn material best for a test if you study it

experimental condition • a situation in which some experimental participants are exposed to a specific set of circumstances, involving a treatment linked to an independent variable

control condition • a situation in which some experimental participants are subjected to a carefully prescribed set of circumstances, which are like those of the experimental condition but do not involve the introduction of the independent variable

basic research • investigations devoted to the study of fundamental underlying relationships and principles, which may not offer any immediate, obvious, or practical value

applied research • investigations that are intended to lead to clear, immediate, obvious, and practical uses, which may not lead to fundamental understandings of the human mind and behavior

TABLE 1.4
Summary of Key Terms in the Experimental Method

Term and definition	Example (in Juana's study)
Independent variable. Aspects of the experiment that are controlled directly by the experimenter	The means of writing a paper (here, pen and paper vs. word processor)
Dependent variable. Outcomes, events, or characteristics that are influenced or affected by the experimental control of the independent variables	The quality of the writing in the paper
Experimental condition (also called *treatment condition*). The condition in which participants are exposed to a particular treatment	The condition in which the participants have access to the use of word processors in writing the paper
Control condition. The condition in which participants are not exposed to the experimental treatment; they may be exposed to an alternative treatment or to no treatment at all	The condition in which the participants do not have access to word processors

over several spaced study sessions rather than in one long session of cramming for the test. For other examples of how to put psychology to work for you, see Putting It to Use 1.2. Basic and applied research provide two alternative pathways to a common goal—psychological understanding—but they are related. Basic discoveries at one time often lead to important applied discoveries later on.

HOW DO PSYCHOLOGISTS DETERMINE CAUSE AND EFFECT?

The preceding section described four different kinds of research methods that psychologists can use. How do researchers choose which method to use? For one thing, the problem being studied may affect the choice of method. Dean Simonton (1988) wanted to find out what makes someone a brilliantly creative and revolutionary scientist. It seems doubtful that he could have used surveys or experiments to find all that he wanted to know. So he collected a great deal of case study information and then quantified it in order to analyze what these scientists had in common.

Another important issue also influences the choice of research method: *causality,* which is the link between a particular cause and a particular effect. A major goal of psychological research is to investigate cause-and-effect relationships. What do researchers need to do to be able to infer that "so-and-so" causes "such-and-such"? They design experiments that allow them to draw *causal inferences,* tentative conclusions about the likelihood that particular events or characteristics of a situation cause other events or characteristics. For example, they might ask whether a particular independent variable (e.g., use of word processors) was responsible for variation in the value of a given dependent variable (e.g., quality of writing). Based on their findings, they might try to infer the likelihood (probability) that the independent variable caused the change observed in the dependent variable.

For various reasons, however, it is not always possible to detect a clear causal relationship between independent and dependent variables. For one

1.2

WHAT ELSE HAVE PSYCHOLOGISTS LEARNED ABOUT HOW TO STUDY?

Psychologists have learned a great deal about how people can learn material in ways that help them to remember it. Following are a few more tips on how you can put psychological findings to work when you study.

5. Check your understanding. Use the Pathways to Knowledge and Pathways to Understanding sections at the end of each chapter in this textbook, to check that you understand and remember the key information in this chapter. In addition, look for opportunities to discuss what you are learning with other students, either in class or after class.

6. Periodically review your lecture notes and review the key points in what you are reading. Take advantage of various opportunities for reviewing key information in this textbook (e.g., the end-of-chapter summary). In addition, create other ways to review what you have read. After you have read a paragraph or two, go back and highlight key terms, concepts, and statements. Make notes in the margins of the book or on separate sheets of paper regarding the key information from each section of each chapter.

7. Make use of various advance organizers, which give you a hint about what information to expect, so that you can better organize the information. In this textbook, advance organizers include chapter outlines, section headings, and introductions to chapter sections. (Note: If you are reading a book that does not have advance organizers, you can create your own by quickly scanning each chapter or section before you actually read it, especially noting information printed in different typefaces.)

---

thing, the ability to draw causal inferences depends on how the research is designed. **Research design** affects two key aspects of the experiment: (a) how variables are chosen and how they relate to each other; and (b) how participants are assigned to the experimental and the control groups.

Next, we consider three basic kinds of designs in psychological research: controlled experimental, quasi-experimental, and correlational designs. In particular, we emphasize the kinds and degrees of causal inference that can be drawn from each. (See Table 1.5 for a summary of the similarities and differences among these three designs, including the advantages and disadvantages of each.)

Controlled Experimental Designs

In a **controlled experimental design** (an experiment in the strict sense, as discussed previously), the experimenter manipulates (controls) one or more independent variables in order to see the effect of these independent

research design • a way of choosing and interrelating a set of experimental variables and of selecting and assigning participants to experimental and control conditions

controlled experimental design • a plan for conducting research in which the experimenter carefully manipulates or controls independent variables in order to see their effects on dependent variables

8. Think critically about the information you hear (in lectures and discussions) and read (in textbooks). Think of questions that you might ask yourself about the information you are reading or hearing.

9. Whenever possible, try to relate what you are reading or hearing (e.g., in a lecture or a discussion) to your own experiences. When reading this textbook, take advantage of the various experiences (called Finding Your Way) and questions (e.g., at the end of each chapter) designed to help you relate what you are reading to your own experiences. In your notes, include comments that help you to relate the new information to what you already know. When you are reviewing your notes (or the chapter summaries), try to think of new ways to relate what you have learned to what you already know, and add those ideas to your notes.

10. Use visual learning techniques. Use the various figures, photos, and tables in this textbook to form mental pictures of key ideas, so that you will be better able to remember them.

11. Monitor your own learning to find out which styles you prefer. For instance, two friends of mine have differing styles of learning. Sally cannot listen to and understand a lecture unless she is taking notes, and she cannot read a book without a pen in her hand for scribbling in the margin (or at least making notes on paper if she is reading a borrowed book). Bernie, on the other hand, is distracted by taking notes and remembers what he hears better if he focuses on listening. When he reads, he sometimes draws pictures in the margins of the book. These pictures capture the key concepts being described. Bernie also finds that he remembers information better if he has a chance to discuss it with other people.

12. If you expect to do well in school, and you try hard to succeed, the chances are that you will succeed!

variables on one or more dependent variables. In any experiment, variables other than the independent variable, including even random variations, may affect the dependent variables. The experimenter must find a way to tell the effects of these other variables apart from the effects of the independent variables. To do so, the experimenter also includes in his or her design one or more control groups of participants who are not in the experimental group, as mentioned earlier. If the experiment involves a particular treatment condition, the participants in the control group do not receive the experimental treatment: They may receive no treatment, or they may receive an alternative treatment.

In a controlled experimental design, participants must be randomly assigned to the experimental and the control groups. This random assignment is important. It ensures that later differences in the results for each group are not due to preexisting differences in the participants. Suppose that Mario designed an experiment in which he assigned men to the treatment group (using word processors) and women to the control group (using pens and paper). No matter what findings resulted, Mario could

TABLE 1.5
Research Designs

Type of design	Advantages	Disadvantages
Controlled experimental design. Experimenter manipulates or controls one or more independent variables and observes the effects on the dependent variable or variables; participants are randomly assigned to control or treatment conditions	Permits conclusions regarding the causal outcomes of the treatment variable(s)	May not apply to settings outside the laboratory; depends on the use of a sample that truly represents the entire population of interest; may involve ethical concerns
Quasi-experimental design. Has many of the features of an experimental design, but participants are not randomly assigned to control versus treatment conditions; in some cases, there is no control group at all *Correlational design.* Researchers observe the degree of association between two or more attributes that occur naturally. Researchers do not directly manipulate the variables themselves, and they do not randomly assign participants to groups.	May be more convenient in some situations; may be used when random assignment of participants is difficult or unethical; may be easier to study larger numbers of participants	Do not typically permit conclusions regarding causal relationships between variable(s)

not be sure whether the results were due to the intended treatment (word processors vs. pens and paper) or to the sex differences between the members of the two groups.

Recall that Juana conducted a similar experiment assessing whether the use of word processors affects the quality of writing. In contrast to Mario, Juana randomly assigned participants to treatment and control conditions. Because Juana randomly assigned participants to each condition, she was able to determine that differences between the treatment group and the control group were due to the treatment variable, not to prior differences between the two groups.

Even very minor differences between groups may affect the outcomes. For instance, suppose that we gave a test of learning early in the day. Suppose also that we assigned the first 20 participants who arrived to the treatment group, and we assigned the second 20 participants to the control group. In this case, we might suspect that differences between the two groups could be associated with promptness (early arrivers might be more hard working), with tiredness (early arrivers might still be tired), or with some other factor associated with whether the participants arrived earlier or later.

In some situations, it is not possible to assign people randomly to a treatment group and a control group. Suppose that Velma wishes to study the effects of long-term alcohol abuse on psychological health. Ethically, she must accept for the alcoholic group those people who already are alcoholics, and she must accept for the control group those people who are not. She cannot randomly assign people to one group or the other and then insist that those assigned to the drinking group become alcoholics.

When it is either unethical or impractical to ensure random assignment of participants to the treatment and the control groups, researchers can use quasi-experimental research designs. In **quasi-experimental designs,** researchers do whatever they can to provide experimental control, but do not assign participants randomly to groups. When using quasi-experimental designs, researchers cannot infer unequivocally the causes of psychological phenomena.

In contrast to quasi-experimental designs, controlled experimental designs allow researchers to draw causal inferences, which are hypotheses about cause–effect relationships. Causal inferences are not final conclusions, however. In experimental research, we can never be sure that the findings we obtain with a group of participants are not due to chance—purely a random accident of the data—because even very remote possibilities sometimes occur. For example, although your chances of winning a major state lottery by purchasing one ticket are about 1 in 5,200,000 (Siskin, Staller, & Rorvik, 1989), you cannot rule out altogether the possibility of winning. You still may win. It is just unlikely. Your chances of dying in a commercial airline crash are extremely small, but as the unfortunate passengers of the September 2, 1998, Swiss Air Flight 111 from New York to Geneva found out in the moments before their death, their chances are not zero.

The only way for psychologists to be 100% sure that particular findings apply to all people is to conduct experiments on an entire *population* (every single person to whom results are supposed to generalize). Unfortunately, it is rarely practical or even possible to study everyone in a population. Therefore, we usually settle for studying what we believe to be a **representative sample,** a subset of individuals from a population, carefully chosen to represent the population as a whole. Alternatively, we may select a random sample of a population, a sample in which each member of the population has an equal chance of being selected.

As you may imagine, some portions of a total population are easier to study than are other portions. Therefore, some people are under- or

How representative is this sample of people? Psychologists try to obtain representative samples of a population. They statistically analyze data based on samples to get some idea about the population of interest.

quasi-experimental design • a plan for conducting research that resembles a controlled experimental design but that does not ensure the random assignment of participants to the treatment and the control groups

representative sample • a subset of a population, carefully chosen to represent the proportionate diversity of the population

overrepresented in research samples. For example, women and nonwhite persons often are underrepresented (too rarely studied), and men, whites, and college students often are overrepresented (commonly studied) in research, relative to their representation in, say, the world population. Samples drawn largely from easily accessible members of a population are termed samples of *convenience* (Lonner & Berry, 1986).

One way to increase the accuracy of causal inferences about a population, based on a particular sample, is to use *sample statistics*, which are numbers that characterize the sample we have tested with regard to the attributes under investigation. Sample statistics represent data for a portion of the entire population. These statistics help researchers to minimize errors in two ways: First, they offer an accurate and consistent means of describing a sample from a population (e.g., the average annual salaries reported by 30-year-olds in the sample). Second, they provide a consistent basis for inferences about the characteristics of an entire population, based on the characteristics of only a sample.

Descriptive statistics, which describe the particular sample of interest, are usually less difficult to determine than are *inferential statistics,* which suggest conclusions about the sample, relative to the population from which it is drawn. For example, to describe the annual salaries of college graduates versus those of high school graduates who did not graduate from college, we would add up all the annual salaries of each group, divide each total by the number of people in each group, and find the average annual salary for each group. Now, suppose that the average annual salaries of college graduates in our sample were far greater than the annual salaries of high school graduates who did not go on to graduate from college. Based on the salary differences we found, we might infer that, in general, graduates from college on average are later earning larger annual salaries.

These graduates have good reasons to smile: First, they have achieved a very difficult task, and second, their financial prospects are now much brighter as a result of their hard work. According to the U.S. Department of Commerce, in 1992, female college graduates earned an average of almost twice as much as female high school graduates who did not enter college; male college graduates earned an average of more than 1$\frac{1}{2}$ times as much as male high school graduates who did not go on to college.

To increase the accuracy of our inferences, we use inferential statistics. Inferential statistics allow us to draw reasoned conclusions about the population based on the descriptive sample data. Such statistics can help us to evaluate the difference between a treatment group and a control group (or even another treatment group). In particular, we can assess how likely it is that the obtained difference is not caused merely by chance variations in the data.

Researchers frequently use the concept of **statistical significance,** which is a probability level agreed on by convention that helps us decide how likely a result would be to occur if only chance factors were operating. If the statistical probability reaches a particular preset point (usually 5% or 1%), we consider the result statistically significant. Why is this finding statistically significant? Think about it. If there were a 5% or a 1% chance that the results would be obtained if only chance were responsible for them, then would it not be reasonable to conclude that something more than chance is at work? Most people would say that this conclusion indeed would be reasonable. Statistical significance is taken to disconfirm the **null hypothesis,** which is the hypothesis of no difference (or relation) between groups.

For example, psychologist Shelley Taylor (1983) was studying how people cope with the stress of having a life-threatening or long-term illness. She hoped to find out what enables some people to cope with stress better than do other people. She noticed that people who cope well with stress seem to have overly favorable views of themselves, to believe they have more control over their lives than they really have, and often to be unrealistically optimistic about the future. That is, people who have an unrealistically positive outlook actually cope better with the stress of having a serious illness than do people who more realistically appraise themselves and their situation.

Taylor then used inferential statistics to determine whether (a) the positive illusions she observed just happened, by chance, to be related to better adaptability; or (b) the relationship between positive illusions and greater ability to cope was likely to be real—that is, statistically significant. She found that the relationship was statistically significant at the 0.05 ("point oh five") level of probability *(p)*. That level of significance means that there is only a likelihood of 5% or less that her results would be obtained if only chance were operating (i.e., there were no systematic phenomenon). Had her results been statistically significant at the 0.01 level of probability, there would have been only a chance of 1% or less that her findings would be obtained due to chance. The smaller the probability is of obtaining a result when only chance factors are operating, the greater is the statistical significance of the result. In other words, the results are more likely to apply not only in the particular sample that was selected, but in the entire population as well. In addition to their statistical significance, Taylor's findings have *practical significance,* in that they have led to various applications in the treatment of persons facing serious illness and other sources of stress.

Two important limitations affect the interpretation of statistical inferences: First, we can never be absolutely certain that a difference is not due to chance. We can be 99% confident (with a 0.01 level of significance) or even more confident, but we can never be 100% confident (with a 0.00 level). Second, we never can prove the null hypothesis. The null hypothesis is the tentative prediction that there is no difference between groups of participants. That is, we cannot prove that a particular variable has no effect or that there is no difference in the population between groups

statistical significance • characterization of a result as unlikely to be true under the null hypothesis

null hypothesis • a proposed expectation of no difference or relation

exposed to two or more different conditions. We only can say that we have not yet found any effect or any difference.

1.1

Watch commercial television, or listen to commercial radio, and choose an advertising claim that you can study (e.g., "New Head-Ex relieves painful headaches faster than the leading brand of pain reliever"). Think about how to design an experiment to test this claim.

FINDING YOUR WAY

Correlational Designs

Some researchers use **correlational designs,** which are designs in which the researchers observe the degree of association between two or more attributes of participants that occur naturally in the group or groups under study. When researchers use correlational research designs, they cannot draw any unequivocal conclusions regarding causation. In general, a **correlation** means that two or more things are related to each other in some way. In a purely correlational design, researchers try to see how strongly two (or more) existing attributes are associated with each other. *Attributes* refer here to the characteristics of the participants, of the setting, or of the situation being studied. In correlational designs, researchers do not directly control the variables themselves, and the researchers do not randomly assign participants to groups. Instead, the researchers usually observe participants in naturally preexisting groups. For example, the researchers may study the relationship between the attributes of individual participants (e.g., age or sex) and particular behavior (e.g., performance on certain tasks). Researchers often study how the speed and accuracy of performing various tasks differs for males versus females or for adults versus children. They also may study the relationship between behavior and particular situations or settings, such as the performance of particular students in two or more classrooms, or of particular employees in two or more work settings.

When two attributes show some degree of statistical relationship to one another, they are *correlated.* Correlation, as a degree of statistical association between two attributes, is expressed as a number on a scale that ranges from −1 to 0 to +1 (see Figure 1.1):

> +1 indicates a perfect *positive correlation* (as A increases, so does B, and vice versa). Example—the amount of air blown into a balloon in relation to the volume (size) of the balloon (until it pops)
>
> 0 indicates no correlation at all. Example—the colorfulness of a balloon in relation to the volume of the balloon
>
> −1 indicates a perfect *negative correlation* (as A increases, B decreases, and vice versa). Example—the amount of air that seeps out of a balloon in relation to the volume of the balloon

correlational design • a plan for conducting research by assessing the degree of association between two (or more) attributes (characteristics of participants, a setting, or a situation)

correlation • the statistical relationship between two attributes, expressed as a number ranging from −1 (a negative correlation) to 0 (no correlation) to +1 (a positive correlation)

Numbers between 0 and +1 indicate some degree of positive correlation (e.g., 0.7, 0.23, 0.01). Numbers between 0 and −1 indicate some degree of negative correlation (e.g., −0.03, −0.2, −0.75). Perfect correlations of +1

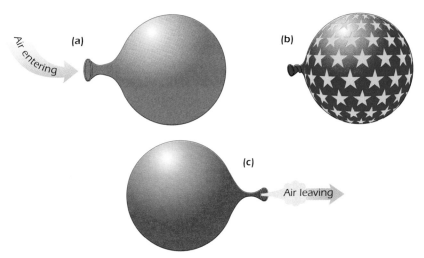

Figure 1.1
Correlation: Positive Versus None Versus Negative
(a) Positive correlation: the amount of air going into a balloon, in relation to the volume (size) of the balloon; (b) no correlation: the colorfulness of a balloon, in relation to the volume of the balloon; (c) negative correlation: the amount of air seeping out of a balloon, in relation to the volume of the balloon.

and −1 are extremely rare. Figure 1.2 shows how correlations appear in graphic form.

For both positive and negative correlations, it usually is difficult to figure out which of two related attributes was the causal attribute. In fact, it may be that neither attribute caused the other one. Instead, perhaps an entirely different attribute caused the relationship. For example, we might gather data about participants' school grades and then give the participants a test of *self-efficacy* (belief in one's own competence) in order to determine whether there is a connection between school grades and self-efficacy. Both variables were having effects before the experiment started, and the experimenters did not (and could not) exercise control over either one. Suppose that we find a correlation between self-efficacy and school grades. We might expect it to be positive in some degree, and it is: Persons with high self-efficacy tend to have better grades in school, and persons with low self-efficacy tend to have poorer grades (Bandura, 1977a, 1996). Does this correlation mean that low self-efficacy causes poor grades, that poor grades cause low self-efficacy, or that both poor grades and low self-efficacy depend on some third variable, which we have not yet identified (such as feelings of rejection in childhood)?

Correlational designs are useful in spotting whether relationships exist and in estimating how strong the relationships are. However, they do not specify exactly what might cause the relationship. Because researchers typically cannot infer causality when they use correlational studies, they generally prefer to use controlled experimental designs whenever possible. Frequently, however, correlational designs are unavoidable. For instance, it would be impossible to design a controlled experiment to study the influence of age on memory. We cannot randomly assign a set of participants to have particular ages. Similarly, ethical considerations would prevent you from randomly assigning participants to engage in dangerous or unhealthful behavior. Several other ethical issues also arise in considering how psychologists conduct research.

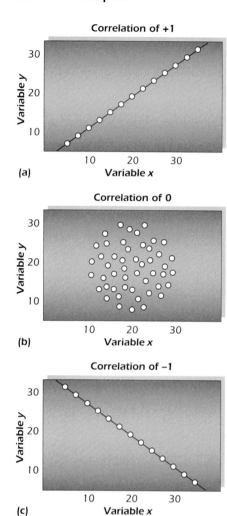

FIGURE 1.2

Graphic Representations of Correlations

These graphs (called scatterplots) show that a given pair of variables may have (a) a positive correlation (i.e., when one variable increases or decreases in value, the value of the other does likewise); (b) no correlation (i.e., the increase or decrease in the value of one variable has no relationship whatsoever to variation in the value of the other variable); or (c) a negative correlation (i.e., when the value of one variable increases, the value of the other decreases, and vice versa).

Sometimes serious errors of interpretation are made on the basis of correlational data. A major national newspaper in the United States carried an article in August of 1998 entitled "Prayer can lower blood pressure." The article claimed that attending religious services lowers blood pressure, and moreover, that it does so more than does listening to religious TV or radio. The article cited a study that noted that people who attended religious services once a week and who prayed or studied the Bible once a day were 40% less likely to have high blood pressure than were people who did not go to church every week and who prayed and studied the Bible less frequently. The article noted that the effect is strongest among African Americans and among people between the ages of 65 and 74. In addition, the authors noted that the study was done in an area of North Carolina that is overwhelmingly Protestant and that there is no way of knowing how far the results would generalize beyond the population in this area. According to the article, the authors believe the study shows that going to religious services is healthy.

Is this conclusion valid, based on the description of the study as provided here? The answer is no. The study shows only a statistical association (correlation) between weekly attendance at church services, Bible study, and prayer, on the one hand, and lower blood pressure, on the other. It is, of course, possible that engaging in religious activity lowers blood pressure, as the article claims. It is also possible, however, that people who engage in religious activities also engage in other activities, not studied, that cause the reduction in blood pressure, such as better eating or reduced use of addictive substances. Or it is possible that the kind of person who would engage in these religious activities is the kind of person who, for whatever reason, would have reduced blood pressure. Or it may be the dedication to religion itself, independent of actual engagement in particular religious activities, that lowers blood pressure. The point is that multiple interpretations are consistent with these data. We do not know that any one or another of these interpretations is correct. Thus it well may be that engaging in organized religious activity lowers blood pressure. But the study as described was not sufficient to show this causal relation. This example shows the value of critical thinking in psychology. The reader needs to apply critical thinking to realize that the data do not support the claims the authors made.

WHAT ETHICAL ISSUES DO PSYCHOLOGISTS FACE?

Psychological researchers constantly must face ethical questions that arise in their research. Almost all research institutions (such as universities) require that researchers get advance approval for their experiments, and special review boards generally check over the plans for research. These boards protect the rights of the people who participate in psychological experiments. Some of the main ethical research issues are deception, confidentiality, and physical or psychological pain.

Sometimes, psychological researchers *deceive* their participants. Usually, when psychologists deceive their participants, they do so by telling the participants before and during the experiment something that is not true. For example, they may say that the true purpose of an experiment is one thing when really it is another.

Why would psychologists try to deceive their own research participants? Generally, when experimenters mislead participants about the purpose of an experiment, they do so in order to get the participants to behave as normally, naturally, and realistically as possible. For some experiments, if participants knew the purpose of the experiment, that knowledge might affect their behavior. After the experiment is over, psychologists always tell the participants the true reason for the research.

Should deception be allowed in psychological research? Some psychologists have argued that it has extremely negative effects (Baumrind, 1985; Kelman, 1982), such as (a) conveying the message that psychologists are liars, (b) sowing the seeds of distrust among people, and (c) causing distress to people who did nothing to deserve to experience such distress. At the same time, some experiments can be done only if a deception is involved.

For example, suppose that you want to study the personality characteristics of people who are helpful. First, you tell your participants the purpose of your experiment, next you give them a personality test, and then you put them in a situation in which they see someone who needs help. Just how normally, naturally, and realistically do you think they will respond?

If, occasionally, psychologists must deceive their participants in order to find out what the psychologists want to know, they also must take two key steps for the benefit of their participants. First, participants in a study are required to give **informed consent** before participating in the research. When participants are asked to give informed consent, they are told (a) what kinds of tasks they may be expected to perform, and (b) what kinds of situations they may expect to face. Participants also must be told that they are free to leave the experiment at any time, without fear of any negative consequences. Informed consent is a necessary part of every study, whether or not there is a deception.

Second, after the research is completed, the participants must be fully debriefed about the research. During *debriefing*, participants are told the true purpose of the experiment, told about any deception that may have been involved, and given the reason for the deception. Most review boards will allow minor deceptions if the research meets three criteria: (a) The proposed research is valuable enough to justify the deception, (b) deception is necessary to fulfill the purpose of the experiment, and (c) the deception is fully explained after the experiment ends. Debriefing is a requirement for all research, regardless of whether or not there has been a deception.

A second major issue in research is **confidentiality,** which is the assurance that information about individual participants will be kept private. The large majority of experiments in psychology are conducted anonymously; participants' names are not associated with their data. Occasionally, however, researchers must keep track of the names attached to the data. For example, research cannot be anonymous when researchers plan to conduct *follow-up work* (in which earlier behavior is linked to later behavior, e.g., when correlating earlier test scores to later grade-point averages). If the research participants are not anonymous, however, experimenters go to great lengths to ensure that the names of participants and their individual data are known only to those persons involved in the investigation who must know the names.

In the past, it was up to individual psychologists to ensure that experimental participants were not exposed to undue physical or psychological discomfort or distress. Nowadays, researchers continue to try to predict whether an experiment possibly might cause any distress, and then they try to reduce that possibility (unless distress itself is the topic being studied).

informed consent • an experimental procedure in which prospective participants are fully informed regarding the general nature of the anticipated treatment procedure and any possible harmful consequences of the treatment

confidentiality • an ethical practice in which researchers ensure the privacy of personal information regarding individual research participants

In addition, however, contemporary research psychologists must obtain the approval of institutional review boards prior to conducting experiments. These institutional review boards generally do not permit studies that may cause any long-lasting pain or harm. Further, if participating in a study might cause short-term pain or distress, participants must be fully informed in advance regarding these possible events.

Animal subjects (participants), of course, cannot give informed consent, and they cannot leave whenever they wish. Nonetheless, most institutions try to protect the health and well-being of animals. The animals must be given all they need in terms of food, shelter, and freedom from harm or discomfort. At the same time, some of our most important discoveries in both medicine and psychology have come from research in which animals were subjected to disease, untested treatments, and the like. The ethical decisions involved in animal research are not easy to make. Review boards and policymakers try to weigh the costs and benefits involved in all research, whether it involves human or animal participants.

The issue of animal participants is particularly troublesome because these participants sometimes are sacrificed at the end of the research in which they are involved. Humans, in contrast, no matter how unpleasant the research may be, do not lose their lives as a result of being research participants. It is therefore especially important that research that involves the loss of life be justified in the most responsible and complete manner possible. The issue remains a contentious one, however, to the point where militant activists have broken into laboratories where animal experiments are conducted. During such break-ins, the militants have destroyed equipment and research journals, as well as "liberating" the animal participants.

Many animal-rights activists strongly feel that animals should never be subjected to scientific experimentation, under any circumstances. In contrast, most scientists believe that as long as animals are provided with the basic resources of food and shelter, and the animals are not subjected to harsh or painful treatment, animal experimentation is justified by the gains in knowledge that result. Do you believe animals should be subjected to experimentation? Why or why not?

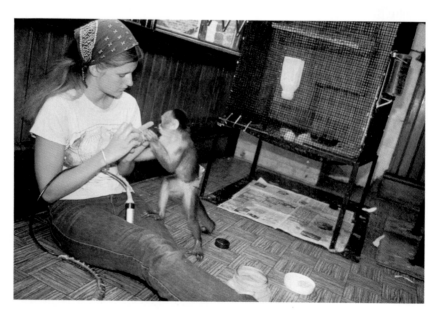

Only since the late 1960s and early 1970s have special review boards become a standard means of evaluating proposed research. In fact, if some of the psychological studies conducted prior to that time were proposed today, they might not pass the scrutiny of contemporary review boards. For example, Stanley Milgram (1974) conducted a series of experiments (see chapter 10) in which participants were falsely led to believe that, by obeying the experimenter, they were inflicting pain on another participant (who was actually a confederate in partnership with the experimenter). Although participants were later debriefed, they nevertheless had to go through their lives realizing that they had been willing to inflict what they thought was great pain on another person. Was such an experiment ethical? Psychologists have differing views. What's yours? Was the benefit of a gain in our understanding of obedience to authority worth the possible psychological costs to the participants? Given the benefit of hindsight, it is now easy to see how researchers should have exerted more care to protect the psychological well-being of participants. Although each of us would prefer to base our knowledge on foresight, we must often rely on what we learn from hindsight. By studying our past, we can more effectively shape our future.

HOW DID PSYCHOLOGY EMERGE AS A SCIENCE?

How do we determine our ethical views and interpret contemporary ideas? In part, what seems reasonable today is shaped by the ideas of both the people around us now and the people who came before us. Most of the i[deas] discussed in this book came from psychologists who are alive now [or recently]. However, to understand what research[ers] ... recently, it will help you to know about the idea[s] ...

Ea[rly Ideas in Psychology]

W[hen] ... dy of psychology begin? Our existing historica[l] ... earliest human efforts to understand the ways in ... feel, and act. In fact, historians now recognize th ... , or think we know, about history reflects the p[eople who] ... have written the accounts of history. Historia[ns] ... nfluenced by the society in which they are writi[ng] ... s. In the field of psychology, the historical r[ecord] ... s were written primarily by Europeans. Theref[ore] ... highlight the contributions of Europeans and t[he contribut]ions of non-Western cultures.

... e the roots of psychology only as far back as an... wever, there were many highly sophisticated civ... [an]cient China) and Africa (e.g., ancient Egypt) for ... ns developed their civilization. Also, many tech... red outside of Europe thousands of years before ... ted these advances or invented them independently. Africans a[nd Asi]ans produced many developments in technology (e.g., agricultural methods and simple machines), medicine (e.g., herbal medications), literature (e.g., legends and a written alphabet), art (e.g., paintings and metalwork), and politics (e.g., hierarchical government and division of labor), among other fields.

At last, centuries later, the seeds of civilization reached the northern shores of the Mediterranean. There, the seeds took root and grew. The ancient Greeks recorded some early ideas about human psychology in their literature. Psychology even takes its name from the ancient Greek myth of *Psyche*.

Although we can learn much about psychology from literature, we usually trace the earliest roots of psychology to two different approaches to human behavior: philosophy and physiology. Persons who study *philosophy* try to understand the general nature of many aspects of the world. They do so mostly through **introspection** (*intro-,* inward, within; *-spect,* look; self-examination of inner ideas and experiences). In particular, the philosopher Plato (ca. 428–348 B.C.) urged his followers to use a **rationalist** (from *ratio,* meaning reason or thought) approach to understanding the world. Rationalists use philosophical analysis (reasoning) in order to understand human behavior, as well as other aspects of the world and people's interactions in the world.

You probably use rationalist approaches in handling many of the everyday situations you face. For instance, when you and a friend disagree regarding where to eat or what to do, you each offer supporting reasons for your choices, and you evaluate each other's arguments according to how well-reasoned they seem to be. You are more likely to go along with your friend's ideas if your friend shows you good reasons for doing so.

An alternative tradition approaches psychology by studying *physiology* (the observation and study of functional processes in living beings). Aristotle (ca. 384–322 B.C.; a biologist as well as a philosopher) disagreed with Plato's rationalist, introspective approach. He preferred to use **empiricism;** that is, he believed that we learn what we want to know by gathering *empirical evidence,* which we can gain through experience and observation. The Aristotelian view is associated with empirical methods for conducting research. We use these methods in laboratories or in the field to observe how people think and behave. Empiricists tend to induce general principles or tendencies, based on observations of many specific instances of a phenomenon.

For example, empiricists might study why people sleep by observing humans and other animals before, during, and after they sleep. From their observations, they might come up with a few ideas about why sleep occurs. They then would devise some experiments to test their ideas. If the tests did not support their ideas, they would reject the ideas, no matter how clever or well-reasoned the ideas seemed to be. A rationalist, in contrast, might either reject the observations, if the ideas seemed well-reasoned, or never make the observations in the first place.

You probably use empirical strategies in solving many of the problems you face. For example, when deciding to buy a car, you probably gather data (e.g., prices and features) about many cars. You even may read consumer reports about the fuel economy, maintenance and repair costs, and safety records of the cars that interest you. When you finally choose a car, your use of empirical data will increase the likelihood that you will be satisfied with your choice.

The conflict between rationalism and empiricism continued in the writings of European and other philosophers who lived long after Plato and Aristotle had died. René Descartes (1596–1650), a French rationalist, argued for the ideas of both mind–body dualism, or the idea that the mind and the body are separate and qualitatively distinct, and of innate (versus acquired) knowledge. Descartes believed that this mind–body dualism is what separates humans from other animals. Descartes also believed,

introspection • self-examination of inner ideas and experiences

rationalist • person who believes that knowledge is most effectively acquired through reasoning

empiricism • approach asserting that knowledge is most effectively acquired through experience and observation

Rationalist Plato (ca. 428–348 B.C.) disagreed with empiricist Aristotle (ca. 384–322 B.C.) regarding the best path to knowledge.

however, that the mind and the body, although separate, interact with each other. In contrast, John Locke (1632–1704), a British empiricist philosopher, believed that the mind and the body are not qualitatively different, that is, different in kind. Thus, Locke did not believe in mind–body dualism. The mind depends on the body, specifically, the experience of the senses, for its information; the body depends on the mind to store processed sense experience for later use. Locke also suggested that the mind is a *tabula rasa* (which means *blank slate* in Latin) at birth. We are born knowing nothing, with no innate knowledge at all. Eventually, German philosopher Immanuel Kant (1724–1804) suggested that we need to use both rationalism and empiricism in our study of the mind and behavior.

Scientific understanding relies on combining both empirical and rational approaches to studying human behavior. We must base our understanding on empirical studies of what is actually happening in the world. However, observations alone are not enough. We also must interpret what we observe in order to understand some of the general principles that govern the observed phenomena. By using rational methods, we can formulate theories and hypotheses that explain what we have observed.

In your everyday experiences, you use both empiricism and rationalism. By observing (empirically) your own actions and those of the people around you, you notice patterns regarding how people think, feel, and act. You probably have noticed that many couples on a first date seem to feel nervous, acting clumsily and speaking awkwardly. You probably also have used reasoning to form your own informal theories regarding why people feel and act as they do on first dates. Both empiricism and rationalism aid you in your study of how people think, feel, and act.

Emergence of Psychology: Diverse Perspectives

From its earliest beginnings, the field of psychology has used both rationalist and empiricist methods in trying to understand the human mind and behavior. Psychologists have forged diverse perspectives and thus followed different pathways in seeking to understand the mind, behavior, and their relationship.

The two main early psychological perspectives were structuralism and functionalism. The goal of **structuralism** was to understand the structure of the mind by studying the mind's parts and contents. Structuralists such as German psychologist Wilhelm Wundt (1832–1920) tried to analyze the contents of the mind into their basic elements. For example, a structuralist analysis of how people perceive a blade of grass might consider the shape, color, texture, and size of each blade. In contrast, **functionalism** focused on the active processes of the human mind and behavior. Whereas structuralists asked, "What are the basic contents [structures] of the human mind?" functionalists such as William James (1842–1910) of Harvard University asked, "What do people do, and how and why do they do it?"

structuralism • the first major school of thought in psychology, which focuses on analyzing the components of the mind, such as particular sensations

functionalism • a school of psychology that focuses on active psychological processes, rather than on passive psychological structures or elements

William James (1842–1910)

A perspective closely tied to functionalism was **pragmatism,** which asserted that knowledge is validated by its usefulness. Pragmatists focused on finding practical uses for the study of the mind and behavior. Thus, pragmatists asked, "What can you do with your knowledge of psychology?" For example, pragmatists might be particularly interested in understanding how to use what we know about perception to help people to perceive situations accurately (e.g., in an air-traffic control tower), rather than in understanding the basic elements people perceive at a given time.

Associationism examined how events or ideas can become associated with one another in the mind, thereby resulting in a form of learning. For example, associationists might seek to discover links between perceptions regarding dangerous situations and particular outcomes of those situations. Some of the main theorists, methods of study, and criticisms of structuralism, functionalism (and pragmatism), and associationism are listed in Table 1.6.

To get an idea of how psychologists from each of these early perspectives might approach a problem differently, suppose that you wanted to understand how you recognize the face of a friend. If you were a structuralist, you might analyze all the elements of your friend's face, including its size, shape, features, colors, and so on. If you were a functionalist or a pragmatist, you might focus on how the process of recognizing a friend's face serves useful purposes for you. If you were an associationist, you might study all the things and events you have associated with the face of your friend, which influence your recognition of your friend's face.

pragmatism • a school of psychology that focuses on the usefulness of knowledge

associationism • a school of psychology that examines how events or ideas can become associated with one another in the mind

TABLE 1.6
Major Early Psychological Perspectives

Perspective	Key methods	Key thinkers	Key criticisms
Structuralism. The nature of consciousness; analysis of consciousness into its constituent components (elementary sensations)	Introspection (self-observation)	Wilhelm Wundt (1832–1920) Edward Titchener (1867–1927)	No means for understanding the processes of thought Lack of application to the world outside the structuralist's laboratory Rigid use of introspective techniques
Functionalism and pragmatism. Mental operations; practical uses of consciousness; the total relationship of the organism to its environment	Whatever works best	William James (1842–1910) John Dewey (1859–1952)	Too vague Too many different techniques Too much emphasis on applications of psychology; not enough study of fundamental issues
Associationism. Mental connections between two events or between two ideas, which lead to forms of learning	Empirical strategies, applied to self-observation and to animal studies	Hermann Ebbinghaus (1850–1909) Edward Lee Thorndike (1874–1949) Ivan Pavlov (1849–1936)	Overly simplistic Doesn't explain well cognition, emotion, or many other psychological processes

WHAT ARE THE MAIN 20TH-CENTURY PERSPECTIVES ON PSYCHOLOGY?

During the 20th century, associationism became much more highly specialized in studying various types of learning through association (e.g., learning as a result of an association between a particular behavior and a particular reward; see chapter 6). An outgrowth of associationism is the 20th-century psychological school of **behaviorism,** which emphasizes the study of observable behavior. Behaviorists such as John Watson (1878–1958) of Johns Hopkins University and later B. F. Skinner (1904–1990) of Harvard University have been especially interested in studying how an event in the environment may be linked to a particular observable behavior. They focus on trying to find ways to study extremely simple events and behaviors, which are much easier to control and to observe than are more complex ones.

As an example of the behaviorist perspective, suppose we train a rat to press a lever or bar, reinforcing (rewarding) the bar-press with food only when a light comes on above the bar. Soon, the rat will learn to press the bar when the light comes on. According to Skinner, the light does not directly elicit the response. Rather, it enables the rat to discriminate a reinforcing situation from a nonreinforcing one. For this reason, Skinner referred to the light as a *discriminative stimulus.* In addition, the stimulus of the light is not necessarily linked with the response of bar-pressing. A rat that has a full stomach may not press the bar in any circumstance. The bar-pressing behavior in this case is voluntary and is thus referred to as an emitted rather than as an elicited response.

Whereas behaviorism takes the whole of human experience and separates it into distinct behaviors, linked to particular events, **Gestalt psychology** emphasizes the importance of seeing certain psychological phenomena (such as anxiety or depression) as wholes, which Gestalt psychologists believe should not and cannot fruitfully be taken apart. To Gestaltists, "the whole [of a psychological phenomenon] differs from the sum of its parts." That is, behaviorists approached psychology *analytically* (breaking a whole psychological phenomenon into various elements), whereas Gestaltists approached it *holistically* (as a whole, without breaking it into parts).

Gestalt psychology is usually traced to the work of German psychologist Max Wertheimer (1880–1943), who collaborated with compatriots Kurt Koffka (1886–1941) and Wolfgang Köhler (1887–1968) to form this new school of psychology. The Gestaltists applied their framework to many areas of psychology. For example, they proposed that problem solving cannot be explained simply in terms of automatic responses to stimuli or to elementary sensations. Instead, new insights often emerge in problem solving; people can devise entirely new ways of seeing problems, ones that are not merely recombinations of old ways of seeing problems.

Another school of psychology, **cognitivism,** uses both analytic and holistic approaches to understanding how people think. To cognitivists such as Ulric Neisser (b. 1928) of Cornell University, even psychological phenomena such as depression and anxiety may be better understood by considering people's thoughts and their thought processes. For instance, cognitivistic treatments for anxiety and depression focus on changing maladaptive thought patterns to more adaptive ones. Cognitivists primarily use experimental methods, but they also use various other methods, such as case studies and tests, in their efforts to understand how and why people think as they do.

behaviorism • a school of psychology that focuses entirely on the association between the environment and emitted behavior

Gestalt psychology • (pronounced "gess-TAHLT") a school of psychology holding that psychological phenomena are best understood when viewed as organized, structured wholes, rather than when analyzed into numerous components

cognitivism • a school of psychology that underscores the importance of perception, learning, and thought as bases for understanding much of human behavior

Mary Whiton Calkins (1863–1930) may be considered a forerunner of cognitivism. In 1913, she wrote an article criticizing Watson's behaviorist approach to psychology and suggested that the study of the human mind was essential.

Whereas cognitivists may use almost any approach to study the phenomena of human thinking, researchers in the field of **psychobiology** (also termed *biological psychology, biopsychology,* or *physiological psychology*) may examine almost any psychological phenomenon by focusing on the physiological foundations underlying human thoughts, feelings, and actions. Psychobiologists interested in anxiety or depression would look for biological changes in the brain that might underlie these psychological states.

A related approach is that of *evolutionary psychology,* which seeks to explain behavior in terms of organisms' evolved adaptations to the changing environment. For example, evolutionary psychologists might seek to explain why people reason better when they need to detect cheaters. They would argue that detection of cheaters was necessary for survival over the course of evolutionary time (Cosmides, 1989). As another example, certain sex differences between women and men are explained in terms of the different challenges women and men have faced over evolutionary time and of how men and women might have adapted differentially to meet these challenges. Men, for example, can impregnate many women in a short period of time, whereas women can give birth to only about one child per year during their reproductive years. In general, those individuals who met these challenges over the course of evolutionary time were more likely to survive long enough to reproduce and pass their genes (hereditary material) on to subsequent generations. The result is that individuals of the present generation still are likely to show in their behavior the adaptations that worked for extended periods of time in the distant past.

psychobiology • a branch of psychology that seeks to understand behavior through studying anatomy and physiology, especially of the brain

Sigmund Freud (1856–1939) developed the first and most influential psychodynamic theory. His daughter, Anna Freud (1895–1982), also became an influential psychodynamic psychologist.

One of the best-known approaches to psychology has biological origins. Early in the 20th century, a *neurologist* (a medical doctor who treats ailments of the brain and nervous system) came up with a very complex and wide-reaching theory based on his study of patients in his medical practice. The neurologist was Sigmund Freud (1856–1939), and his theory of human motivation, personality, and behavior is **psychodynamic psychology.** The clinical practice of Freud's psychodynamic theory is *psychoanalysis,* which is still being practiced by a number of psychiatrists and other psychotherapists today. Freudian theory and therapy emphasize the importance of unconscious forces that influence human motivation and behavior.

In contrast, **humanistic psychology** emphasizes conscious rather than unconscious experiences and psychological processes. Humanistic psychologists such as Carl Rogers (1902–1987) have emphasized that humans have free will and the ability to fulfill their great human potential. Whereas psychodynamic psychologists might treat anxiety and depression by focusing on unconscious forces underlying these psychological states, humanistic psychologists would focus on helping the individual to tap her or his own inner potentials for change, for self-healing, and for creating a sense of well-being.

Yet another perspective emphasizes an appreciation of how humans fulfill their great potential in a variety of ways, depending on the context in which they find themselves: According to **cultural psychology,** human thoughts, feelings, and actions depend largely on the cultural context in

psychodynamic psychology • a school of psychology that emphasizes the importance of (a) conflicting unconscious mental processes and (b) early childhood experiences

humanistic psychology • a school of psychology that emphasizes human potential, as guided by holistic approaches to conscious experiences, rather than analytic approaches to unconscious experience

cultural psychology • a school of psychology that emphasizes the importance of cultural context in the study of the human mind and behavior

Carl Rogers (1902–1987)

Psychologist Kenneth Clark devoted a major portion of his career to studying how schools could be improved in ways that serve minority schoolchildren.

which people find themselves, particularly their culture (e.g., their social patterns and beliefs) and their gender (the social roles they assume, based on whether they are male or female). Cultural psychologists observe that the way in which people express depression and anxiety depends on the social context in which people live and on the social roles they assume. Similarly, the causes of people's feelings of anxiety and depression vary, depending on their social contexts and their social roles.

Cultural psychology makes an important contribution in helping us understand conflicts in the world that, viewed from the outside, seem not to make much sense. For example, many people wonder why Israelis and Palestinians cannot just sit down at a table and resolve their differences. Rouhana and Bar-Tal (1998) have pointed out, however, that conflicts between ethnic groups that take place at a national level have characteristics that make these conflicts particularly difficult to resolve. For example, what in other societies might seem to be wholly intellectual issues quickly can become politically loaded in societies marred by conflict. Furthermore, because such conflicts tend to be long-standing, the animosity that evolves from them often is very deep-rooted and accompanied by severe prejudice. The conflicts also tend to be central to the way people define themselves. Even worse, each side tends to view their differences as irreconcilable, and to view one side's gain as the other side's loss. So, before negotiations even begin, the seeds of discord are well-implanted and growing furiously.

Table 1.7 summarizes some of the main theorists, methods of study, and criticisms of the 20th-century psychological perspectives. In the following chapter, we explore the basics of the psychobiological perspective.

TABLE 1.7
Major 20th-Century Psychological Perspectives

Perspective	Key methods	Key developers	Key criticisms
Behaviorism. Analysis of observable behavior without inferences about mental events	Experiments; often focus on animal subjects	John Watson B. F. Skinner	Doesn't address internal causes of behavior; often slights thoughts and emotions Doesn't explain many aspects of human behavior
Gestalt psychology. Holistic study of behavior; behavior not merely an additive sum of parts	Experiments and observation (focus on whole context, not on controlling separate variables)	Max Wertheimer Kurt Koffka Wolfgang Köhler	Lack of evidence to support theories Lack of experimental control Lack of precise definitions
Cognitivism. Perspective describing how people acquire, store, and use knowledge	Experiments and naturalistic observation	Herbert Simon Ulric Neisser	Many aspects of human behavior (e.g., social and cultural contexts) tend to be neglected
Psychobiology. Biological bases of learning, thought, and emotion; particular emphasis on the workings of the brain and nervous system	Experiments and case studies; examination of brains of people experiencing mental disorders	Roger Sperry and his students	Not all aspects of human behavior are now subject to investigation via biopsychological study; many aspects may not now be studied ethically in humans, and animal investigations sometimes may not generalize to humans
Psychodynamic psychology. Theory of personality development and psychotherapy; focus on unconscious experience in personal development	Psychoanalysis, based on clinical case studies	Sigmund Freud Neo-Freudians (e.g., Carl Jung, Erik Erikson)	Overreliance on case-study research; too little supporting evidence; cannot be disconfirmed Overly comprehensive
Humanistic psychology. Focus on free will and self-actualization of human potential, and on conscious rather than unconscious experience	Clinical practice and case-study observations; holistic rather than analytic approach	Abraham Maslow Carl Rogers	Theories not particularly comprehensive Limited research base
Cultural psychology. Study of how people think, feel, and act in the cultural context in which they find themselves	Naturalistic observations and surveys of people within various cultural and social contexts	Patricia Greenfield Michael Cole	Not enough emphasis on experimentation Not enough emphasis on the role of biological influences on the human mind and behavior Not enough emphasis on individuals and on individual differences

These perspectives are applied throughout a wide range of areas in psychology. To give you an idea of just how wide this range is, note in Table 1.8 a complete list of the divisions of the American Psychological Association. As you can see, psychologists study an incredibly wide range of issues, from general psychology to specializations such as experimental and social psychology to interests such as international psychology and peace psychology. If the topics dealt with by even a few of the divisions interest you, then perhaps the study of psychology is for you.

TABLE 1.8

American Psychological Association—Divisions

Division 1	Division of General Psychology
Division 2	Division on the Teaching of Psychology
Division 3	Division of Experimental Psychology
Division 5	Division on Evaluation, Measurement, and Statistics
Division 6	Division of Behavioral Neuroscience and Comparative Psychology
Division 7	Division on Developmental Psychology
Division 8	Society for Personality and Social Psychology—A Division of the APA
Division 9	The Society for the Psychological Study of Social Issues—A Division of the APA
Division 10	Division of Psychology and the Arts
Division 12	Division of Clinical Psychology
Division 13	Division of Consulting Psychology
Division 14	The Society for Industrial and Organizational Psychology, Inc.—A Division of the APA
Division 15	Division of Educational Psychology
Division 16	Division of School Psychology
Division 17	Division of Counseling Psychology
Division 18	Division of Psychologists in Public Service
Division 19	Division of Military Psychology
Division 20	Division of Adult Development and Aging
Division 21	Division of Applied Experimental and Engineering Psychology
Division 22	Division of Rehabilitation Psychology
Division 23	Society for Consumer Psychology
Division 24	Division of Theoretical and Philosophical Psychology

(Continued)

TABLE 1.8
American Psychological Association—Divisions *(Continued)*

Division 25	Division for the Experimental Analysis of Behavior
Division 26	Division of the History of Psychology
Division 27	The Society for Community Research and Action: The Division of Community Psychology of the APA
Division 28	Division of Psychopharmacology and Substance Abuse
Division 29	Division of Psychotherapy
Division 30	Division of Psychological Hypnosis
Division 31	Division of State Psychological Association Affairs
Division 32	Division of Humanistic Psychology
Division 33	Division on Mental Retardation and Developmental Disabilities
Division 34	Division of Population and Environmental Psychology
Division 35	Division of the Psychology of Women
Division 36	Psychology and Religion
Division 37	Division of Child, Youth, and Family Services
Division 38	Division of Health Psychology
Division 39	Division of Psychoanalysis
Division 40	Division of Clinical Neuropsychology
Division 41	American Psychology-Law Society—A Division of the APA
Division 42	Division of Psychologists in Independent Practice
Division 43	Division of Family Psychology
Division 44	The Society for the Psychological Study of Lesbian, Gay, and Bisexual Issues
Division 45	Society for the Psychological Study of Ethnic Minority Issues—A Division of the APA
Division 46	Division of Media Psychology
Division 47	Division of Exercise and Sport Psychology
Division 48	Division of Peace Psychology
Division 49	Division of Group Psychology and Group Psychotherapy
Division 50	Addictions
Division 51	Society for the Psychological Study of Men and Masculinity
Division 52	Division of International Psychology

The Solution to

The Case of the Messy Roommate

Pedro remembers reading about representative samples in experiments while reading chapter 1 of his *Pathways to Psychology* book. Pedro realizes that the solution proposed by Phil represented the wrong path. The reason is that the test of the other roommates' views was poorly conceived. For one thing, they asked only three individuals for their opinion. More importantly, however, the sample asked may not have been *representative*. Phil chose the three roommates and Pedro could not be assured that the roommates in that particular room were truly representative of other first-year students.

After reading the chapter, Pedro decided to check out the room above his room with Phil. Sure enough, it was a mess. Pedro knew from having visited many other rooms that many rooms were quite neat. Whether intentionally or by accident, Phil had chosen a room full of messy roommates. They, of course, represented their own messy point of view.

Pedro insisted that they ask first-year students in some other rooms what they thought, and most of them did indeed end up supporting Pedro. Phil admitted he was wrong but never said how he had chosen the first group of three. Phil reformed at least partially, enough for Pedro to get through the year and find himself another roommate the subsequent year.

Summary

What Is Psychology? 4

1. *Psychology,* the study of the human mind and behavior, is both a *natural science* and a *social science.* Psychologists try to understand how people think, learn, perceive, feel, interact with others, and understand themselves.

Why Do Psychologists Do What They Do? 8

2. Psychologists seek to describe, explain, predict, and perhaps even sometimes control the human mind and behavior. Often, particular research, however, addresses only one or two of these goals. Scientific research is cumulative, with new studies building on old ones.

Analytical and Other Forms of Higher Order Thinking in Psychology 12

3. Psychologists need to think critically, avoiding such informal fallacies as irrelevant conclusion, composition, personalization, false cause, and ad hominem arguments. Creative and practical thinking, as well as analytical thinking, are important to psychology.

How Do Psychologists Conduct Research? 14

4. Psychologists use various research methods, such as (a) *tests and surveys;* (b) *case studies;* (c) *naturalistic observation;* and (d) *experiments.*
5. In an *experiment,* a researcher studies *cause–effect relations* by controlling one or more *independent*

variables in order to observe the effects on one or more *dependent variables*. Ideally, an experiment should include a *control group* to ensure that differences in results are due to the experimental treatment and not to irrelevant group differences.

How Do Psychologists Determine Cause and Effect?   19

6. Because generally we cannot conduct studies on whole populations, we use *sample statistics* (numbers that characterize the sample we have assessed), generally based on the assumption that the researcher has found a *random sample* of the population under study.
7. We are never able to prove the *null hypothesis* (which states that there is no difference between two or more groups under study). Even so, we can demonstrate that a particular difference has reached a given level *of statistical significance*—that is, the difference is unlikely to have occurred if the null hypothesis were true.
8. Psychological researchers try to draw *causal inferences* (conclusions about cause–effect relationships). *Controlled experimental designs* are better suited to drawing such inferences than are *quasi-experimental designs,* which lack at least one experimental characteristic, or than are *correlational studies,* which show associations between variables.

What Ethical Issues Do Psychologists Face?   28

9. Scientists, including psychologists, must address questions of ethical research procedures. Most questions center on whether human participants or animal subjects are treated fairly. Research institutions today have standard policies that require both *informed consent* and *debriefing*. Most institutions also have set up boards of review to study and approve proposed research; some government agencies also monitor research practices, especially as they pertain to animals.

How Did Psychology Emerge as a Science?   31

10. By studying the historical development in issues of *philosophy* and *physiology,* we can trace the history of the foundations of psychology. Some of the most important questions in the history of psychology are whether *rationalist* or *empiricist* methods are the better way to gain knowledge. In fact, a combination of both methods typically works best.
11. Psychology traces its roots back to archaic Greece. In fact, the word *psychology* (the study of the mind and behavior) is derived from the Greek word *psyche.*
12. The ancient Greek philosophers Plato and Aristotle raised issues that continue to be discussed today. Plato was a *rationalist,* emphasizing the use of reasoning as a way to find knowledge. Aristotle emphasized the world we can see and touch as the route to reality and truth, which made him an *empiricist.* In contrast to Plato, Aristotle believed that knowledge is learned through interactions with and direct observation of the environment. Descartes and Locke continued the argument, and Kant offered a synthesis of these diverging points of view.
13. Over time, psychologists have approached the study of the mind and behavior from different perspectives. At first, *structuralists* tried to analyze consciousness into its constituent components in terms of elementary sensations.
14. *Functionalists* tried to understand what people do and why. A similar outlook was adopted by *pragmatists,* who focus on how to apply knowledge to practice.
15. *Associationism* examines how events or ideas can become associated with one another in the mind to result in a form of learning.

What Are the Main 20th-Century Perspectives on Psychology?   36

16. An offshoot of associationism, *behaviorism* is based on the belief that the science of psychology should deal only with observable behavior.
17. *Gestalt psychology* is based on the notion that the whole differs from the sum of its parts.
18. *Cognitivism* emphasizes the importance of understanding how people think.
19. The basis of *psychodynamic psychology* is that many of the thoughts and feelings that motivate behavior are unconscious.
20. *Psychobiology* studies how human physiology interacts with human behavior.
21. *Humanistic psychology* studies how people consciously fulfill their inner potential.
22. *Cultural psychology* studies how people think, feel, and act in relation to the social context in which they find themselves.

Choose the best answer to complete each sentence.

1. Many psychologists study the behavior of college students
   (a) simply because it is relatively easy to do so.
   (b) because the behavior of college students is typical of that of most intelligent people.
   (c) because the behavior of college students offers a good role model of how people should behave.
   (d) because college students are much more cooperative with experimenters than are other research participants.

2. The four main goals of psychological research are
   (a) description, explanation, control, and verifiability.
   (b) description, assessment, explanation, and manipulation.
   (c) description, assessment, prediction, and manipulation.
   (d) description, explanation, control, and prediction.

3. When psychologists say that a particular research finding is statistically significant, they mean that the finding is
   (a) going to be very important in the field of interest.
   (b) unlikely to have occurred if the null hypothesis were true.
   (c) going to lead to important psychological treatments.
   (d) going to have many widespread applications outside of the psychological laboratory.

4. An independent variable is
   (a) the only variable of interest.
   (b) a variable that is independently verified.
   (c) a variable with a value that depends on the value of the dependent variable.
   (d) a variable that is manipulated by the experimenter.

5. When psychologists notice that two characteristics always seem to go together, they
   (a) usually are able to say which characteristic caused the other one to occur.
   (b) cannot come to any conclusions regarding causality unless they get more information.

(c) determine that the characteristics are multiplicatively correlated.
(d) determine that the characteristics are inversely correlated.

6. An experimental condition differs from a control condition, in that
   (a) participants in the control condition stay the same while participants in the experimental condition vary.
   (b) the experimental treatment is applied in the experimental condition but not in the control condition.
   (c) the experimenter controls the control condition but does not control the experimental condition.
   (d) the treatment varies in the control condition while the treatment stays constant in the experimental condition.

7. Scientists are better able to draw conclusions about the effectiveness of a particular treatment when they
   (a) study people who are not exposed to the experimental treatment, as well as people who are exposed to it.
   (b) expose a group of people to the treatment and then carefully study all of the effects of the treatment only on those people.
   (c) study female volunteers who receive the treatment and compare them with male volunteers who do not receive the treatment.
   (d) give the treatment to people who ask for the treatment and to people who do not ask for it, and then they compare the treatment results for the two groups.

Answer each of the following questions by filling in the blank with an appropriate word or phrase.

8. _____ is a research method in which a participant's behavior is observed in its natural environment.

9. Scientists generate _____, which are predictions or tentative proposals regarding expectations for research outcomes.

10. An _____ is a controlled investigation in which a researcher studies the effects of one or more variables on one or more other variables.

11. An example of a _____ design would be a study examining whether certain personality variables are correlated with criminal behavior.

Match the following theories to their main emphases:

12. Structuralism
13. Functionalism

(a) Functions of thought
(b) Mental connections between two events or between two ideas, which lead to forms of learning

14. Pragmatism

(c) Analysis of conscious experience into its constituent components (elementary sensations)

15. Associationism

(d) The workings of the brain and nervous system, as they affect thoughts, emotions, and actions

16. Behaviorism

(e) Theory of personality development and psychotherapy focusing on unconscious experiences in personal development

17. Gestalt psychology
18. Cognitivism

(f) Practical uses of psychological research
(g) Analysis of observable behavior without considering inferences about mental events

19. Psychobiology

(h) Self-actualization of human potential, based primarily on conscious rather than unconscious experience

20. Psychodynamic psychology

(i) Understanding how people think in order to understand human behavior

21. Humanistic psychology

(j) Holistic study of behavior, rather than of an additive sum of parts

22. Cultural psychology

(k) The cultural contexts in which people think, feel, and act

---

Answers

1. a, 2. d, 3. b, 4. d, 5. b, 6. b, 7. a, 8. Naturalistic observation, 9. hypotheses, 10. experiment, 11. correlational, 12. c, 13. a, 14. f, 15. b, 16. g, 17. j, 18. i, 19. d, 20. e, 21. h, 22. k.

Pathways to Understanding

1. If you could observe naturalistically a psychological phenomenon that differs across cultures, what would you study, and in what cultures would you study it? Why would this phenomenon interest you?

2. If you were heading an ethics committee charged with deciding which experiments should be permitted, what questions about the experiments would you want to have answered?

3. How did early psychological perspectives pave the way for 20th-century perspectives?

Chandra is furious with Tom; she has discovered that Tom has been cheating on her.

Chandra wastes no time dealing with the situation. That afternoon, when Tom comes by her office as usual for lunch, she confronts him right away. She tells Tom that she knows he has been seeing Sharlene, from the marketing department, when he was supposed to have been in meetings and that she now knows precisely what kind of meetings he has been attending. She reminds Tom that she has not seen anyone else in the 2 years they have been going together and that they were supposed to have an understanding that their relationship was exclusive. Chandra also tells Tom that he either can end his relationship with Sharlene, and anyone else he may be seeing, right away, or she is through with him.

CHAPTER 2

BIOLOGICAL PSYCHOLOGY

Tom looks flustered at first. Chandra expects Tom to lie but, to her surprise, he quickly admits to having seen Sharlene. He apologizes and agrees to break off the relationship with Sharlene, who, he assures Chandra, is not important to him. Tom explains to Chandra that she really should not blame him, though. He takes an introductory psychology course 2 nights a week and he has just read that there is an evolutionary difference between men and women. According to what he has read, men and women have different strategies for maximizing their self-interest. Because men can get many women pregnant quickly, it is to be expected that they will seek out multiple women. Women, on the other hand, can give birth to only one child every year or so, with the result that they tend to be more selective and less likely to go out seeking other men. The result is that it is understandable that men sometimes stray. Our ancestors from the distant past lived in societies where men, but not women, were allowed to stray. Tom thus emphasizes that although he immediately will break off with Sharlene, it is important that Chandra understand that "men are men," and that what has happened to him happens to lots of guys and conceivably could happen again.

The argument does not sound right to Chandra but it does seem to fit in with evolutionary theory, which she remembers reading about in her college biology class. She does not want to lose Tom, and does not know what to say in any case, so she drops the matter.

Think about this while you read chapter 2. Is Tom's argument valid? Is Tom using evolutionary theory in an appropriate way, or is he treading down the wrong pathway?

2

*P*sychobiology is the study of the relation between thought, feelings, and behavior on the one hand, and human anatomy and physiology on the other. *Anatomy* is the study of structures of the body and of the interrelationships among these structures; *structures* are the organized physical parts of the body. *Physiology* is the study of the functions and processes of the body; *functions* are processes that serve useful purposes. Thus, psychobiologists study anatomy and physiology, as well as evolution and genetics, in order to discover the biological bases for how we think, feel, and act.

WHAT IS OUR BIOLOGICAL HISTORY?

One way of studying the biological bases of the mind and of behavior is to investigate heredity and evolution: How do your distinctive inherited characteristics affect what you do, think, and feel, and how does our shared human inheritance affect our common human actions, thoughts, and feelings?

Evolutionary Theory

Evolutionary theory describes changes in physiology, thought, emotions, and behavior across many generations of individuals. Organisms can evolve and diversify along many different pathways. In 1859, Charles Darwin (1809–1882) proposed that organisms develop and change over time. These changes occur through **natural selection,** sometimes called "survival of the fittest." In natural selection, at any given time, some members of some species may be able to cope with the conditions in the environment better than do others. The individuals who can cope most effectively are most likely to survive and to reproduce most often, as compared with individuals who are less fit. In contrast, the individuals who are not as fit may die sooner and may produce fewer offspring. In fact, if all members of a particular species are unsuited to the environment, the entire species may become extinct. Diversity of these individuals is thus important for the species' survival. Ultimately, more fit individuals and their descendants are selected by nature for survival, hence, the term *natural selection.*

Diversity ensures that at least some organisms of a given kind will be able to cope with changes in the environment. Diversity does not always work to the advantage of humans. For example, serious diseases such as AIDS continue to plague humankind because the microorganisms that cause these illnesses are so diverse. Medications that kill off most of the viruses that cause AIDS typically fail to work on some of the viruses, perhaps only a small number. But as the viruses that are not resistant to the medications die off, the ones that are resistant grow in numbers until eventually they come to predominate. At the same time, there are some humans who seem to have a natural resistance to the HIV virus that causes AIDS. Should the epidemic become even more widespread, the descendants of these individuals will be at an advantage in the struggle for survival.

The key to natural selection is the relationship between individuals and the environment in which they are trying to survive (and to produce offspring). For example, an individual who was a relatively slow runner

In the late 19th century, a dark and a light variety of moths living in the forests of England illustrated the principle of natural selection. When industrial pollution blackened the forests, the darker moths were less visible to the birds that ate them, so they increased in number. The lighter moths became fewer in number because they were so easily seen against the sooty trees. Recently, however, air-pollution controls have reduced the amount of soot on the trees, and the light moth is making a comeback.

but who had terrific rock-climbing skills would have been unlikely to survive in an environment with large, open plains, in which the ability to run from predators was crucial. On the other hand, that same individual would probably have survived quite well in a very mountainous environment, in which a less skilled climber might have been more likely to fall while trying to climb away from predators on rocky cliffs. Thus, natural selection might lead to the survival of some individuals, with particular characteristics, in one kind of environment but to different individuals, with different characteristics, in another kind of environment. Natural selection affects only those characteristics that help or hinder the individual in surviving until adulthood, finding a mate, and ultimately producing offspring.

Changes in environments spur on evolution. Volcanoes build new land areas, weather changes cause droughts and floods, and so on. These changes lead to changes in the natural selection of plants and animals that will survive in the environment. If a given animal's food source dies away, and the animal cannot find a new food source, that animal will not survive. These constant changes in the environment lead to changes in the natural selection of which individuals will survive. According to Darwin, the changing natural selection of individuals explains evolutionary changes in species, which are now well-documented through fossils.

How have Darwin's ideas about natural selection come to influence psychology? For one thing, the study of evolution has made us more aware of how the human brain affects human behavior. Throughout human evolution, our brains have provided us with greater ability to control what we do voluntarily. Over time, our actions have become more voluntary and less instinctual than the actions of other animals.

Evolutionary theory provides a wonderful, unified framework for understanding many diverse phenomena in psychology. For example, evolutionary frameworks have been applied to the study of phenomena as diverse as intelligence and altruism (helping behavior). Why should anyone ever be altruistic, given that one would seem to be sacrificing one's own self-interest for the sake of others? According to George Williams (1966) and Robert Trivers (1971), there are good reasons. Williams pointed out

natural selection • evolutionary mechanism by which organisms have developed and changed, based on what is commonly called the "survival of the fittest"

that relationships between organisms, including humans, tend to be characterized by reciprocity; we help others in the expectation of being helped. In mutual negotiations, those who reciprocate the kind behavior of others tend to fare the best in the negotiations (A. Rapaport, 1960). Moreover, people who are perceived as selfish often find themselves with few friends and at risk of making enemies, which is clearly not to the individual's advantage in the struggle for survival. An interesting implication of this view, therefore, is that it is being perceived as altruistic, rather than actually being altruistic, that leads to positive outcomes for the individual (R. Wright, 1994).

A number of theorists have suggested that not just organisms, but also ideas may evolve along the lines of a mechanism whereby the "fittest" survive, namely, those that are best adapted to the cultural milieu in which they are proposed and spread (Campbell, 1960; Dawkins, 1989; Perkins, 1995, Simonton, 1995). As cultures change, so might the ideas that are viewed as most adaptive.

Genetics

A key mechanism by which natural selection may occur relates to *genetics,* the study of inherited variations among individuals. Natural selection can occur as a result of genetic *mutation* (a sudden permanent structural change in an inherited characteristic). Genetic mutation permits entirely new characteristics to appear between one generation and the next. In essence, they create a new pathway along which organisms can evolve. Mutations may arise as a result of exposure to radiation, infectious agents (e.g., bacteria or viruses), harmful chemicals, or various other environmental influences. Most mutations are harmful and lead to reduced adaptability to the environment. Occasionally, though, a mutation helps an individual adapt, in which case it favors that individual over others in the struggle for survival. Human intelligence, for example, has developed in part as a result of mutations that have accumulated over the ages.

Genetic mutations occur in the **genes,** the physiological building blocks through which we inherit particular characteristics. Genes are parts of **chromosomes,** rod-shaped bodies containing many genes that are composed of DNA (deoxyribonucleic acid). Humans have 23 pairs of chromosomes, for a total of 46. Almost all of the cells of your body have each of these 23 pairs of chromosomes.

Our genes determine our *genetic traits,* distinctive inherited characteristics that govern everything from our eye color to our blood type. We receive our genes, and therefore our traits, when we are conceived by our parents. The information contained in a specific pair of genes an individual receives for a given trait forms that individual's **genotype** for that trait.

Some genes dominate other genes. Thus, when two different genes are paired, the dominant (stronger) genes appear in an individual's **phenotype,** which is the observable outcome of heredity and which is subject to environmental influences. Whenever a gene for a **dominant trait** (a strong attribute; e.g., brown eyes) is paired with a gene for a **recessive trait** (a weaker, dominated characteristic; e.g., blue eyes), the dominant trait shows up in the phenotype, but the recessive trait does not. That is, when both a dominant gene and a recessive gene are present, the phenotype (the developed physical organism) shows only the dominant trait.

Figure 2.1 illustrates how dominant and recessive traits may be expressed. The first chart (a) shows the possible outcomes when a parent with brown eyes (a phenotype of brown eyes and a genotype with two

---

gene • a basic physiological building block for the hereditary transmission of genetic traits in all life forms

chromosomes • rod-shaped bodies that contain innumerable genes; occur in pairs

genotype • the genetic makeup for inherited traits, which is not subject to environmental influence (except in cases of genetic mutation)

phenotype • the expression of an inherited trait, based on the dominant expression of the trait in the genotype and also subject to environmental influence

dominant trait • the stronger expression of a genetic trait, which appears in the phenotype of an organism when the genotype comprises two dominant expressions of a trait or a dominant and a recessive expression of a trait

recessive trait • the weaker expression of a genetic trait in a pair of traits, which appears in the phenotype when the genotype comprises two recessive expressions of the trait

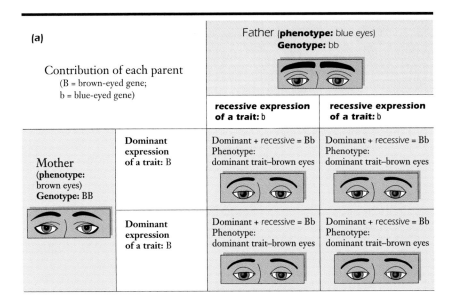

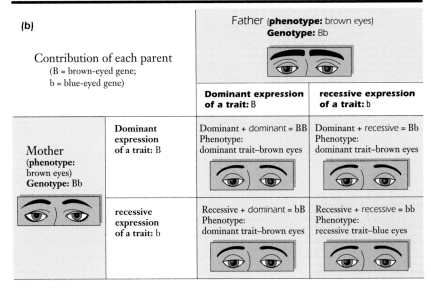

FIGURE 2.1

Inherited Characteristics: Eye Color

(a) What are the possible outcomes when a brown-eyed parent (genotype BB) and a blue-eyed parent (genotype bb) produce children? (b) What are the possible outcomes when two brown-eyed parents with mixed genotypes (Bb) produce children? What are the possible genotypes and phenotypes of the children of these couples?

dominant genes for brown eyes, BB) produces children with a parent who has blue eyes (a phenotype of blue eyes and a genotype with two recessive genes for blue eyes, bb). As the chart shows, all the potential offspring appear to have brown eyes, but all of them have a *mixed genotype* (containing both a dominant and a recessive gene for a given trait) for eye color (Bb). In other words, only the dominant genes (for brown eyes) express themselves in the phenotype, but the recessive genes are lurking in the background of the genotype, even though they are not expressed.

As Figure 2.1(b) shows, when two parents with a mixed genotype (but a phenotype for brown eyes) produce children, any of three outcomes is

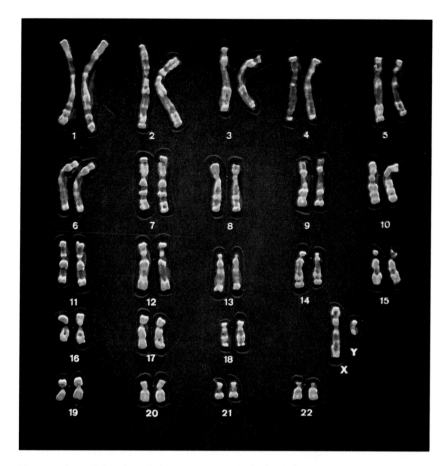

Humans have 23 pairs of chromosomes, including the pair that determines each person's sex.

possible for each of their children: a phenotype for brown eyes with a BB pure genotype (1 chance in 4), a phenotype for blue eyes with a bb pure genotype (1 chance in 4), or a phenotype for brown eyes with a mixed genotype (Bb or bB; 2 chances in 4, or 1 chance in 2).

In fact, the expression of hereditary characteristics is more complicated than this description might lead you to believe. (For instance, more than one gene may be involved in the expression of a given trait.) Moreover, a single genotype can be expressed as a range of phenotypes. For example, a person's height is highly *heritable*—that is, for a given environment, individual differences among people are due largely to differences in genes—but particular individuals may show a range of heights, depending on other factors such as nutrition. Genes help to determine phenotypes, but the environment also influences the expression of our inherited traits.

Many psychologists today are interested in the study of behavior genetics, a branch of psychology that attempts to account for behavior (and often particular psychological characteristics and phenomena, such as intelligence; see e.g., Plomin, 1989, 1997) by attributing behavior in part to the influence of particular genes and their combinations. Behavior geneticists realize, however, that behavior always develops in interaction with the environment. For example, there is substantial evidence in support of a genetic basis for handedness, the preference a person shows for using the right hand, the left hand, or both. But genetic factors alone cannot adequately account for variations in handedness across cultures (J. W. Berry,

Poortinga, Segall, & Dasen, 1992): Some cultures force individuals to use the right hand in activities such as writing; others do not.

Human heredity is highly complex, and many variables influence how heredity is expressed. Therefore, researchers have trouble controlling all the variables necessary to study it effectively in humans. Genetically identical twins provide an effective way to study genetic influences on our biological and psychological makeup. Because identical twins have an identical genetic inheritance, any differences between them can be attributed to environmental influences. Based on twin studies and other evidence, scientists have concluded that both our heredity and our environment are important, and both work together to influence the human mind and behavior.

Studies of twins have revealed that substantially more of human behavior is inherited than previously thought. One way to investigate the effects of genes is through the study of identical versus fraternal twins. It has been found, for example, that identical twins, who share all their genes, are much more similar in how extroverted (outgoing) they are than are fraternal twins, who on average share only half their genes. Indeed, the correlations in scores on measures of extroversion typically exceed .5 for identical twins but do not even reach .2 for fraternal twins (Loehlin, 1992a). Many other traits also show high heritability, including physical ones. For example, both José Canseco and his identical twin Ozzie are professional baseball players, an extremely rare outcome. At the same time, the fact that José has been so much more successful in baseball suggests that environment also plays an important part in who we become.

Twin studies are not the only way of studying the effects of the heritability of traits; family studies provide another way. In such studies, researchers compare people with different degrees of genetic relation (e.g., biological siblings versus adoptive siblings or biological parents and offspring versus adoptive parents and offspring) in an attempt to determine the extent that differences among the people are due to heredity.

FINDING YOUR WAY

2.1

Make a list of 10 of your physical characteristics that are due, at least in part, to inheritance (e.g., eye color; height; ease of developing muscle strength; keen vision; tendency to develop ailments such as diabetes, sickle-cell anemia, or arthritis). Make three columns next to your list: (a) "Adaptive advantage"; (b) "adaptive disadvantage"; and (c) "no adaptive effects." For each item in your list, indicate the adaptive advantages and disadvantages, or indicate no adaptive effects. To what kinds of environments are you well-suited?

The preceding section sketched how our genetic inheritance affects our biological makeup. We also hinted that our inherited anatomy and physiology, our biological makeup, affect many aspects of our mind—how we think, feel, and act. Two physiological systems powerfully affect our mind and behavior: the nervous system and the endocrine (hormonal) system. To many psychologists, the nervous system, discussed next, is the primary system of these two systems.

HOW IS THE NERVOUS SYSTEM ORGANIZED?

The *nervous system* is a physiological network that enables us to interact with the environment. Through it, we receive, process, and respond to information about the environment and about ourselves. Because the nervous system is so complex, the number of biological pathways along which information can be processed by the body is uncountable. In this section, we describe the major subdivisions and specialized structures of the human nervous system. Following this section, we describe the brain in greater detail. We conclude our discussion of the nervous system by noting how information moves through it. (Figure 2.2 shows a diagram of the overall structure of the nervous system.)

FIGURE 2.2
Divisions of the Nervous System
The main divisions of the nervous system are the central nervous system, which comprises the brain and the spinal cord, and the peripheral nervous system, which comprises the somatic nervous system and the autonomic nervous system.

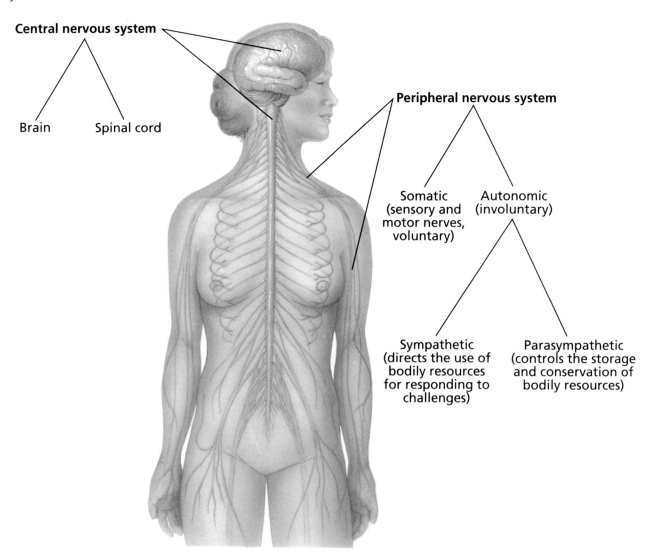

The Central Nervous System

The nervous system is divided into two main parts: the **central nervous system (CNS)**, which comprises the brain and spinal cord, and the peripheral nervous system (PNS), which comprises all the other nerves throughout the body. Both the brain and the spinal cord are protected by an outer, bony covering and by an inner, liquid cushion. The clear, colorless liquid that moves around throughout the brain and the spinal cord is *cerebrospinal fluid (CSF)*. The brain is constantly producing fresh CSF. The CSF also helps to remove waste products from the CNS, as does the rich supply of blood that nourishes the CNS. Another physiological protection for the brain is the *blood–brain barrier*, a dense network of tiny blood vessels that filter the substances that enter or leave the brain.

The Brain and the Spinal Cord

The **brain** is the organ in our bodies that is most directly responsible for our thoughts, emotions, motivations, and actions. The importance of the brain's activity is shown by the fact that it uses up considerably more of the body's resources than would seem to be justified by its size: It accounts for only 2.5% (one fortieth) of the weight of an adult human body, but it uses about 20% (one fifth) of the circulating blood, of the available *glucose* (the blood sugar that supplies the body with energy), and of the available *oxygen* (the gas we pull in from the air through breathing).

There are a huge number of **neurons** (nerve cells) in your brain that are involved in communication within the nervous system. Individual neurons work together to form nerves. **Nerves** are organized strings of neurons that extend from your brain down through the center of your back to the rest of your body, by way of your **spinal cord.** Your spinal cord is a complex tangle of nerves that stretch from your brain to the lower end of the small of your back. Your skull encloses and protects your brain, and your spinal column protects your spinal cord. The *spinal column* consists of a series of interconnected *vertebrae* (the backbone). One function of the spinal cord is to collect information from the outlying nerves (in the peripheral nervous system) and to *transmit* (send) this information to the brain. A complementary function is to relay information back from the brain to the outlying nerves.

The two-directional communication of the nervous system involves two different kinds of nerves and neurons: receptors and effectors. In general, a **receptor** in the human body is a structure of the body that receives a message or a substance from some other structure in the body. In particular, receptor nerves and neurons receive *sensory information* (e.g., sights, sounds, and smells) from the outlying nerves of the body and relay it to the central nervous system. In the opposite direction, **effectors** are neurons and nerves that transmit information from the CNS to the outlying nerves of the body. For voluntary movements, our brains transmit *motor information* (e.g., regarding movements of the muscles) telling our bodies what to do. Sometimes, however, our bodies make involuntary movements.

Spinal Reflexes

The involuntary, automatic reactions of our bodies are termed **reflexes.** During reflexive reactions, the spinal cord transmits a message directly

---

central nervous system (CNS) • the part of the nervous system comprising the brain and the spinal cord, including all of the neurons therein

brain • the organ of the body that most directly controls thoughts, emotions, motivations, and actions and that responds to information received from elsewhere in the body, such as through sensory receptors

neuron • a nerve cell, involved in neural communication within the nervous system

nerve • a bundle of neurons that can be observed as a fiber extending from the central nervous system out to various parts of the body

spinal cord • a slender, roughly cylindrical bundle of interconnected neural fibers, which is enclosed within the spinal column and which extends through the center of the back, starting at the brain and ending at the lower end of the small of the back

receptor • a physiological structure designed to receive something (e.g., a given substance or a particular kind of information), such as sensory information from the sense organs

effector • a physiological structure designed to send something, such as motor information, to the parts of the body that act on the environment

reflex • an automatic physiological response to an external stimulus, which occurs directly through the spinal cord from receptor nerves to effector nerves. On these occasions, the message does not pass through the brain until after the body has responded to the sensory information (see Figure 2.3).

Reflexes offer much faster responses than do voluntary responses. For example, it takes only about 50 *milliseconds* (thousandths of a second) from the time a particular place in your knee is tapped until your calf and foot jerk forward. In comparison, it takes many hundreds of milliseconds for you to move your knee in response to your voluntary decision to move it.

Quick reflexes allow the body to respond immediately to particular sensory information, bypassing the route through the brain. For example, when you touch a very hot oven, you immediately withdraw your hand. You do not pause to think, "Gosh, that hurts. I should probably move away from that." Reflexes do more than just help us to avoid pain. They also help us to minimize any damage that might result from whatever is

FIGURE 2.3
Spinal Reflex
Sometimes, the spinal cord transforms incoming information from receptor nerves directly into outgoing information that is then sent to effector nerves. These direct-connection responses, termed reflexes, *allow for speedy protective reactions.*

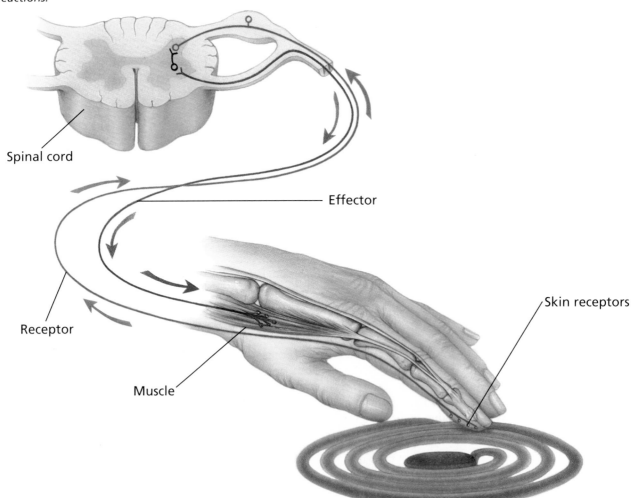

Spinal cord

Effector

Skin receptors

Receptor

Muscle

2.1

PUTTING IT TO USE

HOW TO MASTER DIFFICULT MATERIAL AND HOW TO PREPARE FOR A TEST

1. Make sure that you understand the key terms in the material you are learning. Look up any important words you do not know. In the margins of this textbook are definitions of many of the key terms in each chapter; also, a glossary of terms appears at the end of the book. In addition, you may want to keep a dictionary handy to look up unfamiliar words that may not be defined in the margins or in the glossary.

2. Make a study guide for yourself. Include in your guide some lists of key points, terms, and ideas, as well as any other important information you find difficult to remember. When you rehearse (practice learning) the material, review your own notes, as well as the summaries provided in your textbook.

3. Try to learn the information in a form that matches the form in which you will want to remember the information later. For instance, if your instructor likes to give quizzes that match each structure of the brain or nervous system with the function of each structure, practice matching the structures and their functions while you are studying for the quiz.

4. Make up your own cues for retrieving information. Often, the most effective cues relate the new information to what you already know. Some students make drawings or charts that make it easier for them to remember material. Other students make up little songs or rhymes (e.g., "receptors get clues from the eyes and the nose; effectors cause wiggles in lips and in toes"). Another technique is to make up word games for steps in a process or for parts that make up a whole. (For instance, a word game for linking the lobes in the brain to their functions might be to think of function words that have the same initial letters as the names of the lobes: "forethought [frontal lobe—planning], prickling [parietal lobe—skin sensations], twanging [temporal lobe—hearing], and observing [occipital lobe—vision].")

5. Until you know your own stylistic preferences for studying, use a variety of techniques (e.g., talking with others, writing notes, drawing pictures or charts, making and using flash cards). Once you have tried various techniques, drop the use of techniques that do not work well for you, and increase your use of techniques that seem effective. Tailor your study habits to your own preferred style of learning. Review information in a format that most effectively helps you to recall the information.

6. Overlearn the information that you will want to recall at the time of the test. If you can just barely remember the information when you are reviewing the material, it will probably be difficult to recall it easily when you are experiencing the stress of a testing situation. If you know the material extremely well outside of the testing situation, however, you will probably perform well on the test.

7. If you feel overly anxious as you get ready to take a test, take steps to relax yourself. For example, concentrate on breathing slowly and deeply. While continuing to breathe slowly and deeply, alternately tense and then relax each of your major muscles, starting at the tips of your toes and working your way up to your face muscles.

8. Your efforts to study hard will be rewarded. Even if you do not achieve the grades you hope for, you will come much closer to doing so if you work hard. You are more likely to do well when you recognize that motivation and effort are important to your success (Noel, Forsyth, & Kelley, 1987).

causing the pain (e.g., fires or cuts). Thus, our reflexes better enable us to survive.

Through the reflex response, the spinal cord can act alone. However, the spinal cord has no conscious awareness of pain or of any other sensations. For conscious awareness to occur, the sensation must reach the brain.

In sum, the body is an exceptionally well-organized system. Lower levels in the command system can respond without going through the brain when an immediate need arises. However, higher levels in the system are needed for us to understand and to interact meaningfully with the world around us.

The human body, including the brain, may be exceptionally well-organized, but the human ability to absorb a lot of new information has its limits. Before you read about any more new terms or about any more details of the body and the brain, you may want to take a moment to read the information in Putting It to Use 2.1, which offers some suggestions for mastering difficult and complex material and preparing for taking a test.

The Peripheral Nervous System

The CNS includes the brain and spinal cord; the **peripheral nervous system (PNS)** includes all the other nerve cells, which lie outside of the brain and spinal cord. The PNS even includes the nerves of the face and head that are not part of the brain. Essentially, the PNS helps to get information back and forth between the CNS and the rest of the body. The PNS connects with receptors that receive information from our external sensory organs (e.g., skin and eyes) and from our internal body organs (e.g., stomach and heart). It also connects with effectors in parts of the body that let you wink, wiggle your toes (or your nose), and so on. Most of the PNS nerves lack the surrounding protective bone that encases the brain and spinal cord.

The PNS has two main parts: (a) the *somatic nervous system,* which controls relatively quick, voluntary movements of the muscles attached to our skeleton; and (b) the *autonomic nervous system,* which controls movement of our nonskeletal muscles. Our *nonskeletal muscles* include the heart muscles, the blood vessels, and the muscles of the internal body organs (e.g., the muscles of the digestive tract). We have little or no voluntary control over the muscles of the autonomic nervous system. Usually, we are not even aware of their functioning. In general, the autonomic nervous system responds more slowly and for longer periods of time than does the somatic nervous system.

The autonomic nervous system is divided into two parts: the sympathetic nervous system and the parasympathetic nervous system (see Figure 2.4). Both systems are involved with your metabolism. Through *metabolism,* your body captures, stores, and uses energy and material resources from food, and it gets rid of whatever your body does not use.

The sympathetic and parasympathetic systems often work in tandem, for example, in determining our metabolism. In general, the sympathetic nervous system is activated by situations requiring arousal and alertness. At such times, this system increases the heart rate and diverts blood flow to the muscles, as needed for exercise or emergency. On the other hand, the parasympathetic nervous system becomes active when the body is conserving energy. It promotes the activity of the digestive system and also slows the heart rate, thereby slowing the body and aiding in energy

peripheral nervous system (PNS) • one of the two main parts of the nervous system, comprising the nerve cells that lie outside of the brain and the spinal cord, including the nerves of the face and head

SYMPATHETIC

PARASYMPATHETIC

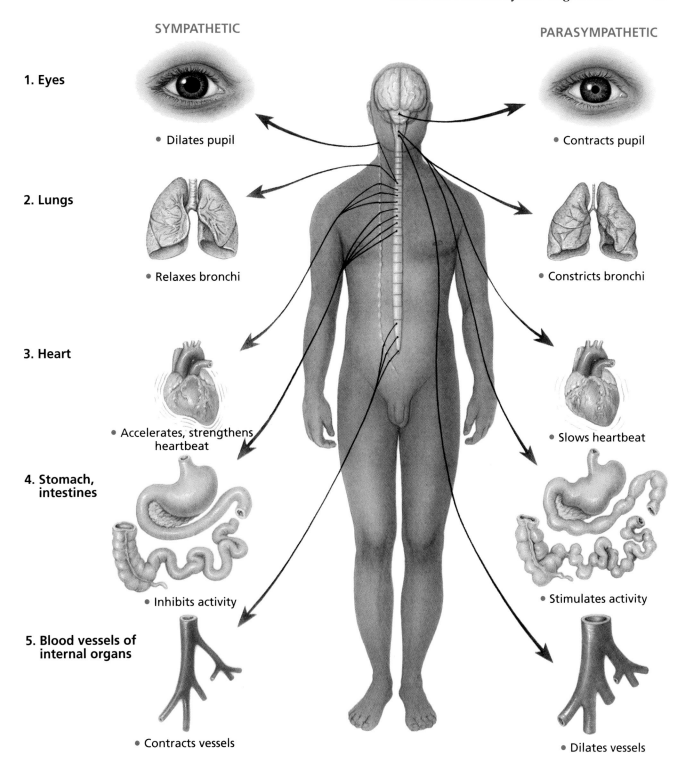

1. Eyes

- Dilates pupil

- Contracts pupil

2. Lungs

- Relaxes bronchi

- Constricts bronchi

3. Heart

- Accelerates, strengthens heartbeat

- Slows heartbeat

4. Stomach, intestines

- Inhibits activity

- Stimulates activity

5. Blood vessels of internal organs

- Contracts vessels

- Dilates vessels

FIGURE 2.4
The Autonomic Nervous System
The two parts of the autonomic nervous system are the sympathetic nervous system (identified with red labels) and the parasympathetic nervous system (identified with blue labels), both of which are involved in metabolism and other self-regulating physiological processes.

storage. Thus, the sympathetic and parasympathetic systems work in parallel, yet also in opposition to one another. If you have a heated argument right after dinner, your sympathetic system will be stirred up, readying you for a fight. Unfortunately, it will end up warring with your parasympathetic system, which will be trying to conserve body energy in order to digest your food. You may end up feeling drained, tired, and even sick to your stomach.

You now have a general idea of the organization of the human nervous system. Next, let us consider how information is processed in the nervous system.

HOW IS INFORMATION PROCESSED IN THE NERVOUS SYSTEM?

Neurons

To understand how the nervous system processes information, we need to know about the major structures and functions of the neurons that form the nervous system (see Figure 2.5). First, we examine the structure of the neuron. Later, we discuss the key function of all neurons, which is to allow for communication within the nervous system.

Three Types of Neurons

There are three types of neurons: sensory neurons, motor neurons, and interneurons. Each type of neuron serves a different function. **Sensory neurons** *receive* information about the internal environment (what is going on

FIGURE 2.5
Neurons
Most humans have more than 100 billion (100,000,000,000) neurons in their nervous system. (If a team of scientists were to count 3 neurons per second, the team would take more than 1,000 years to finish counting.) For the most part, these neurons cannot be replaced, at least in adults: Once a neuron dies, it is gone forever.

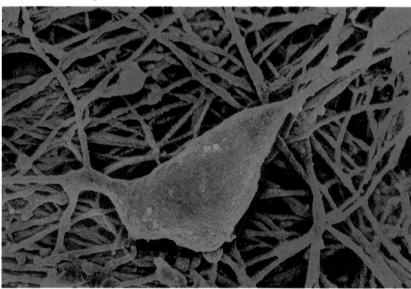

sensory neuron • a nerve cell that receives information from the environment through sensory receptors and then carries that information toward the central nervous system

in the body) and external environment (what is going on in the world). They connect with sensory *receptor cells*, which are specially designed to *receive* a particular kind of information. The receptor cells detect distinctive changes in the sensory organs, such as the skin, ears, tongue, eyes, nose, muscles, joints, and internal organs (see chapter 3). Sensory neurons carry information away from the sensory receptor cells and toward the spinal cord or the brain.

Motor neurons carry information *away from* the spinal cord and the brain and toward the various other parts of the body (e.g., arms and legs). When the body parts receive the information, the information tells the parts to respond in some way. Both motor neurons and sensory neurons are part of the PNS. For example, your sensory and motor neurons may send information to and from your stomach (through your autonomic nervous system) or to and from your toe muscles (through your somatic nervous system).

Interneurons (*inter-*, between) work between the sensory neurons and the motor neurons. They receive signals from either sensory neurons or other interneurons. Then, they send signals either to other interneurons or to motor neurons. In complex organisms such as humans, most neurons are interneurons.

The spinal reflex (see Figure 2.6) illustrates how the neurons interact: (a) Sensory neurons receive a message from specialized sensory-receptor

motor neuron • a nerve cell that carries information *away from* the spinal cord and the brain and toward the body parts that are supposed to respond to the information in some way

interneuron • a type of nerve cell that transmits information between sensory and motor neurons

FIGURE 2.6
The Spinal Reflex Revisited: Three Types of Neurons
In the spinal reflex, sensory neurons receive a message (a sensory stimulus, i.e., a sensation) and then transmit the message to interneurons, which transmit the message through the spinal cord to motor neurons. The motor neurons then send the message to muscles that respond reflexively to the message.

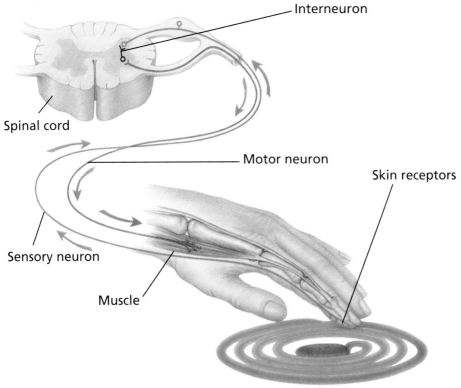

cells; the message arrives in a biological code that can be translated roughly into English as "Yikes! Hot! Hand hurts!" (b) Interneurons receive the message from the sensory neurons. (c) The interneurons translate the sensory message into a motor message. (d) The interneurons send the biologically coded motor message to the motor neurons; the biological code can be translated roughly into English as "Move that hand!" (e) The motor neurons send the message to the muscles responsible for moving the hand. Meanwhile, other interneurons send the incoming message through the spinal cord to the brain. The brain then interprets the incoming message as pain and more deliberately figures out what to do about the situation.

Parts of the Neuron

Not all neurons are alike in their structure, but almost all neurons have four basic parts: a soma, dendrites, an axon, and terminal buttons (see Figure 2.7). We discuss each part in turn, as well as the important junction between neurons, the synapse.

The **soma** (*body;* the body of the cell) sustains the life of the neuron. It contains the cell *nucleus*, which performs metabolic and reproductive functions for the cell. At one end of the neuron, the edges of the soma branch out to the **dendrites** (meaning *trees;* the branching dendrites look

FIGURE 2.7

Parts of a Neuron

Each neuron comprises four basic parts: a soma, dendrites, an axon, and terminal buttons, although the size and shape of these parts may differ, depending on the location and function of the neuron. As these schematics illustrate, the axon may be (a) myelinated or (b) unmyelinated.

(a) Neuron with myelinated axon

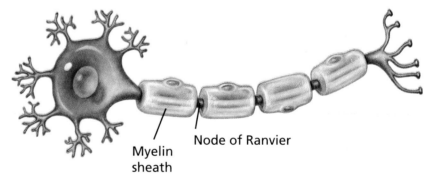

Node of Ranvier

Myelin sheath

(b) Neuron with unmyelinated axon

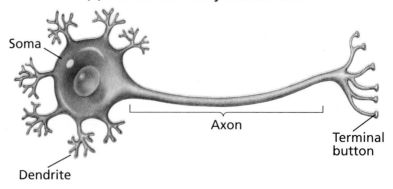

Soma

Axon

Terminal button

Dendrite

soma • the part of the neuron that performs vital functions for the life of the cell

dendrites • the primary parts of the neuron involved in receiving communications from other cells via distinctive receptors on their external membranes

like trees), which are the primary structures for receiving communications from other neurons. On the external *membranes* (thin surface layers) of the soma and the dendrites there are distinctive receptors for chemical messengers. These receptors receive chemical messages from other neurons.

When the soma or dendrites receive a message, they pass the message to the **axon,** which is the long, thin, tubular part of the neuron that responds in one of two ways to the messages received by the dendrites and soma. Usually, the axon seems to ignore the information (for reasons to be described later), but sometimes it sends the information through the length of the neuron. At the opposite end of the neuron from the soma and dendrites is the axon *terminus* (end). At its terminus, the axon can send the message to other neurons.

There are two basic kinds of axons, the myelinated axon and the unmyelinated axon. Both kinds occur in about equal proportions in the human nervous system. The *myelinated axon* is coated with *myelin,* a white, fatty substance, and is surrounded by a **myelin sheath,** which insulates and protects the axon from being disturbed by the *electrochemical* (involving chemicals with electrical charges) activity of nearby neurons. The myelin sheath also speeds up the process of sending information through the axon. Myelinated axons can send messages at 100 meters per second (equal to about 224 miles per hour), or even faster.

Myelin is not spread evenly around the length of the axon. Instead, there are small gaps in the myelin coating along the axon. These gaps in the myelin are termed *nodes of Ranvier.* Somewhat surprisingly, these gaps in the myelin sheath help to speed up *neural transmission* (*neural* means that it has to do with the nervous system, and *transmission* is the process of sending information; in this case, the information travels through the nervous system). It seems that neural impulses save time by leaping from node to node across the myelin sheath.

The second kind of axon, the *unmyelinated axon,* has no myelin sheath. Typically, these axons are narrower and shorter than the myelinated ones. The narrowness of these axons also slows the rate at which they send neural impulses. Because the narrow, unmyelinated axons are also usually shorter, they generally have less distance to travel. Therefore, they do not need to send impulses as quickly as do the long, thick myelinated axons. In unmyelinated axons, the speed of sending impulses is sometimes as relatively slow as 5 meters (a little more than 5 yards) per second. (On the other hand, most of us would be lucky to be able to run that fast!)

The terminus of each axon branches into various *terminal buttons.* The small, knobby terminal buttons do not directly touch the dendrites of the next neuron. Even so, they play a key role in sending information within the nervous system. Specifically, they release a chemical messenger into the synapse, a tiny gap between neurons (see Figure 2.8). The **synapse** is the gap between the terminal buttons of one neuron and the dendrites (or sometimes the soma) of the next neuron.

The width of neuronal somas ranges from about 5 to about 100 *microns* (thousandths of a millimeter, millionths of a meter). Dendrites, too, are tiny, generally a few hundred microns in length. Axons, however, can vary considerably in length. Some axons are as short as a few hundred microns. In fact, some axons are so short that they are almost impossible to find as a separate part of the neuron. However, the axons of some of the longer motor neurons can reach from the spinal cord to the fingers and the toes. To picture the relative size of the parts of a neuron, imagine enlarging a long spinal neuron. You could make the soma the size of an orange.

axon • the long, thin, tubular part of the neuron, which responds to information received by the dendrites and soma of the neuron by either ignoring or transmitting the information through the neuron to the axon's terminal buttons

myelin sheath • a protective, insulating layer of myelin, which coats the axons of some neurons

synapse • the area comprising the interneuronal gap, the terminal buttons of one neuron's axon, and the dendrites (or sometimes the soma) of the next neuron

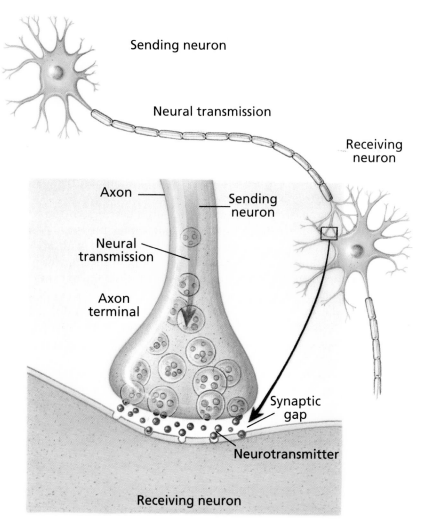

FIGURE 2.8
The Synapse
This simplified drawing shows the neuron-to-neuron transfer of messages in the synapse.

In relative terms, the axon would stretch the length of 240 football fields (roughly 14 miles).

Conduction of Information Within Neurons

For neuronal communication to occur, two interactive processes are needed. First, each neuron must be able to send information from the dendrites and the soma at one end, through the axon, to the terminal buttons at the other end. When information travels through the neuron, it is termed *conduction*. Because this conduction occurs within one neuron, it is *intraneuronal,* which means "within the neuron."

In the second process, information must get from one neuron to another, so that information can travel throughout the nervous system. When information is sent from one neuron to another, it is termed *transmission,* just as radio waves are transmitted from a radio station to the radio receiver in your car or home. Because transmission occurs between two or more neurons, it is *interneuronal,* which means "between the neurons."

In the nervous system, the body does not use electrical wires or radio waves. Instead, it sends the information in the form of electrochemical messages. The electrochemical information takes the form of *ions*, chemical particles that have positive or negative electrical charges, which are both inside and outside of the neurons. We consider intraneuronal conduction first.

Initially, a neuron may be in a state of rest. Sometimes, however, the electrochemical activity surrounding the neuron generates an **action potential** (neural "firing" as a result of a change in the electrochemical balance inside and outside a neuron) along the membrane of the neuron. During an action potential, ions quickly flood in and out of the neuron, across the neuronal membrane. This rapid transfer of ions changes the electrochemical balance inside and outside the neuron. Figure 2.9 shows an action potential.

Although change is essential to neural communication, and to life itself, too much change can be overwhelming. Our neurons are constantly surrounded by the electrochemical activity of our bodies. If our neurons generated action potentials in response to every slight electrochemical charge, chaos would result. Therefore, our neurons are somewhat choosy in reacting to electrochemical activity. Neurons do not respond to electrochemical charges of most levels of intensity and frequency. However, once a charge reaches or surpasses a certain level, the neuron generates an action potential. The required level of electrochemical charge for a neuron to "fire" is its **threshold of excitation.** At or above a neuron's threshold, an action potential is generated. Below that threshold, no action potential occurs. Different neurons require different thresholds of excitation for generating action potentials. For all neurons, however, when an action potential occurs, the neuron fires.

The action potential carries impulses through the axon, from one end to the other. Action potentials are *all-or-none* reactions. Either the electrical

action potential • a change in the electrochemical balance inside and outside a neuron; occurs when electrochemical stimulation of the neuron reaches or exceeds the neuron's threshold of excitation

threshold of excitation • the level of electrochemical stimulation at or above which an action potential may be generated, but below which an action potential cannot be generated

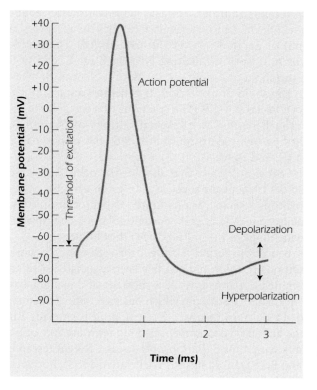

FIGURE 2.9
Action Potential
When electrochemical stimulation reaches a neuron's threshold of excitation, the neuron generates an action potential. During an action potential, ions swiftly cross the membrane of the neuron.

charge is strong enough to generate an action potential or it is not. Once the threshold is reached, the charge travels all the way down the axon without losing strength.

You might compare the firing of a neuron to a sneeze. To generate a sneeze, a substance must irritate the membranes of your nose beyond a certain point. Once the irritating substance crosses that threshold, you definitely will sneeze. Similarly, a neuron definitely will fire once its threshold level has been reached.

To summarize, intraneuronal conduction occurs when a neuron generates an action potential along its axon. Action potentials are set off by an electrical charge at or beyond the neuron's threshold of excitation. This process starts a complex reaction that conducts the electrochemical message through the neuron. Impulses travel especially fast in myelinated axons.

Communication Between Neurons

The conduction of information within each neuron is essential. However, the work of each individual neuron would be useless if there were no way for neurons to communicate with one another. Whenever we think, feel, or act, neurons are communicating with each other. How do they do it?

We already know *where* (in the synapse) and *when* (whenever an action potential triggers release of a chemical messenger) neurons communicate. The *what* of interneuronal communication is a variety of chemical messengers, termed **neurotransmitters** and *neuromodulators*. Neurotransmitters are chemical messengers that carry information from one neuron to the next. Neuromodulators are chemical substances that serve to enhance or diminish the responsivity of neurons to neurotransmitters. (See Table 2.1 for a brief description of both types of chemical messengers.) We still need to explain *how* neurons communicate. Stated simply, this is how they do so (see also Figure 2.8): (a) One neuron (Neuron A) releases a neurotransmitter from its terminal buttons. (b) The neurotransmitter enters and crosses the synapse. (c) The neurotransmitter reaches the receptors in the dendrites (or soma) of another neuron (Neuron B). (d) The neurotransmitters from Neuron A keep stimulating Neuron B until Neuron B reaches its distinctive threshold of excitation. (e) Within Neuron B, when the neuron reaches its threshold of excitation, it generates an action potential that travels down its axon. (f) Within fractions of a second, the action potential of Neuron B reaches the terminal buttons of Neuron B. Neuron B then releases its own neurotransmitter into the next synapse (perhaps with Neuron C); and so on.

In practice, the process is not really that simple. For one thing, large numbers (often hundreds) of neurons meet at any given synapse. Also, various presynaptic neurons release various kinds of neurotransmitters. Carefully review the neurotransmitters and neuromodulators, described in Table 2.1, to see the wide range of mental processes they influence.

The importance of neurotransmitters is shown through research work on schizophrenia. Traditionally, schizophrenia has been associated with an excess of a neurotransmitter, dopamine, while a shortage of dopamine has been associated with Parkinson's disease, in which one experiences tremors, rigidity of limbs, and difficulty in balance. Current drug treatments for schizophrenia block the action of dopamine, but long-term use can cause side effects that resemble symptoms of Parkinson's disease. Recent research by Bita Moghaddam and Barbara Adams (see Wickelgren, 1998), however, suggests that blocking the effect of another neurotransmitter, glutamate,

neurotransmitter • a chemical messenger, released by the terminal buttons on the axon of a presynaptic neuron, which carries the chemical messages across the synapse to receptor sites on the receiving dendrites or soma of the postsynaptic neuron

TABLE 2.1

Common Neurotransmitters and Neuromodulators

Acetylcholine (Ach)	■ *Action in the CNS:* Excites neuronal receptor sites ■ *Action in the CNS:* May be involved in memory (inferred from its concentration in the hippocampus); deficits of acetylcholine may be implicated in some memory disorders (e.g., Alzheimer's disease) ■ *Action in the PNS:* Can cause contraction of the skeletal muscles, leading to movement ■ *Action in the PNS:* Can inhibit the neurons in the muscles of the heart
Dopamine	■ Influences several important activities, including movement, attention, and learning ■ Most receptors are inhibitory, but some receptors are excitatory ■ Deficits (too little) are associated with symptoms of *Parkinson's disease,* such as tremors, rigidity of limbs, and difficulty in balance ■ Excesses (too much) may be associated with symptoms of schizophrenia (see chapter 13)
Norepinephrine and epinephrine *Serotonin*	■ Involved in the regulation of alertness and wakefulness (see chapter 4) ■ Involved in arousal, sleep, and dreaming ■ Affects the regulation of mood, appetite, and sensitivity to pain
Amino-acid neurotransmitters such as glutamate (glutamic acid), aspartate, glycine, and GABA (gamma-aminobutyric acid)	■ About 1,000 times more prevalent in the brain than are acetylcholine, dopamine, norepinephrine, epinephrine, and serotonin ■ Can act as neurotransmitters or as neuromodulators ■ Imbalances have been linked to seizures, Huntington's chorea (a neurological disorder), and the fatal effects of tetanus
Neuropeptides	■ Perhaps the best known are *endorphins* (meaning *endo*genous m*orphine*s) and other neuropeptides linked to pain relief and to stress reactions (see chapter 15) ■ Some serve as specific neurotransmitters such as those involved in hunger, thirst, and reproductive processes (see chapter 11) ■ Others serve as neuromodulators, enhancing or diminishing the responsivity of the excitatory or inhibitory receptors for particular neurotransmitters

may relieve schizophrenia-like symptoms in rats. In addition, this procedure does not seem to yield the unpleasant side effects associated with dopamine blockers. Thus, research on neurotransmitters ultimately can lead to practical applications in helping relieve symptoms of individuals suffering from various kinds of psychological abnormalities.

Just as various neurons produce various kinds of neurotransmitters and neuromodulators, different postsynaptic neurons have different kinds of receptor sites for neurotransmitters. Each kind of neurotransmitter has a distinctive shape, based on its chemical structure. Each kind of receptor site also has a distinctive shape, based on its physiological structure. *Neuroscientists* (psychologists and other scientists interested in studying the nervous system) have come up with a useful metaphor for picturing the interaction of neurotransmitters and receptors: Imagine that the characteristic shape of a given receptor is a keyhole, and the peculiar shape of a given neurotransmitter is a key (Restak, 1984). When the shape of the key matches the shape of the keyhole, the receptor responds.

So far, we know that at any given synapse, countless neurons are sending and receiving neurochemical messages. Neurons are spurting various kinds of neurotransmitters and neuromodulators into the synapse. In response, some neurons are receiving the different kinds of neurotransmitters and neuromodulators. When a particular neurotransmitter matches a particular receptor site, the receptor may respond in either of two ways: The receptor may become either excited or inhibited.

Receptors may be *excited* by some of the neurotransmitters that fit them. The more excited the receptors become, the more likely that the neurons will reach their threshold of excitation and will fire. Other receptors, however, are actually *inhibited* (held back from acting, restrained) by certain neurotransmitters they receive. When postsynaptic receptors are inhibited, neurons are less likely to reach their threshold of excitation. Furthermore, the degree of excitation or inhibition is influenced by the actions of the neuromodulators. These neuromodulators either increase or decrease the responsiveness of the neurons.

A very rough metaphor for how this process might work is to imagine that you are trying to decide whether to transfer to a particular school. You do not have time to visit the school yourself, but someone you know is visiting the school and keeps sending you messages about the school. For you, some of these messages excite your desire to attend the school, and other messages inhibit your desire to attend the school. If you do not become excited enough about the school, you will not take any action to transfer, but the more the messages you hear about the school excite you, the more likely you are to transfer. On the other hand, the more the messages you hear inhibit you, the less likely you are to go to the school.

To summarize, countless presynaptic neurons are squirting neurotransmitters and neuromodulators into the synapse. Some receptors match particular neurotransmitters, and others do not. When a match occurs, some receptors of an affected postsynaptic neuron are excited, and others are inhibited. In addition, neuromodulators strengthen or weaken the responsivity of the receiving neurons. In order for a neuron to fire, the total exciting effects (minus any inhibiting effects) on a neuron must reach the neuron's threshold of excitation.

When you think about all that is involved in getting one neuron to fire, it seems a miracle that any of us can think or act at all. In fact, however, it does not take long for a message to cross the synapse. Sometimes it takes as little as half a millisecond, and it rarely takes longer than a second.

Before we conclude this section, we consider one more process that affects neural communication. Think about all the neurotransmitters and neuromodulators constantly spilling into each synapse. Even when neurons receive these substances, they do not absorb all of the neurochemicals, so what happens to the unused substances? If the extra neurochemicals stayed in the synapse, they would overstimulate the postsynaptic neurons. Fortunately, through the process of *reuptake,* neurons *reabsorb* (take up again) some of the leftover transmitter chemicals that they have released into the synapse.

Under most circumstances, the human nervous system superbly communicates specific sensory and motor information. It quickly sends sensory information from our sense organs to our brains, it processes that information, and then it sends motor information from our brains to our muscles. The speedy communication of specific information enables us to respond immediately to our environments. Sometimes, however, our bodies use a different means of communication. This other communication network is the endocrine system.

HOW DOES THE ENDOCRINE SYSTEM WORK?

The **endocrine system** (*endo-*, inside; *-crine*, referring to secretion; secreting or releasing inside) is a physiological communication system that operates by means of glands. A **gland** is a group of cells that produces and secretes chemical substances. In particular, endocrine glands release their chemical products into the bloodstream. The blood then carries the secreted substances to *target cells*, which respond to the substances. Thus, whereas the nervous system conveys information along relatively well-defined neural pathways, the endocrine system does not use well-defined pathways for the transmission of information. The target cells of various organs usually respond distinctively. (For example, target cells in the heart may react differently than do target cells in the stomach.) Figure 2.10 illustrates the locations of the main endocrine glands and their key functions.

> **endocrine system** • a physiological communication network that operates via glands that secrete hormones directly into the bloodstream
>
> **gland** • a group of cells that secretes chemical substances

FIGURE 2.10
Major Endocrine Glands of the Body
The adrenal glands, thyroid gland, and pituitary gland are among the most important of the endocrine glands, but other glands carry out other important physiological functions as well.

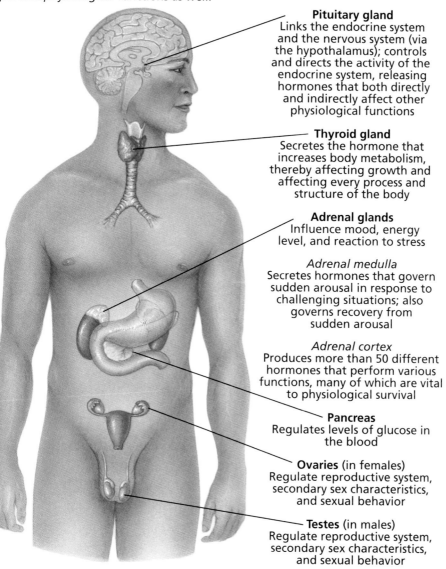

Pituitary gland
Links the endocrine system and the nervous system (via the hypothalamus); controls and directs the activity of the endocrine system, releasing hormones that both directly and indirectly affect other physiological functions

Thyroid gland
Secretes the hormone that increases body metabolism, thereby affecting growth and affecting every process and structure of the body

Adrenal glands
Influence mood, energy level, and reaction to stress

Adrenal medulla
Secretes hormones that govern sudden arousal in response to challenging situations; also governs recovery from sudden arousal

Adrenal cortex
Produces more than 50 different hormones that perform various functions, many of which are vital to physiological survival

Pancreas
Regulates levels of glucose in the blood

Ovaries (in females)
Regulate reproductive system, secondary sex characteristics, and sexual behavior

Testes (in males)
Regulate reproductive system, secondary sex characteristics, and sexual behavior

The chemical substances secreted by endocrine-system glands are **hormones,** which specifically affect the activities of target cells to regulate physiological processes. Hormones work in either of two ways: (a) They can interact with receptors on the surfaces of target cells; or (b) they can enter target cells directly and interact with specialized receptor molecules inside the cells. There are several parallels between neurotransmitters and hormones, as shown in Table 2.2: Both hormones and neurotransmitters (a) are chemical messengers, (b) function within complex communications networks, (c) are secreted by a specific set of cells, (d) communicate information to another set of cells, and (e) affect the receiving cells in different ways, largely depending on the nature of the receptors that receive the chemicals. For instance, as Table 2.2 shows, some substances (e.g., epinephrine and norepinephrine) function as neurotransmitters in the brain and as hormones in the bloodstream. As hormones, however, the chemicals travel a much longer and less direct route to the target cells than they travel as neurotransmitters.

The endocrine system operates largely outside our conscious control, and hormones are released reflexively. The glands generally release hormones in response to a stimulus from either inside or outside the body. Inside the body, the stimulus that prompts the secretion of hormones is often a process by which the body monitors its own activity.

What are the key endocrine glands? The *adrenal glands,* located above the kidneys, are very important in mood, energy level, and reactions to stress. The *thyroid gland,* located at the front of the throat, regulates the metabolic rate of cells. The *pituitary gland,* located above the mouth and sometimes called the *master gland,* is of central importance in controlling many other endocrine glands, which release their hormones in response to hormones released by the pituitary. The pituitary gland also provides a direct link from the endocrine system to the nervous system. The pituitary gland, in turn, is controlled by the hypothalamus.

hormone • a chemical substance secreted by one or more glands; regulates many physiological processes through specific actions on cells, and may affect the way a receptor cell goes about its activities

TABLE 2.2

Parallels Between Hormones and Neurotransmitters

What are some parallels between these chemical messengers?	Hormones	Neurotransmitters
What are some examples of these chemical substances?	Androgen, epinephrine, estrogen, norepinephrine, thyroxine	Acetylcholine, dopamine, epinephrine, norepinephrine, serotonin
What is the communications network within which the substances operate?	Endocrine system	Nervous system
What is the set of cells that secrete the substance, sending the chemical message?	Glands	Presynaptic neurons
Where are the receptors on the cells that receive the chemical message?	Receptors in or on the target cells	Receptors on the dendrites or somas of postsynaptic neurons
What is an example of how the same chemical messages can lead to different specific actions, depending on the receptors that receive the messages?	Receptors in the digestive system respond to hormones differently than receptors in the heart	Inhibitory receptors respond to neurotransmitters by inhibiting the neuron, but excitatory receptors respond by exciting the neuron

Negative-feedback loop

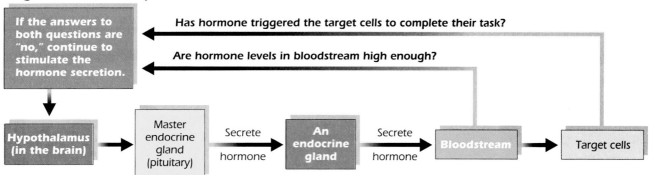

FIGURE 2.11
Negative-Feedback Loop
Through a negative-feedback loop, the body finds out whether the hormones in the bloodstream have reached a desirable level, and it checks to see whether the hormones have accomplished their tasks. If the monitoring processes feed back "yes" responses, the hormone secretion stops.

The body monitors the endocrine system in two ways: (a) It checks the levels of each hormone in the bloodstream; and (b) it checks the effects of hormones on particular bodily processes. Using the first method, the body answers the following question about each hormone: Have the amounts of this hormone in the bloodstream reached a desirable level? The second method seeks answers to this question: Has each hormone completely finished the set of tasks that the hormone was supposed to perform? The answers then are fed back to the glands. If the answer to either question is "yes," the gland stops secreting the hormone. If both answers are "no," the secretion continues. This self-monitoring process is termed a *negative-feedback loop* (see Figure 2.11).

To summarize, the endocrine system secretes hormones into the bloodstream to stimulate various responses in the body. In some ways, the endocrine system is self-regulating. However, it also is subject to control by the nervous system by way of the hypothalamus (see Figure 2.12). Both the endocrine system and the nervous system are essential parts of human physiology.

WHAT ARE THE MAJOR STRUCTURES AND FUNCTIONS OF THE HUMAN BRAIN?

Psychobiologists are particularly interested in the human brain. Before we explore *what* scientists have learned about the brain, it may be helpful to find out *how* scientists have learned what they know.

Viewing the Brain

Scientists can use many methods for studying the human brain. For centuries, investigators have been able to *dissect* (separate into parts for examination) a brain after a person has died. Even today, this method is often used for studying the brain. In particular, researchers look carefully at people whose behavior shows signs of brain damage while they are alive. The researchers document these case studies of patients as

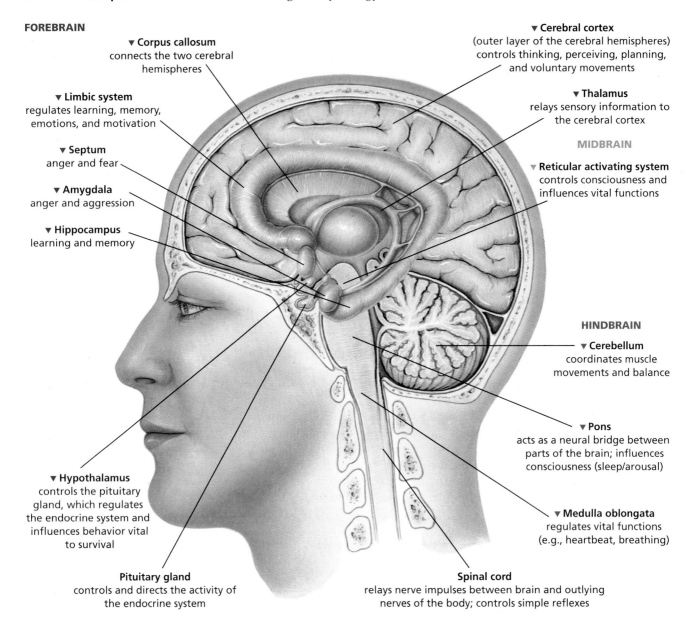

FOREBRAIN

▼ Corpus callosum
connects the two cerebral hemispheres

▼ Limbic system
regulates learning, memory, emotions, and motivation

▼ Septum
anger and fear

▼ Amygdala
anger and aggression

▼ Hippocampus
learning and memory

▼ Hypothalamus
controls the pituitary gland, which regulates the endocrine system and influences behavior vital to survival

Pituitary gland
controls and directs the activity of the endocrine system

▼ Cerebral cortex
(outer layer of the cerebral hemispheres)
controls thinking, perceiving, planning, and voluntary movements

▼ Thalamus
relays sensory information to the cerebral cortex

MIDBRAIN

▼ Reticular activating system
controls consciousness and influences vital functions

HINDBRAIN

▼ Cerebellum
coordinates muscle movements and balance

▼ Pons
acts as a neural bridge between parts of the brain; influences consciousness (sleep/arousal)

▼ Medulla oblongata
regulates vital functions (e.g., heartbeat, breathing)

Spinal cord
relays nerve impulses between brain and outlying nerves of the body; controls simple reflexes

FIGURE 2.12
Major Structures of the Forebrain, the Midbrain, and the Hindbrain
The structures of the forebrain (identified with blue labels), the midbrain (identified with red labels), and the hindbrain (identified with green labels) perform essential functions for survival, as well as for high-level thinking and feeling.

thoroughly as possible. Later, after the patients die, the researchers examine the patients' brains for *lesions* (areas where body tissue has been damaged). Then the researchers infer that the lesioned locations may be related to the behavior that was affected. In this way, they trace an observed type of behavior to a particular location in the brain. (Table 2.3 shows some of the techniques that can be used for studying human brains after death.)

Scientists also want to understand the physiological processes and functions of the living brain. To study the changing activity of the living brain, scientists must use *in vivo* (within living organisms) research. Many in vivo techniques are performed on animals. Because the monkey brain

TABLE 2.3
Techniques for Viewing the Brain

Technique	What questions can be answered by using these techniques?
Techniques performed on a nonliving brain	
Dissection. Separating and observing the structures of the brain with the naked eye, with microscopes, and with various special techniques for studying details about the brain's chemistry and biology	How do the various structures of the brain normally look, and how are they organized in the brain? How do case records of a person's unusual behavior relate to abnormalities in the person's brain?
Techniques performed on living animals	
Surgical procedures. (a) Create specific injuries in particular locations in the animal's brain, then carefully observe how those injuries affect the animal's ability to function. (b) Implant tiny devices that conduct electrical activity to or from body tissues, electrically stimulate particular locations in the brain, and observe the animal's behavior.	What kinds of functions and behaviors are affected by lesions or by electrical stimulation in particular locations in the brain?
Techniques that investigate the living human brain	
Electroencephalograms (EEGs) and *event-related potentials (ERPs)* record changes in electrical activity across large areas of the brain.	How does the brain behave differently when a person is dreaming? Does brain activity appear odd in a person who behaves abnormally?
X-ray photos and *angiograms* use X rays to show the bones or the blood vessels in the head. In *computerized axial tomograms (CT scans),* a computer analyzes a rotating series of X rays and produces images showing detailed cross-sectional slices of the brain.	Is there any damage to the skull that might affect the brain? Are there any abnormalities of the blood flow to the brain? Do the major structures in the brain appear normal?
In *magnetic resonance imaging (MRI),* a computer analyzes the information from a rotating scanner that detects magnetic changes in the molecules of the brain. The computer then generates a picture of the brain, which is much more precise than CT-scan images.	What are some detailed features of the structures of this brain? How do unusual characteristics of a person's behavior relate to unusual features of the person's brain?
Positron emission tomography (PET scan) is based on the notion that areas of the brain that are working the hardest are also using the most glucose. PET scans show much more clearly the active workings of the brain than do studies that measure electrical activity.	Which parts of the brain are working hardest during various kinds of mental and physical activities?

is so similar to the human brain, monkeys are often the subjects in such experiments. (Table 2.3 shows some of the in vivo techniques performed on animals, as well as on humans.)

Some in vivo techniques are used with humans, too. For example, psychologists (and physicians—medical doctors) sometimes record electrical activity in the brain, which appears as waves of various widths (frequencies) and heights (intensities; see Figure 2.13). Psychologists also use various methods of producing a still image of the structures of the brain. Many of these methods are based on the use of X rays (see Figures 2.14a and 2.14b), but more recently, some methods use magnetism (see

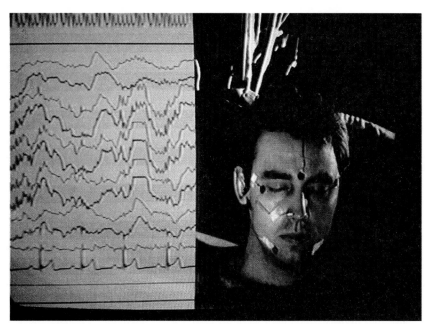

FIGURE 2.13
Electroencephalograms (EEGs)
Psychologists use EEGs to record electrical activity in the brain and translate the data into wave patterns, which can be analyzed.

Figure 2.14c). In addition, psychologists are able to study the behavior of the living brain by examining how the brain uses up a form of radioactive glucose during various activities (see Figure 2.14d). These methods using radioactive glucose have the advantage that they can illuminate not just structures of the brain, but the processing of information by the brain. What are the various regions of the brain that may be using up this glucose?

Structures and Functions of the Brain

The brain can be divided into three major regions: forebrain, midbrain, and hindbrain. These labels describe the front-to-back physical arrangement of the three regions during *prenatal* (before birth) development. However, the physical arrangement of these regions changes so much that by the time of birth, the *forebrain* is above the *midbrain* and the *hindbrain*. Figure 2.12 shows the locations of many of the important structures in these regions.

The forebrain comprises the brain structures that most intrigue psychobiologists: the *basal ganglia* (essential to motor function), the **thalamus** (a two-lobed structure acting as a relay station for transmitting sensory information that enters the brain, projecting the information to the correct regions of the cerebral cortex), the **hypothalamus** (a structure responsible for controlling the endocrine [hormonal] system and for influencing behavior related to survival, consciousness, and emotional reactions, including regulation of internal temperature, appetite, and thirst), and both the cortex and the limbic system. The *cortex* (responsible for most of our thinking and perceiving) is of such great psychological importance that it is discussed at length in a subsequent section. The **limbic system** is also crucial to many aspects of psychological function, such as learning (see

thalamus • a brain structure that primarily serves as a relay station for sensory information

hypothalamus • a brain structure that plays a key role in regulating behavior related to species survival (fighting, feeding, fleeing, and mating)

limbic system • a system of brain structures involved in emotion, motivation, and learning

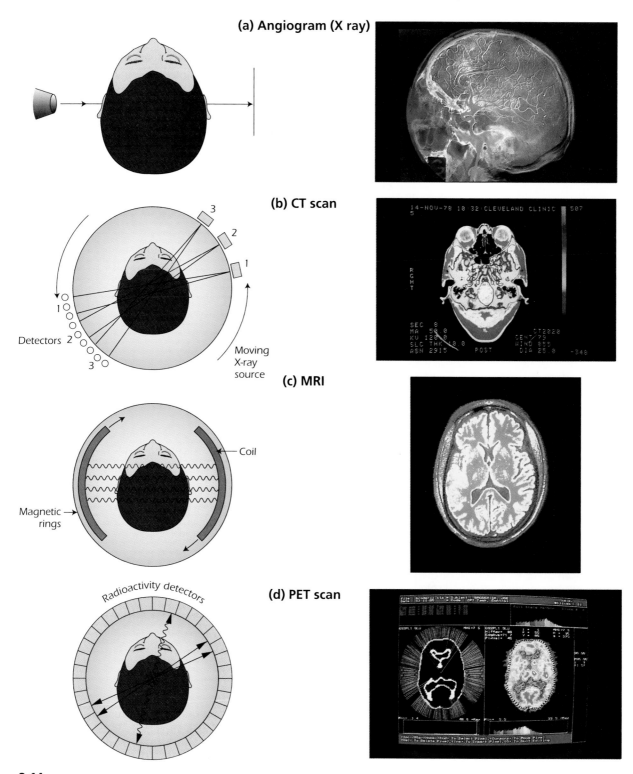

FIGURE 2.14
Images of the Brain
Various techniques have been developed to picture the structures, and sometimes the processes, of the brain. (a) A brain angiogram highlights the blood vessels of the brain. (b) A CT-scan image of a brain uses a series of rotating scans (one of which is pictured here) to produce a 3-D view of brain structures. (c) A rotating series of MRI scans (one of which is pictured here) shows a clearer 3-D picture of brain structures than CT scans show. (d) These still photographs of PET scans of a brain show different metabolic processes during different activities. PET scans permit the study of brain physiology.

chapter 5), memory (see chapter 6), and emotions and motivation (see chapter 11). Within the limbic system, the *amygdala* plays a key role in anger and aggression, and the *septum* influences anger and fear. The **hippocampus** (meaning "seahorse," its approximate shape [Greek]) influences learning and memory and may be implicated in neurological disorders such as Alzheimer's disease. The hypothalamus also is classified sometimes as being part of the limbic system.

The midbrain contains several structures, including most of the **reticular activating system,** which is essential to life, as it partially controls heartbeat, breathing, consciousness (sleep, arousal), attention, and movement. The hindbrain contains the rest of the reticular activating system, as well as the *medulla oblongata* (involved in vital physiological functions such as regulation of heartbeat), the **pons** (a neural bridge from one part of the brain to another and one of several structures influencing consciousness), and the **cerebellum** (a structure that governs many aspects of producing appropriate muscle movements, such as coordination, balance, and muscle tone). Although each of these subcortical (*sub-,* below; *-cortical,* related to the cerebral cortex) structures is important to the human mind and behavior, the cortex deserves special attention.

The Cerebral Hemispheres and the Cerebral Cortex

The **cerebral cortex** (plural, *cortices*) is a thin layer (about 2 millimeters thick) wrapped around the outward surface of the brain. In human beings, the cerebral cortex contains many folds. These folds greatly increase the area covered by the cerebral cortex: If the wrinkly human cerebral cortex were smoothed out, it would cover about 2 square feet. About 80% of the human brain is cerebral cortex (Kolb & Whishaw, 1990). The cerebral cortex is responsible for our being able to think—to plan, to coordinate thoughts and actions, to perceive visual and sound patterns, to use language, and so on. Without it, we would not be human.

The grayish surface of the cerebral cortex, sometimes termed *gray matter,* contains gray nerve cells that process information. *White matter,* the myelin mentioned earlier in the chapter, covers some of the gray matter. Both the white and the gray matter are essential to human intelligence.

The crumpled-looking cerebral cortex forms into the *left* and *right cerebral hemispheres* (*hemi-,* half; *spheres,* 3-D round shapes), which are the two halves of the brain. Although the two hemispheres look similar, they function differently. The left hemisphere is specialized for some kinds of activities, the right for other kinds of activities. For one thing, most sensory information crosses from one side of the body to the opposite hemisphere of the brain: Sensory receptors in the right foot, right ear, and right nostril send information to the left hemisphere. Receptors on the left side generally send information to the right hemisphere. The same crossing occurs when the hemispheres of the brain send motor information to the rest of the body. The left hemisphere directs the motor responses on the right side of the body, and the right hemisphere directs the left side of the body. This crossed pattern is termed *contralateral* (*contra-,* opposite; *lateral,* side) *transmission.* Some *ipsilateral* (same side) *transmission* occurs as well: Visual information from each eye goes to *both* hemispheres.

Despite this general tendency for the hemispheres to be specialized contralaterally, the hemispheres do communicate with one another. The

hippocampus • a portion of the limbic system; plays an essential role in the formation of new memories

reticular activating system • a complex network of neurons essential to the regulation of consciousness and to such vital functions as heartbeat and breathing

pons • a brain structure containing nerve cells that pass signals from one part of the brain to another, thereby serving as a kind of bridge

cerebellum • a brain structure that controls bodily coordination, balance, and muscle tone

cerebral cortex • a thin layer of tissue on the surface of the brain, which is responsible for most high-level cognitive processes

corpus callosum (*dense body*, [Latin]) is a dense collection of nerve fibers that connects the two cerebral hemispheres and thereby permits transmission of information back and forth (refer to Figure 2.12). After information reaches one hemisphere, the information can travel quickly and easily through the corpus callosum to the other hemisphere.

Hemispheric Specialization

In 1861, Paul Broca (1824–1880) noted that he had found a lesion in a particular area in the left cerebral hemisphere of a former patient of his. Before Broca's patient died, the patient had suffered from *aphasia* (impaired or lost ability to speak, due to brain damage). Broca suggested that the left-hemisphere lesion may have caused the aphasia. Since then, research has shown that "Broca's area" (the region of the brain where Broca observed the lesion) does contribute to speech (see Figure 2.15). Curiously, although people with lesions in Broca's area cannot speak fluently, they can use their voices to sing or to shout.

Another important early researcher, Carl Wernicke (1848–1905), studied language-deficient patients who could speak, but whose speech made no sense. He also traced language ability to the left hemisphere, though to a different precise location, now known as Wernicke's area (see Figure 2.15). More recently, researchers have found other areas of the brain to be involved in the comprehension and expression of language, but Broca's area and Wernicke's area are still recognized as key to normal language function.

The early discoveries about the link between the brain and the mind, such as those by Broca and his predecessors, were initially rejected or ignored by the scientific community. Subsequent discoveries have been more readily accepted, and in 1981, Roger Sperry (1920–1994), David Hubel (b. 1926), and Torsten Wiesel (b. 1924) were awarded a Nobel Prize for their work on the physiology of the brain. (The work by Hubel and Wiesel is discussed in chapter 3; in this chapter, we focus on Sperry's work on hemispheric specialization.)

Sperry argued (1964) that each hemisphere behaves in many respects like a separate brain. Sperry and his colleagues developed a technique for studying the brain—a total severing of the corpus callosum. This technique effectively cut the connection between the two hemispheres. Thus, this procedure essentially created two separate specialized brains, which processed different information and performed separate functions.

Epileptic patients can undergo serious and even life-threatening seizures. Sometimes, in order to control these seizures, patients undergo operations that cut through the corpus callosum. These patients are termed *split-brain* patients. Although split-brain patients behave normally in many respects, in a few ways their behavior is bizarre. A split-brain patient, angry at his wife, reached to strike her with his left hand while his right hand tried to protect her and stop his left one (Gazzaniga, 1970). Split-brain research reveals fascinating possibilities regarding the ways we think. Many researchers in this field (Farah, 1988; Gazzaniga, 1985; Zaidel, 1983) have argued that each of the two hemispheres is specialized for distinct kinds of functions. In particular, some researchers have suggested that the left hemisphere specializes in language functions. In contrast, the right hemisphere specializes in *spatial* (involving spatial orientation and perception) functions.

In one kind of study, the participant is asked to focus his or her gaze on the center of a screen. Then a *chimeric face* (a face showing the left side

THE FAR SIDE By GARY LARSON

"Whoa! *That* was a good one! Try it, Hobbs — just poke his brain right where my finger is."

corpus callosum • a dense body of nerve fibers that connect the two cerebral hemispheres

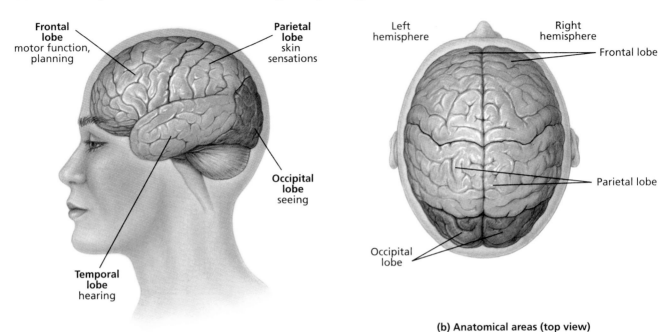

Frontal lobe
motor function, planning

Parietal lobe
skin sensations

Occipital lobe
seeing

Temporal lobe
hearing

(a) Anatomical areas (left lateral view)

Left hemisphere

Right hemisphere

Frontal lobe

Parietal lobe

Occipital lobe

(b) Anatomical areas (top view)

Motor cortex
muscle movement

Association cortex
linkage of sensory and motor information

Broca's area
speech

Auditory cortex

Sensory cortex
sensation and perception

Association cortex

Visual cortex
vision

Wernicke's area
understanding language

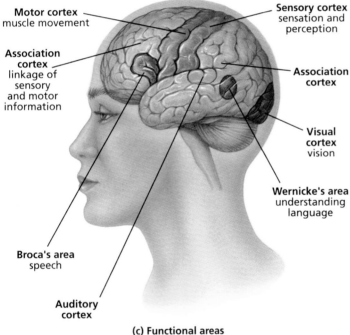

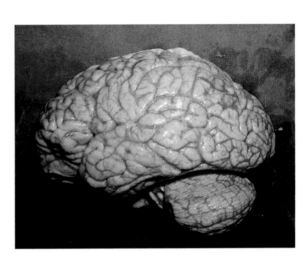

(c) Functional areas

FIGURE 2.15
Lobes of the Cerebral Cortex
The cortical lobes are named for the bones of the skull overlying these regions: the frontal lobe, the parietal lobe, the temporal lobe, and the occipital lobe. Broca's area, in the frontal lobe, and Wernicke's area, in the temporal lobe, play important roles in expressing language.

of the face of one person and the right side of another) is flashed on the screen. The participant is asked to identify what he or she saw, either verbally or by pointing to one of several normal (not chimeric) faces.

Typically, split-brain patients are unaware that they saw conflicting information in the two halves of the picture. When asked to give an answer in words about what they saw, they say that they saw the right half of the picture. Bearing in mind the contralateral association between hemisphere and side of the body, it seems that the left hemisphere controls their verbal processing of visual information (the patients' speaking about what they saw). In contrast, when asked to use their fingers to point to what they saw, participants choose the image from the left half of the picture. This finding indicates that the right hemisphere appears to control spatial processing of visual information (the patients' pointing out of what they saw). Thus, the task that the participants are asked to perform is crucial in determining what image the participant thinks was shown (Levy, Trevarthen, & Sperry, 1972).

At present, other researchers have suggested alternative explanations for many of the findings regarding hemispheric specialization. Currently, we cannot say, with confidence, exactly what each hemisphere does or can do. As always, alternative scientific interpretations of the same data make science both frustrating and exciting. One way to strengthen particular interpretations is to use the method of *converging operations*. In this method, researchers use multiple kinds of procedures for studying a research question. They then look to see whether the various procedures converge (come together) on a single answer or set of answers to the question. In the case of hemispheric specialization, EEG studies have provided converging evidence. These studies show more electrical activity occurs in the left hemisphere during a verbal task, but more occurs in the right hemisphere during a spatial task (Kosslyn, 1988; Springer & Deutsch, 1985).

Another way to approach the hemispheric specialization of language functions is to study the brains and the thinking of people who learn to use languages other than spoken English. Ursula Bellugi and her colleagues have studied individuals whose native language is American Sign Language (ASL). For native signers, the use of ASL is localized in the left hemisphere (Bellugi, Poizner, & Klima, 1989; Corina, Poizner, Bellugi

Ursula Bellugi and her colleagues have had key insights regarding language and the brain by studying persons like this mother and son, whose native language is American Sign Language.

et al., 1992; Corina, Vaid, & Bellugi, 1992; Haglund et al., 1993; Poizner, Bellugi, & Klima, 1990). On the other hand, so to speak, gestures that are not specific ASL signs are localized in the right hemispheres of native signers, just as they are in native speakers of English. Similarly, spatial information seems to be localized in the right hemisphere of native ASL signers (Poizner, Kaplan, Bellugi, & Padden, 1984). These findings support the view that language, not just speech, is localized in the left hemisphere. The following Branching Out box shows another way in which understanding of hemispheric specialization is important in the real world.

Branching Out
HEMISPHERIC SPECIALIZATION AND LANGUAGE SYMBOLS

Cross-cultural research offers yet another way of looking at the contrasting localizations of visuospatial and sound-based language symbols. Based on split-brain research, one would expect the visuospatial system to be based in the right hemisphere and sound-based language symbols to be based in the left hemisphere. In school, Japanese children study two forms of written language: *kanji,* which is based on Chinese ideographs and conveys an entire idea within each symbol, and *kana,* which is based on phonetic syllables and can be used for writing foreign words, such as scientific terms. In the 1970s, Japanese researchers started wondering whether the pictorial versus the phonetic forms might be processed differently in the two hemispheres of the brain. Some researchers concluded, in line with prior expectations, that Japanese children and adults process the phonetic-based *kana* entirely in the left hemisphere but the picture-based *kanji* in both the left and right hemispheres (Shibazaki, 1983; Shimada & Otsuka, 1981; Sibitani, 1980; Tsunoda, 1979). Interestingly, then, research on perfectly normal individuals in Japan confirms findings of research on split-brain patients in the United States. When research on such different populations comes to roughly the same conclusions, we can have more confidence in our results. To explore and understand the diverse abilities and functions of the human brain, researchers should study the rich diversity within the human community.

Lobes of the Cerebral Hemispheres and Cerebral Cortex

Hemispheric specialization is only one way through which to view the various parts of the cerebral cortex. Another way is to divide the cortex into four **lobes** (rounded sections): frontal, parietal, temporal, and occipital (refer to Figure 2.15). The *frontal lobe* handles planning, reasoning, and other high-level thought processes, as well as motor processing (see Figure 2.16); the *parietal lobe* governs somatosensory processing (sensations of feeling in the skin and in the muscles of the body; see Figure 2.17); the *temporal lobe* handles auditory processing (hearing); and the *occipital lobe* oversees visual processing (seeing). In addition to these localized functions, the lobes also interact constantly, and many functions overlap among the lobes.

lobes • each of the four major regions of the cerebral cortex, comprising the frontal lobe (motor, planning), parietal lobe (somatosensory), temporal lobe (auditory), and occipital lobe (visual)

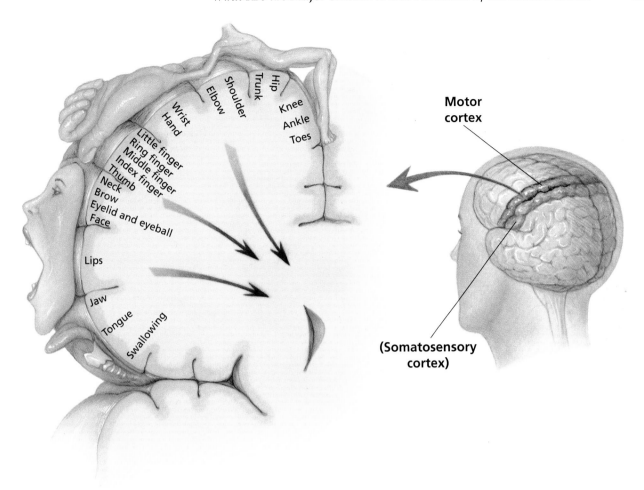

Motor cortex

(Somatosensory cortex)

FIGURE 2.16
Homunculus of the Motor Cortex
A homunculus (little person) resembles a little person. In this case, a map is drawn as a cross-section of the cerebral cortex surrounded by the figure of a small upside-down person, whose body parts map out the parts of the primary motor cortex in the frontal lobe. Note that parts of the body that involve more control of muscle movements (e.g., your hands) take up larger proportions of the areas of the motor cortex.

The frontal lobes and especially the forward portion of them, referred to as *prefrontal*, are particularly important in higher order information processing, such as is done in learning. The temporal lobes also may be important. In a recent study, Anthony Wagner and his colleagues (1998) investigated why some experiences are remembered and others forgotten. Brain activation was measured (using techniques for scanning the brain shown in Table 2.3) while participants were learning verbal material. The measurement was done to examine how neural activation differs for experiences that are subsequently remembered and ones that are subsequently forgotten. The investigators found that the ability later to remember a verbal experience is predicted by the amount of activation in the left prefrontal as well as in the temporal cortices of the brain while that experience is taking place. In a related set of studies, John Brewer and his colleagues (1998) looked at activation in the brain in response to photographs in order to determine what areas "light up" for photos that are subsequently remembered or forgotten. These investigators found that

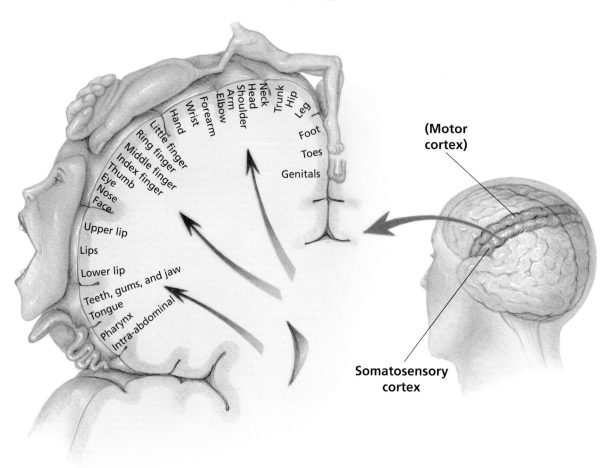

FIGURE 2.17
Homunculus of the Somatosensory Cortex
This homunculus maps the somatosensory cortex in the parietal lobe, identifying the parts of the body from which it receives sensory information. Note that parts of the body that are more highly sensitive (e.g., your mouth and tongue) take up proportionately larger areas of the somatosensory cortex.

activation in the right prefrontal cortex (and elsewhere) was a good predictor of what photographs later would be remembered.

Also in the cerebral hemispheres are projection areas. *Projection areas* are specialized regions of the cortex involved in relaying sensory and motor information within the brain. Receptor nerves transmit sensory information that arrives in the brain from various sensory receptors sending information to the thalamus (in the forebrain; refer to Figure 2.12). There, the thalamus projects the information to the appropriate areas in the lobes. Similarly, motor information from the cortex goes to the projection areas, which then send that information downward through the spinal cord. From the spinal cord, motor information travels through the PNS to reach and direct the movement of the appropriate muscles.

The areas of the lobes that are not just sending or receiving somatosensory, motor, auditory, or visual information are **association areas**. Association areas link sensory and motor information. For instance, when we use

association areas • the regions of the cerebral lobes that are not part of the sensory or motor cortices but that are believed to connect (associate) the activity of the sensory and motor cortices

language, which requires complex links among pieces of information, the association areas of our brains are active. In fact, Broca's area and Wernicke's area, discussed earlier, are both in association areas of the cortex.

The association areas of other animals are relatively small. These animals think very little about the sensations they receive before deciding what actions to take. In humans, association areas make up roughly 75% of the cerebral cortex. We humans do a lot of thinking about our sensations and our actions. If one uses this type of analysis to rank-order the intelligence of various species, we find that humans and dolphins are pretty nearly tied at the top. Under them, in order, come apes, rhesus monkeys, horses, dogs, rats and pigeons about tied, and below them alligators, turtles, and goldfish (Jerison, 1982). These rankings are only rough, however. We cannot strictly rank species because each has to adapt to a different type of environment. Thus, although a fish would not fare well in a human environment, that particular fish might be quite well adapted to its environment, whereas a human would not be.

2.2

Think about your own activities and experiences within the past 24 hours. How have your recent experiences stimulated each lobe of your cortex? How have your experiences stimulated your association areas to link your sensations and actions? What have you done recently that shows off the remarkable mental processing that goes on in your brain?

FINDING YOUR WAY

Thus far, we have discussed the nervous system in terms of the parts that can be seen without using a microscope. We have also discussed briefly what kinds of information are processed in the brain, as well as how and where the brain processes the information it receives.

In the next chapter, we discuss how human physiology and its psychological counterparts manifest themselves through sensation and perception.

The Solution to The Case of the Wrecked Romance

Chandra decides to read for herself the chapter from which Tom got his information. After reading chapter 2 of *Pathways to Psychology,* Chandra realizes that Tom's argument is fallacious. For one thing, Tom's argument is based on an evolutionary hypothesis, not a demonstrated fact. Really, there is no way of knowing what our distant ancestors did or even of knowing for sure whether the evolutionary hypothesis is correct. For another thing, evolutionary theory only can deal in any case with the way things are, not the way they should be. Even if the argument were correct, human beings have free will and can make choices. Their evolutionary history does not dictate the way they must act. Any attributes that result from the genes we have inherited always show themselves *in interaction* with the environment. Tom has not been forced to see someone else nor will he be: He has chosen his actions.

Chandra tells Tom her conclusions and that he has one more chance. Tom replies that Chandra is trying to run his life and that he has to be able to be his own man. Chandra concludes that Tom was using the evolutionary argument as a smoke screen, and she decides to break up with him.

Summary

1. Biological psychology (psychobiology) is the study of how biology affects behavior. By studying the nervous and endocrine systems, psychologists are beginning to answer many questions about how the mind and the body interact.

What Is Our Biological History?   50

2. According to Darwin's notion of *natural selection,* less adaptable organisms tend to become less numerous than organisms that are better able to adapt to the existing and changing environment.
3. A *mutation* occurs when a genetic message is changed.
4. *Genes* are the biological units that contribute to the hereditary transmission of traits. *Genetic traits* are characteristics or patterns of behavior that may be inherited. Genes are located on *chromosomes,* which come in pairs. Humans have 23 pairs of chromosomes in almost every cell of the body.
5. A *genotype* is the genetic code for a trait, and a *phenotype* is the actual visible expression of the trait in the organism. A given genotype may produce a range of phenotypes, depending on the environment in which the organism develops.

How Is the Nervous System Organized?   56

6. The nervous system is divided into two main parts: the *central nervous system (CNS),* consisting of the brain and the spinal cord, and the *peripheral nervous system (PNS),* consisting of the rest of the nervous system (e.g., the nerves in the face, legs, and arms).
7. The *blood–brain barrier* restricts the substances that may enter or leave the brain.

8. *Receptors* are structures that receive something. In particular, receptor neurons receive *sensory information* (e.g., sensations in the eyes, ears, and skin) from the outlying nerves of the body. The sensory neurons then transmit that information back up through the spinal cord to the brain. *Effectors* transmit *motor information* (e.g., movements of the muscles) from the CNS, controlling how the body acts in response to the information it receives.

9. A *reflex* is an automatic, involuntary response to stimulation. In many situations, reflexes can pass directly through the spinal cord, bypassing the brain. The brain is required, however, to assign conscious meaning to stimuli.

10. The peripheral nervous system has two parts: the somatic nervous system and the autonomic nervous system. The *somatic nervous system* controls voluntary movement of skeletal muscles, whereas the *autonomic nervous system* controls the involuntary muscles, such as those of the internal body organs.

How Is Information Processed in the Nervous System?   62

11. A *neuron* is an individual nerve cell. *Nerves* are bunches of neurons.

12. There are three functional types of neurons: (a) *sensory neurons,* through which the CNS receives information from the environment; (b) *motor neurons,* which carry information away from the CNS toward the outlying nerves of the PNS; and (c) *interneurons,* which transmit information between sensory and motor neurons.

13. The *soma* (cell body) of a neuron is responsible for the life of the nerve cell.

14. The branch-like *dendrites* are the structures through which neurons receive chemical messages.

15. *Axons* are the structures through which neurons conduct an action potential, which leads to the transmission of electrochemical messages. Some axons (usually relatively long ones) are covered by segments of *myelin,* a white, fatty substance. Myelin increases the speed and accuracy of conducting information through the neuron.

16. At the end of each axon are branches with knobs termed *terminal buttons.* Each terminal button releases a chemical *neurotransmitter.*

17. Between the terminal buttons of one neuron and the dendrites of the next neuron is a *synapse,* a tiny gap.

18. When a neuron reaches its particular *threshold of excitation,* the neuron generates an *all-or-none action potential.* During an *action potential,* ions quickly flood both ways across the neuronal membrane. This rapid transfer of ions changes the electrochemical balance inside and outside the neuron. Intraneuronal communication (the "firing" of a neuron) depends on generating an action potential.

19. The receptors on postsynaptic neurons can respond to a neurotransmitter in one of two ways: They can become either *excited* (more likely to fire) or *inhibited* (less likely to fire) by the neurotransmitter. In addition, *neuromodulators* may weaken or strengthen the likelihood that a receiving neuron will respond.

20. To avoid having too many neurotransmitters in the synapse, the terminal buttons can reabsorb the excess through *reuptake.*

21. Neurotransmitters include *acetylcholine, dopamine,* and *serotonin,* as well as *glutamate* and *GABA.* Neuropeptides include *endorphins* and many other chemicals involved in physiological regulation.

How Does the Endocrine System Work?   71

22. In the *endocrine system, glands* (organs that secrete a substance into the body) can secrete their products directly into the bloodstream. These endocrine secretions are *hormones.* The release of hormones is regulated by *a negative-feedback loop* (which monitors the levels of hormones in the bloodstream and monitors the effects of the hormones).

23. The nervous and endocrine systems are somewhat parallel: Both are communication systems, and both use chemical substances as messengers, neurotransmitters and hormones, respectively. The brain has some control over the endocrine system, just as hormones can influence the brain.

What Are the Major Structures and Functions of the Human Brain?   73

24. A fundamental way to view the human brain is to *dissect* it (i.e., to separate its tissues for examination).

25. Some psychologists study animal nervous systems.

26. *Electroencephalograms (EEGs)* measure and record electrical activity in the brain.

27. Although X-ray technology allows for X-ray photos and angiograms, a more psychologically revealing use of this technology is the creation of a *computerized axial tomogram (CT scan),* in which a computer analyzes a series of X-ray pictures and then constructs an image of the brain.

28. *Magnetic resonance imaging (MRI)* provides relatively detailed pictures of the brain based on

computer analysis of magnetic changes in the molecules of the brain.

29. *Positron emission tomography (PET scan)* shows the brain in action by tracing the brain's consumption of *glucose* (a simple sugar).

30. There are three main parts of the brain: the *forebrain*, which includes both the cortex and the limbic system, and is important to intelligent human thinking, feeling, and behaving; the *midbrain*, which includes most of the *reticular activating system* controlling heartbeat, breathing, consciousness, attention, and movement; and the *hindbrain*, which controls many vital functions of the body.

31. The highly convoluted *cerebral cortex* is the source of human abilities to reason, think abstractly, plan, and perceive and analyze sensory patterns.

32. The cerebral cortex covers the left and right hemispheres of the brain. The two hemispheres are connected by the *corpus callosum*. In general, each hemisphere contralaterally controls the opposite side of the body.

33. Based on extensive *split-brain* research, many investigators believe that the two hemispheres of the brain have specialized functions.

34. Sometimes, psychologists view the cortex as comprising four separate lobes. Roughly speaking, higher thought and motor processing occur in the *frontal lobe*, somatosensory (skin sensations) processing occurs in the *parietal lobe*, auditory processing in the *temporal lobe*, and visual processing in the *occipital lobe.*

35. *Association areas* also are located in the lobes and appear to link motor and sensory information.

Pathways to Knowledge

Choose the best answer to complete each sentence.

1. Unlike the other two types of neurons, sensory neurons
   (a) carry electrochemical messages from the brain and spinal cord to parts of the body that may respond to the messages.
   (b) receive information from receptor cells and send this information to the brain or spinal cord.
   (c) may be found exclusively in the central nervous system.
   (d) have two functions: to send signals from motor neurons and to receive signals from neurosensory receptors.

2. The four basic parts of a neuron are
   (a) axon, soma, myelin sheath, and dendrites.
   (b) axon, soma, myelin sheath, and nodes of Ranvier.
   (c) axon, soma, dendrites, and terminal buttons.
   (d) axon, soma, myelin sheath, and terminal buttons.

3. A synapse is
   (a) a gap between regions of myelin on an axon.
   (b) a gap between the terminal buttons of some neurons and the dendrites of other neurons.
   (c) a part of the axon, which may or may not be composed of myelin.

   (d) a part of the dendrite, which has terminal buttons for receiving neurotransmitters from other neurons.

4. The reuptake of neurotransmitters allows
   (a) neurotransmitters to be absorbed by the dendrites and soma of a receiving neuron.
   (b) neurotransmitters to be reabsorbed by the terminal buttons of a neuron that previously released the neurochemicals.
   (c) dendrites of receiving neurons to rerelease neurotransmitters back into the synapse.
   (d) dendrites that release one type of neurotransmitter to take up leftover transmitter substances released by neurons that release different types of neurotransmitters.

5. Effector nerves and neurons differ from receptor nerves and neurons, in that
   (a) effectors send information quickly to the central nervous system, whereas receptors send information rather slowly to the central nervous system.
   (b) effectors send information to the brain and spinal cord, but receptors send information to the outlying areas of the body.
   (c) effectors receive motor information from the brain and spinal cord and send it to the outlying areas of the body, but receptors send

information from the sense organs and the outlying areas of the body to the brain and spinal cord.

(d) effectors transmit sensory and motor information to the brain, but receptors receive sensory and motor information from the brain.

Answer each of the following questions by filling in the blank with an appropriate word or phrase.

6. A _____ is a structural change in a gene, which affects a hereditary characteristic.

7. Genes are located on _____.

8. A _____ for a genetic trait is the observable expression of the trait, whereas the _____ is the actual genetic makeup that an individual has for a particular genetic trait.

9. A _____ expression of a genetic trait appears in the phenotype of any individual who has at least one gene for the trait; in contrast, a _____ expression of a genetic trait appears only when a given individual has both genes for that expression of the trait.

10. The _____ of the endocrine system secrete _____ directly into the bloodstream.

11. When a neuron has been stimulated sufficiently to reach its _____ _____ _____, it generates an _____ _____ (and is said to "fire").

12. The two parts of the nervous system are the _____ _____ _____, which comprises the brain and the spinal cord, and the _____ _____ _____, which comprises all the other neurons of the areas lying outside of the brain and spinal cord.

Match the following parts of the brain to their main functions:

13. hippocampus
14. cerebellum

15. cerebral cortex
16. temporal lobe of the cortex

17. hypothalamus
18. corpus callosum

19. occipital lobe of the cortex

20. thalamus
21. parietal lobe

(a) higher order thinking
(b) connects two cerebral hemispheres
(c) bodily coordination
(d) species survival—fighting, fleeing, feeding, and mating
(e) learning
(f) somatosensory processing
(g) main relay station projecting sensory information to the appropriate areas of the cerebral cortex
(h) visual processing
(i) auditory processing

Answers

1. b, 2. c, 3. b, 4. b, 5. c, 6. mutation, 7. chromosomes, 8. phenotype, genotype, 9. dominant, recessive, 10. glands, hormones, 11. threshold of excitation, action potential, 12. central nervous system, peripheral nervous system, 13. e, 14. c, 15. a, 16. i, 17. d, 18. b, 19. h, 20. g, 21. f

Pathways to Understanding

1. Suppose that you were a master bioengineer who could create a genetic breakthrough to enhance the adaptability of humans. What change (or changes) would you make?

2. Suppose that it were possible to make the change (or changes) you suggested in response to the preceding question. What ethical issues would be involved in making that change (or those changes)?

3. Karl Lashley, a pioneering neuropsychologist in the study of brain localization, suffered from migraine headaches. Many scientists have personal reasons for being intensely curious about the phenomena they study. What aspects of human behavior particularly puzzle you? Which areas and structures of the brain might you wish to study to find out about those aspects of behavior? Why?

The Case of The Hearing Test

Liu cannot believe that her husband is insisting that she have a hearing test. She has made the mistake of complaining to her husband that her grades have gone down because she is having trouble hearing her professors, and now, at her husband's insistence, she is stuck having a humiliating hearing test. The last thing she wants to do is get stuck with a hearing aid. She is determined to pass the hearing test, but the problem is that she really is having trouble hearing her professors and sometimes even is having trouble hearing what her husband and friends are saying when they talk to her. Liu is worried that she indeed may have a hearing problem.

Liu and her husband are sitting in the waiting room when the audiologist enters. Liu goes into a soundproof room and is told how the test will work; it is very simple. The test will occur in a series of trials. The audiologist tells Liu that the signals will vary both in their pitch and in how loud they are. On each trial the audiologist will ask Liu if she has heard a tone and all Liu has to do is say "yes" or "no."

CHAPTER 3
SENSATION AND PERCEPTION

Determined not to fail the test, Liu settles on a simple but, she believes, clever strategy. She simply will say "yes" most of the time, even if she does not hear all the tones. But she will not say "yes" so often that she will arouse suspicion. In this way she will pass the hearing test and be done with the threat of the hearing aid.

Liu takes the test and follows through with her plan. During the test the audiologist reminds her to be sure to respond "yes" when she hears signals and "no" when she does not. Liu continues her strategy, however, slightly decreasing the number of "yes" responses just in case the audiologist is suspicious.

After the hearing test, Liu and her husband receive the result. Liu is stunned to hear that the audiologist has determined that her hearing is impaired at several different pitches and that she will, in fact, need a hearing aid. Liu cannot figure out how the audiologist could have made this determination.

Think about this while you are reading chapter 3. How could the audiologist have known that Liu has impaired hearing? Watch for the relevance of signal-detection theory, which provided the pathway for diagnosing the problem with Liu's hearing.

3

A sense is a physical system that collects information and then translates the information into a meaningful form that the brain can understand. A **sensation** is a message that the brain receives from the senses. There are many pathways by which sensory information can enter the body. In this chapter, we will consider each of these pathways, concentrating on the pathways provided by two senses: vision and hearing.

Sensory information may come from the external world or from the internal world of the body. As chapter 2 showed, the sensory system communicates information in an electrochemical form. For example, you might use your eyes and nose to collect sensory information about a pizza as a steaming, circular, flat, red-and-white object. Your eyes then somehow translate this information and send it to your brain through your sensory neurons.

When your brain receives these various sensations, it organizes, interprets, and makes sense of this sensory information. At last, your brain announces, "Pizza for dinner!" The high-level processing of information in your brain is **perception,** which takes up roughly where sensation leaves off. Perception usually refers to the cognitive (thinking) processes through which we interpret sensory messages. During perception, we *synthesize* (selectively combine and integrate) and assign meaning to our sensations. We do so by taking into account our expectations, our prior experiences, and perhaps even our culture.

A few years ago, I was walking down the street in a town abroad. Suddenly someone up ahead, whom I previously had not noticed, started waving frantically at me. "What a clown," I thought to myself, looking directly at him and feeling confident in my belief that I did not know anyone in the town. Finally I recognized a professional colleague whom I had known for at least 15 years and seen on almost a daily basis. It was a face I would have recognized in a fraction of a second at home, but placed out of context and outside my expectations, one that took me several seconds to recognize. Fortunately, he was a psychologist and understood my confusion, or so he said. All the sensations to recognize him were in place, but my different expectations led to a long delay in recognition.

Thus, sensation enables our bodies to receive information from the environment and perception enables us to make sense of this information. Clearly, sensation and perception are highly interrelated. Even so, psychologists separate the two processes in order to study each more closely.

Learning about sensation and perception can be very practical. For example, are you one of the people who slow down considerably when it is foggy outside, or are you one of the people who get annoyed at those who do slow down and keep you from getting where you want to go? The principles of perception teach you that you are much better off slowing down. The reason is that, when it is foggier, objects are substantially closer than they appear to be. You therefore are much more likely to have an accident, not just because you cannot see other cars or because they cannot see you, but because it is so easy to misjudge distances. You easily can end up rear-ending the car in front of you or end up being rear-ended by the car in back of you. At the opposite extreme, did you ever look out on a clear day and see a mountain in the distance? Did you maybe try driving toward that mountain? On an exceptionally clear day, objects are farther away than they appear to be. It has happened to many people; the mountain that seems to be an hour or so off in the distance is more like four hours off in the distance. These are just two of the many cases in which understanding principles of sensation and perception can help you in your daily life.

In this chapter, we examine sensation before we study perception. Hence, the first part of this chapter describes how our senses provide us with the sensations of light, color, sound, taste, scent, pressure, temperature, pain, balance, and movement. The second part of this chapter describes how we meaningfully synthesize our sensations.

Even before we examine each sense individually, however, we discuss some phenomena that apply to all our senses. First, we explore how to study and measure the functioning of the senses. Second, we probe some biological properties common to all our senses.

HOW DO PSYCHOLOGISTS STUDY THE SENSES?

Psychophysics is the study and measurement of the functioning of the senses. Specifically, psychophysicists first observe particular forms of *physical stimulation* of the senses (e.g., light going to the eye or sound going to the ear). Then they observe what people seem to experience in their minds as *psychological sensations* (i.e., their form of awareness of the physical stimulation). Finally, and most importantly, psychophysicists try to measure the relationship between a particular form of physical stimulation and the psychological sensations it produces. For example, a psychophysical experiment might measure the relationship between how quickly a light is flashed on and off and how easily you can detect separate flashes. Another experiment might measure the relationship between the physical *intensity* of a sound (the actual amount of stimulation that reaches your ears) and how loud you hear that sound to be.

The relationship between physical intensity and psychological experience is an important one. Consider this example: Many young people are permanently damaging their hearing by listening to very loud music, whether by listening to the music through earphones or by listening to it at concerts. For the rest of their lives, they will have difficulty hearing sounds at certain frequencies or they may not hear at these frequencies at all. The problem is that the psychological experience they are having is not sufficient to make them aware of the damage they are doing to themselves, and as they start to lose their hearing, the problem only will get worse. It would be as though the pain of a hot iron were insufficient for a person to withdraw his or her hand, rendering the person susceptible to tissue damage. It is therefore important for psychologists to understand where and when psychological experience is insufficient to lead people to withdraw from activities, such as listening to loud music, that can cause permanent damage.

Psychophysical measurements can be used in many practical ways. A common use involves testing whether people's senses are functioning normally. For example, the eye doctor who checks your vision determines how large the letters must be for you to see them clearly (see Figure 3.1).

Psychophysics is also useful in engineering psychology, such as in the design of instrument panels. How brightly should a car's dashboard gauges glow in order to be visible, but not distracting, at night? For that matter, in the development of almost any product, psychologists may be asked to provide psychophysical information regarding both the usefulness and the appeal of the product. For example, consumer psychologists tackle questions such as "How strong can a perfume be without seeming to be overpowering?" Fundamentally, the key question asked by psychophysicists is "How easily can people detect particular sensory stimuli?" Detection is considered next.

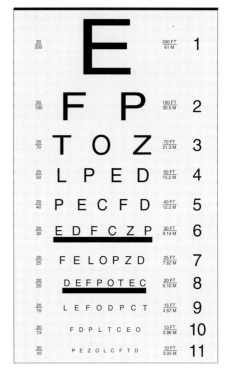

FIGURE 3.1
The Snellen Vision Chart
This familiar chart shows a psychophysical test used in measuring one aspect of visual sensation.

sense • a physical system for receiving a particular kind of physical stimulation and translating that stimulation into an electrochemical message

sensation • a message regarding physical stimulation of a sensory receptor

perception • the mental processes that organize and interpret sensory information that has been transmitted to the brain

psychophysics • the systematic study of the relationship between the physical stimulation of a sense organ and the psychological sensations produced by that stimulation

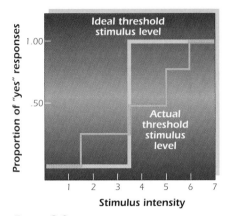

FIGURE 3.2
Sample Ideal and Real Absolute Thresholds
Because it is impossible to determine an ideal absolute threshold, psychologists define an absolute threshold *as the level of stimulation that an individual can detect 50% of the time.*

Detection

Absolute Threshold

Detection is the active psychophysical sensing of a stimulus, knowing that the stimulus is there. In sensory-detection studies, researchers ask how much light, sound, taste, or other sensory stimulation is needed in order for the human senses to detect it. For each kind of sensory stimulation, there is a minimum amount of physical energy that your senses can detect. This minimum detectable amount is your **absolute threshold** for that kind of sensory stimulation. In theory, you would never sense the stimulus below your absolute-threshold level, and you would always sense the stimulus above that level.

Low absolute thresholds have important survival value. The ability to detect the sound, sight, or smell of an approaching predator can mean the difference between life and death to an animal in the wild. Absolute thresholds also can make the difference between life and death to soldiers in a war zone who are being hunted by the enemy. The ability to detect a noxious or bitter taste can lead either to a person's dying of poisoning or to that same person's spitting out a noxious substance before it is too late.

In reality, however, our sensations do not detect particular sensory stimuli at exactly the same levels all of the time. Thus, an absolute threshold really cannot be measured directly. To come up with a way to describe phenomena that cannot be measured directly, psychologists use **operational definitions,** which specify how to figure out a best guess about these phenomena. In psychophysics, psychologists operationally define the *absolute threshold* as the level of stimulation at which a stimulus is first detected 50% of the time during many attempts to detect the stimulus (see Figure 3.2). Knowing the absolute thresholds for people enables doctors to determine whether these people show hearing loss. But people's responses in hearing tests do not always accurately reflect what they hear. How can we determine any kind of sensitivity to auditory or other forms of stimulation, given that people's responses do not always reflect their sensory experiences? Signal detection theory provides a method.

detection • the awareness of the presence of a sensory stimulus

absolute threshold • a hypothetical minimum amount of physical energy that an individual can detect for each kind of sensory stimulation; operationally defined as the level at which a stimulus is first detected 50% of the time during many attempts to detect the stimulus

operational definition • a means for researchers to specify exactly how to test or to measure particular phenomena being studied

signal detection theory (SDT) • a method of measuring the detection of a sensation, which takes into account the influence of expectations and decision making on detection

Signal Detection Theory

Often, people's expectations regarding a sensation affect the likelihood that the people will detect it. For example, are you more likely to notice someone approaching your door when you expect a guest or when you do not expect one? **Signal detection theory (SDT)** is a systematic method of measuring detection, which considers expectations and other thought-related influences on the detection of sensations.

According to SDT, there are four possible combinations of stimulus and response (Green & Swets, 1966; Swets, Tanner, & Birdsall, 1961). Suppose you are a spy waiting to get a signal from your confederate letting you know when it is safe to deliver your coded message (or your microfilm). The signal for safe delivery is the flicker of a light. One possibility is that the *signal* (the stimulus; in this case, the flicker of the light) is present, and you detect it (your response); this pairing is a *hit.* You correctly deliver the message. Another possibility is a *miss:* The light flickers, but you do not detect it. You should deliver the message, but you fail to do so, thereby endangering the well-being of your fellow agents and perhaps imperiling your country. A third possibility is a *false alarm:* The

TABLE 3.1
Signal Detection Matrix

Signal detection theory	Detect a signal	Do not detect a signal
Signal present	Hit	Miss
Signal absent	False alarm	Correct rejection

light does not flicker, but you think you see it flicker. You deliver the message when you should not; once again, your country is endangered. The fourth possibility is a *correct rejection:* The light does not flicker, and you do not think it does. You wait longer for an opportunity to deliver your message safely into the right hands. These combinations of stimuli and responses are summarized in Table 3.1. The ratio of hits to false alarms provides a measure of sensitivity to stimuli: the higher the ratio, the more sensitive the organism. Organisms need to be sensitive not only to minimal levels of stimuli, but to small differences in stimuli. Discrimination of differences is considered next.

Discrimination: The Just Noticeable Difference

Being able to detect a single stimulus is certainly crucial in many circumstances, such as in the case of a police officer searching for a lawbreaker in hiding. Often, however, the problem is not how strong or intense a stimulus must be in order for a person to detect it. Rather, the problem involves *discrimination* (the ability to detect the difference between one stimulus and another). For example, suppose that you were looking quickly at a digital timepiece. Were you seeing 1:11 or 1:17? Were the last two numerals alike (11) or different (17)?

The minimum amount of difference that can be detected between two stimuli is the **difference threshold.** A more common term for the difference threshold is the **just noticeable difference (jnd).** Just as our ability to detect sensory stimuli varies, so does our ability to detect differences between stimuli. For this reason, psychologists try to measure a jnd many times for a given kind of stimulus (e.g., different musical tones or different color chips), and then they average the data from all of their attempts. In practical terms, psychologists operationally define the *jnd* as the difference between two stimuli that can be detected at least 50% of the time.

Sensory-difference thresholds are important in everyday life and even in some professions. A coffee taster must be able to taste and smell the differences among various blends, grinds, and roasts of beans. Musicians must be able to hear whether their instruments are just a fraction of a note off-key. Engineering psychologists use jnds to help determine various aspects of product design. For example, each notch on a sound-volume dial of a stereo system must represent at least some jnd in loudness, or the dial is not effective.

An interesting phenomenon affects our sensation of the jnd. Physiologist Ernst Weber (1795–1878) noticed that the change needed to cause a jnd increases proportionally with increases in the intensity of a stimulus. That is, you may be able to detect a small difference in a low-intensity

difference threshold • a hypothetical minimum amount of difference that can be detected between two stimuli (see also *just noticeable difference*)

just noticeable difference (jnd) • a term operationally defined as the point at which an individual can detect the difference between two stimuli at least 50% of the time over a series of attempts to detect the difference stimulus, but a much larger difference is needed for you to detect a difference in a high-intensity stimulus. For example, with your eyes closed, you could probably sense the difference in weight between a 5-ounce (141.75-gram) bag of cherries and an 8-ounce (226.80-gram) bag of cherries. However, you probably would find it almost impossible to detect the difference between a 20-pound (9.07-kilogram) bag of potatoes and a bag of potatoes weighing 20 pounds and 3 ounces (9.16 kilograms). Why would you sense the extra 3 ounces (98.31 grams) the first time but not the second? As the stimulus intensity (here, the weight of the bag) increases, the amount of change needed to produce a jnd also increases. Therefore, the difference in weight would have to be much greater for you to sense the difference in the 20-pound bags. Similarly, when you carry suitcases in an airport, you notice the difference between, say, 10 and 20 pounds more than you notice the difference between 30 and 40 pounds.

So far, we have explored how psychologists measure sensory functioning. Next, we study what psychologists have discovered, based on those measurements.

WHAT ARE SOME BIOLOGICAL PROPERTIES COMMON TO ALL SENSES?

Receptor Cells and Transduction

Various forms of physical energy, such as light and sound, stimulate our sense organs. **Receptor cells** are the structures of our sense organs that receive these various forms of energy. These cells are specialized to detect particular kinds of energy within the receptive fields of the cells. A *receptive field* is the area of the external world from which each receptor cell receives messages.

Different kinds of receptor cells are sensitive to different forms of energy. Our visual system has receptors sensitive to *light waves* (visible electromagnetic radiation). Our *gustatory* (taste) and *olfactory* (smell) systems have receptors for chemicals from foods and other substances. Our other senses (e.g., hearing, touch, and balance) have specialized receptors for mechanical energy from the air, from other objects, or even from within our own bodies.

Each of our sensory receptors **transduces** (converts) an incoming form of energy (mechanical, chemical, electromagnetic, etc.) into the electrochemical form of energy that is used by our nervous system. In general, for each sense, the set of specialized receptor cells transduces only the particular kind of stimulus energy the sense is designed to receive. For example, our *auditory* (hearing), *tactile* (touch), *kinesthetic* (motion), and *vestibular* (balance) systems transduce mechanical energy into electrochemical energy. (They are insensitive to light energy, however.) The sensory neurons then carry those electrochemical messages to our brains for information processing. Such processing is possible only if the brain has some way to code sensory information.

receptor cell • a body cell that is especially suited to detecting and transforming a particular kind of energy that reaches the cell

transduce • the conversion of incoming energy from one form (e.g., mechanical, chemical, electromagnetic) into an electrochemical form of energy for use within the nervous system

Sensory Coding

How do our brains distinguish among assorted stimuli? The trill of a flute does not sound like the wail of an electric guitar. An onion's strong odor is noticeably distinct from a violet's mild scent. Each set of receptors must somehow be able to convey to the brain a range of information about individual stimuli. Otherwise, we would not know a loving caress from a hostile punch; we would only know that we felt something. **Sensory coding** is the means by which sensory receptors convey this range of information about stimuli. Receptors and neurons use electrochemical codes to express shades of meaning in their messages.

For a given stimulus, sensory coding must convey a range of physical properties that affect our psychological perception of the stimulus. In particular, each sensory stimulus has at least two main features: (a) *intensity,* the amount of energy sensed (e.g., the strength of an odor), and (b) *quality,* the nature of the stimulus (e.g., the particular kind of smell, such as a skunk vs. a rose). For seeing and hearing, we can measure the physical intensity of the stimulus in terms of *amplitude.* For light waves, the psychological experience of greater amplitude is increased brightness; for sound waves, it is increased loudness. For seeing and hearing, we also measure *wavelength,* the distance from the peak of one sound wave or light wave to the peak of the next wave. For light waves, the physical wavelength is associated with the psychological experience of color. For sound waves, the physical wavelength is associated with *pitch* (how high or low we sense the tone to be). Actually, sound waves are usually described in terms of the frequency of the waves, rather than in terms of the length of the waves.

For all of the senses, intensity is usually coded in the form of how many neurons fire or how frequently they fire in response to a transduced sensory stimulus. The coding of sensory quality (e.g., color [vision], pitch [hearing], or saltiness [taste]) is more complex, and psychologists are continually making new discoveries regarding how we can sense various qualities of a stimulus. We more fully explore how our senses code the qualities of stimuli in the discussion of each sensory system. Meanwhile, let's consider how these sensory systems can detect changes in stimuli.

Detection of Changes in Stimuli

In addition to energy transduction and sensory coding, another process is common to all the senses: how we detect changes in stimuli. Our senses readily detect changes in stimulus energy. When the stimulus energy changes, the sensory neurons alert the brain to the change. The ability to detect change is essential to survival; it is what enables you to know that you are getting too warm or too cold or to know that a car in back of you has speeded up and is now getting dangerously close. It is also what enables you to detect that what might before have been a faint background smell of gas from an oven is quickly becoming stronger and therefore signaling the potential danger of a gas leak.

The sensory system also makes physiological adjustments to the change in the sensed stimulus. These adjustments occur through the process of **adaptation.** Sensory adaptation is a temporary physiological response to a sensed change in the environment. For example, your eyes automatically and unconsciously adapt to changes in light intensity (increases or decreases in brightness). Similarly, your sense of smell adapts to having a particular odor in the environment. A smell that you hardly can stand in the first minute, such as of decaying fruit, may be much less detectable after a while. You need no training or previous experience to make these adaptations, and you will adapt almost exactly the same way the first time and every time thereafter. The degree to which your senses

sensory coding • the physiological form of communication through which sensory receptors convey a range of information about stimuli within the nervous system

adaptation • a temporary physiological response to a sensed change in the environment, which is neither learned nor consciously controlled; the degree of adaptation depends directly on the degree of change in the stimulus, with greater changes producing greater adaptation

adapt relates directly to the intensity of the stimulus in the environment. It does not matter how many times you previously were exposed to the stimulus or how long it was between your last exposure and your present exposure. Furthermore, when the stimulus in the environment changes back again, your physiological mechanisms for adaptation change back again, too. All of these common properties are of interest because they apply to each sense individually. In the next section, we consider each of the senses individually.

HOW DO WE SEE?

Have you ever wakened to total darkness? If you get out of bed, you stumble into and over things you did not remember noticing before you went to bed. In the dark, you appreciate your vision in a way that you do not when you see well. In order to understand vision, we need to know something about light, about the structure of the eye, and about how the eye interacts with light to enable us to see.

The Nature of Light

The receptors of our eyes seem well designed for receiving *light* (a form of electromagnetic energy). The qualities of light energy take the form of varying wavelengths, which together make up the *electromagnetic spectrum* (see Figure 3.3). Human eyes sense only a very narrow range of wavelengths within this broad spectrum. For example, humans cannot see wavelengths in the infrared or ultraviolet bands of the electromagnetic spectrum, although some other animals can. What is the anatomy of the eye that enables us to see the wavelengths we can see?

FIGURE 3.3
The Electromagnetic Spectrum
Within the wide range of the electromagnetic spectrum, humans are able to detect only a narrow band of wavelengths of light.

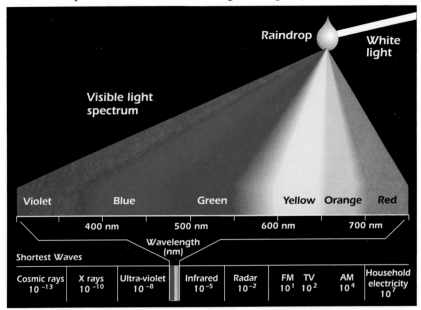

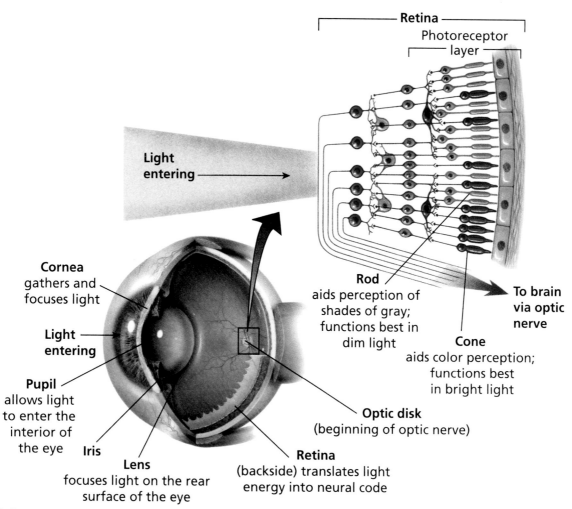

FIGURE 3.4

Anatomy of the Eye: How the Eye Adjusts to Focus Visual Images

The cornea of the eye makes gross adjustments of its curvature when light enters, and the lens makes finer adjustments of its curvature, to provide the best angle of focus for the entering light. Flatter lenses and corneas bend the light less and focus on more distant objects, whereas more curved lenses and corneas more clearly focus on closer objects. The various structures and processes of the human eye focus entering light on the retina, located on the rear surface of the eye.

Anatomy of the Eye

Light beams enter the eye through the **cornea,** a curved, clear outer surface that gathers the entering light and bends it toward the center of the eye. Next, the light passes through the **pupil,** a hole in the center of a circular muscle, namely, the **iris.** The light bends further as it passes through the eye's curved inner **lens** (see Figure 3.4).

If light rays are not bent sharply enough by the cornea, distant objects are seen quite clearly but it is harder to bring near objects into good focus. In this case, the individual is labeled as farsighted. If, on the other hand, the light rays are bent too sharply by the cornea, near objects are sharply

cornea • the clear, dome-shaped window through which light passes, serving primarily as a curved exterior surface of the eye that gathers and focuses the entering light

pupil • the hole in the iris (roughly in its center) through which light gains access to the interior of the eye, particularly the retina

iris • a circular membrane that reflects light beams outward and away from the eye and surrounds the pupil

lens • a curved interior structure of the eye, which bends light slightly to focus it on the center of the rear surface of the eye

in focus but distant objects look blurry. This condition results in near-sightedness.

The lens and cornea focus the entering light on the **retina**, a network of neurons on the back surface of the eye. Even though the retina only is about as thick as a single page in this book, it includes three main layers. The most important of the three layers is a layer of photoreceptors. **Photoreceptors** *(photo-,* light) transduce light energy into electrochemical energy.

There are two kinds of photoreceptors: rods and cones. The **rods** are long, thin, and very numerous; the **cones** are relatively short, thick, and less numerous. Rods and cones also differ in their locations in the retina. Cones are more densely concentrated in the center of the retina, and rods are more densely concentrated in the outer region of the retina. Together, they enable us to see. Messages from the rods and the cones are sent primarily to the occipital lobe of the brain.

How We See

It appears that rods and cones also differ in their responses to light. This observation led biologist Max Schultze (1825–1874) to propose that there are two separate visual systems. One system, responsible for vision in dim light, depends on the rods. The other system, responsible for vision in brighter light and for the ability to see colors, depends on the cones. The cones provide much sharper and clearer vision than the rods. One reason for the greater clarity of cone vision over rod vision is that each cone gets more direct representation in the visual cortex, the part of the brain that controls vision, than does each rod.

Cones are more involved when you undergo **light adaptation**, which is an adjustment to increases in light intensity, such as when you walk from a dark room into bright sunlight. In contrast, when you go from the bright outdoors into a dim or dark room, you undergo **dark adaptation**, in which your rods must become active enough to permit you to see relatively well in dim light. The phenomena of light and dark adaptation have important practical applications, as shown in Putting It to Use 3.1. But perhaps most practical of all, as anyone who has ever obeyed a traffic light will affirm, is our ability to see in color.

Color

Psychologists have a relatively clear view of how people sense differing intensities of light. However, there is considerable controversy regarding how people sense the qualities of light related to color. Some of light's physical properties make colors psychologically appear the way they do to us. Wavelength produces the most basic quality for us: *hue,* which is the physical property corresponding to the psychological property we call *color.* We sense colors based on how our nervous systems react to particular wavelengths of the visible spectrum.

A second physical property of color is *purity,* which is the mixture of wavelengths of light that reaches the senses. The psychological property of *saturation* corresponds to purity. Highly saturated colors look rich and lively, with no hint of dull gray or flat brown. The third physical property of color is *intensity* (amplitude), which corresponds to the psychological property of *brightness.*

Colors can be mixed either additively or subtractively; the two processes work quite differently and result in different colors. When light

retina • a network of neurons covering most of the rear surface inside the eye; contains the photoreceptors that transduce light energy into electrochemical energy

photoreceptor • a receptor cell that receives and transduces light *(photo-,* light) energy into electrochemical energy

rod • a long, thin, and abundant type of photoreceptor, responsible mostly for vision in dim lighting

cone • a relatively short, thick, and less abundant type of photoreceptor, responsible mostly for very clear color vision in bright lighting

light adaptation • the physiological adjustment to increases in light intensity, during which the cones become more active

dark adaptation • the physiological adjustment to decreases in light intensity, during which the rods become more active

3.1

DESIGNS IN LIGHT AND DARK

PUTTING IT TO USE

Engineering psychologists consider light and dark adaptation in the design of products and settings in which people work, play, and reside. When people go to and from extreme brightness or darkness, they cannot see as well. Hence, exit signs in darkened movie theaters must be easy to observe even before dark adaptation takes place. Stairs in the paths leading into or out of darkness or glaring light should have handrails, special illumination, or some other means of alerting people to their presence until adaptation takes place. Although adaptation occurs in almost the same way from our first entrance into bright light until our final exit into darkness, we lose some of our ability to adapt to darkness as we age. Hence, buildings designed particularly for use by older persons should allow for slower adaptation to changes in lighting.

waves of varying wavelengths are mixed, as when aiming spotlights of different colors (e.g., red, green, and blue) toward one point, we obtain an **additive mixture** (see Figure 3.5a). You are probably more familiar with **subtractive mixture**. When paints or other light-reflecting colors are mixed, they *absorb (subtract* from our vision) more wavelengths of light than each one absorbs individually. The more wavelengths of light that are subtracted, the darker the result looks. Figure 3.5b shows what happens

additive mixture • the mixture of light waves of varying wavelengths, in which each wavelength of light adds to the other wavelengths

subtractive mixture • the remaining combined wavelengths of light that are reflected from an object after other wavelengths of light have been absorbed (subtracted from the reflected light) by the object

FIGURE 3.5
Color Mixtures
(a) In additive color mixtures, *each light* adds *its wavelength to the color mixture, and the resulting sum of the wavelengths is what we see. When red light, blue light, and green light are mixed in different combinations, different colors appear. The additive mixture of all three colors of light produces white light. (b) Subtractive color mixtures may be obtained with various mixtures of pigments or filters. Most colored objects do not generate light; they reflect it. That is, the sky appears blue to us because it reflects blue light and absorbs all wavelengths other than blue, subtracting those colors from our sight. In subtractive mixtures, colors may be combined to subtract (absorb) more colors, reflecting fewer colors when more pigments are mixed.*

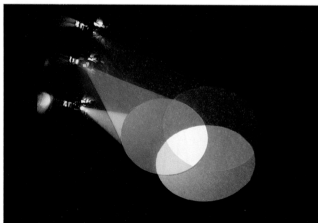

(a)

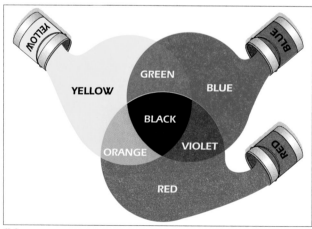

(b)

when subtractively mixing together pigments of yellow, *cyan* (greenish-blue as a pigment, but deep blue when used as an additive color), and *magenta* (purplish-red).

Not everyone can see all or even some colors. People who are either partially or fully color-blind often have an inability to distinguish red from green. Some people are fully color-blind and can distinguish only various shades of gray.

Up to this point, visual sensations have dominated our discussion of sensation. Through visual sensations, we can gain information from places far removed from the grasp of our hands, from mountains at the edge of the horizon and even from the moon, the sun, and the stars. Through auditory sensations, we can gain information from behind our backs, from around corners, and sometimes even through doors and walls. Our sense of hearing readily complements our sense of sight; the two together provide far more information than either alone can offer.

HOW DO WE HEAR?

To understand hearing, you need to know about the structures (anatomy) and processes (physiology) that permit us to hear: the interaction between sound and the ear.

FIGURE 3.6
Properties of Sound Waves
Sound waves are generally measured in terms of amplitude, *which corresponds to the psychological sensation of loudness, and* frequency, *which corresponds to the psychological sensation of pitch. A third psychological dimension of sound is* timbre *(not shown here).*

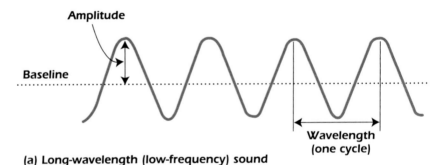

(a) Long-wavelength (low-frequency) sound

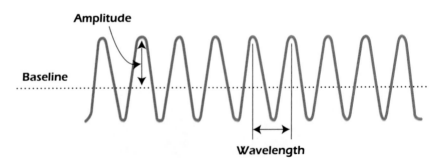

(b) Short-wavelength (high-frequency) sound

The Nature of Sound

Physical Properties of Sound

Sound results from mechanical pressure on the air. To get a feel for the physical force of sound, place your hand gently over your throat, in the front of your neck, and speak aloud. The sound you produce will vibrate your hand. Similarly, when you pluck the string of a guitar, or clap your hands together, you are pushing on air molecules.

When sounds push on air molecules, the pushed molecules briefly crash into other air molecules, which then crash into still other air molecules. The result is a three-dimensional wave of mechanical energy. The air particles themselves do not move much; it is the wave of pressure that covers the distance. Compare this effect to a line of cars waiting at a stoplight. Along comes a speeder who fails to stop in time, rear-ending the last car in line. That car then hits the car in front of it, and so on. The mechanical pressure spreads in a forward wave through the line of cars. However, the car that started the wave does not move much at all.

Corresponding Physical and Psychological Properties of Sound Waves

The physical properties of sound waves affect how we sense and process these waves psychologically. The first two properties are familiar: the amplitude (height) and the frequency (length; see Figure 3.6). Sound amplitude (intensity) corresponds to our sensation of loudness: the higher the amplitude, the louder the sound. The usual unit of measurement for the intensity of sound is the *decibel (dB)*. Zero decibels is the absolute threshold for normal human hearing, at which most people can detect a sound at least 50% of the time. Table 3.2 shows the decibel levels of various common sounds.

TABLE 3.2
Decibel Table

Decibel level	Example	Dangerous time exposure
0	Lowest sound audible to human ear (threshold)	
30	Quiet library, soft whisper	
40	Quiet office, living room, bedroom away from traffic	
50	Light traffic at a distance, refrigerator, gentle breeze	
60	Air conditioner at 20 feet, conversation	
70	Busy traffic, noisy restaurant (constant exposure)	Critical level begins
80	Subway, heavy city traffic, alarm clock at 2 feet, factory noise	More than 8 hours
90	Truck traffic, noisy appliances, shop tools, lawnmower	Less than 8 hours
100	Chain saw, boiler shop, pneumatic drill	2 hours
120	Rock concert in front of speakers, sandblasting, thunderclap	Immediate danger
140	Gunshot blast, jet plane	Any exposure is dangerous
180	Spacecraft launch	Hearing loss inevitable

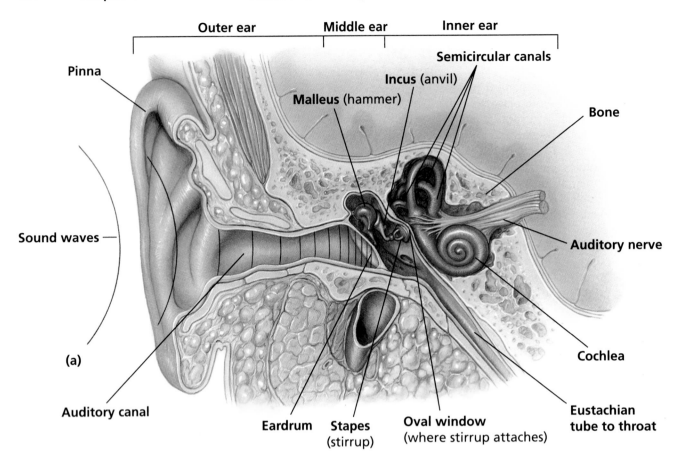

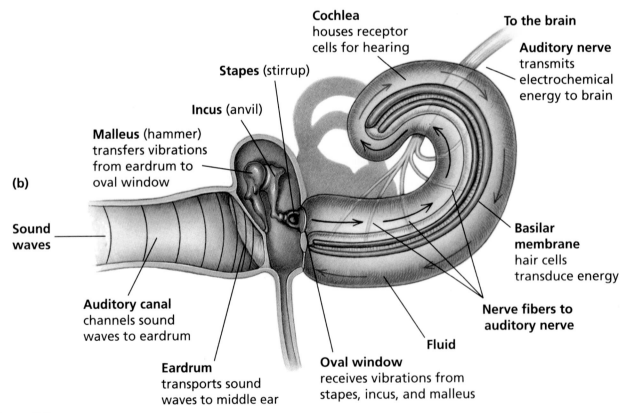

FIGURE 3.7
Anatomy of the Ear
Shown here are (a) the various physical structures of the ear and (b) a close-up view of the cochlea.

The frequency (Figure 3.6) of sound corresponds to our psychological sensation of *pitch* (how high or low a tone sounds). A frequency of one cycle per second is 1 *hertz (Hz)*. The third psychological dimension of sound is timbre. *Timbre* is the quality of sound that allows us to tell the difference between a note played on a piano and the same note played on a harmonica. How can we hear timbre or any other property of sound?

How We Hear

When sound waves enter the ear, they pass through three regions: the outer ear, the middle ear, and the inner ear. The key mechanism for hearing the properties of sound lies deep inside the inner ear, in a set of fluid-filled canals. One of the membranes separating two of these canals is the **basilar membrane** (see Figure 3.7). On the basilar membrane are thousands of **hair cells,** which are our auditory (hearing) receptors. When sound vibrations reach the hair cells, the sound waves move parts of the hair cells. The hair cells then transduce the mechanical energy of the sound waves into electrochemical energy. The electrochemical energy is transmitted through the neurons primarily to the temporal lobe of the brain.

Humans can generally hear sound waves in the range from about 20 to 20,000 Hz. Within this broad range, we are most sensitive to sounds in the middle of the range, roughly corresponding to the range of human voices. We are especially sensitive to changes in sounds, such as changes in pitch. We also need to be able to locate sounds.

Locating Sounds

How do we figure out where sounds are coming from? The way we locate sounds is based on a very simple physiological fact: Our two ears are located about 6 inches apart on opposite sides of our heads. When a sound comes from our right, it has less distance to travel to reach the right ear than the left ear, so it reaches the right ear a little sooner than it reaches the left ear. We can detect differences in arrival times that are as brief as 10 microseconds (millionths of a second; Durlach & Colburn, 1978). Another way we process sound location is by comparing the differences in the intensities of the sounds reaching our ears. The farther ear receives a lower intensity sound than does the closer ear because the head absorbs some of the sound going to the farther ear. Apparently, the *time-difference method* works best for locating the source of low-frequency sounds, and the *intensity-difference method* works best for locating high-frequency sounds (see Figure 3.8).

Most of us rely on our sensations of sights and sounds to comprehend our environment and to monitor the events taking place around us. It is largely through hearing and seeing that we adapt to and shape our environment. Because of the power of these sensory systems, we sometimes fail to appreciate all we learn from our other senses. However, people who cannot see or hear are able to adapt quite well to their surroundings by making the most of the other senses they have available. To find out more about how people adapt to a world without sights or sounds, see the following Branching Out box.

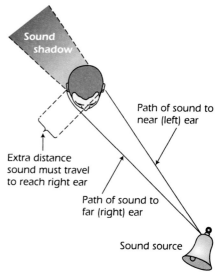

FIGURE 3.8
Locating Sounds
We locate the sources of sounds by using two methods: (a) In the time-difference method, we note the time that a given sound arrives at each ear, and we figure out that the sound comes from somewhere nearer to the ear that heard the sound first. (b) In the intensity-difference method, we note the loudness of a given sound in each ear, and we conclude that the sound comes from somewhere nearer to the ear that heard the sound more loudly.

basilar membrane • one of the membranes separating two of the fluid-filled canals of the inner ear; on this membrane are the hair cells that transduce sound waves

hair cell • an auditory receptor that transduces sound waves into electrochemical energy

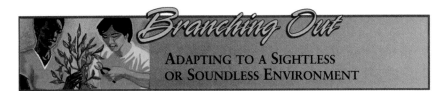

ADAPTING TO A SIGHTLESS
OR SOUNDLESS ENVIRONMENT

All of us rely on our senses for adapting to the world around us. When we lack information from one or more of our senses, we rely even more heavily on the remaining senses. We also depend on help from other people, from various kinds of technologies, and from learning various techniques to make the most of the sensory information we have. For instance, Helen Keller's relationship with her nurse, Anne Sullivan, made it possible for the blind and deaf Keller to become a world-renowned lecturer and author. She was also able to benefit from the technological aids that were available around the turn of the century: She learned to read both raised letters and Braille (raised dots) letters, and she learned to write, using a Braille typewriter. (Keller could also lip-read pretty well by placing her hand on the mouth and neck of the speaker.) Through reading, Keller explored a vast world of experience extending far beyond the limitations of her sensory world.

Almost a century after Keller wrote the story of her life, many more options have become available to extend the experiences of deaf and blind individuals. Well-trained hearing-ear dogs and seeing-eye dogs, and other animal assistants, ably can provide needed sensory information for independent living. In addition, technological aids can translate information from one sensory modality to another. Sounds can be translated into other sensations, such as sights or vibrations, enabling deaf persons to see "doorbells," feel the vibrations of an "alarm clock," and read the "voices" of a telephone caller or a television show. Similarly, sights can be translated into sounds: Speech-synthesis technologies can transform printed material into spoken words. Many blind students can now have access to almost any reading material of interest to them, through various reading services and technologies. Technological assistance for enhancing and supporting independent living are increasing almost daily: Voice-recognition systems can implement voiced commands, motion-detection systems can signal the presence of other persons, and so on.

Cultural changes, too, have widened the perceptible world of persons who cannot sense sights or sounds. Less than a century ago, most deaf children had little or no formal education. Many such children were not identified as being deaf or were not given adequate opportunities to learn language until it was too late for them to acquire a native or native-like mastery of language. Through the early detection of deafness and the increasingly widespread use of natural languages, such as American Sign Language (ASL), children who might otherwise be deprived of language and of rich educational opportunities have been able to acquire language early enough to become fluent users (Sacks, 1990). Although it may be surprising to hearing persons, many persons who are deaf from birth are quite content with their soundless world and do not seek to hear. Even persons who become deaf later in life may come to feel that their soundless world is complete (Sacks, 1990), so that when asked whether they would choose to restore their hearing, they say they would not.

This wariness of restored hearing (or vision) may not be unfounded. For people who have been blind or deaf from birth, the introduction of sight or of sound in adulthood may be more confusing than it is rewarding (Gregory, 1987; Sacks, 1995). To make sense of their sensations, they rely on the senses they have fine-tuned over a lifetime for constructing a coherent and comprehensible perceptual world. Only through tremendous effort and persistent practice can they adjust to regaining their vision or their hearing.

HOW DO WE SENSE TASTE, SMELL, TOUCH, MOVEMENT, AND OTHER SENSATIONS?

Taste

We can see objects and hear events that occur at some distance from our bodies. In contrast, to use our sense of taste, we must come into physical contact with the things we taste. Just how does this intimate sensory system work?

There are two main requirements for being able to taste a stimulus: (a) The stimulus must contain chemical molecules that can dissolve in saliva, and (b) we must have enough saliva in our mouths to dissolve those chemicals. From these dissolved chemicals, we detect the four primary psychological qualities of saltiness, bitterness, sweetness, and sourness. Other tastes are produced by combinations of the four primary tastes, much as colors can be produced by a combination of the three primary colors.

As tasty substances enter the mouth, they land on the tongue, where they are detected by one or more taste buds. **Taste buds** are clusters of taste receptor cells located on the small visible bumps, or *papillae*, on the tongue (see Figure 3.9). Although there may be an average of about 10,000 taste buds on each person's tongue, according to Linda Bartoshuk and her colleagues (Bartoshuk, Duffy, & Miller, 1994), the actual number of taste buds on the tongue varies widely across individuals, so that some people are much more sensitive to tastes than others. The taste receptors seem specially tailored to receive particular kinds of chemicals (e.g., salts or acids). Contact with these tasty chemicals activates the taste buds, thereby beginning the transduction process.

Much of the food that we believe we taste we do not taste at all. Rather, we are experiencing the food through our sense of smell, considered next.

Smell

The sense of smell, **olfaction,** enhances our ability to enjoy food (see Figure 3.10). In addition, it works independently of taste. Like taste, smell is chemically activated. When molecules in the air can dissolve in either water or fat, they can be sensed by our olfactory system.

Once our olfactory system detects scent-bearing molecules, we sense the odor. It is hard to specify absolute thresholds for smell, and we have different thresholds for detecting different substances. Also, the smell receptors of different people have differing thresholds, and the sense of smell generally decreases with age. These differences have practical implications. People who have limited sensations of smell cannot rely on their ability to detect odors such as smoke, leaking gas, or contaminated food so they must find other means of protecting themselves from such dangers (e.g., using smoke detectors, replacing gas heaters and stoves with electric ones, and discarding even remotely questionable foods).

taste bud • clusters of taste receptor cells located on the tongue

olfaction • the sense of smell

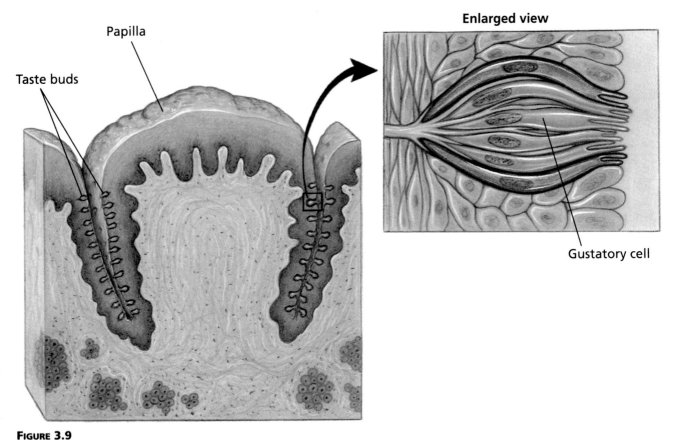

Enlarged view

Papilla

Taste buds

Gustatory cell

FIGURE 3.9
Taste Buds
This enlarged view shows a papilla and some of the thousands of taste buds on a person's tongue.

For smell to occur, odorous molecules must be carried through the air into the nasal cavity, either through the nostrils or through air passages leading from the mouth. There, the molecules reach the olfactory receptors in the skin of the nasal cavity (see Figure 3.11). This skin is referred to as the *olfactory epithelium*. An electrochemical signal is produced. This signal travels along fibers of the *olfactory nerve* to the *olfactory bulb*,

FIGURE 3.10
The Importance of Smell to Perceived Taste
Many foods are much less easy to identify when they cannot be smelled.

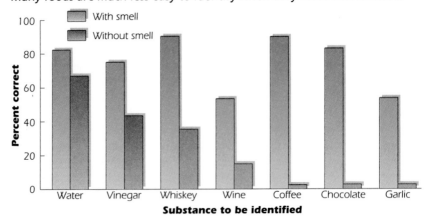

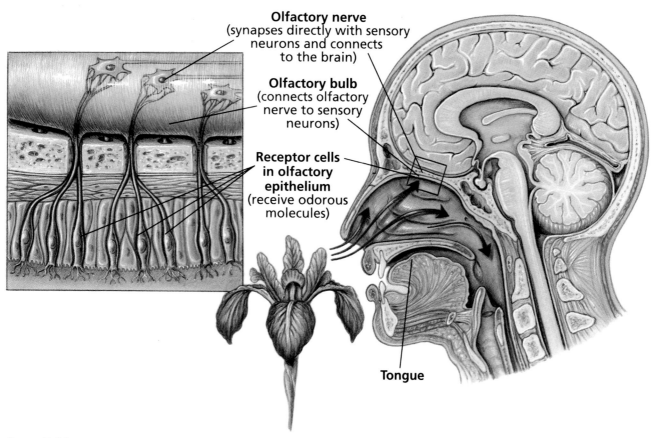

Olfactory nerve
(synapses directly with sensory neurons and connects to the brain)

Olfactory bulb
(connects olfactory nerve to sensory neurons)

Receptor cells in olfactory epithelium
(receive odorous molecules)

Tongue

FIGURE 3.11
The Nasal Cavity
Airborne molecules are drawn into the nasal cavity when we breathe. The sensitive skin in the nasal cavity houses the receptor cells that transduce the chemical energy of smell into the electrochemical energy understood by the nervous system.

which is analogous in function to the retina of the eye. It processes the signals and carries the processed signals to the brain.

Skin Senses

We often think of the **skin senses** as simply the sense of touch. The term *touch,* however, does not adequately describe the various sensations of pressure, temperature, and pain that we feel through our skin. We can feel various sensations through our skin because its many layers contain various kinds of sensory receptors.

Each different kind of sensory receptor in our skin can respond to a different kind of physical stimulus. When we sense these differing physical stimuli, our brains interpret these stimuli as psychological sensations of pain, warmth, vibration, pressure, and so on. Objects pressed against the skin change the skin's shape, causing the sensation of pressure. When even a single tiny hair on our skin is moved, we feel pressure from its movement. The temperature of whatever touches our skin leads to a sensation of warmth or cold. Slight electrical stimulation of our skin usually results in a sensation of pressure and perhaps of temperature.

skin senses • the means by which we become sensitive to pressure, temperature, and pain stimulation directly on the skin

Too much of any kind of stimulation generally causes pain sensations. Pain serves an important role in alerting us that tissue damage has occurred for some reason (see chapter 15). Even damage to internal tissues may lead to sensations of pain, particularly if the damage is severe and is located where there are pain receptors. (Ironically, there are no pain receptors located in the brain itself.)

Different parts of the body are differentially susceptible to pain. The back of the knee, for example, is much more susceptible than the sole of the foot. Moreover, people differ widely in their apparent sensitivity to pain. In extreme cases, some individuals feel no pain at all. Although such insensitivity might seem to be an ideal state, many of these individuals die early deaths due to accidental injury.

Pain is unpleasant, but it serves a functional, evolutionary purpose; it prompts us to remove ourselves from dangerous or stressful situations or to seek a quick remedy for injuries. It is important to realize, however, that factors that go beyond the individuals' mere sensory physiology, such as cultural influences, personal expectations, and adaptation levels, seem to affect how much pain a person experiences. For example, Asians report more pain than do Caucasians and other groups in response to having their ears pierced (V. J. Thomas & Rose, 1991).

Body Senses

Pain is not the only sensation that can be created by stimulation from inside our bodies. Your ability to walk or to make almost any intentional movement depends on your sense of kinesthesis and your vestibular sense (sense of balance). **Kinesthesis** is the sense that helps you to be aware of your skeletal muscle movements.

Kinesthetic receptors are in the muscles and other tissues connecting your muscles and your bones. When these receptors detect changes in positions, they transduce this mechanical energy into electrochemical energy. This information is sent up the spinal cord and eventually reaches the brain.

3.1

Not seeing is believing: Close your eyes, and move your arms and your legs, changing their positions. Stop moving, but keep your eyes closed. Where are the various parts of your body in respect to one another? Open your eyes, and check to see whether you answered the question correctly. How did you do that?

FINDING YOUR WAY

kinesthesis • the sense through which receptors within our muscles and connective tissues inform us about the positions and movements of our skeletal muscles

vestibular system • the sense of balance, governed by receptors in the inner ear, which detect the position and movement of the head, relative to a source of gravity

The *vestibular* sense is, roughly speaking, the sense of balance. The vestibular sense is determined by the position and movement of the head relative to the source of gravity. The vestibular receptors for balance are located in the inner ear, in the vestibular system. The **vestibular system** tells the visual system how to control eye positions to adjust for head movements. This system also uses information from our eyes to help us sense motion and balance. In fact, input from the kinesthetic, vestibular, and visual systems comes together in the cerebral cortex.

Our senses are our gateways to thoughts, feelings, and ideas; they serve as our bridges from the external world, through our bodies, to our minds. Once we have gathered sensations into our minds, we must assign meaning to them; this calls for perception, the following topic.

HOW DO WE MAKE SENSE OF WHAT WE SENSE?

As the following passage shows, *perception* (the set of processes by which we recognize, organize, and make sense of our sensations) is no easy task. The passage describes the experiences of Virgil, a 50-year-old man whose sight was newly restored after a lifetime of blindness. Because he lacked the extensive visual experiences that usually pave the way for normal visual perception, Virgil had great difficulty in making sense of what he was newly able to see.

> In general, . . . if Virgil could identify an animal, it would be either by its motion or by virtue of a single feature—thus, he might identify a kangaroo because it leapt, a giraffe by its height. . . . [Virgil] thought that [the gorilla] looked just like a man. Fortunately, there was a life-size bronze statue of a gorilla in the enclosure. . . . Exploring it swiftly and minutely with his hands, [Virgil] had an air of assurance that he had never shown when examining anything by sight. It [became apparent] how skillful and self-sufficient he had been as a blind man, how naturally and easily he had experienced his world with his hands. . . .
>
> His face seemed to light up with comprehension as he felt the statue. "It's not like a man at all," he murmured. The statue examined, he opened his eyes, and turned around to the real gorilla standing before him in the enclosure. And now, in a way that would have been impossible before, he described [observable details of] the ape's [appearance].
>
> —Oliver Sacks

In middle adulthood, Virgil readily recognized, organized, and made sense of his auditory, tactile, and other sensations, but he could not do so with his new visual sensations. When surgeons restored Virgil's sight, they could not give him a lifetime of visual experience. Instead, Virgil had to gradually construct visual perceptions by translating information from the tactile and auditory world of his experience to apply it to the new visual sensations assaulting him from all directions.

Most of us begin to organize our sensory experiences from the moment we emerge from the womb. Over time, we mentally construct objects (e.g., the talking face and warm, soft skin of a parent) and settings (e.g., the sensations that characterize the crib, the kitchen, or the living area). Gradually, we build a perceptual world in which we can make sense of our sensations.

Because the scope of this chapter prohibits exploration of all aspects of perception, in the following section, we focus on how we use our knowledge and understanding of the world to give meaning to our visual sensations, in particular. Vision is the sense system on which we rely the most, and usually it is controlled more easily experimentally, so there has been more research on visual perception than on other aspects of perception. Even within the field of visual perception, the possibilities for exploration are vast. In this discussion, we focus on visual perception of space, of forms, and of perceptual constancy.

FIGURE 3.12
False Perspective
At first, this engraving by English painter and engraver William Hogarth (1697–1764) seems realistic, but after closer inspection, conflicting personal cues become apparent. What are the perceptual cues and miscues the artist has used?

3.2

Before you read the following section, look closely at the engraving by William Hogarth in Figure 3.12. What kinds of cues did Hogarth use to influence viewers' perceptions of his picture? Which cues are not consistent with some other cues? (For example, notice some oddities about the sign hanging in front of the building.)

FINDING YOUR WAY

HOW DO WE PERCEIVE WHAT WE SEE?

Space Perception

As you move through space, you constantly look around and visually orient yourself in three-dimensional space, which includes the dimensions of length, width, and depth. As you look forward into the distance, you look into the third dimension of *depth*. You must make frequent judgments regarding depth, such as whenever you transport your body, reach for or manipulate objects, or otherwise position yourself in your three-dimensional world. Generally, depth cues are either *monocular* (one-eyed) or *binocular* (two-eyed).

Monocular Depth Cues

One way of judging depth is through monocular depth cues. **Monocular depth cues** can be represented in just two dimensions, as in a picture. These depth cues are referred to as "monocular" because you need only

monocular depth cue • the perceived information about depth, which can be gained by using only one eye (*mon-*, one; *-ocular*, related to the eyes)

FIGURE 3.13
Monocular Depth Cues in Art
The Annunciation, *by Venetian artist Carlo Crivelli (1430–1494), illustrates several monocular depth cues: texture gradients, relative size, interposition, linear perspective, and location in the picture plane.*

one eye to perceive them. In contrast, you need two eyes to perceive binocular depth cues (discussed later). Figure 3.13 beautifully shows the following monocular depth cues:

1. *Relative size* is the perception that things that are farther away (such as the rear tiles on the floor in Figure 3.13) appear to be smaller on your retina; the farther away an object is, the smaller its image is on the retina.

2. *Texture gradient* is a change in both the relative sizes of objects and the *densities* in the distribution of objects when viewed at different distances. The distributional density of objects is the distance among particles, parts, or objects, such as distances among various parts of the grating on the window to the right of the corridor in Figure 3.13.

3. *Interposition* is the positioning of objects, whereby an object that is perceived to be closer partially blocks the view of an object that is perceived to be farther away. The blocking object (e.g., the peacock in Figure 3.13) is perceived to be in front of the blocked object (e.g., the decorated wall in Figure 3.13).

4. *Linear perspective* helps us to make judgments about distance on the basis of our perceiving that parallel lines (such as the lines along the sides of the walls in Figure 3.13) seem to be coming together as they move farther into the distance.

5. *Location in the picture plane* indicates depth, in that objects that are farther from the observer are viewed as higher in the picture plane if below the horizon (such as the higher position of the

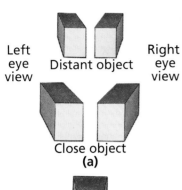

Left eye view   Distant object   Right eye view

Close object
(a)

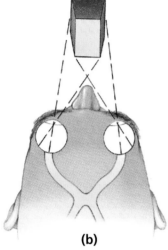

(b)

FIGURE 3.14
Binocular Disparity and Binocular Convergence
One of the reasons you are able to see a three-dimensional world is because your two eyes are in slightly different places on your head. (a) Binocular disparity: Each of your eyes sees a slightly different visual field. The disparity in the view from each eye is greater for objects that are closer to you. (b) Binocular convergence: As objects approach you, you adjust the focus of each eye inward, toward your nose. The closer the object is to you, the more your two eyes must turn inward (converge) to focus the image. Your brain uses both convergence and disparity information as depth cues.

binocular depth cue • the perceived information about depth, which can be gained only by using two eyes *(bin-, both; two)*

feature-detector approach • an approach to form perception based on observing the activity of the brain; apparently, specific neurons of the visual cortex respond to specific features detected by photoreceptors

people at the rear of the corridor, as compared with the woman kneeling in the cubicle to the right of the corridor in Figure 3.13), and lower in the picture plane if above the horizon.

6. *Aerial perspective* is perceived by observing the relative distribution of moisture and dust particles in the atmosphere as a means to judge distance. Objects close to us are relatively unaffected by these particles, but as we view objects that are at increasing distances from us, we are looking through increasing numbers of these particles. This greater density of particles makes objects that are farther away appear to be hazier and less distinct.

Another way of perceiving our three-dimensional world involves binocular depth cues.

Binocular Depth Cues

Binocular depth cues depend on the use of two eyes. Each of your eyes views a scene from slightly different angles; the two different viewing angles provide information about depth. The term for three-dimensional perception of the world through the use of binocular (two-eyed) vision is *stereopsis*. With stereo sound, you hear slightly different sounds coming to each ear, and you combine those sounds to form realistic auditory perceptions. With stereopsis, you receive slightly different visual images in each eye, and you *fuse* (fully combine to make a single image) those two images to form realistic visual perceptions. You rely on this fusion to give you a whole visual representation of what you see. Figure 3.14 illustrates two phenomena that lead to stereoscopic vision: *binocular disparity* (slight discrepancy in the viewpoint of each eye) and *binocular convergence* (merging focus of the two eyes). Binocular disparity functions because the brain uses it to integrate two slightly different sets of information that together, but not singly, provide information about depth. Binocular convergence functions because the brain uses information about how the eyes must focus together to figure out the depth at which perceived objects lie.

Another aspect of vision seems to be at least as important as depth perception—form perception—our perception of the shapes of things.

Form Perception

Two of the main attributes of form are size and shape. How, exactly, do we perceive size and shape? One approach to form perception tries to link form perception to the functioning of neurons in the brain. This psychophysiological approach is the **feature-detector approach,** developed by Nobel laureates David Hubel and Torsten Wiesel (1963, 1968, 1979). The research of Hubel and Wiesel focused on specific neurons of the visual cortex. These investigators found that specific cortical neurons respond to varying kinds of visual stimuli, which they presented to the specific retinal regions connected to the cortical neurons. A disproportionately large amount of the visual cortex is devoted to neurons mapped to receptive fields in the central regions of the retina. This overrepresentation of the central fields of vision in the cortex corresponds to the overrepresentation of cones in the center of the retina.

Most of the cells in the cortex respond to "specifically oriented line segments" (Hubel & Wiesel, 1979, p. 9). These specifically oriented line segments (e.g., vertical, horizontal, or diagonal lines) are the features for which the feature-detector approach is named. In addition, other cells in the visual cortex respond to other stimuli, which vary in their degree of complexity. These other cells seem to be organized into a hierarchy: In general, as a stimulus proceeds through the visual system to higher levels in the cortex, the size of the receptive field increases, as does the complexity of the stimulus required to prompt a response in the neurons of the cortex.

Generally speaking, a feature-detector approach to perception makes evolutionary sense. Suppose that an animal is being stalked by a predator. If the animal that is the potential prey had to wait to detect the predator until the predator came into full view, the recognition by the potential prey likely would be too late for the animal to escape. But if the prey can recognize just a small number of features of the predator, and use these features to do further cognitive operations to identify the stalker as a predator, its chances of saving itself are greater. Note that here, as almost always, perception works in conjunction with other mental processes to enhance adaptation to the environment.

A different approach to form perception focuses on the integration of various features into a whole configuration. Specifically, the **Gestalt approach** is based on this notion: The whole differs from the sum of its individual parts. Gestalt principles are particularly relevant to understanding how we perceive an assembly of forms, which is a grouping that fits together various parts or elements into a whole unit. Figure 3.15 shows some illusions for which it is difficult to integrate parts and whole.

When you walk into a familiar room, you perceive that some things stand out (e.g., faces in photographs or posters) and that others fade into the background (e.g., undecorated walls and floors). The way in which you perceive each aspect depends on your perception of the whole. A **figure** is any object perceived as being highlighted. Figures are perceived against, or in contrast to, some kind of receding, unhighlighted (back)**ground** (refer to

FIGURE 3.15
Gestalt Principles of Perception
The Gestalt principles of (a) figure–ground, (b) proximity, (c) similarity, (d) continuity, (e) closure, and (f) symmetry aid in our perception of forms.

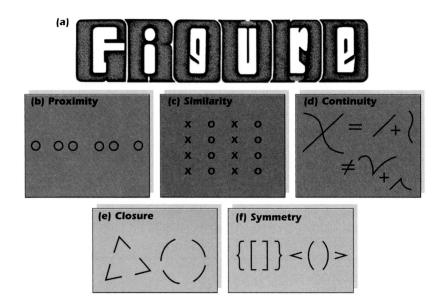

Gestalt approach • an approach to form perception, based on the notion that the whole differs from the sum of its parts

figure • a highlighted feature of the perceived environment

ground • the features of the perceived environment that are not highlighted, which serve as a background for highlighted features

Figure 3.15a). Table 3.3 summarizes and defines some of the Gestalt principles of form perception, including *figure-ground, proximity, similarity, continuity, closure,* and *symmetry* (see also Figure 3.15).

According to the *figure–ground principle,* some objects tend to stand out (figures) from others (grounds), which recede into the background. The *proximity principle* asserts that elements that are close to each other are grouped together. The *similarity principle* holds that elements that resemble each other are grouped together. The *closure principle* states that gaps in what otherwise would be viewed as a continuous border are ignored. According to the *good continuation principle,* those segments of intersecting lines that would form a continuous line with minimal change in direction are grouped together. The *symmetry principle* maintains that elements are grouped together so as to form figures that comprise mirror images on either side of a central axis. These principles can have practical importance. For example, camouflage in military operations is more effective if the uniforms create good continuation with the background against which they are viewed, making it harder to distinguish figure (the uniform) from ground (the background).

The Gestalt principles of form perception describe *how* we perceive many aspects of what we see. The feature-detector approach complements the Gestalt approach, explaining *why* we are able to perceive various forms as we do. Other approaches address the perception of forms that fall into various kinds of *patterns* (sets of characteristics that can be detected across various instances; e.g., the set of characteristics of a particular letter or numeral).

TABLE 3.3
Gestalt Principles of Visual Perception

Gestalt principles	Figure illustrating the principle
Figure–ground. When we perceive a visual field, some objects (figures) seem prominent, and other aspects of the field recede into the background (ground).	In viewing Figure 3.15a, we tend to see the word "figure" as the foreground, against a background of the word "ground." (After Shepard, 1990)
Proximity. When we perceive an assortment of objects, we tend to see objects that are close to each other as forming a group.	In viewing Figure 3.15b, we tend to perceive the circles that are the closest together as belonging together.
Similarity. We tend to group objects on the basis of their similarity.	In viewing Figure 3.15c, the similarity of the items in each column leads us to perceive alternating columns of Xs and Os, rather than horizontal rows of unlike items.
Continuity. We tend to perceive smoothly flowing or continuous forms rather than disrupted or discontinuous ones.	In viewing Figure 3.15d, we perceive a line and a curve that intersect, rather than disjointed curves that touch in the middle.
Closure. We tend to perceptually close up or complete objects that are not, in fact, complete.	In viewing Figure 3.15e, we tend to close up disjointed line segments to perceive a triangle and a circle.
Symmetry. We tend to perceive objects as forming mirror images about their center.	In viewing Figure 3.15f, we perceive an assortment of brackets as forming four sets of brackets rather than eight individual lines because we integrate the symmetrical elements into coherent pairs.

Psychologists have had trouble figuring out how people recognize patterns, such as letters, numbers, or faces. Some aspects of pattern recognition are tricky. For example, you might be able to specify in a reasonably complete way the features of a letter. However, how do you specify completely the features that allow you to recognize a familiar face? What you may take for granted, such as the ability to recognize the face of your friend, is not something that everyone can do easily.

Some people have severe problems in perceiving sensory information; these people are said to suffer from **agnosia.** People with visual agnosia have normal sensations of whatever sights are in front of them. However, they cannot recognize and understand those sights. In many ways, Virgil's difficulties with visual perception appear similar to the difficulties of agnosics. Agnosics see perfectly well, but they cannot organize and interpret what they see.

The perceptual difficulties of agnosics are generally caused by some type of trauma that produces *lesions* (areas damaged by injury or disease) in the agnosics' brains. For example, lesions in particular areas of the visual cortex may be responsible for the inability to identify familiar objects, such as a cat or the face of a loved one. There are many kinds of agnosias, and not all are visual. As we become better able to understand agnosias and other problems in perception, we may be able to understand more fully how normal perception works.

In viewing agnosia, many psychologists are puzzled by the observation that some people cannot recognize patterns. Perhaps even more puzzling, however, is the observation that most of us can do so. How do you know the letter *A* when you see it? What makes it look like an *A* instead of an *H?* Look at Figure 3.16 to see how difficult it is to answer this question. You will probably see the image in Figure 3.16 as the words, "THE CAT," and yet the *H* of *THE* is identical to the *A* of *CAT.* What subjectively feels like a simple process of pattern recognition is almost certainly quite complex.

Context effects are the perceptual effects due to the surrounding information in the environment. For example, because of context effects, we perceive "THE CAT," even though what we perceive as two different letters are actually physically identical. Gestalt psychologists would point out that the whole perception of "THE CAT" differs from the sum of its parts.

Psychologists do not yet understand exactly how people perceive forms. Another puzzling aspect of perception is perceptual constancy.

FIGURE 3.16
How Do You Recognize These Letters?
When you read these words, you probably have no difficulty differentiating the A *from the* H. *Look more closely at each of these two letters: Do any features differentiate the two letters? (After Selfridge, 1959)*

THE CAT

agnosia • severe problems in recognizing and interpreting information sent to the brain from one or more sense organs (*a-,* lack; *gnosis,* knowledge)

context effects • the influences on perception that come from information in the surrounding environment

Perceptual Constancies

3.3

Tilt this book back and forth, so that you observe it from a top view, a side view, and the forward view you normally use for reading. Next, move the book close enough to your face to have it completely block out your view of everything else. Now, move the book away from you, rest it on a surface such as a desk or the floor, and back away from the book, continuing to look at its size and shape. Move back toward the book, pick it up, and hold it at the normal distance for reading. Does it always look like a book?

FINDING YOUR WAY

(a)   **(b)**   **(c)**

Front view

Top view

Viewer

FIGURE 3.17
Perceptual Constancy
(a, b) The Ames room *has been carefully constructed to give us the impression of a normally constructed room in which people take on bizarre sizes. (c) As you can see, however, the room is actually quite distorted, and if you were to view it from an angle other than the one for which it was designed, the room, not the people in it, would seem to be oddly formed. (Copyright © Norman Snyder, 1995)*

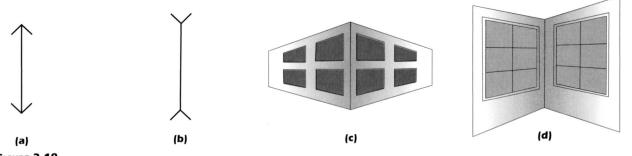

(a)   **(b)**   **(c)**   **(d)**

FIGURE 3.18
Size-Constancy Illusion
In the Müller-Lyer illusion, we tend to view two equally long line segments as being of different lengths. In particular, the vertical line segment in (a) and the central segment in (c) appear shorter than the line segment in (b) and the central segment in (d), even though all the line segments are the same length. We are not yet certain why such a simple illusion occurs.

Just now, in Finding Your Way 3.3, you watched your book change its shape from a wide rectangle to a very thin one. You also observed it enlarge and shrink in size before your very eyes. Somehow, though, despite this clear sensory evidence that your book was transforming its shape and size, you probably continued to believe that your book retained its distinctive shape and size. Why is that?

Your perception of this apparent constancy in size is an example of perceptual constancy. **Perceptual constancy** occurs when our perception of an object remains the same even when our immediate sensation of the object changes. For example, as objects recede into the distance, their representation on the retina becomes smaller, but we do not see them as becoming smaller but rather as perceptual constants. Some of the main kinds of perceptual constancies are size, shape, lightness, and color constancies.

Size constancy is the perception that an object maintains the same size despite changes in the size of the stimulus on our retinas. The size of an image on the retina directly depends on the distance of that object from the eye, as well as the size of the object, of course. The same object at two different distances projects different-sized images on the retina. Usually, size constancy helps us to make sense of the changing stimuli we see. For example, an approaching automobile on the highway does not appear to increase in size. Sometimes, however, our perceptual system is fooled by the very same information that usually helps us to achieve size constancy. We often are tricked by various visual illusions. (Compare the three-dimensional illusion shown in Figure 3.17 with the two-dimensional illusions created by painters such as Carlo Crivelli.) An illusion often described in books for engineers, architects, designers, and painters is the *Müller-Lyer illusion* (see Figure 3.18). Which line in Figure 3.18 is longer, (a) or (b)? Is the central line segment of (c) or (d) longer? The illusion makes two lines that are of the same length appear to be of different lengths.

Another form of perceptual constancy is shape constancy. In *shape constancy*, we perceive that the shape of an object remains the same despite changes in our sensations of the object. For example, when a door opens, the shape that is presented to the retina is constantly changing, but we do not see the shape of the door as changing, despite the change in what the retina "sees." These sensations may result from changes in our orientation toward the object. Although the changes in orientation cause changes in the shape of its retinal image, we perceive the object as unchanging (see Figure 3.19).

Lightness constancy is our perception that objects have an even appearance of brightness, despite differences in the actual amount of physical light reaching our eyes. Similarly, *color constancy* is the perception that objects remain the same color, even when our senses tell us that a hue (color) is changing. Artists have used lightness and color constancy for centuries.

In concluding our look at sensation and perception, we find that the whole differs from the sum of its parts. As Gestalt psychologists have pointed out, our sensory and perceptual systems accomplish amazing work as an intact whole. As subsequent chapters show, these systems fit into an even larger framework of thoughts, feelings, and actions. Although many aspects of perception occur at an unconscious level, other aspects are subject to conscious manipulation. Just what constitutes consciousness, and what mental processes occur in different states of consciousness, is the subject of the next chapter.

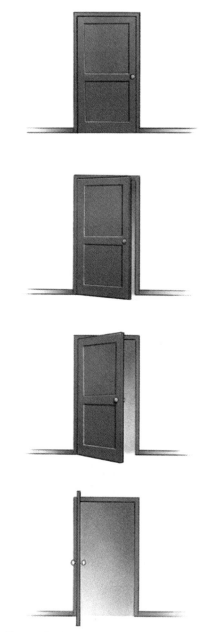

FIGURE 3.19
Shape Constancy
When you view a door, you perceive it as retaining the same shape, even though your sensations of the shape change as the door shifts in relation to your viewpoint. (After Gibson, 1950)

perceptual constancy • the perception that stimuli remain the same even when immediate sensations of the stimuli change

The Case of the Hearing Test

The following week, while reading chapter 3 of *Pathways to Psychology*, Liu suddenly realizes how the audiologist knew that Liu's hearing was impaired. The audiologist used *signal detection theory* to evaluate Liu's hearing abilities.

The audiologist knows that people sometimes intentionally or mistakenly respond in a way that does not reflect what they actually have heard. Thus, the audiologist computes the number of signals that Liu has heard (hits) as well as the number of signals that she has not heard (misses). But on a number of the trials, there was no signal. And Liu's score also takes into account trials in which she said she heard a signal when in fact none was presented (false alarms) as well as trials in which she said she heard no signal when there was no signal (correct rejections). Using a scoring formula that takes into account all four kinds of responses, the audiologist is able to determine that Liu has set her criterion for saying "yes" very low, intentionally or unintentionally, but the bottom line is that Liu's hearing is sufficiently impaired that it would be in her best interest to have a hearing aid.

Things work out happily. Liu agrees to get a hearing aid. Her main concern was with regard to her appearance, but she gets a model so small that it is unnoticeable. She now is better able to hear lectures and her grades improve. Additionally, she is better able to hear what her husband and friends are saying to her and both her marriage and social life are improving as well.

Summary

1. A *sensation* is a message that the brain receives from a sense. A *sense* is a physical system that collects information for the brain and transduces it from one form of energy into electrochemical energy, which the brain can use for making sense of the sensation.

How Do Psychologists Study the Senses?   93

2. *Psychophysics* is the study of the relationship between physical stimulation of a sense organ and its psychological effects.
3. *Detection* refers to the ability to sense a stimulus. The smallest amount of physical energy of a given kind that can be *sensed* (detected) 50% of the time is operationally defined as the *absolute threshold* for that kind of stimulus.
4. *Signal detection theory (SDT)* is used for analyzing responses in terms of *hits* (true positive responses),

false alarms (false positives), *correct rejections* (true negatives), and *misses* (false negatives).

5. *Discrimination* involves distinguishing between one stimulus and another. The *just noticeable difference (jnd;* also termed the *difference threshold)* is the minimum amount of difference that can be detected between two stimuli at least 50% of the time.
6. As the intensity of a stimulus increases, larger and larger differences between stimuli are needed to generate a jnd.

What Are Some Biological Properties Common to All Senses?   96

7. All of the senses share particular biological properties, such as psychophysical *thresholds, transduction, sensory coding,* and *adaptation.*
8. Each sense has specialized sensory *receptor cells.* These cells take in a particular form of energy and

transduce it into an electrochemical form that sensory neurons can transmit to the brain.

9. Through sensory coding, *sensory receptors* convey a range of information, such as *the intensity* (amplitude) and the *quality* (e.g., wavelength) of a stimulus.

10. When our senses detect changes in energy, receptor cells send an alert to the brain. *Adaptation* is the temporary physiological response to a change in the environment; it varies according to the intensity of the change stimulus.

How Do We See?   98

11. We can see because the receptors of our eyes receive and transduce energy from a portion of the electromagnetic spectrum of light.

12. The *cornea* and the *lens* of the eye bend light and focus it on the retina. *Accommodation* is the process by which the focusing of the lens enables us to see objects clearly at varying distances from us.

13. The *retina* is the structure in which photoreceptors transduce the electromagnetic energy in light into the electrochemical energy of neural impulses.

14. There are two separate visual systems of photoreceptors. The *rod* system is used primarily for vision in dim light, and the *cone* system is used primarily for vision in bright light.

15. Three properties of color are *hue*, which matches the psychological sensation of *color; purity*, which matches the psychological sensation of *saturation*, the richness of a color; and *intensity*, which matches the psychological sensation of *brightness*. Color, saturation, and brightness are psychological, rather than physical, phenomena.

How Do We Hear?   102

16. In the inner ear there is a *basilar membrane*. On the surface of this membrane are *hair cells*, which transduce the mechanical energy of sound waves into electrochemical energy that can be processed by the brain.

How Do We Sense Taste, Smell, Touch, Movement, and Other Sensations?   107

17. We are able to taste because of interactions between chemical substances and *taste buds*, which are sensory receptors on the bumps on our tongues.

18. We are able to smell because of interactions between chemical substances and sensory receptors in our nasal cavities.

19. *Skin-sense* nerves respond to pressure, pain, and temperature information.

20. Through *kinesthesis*, we can sense whether we are moving or stationary, where our various body parts are, and how (if at all) the parts are moving.

21. Receptors of the *vestibular system,* located in the inner ear, allow us to maintain our sense of balance.

How Do We Make Sense of What We Sense?   111

22. From the moment we emerge from the womb, we begin trying to make sense of our sensations, organizing our sensory experiences into specific objects and settings. These sensory experiences form the basis for perception.

How Do We Perceive What We See?   112

23. Two kinds of depth cues enable us to perceive three-dimensional space. *Monocular depth cues,* which can be noted by just a single eye, include relative size, texture gradients, interposition, linear perspective, location in the picture plane, and aerial perspective.

24. *Binocular depth cues* depend on using both eyes at the same time. *Binocular disparity* cues capitalize on the fact that each of the two eyes receives a slightly different image of the same object being viewed. *Binocular convergence* cues depend on the degree to which our two eyes must turn inward toward each other as objects get closer to us.

25. Two main approaches to form perception are the feature-detector approach and the Gestalt approach. According to the *feature-detector approach* to form perception, various neurons in the visual cortex can be mapped to specific receptive fields on the retina. Differing cortical neurons respond to different kinds of forms, such as line segments in various spatial orientations. Visual perception seems to depend on increasing levels of complexity in the cortical neurons. Complexity seems to increase as it is farther removed from the incoming information from the sensory receptors.

26. According to the *Gestalt approach,* the whole of form perception differs from the sum of its parts. *Gestalt principles of form perception* include *figure–ground, proximity, similarity, closure, continuity, and symmetry.*

27. *Agnosia* is an inability to recognize and understand what the senses are receiving. Visual agnosics cannot recognize objects that their visual senses transmit to their brains.

28. *Perceptual constancies* result when our perceptions of objects remain constant despite changes in the stimuli being sensed. Examples of perceptual constancies are size, shape, lightness, and color constancies. A size-constancy illusion is the Müller-Lyer illusion, which may be affected by cultural experiences.

Choose the best answer to complete each sentence.

1. Psychophysics is the study of
   (a) how physics and psychology combine to allow understanding of the movement of particles.
   (b) why particle movements may be psychologically undetectable.
   (c) the measurement of the relationship between a form of physical stimulation and the psychological sensations it produces.
   (d) how psychological functions can be broken down into discrete components.

2. Signal detection theory attempts to
   (a) assess the intensity of a given stimulus.
   (b) eliminate possible errors in psychological measurement.
   (c) control measurement error in detection experiments.
   (d) explain how a person's expectations influence his or her perception of a stimulus.

3. The minimum amount of difference that can be detected between two stimuli is called the
   (a) detection threshold.
   (b) just noticeable difference.
   (c) discriminatory level.
   (d) perceivable difference.

4. The electromagnetic spectrum refers to
   (a) a range of varying wavelengths of electromagnetic energy.
   (b) wavelengths of light visible to the naked eye.
   (c) a range of all the colors visible to the naked eye.
   (d) the spectrum of energy variations that result from exposure to light.

5. Rods and cones are two types of photoreceptors that are
   (a) responsible for the transduction of neural energy into a form that can be received in the sensory receptors.
   (b) more activated in bright sunlight (rods) or in dim light (cones).
   (c) both highly sensitive to the color and the brightness of visible light.
   (d) responsible for transducing electromagnetic energy into electrochemical energy.

6. The psychological experience of color relates most closely to
   (a) a physical property of wavelengths of light.
   (b) the actual brightness of what we observe.
   (c) a physical property of intensity of light.
   (d) an interaction between a physical stimulus and the eye.

7. Perceptual constancy refers to our
   (a) perception of an object as remaining the same even when our immediate sensation of the object changes.
   (b) tendency to perceive objects as being grouped together, based on their similarity.
   (c) perception of an object as changing even when our immediate sensation of the object remains the same.
   (d) tendency to perceive a constant closed-up shape of an object even when our perception of it is incomplete.

Answer each of the following questions by filling in the blank with an appropriate word or phrase.

8. _____ is the process whereby energy is converted from a form that enters the sensory receptors to a form that the brain can process.

9. The _____, a thin layer on the rear surface of the eye, contains the photoreceptors responsible for transducing electromagnetic energy into electrochemical energy.

10. The four primary psychological qualities of taste are _____, saltiness, _____, and bitterness.

Match the following depth cues to their descriptions:

11. linear perspective

    (a) objects farther away from the observer appear higher in the picture plane (as long as the objects are below the horizon)

12. interposition

    (b) objects that are farther away are viewed through a greater density of dust and moisture particles

13. relative size

    (c) objects that are closer present more noticeably different images to each of the two eyes

14. aerial perspective

    (d) as parallel lines move farther into the distance, they appear to come together at the horizon

15. location in the picture plane

    (e) objects that are farther away appear to be smaller

16. binocular convergence

    (f) objects that are closer may block the view of objects that are farther away

17. binocular disparity

    (g) objects that are closer require the eye muscles to pull more strongly inward toward the nose

Answers

1. c, 2. d, 3. b, 4. a, 5. a, 6. d, 7. a, 8. Transduction, 9. retina, 10. sweetness, sourness, 11. d, 12. f, 13. e, 14. b, 15. a, 16. g, 17. c

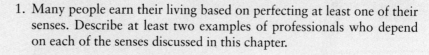

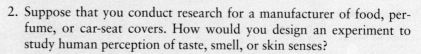

Pathways to Understanding

1. Many people earn their living based on perfecting at least one of their senses. Describe at least two examples of professionals who depend on each of the senses discussed in this chapter.

2. Suppose that you conduct research for a manufacturer of food, perfume, or car-seat covers. How would you design an experiment to study human perception of taste, smell, or skin senses?

3. If you had to memorize a long list of terms and definitions, would you be better off trying to remember them by seeing them (e.g., reading printed flashcards) or by hearing them (e.g., by having someone drill you by saying the words aloud)? Do you seem to be able to remember material better if it is presented visually (e.g., in a book) or auditorily (e.g., in a lecture)? How do you tailor your studying to your sensory preferences?

The Case of The Dangerous Drinker Who Wanted to Drive

Barry and Martha are having a great time at a fraternity party. There is a terrific band, and Barry has been celebrating fully. He especially has been self-indulgent because he just aced a math test that he had expected to bomb. Barry has his first beer at 10:00 p.m. and his last at 2:00 a.m. In between, he has had four more beers, for a total of six. Martha has not been drinking and has told Barry to control his drinking, but he has not paid much attention to her. Now he realizes that he is drunk. He finds it difficult to believe that he allowed himself to have six beers, but at 2:00 a.m. it is too late to scold himself for getting carried away. Barry does not want to embarrass himself by admitting to Martha that he has let himself get drunk. He knows that she will react badly and that, given the way things have been going lately, he just cannot afford to have her disappointed in, or angry at, him. Martha suggests that she drive them both home, a suggestion that embarrasses Barry.

CHAPTER 4
CONSCIOUSNESS

As things wind down, Barry decides to take control of matters. He drinks down an enormous mug of coffee and quickly finds himself feeling much more awake. He tells Martha that, after drinking the mug of coffee, he is fully prepared to drive them both home. Martha insists that she drive. Barry sees no reason why he should not drive.

Is Barry correct? Think about this while reading chapter 4. Will the coffee adequately enable Barry to drive; or will driving put Barry and Martha at risk for following a pathway to disaster?

4

Consciousness is the complex process of evaluating our environment and then filtering that information through our minds. Consciousness seems to serve various essential and interrelated purposes. For one thing, consciousness aids in survival by allowing us to obtain, manipulate, and apply information for adapting to the environment. Through consciousness, we can make sense of the world and can act accordingly in order to avoid danger, to find mates, to plan for future successes, and to fulfill countless other purposes we determine for ourselves. For example, no matter what kind of relationship we form with a significant other, the relationship began in the same way, with our becoming conscious of that person's existence and the relationship's potential relevance to our lives. It is incredible that our brains can do all this and more!

Consciousness provides both monitoring and controlling functions (Kihlstrom, 1984). We can *monitor* (keep track of) our sensations from the external environment, as well as our own internally generated thoughts, feelings, and desires. Through consciousness, we can *control* (direct and shape) our lives. For example, suppose we become conscious of potential danger coming our way, such as a seedy-looking character on a poorly-lit street in a bad neighborhood, who looks like he is about to mug us. Our consciousness of his presence enables us to take preventive action, such as getting out of his path, and preferably out of his line of sight, as quickly as possible.

Consciousness actively processes and integrates everchanging information from various pathways that reach it: from our varied senses (e.g., visual or auditory stimuli in the environment), from memory (e.g., stored information gained from previous experiences), and from mental processing itself (e.g., beliefs, dreams, strategies, plans). Although the information is constantly changing, consciousness provides us with a sense of continuity, of a unique self that continues to exist throughout these processes.

Through consciousness, we can control the flow of perceived, remembered, and mentally produced information. It is impossible to process actively all of the information available to us, so consciousness restricts the flow of information being processed at one time. It screens out some information and selectively allows in the most noticeable and relevant information for processing. While you are dreaming about waterfalls, you are probably not dreaming about desert wastelands. Although you have a wealth of memories on which you can draw at will, you are not remembering everything you know all at once. Nor are you actively processing all of the sensory stimuli, or all of the thoughts, beliefs, hopes, or plans that may be available for use by your conscious mind.

A phenomenon related to consciousness is **attention,** which serves as the link between the enormous amount of information that reaches our consciousness and the limited amount of information that we actually are aware of processing. If you are having a hard time figuring out the difference between attention and consciousness, you are not alone. At one time, psychologists also believed that consciousness was the same thing as attention. To get an idea of how they came to believe that the two phenomena are different, try the following activity.

Repeatedly write your name on a piece of paper while you picture everything you can remember about the room where you slept when you were 10 years old. While continuing to write your name and picturing your old bedroom, take a mental journey through your bodily sensations. Start by noticing the sensations in one of your big toes, and continue by proceeding up your leg, across your torso, to the opposite shoulder, and down your arm. What sensations do you feel (pressure from the ground, your shoes, your clothing; or even pain anywhere)? Are you still managing to write your name while retrieving remembered images from memory and continuing to pay attention to your current sensations?

You may have found the preceding activity awkward but not impossible. Why is it difficult, yet possible? It is difficult because it places a heavy workload on your active mental processing (i.e., your consciousness). It is possible because you do not have to pay attention to all of the mental processes involved. When you started to write your name, you paid attention to doing so. However, at this time in your life, writing your own name requires no active awareness and very little attention. Hence, you may write it while focusing your attention on other activities. Similarly, once you started picturing your old bedroom, you could continue to cruise mentally around the room while shifting some of your attention to the next task.

In this particular activity, each time you started a new task, you had to focus your attention on the new task. Once the task was started, however, the task did not require your full attention, so you had some attentional resources available for other mental processing. Note that when you were paying attention, you were not only processing information actively, but also were aware of doing so. What allowed you to continue the other tasks? It was your consciousness, in which the active processing of information may proceed with or without your awareness of doing so. You do not have to pay attention to information in order for conscious processes to act on the information.

HOW DOES ATTENTION WORK?

As you read these words, you are paying attention to the words on the text page, and you are probably disregarding all the other visual sensations reaching your eyes. If you paid attention to all the sensory information available to you at any one time, you would never be able to concentrate on the important and ignore the unimportant.

In **selective attention**, we attempt to track one message and to ignore another. Psychologist Colin Cherry (1953) was interested in how we follow one conversation even when we are distracted by other conversations. Cherry referred to this phenomenon, of trying to track one conversation while apparently listening to another, as the *cocktail party problem*, based on his observation that cocktail parties provide an excellent setting for observing selective attention.

consciousness • the complex phenomenon of actively processing perceptions, thoughts, feelings, wishes, and memories to create a mental reality for adapting to the world

attention • the process by which we focus our awareness on some of the information available in consciousness and screen out other information

selective attention • the conscious attempt to perceive some stimuli (e.g., the voice and gestures of a speaker) and to ignore others (e.g., background noises and sights)

Cherry did not actually study conversations by hanging out at cocktail parties. Rather, he studied selected messages spoken in a more carefully controlled experimental setting. He used *shadowing,* in which each of your ears listens to a different message, and you are required to repeat back the message from only one of the ears as soon as possible after you hear it. In other words, you are to follow one message (think of a detective "shadowing" a suspect) but to ignore the other. This form of presentation is often referred to as dichotic presentation. In **dichotic presentation,** each ear receives a *different* message. When the two ears receive the *same* message (or messages), it is referred to as *binaural presentation* (see Figure 4.1).

Cherry's research prompted additional work in this area. For example, Anne Treisman (1960) noted that participants shadowing the message presented to one ear heard almost nothing of the message presented to the other ear. Participants were not, however, totally ignorant of what they heard in the other ear. For instance, they could hear whether the voice in the unattended ear was replaced by a tone, or they could hear whether a man's voice was replaced by a woman's. Moreover, if the unattended

FIGURE 4.1
Selective Attention
Colin Cherry studied both (a) dichotic presentation, in which a different message is presented to each ear; and (b) binaural presentation, in which the same message is presented to both ears.

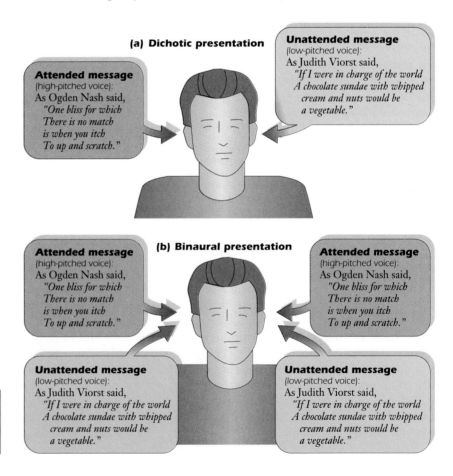

dichotic presentation • a perceptual experience in which each ear receives a different message (*dich-,* in two parts; *-otic,* related to the ears [Greek])

message was identical to the attended one, all participants noticed it, even if one of the messages was not matched perfectly in timing with the other.

Much of the research on selective attention has focused on auditory processing. However, researchers also have studied selective attention through visual processing. One of the most common tasks used for studying selective visual attention was first formulated by John Ridley Stroop (1935), which is described in Finding Your Way 4.2. The **Stroop effect,** which occurs in the Stroop task, refers to the psychological difficulty that occurs when a person attempts to name the colors of ink in which are printed color words that identify a color other than the color of the ink. For example, in this task, the word "blue" might be printed in red ink. The participant would be presented with a series of such words and have to identify the colors of the inks in the face of interference from words identifying colors other than those of the inks in which the words are printed. Stroop's task highlights the difficulty of selectively attending to some visual stimuli and not to others. Compare the ease of performing the first of the following two tasks with the second of the tasks.

FINDING YOUR WAY

4.2

First, quickly identify aloud the ink colors of the printed color names in Figure 4.2a, in which the color of the ink matches the name of the color word. Easy, isn't it? Now, look at Figure 4.2b, in which the colors of the inks differ from the color names that are printed with those inks. Quickly identify aloud the colors of the inks in that figure. You probably will find the second task very difficult: Each of the written words interferes with your naming the color of the ink. This interference is the Stroop effect.

FIGURE 4.2
The Stroop Effect
Quickly identify aloud the names of the colors of the inks *in each set of words,* disregarding the words *showing the various colors of ink.*

(a) Name as quickly as possible the color of ink in which each word is printed. Name from left to right across each line.

Red	Yellow	Blue	Green
Blue	Red	Green	Yellow
Yellow	Green	Red	Blue

(b) Name as quickly as possible the color of ink in which each word is printed. Name from left to right across each line.

Red	Blue	Green	Yellow
Yellow	Red	Blue	Green
Blue	Yellow	Green	Red

Stroop effect • the interference experienced in selectively attending to one sensory stimulus (e.g., the color of the ink) while trying to ignore another sensory stimulus (e.g., the word that is printed with the ink of a different color)

WHAT LEVELS OF CONSCIOUSNESS DO WE EXPERIENCE?

Generally, when we are paying attention to stimuli, we see ourselves as being at a fully conscious level of awareness. In addition to full conscious awareness, there are lower levels of consciousness, two of which are described here: the preconscious and the subconscious.

The Preconscious Level

The **preconscious level** of consciousness includes information that can become conscious readily, but that is not continuously available at the conscious level. This information includes stored memories that we are not using at a given time, but that we can call to mind when needed. For example, if prompted, you can remember what your bedroom looks like. Obviously, however, you are not always thinking about your bedroom. Also stored at the preconscious level are automatic behaviors. **Automatic behaviors** require no conscious decisions regarding which muscles to move or which actions to take. For instance, automatic behaviors include signing your name, dialing a familiar telephone number, or driving a car to a familiar place by way of empty roads. In the driving task, for example, you may be watching the road, pressing your foot on the gas pedal, putting on a turn signal, starting to turn, listening to the radio, and talking to someone all at the same time. You are able to do all these tasks at once because driving has become so automatic for you. When driving was not automatic for you, when you first learned to drive, it is unlikely you could have done all these things at once without inviting an accident.

Perhaps our most common experience of preconsciousness is the **tip-of-the-tongue phenomenon**. This phenomenon occurs when we are trying to remember something we already know but cannot quite pull from memory. Psychologists have tried to come up with experiments that measure this phenomenon. For example, they have tried to find out how much people can draw from information that seems to be stuck at the preconscious level. In one study (R. Brown & McNeill, 1966), participants were read a large number of dictionary definitions of uncommon words. For each definition, the participants then were asked to supply the corresponding words having these meanings (similar to the game on the television show *Jeopardy!*). For instance, they might have been given this clue: "an instrument used by navigators to measure the angle between a heavenly body and a horizon."

In the study, some participants could not come up with the word but thought they knew it. These participants then were asked to perform various tasks related to the word. For instance, they were asked to identify the first letter, indicate the number of syllables, or make a guess about the word's sounds. The participants often answered these questions correctly. In this example (of the navigation instrument), the participants might have been able to say that the appropriate word for the instrument begins with an *s*, has two syllables, and sounds like "sextet." Eventually, some participants realized that the proper word was *sextant*. These results indicate that particular preconscious information may be hard to recall but still be available to consciousness.

Other researchers have shown evidence of preconscious processing (Greenwald, Klinger, & Schuh, 1995; Marcel, 1983). In one of a series of experiments (Marcel, 1983), participants were shown words very

preconscious level • a level of consciousness comprising information that is accessible to, but not continuously available in, awareness

automatic behavior • conduct that requires no conscious decisions regarding which muscles to move or which actions to take

tip-of-the-tongue phenomenon • an experience of preconsciousness, in which a person cannot successfully retrieve information known to be stored in memory

briefly (20–110 *milliseconds* [thousandths of a second]). After each word was presented, it was replaced by a visual mask to remove any visual trace of the word. A *visual mask* blocks an image from staying on the retina at the back of the eye. The rate at which the words were shown was so fast that observers could not guess whether they even had seen a word at better than chance levels; that is, they made correct guesses only as often as would be expected if they were basing their guesses on the toss of a coin.

Next, the participants were shown a series of letters, and they were asked to do a classification task whereby they had to indicate whether the letters did or did not form a word. For example, participants might be expected to indicate that "MARD" is not a word, but that "HARD" is. It turned out that the participants could classify this second string of letters more quickly when it related to the first word than when it did not. For example, "BUTTER" is typically classified as a word faster in the classification task if it follows the very rapidly presented word "BREAD" than if it follows the very rapidly presented word "NURSE" (Marcel, 1983, p. 219). In other words, the very rapid presentation of "BREAD" but not of "NURSE" prepares the individual to see "BUTTER."

How could the presentation of associated words enhance people's speed of response when they were not even aware that they had seen these words? Clearly, some kind of preconscious recognition of the rapidly presented word must have taken place. In this kind of preconscious processing, people can detect information without being aware that they are doing so. This preconscious processing is termed **subliminal perception.**

Recently, various companies have produced an assortment of self-help audiotapes conveying subliminal messages designed to improve almost any aspect of your life, from your love life to your work life. The idea is that when you play these tapes, while you consciously listen to soothing music or nature sounds, the subliminal messages miraculously will change how you think, feel, or act, thereby changing your life. You will become more assertive or more self-disciplined; you will improve your memory, or you will lose weight.

Anthony Greenwald, Anthony Pratkanis, and their colleagues (Greenwald, Spangenberg, Pratkanis, & Eskenazi, 1991; Pratkanis, Eskenazi, & Greenwald, 1994) have tested the effectiveness of these tapes. They recruited volunteers interested in memory enhancement or in improving their self-esteem. All of the participants were given tests of self-esteem and of memory.

The researchers then divided the participants into four groups: (a) participants who were told that they were being given a memory-enhancement tape and who were indeed given such a tape; (b) participants who were told that they were being given a memory-enhancement tape but who were given a self-esteem-enhancing tape instead; (c) participants who were told that they were being given a self-esteem-enhancing tape and who were indeed given such a tape; and (d) participants who were told that they were being given a self-esteem-enhancing tape but who were given a memory-enhancement tape instead. The experiment was administered using a **double-blind procedure,** so that both the participants and the experimenters who gave the instructions to the participants were kept in the dark as to which participants actually received which tapes. (Of course, the researchers used a coding technique so that they later could figure out which participant received which tape, and the researchers could analyze the results at the end of the study.) All participants were instructed to use the tapes at home for 5 weeks.

subliminal perception • a form of preconscious processing in which people may have the ability to detect information without being fully aware that they are doing so

double-blind procedure • an experimental technique whereby neither the experimenters nor the participants know which participants will have received which kind of treatment, or even any treatment at all (e.g., in a control condition)

When the participants returned, they were again tested for memory and for self-esteem. How did participants feel about the effectiveness of the tapes? The participants reported experiencing the improvements they expected (memory or self-esteem enhancement), regardless of which tape they received (the memory tape or the self-esteem tape). However, their actual scores on the tests of memory and of self-esteem showed no such improvements. What can we conclude? The tapes do not work. It is not even clear they really have subliminal messages. The tapes will, however, produce a **placebo effect**; they will make people believe the treatment worked, as long as the people strongly expect it to do so.

To summarize, automatic behaviors, tip-of-the-tongue phenomena, subliminal perception, and other preconscious knowledge are outside our conscious awareness. Nevertheless, the preconscious information is available for use by our conscious minds under many circumstances. At the same time, tapes based on subliminal perception appear to be ineffective in influencing people to change their behavior, their mental abilities, or their personal characteristics.

The Subconscious Level

Unlike knowledge stored at the preconscious level, information stored at the **subconscious level** is not easily pulled into the conscious mind. In this chapter, the terms *subconscious* and *unconscious* are used interchangeably. However, the term *unconscious* usually is preferred by followers of Sigmund Freud. Freud believed that many of our most important memories and impulses are unconscious, but that they nonetheless deeply and powerfully affect our behavior. For example, Freud believed that our early relationships with our parents affect our views of ourselves, and thus our lifelong behavior. Despite their importance, we cannot easily remember every aspect and interaction of those relationships.

According to Freud, the reason we remember so little about these crucial early experiences is because we often find some memories too difficult to handle at a conscious level. We therefore repress (never let it enter consciousness) this information through the defense mechanism called **repression.** In Freud's view, although these difficult experiences, feelings, and desires are not conscious, their effects can be seen through careful observation. For instance, according to Freud, our dreams and slips of the tongue actually indicate unconscious processing. As an example, suppose that you are introduced to someone against whom you are competing for something you want. You say, "I'm glad to beat you," when you intended to say, "I'm glad to meet you." Freud would interpret the slip as being psychologically significant. This sort of verbal error is still sometimes called a "Freudian slip."

To a large extent, classical Freudian theory can be neither proved nor disproved: It focuses on concepts of the unconscious mind that are affected by variables that psychologists cannot control in experiments. Without control of the variables, psychologists cannot test these concepts; thus, there is little experimental evidence for Freud's theories of the mind. Nonetheless, Freud's theories of the levels of consciousness were groundbreaking when first proposed. Even now, his theories continue to influence many people. Another innovative idea of Freud's that continues to be influential is the probing of the unconscious through psychological treatments involving altered states of consciousness, such as hypnosis and dreams.

placebo effect • a perceived improvement that occurs simply because people believe that they have received a given treatment, even when they did not actually receive the treatment

subconscious level • a level of consciousness that involves less awareness than full conscious awareness and from which information is not easily pulled into the conscious mind

repression • a Freudian defense mechanism, by which a person keeps troublesome internally generated thoughts and feelings from entering consciousness and thereby causing internal conflicts or other psychological discomfort

WHAT HAPPENS DURING ALTERED STATES OF CONSCIOUSNESS?

In an altered state of consciousness, awareness somehow is changed from our normal, waking state. In this chapter, we discuss several forms of altered consciousness: sleep and dreams, hypnosis, meditation, and drug-induced altered states of consciousness. There are some *quantitative* (involving increases or decreases in amounts) changes associated with states of consciousness, such as increases or decreases in alertness and awareness. For example, when a person is under the influence of drugs that cause hallucinations, the person's awareness of the external environment undergoes a quantitative decrease. However, the key features of the various states of consciousness are *qualitative* changes, which involve changes in the characteristics (qualities) that are present in a given state. That is, some qualities that are very important in one state of consciousness are either absent altogether or just not important in another state. Thus, the person undergoing hallucinations experiences a qualitative alteration, believing him or herself to be experiencing sounds, sights, or other sensory experiences that correspond to no actual stimulation from the environment.

Altered states of consciousness have several common characteristics related to changes in thinking, in perception, and in behavioral self-control (Martindale, 1981). First, during altered states, you may not think as deeply or as carefully as usual. For example, during sleep, you accept unrealistic dream events as being real, although you never would accept those events as realistic while you are awake. Second, your perceptions of yourself and of the world may change from what they are during wakefulness. Under the influence of particular kinds of drugs, for example, you may perceive illusions or hallucinations. **Illusions** are distorted perceptions of objects (e.g., surfaces of objects may appear to quiver or to take on bizarre forms). **Hallucinations** are perceptions of objects that do not exist (e.g., the floor may appear to be covered with nonexistent spider webs). Third, your normal inhibitions and level of control over your own behavior may weaken. People under the influence of alcohol, for example, may do things they normally would not do when sober.

The most common altered state of consciousness is sleep, to which we now turn.

WHAT HAPPENS WHEN WE SLEEP AND DREAM?

Scientists do not know why we sleep. There are several theories of sleep, however. One theory derives from an evolutionary viewpoint as to why the need to sleep might have emerged. According to this *preservation and protection theory of sleep,* we sleep to protect ourselves during that portion of the 24-hour day in which being awake, and hence roaming around, would place us at greatest risk. A second theory, the *restorative theory of sleep,* holds that we sleep to restore used-up resources and to get rid of accumulated waste products in the body. These theories are not mutually exclusive: Perhaps we sleep for the reasons proposed by both of the theories.

One way to study sleep is to study carefully the physiology of animals before, during, and after sleeping, as well as when the animals are unable

illusion • the distorted perception of physical stimuli, sometimes due to altered states of consciousness, to psychological disorder, or to misleading cues in the objects themselves

hallucination • the perception of sensory stimulation (usually sounds, but sometimes sights, smells, or tactile sensations) in the absence of any actual corresponding sensory input from the physical world

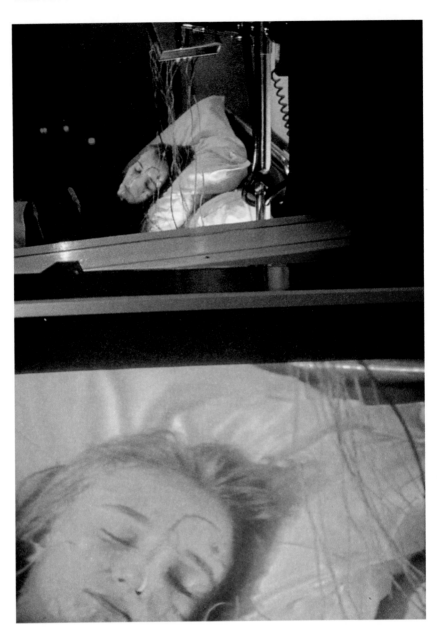

Sleep researchers monitor the patterns of brain-wave activity throughout the sleep cycle of their participants.

to sleep for various reasons. These studies have led some psychologists to conclude that there are chemical causes of sleep. Not all psychologists agree with this conclusion, however. To find out more about human sleep, most sleep researchers study people.

Stages of Sleep

How do psychologists study sleep in people? For one thing, they often test people's thought processes and their moods during various degrees of sleepiness and wakefulness. Psychologists also observe people's natural sleeping and waking behaviors. Another common method of studying sleep is to examine people's brain-wave patterns, as recorded on electroencephalograms. **Electroencephalograms (EEGs)** are recordings that show the electrical activity of the brain as patterns of waves (see Figure 4.3). The EEGs of sleeping people have shown that sleep occurs in stages common to almost everyone (see Figure 4.3). The first four stages of sleep make up **N-REM sleep** (non-rapid eye movement sleep). During these four stages, as the name "N-REM" implies, people's eyes do not move much.

During a fifth stage of sleep, however, our eyes roll around in their sockets (Kleitman, 1963). When sleep researchers rouse sleepers during this eye-rolling stage of sleep, the sleepers usually report being wakened in the middle of a dream (Dement & Kleitman, 1957). The distinctive kind of sleep that occurs during this stage has become known as **REM sleep,** for "rapid eye movement" sleep. REM sleep is the stage of sleep most often associated with dreaming, although dreaming is not limited to this stage. (Dreaming is discussed later in this chapter.)

EEG patterns become extremely active during REM sleep. The EEG of REM sleep somewhat resembles the EEG of the awake brain (refer to Figure 4.3), although REM sleep is so deep that it is usually difficult to waken a person from it. During this period of sleep, muscle activity is largely suppressed. Because this sleep stage is both the deepest in terms of how difficult it is to waken people and the most like wakefulness in terms of people's EEG patterns, REM sleep is sometimes called "paradoxical sleep." Here, as always, the paradox seems self-contradictory, but is nevertheless true.

The paradox of REM sleep points out an important aspect of psychophysiological measurements. In this case, a measurement (EEG) recorded very similar physiological data from two different states of consciousness (REM sleep and waking). What would have happened if psychologists had relied only on EEGs for assessing the two states? They might have concluded that REM sleep is very similar to the waking state. Fortunately, psychologists and other scientists also searched for supporting evidence based on observations of behavior. In this way, they discovered the paradoxical nature of REM sleep. Neither psychophysiological nor behavioral measurement tells the full story. However, each method of measurement provides a kind of information that adds to the other kind of information.

Using both EEG studies and behavioral measurements, psychologists have found out more about sleep stages: The stages of N-REM sleep and REM sleep alternate throughout the night, roughly in 90-minute cycles. As the night progresses, the length and sequence of the sleep stages may vary.

Sleep Deprivation

In addition to studying how people sleep, scientists study what happens when people are deprived of sleep. In *sleep deprivation,* participants are not allowed to sleep for fixed amounts of time. The scientists then measure the resulting changes in mood, motor activity, thought patterns, task performance, and brain-wave patterns (e.g., Borbely, 1986; Dement, 1976). Participants usually have few problems after the first sleepless night, and they appear to be relaxed and cheerful. They have more difficulty staying awake during the second night. Usually, they are severely tired by 3:00 a.m. of the second day. If they are given long test problems to solve, they may fall asleep but will deny having done so.

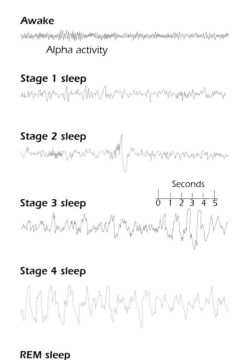

Awake

Alpha activity

Stage 1 sleep

Stage 2 sleep

Seconds
0 1 2 3 4 5

Stage 3 sleep

Stage 4 sleep

REM sleep

FIGURE 4.3
EEG Patterns Showing the Stages of Sleep
These EEG patterns show changes in brain waves. The brain-wave changes reflect changes in consciousness during REM sleep and during the four stages of N-REM sleep. (a) Alpha waves typify relaxed wakefulness. (b) More rapid, irregular brain waves typify Stage 1 of N-REM sleep. (c) During Stage 2, large, slow waves are interrupted by bursts of rapid brain waves. (d) During Stages 3 and 4, extremely large, slow brain waves are the most common. (e) During REM sleep, the brain waves look very much like those of the waking brain.

electroencephalogram (EEG) • a recording of the electrical activity of the living brain, as detected by various electrodes (*en-,* in; *cephalo-,* head; *-gram,* record [Greek])

N-REM sleep • the four stages of sleep that are not characterized by rapid eye movements (REMs) and that are less frequently associated with dreaming

REM sleep • the distinctive kind of sleep that is characterized by rapid eye movements (REMs) and that is frequently associated with dreaming

By the third day, the participants appear tense. Increasingly, they are irritable when disturbed. They may follow the instructions of the experimenter, but they do very little that they are not specifically told to do. Their moods can swing wildly. By the third night, they cannot stay awake unless special steps are taken to keep them awake.

Starting with this third night, periods of *microsleep* are observed: Participants stop what they are doing for periods of several seconds and stare into space. During these periods, their EEGs show brain-wave patterns similar to the patterns typical of sleep. Participants may start to experience illusions and hallucinations. For instance, they may perceive auditory hallucinations, such as hearing voices in the sound of running water. Microsleep is of minor consequence in the laboratory, but on the road, it could have fatal consequences. This is one reason that people who are overtired simply should not drive.

Things really start to fall apart after 4 days. Beyond 4 days, participants typically become *paranoid,* sometimes believing that the experimenters or other people are planning to harm them in some way. It is possible to keep sleep-deprived participants awake for longer than 4 days. Clearly, however, prolonged sleep deprivation is serious. It can lead to a suppression of the proper functioning of the immune system. More importantly, it even can be fatal, as when people fall asleep at the wheel when they are driving.

Circadian Rhythms

People go through periods of sleeping and waking even before birth. Usually, newborn humans switch back and forth often between sleep and wakefulness, for a total of about 17 hours of sleep per day. Within the first 6 months, however, their sleep patterns change. Most infants have about two short naps and one long stretch of sleep at night, for a total of about 13 hours per day. By about 5 to 7 years of age, most children follow about the same pattern of sleep as adults (Berger, 1980). Adults sleep about 8 hours each night and remain awake about 16 hours each day.

Regardless of the average, the actual range of sleep needed varies widely across individuals. Some people need as little as 1 hour of sleep each day, and others need 10 to 12 hours of sleep per day. *Long sleepers* regularly sleep more than 9.5 hours per day. *Short sleepers* regularly sleep less than 4.4 hours per day. Studies of long sleepers and short sleepers show no differences in their average relative health (Kolb & Whishaw, 1990).

Despite individual differences, the typical pattern roughly corresponds to our planet's cycle of darkness and light. Humans go through physiological changes that can be measured according to this daily rhythm. For example, our body temperature generally lowers at night. The term for these cyclical daily changes is **circadian rhythm.**

Several investigators have studied circadian rhythms (see Hobson, 1989; Wever, 1979). Participants in one study were placed in a specially built underground living environment. In this environment, the participants were deprived of all the cues people normally use for telling the time of day—the rising and setting of the sun, clocks, scheduled activities, and so on (Wever, 1979). For 1 month, participants were told that they could create their own schedules. They could sleep whenever they wished to, but they were asked not to nap.

The results were striking and since have been shown many times. As participants became used to having no time cues, their internally determined

circadian rhythm • the usual sleeping–waking pattern of physiological changes corresponding roughly to the cycle of darkness and light associated with a single day (*circa-*, around; *-dies*, day [Latin])

French geologist Michel Siffre (left) was shielded from all time cues for 6 months in an underground cavern (shown on right). When people have no external time cues, their natural circadian rhythms gradually shift from a 24-hour day to a 25-hour day. When they return to a normal environment, their circadian rhythms return to a 24-hour day, cued by clocks and by the daily cycle of our planet.

days became longer, averaging about 25 hours. Participants showed stable individual circadian rhythms, although the rhythms differed somewhat from person to person. When returned to the normal, time-cued environment, the participants reestablished a 24-hour cycle. The ability of people to maintain a 24-hour cycle when their normal cycle appears to be 25 hours is an excellent example of how people can adapt flexibly to environments that do not ideally suit them.

Anything that changes our circadian rhythm can interfere with sleep. Many of us have experienced jet lag. *Jet lag* is a disturbance in circadian rhythm caused by changing the light–dark cycle when we travel through time zones. Even if you never have flown out of your own time zone, however, you may have experienced a mild case of jet lag: Recall what happens when you change to and from daylight savings time. Think about how you feel that first Monday morning after setting your clocks forward an hour. You may have trouble adjusting to waking up and going to sleep an hour earlier than usual. More troubling than jet lag, however, are full-fledged sleep disorders.

Sleep Disorders

Sleep disorders can be very troublesome: Lack of sleep (caused by insomnia) can wreak havoc on a person's life. Snoring can cause distress to both snorers and those close to them. Talking in one's sleep also can present a problem, especially to those who end up having to listen. Frequent nightmares can cause great distress for both those who experience the nightmares and for those who are close to them. Likewise, sudden uncontrollable sleep (caused by narcolepsy), breathing difficulties during

"Wait! Don't! It can be dangerous to wake them!"

Copyright © Joe Dator/The Cartoon Bank, Inc.

This cartoon makes light of the potentially disastrous consequences of sleepwalking. In reality, however, sleepwalkers sometimes are endangered by their somnambulism.

PUTTING IT TO USE

4.1

HOW TO GET A GOOD NIGHT'S SLEEP

Physicians often recommend the following steps to sleep well and to avoid medication (Borbely, 1986):

- Establish a regular bedtime, and try to keep to it. If you occasionally go to bed late, still try to get up at the same time the following morning.
- Avoid taking occasional naps. Either take naps regularly, or do not nap at all.
- Establish a regular bedtime routine. Include in your routine some restful, relaxing activities (e.g., reading, taking a warm bath, or listening to soothing music).
- Avoid engaging in strenuous mental or physical activities in the evening. Although a regular program of exercise will help you to sleep well in general, if you are highly active just before you go to bed, you may have trouble getting to sleep.

insomnia • any of various disturbances of sleep, such as difficulty in falling asleep or in staying asleep

narcolepsy • a disturbance of the pattern of wakefulness and sleep, in which the narcoleptic periodically experiences an uncontrollable urge to fall asleep and then briefly loses consciousness

sleep apnea • a breathing disturbance that occurs during sleep, in which the sleeper repeatedly stops breathing during sleep; a sleep disorder

somnambulism • a disorder characterized by sleepwalking

sleep (caused by sleep apnea), and sleepwalking (somnambulism) can cause serious problems.

Insomnia is a sleep disorder that may involve difficulty in falling asleep, waking up during the night and being unable to go back to sleep, or waking up too early in the morning (without feeling well-rested). Insomnia is often upsetting to the millions of people who are affected by it. Almost everybody has trouble falling asleep occasionally, but about 6% of adults surveyed have tried to get medical help because of sleeplessness (Borbely, 1986). Insomnia is more common among women than among men and is also more common among persons who are past middle age than among younger people (Borbely, 1986).

What appears to be the opposite problem to insomnia is **narcolepsy,** which is a disorder causing an uncontrollable urge to fall asleep periodically during the day. Narcolepsy affects about 1 or 2 people in 1,000 (Borbely, 1986). The loss of consciousness can occur at any time. It even may occur when the person is driving or otherwise doing something in which sudden sleep can be dangerous. Fortunately, medication usually can control the symptoms of this disease.

Another sleep disorder is **sleep apnea,** a breathing disturbance in which the *apneic* (person who has apnea) repeatedly stops breathing during sleep. These attacks can occur hundreds of times per night. The episodes usually last only a few seconds, but they may last as long as 2 minutes in severe cases.

Somnambulism (sleepwalking) combines aspects of waking and sleeping. Sleepwalkers can see, walk, and perhaps even talk, but they usually cannot remember the sleepwalking episodes after they waken. For many years, scientists believed that sleepwalkers were merely acting out their dreams. In fact, however, sleepwalking usually begins during N-REM sleep, when dreaming is rare. If the sleepwalking episode is short, sleepwalkers

- Avoid eating too much before going to bed. If you eat at all, eat only a light snack. Also, there is some support for the old wives' tale that a glass of warm milk may help you to get to sleep.

- Avoid alcohol, caffeine, and nicotine (e.g., in cigarettes). Alcohol probably will not prevent you from getting to sleep, but it may keep you from staying asleep throughout the night. Caffeine and nicotine may make it difficult for you to get to sleep in the first place.

- Avoid taking sleeping pills. They provide some short-term help for some people, but over the long term, they actually can cause insomnia. Also, the effects of sleeping pills often carry over through at least part of the day after their use.

- Try to sleep in a quiet, dark room with adequate circulation and a comfortable temperature.

- If you wake up during the night, and you do not go back to sleep quickly and easily, try getting out of bed and doing something restful, such as reading a relaxing book or listening to soothing music. Do not stay in bed, tossing and turning, worrying about not sleeping. (The frustration will increase your anxiety level, which can in turn make your insomnia worse.)

may stay in deep sleep. If the episode is long, the EEG patterns begin to look like those of light sleep or even those of the waking state.

Scientists have not found a cause or a cure for sleepwalking. Sleepwalking puzzles us because it occurs completely outside our conscious control. Similarly, dreams come in the night, when we are asleep and have no conscious control over our thoughts.

Dreams

All of us have dreams every night, whether or not we remember them (Ornstein, 1986). Dreams fill our heads with fantastic ideas, sometimes pleasant, sometimes frightening, and frequently creative. Many of the fantastic events of our dreams are implausible to our waking minds, but they may seem reasonable to us as we sleep.

Dreams can cover a wide variety of topics. In one study, college students were asked about the content of their dreams (R. M. Griffith, Miyago, & Tago, 1958). Common themes of dreams, and the percentages of students responding that they had experienced each of the various types of common dreams, were failing (83%); being attacked or pursued (77%); trying repeatedly to do something (71%); school, teachers, and studying (71%); sexual experiences (66%); arriving too late (64%); eating (62%); being frozen with fright (58%); the death of a loved one (57%); being locked up (56%); finding money (56%); and swimming (52%).

Why do we dream? Consider several theories. Perhaps the best-known theory of dreaming was proposed by Sigmund Freud (1900/1954). According to Freud, dreams are the "royal road to the unconscious": They are one of the few ways in which we allow the hidden contents of the unconscious (e.g., sexual desires) to be expressed. These contents are expressed in a disguised form, however. How do we achieve such a disguise? Freud proposed a mechanism by distinguishing between two kinds of contents of dreams. The *manifest content of dreams* is the overt content that we experience when we dream. The *latent content of dreams* is the disguised meaning of the dreams, the means by which we hide from ourselves the wishes that we try to fulfill via our dreams. We need these disguises because our unconscious wishes would be so threatening if expressed directly and clearly that we might awaken every time we dreamed. Freud applied his psychodynamic theory to the interpretation of the disguised meanings expressed in dreams. Freudians spend a lot of time trying to detect the hidden meanings in the contents of dreams.

Other theorists, however, have suggested that many of the events and symbols of dreams are not mysteriously disguised longings. In fact, sometimes the meaning underlying dream content is interpreted easily (Dement, 1976). For example, William Dement (1976) studied the dreams of participants who were prevented from drinking liquids before they fell asleep. Unsurprisingly, many of their dreams involved wanting to drink liquids (Dement, 1976, p. 69): "Just as the bell went off, somebody raised a glass and said something about a toast. I don't think I had a glass."

An alternative cognitive view of dreams is the **activation–synthesis hypothesis** (McCarley & Hobson, 1981). According to this hypothesis, dreaming represents our attempts to interpret the neural activity of our brains during sleep. Just as our brains organize sensory information during wakefulness, our brains also organize sensory information during sleep. For example, while we dream, our ability to command the movements of our skeletal muscles is blocked. According to the activation–synthesis hypothesis, our brains may interpret this inability to move as a dream of being unable to escape from some danger. Another somewhat more widely accepted cognitive view of dreaming is that it is a cognitive ability that develops with age that serves a problem-solving function, as does much of waking cognition. Dreaming, however, is generally involuntary in this function, unlike waking cognition (Antrobus, 1978, 1991; Foulkes, 1985; see Squier & Domhoff, 1997).

Yet another theory of dreaming is nearly the opposite of Freud's. According to this theory (Crick & Mitchison, 1983), dreaming is the mind's attempt to get rid of mental garbage. Thus, whereas Freud suggested that we should examine our dreams closely, Francis Crick and G. Mitchison suggested that we should ignore the mental garbage being tossed out by our brains. This theory is sometimes called the *reverse-learning theory of dreams,* because it proposes that dreams have no meaning in themselves but rather help us to rid ourselves of the unnecessary information that we have accumulated during the course of the day.

Scientists may never be able to come up with a theory of dream interpretation that applies to all people in all situations. Dreams are highly personal, so many people can and do freely interpret their own dreams as they choose to do so. Within the context of their current lives and past memories, they draw whatever conclusions seem appropriate to them.

Daydreams

activation–synthesis hypothesis • a belief that dreams result from subjective organization and interpretation (synthesis) of neural activity (activation) that takes place during sleep

A phenomenon related to dreaming is *daydreaming,* a state of consciousness somewhere between waking and sleeping that permits a shift in the focus of conscious processing toward internal thoughts and images and away from external events. Daydreaming can be useful in cognitive processes that involve the generation of creative ideas. But it also can be disruptive, as anyone knows who ever has been questioned while day-dreaming in class, in cognitive processes requiring focused attention on environmental events. Hyponosis is another state that can be helpful or disruptive.

4.3

This is probably the first time you have seen this instruction in a textbook: Stop reading your textbook and take a few minutes to daydream. When you return to studying, think about both the content and the process of your daydreaming. How does daydreaming seem to differ from what you know about the content and the process of dreams that come to you during your sleep?

IS HYPNOSIS AN ALTERED STATE?

The Phenomenon of Hypnosis: Real or Fake?

An altered state of consciousness that somewhat resembles sleep is **hypnosis.** Historically, the man credited with introducing hypnotism as a psychological phenomenon is Franz Anton Mesmer (1734–1815), who referred to the phenomenon he discovered as *mesmerism.* In his own lifetime, Mesmer came to be considered a fraud, perhaps because he had some strange beliefs, such as that "animal magnetism," a never well-defined construct, could cure illnesses.

A person undergoing hypnosis usually is deeply relaxed and extremely sensitive to suggestion. For example, hypnotized people may imagine that they see or hear things when they are prompted to do so (Bowers, 1976). Hypnotized people also may receive a posthypnotic suggestion. In a **posthypnotic suggestion,** participants are given instructions during hypnosis to carry out after they awake from the hypnotic state. Participants often do not remember receiving the instructions, and many do not even recall having been hypnotized (Ruch, 1975). People differ in their susceptibility to hypnotism, and scales can be used to measure this susceptibility. These scales largely measure the extent to which a person is susceptible to actual suggestions made when the individual is under hypnosis.

Hypnotized research participants also may not sense things that they otherwise would sense. For example, a hypnotized person may not feel pain when dipping an arm into icy cold water. Hypnosis has been particularly effective in relieving pain for which physical causes have not yet been found (e.g., Siegel, 1979).

Some scientists have argued that the very phenomenon of hypnosis is phony (Meeker & Barber, 1971; also described in Barber, 1964a, 1964b). According to this view, hypnotized research participants actually only pretend to be hypnotized. Some people may participate in the hoax even without realizing that they are doing so. These people may believe so strongly in the powers of the hypnotist that they believe that they are hypnotized, even when they are not. Some people in stage demonstrations may only pretend or may believe they are hypnotized when they are not.

hypnosis • an altered state of consciousness that usually involves deep relaxation and extreme sensitivity to suggestion and appears to bear some resemblance to sleep

posthypnotic suggestion • an instruction received during hypnosis, which the individual is to implement after having wakened, often despite having no recollection of having received the instruction

Franz Anton Mesmer (1734–1815) was one of the first to discover hypnosis. Here, he is shown supposedly helping his patients to recover from any number of mysterious illnesses, through his healing powers of hypnosis. Mesmer was apparently sincere in believing that he could cure the illnesses of his patients. However, most physicians and scientists doubted his abilities. Eventually, he was prevented from practicing his mesmerizing treatments.

But the consensus among most psychologists is that hypnosis is a genuine altered state of consciousness.

How can psychologists tell whether hypnotism is genuinely affecting people who appear to be hypnotized? One way is to use the simulating paradigm (Orne, 1959). In the **simulating paradigm,** one group of participants is hypnotized, and another group (a control group) is not. The participants in the unhypnotized group then are asked to *simulate* being hypnotized, that is, to behave as though they were hypnotized. Experimenters then must try to distinguish the behavior of the hypnotized group from the behavior of the control group. As it turns out, simulators can imitate some, but not all, of the behavior of hypnotized participants (Gray, Bowers, & Fenz, 1970).

Some psychologists have become convinced that hypnosis can be used to dredge up old memories of events that otherwise would appear to be forgotten, even memories of past lives! For example, in one study, a full third of the hypnotized college students who were instructed to remember events from previous lives were able to do so (Spanos, DuBreuil, & Gabora, 1991). While they were recalling these past lives, they were asked questions about their lives and surrounding events. Their recall cast serious doubt on the validity of their assertions. One student, for example,

simulating paradigm • a research technique for determining the true effects of a psychological treatment (e.g., hypnosis); one group of participants is subjected to the treatment and another group (a control group) does not receive the treatment but is asked to simulate the behavior of persons who do; observers try to distinguish the behavior of the treatment group from that of the control group trying to simulate the treatment group's behavior

recalled his life as Julius Caesar in A.D. 50, when he was Emperor of Rome. Caesar died in 44 B.C. and never was crowned Emperor of Rome.

The evidence suggests that people under hypnosis are highly suggestible and that at least some of their recall may be induced inadvertently by their hypnosis (Newman & Baumeister, 1994). For example, hypnotists' questions about events during reported abductions by extraterrestrial aliens often contain suggestions, which then are picked up by the hypnotized individual and "recalled" as having happened. An example is being asked whether one was injected with a needle by the extraterrestrials, and then "remembering" that one was, indeed, injected (Fiore, 1989).

Some recollections under hypnosis may be correct (Geiselman, Fisher, MacKinnon, & Holland, 1985). But the current weight of the evidence is that recollections made under hypnosis need to be treated with skepticism, and that corroborating sources of evidence for these recollections should be obtained before they are accepted as true memories.

Theories of Hypnosis

Suppose that we accept hypnosis as a potentially genuine psychological phenomenon. We still need to determine exactly what goes on during hypnosis. One theory holds that hypnosis is a form of deep relaxation (Edmonston, 1981). Although EEG patterns obtained during hypnosis are different from those for sleep, there may be a close connection between hypnosis and deep relaxation, which sometimes precedes or resembles sleep.

Psychoanalysts have suggested that during hypnosis, we partially return to a way of thinking that is like that of infants or young children. According to this view, hypnotized persons act in ways that adults normally would avoid because their mature thought processes would rule out those actions (Gill, 1972). Empirical studies have shown, however, that hypnotized participants who show what appear to be childlike ways of speaking or acting still retain adult modes of thinking and speaking, as well as adult capabilities (Nash, 1987).

A widely accepted view of hypnosis is neodissociative theory. According to the **neodissociative theory**, some people can *dissociate* (separate) one part of their minds from another. In effect, when hypnotizable participants are hypnotized, their consciousness splits. One part of the conscious mind responds to the hypnotist's commands, while another part becomes a hidden observer. This hidden observer monitors everything that is going on. In the responding part of the hypnotized participant's mind, some of the events taking place may fail to be observed consciously (Hilgard, 1977).

For example, studies of pain relief through hypnosis have found an interesting paradox: Some participants respond to a hypnotist's suggestion and agree that they feel no pain (as reported by the responding part of the mind). At the same time, if they are asked to describe how the pain feels, they can do so (as reported by the observing part of the mind). In other experiments, participants can be made to do one task consciously and another without realizing they are doing it. For example, while they are consciously engaged in a task, they can write down messages that they do not consciously realize they are writing (see Kihlstrom, 1985; Knox, Crutchfield, & Hilgard, 1975; Zamansky & Bartis, 1985). Thus, it seems that part of the participant's consciousness is unself-consciously involved in the hypnosis. Meanwhile, another part of the person's consciousness observes and thereby knows, at some level, what is going on.

neodissociative theory • a view of hypnosis asserting that some individuals can separate one part of their conscious minds (which responds to the hypnotist's instructions) from another part (which observes and monitors the events and actions taking place)

People differ in their susceptibility to hypnosis (Hilgard, 1965), with some people readily becoming deeply hypnotized, others less so, and still others appearing invulnerable to hypnotism. Unsurprisingly, hypnosis is more successful as a clinical treatment with highly hypnotizable individuals. Today, hypnosis is used in clinical settings to control smoking and to treat a variety of health-related problems such as asthma, high blood pressure, and migraine headaches. The effects of hypnosis, however, appear to be temporary. For this reason, hypnotism generally is used in conjunction with other therapeutic techniques. Still, hypnosis appears to have an effect that goes beyond other treatment techniques, whether in relieving pain or in changing behavior. Other uses of hypnosis appear rather dubious, such as its use for recovering lost memories.

To conclude this discussion, the results are inconclusive. Psychologists do not all agree about what hypnosis is, or even whether it is a genuine phenomenon. There is persuasive evidence that hypnosis is more than fakery. Some people, apparently those who are more susceptible to suggestion, easily become deeply hypnotized. Others are less likely to be hypnotized, and still others appear incapable of being hypnotized (Hilgard, 1965).

WHAT HAPPENS WHEN WE MEDITATE?

Meditation, another means of achieving an altered state of consciousness, also may offer possible therapeutic benefits. Many forms, but not all forms, of meditation have their origins in Eastern religions. During **meditation,** people shift away from focusing their thoughts on actions and events in the external world. Instead, they shift toward allowing their thoughts and sensations to float and drift through their minds, including sensations and impressions from the internal world of their bodies and minds. Meditation can be soothing and calming, allowing a person to stop thinking about past actions and future plans, as well as present events taking place in the world outside the person's body.

What happens during meditation? In general, breathing rate, heart rate, blood pressure, and muscle tension decrease (D. H. Shapiro & Giber, 1978; Wallace & Benson, 1972). Meditation also seems to help patients with bronchial asthma (Honsberger & Wilson, 1973), with high blood pressure (Benson, 1977), with insomnia (Woolfolk, Carr-Kaffashan, McNulty, & Lehrer, 1976), and with some symptoms of psychiatric problems (Glueck & Stroebel, 1975). EEG studies suggest that meditation tends to produce a concentration of brain waves associated with relaxation and the beginning stages of sleep (Ornstein, 1977). Many drug-induced alterations in consciousness also are related to sleep and relaxation.

meditation • a set of techniques, used for altering consciousness, to become more contemplative

psychoactive drug • a drug (e.g., depressants, stimulants, opiates and opioids, or hallucinogenics) that produces a psychopharmacological effect, thereby affecting behavior, mood, and consciousness

psychopharmacological • a drug-induced influence on behavior, mood, and consciousness

HOW DO DRUGS INDUCE ALTERATIONS IN CONSCIOUSNESS?

Various drugs introduced into the body may destroy bacteria, ease pain, or alter consciousness. Taken in excess, almost any drug can be dangerous. For example, two commonly used nonprescription painkillers can be dangerous when taken without adequate restraint. Aspirin taken in large quantities can induce internal bleeding in the stomach; acetaminophen taken in excess can cause liver damage. However, in this chapter, we are concerned primarily with psychoactive drugs. **Psychoactive drugs** achieve a **psychopharmacological** effect whereby they affect behavior, mood, and consciousness. Psychoactive drugs can be classified into four basic categories (Seymour & Smith, 1987): opiates and opioids, central nervous system depressants, central nervous system stimulants, and hallucinogenics. Table 4.1, at the close of this chapter, summarizes the drugs in each category.

In addition to these four categories of psychoactive drugs, two other kinds of drugs produce psychoactive effects: antipsychotic drugs (discussed in chapter 14) and mild **analgesics** (painkillers). Mild analgesics include acetaminophen (the active ingredient in Tylenol), ibuprofen (the active ingredient in Advil), and salicylic acid (the active ingredient in aspirin); pain relief is discussed more fully in chapter 15. Before we discuss each of the four main categories of psychoactive drugs, we consider the general pattern of the body's reactions to a psychoactive drug.

Pattern of Drug Use

The use of psychoactive drugs typically follows a particular pattern: When the person starts using the drug, the person has an initial psychoactive reaction to the drug. The particular psychoactive reaction depends on the particular drug being used. For some drugs, the person may appear to be **intoxicated.** *Toxic* means poisonous, and psychoactive drugs act as poisons when taken into the body at high levels. At low levels, intoxication produces trouble in thinking clearly and in making reasoned judgments.

If a person repeatedly and regularly uses a given drug, the person develops a **tolerance** for the drug. When tolerance occurs, increasingly high doses of the drug are required to produce the same psychoactive effect. Eventually, the person's tolerance reaches a very high level. At this level, the dose that would be required to produce a psychoactive effect also would produce an overdose. An **overdose** occurs when a person takes a life-threatening or lethal dose of a drug.

Once tolerance reaches this high level, the person clearly has an **addiction** to the drug. How many uses of a drug are required before developing a drug abuse problem? That number depends on the characteristics of the particular drug and of the drug user. Some drugs are rapidly addictive, and others are less so. The rate of forming a dependence on drugs also varies from person to person. In any case, as the level of tolerance increases, the level of psychoactive effect from using the drug decreases.

When an addict stops using a drug, the addict experiences symptoms of withdrawal. During **withdrawal,** the body must adjust to being without the addictive drug. The particular symptoms of withdrawal vary for different persons and different drugs.

Treatment of drug dependence is based on whether the patient suffers from medical problems that are acute or chronic. **Acute toxicity** is the injury to health resulting from a particular overdose. **Chronic toxicity** is the damage caused by long-term drug dependency.

Most forms of treatment address the problems of acute toxicity first. Once the acute toxicity is managed, the treatment of chronic toxicity begins. This treatment generally involves some form of withdrawal from the drug, which is supervised by a doctor or other therapist. For many psychoactive drugs, medical supervision is needed because of the potentially deadly consequences of drug withdrawal. In general, substance abusers need to do the following:

- Become drug-free.
- Develop a lifestyle that will enable them to stay drug-free.

analgesics • pain-relieving drugs (e.g., acetaminophen, ibuprofen, and salicylic acid [aspirin])

intoxicated • characterized by grogginess, insensibility, or temporary trouble thinking clearly and making reasoned judgments due to the effects of toxins such as alcohol or sedative–hypnotic drugs

tolerance • a consequence of prolonged use of psychoactive drugs, in which the drug user feels decreasing psychopharmacological effects of a given drug at one level of dosage and must take increasing amounts of drugs in order to achieve the same effects, eventually reaching such a high level that further increases will cause overdose

overdose • ingestion of a life-threatening or lethal dose of drugs, often associated with the use of psychoactive drugs

addiction • a persistent, habitual, or compulsive physiological or at least psychological dependency on one or more psychoactive drugs

withdrawal • the temporary discomfort, which may be extremely unpleasant and sometimes even life-threatening, associated with a reduction or discontinuation of the use of a psychoactive drug, during which the drug user's physiology and mental processes must adjust to an absence of the drug

acute toxicity • the negative health consequences of a single instance of ingesting a poisonous substance, such as a single overdose of a psychoactive drug

chronic toxicity • the negative health consequences of repeated ingestion of one or more poisonous substances, such as opiates and opioids

If users of illicit drugs share needles for injecting drugs into the bloodstream, they risk developing AIDS (acquired immune deficiency syndrome), hepatitis, and various other infections. Infections acquired through the bloodstream have much more serious consequences, because they bypass many of our body's protective responses.

FIGURE 4.4
Chemical Twins
The molecules of some psychoactive drugs (e.g., heroin) and some natural brain substances (e.g., endorphins) have very similar shapes. Because the molecules have similar structural shapes, these drugs easily fit into the places (receptor sites) in the brain where the natural substances usually belong.

- Understand what got them addicted in the first place.
- Take proactive steps to stay off drugs and to avoid situations that may lead to drug use.

What happens in the brain to cause the actions of psychoactive drugs? How do neuroscientists explain the initial effects, the prolonged effects, and the withdrawal symptoms of psychoactive drugs? Many psychoactive drugs behave like the body's natural *neurochemicals* (neurotransmitters and related substances that are naturally produced in the brain; see chapter 2, see also Figure 4.4). Some neurochemicals are relaxing, others are stimulating, and some neurochemicals (known as "endorphins") are even associated with pain relief and, potentially, with feelings of *euphoria* (intense happiness and a sense of well-being).

Initially, the use of psychoactive drugs tricks the body into behaving in ways that exaggerate normal, natural processes of the brain. As Figure 4.4 shows, these drugs manage to trick the brain because their molecular shape is very similar to the molecular shape of naturally occurring neurochemicals. For example, drugs that have a molecular shape similar to that of endorphins may provide pain relief and feelings of euphoria. If psychoactive drugs have a molecular shape similar to that of a neurochemical with a calming effect, those drugs may produce a calming effect. Drugs with a molecular shape similar to that of a stimulating neurochemical may produce stimulating effects. Psychoactive drugs produce intense levels of psychoactive symptoms that the brain may produce naturally, and usually less intensely, from time to time.

Unfortunately, the brain seems to react to prolonged use of these drugs by slowing down the body's natural production of these neurochemicals. Hence, over time, the brain becomes less able to produce its own calming, pain-relieving, stimulating, or euphoria-inducing effects. This slowing down of production leads to tolerance. Gradually, the body stops producing much of the natural substances at all. It also stops reacting as strongly to the psychoactive drugs. At this point, the person is dependent on the drug. It is very hard to stop using the drug because of the dependence and because the body is no longer creating the neurochemicals that it should be creating. If the person withdraws successfully from the drug, the brain gradually begins again to produce more of the natural substances. Usually, the brain eventually returns to its normal neurochemical balance: It produces and reacts normally to the endorphins, neurotransmitters, and related substances in the brain.

Opiates and Opioids

The term *opiate* originally was used to describe only opium and drugs derived from opium, such as codeine, morphine, and heroin. These drugs also sometimes are referred to as **narcotics.** More recently, chemists have been able to produce drugs either naturally from opium or synthetically from combinations of chemicals. Drugs made from the opium poppy bulb are termed *opiates*. Opiate-like drugs that are produced synthetically are termed *opioids*. Both opiates and opioids may be injected intravenously (using needles to get the drug into the bloodstream), smoked, inhaled nasally (snorted), or ingested orally (eaten as pills or syrups). These drugs generally produce some degree of numbness or stupor and lead to drug dependency. The psychopharmacological effects are like the effects produced by endorphins, such as euphoria or analgesia.

Because opiates and opioids are highly addictive and potentially harmful, they usually either are regulated by prescription or are banned outright. These drugs primarily affect the functioning of the brain and of the bowel (the intestines). With respect to the former, they bring about pain relief, relaxation, and sleepiness. With respect to the latter, they produce constipation. They also slow down other physiological processes, such as breathing. Opiates and opioids may be prescribed for acute pain, and very low doses sometimes are prescribed for severe diarrhea. Because of the dangers of drug dependency, these drugs usually are not prescribed for chronic pain or mild diarrhea. Typically, users of opiates and opioids have trouble concentrating and feel mentally clouded and fuzzy. Typical withdrawal symptoms are chills, sweating, intense stomach cramps, diarrhea, headache, and repeated vomiting, symptoms similar to those of a really horrible case of intestinal flu.

For opiates and opioids, acute toxicity is usually treated with *naloxone,* which blocks the effects of the drugs (see Figure 4.5). For chronic toxicity, the addict is given one of two treatments: (a) The addict is weaned from the drug; or (b) the addict is allowed to switch to using a legal substitute for the drug, from which the addict is, in theory, eventually weaned. The eventual weaning may or may not occur in practice. For example, many addicts are treated with methadone, which can be taken orally (not intravenously) and which has more long-lasting effects than heroin, so that the user can wait longer between doses without experiencing withdrawal.

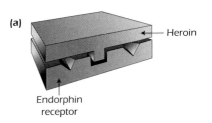

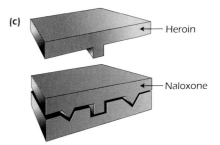

Figure 4.5
Chemical Mate
(a) Opiate (heroin) and (b) opioid (methadone) drugs, which have molecular shapes similar to the molecular shapes of endorphins, can trick the brain into intense levels of response, based on the brain's natural responses to endorphins. (c) The molecular shape of naloxone fits the receptor site so well that it effectively blocks the ability of opiates, opioids, and endorphins, but it does not trigger the pain-relieving and euphoric effects that these substances produce. Hence, naloxone can provide life-saving blockage of the effects of opiate or opioid overdose.

narcotic • any drug in a class of drugs derived from opium or synthetically produced to create the numbing, stuporous effects of opium and that lead to drug dependency

Central Nervous System Depressants

General Drug Actions

Relatively few people regularly use opiates and opioids; many people, however, regularly use **central nervous system (CNS) depressants** such as alcohol and the sedative–hypnotics (which usually are sleeping pills or pills that produce a calming effect). Depressants, like opiates and opioids, slow the operation of the CNS. In general, CNS depressants reduce *anxiety* (general feelings of uneasiness or even fear) and guilt and they relax normal inhibitions. However, intoxicated persons also may show sudden shifts in mood and experience *increased* anxiety and irritability. High doses of depressants can cause slow reflexes, unsteady walking and other movements, slurred speech, and impaired judgment. Overdoses can slow physiological responses to the point of causing death.

Alcohol

Alcohol is the most well-known and widely used CNS depressant. Alcoholism, now widely regarded as a disease, is one of the most common afflictions in the United States. Many factors influence the effects of alcohol: the amount a person drinks, the rate at which the person drinks, the amount and kind of food the person has consumed before starting to drink or while drinking, and the person's body weight, tolerance, and *metabolism* (use and storage of energy and other resources). About 10% of the people who use alcohol have problems in their lives related to alcohol use. About 90% of all assaults, 50% to 60% of all murders, and more than 50% of the rapes and sexual attacks on children are alcohol-related. Alcohol also impairs health, and alcoholics generally have their life expectancy

Many criminal prosecutions are related to the use and sale of illicit drugs, but the psychoactive drug that most often is linked to assaults, homicides, suicides, and accidents is alcohol. This accident, caused by a drunk driver, shows the deadly effects of alcohol.

central nervous system (CNS) depressant • a drug that slows the operation of the CNS and is often prescribed in low doses to reduce anxiety and in relatively higher doses to combat insomnia

4.2

IS SOMEONE YOU KNOW AN ALCOHOLIC?

PUTTING IT TO USE

The National Institute on Alcohol Abuse and Alcoholism has developed the following seven questions for you to use to check whether you (or someone you know) may be having problems due to alcoholism. If you answer "yes" to even one question, alcohol may be a problem in your life (or in the life of someone you know). If you answer "yes" to several questions, you (or someone you know) may be an alcoholic. Most of these questions boil down to a central issue: Is the use of alcohol creating problems in one or more areas of your life?

1. Has someone close to you expressed concern about your drinking?

2. When faced with a problem, do you often turn to alcohol for relief?

3. Are you sometimes unable to meet home or work responsibilities because of drinking?

4. Have you ever required medical attention as a result of drinking?

5. Have you ever experienced a blackout, which is a total loss of memory while still awake, when drinking?

6. Have you ever come in conflict with the law in connection with your drinking?

7. Have you often failed to keep the promises you have made to yourself about controlling or cutting out your drinking?

cut short by an average of 10 to 12 years (M. A. Block, 1970; Ciompi & Eisert, 1969). Overuse of alcohol also can lead to many health problems, including increased risk of cancer (Herity, Moriarty, Daly, Dunn, & Bourke, 1982; Heuch, Kvale, Jacobsen, & Bjelke, 1983). To help detect the signs of alcoholism, see Putting It to Use 4.2.

The effects of alcohol depend upon concentrations in the bloodstream. When concentrations are around 0.03% to 0.05%, people often feel relaxed, uninhibited, and have a general sense of well-being. At a blood-alcohol level of 0.10%, sensorimotor functioning is impaired markedly. Many states consider people to be legally drunk at this level. People may exhibit slurred speech and grow angry, sullen, or morose. At a concentration of 0.20%, people show grave dysfunction. With concentrations of 0.40% or more, there is a serious risk of death. College students may underestimate the risks they are taking. Recently, a first-year student at MIT died from alcohol intoxication. Unfortunately, such incidents are not uncommon. Drinking coffee or other stimulants does not cure drunkenness: It creates an awake drunk.

Sedative–Hypnotics

Sedative–hypnotics are depressant drugs that are used to calm anxiety and to relieve insomnia. The two most widely used sedative–hypnotics

sedative–hypnotics • one of the two primary types of CNS depressants, used to calm anxiety and to relieve insomnia

are barbiturates and tranquilizers. When used properly, **barbiturates** are effective sedative–hypnotics. However, barbiturates are also highly addictive and dangerous. **Tranquilizers** are generally safer than barbiturates: They do not cause as much sleepiness, they are effective at low dosages, and they cause fewer risks to normal breathing. Still, tranquilizers also can be addictive.

Treatment for drug dependency or overdose varies according to the sedative–hypnotic drug. In any case, both a psychological and a physiological dependence must be addressed. Recall that withdrawal from opiate and opioid drugs is extremely uncomfortable but usually not life-threatening. In contrast, withdrawal from sedative–hypnotic drugs can be both painful and life-threatening. Therefore, medical professionals should supervise withdrawal, carefully watching for symptoms of acute and chronic toxicity. Withdrawal symptoms can include anxiety, *tremors* (uncontrollable shaking), nightmares, insomnia, *anorexia* (unwillingness to eat despite the need for food), nausea, vomiting, fever, *seizures* (attacks that may affect both consciousness and muscular control), and *delirium* (mental disturbance involving distortions of thinking and of perception; Seymour & Smith, 1987).

Other sedative–hypnotics also can have marked effects. One such drug, rohypnol, recently was made illegal for sale in the United States, because it was being used by some men for the purpose of date-rape: Women would be knocked out by the drug and then raped, after which they typically did not remember what had happened to them.

Central Nervous System Stimulants

In contrast to CNS depressants, **central nervous system (CNS) stimulants** excite the CNS. They do so either by *stimulating* the heart (making it work harder) or by reducing the activity of natural compounds that slow down brain activity. One way to picture how stimulants work in the brain is to think of stimulants as substances that limit the effectiveness of chemical "brakes" in the brain. When these natural chemical brakes do not work properly, brain activity races ahead, sometimes out of control. Common CNS stimulants include caffeine, nicotine (found in tobacco), amphetamines, and cocaine. Short-term use of mild CNS stimulants can increase the user's alertness, increase the user's ability to continue activity despite being physically tired, help the user to stave off hunger pains, and create a sense of euphoria in the user. In stronger doses, the drugs can cause anxiety and irritability.

Overdoses of stimulants may produce intoxication, *paranoia* (false perceptions that other people are trying to harm the drug user), confusion, hallucinations, and death due to breathing failure or wild and rapid changes in body temperature. Withdrawal symptoms may include extreme tiredness and depression. Occasional on-again, off-again use of amphetamines also seems to produce the paradoxical effect of sensitization. In **sensitization,** the rare or occasional user of stimulants actually becomes *more* sensitive to low doses of the drug.

Nicotine is the psychoactive ingredient in tobacco. At present, nicotine is believed to be among the most addictive substances known: Nine out of 10 people who start smoking become addicted. Compare that number to 1 in 6 people who become addicted after trying crack cocaine and to 1 in 10 people who become alcoholics after experimenting with alcohol. In

barbiturates • the most widely used type of sedative–hypnotic drug; prescribed to reduce anxiety but may lead to grogginess that can impair functioning in situations requiring alertness

tranquilizers • one of the sedative–hypnotic drugs used to combat anxiety; considered to be safer than barbiturates, although the potential for drug dependency remains problematic

central nervous system (CNS) stimulant • a drug that arouses and excites the CNS, either by stimulating the heart or by inhibiting the actions of natural compounds that depress brain activity (thereby acting as a "double-negative" on brain stimulation)

sensitization • the paradoxical phenomenon in which an intermittent user of a drug actually demonstrates heightened sensitivity to low doses of the drug

pregnant women, smoking has been linked both to preterm birth and to low birth weight. Both problems can pose serious risks for newborns. In addition, tobacco users often produce direct effects on other people in the environment through secondary smoke.

Nicotine and other ingredients in tobacco have complex effects on the body. They can act as both stimulants and depressants, increasing respiration, heart rate, and blood pressure, but decreasing appetite. Intoxication is characterized by euphoria, light-headedness, giddiness, dizziness, and a tingling sensation in the extremities (Seymour & Smith, 1987). Tolerance and dependence develop relatively quickly, so that the intoxication effect typically is experienced only by new initiates to smoking. People who habitually use tobacco usually stabilize at some point that becomes a maintenance dosage for them.

The most common treatment for drug dependency on stimulants is psychotherapy. Acute toxicity from stimulants must be treated medically. The exact treatment depends on the particular stimulant. Drug-substitution therapy is generally not used except in the case of nicotine. However, for acute nicotine withdrawal, nicotine gum and epidermal (skin) patches appear to be effective, when used in combination with some other form of therapy.

Hallucinogenics

Hallucinogenic drugs (also known as "psychedelics") alter consciousness by inducing hallucinations and affecting the way the users perceive both their inner worlds and their external environments. To some clinicians, these drugs seem to mimic the effects produced naturally in *psychosis* (very serious psychological disturbances). Other clinicians, however, suggest that these drug-induced hallucinations have different qualities than do the hallucinations produced by psychosis. Mescaline, LSD, and marijuana (the most commonly used) are a few of the hallucinogenic drugs. Hallucinogenic drugs seem to produce different effects, depending on the type of situation in which they are used.

Acute overdoses of hallucinogenics normally are treated by a therapist who uses talk therapy. Typically, the therapist attempts to talk to the user in order to reduce any anxiety and to make the user feel as comfortable as possible ("talking the user down"). Tranquilizers also can be used; a final alternative is the use of *antipsychotic drugs* (drugs used for treating psychosis; see chapter 14). Chronic use of hallucinogenics can lead (in rare cases) to prolonged psychotic reactions; severe and sometimes life-threatening depression; a worsening of psychiatric problems that existed before the drug was taken; and *flashbacks,* in which the drug user reexperiences hallucinations or distortions associated with past drug use, without actually taking the drug again (Seymour & Smith, 1987). Scientists do not yet understand how flashbacks occur because no physiological mechanism has been found that can account for them.

Treatment of Drug Abuse

Table 4.1 briefly summarizes the four categories of drugs and lists some of the common drugs in each category. It does not, however, address the central question of interest to psychologists: Why do people use psychoactive drugs at all? The reasons are various and are not well-understood yet.

hallucinogenic • a type of psychoactive drug that alters consciousness by inducing hallucinations and by affecting the way the drug users perceive both their inner worlds and their external environments

TABLE 4.1

Four Basic Categories of Drugs

Psychoactive drugs can be sorted into four basic categories, each of which produces distinctive psychoactive effects.

Category	Effect	Drugs in this class
Narcotics	Produce numbness or stupor, relieve pain	■ Opium and its natural derivatives: morphine, heroin, and codeine ■ Opiods (synthetic narcotics): meperidine (Demerol), propoxyphene (Darvon), oxycodone (Percodan), methadone

CNS depressants ("downers")	Slow (depress) the operation of the central nervous system	■ Alcohol
		■ Sedative–hypnotics
		  Barbiturates: secobarbital (Seconal), phenobarbital (Dilantin)
		  Tranquilizers (benzodiazepines): chlorpromazine (Thorazine), chlordiazepoxide (Librium), diazepam (Valium), alprazolam (Xanax)
		■ Methaqualone (Quaalude)
		■ Chloral hydrate

CNS stimulants ("uppers")	Excite (stimulate) the operation of the central nervous system	■ Caffeine (found in coffee, teas, cola drinks, chocolate) ■ Amphetamines: amphetamine (Benzedrine), dextroamphetamine (Dexedrine), methamphetamine (Methedrine) ■ Cocaine ■ Nicotine (commonly found in tobacco)
Hallucinogens (psychedelics, psychotomimetics)	Induce alterations of consciousness	■ LSD ■ Mescaline ■ Marijuana ■ Hashish ■ Phencyclidine (PCP)

Many behaviorally oriented psychologists have suggested that these drugs are linked to rewarding feelings or mental states. Drug users learn to use drugs because they receive this reward. Other psychologists disagree. They point out that the strength of the reward lessens (as a result of increasing tolerance), but the drug use continues anyway.

Given our ignorance about what causes people to engage in the abuse of psychoactive drugs, does it do any good to try to treat people addicted to these drugs? Yes. According to a study by the Institute of Medicine of the National Academy of Science (Gerstein & Harwood, 1990), the cost of drug-treatment programs is more than offset by their success in reducing the much higher costs related to drug abuse, including drug-related crime, health care, and lost productivity.

Each of the preceding sections on psychoactive drugs has included a brief mention of treatment for acute or chronic toxicity related to specific drugs. What, if anything, is likely to increase the probability that drug treatment of any kind will be successful? The single most important factor that seems to enhance the likelihood of treatment success is to increase the length of time in treatment (Gerstein & Harwood, 1990). About one third of recovering addicts who remain in treatment for 3 months or more continue to resist drugs a year later, and about two thirds of recovering addicts who remain in treatment for a year or more manage to stay drug free long afterward (Falco, 1992). Also, even when individuals do not fully succeed in remaining drug free following initial treatment, there still may be gains from treatment, such as reduced use, reduced criminal activity, and increased likelihood of returning to treatment, thereby leading to future possibilities for success (Falco, 1992).

Other factors that improve the likelihood of treatment success include having a stable family, being employed, and having access to other rewarding activities. Having adequate financial resources also may be helpful. For example, a 70% success rate was achieved with affluent cocaine addicts in a Beverly Hills treatment program. However, when the same program was implemented with impoverished crack addicts, the success rate plummeted to 30% (Falco, 1992). The approach used in this particular program is to help addicts to understand both the physiological and the psychological processes of drug dependency and recovery. The program encourages addicts to focus on the drug-using behavior and on the many environmental stimuli that contribute to whether the person will be able to resist using drugs. Other programs for treating drug use include Alcoholics Anonymous and Narcotics Anonymous. The behavioral view of drug dependencies and other learned behavior is described more fully in the following chapter.

The Solution to The Case of the Dangerous Drinker Who Wanted to Drive

Martha remembers from reading chapter 4 of *Pathways to Psychology* that drinking coffee does nothing to alleviate a state of drunkenness. What it does is to create an "awake drunk." Barry may feel more awake, but the effects of alcohol on his sensorimotor abilities will continue for awhile, regardless of how much coffee he drinks. In a way, the coffee has an unfortunate effect, because it falsely convinces Barry that he is now in control. Martha explains to Barry what she has read and Barry, realizing that Martha is right, decides that the embarrassment of being out of full control is a much better outcome than would be a motor vehicle accident. Barry lets Martha drive. Although she is unhappy that Barry drank too much, she gives him credit for not insisting that he drive when he is impaired. At the next party, Barry controls his drinking.

Summary

1. *Consciousness* is a stream of active mental processing. It is the state of mind through which we obtain, manipulate, and apply information available from our senses, from memory, and from our ongoing mental processes.
2. *Attention* is the process by which we focus mental awareness on particular information available in consciousness, allowing other information to remain outside of our awareness.

How Does Attention Work?   127

3. People use *selective attention* to track one message while ignoring other messages.
4. In *dichotic presentation,* each of the ears receives a *different* auditory message. In contrast, during *binaural presentation,* both ears receive the *same* message.

5. The *Stroop effect* occurs when a person is asked to identify the ink color of color words when the ink color of the words differs from what the printed word means (e.g., the word "red," printed in blue ink).

What Levels of Consciousness Do We Experience?   130

6. Consciousness occurs on *multiple levels.*
7. Information in the *preconscious level* is just outside of consciousness and is usually available for conscious retrieval or use. *Subliminal perception* occurs at the preconscious level.
8. Information in the *subconscious level* is normally not available to consciousness, except with great difficulty or perhaps through dreams.

What Happens During Altered States of Consciousness? 133

9. Altered states of consciousness can involve *illusions,* which are distorted perceptions of objects, or *hallucinations,* which are perceptions of objects that do not exist.

What Happens When We Sleep and Dream? 133

10. There are two basic kinds of sleep, *REM sleep* and *non-REM* (N-REM) sleep. In REM sleep, the eyes move rapidly, and the sleeper usually is dreaming. N-REM sleep usually is divided into four stages of successively deeper sleep, which seldom involve dreaming. The stages of N-REM sleep and REM sleep cycle repeatedly through the night.

11. If people are subjected to *sleep deprivation* for several days, they show increasingly serious symptoms of being mentally disturbed.

12. People seem to show a *circadian* (daily) *rhythm* that corresponds to the night–day pattern of our planet.

13. In *insomnia,* individuals have trouble falling asleep, wake up during the night, or wake up too early in the morning. Persons with *narcolepsy* feel sudden, overwhelming impulses to sleep when they do not really want to. In *sleep apnea,* breathing is temporarily interrupted during sleep. *Somnambulists* (sleepwalkers) typically do not dream while they are acting out wakeful-seeming behaviors in their sleep.

14. Several different theories of dreaming have been proposed. According to Freud, dreams express the hidden wishes of the unconscious. According to McCarley and Hobson's *activation–synthesis theory,* dreams represent our own interpretations of our brain activity during sleep. According to Crick and Mitchison, dreams are the brain's way of clearing itself during the night, essentially, for disposing of "mental garbage."

Is Hypnosis an Altered State? 141

15. During *hypnosis,* some people become extremely responsive to whatever the hypnotist tells them, and they often are quite willing (within limits) to obey the hypnotist's instructions to do things or even to feel things they normally would not do or feel. A *posthypnotic suggestion* is a means by which hypnotized participants can be asked to do something after the hypnotic trance is removed.

16. Various theories of hypnosis have been proposed. One theory views hypnosis as a form of deep relaxation. Another views it as a return to childlike ways of thinking. Still another theory views hypnosis as a set of play-acted roles, and the actors may be sincere or insincere in acting out their roles. Research has not supported the return-to-childhood view, and findings from research on the play-acting view are mixed. A fourth theory, which now is widely accepted, views hypnosis as a form of split consciousness: There is a hidden observer in the person who observes what is going on, as though from the outside, at the same time that the person responds to hypnotic suggestions.

What Happens When We Meditate? 144

17. *Meditation* is a set of techniques used to alter state of consciousness; the person becomes more relaxed, inner directed, and calm, as well as less tense, goal oriented, and outer directed.

How Do Drugs Induce Alterations in Consciousness? 144

18. State of consciousness can be altered by four kinds of *psychoactive drugs: opiates and opioids, central nervous system (CNS) depressants, central nervous system (CNS) stimulants,* and *hallucinogenics.* The *psychopharmacological* effects of these drugs are related to similar effects produced by naturally occurring neurochemicals in the brain.

19. A typical pattern of drug use involves *intoxication, tolerance,* and *drug dependency,* as well as the possibilities for *withdrawal* and even for *overdose.* Drug treatment must address either *acute toxicity* or *chronic toxicity.*

20. *Narcotics* include natural opiates and synthetic opioids. These drugs produce some degree of numbness or stupor and often a feeling of euphoria or pain relief.

21. *Depressants,* including alcohol and *sedative–hypnotic* drugs, slow the operation of the CNS. In contrast, *stimulants,* including caffeine, nicotine, cocaine, and amphetamines, speed up the operation of the CNS.

22. *Hallucinogenics,* including LSD, mescaline, and marijuana, produce distorted perceptions of reality.

Pathways to Knowledge

Choose the best answer to complete each sentence.

1. Tolerance to a psychoactive drug occurs when
   (a) drug users no longer care whether they receive the drug.
   (b) drug users need successively greater doses of a drug to achieve the same effect.
   (c) drug users stop having withdrawal symptoms.
   (d) people get used to the idea that an addict is not likely to stop taking drugs.

2. The purpose of the simulating paradigm in studies of hypnosis is to determine whether
   (a) hypnotized people can act as though they were not hypnotized.
   (b) nonhypnotized people can act as though they were hypnotized.
   (c) hypnotized people know that they are hypnotized.
   (d) hypnotized people can act as though they received a posthypnotic suggestion.

3. Which of the following is typically a symptom of severe sleep deprivation?
   (a) illusions or hallucinations
   (b) apnea
   (c) hunger
   (d) thirst

4. Subliminal perception occurs
   (a) only at night.
   (b) in persons who are successfully hypnotized.
   (c) without full-conscious awareness.
   (d) during dreams.

Answer each of the following questions by filling in the blank with an appropriate word or phrase.

5. The stage of sleep during which much dreaming occurs is called _____ _____.
6. A syndrome in which the sleeper has difficulty in breathing is called sleep _____.
7. The hypothesis that dreaming represents a person's subjective awareness and interpretation of neural activity during sleep is called the _____–_____ hypothesis.
8. According to Freud, people _____ information that they find too threatening to permit to enter conscious awareness, but this information may be revealed through slips of the tongue or through _____.

Match the following drugs to their descriptions:

9. nicotine
10. barbiturates
11. cocaine
12. CNS depressants
13. CNS stimulants
14. narcotics
15. heroin
16. methadone
17. alcohol
18. naloxone
19. LSD
20. hallucinogenics
21. sedative–hypnotic drugs

(a) a type of sedative–hypnotic drug
(b) an opiate
(c) the most commonly used CNS depressant
(d) a category of drugs associated with symptoms that may appear similar to those of psychosis
(e) a category of drugs that produces psychopharmacological effects related to the effects of endorphins
(f) an opioid
(g) a highly addictive substance found in tobacco
(h) a category of CNS depressants, including tranquilizers
(i) a category of drugs that slows down the activity of the central nervous system
(j) a strong CNS stimulant
(k) a category of drugs that speeds up the activity of the central nervous system
(l) a drug that effectively blocks the psychopharmacological effects of opiates and opioids
(m) a hallucinogenic

1. b, 2. b, 3. a, 4. c, 5. REM sleep, 6. apnea, 7. activation–synthesis, 8. repress, dreams, 9. g, 10. a, 11. j, 12. i, 13. k, 14. e, 15. b, 16. f, 17. c, 18. l, 19. m, 20. d, 21. h

1. Freud suggested that particular imagery in dreams has particular symbolic meanings. Think of a recent dream you have had, or make up a fanciful dream. Try to analyze the symbolic meanings for the objects and events in your dream. What would you say that your dream meant? What are some more ordinary interpretations of your dream?

2. What are your normal sleep patterns? How do you react when your normal patterns are interrupted? How do your experiences compare with the experiences of participants in sleep-deprivation research?

3. What are some of the factors that you believe can lead people to abuse psychoactive drugs? In your opinion, how can we help people to avoid becoming involved in the abuse of these drugs?

The Case of The Helpful Ex-Friend

*J*illian feels very badly about having ended her friendship with Phoebe. Jillian and Phoebe had been fairly good friends for 6 months and things were going reasonably well. But then Jillian realized that Phoebe's dependency on her was driving her crazy. The worst part was that Phoebe really had done nothing wrong. She was decent, caring, and warm. But Phoebe constantly was calling and making demands on Jillian at all hours of the day and night. Jillian had tried to communicate to Phoebe that her intense dependency was too much for Jillian, but Phoebe seemed unwilling or unable to change. Jillian had concluded that even though she and Phoebe got along, they just did not click as friends. In the long run, Jillian figured she was doing Phoebe a favor by allowing her to find someone who would be able to better tolerate her intense dependency needs.

CHAPTER 5
LEARNING

Not wanting to let Phoebe down, Jillian was still trying to be helpful to her. She saw Phoebe as much as possible and tried to be supportive. Once or twice, when Phoebe had seemed desperate, Jillian even tried spending a lot of time with her because Jillian felt sorry for her. But Phoebe did not seem to be getting over the friendship, despite Jillian's efforts to help her out, and Jillian was at a loss as to what to do. She just did not see how she could be any more helpful than she was being.

What should Jillian do? Think about this as you read chapter 5 and discover the processes of learning. Consider the possibility that perhaps Jillian's attempts to help actually are backfiring and that Jillian is following the wrong pathway to solving her problem. Pay special attention to the nature of intermittent reinforcement.

5

Stop for a moment, and think about all the simple things you have learned in order to get through a single day. What do you do when you feel hunger pangs? What foods do you like to eat, and what foods do you dislike eating? Why do you like some foods and not others? What other simple things have you learned about adapting to your environment?

Psychologists generally define **learning** as any relatively permanent change in the behavior, thoughts, or feelings of an individual that results from experience. This chapter considers relatively simple forms of learning. More complex forms of learning (e.g., the learning that enables you to understand and remember the concepts in this chapter) are considered in other chapters. Through learning, we may adapt to our environment more effectively.

There are various pathways to learning information. In this chapter, we will consider three such pathways: classical conditioning, operant conditioning, and social learning. But first, we will consider preprogrammed responses, which are ways of dealing with environmental challenges that are available from birth.

WHAT ARE SOME PREPROGRAMMED RESPONSES?

Although we must learn a great deal in order to adapt effectively to our environments, we seem to know some things, like how to blink, even at the moment we are born, without having to learn them. These things are biologically preprogrammed into us rather than learned.

One kind of preprogrammed response is **habituation,** in which we tune out relatively familiar stimuli about which we are not trying to learn more information. That is, based on prior experience, particular stimuli become familiar to us, and we generally tune out those familiar stimuli. As I am typing these words, countless stimuli are available to my senses, the steady drone of my old air conditioner; the sights of photos, books, and office supplies surrounding my desk; the feel of my hands on the keyboard; the changing tensions of the muscles in my arms; and so on. One paragraph ago, I was habituated to these familiar stimuli, so I paid no attention to any of them. Habituation is useful because it enables us to do what we need to do without being distracted by all of the competing stimuli that could interfere with our getting things done. If you were distracted by all the stimuli around you, you would hardly be able to concentrate on this exciting textbook.

With a little conscious effort, however, any of these stimuli are available to my awareness. That is, simply by deciding to pay attention to these stimuli, I can notice them again. A complement to habituation is *dishabituation,* in which we tune in to relatively unusual stimuli or to changing stimuli about which we are trying to learn more: If one of my books falls onto the floor, I will become dishabituated and will pay attention to the book. Notice that although habituation is a preprogrammed response, its use is under the control of the individual in interaction with the environment. It does not satisfy our definition of learning because it is not a *relatively permanent* change in behavior.

To see how habituation and dishabituation work together, think about this example: Suppose that a radio was playing instrumental music while you were studying your psychology textbook. At first, the sound might have distracted you, but after a while, you might have become habituated to the familiar sound and scarcely noticed it. However, if the style of music changed dramatically (e.g., from classical to hard rock), you might have dishabituated to the sound, at least temporarily. In this case, the pattern of sound that had been familiar would have entered your awareness as an unusual sound. Similarly, if someone were to ask you a question about the music, you might dishabituate to the music in order to answer the question.

Habituation and dishabituation may seem somewhat similar to sensory adaptation (see chapter 3), which is a temporary physiological response to a sensed change in the environment that is generally not subject to conscious manipulation or control. But sensory adaptation differs from habituation in several key ways (see Table 5.1). The chief difference is that habituation and dishabituation depend on prior experiences with stimuli, and thereby relate closely to learning, whereas sensory adaptation does not. Instead, the degree to which sensory adaptation occurs depends on the intensity of the stimulus. There essentially is no difference in sensory adaptation between the first exposure to a given stimulus and the millionth exposure to the stimulus. For example, people who live in apartments on noisy city blocks learn to habituate to the noise, but it may take awhile. In contrast, if the city block also smells of pollution, sensory adaptation will occur the very first time new residents experience these smells, regardless of previous experience with these or similar smells.

Habituation and dishabituation also serve a helpful purpose for learning: By using these two processes, we turn our attention to novel stimuli about which we can learn a great deal, and we ignore relatively familiar stimuli about which we can learn very little. (Actually, some psychologists consider habituation to be a simple form of learning, rather than a preprogrammed

learning • any relatively permanent change in the behavior, thoughts, or feelings of an individual that results from experience

habituation • a phenomenon in which a person gradually becomes more familiar with a stimulus and notices it less and less; in *dishabituation,* a once-familiar stimulus changes to become unfamiliar, so the person notices the stimulus once again

TABLE 5.1

Differences Between Adaptation and Habituation

Responses involving physiological adaptation take place mostly in our sense organs, whereas responses involving cognitive habituation take place mostly in our brains (and relate to learning).

Adaptation	Habituation
Not accessible to conscious control	Accessible to conscious control
Example: You cannot decide how quickly to adapt to a particular smell or a particular change in light intensity.	*Example:* You can decide to become aware of background music to which you have become habituated (dishabituation).
Tied closely to stimulus intensity	Not tied very closely to stimulus intensity
Example: The more the intensity of a bright light increases, the more strongly your senses will adapt to the light.	*Example:* Your level of habituation will not differ much in your response to the sound of a loud fan and to that of a quieter air conditioner.
Unrelated to the number, length, and recency of prior exposures	Tied very closely to the number, length, and recency of prior exposures
Example: The sense receptors in your skin will respond to changes in temperature in basically the same way, no matter how many times you have been exposed to such changes, and no matter how recently you have experienced these changes.	*Example:* You will become more quickly habituated to the sound of a chiming clock when you have been exposed to the sound more often, for longer times, and on more recent occasions.

Ethologist Konrad Lorenz had young goslings imprint to him, waddling behind him on the ground and swimming behind him in the water. Canadian ethologist Bill Lishman was able to go beyond Lorenz, leading his imprinted goslings into the air, as he flew in his ultralight plane.

response, because it involves change that results from experience; in this chapter, however, because habituation does not involve *relatively permanent change,* we do not consider it to be a form of learning.)

Although habituation can pave the way for complex learning (such as when you learn psychology from a textbook), it involves a relatively simple form of preprogrammed response (ignoring a stimulus). In many species of animals, however, even fairly complex responses may be preprogrammed. These more complex forms of preprogrammed responses are **instincts,** or fixed-action patterns. These patterns of action are inborn. For example, if a male stickleback fish swims too close to the nest of another male, the second male stickleback will warn and possibly attack the first male. The preprogrammed defensive pattern of the second stickleback is automatic, and it is triggered by a red area on the belly of the first (or any other) male stickleback (Tinbergen, 1951). In general, organisms more dependent on instincts are able relatively more quickly to separate themselves from the care of their parents or other caretakers and to be on their own. Organisms more dependent on learning need a longer amount of time being nurtured by their caretakers. But the advantage of these latter organisms is that they acquire a level of flexibility in response to environmental challenges that organisms more highly dependent on instincts do not acquire.

Some instinctive behaviors also involve a degree of learning. In particular, during **imprinting,** a newborn animal seeks out a particular kind of stimulus and then responds with a preprogrammed behavior when it senses the right kind of stimulus. Although both the particular response and the general kind of stimulus are preprogrammed, the animal learns from experience the specific stimulus to which it will respond. For example, Konrad Lorenz (1937, 1950) watched newly hatched goslings form an immediate attachment to the first moving object near them, whether the moving object was the mother or even a human researcher.

There are many variations of imprinting. The stimulus for imprinting may be seen (e.g., the movement of a mother duck), smelled (e.g., the odor of a salmon's native stream), or otherwise sensed (e.g., hearing a mother's call or tasting a mother's milk). Although the imprinted behaviors can vary widely, they usually are associated with survival either for

instinct • an inherited, species-specific, stereotyped, and often relatively complex pattern of behavior

imprinting • a preprogrammed response in which a newborn animal looks for a particular kind of stimulus and then carries out the response; the specific stimulus that prompts the response is learned

the individual (e.g., following a parent who will provide food and will help in avoiding or defending against predators) or for the species (e.g., finding a mate, such as becoming imprinted on the sight or the smell of opposite-sex members of the same species). Although there is generally a critical period for imprinting, imprinted behavior occasionally may be modified somewhat later on. For example, it has happened that a gosling that is not offered a moving object to follow during the critical period for imprinting has imprinted on a moving mother duck at a somewhat later time.

Are preprogrammed responses a help or a hindrance? On the one hand, preprogrammed responses can be adaptive, such as when a duckling learns to follow its mother. On the other hand, preprogrammed responses do not allow for much flexibility. If the environment changes, and the old preprogrammed responses are no longer adaptive in the newly changed environment, the individual has no way to adapt effectively to the changes.

For instance, newly hatched salmon imprint to the odor of their native stream as they swim downstream to the ocean. As long as their natural environment remains essentially the same, the adult salmon, ready to mate, masterfully follow the imprinted odor upstream through complex waterways to their spawning grounds. However, when a salmon's native stream is altered by loggers, hikers, or adventurers the salmon's imprinting does little to help the salmon find its way to its native spawning ground. A more flexible alternative to preprogrammed behavior is learned behavior. If individuals can learn new responses to a changing environment, they have a much better chance of adapting to and surviving in a changing world. One kind of learning of new responses is classical conditioning, which is considered next.

WHAT IS CLASSICAL CONDITIONING?

Do the smells of particular foods turn your stomach? Do the sounds of barking or growling dogs make your heart pound? Do you feel delight at the mere mention of a particular person you know? These common responses result from classical conditioning. In **classical conditioning**, an individual learns to associate a stimulus that causes a particular physiological or emotional response with a second stimulus, which produces no particular response before the two stimuli are linked. After the individual learns to associate the two stimuli, however, the second stimulus alone starts to produce the same physiological or emotional response as the first stimulus.

For instance, if the smell of a particular food sickens you, you probably learned to associate the smell of that food with feeling ill or at least uncomfortable after eating that food. If the mention of a particular person delights you, you probably associate that person with a very pleasant experience (or set of experiences). In each of these examples, you were classically conditioned to learn an association between stimuli.

Pavlov's Discovery of Classical Conditioning

How was classical conditioning discovered? Did a group of psychologists go to a smelly restaurant, eat some sickening, bad-smelling food, and jointly discover the mechanisms of classical conditioning as a form of

classical conditioning • the learning process whereby an originally neutral stimulus becomes associated with a particular physiological or emotional response that the stimulus did not originally produce

After using a buzzer in his first experiments, Ivan Pavlov went on to investigate whether other sound cues and even cues to other sensory modalities, such as sight and touch, could be systematically manipulated to prompt the associative learning. His creative exploration of alternative stimuli illustrates well the scientific method at work. For example, to study the effects of touch stimulation, he rigged a device for touching various parts of the dog's body so that each part could be touched without introducing other sensory stimuli, such as the sight or sounds of an experimenter.

learning? No, but food did play an important role in this discovery. Ivan Pavlov (1849–1936), a Nobel Prize–winning physiologist, accidentally noticed this form of learning while he was studying how saliva influenced the digestion of food in dogs.

In one set of studies, Pavlov was measuring the saliva dogs produced when the dogs were given food (meat powder). After running a few experiments, however, Pavlov noticed that the dogs started to produce saliva even before they were given the meat powder. In fact, the dogs would start salivating in response to the sight of one of his lab technicians or even to the sound of the lab technician's footsteps. What a nuisance! If Pavlov could not keep the dogs from salivating *before* they smelled the meat powder, he would not be able to measure accurately how much saliva they produced *after* smelling it. He would end up with ambiguous results that would be of no use to him or to anyone else. For a while, Pavlov tried to invent ways to keep this annoying problem from interfering with his important research on digestion.

Happily for psychology, however, Pavlov was open to new discoveries. Soon, he saw a startling implication of the dogs' behavior. Some kind of *associative learning* (learning of the nature of some kind of connection between one thing and another) must have taken place. Originally, only the food led to the physiological response (salivation). After repeated experience, however, other stimuli came to be associated with the food, and these other stimuli also led to the salivation response. Psychologists refer to this form of learning as *classical conditioning* (or sometimes *Pavlovian conditioning,* in honor of Pavlov).

After making his discovery, Pavlov set out systematically to study classical conditioning. First, he showed that a dog naturally salivated only when it tasted food, not when it sensed a nonfood stimulus, such as a buzzer. Second, Pavlov rigged his equipment so that a buzzer would sound, and then soon after, meat powder would be placed on the dog's tongue. After this procedure was repeated many times, the buzzer was sounded, but no meat powder was placed on the dog's tongue. The dog still salivated. By pairing the buzzer with the food, Pavlov had classically conditioned the dog to salivate in response to the buzzer alone (see Figure 5.1).

The Basics of Classical Conditioning

The particular stimuli and responses used in classical conditioning can vary, but the basic structure of classical conditioning does not change. If

FIGURE 5.1
Pavlov's Classic Experiment
The first classical-conditioning experiment began as an accidental discovery, developed through a simple procedure, and started an entirely new way of looking at learning. Before the experiment, the sound was a neutral stimulus that yielded no response from the dog, whereas the food (US) made the dog salivate (UR). During the experiment, Ivan Pavlov paired the sound (which now became the CS) with the food (US) to prompt the dog to salivate (UR). After many repetitions, the sound (CS alone) prompted the dog to salivate (CR).

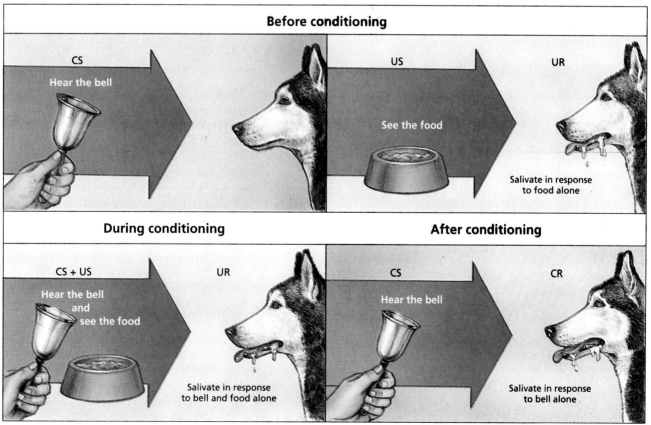

you were to create a classical-conditioning experiment like the ones Pavlov conducted, you would do (more or less) as follows:

1. Start with an **unconditioned stimulus (US;** e.g., the meat powder), which elicits a physiological or emotional response.
2. Note your participant's **unconditioned response (UR)**—the automatic physiological response (e.g., salivation) to this stimulus.
3. Choose a stimulus (e.g., a buzzer) that originally produces no particular response. This **conditioned stimulus (CS)** is originally neutral but later will elicit the physiological response.
4. Pair your CS and your US, so that the CS and the US become associated. Eventually, you may obtain from this CS a **conditioned response (CR;** e.g., salivation). The CR is similar to the UR, but it is elicited by the CS rather than by the US. Classical conditioning would probably occur, but why?

Why Does Classical Conditioning Occur?

Since classical conditioning was first discovered, psychologists have tried to explain why it occurs. An obvious explanation for classical conditioning is *temporal contiguity,* or closeness in time between the occurrence of events: Simply because the CS and the US occur close together in time, conditioning occurs. At one time, many researchers believed that temporal contiguity was the basis for classical conditioning, and a few researchers (e.g., Papini & Bitterman, 1990) continue to hold this view. Indeed, research has shown that temporal contiguity does facilitate learning; if too long a time period passes between the end of the CS and the start of the US, classical conditioning will not take place.

5.1

Think about the last time you felt frightened. What are all the sights and sounds you now associate with that experience? How many of those sensations occurred during or close to the time when you felt frightened? (If you are like most people, those sensations occurred at about the same time as when you were frightened.)

FINDING YOUR WAY

unconditioned stimulus (US) • a stimulus that elicits a physiological or emotional response

unconditioned response (UR) • an automatic physiological or emotional response to a US

conditioned stimulus (CS) • an originally neutral stimulus that later will elicit a physiological or emotional response

conditioned response (CR) • a response that is similar to the UR, but that is elicited from the CS rather than from the US

contingency • a phenomenon in which one or more stimuli *depend on* the presence of another stimulus

Although temporal contiguity clearly plays a role in conditioning, most psychologists now believe that temporal contiguity alone does not lead to learning. Think again about a frightening experience you have experienced. Do you associate absolutely everything you were doing, wearing, and saying with the experience? Do you associate all aspects of where you were living, working, or attending school with the experience? If the frightening experience lasted only a short time, you probably associate some things, but not others, with the experience.

If temporal contiguity does not explain how classical conditioning works, what does explain it? A classic study by Robert Rescorla (1967) suggests that the key to conditioning is contingency, not just temporal contiguity. In **contingency,** one or more actions or events *depend on* either the occurrence of an event or the presence of a stimulus. For example, suppose that you eat a rotten tuna sandwich, and you feel sick afterward.

In this case, feeling sick is contingent on (depends on) having eaten a rotten tuna sandwich. Feeling sick is not contingent, however, on what you were wearing at the time you ate the sandwich. Although your having felt sick was temporally contiguous with both your wearing of particular clothes and your eating of the rotten sandwich, your sick feelings were contingent only on your eating of the sandwich. You can wear those clothes again safely without worrying about becoming ill (as long as you steer clear of other things that make you sick).

Of course, Rescorla did *not* study contingency by recruiting human volunteers who were eager to eat rotten tuna sandwiches and to feel ill afterward. Instead, Rescorla followed Pavlov's example and tested his notion of contingency by studying dogs. Rescorla designed a complex experiment with dogs to test the notion that contingency is the basis for classical conditioning. The results of Rescorla's experiment confirmed the contingency point of view: Rescorla found that fear conditioning took place when the occurrence of a shock was contingent (i.e., dependent) on the occurrence of a tone. That is, when the tone provided information helpful in predicting the appearance of the shock, conditioning occurred. However, conditioning did *not* occur if the shock and the tone were associated in time (were temporally contiguous) but the occurrence of the tone did not predict the occurrence of the shock.

In his experiment, Rescorla showed that classical conditioning is based on contingency rather than on contiguity. He also suggested that the basis for classical conditioning involves phenomena of a kind different from what most behaviorists previously had believed. According to Rescorla, individuals try to make sense of the stimuli in their environments that affect them. When the US first appears, it is unexpected and is therefore surprising. This element of surprise sets the stage for learning.

In Rescorla's view, when individuals are surprised by the appearance of the US, they try to figure out how to predict when the US may appear again. If they succeed in predicting the US, it will not surprise them in the future. Being able to predict the appearance of the US makes it easier to understand the environment.

For example, suppose that Irena notices that every time Professor Badman is about to give a pop quiz, he enters the classroom with a twisted smile on his face. When a CS contingently predicts the occurrence of the US, learning occurs easily and rapidly. For Irena, seeing that twisted smile becomes a predictor of Professor Badman's pop quizzes. To summarize, individuals learn to associate a CS (e.g., a twisted smile) with a US (e.g., a pop quiz) because the first stimulus accurately predicts the occurrence of the second stimulus. What are the phases through which the association of CS and US develop, and what are some of the main features of this kind of learning?

Phases and Features of Classical Conditioning

Phases of Classical Conditioning

Given a contingent relationship between the CS and the US, the likelihood that learning will occur increases over learning trials. The time when the probability of learning increases is the **acquisition** phase of learning, when learning first occurs. During this phase, the individual acquires the CR to the CS. Eventually, at the peak of the acquisition phase, the CR reaches its most stable probability of occurrence (see Figure 5.2).

acquisition • a phase of learning during which the probability of learning increases

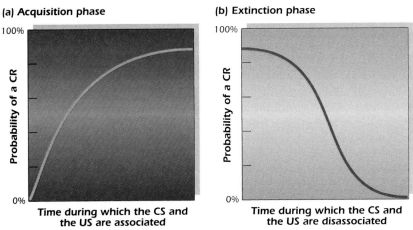

FIGURE 5.2

Phases of Classical Conditioning

Once a learner acquires a CR (during the acquisition phase), if the CS and the US are uncoupled, the CR may be extinguished (during the extinction phase).

After the individual acquires the CR to the CS, what happens if the CS and the US become unlinked? That is, what would happen if the CS were to continue to be presented, but in the absence of the US? For example, suppose that a buzzer (CS) that previously had gone off before a shock (US) no longer was followed by a shock. What would happen at this time? Gradually, the probability of the CR occurring would decrease until it vanished almost completely. This phase of learning is the **extinction** phase: The probability of the CR decreases over time, eventually approaching zero. A curve showing the CR during extinction would start out at high levels, then it would go down gradually until the CR seemed to disappear altogether (refer to Figure 5.2).

The term *extinction* may be somewhat misleading. It might seem that an extinguished CR would completely disappear forever, as if the CR never had existed at all. That is not quite the case. The CR may be extinguished, but the memory of the learning has not been erased completely, and an individual still can be stimulated to show the behavior again. This phenomenon is called *spontaneous recovery,* and it refers to the reappearance of a CR after extinction followed by a rest period. The individual seems to recover some level of responding spontaneously during the rest period, even though the CS was already absent (during extinction) before the rest period.

Features of Classical Conditioning

extinction • a phase of learning when the probability of the CR decreases over time, eventually approaching zero

stimulus generalization • a response to the observed similarity of a stimulus to the CS, which increases the likelihood that the CR will occur following presentation of the stimulus

Sometimes, when an individual acquires a CR to one particular CS, stimuli that are similar to the original CS also lead to the CR. When stimuli similar to the CS also lead to the CR, **stimulus generalization** has occurred. For example, suppose that particular ice cream-loving participants are classically conditioned to learn that a particular bell always rings before the appearance of ice cream. Even if the pitch of the bell is changed very slightly, the ice cream-loving participants probably will be about as likely to show the CR as if they had heard the original CS bell. In other words, they have generalized the appearance of the ice cream to a stimulus that is similar but not identical to the original stimulus.

Diane Berry and Leslie McArthur (1986; McArthur & Berry, 1987) have found an interesting illustration of stimulus generalization. It appears that both Korean and American adults expect that adults with childlike facial qualities (i.e., baby-faced adults) will show childlike psychological qualities. That is, we generalize from one stimulus (infants' and young children's faces) to similar stimuli (i.e., adult faces with features similar to those of infants and young children).

However, as the bell's sound is changed more and more so that the sound is less and less like the sound of the original bell, the participants are less and less likely to show the CR to the sound of the new bell. The process by which an individual increasingly is able to distinguish the new stimulus from the original CS is **stimulus discrimination.** The more the new stimulus differs from the original CS, the less likely it is that the new stimulus will lead to the CR.

As stimuli become less similar to the CS, stimulus discrimination becomes more likely, stimulus generalization becomes less likely, and the likelihood of a CR decreases. Conversely, as stimuli become more similar to the CS, stimulus generalization becomes more likely, stimulus discrimination becomes less likely, and the likelihood of a CR increases. To summarize, increased stimulus similarity leads to increased stimulus generalization, which leads to an increased likelihood of a CR; in contrast, decreased stimulus similarity leads to increased stimulus discrimination, which leads to a decreased likelihood that a CR will occur.

Sometimes, stimulus generalization and discrimination can have telling effects on our relationships. Suppose you have come to love your significant other's long hair and now, every time you see that hair, you still feel a thrill. One day your significant other appears with a minor reshaping of that long hair. You notice the reshaping but stimulus generalization is at work and you feel the usual thrill, nevertheless. Two weeks later, your significant other appears with a crew cut. Stimulus discrimination goes to work and the thrill—the conditioned response—is definitely gone.

| more | **more** | higher |
| stimulus similarity → **stimulus generalization** → likelihood of CR |

| less | **more** | lower |
| stimulus similarity → **stimulus discrimination** → likelihood of CR |

Surprising Relationships Between the Stimulus and the Response

Up to this point, we have described conditioned and unconditioned stimuli that have had only an arbitrary relationship to each other. In these

stimulus discrimination • a response to the observed difference between a new stimulus and the original CS, which makes it less likely that the new stimulus will lead to the CR

Although John Garcia and Robert Koelling's findings may not have been welcomed with open arms by their fellow behaviorists, sheep ranchers soon learned to appreciate their findings (Gustavson & Garcia, 1974; Gustavson & Nicolaus, 1987). Coyotes, such as the one shown here, normally love to prey on sheep. On the other hand, the coyotes also prey on the rabbits that gobble up the sheep's grass, so it is counterproductive to wipe out the coyote population altogether. Instead, ranchers can taint the lamb meat with lithium chloride, which sickens but does not kill the coyotes. After a sickening feast of tainted lamb, the coyotes turn their attention away from the sheep and toward the grass-munching rabbits. Similar strategies have been used to deter mongooses from eating the eggs of endangered species (Nicolaus & Nellis, 1987), crows from eating chicken eggs (Nicolaus, Cassell, Carlson, & Gustavson, 1983), and even rats from eating food grains (Nicolaus, Farmer, Gustavson, & Gustavson, 1989).

instances, prior to classical conditioning, there is no meaningful connection between the conditioned stimuli and the unconditioned stimuli. For example, there is no particular reason to link a tone with an electric shock, except when the presence of one appears to be contingent on the presence of the other. Does it make any difference if the CS and the US also seem to have some natural or meaningful relationship to each other, in addition to their contingently conditioned relationship? The answer is *yes*.

John Garcia and Robert Koelling (1966) surprised other behaviorists when they showed that some CS–US pairs seem to have a natural relationship that makes it easier to link the two through classical conditioning. At first, Garcia and Koelling rigged their equipment so that whenever a group of experimental rats licked a drinking spout, the rats sensed two types of conditioned stimuli: The rats tasted some flavored liquid, and they also heard a clicking noise accompanied by a flash of light. After licking the spout, some of the rats were mildly poisoned (US), causing them to vomit, whereas other rats were shocked (an alternative US). After a number of learning trials for both the poisoned rats and the shocked rats, a new procedure was introduced: The CS of the flavoring was separated from the combined CS using the clicking noise and the flash of light. For each group of rats, on one day, when the rats licked the spout, they tasted the flavored liquid without the light and noise. On another day, when the rats licked the spout, they experienced the light and the noise, but they tasted only regular tap water instead of the flavored liquid.

The critical finding was that when poison was the US, taste was a more effective CS than was the combination of light and noise. In contrast, when electric shock was the US, the "bright, noisy water" was a more effective CS than was the flavored liquid. In other words, there was a natural association between taste and poison. Similarly, there was a natural link between electric shock and the combination of the light and sound.

Subsequent research (e.g., Holder, Bermudez-Rattoni, & Garcia, 1988; Holder, Yirmiya, Garcia, & Raizer, 1989) has confirmed that taste and illness are easily linked, as are noise and shock, but noise and illness generally fail to produce learned associations.

When Garcia and Koelling (1966) found that a natural association between the CS and the US could affect classical conditioning, they surprised the scientific community. Garcia had yet another surprise for fellow psychologists: Conditioning could occur after only a single learning trial. Garcia found that rats showed a CR to the flavored liquid after just one experience in which they were poisoned after drinking the liquid. Garcia's finding was so unexpected that many people did not want to believe, and did not believe, his results (Garcia, 1981). As someone outside the field of behaviorism, how surprising do you consider Garcia's findings to be? Think about your own reactions to foods that have made you ill. Have you ever experienced the *Garcia effect,* in which you have learned to avoid a particular food because of a past, single unpleasant association?

The Garcia effect illustrates how classical conditioning may have served an adaptive purpose for animals across the span of evolutionary history: Suppose that two animals, let's call them Bobo and Bibi, get sick after eating rotten fruit; Bibi learns to stop eating rotten fruit, but Bobo does not. Bobo therefore is ill much of the time and thus becomes unattractive to other animals. Bibi, on the other hand, is healthy and attractive to mates. Bobo is more likely to not end up mating and therefore is likely to produce no offspring, or at least fewer than Bibi does. Thus, the animal that learned from experience is in a better position to pass on its genes to subsequent generations.

Classical conditioning also seems to serve some other adaptive purposes, such as helping some animals to perform more effectively some behaviors related to survival. For example, Karen Hollis and her colleagues (Hollis, 1990; Hollis, Cadieux, & Colbert, 1989; Hollis, Martin, Cadieux, & Colbert, 1984; Hollis, ten Cate, & Bateson, 1991) have observed that, through classical conditioning, animals may become more alert to cues signaling the presence of territorial intruders or of potential reproductive partners.

Psychologists have found that, in addition to classical conditioning, an entirely different type of conditioning further lends itself to a wide assortment of practical uses. This other type of associative learning, when understood and applied appropriately, further expands the possibilities for improving people's lives.

**CLASSICAL CONDITIONING
AND EMOTIONAL RESPONSES**

Although the principles of classical conditioning have been studied mostly in the laboratory, using animal subjects, these principles also apply to humans in everyday situations outside of the laboratory. Psychologists have explained many psychological phenomena, such as emotional responses, in terms of classical conditioning. For instance, we can become conditioned to feel both fear (a specific frightened feeling about a particular object, such as an injection needle) and anxiety (a more generalized

(CONTINUED)

feeling of unease about a situation or an experience, such as feeling anxious in the dark). When a conditioned stimulus (e.g., the sight or sound of a dog) is linked to a fearsome unconditioned stimulus (e.g., a dog's bite), we begin to feel fearful of the conditioned stimulus, too. Classical conditioning may account for many of our other emotional responses as well, such as disgust, anger, or joy.

Most conditioned emotional responses (sometimes called *CERs*) are linked to distinctive physiological (bodily) feelings. For example, most of us have experienced something akin to the *Garcia effect*. We are especially likely to consider a particular food distasteful if we feel nauseated after eating it, although other responses (e.g., breathing difficulties, diarrhea, or rashes) also may motivate us to avoid eating the particular food (Pelchat & Rozin, 1982). The mere sight or smell or even mention of the offending food disgusts us (an emotional reaction), making our stomachs queasy (a physiological reaction).

CERs need not be negative. For example, as you see your loved one approach, you may feel joyful, tingling from head to toe, due to previous pleasurable experiences with that person. Positive emotions also are frequently prompted by catchy television advertisements, which use classical-conditioning techniques for associating positive emotions with particular products or services. TV advertisers know how to use classical conditioning to appeal to our appetites for food and for sexual gratification, leading us to associate satisfaction with new cars, perfumes, cosmetics, and foods of every shape, smell, texture, and color. What do advertisers expect you to learn about a product by watching a sexy driver steering a flashy convertible on a narrow road winding around a cliff?

WHAT IS OPERANT CONDITIONING?

Imagine a hungry cat in the puzzle box shown in Figure 5.3. The cat inside the puzzle box can see and smell a piece of fish just outside the box. The cat tries to reach the fish through the openings in the box, but its paws cannot reach the fish. At first, the cat starts scratching, bumping, and jumping around the box, with no luck. Eventually, however, it happens to release the latch, simply through trial and error. When the latch gives way, the door to the puzzle box opens, and the cat runs to get the fish. Later, the cat is placed again in the box, and the whole process is repeated. This time, the scratching and jumping around do not last very long before the cat manages to open the box. "After many trials, the cat will, when put in the box, immediately claw the button or loop in a definite way" (Thorndike, 1898, p. 13) to release the latch, thereby opening the puzzle box to get the fish.

Now imagine another situation. In the past, Joe has had very mixed experiences when he has opened his mouth in seminars. Often when he had an idea he believed to be interesting and creative, other students seemed either to ignore the idea or to ridicule it. Joe has learned to keep his mouth shut so that he does not appear ridiculous. Professor Kane, noticing that Joe is silent in class, takes him aside after class and asks him why he is so silent. Joe explains why. Professor Kane encourages Joe to speak out and promises that he will actively speak up and support Joe when he makes insightful comments so that not only Joe, but other

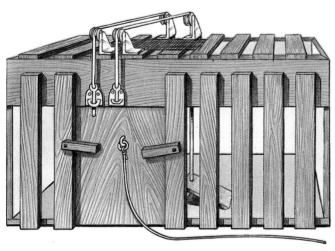

FIGURE 5.3
Thorndike's Puzzle Box
Imagine being a hungry cat, trapped inside one of Edward Lee Thorndike's various puzzle boxes. Outside your puzzle box, just out of reach, is some delicious fish. Unfortunately, the door is held tightly shut by a simple latch. After many attempts to get the puzzle box to burst open, you accidentally release the triggering device (a button, a loop, a string, or whatever else Thorndike thought to use), and the door to your puzzle box opens easily, allowing you to leap to the fish. The next time you are trapped in the puzzle box, what will you do?

students as well, will see that he encourages students to present creative ideas in class. Joe promises he will give it a try. He does, and Professor Kane is true to his word. Soon, not only Joe, but other students as well start taking risks in class, speaking their minds. By reinforcing students for their creative ideas, Professor Kane has changed the reinforcement system to which some of the students previously were accustomed.

Thorndike's Law of Effect

Both of the preceding situations, with the hungry cat and with Professor Kane's classroom, involve operant conditioning. The study of operant conditioning usually is viewed as starting with Edward Lee Thorndike (1874–1949). Through his experiments, such as the one with the cat in the puzzle box, Thorndike (1898, 1911) discovered the basic phenomenon of operant conditioning, although the term *operant conditioning* came into use after Thorndike's time. **Operant conditioning**, which is the same as and also is called by Thorndike's original term, *instrumental conditioning*, is learning that occurs when an individual produces an active behavioral response (an *operant*), which is followed by an environmental stimulus, which influences the likelihood that the response will be repeated again in the future. In operant conditioning, some environmental outcomes tend to strengthen active behavior (making it more likely to occur again in the future) and other outcomes tend to weaken it (making it less likely to occur again in the future). For the hungry cat, getting to reach the fish strengthened the cat's operant behavior, namely, opening the puzzle-box latch. For Joe, getting reinforced positively for making constructive comments in class strengthened his operant behavior, namely, making such statements in the classroom situation.

operant conditioning • the process of increasing or decreasing the likelihood that an individual will produce an active behavior (an operant) as a result of interacting with the environment

Thorndike proposed a mechanism to account for (what later came to be called) operant conditioning, which he termed the *law of effect*. According to Thorndike, much of our behavior constitutes random, trial-and-error exploration of the environment. Occasionally, our actions result in a *reinforcement* (an outcome with pleasurable consequences). At other times, our actions result in a *punishment* (an outcome with unpleasant and unwanted consequences). According to Thorndike's law of effect, the outcomes of particular actions will influence the likelihood that the actions will be repeated again in the future. Actions that are reinforced will tend to be strengthened and thereby will become more likely to occur in the future; in contrast, actions that are punished will tend to be weakened and thus will be less likely to occur in the future.

How might you apply the law of effect to your own experiences? If you reinforce your friend for doing you a favor, your friend is more likely to do you a favor again in the future. For example, if your friend helps you move into a new apartment, you might reinforce your friend by treating her or him to a meal or to a fun activity as soon as you finish moving in. Your hope well may be that the next time your friend thinks of helping you, he or she once again will do so.

One difference between classical and operant conditioning is in the role of the individual:

- In classical conditioning, the individual is largely *passive:* The experimenter or the environment controls the situation; for example, by repeatedly pairing a CS with a US.

- In operant conditioning, the individual is largely *active:* The individual operates on the environment in order to create reinforcement.

In addition, each of the two kinds of conditioning (also known as *associative learning*) centers on a different key association:

- In classical conditioning, the crucial association for conditioning is between the *conditioned stimulus* (something you sense; e.g., the smell of coffee) and the *unconditioned stimulus* (something that prompts a physiological or emotional response; e.g., the caffeine in coffee).

- In operant conditioning, the fundamental association is between an *active behavioral response* (operant—something you do; e.g., calling a pizza-delivery service) and a *reinforcement* that increases the probability that the behavior will be repeated (e.g., receiving a pizza to eat).

Operant conditioning is of great importance in our lives, literally from the day we are born: Parents reinforce some actions and punish others in order to get their children to behave in ways that the parents prefer. Parents hope that reinforcements will strengthen the behavior they like and that punishments will weaken the behavior they do not like. The same basic procedures are used in school: Some kinds of behavior are reinforced by nods, good grades, and so on, whereas other kinds of behavior result in a student's being kept away from other students, being sent to the principal's office, and so on.

Reinforcement

operant • a kind of *response* that has some effect on the world

In the study of operant conditioning, an **operant** is a kind of *response* that has some effect on the world. Asking for help, drinking a glass of water, threatening to hurt someone, kissing your lover—all of these are operants. Operant conditioning leads to either an increase or a decrease in the probability that these operant behaviors will be performed again.

A **reinforcer** is a *stimulus event* that increases the probability that the operant associated with the stimulus will happen again. (Usually, the response has occurred immediately or almost immediately before the reinforcing stimulus.) Reinforcers can be either positive or negative. A **positive reinforcer** is a *positive* stimulus event that follows an operant and whose occurrence strengthens the associated behavioral response. Examples of positive reinforcers are a smile or a compliment following something we say or do or a candy bar released by a vending machine after we put in the required change. When a positive reinforcer (stimulus event) occurs soon after an operant (response), the effect of the pairing of the two is termed **positive reinforcement.**

Negative reinforcement is the effect that results from the removal or the stopping of an unpleasant stimulus, such as physical or psychological pain or discomfort. Examples of negative reinforcements are the relief you feel when someone stops hurting you or the reinforcement of being allowed to escape from an uncomfortable or unpleasant situation. The **negative reinforcer** is the cessation of the unpleasant stimulus. Negative reinforcement leads to an increased probability that an operant will be repeated. Whether it is negative or positive, reinforcement always strengthens a response.

Punishment

Punishment is the result of a stimulus event that *decreases* the probability of an associated operant; punishment results from either presenting an unpleasant stimulus or removing a pleasant one. (In contrast, negative reinforcement *increases* the likelihood of a response by removing or at least reducing the impact of an unpleasant stimulus.) Examples of punishment include being hit, scolded, humiliated, or laughed *at* (not *with*); being restricted from an enjoyable activity such as viewing television or visiting with friends; or receiving a failing grade in a course or a negative evaluation from a work supervisor. The aversive stimulus event is called a *punisher.*

Psychologists sometimes distinguish between *positive punishment,* which is the kind of aversive stimulation described above (e.g., being scolded) and *negative punishment,* which is the withholding of desirable stimulation (e.g., the opportunity to watch television). Negative punishment is also called a *penalty.*

Frequently, punishment is used for **aversive conditioning,** a means of encouraging an individual to try to escape from or to avoid a situation. The goal of aversive conditioning is **avoidance learning,** whereby an individual learns to stay away from something. Individuals can learn to avoid a particular behavior by being aversively conditioned to avoid that behavior. For example, rats can learn to avoid scratching at a door latch if they are shocked every time they scratch at the latch. Sometimes, the aversive conditioning that leads to avoidance learning also may lead to classical conditioning. Specifically, the object or situation that the individual is being conditioned to avoid may serve as a conditioned stimulus for a fear response. For example, in the case of rats that learn to avoid scratching at a latch, the rats also may learn to feel fearful of the latch or even of the area near the latch. Operant conditioning through the use of punishment

"Remember, every time he gives you a pellet reinforce that behavior by pulling the lever."

Copyright © 1994 Joe Dator/The Cartoon Bank, Inc.

reinforcer • a *stimulus event* that increases the probability that the operant associated with it will be repeated

positive reinforcer • a positive stimulus event that follows an operant and strengthens the associated behavioral response

positive reinforcement • the effect of a positive reinforcer (stimulus event) soon after an operant (response)

negative reinforcement • the effect of the removal or cessation (stopping) of an unpleasant stimulus, such as physical or psychological pain or discomfort

negative reinforcer • an unpleasant stimulus event that is removed following an operant response, thereby leading to an increased probability that the operant will be repeated

punishment • the effect of the delivery of a stimulus event that *decreases* the probability of an associated response; results from either presenting an unpleasant stimulus or removing a pleasant one

aversive conditioning • the use of punishment as a means of encouraging an individual to try to escape from or to avoid a situation

avoidance learning • the goal of aversive conditioning; an individual learns to stay away from something

leads to the *behavioral outcome of avoidance,* and the classical conditioning that may accompany it leads to an *emotional and physiological response of fear.* Thus, the two forms of learning may interact cooperatively to strengthen the outcome.

Consequences of Punishment: Intended and Unintended

In general, punishment is less effective in achieving behavioral change than is positive reinforcement (Sulzer-Azaroff & Mayer, 1991). Used by itself with no other interventions, it typically is not successful. In addition, punishment may lead to several unintended consequences (Bongiovanni, 1977), such as the following consequences:

1. Although punishment does lead a person to try to avoid punishment, the person may find some way to avoid the punishment or to reduce its effects, without necessarily avoiding the undesired behavior.

2. Punishment can increase the likelihood that the person being punished will show an increase in aggressive behavior. That is, the person being punished may imitate the punishing behavior in other interactions, such as through physical aggression (Vissing, Straus, Gelles, & Harrop 1991). For example, parents who are overly punishing with their children risk having children who become punishing themselves—in other words, bullies.

3. The punished person may be injured. Punishment becomes child abuse when the child is damaged, physically or psychologically, an unfortunately too common occurrence (Gelles & Straus, 1988).

4. Punishment may lead to extreme fear of the punishing person and context. This fear may in turn lead to problems in the relationship between the punished person and the punishing person or situation. Sometimes, the fear even worsens the unwanted behavior. For example, screaming at a child who scores poorly on a test may increase the child's feelings of test anxiety, which may cause further lowering of the child's test scores.

Despite the potential problems of using punishment, punishment can be made more effective by using it carefully (Park & Walters, 1967; Walters & Grusec, 1977).

Learned Helplessness

An additional possible consequence of punishment deserves special attention because of its far-reaching implications. This consequence is the phenomenon of **learned helplessness,** in which an individual is operantly conditioned to act (and perhaps to feel) helpless to do anything to avoid an unpleasant situation. Martin Seligman and Steven Maier (Seligman, 1975; Seligman & Maier, 1967) discovered learned helplessness when studying two groups of dogs. The dogs were placed in an electrified chamber where they received painful (but not harmful) electric shocks. In the first group, the dogs were unable to escape the shock, despite their efforts to do so. Later, the chamber was divided into two parts, with a barrier separating the two parts. In this divided chamber, only one part was electrified to

learned helplessness • a learned behavior in which an individual gives up trying to escape from a painful situation after repeatedly failing to escape

5.1

ENHANCING THE EFFECTIVENESS OF PUNISHMENT

PUTTING IT TO USE

Although there are many potential problems of using punishment, punishment can be made more effective by taking the following steps.

- Make it easy for the punished individual to choose other responses to replace the responses that are being punished. A Kenyan proverb suggests the intuitive wisdom of this strategy: "When you take a knife away from a child, give him a piece of wood instead."
- In addition to using punishment, use positive reinforcement to encourage the punished individual to choose to repeat a more desirable operant behavior.
- Make sure that the individual being punished knows exactly what behavior is being punished and why.
- Carry out the punishment *immediately* after the undesirable operant behavior.
- Choose a punishment that is strong enough and that lasts long enough to stop the undesirable behavior but that is no stronger and lasts no longer than is necessary.
- Try to ensure that it is impossible to escape punishment any time that the individual shows the operant behavior.
- Prefer the use of *penalties* (removal of a pleasant stimuli) to the use of physical or emotional pain as punishments.
- Take advantage of the natural tendency to try to escape from and to avoid punishment: Use punishment when you want the punished person to try to escape from or to avoid a particular situation (e.g., teaching a child to seek escape from dangerous places or to avoid dangerous objects).

deliver shocks, so that the dogs could have escaped the shocks simply by jumping over the barrier into the nonelectrified part of the chamber. However, because these dogs had previously learned that they could not escape, they did not even try to escape. They just whined helplessly. They appeared to believe that escape from pain was impossible.

In contrast, a second group of dogs was not forced to stay in an undivided chamber in which the dogs were unable to escape shocks. Rather, these other dogs were placed only in the divided chamber, and the shock was turned on in only one part of the chamber. As soon as the dogs in this second group saw the barrier, they jumped over it, escaping the shocks. Whenever the shock was turned on, these dogs quickly jumped the barrier, thereby spending as little time as possible feeling any pain.

Apparently, the first group of dogs had learned to feel helpless to do anything about their situation. For these dogs, their learned feelings of helplessness were caused by their previous inability to escape the pain. In contrast, the second group of dogs, which had not learned to feel helpless, quickly learned how to escape the painful shocks. Observers of just this second group of dogs might leap to the conclusion that virtually all animals would try to escape from pain, without considering their previous experiences. The observers would be wrong.

Humans also are subject to the effects of learned helplessness. We try something; we fail. Maybe we try again and fail again. Soon we have learned that we cannot perform that task or master that skill; as a result, we never try again. The child who fails in school and the adult who fails on the job may learn to feel helpless. Our past conditioning may tell us that we cannot succeed. Some people stop accepting new challenges because they have learned to feel helpless to avoid any unwanted consequences of challenging situations.

Both Maier and Seligman have extended their work in learned helplessness, exploring how learned helplessness may influence other psychological phenomena. Maier and his colleagues (Maier, Watkins, & Fleshner, 1994) have studied how learned helplessness may influence the immune system, suppressing its defensive responses against disease. Seligman (1989) has suggested that learned helplessness may play a key role in depression, and other researchers have expanded Seligman's notion by proposing a specific type of depression known as *hopelessness depression* (Abramson, Metalsky, & Alloy, 1989).

Seligman (1991) believes that just as we can learn to feel helpless, so can we learn to feel optimistic. Seligman's research shows that optimistic people fare better in life, not only in terms of the outcomes they achieve, but also in terms of how they feel about attaining these outcomes. Thus, when you are feeling helpless, one of the most useful things you can do is simply to change your attitude and try to see or create a positive side to the situation you are in.

How Is Operant Conditioning Implemented?

Discriminating Between Reinforcement and Punishment

To summarize what we know about reinforcement and punishment, reinforcement *increases* the probability of some future response; punishment *decreases* it. Reinforcement can involve presenting a rewarding stimulus (positive reinforcement; e.g., presentation of smiles or candy) or removing an unpleasant stimulus (negative reinforcement; e.g., relief from pain or discomfort). Similarly, punishment can involve the presentation of an unpleasant and unwanted stimulus (e.g., a scolding) or the removal of a rewarding one (i.e., a penalty; e.g., the revoking of driving privileges). In other words, both forms of reinforcement (positive or negative) teach the person what to do, whereas punishment teaches the learner what not to do. Table 5.2 summarizes these differences.

The Gradient of Reinforcement: Effects of Delays

gradient of reinforcement • a phenomenon in which increases in the length of time between an operant and a reinforcer directly decrease the effect of the reinforcement

When implementing either reinforcement or punishment, an important consideration is the **gradient of reinforcement**: The longer we wait to reinforce (or to punish) a given operant, the weaker the effect of the reinforcement (or punishment) will be. This principle is important both for establishing behavior and for suppressing it. For example, if parents want

TABLE 5.2
Summary of Operant Conditioning

Operant conditioning technique	Stimulus introduced in the environment as an outcome of operant behavior	Effect of stimulus operant response
Positive reinforcement	*Positive reinforcer.* Pleasant stimulus event	Strengthens and increases the likelihood of the operant behavior
Negative reinforcement	*Negative reinforcer.* Unpleasant stimulus event (that is removed)	Strengthens and increases the likelihood of the operant behavior
Punishment	*Punisher.* Unpleasant stimulus event	Weakens and decreases the likelihood of the operant behavior

to change their children's behavior (e.g., to get a child to put away toys), the parents should reinforce the desired behavior immediately after it occurs. If, instead, the parents reinforce the children for the desired behavior long after it occurs, the parents will be ineffective in changing it. Hence, a father who tells a child that she will be rewarded for her excellent behavior when her mother comes home is reducing the effectiveness of the reinforcement by having the child wait for hours before receiving the reward.

The effectiveness of reinforcement generally *decreases* rapidly as the time between the response and the reinforcement *increases*. This decreased effectiveness may be because the passage of time quickly weakens the link between the reinforcement and the behavior it reinforces. As time passes, many other stimuli may appear between the response and the reinforcing stimulus.

The gradient of reinforcement seems to play a key role in the sexual behavior and contraceptive practices of adolescent girls (Loewenstein & Furstenberg, 1991). Specifically, when adolescent girls are making decisions regarding their own behavior, they may find the reinforcing benefits of unprotected sexual activity to be immediate and certain (e.g., getting and perhaps keeping the attention of an attractive member of the opposite sex). On the other hand, the reinforcing benefits of contraception and of abstinence are delayed and uncertain (e.g., avoiding unwanted pregnancy or sexually transmitted disease). A consequence of the gradient of reinforcement, therefore, is that adolescent girls may go for the immediate reinforcements and later end up paying for doing so with an unwanted pregnancy or a sexually transmitted disease.

For people of all ages, *increases* in the delay time between an operant behavior and an environmental reinforcer lead to *decreases* in the strength of the conditioning. Children have particular difficulty with tolerating delays between the operant behavior and the presentation of the reinforcement. When offered access to immediate reinforcers, such as food or toys, children often find it particularly difficult to *delay gratification;* that is, they do not easily postpone their enjoyment of immediate reinforcers in order to receive some other (usually greater) reinforcement at a future time. Even when a future reinforcement is much more appealing than a present one, children often have difficulty delaying gratification (Rodriguez, Mischel, & Shoda, 1989). Children who can divert their attention away from attractive items seem better able to delay gratification. Similarly, children are better able to delay gratification when they know that it is easier to delay their gratification if they avoid thinking about the desirable characteristics of the coveted items.

Until children develop their own strategies for delaying gratification, adults may need to help them to divert their attention away from appealing immediate reinforcers and toward other activities or objects. An additional means of enhancing self-control in delaying gratification is to increase the perceived difference between the delayed reinforcer and the immediate reinforcer. Even adults will be more likely to delay gratification when they perceive that a delay will lead to a much greater reinforcement (King & Logue, 1987; Logue, King, Chavarro, & Volpe, 1990).

Primary and Secondary Reinforcers

In the laboratory, researchers can provide **primary reinforcers,** which are immediately satisfying or enjoyable reinforcements, such as food, water, or comfort. In most situations outside the laboratory, however, it is not practical to provide primary reinforcers for every operant behavior we want to encourage. At the very least, primary reinforcement often must be delayed. How do we use operant conditioning when we cannot provide immediate primary reinforcers? We offer **secondary reinforcers,** which have reinforcing value only through their association with primary reinforcers. Secondary reinforcers may include money, good grades, high-status objects, praise, and other reinforcements that have become attached to primary reinforcers.

A secondary reinforcer that works well for people of all ages is sincere praise. In a study of elementary and junior-high students, researchers were able to reduce school vandalism by an average of more than 75%, and to obtain significant improvements in classroom behavior, simply by increasing the reinforcing properties of the school, such as the rates at which teachers praised their students at treatment schools, as compared with control schools where extra praise was not given (G. R. Mayer, Butterworth, Nafpaktitis, & Sulzer-Azaroff, 1983). In contrast, the use of *destructive criticism* (which is inconsiderate and nonspecific, and which attributes poor performance to intrinsic characteristics of the individual) leads to anger, tension, resistance, and avoidance in college students and other adults (J. Baron, 1988). Another use of secondary reinforcers is in a *token economy,* in which tokens are used as a means of reinforcing certain operant behaviors, thereby encouraging prosocial behavior.

Token economies have shown some success in facilitating language development and behavioral control in autistic persons, who are otherwise largely out of touch with their environments (Lovaas, 1968, 1977). Researchers and clinicians have become interested in using similar reinforcement systems with nonautistic children. A danger of such systems, however, is that under some circumstances they can undermine children's natural interest in performing the behaviors that are being reinforced (Eisenberger & Cameron, 1996; Lepper, Greene, & Nisbett, 1973).

Token economies represent only one way in which adults use conditioning to try to shape children's and others' behavior.

primary reinforcer • a stimulus that provides an immediate reinforcement that satisfies the senses

secondary reinforcer • a stimulus that gains reinforcing value through association with a primary reinforcer

Successive Approximations: The Shaping of Behavior

Sometimes, it is easy to see how to encourage an individual to behave in a particular way: Just wait for the desired behavior to occur, and then reinforce it immediately and powerfully. However, not all desirable behavior is likely to occur by chance. For example, how do you get someone to start washing the dishes when the person never goes near the kitchen? When the behavior is complex or is very different from the normal behavior of the individual, we cannot realistically expect the behavior to occur by chance. Instead, we can **shape** behavior through the method of **successive approximations,** in which we gradually reinforce a series of actions that increasingly approach the behavior we want to obtain. This method is used for training animals, such as in circuses and other shows.

To implement this method, you first reinforce a very rough beginning step for performing the behavior of interest (e.g., praising a reluctant dishwasher for putting a dish in the sink). After a while, that first rough step toward the behavior is established. Next, you begin to look for some changes so that the observed behavior comes a little closer to the desired behavior, and you reinforce only those closer steps toward the desired behavior (e.g., praising the reluctant individual for rinsing out the dish). You continue with this procedure, getting closer and closer to the desired behavior until you finally condition the individual to show the desired behavior (e.g., actually washing a few grimy dishes).

Schedules of Reinforcement

Up to now, we have discussed **continuous reinforcement,** whereby a reinforcement always follows a particular operant behavior. A continuous **schedule of reinforcement** (timing of reinforcers in relation to operants) is fairly easy to establish in a laboratory, but it is actually quite rare in everyday life. People who behave in desirable ways are not always reinforced, and people who misbehave are not always punished. In normal everyday life, we are much more likely to face a **partial-reinforcement schedule** (also termed an *intermittent-reinforcement schedule*), in which an operant is reinforced only part of the time. Luckily, operant responses that are strengthened by partial-reinforcement schedules are less easily extinguished than are operant responses that rely on continuous schedules of reinforcement.

Partial reinforcement may be given either after a particular number of operant responses (e.g., treating yourself to a rest break after you read 20 pages of your chemistry textbook) or after a particular amount of time has passed during which an operant response has been shown (e.g., treating yourself to a rest break after you read your physics textbook for 30 minutes). In general, a higher rate of responding occurs when the reinforcement is tied to the number of responses, rather than to an interval of time. In addition, the strength of an operant response will be at a more consistently high rate if the reinforcement is given after a variable number of responses (e.g., winning a bet after placing between 1 and 50 bets), rather than after a fixed number of responses (e.g., receiving 1 free item for buying 25 items). Let's be specific.

In ratio schedules, a proportion (ratio) of operant responses is reinforced, regardless of the amount of time that has passed. There are two principal ratio schedules. In a *fixed-ratio reinforcement schedule,* reinforcement always occurs after a certain number of operant responses, regardless of the amount of time it takes to produce that number of responses. Many factory workers get piecework wages, meaning that they get paid a flat rate for completing a set number of tasks or crafting a set number of products. In a *variable-ratio reinforcement schedule,* reinforcement occurs, on average, after a certain number of operant responses, but the specific number of responses varies from one reinforcement to the

shape • bring behavior under control by providing a program of reinforcement

successive approximations • a method for shaping behavior by gradually reinforcing operants that are increasingly more similar to the desired behavior

continuous reinforcement • a learning program in which reinforcement always follows a particular operant behavior

schedules of reinforcement • the patterns by which reinforcements follow operants

partial-reinforcement schedule • an operant-conditioning program in which a given operant is reinforced at some times but not at other times

next. The classic example of a variable-ratio reinforcement schedule in the real world is provided by the slot machine. Gamblers are reinforced by winning coins or tokens after varying numbers of pulls on the handle, with each machine set to require a certain number of pulls, on average, before it "pays off."

In interval schedules, reinforcement occurs for the first response after a certain amount of time has passed, regardless of how many operant responses have taken place during that time.

In a *fixed-interval reinforcement schedule,* reinforcement always occurs after a certain amount of time has passed, as long as the operant response has occurred at least once during a particular time period. Many aspects of our lives are tied to fixed-interval reinforcements. In most salaried jobs, for example, workers are reinforced with paychecks at regular intervals. In a *variable-interval reinforcement schedule,* reinforcement occurs, on average, after a certain period of time, assuming the operant behavior has occurred at least once during the time period, but the specific amount of time preceding reinforcement changes from one reinforcement to the next. For example, some libraries allow you to reserve popular books. The amount of time you need to wait to get the books can vary from one book to the next.

Skinner and the Experimental Analysis of Behavior

The psychologist who may have done the most to promote the study and application of operant conditioning was B. F. Skinner (1904–1990), who developed the theory and methods for the experimental analysis of behavior. Skinner (e.g., 1988) believed that all behavior should be studied and analyzed in terms of reinforcement contingencies. He particularly valued the observation of animal behavior, which can be analyzed experimentally more easily than can human behavior, often using a box (known as an *operant chamber,* or later, a *Skinner box*) in which to study animals' behavior.

To Skinner (e.g., 1986), what mattered were the contingent reinforcements that produce various patterns of behavior, regardless of what might go on inside the head of the individual producing the behavior. When Skinner defined the problem of understanding human behavior only in terms of reinforcement contingencies, he more narrowly limited the field of psychology than do most psychologists. In fact, even many contemporary behaviorists find Skinner's radical behaviorism to be too extreme (e.g., Amsel, 1992).

On the other hand, many present-day psychologists still agree with Skinner's belief that behaviorism can be applied to many of society's problems. For instance, operant conditioning continues to offer many practical uses in managing the behavior of persons in institutional settings (e.g., prisons, mental hospitals, and custodial or residential facilities for persons who cannot care for themselves for various reasons). Caregivers have used operant conditioning successfully to decrease the frequency with which some individuals engage in self-injurious behavior (e.g., head-hitting; Linscheid, Hartel, & Cooley, 1993). Surprisingly, when mildly aversive shocks are administered after an individual attempts to engage in self-injurious behavior, the likelihood of further attempts seems to decrease, at least for some people.

Behavioral psychologists also have addressed a broad range of psychological problems among people outside of institutional settings. Behavioral

5.2

PUTTING OPERANT CONDITIONING INTO PRACTICE

What do we know about how to use operant conditioning? Briefly, to get the greatest benefit from operant conditioning, do the following:

1. To get someone to do something, use reinforcement; to get someone not to do something, use punishment, but be aware that punishment may also lead to some unwanted additional outcomes.

2. To reinforce behavior effectively, offer reinforcers as soon as possible after the desired behavior.

3. When you cannot avoid delay of gratification, try to divert attention away from the desired object, and try to avoid thinking about the object's desirable features.

4. Use successive approximations to shape complex or highly unusual behaviors.

5. Provide reinforcement after particular numbers of operant responses, rather than after particular intervals of time, in order to produce high rates of response. Use variable rather than fixed schedules of reinforcement to obtain more constant rates of response and to encourage greater self-control. Avoid using continuous reinforcement schedules, which are easily subject to extinction.

treatments have been devised for such diverse disorders as depression, anxiety disorders, *schizophrenia* (a serious psychological disorder associated with a drastic break from reality), obesity, *anorexia nervosa* (an eating disorder), sexual dysfunction, abuse of children or spouses, and substance abuse (Bellack, Hersen, & Kazdin, 1990). In each case, the behavioral psychologist analyzes the behavior of the patient and then determines appropriate ways to reduce the reinforcement of (or even to punish) unwanted behavior and to use reinforcement to increase the frequency of desirable behavior.

Many psychologists believe that whether a child develops normally or abnormally will depend in part upon the kinds of learning experiences that child has had. For example, a newspaper carried an article on a group of individuals who are taught, from when they are fairly young, to make a living swindling others who are not members of this group. It is little surprise that, with this kind of training, many children grow up to be swindlers as adults.

To reinforce what you have learned about operant and classical conditioning, before we proceed to considering social influences on learning, it may be helpful to review Table 5.3, which briefly summarizes the features of each type of conditioning.

Latent Learning

Up to this point, we have described conditioning in terms of the observable changes that occur as a result of learning. However, what we learn is

TABLE 5.3

Comparison of Classical and Operant Conditioning

Characteristics	Classical (or Pavlovian)	Operant (or instrumental)
Key relationship	Conditioned stimulus *and* Unconditioned stimulus	Organism's response *and* Environment's stimulus (reinforcement or punishment)
Organism's role	Passively (emotionally or physiologically) responds to stimuli (CS or US)	Actively operates on environment
Sequence of events	Initiation of conditioning: CS → US → UR	Operant response → Reinforcement → Increases response probability
	Peak of acquisition phase: CS → CR	Operant response → Punishment → Decreases response probability
Extinction techniques	Uncouple the CS from the US, repeatedly presenting the CS in the absence of the US	Uncouple the operant response from the stimulus reinforcer or punisher; repeatedly fail to reinforce or to punish the operant behavior

not always evident. In 1930, long before other researchers acknowledged internal mechanisms that affect conditioning, Edward Tolman and C. H. Honzik did research that showed that performance may not be a clear reflection of learning. In so-called *latent learning,* acquired knowledge is not presently reflected in performance. Tolman even suggested that the participants in his studies, rats, could form a *cognitive map,* whereby they internally represented patterns they encountered during maze learning. He argued that those learned cognitive maps can exist even when they are not reflected in performance. This contribution was important because, at the time he was working, cognitive interpretations of learning were widely rejected.

WHAT IS SOCIAL LEARNING?

Suppose that you wanted to teach someone how to do something: to type, to tie her or his shoes, to write a term paper, or whatever. What is the first thing you would do? If you are like most of us, neither classical nor operant conditioning techniques would leap to mind. Instead, you probably would *show* the person what to do, using your own actions as a model for what you wanted the other person to do.

In our everyday lives, we often learn by observing what other people are doing. Through **social learning,** we do not learn directly, but rather by observing others. Is there really any empirical evidence that supports the concept of social learning (also termed *vicarious learning* or *observational learning*)?

Albert Bandura (1965, 1969, 1986) and his colleagues have performed numerous experiments showing that social learning is an effective way of learning. In a typical experiment, preschool children were shown a film featuring an adult who punched, kicked, hit, and threw things at a large, inflatable *Bobo doll* (see Figure 5.4). The given film ended in one of three

social learning • the learning that occurs by observing the behavior of others, as well as by observing any environmental outcomes of the behavior

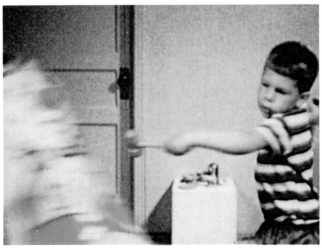

FIGURE 5.4
Social Learning
In numerous experiments, Albert Bandura has shown that children learn to imitate the behavior of adult models. By observing a video of a woman behaving aggressively toward a Bobo doll, this girl and boy have learned to kick and punch the doll. The doll has a weighted bottom that causes it to bounce back to an upright position after being tipped off balance.

different ways, depending on the group to which a particular child viewer was assigned. In one group, the adult model was rewarded for the aggressive behavior. In a second group, the adult model was punished. In a third (control) group, the adult model was neither rewarded nor punished. After seeing the film, the children were allowed to play with a Bobo doll. Those children who had seen the adult model rewarded for aggressive behavior were more likely than the controls to behave aggressively with the doll, whereas those who had observed the adult model being punished were less likely than the controls to behave aggressively with the doll. Clearly, social learning had taken place.

Other studies show that behavioral reinforcement is not needed for social learning to take place. In another experiment (Bandura, Ross, & Ross, 1963), preschool children watched an adult model either sit quietly next to the Bobo doll or attack it. The adults were neither rewarded nor punished for their behavior. Later, these children were left alone with the doll. As expected, those children who had observed aggressive behavior were more likely to behave aggressively than were the children who saw no aggressive behavior.

What conditions are necessary for social learning to occur? There appear to be four (Bandura, 1977b):

1. *Attention* to the behavior on which the learning might be based

2. *Retention* (memory) of the observed scene when the chance arises later to apply the learning

3. *Motivation* to imitate the observed behavior

4. *Potential reproduction* of the behavior; in other words, the observer must be able to do whatever he or she observed being done

In addition, four factors can increase the likelihood that observers will imitate the behavior of a given model: (a) The model stands out in contrast to other competing models; (b) the model is liked and respected by the observer (or by others in the environment); (c) the model is perceived to be similar to the observer, in the eyes of the observer; and (d) the model's behavior is reinforced. Although each of these factors increases the likelihood of social learning, such learning can occur even when these factors are absent.

Social learning is not limited to scenes with Bobo dolls, of course. Many people of all ages spend countless hours in front of televisions watching violent behavior. Considerable evidence suggests that exposure to violent activity on television is linked to aggressive behavior in real life (e.g., Friedrich-Cofer & Huston, 1986; Huesmann, Lagerspetz, & Eron, 1984; Park, Berkowitz, Leyens, West, & Sebastian, 1977). In addition, social learning extends to the development of many other behaviors, such as gender-role behavior, gender expectations, and even gender identity (described in Basow, 1986; Gilly, 1988). Such learning is based on both media images and the behavior of same-sex parents and peers.

Social learning also may lead to behavior that is highly *prosocial* (favorable to society). For instance, during the Nazi Holocaust, many German rescuers showed altruism, risking their own lives and well-being to protect and aid Jews and members of other persecuted groups. In a study of more than 100 such rescuers (Oliner & Oliner, 1993), a common theme emerged, in which the rescuers' early family experiences served as models for their subsequent altruism.

Social learning also seems to influence much more mundane, ordinary behavior, and it occurs in children as young as 9 to 24 months of age. In a pair of studies, children watched adult models demonstrate how to pull apart and put back together a toy designed specifically for these experiments. After observing the adult either in person (9-month-olds) or on television (14- and 24-month-olds), the children imitated the behavior they observed. Even when the children did not have an opportunity to imitate the observed behavior until the next day, they correctly imitated the behavior they had observed (Meltzoff, 1988a, 1988b).

Bandura's work suggests that learning is much more complicated than it once appeared to be. This complexity is reflected in Bandura's concept of *reciprocal determinism,* according to which all human functioning, including learning, represents an interaction among behavior, personal variables such as cognitive functioning, and the environment. In other words, human functioning can be understood fully only if all of these variables and the ways they interact with each other are taken into account. Memory, considered in the next chapter, also depends on a whole array of interacting variables.

Humans are born with a variety of preprogrammed responses (e.g., habituation and instincts, such as in imprinting), but much of what we know we learn as a result of experience, through classical conditioning, operant conditioning, and social learning. In order to learn from experience, we must have some means of remembering our experiences. The many factors that influence our ability to remember what we have learned from experience are the subject of the next chapter.

The Solution to The Case of the Helpful Ex-Friend

After reading chapter 5 of *Pathways to Psychology*, Jillian realized that her efforts to help Phoebe were backfiring. Rather than helping Phoebe get over the intense friendship, Jillian actually was making it harder for her. The reason was that, inadvertently, she was *intermittently reinforcing* Phoebe. By maintaining close contact and support at the same time that she wanted to terminate the unsatisfactory friendship, she was giving Phoebe just enough hope to keep her on a string. She meant well, but the results were predictable. Intermittent reinforcement is the kind of reward system that most sustains an established pattern of behavior.

Jillian realized that the best thing she could do for Phoebe at this point would be to leave her alone for awhile so that Phoebe could move on with her life, rather than cling to Jillian. Jillian told Phoebe as much, and although Phoebe resisted Jillian's plan, Jillian carried it out. Phoebe eventually did get over her intense dependency on Jillian and, 2 years later, Phoebe and Jillian became friends again, but on a more mutual basis.

Summary

What Are Some Preprogrammed Responses? 160

1. *Learning* is a relatively permanent change in behavior, thoughts, or feelings as a result of past experience.
2. *Habituation* and *instincts*, such as *imprinting*, are preprogrammed responses that are mainly determined by biology (nature), although learning (nurture) also may play a role.

What Is Classical Conditioning? 163

3. Pavlov identified *classical conditioning* when he observed that dogs produced saliva when they sensed stimuli that came before the arrival of meat powder. For example, Pavlov realized that he could condition dogs to produce saliva in response to a sound, a response that would not occur naturally.

4. In classical conditioning, an individual pairs a neutral stimulus with a stimulus that produces an unconditioned physiological or emotional response.
5. In Pavlov's experiment, the dog's salivating for the meat powder was the *unconditioned response (UR)*, the meat powder was the *unconditioned stimulus (US)*, the buzzer (an originally neutral stimulus) became the *conditioned stimulus (CS)*, and the salivation (originally the UR) in response to the buzzer became the *conditioned response (CR)*.
6. In the standard classical conditioning experiment, the start of the CS comes soon before the start of the US.
7. *Temporal contiguity* alone does not lead to classical conditioning; in addition, a contingency must be established between the stimulus and the response if conditioning is to occur.

8. The phase during which the probability of a CR increases is the *acquisition* phase of learning. If the US is not presented with the CS over many learning trials, eventually, the learned response, the CR, is *extinguished*.

9. When individuals respond to stimuli that are similar to the CS, they show *stimulus generalization*. When individuals do not respond to stimuli that differ from the CS, they show *stimulus discrimination*.

10. Individuals seem to be predisposed toward making some associations and not others. For example, for rats who were exposed to poison as the US, taste was a more effective CS than was the combination of light and noise.

11. Classical conditioning applies to everyday human experiences. Many of our conditioned emotional responses, such as fear, anxiety, or even joy, are linked to distinctive physiological feelings (e.g., increased heart rate).

What Is Operant Conditioning?   172

12. *Operant conditioning* is learning produced by the active behavior (i.e., an *operant*) of an individual. According to the *law of effect*, operant actions that are reinforced will tend to be strengthened and thus to be more likely to occur in the future, whereas operant actions that are punished will tend to be weakened and thus to be less likely to occur in the future.

13. A *reinforcer* is a stimulus event that increases the probability that the operant associated with it will happen again.

14. A *positive reinforcer* is a positive stimulus event whose occurrence strengthens an associated response. A *negative reinforcer* is an unpleasant stimulus event whose removal strengthens an associated response. *Positive reinforcement* refers to the effect of the pairing of a positive reinforcer with an operant. *Negative reinforcement* refers to the effect of the pairing of the removal of a negative reinforcer with an operant. Both types of reinforcement are welcomed by the individual and strengthen the associated operant response.

15. *Punishment* is the administration of a stimulus event that decreases the probability of a response. Punishment should be administered carefully because it can lead to unwanted consequences.

16. *Avoidance learning* occurs when an individual learns to stay away from something. Under some circumstances, avoidance learning can occur after just a single trial of *aversive conditioning*.

17. Individuals show *learned helplessness* when they feel helpless to escape a painful or otherwise unpleasant stimulus. Individuals learn to feel helpless after they repeatedly fail to escape unpleasant stimuli.

18. The *gradient of reinforcement* is a feature of operant conditioning: the longer the time between the operant behavior and the reinforcement, the weaker the reinforcement.

19. Often, it is not easy to provide *primary reinforcers* (e.g., food and other immediately satisfying or enjoyable things). *Secondary reinforcers* (e.g., money, sincere praise, good grades, high-status objects) can provide reinforcement after being associated with primary reinforcers.

20. When *shaping* behavior, the method of *successive approximations* reinforces operant behaviors that are successively closer to the desired behavior.

21. In operant conditioning, *partial reinforcement* may occur after a particular number of operant responses or after a particular interval of time during which operant responses have occurred. Four schedules of partial reinforcement are fixed-ratio, variable-ratio, fixed-interval, and variable-interval.

What Is Social Learning?   184

22. When we watch the behavior of others, as well as the outcomes of that behavior, we engage in *social learning*. A classic example of social learning is Bandura's experiment with children who watched and mimicked aggressive behavior toward a Bobo doll.

23. Learning by observation seems to take place when the potentially learnable behavior is attended, retained, and reproducible by the observer, and when the individual is motivated to reproduce that behavior.

Choose the best answer to complete each sentence.

1. Instincts
   (a) are preprogrammed responses.
   (b) are patterns of behavior that bypass normal neuronal-brain pathways.
   (c) can be learned.
   (d) are actions that are performed without conscious awareness.

2. Classical conditioning is a process whereby
   (a) certain physiological or emotional responses accurately predict the appearance of particular stimuli.
   (b) actions that are desirable are strengthened, and actions that are undesirable are weakened.
   (c) actions that are reinforced tend to be strengthened.
   (d) learning occurs when one stimulus accurately predicts the appearance of another stimulus, which prompts a physiological, emotional, or other response.

3. A mechanism whereby a new stimulus is distinguished from a similar, older one so that conditioning does not take place is termed stimulus
   (a) selectivity.
   (b) degeneralization.
   (c) discrimination.
   (d) extinction.

4. In order to be most effective, punishment should not be
   (a) delivered immediately after the undesirable response.
   (b) used as the only means for eliciting behavioral change.
   (c) inescapable when the operant is demonstrated.
   (d) delivered with sufficient intensity to stop the undesirable behavior.

5. Albert Bandura's social-learning theory holds that
   (a) learning is greatest in group settings.
   (b) learning can be achieved by observing and modeling another person's behavior.

(c) exposure to an aggressive scene for a fraction of a second later can elicit aggressive behavior.
(d) social learning takes place at an unconscious level.

Answer each of the following questions by filling in the blank with an appropriate word or phrase.

6. In Pavlov's historic experiment on classical conditioning, the unconditioned response was _____.

7. An unpleasant stimulus event that is presented immediately after a response, in the hope of decreasing the probability of that response, is called a _____.

8. In order to shape a complex behavior, a behaviorist may use _____ _____, which involve continually reinforcing behavior that comes closer and closer to the desired behavior.

9. _____ and _____, such as _____, are preprogrammed responses that are mainly determined by biology (nature), rather than as a result of learning.

10. In classical conditioning, the conditioned response is _____ upon the occurrence of the conditioned stimulus.

11. When a person who is afraid of rats also shows fear of any small furry animals, this person is showing _____ _____.

12. When a mother smiles back at her laughing baby, she is providing a positive _____ for the infant's laughter.

13. A battered wife decides to stay with her husband, although he continually beats her. At one time, when she tried to leave him, she was repeatedly prevented from doing so. She now no longer even tries to leave. This wife is showing _____ _____.

14. When a student drops out of school after being humiliated in front of the whole class, this student is showing _____ learning.

15. In operant conditioning, the _____ of _____ refers to the observation that the strength of a reinforcer *decreases* as the length of time between the operant and the reinforcement *increases*.

Match the following forms of learning to the examples of each kind.

16. imprinting

(a) Shareen once got sick after eating raw fish, and now the smell of fish makes her feel nauseous.

17. habituation

(b) After a while, Jaime got used to the country-western music playing in the background and did not even notice it was there.

18. classical conditioning

(c) Goslings followed Lorenz wherever he went because he was the first moving object they saw.

19. operant conditioning

(d) Sarah's mother participated in civil rights, ban-the-bomb, and other protest marches ever since Sarah was a little girl; when the Gulf War started, Sarah was on the front lines to protest against the war.

20. social learning

(e) Buffy gets paid for every part she solders together, and she now solders many parts per hour.

Answers

1. a, 2. d, 3. c, 4. b, 5. b, 6. salivation, 7. punisher, 8. successive approximations, 9. Habituation, instincts, imprinting, 10. contingent, 11. stimulus generalization, 12. reinforcer, 13. learned helplessness, 14. avoidance, 15. gradient, reinforcement, 16. c, 17. b, 18. a, 19. e, 20. d

Pathways to Understanding

1. Suppose that you were a storyteller or a moviemaker. How might you use classical conditioning to influence your audience's emotions? (Use a real story or movie plot for your example.)

2. What is something (a skill, a task, or an achievement) that you think is worthwhile but that you feel a sense of learned helplessness about successfully accomplishing? How could you design a conditioning program for yourself to overcome your learned helplessness?

3. Given the powerful effects of social learning, how might the medium of television be used as a medium for *lowering* the rate of violent crimes in our society?

The Case of The Cram Man

In high school, José was more interested in parties than he was in studying. He tried to make sure he got to every party he could possibly find. In order to keep up his grades, he developed a series of strategies for succeeding on exams. Foremost among these strategies was cramming the night before the exam. José usually crammed for exams and it almost always worked. He could study the night before, go into the exam, and get a good, if not a perfect, grade. In this way, José could put off studying until the last minute, using the time before the last minute attending to his social life. José perfected his strategy for cramming in high school and went to college confident he could make the same strategy work for him.

The strategy was not working. José was pulling Cs instead of As and he was confused. The strategy had always worked for him before but the strategy no longer was working. He did not understand why; but he knew that if he wanted to reach his goal and gain admission to law school he would have to improve his grades.

What should José have done? Think about this while you are reading chapter 6. Will the pathway to studying that José is following lead him to reach his goals? Pay special attention to the issue of massed learning versus distributed learning.

CHAPTER 6
MEMORY

6

What do we do when we decide to try to remember something? In fact, just what is memory anyway? How does memory work? Are there different kinds of memory and, if so, what are they? How is memory organized? How are different kinds of memories related? How can we measure memory, and how can we improve it? We start to answer these questions by investigating how psychologists study memory.

HOW DO PSYCHOLOGISTS STUDY MEMORY?

Memory is the means by which we use information that we gained in the past. Through memory, we store and retrieve information about past experience (Crowder, 1976). One of the ways that psychologists study memory is by examining case studies of people with exceptional memory, such as people who lack the normal ability to store and retrieve information. A second way of studying memory, considered later, is through experimental methods.

Case Studies of Memory Deficiencies: Amnesia

One of the most famous cases of **amnesia** (severe loss of memory function) is the case of Henry M., reported by Brenda Milner, Suzanne Corkin, and Hans-Lukas Teuber (1968). Following an experimental surgery performed by neurosurgeon William Scoville (Scoville & Milner, 1957), Henry suffered severe **anterograde amnesia**: He had difficulty deliberately forming new memories of factual information (e.g., the names and faces of people who cared for him following his surgery) and he was unable to store memories of events that took place after the surgery (e.g., what he had done even minutes earlier if he was distracted from an activity). Nonetheless, he remembered whatever he had known before his operation.

I apologise for the non-arrival of the guest speaker—who I'm almost sure I invited.

Reproduced with the permission of the South Wales Echo, U.K.

After his surgery, Henry's intelligence test score was somewhat above average; however, his score on the memory portion of the test was far below average. Moreover, shortly after taking one of the tests, he could no longer remember that he had even taken the test. Henry once remarked on his situation: "Every day is alone in itself, whatever enjoyment I've had, and whatever sorrow I've had" (Scoville & Milner, 1957, p. 217).

Another type of memory loss is **retrograde amnesia,** in which individuals lose their ability purposefully to recall events that occurred before the event that led to the memory loss. W. Ritchie Russell and P. W. Nathan (1946) reported a case of retrograde amnesia following a motorcycle accident: A 22-year-old man suffered severe memory loss due to *trauma* (an event that causes injury). By 10 weeks after the accident, however, the accident victim had recovered most of his memory. His recovery of memory started with the events in the most distant past and gradually progressed to more recent events. Eventually, he was able to recall everything that happened up to a few minutes before the accident. As is often the case, the events that occurred immediately before the accident were never recalled.

Case Studies of Outstanding Memory: Mnemonists

In contrast to amnesia, **mnemonism** is the use of special techniques for enhancing memory skill. Perhaps the most well-known mnemonist was a man whom Alexander Luria (1902–1977) called "S." Luria (1968) reported that S., a newspaper reporter, showed up in his laboratory and asked to have his memory tested. Luria tested him and discovered that the man's memory appeared to have no limits. S. could recall series of words of any length, regardless of the span of time before the words were presented to him again. Luria studied S. over a period of 30 years and found that even when he tested S.'s memory for a list of words 15 or 16 years after S. had learned the list, S. could still recall the list. S. eventually became a professional entertainer, amazing audiences with his ability to recall whatever was asked of him.

What was S.'s trick? How did he remember so much? Apparently, he seemed automatically to convert words and other information that he needed to remember into visual images. For example, he reported that for remembering numbers, "One is a proud, well-built man, two is a high-spirited woman," and so on (Luria, 1968, p. 31). S. often used his "graphic thinking" (p. 112) to solve problems (visually manipulating various concrete objects in his mind) or to recall what he read (visualizing the words and phrases in a text). Sometimes, however, his automatic construction of images would interfere with his ability to grasp lengthy passages: "A point is . . . reached at which images begin to guide one's thinking, rather than thought itself being the dominant element" (p. 116). In addition, when S. tried to understand abstract concepts that are not easily visualized, such as *infinity* or *nothing,* S. observed, "I can only understand what I can visualize" (p. 130).

In contrast to Luria's S., S. F. (a mnemonist studied by Ericsson, Chase, & Faloon, 1980) started out with relatively ordinary memory abilities when he was first tested. He developed his mnemonic abilities during 200 memory-testing sessions in a 2-year period. S. F. learned to use information with which he was already familiar (running times for various races) as a tool for remembering new and unfamiliar information (long strings of numbers). He did so by breaking down the long numbers into groups of three or four digits each and then memorizing the number

Frequently, amnesia occurs as a result of some kind of traumatic injury to the head (and the brain).

memory • the process by which past experience and learning can be used in the present

amnesia • the loss of partial or total explicit memory

anterograde amnesia • the difficulty in purposefully forming new memories after an injury to memory function without any effect on the ability to retrieve memories stored prior to the injury; one meaning of *antero-* is "before"; people with anterograde amnesia forget new information before they even have a chance to store it

retrograde amnesia • a memory loss that affects the purposeful retrieval of events that occurred before an injury causing memory loss, without any effect on the ability to form new memories; one meaning of *retro-* is "backward"; people with retrograde amnesia forget information stored prior to the injury

mnemonism • the use of special techniques for improving memory skill (see also *mnemonic devices*)

groups as running times for different races. His memory skill was severely limited, however, when the experimenters purposely gave him sequences of digits that could not be translated into running times.

The work with S. F. suggests that people with ordinary memory abilities can greatly increase their abilities if they put considerable effort into doing so. Similarly, Luria observed that people with ordinary memory abilities can intentionally find ways to use visual imagery as a means for remembering information. On the other hand, the work with both S. and S. F. indicates that mnemonic techniques that are successful in certain situations do not necessarily work under all circumstances.

Using Mnemonics

You can use many of the same techniques mnemonists use. The memory performance of mnemonists is quite rare, but you can use several similar mnemonic devices to improve your learning of new material. **Mnemonic devices** comprise a variety of specific techniques for aiding in the memorization of various isolated items by adding meaning or imagery to an otherwise arbitrary listing of isolated items that may be difficult to remember. Of the many mnemonic devices, the ones described here rely on organization of information into meaningful chunks, such as categorical clustering, acronyms, and acrostics; or on visual images, such as interactive images, a pegword system, the method of loci, and the keyword system.

In *categorical clustering*, various items are grouped into categories in order to facilitate recall of the items. For example, if you need to remember to buy apples, milk, grapes, yogurt, Swiss cheese, and grapefruit, try to memorize the items by categories: fruits—apples, grapes, grapefruit; dairy products—milk, yogurt, Swiss cheese. *Acronyms* are another type of memory device, where a set of letters forms a word or phrase, in which each letter stands for a certain other word or concept (e.g., U.S.A., IQ, and laser). For example, you could try to remember the names of these mnemonic devices by using the acronym I AM PACK: Interactive images, Acronyms, Method of loci, Pegwords, Acrostics, Categories, and Keywords.

Acrostics, on the other hand, are the initial letters of a series of items that are used in forming a sentence, such that the sentence prompts the recall of the initial letters and the letters prompt the recall of each of the items. Music students use the acrostic "Every Good Boy Does Fine" to memorize the notes on the lines of the treble clef.

When using *interactive images* to enhance memory, you can link a set of isolated words by creating visual representations for the words and then picturing interactions among the items. For instance, if you needed to remember a list of unrelated words such as *aardvark, table, pencil,* and *book,* you could imagine an aardvark sitting on a table holding a pencil in its claws and writing in a book.

A system that uses interactive images is the pegword system. With a *pegword system,* memorization of a familiar list of items can be linked (via interactive images) with unfamiliar items on a new list. Using a pegword system, you might take advantage of this nursery rhyme: One is a bun, two is a shoe, three is a tree, four is a door, five is a hive. Then you imagine, say, an aardvark ready to be eaten on a bun, a shoe resting on a table, a tree that has pencils for branches, and a large book serving as a door, complete with doorknobs and hinges.

Still another method, the *method of loci,* consists of visualization of a familiar area with distinctive landmarks that can be linked (via interactive

mnemonic devices • the methods or "tricks" for improving memory by combining unrelated bits of information into meaningful verbal information or into visual images (see also *mnemonism*)

images) with items to be remembered. In using this method, you could mentally walk past each of the landmarks and visualize an image incorporating a new word and a landmark. For example, you could envision an aardvark digging at the roots of a familiar tree, a table sitting on a familiar sidewalk, and a pencil-shaped statue in the center of a familiar fountain. To remember the list, you take your mental walk and pick up the words you have linked to each of the landmarks along the walk.

A *keyword system* for learning isolated words in a foreign language forms an interactive image that links the sound and meaning of the foreign word to the sound and meaning of a familiar word. For instance, to learn that the French word for *butter* is *beurre,* you might note that *beurre* sounds like *bear.* Next, you would associate the keyword *bear* with butter in an image or sentence, such as a bear eating a stick of butter. Later, *bear* would provide a retrieval cue for *beurre.*

Of the many mnemonic devices available, the ones described here rely on two general principles of effective recall that we covered earlier. Categorical clustering, acronyms, and acrostics involve organizing information into meaningful chunks, which we have seen can help with both short-term and long-term memory. Storing items as visual images can help with retrieval from long-term memory and is the basis of mnemonic techniques such as interactive images, the pegword system, the method of loci, and the keyword system.

Experimental Study of Memory

Clearly, psychologists learn a great deal by examining case studies of exceptional individuals such as Scoville and Milner's Henry M. and Luria's S. By carefully observing and describing how exceptional memory works, we may gain insight into how normal memory works. Another obvious way in which to probe the depths of normal memory functions is to study normal memory directly. One of the first psychologists to study normal memory functions was Hermann Ebbinghaus (1850–1909). Although Ebbinghaus had no support from a university and no formal laboratory in which to conduct his research, his research continues to be cited and discussed a century later. Astonishingly, this pioneer in memory research studied the memory performance of a single individual, whom he could observe 24 hours a day, 7 days a week: himself.

One of the most difficult problems Ebbinghaus faced is one that continues to plague researchers today: How do you study a phenomenon that cannot be photographed, measured, or otherwise observed directly? Like other psychological phenomena, memory is a **hypothetical construct.** Its functions and processes can be observed and measured only indirectly. Its very existence can only be inferred by observing the outcomes it produces. One way to observe the outcomes of memory is to find situations where people use memory and then to record what happens. Another way is to design controlled experiments, using specialized memory tasks, and to record the outcomes in a relatively controlled manner.

Ebbinghaus pioneered the use of various kinds of tasks for studying memory. He carefully recorded his own responses to each task, noting such outcomes as the number of errors, the time it took to make each response, and so on. From these careful self-observations, he could infer conclusions about what factors impeded memory and what factors enhanced memory. For one thing, he found that the number of items he could recall decreased over time (see Figure 6.1a). On the other hand, he noted

hypothetical construct • a phenomenon that is believed to exist but that cannot be measured or perceived directly; that is, we cannot directly see, hear, touch, smell, or taste these constructs, however, we believe they exist—a hypothetical construct (e.g., memory or intelligence) is *constructed* (built) from *hypotheses* (beliefs)

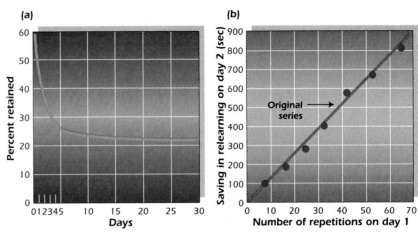

FIGURE 6.1

Ebbinghaus: Pioneer in Memory Research

Hermann Ebbinghaus's investigation of his own memory processes blazed a trail followed by countless other researchers. (a) Memory researchers have confirmed Ebbinghaus's observation of the "forgetting curve," which shows that the number of items that can be recalled decreases over time. (b) One of the main techniques Ebbinghaus developed involved "relearning," in which he memorized some material in one learning session, and then in a subsequent session, he observed how quickly he could relearn the material from the first session. As this graph shows, the more frequently he had repeated (rehearsed) a particular list of items on the first day, the less time it took him to relearn the list of items on the second day.

that the more frequently he rehearsed (repeated) a particular set of items, the more easily he could recall the items (see Figure 6.1b).

Since Ebbinghaus's day, we have learned a great deal about memory, as well as about effective techniques for psychological experimentation. Most psychologists now would question research findings based solely on self-observation. In addition, psychologists now view memory as comprising multiple aspects, not just one. Hence, to study memory, psychologists observe people performing tasks that call on different aspects of memory (e.g., recall vs. recognition memory, implicit vs. explicit memory, and declarative vs. procedural memory). By studying how people use memory to perform various tasks, psychologists learn new information about how memory works.

If you were to be given a task that requires **recall** from memory, you would be asked to produce a fact, a word, or another item from memory. On the other hand, if you were given a task that required **recognition,** you would have to select or otherwise to identify an item as being one that you had learned previously. Three types of recall tasks used in experiments are *serial recall, free recall,* and *cued recall.* (To try each kind of task for yourself, see Table 6.1.) By using both recognition tasks and recall tasks, psychologists have found that recognition memory is usually much better than recall memory. For example, one study found that research participants could recognize close to 2,000 pictures in a recognition-memory task (Standing, Conezio, & Haber, 1970). Can you imagine anyone recalling 2,000 pictures they were just asked to memorize?

Ebbinghaus and other researchers focused on memory tasks involving lists of individual items (e.g., the tasks described at the top of Table 6.1). More recently, many psychologists have become increasingly interested in

recall • the production of an item from memory

recognition • the identification of an item as one that was previously stored in memory

TABLE 6.1
Tasks Used for Measuring Memory

Measuring explicit memory about declarative knowledge	Examples: Try the following tasks for yourself
Explicit memory tasks: You must consciously recall information. *Declarative-knowledge tasks: You must recall facts.*	
Recall tasks. Produce a fact, a word, or other item from memory.	What is the kind of amnesia in which a person is unable deliberately to recall information, going backward from the time of the trauma that causes the amnesia?
Serial-recall task. Repeat the items in a list in the exact order in which you heard or read them.	Look at the following digits, and then look away and write down the digits in the exact order in which you see them: 2-8-7-1-6-4-3.
Free-recall task. Repeat the items in a list in any order in which you can recall them.	Look at the following list of words, and then look away and write down the words in any order at all: *dog, pencil, time, hair, monkey, restaurant.*
Cued-recall task. Memorize a list of paired items, then when you are given a cue of one item in the pair, you must recall the mate for that cued item.	Memorize the following list of word pairs: "time–city, mist–home, switch–paper, credit–day, fist–cloud, number–branch." On a sheet of paper, write the following words, one word per line: *time, mist, switch, credit, fist, number.* Next, recall the word pairs, and write the corresponding words for each pair.
Recognition tasks. Select or otherwise identify an item as being one that you learned previously.	Which is the kind of amnesia in which a person is unable deliberately to form new memories of events: (a) reactive amnesia; (b) anterograde amnesia; (c) traumatic amnesia; or (d) retrograde amnesia?
Measuring implicit memory and procedural knowledge	**Examples: Try the following tasks for yourself**
Implicit memory tasks. Draw on information in memory, without consciously realizing that you are doing so.	Fill in the blanks for the following words: imp _ _ _ _ _, am _ _ _ _ _. You are more likely to fill in these blanks with words you have read recently than with other words that you know.
Tasks involving procedural knowledge. Remember learned skills and automatic behaviors, rather than facts.	Practice "mirror writing," by writing words that you see only as they are reflected in a mirror. Over time, you will improve your ability to use mirror writing; even if you could not recall ever having practiced this skill (e.g., as in persons who suffer from amnesia), your performance would improve.

studying how people recall or recognize integrated, context-rich information, such as information from lengthy text passages, lectures, experiences and events, and so on. Usually, when people are performing recall or recognition tasks, they are expected to use **explicit memory**, in which they consciously try to recall or to recognize information.

In addition to studying explicit memory, many psychologists seek to understand **implicit memory** (Graf & Schacter, 1985), in which we use remembered information, even when we are not consciously aware of recalling the information. Every day, you do many things that involve your implicit memory. As you read this book, you unconsciously remember the meanings of words, as well as how to read in the first place. Surprisingly,

explicit memory • remembering that requires a conscious effort at recollection of information

implicit memory • remembering information from prior experience to enhance performance, without being consciously aware of retrieving that information

People with amnesia may be unable to learn to remember the names of new musical works, which requires explicit memory, even if they are repeatedly told those names. Nonetheless, their ability to play new pieces shows improvement as a result of repeated experience in playing those pieces, which shows their use of implicit memory.

the use of implicit memory improves your performance even when you have not been instructed to use implicit recollections and when you are not aware of doing so. In fact, people who suffer from amnesia seem to benefit from using implicit memory (Baddeley, 1989).

Amnesia victims also show puzzling abilities in regard to tasks that involve **procedural knowledge** (e.g., how to ride a bicycle or how to sign their names). Even when amnesia sufferers have great difficulty in remembering **declarative knowledge** (e.g., the terms in a psychology textbook), they still remember procedural knowledge. For example, amnesia victims usually perform very poorly on traditional memory tasks requiring recall or recognition memory of declarative knowledge. On the other hand, they seem to be able to learn from previous experience in performing skill-based tasks that depend on procedural knowledge. Their remembered practice helps them to improve their performance, even when they do not remember having seen the task before (Baddeley, 1993). For instance, Henry M. showed improvement in his skill in doing *mirror writing* (tracing words seen only in a mirror), but he had no recollection of ever having performed the task relatively soon after completing it (described in Hilts, 1995).

When psychologists study persons who have amnesia, the psychologists learn more than just how memory works in cases of amnesia. They also get ideas about how memory works in general. For one thing, by studying amnesia victims, psychologists have found that the ability to retrieve information consciously from memory about prior experience seems to differ from the ability to use remembered information without being aware of doing so (Baddeley, 1989). Thus, persons with amnesia may show relatively normal use of implicit memory and procedural knowledge, even when they show very poor use of explicit memory and declarative knowledge.

procedural knowledge •
"knowing how"; skills that require a person to follow a set of steps to carry out a task

declarative knowledge •
"knowing that"; factual information that a person can state in words

What is the structure of memory, whether for mnemonists, amnesics, or typical people? We consider this question next.

6.1

Carefully read over the following passage, and think about how you can help yourself to remember as much as possible of this passage. Later in this chapter, you will be asked to recall this passage.

WAR OF THE GHOSTS

One night two young men from Egulac went down to the river to hunt seals, and while they were there it became foggy and calm. Then they heard war-cries, and they thought, "Maybe this is a war-party." They escaped to the shore, and hid behind a log. Now canoes came up, and they heard the noise of paddles, and saw one canoe coming up to them. There were five men in the canoe, and they said:

"What do you think? We wish to take you along. We are going up the river to make war on the people."

One of the young men said, "I have no arrows."

"Arrows are in the canoe," they said.

"I will not go along. I might be killed. My relatives do not know where I have gone. But you," he said, turning to the other, "may go with them."

So one of the young men went, but the other returned home.

And the warriors went on up the river to a town on the other side of Kalama. The people came down to the water, and they began to fight, and many were killed. But presently the young man heard one of the warriors say: "Quick, let us go home; that Indian has been hit." Now he thought: "Oh, they are ghosts." He did not feel sick, but they said he had been shot.

So the canoes went back to Egulac, and the young man went ashore to his house, and made a fire. And he told everybody and said: "Behold I accompanied the ghosts, and we went to fight. Many of our fellows were killed, and many of those who attacked us were killed. They said I was hit, and I did not feel sick."

He told it all, and then he became quiet. When the sun rose he fell down. Something black came out of his mouth. His face became contorted. The people jumped up and cried.

He was dead.

(Bartlett, 1932, p. 65)

HOW HAVE PSYCHOLOGISTS TRADITIONALLY VIEWED MEMORY?

What have psychologists learned about memory and its structure by conducting case-study and experimental research? Just what is memory, and how does it work? The answers to these questions depend on whom you ask. For years, the most common way to view memory has been one that was originally proposed by Richard Atkinson and Richard Shiffrin

(1968). Although other models have since been proposed and are gaining acceptance, the Atkinson–Shiffrin model is still widely accepted, so it is the primary model discussed in this chapter. Later in this chapter, however, some other views are described.

Atkinson and Shiffrin thought of memory in terms of three different memory *stores* (containers for holding what we remember): sensory memory (the sensory store), short-term memory (the short-term store), and long-term memory (the long-term store). (a) **Sensory memory** can very briefly (for less than 1 second) store very limited amounts of information. (b) **Short-term memory** can store information for somewhat longer periods of time (up to a couple minutes under most circumstances), but it also has a relatively limited capacity. (c) **Long-term memory** has a very large capacity (perhaps limitless) and can store information for very long periods of time (perhaps indefinitely).

Psychologists do not believe that these three stores are distinct physiological structures. Rather, the stores are metaphors for hypothetical constructs of memory processes. Figure 6.2 shows a simple model of these stores (e.g., R. C. Atkinson & Shiffrin, 1968). Notice that in this model, all information that we remember over the long term follows a common pathway: from the sensory store to the short-term store to the long-term store.

In the three-stores model, all three memory stores process information by using three mental operations: encoding, storage, and retrieval. First is **encoding,** in which you transform sensory information into an understandable mental representation that can be used in memory. For example, when you meet someone new, you encode the person's name and face into a form of mental representation. Next is **storage,** in which you keep the encoded information in memory. For example, if you expect to have future dealings with a person you have just met, you will probably try to store the person's name and face in memory. Last is **retrieval,** in which you pull the information from a memory store into active use or awareness. For instance, if you meet someone again whom you have met previously,

sensory memory • the storage of very limited amounts of information for about a fraction of a second

short-term memory • the relatively brief memory storage of about seven items

long-term memory • the storage of a practically limitless amount of information for unknown lengths of time

encoding • the transformation of sensory information into an understandable mental representation that can be stored in memory

storage • the keeping of encoded information in memory

retrieval • the recovery of information from memory for active use or awareness

FIGURE 6.2

The Three-Stores View

In Richard Atkinson and Richard Shiffrin's model of memory, information flows from sensory to short-term to long-term memory stores. Atkinson and Shiffrin's metaphor for memory has long served as a basis for research on memory processes. (Adapted from "The control of short-term memory" by R. C. Atkinson and R. M. Shiffrin (1971). In Scientific American, 225, 82–90.)

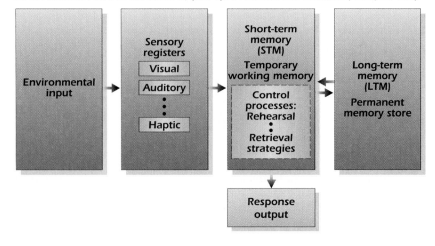

you will probably try to retrieve the person's name to go with the face, which may not always be easy to do! Although encoding, storage, and retrieval are usually viewed as sequential stages, the processes interact with and depend on each other. Next, we investigate each memory store, starting with the sensory store.

Sensory Memory

The sensory store is considered the first mental storage area for much of the information that eventually enters the other two stores. Excellent evidence has shown the existence of a separate visual sensory store, termed an **iconic store**. It is called an "iconic store" because information may be stored there in the form of *icons* (visual images that look somewhat like the things that they represent). The notion of the iconic store came from the PhD dissertation of George Sperling (1960), a graduate student at Harvard who revealed the existence of this sensory store.

Sperling found that the iconic store can hold about nine items, but that these items fade very rapidly (see Figure 6.3). We normally are not aware of any fading at all, however. What we see in iconic memory we believe to be in the environment. Visual information appears to enter our memory system through the iconic store, which holds the visual information for fractions of a second. In the normal course of events, this information may be either transferred to another store or erased. The sensory information is erased if other information replaces it before the information can be transferred to another memory store.

Short-Term Memory

Although most of us have little or no ability to control our sensory memory, we all have some control over our short-term memory. In short-term memory, we can hold information for matters of seconds and, occasionally, up to a minute or two. Whenever we look up a phone number in the phone book and remember it long enough to make our call, we are using our short-term memory.

You may also have had this experience: After you entered a number, the phone line was busy, and then you had to look up the number again in order to enter it again. Why do we forget such simple information so easily? It appears that our ability to hold information in short-term memory is quite limited.

George Miller (1956) noted that our short-term memory capacity for a wide range of items appears to be about 7 items, plus or minus 2. An item can be something simple, such as a digit, or something more complex, such as a word. If we were to **chunk** a string of 20 items (e.g., letters or numbers) into 7 meaningful items, we could remember them. If we did not chunk the items, we could not remember 20 items and repeat them immediately. For example, most of us could not easily hold in short-term memory this string of 20 letters: *t, s, x, r, q, n, m, n, a, f, s, y, w, e, i, u, e, o, e, u.* However, if we chunked this series into larger units, such as *foxes, yams, quiet, new,* and *run,* we would easily be able to reproduce the 20 letters as 5 items. Once we have formed mental chunks of new information, we can store the information in memory. With a little effort, we can then move the information into long-term memory.

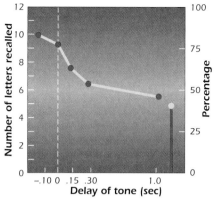

FIGURE 6.3
Effects of Delay on Visual Recall
The line graph shows the average number of letters available (left axis; percentage equivalents indicated on right axis) to a participant using a partial-report procedure, as a function of the delay between the presentation of the letters and the tone signaling when to show recall. As the delay interval approaches 1 second, recall ability falls sharply. At the far right is shown a bar graph for recall from a whole-report procedure. (From "The information available in brief visual presentations," by G. Sperling (1960). In Psychological Monographs, 74 (Whole No. 11).)

iconic store • sensory memory for very brief storage of visual images

chunk • a grouping, by which a collection of items is organized into a coherent whole

What is 119 divided by 7? To figure out the answer to this question, you must use your short-term memory to remember the problem, retrieve what you know about division from long-term memory, apply what you know to this problem, and then come up with an answer.

Long-Term Memory

According to the Atkinson–Shiffrin model, the long-term store is where we keep memories that stay with us over long periods of time, perhaps indefinitely.

Organization of Information in Long-Term Memory

It appears that we organize declarative knowledge stored in memory differently, depending on whether it is tied to our own particular experiences. Information in **semantic memory** is general world knowledge, our memory for facts that are not unique to us and that are not recalled in any particular time-bound situation (Tulving, 1972). Information in **episodic memory** is tied to personally experienced events or episodes. We use episodic memory when we learn meaningless lists of words or when we need to recall something that occurred to us at a particular time or in a particular situation. For example, if I need to remember that I saw Hector Hinklemeyer in the lunchroom yesterday, I must draw on episodic memory. However, if I need to remember the name of the person I now see in the lunchroom again today ("Hector Hinklemeyer"), I must draw on semantic memory. There is no particular time tag associated with the fact that this individual is named Hector, but there is a time tag associated with my having seen him at lunch yesterday. Semantic and episodic memory may not be two distinct systems, but they do appear to function, at times, in different ways. Some physiological evidence also suggests that episodic memories are stored separately from semantic memories (described in Schacter, 1989a).

Semantic memory operates on **concepts,** which are ideas about things; our concepts may be about concrete things, such as cars or apples, or about abstract things, such as truth or justice. People mentally organize

semantic memory • the memory for general knowledge of facts that are not linked to particular personal experiences and that organizes internal representations of concepts

episodic memory • the memory for particular events that an individual has experienced, as well as for information that is linked to those experiences

concept • an idea to which a person may attach various characteristics and with which a person may connect other ideas into a single notion

Most of us have stored a lot of information in semantic memory that relates to cars (e.g., various makes and models of cars, automotive parts and systems, traffic laws to be obeyed). In addition, most of us have episodic memories of particular experiences related to cars, such as when learning to drive or when taking car trips.

concepts in various ways, such as in categories (e.g., types of fruits), in ranked orderings (e.g., degrees of truthfulness), or in sets of features (e.g., the attributes of cars). We can better understand memory by understanding how information is organized in memory.

Psychologists often use the term **schema** to describe the cognitive framework for how people pull together and organize an assortment of information in memory. For example, a schema for having lunch might associate all the things you have personally experienced regarding lunch, as well as what you have learned about lunch from other information sources. When you think about all that you know about one simple meal, and then you consider all of the schemas for information you have stored in memory, you may begin to realize the great extent of your long-term memory capacity.

The Capacity of Long-Term Memory

How much information can we hold in long-term memory, and just how long does the information stay in memory? Unfortunately, to date, we do not know how much information can be stored in long-term memory. In fact, we do not even know how we would find out its capacity. Some theorists have suggested that there is no practical limit to long-term memory capacity (Hintzman, 1978).

At present, it is also hard to know how long information can be stored because we have no proof that there is any absolute outer limit to the time that information stays in long-term memory. Some researchers have found evidence in support of the durability of long-term memories. An interesting study on memory for names and faces was conducted by Phyllis Bahrick, Harry Bahrick, and Roy Wittlinger (1975). They tested how well people remember names and photographs of their high school classmates.

schema • the cognitive framework for organizing information about a particular concept

What is the name of the person in this photo? You might not recognize the face of this person from her high school photo, but her high school classmates probably would. Most of us show surprisingly good memory for the faces of people we knew many years before now. Have you figured out who this is yet? It is a photo of the singer Madonna when she was in high school.

Even after 25 years, people showed pretty good memory for recognizing names and faces. They tended to recognize names as belonging to classmates rather than to outsiders, and they could match the names of many classmates to the classmates' graduation photos. As you might expect, recall of names showed a higher rate of forgetting than did recognition of names. According to Harry Bahrick, we keep some information in *permastore,* which offers permanent or at least very long-term storage of memories.

Research such as Bahrick's can give some idea of how much information we remember. However, it cannot really show how much information we have forgotten. After all, how do we know that we are no longer storing information that we cannot retrieve? Instead of losing information from storage, perhaps we just do not know how to find and retrieve the stored information. For the present, it seems impossible to ascertain any limits to long-term memory.

Thus far, we have discussed memory within the context of the three-stores model of memory. Next, we consider whether there are reasonable alternative ways to view what we know about memory.

WHAT ARE SOME ALTERNATIVE WAYS TO VIEW MEMORY?

The Atkinson–Shiffrin model is only one of several ways of viewing memory. Because memory is a hypothetical construct (and therefore cannot be observed directly), different psychologists can look at the same data about memory and can interpret those data in different ways, depending on their point of view. The main differences among these various points of view center on the metaphor they use for thinking about memory (Roediger, 1980).

Why do psychologists use metaphors for thinking about memory and other hypothetical constructs? Metaphors often make it easier to form a mental picture of ideas that are highly abstract and difficult to think about. They provide a way to organize ideas about hypothetical constructs. Once psychologists have organized their ideas, they can more easily figure out how to study the construct. As the research progresses, they may need to change the metaphor to fit the new data, or other researchers may propose new metaphors that seem better to fit the new information. Next, we consider some alternatives to the Atkinson–Shiffrin metaphor for thinking about memory.

Alternative Views of Memory Processes

Some psychologists (e.g., Baddeley, 1990a, 1990b; Cantor & Engle, 1993; Daneman & Carpenter, 1980; Daneman & Tardif, 1987; Engle, 1994; Engle, Cantor, & Carullo, 1992; Engle & Oransky, 1999) view short-term and long-term memory from a different perspective than that of the three-stores model. Table 6.2 contrasts the Atkinson–Shiffrin model with this alternative perspective. Note the differences in the *terminology* (choice of words), in the choice of metaphors, and in the emphasis of each view.

The key feature of the alternative view is the emphasis on working memory. **Working memory** may be viewed as a specialized, highly active part of long-term memory. Within working memory is short-term memory, which is the small pool of information in conscious awareness at any

working memory • an activated portion of long-term memory, as well as a means for moving activated elements into and out of short-term memory

TABLE 6.2
Traditional Versus Nontraditional Views of Memory

Different kinds of choices	Traditional three-stores view	Alternative view of memory*
Terminology	*Working memory* is another name for short-term memory (STM), which is distinct from long-term memory (LTM).	*Working memory* (active memory) is the part of LTM that includes all the knowledge (both facts and procedures) that has been recently activated in memory, including the brief, fleeting STM and its contents.
Relationships of stores	STM is viewed as being distinct from LTM, perhaps either alongside it or hierarchically linked to it.	STM, working memory, and LTM may be viewed as nested concentric spheres, in which working memory encompasses only the most recently activated portion of LTM, and STM encompasses only a very small portion of working memory.
Movement of information	Information moves directly from STM to LTM, or vice versa, and is never in both locations at once.	Information remains within LTM; when activated, information moves into working memory, a specialized portion of LTM. The working memory actively moves information into and out of STM.
Emphasis	This view distinguishes between LTM and STM.	This view emphasizes the role of activation in moving information into working memory and the role of working memory in memory processes.

Note. *View of working memory suggested by Cantor & Engle, 1993; Engle, 1994; Engle, Cantor, & Carullo, 1992.

given moment. From this perspective, working memory holds only the portion of long-term memory that has become active recently, and it moves both the active elements and any new information into and out of brief, temporary memory storage.

Whereas the three-stores view emphasizes a single pathway of successive structural containers for stored information, the working-memory view focuses on the functions and processes of memory. One way of picturing the two views of memory is to suppose that a metaphor for the three-stores view is in terms of the pathways things follow in a warehouse, in which information is passively stored. Sensory memory is the loading dock, and short-term memory is the area surrounding the loading dock, where information may be stored temporarily until it is moved into a permanent location in the body of the warehouse, the long-term memory store.

In contrast, a metaphor for the working-memory model may be a multimedia production house, which continually generates and manipulates images and sounds, integrating them into meaningful arrangements for storage and use. These stored images and sounds are frequently reformatted and rearranged, as new demands and new information become available to working memory.

In the working-memory model, memory activity involves **parallel processing**, in which multiple operations are all occurring at once. For example, when you draw from memory information about your best friend, you simultaneously activate many things you know about your friend (e.g., appearance, voice, facial expressions, pet peeves, favorite activities).

parallel processing • information processing during which multiple operations occur simultaneously

The working-memory model has gained support from the use of computer models (artificial intelligence) of memory processes, as well as from experiments with people and from neuropsychological research.

A more radical departure from the three-stores view of memory is the **levels-of-processing framework,** originally proposed by Fergus Craik and Robert Lockhart (1972). In their framework, memory is not made of any specific number of separate stores. Rather, memory storage varies continuously in terms of the depth at which information is encoded.

Different levels of encoding are based on different kinds of encoding. For example, the authors noted the following three different levels of processing: *physical* (based on physical appearance; e.g., the letters of the word *fizz*), *acoustic* (based on sounds; e.g., the sounds of the word *fizz*), and *semantic* (based on word meanings; e.g., the meaning of the word *fizz*). At first, it seemed that some levels (e.g., semantic) were better than others (e.g., physical or acoustic) for remembering information. It turns out that the key to remembering is a match between the level of encoding and the form of the recall. In addition, when information is encoded at more than one level, it appears to be more easily retrieved later on.

This framework has immediate practical applications: In studying, the more ways in which you encode material, the more readily you are likely to recall it later. Just looking at material again and again in the same way is less likely to be productive for learning the material. Instead, find more than one way in which to learn the material. On the other hand, you may want to give particular emphasis to encoding information at a level that closely matches the level at which you will want to retrieve it. If you will be given a test on rhyming words, for instance, you should focus on acoustic encoding. If you will be tested on meanings (more likely in most college classes), you should give extra time to semantic encoding.

A Neuropsychological View of Memory

Another way of viewing memory is to observe the cerebral processes and structures involved in memory. Some structures of the brain, such as the hippocampus and other nearby structures (see chapter 2), clearly play a vital role in memory (Squire, 1987). Damage to these areas causes severe memory problems. Studies of brain-injured patients such as Henry M. (mentioned earlier in this chapter) offer distinctive insights into memory not available by observing normal research participants. It appears that different structures of the brain may be involved in different kinds of memory (Squire, 1987). For example, the importance of the hippocampus for forming new memories of declarative knowledge largely started with studies of the amnesic Henry M., as the portion of Henry's brain that was removed by Scoville included chiefly the hippocampus. Once psychologists noticed that the removal of the hippocampus tragically destroyed some of Henry's memory abilities, they were able to infer the role of the hippocampus in memory formation. In addition to the hippocampus, the cortex is also involved in the memory for declarative knowledge (Zola-Morgan & Squire, 1990), and the basal ganglia are primarily involved in memory for procedural knowledge (Mishkin & Petri, 1984).

When trying to figure out what brain structures and regions are involved in which functions, neuropsychologists often look for dissociations. In *dissociations,* people with lesions in particular areas of the brain show particular deficits of brain function, but people without lesions in those areas do not show those deficits of function. Whenever possible, neuropsychologists try to find *double dissociations,* in which people with

levels-of-processing framework •
a view of memory that suggests that the extent to which an experience is remembered is determined by the degree and depth of information processing that takes place

The hippocampus is crucial for moving new declarative information into long-term memory. Both this elderly woman and this young toddler do not readily move declarative information into long-term memory. Whereas the hippocampus of the woman is deteriorating (possibly due to repeated strokes) and is decreasingly able to aid in storage of declarative information, the hippocampus of the toddler is maturing and is increasingly able to do so.

lesions in different areas of the brain show opposite patterns of deficits. For example, people with lesions in the left parietal lobe show impairments of short-term memory, but not of long-term memory (Warrington & Shallice, 1972). People with lesions in the temporal lobe, however, show impairments of long-term memory but not of short-term memory (Warrington, 1982). Both single and double dissociations help psychologists to confirm or to disconfirm their present hypotheses regarding how memory works; in addition, dissociations lead psychologists to discover new insights about memory.

Larry Squire, using his own research and that of fellow psychologists and neuropsychologists, has proposed a *taxonomy,* or classification schemas, for memory (see Figure 6.4). His taxonomy distinguishes declarative from nondeclarative memory. Nondeclarative memory includes procedural memory, as well as simple learning (operant and classical conditioning; see chapter 5), habituation (see chapter 5), some memory phenomena related to perception (see chapter 3), and priming. In **priming,** information stored in memory becomes activated by stimuli that are identical to or related to the primed information. For example, hearing the word "palm" may prime the word *palm* itself, stored in memory, and it may prime information related to parts of the hand or to various kinds of trees. If you have recently visited a palm-studded beach, your memories of the trip may also be primed.

In addition to learning about the macroscopic structures involved in memory (e.g., the hippocampus or areas of the cortex), we are starting to understand how memory works at the microscopic level. The synapses between neurons seem to be particularly important for forming, keeping, and strengthening memories (e.g., Kandel & Schwartz, 1982). For one

priming • the enhanced access to a particular stimulus or item of information as a result of recent activation of, or exposure to, the same stimulus or a related one

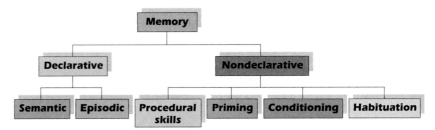

FIGURE 6.4
Squire's Types of Memory
Based on extensive neuropsychological research, Larry Squire has proposed that memory includes two fundamental types: declarative memory and various forms of nondeclarative memory. Each type of memory may be associated with distinct cerebral structures and processes.

thing, chemical neurotransmitters powerfully affect how and how well memory works. Both serotonin and acetylcholine seem to be important to normal memory processes. If these processes are disrupted by drugs (e.g., alcohol; Shimamura & Squire, 1986) or by disease (e.g., Alzheimer's disease; Squire, 1987), memory does not function properly. Even hormones have been found to affect memory under some circumstances, either enhancing or inhibiting memory functions. These functions include encoding, storage, and retrieval and are considered next.

HOW IS INFORMATION ENCODED, STORED, AND RETRIEVED?

Neurotransmitters, hormones, and other substances influence memory by affecting the three main memory processes: *encoding* (in which we move information into memory), *storage* (in which we keep information in memory), and *retrieval* (in which we gain access to stored information). In this section, we discuss each of these processes.

Encoding of Information

Encoding for Temporary Storage of Information

When you encode information to move it into temporary memory storage, what kind of code do you use? That is, in what form is the mental representation that is used for moving information into short-term (or working) memory? R. Conrad (1964) found the answer to this question: The mental representation in temporary memory storage is based on sounds, rather than on icons or some other form.

Conrad found the answer through a serial-recall task. He quickly showed participants various lists of six letters each. Immediately after each list was shown, participants had to write down the correct sequence of items in the list. Conrad was particularly interested in the kinds of recall errors participants made. The pattern of errors was clear. Even though the letters were presented *visually*, errors tended to be based on how easily the sounds of the letters could be confused. Sometimes, instead of recalling the letters they were supposed to recall, participants substituted letters that sounded like the correct letters. Thus, the participants were likely to confuse *F* for *S, B* for *V, P* for *B,* and so on. These confusions are the same ones shown when people simply listen to single letters in a noisy setting. Alan Baddeley (1966) expanded on Conrad's work by using words instead of letters to study encoding in short-term memory. His work confirmed that such encoding relies primarily on an *acoustic code* (based on sounds) rather than on a *semantic code* (based on word meanings).

Encoding for Long-Term Storage

Information in short-term memory is encoded primarily based on sounds, so encoding errors are often based on confusions of sounds. In contrast, information in long-term memory seems to be primarily encoded *semantically*, based on the meanings of words, and errors are based on confusions of word meanings. In addition, however, we also can hold visual (sight) and acoustic (sound) information in long-term memory. Some researchers (e.g., J. R. Anderson & Bower, 1973; Clark & Chase, 1972) have proposed that we store all information in terms of underlying meanings of the information, rather than in terms of word meanings or any other form of mental representation. Other researchers (e.g., Kosslyn, 1975, 1988; Paivio, 1971) have suggested that we store some information in terms of mental images. There is some evidence for mental storage of both underlying meanings and mental images.

Using Techniques for Encoding Information

So far, we know that we encode information in the form of underlying meanings and mental images. How can we apply what we know to develop our own memory skills? A clear application is that when we wish to remember information, we should find ways to encode information by enriching or deepening its meaning or by forming mental images of the information.

FINDING YOUR WAY

6.2

Consider, for example, the following passage from an experiment by John Bransford and Marcia Johnson (1972, p. 722). As you read the following passage, try to memorize the information so that you can recall it effectively.

The procedure is actually quite simple. First you arrange items into different groups. Of course one pile may be sufficient depending on how much there is to do. If you have to go somewhere else due to lack of facilities that is the next step; otherwise, you are pretty well set. It is important not to overdo things. That is, it is better to do too few things at once than too many. In the short run this may not seem important but complications can easily arise. A mistake can be expensive as well. At first, the whole procedure will seem complicated. Soon, however, it will become just another facet of life. It is difficult to foresee any end to the necessity for this task in the immediate future, but then, one can never tell. After the procedure is completed one arranges the materials into different groups again. Then they can be put into their appropriate places. Eventually they will be used once more and the whole cycle will then have to be repeated. However, that is part of life.

Cover the preceding passage with your hand, and try to recall as much as possible of the information. If you are like the people studied by Bransford and Johnson, you will have found it hard to understand and will have had trouble recalling the steps involved. The information seems meaningless, and you have no way to organize the information into a mental representation. You (and Bransford and Johnson's research participants) therefore may have found it hard to encode the information and then to store and retrieve it. However, a simple verbal label can make it easier to encode, store, and retrieve this information. Research participants did much better with the passage when given its title, "Washing Clothes." Once they had the verbal label, they could easily encode, and therefore remember, a passage that otherwise seemed to make no sense. Similarly, once you have encoded information into a form that can be represented in memory, you can store the information.

Storage and Forgetting

How We Keep Information in Storage

Psychologists largely agree about how information is kept in short-term memory. The key technique people use for keeping information in short-term memory is **rehearsal.** An obvious method of rehearsal is simply to repeat the information over and over again, in order to remember it. Effective rehearsal leads to **practice effects,** in which recall is enhanced as a result of repeating the information. Although simple repetition helps to keep information in short-term memory, it does not help in moving the information from short-term memory to long-term memory or in keeping it in long-term memory.

To transfer information into long-term memory, an individual must use elaborative rehearsal. In *elaborative rehearsal,* the person somehow elaborates the information to be remembered in a way that makes the information either more meaningfully integrated into what the person already knows or more meaningfully connected as a whole and therefore more memorable. For example, once you had the label for the "Washing Clothes" passage, you could integrate it into a whole and more easily remember the passage. Recall, too, the effects of chunking, in which people can chunk many smaller units of information into larger units of integrated information, to remember the information more easily. You could also easily integrate the new information into what you already know about washing clothes, further enhancing your ability to remember the information.

Although most adults and older children seem to use rehearsal naturally for keeping information in memory, young children do not. That is, unlike older children and adults, younger children do not understand that to keep information in memory they need to rehearse the information. In fact, the major difference between the memory abilities of younger children and the abilities of older children and adults may lie in the use of learned memory strategies, such as rehearsal (Flavell & Wellman, 1977). Young children have not yet developed *metamemory* skills; that is, knowledge and understanding of their own memory abilities.

Metamemory is one aspect of **metacognition,** in which you think about and try to understand your own thought processes. For example, if you were given a list of items to remember (perhaps you wanted to recall key concepts from a psychology lecture), you might think about your own

rehearsal • the repeated reciting of information or the repetition of a procedure

practice effect • the outcome of rehearsal, usually involving an improvement in recall or skill

metacognition • the process of knowing or thinking about how we use strategies and skills to enhance our thought processes; thinking about how we think

This storyteller elaboratively rehearses each story in her repertoire during each retelling of a narrative. At each retelling, the storyteller reconstructs the story from a known set of characters and events, using rhythm and perhaps rhyme as cues for retelling the same sequence of events in about the same way.

thinking and decide to use a mnemonic device to help you form mental images or meaningful relationships among the items. If you were given a passage of text to learn (e.g., a psychology chapter you were asked to read), you might try to find ways to relate the information to what you already know and to your own experiences.

The way in which you rehearse new information clearly affects how well you will remember it. In addition, the amount of time you spend on rehearsal will affect your ability to remember the rehearsed information. According to the widely accepted *total-time hypothesis,* the amount of information you will remember depends mainly on the total amount of time you spend studying the material in each study session, regardless of how you budget your time within a given session.

On the other hand, although it makes little difference how you divide up your time in any one session, it makes a lot of difference how you divide up your time across study sessions. More than a century ago, Hermann Ebbinghaus (1885/1964, cited in Schacter, 1989a) noticed that the distribution of study (memory rehearsal) sessions over time affects how well you will recall the information later on. Much more recently, Harry Bahrick and Elizabeth Phelps (1987), while studying people's long-term recall of information, have offered support for Ebbinghaus's observation: **Distributed learning** (which is spaced over time) is more effective than **massed learning** (i.e., learning that is crammed together all at once). The more widely the learning trials are distributed over time, the more ably people remember the information. The enhancement of recall due to distributed learning has been termed the *spacing effect* (Glenberg, 1977, 1979).

What might explain the spacing effect? Arthur Glenberg (1977, 1979) has studied this effect extensively, and he and others (e.g., Leicht & Overton, 1987) have linked the spacing effect to the process by which memories

distributed learning • the storage of information in memory that occurs over a long period of time rather than all at once

massed learning • the storage of information in memory that occurs over a brief period of time

PUTTING IT TO USE

6.1

A BAKER'S DOZEN TIPS FOR IMPROVING YOUR MEMORY

1. Be aware of constructive memory processes. If others remember information differently than you do, their memories may be vividly recalled but still inaccurate, just as yours may be.

2. Use external memory aids, such as shopping lists, calendars (for noting key appointments and dates), and alarms and timers. Make lists of things you need to do; designate specific customary locations for things you tend to misplace often (e.g., keys or sunglasses); and place important items and reminders where you cannot miss noticing them.

3. Use either of two basic strategies often used by mnemonists such as S. and S. F.: When you are asked to remember many isolated items of information, you should either (a) translate the items into visual images or (b) try to find ways to connect the items to one another so that you can recall them more easily. You also may want to use particular mnemonic devices (e.g., categorical clustering, interactive images, pegwords, method of loci, acronyms, and acrostics) that take advantage of these strategies.

4. Along the same lines, use chunking to group a large number of unconnected items into a smaller number of interconnected items.

5. Rehearse (practice learning) information that you want to remember. For instance, suppose that you have trouble remembering the names of people you meet. Pay close attention to people's names when they first say their names, and then address them by name several times during your initial meeting.

6. Recall that the more time you spend trying to learn information, the better you will learn that information. Make use of

are consolidated in long-term memory. In memory **consolidation,** we integrate new information into stored information. This process of consolidation can continue for many years (Squire, 1986).

Hence, the spacing effect may occur because at each learning session you have new opportunities for consolidating the information in long-term memory. The principle of the spacing effect is important to remember in studying: You will recall more information for a longer time, on average, if you space out your learning of subject matter, rather than trying to cram your learning into a short period of time. In addition, if you use various strategies for integrating the new information into what you already know, you will help yourself to consolidate the information in long-term memory.

consolidation • a process by which people integrate new information into existing information stored in long-term memory

How We Forget Information

What we have learned about consolidation in long-term memory suggests the way in which we forget information. Before information is consolidated,

your spare moments (e.g., while waiting in line or while waiting for an event to begin) as opportunities for learning whatever information you wish to remember.

7. Try to avoid cramming your study sessions all together. Spread them out as much as possible.

8. When trying to remember information (e.g., when studying), try to find more than one way in which to encode the information, so that you may recall it better later. On the other hand, give particular emphasis to encoding information at the same level (e.g., physical, acoustic, semantic) at which you will be asked to recall it.

9. As much as possible, try to encode information in a context that matches as closely as possible the context in which you expect to need to retrieve it. Along the same lines, if you are having trouble retrieving information (e.g., where you put your keys), try to put yourself in about the same context in which you encoded the information. (If you cannot put yourself physically in the same context, use your imagination to recreate the same context as much as possible.)

10. Use metamemory to think about your own memory processes. Monitor your own experiences with memory, to find the circumstances that enhance, as well as those that hinder, your own memory abilities.

11. Look for ways to find meaning in the information you want to remember. If the meaning of the information does not seem obvious, find ways to relate it to your own experiences as much as possible.

12. Organize information you want to remember and make up your own cues for retrieving the information.

13. Be wary of using drugs (e.g., alcohol or marijuana) that may impair your memory.

it is unstable and is easily forgotten. If the information is not used or reinforced during consolidation, the somewhat shaky information may simply be lost. In addition, during consolidation of information, new information may distort the consolidation of information that is not yet established. Of course, if something happens to disrupt the consolidation process (e.g., a trauma, such as a blow to the head), the information may very well be forgotten altogether.

We have yet to discuss how we forget information in short-term memory, but the experience of forgetting is familiar to all of us. If we do not use rehearsal or other strategies to keep information in short-term memory, the information seems to disappear. Why do we forget information, such as a phone number, after a brief period of time?

Several theories of forgetting have been proposed. The two most well-known theories are *interference theory* and *decay theory*. In **interference**, competing information causes us to forget something. For example, suppose that you are in a phone booth, dialing a phone number you have just looked up. Someone taps you on the shoulder and asks you for the correct

interference • a process by which competing information causes people to forget already stored information

time. It takes you just a few seconds to answer, but when you turn back to the phone dial, you no longer remember the number you were dialing. This example illustrates *retroactive interference,* which occurs *after* the memorable information is stored.

In addition to our being affected by retroactive interference, we may be affected by *proactive interference,* which occurs *before* the memorable information is stored. For example, if you were trying to remember a list of details to tell a mechanic whom you were calling from the phone booth, the list of details might proactively interfere with your ability to remember the mechanic's phone number. The evidence for interference is rather strong (J. A. Brown, 1958; Peterson & Peterson, 1959), but at present, it is unclear as to the extent to which the interference is retroactive, proactive, or both (Keppel & Underwood, 1962).

An alternative means for forgetting is **decay,** in which simply the passage of time causes us to forget. The evidence for decay is not airtight, but it is certainly suggestive (Reitman, 1974). Hence, it appears that both interference and decay affect short-term memory, and whether we can retrieve information from it.

Retrieval

Retrieval From Temporary Storage

Once information is encoded and stored in short-term memory, how do people retrieve that information? Saul Sternberg carried out a classic series of experiments on the issue of retrieval from short-term memory. The phenomenon he studied is short-term memory scanning. In *memory scanning,* a retrieval task, you check the items contained in your short-term memory to see whether any of the items accomplishes a particular goal. For example, suppose that you were asked to remember these digits: 1, 7, 8, 5, 2, 6, 9. You might then be asked to scan your memory to determine whether the digit 6 was in the list of digits you were asked to remember.

Saul Sternberg and other psychologists wondered whether we retrieve items all at once, using *parallel processing,* or one by one, using **serial processing.** If we retrieve the items serially (one by one), the question then arises, do we use *exhaustive serial processing,* always retrieving all of the items? Or instead, do we use *self-terminating serial processing,* stopping retrieval of items as soon as an item seems to accomplish our goal? If we use exhaustive serial processing, we retrieve the wanted item only after checking all of the items in short-term memory. If we use self-terminating serial processing, we stop retrieval as soon as we find a suitable item that accomplishes our goal. As a result of his research, Sternberg (1966, 1969) concluded that exhaustive serial processing is probably the method used for retrieval from short-term memory. To return to the example, if you were given the digits 1, 7, 8, 5, 2, 6, 9, you would scan your memory of all the digits, one by one. After you had scanned all seven digits, you would determine that one of the digits was indeed 6. Although there have been other interpretations of Sternberg's data (see, e.g. Townsend, 1971), Sternberg's interpretation is still probably the most widely accepted.

Retrieval From Long-Term Memory

If we cannot retrieve particular information from short-term memory, we can infer that the information is no longer present in short-term memory.

decay • the forgetting of unused stored information due to the passage of time

serial processing • information processing in which operations occur sequentially

We cannot reach similar inferences regarding long-term memory. That is, information may still be stored in long-term memory even if we find it difficult, or impossible, to retrieve the information. Psychologists distinguish between *availability* of information (whether information is permanently stored in long-term memory) and *accessibility* of information (the degree to which we can gain access to stored information). What helps us, and what hinders us as we try to gain access to information stored in long-term memory?

What we can retrieve from memory depends on what we know and how we organize what we know. Our existing knowledge and schemas provide an internal context that affects memory retrieval. Because adults have greater knowledge and more elaborate schemas than children do, adults have more diverse internal contexts for retrieving information than children have. Diversity and richness of context may offer one reason why adults generally perform better on memory tests than children do.

Even our moods and our states of consciousness may provide an internal context for encoding and retrieving information. That is, we may more readily retrieve information that we encode during a particular mood or state of consciousness when we are in the same state again (Baddeley, 1993; Bower, 1983). For example, some (e.g., Baddeley, 1989) have suggested that memory processes may play a role in maintaining depression: Persons who feel depressed may more readily retrieve memories of previous sad experiences, which may further prolong the depression. If this vicious cycle can somehow be stopped from continuing, the person may begin to feel happier. This happier mood will then lead to retrieval of happier memories, thus leading to further relief from the depression, and so on. Perhaps the folk wisdom to "think happy thoughts" is not entirely unfounded.

Other aspects of consciousness and mood also affect memory. For example, when people encode information while under the influence of alcohol or other drugs, they can often more readily retrieve that information when in the same state again. Thus, a person who feels anxious as a result of the psychoactive effects of stimulants may more easily retrieve anxiety-related memories, which may lead to further feelings of anxiety.

External contexts also may affect our ability to recall information. We appear to be better able to recall information when we are in the same context as the one in which we learned the material. In one experiment, 16 underwater divers were asked to learn a list of 40 unrelated words, either while they were on shore or while they were 20 feet beneath the sea (Godden & Baddeley, 1975). Later, the divers were asked to recall the words either when in the same environment as where they had learned them, or in the other environment. Recall was better when it occurred in the same place as did the learning.

To summarize, internal contexts (such as schemas and moods) and external contexts (such as locations and situations) affect recall. Each of the preceding context effects involves a match between what is encoded and what is recalled. Many other experiments confirm that the way in which items are encoded powerfully influences how and how well the items are retrieved. Endel Tulving and Donald Thomson (1973) have termed the relationship between encoding and retrieval, **encoding specificity:** What is recalled depends on what is encoded.

Another influence on recall of information is the degree to which the information is organized into mental categories. In general, better organization leads to easier recall. Some tasks requiring recall do not lend themselves to the use of categories, however. In such situations, people often

Even infants show the effects of context on memory: When given an opportunity to kick a mobile in the same context in which they first learned to kick it (e.g., the patterned crib bumper shown here) or in a different context (e.g., a crib bumper with a different pattern), the infants kicked more strongly when in the same context (Butler & Rovee-Collier, 1989).

encoding specificity • the phenomenon by which the retrieval of information depends on the form of representation of the information during encoding

According to Endel Tulving and Donald Thomson (1973), we can retrieve information from memory more readily when the context for encoding closely matches the context for retrieval. Given the notion of encoding specificity, which of these students will more readily retrieve the information they are now encoding, when the need arises: the student in a simulated air traffic control center (left) who is responding to realistic situations, or the student in this language laboratory (right) who is parroting back phrases from a predetermined dialogue?

WELL, FOR CRYING-OUT LOUD! AL TOWBRIDGE! WHAT IS IT, NINE YEARS, SEVEN MONTHS, AND TWELVE DAYS SINCE I LAST RAN INTO YOU? TEN-THIRTY-TWO A.M., A SATURDAY, FELCHER'S HARDWARE STORE. YOU WERE BUYING SEALER FOR YOUR BLACKTOP DRIVEWAY. TELL ME, AL, HOW DID THAT SEALER WORK? DID IT HOLD UP?

MR. TOTAL RECALL

Drawing by W. Miller. Copyright © 1987 The New Yorker Magazine, Inc.

reconstructive memory • the phenomenon by which people encode, store, and retrieve only the sensations and events they have experienced

constructive memory • the phenomenon by which people build stored memories, based on existing schemas, sensations, experiences, and other stored information

make up their own memory cues for recalling information. These self-generated cues can be quite effective. For example, Timo Mantyla (1986) found that when people made up their own retrieval cues they were able to remember, almost without errors, lists of 500 and even 600 words. People thereby help construct their own memories.

HOW DO WE CONSTRUCT OUR OWN MEMORY?

We more readily recall meaningful than meaningless information, and sometimes we even create the meaning that we later recall. During consolidation, we integrate new information into what we already know, and new information sometimes even changes existing information that is still being consolidated. Hence, memory is not just **reconstructive** (based only on actual events and experiences); it is also **constructive** (based also on expectations, existing schemas, and even information gained after memory consolidation begins; see Figure 6.5). The influence of existing schemas was shown in the Bransford and Johnson (1972) study mentioned earlier: Participants could remember a passage quite well once they realized that the passage fit their existing schemas about washing clothes. Before then, however, they had trouble remembering or understanding the passage.

Some cross-cultural work (Tripathi, 1979) shows how schemas may serve as a mental framework for constructive memory. For example, Indian children were asked to read several stories from *The Panchatantra*, a collection of ancient Hindi fables and folktales. The stories contain unusual names and settings that seem strange to contemporary Indian schoolchildren. After hearing these stories, the children were asked to recall the stories. Over time, the children added words and sentences not originally presented in the stories. In general, their reconstructions changed the stories from unfamiliar to more familiar forms, as well as from complex to

(a)   (b)

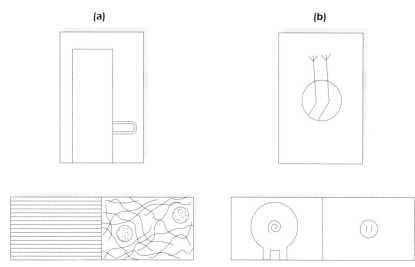

FIGURE 6.5
Droodles

Droodles are nonsense pictures that can be given funny interpretations. (a) Quickly glance at the droodles on the left: The top droodle depicts "a [very short person] playing a trombone in a telephone booth," and the bottom droodle depicts "uncooked spaghetti, then cooked spaghetti and meatballs." Now, look away and draw the droodles. (b) Quickly glance at the unlabeled droodles on the right, then look away and draw the sets of droodles. If you are like the research participants studied by Gordon Bower, Martin Karlin, and Alvin Dueck (1975), you will have found it easier to recall the droodles that were labeled (giving you a schema for the droodles) than the droodles that were not labeled. (In this demonstration, order of looking may affect recall. By the way, the labels for the droodles on the right are printed upside-down here.)

The top droodle depicts "an early bird who caught a very strong worm," and the bottom droodle depicts the "rear end of a pig disappearing into a fog bank, and his nose coming out the other side of the fog."

more simple forms. Decades before the Indian study, Frederic Bartlett (1932) had found similar results when he studied the effects of schemas on recall in British students who read a passage of text from a native North American legend, the full text of which you will now read again in Finding Your Way 6.1.

FINDING YOUR WAY

6.3

Stop for a moment, and jot down everything you remember about Bartlett's "War of the Ghosts." Now, flip back to Finding Your Way 6.1 and compare what you recalled with what the legend actually described. Bartlett found that British readers had trouble recalling this traditional North American legend. They frequently distorted their recall in ways that fit with their own existing schemas. How easily were you able to recall the information in Bartlett's passage? How did your existing schemas affect your recall?

When Simon Rodia built the Watts Towers in East Los Angeles (c. 1921–1954) he assembled it from fragments of realistic objects (such as the broken plates and cups shown here), according to his own preexisting ideas. Similarly, we construct our memories from fragments of realistic events according to our own preexisting schemas.

Some of the strongest evidence for the constructive nature of memory recall has come from studies on eyewitness testimony. In one such study, Elizabeth Loftus, David Miller, and Helen Burns (1978) showed participants a series of 30 slides, in which a red Datsun appeared to go down a street, stop at a stop sign, turn right, and then knock down a pedestrian who was crossing at a crosswalk. As soon as the participants finished seeing the slides, they had to answer 20 questions about the accident. One of the questions contained information that was either consistent or inconsistent with what they had been shown. Half of the participants were asked: "Did another car pass the red Datsun while it was stopped at the stop sign?" This question was consistent with what they saw. The other half of the participants received the same question, except that the word *yield* replaced the word *stop*. For the second group of participants, the information in the question was inconsistent with what they had seen.

Later, after a different activity, all participants were shown the two slides and were asked which they had seen. One slide showed a stop sign, the other a yield sign. Accuracy on this task was 34% better for participants who had received the consistent (stop sign) question than for participants who had received the inconsistent (yield sign) question. This experiment and many others (e.g., Loftus, 1975, 1977; described in Loftus & Doyle, 1992) have shown how easily eyewitness accounts can become distorted. We can easily be led to construct a memory that differs from what we really observed (see Figure 6.6).

Loftus (e.g., Loftus & Ketcham, 1991; Loftus, Miller, & Burns, 1987) has been instrumental in pointing to the potential problems of wrongful

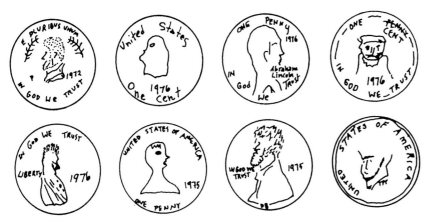

FIGURE 6.6
What's Wrong With This Picture?
Eight different American adults drew these eight depictions of the U.S. penny (Nickerson & Adams, 1979). Can you tell what is right or wrong about each one? Clearly, many people have trouble recollecting the appearance of an object as common as the penny. Given this difficulty, how easily can people recall the appearance of a person whom they see only briefly, during a time of great psychological stress, such as during eyewitness observation of a crime?

By the way, in case you're penny-less but curious, the drawing with the most accurate features is the far left one on the bottom row.

conviction when eyewitness testimony is used as the sole or even the primary basis for convicting people accused of crimes. Further, she has noted that eyewitness testimony is often a strong determinant of whether a jury will convict an accused person. The effect is particularly pronounced if eyewitnesses appear to be highly confident of their testimony, even if the eyewitnesses can provide few perceptual details or offer apparently conflicting responses. John Brigham, Roy Malpass, and others (e.g., Bothwell, Brigham, & Malpass, 1989; Brigham & Malpass, 1985; P. Shapiro & Penrod, 1986) have pointed out that eyewitness identification is particularly suspect when witnesses identify persons of a race other than their own. Astonishingly, even infants seem to be influenced by postevent information when recalling an experience, as shown through their behavior in operant-conditioning experiments (Rovee-Collier, Borza, Adler, & Boller, 1993).

Branching Out
**EYEWITNESS TESTIMONY—
WHAT IS YOUR JUDGMENT?**

In 1986, Timothy was convicted of brutally murdering a mother and her two young daughters (Dolan, 1995). For committing this gruesome crime he was sentenced to die, and for 2 years and 4 months Timothy lived on death row. Although the physical evidence did not point to Timothy, eyewitness testimony placed him near the scene of the crime at the time of the murder. Subsequently, it was discovered that a man who looked like
(CONTINUED)

Branching Out   (CONTINUED)

Timothy was a frequent visitor to the neighborhood of the murder victims, and Timothy was given a second trial. After Timothy's family spent more than $100,000 on legal fees, Timothy was acquitted. Although Timothy is now deeply in debt, he was lucky to be able to return to his wife and child and to his job in the U.S. Army.

A survey of U.S. prosecutors estimated that about 77,000 suspects are arrested each year, based primarily on eyewitness identification (Dolan, 1995). Studies of more than 1,000 known wrongful convictions have pointed to errors in eyewitness identification as being "the single largest factor leading to these false convictions" (Wells, 1993, p. 554). What proportion of eyewitness identifications are mistaken? The answer to that question varies widely ("from as low as a few percent to greater than 90%"; Wells, 1993, p. 554), but even the most conservative estimates of this proportion suggest frightening possibilities. Clearly, there are tragic consequences for the falsely convicted, but another outcome of wrongful conviction is that the police stop searching for the true criminal, who is then free to continue committing further crimes.

Steps can be taken to enhance eyewitness identification (e.g., using methods to reduce potential biases, to reduce the pressure to choose a suspect from a limited set of options, and to ensure that each member of an array of suspects fits the description given by the eyewitness, yet offers diversity in other ways; described in Wells, 1993). In addition, some psychologists (e.g., Loftus, 1993a, 1993b) and many defense attorneys feel that jurors should be advised that the degree to which the eyewitness feels confident of her or his identification does not necessarily correspond to the degree to which the eyewitness is actually accurate in her or his identification of the defendant as being the culprit. On the other hand, some psychologists (e.g., Egeth, 1993; Yuille, 1993) and many prosecutors feel that the existing evidence, based largely on simulated eyewitness studies rather than on actual eyewitness accounts, is not strong enough to risk attacking the credibility of eyewitness testimony when such testimony might send a true criminal to prison, thereby preventing the person from committing further crimes. Still others (e.g., Bekerian, 1993; described also in LaFraniere, 1992) suggest that there are no typical eyewitnesses, and conclusions based on an average case should not necessarily be applied to all other cases.

Suppose that you were a juror in a case of murder, for which the defendant would be sentenced to death or to life in prison if convicted. How would you weigh eyewitness testimony in such a case? How would your views change if you were not a juror, but rather the family member or close friend of the defendant? What about if you were a close friend of the victim of the crime?

Not everyone views eyewitness testimony with such skepticism, however (e.g., see Zaragoza, McCloskey, & Jamis, 1987). Judith McKenna, Molly Treadway, and Michael McCloskey (1992) have argued that psychologists need to know a great deal more about the circumstances that impair eyewitness testimony before opposing such testimony before a jury. At present, the verdict on eyewitness testimony is still not in. Children's

(a)

(b)

(a) Witnesses to accidents often forget crucial details or misremember what they saw. (b) Although the accuracy of eyewitness identification may be questionable in various cases, prosecutors note that jurors find eyewitness testimony very convincing: "Everybody in the jury box looks at the witness, looks at the finger and follows the line right to the defendant, and just about every defendant squirms," said former federal prosecutor John Shepard Wiley Jr. (cited in Dolan, 1995, p. A1).

recollections are particularly susceptible to distortion, especially when the children are asked leading questions, as in a courtroom setting. Stephen Ceci and Maggie Bruck (1993, 1995) have reviewed the literature on children's eyewitness testimony and come to a number of conclusions. First, the younger the child, the less reliable the testimony. In particular, children of preschool age are much more susceptible to suggestive questioning that tries to steer them to a certain response than are children of school age or adults. Second, when a questioner is coercive or seems to want a particular answer, children can be quite susceptible to providing the adult what he or she seems to want to hear. Given the pressures involved in court cases, such forms of questioning may be unfortunately prevalent. Third, children may believe that they recall observing things that others said they observed. In other words, they hear a story about something that took place, and then believe that they have observed what allegedly took place. Perhaps even more than eyewitness testimony from adults, the testimony of children must be interpreted with great caution.

Future studies of memory will help us to understand memory better than we do now. Although we still have much to learn, we have already learned a great deal.

Many of the suggestions for enhancing your memory involve the use of language and thought. We depend on language and thought in order to meaningfully encode, store, and retrieve information. On the other hand, we cannot think or use language without depending on our memory. Now that we have probed the workings of memory, we are ready to examine the processes of language and thought, discussed in the next chapter.

The Solution to The Case of the Cram Man

After reading chapter 6 of *Pathways to Psychology,* José realized that his method of studying for exams constituted *massed learning,* a form of practice that is relatively ineffective in studying or otherwise learning material. If he wanted to improve his performance on the exams, José realized, he would have to switch to *distributed learning,* which would not necessarily involve more time studying, but would involve distributing the time over several days rather than just putting in all the study time the night before. Although José wanted to improve his grades, he was not eager to disrupt his active social life.

José knew the solution but he chose not to follow it. We do have free will and knowing what will help us achieve our goals does not mean we will follow through on what we know. José continued to cram and continued to receive low grades. He graduated, just barely, but then was unable to gain admission to law school. José decided to retake some of the classes he bombed and then to reapply to law school the subsequent year. He was accepted the following year at the law school of his choice.

Summary

How Do Psychologists Study Memory?   194

1. *Memory* (a *hypothetical construct*) is the means by which we use our knowledge gained from past experiences in handling our present experiences.

2. Severe loss of memory is referred to as *amnesia. Anterograde amnesia* refers to difficulty in purposefully remembering facts about events that occurred after the loss of memory function (i.e., in anterograde amnesia, people seem to forget facts *before* they have a chance to store the facts), whereas *retrograde amnesia* refers to severe difficulty in purposefully remembering facts about events that occurred before the loss of memory function (i.e., in retrograde amnesia, people seem to forget information, going *backward* from the time of the trauma).

3. *Mnemonists* rely on special techniques, such as imagery, for greatly improving their memory; anyone can use these techniques.

4. *Mnemonic devices* (e.g., categorical clustering, in-

teractive imagery, acronyms, and acrostics) are used to improve memory recall.

5. Two of the main kinds of tasks used for studying memory are *recall,* in which a person is asked to produce items from memory, and *recognition,* in which a person must indicate whether presented items have been observed previously.

6. In addition to recall and recognition tasks, which involve *explicit memory* (participants are asked to recall information intentionally), memory researchers study *implicit memory* (in which participants show that they are using information stored in memory without necessarily trying to do so or even realizing that they are doing so). Psychologists also study *procedural knowledge* ("knowing how"; skills, such as how to ride a bicycle) and *declarative knowledge* ("knowing that"; factual information, such as the meanings of terms in a psychology textbook).

How Have Psychologists Traditionally Viewed Memory?   201

7. Memory is often viewed as involving three stores: (a) *sensory memory,* capable of holding up to about nine images in memory for fractions of a second; (b) *short-term memory,* capable of holding about five to nine items of information for a minute or two; and (c) *long-term memory,* capable of storing large amounts of information almost indefinitely.

8. Three operations that occur in all three kinds of memory are (a) *encoding,* by which information is placed into memory storage; (b) *storage,* by which information is kept in storage; and (c) *retrieval,* by which information is pulled from memory into consciousness.

9. The *iconic store* refers to visual sensory memory.

10. We often organize lengthy or complex information into smaller and simpler *chunks,* which we can remember more easily.

11. Some theorists distinguish between (a) *semantic memory,* our memory for facts that are not tied to any particular previous experiences, and (b) *episodic memory,* our memory for events that are tied to particular previous experiences. Semantic memory operates on *concepts,* organized in the form of *schemas.*

What Are Some Alternative Ways to View Memory?   206

12. From one perspective, *working memory* usually is defined as being part of long-term memory, and it also includes short-term memory. Working memory holds only the most recently activated portions of long-term memory, and it moves these activated elements, via *parallel processing,* into and out of short-term memory.

13. The *levels-of-processing framework* suggests that memory involves a continuum of successively deeper levels at which information can be processed.

14. According to Squire's taxonomy, there are several kinds of memory: declarative (including semantic and episodic memory) and nondeclarative (including procedural memory, conditioning, habituation and some other simple forms of memory, and *priming,* in which information in memory becomes activated by stimuli).

15. Although researchers have yet to identify particular locations for particular memories, they have been able to learn a great deal about the specific structures of the brain that are involved in memory (e.g., the hippocampus, the cortex, and the basal ganglia). In addition, researchers are studying microscopic physiological processes involved in memory, such as the role of some specific neurotransmitters (e.g., serotonin and acetylcholine) and hormones.

How Is Information Encoded, Stored, and Retrieved?   210

16. Encoding of information in short-term memory appears to be largely based on sounds.

17. Information in long-term memory is encoded primarily in a *semantic* form, based on the meanings of words.

18. Theorists disagree as to whether all information in long-term memory is encoded in terms of underlying meanings or whether some information is also encoded in terms of *images* (mental pictures).

19. How we *rehearse* information influences how well we keep it in memory. When we use elaborative rehearsal, connecting new information to what we already know, we are better able to remember the new information.

20. Using *metacognition,* we think about our thinking and how to use strategies to improve it. Through metamemory, we use strategies to influence our memory processes.

21. People tend to remember better when they use *distributed learning* (learning that is spaced over time), rather than *massed learning* (learning that occurs within a short period of time). This spacing effect may occur as a result of the process of *consolidation,* by which we gradually integrate new information into long-term memory.

22. Two of the main theories of forgetting are (a) *interference theory,* in which information is forgotten when new information replaces the information that was to be remembered; and (b) *decay theory,* in which information is lost over time.

23. Information retrieval from short-term memory appears to be handled through *serial processing* (each item in short-term memory is processed one at a time) that is exhaustive (all items in short-term memory are checked before the desired item is retrieved).

24. According to *encoding specificity,* how information is encoded at the time of learning will greatly affect how it is later recalled. The context of encoding and the organization of information also influence encoding and later retrieval of information.

How Do We Construct Our Own Memory?   218

25. Memory appears to be not only *reconstructive* (a reproduction of what was learned), but also *constructive* (influenced by existing expectations and schemas).

Choose the best answer to complete each sentence.

1. Ellen was in a car crash and subsequently had difficulty recalling events that occurred prior to the crash. She is showing signs of
   (a) retrograde amnesia.
   (b) anterograde amnesia.
   (c) automotive amnesia.
   (d) concussive amnesia.

2. Implicit memory differs from explicit memory in that
   (a) implicit memory involves conscious awareness of memory retrieval, whereas explicit memory does not.
   (b) explicit memory involves conscious awareness of memory retrieval, whereas implicit memory does not.
   (c) explicit memory is primarily procedural, whereas implicit memory is primarily declarative.
   (d) explicit memory involves a deeper level of processing.

3. The short-term store
   (a) encodes primarily visual information.
   (b) holds information for just a few days at a time.
   (c) holds information for about 2 minutes or less.
   (d) registers discrete visual images for fractions of a second.

4. Metamemory refers to
   (a) the ability to increase your long-term memory capacity through extensive training.
   (b) memories of experiences that occurred prior to the age of 4 years.
   (c) individuals' understanding of and control over their own memories.
   (d) a reserve source for memory enhancement.

5. Which of the following is *not* one of the ways in which interference affects short-term memory?
   (a) New information makes it more difficult to remember previously learned information.
   (b) Old information makes it more difficult to remember new information.
   (c) What you have already memorized makes it more difficult to memorize new information.
   (d) Information decays through time and subsequent learning.

6. Researchers studying long-term memory have suggested that information is encoded in three of the following ways. Which of the following is *not* one of the ways in which information is encoded in long-term memory?
   (a) in underlying meanings
   (b) in words
   (c) in images
   (d) in completely accurate reconstructions of events

7. Memories for personally experienced events with associated time tags are referred to as
   (a) episodic.
   (b) semantic.
   (c) reconstructive.
   (d) schematic.

8. Which of the following does *not* influence the ease of recall of information from long-term memory?
   (a) what a person already knows
   (b) the person's mood or state of consciousness (e.g., influence of drugs)
   (c) the environmental context in which the person is recalling the information
   (d) the use of retroactive-interference strategies

9. Studies of eyewitness testimony by Elizabeth Loftus have shown that
   (a) the accuracy of participants' recall of events is, on average, about 95%.
   (b) participants' memories are influenced by prior experiences, which shape their recall of events.
   (c) if research participants are given certain retrieval cues, particularly while under the influence of hypnosis, they will reproduce events with extraordinary detail.
   (d) visual memories have high permanence and are not easily manipulated by external probing.

10. Which of the following is *not* a primary reason that adults perform better on memory tasks than do 6-year-old children?
    (a) Adults know to use specialized strategies for remembering information.
    (b) Adults have much bigger brains than children do.
    (c) Adults simply know more and can therefore more easily integrate new information into what they already know.
    (d) Adults generally have much more elaborate schemas for organizing what they know than children do.

11. If you want to remember the contents of this chapter, you should probably
    (a) spread out your studying over many study sessions, across an extended period of time.
    (b) study as much as possible at one study session, instead of scattering your attention by spreading out your study sessions.
    (c) repeat the important information over and over as many times as possible, being careful to use exactly the same words, sequences, and methods for repeating the information each time.
    (d) avoid getting side-tracked by seeing how the information in the chapter relates to your own experiences and to what you already know.

Answer each of the following questions by filling in the blank with an appropriate word or phrase.

12. _____ _____ are used to aid in memory retrieval.
13. _____ is an effective way of maintaining information in short-term memory, perhaps even for eventual transfer to long-term memory.
14. _____ _____ is the term used by Tulving to describe the effects of a close match between the context of encoding and the context of retrieval.
15. An alternative to the three-stores view of memory suggests that there is not any particular number of memory stores, but rather that memory occurs at multiple _____ of _____.

Match the following descriptions to the type of memory being described:

16. primarily involves acoustic encoding
17. very briefly holds iconic images
18. primarily involves semantic encoding
19. holds an almost limitless number of items virtually indefinitely
20. involves consolidation of memories
21. generally holds information for up to 2 minutes

(a) long-term memory
(b) short-term memory
(c) sensory memory

Answers

1. a, 2. b, 3. c, 4. c, 5. d, 6. d, 7. a, 8. d, 9. b, 10. b, 11. a, 12. Mnemonic devices, 13. Rehearsal, 14. Encoding specificity, 15. levels, processing, 16. b, 17. c, 18. a, 19. a, 20. a, 21. b.

Pathways to Understanding

1. How might constructive memory processes help to support a person's prejudices? How might prejudices lead to greater distortions in constructive memory?

2. Suggest an experiment to show that memory is not just reconstructive, but also very much constructive.

3. How might you increase the likelihood that you would remember the meanings for the key terms in this or any other chapter?

The Case of **The Grumpy Gambler**

*D*oreen is short of money again. She makes more money at her new job but not enough to meet her expenses. Doreen has maxed out all her credit cards, and her debts are out of control. She always has considered herself lucky, but lately that has been her problem.

Precisely because she does consider herself lucky, Doreen has started visiting an upstate gambling casino in the hope that she can take what money she has and turn it into a lot more. The first time she went to the casino she actually came out well ahead, but since then things have not gone so well. She has been losing money steadily and had to go even more deeply into debt than she was when she started. She is worried that her negative attitude may be doing her in. The first time she went she had a positive, upbeat attitude and she won. The second time her attitude was positive, too, but things did not go quite so well and she lost some money. The third time she tried not to think about it, but doubts were gnawing away at her; and from that time on she has been steadily losing. When she arrives at the casino she tries to have a positive attitude, especially when she hears the bells of the slot machines ringing away as winners scoop up their earnings. But somehow she has not been able to repeat her early success. She knows that according to the laws of probability her luck has to change, but so far it has not, and the money is fast running out. Doreen is not sure of what to do, and her mood is turning very bad.

What should Doreen do? Think about this while you read chapter 7. Does Doreen properly understand the laws of probability; or is she following a pathway to poverty? Pay special attention to the notion of the gambler's fallacy.

CHAPTER 7
THOUGHT AND LANGUAGE

7

When we think, we process information in our minds. **Thinking** involves the creation and organization of mental images, statements, or underlying meanings of information. Generally, our meanings involve **language**, the use of an organized way of combining words in order to communicate. Nonetheless, it is entirely possible to think without using language. For example, if you were putting together a jigsaw puzzle, you might use some language as you thought about solving the puzzle (e.g., "Is this blue piece part of the sky or part of the water?") but you probably could put a puzzle together perfectly well without using language. Recall from chapter 6 that memories and thoughts may be represented in visual or other sensory images, or they may be represented in the form of language or underlying meanings. Later in this chapter, we focus specifically on how we think in terms of language, and we consider some of the ways in which language and thought interact. First, however, we focus on thinking.

Usually, when psychologists talk about thinking, they are talking about critical thinking. In **critical thinking,** we consciously direct our mental processes to reach particular goals, such as solving problems, making judgments or decisions, and reasoning. In everyday thinking, these three kinds of goals overlap somewhat. Nonetheless, the goal of thinking differs for each one. The goal of **problem solving** is to overcome obstacles (e.g., not having enough money to buy a car) in order to reach a solution: to find a pathway by which one can go from a statement of a problem to the formulation of a solution. Often, there are many pathways to solving a single problem. The goal of **judgment and decision making** is to evaluate various possibilities and to choose one or more of them (e.g., choosing the car that would please you the most for the amount of money you have to

When trying to find a suitable place to live, you may use three kinds of critical thinking: (a) problem solving (e.g., finding a way to get enough money together for moving expenses and for deposits and rent on an apartment); (b) reasoning (e.g., gathering information about various neighborhoods and apartment features to determine the likely amount you will have to pay to get the features you want in an area you like); and (c) decision making (choosing an apartment that best suits your needs for the amount of money you have available to spend).

spend). The goal of **reasoning** is to draw conclusions from evidence (e.g., infer the relative safety of a given model after reviewing the safety records of various cars). All of these processes may be used in a social context, such as when we make judgments about the effects of our actions on other people. Our prior beliefs and values may affect the kinds of judgments we make. First, we consider problem solving.

WHAT IS PROBLEM SOLVING?

Psychologists have noticed that the way in which we solve problems depends on whether we face **well-structured problems,** for which there is a clear path for finding a solution, or **ill-structured problems,** for which there is no obvious path to a solution. When we face well-structured problems (sometimes called "routine problems"), we usually can reach a solution by following an orderly series of steps.

You probably have extensive experience in solving countless well-structured problems. In school, you have tried to solve numerous problems in specific content areas (e.g., math, history, geography). These problems had clear, if not necessarily easy, paths to their solutions. For example, you can probably see a clear path for solving each of the following problems: "What is 98,453,179,305 divided by 413,253,763?"; "How did scientific, medical, and technological advances influence the outcome of the Civil War?"; "How does the climate and topography of India influence Indian agriculture?" Although you may not know the answers to these questions off the top of your head, you can use paths for solving these problems that are similar to paths you have used in problem solving before.

When solving ill-structured problems (sometimes called "insight problems"), on the other hand, we may have no idea of how to find a solution. We may struggle with the problem for a long time, feeling that we are getting no closer to a solution, when the solution suddenly becomes clear to us. Once we see a solution, we may consider it so simple and so obvious that we cannot believe that we did not see it before. To get an idea of how difficult it is to see a path for solving an ill-structured problem, find an answer to the following problem (after M. Gardner, 1978, cited in Weisberg, 1995), for which the solution will be given later.

7.1

The Schneeville Wolverines won the championship basketball game 72–49, yet not one man on the team scored as much as a single point. How is that possible?

FINDING YOUR WAY

Well-Structured Problems: Heuristics and Algorithms

In solving the preceding ill-structured problem, either you will realize suddenly the correct answer or you will find it very difficult to see a path for solving the problem. In contrast, the paths for solving well-structured

---

thinking • a psychological function that involves the creation and organization of information in the mind

language • the use of an organized means of combining words in order to communicate

critical thinking • the conscious direction of mental processes toward representing and processing information, usually in order to find thoughtful solutions to problems, make judgments or decisions, or to reason

problem solving • a set of processes for which the goal is to overcome obstacles obstructing the path to a solution

judgment and decision making • cognitive processes by which an individual may evaluate various options and select the most suitable option from among various alternatives

reasoning • a set of cognitive processes by which an individual may infer a conclusion from an assortment of evidence or from statements of principles

well-structured problem • a problem with a well-defined path to a solution

ill-structured problem • a problem with no clear, obvious, readily available path to solution

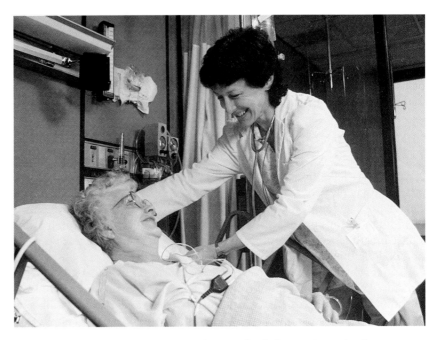

Computer programs, used as an aid to medical diagnosis, make frequent use of algorithms to carry out routine operations during problem solving. On the other hand, physicians and pathologists often use heuristics when trying to diagnose the source of a medical problem.

problems are generally clear, if not easy to follow. In fact, most well-structured problems can generally be solved using one of two kinds of strategies: heuristics or algorithms. **Heuristics** are informal strategies, often described as "rules of thumb," for solving problems. They can be seen as mental shortcuts, which sometimes work and sometimes do not. In fact, one heuristic strategy is simply trial and error, try whatever solution comes to mind and see whether it works; if it does not work, try something else. For example, in solving the history problem mentioned previously, you could look up various scientific, medical, and technical advances that occurred before the end of the Civil War and then check to see which ones may have influenced the outcome of the war.

In solving the long-division problem, you probably could try to find a more formal way of finding an answer, rather than just guessing at solutions and then checking to see whether they are correct. For this problem and many others, you might prefer to use **algorithms,** which are much more formal strategies than are heuristics. To use algorithms, you repeatedly follow a particular series of steps until you reach the correct solution. For example, to figure out a long-division problem, you repeatedly divide the digits of one number (the dividend) by another number (the divisor). Algorithms work quite well for solving some kinds of problems. In fact, if you can find an algorithm that applies to your problem, and you accurately carry out all the steps of the algorithm, you are virtually guaranteed to reach an accurate solution to the problem. Thus, algorithms can be slow in application, but they always reach a solution; heuristics generally are faster, but may not lead to a solution.

What are the pros and cons of using algorithms versus heuristics? If you can find the right algorithm and then follow it correctly, you will feel much more confident of reaching an accurate solution than you will if you

heuristics • the informal, speculative, shortcut strategies for solving problems, which sometimes work and sometimes do not

algorithm • the formal path for reaching a solution, which involves one or more successive processes that usually lead to an accurate answer to a question

use heuristics. On the other hand, heuristics generally apply to a wider variety of problems. Many problems that can be solved by using a heuristic have no obvious algorithm for reaching a solution. Can you think of an algorithm for figuring out how the climate and topography of India influence Indian agriculture? Probably not. Even if you could think of one, it would probably be so complicated and take so long to apply that you might give up before finding an answer. Some algorithms may be so complex and may take so long to carry out that it is just not practical to use them. For instance, an algorithm for cracking a safe would be to try all possible combinations of numbers; this is not a practical strategy for the safecracker in a hurry.

Before we move from well-structured problems to ill-structured ones, we should consider two complementary processes that greatly enhance our ability to see a path to the solution of a problem: **analysis,** in which we break down wholes into various parts, and **synthesis,** in which we put parts together into wholes. For example, to find a solution for a mechanical problem with a car, you would use analysis. Suppose that your car will not start. You would *analyze* (break down) the whole car-starting process into its various parts, then you would look for the origin of the problem in each of those parts. On the other hand, you probably would use synthesis to create a new type of sauce for pasta. You would take various ingredients (your parts) and combine them to make a delicious sauce (the whole).

Analysis and synthesis can also work together to serve various purposes. As any good mechanic knows, once you have broken down the problem, you must still put the car back together. As any good cook knows, if the sauce does not taste good, you must analyze the problem to figure out which ingredients or which steps in cooking led to the unpleasant taste.

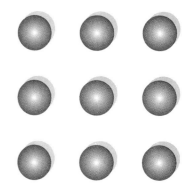

FIGURE 7.1
The Nine-Dot Problem
Pictured here are nine dots. Try to connect all nine dots with no more than four line segments. Do not lift your pencil off the page, do not go through a dot more than once, and do not use more than four straight-line segments. Can you connect the nine dots without ever taking your pencil off the page? (After R. J. Sternberg, 1986a)

Ill-Structured Problems: Insight

Some problems just do not lend themselves to either analysis or synthesis. Recall the earlier example, in which the Schneeville Wolverines won the game 72–49, but not one single man scored a single point. Were you able to figure out how that was possible? If you were, you probably did not follow a clear path to find the answer; instead, you realized the answer suddenly: The Schneeville Wolverines are all women. This problem is a good example of an ill-structured problem. Now that you have an idea of how puzzling ill-structured problems can be, stop for a minute and try to solve another ill-structured problem, shown in Figure 7.1 (R. J. Sternberg, 1986a).

Like other ill-structured problems, the nine-dot problem requires **insight:** In order to solve it, you need to see the problem in a new way—different from the way you would probably see the problem at first, and different from the way you would probably solve problems in general. You will not find a clever algorithm or even a handy heuristic for solving insight problems. When you have an insight, you form a new idea about a problem, which helps you to understand either the problem or a strategy for solving the problem. Frequently, insight leads you to see how to put together old and new information to come up with a solution. You are more likely to have an insight when solving ill-structured problems than when solving well-structured problems. Insights usually seem to be sudden. However, they often appear following a lot of thought and hard work, without which the insight would never have occurred (R. J. Sternberg & Davidson, 1995).

analysis • the process of breaking down a complex whole into smaller elements

synthesis • the process of integrating various elements into a more complex whole

insight • a seemingly sudden understanding of the nature of something, often as a result of taking a novel approach to the object of the insight

Insight problems have interested many psychologists, particularly Gestalt psychologists, for decades. According to Gestalt psychologists, insight problems require problem solvers to perceive the problems as wholes. Gestalt psychologist Max Wertheimer (1945/1959) observed that, to solve insight problems, you have to break away from the associations and information you already know, and you have to see the problems from a new outlook. For example, to solve the Wolverines problem, you had to break away from your expectations regarding arithmetic word problems to see the problem in a different way. It is for this reason that psychologists use problems like the Wolverines problem to measure people's ability to break away from their usual ways of thinking. People who more easily are able to break away from their traditional ways of thinking are more quickly or better able to solve problems like this one.

To Gestalt psychologist Wolfgang Köhler (1927), insight involves suddenly becoming aware of a whole strategy for solving a problem. To study the emergence of insight, Köhler observed how apes reacted to ill-structured problems. As you can see in Figure 7.2, Köhler's ape showed sudden insight by stacking a set of boxes to reach a luscious bunch of bananas. In other studies, Köhler's ape figured out how to connect two short sticks to make one long stick to reach bananas lying just outside the cage. In each case, the ape appeared to grapple with the problem for a while and then suddenly, in a flash of insight, to see a path to the solution.

More recently, Janet Metcalfe (1986; Metcalfe & Wiebe, 1987) has studied insight in humans and has found that people, too, show a distinctive pattern of insight during problem solving. In her experiments, she asked people to rate their own progress in solving routine (well-structured) problems and insight (ill-structured) problems. When solving routine problems, people perceive steady progress toward solving the problems. In contrast, when solving insight problems, they do not feel that they are making progress at all until moments before they solve the problems. Finding Your Way 7.2 enables you to try an insight problem for yourself.

FIGURE 7.2
Insightful Problem Solving
Wolfgang Köhler, a Gestalt psychologist, studied insight by observing problem solving in apes. In the study depicted here, he placed an ape in a cage with a few boxes. At the top of the cage, just out of reach, was a bunch of bananas. After trying to grab the bananas, the ape showed sudden insight: The ape realized that the boxes could be stacked on top of one another to make a structure tall enough to reach the bunch of bananas.

7.2

FINDING YOUR WAY

Try your own hand at solving one of the insight problems Metcalfe used (Metcalfe & Wiebe, 1987): "A prisoner was attempting to escape from a tower. He found in his cell a rope which was half long enough to permit him to reach the ground safely. He divided the rope in half and tied the two parts together and escaped. How could he have done this?" Record your own progress toward reaching the answer.

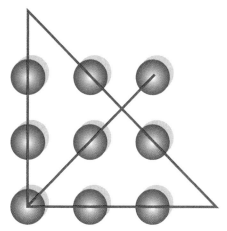

FIGURE 7.3
A Solution to the Nine-Dot Problem
Most people assume that the line segments must stay within the square that seems to be formed by the nine dots. Therefore, they do not allow their solution to go beyond the boundaries of the dots. The problem does not state this limitation. In fact, the problem cannot be solved if the four line segments must stay inside the dotted figure.

Now that you have an idea of how insight works in solving ill-structured problems, we return to the nine-dot problem. Did you have an insight when trying to solve that problem? Most people find the problem extremely hard to solve, and many very bright people never solve it. One common difficulty is a mistaken assumption. Figure 7.3 shows the solution to the nine-dot problem. Before you read the figure caption, can you guess the mistaken assumption that many people make?

As the solution to the nine-dot problem shows, many people make mistakes when defining the problems they face. Speaking of solutions and problem definitions, the solution to Metcalfe's rope problem is that the man divided the rope lengthwise, separating the strands into two parts, then using the two sets of strands to make the rope long enough. You may not have considered this solution because you defined "divided" as meaning that the rope had to be cut across its diameter. Such a cut would divide the rope into two segments, but not change the length of the rope. You might not have considered that the lengthwise strands of the rope could also be divided. Sometimes a misdefined problem can be hard, if not impossible, to solve. When solving problems, it helps to try to free ourselves of assumptions that can get in the way of solving the problems.

Hindrances to Problem Solving

Many insight problems are hard to solve because problem solvers tend to bring old mental sets to new problems. **Mental sets** are frames of mind in which we carry old ways of thinking to new situations, and in which the old ways do not fit the new situations. The old ways of thinking often involve methods for solving problems that may have worked for solving many problems in the past, but that do not work for solving the present problem. For example, in the nine-dot problem, many people use an old way of seeing the problem ("Stay within the dots"). They carry the old information from a situation where the information helped (e.g., when solving dot-to-dot problems) to a situation where it actually makes problem solving more difficult. The carryover of information that makes problem solving more difficult is termed **negative transfer**. (A related process, *positive transfer,* is discussed later.)

One type of mental set that leads to negative transfer involves fixation on a particular use (function) for an object: Specifically, **functional fixedness** is the inability to realize that something known to have a particular use may also be used for performing other functions. Functional fixedness prevents us from using old tools in novel ways to solve new problems. Becoming free of functional fixedness is what first allowed people to use a

mental set • a cognitive phenomenon in which an individual is predisposed to use an existing model for representing information, even when the existing model inadequately represents the information in a new situation

negative transfer • the hindrance of problem solving as a result of prior experience in solving apparently related or similar problems

functional fixedness • a mental set in which an individual fails to see an alternative use for something that previously has been known to have a particular use

reshaped coat hanger to get into a locked car, and it is what first allowed thieves to pick simple spring door locks with a credit card. It is also what might allow you to think of an introductory psychology textbook as a resource for criminal ideas.

Aids to Problem Solving

If mental sets and negative transfer make problem solving harder, what might make problem solving easier? Among other things, cognitive psychologists have noticed two positive influences on problem solving: positive transfer and incubation.

Positive Transfer

As you may have guessed, based on the meaning of negative transfer, **positive transfer** occurs when what you know about solving an old problem helps you to solve a new problem. Mary Gick and Keith Holyoak (1980, 1983) have studied positive transfer involving *analogies,* in which some similarities are observed between things that appear dissimilar in other ways. To do their work, they used the "radiation problem," a problem first studied by Karl Duncker (1945). Try the following problem.

7.3

Imagine that you are a doctor treating a patient with a cancerous stomach tumor. You cannot operate on the patient, but unless you destroy the tumor somehow, the patient will die. You could use X rays to destroy the tumor. If the X rays are strong enough, they will destroy the tumor. Unfortunately, the X rays that are strong enough to destroy the tumor will also destroy healthy cells of the body, and the X rays must pass through healthy cells to get to the tumor. X rays that are not strong enough, however, will not destroy the tumor. Your problem is to figure out how to destroy the tumor without also destroying the healthy cells surrounding the tumor.

What solutions would you suggest for solving this problem? Duncker had an insightful solution for this problem. This solution involves dispersion: Direct many weak X rays toward the tumor from different points outside the body (see Figure 7.4). No single X ray will be strong enough to destroy either the healthy tissue or the tumor. However, the rays will be aimed so that they will all *converge* (come together) on the tumor. This idea is used today in some X-ray treatments.

Before Gick and Holyoak showed Duncker's radiation problem to research participants, they presented another problem, called the "military problem" (after Holyoak, 1984, p. 205). This problem involved a somewhat similar convergence solution, applied to the capture of a fortress by way of various roads. The correspondence between the radiation and the military problems was quite close, although not perfect. The question is this: When participants were shown a convergence solution to the military problem, were they helped in solving the radiation problem? If research

positive transfer • the facilitation of problem solving as a result of prior experience in solving related or similar problems

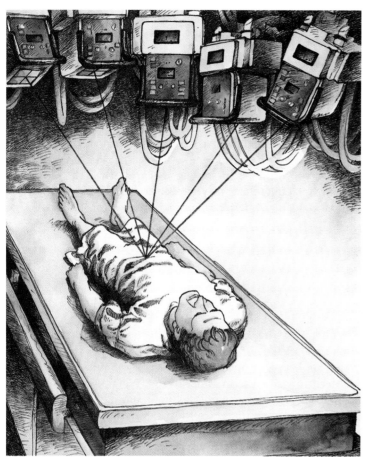

FIGURE 7.4
The X-Ray Problem
Karl Duncker's X-ray problem requires an insightful solution: Issue several weak X rays from different directions, which converge on a single point, in this case, the tumor. Duncker and other psychologists have studied whether insight into one problem involving convergence paves the way for positive transfer to other problems involving convergence. (After Duncker, 1945)

participants received the military problem with the convergence solution and then were given a hint to apply it in some way to the radiation problem, about 75% of the participants reached the correct solution to the radiation problem. In comparison, fewer than 10% of the research participants who did not first receive the military story reached the correct solution to the X-ray problem.

Incubation

Another aid to problem solving is incubation. In **incubation,** you simply put the problem aside for a while. For example, suppose that you find yourself unable to solve a problem, and none of the strategies you can think of seem to work. Try setting the problem aside for a while to incubate. During incubation, you do not consciously think about the problem. Still, you may be processing the solution to the problem subconsciously. Some cognitive psychologists even say that incubation is an essential stage of problem solving (e.g., Cattell, 1971; Helmholtz, 1896; Poincaré, 1913).

incubation • a period of rest, following a period of intensive effort in problem solving, during which the problem solver puts aside the problem for a while

Often incubation works well when you are trying to have an insight to the solution of a problem but the insight just seems to be escaping your conscious awareness.

Craig Kaplan and Janet Davidson (1989) have reviewed the literature on incubation and have found that the benefits of incubation can be enhanced in two ways: (a) Invest enough time in the problem initially; perhaps explore all aspects of the problem, and investigate several possible avenues of solving it. (b) Allow sufficient time for incubation to permit your old associations due to negative transfer to weaken somewhat. A drawback of incubation is that it takes time. If you have a deadline for the problem solution, you must begin solving the problem early enough to meet the deadline, including the time you need for incubation. The strategic use of incubation can be one characteristic of expert problem solvers.

Useful Heuristics

Several useful heuristics also can help you in your problem solving. Four such heuristics are forming subgoals, working backwards, searching for analogies, and modifying your representation of the problem.

In forming subgoals, you set a series of goals on the way to your final goal. When you have a difficult task in front of you, rather than trying to think about the whole task at once, you break it down into parts. For example, if you need to write a term paper on the topic of depression, you could have the term paper as a whole as your ultimate goal, and then break down the process of getting the term paper done into subgoals. The first subgoal might be narrowing down the topic. As you cannot write everything there is to know about depression, you need to decide what aspect or aspects of depression to consider. A second subgoal might be obtaining a reference list. A third subgoal might be drafting an outline. By forming subgoals, you take what might have seemed like an unmanageable task, or at least a difficult-to-manage task, and make it manageable.

In working backwards, you start at the end of the problem and try to go back to the beginning. For example, if you are asked to provide a geometric or algebraic theorem and find it very challenging, rather than starting at the beginning with the axioms (or assumptions) and working forward to the conclusion, you might start with the conclusion and work backward to the assumptions. Detectives use this heuristic all the time. They know the conclusion (e.g., the heiress was murdered). They then have to work backward to figure out who did it and why (e.g., the butler because he hoped to cash in on her fortune).

In searching for analogies, you ask whether the solution or solution path to a problem similar to the one you are trying to solve will help you solve your problem. For example, the detective may remember a similar case of a mysterious death and recall that in that case a butler had hoped to profit from the death of an heiress. Or in trying to deal with a problem in a relationship with a friend, you may remember a similar problem you had in the past that involved another friend and that you solved successfully. You may then choose to apply the solution you used there to the present problem.

In modifying your representation of the problem, you ask whether there is some other way of conceiving the problem, different from the one that you are using, that makes the problem easier to solve. For example, suppose you have been having serious problems with a girlfriend or boyfriend and keep trying to resolve these problems without success. You might ask whether the problem you should be solving is that of how to patch up your relationship, or whether it should be that of how to end the relationship and find another, better one.

Expertise: Knowledge and Problem Solving

Experts solve problems in their areas of expertise more readily than novices solve such problems. What can explain the benefits of expertise for problem solving? The research that launched the study of expertise was a study of chess experts and novices conducted by William Chase and Herbert Simon (1973). Chase and Simon found that chess experts were better able to recall positions of chess pieces on a chessboard, but only if the chess pieces were arranged in a way that they might be in an actual chess game. Chase and Simon therefore suggested that experts differed from novices in their amount and organization of knowledge. In the Chase and Simon study, the experts' knowledge of positions of pieces in chess games helped during the recall of positions from actual games.

Many psychologists, such as Michelene Chi and her colleagues, have studied large numbers of experts in various fields (e.g., see Chi, Glaser, & Farr, 1988). What most clearly separates experts from novices is that experts know more, and they can better organize what they know. For example, Jill Larkin and her colleagues compared experts with novices in physics. Because the experts knew more than the novices, the experts could more effectively represent physics problems in their minds (Larkin, McDermott, Simon, & Simon, 1980).

People in different cultures may have different notions of the kind of knowledge that is worthy of being considered as "expert" and what

Psychologists are not the only people interested in problem solving. In fact, one of the rare points about which almost all psychologists can agree is that all people face problems to be solved.

7.1

PROBLEM SOLVING ON THE JOB

A problem almost all of us face at one time or another is the need to find a job we enjoy, at which we feel both competent and useful. According to career consultants (described in V. M. Cooper, 1994), a good way for you to get a job is to think in terms of finding out the problems faced by potential employers and then to show how you can help them solve their problems. If you have good organizational skills, search for potential employers who need help with organizing large quantities of things or facts (e.g., parts distributors or libraries). If you know how to make strangers feel at ease, think about potential employers who need help in getting strangers to feel relaxed and comfortable (e.g., hospitals and lawyers' offices). Whatever your skills may be, the key to solving your problem of the need to find a job is to shift your perspective and to think of yourself as a problem solver who can put your talents to work in solving the problems faced by your potential employers.

If you enjoy solving problems of all kinds, you may even enjoy being an independent consultant or a corporate troubleshooter, helping companies to solve a variety of problems, from product development to manufacturing to marketing (described in Corcoran, 1993). Some companies even use problem solving as a strategy for fostering team spirit and company morale and for enhancing the collaboration and productivity among team members (described in K. Johnson, 1994). For example, in 1994, ITT Hartford Insurance Group tackled a community-wide problem, homelessness, by assigning 60 of its white-collar employees the task of painting 20 rooms in a homeless shelter within 7 hours (K. Johnson, 1994). Various participants in the project gave mixed reviews regarding how well this particular effort would affect their performance on the job, but most seemed to support the general idea of addressing community problems as a means of enhancing productivity and cooperation at work.

constitutes worthwhile expertise. For example, in research conducted in rural Kenya (R. J. Sternberg & Grigorenko, 1997b), it was found that healers who use natural herbal medicines, which the Kenyans believe cure illnesses, are considered valuable experts in a community. In certain Caribbean cultures, practitioners of voodoo might be considered valuable experts, whereas in other parts of the world they might be considered, correctly or incorrectly, to be outright frauds. We need to be careful, however, in applying our own standards to other cultures. In the West, we might consider a seasoned lawyer to be a valuable expert to consult. In rural Kenya, the expertise of that lawyer probably would be of no use at all.

To summarize this section, problem solving involves inventing or discovering strategies in order to overcome obstacles (see Putting It to Use 7.1). Another kind of thinking involves evaluating various possibilities and then choosing one, or several possibilities. The next section deals with how we make judgments and decisions.

WHAT ARE JUDGMENT AND DECISION MAKING?

What career should you choose? In what subject area should you major in college? What courses should you take? Whom should you choose as friends, as dates, as lifetime partners? Many of the decisions and judgments we make have long-term consequences. More often, in the course of our everyday lives, we make less-crucial judgments (e.g., "Which of my friends is the most reliable and supportive if I need help?") and decisions (e.g., "Which menu item do I want to eat now?").

Decision-Making Strategies

Just how do people make judgments and decisions? Early theorists, many of whom were economists rather than psychologists, assumed that decision makers operate in ideal circumstances and make ideal decisions. Since then, theorists have recognized that we humans may not make ideal decisions, although we often try to do so. More often than not, we make decisions based on personal preferences, biases, and mental shortcuts.

Leading the way in this realization was Herbert Simon (1957), who went on to win the Nobel Memorial Prize in Economic Science. Simon noted that we often show **bounded rationality:** We are rational, but within limits. Simon then described one of the most common decision-making strategies: satisficing. In **satisficing,** we *do not* first consider all possibilities and then carefully compute which one will give us the most gains, with the fewest losses. Instead, we consider various possibilities one by one, and we choose the first one that is satisfactory, that is just good enough. In this way, we satisfy our minimum requirements, but we do so by considering as few choices as we can. For example, you may use satisficing when considering research topics for a term project or paper. Of the countless possible topics, you probably consider quite a few, but then you may settle on the first satisfactory or even fairly good topic you think of, without continuing your search endlessly. Satisficing has advantages as well as disadvantages. Although it may not yield an optimal solution, it can save a great deal of time and still yield a satisfactory decision.

In the 1970s, Amos Tversky (1972a, 1972b) built on Simon's notion of bounded rationality and observed that we sometimes use a different strategy when we are faced with far more alternatives than we feel that we can reasonably consider in the time we have available. In such situations, we do not try to manipulate mentally all the important attributes of all the options available to us. Rather, we use a process of **elimination by aspects:** We focus on one aspect (attribute) of the various options, and we form a minimum criterion for that aspect. We then eliminate all options that do not meet that criterion. Then, for the remaining options, we select a second aspect for which we set a minimum criterion by which to eliminate additional options. We continue using a sequential process of elimination of options by considering a series of aspects, until eventually only a single option remains.

For example, in choosing a car to buy, we may focus on total price as an aspect, dismissing factors such as maintenance costs, insurance costs, or other factors that realistically might affect the money we will have to spend on the car in addition to the sale price. Once we have weeded out the alternatives that do not meet our criterion, we choose another aspect, set a criterion value, and weed out additional alternatives. We continue in

bounded rationality • the recognition that although humans are rational, there are limits to the degree to which they demonstrate rational cognitive processes across situations

satisficing • a decision-making strategy in which an individual chooses the first acceptable alternative that becomes available, without considering all possible alternative options

elimination by aspects • a decision-making strategy in which an individual focuses on one attribute of an overabundance of options, forms a minimum criterion for that attribute, and then eliminates all options that do not meet that criterion; the process is repeated until either a single option remains or few enough remain that a more careful selection process may be used

Whatever your age and experience, making a decision can be difficult. As much as possible, we may try to make ideal choices, but we frequently settle for using shortcut methods that make the selection process easier and less time consuming.

this way, weeding out more alternatives, one aspect at a time, until we are left with a single option. In practice, it appears that we may use some elements of elimination by aspects or satisficing to narrow the range of options to just a few; then we use more thorough and careful strategies for selecting among the few remaining options (Payne, 1976). You can improve your decision making in buying a car, or anything else, if you consider as many options as possible and carefully weigh all your considerations in the purchase.

Heuristics and Biases of Judgment

Amos Tversky was not content just to observe that we often make decisions based on less than optimal strategies. Adding insult to injury, Tversky and his associate Daniel Kahneman (1973) observed that we often use mental shortcuts and even biases that limit and sometimes distort our ability to make rational decisions. Tversky and Kahneman have studied several *heuristics* (mental shortcuts) and biases of decision making and other judgments.

Availability

One of the heuristics studied by Tversky and Kahneman is the availability heuristic. According to the **availability heuristic** (Tversky & Kahneman, 1973), people make judgments on the basis of how easily they can call to mind what they perceive as relevant instances of a phenomenon. In one study of this heuristic, Tversky and Kahneman (1973) asked people the following question: "Are there more words in the English language that begin with the letter *R*, or are there more words that have *R* as their third letter?" Most people could more easily think of words beginning with *R* than they

availability heuristic • a cognitive shortcut in which an individual makes judgments on the basis of how easily he or she can call to mind what are perceived as relevant instances of a given phenomenon

could of words having *R* as the third letter (Tversky & Kahneman, 1973), but there are actually more English words with *R* as the third letter.

Note that heuristics, such as availability, do not always lead to wrong judgments. Indeed, we use heuristics because they so often are right. For instance, one of the factors that makes particular events more available in our minds is that these events may occur more frequently. However, availability also may be influenced by how recently we observed the event, as well as how unusual, distinctive, or salient the particular event is for us. Because we generally make decisions in which the most common instances are the most relevant and valuable ones, the availability heuristic is often a convenient shortcut with few costs. However, when particular instances are better recalled because of biases (e.g., the media has sensationalized a particular event), the availability heuristic may lead to less than optimal decisions.

For example, suppose that someone were to ask you, "What is the likelihood that a former football star and likable actor would be accused of murdering his ex-wife?" You might well give a higher estimate now than you would have in 1990. In many situations, however, the answer that first comes to mind is correct because common answers are often more likely to be correct than are uncommon ones. Thus, availability can lead one to erroneous responses, but much of the time it can lead to correct responses.

Representativeness

Another heuristic studied by Tversky and Kahneman, the *representativeness heuristic,* is essentially a mental shortcut most of us use when we try to guess about the likelihoods of particular occurrences. For instance, suppose that you had been talking to someone while standing in line at a supermarket. This stranger said to you, "Did you see that big burly guy that just left? I know that he has rough hands and that he likes to watch sports on TV. One of the clerks told me that he's a lawyer, and someone else told me that he's a bus mechanic. Which one do you think he is?" In your opinion, which occupation is this person more likely to have? Why do you think this occupation is more likely to fit the description?

The stranger's description seems better to *represent* bus mechanics than to represent lawyers, so most people would answer that the burly man is a bus mechanic. That may seem like a good first guess, but it leaves out important information that should be considered: In general, there are more lawyers than there are bus mechanics. This information suggests that this person is more likely to be a lawyer than to be a bus mechanic, so "lawyer" might be a better guess. Thus, representativeness can lead to errors, but keep in mind that one reason people probably use the heuristic so often is that it leads them to correct answers much, and possibly most, of the time.

This last point shows that in order fully to understand the representativeness heuristic, you need to understand the concept of base rate, which is the prevalence of an event or characteristic within its population of events or characteristics. People often ignore base-rate information, even though it is important to effective judgment and decision making. In many occupations, the use of base-rate information and the representativeness heuristic are essential for adequate job performance. For example, if a doctor was told that a 10-year-old girl was suffering from chest pains, the doctor would be much less likely to worry about the risk of a heart attack than if told that a 50-year-old man had the identical symptoms. Why? Because the base rate of heart attacks is much higher in 50-year-old men than in 10-year-old girls. Of course, a risk any doctor or anyone else takes in such judgments is one of being overly confident and then proving to be wrong.

Overconfidence

Most of us occasionally fall prey to **overconfidence,** being overly trustful of personal skills, knowledge, or judgment. In one study (Fischhoff, Slovic, & Lichtenstein, 1977), people were given 200 two-choice statements. For example, choose the correct answer to complete this statement: "Absinthe is (a) a liqueur, (b) a precious stone." People were asked to choose the correct answer and to give the probability that their answer was correct. People were strangely overconfident. For example, when people were 100% confident of their answers, they were right only 80% of the time! (Absinthe is a liqueur.)

Anchoring and Adjustment

If you are going to give an oral presentation in class, would you rather follow someone whose oral presentation was wonderful or someone whose oral presentation was awful? Chances are that you would rather follow someone whose oral presentation was worse than you hope yours will be. The reason is that you look good in comparison, whereas if the last speaker was exceptionally good, you may look bad in comparison. Anchoring refers to the use of a baseline in evaluation to make further evaluative decisions. For example, you are more likely to like a so-so movie if recently you have seen a whole string of bad movies than if recently you have seen a whole string of good movies. In this case, as in the case of the oral presentations, the recent experiences serve to anchor evaluations of the new experiences. Anchoring becomes a bias when you make insufficient adjustment and are unduly influenced by your recent experience.

Gambler's Fallacy

Another common error is gambler's fallacy, an intuitive and fallacious inference that when a sequence of coincidental events appears to be occurring in a nonrandom pattern, subsequent events are more likely to deviate from the apparent pattern than to continue in the same apparent pattern. For example, someone might believe that if they have lost in the state lottery seven times, they are more likely to win on their eighth try because they have already lost seven times in a row.

Actually, the probability of each event continues to be the same at each occurrence. In other words, just by the nature of things, a person's luck does not necessarily change over time. It may or may not. No matter how many times you gamble, the probability of your winning the next time is the same, assuming a fair game. For example, slot machines are adjusted to yield winnings a certain proportion of the time. Over the long run, all slot machines with the same adjustment will perform the same. If you lose money at one particular slot machine, you are no more likely to start winning at that slot machine now, nor at any other slot machine, for that matter.

overconfidence • a bias affecting decision making, in which individuals overestimate the probability that their own responses are accurate or even more broadly overvalue their own skills, knowledge, or judgment

Branching Out

DECISION MAKING
AND RISK ASSESSMENT

"More than 30% of regular smokers will die from some diseases connected to their habit, losing an average of 8.3 years from normal life expectancy" (Specter, 1989, p. A20). Surprisingly, however, many smokers have a greater fear of dying in a plane crash, dying of AIDS, or dying from some other cause that is much less likely because these less probable outcomes are nonetheless more readily available in their minds.

The consequences of decision making extend through all aspects of our lives, at every age, but the decisions we make early in life often have more long-term consequences than the decisions we make later on. "Adolescents are the only age group in which mortality has risen since 1960. Three-quarters of adolescent deaths are caused by accidents, homicide and suicide, all of which indicate a lethal propensity for risk-taking" (Goleman, 1987, p. 13 [N]). One reason that many adolescents seem to engage in risky behavior is that they do not understand how to evaluate the probabilities associated with a given risk. For example, if a particular teen couple engages in unprotected sexual behavior, and pregnancy or sexually transmitted diseases do not result from a first encounter, they may actually believe that because they beat the odds the first time, the cumulative probability of these outcomes goes *down*, rather than *up*, for each subsequent unprotected sexual encounter.

Some psychologists (e.g., Elkind, 1967) have suggested that many adolescents irrationally believe that they are *invincible:* The dangerous situations that bother, injure, or even kill other persons will not harm them. Perhaps the invincibility fallacy is one reason for adolescents' false belief that when they take more chances, their risks go down rather than up: Each time they beat the odds, their belief in their own invincibility is strengthened.

Another reason for risk-taking among adolescents may be their tendency to grossly under- or overestimate the number of their peers who engage in particular behaviors. For instance, although only 15% of 10- to 14-year-olds reported occasionally smoking, adolescents guessed that almost 80% of 10- to 14-year-olds occasionally smoke (described in Goleman, 1987). Yet another consideration simply may be that adolescents give differing emphasis to particular risks than adults would give to these risks. For example, most adults would give far more weight to the risk of death, disease, or unwanted pregnancy than to the risk of social rejection; many adolescents, however, would not do so.

On the other hand, adults are not entirely rational in their assessment of risk either. For example, the risk of contracting AIDS from a dentist who has the disease is between 1 in 263,000 and 1 in 2,600,000 (J. Scott, 1991). Nonetheless, many adults who think nothing of driving a car to work each day (thereby facing much greater odds of confronting death) will shun an AIDS-infected dentist, even if the dentist wears protective gear and rigorously follows sterile techniques. Similarly, many adults grossly overestimate the health risks associated with artificial sweeteners, traces of pesticides remaining on fruits and vegetables, occasional medical or dental X rays (Specter, 1989), and immunizations.

Much of the work on judgment and decision making has focused on the mistakes people make. As Jonathan Cohen (1981) has pointed out, however, people do act rationally much of the time, even though they do not act rationally all of the time.

WHAT IS REASONING?

As this chapter has shown, people often make decisions and other judgments based on very informal methods. *Reasoning* involves a more formal process, in which we draw conclusions based on evidence (Johnson-Laird, 1999; Wason & Johnson-Laird, 1972). Reasoning is often classified as either deductive or inductive. **Deductive reasoning** is the process of drawing conclusions based on one or more general statements regarding what is known; through deductive reasoning, we can reach a logically certain conclusion, which usually involves a specific application of the general statements. In contrast, **inductive reasoning** proceeds from specific facts or observations in order to reach a probable general conclusion that may explain the facts. Inductive reasoning cannot lead to a logically certain conclusion, it can lead only to a particularly well-founded or likely conclusion. Thus, inductive reasoning proceeds from specifics to an uncertain but probable general conclusion, but deductive reasoning proceeds from a set of general premises to a specific and logically certain conclusion.

For example, given the statements "If Joan is a college student, then Joan can read; Joan is a college student," we can deduce with certainty, "Therefore, Joan can read." Of course, the truthfulness of the statements influences the accuracy of the deductive inference. Nonetheless, this conclusion is unequivocally certain, given that we accept the initial statements as being true. In contrast, when given a set of observations, such as "Every person we've seen carrying books is able to read; Jim is carrying books," we can induce a probable conclusion, such as "Jim can probably read." An inductive conclusion is probable, but it is not certain. (For instance, Jim might be illiterate and carrying the books for someone else.)

Deductive Reasoning

Deductive reasoning is based on *logical propositions,* which are assertions that may be either true or false. For example, you can judge for yourself whether the following propositions are true or false: "All politicians are dishonest"; "Some students like peanut butter"; "No students are illiterate." Each isolated proposition states what already is believed to be true. What intrigues psychologists (and other people) is that when you relate two or more propositions through deductive reasoning, you can infer new information that was not stated in the propositions. For example, "If all politicians are dishonest, and John is a politician, then John is dishonest"; "If some students like peanut butter, and no students are illiterate, and Joaquim is a student, then Joaquim is not illiterate." (We cannot infer that Joaquim likes peanut butter because only some students like it.) Thus, by making inferences from a set of general premises stating what is known, deductive reasoners can reach a specific new conclusion.

Inductive Reasoning

Suppose that you are not given a neat set of logical propositions from which you can draw a conclusion. Instead, you are given a set of observations. For example, suppose that you notice that all the cars you have observed run on gasoline fuel. From these observations, you might inductively reason that all cars run on gasoline fuel. However, unless you can observe all the cars that ever have existed or ever will exist, you will be unable to prove your conclusion. Even one car that ran on a fuel other than

deductive reasoning • a set of processes by which an individual tries to draw a logically certain and specific conclusion from a set of general propositions

inductive reasoning • a set of processes by which an individual attempts to reach a probable general conclusion, based on a set of specific facts or observations

gasoline would disprove your conclusion. Still, after you made many observations, you might conclude that you could draw a reasonable inductive inference.

In the preceding situation, and in many other situations requiring reasoning, we are not given clear premises from which to deduce a surefire conclusion. In these types of situations, we simply cannot deduce logically valid conclusions. An alternative kind of reasoning is needed. Inductive reasoning involves gathering specific facts or observations to infer a general conclusion that may explain the facts. For example, when Jessica Fletcher (of the TV show *Murder, She Wrote*) uses inductive reasoning to solve crimes, she gathers clues (many specific observations) and develops a general idea about what probably happened at the scene of a crime.

Scientific research is based on inductive reasoning. A key feature of this method is that we cannot reasonably leap from saying, "All observed instances of X are Y," to saying, "Therefore, all X are Y." For example, suppose that a child has seen many different kinds of birds flying in the sky. She may reasonably conclude, "All birds fly." However, when she visits the zoo and meets penguins and ostriches for the first time, she sees that her inductive conclusion is false. She finds that her inductive conclusion, based on many observations, can be disproved by just one observation that differs from her conclusion.

Furthermore, inductively based conclusions can never be proved, regardless of how many observations are made or how well-reasoned the conclusions are. Such conclusions can only be supported, to a greater or lesser degree, by what is known at the time. Thus, inductive reasoners must state any conclusions about a hypothesis in terms of likelihoods, such as "There is a good chance of rain tomorrow," or "There is a 99% probability that these findings are not a result of random events."

Thus far, in this chapter, we have focused on various kinds of thinking. Throughout this discussion, we have alluded to processes that involve our use of language, but we have not addressed the ways in which language and thought interact. Psychologists have long recognized that thought and language interact, and Russian psychologist Lev Vygotsky (1934/1962) wrote an entire book devoted to this topic. In discussing language separately from thought, it is as if we were discussing various aspects of how

Weather prediction is based on gathering a large quantity of data and then inductively inferring the likelihood of particular weather patterns, given the current conditions. As the people on the right have discovered, inductive reasoning does not lead to 100% certain conclusions.

fish swim without mentioning the watery environment in which fish do so. Many psychologists believe that language and thought are so thoroughly intertwined that it is difficult to separate them, even in a chapter dedicated to understanding language and thought as distinct phenomena. The language we hear and read shapes our thoughts, and our thoughts shape what we say and write. Hence, if we are to understand thinking, we must know more about language, a point made by Vygotsky in his book, aptly entitled, *Thought and Language*.

WHAT IS LANGUAGE?

It is difficult to imagine how we might be able to think without using *language*, an organized way of combining words in order to communicate. It is not impossible to think without using language, however. As was mentioned in chapter 6, we may be able to represent information in the forms of images and of abstract underlying codes that may be viewed as a sort of "mentalese" for representing the meanings underlying our thoughts (Pinker, 1994).

Essentially, there are two fundamental aspects of using language to communicate: (a) understanding the language we hear (or see signed) and read, and (b) speaking (or signing) and writing. Psycholinguists often describe these two aspects as (a) **verbal comprehension,** the ability to understand written and spoken (or signed) language, such as words, sentences, and paragraphs; and (b) **verbal fluency,** the ability to produce language.

The great diversity of languages around the world all serve these fundamental communicative functions. Surprisingly, however, many people believe that their own language is somehow better than other languages. Although this belief is quite popular, no evidence supports the notion that any language is meaningfully better than any other language. Based on observations of countless languages, psychologists, *psycholinguists* (who study the interaction of language and thought), *linguists* (who study language), and anthropologists have observed that all languages seem to have the following six general properties (e.g., R. Brown, 1965; Clark & Clark, 1977; Glucksberg & Danks, 1975): Language is

1. *Communicative.* Language lets us communicate with one or more persons who share our language.
2. *Arbitrary.* Language creates an arbitrary (not based on any meaningful pattern) relationship between a symbol (such as a word) and whatever the symbol represents—an idea, a thing, a process, a relationship, a characteristic, or a description.
3. *Productive.* Although language users must stick to the general patterns of a given language, they can produce their own original and new combinations of words; in fact, the possibilities for creating new combinations are virtually limitless.
4. *Dynamic.* Languages constantly change.
5. *Meaningfully structured.* Language has a structure; only particular patterns of symbols have meaning. Different arrangements lead to different meanings.
6. *Multiply structured.* Language can be analyzed at more than one level (e.g., sounds, words, and sentences).

verbal comprehension • the ability to comprehend written and spoken (or signed) linguistic input, such as words, sentences, and paragraphs

verbal fluency • the ability to produce written and spoken linguistic output, such as words, sentences, and paragraphs

linguistics • the study of language structure and change

The ability to analyze language at more than one level has made the science of **linguistics,** the study of language structure and change, quite

Sounds and gestures can be used to communicate without language. However, both spoken and signed languages involve far more complexity than simple communication. For instance, both spoken English and American Sign Language (ASL) have all the properties of any other language: They involve arbitrary symbols; they are communicative, productive, dynamic, and meaningfully structured; and they can be analyzed at more than one level.

complex. For starters, language may be analyzed in terms of sounds, words, phrases, sentences, and even larger units of language such as conversations, stories, or discussions in textbooks. At the level of sounds, the smallest distinguishable unit of all possible human speech sounds is the *phone,* of which there are more than 100. No known language uses all of the possible phones, however. Each language uses only some of these possibilities; the particular speech sounds that the users of a particular language can identify are *phonemes*. In English, phonemes are generally identifiable as vowel or consonant sounds.

For example, in English, the difference between the /p/ and the /b/ sound is an important phonemic distinction. We hear a difference between "they bit the buns from the bin" and "they pit the puns from the pin" (a meaningless sentence). On the other hand, we ignore the differences between some phones. (Figure 7.5, a diagram of a human vocal tract, shows where and how some phones, human speech sounds, are produced.) Try an activity that shows how sounds that may seem to be the same actually differ:

7.4

FINDING YOUR WAY

Put your open hand about 1 inch (about $2\frac{1}{2}$ cm) from your lips. Now, use your normal speech, without trying to add any sounds you do not normally pronounce, and say aloud, "Put the paper cup to your lip." If you are like most English speakers, you felt a tiny puff of air when you pronounced the /p/ in Put and paper and no puffs of air when you pronounced the /p/ in cup and lip.

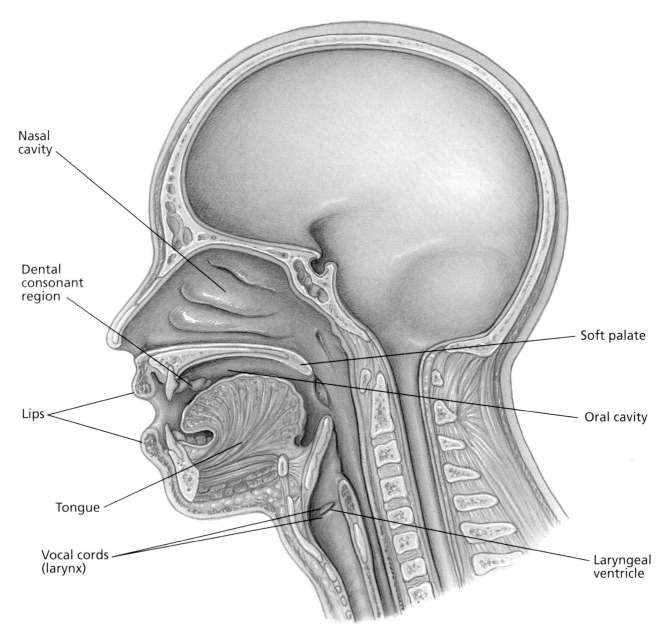

FIGURE 7.5
The Human Vocal Tract
The human vocal tract enables us to produce the various phonemes (speech sounds), many of which other animals cannot produce.

morpheme • the smallest unit of single or combined sounds denoting meaning within a given language

lexicon • the entire set of morphemes in a given language or in a given person's linguistic repertoire

One or more phonemes can become a **morpheme,** the smallest unit of individual or combined phonemes (sounds) that gives meaning within a particular language. You may already know two forms of morphemes: (a) *root words,* to which we add (b) *affixes*—both *suffixes,* which follow the root word, and *prefixes,* which come before the root word. The word *affixes* itself comprises (a) the root word *fix;* (b) the prefix *af-,* which is a variant of the prefix *ad-,* meaning "toward," "to," or "near"; and (c) the suffix *-es,* which indicates the plural form of a noun.

Linguists use the term **lexicon** to describe the entire set of morphemes in a given language or in a given person's vocabulary. The average English-speaking high school graduate has a lexicon of about 60,000 root morphemes, and most college students have lexicons about twice that large (G. A. Miller, 1990).

The next level of analysis is **syntax,** which refers to the way in which users of a particular language put words together into sentences. A sentence has at least two parts: (a) a *noun phrase,* which contains at least one noun (usually the subject of the sentence), and (b) a *verb phrase,* which contains at least one verb and whatever the verb acts on. The verb phrase states something about the subject, usually an action or a characteristic of the subject. Linguists consider the study of syntax to be basic to understanding the structure of language.

The final level of linguistic analysis is **discourse,** which encompasses language use at the level beyond the sentence, such as in conversation, in paragraphs, in stories, and in textbooks. When linguists analyze discourse, they consider many features of the social context in which language occurs. Table 7.1 summarizes these aspects of language. Next, we discuss how people learn to use language.

FINDING YOUR WAY

7.5

Write a paragraph, or choose one in this book, containing at least three sentences. Using this paragraph, find an example for each level of linguistic analysis shown in Table 7.1.

syntax • a level of linguistic analysis, which centers on the patterns by which users of a particular language put words together at the level of the sentence

discourse • the most comprehensive level of linguistic analysis, which encompasses language use at the level beyond the sentence, such as in conversation, in paragraphs, and so on

TABLE 7.1
Summary of a Description of Language

Language input			Language output
↓ D e c o d i n g ↓	*Phonemes* (distinctive subset of all possible phones)	. . . /t/ + /ā/ + /k/ + /s/ . . .	↑ g n i d o c n E ↑
	Morphemes (from the distinctive lexicon of morphemes)	. . . take (content morpheme) + s (plural function morpheme) . . .	
	Words (from the distinctive vocabulary of words)	It + takes + a + heap + of + sense + to + write + good + nonsense.	

	Phrases
	    Noun phrases (NP: a noun and its
	    descriptors)
	    Verb phrases (VP: a verb and
	    whatever it acts on)
		NP = It
		    +
		VP = takes a heap of sense to write good nonsense.	

	Sentences (based on the language's syntax—syntactical structure)	It takes a heap of sense to write good nonsense.	
	Discourse	"It takes a heap of sense to write good nonsense," was first written by Mark Twain (Lederer, 1991, p. 131).	
Comprehend language			Produce language

"No, Jimmy, it's not 'I sawed a chair'—it's 'I have seen a chair' or 'I saw a chair'."

Copyright © Glenn Bernhardt

cooing • an oral expression that explores the production of all the phones that humans can possibly produce

babbling • a prelinguistic preferential production of only those distinct phonemes characteristic of the language being acquired

overextension error • an overapplication of the meaning of a given word to more things, ideas, and situations than is appropriate for the word; usually made by children or other persons acquiring a language

telegraphic speech • the rudimentary syntactical communications of two or more words, which are characteristic of very early language acquisition, and which seem more like telegrams than like conversation because function morphemes are usually omitted

HOW DO WE ACQUIRE LANGUAGE?

Around the world, people seem to *acquire* their first language in just about the same way. As revolutionary linguist Noam Chomsky (1959) hypothesized, and numerous cross-cultural and naturalistic studies have suggested, humans may have an innate *language-acquisition device (LAD)*, which helps people to acquire language. Within the first years of life, we start out listening and responding to language, and then we become able to produce the language ourselves.

Before birth, fetuses may be sensitive to the sounds spoken by their mothers, as shown by their responses to her voice immediately after birth (DeCasper & Fifer, 1980; DeCasper & Spence, 1986). After birth, newborns seem to move rhythmically in response to the speech of their caregivers (Field, 1978; J. A. Martin, 1981; Schaffer, 1977; Snow, 1977; D. Stern, 1977). The emotional expressions of infants also respond to and match those of their caregivers (Fogel, 1992). Although crying may be the most obvious sound produced by infants, linguists are more interested in their **cooing.** When infants coo, they try making all the possible phones that humans can make. The cooing of infants around the world, including that of deaf infants, is about the same for all babies and all languages.

As infants progress to the babbling stage, they gradually become unable to tell the differences among all phones, and deaf infants generally stop making playful sounds. When infants are **babbling,** they start producing and perceiving only the phonemes of their own language. Thus, although the cooing of infants around the world is pretty much the same, infant babbling is different for different languages.

Eventually, the child's first wondrous word is spoken (or signed), followed shortly by 1 or 2 more words, and so on, until by age 18 months, children typically have vocabularies of 3 to 100 words (Siegler, 1991), most of which are nouns that identify familiar objects. Because young children's vocabulary cannot yet communicate all they wish to say, children often overextend the meanings of the words they know to cover things and ideas for which they do not yet have distinct words. This overly broad use of a few words to cover many concepts is an **overextension error.** For example, the general term for any man may be "Dada," which can be quite upsetting to a new father in a public place.

Gradually, by about 2½ years of age, children begin to combine single words to produce two-word phrases. At this time, they begin to understand syntax. These early phrases seem more like telegrams than like conversations: The articles, prepositions, and so on, are usually left out. Hence, linguists refer to these early phrases as **telegraphic speech.** In fact, telegraphic speech can be used to describe three-word phrases and even slightly longer ones if the phrases include only nouns or verbs, leaving out prepositions, articles, conjunctions, and so on. Vocabulary grows rapidly, more than tripling from about 300 words at about 2 years of age to about 1,000 words at about 3 years of age. Almost incredibly, by age 4, children learn the basics of adult syntax and language structure. By age 5, most children can also understand and produce quite complex and uncommon sentence constructions, and by age 10, children's language is basically the same as that of adults.

Lev Vygotsky (1934/1962) had further insights about the development of speech. He pointed out that at about 3 to 4 years of age, children begin to differentiate between the speech they direct toward themselves (e.g., when playing alone) and the speech they direct toward others (e.g., when talking to a parent). Eventually, inner-directed speech becomes internal and silent; it becomes thought.

In general, there seem to be critical periods for acquiring language—times of rapid development, during which a particular ability must be developed if it is to ever develop adequately. Perhaps the greatest support for this comes from studies of adult users of American Sign Language (ASL). Among adults who have signed ASL for 30 years or more, researchers could discernibly differentiate among those who acquired ASL before age 4, between ages 4 and 6, and after age 12. Despite 30 years of signing, those who acquired ASL later in childhood showed less profound understanding of the distinctive syntax of ASL (Meier, 1991; Newport, 1990). Studies of linguistically isolated children seem to provide additional support for the notion of the interaction of both physiological maturation and environmental support. Of the rare children who have been linguistically isolated, those who are rescued at younger ages seem to acquire more sophisticated language structures than do those who are rescued when they are older.

HOW DO WE UNDERSTAND AND ARRANGE WORDS?

Semantics: The Study of Meaning

One way to analyze the structure of language is through **semantics,** the study of the meanings of words. Linguistic meanings can take two forms: (a) The strict, dictionary definition of a word is its **denotation;** and (b) the emotional overtones and other less well-defined meanings of a word are its **connotations.** For example, when you look up "good" in the dictionary, you see many meanings for the word. In addition, when you use "good" in conversation, you may suggest many shades of meaning that are not listed in the dictionary.

In addition to understanding words based on dictionary meanings of words, we may also come to understand the meanings of words based on typical examples that represent these words. For instance, when we hear the word *bird,* we base our understanding of the word on typical examples of birds, such as robins or sparrows, rather than on unusual instances, such as vultures, penguins, or ostriches.

Psychologists learn a lot about how we figure out the meanings of words through the study of semantics. Language involves more than just word meanings, however. We also need to understand another aspect of language in order to understand what we hear and read. For example, the word *read* may be used to describe present or past actions. (I *read* now, and I *read* yesterday.) The word *run* can be used as a noun (e.g., home *run*) or as a verb (e.g., *run* home). To figure out the meanings of some words, we must understand syntax.

semantics • the study of the meanings of words in language

denotation • the strict dictionary definition of a word

connotation • an emotional overtone, presupposition, or other nonexplicit meaning of a word

grammar • the study of language in terms of regular patterns that relate to the functions and relationships of words in a sentence, extending as broadly as the level of discourse and as narrowly as the pronunciation and meaning of individual words

Syntax: The Study of Structure

Syntax is the systematic way in which words can be put together in a particular order to make meaningful phrases and sentences (D. W. Carroll, 1986). The meaning of a sentence depends not only on the meanings of the words in the sentence, but also on how those words are put together. Syntax begins with the study of the grammar of phrases and sentences.

Most English teachers use the word *grammar* to refer to how people *should* structure their sentences. In contrast, psycholinguists use **grammar**

PUTTING IT TO USE

7.2

TAKE MY DISK, MAKE ME A HARD COPY, AND XEROX IT FOR ME!

Many people find it impossible to graciously welcome changes in a language's syntax, and many people consider such changes hard to put up with. For example, most contemporary grammar books now say that it is okay to split an infinitive (e.g., "to graciously welcome") or to end a sentence with a preposition (e.g., "to put up with"). However, many people still find these usages distressing.

The same people who resist syntactical changes in language, however, often welcome new words into the lexicon. For example, who among us does not recognize the verb "to xerox" (first entered the lexicon in 1965), the noun "hard copy" (first entered in 1954), and the use of the noun "disk" as meaning a flat magnetic medium for storing computer data (first entered in 1972)? What new words have entered your lexicon recently? (Many additional examples are described in Levine, 1993, and Roark, 1992; also, *Merriam-Webster's Collegiate Dictionary* [10th edition] lists the years when many words entered the American English lexicon.)

to mean the study of the regular patterns of language. Although these patterns relate to the uses and relationships of words in a sentence, they also extend to larger and smaller units of language (such as whole conversations and the pronunciation of individual words). Your English teachers may have taught you *prescriptive grammar,* which prescribes the "correct" ways in which to pattern your use of language. Psycholinguists study *descriptive grammar,* which describes the existing patterns in the language that you use. In particular, linguists are interested in syntax.

To assure yourself that you are, indeed, highly proficient in using English syntax, try the following activity.

FINDING YOUR WAY

7.6

Using the following 10 words, create (a) five strings of words that make grammatical sentences and (b) five sequences of words that violate the syntax rules of English grammar: ball, hoop, rolled, into, put, round, bounced, big, the, girl.

Linguists have found that every known language in the world has a grammatical syntax. No one has ever discovered a human language that has no grammatical structure. Similarly, variations of some languages may have differing grammatical structures. For example, some variations of English have a grammar that differs from the grammar of standard English. These various grammars fulfill the purposes of grammar about equally well; they just do so in different ways. For example, in the United States, it is common to use a singular verb with a collective noun. People would say, "The group is here." In some places, however, the acceptable grammatical form is the plural form of the verb, yielding, "The group are here."

Many psycholinguists believe that even the combined study of syntax and semantics does not fully explain our use of language. According to these psycholinguists, to understand language, we must also study language in a social context.

HOW DO WE USE LANGUAGE IN A SOCIAL CONTEXT?

In recent decades, linguists have become increasingly interested in pragmatics and sociolinguistics. **Pragmatics** is the study of how people use language to communicate, sometimes effectively and sometimes not. More specifically, *sociolinguistics* is the study of how people use language in the context of social interaction. Sociolinguists study how people use language to tell others about themselves. Some sociolinguists even study how people use nonverbal (wordless) communication in conversational contexts. For example, when you use language in conversations, you use gestures and *vocal inflections* (the natural rise and fall in the pitch of your voice).

During job interviews, and perhaps first dates, you may be painfully aware of how you use nonverbal and verbal communication in context. Under most circumstances, however, you change how you use language to fit your context without giving these changes much thought. For example, imagine yourself in the following situations.

FINDING YOUR WAY | **7.7**

Suppose that you and your friend are going to meet right after work. Suppose also that something comes up, so you must call your friend to change the time or place for your meeting. When you call your friend at work, your friend's supervisor answers and offers to take a message. Exactly what will you say to your friend's supervisor, to ensure that your friend will know about the change in time or location? Suppose, instead, that the 4-year-old son of your friend's supervisor answered. Exactly what would you say in this situation? Finally, suppose that your friend answered directly. How would you have changed your language to suit each context? Note that you would have made these changes even though your purpose in all three contexts was the same.

Conversational Postulates

In speaking to each other, we implicitly set up a cooperative enterprise. Indeed, if we do not cooperate with each other when we speak, we often end up talking past rather than to each other, and we do not communicate what we intended. H. P. Grice (1967) has proposed that conversations thrive on the basis of a **cooperative principle**, whereby people seek to communicate in ways that make it easy for the listener to understand what a

pragmatics • the study of how people use language, emphasizing the contexts in which language is used

cooperative principle • the principle of conversation in which it is held that people seek to communicate in ways that make it easy for a listener to understand what a speaker means

TABLE 7.2

Conversational Postulates

In order to maximize the communication that occurs during conversation, speakers generally follow four maxims.

Postulate	Maxim	Example
Maxim of quantity	Make your contribution to a conversation as informative as required, but no more informative than is appropriate.	If someone asks you the temperature outside, and you reply, "It's 31.297868086298 degrees out there," you are violating the maxim of quantity because you are giving more information than was probably wanted.
Maxim of quality	Your contribution to a conversation should be truthful; you are expected to say what you believe to be the case.	Clearly, there are awkward circumstances in which each of us is unsure of just how much honesty is being requested, such as for the response to "Honey, how do I look?" Under most circumstances however, communication depends on an assumption that both parties to the communication are being truthful.
Maxim of relation	You should make your contributions to a conversation relevant to the aims of the conversation.	Almost any large meeting I attend seems to have someone who violates this maxim. This person inevitably goes into long digressions that have nothing to do with the purpose of the meeting and that hold up the meeting. "That reminds me of a story a friend once told me about a meeting he once attended, where . . . "
Maxim of manner	You should try to avoid obscure expressions, vague utterances, and purposeful obfuscation of your point.	Nobel Prize–winning physicist Richard Feynman (1985) described how he once read a paper by a well-known sociologist, and he found that he could not make heads or tails of it. One sentence went something like this: "The individual member of the social community often receives information via visual, symbolic channels" (p. 281). Feynman concluded, in essence, that the sociologist was violating the maxim of manner when Feynman realized that the sentence meant, "People read."

speaker means. According to Grice, successful conversations follow four maxims: the *maxim of quantity*, the *maxim of quality*, the *maxim of relation*, and the *maxim of manner* (described in Table 7.2). Basically, the maxim of quantity states that you say what is required by a conversation but no more. The maxim of quality states that what you say is true. The maxim of relation states that your contributions to a conversation should be relevant. Finally, the maxim of manner states that your contributions to a conversation should be stated clearly.

Linguistic Relativity and Linguistic Universals

Different languages use different lexicons and different patterns of syntax. These differences often relate to differences in the environments in which the languages developed. For example, in terms of lexicon, the Garo of Burma distinguish among many different kinds of rice, which is understandable, because they are a rice-growing culture. Clearly, the Garo have more words for rice than do most other people. The question is this: As a result of these linguistic differences, do the Garo think about rice differently than other people do?

Does the bedouin think about sand differently than other people do? If so, do these cognitive differences influence language or do linguistic differences lead to differences in thinking?

Although some linguists say that language differences do not relate to differences in thinking, others disagree. Many linguists believe in the hypothesis of **linguistic relativity,** which states that the speakers of different languages have differing *cognitive systems* (systems for thinking). In turn, these different cognitive systems influence how people think. According to the linguistic-relativity view, the Garo think about rice differently than do other people. For example, when the Garo think about rice, they may think about it in more complex ways than may persons who have only a few words for rice. Thus, according to the linguistic-relativity view, language shapes thought, at least to some extent. The linguistic-relativity hypothesis is sometimes referred to as the *Sapir–Whorf hypothesis,* named after the two people (Edward Sapir and Benjamin Lee Whorf) who first defended it. The Sapir–Whorf hypothesis has been one of the most widely mentioned ideas in all of the social and behavioral sciences (Lonner, 1989).

Perhaps because of its widespread acceptance, however, some people have distorted the interpretation of this hypothesis. Even some of the facts that are believed to support the hypothesis have been found false. For example, many social scientists have said that Eskimos have a huge number of words for the single English word *snow.* These social scientists have been wrong. Anthropologist Laura Martin (1986) has firmly stated that Eskimos do *not* have numerous words for snow. Martin understands why her colleagues might think the snow-word myth charming, but she has been quite "disappointed in the reaction of her colleagues when she pointed out the fallacy; most, she says, took the position that true or not 'it's still a great example'" (J. Adler, 1991, p. 63; described also in Pullum, 1991).

Based on Martin's findings, we can see that it is very hard to find accurate, unbiased information about cultures other than our own. Therefore, we should be careful when drawing conclusions based on cross-cultural studies of language. Sometimes, cross-cultural research distorts both the data and the conclusions, overemphasizing cultural differences.

linguistic relativity • a proposition regarding the relationship between thought and language, which asserts that the speakers of different languages have differing cognitive systems, based on the languages they use, and that these different cognitive systems influence the ways in which people speaking the various languages think about the world

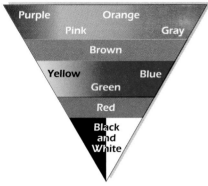

FIGURE 7.6
A Color Hierarchy
Brent Berlin and Paul Kay (1969) found some linguistic universals regarding color naming. Many languages use a set of 11 color names: black, white, red, yellow, green, blue, brown, purple, pink, orange, and gray. When only some of the color names are used, the naming of colors falls into a hierarchy of five levels, as shown here: (1) black, white; (2) red; (3) yellow, green, blue; (4) brown; and (5) purple, pink, orange, gray. Thus, if a language names only two colors, they will be black and white. If it names three colors, they will be black, white, and red. A fourth color will be taken from the set of yellow, green, and blue, and so on until all 11 colors have been labeled.

linguistic universals • the characteristic patterns of language that apply across all the languages of various cultures

bilingual • a person who can speak two languages

One way to offset an overemphasis of cultural differences is to study cultural similarities. Some cross-cultural research has focused on **linguistic universals,** the characteristic patterns that seem to be true of all languages. One area of research has examined the use of color names. At first glance, color words seem to be an ideal focus of research because people in every culture can be expected to be exposed to about the same range of colors.

Although the color ranges people see are about the same, different languages name colors quite differently. Does this finding mean that there are no linguistic universals? No. It appears that there is a systematic pattern for naming colors across languages, even though the system is used somewhat differently in different languages. Two anthropologists (Berlin & Kay, 1969; Kay, 1975) found what seem to be two linguistic universals about color naming across languages. First, all of the languages surveyed took their basic color terms from a set of just 11 color names: black, white, red, yellow, green, blue, brown, purple, pink, orange, and gray. Languages ranged from using all 11 color names, as in English, to using just 2 of the names, as in New Guinean Dani. Second, when only some of the color names are used, the naming of colors falls into a hierarchy of five levels, as shown in Figure 7.6.

Bilingualism

Cross-cultural research offers one way to study the interactions among language, thought, and social context. Another way is to study **bilinguals,** people who can speak two languages. If a person can speak and think in two languages, does the person think differently in each language? In fact, do bilinguals think differently from *monolinguals,* people who can speak only one language? What differences, if any, arise from being able to speak two languages instead of just one?

Some bilinguals seem to benefit from knowing two languages well, but other bilinguals suffer when they try to master a second language before they have a firm grasp of their first language. In particular, persons who are highly skilled in each language profit from having more than one language (Hakuta, 1986). However, bilinguals suffer ill effects if they are less skilled in their first language, and the second language partially replaces the first.

James Cummins (1976) has suggested that we note a difference between additive and subtractive bilingualism. In *additive bilingualism,* a second language is taught in addition to a relatively well-developed first language. In *subtractive bilingualism,* parts of a second language replace parts of the first language. Cummins believes that the additive form improves people's ability to think. However, the subtractive form harms people's ability to think. In particular, individuals may need to have reached a relatively high level of skill in both languages for bilingualism to improve people's thinking.

Ellen Bialystok and Kenji Hakuta (1994) have found that there probably is no one best way for acquiring a second language. Rather, the kinds of learning experiences that facilitate second-language acquisition should match the context and uses for the second language once it is acquired. For example, the language-acquisition experiences needed by an 8-year-old immigrant who wants to play with nonimmigrant school- and playmates differ from those of a 38-year-old American businesswoman who wants to conduct business in Japan.

In a 1992 poll of U.S. citizens of Hispanic descent (Mexican, Puerto Rican, and Cuban), 90% asserted that all residents and citizens of the United States should learn to speak English (Duke, 1992). This task is often more readily accomplished by children of immigrants than by adult immigrants. Frequently, children born of adult immigrants are fully bilingual, acquiring native fluency in their parents' language, as well as native (or native-like) fluency in the language of their new country. Sadly, subsequent generations of immigrants all too often fail to become fluent in languages other than English.

ARE HUMANS THE ONLY SPECIES TO USE LANGUAGE?

The philosopher René Descartes suggested that language is what qualitatively distinguishes human beings from other species. Using the definitions and qualities of language described in this chapter, we can consider whether Descartes was correct.

Primates, especially chimpanzees, offer our most promising insights into nonhuman language. Perhaps the most internationally well-known investigator of chimpanzees in the wild has been Jane Goodall. She has studied many aspects of chimp behavior, including chimps' vocalizations, many of which she considers to be clearly communicative, although not necessarily indicative of full language. For example, chimps have a specific cry indicating that they are about to be attacked and another vocalization calling together their fellow chimps. Nonetheless, their repertoire of communicative vocalizations seems to be small, nonproductive (new utterances are not produced), limited in structure, lacking in multiplicity of structure, and relatively nonarbitrary. Their repertoire thus does not satisfy the criteria given earlier for language.

Initial attempts to teach language directly to chimpanzees did not succeed. Early investigators (e.g., C. Hayes, 1951; Kellogg & Kellogg, 1933) attempted to teach chimpanzees to communicate vocally and failed rather miserably. R. Allen Gardner and Beatrice Gardner (1969) suggested that a better way to teach language to chimpanzees might be through the use of American Sign Language (ASL). By using sign language, the Gardners were able to teach their chimp, Washoe, rudimentary language skills (R. Brown, 1973), although her development never went beyond the stages of language a human infant could reach. Subsequently, David Premack (1971) had even greater success with his chimpanzee, Sarah, who picked up a vocabulary of more than 100 ASL words of various parts of speech and who showed at least rudimentary language skills.

Susan Savage-Rumbaugh and her colleagues (1986) have found the best evidence yet in favor of language use among chimpanzees. Their pygmy chimpanzees spontaneously have combined the visual symbols (such as red triangles, blue squares, etc.) of an artificial language the researchers taught them. One chimpanzee even seemed to have some grasp of the structure of language.

Not all researchers agree that chimps show language skills, however. Herbert Terrace (1979), who studied a chimpanzee whom he named Nim Chimpsky (a takeoff on the name of the great linguist Noam Chomsky), concluded that chimpanzees can show impressive accomplishments, but that among them is not the complete set of skills that constitute use of language. For example, his chimpanzee did not even show elementary use of syntax. Thus, although there is some evidence that animals may show some language skills, researchers have not reached a consensus regarding whether they show all the skills that are shown by human users of language.

This chapter has briefly skimmed the surface of the many issues involved in how we think and how we use language. Many of our most remarkable thoughts and our most appealing uses of language reflect both intelligence and creativity, the subjects of the next chapter.

The Case of the Grumpy Gambler

A friend suggests that Doreen read chapter 7 of *Pathways to Psychology*, and Doreen realizes that her understanding of the laws of probability has been wrong and has led her seriously astray. In fact, her luck is not likely to change and, in the long run, if she continues to gamble she will almost certainly continue to lose even more money. All gambling games are stacked in favor of the house. If they were not, then the gambling house quickly would go out of business. Instead, the house typically makes huge profits because with enough gamblers the house has to win over the long run. In thinking that her luck will change, Doreen is committing the *gambler's fallacy*, which is the mistaken belief that if one has a string of one kind of luck, one's luck has to change. This kind of reasoning is a fallacy when each event is independent, as it is in a gambling situation. In other words, each event is like the first in the sense that it is uninfluenced by prior events. The chances of Doreen's losing in her next trip to the gambling casino are the same as they were in the last trip and every other trip. Doreen realizes she has been a fool and stops gambling. Instead, she scales down her spending and eventually gets out of debt.

Summary

What Is Problem Solving? 231

1. *Problem solving* involves working to overcome obstacles.
2. It is easy to see how to find a solution to *well-structured problems*, although it may not be easy actually to solve them. For *ill-structured problems*, such as insight problems, it is hard to see how to find a solution.
3. *Heuristics* are informal strategies for solving problems, which sometimes work and sometimes do not. Heuristics are often contrasted with *algorithms*, which are more formal strategies that generally can guarantee an accurate solution to the problem if they are applied and implemented correctly.

4. *Mental set* refers to the use of a strategy that has worked in the past but that may not work for a particular problem to be solved in the present.
5. *Transfer*, which may be either *positive* or *negative*, refers to the carryover of knowledge or skills from one problem, or kind of problem, to another.
6. *Incubation*, which follows a period of working hard to solve a problem, involves putting aside the problem for a while. During incubation, you may subconsciously work on the problem while you consciously ignore it.
7. Experts differ from novices in both the amount and the organization of knowledge that they can use for solving problems.

What Are Judgment and Decision Making?   241

8. *Satisficing* involves choosing the first acceptable possibility that comes to mind. *Elimination by aspects* involves gradually eliminating various options, based on a ranked set of criteria. Both methods involve *bounded rationality*.

9. People using the *availability heuristic* make judgments based on how easily they can think of relevant instances of a phenomenon.

10. People using the *representativeness heuristic* make judgments on the basis of how representative something appears to be of a class of phenomena.

11. People often show *overconfidence*, appearing overly trusting of their own abilities or judgments.

What Is Reasoning?   246

12. *Reasoning* is the process of drawing conclusions from evidence.

13. In *deductive reasoning*, a person tries to figure out whether one or more logically certain conclusions can be drawn from a set of logical propositions.

14. *Inductive reasoning* involves reasoning from specific facts or observations to reach a general conclusion that may explain the specific facts or observations. Such reasoning is used when it is not possible to draw a logically certain conclusion from a set of premises.

What Is Language?   248

15. *Language* is the use of an organized way of combining words in order to communicate. *Communication* is the exchange of thoughts and feelings, which may or may not include language. Language and thought constantly interact.

16. Language involves (a) *verbal comprehension*, the ability to comprehend written and spoken (or signed) language, such as words, sentences, and paragraphs; and (b) *verbal fluency*, the ability to produce language.

17. *Psycholinguistics* is the psychology of language use, and *linguistics* is the study of language structure and change.

18. There are at least six properties of language: (a) Language lets us communicate with one or more persons who share our language. (b) Language creates an arbitrary relationship between a symbol and its referent—an idea, a thing, a process, a relationship, or a description. (c) Language has a structure; only particularly patterned arrangements of symbols have meaning, and different arrangements lead to different meanings. (d) Languages constantly change. (e) Language users can produce new combinations of words, and the possibilities for new combinations are almost limitless. (f) The structure of language can be analyzed at more than one level (e.g., phonemes and morphemes).

19. The smallest distinguishable unit of all possible human speech sounds is the *phone*. The particular set of distinctive speech sounds in a particular language are *phonemes*. The smallest semantically meaningful unit in a language is a *morpheme*. The entire set of morphemes in a given language is the *lexicon* of the language. *Discourse* encompasses language at a level beyond that of the sentence.

How Do We Acquire Language?   252

20. Humans seem to progress through the following stages in acquiring language: (a) prenatal responsiveness to human voices; (b) *cooing*, which includes all possible phones; (c) *babbling*, which includes only the distinct phonemes that characterize the primary language of the infant; (d) one-word expressions; (e) two-word expressions; (f) *telegraphic speech*; (g) basic adult sentence structure (present by about age 4).

21. During language acquisition, children make *overextension errors*, in which they extend the meaning of a word to cover more concepts than the word is intended to cover.

22. Children seem to have an innate *language-acquisition device (LAD)*, which makes it easier to acquire language.

How Do We Understand and Arrange Words?   253

23. *Semantics* is the study of the meanings of words.

24. *Syntax* is the study of the structure of language in sentences.

25. In linguistics, *grammar* refers to regular patterns in the usage of language. The grammar taught in schools is *prescriptive grammar*.

How Do We Use Language in a Social Context?   255

26. *Pragmatics* is the study of how language is used. Sociolinguistics is the study of the relationship between social interaction and language.

27. The *linguistic-relativity hypothesis* states that differences in thinking arise from different languages, and that these differences cause people who speak the various languages to perceive the world differently.

28. *Bilinguals* can speak two languages. *Additive bilingualism* occurs when a second language is taught in addition to a relatively well-developed first language; in contrast, *subtractive bilingualism* occurs when a second language partially replaces a first language.

Are Humans the Only Species to Use Language? 259

29. There is some evidence that at least one other species, that to which chimpanzees belong, uses rudimentary language, but the evidence is not yet conclusive.

Pathways to Knowledge

Choose the best answer to complete each sentence.

1. Ill-structured problems
   (a) have no solutions.
   (b) are commonly found in textbooks.
   (c) are formulated so that efforts to answer them are futile.
   (d) have no obvious path to solution.

2. Negative transfer in problem solving refers to
   (a) the transfer of knowledge that was useful in solving a previous problem to a new problem for which the knowledge interferes with the solution.
   (b) the transfer of negative information from one problem to another.
   (c) the transfer of nonconstructive problem-solving strategies that were useless in solving an earlier problem.
   (d) the habitual use of a poor problem-solving strategy.

3. Researchers have found that expert problem solvers differ from novice problem solvers primarily in that
   (a) experts can solve problems more quickly, as a result of greater motivation to solve the problems rapidly.
   (b) experts always have been good problem solvers, even at a young age.
   (c) experts have a wider and better organized knowledge base.
   (d) novices' problem solving has become more automatized, so that the novices can avoid the unnecessary, methodical steps in problem solving.

4. If all the news stations repeatedly report the appearance of a horrendous case of leprosy, and viewers conclude that leprosy has become rampant, the type of cognitive strategy that the viewers are using is

   (a) the availability heuristic.
   (b) the overconfidence algorithm.
   (c) bounded rationality.
   (d) the top-of-the mind heuristic.

5. The smallest meaningful unit in a language is called a(n)
   (a) morpheme.
   (b) phoneme.
   (c) root word.
   (d) affix.

6. The analysis of language, proceeding from the most elementary to the most complex level of sophistication is
   (a) phoneme, morpheme, syntax, discourse.
   (b) phoneme, morpheme, lexicon, vocabulary.
   (c) morpheme, phoneme, syntax, discourse.
   (d) morpheme, phoneme, vocabulary, discourse.

7. Semantics is the study of
   (a) culture and its effects on language.
   (b) the origins of words.
   (c) how words are organized into meaningful sentences.
   (d) the meanings of words.

Answer each of the following questions by filling in the blank with an appropriate word or phrase.

8. A person shows _____ _____ when she or he views a wine bottle exclusively as a container to hold wine.

9. A _____ is composed of an individual's repertoire of morphemes.

10. The period of time during which a problem solver temporarily stops consciously working on a problem, in order to work on it subconsciously, is called _____.

11. _____ is a level of linguistic analysis, focused on the organized arrangement of words into meaningful sentences.

12. _____ is a seemingly sudden understanding of the nature of something, often as a result of taking a novel approach to a problem.

13. _____ _____ involves the recognition that although humans are rational, there are limits to the degree to which humans demonstrate rational cognitive processes across situations.

Match the following linguistic terms to their descriptions:

14. phoneme

15. pragmatics

16. morpheme

   (a) the study of the interaction of language and thought

   (b) a unit of speech sound in a given language

   (c) the study of how words have meaning in a language

17. semantics

18. lexicon

19. psycholinguistics

20. discourse

   (d) the level of linguistic analysis that encompasses linguistic units beyond the level of the sentence

   (e) the smallest semantically meaningful unit in a language

   (f) the entire repertoire of morphemes in a given language (or a given person's repertoire of morphemes)

   (g) the study of how people use language, such as in social interactions

---

Answers

1. d, 2. a, 3. c, 4. a, 5. a, 6. a, 7. d, 8. functional fixedness, 9. lexicon, 10. incubation, 11. Syntax, 12. Insight, 13. Bounded rationality, 14. b, 15. g, 16. e, 17. c, 18. f, 19. a, 20. d

Pathways to Understanding

1. If you were the head of a problem-solving team, and your team members seemed to be running into a block in their approach to the problem being addressed, what would you have the team members do to get around the block?

2. How do advertisers use invalid reasoning to influence people? Give some specific examples of ads, and compare and contrast their means of persuasion.

3. What are some heuristics you use for figuring out what things to study for an upcoming examination?

The Case of The Low Grades

From the time she was a young girl, Moira wanted to start a business. She thought of herself as a natural-born entrepreneur. At 6 years of age, Moira had a lemonade stand. By the time she was 10, Moira was selling whatever food she or her mother could bake. She became interested in rare books and started carefully choosing books from local bookshops in her city, selling books to collectors for more than she had paid to buy them.

When Moira went to college, she took an introductory course in business administration her first year. She was confident at first, but then the grades started to come in. Moira was shattered. After planning her whole life to go into business, she was getting low grades in her introductory business course. Oddly enough, at the same time that Moira was barely passing the course she had expanded her book business and was taking in substantial amounts of money. Moira seriously considered dropping out of business and perhaps dropping out of college altogether. She could not see the point of staying in college if it would not help her prepare for a career in business. Moira was stumped.

What should she do? Think about this while you read chapter 8. Is it possible that Moira is more able than she believes herself to be? Is it possible that business represents a good pathway for her after all? Pay special attention to the notion of practical intelligence.

CHAPTER 8
INTELLIGENCE AND CREATIVITY

Many psychologists (myself included) spend a lifetime trying to answer questions about intelligence in order to gain a clear understanding of it. I define **intelligence** as comprising the abilities needed to engage in goal-directed adaptive behavior, but other psychologists who study intelligence may define it somewhat differently. In fact, there are many pathways toward the understanding of intelligence. We begin this chapter with a discussion of two traditional approaches to the study of intelligence, those of Sir Francis Galton and of Alfred Binet, and then discuss some more recent and modern approaches to the study of intelligence.

WHAT ARE TWO TRADITIONAL APPROACHES TO STUDYING INTELLIGENCE?

Almost a century ago, two highly intelligent men came up with two completely different answers to the question *What is intelligence?* According to Francis Galton (1822–1911), *intelligence* comprises two general qualities: *energy* (the capacity for labor) and sensitivity to physical stimuli (Galton, 1883). That is, Galton held that intelligence is based on physical strength (e.g., muscular strength, speed, and accuracy) and psychophysical abilities. Recall from chapter 3 that psychophysical ability involves *sensory acuity* (e.g., keen ability to see, hear, smell, taste, touch). Galton actually set up a laboratory to test the psychophysical abilities of people who visited his lab.

Think about how various people might have scored on Galton's tests: heavyweight champion George Foreman versus scientist Albert Einstein, Olympic speed skater Bonnie Blair versus Nobel Prize–winning author Toni Morrison. It is likely that Foreman would be considered a genius in comparison with Einstein. Similarly, although I am sure that Toni Morrison has perfectly good psychophysical abilities, I suspect that Bonnie Blair would have outshined her on Galton's tests.

Although Galton's tests might still be considered useful by Olympic committees, athletic teams, and a few others who value physical prowess, few (if any) colleges or other educational institutions would consider his tests highly useful in assessing a person's intelligence. An alternative to Galton's approach to intelligence emerged from a need to use measures of intelligence as a guide for predicting success in school. In the early 1900s, the Minister of Public Instruction in Paris, France, asked Alfred Binet (1857–1911) and his collaborator, Théodore Simon (1873–1961), to come up with tests that could distinguish children who were truly mentally retarded from children who were not succeeding in school for other reasons. Based on this practical concern for educating children who were likely to succeed in school, Binet and Simon launched the **psychometric** (psychological measurement) tradition of intelligence theory and research.

For Binet and Simon (1916), the core of intelligence is "judgment, otherwise called good sense, practical sense, initiative, the faculty of adapting one's self to circumstances" (pp. 42–43). The test they devised was intended to tap intellectual abilities as expressed through judgment and adaptation.

On Francis Galton's psychophysical tests of intelligence, boxer George Foreman (top, left) would probably have fared far better than scientist Albert Einstein (top, right), and Olympic athlete Bonnie Blair (bottom left) would probably have surpassed writer Toni Morrison (bottom, right). Do you agree with Galton that these tests would accurately indicate the differences in intelligence among these individuals? Why or why not?

HOW DO PSYCHOLOGISTS ASSESS INTELLIGENCE?

Mental Age and the Intelligence Quotient

Schools have usually classified children according to their chronological age (i.e., the amount of time they have lived since birth), with this criterion

intelligence • comprises the abilities needed to engage in goal-directed adaptive behavior

psychometric • characterized by psychological measurement (*psycho-*, pertaining to the mind or mental processes; *-metric*, measurement) serving as a basis for separating children into 12 or 13 (counting kindergarten) school grades. One rationale for using this criterion is the assumption that most children of the same chronological age have about the same general mental abilities. The schools may then compare children of the same general age and may assign different evaluations (grades such as *A, B, C,* etc.) to children who show different levels of academic performance.

Binet suggested an alternative to comparing and classifying children based on their chronological age. Instead, according to Binet, a better way to compare children's intelligence (and to sort them into appropriate school classes) is based on their **mental age,** their level of intelligence based on the mentally "average" person of a given chronological age. If a person performs on a test at about the same level as an average 12 year old, the person's mental age will be 12, regardless of the person's chronological age. For example, suppose that José's chronological age is 10 years. However, his performance on a test of intelligence equals that of the average 12 year old. His mental age will be 12.

William Stern (1912) noted that mental age is less useful when comparing children of differing chronological ages. A mental age of 12, for example, is more impressive in a 10 year old than in a 14 year old. Stern suggested that instead of measuring intelligence in terms of mental age, we should measure intelligence by using an **intelligence quotient (IQ):** a ratio of mental age (MA) to chronological age (CA), multiplied by 100. This ratio can be expressed mathematically as follows: $IQ = (MA \div CA) \times 100$. For example, José's mental age is 12, and his chronological age is 10. Therefore, his ratio IQ is 120, because $(12 \div 10) \times 100 = 120$. A **ratio IQ** expresses intelligence as the ratio of mental age to chronological age, times 100.

Unfortunately, ratio IQs have their problems, too. It turns out that calculations based on mental age just do not work very well for people over 16 or so years of age. Up to about age 16, children's measured intelligence goes up each year. After that time, however, measured intelligence does not go up as much, and some measurements of intelligence actually go down as people approach the end of the life span. To get an idea of the problem, think about the likely differences in intellectual ability among a 4 year old, a 10 year old, and a 16 year old, and compare those differences with the likely intellectual differences among a 40 year old, a 46 year old, and a 52 year old. You probably would notice big differences between ages 4 and 16, but few differences between ages 40 and 52.

Deviation IQ Scores

Once many psychologists gave up on comparing people based on mental age, they needed some other way of comparing people's scores on intelligence tests. The solution that occurred to them was to give each test to a huge number of people of various ages and then to compare a given person's test scores with the scores of people of about the same chronological age as that individual. When tests are given to thousands of people, the scores obtained generally approximate a *normal distribution,* in which most people score somewhere near the middle, and fewer people score on either side of the middle. Only a very few people have extremely high or extremely low scores. A normal distribution is generally based on measuring the characteristics (e.g., test scores) of a large number of individuals.

The actual number of items that a person answers correctly is the person's raw score for the test. If Jeanie answers 48 questions correctly on a test, her raw score will be 48. To make it easy to compare a particular

mental age • a means of indicating a person's level of intelligence (generally in reference to a child), based on the individual's performance on tests of intelligence, by indicating the average chronological age of persons who typically perform at the same level of intelligence as the test-taker

intelligence quotient (IQ) • broadly, a normative score on an intelligence test, with a mean of 100 and a standard deviation of 15 or 16

ratio IQ • a means of indicating performance on intelligence tests; expressed as a quotient of mental age divided by chronological age, times 100

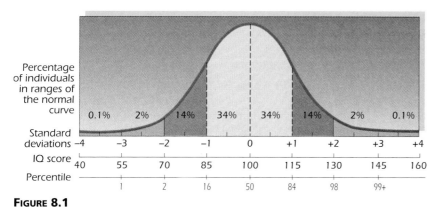

FIGURE 8.1
Normal Distribution of Deviation IQs
This figure shows a normal distribution as it applies to IQ, including percentile equivalents for various levels of IQ.

person's score with the scores of other people, the raw scores for many psychological tests are converted into **normative scores,** scores based on a normal distribution of many individual scores, which show how various test-takers scored in relation to one another. For most IQ tests, the normative scores are calculated so that the middle score is 100. (For example, if the average person scored 19 out of 55 on a given test, a raw score of 19 would be converted to a score of 100, and the other scores on each test would be converted in a similar way.)

In a normal distribution of IQ scores for a large population, roughly two thirds of the normative scores fall between 85 and 115, and about 95% of the scores fall between 70 and 130. From this distribution of normative scores, psychologists can calculate **deviation IQs,** based on degree of difference from the average score. The deviation IQ scores lend themselves to comparisons among individual test-takers, based on how the individual's scores deviate from the average scores. Figure 8.1 shows an example of how a normal distribution of scores can be plotted on a graph. IQ scores are typically computed on the basis of scores on tests of intelligence. One such test is the Stanford-Binet.

The Stanford-Binet Intelligence Scales

Scores on Binet and Simon's original intelligence test were calculated based on mental age alone. Next, Lewis Terman, a Stanford University professor, together with Maud Merrill, modified Binet and Simon's test, using ratio IQs for comparing intelligence across different individuals. Terman and Merrill thereby developed the earliest versions of the *Stanford-Binet Intelligence Scales* (Terman & Merrill, 1937, 1973; see Figure 8.2). In psychological assessment, a *scale* is a test or subtest that includes a graded series of questions or problems that measure an ability or another psychological construct (e.g., a personality trait). The idea is that a greater amount of skill, ability, or some other characteristic is required to reach each of the graded levels of the scale. Most modern intelligence tests include a set of scaled subtests.

For years, the Stanford-Binet test was the most widely used intelligence test, and it is still widely used. In recent years, however, another test, authored by psychologist David Wechsler, has become even more widely used than the Stanford-Binet.

normative scores • the set of normative equivalents for a range of raw test scores that represent the normal distribution of scores obtained by giving a test to a huge number of individuals

deviation IQs • a means of determining intelligence-test scores, based on deviations from an average score, calculated such that the normative equivalent for the median score is 100; not IQs, strictly speaking, because no quotient is involved

Content area	Explanation of tasks/questions	Example of a possible task/question
Verbal reasoning		
Vocabulary	Define the meaning of a word	What does the word **diligent** mean?
Comprehension	Show an understanding of why the world works as it does	Why do people sometimes borrow money?
Absurdities	Identify the odd or absurd feature of a picture	(Point out that ice hockey players do not ice-skate on lakes into which swimmers in bathing suits are diving.)
Verbal relations	Tell how three of four items are similar to one another yet different from the fourth item	(Note that an apple, a banana, and an orange can be eaten, but a cup or mug cannot be.)
Quantitative reasoning		
Number series	Complete a series of numbers	Given the numbers 1, 3, 5, 7, 9, what number would you expect to come next?
Quantitative	Solve simple arithmetical-word problems	If Maria has six apples, and she wants to divide them evenly among herself and her two best friends, how many apples will she give to each friend?
Figural/abstract reasoning		
Pattern analysis	Figure out a puzzle in which the test-taker must combine pieces representing parts of geometric shapes, fitting them together to form a particular geometric shape	Fit together these pieces to form a rectangle. 
Short-term memory		
Memory for sentences	Listen to a sentence, then repeat it back exactly as the examiner said it	Repeat this sentence back to me: "Harrison went to sleep late and awoke early the next morning."
Memory for digits	Listen to a series of digits (numbers), then repeat the numbers either forward or backward	Repeat these numbers backward: "9, 1, 3, 6."
Memory for objects	Watch the examiner point to a series of objects in a picture, then point to the same objects in exactly the same sequence as the examiner	(Point to the carrot, then the hoe, then the flower, then the scarecrow, then the baseball.) 

FIGURE 8.2
Stanford-Binet Intelligence Scales
The above sample questions illustrate each of the subtests in the Stanford-Binet; each subtest measures abilities Lewis Terman, one of the authors of the first edition of the test, included in his overall view of intelligence. The sample questions used throughout this chapter are not actual questions from any of the scales; they are intended only to illustrate the types of questions that might appear in each of the main content areas of the tests. How would you respond to these questions? What do your responses indicate about your intelligence?

The Wechsler Scales

The Wechsler intelligence scales include the *Wechsler Adult Intelligence Scale—Revised (WAIS-R)*, the third edition of the *Wechsler Intelligence Scale for Children (WISC-III)*, and the *Wechsler Preschool and Primary Scale of Intelligence (WPPSI)*. Each of the Wechsler tests yields three scores, all of which are based on deviation IQs: a verbal score, a performance score,

Content area	Explanation of tasks/questions	Example of a possible task/question
Verbal scale		
Comprehension	Answer questions of social knowledge	What does it mean when people say, "A stitch in time saves nine"? Why are convicted criminals put into prison?
Vocabulary	Define the meaning of a word	What does **persistent** mean? What does **archaeology** mean?
Information	Supply generally known information	Who is Chelsea Clinton? What are six New England states?
Similarities	Explain how two things or concepts are similar	In what ways are an ostrich and a penguin alike? In what ways are a lamp and a heater alike?
Arithmetic	Solve simple arithmetical-word problems	If Paul has $14.43, and he buys two sandwiches, which cost $5.23 each, how much change will he receive?
Digit span	Listen to a series of digits (numbers), then repeat the numbers either forward or backward or both	Repeat these numbers backward: "9, 1, 8, 3, 6."
Performance scale		
Object assembly	Put together a puzzle by combining pieces to form a particular common object	Put together these pieces to make something. 
Block design	Use patterned blocks to form a design that looks identical to a design shown by the examiner	Assemble these blocks to make this design. 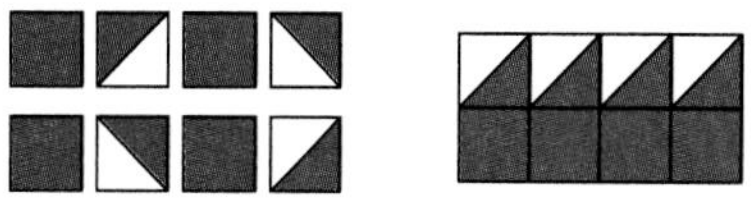
Picture completion	Tell what is missing from each picture	What is missing from this picture? 
Picture arrangement	Put a set of cartoonlike pictures into a chronological order, so they tell a coherent story	Arrange these pictures in an order that tells a story, and then tell what is happening in the story. 
Digit symbol	When given a key matching particular symbols to particular numerals, copy a sequence of symbols, transcribing from symbols to numerals, using the key	Look carefully at the key. In the blanks, write the correct numeral for the symbol above each blank.

FIGURE 8.3
Wechsler Adult Intelligence Scale—Revised (WAIS-R)
The Wechsler scales are based on deviation IQs. Given the content areas and the kinds of questions shown here, how does the Wechsler differ from the Stanford-Binet?

and an overall score. The *verbal score* is based on subtests that tap the ability to understand and to use words, such as vocabulary tests. The *performance score* is based on subtests that, for the most part, require test-takers to perform physical manipulations of materials, rather than to supply verbal responses. For example, one of the performance subtests involves *picture completion,* in which test-takers are asked to find a missing part in a picture of an object. The overall score is a combination of the verbal and the performance scores. Figure 8.3 shows various types of items from each of the Wechsler adult-scale subtests. You may wish to compare sample items from the Wechsler with sample items from the Stanford-Binet.

Wechsler did not limit his thinking about intelligence to test scores. Although Wechsler (1974) clearly considered test scores important, he believed that intelligence involves more than just what is measured on tests. Intelligence affects our everyday life, as when we take tests and do homework, or relate to people and do our jobs effectively. In Wechsler's view, a person's intelligence is that person's ability to adapt to the environment in all aspects of her or his life.

Additional Tests Related to Intelligence Testing

In the United States today, hundreds of intelligence tests are in everyday use. Some of these tests are given to just one person at a time by a highly trained psychologist; other tests are group tests, which can be given to large numbers of people at once. Tests of intelligence are not the only tests of abilities being used today; many tests are designed to measure abilities not normally assessed on intelligence tests, such as musical or athletic abilities. Most of these tests are intended to measure **aptitudes,** a person's capabilities for learning new information or for mastering skills in a specific area of knowledge (e.g., language, mathematics, athletics, or music).

8.1

What is a skill or an area of knowledge that you have mastered pretty well by now? Stop for a moment to think about how you could assess another person's aptitude for learning what you have learned or for mastering the skill you have mastered. What are some of the questions or tasks you would include on an aptitude test for this area of knowledge? Jot down a few ideas for the kinds of test items you would include.

As you have probably discovered, it is difficult to come up with legitimate ways in which to assess a person's aptitude for learning new information or for mastering a skill. In contrast, it is much easier to find ways to assess a person's **achievement,** what the individual has already accomplished or learned in a given area of knowledge, by the time of the test.

Characteristics of Intelligence Tests

Once test developers know what it is they want to assess, they must develop questions and tasks that effectively measure what they want to assess. Test developers evaluate their tests to see whether the tests show three key properties:

1. **Validity** is the extent to which a test measures what it is supposed to measure. For example, do people who score high on a test of intelligence actually show greater intelligence, as measured by other tests or other kinds of outcomes such as school grades?

aptitude • a capability for accomplishing something, for attaining a level of expertise on performance of a task or a set of tasks, or for acquiring knowledge in a given domain or set of domains

achievement • an accomplishment; an attained level of expertise on performance of a task, or an acquired base of knowledge in a domain or a set of domains

validity • the extent to which a given form of measurement assesses what it is supposed to measure

There are several different kinds of validity. Construct-related validity is an evaluation of the degree to which a test or other measurement actually reflects the hypothetical construct (e.g., intelligence) that the test or other measurement is designed to assess. For example, a test of intelligence that measured how fast a person could tap his or her finger on a desk would have low construct-related validity, whereas a test that measured reasoning about numbers presumably would have higher construct-related validity. Content-related validity reflects expert judgments of the extent to which the content of a test measures all of the knowledge or skills that are supposed to be included within the domain being tested. For example, if a test of intelligence only measured reasoning about numbers, that test would probably be judged as having low content-related validity because so many other aspects of intelligence would be ignored. Criterion-related validity assesses the extent to which a test correlates with other measures with which it is supposed to be related. For example, if a test of intelligence did not predict school grades at all, the test of intelligence would be judged to have low criterion-related validity. This kind of validity is often itself divided into two types. Predictive validity is assessed when the test that is supposed to predict performance (e.g., an intelligence test) is administered before the criterion data (e.g., school grades) are collected. When a college-admissions test is given during the senior year of high school, its correlation with first-year grades is a measure of predictive validity. Concurrent validity is assessed when the test that is supposed to correlate with performance (e.g., an intelligence test) is administered at roughly the same time that the criterion data are collected. For example, if the ability test to predict first-year performance were given in the first year of college, rather than the senior year of high school, the ability test would then be used in a way that would assess concurrent validity.

2. **Reliability** is the extent to which a test consistently measures whatever it actually measures in just the same way every time. For example, will the people who had relatively high (or low) scores on April 27 be the same people who have relatively high (or low) scores on May 13?

3. **Standardization** is the extent to which the conditions for taking a test are the same for all test-takers. For example, do all people taking the test have the same amount of time to answer the questions, and will they answer these questions under the same conditions (e.g., temperature in the room, freedom from distractions, etc.)?

HOW SHOULD WE TRY TO UNDERSTAND THE NATURE OF INTELLIGENCE?

In designing tests of intelligence, test designers spend more time deciding how they will measure intelligence than they do studying just what is the nature of intelligence. Some researchers, however, spend much of their time trying to understand the nature of intelligence. One way to try to understand the nature of intelligence is to start with tests of intelligence, an approach considered next.

reliability • the dependability of a measurement instrument (e.g., a test), indicating that the instrument consistently measures the outcome being measured

standardization • the administration of a test in a way that ensures that the conditions for taking the test are the same for all test-takers

Structures and Processes of Intelligence

Factor Analysis: Exploring the Structure of the Mind

During the first half of the 20th century, psychologists studied intelligence by trying to map out the abilities that make up intelligence. These psychologists tried to chart the innermost regions of the mind. To chart the territory of intelligence, they needed tools. The tool they found the most valuable for this work was *factor analysis*, which is a statistical method for separating an overall concept or phenomenon (e.g., intelligence) into a number of distinct aspects (abilities, in the case of intelligence).

Both the overall phenomenon and the numerous distinct abilities are hypothetical constructs. Recall from chapter 6 that a hypothetical construct is a phenomenon that is believed to exist even though the phenomenon (e.g., intelligence) cannot be observed directly. Because the hypothetical construct of intelligence cannot be observed directly, researchers must devise other means to find out about it.

One way to find out about the hypothetical construct of intelligence is to give tests to people that require them to use the abilities believed to constitute intelligence. Researchers who use the tool of factor analysis believe that these hypothetical abilities form the bases of individual differences in test performance. Charles Spearman (1863–1945) is generally considered to have invented factor analysis. Using this technique, Spearman (1927) concluded that intelligence could be understood in terms of both a single general factor (which he believed to be "mental energy") and a set of specific factors. Later, Louis Thurstone (1887–1955) and others suggested that intelligence comprises various separate factors (e.g., Thurstone, 1938), such as verbal comprehension (measured by vocabulary), number skills (measured by simple arithmetic problems), and memory (measured by recall of words).

John Carroll (1993) proposed a hierarchical model of intelligence, based on his extensive analysis of data obtained between 1927 and 1987. Carroll's model involves a hierarchy comprising three levels: At the top of the hierarchy is general ability; at the bottom of the hierarchy are many narrow, specific abilities (e.g., spelling ability, speed of reasoning); and in the middle are various broad abilities (e.g., learning and memory processes, effortless production of many ideas, and the ability to cope with novel tasks and situations). Other theorists have accepted similar models, often emphasizing the importance, in their view, of the general factor at the top of the hierarchy (Brand, 1996; Jensen, 1998). It has been found that abilities involving knowledge-based skills tend to increase with age throughout almost the entire life span, whereas abilities involving rapid and abstract reasoning tend to decrease in old age (Horn, 1994).

In general, the factor-analytic model does a pretty good job of describing the mental abilities that make up intelligence. Although it describes *what* structures characterize intelligence, it does not say much about *how* intelligence works in the mind of an individual. That is, factor-analytic models say little about the mental processes underlying intelligence. Information-processing approaches, in contrast, say a lot about these mental processes.

Intelligence and Information Processing

information processing • the operations by which people mentally manipulate what they learn and know about the world

Information processing is the set of mental actions by which people manage and use knowledge. Information-processing investigators study intelligence in various ways. Most of these differences relate to the processes being studied. Some of these processes are extremely simple, and others are quite complicated. Among the main information-processing theorists are Earl Hunt (1978), who believes that an important aspect of intelligence is the ability to retrieve information quickly about words from memory, and Herbert Simon (1976), who believes that complex problem solving is central to intelligence. Each has studied both the speed and the accuracy with which people process information.

Although the information-processing approach offers more understanding of the processes of intelligence than does the psychometric approach, it often does not link the processing of information directly to specific biological aspects of brain function. Some investigators who study intelligence try to understand just how our brains work while engaging in activities that require intelligence. They take a biological approach.

The Biology of Intelligence

Biological psychologists try to understand intelligence by studying the brain directly (see chapter 2). Through such studies, researchers have found that intelligence correlates with complex patterns of electrical activity (Barrett & Eysenck, 1992), with speed of neuronal conduction (e.g., McGarry-Roberts, Stelmack, & Campbell, 1992; Reed & Jensen, 1992; Vernon & Mori, 1992), and with particular ways of using a simple sugar, glucose, during mental activities (e.g., Haier, Siegel, Tang, Abel, & Buchsbaum, 1992). As an example, it appears that the brains of more intelligent people use up less glucose (and spend less energy) than do the brains of less intelligent persons performing the same task. The reason for this difference in energy use may be that the brains of more intelligent people may find the tasks easier than do the brains of less intelligent people. Further, Richard Haier and his colleagues have found that the efficient use of glucose increases as a result of learning. Perhaps persons who are more intelligent have learned how to use their brains more efficiently than have persons who are less intelligent. Some psychologists (e.g., Matarazzo, 1992) believe that we will be able to find practical uses for the information from this research in the near future.

The biological approach certainly offers promising insights into intelligence, but many psychologists question whether we can fully understand intelligence by studying the human brain in isolation. They believe that we also must consider the entire human being and the entire environment within which the person engages in intelligent actions. Such researchers and theorists would urge us to take a more *anthropological* (culture-based) view of intelligence.

Context and Intelligence

Up to now, we have discussed models of intelligence with an internal orientation: The psychologists we have discussed view intelligence as something occurring inside the head. In contrast, **contextualist** theorists of intelligence prefer an externally oriented approach to intelligence. The idea is that intelligence cannot be understood outside its real-world context. Take, for example, the following hypothetical dialogue (from Chieh Li, personal communication, September 28, 1995).

> Jane is a student in the classes of Professor Blaine, a European American educated in Western schools influenced by Judeo-Christian religious traditions, and of Professor Chang, an Asian

contextualist • a psychologist who theorizes about a psychological phenomenon (e.g., intelligence) strictly in terms of the context in which an individual is observed, and who suggests that the phenomenon cannot be understood, let alone measured, outside the real-world context of the individual

American educated in traditional Chinese schools influenced by Buddhism, Confucianism, and Taoism. By chance, Jane passed by and greeted the two professors as they were discussing what constitutes intelligence.

"There," said Dr. Blaine, "Jane is an excellent example of an intelligent student. She always responds quickly and accurately to questions I ask, and I hear that she is an excellent chess player. Is she an *A* student in your class, too?"

"Yes," responded Dr. Chang.

"Well, wouldn't you say that Jane is intelligent?"

"I don't know yet. She seems to be a quick learner, but she has not shown me her wisdom yet."

"What do you mean when you say 'her wisdom'?"

"A quick learner may not be wise. A wise person does not always show her smartness but rather her modesty. A wise student listens, observes, and tries to learn from others. When solving a problem, a wise person considers all factors involved and considers the immediate, short-term and long-term outcomes of various possible solutions."

The preceding dialogue illustrates the importance of cultural context in what people value as reflecting intelligence. Contextualists believe that each culture creates its own conception of intelligence in order to serve two purposes: (a) to define the nature of adaptive behavior; and (b) to explain why some people perform better than others on the tasks that the culture values (e.g., in U.S. society, getting good grades in school). Contextualist psychologists study how intelligence relates to the context in which intelligence is being studied.

As an example, Michael Cole and his colleagues (Cole, Gay, Glick, & Sharp, 1971) conducted an interesting cross-cultural study of intelligence. These investigators asked adult members of the Kpelle tribe in Africa to sort various terms (such as names of fruits or vegetables). In Western culture, when adults are asked to sort terms, more intelligent people typically sort the terms hierarchically (i.e., sort the terms into various categories, with various levels being more specific or less so). Less intelligent people sort the terms functionally (in terms of the uses of the terms). In hierarchical sorting, for example, people may sort names of different kinds of fruit together. Then they may place the word "fruit" over the names of the particular kinds of fruit, and so on. In functional sorting, people may sort "fruit" with "eat," for example, because we eat fruit. The Kpelle sorted functionally, even after investigators unsuccessfully tried to get the Kpelle to sort hierarchically.

Finally, in desperation, one of the experimenters (Joseph Glick) asked a Kpelle person to sort the way a foolish person would. When asked to sort in this way, the Kpelle had no trouble at all sorting hierarchically. This individual and others had been able to sort this way all along. They just had not done so because they believed that hierarchical sorting is not intelligent. They may also have considered the questioners rather unintelligent for asking what may have seemed like stupid questions. Why would the Kpelle view functional sorting as intelligent? Simple; in ordinary life, we normally think functionally. When we think of a fruit, we think of eating it. However, in Western schooling, we learn what is expected of us on tests. The Kpelle did not have Western schooling and had not been exposed to Western testing. As a result, they solved the problems the way

When Michael Cole and other researchers asked Kpelle adults to sort items intelligently, the Kpelle sorted the items according to the functional uses of the items. When asked to sort items as a foolish person would sort them, Kpelle adults sorted the items hierarchically, according to attribute categories. In contrast, the majority of Western researchers generally consider hierarchical sorting to reflect greater intelligence than does functional sorting. What conclusions would Kpelle researchers have drawn regarding the intelligence of Westerners if they had administered intelligence tests to Cole and his colleagues? What should we infer regarding cultural definitions of intelligence?

Western adults might solve them in their everyday lives, but not on a test of cognitive abilities.

The Kpelle people are not the only ones who might question Western understandings of intelligence. In the Puluwat culture of the Pacific, for example, sailors figure out how to travel incredibly long distances to precise locations. They do so without using any of the special equipment that sailors from technologically advanced countries need in order to get from one place to another (Gladwin, 1970). If Puluwat sailors were to design intelligence tests for us, we might not seem very intelligent. Similarly, the highly skilled Puluwat sailors might not do well on Western tests of intelligence. Because of these and other observations, several theorists have suggested the importance of considering cultural context when measuring intelligence.

The preceding examples make it clear that it is very difficult, if not actually impossible, to come up with a test that everyone would consider culture-fair (Greenfield, 1997; R. J. Sternberg, 1997c). A **culture-fair** test is equally appropriate and fair for members of all cultures. Finding test items for such a test is almost impossible if members of different cultures have different ideas of what it means to be smart. That is, the very behaviors that may be considered intelligent in one culture may be viewed as unintelligent in another. For example, Americans often put a premium on mental quickness, but other cultures may put a higher value on careful and

culture-fair • describes the assessment that is equally appropriate for members of all cultures and that comprises items that are equally fair to members of all cultures; probably impossible to attain

"YOU CAN'T BUILD A HUT, YOU DON'T KNOW HOW TO FIND EDIBLE ROOTS AND YOU KNOW NOTHING ABOUT PREDICTING THE WEATHER. IN OTHER WORDS, YOU DO TERRIBLY ON OUR I.Q. TEST."

Copyright © 1996 Sidney Harris.

deliberate decision making, considering hasty decisions to be unwise (R. J. Sternberg, 1985a, 1990). Because various cultures conceive of intelligence differently, it is probably unrealistic to expect that a truly culture-fair test of intelligence will be developed. Indeed, in a rural village in Kenya, we found that children who did better on a test of practical, adaptive intelligence for their environment actually did worse on several conventional Western tests of intelligence (R. J. Sternberg & Grigorenko, 1997a). Western tests are biased with respect to the kind of education many of these rural Kenyans receive, just as the Kenyan test we used (a measure of the use of knowledge about natural herbal medicines that the Kenyans use to fight infection) would be biased with respect to the kind of education Westerners receive.

It used to be thought that tests of intelligence that contain only geometric types of items (such as matrix problems, where one element of the matrix is missing and the test-taker has to fill it in) were culture-fair and not susceptible to differences in education and environment. Yet we now know that this belief was incorrect. For one thing, tests of geometric reasoning show greater differences between cultures than do verbal tests (see R. J. Sternberg, 1985a). For another, we know that scores on tests of abstract reasoning skills have been rising steadily around the world and that the rate of increase is greater for such tests than it is for verbal tests (Flynn, 1987; Neisser, 1998). This finding, that scores on IQ tests have been rising and that they have been rising more quickly for geometric than for verbal types of items, indicates that exposure to culture, in general, and education, in particular, actually has more of an effect on abstract-reasoning tests than on verbal tests. This result is counterintuitive, and no one is quite sure of the cause. The gains on these abstract-reasoning tests are substantial—more than one standard deviation (15 points of IQ) per generation (30 years). So, we now know that all currently used measures of intelligence are affected by cultural contact.

INTELLIGENCE TESTING AND IMMIGRATION POLICIES

Even though it may not be possible to provide culture-fair tests of intelligence, a study by Seymour Sarason and John Doris (1979) illustrates the importance of looking for ways to allow for cultural differences in the design and use of intelligence tests. Sarason and Doris tracked the IQs of an immigrant population: Italian Americans. Less than a century ago, first-generation Italian-American children showed a median IQ of 87 (low average; range 76–100), even when nonverbal measures were used and when so-called mainstream American attitudes were considered. Some social commentators and intelligence researchers of the day pointed to heredity and other nonenvironmental factors as the basis for the low IQs, much as they do today for other minority groups.

For example, a leading researcher of the day, Henry Goddard, pronounced that 79% of immigrant Italians were "feeble-minded." He also asserted that about 80% of immigrant Jews, Hungarians, and Russians were similarly dull-witted (Eysenck & Kamin, 1981). Goddard (1917) also said that moral decadence accompanied this deficit in intelligence. He recommended that the intelligence tests he used be administered to all immigrants and that the U.S. authorities prevent the entry of any persons found to be below a reasonable minimum level of intelligence, as measured by these tests.

Stephen Ceci (1996) has noted that the present generation of Italian American students who take IQ tests show slightly above-average IQs. Other immigrant groups that Goddard had wanted to bar from admission to the United States have shown similar "amazing" increases. The kinds of genes possessed by Italian Americans have probably not changed much in just a few generations. Instead, it seems much more likely that the dramatic gains in IQ scores can be explained by cultural assimilation and education.

The observations of Ceci and others suggest a specific question of public policy: Should intelligence tests be used as a means of determining who should or should not be permitted to immigrate to the United States? What do you think?

A broader question posed by these findings is this one: Should researchers try to influence public policy? Was Goddard correct to try to use his findings to influence who should or should not be allowed to immigrate to the United States? Should Ceci speak up regarding his observations to influence public policy regarding immigration?

Many psychologists believe that research findings should be used when determining issues of public policy, such as decisions regarding immigration or regarding the use of intelligence tests. To these psychologists, people who shape public policy should be provided with research findings, so that policy issues can be based on the best available data. Other psychologists, however, warn that researchers should not concern themselves with issues of public policy and should leave policy matters outside the laboratory door. To these other psychologists, as soon as researchers begin to think about public policy, they become less concerned with objective observation of what does exist and more concerned with subjective evaluation of what should exist.

What do you think? Should researchers always avoid concerning themselves with issues of public policy? Should researchers always speak up about issues of public policy? What considerations should influence a researcher's decision regarding whether to speak up about issues of public policy?

Context Effects in Intelligence

Although we probably cannot design culture-fair tests of intelligence, we may be able to design culture-relevant tests. **Culture-relevant** tests tap skills and knowledge that relate to the cultural experiences of the test-takers. For example, memory abilities are one aspect of intelligence, as Western culture defines it. Daniel Wagner (1978) studied memory abilities in Western culture versus Moroccan culture. Wagner found that the level of recall depended on the content that was being remembered. Culture-relevant content was remembered more effectively than was nonrelevant content. For instance, Moroccan rug merchants were better able to recall complex visual patterns on black-and-white photos of Oriental rugs than were Westerners.

Stephen Ceci (Ceci & Roazzi, 1994) has found similar context effects in performance on various tasks. For example, Ceci and his associates

culture-relevant • describes the assessment of skills and knowledge that relate to the cultural experiences of the test-takers, by using content and procedures that are appropriate to the cultural context of the test-takers

Early in the 20th century, some experts on intelligence attempted to bar many European immigrants from entering the United States because these immigrants scored poorly on group intelligence tests. Subsequent generations of Americans descended from these immigrants have IQs slightly above the national average. If IQ scores are not used as immigration criteria, what criteria should be used to determine who should be allowed to enter and remain legally in this country?

(Ceci, Bronfenbrenner, & Baker, 1988) compared children's ability to learn to predict where an image would end up on a video screen. Children learned more easily if they believed the images were butterflies to be captured than if they believed the images were abstract geometric figures. Brazilian women had no difficulty with *proportional reasoning* (figuring out how various amounts relate to each other) when they were asked to pretend they were buying food, but they had great difficulty with such reasoning when they were asked to pretend they were buying medicinal herbs (Schliemann & Magalhües, 1990). Brazilian children who had become street vendors showed no difficulty in doing complicated arithmetic computations when selling things, but they had great difficulty doing similar calculations in a classroom (Carraher, Carraher, & Schliemann, 1985; Nuñes, 1994). In these studies, the context in which people act clearly affects how intelligently they perform.

Some psychologists have criticized the contextual approach because it fails to define exactly what a context is, and it fails to specify exactly how context affects intelligence. In addition, whereas the internal approaches to intelligence perhaps place too much emphasis on what goes on in a single person's head, the contextual (external) approach may say too little about what goes on in an individual's mind. Some theorists have sought a more comprehensive approach to try to understand intelligence

Intricate patterns on Moroccan rugs were more easily remembered by Moroccan rug merchants than by Westerners. In contrast, Westerners more easily remembered information unfamiliar to Moroccan rug merchants.

in terms of its relationship to both the internal and the external worlds of the individual.

Intelligence as a System

Some theorists view intelligence as a complex system. They try to combine the best aspects of the various theories of intelligence, such as by specifying both the structure and the function of intelligence, rather than just one or the other.

Multiple Intelligences

Howard Gardner (1983, 1993b, 1999) has proposed a **theory of multiple intelligences,** which comprises eight distinct intelligences (linguistic, logical–mathematical, spatial, musical, bodily–kinesthetic, interpersonal, intra-personal, and naturalist), each of which is relatively independent of the others (see Table 8.1). Gardner also has proposed spiritual intelligence and existential intelligence as possible, or "candidate," intelligences. Each intelligence is a separate system of functioning, although the systems can interact to produce what we see as intelligent performance.

Gardner's theory is counter to the popular theory in psychology that there is a general factor, sometimes called *g*, which pervades all intelligent performance (Jensen, 1998; Spearman, 1927). Gardner claims that the evidence in favor of the general factor is biased by the fact that all of the tests typically used to measure general intelligence are paper-and-pencil types of tests, or at least are of an academic variety. Gardner believes that an expanded range of tests would show that the general factor is much more limited than it appears; in other words, that it is not truly general.

Gardner (1983, 1993b) based his theory on evidence that goes well beyond factor analysis. He put together various sources and types of data.

theory of multiple intelligences • a theory suggesting that there are eight distinct intelligences that function somewhat independently: linguistic, logical–mathematical, spatial, musical, bodily–kinesthetic, interpersonal, intrapersonal, and naturalist intelligence

TABLE 8.1

Gardner's Eight Intelligences

On which of Howard Gardner's eight intelligences do you show the greatest ability? In what contexts can you use your intelligences most effectively? (After H. Gardner, 1983, 1993b, 1999)

Type of intelligence	Tasks reflecting this type of intelligence
Linguistic intelligence	Reading a book; writing a paper, a novel, or a poem; and understanding spoken words
Logical–mathematical intelligence	Solving math problems, balancing a checkbook, doing a mathematical proof, and logical reasoning
Spatial intelligence	Getting from one place to another, reading a map, and packing suitcases in the trunk of a car so that they all fit into a compact space
Musical intelligence	Singing a song, composing a sonata, playing a trumpet, or even appreciating the structure of a piece of music
Bodily–kinesthetic intelligence	Dancing, playing basketball, running a mile, or throwing a javelin
Interpersonal intelligence	Relating to other people, such as when we try to understand another person's behavior, motives, or emotions
Intrapersonal intelligence	Understanding ourselves—the basis for understanding who we are, what makes us tick, and how we can change ourselves, given the existing constraints on our abilities and our interests
Naturalistic intelligence	Understanding patterns in the natural world

Among the diverse kinds of support Gardner used was evidence from studies of brain damage, from observed patterns by which a given ability develops, from the behavior of exceptional individuals (at both ends of the spectrum), and from evolutionary history (in which increases in intelligence are associated with enhanced adaptation to the environment). In addition, Gardner has cited supporting evidence from psychometric and experimental research. Since Gardner's theory was proposed, however, there have been no overall empirical tests of the theory.

The Triarchic Theory

Gardner's theory emphasizes the separateness of the various aspects of intelligence. In my **triarchic theory of human intelligence** (R. J. Sternberg, 1985a, 1988b, 1997c), I tend to emphasize the extent to which the aspects of intelligence work together. According to the triarchic (*tri-*, three; *-archic*, governed) theory, there are three main aspects of intelligence: analytical, creative, and practical. You use the analytical aspect of intelligence when you compare and contrast ideas or when you evaluate them. You use the creative aspect of intelligence when you think in new ways and when you cope with new kinds of situations. You use the practical aspect of intelligence when you adapt to the various demands of your everyday environment. For example, comparing two theories of visual perception would involve analysis, coming up with your own theory would involve creativity, and applying the theory to helping people see better in dark places would involve practical intelligence. Figure 8.4 illustrates the parts of the theory and their interrelationships.

**triarchic theory of human intelligence • ** a theory of intelligence, which asserts that intelligence comprises three aspects (analytical, creative, and practical)

According to the triarchic theory, people may differ in how well they apply their intelligence to different kinds of problems. For example, some people may be more intelligent when they face problems in their studies in school, whereas others may be more intelligent when they face practical problems. The theory does not define an intelligent person as someone who necessarily is excellent in all aspects of intelligence. Rather, intelligent people know their own strengths and weaknesses. They then find ways to make the most of their strengths, and they either try to fix or to make up for their weaknesses. For example, suppose that a person is strong in psychology but weak in physics. This person might choose a physics project that uses psychology, such as creating a physics aptitude test (which I did when I took physics). In whatever you do, you should make the most of your strengths and find ways to improve upon or at least to make up for your weaknesses.

Over the years, we have conducted a research program studying people's practical intelligence as indicated by their adaptive behavior (see e.g., R. J. Sternberg, Wagner, Williams, & Horvath, 1995). We have asked people to solve the kinds of problems they might face on the job. For example, salespeople might be asked to evaluate different strategies for selling a slow-moving copy machine, or managers might be asked to evaluate procedures for awarding contracts to suppliers. We have found in these studies that practical intelligence, as measured by our tests, does not correlate with the more academic form of intelligence, as measured by conventional tests.

The systems theories of intelligence are broader and more comprehensive than the theories of intelligence considered earlier. Some psychologists (e.g., Eysenck, 1984; Jackson, 1984; Yussen, 1984) say that the systems

FIGURE 8.4
Triarchic Theory of Intelligence
According to Robert Sternberg, intelligence comprises analytical, creative, and practical abilities. In analytical thinking, we try to solve familiar problems by using strategies that manipulate the elements of a problem or the relationships among the elements; in creative thinking, we try to solve new kinds of problems that require us to think about the problem and its elements in a new way; in practical thinking, we try to solve problems that apply what we know to everyday contexts.

According to Howard Gardner's theory of intelligence, gifted musicians such as Itzhak Perlman show high levels of musical intelligence.

theories are too broad and that these theories are therefore difficult to test. Nonetheless, the trend in the coming years seems to be toward broader theories of intelligence, which encompass abilities that earlier theorists downplayed or even neglected.

WHAT HAVE WE LEARNED ABOUT EXTREMES OF INTELLIGENCE?

Every theory of intelligence must somehow address the extremes of intelligence. Although most people fall within the broad middle of the range of intelligence, some people fall at the upper and lower extremes. People at the upper extreme are often labeled as *intellectually gifted,* whereas those at the lower extreme are often labeled as *mentally retarded.*

Intellectual Giftedness

Psychologists disagree regarding how to define intellectual giftedness. For example, some school programs for the gifted choose candidates largely on the basis of several tests of intelligence. Such programs may take children in the top 1% (IQ roughly equal to 135 or above) or 2% (IQ roughly equal to 132 or above) of IQ scores. Other programs also use other measures for determining giftedness, such as school achievement or motivation.

Lewis Terman, developer of the *Stanford-Binet Intelligence Scales,* conducted a longitudinal study of gifted individuals. A *longitudinal study* is research that follows a particular group of individuals across many years. Terman and his collaborators followed particular gifted individuals over the course of their life span (Terman, 1925; Terman & Oden, 1959). The longitudinal study has continued, even after Terman's death. The core of Terman's sample was 621 children from California under age 11 years with IQs over 140. The average IQ of the entire sample of participants was 151.

The later accomplishments of the children were extraordinary. By 1959, 70 were listed in *American Men of Science,* 3 were members of the prestigious National Academy of Sciences, 31 were listed in *Who's Who in America,* and 10 appeared in the *Directory of American Scholars.* Numerous others were highly successful in businesses or professions. One of the people studied by Terman, Robert Sears, became a professor at Stanford and even took over the Terman study for some time. During the time of Terman's study, most of the women in Terman's study became housewives. Thus, it is impossible to compare meaningfully the accomplishments of the men and the women in Terman's sample.

Many factors other than IQ also could have contributed to the success of Terman's sample. Among the most important of these factors are familial socioeconomic status (SES; income, education, etc.) and the final educational status of these individuals. As with all correlational data, we cannot infer what caused what.

Today, many psychologists believe that intellectual giftedness involves more than a high IQ (R. J. Sternberg & Davidson, 1986). For example, Joseph Renzulli (1986) believes that high commitment to tasks (motivation) and high creativity are important to giftedness, in addition to above-average (although not necessarily outstanding) intelligence, as measured by IQ tests.

How can we identify intellectual giftedness? Stephen Hawking is widely regarded as extremely gifted because of his creative insights regarding time and space, as well as for his depth of knowledge of physics. How are we able to identify Hawking as being intellectually gifted?

I believe that there are many ways to be gifted, and scores on standard intelligence tests represent only one of these ways. Indeed, some highly gifted persons, such as Albert Einstein or Thomas Edison, were not outstanding students or test-takers during their early years. Moreover, Einstein did not even speak until he was 3 years old. Einstein was near the top of the scale of intellectual performance; many individuals are closer to the opposite extreme.

Mental Retardation

Mental retardation refers, simply, to very low levels of intelligence. Much less simple is determining whom to label as mentally retarded. Different viewpoints lead to different conclusions. The American Association on Mental Retardation includes two main parts in its definition of mental retardation: low IQ and low adaptive competence. *Adaptive competence* refers to how a person gets along in the world. In other words, to be labeled as retarded, an individual would have to meet two criteria: (a) poor performance on an intelligence test, and (b) problems in adapting to the environment. By this definition, a child with a low IQ would not be classified

mental retardation • a very low level of intelligence, usually reflected by both poor performance on tests of intelligence and poor *adaptive competence* (the degree to which a person functions effectively within a normal situational context)

as mentally retarded if the child performed normally in all or most other ways. Table 8.2 illustrates some of the ways in which particular IQ scores have been related to particular adaptive life skills.

It is not always easy to measure adaptive competence, however, as the following example (Edgerton, 1967) shows. A retarded man (who had scored low on tests of intelligence) was unable to tell time, an indication of some kind of thinking problem. However, the man figured out a clever way to find out the time: He wore a nonfunctional watch, so that whenever he wanted to know the time, he could stop, look at his watch, pretend to notice that his watch did not work, and then ask a nearby stranger (who would have observed his behavior) to tell him the correct time. How should we measure this man's adaptive competence, in terms of his strategy for determining the time or in terms of his inability to tell time by looking at a watch?

Some individuals are mentally retarded and yet show a high level of an unusual skill that sets them apart from other mentally retarded individuals. Those individuals whose general level of mental functioning is very low but who have such a high level of a skill are referred to as *savants*. The skills can vary. Some are calendar calculators and can tell others the day on which virtually any date in the future or past will occur or has occurred. Others, such as a well-known child savant named Nadia, show extraordinary artistic talent. Scientists still do not understand why savants have these extraordinary skills or how the savants acquire them.

Where does mental retardation come from? Is it hereditary, environmental, or both? We consider this question next.

TABLE 8.2
Levels of Mental Retardation

Degree of retardation	Adaptive life skills
Mild. (IQ score 50–70; ≈ 85% of retarded persons; about 2% of general population)	May acquire and demonstrate mastery of academic skills at or below the sixth-grade level, particularly if given special education. Likely to acquire various social- and vocation-related skills, given adequate training and appropriate environment. Given appropriate environmental support and assistance (especially during times of stress), may achieve independent living and occupational success.
Moderate. (IQ score 35–55; ≈ 10% of retarded persons; 0.1% of the general population)	Have considerable difficulty in school, but may acquire and demonstrate mastery of academic skills at or below the fourth-grade level if given special education. Given appropriate very structured environmental support and supervision, may be able to engage in unskilled or possibly highly routinized semiskilled vocational activities that contribute to self-support. Able to engage in many personal self-maintenance activities. A sheltered home and work environment, in which supervision and guidance are readily available, often works well.
Severe. (IQ score 20–40; ≈ 4% of retarded persons; <0.003% of the general population)	May learn to talk or at least to communicate in some manner. Unlikely to profit from vocational training, but given adequate full supervision and highly structured environmental support, may be able to perform simple tasks required for personal self-maintenance (including toileting) and possibly even some limited vocational activity. Some custodial services may be required, in addition to a carefully controlled environment.
Profound. (IQ score below 25; <2% of retarded persons)	Limited motor development and little or no speech. Generally unresponsive to training, but may be trained to participate in some self-maintenance activities (not including toileting). Constant supervision and assistance in performing fundamental self-maintenance within a custodial setting are required.

IS INTELLIGENCE INHERITED?

Psychologists believe that, in general, both heredity and environment can contribute to mental retardation and to individual differences in intelligence (R. J. Sternberg & Grigorenko, 1997b). For example, environmental contributions to low intelligence may involve limited opportunities for learning. Even the prenatal environment may cause permanent retardation. For instance, retardation may result if a pregnant mother is poorly nourished or if she consumes teratogenic substances (which can cause damage to the prenatal child), such as alcohol, during the child's prenatal development. Even a brief trauma (e.g., an injury caused by a car accident or a fall) can damage the functioning of the brain, leading to mental retardation.

We do not yet have a clear understanding of how heredity influences intelligence. Even so, we do know of several genetic syndromes that cause mental retardation. One of the more common ones is *Down's syndrome,* a genetic disorder causing mental retardation.

Sometimes, heredity interacts with the environment to produce mental retardation. Although we cannot prevent the inheritance of genetic disorders or diseases once a child is conceived, we can try to keep the environment from contributing to the retardation. For example, we now know how to prevent serious mental retardation resulting from *phenylketonuria (PKU).* PKU is a rare hereditary disease that results in mental retardation if nothing is done to prevent retardation from occurring. With a special diet, however, damage to the brain can be avoided or at least limited, and serious retardation can be avoided altogether. In PKU, the interaction of nature and nurture is clear. For most of us, however, the distinctive influences of nature and nurture are less clear.

How do psychologists try to determine the relative influences of nature and nurture? Several methods have been used for determining the *heritability of intelligence* (the degree to which variation in levels of intelligence is due to heredity, assuming that environmental factors are held constant). The main methods involve studies of separated identical twins, studies of identical versus fraternal twins, and studies of adopted children. These kinds of studies have led to uncertain, mixed results. For example, the Minnesota Study of Twins Raised Apart (Bouchard, 1997; Bouchard & McGue, 1981) suggested a fairly high heritability estimate. Many psychologists now believe that heredity and environment each contribute about equally to intelligence. However, many variables can change these estimates. For example, Sandra Scarr (1997) has reported that the heritability of intelligence is greater for white than for black Americans, meaning that environmental factors appear to play a greater role in influencing the observed intelligence of black Americans, as compared with white Americans. Also, the distributions of genes or environments may vary across persons of different ages. There is some evidence that the apparent heritability of intelligence increases with age (Plomin, 1997), which means that environmental effects become less influential and genetic effects more influential in contributing to differences in observed intelligence as people grow older. Apparently, differential effects of early environment start to moderate with age, leaving more room for genes to express their relative effects as people age.

Research has shown that most of the effects of environment are *within family* rather than *between family.* In other words, to the extent environment affects intelligence, most of the effect is not due to differences in environment children experience from one family to another, but rather, is due to differences in environment that children within the same family

These identical twins were separated at birth and were not reunited until they were 31 years old, when the two firefighters met and discovered striking similarities in their personal habits and interests. Studies of twins reared apart reveal a great deal about how much of our intelligence is due to our nature and how much is due to our nurture.

"Actually, Lou, I think it was more than just being in the right place at the right time. I think it was my being the right race, the right religion, the right sex, the right socioeconomic group, having the right accent, the right clothes, going to the right schools . . ."

Drawing by W. Miller. Copyright © 1992 The New Yorker Magazine, Inc.

experience (Plomin, 1997). For example, Zajonc and his colleagues (Zajonc & Markus, 1979; Zajonc & Mullally, 1997) have suggested that children with different birth orders are treated differently by parents. According to their *confluence theory,* older children serve as teachers for younger children. Thus, an eldest sibling can serve as a teacher for younger siblings. Serving as a teacher actually helps raise the eldest child's level of cognitive abilities. But as the number of siblings increases substantially, the amount of intellectual stimulation any child can get decreases so that average levels of intelligence actually go down. Thus, the intellectual level of the children will be higher in a two-child than in a one-child family, but soon will start to decrease as the number of children becomes so large that the children receive less, not more, intellectual stimulation. The evidence on the confluence theory is mixed, and only some theorists of intelligence accept this theory.

Recently, Judith Rich Harris (1998) has suggested that to the extent that nurture has an effect, it is overwhelmingly due not to the effects of parents but to the effects of peers. Harris probably overstates her case, but makes the important point that a child's peers can have a substantial influence on how the child develops. Harris also correctly observes that as parents typically choose where the children will live and may choose the school the children attend, these effects of peers can be influenced by choices the parents make.

When we consider intelligence and other characteristics, we must be careful to recognize the role of the environment, as well as of heredity. Even if a characteristic is highly heritable, it can be developed. For example, height is highly heritable, yet heights have been increasing over the past several generations. Clearly, better environments can lead to growth, physical as well as intellectual.

One of the most powerful environmental factors affecting intelligence is societal status. It appears that intelligence may be hindered when individuals are assigned an inferior status within a given society. Across cultures, disadvantaged groups (e.g., native Maoris vs. European New Zealanders) have often shown lower scores on tests of intelligence and aptitude (Steele, 1990; Zeidner, 1990). Such was the case of the Buraku-min tanners in Japan, who, in 1871, were granted emancipation but not full acceptance into Japanese society. Although they generally have low status and show poor academic performance in Japan, those who immigrate to America, and are treated like other Japanese immigrants, perform on IQ tests and in school at a level comparable to that of their fellow Japanese Americans (Ogbu, 1986). Once they are relieved of their lower societal status, their measured intelligence improves.

Some investigators believe that individual differences in intelligence can themselves play a role in determining social status (Herrnstein & Murray, 1994). They argue that more intelligent people tend to rise to the top of a meritocratic society such as the United States, whereas less intelligent people tend to sink toward the bottom. There may be some truth to this argument, but the causation of this divergence is very much in dispute. It has been argued, for example, that this pattern must occur in any society that uses intelligence-type tests as vehicles for deciding who will be given the opportunities society has to offer (R. J. Sternberg, 1995, 1997c). In effect, people who do not score well on these tests are denied the access routes to many of the highest paying and most prestigious jobs, and so they may find that the society has created a system that propels them downward in socioeconomic status.

In the United States, average scores on intelligence tests are about 10 to 15 points higher for whites than for blacks. We cannot say whether the differing societal status of blacks versus whites explains this difference in average test scores. In fact, at present, there are no conclusive explanations for this difference in test scores, although various interpretations have been offered (e.g., Herrnstein & Murray, 1994; Ogbu, 1982). We can say, however, that there is no compelling evidence for a genetic basis underlying apparent racial differences in intelligence-test scores (described in Loehlin, Lindzey, & Spuhler, 1975; Nisbett, 1995). There is compelling evidence, however, that intelligence can be increased, at least to some extent, in people of all races.

Although males and females show similar overall levels of scores on tests of cognitive abilities, they show somewhat different patterns of abilities, on average. Table 8.3, from a review article by Diane Halpern (1997), summarizes some of the main sex differences in patterns of performance.

TABLE 8.3
Sex Differences in Intelligence

Males score higher on tasks with the following requirements	Females score higher on tasks with the following requirements
Transformation in visual–spatial working memory	Rapid access to and use of phonological and semantic information in long-term memory
Motor skills involved in aiming	Production and comprehension of complex prose
Spatiotemporal responding	Fine motor skills
Fluid reasoning (especially in abstract mathematical and scientific domains)	Perceptual speed

Based on Halpern, D. F. (1997). Sex differences in intelligence: Implications for education. *American Psychologist, 52,* 1091–1102.

Note that although males tend to do better on many spatial tasks and women tend to do better on many verbal tasks, the actual patternings of abilities are more complex than would be accounted for by any kind of simplistic explanation. In fact, we still do not know why we get these differences.

CAN WE IMPROVE INTELLIGENCE?

At one time, it was believed that intelligence is fixed; that is, we are stuck forever with whatever level of intelligence we have at birth. Today, many researchers believe that intelligence is malleable: It can be shaped and even increased (Detterman & Sternberg, 1982; Perkins & Grotzer, 1997; Ramey, 1994; R. J. Sternberg, Okagaki, & Jackson, 1990). For one thing, intelligence can be increased simply by using intellectual skills as much as possible in everyday life. Just as musicians may improve their musical abilities through practice, all of us can enrich our intellectual abilities through practice in thinking intelligently in our daily experiences. Another way to increase intelligence is to be involved in an educational setting that fosters the development of intelligence (Ceci, 1996). When teachers emphasize the use of thinking skills in the classroom, the teachers enhance their students' intelligence. In addition, various programs have been designed specifically to help people increase their intelligence.

Teaching in ways that utilize modern theories of intelligence can also enhance children's learning of subject matter. In one study, investigators found that when high school students are taught in a way that enables them maximally to utilize their patterns of analytical, creative, and practical abilities, their achievement in a psychology course increased (R. J. Sternberg, Ferrari, Clinkenbeard, & Grigorenko, 1996; R. J. Sternberg, Grigorenko, Ferrari, & Clinkenbeard, 1999). In a psychology course, for example, analytical instruction might require students to analyze a theory of intelligence or to compare and contrast two theories of intelligence. Creative instruction might encourage students to create their own theory of intelligence. Practical instruction might require students to think about how intelligence tests are used properly and improperly in U.S. society or other societies. In another study, investigators showed that third-grade students (of about 8 years of age) who were taught social studies and eighth-grade students (of about 14 years of age) who were taught psychology in a way that enabled them to utilize analytical, creative, and practical thinking skills were at an advantage in their school work. In particular, these students outperformed students in these grades who were taught in a way that encouraged them to use primarily memory abilities or primarily memory and analytical abilities, but not creative and practical abilities as well (R. J. Sternberg, Torff, & Grigorenko, 1998).

Head Start is a program intended to provide preschoolers with an edge on intellectual abilities and accomplishments that would serve the children well when they started school. Studies checking the progress of Head Start children have included matched controls. Matched controls are research participants who are in the control condition, but who have been matched to the participants in the treatment condition as closely as possible. For example, the researchers try to ensure that the ages, family backgrounds, income levels, and other characteristics of participants in the control group match those of participants in the treatment group. In the case of the Head Start studies, the treatment group would participate in the Head Start program, and the control group would not.

Long-term follow-ups have indicated that by midadolescence, performance of children who participated in the program was more than a grade ahead of matched controls who did not participate in the program (Lazar & Darlington, 1982; Zigler & Berman, 1983). The children in the Head Start program also showed other advantages: They scored higher on various tests of scholastic achievement, were less likely to need remedial attention (involving remedies or treatments for educational problems), and were less likely to show behavioral problems. Although these outcome measures are not direct measures of intelligence, they do show a strong positive correlation with measures such as intelligence tests. Many newer programs in schools or other community settings have also shown some success (see Adams, 1986; Ramey, 1994).

We now know that people's environments (e.g., Ceci, Nightingale, & Baker, 1992; Reed, 1993; R. J. Sternberg & Wagner, 1994), their motivation (e.g., Collier, 1994; R. J. Sternberg & Ruzgis, 1994), and their training (e.g., Feuerstein, 1980; R. J. Sternberg, 1987) can powerfully affect their intellectual skills. Heredity may set some kind of upper limit on how intelligent a person may become. However, for any attribute that is partly genetic, there is a reaction range. In a **reaction range,** the attribute can be expressed in various ways within broad limits of possibilities. Thus, each person's intelligence can be developed further within this broad range of potential intelligence. People have yet to reach their upper limits in developing their intellectual skills. Evidence suggests that we can do quite a bit to help people become more intelligent.

Intelligence is also linked to another ability that appears to be highly malleable: creativity. Surprisingly, perhaps, extremely high intelligence is not necessary for great creativity. Beyond a given level of intelligence, further increases in intelligence do not necessarily correlate with increases in creativity. Thus, to be creative, an individual must be bright but not necessarily brilliant. If extreme brilliance is not necessary for creativity, what characteristics are needed?

WHAT IS CREATIVITY AND HOW DOES IT EMERGE?

Although specialists on creativity often disagree about how to define creativity precisely, most psychologists would generally agree that **creativity** is a process of producing something that is both original and worthwhile. The something may be a theory, a dance, a chemical, a process or procedure, or almost anything else.

Just what does it mean for that something to be original? Almost everything we do is based on the ideas and the work of those who have come before us. Still, we recognize that composers, choreographers, poets, and other artists create original somethings, even if they learn from the techniques, styles, and subjects of other people. Can scientists and other nonartists create anything original?

When Nicolaus Copernicus (1473–1543) proposed his heliocentric *(helio-,* sun; *-centric,* centered) view of our solar system, he based his idea on the work of other people, as well as on his own observations. What makes his work creative? He analyzed and then synthesized (combined) the existing information in an unusual way. Through his creative work, he completely changed the way we see our planet in relation to the universe.

That Copernicus's creation was worthwhile seems doubtless now, but during his lifetime, many people doubted the worth of his idea. Sometimes,

reaction range • the broad limits within which a particular attribute (e.g., intelligence) may be expressed in various possible ways, given the inherited potential for expression of the attribute in the particular individual

creativity • the process of producing something that is both original and valuable

How can we tell a highly creative person from someone who is relatively less creative? Shown here are three highly creative individuals: Salvador Dali, Alice Walker, and Elton John.

people do not appreciate the value of the creative work until long after the creator dies. This fact is not as odd as it might seem: By definition, creative work moves away from what has already been done by others. It may take awhile for other people to see that the unusual can have great value. Even after quite some time, a creative product may not be considered valuable by everyone. For example, almost anyone would recognize Giuseppe Verdi's operas as original. However, not everyone considers these works to be worthwhile. What makes something worthwhile is that it is significant, useful, or valuable in some way to some people.

What does it take to create something original and worthwhile? What are creative people like? Almost everyone would agree that creative individuals show *creative productivity*. Creative people produce inventions, insightful discoveries, artistic products, or other creative products that are both original and worthwhile. Conventional wisdom suggests that highly creative individuals also have creative lifestyles: Their lifestyles are characterized by flexibility, unusual behaviors, and uncommon attitudes.

Some psychologists have taken a *psychometric* approach to creativity, such as Joy P. Guilford (1950). They have emphasized performance on tasks involving specific aspects of creativity, such as *divergent production,* which involves the generation of a diverse assortment of appropriate responses to a problem question or task. Using this and similar notions, Paul Torrance (1988) and other researchers have devised tests of creativity, such as the *Torrance Tests of Creative Thinking* (Torrance, 1974, 1984). On such tests, high scores reflect diverse, numerous, appropriate responses to open-ended questions, such as thinking of all the possible ways in which to use a paper clip or a ballpoint pen.

Many different factors contribute to creativity. Perhaps the most important is a willingness to defy convention, to separate oneself from the crowd in terms of one's ideas (R. J. Sternberg & Lubart, 1995, 1996). Other factors are important as well, including intelligence, knowledge, personality, motivation, and the environment (R. J. Sternberg & Lubart, 1991, 1995, 1996).

With respect to intelligence, it appears that highly creative people are above average, but not necessarily exceptionally intelligent (Renzulli, 1986). Thus, you do not need sky-high scores on conventional tests of abilities in order to do highly creative work. Knowledge is important also: To move beyond what is known, you have to be aware of what is known. However, knowledge can be a double-edged sword: Sometimes, knowledge can interfere with thinking flexibly and in new ways about a problem (Frensch & Sternberg, 1989). Several aspects of personality are also important for creativity, such as openness to new ways of seeing things, alertness to opportunities, willingness to take sensible risks, and willingness to overcome obstacles (Barron, 1988; R. J. Sternberg & Lubart, 1995, 1996). Motivation is important, too. Creative people virtually always love what they do and they work hard at it for the sheer enjoyment of the work (Hennessey & Amabile, 1988). Finally, the environment matters. Even if you have all the attributes of a creative person, you need a supportive environment that will encourage and recognize your creativity, rather than discourage or even actively suppress it (Csikszentmihalyi, 1988, 1996; H. Gardner, 1993a; Simonton, 1994; R. J. Sternberg, 1999).

David Perkins (1995) and Dean Simonton (1995) have both suggested that some evolutionary principles may be applied to the understanding of human creativity. According to these investigators (see also Campbell, 1960), many new ideas are generated more or less blindly, without any foreknowledge of whether they will be well received or not. In this respect, the generation of ideas is somewhat like mutations of genes, which may or may not receive a favorable reception from the environment (and usually do not). These ideas, like mutations, must undergo a selection process. Most of the ideas serve no particularly useful purpose and are quickly discarded. But a few ideas may be not only novel, but useful, and those ideas will be selected by a society as ones of value. They then become a part of society's ways of thinking, much as useful genetic mutations can become part of humanity's genetic makeup.

Some researchers believe that only a few rare persons can be creative. However, most psychologists believe that almost anyone can become more creative by working to become so. Quite a few also believe that many more of us could become exceptionally creative if we wished to become so (see Putting It to Use 8.1).

There is some agreement that each of the Putting It to Use suggestions may play a role in creative productivity. Even so, many psychologists and other researchers might disagree about one or more of these suggestions, and many creative individuals do not follow all of these general recommendations. In fact, we might say that, as a group, creative people are defined by their differences. Extraordinary creative productivity may be rare

8.1

HOW CAN YOU BECOME MORE CREATIVE?

To increase your own creativity, take the following steps:

1. Become highly motivated to be creative in a particular kind of work. Under most circumstances, however, try to avoid being tempted by extrinsic motivators related to an outcome of your creative work. In general, your primary motivation should be intrinsic, related to the creative work itself.

2. Show some nonconformity, as necessary, to promote your creative work. Boldly question and possibly violate rules or conventions that senselessly inhibit your creative work. Avoid getting sidetracked by the struggle against conventions, however. Remember also that some conventions can be useful. Maintain tough standards of excellence in your performance and your work habits. Demonstrate strong self-discipline as it relates to your creative work.

3. Deeply believe in the value and importance of your creative work; do not let others discourage you from pursuing this work. On the other hand, you should constantly monitor and criticize your own work, seeking always to improve it.

4. Carefully choose the problems or subjects on which to focus your creative attention. Find problems that appeal to you. At first, some creative ideas may be considered distasteful and unappealing by others.

5. Actively seek out information that other people ignore and seek novel combinations of the pieces of information. Think in terms of many possibilities, rather than in terms of limited options.

6. Choose friends who will encourage you to take sensible intellectual risks and who do not conform just for the sake of conforming.

7. Gain as much of the available knowledge as possible in your chosen field. In this way, you can avoid reinventing the wheel or producing the same old stuff being produced by others in your field. Find the interesting gaps in the existing information. On the other hand, avoid becoming trapped by mental sets or negative transfer (see chapter 7). One way in which to get as much knowledge as you need, yet to avoid mental sets, is to study various phenomena that interest you. This variety of interests helps you to avoid getting bogged down in the conventional thinking about one particular phenomenon.

8. Commit yourself deeply to your creative work.

because so many variables must come together, in the right amounts, in a single person. For a highly creative person to express great creativity, that person must find a supportive developmental context. The influence of the developmental context is the topic of our next chapter.

The Case of the Low Grades

After reading chapter 8 of *Pathways to Psychology,* Moira realized that dropping out of college was not a good option, nor was dropping out of the business major. In reading about the importance of *practical intelligence* to success in life, Moira realized that many of her greatest skills simply were ones that would not show up in an introductory course in business. Moira believed that she did have the practical intelligence to succeed in business, whether or not she had the skills needed to get a high grade in the introductory business course. Moira was correct. In fact, her skills proved more relevant to upper-level courses and her average improved considerably as she advanced in the study of business. Today, she is successfully running several businesses, including the book business she started in high school.

Summary

What Are Two Traditional Approaches to Studying Intelligence? 268

1. Two traditions in the study of intelligence are those of Francis Galton and of Alfred Binet. The tradition of Galton emphasizes *psychophysical* abilities, whereas that of Binet emphasizes *judgmental* abilities.

How Do Psychologists Assess Intelligence? 269

2. *Mental age* refers to a person's level of intelligence, as compared with the average person of a given chronological age. Because of conceptual and statistical problems, mental age is rarely used today as a means of expressing intelligence test scores.
3. The *intelligence quotient (IQ)* originally represented the ratio of mental age to chronological age, multiplied by 100. It was intended to provide a measure of a child's intelligence, relative to his or her agemates.
4. Today, *IQ*s typically are computed to have an average score of 100. IQs that are computed based on deviations from the average are *deviation IQs. Normative scores* represent a translation of raw scores into scaled equivalents; these scaled equiva-

lents reflect the relative performance of individual test-takers, thereby permitting comparison.
5. Two of the most widely used intelligence tests are administered individually. They are the *Stanford-Binet Intelligence Scales* and the *Wechsler Adult Intelligence Scale—Revised (WAIS-R).*
6. Test *validity* indicates the degree to which a test measures what it is supposed to measure. Test *reliability* indicates how dependably and consistently a test measures whatever it measures.
7. Test *standardization* refers to the steps taken to ensure that the conditions for taking a test are the same for all test-takers.

How Should We Try to Understand the Nature of Intelligence? 275

8. *Intelligence* can be understood in terms of its many different aspects. Some investigators focus more on mental structures, others on mental processes. Some investigators seek to understand intelligence in relation to the brain; others study its relation to culture. Systems theories, such as those of Howard Gardner and Robert Sternberg, integrate a number of these different aspects.
9. In an approach focusing on structure, intelligence is studied via *factor analysis,* a statistical technique

for identifying the underlying sources of individual differences in performance on tests.

10. An alternative approach to intelligence (a computational one) emphasizes *information processing*—the mental manipulation of symbols.

11. Biologically oriented psychologists use sophisticated means of viewing the brain while the brain is engaged in performing tasks that require intelligence.

12. Psychologists taking a *contextual approach* view intelligence as wholly or partly determined by cultural surroundings.

13. What is considered to be intelligent behavior is, to some extent, culturally relative: The same behavior that is considered to be intelligent in one culture may be considered to be unintelligent in another culture.

14. *Culture-fair* tests, in theory, are equally fair for members of all cultures. It is probably impossible to create a test of intelligence that is truly culture-fair. Such tests cannot exist because members of different cultures have different conceptions of what constitutes intelligent behavior. The development of *culture-relevant* tests, however, is both realistic and desirable.

15. A useful approach to understanding intelligence is to understand it as a system. Gardner's *theory of multiple intelligences* specifies that there are eight distinct intelligences, each relatively independent of the others. Sternberg's *triarchic theory of human intelligence* conceives of intelligence as a unified system that integrates information processing with cultural context. Intelligence is seen as having analytical, creative, and practical aspects.

What Have We Learned About Extremes of Intelligence?   286

16. *Intellectual giftedness* refers to a very high level of intelligence and is often believed to involve more than just high IQ. For example, it may be seen as also involving high creativity and high motivation.

17. The contemporary definition of *mental retardation* includes two components: low IQ and low adaptive competence for getting along in the world.

Is Intelligence Inherited?   289

18. Mental retardation can be caused by either hereditary or environmental factors, or by both kinds of factors in interaction.

19. The *heritability of intelligence* refers to the degree to which variation in levels of intelligence is due to heredity, assuming that environmental factors are held constant. Heritability can differ both across populations and within populations, across different times and places.

Can We Improve Intelligence?   292

20. Intellectual skills can be taught. Thus, intelligence is *malleable* rather than fixed.

What Is Creativity and How Does It Emerge?   293

21. *Creativity* involves producing something that is both original and worthwhile. Various researchers have suggested a diverse assortment of views regarding how creativity emerges. For example, one theory suggests that creative individuals produce ideas that are typically undervalued at the time they are produced but that are eventually considered to be highly valuable.

22. The following factors characterize highly creative individuals: (a) extremely high motivation to be creative in a particular field (e.g., for the sheer enjoyment of the creative process); (b) nonconformity in questioning senseless conventions that inhibit creative work, dedication in maintaining standards of excellence, and self-discipline related to creative work; (c) a deep belief in the value of creative work, as well as a willingness to criticize and improve one's own creative work; (d) careful choice of the problems or subjects on which to focus creative attention; (e) thought processes characterized by both insight and divergent thinking; (f) associates who encourage sensible intellectual risk taking; (g) extensive knowledge of the relevant domain; and (h) profound commitment to the creative endeavor.

Choose the best answer to complete each sentence.

1. Alfred Binet devised a battery of tests primarily to
   (a) differentiate average from above-average intelligent individuals.
   (b) identify the brightest individuals for future government service.
   (c) test his hypothesis that there is no great range in intellectual ability.
   (d) differentiate students who were mentally retarded from students who had behavioral problems.

2. Aptitudes are
   (a) preferences and tendencies to perform certain activities.
   (b) accomplished achievements in an area of endeavor.
   (c) individuals' abilities to learn in specific areas of endeavor.
   (d) skills that can be focused only on single tasks.

3. In one study, Kpelle individuals had difficulty in performing a classification task until one of the experimenters
   (a) showed the chief how to perform the task.
   (b) used objects with which the Kpelle were familiar.
   (c) asked the Kpelle to perform the task the way the chief would perform it.
   (d) asked the Kpelle to perform the task the way a foolish person would perform it.

4. IQ means intelligence quotient,
   (a) and psychologists figure out a person's IQ score by dividing the total number of correct answers by the total number of incorrect answers on an intelligence test.
   (b) but nowadays, the IQ scores computed from the most widely used intelligence tests are not quotients at all.
   (c) which offers an exact indication of a person's intelligence.
   (d) which is determined by using tests that are culture-fair when administered by a competent professional.

5. According to Robert Sternberg's triarchic theory, if you were designing a theoretical model explaining how individuals use memory in solving problems, the aspect of intelligence you would be using, for the most part, in designing the model would be

(a) creative.
(b) practical.
(c) memorial.
(d) analytic.

6. According to Robert Sternberg's triarchic theory, if you were skillfully applying what you learned in school to the problems you face at work, the aspect of intelligence you would be using, for the most part, would be
   (a) creative.
   (b) practical.
   (c) memorial.
   (d) analytic.

7. If psychologists were giving an intelligence test to a large group of people, they would probably want to make sure that
   (a) the test items included equal numbers of arithmetic problems and vocabulary problems.
   (b) if one test-taker had to listen to an annoying cuckoo clock while taking the test, all other test-takers would have to listen to the clock, too.
   (c) the test administrators endorsed only the theoretical approach preferred by the test designers.
   (d) the test was completely reliable, valid, and culture-fair.

Answer each of the following questions by filling in the blank with an appropriate word or phrase.

8. William Stern originated the concept of the _____ _____, which was later abbreviated as _____, and which is defined as the ratio of mental age over chronological age, multiplied by 100.

9. An individual's _____ _____ is defined as his or her level of intelligence expressed in terms of the performance of an average person of a given age.

10. Two of the more popular adult-level intelligence tests in use today are the _____-_____ *Intelligence Scales* and the _____ _____ *Intelligence Scale*.

11. Psychometric theories of intelligence often use the statistical technique of _____ _____ in order to come up with underlying factors that differentiate individuals.

12. _____ is the process of producing something that is both original and valuable.

13. Intelligence is partly inherited, within a _____ _____, which is the expression of intelligence within broad limits and possibilities.

14. According to Howard Gardner, an individual who is very adept at evaluating and analyzing him or herself is high in _____ intelligence.

15. In order for an individual to be classified as mentally retarded, he or she must show low _____ _____, as well as having a low score on a typical intelligence test.

16. The type of IQ we use today is referred to as a _____ _____ because it is calculated on the basis of deviations in the normal distribution of scores.

17. Whereas _____ is the extent to which a given form of measurement assesses what it is supposed to measure, _____ is the consistency of a measurement instrument (e.g., a test).

Match each of the following theories to the appropriate theorist:

18. There are eight distinct intelligences.

19. Intelligence consists of a hierarchy of variables, varying in their levels of generality.

20. Intelligence involves analytical, creative, and practical aspects.

(a) Charles Spearman
(b) Robert Sternberg
(c) Howard Gardner
(d) John Carroll
(e) Stephen Ceci

Answers

1. d, 2. c, 3. d, 4. b, 5. a, 6. b, 7. b, 8. intelligence quotient, IQ, 9. mental age, 10. *Stanford-Binet, Wechsler Adult,* 11. factor analysis, 12. Creativity, 13. reaction range, 14. intrapersonal, 15. adaptive competence, 16. deviation IQ, 17. validity, reliability, 18. c, 19. d, 20. b.

Pathways to Understanding

1. Suppose that you were to select a job for yourself solely on the basis of your abilities. What might that job be?

2. How should educators foster the intellectual gifts of their students? Give at least one concrete suggestion.

3. In your view, to what extent are different people born with differing levels of intelligence? To what extent do differences in children's environments affect the development of their intelligence?

The Case of The Unhappy Lawyer

Felicia is holding down a job that pays her a six-figure income. As an undergraduate more than 25 years ago, she majored in English literature. Not sure of what she wanted to do with her specialization, Felicia went to law school and later became a lawyer in a good firm. She has spent her life practicing family law, representing contestants in divorce cases. After roughly two decades representing clients, Felicia has found herself remarkably unfulfilled. Her job consists of helping one side, in usually contested divorces, receive the best possible deal. But she realizes she has become unhappy with herself. What Felicia wishes she had learned to do is to help people hold marriages together and instead she is helping people break them apart. Although Felicia felt satisfied early in her career, now she feels as though she has entered a rut where she helps people break apart their marriages, some of which could be saved, in a way that optimally favors one party to the divorce but not the other. She is uncertain about what to do.

What should Felicia do? Think about this while you read chapter 9. Might she find an alternative pathway to fulfillment? Pay special attention to the theory of Erik Erikson.

CHAPTER 9
LIFE-SPAN DEVELOPMENT

9

Developmental psychologists look for both constancies and changes in how people think, feel, and act as a result of their increasing maturity and their accumulating experiences. **Development** involves pathways of both quantitative and qualitative changes associated with increasing physiological maturity and experience. Quantitative changes in the individual include increases in size (e.g., height or weight) and in amount (e.g., number of brain cells). Qualitative changes usually involve increasing complexity, organization, and sophistication. Development can involve both increases and decreases in quantity and quality of functioning.

Psychological development includes both cognitive development and socioemotional development. **Cognitive development** is the set of processes by which people's mental skills change and, in some cases, remain stable with increasing age and experience. **Socioemotional development** is the set of processes involved in change as well as stability in a person's emotions, personality, interpersonal (social) relationships, and moral beliefs and actions. This chapter deals with both of these kinds of development, as well as with physical development, for each major period of the life span: infancy, childhood, adolescence, and adulthood.

WHAT DEVELOPMENTAL TRENDS HAVE PSYCHOLOGISTS OBSERVED?

Psychologists have noticed several trends that characterize development across the life span. Some of these trends are obvious. For example, humans grow taller and heavier between infancy and adulthood. Other trends are more subtle, such as the trend toward **differentiation,** in which

the *few* become *many* (e.g., a few neural connections in the brain develop into many connections);

the *simple* becomes more *complex* (e.g., one-word expressions become grammatical speech);

the *general* becomes more highly *specialized* (e.g., walking becomes running, climbing, and skipping);

and the *homogeneous* (having a uniform makeup of identical elements) becomes more *diverse* (e.g., identical newly conceived cells become various kinds of cells for making bones, nerves, or muscles).

Researchers use two main methods for detecting developmental trends. The first is to observe individuals *longitudinally* (noting the characteristics of particular persons as they change over time); the second is to observe individuals *cross-sectionally* (noting at a given time the characteristics of various people of different ages). Sometimes, researchers combine the two methods. Psychologists seek not only to *describe* various developmental trends but also to *understand* these trends by asking how and why particular changes occur.

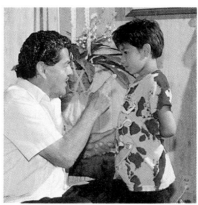

Socioemotional development involves emotional, personality, interpersonal (social), and moral development.

WHAT ARE THE ROLES OF MATURATION AND LEARNING?

The Nature–Nurture Controversy: Maturation Versus Learning

How and why do developmental changes occur? Developmental psychologists often disagree about exactly how to answer this question. A main point of disagreement centers on the **nature–nurture controversy.** This controversy concerns why we develop as we do. Do we develop in particular ways because of our inherited characteristics (our *nature*) or because of our interactions with the environment (our *nurture*)? It seems that as soon as some psychologists find data to support the importance of nature, other psychologists find new information emphasizing the importance of

development • the changes that are associated with increasing physiological maturity, experience, or an interaction of physiological changes and experiences with the environment

cognitive development • the process by which people's thinking changes across the life span

socioemotional development • the process by which people learn about themselves as human beings, as well as the process by which they learn to interact with each other, across the life span; may be viewed as including emotional, personality, interpersonal (social), and moral development

differentiate • to become more highly specialized into distinct parts or types

nature–nurture controversy • a debate regarding whether our psychological makeup arises from our inherited characteristics (our *nature)* or from our interactions with the environment (our *nurture)*

This child's innate musical talent (his nature) might never have been discovered if he had been raised in a home in which music was not an important part of his environment (his nurture).

nurture (e.g., Plomin, 1997; Plomin & McClearn, 1993; R. J. Sternberg & Grigorenko, 1997b). Many developmental psychologists have concluded that there is really no conflict at all, that in fact most of development can be viewed in terms of the interaction between the two. For example, human intelligence certainly represents such an interaction.

How are nature and nurture expressed in the developmental pathways of the growing organism? Development can occur in two different ways: by maturation (developmental pathways linked to nature) and by learning (developmental pathways linked to nurture). **Maturation** is any relatively permanent change in an individual that occurs as a result of internally (biologically) prompted processes of development, without regard to personal experiences or any other environmental considerations. Physical growth in height, for example, occurs as a result of maturational processes (although some environmental influences, e.g., diet, may influence these processes). *Learning* is any relatively permanent change in thought or behavior that occurs because of interactions with the environment. If you learn how to swim or to ride a bicycle, you will do so chiefly as a result of learning, assuming, of course, that you are mature enough to learn these skills (e.g., 1-year-olds do not learn to ride bicycles regardless of how skillfully they are taught).

Maturation is preprogrammed; it will happen for the most part regardless of the environment. In contrast, learning will take place only if the individual has particular experiences. Almost all psychologists recognize that both maturation and learning interactively influence our development, but some psychologists may more strongly emphasize one process or the other.

The Roles of Maturation and Learning: The Developmental Theories of Piaget and Vygotsky

The theories of Jean Piaget (1896–1980) and of Lev Vygotsky (1896–1934) illustrate how two different theorists give different emphases to maturation versus learning in explaining the processes of cognitive development. Piaget suggested that cognitive development occurs largely as a result of internal processes of maturation. Piaget's theory does not discount environmental influences, but it emphasizes internal developmental processes that gradually unfold from the inside out. To Piaget, development is chiefly a biological process by which the individual adapts to the environment.

Piaget (1972) believed that cognitive development occurs in stages that evolve as children develop increasingly complex *schemas* (also called *schemata*), which are mental frameworks for children's organizing what they know about the world. In many situations, the child's existing way of thinking and the child's existing schemas are well-suited for adapting to the challenges of the environment; the child is thus in a state of cognitive equilibrium (balance). For example, suppose that 2-year-old Howie uses the word *doggie* to embrace all the four-legged creatures that he believes are like his own dog. As long as all the four-legged creatures that Howie sees are like the dogs he has already seen, Howie remains in a state of cognitive equilibrium.

At other times, however, the child is presented with information that does not fit with the child's existing schemas, so cognitive disequilibrium arises. The imbalance comes from shortcomings in thinking as the child

**maturation • **any relatively permanent change in an individual that occurs strictly as a result of the biological processes of getting older

faces new challenges. When imbalances occur, the child tries to restore equilibrium through one of two equilibrative processes: assimilation and accommodation. In **assimilation,** the child adapts to new information by incorporating it into her or his existing schemas. For example, suppose that Howie's dog is a Great Dane and Howie goes to the park and sees a poodle, a cocker spaniel, and a Siberian husky. Howie must assimilate the new information into his existing schema for *doggies*—not a big deal.

Suppose, however, that Howie also visits a small zoo and sees a wolf, a rhinoceros, a bear, a lion, a zebra, and a camel. Howie cannot assimilate these diverse creatures into his existing schema for *doggies*. Instead, he must somehow modify his existing schemas to allow for the new information. Piaget would suggest that Howie modifies existing schemas through **accommodation**—adapting to new information by changing the existing schemas to fit the relevant new information about the environment. Together, the processes of assimilation and accommodation result in a more sophisticated level of thought than was previously possible. As children become more adept thinkers, they become less **egocentric;** that is, they become increasingly able to see how others may view a situation.

Although Piaget's theory is comprehensive and attractive, it has been criticized on a number of grounds, including critiques of the ages at which Piaget believed children could first perform various kinds of cognitive

> **assimilation** • the process of trying to restore cognitive equilibrium by incorporating new information into existing schemas
>
> **accommodation** • the process of trying to restore cognitive equilibrium by modifying existing schemas or even creating new ones to fit new information
>
> **egocentric** • focused on one's own views without being able to see how others may view a situation

Jean Piaget (left) learned a great deal about how children think by observing children (including his own) and paying a great deal of attention to what appeared to be errors in their reasoning. Lev Vygotsky (right, with his daughter) also observed children closely, but paid special attention to the role of society in molding their behavior.

tasks (Baillargeon & DeVos, 1991; R. Gelman & Baillargeon, 1983) and of the cross-cultural generality of aspects of the theory (Werner, 1972). Thus, the theory is helpful but not definitive. Another theory that has received a great deal of recent attention is that of Lev Vygotsky.

Unlike Piaget, Vygotsky strongly emphasized the role of learning in his theory of cognitive development. In Vygotsky's theory, social influences are more important to cognitive development than are biological influences. To Vygotsky (1962, 1978), development proceeds from the outside in, rather than from the inside out. Specifically, cognitive development occurs through **internalization,** whereby individuals absorb knowledge from their social context and make it their own. When children interact with the people in their environment they re-create within themselves the interactions they observe. Thus, in Vygotsky's view, the people in a child's world can help or hinder the child's development of thought and knowledge.

Although Vygotsky emphasized the role of the environment, he also appreciated the importance of what each child brought to interactions with the environment. According to Vygotsky, children develop their intellect within a **zone of proximal development (ZPD).** The ZPD is the range of ability between a child's developed, observable level of ability and the child's full, potentially hidden, capacity for developing further at a given time through the benefit of instruction. When we observe children, what we observe typically is the ability that they have developed through the interaction of heredity and environment. To a large extent, however, we are interested truly in what children are capable of doing, what their potential would be if they were freed from the confines of an environment that is never truly optimal. Vygotsky inferred the difference between latent capacity and developed ability by observing children's ability to learn while they were being tested through a series of graded and carefully structured learning experiences.

To summarize, whereas Piaget emphasized maturation (nature), Vygotsky emphasized learning (nurture). Nonetheless, both theorists recognized that development involves an interaction of nature and nurture.

WHAT HAPPENS DURING PRENATAL DEVELOPMENT?

The influence of nature begins at the moment of conception, when the father's sperm fertilizes the mother's *ovum* (human egg). Once the one-celled ovum is fertilized, it is termed a **zygote,** the name for the first of three stages of prenatal development. The single-celled zygote immediately begins dividing into hundreds of virtually identical cells. While the zygote divides, it travels downward to the uterus (about a 3- to 7-day trip to travel several inches). The zygote takes about another week to become firmly *implanted* (deeply embedded) in the internal wall of the uterus. During implantation cell division continues, but some of the cells begin to differentiate into specialized types of cells with distinctive functions. For example, some cells of the zygote begin to form a placenta. The **placenta** lines the wall of the uterus and provides nourishment through the umbilical cord, which attaches the placenta to the developing individual.

Once implanted (at about 2 weeks after conception), the individual is considered an **embryo,** the second of the three stages of prenatal development. The embryo stage lasts from about the end of the 2nd week until about the beginning of the 9th week. During the development of the embryo, the cells further differentiate: One type of cell becomes the nervous

internalization • the process of absorbing knowledge from a given social environmental context

zone of proximal development (ZPD) • a range between the developed abilities that a child clearly shows and the latent capacities that the child might be able to show, given the appropriate environment in which to do so

zygote • an individual in the first of three stages of prenatal development (from the time of conception to implantation and cell differentiation)

placenta • a protective membrane containing a dense network of blood vessels through which the mother's body supplies needed resources (e.g., oxygen, sources of energy, and material resources such as protein and minerals) and removes waste products

embryo • an individual in the second of the three stages of prenatal development (from about 2 weeks after conception until about the end of the 8th week); the individual undergoes tremendous differentiation and rapid growth and is easily influenced by the maternal environment

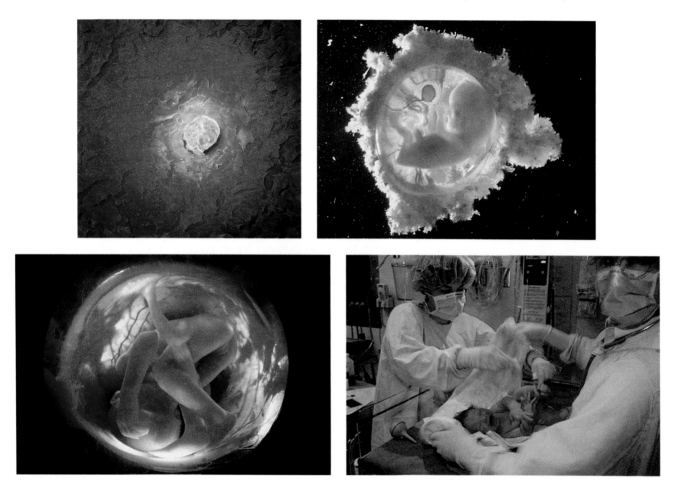

During prenatal development, the internal organ systems develop before the outer parts of the body develop, and development generally proceeds from the head downward.

system, sense organs, and skin; another type becomes the internal organs (e.g., intestines); and a third type becomes the muscles, skeleton, and blood vessels. By the end of this stage (at about 8 weeks after conception), the cells of the inch-long embryo have differentiated in many ways, including the formation of a distinct heart (which begins beating at about 1 month after conception), a primitive brain and intestinal tract, a face, eyes, ears, fingers, toes, and even male or female genitals. Early development proceeds from head to tail and from the center of the body to the outer extremities. Thus, legs and arms, as well as feet and hands, develop later than internal structures do. For many systems of the body, the embryo stage is a **critical period** of rapid growth and development. For instance, the systems governing blood circulation and the function of the brain develop rapidly in the embryo. During critical periods of embryonic development essential changes occur and after critical periods such changes are less likely to occur easily, fully, or adequately, if they can occur at all.

Nurture, through the maternal environment, most dramatically can affect the course of embryonic development during critical periods. If the mother smokes (Frazier, David, Goldstein, & Goldberg, 1961; Golbus, 1980), drinks alcohol (Abel, 1984; Barr, Streissguth, Darby, & Sampson, 1990), or consumes any other toxic drugs or other substances (T. Adler, 1989; Chasnoff, Griffith, MacGregor, Dirkes, & Burns, 1989; Finnegan,

critical period • a time of rapid growth and development, during which particular changes typically occur if they are ever to occur; that is, such changes typically do not occur after the critical period

1982; D. R. Griffith, Azuma, & Chasnoff, 1994), the embryo she carries may not develop properly (Bornstein & Bruner, 1989; Bornstein & Krasgenor, 1989).

The brain and other parts of the nervous system may fail to develop properly if the mother consumes alcohol during her pregnancy. Unfortunately, many women are not even fully aware of their pregnancy during this time, and they may unwittingly harm their unborn children. When mothers consume alcohol there is a risk of fetal alcohol syndrome, which is represented by an assemblage of disorders, chief among which are permanent and irreparable mental retardation and facial deformities, including deformed limbs and malformed genitals. Because it is not known what quantity of alcohol can lead to fetal alcohol syndrome, pregnant women should drink no alcohol at all. Learning disabilities and behavioral problems also can result (Streissguth et al., 1984; Streissguth, Sampson, & Barr, 1989). Exposure to drugs (D. R. Griffith, Azuma, & Chasnoff, 1994; Lester et al., 1991), as well as to dangerous chemicals in the environment, such as PCBs (polychlorinated bipheryls) also can cause damage that will affect development after birth (J. L. Jacobson, Jacobson, & Humphrey, 1990; J. L. Jacobson, Jacobson, Padgett, Brunitt, & Billings, 1992). In addition, a pregnant woman may be exposed to harmful influences against her will. For example, she may be unable to avoid breathing polluted air, or she may become infected with a virus such as rubella (German measles). Acquired immune deficiency syndrome (AIDS) is also a risk factor for development.

The final period of prenatal development is the stage of the **fetus,** which lasts from about the 9th week after conception until the time of birth. During this stage, the fetus continues to grow larger and heavier (to about 7–7½ pounds, 20 inches at birth), and the systems of the body grow more complex. For instance, the brain develops many neural connections, and many of the cells in the nervous system develop myelin sheaths (see chapter 2). Throughout the entire prenatal period, the mother's attention to her own health and nutrition strongly affects the health and development of her unborn child.

After 9 or so months of enjoying the most intimate of human relationships, mother and fetus work together to deliver the infant out of the womb and into the less-protected, and far more interesting, world outside. In this world, the infant must breathe, maintain a stable body temperature, obtain and digest food, eliminate waste, and perform many other independent activities for the rest of its natural life. Fortunately, most newborns arrive well-equipped to do so.

HOW DO INFANTS AND YOUNG TODDLERS DEVELOP?

What Can Newborns Do?

In recent decades, psychologists have recognized the remarkable capabilities of the **neonate** (newborn). Just what can newborns do? To start with, although newborns are very nearsighted, they seem to have a set of inborn rules that guides how they scan the environment (Haith, 1979). For example, infants seem to have a general rule to scan the environment broadly but to stop scanning and explore in depth if they see an edge. Quite conveniently, edges are more likely to contain interesting information than are uninterrupted surfaces.

fetus • an individual in the third of the three stages of prenatal development (from about the 9th week until birth); a time during which the individual develops enough sophistication to be able to survive outside the mother's uterus

neonate • newborn (*neo-*, new; *-nate,* born)

Newborns seem to have an inborn knack for imitating some of the facial expressions of their caregivers (e.g., a smile, a pout, an open-mouthed expression of surprise, or tongue protrusion).

Infants also prefer to look at particular kinds of objects; these objects are characterized by a high degree of complexity (e.g., many narrow stripes vs. a few wide ones), many visual contours (e.g., edges and patterns vs. solid regions of color), curved rather than straight contours, high contrast between light and dark (e.g., black and white vs. gray), and frequent movements (described in Banks & Salapatek, 1983). Quite conveniently, every parent has available a highly stimulating object that perfectly matches these criteria: a human face. In fact, infants as young as 4 days of age prefer looking at a human face to looking at other visual patterns (Fantz, 1958, 1961).

Within just a few days after birth, infants can hear voices clearly, and they seem to prefer listening to the human voice. They particularly notice the child-directed speech (formerly called "motherese"), which involves higher pitch, exaggerated vocal inflections, and simple sentence structures that characterizes the way in which adults communicate with infants. Some psychologists suggest that newborns seem custom designed to gain the attention, and perhaps even the love, of their caregivers. Infants can also detect smells; breast-fed 6-day-olds seem to prefer the smell of their own mothers' milk to that of other breast-feeding women, and breast-fed 3-month-olds seem to prefer the body smells of their own mothers over those of other mothers (MacFarlane, 1975; M. J. Russell, 1976).

In comparison with the senses of vision, hearing, and smell, the sensory system that appears most fully developed at birth is that of touch. For instance, Jean Mandler (1990) found that 1-month-old infants can link some visual and tactile (touch) sensations. When infants were given a chance to suck on either a bumpy or a smooth pacifier (see Figure 9.1), the infants seemed to recognize which type of pacifier they had been sucking, suggesting that their sense of touch was exceptionally well developed at a very early age. Recall that early development proceeds from the head downward (and from the center of the body to the outer extremities), so infants' sensory and motor skills are highly developed in the sensory

FIGURE 9.1
Familiar Versus Unfamiliar
Even 1-month-old infants can readily integrate their senses of touch and of vision when given the chance to use the well-developed sensory and motor skills of their mouths. For example, after sucking on one of the two types of pacifiers shown here, 1-month-olds looked longer at the kind of pacifier on which they had sucked (Mandler, 1990).

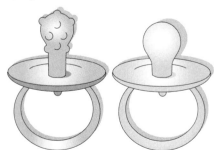

receptors and muscles of their mouths before they develop in regions of the body farther from the head and from the center of the body (e.g., in the hands or feet).

Physical Development During Infancy

Maturational changes in physical abilities were among the first aspects of development to be studied extensively. For example, Nancy Bayley's (1968, 1993) *Bayley Scales of Infant Development* specify the ages at which infants normally begin performing various kinds of physical **motor** tasks (involving movements of the muscles; see Figure 9.2). Usually, the ages at which children develop particular motor skills (or particular reflexes) bear little direct relationship to the children's cognitive or socio-emotional development or to their future intelligence or adult personality (B. S. Bloom, 1964). The exception to this rule occurs when the development of these skills falls far below the normal age range. Neonatal reflexes are also important as bases for determining the integrity of the nervous system during infancy.

Perceptual abilities develop rapidly during infancy to ensure that infants learn a great deal about the world. For example, in one study, children as young as 4 months of age were shown two movies (Spelke, 1976). In one film, a woman was playing and saying "peek-a-boo." In the other film, the child saw a hand holding a stick and rhythmically striking a wooden block. The catch was that the baby was shown the film either with its corresponding sound track or with the other movie's sound track. Infants spent more time looking at the picture if the sound corresponded

motor • related to moving the muscles

FIGURE 9.2
Bayley's "Landmarks of Motor Development and Ages of Occurrence"
These landmarks served as the basis for the Bayley Scales of Infant Development. *Particular motor accomplishments do not directly correlate with particular cognitive changes. However, these accomplishments do alter how the child can interact with the environment. Also, the child's interactions may facilitate cognitive development.*

1 MONTH	2 MONTHS	3 MONTHS	4 MONTHS	5 MONTHS	6 MONTHS
▪ Prefers to lie on back ▪ Cannot hold head erect; head sags forward ▪ Hands usually tightly fisted	▪ When lying on stomach, can lift head 45° and extend legs ▪ Head-bobbing gradually disappears; may hold head erect		▪ Can roll from back to side ▪ When lying on stomach, can lift head 90°, arms and legs lift and extend ▪ Can sit propped up for 10–15 minutes		▪ Can roll from back to stomach ▪ May "bounce" when held standing

to the picture. In other words, even at 4 months of age, children can match visual and auditory stimuli. This skill is important to all of us in our making sense of the world through our integration of sensory inputs.

Cognitive Development During Infancy

During infancy, physical development provides the foundation and the framework for all other aspects of development. In fact, according to developmental psychologist Jean Piaget (1969, 1972), infant cognitive development is in a **sensorimotor stage**, characterized by *sensory* (involving the senses) and *motor* (involving muscle movements and coordination) development.

According to Piaget, during the sensorimotor stage of cognitive development, infants gradually adapt their reflexive actions (e.g., random kicking or arm movements) to bring those actions under conscious control. For example, if a young infant accidentally kicks a mobile and makes it move in an interesting way, the infant will purposely try to control the muscles that kicked the mobile, to make the interesting movements of the mobile continue or occur again. Hence, as infants gain mastery over their motor system, they gain increasing control over (a) their interactions with their environment, and (b) the sensations they will experience because of these interactions.

Just what kinds of sensations do infants consider interesting? They tend to be most interested in stimuli that are moderately unfamiliar. That is, they are more interested in stimuli that are somewhat unusual than in stimuli that are either highly familiar or highly unusual (and perhaps

sensorimotor stage • Piaget's first stage of development (about the first 2 years after birth), during which the child builds on reflexes and develops the first mental representations of things that are not being sensed at the moment

7 MONTHS	8 MONTHS	9 MONTHS	10 MONTHS	11 MONTHS	12 MONTHS

7 MONTHS	8 MONTHS	9 MONTHS	10 MONTHS	11 MONTHS	12 MONTHS
	• When lying on back, can lift feet to mouth • Can sit erect for a few minutes • May crawl • Can stand supporting full body weight on feet, if held up	• Creeps on hands and knees • Can sit indefinitely • Can pull self to standing position and may "cruise" by moving feet • By 10 months may be able to sit down from standing position		• Pulls self actively to feet and "cruises" along table or crib • May stand momentarily without support • Can walk if one hand is held; may take a few steps alone	• Can get up without help and may take several steps alone • Can creep upstairs on hands and knees • May squat or stoop without losing balance • Can throw ball

 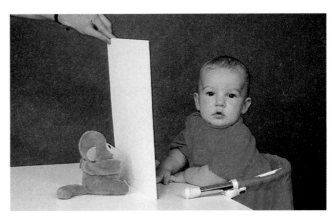

FIGURE 9.3
Object Permanence
As this sequence of pictures shows, younger infants (at about 4 months of age) and older infants (by about 9 months of age) react quite differently to tasks requiring a sense of object permanence. In the object-permanence demonstration, an object is hidden under a blanket or behind a screen. An older infant realizes that the object continues to exist even when it is out of sight, and the infant pursues the hidden object. In contrast, as shown here, the younger infant looks away as soon as the object disappears from sight. Once the young infant cannot sense the object's presence, the object no longer exists in the mind of the infant.

therefore overwhelming). Infants who prefer more relative novelty show higher intelligence during middle and later childhood than do infants who prefer less relative novelty (Bornstein & Sigman, 1986; Fagan & Montie, 1988; Lewis & Brooks-Gunn, 1981).

If infants can distinguish unfamiliar from familiar stimuli in their environments, they must be able to remember something about their environments, at least for short periods of time. On the other hand, throughout infancy and even the first few years after birth, children's long-term memories are highly unstable. Researchers have found little evidence that anyone can remember large numbers of specific experiences from their first few years of life (see chapter 6), a phenomenon sometimes referred to as infantile amnesia.

Despite young children's apparent inability to form lasting memories of specific experiences, young children do learn a great deal. In fact, much of what people learn during those early years continues to serve as a solid foundation for subsequent learning. For example, through their experiences and interactions with objects and people in their environment, infants achieve a major cognitive milestone: They develop a sense of object permanence. **Object permanence** is the ability to form mental representations of objects (and people) that can continue to be held in mind even when those objects cannot be seen, heard, or otherwise sensed (see Figure 9.3). Basically, what infants 4 months old or younger see is what they get (what they know to exist). These infants have not developed a way of mentally representing anything they do not sense at the moment. Anything that young infants cannot sense directly simply ceases to exist for them. Over the following months, infants begin to form stable, permanent mental representations of objects and people, which the infants can continue to hold in mind even when those objects and people are not immediately perceptible to them. By age 9 months, infants have developed a sense of object permanence.

The development of object permanence means that when young infants can neither see nor hear their parents they have no mental representation of their parents to carry in their minds until their parents reappear. Hence,

object permanence • the cognitive realization that objects may continue to exist even when they are not currently being sensed

they may need more frequent assurance of their parents' presence, at least until they develop a sense of object permanence. In addition to influencing children's interactions with their parents, cognitive development influences socioemotional development in other ways. Recall, for example, that newborns seem to be mentally tuned in to human faces and voices. This innate interest in people seems to continue throughout infancy.

Socioemotional Development During Infancy

The socioemotional development of infants centers on emotional development, interpersonal (social) development, and personality development.

Emotional Development

We start our discussion of infant socioemotional development by considering the development of emotions. Infants show increasing emotional differentiation (Brazelton, 1983; Izard, Kagan, & Zajonc, 1984; Sroufe, 1979), as well as increasing cognitive control over their emotions. For example, young infants show a generalized response (a startle reflex) to such stimuli as loud noises. Older infants, however, show more specific emotional responses, which tend to involve more cognitive processing, such as when the infants show a fear of strangers.

Emotional development also involves increasing awareness of, sensitivity to, and interaction with other people. For one thing, infants form an **attachment,** which is a strong and relatively long-lasting emotional tie, to their parents and to other significant persons in their lives. Attachment is a mutual process of emotional bonding; parents help to cement this bonding by providing emotional and physical nurture to their infants. Infants encourage their parents' attachment through social smiles and through social referencing. *Social smiles* are the toothless grins that infants start

At about 8 months of age (give or take a month or 2), infants start to show separation anxiety, *a fear of being separated from their mothers or other familiar adults.*

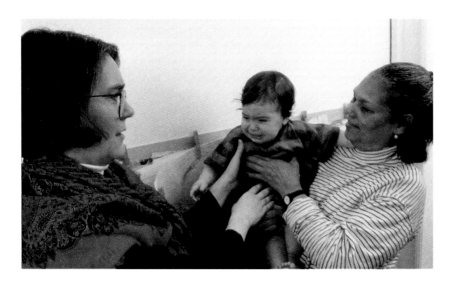

attachment • a strong and relatively long-lasting emotional tie between people

flashing a few weeks after birth. Through *social referencing*, infants observe how their parents and other trusted adults react to new or ambiguous situations; then the infants figure out how they themselves should respond emotionally to these situations. For instance, if infants observe that their parents feel emotionally distressed when leaving the infants with a caregiver, the infants are also more likely to feel emotionally distressed.

At about the same time that infants are beginning to develop a sense of object permanence, the infants start to show separation anxiety. In **separation anxiety,** infants show varying degrees of fearfulness when briefly separated from their parents (or other primary caregivers). Infants also start to show *stranger anxiety* (a wariness of strangers). The ways in which infants show social and emotional developments (e.g., separation anxiety and stranger anxiety) depend partly on their personalities and partly on their relationships with significant persons (e.g., their parents).

Attachment

Attachment refers to a strong and relatively long-lasting emotional tie between two humans. Our first attachment begins at birth (although some mothers contend that it begins even earlier) and is usually fully cemented within several years. Babies form long-term emotional attachments to their parents, especially their primary caregivers, usually their mothers. Mary Ainsworth and her colleagues (Ainsworth, Bell, & Stayton, 1971; Ainsworth, Blehar, Waters, & Wall, 1978) have conducted some of the best-known work on attachment. In particular, Ainsworth and her colleagues have studied attachment by using a research paradigm called the **strange situation:** In this paradigm, the research participants are usually a toddler, 12 to 18 months of age, and the toddler's mother. The mother and her infant enter a room containing a variety of toys. The mother puts the infant down and sits in a chair. A few minutes later an unfamiliar woman enters the room, talks to the mother, and then tries to play with the child. While the stranger is trying to engage the child, the mother quietly walks out of the room, leaving her purse on the chair to indicate that she will return. Later, the mother returns. An observer positioned behind a one-way mirror records the child's reactions to the mother's return. Still later, the mother leaves yet again, but this time the child is left alone. The mother returns once more and the observer records the child's reactions again.

Ainsworth noticed that children's reactions tend to fit one of three different patterns: avoidant, secure, and resistant. In the **avoidant-attachment pattern** ("Type A"), the child generally ignores the mother while she is present, and the child shows minimal distress when the mother leaves. If the child does show distress, the stranger is about as effective as the mother in providing comfort.

In the **secure-attachment pattern** ("Type B"), the child generally shows preferential interest in, but not excessive dependence on, the attention of the mother while she is present. The child shows some distress when the mother leaves but can be calmed and reassured by her when she returns, usually through holding and hugging. The secure child is friendly with the stranger but shows an obvious preference for the mother.

In the **resistant-attachment pattern** ("Type C"), the child generally shows ambivalence toward the mother while she is present, seeking both to gain and to resist physical contact with her when the mother returns after being gone a short time. For example, the child might run to the mother when she returns, but then, when held, tries to extricate him- or herself.

Attachment does not end in childhood. It has been shown to be important to adult relationships and to general adjustment in adulthood

separation anxiety • the fear of being separated from a primary caregiver, such as a parent

strange situation • an experimental technique for observing attachment in young children

avoidant-attachment pattern • a pattern in which a child generally ignores the mother while she is present and in which the child shows minimal distress when the mother leaves; one of three major attachment patterns observed in the strange situation

secure-attachment pattern • a pattern in which a child generally shows preferential interest in, but not excessive dependence on, the attention of the mother while she is present and in which the child shows some distress when the mother leaves but can be calmed and reassured by her when she returns; one of three attachment patterns observed in the strange situation

resistant-attachment pattern • a pattern in which a child generally shows ambivalence toward the mother while she is present, seeking both to gain and to resist physical contact with her when the mother returns after being gone a short time; one of three attachment patterns observed in the strange situation

(Hazan & Shaver, 1994; Main, Kaplan, & Cassidy, 1985; Scharfe & Bartholomew, 1994). Thus, when researchers study attachment in infants and young children, they are studying an aspect of behavior that will continue to be important throughout the life span.

Infant Personality Development

Temperament. When psychologists study social and emotional development, they often emphasize likenesses in development across all or most individuals (e.g., the emergence of attachment, of separation anxiety, and even of social smiles). In contrast, when psychologists study personality development, they often emphasize individual differences in development. For example, some researchers have studied **temperament,** differences in an individual's characteristic mood and typical intensity and duration of emotions and motivations. Temperament influences the development of personality and of relationships with other people. Studies of temperament have looked at children even in their infancy.

Alexander Thomas and Stella Chess conducted a well-regarded longitudinal study of temperament in children from birth through adolescence (e.g., A. Thomas & Chess, 1977; A. Thomas, Chess, & Birch, 1970). They found that infants showed individual differences in the nine distinctive temperamental characteristics shown in Putting It to Use 9.1, such as activity level and adaptability. In addition, these investigators noted the importance of the **person–environment interaction,** the distinctive match between an individual's temperament and the treatment of the individual by other persons in the environment. For example, a highly active child might be well suited to a rowdy family environment with many siblings, but such a child might not be as well-suited to a quiet family environment in which children are expected to engage only in restful activities.

Erikson's Psychosocial Theory of Personality Development. Whereas Thomas and Chess focused on stable characteristics of temperament, Erik Erikson focused on changes in personality development across the life span. For Erikson, infant personality development centers on the establishment of a fundamental sense of trust or of mistrust. In Erikson's view, infants come to establish a basic sense of trust through their relationship with their primary caregiver, who continually meets their basic physical and emotional needs for loving nurturance (e.g., food and drink), for physical and emotional comfort, and so on. Hence, infants learn either to *trust* or to *mistrust* that their needs will be met. They come to view the world as basically either friendly or hostile. Successful passage through this stage leads to the development of a hopeful attitude toward life.

HOW DO CHILDREN DEVELOP?

Cognitive Development During Childhood

Preoperational Thinking

According to Piagetian theory, young children (of ages 1½ or 2 to 6 or 7 years) are in a **preoperational stage** of cognitive development, during which the young child becomes increasingly able to develop mental representations of familiar objects and events and to manipulate these representations at a rudimentary level. *Representations* are things or ideas that stand for other things or ideas. The earliest mental representations

temperament • a person's distinctive tendency to show a particular mood and a particular intensity and duration of emotions

person–environment interaction • the distinctive fit between a given person and his or her environment

preoperational stage • Piaget's second stage of development (about age 2 years until the age of starting elementary school), during which the child develops language and concepts about physical objects

9.1

WHAT IS YOUR TEMPERAMENT?

PUTTING IT TO USE

According to Thomas and Chess, individual differences in nine distinctive characteristics of temperament have been observed to begin in infancy and to remain relatively stable at least through adolescence (A. Thomas & Chess, 1977; A. Thomas, Chess, & Birch, 1970). In the following chart, ask yourself the questions in the left-hand column (a possible range of answers is given in the right-hand column). At your next opportunity, ask someone who knew you as an infant (e.g., a parent, grandparent, or older sibling) to describe your temperament during infancy. (You may have to rephrase the questions. For instance, instead of "How active are you?" you might ask this person, "How active was I when I was an infant?") How stable do your temperament characteristics appear to be?

What temperament characteristics do you observe in yourself?*	Characteristic (range of responses)
How active are you?	*Activity level* (very active to very inactive)
How predictable are your patterns of eating, sleeping, and so on?	*Rhythmicity* or regularity of biological cycles (very predictable to very unpredictable)
How outgoing are you?	*Approach/withdrawal* (very outgoing to very shy)
How ably do you adapt your responses to new situations?	*Adaptability* (very adaptable to very unadaptable)
How high a level of stimulation is needed to prompt you to respond?	*Threshold of reactivity* (very high to very low threshold)
How strongly and energetically do you respond to stimuli?	*Intensity and energy of reaction* (very strongly and energetically to very mildly and calmly)
In what kind of mood are you most of the time?	*Quality of dominant mood* (very happy and pleasant to very sad and unpleasant)
How easily are you distracted from pursuing activities in which you were already interested?	*Distractibility* (highly distractible to highly engaged)
How willing are you to continue to attempt activities or to solve problems in the face of obstacles?	*Attention span and persistence* despite obstacles (highly persistent to lacking in persistence)

* Can someone you know help you to answer these questions about yourself when you were an infant?

are highly concrete (e.g., mental representations of parents who are out of sight).

Eventually, however, these mental representations include *signs* (e.g., the familiar signs for men's and women's restrooms), which somewhat resemble what they represent, and *symbols,* which do not resemble what they represent and are chosen arbitrarily. For example, the words on this page are very abstract symbols, in which particular letters (symbols) are associated with particular sounds (more symbols), to be linked into words, phrases, and sentences (still more symbols), which have arbitrary meanings. (For example, there is only an arbitrary relationship between the words "rat," "cat," and "bat" and the particular kinds of mammals that those words represent.)

The original meaning of *infant* is "incapable of speech" *(Merriam-Webster's Collegiate Dictionary,* 1993). By definition, therefore, the emergence of language and linguistic communication signals the end of infancy. With the development of language comes the increasing development of concepts. According to Piaget, children develop conceptual schemas through the processes of assimilation and accommodation. Over time, young children use increasingly complex **representational thought** as they acquire more sophisticated concepts and language. Such thought enables them to characterize objects as well as concepts mentally. Early and highly concrete representations pave the way for later, less concrete representations. Additional characteristics of preoperational thinking include the following:

"How come PJ got 4 sandwiches and I only got 2?"

1. Initially, preoperational children tend to focus on only one aspect of a situation at a given time; they cannot *decenter* (consider more than one aspect of the situation at a time). For example, they cannot focus simultaneously on both the width and the height of a glass of milk; if they see a glass of milk poured from a short, wide glass into a tall, thin glass, they do not consider both the width and the height of the glass in thinking about the quantity of milk in each glass. Typically, they focus on the height of the glass. They believe that the *tall,* thin glass contains more milk than did the *short,* wide glass.

2. They also focus on *static* (unchanging) conditions rather than on *dynamic* (changing) processes. For example, in observing someone pour milk from a short, wide glass into a tall, thin glass, they give less thought to the process of pouring than to the states before and after the milk was poured.

3. Preoperational children find it difficult or impossible mentally to *reverse* (imagine undoing) a process. For example, after observing someone pour milk from a short, wide glass into a tall, thin glass, these children do not seem able to consider what would happen if the milk in the tall, thin glass were poured back into the short, wide glass, reversing the process.

To summarize, preoperational children show the developmental characteristics of *centration* (inability to focus on more than one aspect of a situation), an *emphasis on states* rather than on processes, and *irreversibility of thought* (inability mentally to reverse a process). These characteristics combine to make it virtually impossible for preoperational children to comprehend conservation of quantity. **Conservation of quantity** is the ability to recognize that the quantity (amount) of something remains the same, despite changes in appearance, as long as no amount of the substance was added or taken away. Figure 9.4 shows several examples of how preoperational children respond to tasks involving conservation of quantity.

Preoperational children also have difficulty with their understandings of causal relationships. On the one hand, when observing events with which they are highly familiar, young children demonstrate a pretty clear understanding of causal relationships (S. Gelman, Bullock, & Meck,

representational thought • the thinking that involves mental images, such as images of tangible objects

conservation of quantity • the principle that the quantity of something remains the same as long as nothing is removed or added, even if the appearance of the substance changes in form

Type	The child is shown	The experimenter	The child responds
Liquid	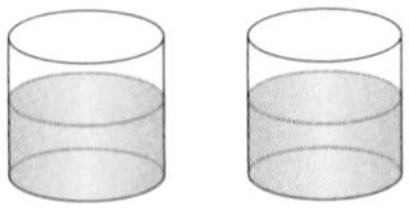 two equal short, wide glasses of water and agrees that they hold the same amount.	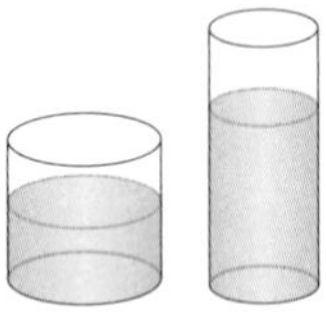 pours water from the short, wide glass into the tall, thin glass and asks if one glass holds more water than the other or if both are the same.	**Preoperational child:** The tall glass has more. **Concrete-operational child:** They hold the same amount.
Matter	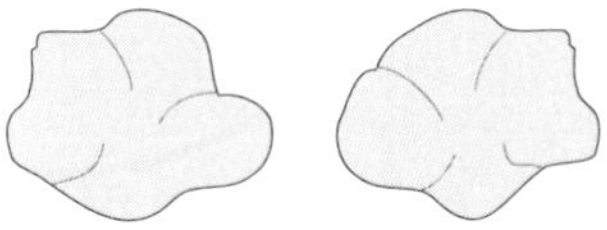 two equal balls of clay and agrees they are the same.	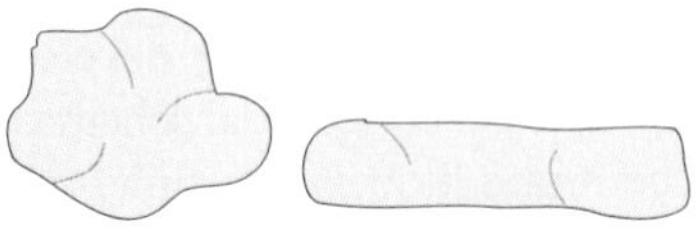 rolls one ball of clay into a sausage and asks if one has more clay or if both are the same.	**Preoperational child:** The long one has more clay. **Concrete-operational child:** They both have the same amount.
Number	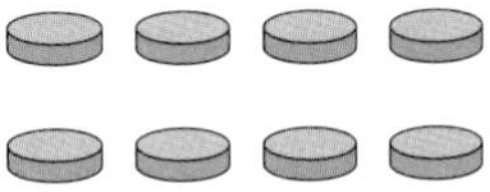 two rows of checkers and agrees that both rows have the same number.	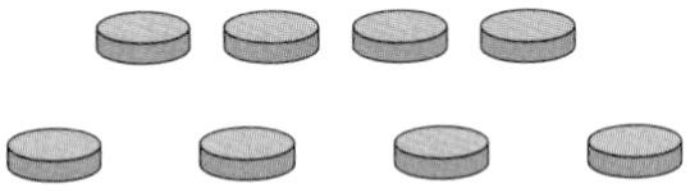 spreads out the second row and asks if one row has more checkers than the other or if both are the same.	**Preoperational child:** The longer row has more checkers. **Concrete-operational child:** The number of checkers in each row has not changed.
Length	 two sticks and agrees that they are the same length.	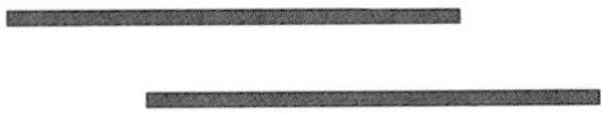 moves the bottom stick and asks if they are still the same length.	**Preoperational child:** The bottom stick is longer. **Concrete-operational child:** They are the same length.
Volume	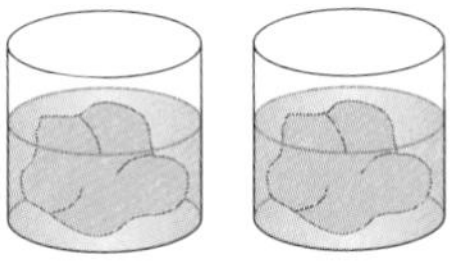 two balls of clay put in two glasses equally full of water and says the level is the same in both.	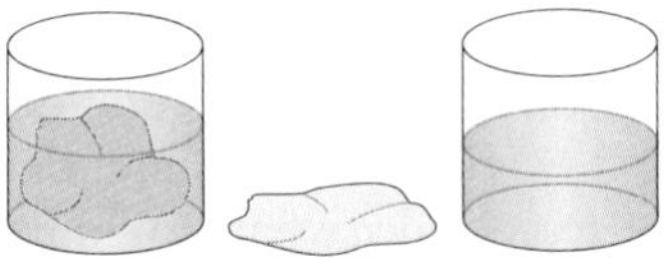 flattens one ball of clay and asks if the water level will be the same in both glasses.	**Preoperational child:** The water in the glass with the flat piece won't be as high as the water in the other glass. **Concrete-operational child:** Nothing has changed; the levels will be the same in each glass.

FIGURE 9.4

Conservation of Quantity

During the preoperational stage, children have difficulty conserving quantity when perceptible changes occur. When viewing an experimenter transform the shape of a ball of clay, preoperational children tend to assert that there is more clay when the amount of matter of the clay appears to be greater (e.g., in a long sausage shape, as opposed to a ball of clay). When viewing an experimenter change the arrangement of checkers from a more dense pattern to a more scattered pattern, preoperational children tend to assert that there are more checkers in a dispersed arrangement than in the dense arrangement. When viewing an experimenter change the relative positions of sticks, preoperational children tend to assert that the moved stick is longer when it protrudes beyond the end of the other stick.

1980; Mandler, 1990). For example, if you were to ask 3-year-olds, "Why is the sidewalk wet?" most 3-year-olds (who have had experience with wet sidewalks) would probably suggest plausible causes (e.g., rain, sprinklers, water being poured or spilled). On the other hand, young children do not consistently reason *deductively* (from general principles to particular instances) or *inductively* (from many specific instances to some general principles). Instead, they frequently reason *transductively:* They reason based on associations due to *coincidence* (things happening to occur at about the same time) or due to *functional relationships* (things that are part of the same process, thing, or event; e.g., cats both have fur and drink milk, but neither of these functional cat-related features causes the occurrence of the other; see chapter 7 for a further discussion of reasoning). As an example of transductive thinking, young children may observe that in American culture, carrying a purse and wearing facial makeup are associated with being a woman. Hence, they may reason transductively that carrying a purse and wearing facial makeup cause a person to be a woman.

Concrete-Operational Thinking

After many experiences interacting with and observing their environment, children enter the **concrete-operational stage** (Piaget, 1972), in which children begin to form mental rules about what they experience and to engage in mental manipulations of internal representations of *tangible* (concrete) objects. We may characterize the shift from preoperational to concrete-operational thinking in terms of the following trends:

1. Through experiences with realistic events, children gradually differentiate reality from fantasy.

2. Through experiences with cause–effect relationships, children gradually come to infer principles regarding what cause will lead to a particular effect.

3. Through experiences with physically manipulating various numbers of concrete objects, children gradually can manipulate concepts about numbers (e.g., adding or subtracting).

4. Through their experiences in manipulating various kinds of quantities of substances, children can eventually *conserve quantity,* recognizing that the quantity of a substance stays the same despite changes in the appearance of the substance.

In Piaget's classic experiment on the conservation of quantity, the experimenter shows the child two short, stout beakers with liquid in them (see Figure 9.5). The experimenter has the child confirm that the two beakers contain the same amounts of liquid. Then, as the child watches, the experimenter pours the liquid from one beaker into a third beaker, which is taller and thinner than the other two. In the new beaker, the liquid in the narrower tube rises to a higher level than in the other, still-full, shorter beaker. When asked whether the amounts of liquid in the two full beakers are the same or different, the preoperational child says that there is now more liquid in the taller, thinner beaker because the liquid in that beaker reaches a perceptibly higher point. The child does not conceive that the amount is conserved despite the change in appearance. The concrete-operational child, on the other hand, says that the beakers contain the same amount of liquid, based on the child's internal schemas regarding the conservation of liquid.

concrete-operational stage •
Piaget's third stage of development (about the period of elementary school), during which the child can mentally manipulate images of concrete objects

FIGURE 9.5
Conservation of Liquid Quantity
Can this child conserve matter, recognizing that the quantity is conserved (stays the same) despite superficial changes in the liquid's appearance?

During the concrete-operational stage most children have entered school, and they spend large portions of their days engaged in learning to read and write, to understand various concepts, and to solve an array of problems involving the mental manipulation of concrete objects and ideas. In recent years, in addition to "reading, 'riting, and 'rithmetic," "reasoning" has become a fourth "R" of formal education. Children in the concrete-operational stage are developmentally ready to explore how reasoning may aid them in their thinking processes. In fact, a key characteristic of concrete-operational children, as opposed to preoperational children, is their readiness to engage in *metacognition* (thinking about their own thought processes). Their increasing ability to think about their own thought processes accompanies an increasing ability to think about how other people think and feel. This ability to consider the perspectives of other people influences the children's social interactions, as well as their emotional and personality development.

Socioemotional Development

Emergence of Personality and Identity During Childhood

The personality and identity development of children centers on their development of independence, mastery, and a sense of personal competence;

on their development of self-understanding and self-esteem; and on their development of gender identity.

Erikson's Theory of Personality and Identity Development. According to Erikson, during early childhood (about ages 1–3 years), the main crisis young children face centers on the issue of *autonomy* versus *shame* and *doubt*. Children who do not master this stage doubt themselves and feel shame about themselves and their abilities in general. Children who master the challenge become autonomous (self-sufficient in walking, talking, eating, using the toilet, etc.).

A little later in childhood (at about ages 3–6 years), children face the difficult challenge of learning how to take initiative, to avoid guilt, and to assert themselves in socially acceptable ways. Somewhat older children (about ages 6–12 years) must face a crisis centered on the issue of *industry* versus *inferiority*. At this time, children learn a sense of capability and of industriousness in their work. Those who do not develop this sense develop instead feelings of incompetence, inferiority, and low self-worth.

Self-Concept. The development of feelings of self-worth is one aspect of the emergence of the self-concept. A broad, general definition of **self-concept** is that it is the way we view ourselves, which may or may not be realistic. Cross-cultural developmental psychologists such as Patricia Greenfield (1994) have suggested that our self-concept often depends on our sense of *independence* (i.e., our autonomy and individuality) and of *interdependence* (i.e., our sense of belongingness and collectivity; e.g., described in Greenfield & Cocking, 1994; Markus & Kitayama, 1991). Although both of these aspects of self are important to all persons, the influence of culture determines how the two combine to characterize a specific individual. For example, some Asian and Latin American societies (such as in China, Japan, and Mexico) tend to emphasize the socialization of individuals to be interdependent and collectivistic, whereas most Western societies tend to emphasize the fostering of independence and individualism. According to Greenfield, the orientation toward interdependence versus independence profoundly influences socioemotional and intellectual development at home, in the community, and at school.

Home, community, and school contexts also seem to influence two distinctive aspects of self-concept: self-understanding and self-esteem. Self-understanding is mainly cognitive, whereas self-esteem is mainly emotional. In particular, *self-understanding* refers to how we comprehend ourselves—as good students, as fair athletes, as thoughtful friends, and so on (Damon & Hart, 1982). *Self-esteem* refers to how much a person values him- or herself. According to research by Susan Harter (1990), our self-concepts become increasingly differentiated over the course of development. As we explore our abilities and learn more skills, we also have more arenas in which to gauge our self-worth. For example, during the elementary-school years, children's self-concept increasingly focuses on what children can do—dance, play soccer, achieve high grades.

In addition, the influence of other people in the development of self-concept changes across the course of development. During early childhood, children's self-concept often reflects children's views of how their parents perceive them. Once children start school, the perceived opinions of their peers increasingly influence children's self-concepts.

Many observable characteristics of an individual can affect the development of self-esteem. The characteristics may include racial differences, regional or cultural accents, physical differences (e.g., weight, height, unusual

self-concept • an individual's beliefs, understandings, and judgments about her- or himself

At an early age, children believe that particular hair styles and clothing determine gender instead of merely signaling gender according to a particular society. If young children were to see this photo of Ernest Hemingway and were told that he grew up to be a man and a father, they might still believe that in this photo he was a girl, but that he may have changed later to become a man.

features, or physical handicap), and the distinction of being male or female. (*Sex* is a person's biological distinction as being male or female, and *gender* is the social and psychological distinction as being male or female.) For example, self-esteem has been linked to gender differences. A report by the American Association of University Women (AAUW) Education Foundation has found that girls, who enter school roughly equal to boys in their abilities and self-esteem, leave school relatively deficient in mathematical ability and in self-esteem (AAUW, 1992). Why does this change occur? Among other things, research has shown that girls receive less attention from teachers and that curricula in schools heavily emphasize male achievements (Nelson, 1990; Sadker & Sadker, 1984). The differences in self-esteem become greatest during adolescence, when issues of sexuality and gender identity are highlighted.

Development of Gender Identity.   Although most of us think of sexual-identity development as beginning some time in adolescence, children actually start to form their gender identifications by the age of 2 or 3 years (Thompson, 1975). **Gender typing,** the acquisition of roles and associations related to the social and psychological distinction of being masculine or feminine, begins early, too. From ages 2 to 7 years, children seem to have rather rigid sex-role stereotypes. They use rigid stereotypes because they see gender identity as being determined by superficial characteristics, which can be changed, rather than as being characterized by biological distinctions, which cannot be changed. By the end of childhood, young people develop a sense that a person's sex cannot be changed just by changing superficial characteristics (e.g., hair length) or behaviors (e.g., carrying a purse).

There are many theories of gender typing (described in Beall & Sternberg, 1993; e.g., Bandura, 1977b; S. L. Bem, 1981; Benbow & Stanley, 1980; Huston, 1983, 1985; Kenrick & Trost, 1993). Some theorists more strongly emphasize the role of nature (physiological differences between the sexes), and others more strongly emphasize the role of nurture (differences due to socialization). Some theorists have also suggested the concept of *androgyny,* in which a person shows about equal degrees of feminine and masculine characteristics and behavior. Such a person acts in ways that seem appropriate to the situation, regardless of society's gender stereotypes as to how people of a particular sex should react. A key aspect of gender identity is the way in which people form and develop interpersonal relationships.

Development of Interpersonal Relationships

Interpersonal development encompasses qualitative changes in how people relate to other people. For one thing, although parents continue to be important to people throughout the life span, particularly during childhood, friendships and other interactions with peers become increasingly important. Relationships with peers during childhood are important not only for the child's well-being, but eventually, for the well-being of the adult whom the child will become. During this time, children develop increasing awareness of others and increasingly consider the perspectives of other persons. These changes influence and are influenced by children's relationships with friends. Robert Selman (1981) has identified successive stages of friendship during childhood. These stages are marked by the increasing ability to consider the views of another person and the increasing willingness to give, as well as to take.

gender typing   •   the process of acquiring gender-related roles for a given society

interpersonal development   •   the process by which people change across the life span in the way they relate to other people

Early in this century, families tended to include more children, so children spent a lot of time in the company of other children. During the 1950s, however, when families tended to be smaller and many mothers worked mostly at home, children spent a lot of time with one or two parents and one or two siblings. Nowadays, the trend seems to be for children to spend more time with other children once again. By the time this book reaches your hands, an estimated three fourths of the mothers with school-age children will be working outside the home (U.S. Department of Labor, Bureau of Labor Statistics, 1994). At present, an extensive body of research (Andersson, 1989; Belsky, 1990; Clarke-Stewart, 1989; Field,

PUTTING IT TO USE

9.2

WHAT SHOULD PARENTS LOOK FOR IN HIGH-QUALITY CHILD CARE?

The National Association for the Education of Young Children has suggested a long list of appropriate versus inappropriate child-care practices, from which we can summarize the following key features of high-quality child care.

1. Staff members try to facilitate both intellectual and socioemotional development of children.

2. Children are valued as individuals whose distinctive abilities and preferences for activities are recognized and appreciated.

3. Children are offered a wide variety of hands-on explorations of materials and diverse kinds of activities from which they may choose to work individually or in small groups.

4. Children are given meaningful experiences with language, both spoken and written. Literacy-related activities are naturally incorporated into the whole curriculum.

5. Teachers work with small numbers of children, with whom they frequently interact to facilitate, extend, and explore each child's interests.

6. Teachers set clear but reasonable age-appropriate limits and help children to regulate their own behavior. Teachers encourage and support children's social interactions, suggesting alternatives for conflict resolution when children cannot satisfactorily resolve conflicts unaided.

In addition to these practices, two factors also strongly influence the quality of the care given to children: *low staff:student ratios* (i.e., each adult caregiver is responsible for only a small number of children) and *low turnover of staff* (i.e., most staff persons continue working in the same site, with the same children, over an extended period of time). When each staff person has fewer children to supervise, each child receives better social and educational stimulation, as well as the fundamental assurance of safety. When there is low turnover of staff, children can establish secure relationships with the people who provide care to them. In addition, low staff turnover generally indicates that the care facility provides a pleasant work environment and that the staff members enjoy their work.

1990; Gottfried & Gottfried, 1988; Hoffman, 1989) has not led to definite conclusions regarding the effects of child care on preschoolers and school-aged children. Clearly, the quality of the child-care program influences the outcomes. What seems to matter most is not *whether* children are in a child-care program, but *which* child-care program they are in (see Putting It to Use 9.2).

WHAT DEVELOPS DURING PUBERTY AND ADOLESCENCE?

Physical Development During Adolescence

The end of childhood is signaled by the onset of **puberty,** which is the stage of development where males and females reach sexual maturity, their reproductive systems begin to function (*primary sex characteristics*), and they develop *secondary sex characteristics* (e.g., male voice, female breasts and hips, and pubic and underarm hair). **Adolescence** is the period of time between the onset of puberty and the time the individual accepts the full responsibilities of being an adult.

During adolescence, people change from being seen as children to being seen as adults, both by themselves and by other persons. Although the change from childhood to adulthood occurs in all cultures, the form and the timing of the change vary cross-culturally (J. W. Berry et al., 1992). Thus, whereas puberty involves physiological changes largely affected by nature (e.g., development of secondary sex characteristics), adolescence often also involves psychological changes largely affected by nurture (e.g., social attitudes toward the appearance of secondary sex characteristics at particular ages).

Cognitive Development During Adolescence

The obvious changes in physical development that occur during adolescence are accompanied by striking changes in cognitive development. Clearly, adolescents know a lot more than younger children know, so they have a larger knowledge base; their thinking differs *quantitatively* from the thinking of younger children. In addition, many researchers agree that adolescent thinking differs *qualitatively* from earlier kinds of thinking (Andrich & Styles, 1994; Byrnes, 1988; Inhelder & Piaget, 1958; Kitchener & Brenner, 1990; Overton, 1990; Siegler, 1991; see also chapter 7). A major change centers on their ability to reason both *inductively* (formulating and testing hypotheses about what causes what, based on observing specific instances of a phenomenon) and *deductively* (applying known general principles to specific instances). According to Piaget's theory, these and other qualitative changes in thinking indicate that adolescents have reached the highest level of cognitive development, the **formal-operational stage,** in which they are able to manipulate abstract symbols mentally (Inhelder & Piaget, 1958).

An exciting aspect of adolescent thinking is the adolescent's ability to move beyond concrete, practical considerations. Unlike younger children, who chiefly conceive only of what they previously have seen, heard, or otherwise sensed, adolescents can conceive of what they *never* have seen, heard, or experienced. A whole world of possibilities opens up to them as they consider options that they never have observed before.

puberty • the period of physiological development during which males and females develop primary (i.e., functioning sex organs) and secondary sex characteristics (e.g., body hair and distinctive shape), thereby reaching sexual maturity

adolescence • the stage of psychological development between the start of puberty and the time the individual accepts the full responsibilities of being an adult in a given society

formal-operational stage • Piaget's fourth stage of development (about the time of adolescence), during which the child becomes able to manipulate abstract ideas and formal relationships

In addition to being able to explore possible options, adolescents reasonably can evaluate the options, thereby differentiating the possible from the impossible. Although adolescents can conceive of pixies, fairies, witches, and dragons, they also can realistically evaluate the improbability of the existence of such creatures, based on their own reasoning. Furthermore, they can consider logical reasons for beliefs that differ from their own. If asked to offer convincing evidence of Santa Claus's existence (e.g., to a young child), adolescents can do so, despite their own beliefs to the contrary. Adolescents' ability to consider viewpoints other than their own also enhances the flexibility and complexity of their thought processes. This is not to say that adolescents never use flawed reasoning, such as circular thinking (e.g., "We know that poor people are lazy because they don't have any money") or overgeneralization ("I know that smoking isn't really bad for your health because my Uncle Mort lived to be 100, and he smoked like a chimney from the age of 8").

Although adolescents are better able to consider the feelings and thoughts of other persons than are younger children, the adolescents continue to engage in some fallacies related to egocentrism (Elkind, 1967, 1985). A common fallacy of adolescent thinking centers on the *personal fable,* in which adolescents believe that they, as opposed to other persons, are somehow unique, destined for fame, fortune, or perhaps even heroism. Unfortunately, the personal fable usually accompanies an *invincibility fallacy,* in which the adolescent believes that he or she is not vulnerable to the same risks of tragic outcomes that affect other people. Hence, adolescents may continue to engage in unprotected sexual activity, unsafe driving, or the use of alcohol, cigarettes, or other drugs because they unreasonably believe that the undesirable outcomes that affect others will not affect them.

Socioemotional Development

Personal Identity

Many aspects of identity development (e.g., the development of gender identity) precede adolescence. Still, according to Erik Erikson (1968) and many other developmental psychologists, adolescence typically is characterized by a profound search for identity and by huge leaps in the development of the individual's awareness of her or his own personal identity. In Erikson's theory, adolescents face a crisis of *identity* versus *role confusion*. Adolescents try to figure out who they are, what they value, and who they will grow up to become. They try to integrate intellectual, social, sexual, ethical, and other aspects of themselves into a unified self-identity. Because of the tremendous importance of identity, other theorists have focused their attention specifically on the development of identity.

Erikson's theory highlights adolescence as a time when individuals face a *crisis* (turning point) in developing a sense of personal identity. James Marcia builds on the concept of personal identity and indicates in more detail the specific kinds of coping patterns that an adolescent can utilize on the way to adulthood. Specifically, Marcia (1966, 1980) has proposed that four patterns of coping can emerge as a result of internal conflicts and decision making. These patterns add another dimension to Erikson's stage of identity development, not a separate series of stages or substages. These four patterns are (a) *identity achievement,* in which the person has searched for an identity and found it; (b) *foreclosure,* in which

TABLE 9.1

Marcia's Coping Patterns for Achievement of Personal Identity

		Do you make commitments (e.g., to a career, to a mate, to your values)?	
		Yes	*No*
Have you engaged in a period of active search for identity?	*Yes*	Marcia would describe you as having reached *identity achievement,* having a firm and relatively secure sense of who you are. You have made conscious and purposeful commitments to your occupation, religion, beliefs about sex roles, and the like. You have considered the views, beliefs, and values held by others in achieving this identity, but you have branched out to achieve your own resolution.	Your identity is in *moratorium,* and you currently are having an *identity crisis* (i.e., turning point). You do not yet have clear commitments to society or a clear sense of who you are, but you are actively trying to reach that point.
	No	Your identity is in *foreclosure,* in which case you have committed yourself to an occupation and various ideological positions, but you show little evidence of having followed a process of self-construction. You simply have adopted the attitudes of others, without serious searching and questioning. In essence, you have foreclosed on the possibility of arriving at your own unique identity.	You are experiencing *identity diffusion,* and you lack direction. Moreover, you do not seem to care that you have no strong identity. You are unconcerned about political, religious, moral, or even occupational issues. You go your own way, not worrying about why you are doing what you are doing.

the person has settled on an identity without having earnestly searched for it; (c) *moratorium,* in which the person currently is involved in searching for an identity; and (d) *identity diffusion,* in which the person has no identity and has no interest in searching for one. Table 9.1 summarizes the four coping patterns and the criteria for each pattern.

People who have reached identity achievement would move beyond Erikson's stage of development for identity, but people with any of the other coping patterns would be blocked from progressing beyond that stage.

Peer Relationships

As the theories of Erikson and Marcia show, by late adolescence, young people have turned their attention to understanding who they are as people. They consider their beliefs, values, thoughts, and attitudes important to who they are. At the same time, adolescents also become keenly aware of how others view them. Their friendships and their relationships with their peers become central to how they spend their time and how they view themselves.

In fact, adolescents so greatly exaggerate the importance of how their peers view them that they come to develop a form of egocentrism in which they create within themselves an **imaginary audience** (Elkind, 1967, 1981, 1985): For a time, they feel themselves to be the constant object of the thoughts, judgments, and observations of other people. When adolescents believe that these other people judge their appearance or behavior harshly, their self-esteem suffers.

A more positive outcome of adolescents' awareness of what other persons think and feel is their increasing ability to view situations from the perspective of another person. Although none of us always can see how

imaginary audience • an adolescent's unfounded belief that other people are constantly observing, paying attention to, and judging the adolescent

others view a situation, adolescents increasingly become able to do so, far more than they could have just a few years earlier. According to Piaget, this ability is related to decreasing egocentrism and increasing ability to decenter from just their own points of view. Lawrence Kohlberg built on Piaget's ideas to propose his own theory of moral development, which made use of moral dilemmas.

Kohlberg's Model of Moral Reasoning

Scenarios such as the following one form the basis for measuring the development of moral reasoning in Kohlberg's influential theory (1963, 1983, 1984). According to Kohlberg, your answers to the dilemma will depend on your level of moral reasoning, which progresses through six specific stages, embedded within three general levels. Your solutions do not determine your stage of moral reasoning; rather, the kinds of reasons you give to justify your solutions determine your moral stage (see Table 9.2 and Figure 9.6). The accompanying Finding Your Way box will help you better understand Kohlberg's theory.

9.1

FINDING YOUR WAY

In Europe, a woman was near death from a rare form of cancer. The doctors thought that one drug might save her: a form of radium a druggist had recently discovered. The drug was expensive to make, but the druggist was also charging 10 times the cost of the drug; having paid $400 for the radium, the druggist charged $4,000 for a small dose. The sick woman's husband, Heinz, went to everyone he knew to borrow the money, but he could gather only $2,000. He begged the druggist to sell it more cheaply or to let him pay the rest later, but the druggist refused. So, having tried every legal means, Heinz desperately considered breaking into the drugstore to steal the drug for his wife (adapted from Kohlberg, 1963, 1983, 1984).

Suppose that you are Heinz. Should you steal the drug? Why or why not?

Other psychologists also have found that the complexity of moral reasoning increases with age, roughly along the lines Kohlberg suggested (e.g., Rest, 1983). Moreover, even research in other cultures has been rather supportive of Kohlberg's theory in places such as Turkey (Nisan & Kohlberg, 1982), Israel (Snarey, Reimer, & Kohlberg, 1985a, 1985b), South Africa (Maqsud & Rouhani, 1990), Iceland (M. Keller, Eckensberger, & von Rosen, 1989), and Poland (Niemczynski, Czyzowska, Pourkos, & Mirski, 1988), although some of the stages of morality do not apply without modification across cultures (e.g., studies in China; described in Ma, 1988). Not everyone agrees with Kohlberg's theory, however. The theory has been criticized for difficulties of subjectivity in assigning people to stages (Rest, 1979, 1983), for artificiality of the moral dilemmas Kohlberg used (Yussen, 1977), and for its postulation of a fixed and unalterable progression of stages (Kurtines & Greif, 1974). One of the most striking criticisms of his theory comes from a former student of Kohlberg's, Carol Gilligan.

FIGURE 9.6
Development of Moral Reasoning: Ages and Stages
The percentages of individuals (ages 10 through 36 years) who responded in terms of Lawrence Kohlberg's preconventional, conventional, and postconventional moral reasoning are summarized graphically here. Clearly, preconventional reasoning declines, conventional reasoning sharply increases, and postconventional reasoning increases slightly across the span of middle childhood through early adulthood. Note the absence of individuals in Stage 6.

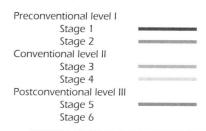

Preconventional level I
    Stage 1
    Stage 2
Conventional level II
    Stage 3
    Stage 4
Postconventional level III
    Stage 5
    Stage 6

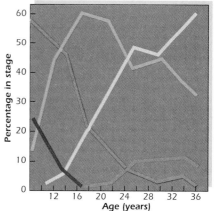

TABLE 9.2
Kohlberg's Theory of the Development of Moral Reasoning
How did you respond to Heinz's dilemma, and on what basis did you reason your answer?

Level/Stage	Basis for reasoning
Level I: Preconventional morality	The reasons to behave in ways that please other people or that avoid displeasing them are to avoid punishment or to obtain rewards. (Often characteristic of children's behavior between ages 7 and 10 years; 95% of 7-year-olds show judgments at this level.)
Stage 1: Heteronomous morality (i.e., Don't get caught)	Egocentric consideration of whether the behavior leads to punishment or to reward for self, not considering the outcomes, interests, or well-being of others. That is, reasoning is based on the principle that might makes right, so people should obey authority.
Stage 2: Individualistic, instrumental morality (i.e., What's in it for me?)	Give-and-take exchanges guide behavior. In recognition that others, too, have their own interests and considerations, the reasoner in this stage tries to strike deals that serve the reasoner's interests and also the other party's interests.
Level II: Conventional morality	Social and societal rules have become internalized, and the individual conforms to those rules and expectations because it is right to do so. (Often characteristic of children's behavior between ages 10 and 16 years and usually even beyond that age; moral judgments at this level were shown in no 7-year-olds, 20% of 10-year-olds, and most 13- and 16-year-olds.)
Stage 3: Interpersonally normative morality (i.e., I'm being good/nice)	Mutual interpersonal expectations and interpersonal conformity guide reasoning. Rules of behavior become internalized, so that individuals seek to perceive themselves as behaving in ways that other people consider to be good, appropriate, or nice. These individuals conform to particular behaviors to please others.
Stage 4: Social-system morality (i.e., Preserve the social order)	Societal rules form the basis of moral reasoning, and the development of an internal conscience and a recognition of the importance of the social system guides moral reasoning. You have entered into social contracts, which you are morally obligated to fulfill.
Level III: Postconventional morality	The person accepts society's rules as a basis for most behavior, but the person has also formulated an internal set of moral principles; when there is a conflict between the internal rules and society's rules, the person will follow the internal moral principles. (Stage 5 is rare before age 16, apparent in about 20% of 16-year-olds, and still not common after that age. Stage 6 is almost never evident in people under age 20 years, and still is unusual even in adults.)
Stage 5: Human-rights and social-welfare morality (i.e., What ensures the rights and well-being of each person?)	Social contracts and individual rights form the basis of moral reasoning in this stage.
Stage 6: Morality of universal, reversible, and prescriptive general ethical principles (i.e., What's best from the point of view of each person involved, including the broadest ramifications of individual actions?)	An orientation toward universal principles of justice guides moral reasoning in this stage.

Gilligan's Model

According to Gilligan (1982), although women *can* conceive morality as men do, women tend *not* to do so. Whereas men focus on abstract, rational principles, such as justice and respect for the rights of others, women see morality more as a matter of caring and compassion. Gilligan has proposed that women pass though three basic levels of morality, although not all women reach the third level. The first level involves the individual's concern only for herself; the second level involves self-sacrifice, in which concern for others predominates; and the third level involves integrating the responsibilities to both self and others. There is a lack of definitive evidence supporting this theory.

Other psychologists (e.g., Baumrind, 1986; Gibbs, Arnold, Ahlborn, & Cheesman, 1984; as well as Gilligan & Attanucci, 1988) have found similar sex differences in responses to moral dilemmas. At the same time, Lawrence Walker (1989), using a relatively large sample, found that most men and women, as well as girls and boys, used considerations of both caring and justice in their responses to moral dilemmas. However, although women were more likely to express a caring orientation than were men, girls were not more likely to do so than were boys. Although Gilligan's theory is attractive, at present the empirical evidence in support of her theory remains quite weak.

Thus far, this chapter has focused primarily on development in people who have not yet reached adulthood. The field of psychological development, however, does not stop at adolescence. Many psychologists study **life-span development,** which refers to the changes in a person that occur over a lifetime.

HOW DO ADULTS DEVELOP AND AGE?

Cognitive development during adulthood involves a continuing increase in knowledge and skill, but after middle adulthood people's speed of performing various mental operations (e.g., mental arithmetic) seems to decline somewhat (Bashore, Osman, & Hefley, 1989; Cerella, 1985; Denny, 1980; Poon, 1987; Schaie, 1989). Nevertheless, older people show remarkable plasticity, or modifiability, in old age, finding ways to compensate for declines in speed and other cognitive functions (Salthouse, 1996; Salthouse & Somberg, 1982).

Although there is some question as to how much decline individuals show with age, three basic principles of cognitive development in adulthood seem to capture much of what happens (Dixon & Baltes, 1986). First, although the ability to think quickly and flexibly and other aspects of information processing may decline in late adulthood, this decline is balanced by stabilization and even advancement of well-practiced and practical aspects of mental functioning. Thus, when adults lose some of their speed and physiology-related efficiency of information processing, they often compensate with other knowledge and expertise-based information-processing skills. Second, despite the age-related decline in information processing, sufficient reserve capacity allows at least temporary increases in performance, especially if the older adult is motivated to perform well. Third, at all times throughout the life span, there is considerable plasticity of abilities. None of us is stuck with a particular level of performance: Each of us can improve.

What form does the development of personality and identity take that occurs during adulthood? In young and middle-aged adults, identity development centers mainly on family and work. Within the family, adults usually form intimate relationships with a partner (or a series of partners) and they come to identify themselves as part of this partnership.

According to Erikson, during early adulthood, adults must resolve a crisis of *intimacy* versus *isolation*. The emerging adult tries to commit

Psychologist Carol Gilligan has suggested that women, more than men, focus on the special obligations of their close relationships and that women resolve moral issues with sensitivity to the social context, more than in regard to abstract principles. Also, whereas men are more likely to be competitive, women are more likely to be cooperative.

life-span development • the changes that occur within a person over the life span

him- or herself to a loving intimate relationship. The adult who succeeds will learn how to love in a giving and nonselfish way. The adult who fails will develop a sense of isolation and may fail to connect with the significant others in his or her life. Most adults also eventually become parents and, for many years, their identity is at least partly shaped by their roles as parents.

In addition, adult identity usually relates to adults' roles as workers in particular careers. Patterns of career choice and development have been described as having an *exploration phase,* in which individuals search for a career that is compatible with their interests, values, and abilities; an *establishment phase,* in which individuals begin to be identified with a particular career; a *midcareer phase,* in which individuals have established and seek to maintain their chosen careers; and a *late-career phase,* in which individuals are fully established and may even be viewed as leaders or mentors to others in their chosen career.

According to Erikson, during middle adulthood, adults face a crisis of *generativity* versus *stagnation.* Adults try to be productive in their work and to contribute to the next generation. They may do so by formulating ideas, creating products, or raising children. People face seven major developmental tasks during middle adulthood (Havighurst, 1967): (a) reaching and then maintaining satisfactory performance in a career; (b) accepting and adjusting to the physical changes of the middle years; (c) adjusting to parents who are aging and sometimes needing increasing care and supervision; (d) assisting adolescent children in their transition to adulthood; (e) achieving adult social responsibilities (e.g., with family and friends); (f) relating to a spouse; and (g) developing leisure-time activities.

Satisfaction in marriage tends to be greatest in the early years, to fall during the raising of children, and then to increase again in the later years when children grow older and, especially, when they start their own lives away from their families. Thus, the empty-nest syndrome, whereby parents adjust to having their children grow up and move out of the family home, can be partially offset by their own newfound happiness with each other.

What actually makes for a happy marriage? According to Gottman (1994), the key is in the way a couple resolves the conflicts that are inevitable in any marriage. Gottman has found that three different styles can succeed in resolving conflict. In a *validating marriage,* couples compromise often and develop relatively calm ways of resolving conflicts. In a *conflict-avoiding marriage,* couples agree to disagree and avoid conflicts to the extent possible. In a *volatile marriage,* couples have frequent conflicts, some of them antagonistic. Any one of these styles can work, as long as the number of positive moments the couple has together is at least five times as great as the number of negative moments. What destroys a marriage, according to Gottman, are (a) attacking the partner's personality or character, rather than his or her particular behavior; (b) showing contempt for a partner; (c) being defensive in response to constructive criticism; and (d) stonewalling, failing to respond at all to the concerns of the partner. Careers are important too, of course, but of differing importance at different points of life.

During later adulthood, most people retire or otherwise reduce their involvement in their careers, and they watch their own children become adults. They must again think about who they are now that their identities are not centered on raising children or on succeeding at work. According to Erikson, during late adulthood, adults confront a crisis of *integrity* versus *despair*. As they come to terms with their own mortality, people try to make sense of the lives they have led and, in particular, of the choices they have made. They may not feel as though every decision was right, in which case they must come to terms with their mistakes. Adults who succeed in this stage gain the wisdom and integrity of older age. Adults who fail may approach death with a sense of despair over mistakes or lost opportunities.

In humans, the process of development continues throughout life. Table 9.3 summarizes some of the developmental changes that occur across the life span, according to four developmental theorists. Although each theorist focuses on just one aspect of development (i.e., cognition, personality, friendship, or moral reasoning), each aspect of development influences and is influenced by the others. We view the world differently at each phase of life, based on both our maturational processes and our experiences. However, despite differences in development that influence how we perceive the world, we all must rely on similar fundamental processes of social psychology, the topic of the next chapter.

TABLE 9.3

Summary of Cognitive and Socioemotional Development

Period of development	Aspect of development: Theorist			
	Cognitive: Piaget	*Personality: Erikson*	*Friendship: Selman*	*Moral: Kohlberg*
Infancy	Sensorimotor	Trust versus mistrust		
Toddler period	Preoperational	Autonomy versus shame and doubt		Preconventional morality
Preschool years		Initiative versus guilt	Playmateship	
Middle childhood	Concrete operations	Industry versus inferiority	One-way assistance	Preconventional and conventional morality
			Fair-weather cooperation	
			Intimate and mutually shared relationships	
Adolescence	Formal operations	Identity versus role confusion		Conventional morality
Early adulthood		Intimacy versus isolation		Conventional morality (and in rare cases, postconventional morality)
Middle adulthood		Generativity versus stagnation		
Late adulthood		Integrity versus despair		

The Solution to The Case of the Unhappy Lawyer

Felicia picks up a copy of *Pathways to Psychology* in order to learn more about the psychology behind what is happening to her. After reading chapter 9, she realizes that, in the terms of Erik Erikson, she is facing a crisis of generativity versus stagnation. Felicia feels like she is stagnating. Because she has been paid well for a number of years, Felicia is able to redefine her priorities. She decides that although others may find fulfillment in law in general, and family law in particular, she no longer can. Felicia therefore takes an extended leave of absence from her firm to explore training in counseling psychology that will enable her to become a marriage counselor. Felicia returns to school first as a special student to pick up the undergraduate courses she will need to be admitted to a graduate program, and then as a graduate student to get a degree in counseling psychology. She eventually decides to resign from her law firm to become a full-time marriage counselor. Her income is less than half of what it was before, but she has found the fulfillment she personally was unable to find as a lawyer.

Summary

What Developmental Trends Have Psychologists Observed? 304

1. Trends in *development* include qualitative changes, such as differentiation, and quantitative changes, such as growth. *Cognitive development* involves changes in thinking across the life span, and *socioemotional development* involves changes in people's emotions, personality, interpersonal (social) interactions, moral beliefs, and behavior.

What Are the Roles of Maturation and Learning? 305

2. *Learning* refers to any relatively permanent change in thought or behavior, as a result of experience. *Maturation* refers to any relatively permanent change in thought or behavior that occurs simply as a result of aging, without regard to par-

ticular experiences. Today, almost all psychologists believe that both maturation and learning interact in influencing the course of development.

3. Jean Piaget proposed that cognitive development occurs largely through two processes of *equilibration:* (a) *assimilation,* whereby the child incorporates new information into the his or her existing cognitive *schemas;* and (b) *accommodation,* whereby the child attempts to change his or her cognitive schemas to fit relevant aspects of the new environment.

4. As children grow older, they become less *egocentric,* that is, they become less focused on themselves and more able to see things from the perspectives of others.

5. Lev Vygotsky's theory of cognitive development stresses the importance of (a) *internalization,* whereby we incorporate into ourselves the knowledge we gain from social contexts; and (b) the *zone of*

proximal development (ZPD), which is the range between a child's existing undeveloped potential capacity and the child's developed ability.

What Happens During Prenatal Development?   308

6. Prenatal development is characterized by increasing differentiation during the stages of the *zygote*, the *embryo*, and the *fetus*. During the stage of the embryo, the maternal environment strongly influences the course of development because that stage is a time during which many systems of the body undergo *critical periods* of development.

How Do Infants and Young Toddlers Develop?   310

7. We know that infants possess many more abilities than we recognized previously. As we become smarter observers of infants, infants appear smarter to us.

8. Piaget's *sensorimotor stage* centers on the development of sensory and motor skills during the first 2 years after birth. At the end of the sensorimotor stage, children start to develop *internal representations* (thoughts about people and objects that the children cannot see, hear, or otherwise perceive). The schema for *object permanence* develops during this stage.

9. Emotional development involves increasing specialization and sensitivity to the feelings of others.

10. *Temperament* refers to individual differences in the characteristic mood and in the typical intensity and duration of emotions. Temperament must be taken into account in observing the fit between a person and his or her environment.

11. According to Erikson, a crisis of trust versus mistrust occurs during infancy.

12. *Attachment* is a long-lasting emotional tie between two individuals, such as parent and child.

How Do Children Develop?   317

13. According to Piaget, young children (ages 1½ or 2 through 6 or 7 years) are in a *preoperational stage* of cognitive development. During this stage, they demonstrate *centration*, which is the tendency to center all thoughts on just one aspect of an object or concept. Somewhat older children (ages 6 or 7 to about 12 years) enter the *concrete-operational stage* of cognitive development and start to show *conservation of quantity*; they can recognize that two quantities remain the same, despite transformations on them that may change

their appearance. They also begin to show *inductive* and *deductive reasoning*, although they still continue to show *transductive reasoning*.

14. According to Erikson, crises that occur during childhood include autonomy versus shame or doubt, initiative versus guilt, and industry versus inferiority.

15. *Self-concept* consists of *self-understanding*, which is an individual's definition of *self*, and *self-esteem*, which is the person's sense of self-worth. Self-understanding often depends on different aspects of the self, such as physical attributes, behavior, and social relationships. Self-esteem is based on self-judgments about personal worth in various realms.

16. Development of gender identity involves the growth of self-perceptions about sexuality and gender identifications. *Gender typing* is the acquisition of specific gender-related roles.

17. Research results on the effects of *child care* are somewhat contradictory, but most studies show that high-quality child care does children little harm and may offer some benefits.

18. Learning how to make friends is important to a child's development. Developmental patterns of friendship show children's increasing ability to look for more than immediate material rewards from friends and to see the perspective of other persons across the course of development.

What Develops During Puberty and Adolescence?   326

19. *Puberty* is the onset of developing sexual maturity. *Adolescence* is the period from the onset of puberty until the time the individual is recognized as an adult, assuming the full adult responsibilities of the given society.

20. According to Piaget, adolescents are in the *formal-operational stage* of cognitive development, which is characterized by an increasing ability to manipulate abstract symbols, to carry out formal reasoning, and to consider hypothetical situations.

21. Adolescents commonly believe in the *personal fable* and the *invincibility fallacy*.

22. According to Erikson, adolescents confront the psychosocial crisis of identity versus *role confusion*.

23. According to Marcia, people's sense of *identity* can be categorized as being in a state of (a) *identity achievement*, if they have made their own decisions and have a firm sense of who they are; (b) *foreclosure*, if they have chosen their path with little thought; (c) *moratorium*, if they are still seeking an identity; or (d) *identity diffusion*, if they lack direction or commitment.

24. *Kohlberg's stage theory of moral development and reasoning* is the most widely accepted of such theories, although it has been criticized for several reasons. In the *preconventional stage,* people reason to avoid punishment and to seek self-interest; in the *conventional stage,* they reason according to family and social rules; and in the *postconventional stage,* they reason according to universal ethical requirements.

25. Carol Gilligan has suggested an alternative series of moral–developmental stages for women, involving an orientation toward caring relationships more than toward an abstract notion of justice.

How Do Adults Develop and Age?   331

26. According to Erikson, adults face the psychosocial crises of *intimacy* versus *isolation, generativity* versus *stagnation,* and *integrity* versus *despair.*

27. Adult identity more strongly centers on family and career than on sexuality. Thus, the assumption of roles as a partner and as a parent is important to adult identity, as is the development of a career.

Pathways to Knowledge

Choose the best answer to complete each sentence.

1. Maturation refers to
   (a) the attainment of successive stages of cognitive development.
   (b) changes in an individual's thoughts or behavior as a result of biological processes of aging.
   (c) changes in an individual's thoughts or behavior as a result of accumulating experience.
   (d) the development of an individual's thoughts and behavior due to the interactions of biological and environmental factors.

2. Learning refers to
   (a) the attainment of successive stages of cognitive development.
   (b) relatively stable changes in an individual's thoughts or behavior as a result of biological processes of aging.
   (c) relatively stable changes in an individual's thoughts or behavior as a result of accumulating experience.
   (d) the development of an individual's thoughts and behavior due to the interactions of biological and environmental factors.

3. Piaget described *accommodation* as a process whereby
   (a) individuals modify their existing schemas to incorporate new information from the environment.
   (b) individuals add new information from the environment to their existing schemas, without modifying their schemas.
   (c) infants eventually realize that objects not immediately available to their senses still continue to exist.

   (d) infants maintain abstract, complex cognitive representations of events.

4. According to Erik Erikson, individuals confront the following crises during personality development
   (a) trust versus mistrust, autonomy versus shame and doubt, identity versus role confusion.
   (b) initiative versus guilt, industry versus inferiority, intimacy versus isolation.
   (c) trust versus mistrust, optimism versus pessimism, extroversion versus introversion.
   (d) a and b.
   (e) b and c.

5. James Marcia has addressed the notion of identity development by suggesting four specific kinds of coping patterns:
   (a) diffusion, moratorium, internal, external
   (b) achievement, foreclosure, delayed, advanced
   (c) internal, external, delayed, advanced
   (d) diffusion, moratorium, achievement, foreclosure

6. Temperament is best described as an individual's
   (a) moods that are dependent on situational factors.
   (b) disposition and characteristic level of emotional reactivity.
   (c) stable personality characteristics in a given culture.
   (d) generalized mood state during a particular stage of development.

Answer each of the following questions by filling in the blank with an appropriate word or phrase.

7. According to Vygotsky, in the process of _____, people absorb knowledge from their surrounding social contexts.

8. Piaget's stages of cognitive development included the _____ stage (infancy and a little beyond), the preoperational stage (early childhood), the _____-_____ stage (middle childhood), and the formal-operational stage (adolescence and beyond).

9. According to Vygotsky, children can learn best when given opportunities for learning within their zone of _____ _____.

10. Lawrence Kohlberg's stages of moral reasoning are the _____ stage, the _____ stage, and the _____ stage.

11. According to Erik Erikson, the psychosocial crises people face in middle and late adulthood are the crises of _____ versus stagnation and _____ versus despair.

12. Self-concept comprises two aspects: _____ and _____.

Match the following developmental achievements or characteristics to the period of development with which they are most strongly associated:

13. conservation of quantity
14. object permanence
15. crisis of intimacy versus isolation
16. invincibility fallacy
17. sensorimotor stage
18. generativity
19. formal-operations stage
20. concrete-operations stage

(a) infancy
(b) childhood
(c) adolescence
(d) adulthood

Answers

1. b, 2. c, 3. a, 4. d, 5. d, 6. b, 7. internalization, 8. sensorimotor, concrete-operational, 9. proximal development, 10. preconventional, conventional, postconventional, 11. generativity, integrity, 12. self-esteem, self-understanding, 13. b, 14. a, 15. d, 16. c, 17. a, 18. d, 19. b, 20. b

Pathways to Understanding

1. What are some of the ways in which our limitations as researchers (i.e., limited tools, imaginations, resources, methods, etc.) limit our ability to identify some of the cognitive abilities of children? What steps should researchers take to avoid interpreting our own limitations as investigators as being limitations in the cognitive abilities of children?

2. Choose one of the ages or stages of development that differs from your own, and imagine being at that age or in that stage of development. Describe how you view the world, as well as how you think, feel, and act.

3. Give examples of your own gender-role development. In what ways do you conform to traditional gender roles, and in what ways have you departed from traditional gender roles?

The Case of The Rapidly Developing Relationship

Tyrone is almost everything Janet had hoped for. She has experienced love at first sight with him. He is handsome, athletic, intelligent, and successful. If Tyrone has one flaw, it is probably that he is a little quiet for her taste. But he explains that it goes with the turf in his family: The whole family is quiet. Janet has gone out with Tyrone five times and has never found herself so attracted to a man. She thinks about him most of the time now and about what they will do the next time they see each other. Janet also thinks about how passionate she feels toward Tyrone. She likes to get him little gifts, which he always appreciates. Tyrone in turn buys Janet gifts, expensive ones, and seems taken with her. So far they haven't really had much in the way of conversation, but they have been so busy with having fun that conversation has seemed like something that could wait. Now, to Janet's surprise, Tyrone has asked her to go steady, and she is trying to figure out what to do. The problem is that Janet feels that she hardly knows Tyrone. They have been dating for only a little over a month and his request seems premature to her. Also, the more Janet thinks about the situation, the more she feels like something is wrong; she just is not sure what is wrong. Janet is totally taken with Tyrone but something is gnawing at her.

What should Janet do? Think about this while you are reading chapter 10 on social psychology, which includes the topic of love and close relationships. Is a steady relationship with Tyrone a good pathway for her to take? Pay special attention to the triangular theory of love.

CHAPTER 10
SOCIAL PSYCHOLOGY

10

According to influential social psychologist Gordon Allport (1897–1967), **social psychology** is the attempt "to understand and explain how the thoughts, feelings, and behavior of individuals are influenced by the actual, imagined, or implied presence of others" (1985, p. 3). For instance, it appears that (a) the *actual* presence of other persons may lead people to go along with decisions that they would be less likely to agree with otherwise; (b) the *imagined* presence of other persons may lead people to change how hard they work at a task; and (c) the *implied* presence of other persons may influence whether people will go out of their way to help during an emergency. This chapter briefly elaborates on these and other findings discovered by social psychologists during their search for understanding and explanation.

Most of the studies in this chapter, like the studies cited in similar chapters in other textbooks (Moghaddam, Taylor, & Wright, 1993; P. B. Smith & Öngel, 1994; Triandis, 1994), have been conducted in the United States, involving American psychologists and research participants. Many social psychologists question whether findings based on American studies alone can be generalized to other countries and other cultures (M. H. Bond, 1988). Different cultures provide a different context for people's thoughts, feelings, and actions so we must be careful not to overgeneralize findings from one culture to another (Amir & Sharon, 1987). Moreover, the pathways connecting thoughts, feelings, and actions can differ from one culture to the next. For example, adulterous behavior on the part of a spouse may be ignored by one culture but lead to execution of the adulterous party in another culture. At the same time, many of the questions we ask about how people think, feel, and act are the same across cultures. First, we consider how we think about ourselves and other people.

WHAT IS SOCIAL COGNITION?

Social cognition refers to the thought processes through which people perceive and interpret information from and about themselves and other people. In this chapter, we discuss two interrelated theories of social cognition: cognitive-consistency theory and attribution theory.

Cognitive-Consistency Theory

Imagine that you are a research participant in a classic experiment by Leon Festinger and J. Merrill Carlsmith (1959). The experimenter asks you to perform two mind-numbingly simple tasks of eye–hand coordination. After you have performed these painfully boring tasks for a full hour, the experimenter finally lets you stop. If you are in the control group, you are asked to report how interesting you found the tasks, and that is the end of the experiment.

If you are in one of the experimental groups, however, you are asked to fill in for the research assistant, who has not arrived in time to prepare the next research participant. The experimenter promises to pay you to prepare the next research participant, telling her or him that you thoroughly enjoyed the experimental task. You are told that the experiment is designed to see whether research participants who expect to enjoy the task will perform better. Now you have the chance to become a part of the administration of the experiment, as an experimenter rather than merely as a participant.

Culture provides a context within which we "are influenced by the actual, imagined, or implied presence of others" (Allport, 1985, p. 3).

You agree to fill in for the missing research assistant, and you work hard to convince the next research participant that the task is great fun. Afterward, you are paid either $1 or $20, depending on the experimental condition to which you are assigned. Finally, a secretary asks you how much you actually enjoyed the task. How will you respond?

The true experiment was designed to measure the relationship between the amount of money the research participants were paid and the amount of enjoyment reported afterward. Surprisingly, research participants paid $1 rated the boring task as much more interesting than did either the participants who were paid $20, or the control participants (see Figure 10.1; Festinger & Carlsmith, 1959). Why did they do this?

Cognitive-Dissonance Theory

Festinger and Carlsmith explained the surprising results by suggesting that research participants' responses could be understood in terms of their efforts to achieve cognitive consistency between their beliefs (cognitions) and their behavior. **Cognitive consistency** refers to a match between the cognitions (thoughts) and the behavior of a person, as perceived by the person who is thinking and behaving. Cognitive consistency is extremely important to our mental well-being. Without it, we feel nervous, irritable, and uncomfortable.

social psychology • the study of how each person's thoughts, feelings, and behaviors are affected by the presence of others, even if that presence is only implied or imagined

social cognition • the thoughts and beliefs we have regarding ourselves and other people, based on how we perceive and interpret information that we either observe directly or learn from other people

cognitive consistency • the reassuring presence of a match between an individual's thoughts (cognition) and that person's behavior

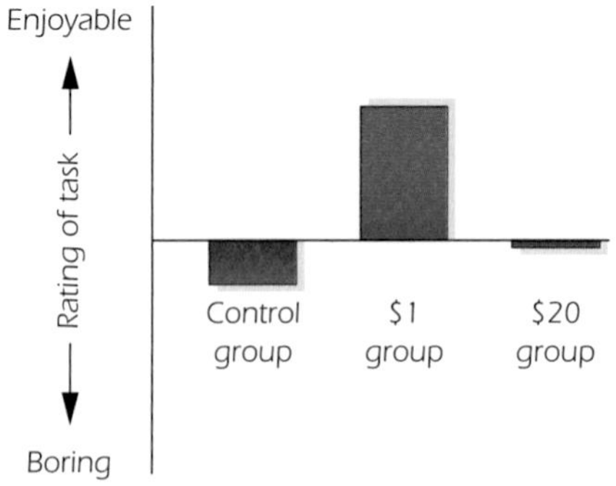

Enjoyable ↑

Rating of task

Boring

| Control group | $1 group | $20 group |

FIGURE 10.1
When Less Leads to More
The research participants who were paid less money ($1 instead of $20) to convince someone else that the boring task was interesting reported that they actually liked the task more (Festinger & Carlsmith, 1959). Why would research participants who were paid less say that they actually liked the task more?

Now, reconsider the experiment: The research participants who were paid $20 performed an extremely boring task and then encouraged someone else to believe that the task was interesting. They were well-compensated for doing so, however, so they could achieve cognitive consistency easily by saying to themselves: "I said that the boring task was interesting because I was paid well to do so."

Now consider the research participants who were paid $1. They performed a boring task, and then they tried to convince someone else that it was interesting. These participants experienced **cognitive dissonance** because their beliefs and their behavior did not agree. People need to feel that they have good reasons for behaving as they do. When the participants saw their own behavior in this situation, they needed to find some reason for their behavior. Clearly, money was not the reason in this case. They needed to find a way to bring their behavior and their beliefs more closely into agreement. Therefore, they came to believe that the task must not really have been quite as boring as they had previously thought. That is, they gave themselves reasons for their own behavior by changing their beliefs about the task. Several conditions make cognitive dissonance more likely to occur (see Figure 10.2).

FIGURE 10.2
Conditions for Cognitive Dissonance
Cognitive dissonance seems more likely to occur when (a) you have freely chosen the action that causes the dissonance, (b) you have committed yourself to that behavior and cannot undo your commitment, and (c) your behavior has important consequences for other people.

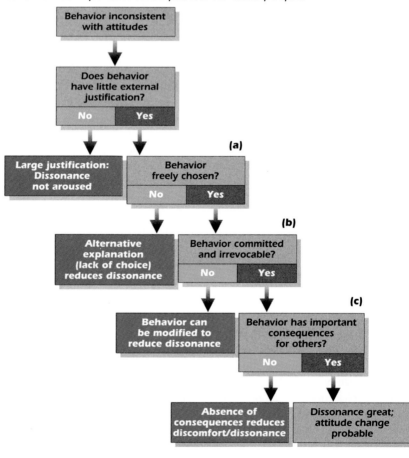

cognitive dissonance • the discomforting conflict between an individual's thoughts (cognition) and that person's behavior; often as a result of the person's having acted in a way that does not agree with her or his existing beliefs

Festinger and Carlsmith (1959) mapped out new territory with their interpretation of their experiment in terms of cognitive-dissonance theory. Since their landmark research and interpretation, other social psychologists have suggested alternative interpretations of their findings. Consider now the rather different analysis suggested by self-perception theory, an alternative view of cognitive consistency.

Self-Perception Theory

Most of us assume that our behavior is caused by our beliefs. **Self-perception theory** (Bem, 1967, 1972) suggests essentially the opposite: When we are not sure of what we believe, we *infer* our beliefs *from* our behavior. We perceive our actions much as an outside observer would, and then we draw conclusions about ourselves, based on our actions. We form beliefs about ourselves, based on our behavior. For example, if you meet someone and act in a friendly manner to the person, even though you do not have to, you might perceive your own behavior and conclude that you like the person. You have decided you like the person by observing your own behavior toward that person.

Consider how self-perception theory might interpret the findings of the Festinger and Carlsmith (1959) experiment. As you find yourself explaining to another research participant how much you enjoyed the task, you wonder, "Why in the world am I doing this?" If you are not sure why, then how can you understand your own behavior? If you have been paid $20, an explanation is easy: You are doing it for the money. However, if you have been paid only $1, you cannot be doing it for the money. So, looking at the situation as an outside observer, you conclude that you must have liked the task. Note that according to self-perception theory, you *form* beliefs about yourself based on your actions. According to cognitive-dissonance theory, you *modify* your beliefs, including your beliefs about yourself and your experiences, when your actions seem to conflict with your existing beliefs.

The results of research on cognitive-dissonance theory and self-perception theory (e.g., Bem, 1967; J. Cooper, Zanna, & Taves, 1978) are mixed, with some support for each interpretation. Russell Fazio, Mark Zanna, and Joel Cooper (1977) have suggested that dissonance theory seems better to explain *attitude change,* discussed below, particularly when the change is dramatic and the original beliefs and attitudes are obvious and well defined. Self-perception theory seems better to explain *attitude formation,* when the person's attitudes are still unclear and poorly defined.

For example, suppose you find yourself working in a political campaign in order to meet some new people, but you find yourself uncomfortable with what you are doing because in the past you have lacked enthusiasm for the candidate. You now find yourself feeling more positively toward the candidate. Why? If your attitude toward the candidate was not well formed or just in the process of forming, you might explain your behavior by self-perception theory, taking your working for the candidate as evidence that you really are starting to like the candidate after all. If, however, your attitude in the past was more well formed, you might adopt a more positive attitude toward the candidate to justify your work for the candidate, and thereby reduce cognitive dissonance. In general, self-perception theory is a special case of a more general kind of theory called *attribution theory* (the case in which one makes attributions about oneself).

self-perception theory • the suggestion that when we are not sure of what we believe, we view our behavior much as an outsider might view our behavior, and then infer our beliefs, based on our actions

Attribution Theory

One of the ways in which we may resolve cognitive dissonance to achieve cognitive consistency is to make attributions regarding the causes of our own behavior. An **attribution** is an explanation that points to the cause of a person's behavior (including the behavior of the individual devising the explanation). Such attributions are not needed in cognitive-dissonance theory, but they are essential to self-perception theory. In self-perception theory, we must make a self-attribution regarding our behavior in order to form our beliefs and attitudes.

Because self-perception theory focuses on making attributions, it is an *attribution theory,* a broad class of social-psychological theories. Attribution theories address how people explain not only their own behavior, but also the behavior of others. People make attributions so that they can understand their social world and can answer questions such as "Why did I act that way?"; or "Why did she do that?"

Fritz Heider (1958), an early leader in attribution theory, held that we explain observed behavior by making causal attributions. Then, we often base our own later behavior on the causal attributions we have made. For example, suppose that someone bumps into us. If we attribute the behavior to the person's having been preoccupied or in a hurry, we may be gracious about having been bumped. Instead, however, if we attribute the person's behavior to that person's natural disposition as a rude individual, we may behave more rudely toward that person in turn.

Heider pointed out that people make two basic kinds of attributions: personal attributions and situational attributions. **Personal attributions** (sometimes called "dispositional attributions") are based on internal factors in a person ("My stubbornness got us into this argument."). **Situational attributions** point to causes in external factors such as settings, events, or other people ("If my neighbors hadn't been partying the whole night before my final, I probably wouldn't have flunked my exam.").

When people make attributions, they often use mental shortcuts. These shortcuts may save time and energy but they can lead to distortions and other errors in judgment. What are some of the common shortcuts and biases that affect how people make causal attributions? They include **social desirability bias, common and uncommon effects, personalism,** the **fundamental attribution error, actor–observer effects, self-serving biases,** and **self-handicapping.**

Heuristics and Biases of Attribution

None of us carefully weighs every factor each time we make an attribution. Instead, we sometimes use *heuristics* (mental shortcuts) to help us make decisions. Unfortunately, these shortcuts sometimes lead to biases and other distortions in our thinking, such as in our thinking about the causes of behavior.

Social Desirability.   We tend to give undeservedly heavy weight to socially undesirable behavior (Jones & Davis, 1965), and we sometimes fail to notice even highly socially desirable behavior. For example, someone who belches and drools at the dinner table is likely to make a bad impression, despite the person's witty, insightful, thought-provoking conversation.

---

attribution • a mental explanation pointing to the cause or causes of a person's behavior, including the behavior of the person making the attribution

personal attribution • a mental explanation pointing to the cause of behavior as lying within the individual (internal) who performs the behavior (also termed *dispositional attribution*)

situational attribution • a mental explanation pointing to the cause of behavior as lying within the situation (external) in which the individual shows the behavior

social desirability bias • the tendency, when trying to infer the dispositions of people, to give undeservedly heavy weight to socially undesirable behavior

common and uncommon effects • the tendency to infer attributions based on whether the effects of a behavior are ordinary (situational attributions) or are unusual (personal attributions)

personalism • the tendency to make more personal attributions when the behavior of someone affects us directly but to make more situational attributions when the behavior affects us less directly

fundamental attribution error • the tendency to overemphasize internal causes and personal responsibility and to deemphasize external causes and situational influences when observing the behavior of other people

actor–observer effect • the tendency not only to attribute the actions of others to stable internal personal dispositions but also to attribute our own actions to external situational variables

self-serving biases • the tendency to be generous to ourselves when interpreting our own actions, pointing to personal causes when we do well and to situational causes when we do poorly

self-handicapping • the tendency to take actions to undermine our own performance in order to have an excuse in case we fail

Common and Uncommon Effects. We tend to infer attributions based on whether the effects of a behavior are common (in which case, we would infer situational attributions) or uncommon (in which case, we would infer personal attributions; Jones & Davis, 1965). For example, if a literature professor asks someone to recite poetry, we tend to infer that situational factors led to the request, but if a physics professor does so, we tend to infer that personal factors led to the request.

Personalism. We tend to make personal, rather than situational, attributions for the behavior of someone who affects us directly but to be more willing to attribute the cause to situational factors when behavior affects us less directly. For example, each of us tends to believe that a person who bumps into us is probably a rude jerk by nature but a person who bumps into somebody else is probably just preoccupied or in a hurry.

Fundamental Attribution Error. We tend to overemphasize internal causes and personal responsibility and to deemphasize external causes and situational influences when observing the behavior of other people (L. Ross, 1977). For example, we are more likely to attribute a person's generous donations to charity to the person's nature, rather than to the person's circumstances.

Actor–Observer Effects. We tend not only to attribute the actions of others to stable internal personal dispositions, but also to attribute our own actions to external situational variables (Jones & Nisbett, 1971; Nisbett, Caputo, Legant, & Marecek, 1973). For example, if I kick a dog, it is because the dog was about to bite but if I see someone else kick a dog the action shows just how mean and nasty that person really is.

Self-Serving Biases. We tend to be generous to ourselves when interpreting our own actions. For example, when students study for examinations and do well, they are likely to take credit for the success. However, when students study and do poorly, they are more likely to attribute the low grade to the examination ("That test was unfair!") or to the professor ("His grading is so strict!"; Whitley & Frieze, 1985).

Self-Handicapping. Often, we tend to undermine our own performance so that we will have an excuse in case we fail to perform well (Berglas & Jones, 1978; Sheppard & Arkin, 1989). For example, a student might not make the time to study for a test. Later, if she does badly on the test, she then may attribute the failure to not being able to study, thereby avoiding the need to attribute her failure to her own inability to do well.

These shortcuts can lead us to form attitudes toward ourselves and others, some of which are based on faulty information. In the next section, attitudes are considered in more detail.

HOW DO WE FORM AND CHANGE OUR ATTITUDES?

Which is more important: devotion to helping other persons or the accumulation of wealth? The way that you answer this question depends on your attitudes toward helpfulness and toward wealth. An **attitude** is a learned, stable, and relatively enduring evaluation of a person, object, or

attitude • a learned, stable, and relatively enduring evaluation (e.g., of a person or an idea); such an evaluation can affect an individual's thoughts, feelings, and behavior

Children learn many of their attitudes about race and gender through observation. Children's TV programs show more than twice as many male roles as female roles. Males are more likely to be shown as the doers who make things happen and who are rewarded for their actions, and females are more likely to be the recipients of actions. The females who do take action are more likely than males to be punished for their activity (Basow, 1986). On prime-time TV, about three fourths of the leading characters are white males. What attitudes are children learning by watching TV?

idea that can affect an individual's behavior (Allport, 1935; Petty & Cacioppo, 1981). This definition covers several points. First, we are not born with the attitudes we have; we acquire them through experience. Second, attitudes tend to be stable and relatively enduring; they tend not to change easily. Third, attitudes are evaluative; we use them for judging things positively or negatively, and in varying degrees. Some issues may not concern us much one way or the other, whereas other issues may lead to strong opinions. Finally, attitudes can influence behavior, such as when they cause people to act—to vote, protest, work, make friends, and so on. (As you may have guessed from the earlier discussion of cognitive-consistency theories, behavior may also influence attitudes.)

Some psychologists view attitudes as having components that are *cognitive* (thought-based), *behavioral* (action-based), and *affective* (emotion-based): Your attitude toward someone or something depends on what you think and feel about the person or thing, as well as on how you act toward the person or thing (Katz & Stotland, 1959). Attitudes are central to the psychology of the individual.

Research has shown that learning influences the formation of our attitudes. For instance, when we are rewarded for expressing particular attitudes, those attitudes are strengthened (Insko, 1965). Similarly, observational learning (also called "social learning"; see chapter 5) seems to influence both behavior (as shown in Figure 5.4) and attitude formation. Do these same processes underlie changes in our attitudes or do other processes influence such changes? It appears that changes in people's attitudes are influenced by various characteristics of the person who receives the message (e.g., motivated, interested, knowledgeable, and able to use reasoning skills); of the person who sends the message (e.g., likable and credible);

10.1

CHARACTERISTICS AFFECTING ATTITUDE CHANGE

Would you like to know how to influence other people to change their attitudes to resemble more closely the attitudes you favor? The following list outlines the ways that you can increase your effectiveness in persuading other people to change their attitudes:

1. Tailor your persuasive message to the characteristics of the person to whom you are addressing your message. Is your message recipient highly motivated, interested, knowledgeable, and able to *think* about the issues related to the attitude you wish to change? If so, appeal to this person by emphasizing the use of thoughtful, well-reasoned arguments. If not, appeal to this person by emphasizing the use of inviting messages (e.g., colorful photos), attractive and rewarding message senders (e.g., beautiful or sexy models or entertainers), and rewarding message formats (e.g., appealing videos or catchy jingles).

2. Tailor your persuasive message to the situation of the message recipient. Is your message recipient likely to think of, or perhaps to hear about, counterarguments to your persuasive message? If so, use balanced, two-sided arguments when giving your persuasive message (Lumsdaine & Janis, 1953). If not, one-sided arguments will probably do the trick. For message recipients who will neither think of nor face counterarguments, one-sided arguments may even be more effective than two-sided ones, and one-sided arguments will probably take less time and effort on your part.

3. Use strong arguments, rather than weak arguments, and repeat the arguments often, so that the arguments become familiar to the recipients of your message. Sheer repetition of a persuasive message seems to increase its familiarity and its appeal. (Watch commercial television if you wonder whether most advertisers know about this persuasive technique.)

4. Have the attitude-change message delivered by someone who is both believable (Hovland & Weiss, 1951) and appealing (Chaiken & Eagly, 1983; Eagly & Chaiken, 1975).

and of the message itself (e.g., familiar and strong arguments; one-sided vs. two-sided [balanced] arguments), as shown in Putting It to Use 10.1.

You may be saying to yourself, "I don't really want to change other people's attitudes very often, if at all. I have a live-and-let-live attitude." Even if you do not wish to know how to persuade other people to change their attitudes, you still may want to be aware of methods for attitude change, however. Why? Because other people, such as politicians and advertisers, are constantly trying to influence you to change your attitudes, and not all of those people necessarily will have your best interests at heart. If you examine some of the variables likely to influence attitude change, you may become more aware of such attempts. Thereby, you may become better able to decide when, or even if, you choose to change your own attitudes.

Recall an effective advertisement that you have recently seen (e.g., on television or in print) or heard (e.g., on the radio). What factors do you believe made this ad effective in leading to attitude change? What is it about this advertisement that would lead you to have a more positive attitude toward the product or service being advertised? Using a scale of 1 (low) to 7 (high), rate the attitude-change characteristics of this advertisement.

- *Characteristics of the message giver (the source of the attitude-change message):*

  Credibility
  1. *Knowledge*　　1 2 3 4 5 6 7
  2. *Trustworthiness*　　1 2 3 4 5 6 7

  Likability and appeal
  3. *Familiarity*　　1 2 3 4 5 6 7
  4. *Attractiveness*　　1 2 3 4 5 6 7
  5. *Similarity to you*　　1 2 3 4 5 6 7

- *Characteristics of the advertising message:*

  Likability and appeal
  6. *Familiarity*　　1 2 3 4 5 6 7
  7. *Attractiveness*　　1 2 3 4 5 6 7
  8. *Similarity to your own experiences*　　1 2 3 4 5 6 7

  Informativeness
  9. *Balance (one- vs. two-sided arguments)*　　1 2 3 4 5 6 7
  10. *Reasoning*　　1 2 3 4 5 6 7
  11. *Factual information*　　1 2 3 4 5 6 7

  Emotional appeal
  12. *Appeal to emotions (e.g., fear of social rejection due to bad breath)*　　1 2 3 4 5 6 7

- *Characteristics of the message receiver (you):*
  13. *Interest*　　1 2 3 4 5 6 7
  14. *Knowledge*　　1 2 3 4 5 6 7

Overall, which of the preceding characteristics were most important in making the advertisement effective? What other characteristics of this advertisement helped to make it effective?

Once people's attitudes have changed, do their actions always change as well? Not necessarily. Although attitudes and behaviors are strongly linked, we cannot safely assume that people's behavior always accurately demonstrates their attitudes. Several factors increase the likelihood that people's attitudes will show up in their behavior (described in R. A. Baron & Byrne, 1991; S. S. Brehm & Kassin, 1990). Attitudes that are more likely to be tied to behavior are stronger and more highly specific and are based on more information and more experience, as compared with attitudes that are less likely to be reflected in people's behavior.

For example, you are more likely to vote to spend tax money on public education if you strongly believe in the value of public education, if you specifically believe that tax money should be spent for public education, and if you have a great deal of information and experience regarding public education as compared with someone who does not believe strongly in the value of public education, who sees only a vague link between voting to spend tax money on public education and the quality of the public education system, and who has very little information and experience regarding public education.

One set of attitudes we have is toward others who are especially important to us in our lives, in particular, people whom we like or love, or people to whom we are attracted. Consider now the nature of liking, loving, and interpersonal attraction, all of which are affected by and affect our attitudes.

WHAT ARE LIKING, LOVING, AND INTERPERSONAL ATTRACTION?

The preceding section of this chapter described several strategies for persuading people to change their attitudes. One factor that affects the likelihood of being persuaded is the likability of the persuader: We tend to be more easily persuaded by people who are likable. Just what does it mean to be "likable"? Why are we more attracted, and more attractive, to one person rather than to another?

Each of us needs friendship and love, and each of us feels physical attraction to other persons. In addition, our perceptions of ourselves are partly shaped by our friendships, our loving relationships, and our feelings of attractiveness and attraction to others. Social psychologists have asked, "What is going on in the mind of a person who feels attracted to someone?"

Theories of Liking and Interpersonal Attraction

Suppose that you are introduced to someone. This person immediately, and quite sincerely, compliments you on your looks, your brains, your physical strength, or something else of which you are proud. Chances are that you will like that person all the more for the compliment. In terms of *learning theory,* you will have been positively reinforced by the complimenter, so you will feel more attracted to him or her. Similarly, you will like a person when you are rewarded in the presence of that person (Clore & Byrne, 1974). For example, if you always see a particular person at a particularly enjoyable type of event, you may feel more attracted to that person by virtue of the person's association with the rewarding event.

An alternative view of attraction combines ideas from learning theory and from cognitive-dissonance theory. According to **equity theory** (Walster, Walster, & Berscheid, 1978), people will be more attracted to those with whom they have an equitable (fair) relationship. We are attracted to people who take from us in proportion to what they give to us. How does equity theory draw on ideas from learning theory and from cognitive-consistency theory? It suggests that we usually expect to receive rewards and punishments in about equal proportion to what we give in relationships, and we try to maintain cognitive consistency by ensuring that what we give is in balance with what we get in relationships.

Other theories of attraction depend more heavily on cognitive-consistency theories. For example, according to **balance theory** (Heider, 1958), we try to maintain a sense of balance (equilibrium) in our personal

equity theory • a theory of attraction suggesting that people feel more strongly attracted to those with whom they have more equitable (fair) relationships of giving and taking

balance theory • a cognitive-consistency theory of attraction, suggesting that people who like each other try to maintain a balance (reciprocity) regarding the mutual give and take in the relationship and that they try to maintain similar likes and dislikes

relationships. One aspect of maintaining balance has to do with reciprocity. Similar to the notion of equity, *reciprocity* refers to the balance of give and take in a relationship. Another aspect of maintaining balance is *similarity:* We expect our friends to have the same positive or negative attitudes that we have, liking the people and ideas that we like, and disliking the people and ideas we dislike.

Theories of Love

Do we like all the people we love and love all the people we like? Are liking and loving the same thing? Most of us distinguish between liking and loving but we also admit that it is difficult to define precisely all the differences between liking and loving, not to mention the difficulty in trying to define precisely the two terms themselves. To avoid wrestling with this question, we assume here that *love* is a deeper, stronger emotion than is liking. Both feelings are rooted in attraction, but love stems from more powerful, perhaps even instinctual, emotional and physical attractions than does liking. Maybe an even more difficult question is why do people feel love? Of the many different answers to that question are the three theories discussed here: evolutionary theory, attachment theory and the triangular theory of love.

One way to understand love is in evolutionary terms. According to *evolutionary theory,* the ultimate function of romantic love is to create new generations of individuals who will carry on the genotypes of past generations. Unfortunately, however, romantic love generally does not last long, sometimes just long enough to commit the procreative act. Were romantic love the only force keeping couples together, children might not be raised in a way that would enable them to develop their potential. Fortunately, just plain liking can also contribute to the maintenance of a relationship.

The evolutionary point of view suggests that females and males will value somewhat different things in love (D. M. Buss & Schmitt, 1993; Kenrick & Keefe, 1992). In particular, females, from this point of view, have more investment in their offspring because (a) they must carry the offspring during pregnancy, (b) they know that the offspring they bear is their own, and (c) they tend to be more involved in raising the offspring. Because of their greater investment, they are particularly interested in males who have considerable resources to bring to the relationship. Males, on the other hand, (a) can impregnate many females in a short period of time, (b) cannot be certain that the offspring is theirs, and (c) tend to be less involved, on average, in the offspring's upbringing. Evolutionarily, their best strategy may be to find a female who will bear the healthiest possible offspring. As a result, males, according to evolutionary theory, tend to be attracted to females who have signs of good health, such as youth and beauty. Across cultures, these predictors seem to hold up.

According to the **attachment theory of love** (Hazan & Shaver, 1987), how we relate to other people in loving relationships derives from how we related to our parents, and especially our mother, as an infant (Shaver, 1994). *Securely attached* lovers tend to be confident in their relationships and tend not to worry about being abandoned. *Anxious–ambivalent* lovers, on the other hand, tend to worry about being abandoned, tend to be prone to jealousy, and often feel like their partner is more distant than they would like. *Avoidant* lovers actually seek distance and become uncomfortable when their partner tries to get very close.

attachment theory of love • a view that how we relate to loved ones as adults stems from the way in which we attached to our parents, and particularly our mothers, as infants

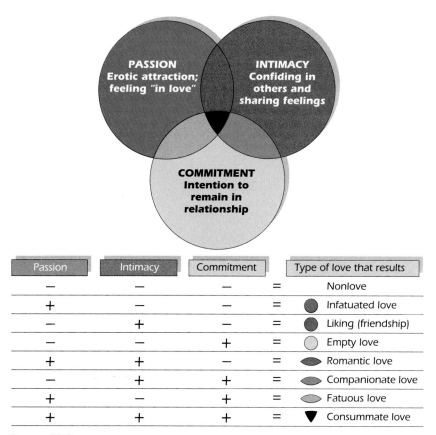

Passion	Intimacy	Commitment		Type of love that results
−	−	−	=	Nonlove
+	−	−	=	⬤ Infatuated love
−	+	−	=	⬤ Liking (friendship)
−	−	+	=	⬤ Empty love
+	+	−	=	⬬ Romantic love
−	+	+	=	⬬ Companionate love
+	−	+	=	⬬ Fatuous love
+	+	+	=	▼ Consummate love

Figure 10.3
Triangular Theory of Love
According to this theory, love has three main components: intimacy, passion, and commitment.

An additional view of love is my own **triangular theory of love** (R. J. Sternberg, 1986b, 1997b, 1998a), according to which love has three basic components: (a) *intimacy*, feelings that promote closeness and connection; (b) *passion*, the intense desire for union with another person (Hatfield & Walster, 1978); and (c) *commitment*, the decision to maintain a relationship over the long term. Different combinations of these three components lead to different kinds of love, as shown in Figure 10.3. The integration of all three components is *consummate love*, in which the loved ones share great intimacy and passion, as well as deep commitment to the relationship. These various kinds of love develop as a result of the kinds of stories we bring to loving relationships (R. J. Sternberg, 1996, 1998b). For example, stories may emphasize the importance of intimacy, as when we view a story of love as one of a couple's journeying through life together, at each other's side; of passion, as when we have a highly romantic story, perhaps emphasizing the fantasy qualities of a relationship; or of commitment, as when we view love as a story about staying with a partner, come what may.

Attraction

According to this theory, each of us creates our own personal idealized love stories, in which we formulate particular roles for ourselves and for the partners to whom we are attracted (R. J. Sternberg, 1998b). We are

triangular theory of love • a theory suggesting that love has three basic components: intimacy, passion, and commitment

What attracts these people to each other? According to social-psychological research, they probably know each other pretty well, live or work near each other, and have similar attitudes, temperaments, and social and communication skills. They probably also are physically aroused in each other's presence and find each other physically attractive.

typically unaware, or only vaguely aware, of the stories we create. Each of us is attracted to prospective partners who closely match the leading characters in our personal love stories (e.g., the cop and the criminal in a police story, or the prince and the princess in a fairy tale). Further, we continue to find happiness with a given partner as long as we continue to perceive the partner as matching our desired personal love story.

What factors lead people to be attracted to one another? Psychologists have observed that several variables seem to contribute to whether particular people will be attracted to one another. The variables underlying attraction include the following:

- *Arousal* (how excited we become about a person)

    Arousal seems to play an important role in interpersonal attraction. The role of arousal was demonstrated in a famous and creative study (Dutton & Aron, 1974) conducted in a scenic spot with two bridges in different places. The first bridge extended over a deep gorge and swayed from side to side when people walked across the bridge. For most people, walking across the bridge was sufficient to arouse fear. The second bridge was stable, solid, and near the ground. As the men walked across the bridge they were met by a female research assistant who requested that they write a story about a picture and who also gave them her home phone number in case they had any questions about the study. The researchers found that male participants who walked across the unstable bridge were more likely than males who walked across the stable bridge to show signs of attraction to the female research assistant. The fearfully aroused males wrote stories in response to the picture shown to them that contained high levels of sexual imagery, and they also were more likely later to call the female research assistant at home.

- *Familiarity* (mentioned as a persuasive feature of a message source)

  Research shows that simply exposing people to a stimulus many times tends to increase people's liking for that stimulus (Arkes, Boehm, & Xu, 1991). This positive effect on attitudes that results from repeated exposure to a stimulus is called the *mere-exposure effect* (Zajonc, 1968). For example, many people find that their liking for a piece of music, a work of art, or a person increases with repeated exposure. However, if repetition becomes boring or annoying it can backfire, decreasing the likelihood of liking or of attitude change (Cacioppo & Petty, 1979, 1980). Thus, repetition is useful to make sure that people get the message, but after a point it may hurt. Mere exposure to people tends to increase attraction to them, unless they become boring.

- *Proximity* (geographical nearness of the person toward whom we are attracted; Festinger, Schachter, & Back, 1950)

  We meet only a small proportion of all the people to whom we might be attracted. Thus, some kind of proximity is needed for attraction even to take place. Researchers studying life in married-student housing at the Massachusetts Institute of Technology found that the closer people lived to each other in the housing, the more likely they were to become friends (Festinger, Schachter, & Back, 1950).

- *Physical attractiveness* (e.g., Walster, Aronson, Abrahams, & Rottman, 1966)

  Whether we like to admit it or not, we are very much affected by physical attractiveness in many ways. For example, Kenneth Dion, Ellen Berscheid, and Elaine Walster (1972) found that more physically attractive people are judged to be kinder and stronger; to be more outgoing, nurturant, sensitive, interesting, poised, sociable, and sexually warm and responsive; to be more exciting dates, and to have better character. Moreover, Langlois, Ritter, Casey, and Savin (1995) have shown that mothers are more affectionate toward and more playful with attractive infants than with unattractive infants. Our generalized judgments solely on the basis of physical attractiveness are often overly positive (Feingold, 1992).

  Another important consideration in regard to physical attractiveness is the cultural context of the beholders of beauty. Cross-cultural studies of beauty have clearly documented that different cultures have strikingly different views of what constitutes a standard of beauty. We have known for decades that different societies have sharply different views of physical attractiveness. An early review of more than 200 widely divergent cultures (Ford & Beach, 1951) found that societies differ not only in what they consider beautiful, but also in the parts of the body (e.g., eyes, pelvis size, overall height and weight) they emphasize in evaluating beauty. More recent reviews (e.g., Berscheid & Walster, 1974) support this diversity of cultural views of attractiveness.

- *Similarity* (Murstein, 1986; R. J. Sternberg, 1988b; mentioned also in the balance theory of liking)

  Several aspects of similarity have been found to increase attraction, such as similar attitudes and temperament (Hatfield & Rapson, 1992), social and communication skills (Burleson & Denton, 1992), and even sense of humor (Murstein & Brust, 1985). We are attracted to people like ourselves, almost without regard to the dimension of personality, motivation, or cognition under consideration.

Attraction also is more likely to develop in relationships where there is good communication, the topic considered next.

HOW DO WE COMMUNICATE IN OUR PERSONAL RELATIONSHIPS?

In personal relationships of many kinds, communication appears to be an important key to success. Couples in happy marriages truly listen to each other and affirm the value of each other's points of view, whereas couples in unhappy marriages are less likely to do so (Gottman, 1979, 1994). Other factors also contribute to unsuccessful communication in couples (Gottman, Notarius, Gonso, & Markman, 1976): One or both partners (a) feel hurt and ignored, (b) feel that the other person does not see her or his point of view, (c) neglect to stay on one problem long enough to resolve the problem, (d) frequently interrupt one another, and (e) drag many irrelevant issues into the discussion.

Another consideration is that there appear to be gender differences in communication patterns, content, and styles. In general, women seem to disclose more about themselves than do men (Morton, 1978). Based on her extensive research on male–female conversation, Deborah Tannen (1986, 1990) suggests that the conversational differences between men and women largely center on their differing understanding of the goals of conversation. According to Tannen (1990), men see the world as a ranked social order in which the purpose of communication is to negotiate for the upper hand, to preserve independence, and to avoid failure. Each man tries to one-up the other and to "win" the contest. Women, in contrast, try to establish a connection between the two participants, to give support and confirmation to others, and to reach agreement through communication.

Tannen states that when men and women become more aware of their differing styles and traditions they may be less likely to misinterpret one another's conversational interactions. In this way, they can both work toward achieving their own individual aims, as well as the aims of the relationship. Just as verbal communication is a key aspect of close personal relationships, it is also vital to interactions within larger groups of people, such as in work groups.

HOW DO WE INTERACT IN GROUPS?

A **group** is a collection of individuals who interact with each other, often for a common purpose or activity. What actually happens when members of a group interact? Robert Bales (1950, 1970) suggested that groups serve two basic functions: to get work done and to handle relationships among group members. Different kinds of groups, and different group leaders, give differing emphasis to each of these functions.

How do groups of people reach agreement as to what they will do? What factors influence the route to agreement and the kind of agreement achieved? What makes individuals within a group conform to a group decision, even if they do not believe in it? We consider some of these questions here.

Social Facilitation and Social Interference

Having other people around can affect the quality of the work you do (Triplett, 1898). In **social facilitation,** having other people around improves

group • a collection of individuals who interact with each other, usually either to accomplish work or to promote interpersonal relationships (or both)

social facilitation • the phenomenon in which the presence of other people positively influences the performance of an individual

Successful entertainers seem to respond particularly to social facilitation, especially if they have rehearsed well enough to be thoroughly familiar with the material they plan to perform.

the performance of an individual. For example, many athletes, actors, and singers find that they perform better when other people are present than when they are alone.

On the other hand, the presence of people can sometimes hurt performance, through the phenomenon of **social interference.** Have you ever had to speak or perform in front of others and found yourself too nervous to perform well? The question then becomes, when do other people facilitate performance, and when do they interfere with it? In general, for familiar, well-learned behavior, the presence of people may lead to facilitation. In contrast, for unfamiliar, poorly learned behavior, the presence of people may lead to interference. The interference may occur because other people are distracting (R. S. Baron, 1986) or because the other people cause heightened arousal (Zajonc, 1965, 1980).

Social Loafing

What happens to our performance when we perform not only in front of others but also in cooperation with them? Apparently, as the number of people increases, the average amount of effort put forth by each individual decreases (Ringelmann, 1913). This reduced effort is termed **social loafing** (Latané, Williams, & Harkins, 1979).

Bibb Latané and other social psychologists (1979) studied whether it was the actual presence of others or merely the perceived presence of others that caused social loafing. To assess the influence of social loafing, the experimenters asked research participants either to clap as loudly as they could or to cheer at the top of their voices. They assigned some participants to perform the task alone, others to perform the task in groups, and still others to perform the task in *pseudogroups,* in which the participants believed that they were working with other people, but they were actually working alone. (To create the impression of the pseudogroup, the participants were blindfolded, and they were provided with headphones that produced static, drowning out any other sounds in the surrounding environment.) As Figure 10.4 shows, the research participants put forth more effort when they knew that they were alone, as compared with when they really were working with other people or incorrectly perceived that they were working with other people.

social interference • the phenomenon in which the presence of other people negatively influences the performance of an individual

social loafing • the phenomenon in which each individual member of a group puts forth less effort as the size of the group increases

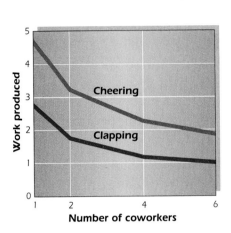

FIGURE 10.4
Social Loafing
When the number of coworkers believed to be in the work group increases, the amount of effort each research participant puts forth decreases (Latané, Williams, & Harkins, 1979). How can social loafing be kept to a minimum? Find a way to inform individual participants of how well they are performing as individuals (Harkins, 1987; Harkins & Szymanski, 1987).

It also appears that social loafing is affected by cultural orientation toward either individualism or collectivism. In **individualism,** we tend to put the interests and well-being of the individual above those of the group, such as the family, the corporation, or the nation. In **collectivism,** we tend to put the welfare of the group ahead of the well-being of the individual. It appears that social loafing may commonly occur in highly individualistic societies, such as in the United States, but it may be less common in societies with a more collectivistic orientation, such as in China and Taiwan. For instance, studies involving Chinese research participants have shown that individuals work *harder* when they are in a group than when they are alone (Early, 1989; Gabrenya, Latané, & Wang, 1983; Gabrenya, Wang, & Latané, 1985). Cross-cultural psychologists (e.g., Triandis et al., 1993; Triandis, McCusker, & Hui, 1990) frequently note that many other social-psychological phenomena also are influenced by the degree to which a given culture tends toward individualism or toward collectivism.

Group Polarization

In addition to social facilitation, social interference, and social loafing, in what other ways do people change their behavior when participating in groups rather than acting alone? Are people in groups more or less likely to take risks than individuals? Actually, groups tend to exaggerate the initial views of group members, so that they become more extreme, a phenomenon referred to as **group polarization** (Moscovici & Zavalloni, 1969; Myers & Lamm, 1976). Thus, if the members of a group, on average, initially tend toward taking risks, the group process will tend to move the decision of the group in a direction that exaggerates this risk-taking tendency. However, if the members of a group originally tend toward

individualism • the tendency to emphasize the personal interests and welfare of the individual over those of the group

collectivism • the tendency to emphasize the interests and well-being of the group over those of each individual

group polarization • the tendency to exaggerate the initial views of group members, so that the views become more extreme

conservatism, the group discussion will usually lead the group to a more conservative response than that of the individual members. For instance, participants in meetings of a local bungee-jumpers club will be more likely to shift toward making risky decisions, but bank executives at a board meeting will be more likely to shift toward making conservative decisions.

Why does group polarization occur? Two factors appear to be responsible: *new information* and *movement toward the group norm*. When people hear new arguments supporting their point of view, they become even more extreme in their conviction (Burnstein & Vinokur, 1973, 1977). In addition, as people meet other people supporting their point of view, and they receive social approval from these other people, they begin to move in the direction of the group norm. **Norms** are standards of behavior and expressed attitudes, based on the common trends of the majority in a group. When the information and reactions are expressed by people whom the group member identifies as members of his or her respected "in-group," the movement toward agreement is even stronger than usual (J. C. Turner, 1987). Through the process of group polarization, the group members may become more and more unified as their position becomes more extreme. However, this unification sometimes occurs at the expense of rational decision making.

Groupthink

Irving Janis (1972) has given special attention to **groupthink,** in which a striving for unanimity within a group overrides the motivation of people in the group to appraise realistically alternative courses of action (Janis, 1972, p. 9). In other words, people in the group are so intent on pleasing each other that they lose sight of what would be the best decision for the group to make. Janis analyzed a number of foreign-policy decisions that he believed reflected groupthink. For example, Janis noted that the U.S. failure to anticipate the attack on Pearl Harbor during World War II may have resulted partly from groupthink at the top levels of defense and government. During the John F. Kennedy administration, the high-level decision making that led to the disastrous Bay of Pigs invasion of Cuba may have been the result of groupthink. In these and other examples cited by Janis, highly intelligent people managed to make appallingly stupid decisions because they fell into the trap of groupthink.

What conditions lead to groupthink? Janis has cited three kinds of conditions: (a) a group with the power to make decisions that is isolated, *cohesive* (sticks together), and *homogeneous* (composed of similar, like-minded individuals); (b) a lack of objective and impartial leadership, either within the group or outside of the group; and (c) high levels of stress imposed on the group decision-making process. The groups responsible for making foreign-policy decisions are excellent candidates for groupthink: The group members are often like-minded, and they frequently isolate themselves from what is going on outside of their own group. They generally are trying to meet foreign-policy aims set by the president or the prime minister; hence, they probably believe that they cannot afford to be impartial and objective. Also, of course, they are under very high levels of stress: The consequences of their decisions can be tremendously wide reaching.

Janis has also spelled out six symptoms of groupthink: (a) *closed-mindedness*—the group is not open to a variety of alternative conceptualizations; (b) *rationalization*—the group goes to great lengths to justify

norm • a standard of behavior, or an expressed attitude, based on the shared trends of the majority in a group

groupthink • a group process in which group members work so hard to achieve unanimous agreement that they fail to consider realistically the various alternative courses of action available to them

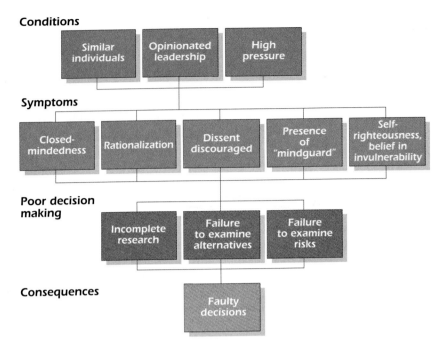

Conditions

Similar individuals

Opinionated leadership

High pressure

Symptoms

Closed-mindedness

Rationalization

Dissent discouraged

Presence of "mindguard"

Self-righteousness, belief in invulnerability

Poor decision making

Incomplete research

Failure to examine alternatives

Failure to examine risks

Consequences

Faulty decisions

FIGURE 10.5
Janis's Groupthink
This chart summarizes the conditions, symptoms, weak decision making, and results of groupthink (Janis, 1972).

both the process and the product of its decision making, distorting reality where necessary in order to accomplish this justification; (c) the *squelching of dissent*—those who do not agree are ignored, criticized, or even rejected; (d) the *formation of a "mindguard" for the group*—a self-appointed keeper of the group norm, who makes sure that people stay in line; (e) the *feeling of invulnerability*—the group believes that it must be right, given both the intelligence of its members and the information available to them; and (f) the *feeling of unanimity*—the group members feel that all members of the group are unanimous in sharing the opinions expressed by the group. Due to groupthink, members fail to examine all reasonable alternatives, to assess fully the risks involved in carrying out the recommended decision, and to search adequately for information about alternatives. The result of groupthink is defective decision making, chiefly due to overeagerness to conform to the thinking of the group (see Figure 10.5). Conformity, as well as compliance and obedience, are considered next.

WHAT ARE CONFORMITY, COMPLIANCE, AND OBEDIENCE?

Based on what we now know, it appears that in 1993, more than 80 members of the Branch Davidian religious sect obeyed their leader by intentionally setting fire to their small fortress and shooting their loved ones, effectively committing group suicide. Unfortunately, numerous other astonishing examples of self-destructive obedience exist, such as the mass suicide of more than 900 followers of a religious sect in Jonestown, Guyana, in 1978. Similar examples can be found in which people showed horrifying obedience in committing genocide, rather than suicide: Nazi soldiers during World War II and Serbian soldiers in the 1990s.

Why are people willing to modify their own behavior in order to conform to the norms of a group, to comply with the request made by a peer, or to obey the command of a person with authority? What are the benefits of doing so? What are the consequences of not doing so?

Conformity, compliance, and obedience all involve changes in one person's behavior, due to the social influence of another individual or group of people. Through **conformity**, people shape their own behavior to make it consistent with the norms of the group. Through **compliance**, one or more persons shape their behavior in response to a request by one or more other persons. Through **obedience**, people shape their behavior in response to the command of an actual or perceived authority. We consider each of these three kinds of social influence in turn. For each form of social influence, the individual may experience both changes in behavior and changes in perceptions, beliefs, and attitudes.

Conformity

Conformity refers to the modification of behavior in order to bring the behavior into line with the norms of a social group. Solomon Asch (1951, 1956) conducted several classic studies on conformity, although the extent to which these studies are replicable is uncertain. In Asch's studies, research participants believed that they were participating in an experiment on perceptual judgment. Imagine that you are the sixth of seven participants in one such experiment (see Figure 10.6). The first five members of the group choose an answer that is clearly wrong. What do you say when it is your turn to give your answer?

conformity • the process in which an individual shapes her or his behavior to make it consistent with the norms of a group

compliance • the process in which an individual goes along with a request made by one or more other persons

obedience • the process in which an individual follows the command of an actual or perceived authority figure

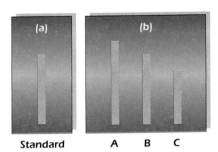

FIGURE 10.6

Line Length and the Norm

Asch's research participants were shown a standard line (on the left). Then they were asked to say which of the comparison lines (Lines A, B, or C) matched the standard line. Seem easy? What would you say if all of the other observers who spoke before you chose Line A (or Line C)? Check the facial expression of research participant number 6. Although he may decide to conform to the group norms in terms of his behavior, agreeing publicly that an incorrect match is correct, his own private beliefs clearly do not conform to the group norm. In fact, if he is given a chance to express his beliefs privately, he is quite likely to disagree with the group norms.

It is not easy to know what to say, as shown by the look on the face of research participant number 6 from one of Asch's actual studies (see Figure 10.6). In fact, about three fourths of Asch's research participants went along with the majority, stating obviously wrong answers about one third of the time, on average. It turns out that all of the other participants were really confederates who purposely were giving wrong answers.

Why did Asch's research participants go along with the majority? Did they really believe that their own perceptions were wrong, or did they bend to the pressure of the social group? In interviews and in a separate set of experiments, Asch's research participants showed that when they

Because this person is deviating from group norms, members of the group are likely to ridicule this person.

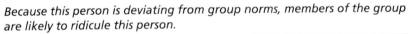

went along with the group, they generally did not believe the incorrect responses they announced. Rather, the research participants felt group pressure to conform. Later work (Asch, 1952) showed that Asch's research participants had good reason to want to conform. Participants who deviate from the group norm are indeed put down when in a group of genuine experimental research participants.

Several factors seem to affect the likelihood of conformity. These factors are group size, cohesiveness, social status (see Figure 10.7), culture, and the appearance of unanimity.

Factors Affecting Conformity

Which of the following factors most surprises you? Of which factors were you already intuitively aware?

1. *Group size.* Increases in group size lead to increases in conformity until a size of three or four is reached; further increases have little effect under most circumstances (Asch, 1955; Latané, 1981; Tanford & Penrod, 1984).

2. *Cohesiveness.* In cohesive groups, group members feel very attracted to the group and feel very much a part of the group; increases in cohesiveness lead to increases in conformity (e.g., Newcomb, 1943).

3. *Social status.* Persons who are viewed as being average in social desirability tend to be more likely to conform than persons who are rated as being high, low, or very low in social desirability (Dittes & Kelley, 1956).

4. *Culture.* People in individualistic societies tend to conform less than do people in collectivistic societies (P. B. Smith & Bond, 1994).

5. *Appearance of unanimity.* Conformity is much more likely when the group norm appears to be unanimous. Even a single dissenter can seriously diminish conformity (Asch, 1951). Surprisingly, this effect occurred even if the dissenter offered an answer that was even farther off the mark than the response of the group.

Perhaps the most surprising of these factors is the effect of having even one person disagree with the majority view. Even if the disagreeing person is obviously wrong, the fact of having someone model disagreement strongly reduces the likelihood of conformity based on normative influence. Thus, another consideration in determining your degree of conformity is whether you believe your views to be (a) in the *majority* (most others agree), (b) in the *minority* (one or more others agree, but most disagree with you), or (c) altogether *unique* (one of a kind; everyone else disagrees with you) within the group. In conformity, you shape your behavior to go along with group norms. Another type of social influence is compliance, in which you shape your behavior in response to a request.

Compliance

Do you know somebody who always seems to get his or her way? Do you ever wonder how con artists and cheats manage to trick their marks (persons who are the targets of the con artists' compliance-seeking techniques)? Have you ever bought something that you really did not want to buy because you were talked into it by a persuasive salesperson? These

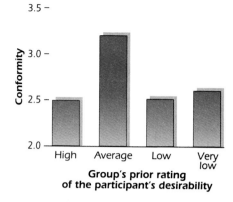

FIGURE 10.7
Social Status and Conformity
When research participants were told that they had been rated by the group as being high, low, or very low in social desirability, they showed less conformity to the group than when they were told that they had been rated by the group as being average in social desirability (Dittes & Kelley, 1956).

questions address the issue of compliance—going along with other people's requests. Robert Cialdini (1988) has studied compliance-seeking techniques extensively in the laboratory, but he also did some preliminary fieldwork by studying how professional compliance-seekers operate: He attended countless training seminars for sales personnel. Of the various techniques for eliciting compliance, the following seven are particularly important: justification, reciprocity, low-balling, foot-in-the-door, door-in-the-face, that's-not-all, and hard-to-get techniques.

Techniques for Eliciting Compliance

1. *Justification.* You justify your request (Langer, Blank, & Chanowitz, 1978). Someone asks to be allowed to go ahead of you in a line at a copying machine, giving you the incredibly weak justification, "because I have to make some copies" or you are told to buy something "because you need it."

2. *Reciprocity.* You appear to be giving your target something, so that the target thereby is obliged to give you something in return (Regan, 1971). Someone hands you a flower at an exit to a zoo and then asks you to make a contribution to a religious organization.

3. *Low-ball technique.* You get the target to commit to a deal under misleadingly favorable circumstances, and then you add the hidden costs or reveal the hidden drawbacks (Cialdini, 1988; Cialdini, Cacioppo, Bassett, & Miller, 1978). A car salesperson obtains your agreement to a deal, then disappears to ask the manager "for approval," only to return with a deal that is less favorable to you.

4. *Foot-in-the-door technique.* You ask for compliance with a smaller request, which is designed to "soften up" the target for the big request (De Jong, 1979; Freedman & Fraser, 1966). Someone asks you if you have time to answer a few questions and then follows that request by asking you to participate in a half-hour interview.

5. *Door-in-the-face technique.* You make an outlandishly large request that is almost certain to be rejected, then you make a more reasonable request (Cialdini et al., 1975). Someone asks you to contribute $100 to a charitable cause and then says that if you can only afford $5, that would be fine.

6. *That's-not-all technique.* You offer something at a high price, and then, before the target has a chance to respond, you throw in something else to sweeten the deal (Burger, 1986). A late-night television advertiser offers you a complete set of golden-oldie CDs for only $29.95 and then says that you also will receive a free CD of Elvis Presley's first hits.

7. *Hard-to-get technique.* You convince your target that whatever you are offering is very difficult to obtain (J. Brehm, 1966; see also S. S. Brehm & Brehm, 1981; Hatfield & Walster, 1978). Another late-night TV advertiser offers you a set of 10 automatic electric slicers and dicers, but you must phone now, while the supplies last.

Each of the preceding techniques involves having someone you consider more or less a peer ask you to comply with a request. Not all requests come from peers, however. At times, those who make requests of us are in a position of authority. Their superior authority may stem from actual or perceived greater relative power, expertise, or desirability in terms of some criterion we consider important, such as physical attractiveness or social skill. When we go along with the requests of persons who have authority over us, we are being obedient.

Obedience

Consider what you would do if you were a research participant in the following experiment. An experimenter wearing a lab coat and carrying a clipboard meets you in the laboratory and tells you that you are about to participate in an experiment on the effects of punishment on learning. You and another research participant, Mr. Wallace (see Figure 10.8), agree to draw lots to determine who will be the "teacher" in the experiment, and who will be the "learner."

You draw the "teacher" lot, so it will be your job to teach the learner a list of words that he must remember. You watch the experimenter strap Mr. Wallace into a chair, roll up Mr. Wallace's sleeves, and swab electrode paste onto his arms, "to avoid blisters and burns" from the shocks (Milgram, 1974, p. 19). The experimenter warns that the shocks may become extremely painful, but he assures Mr. Wallace that they will "cause no permanent tissue damage" (p. 19). You are then shown the machine you will use to deliver shocks, ranging from a mere 15 volts (labeled "slight shock") to a full 450 volts (labeled "XXX," beyond the setting for "danger: severe shock"; see Figure 10.8). Before beginning, the experimenter also gives you a rather painful shock, which he describes as a mild shock, just to give you an idea of what the shocks are like.

FIGURE 10.8

The Shocking Treatment of Mr. Wallace

Mr. Wallace, pictured here, as he was being strapped into the chair where he was expected to receive the shocks being sent by Milgram's research participants. It appeared that Mr. Wallace could not possibly escape the shocks that were given during the experiment.

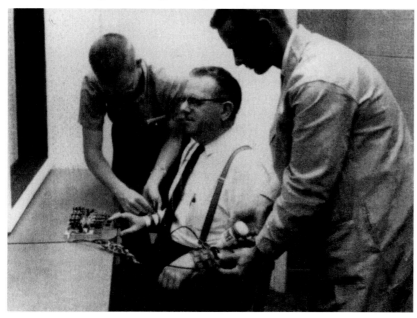

The experiment now begins. If Mr. Wallace correctly answers your questions, you move on to the next question. If he answers incorrectly, you tell him the correct answer and administer a shock. Each time Mr. Wallace makes a mistake, you are told to increase the intensity of the shock by 15 volts.

Soon, he makes his first mistake, so you pull the appropriate shock lever. A loud buzzer sounds, and a red light flashes, indicating that the shock has been delivered to Mr. Wallace in the next room. When you reach the level of 75 volts, Mr. Wallace grunts in pain. Grunts are followed by shouting at 120 volts. At 150 volts, Mr. Wallace screams in agony and protests, "Experimenter! That's all. Get me out of here. I refuse to go on!" Mr. Wallace refuses to continue at 300 volts, and at 315 volts, following an intense scream, he shouts, "I told you I refuse to answer. I'm no longer a part of this experiment." At 330 volts, there is an intense, long scream of agony, and Mr. Wallace shouts, "Let me out of here. Let me out of here. Let me out, I tell you. . . . You have no right to hold me here. Let me out! . . ." After 330 volts, there is only silence.

Would you continue administering shocks until the end, up to 450 volts? Perhaps at some point, it would occur to you that something is very wrong with this experiment, and that you simply do not want to continue. If you tell the experimenter your concerns, he only responds, "Please continue." If you protest further, he tells you, "The experiment requires that you continue." If you continue to argue, he says, "It is absolutely essential that you continue." If you still protest, he replies, "You have no other choice, you *must* go on." What would you do? Before you read on, guess how most people would have responded to this experiment.

Before conducting his experiments, psychologist Stanley Milgram (1974) had expected that very few research participants would fully obey the commands of the experimenter and that many might refuse to obey even the early requests of the experimenter. As he was planning the design for the experiment, he consulted with many other colleagues, all of whose expectations were similar to his. Instead, an astonishing two thirds of the research participants tested in this procedure continued up to the very end, delivering shocks at the level of 450 volts. Not one participant stopped giving the shocks before 300 volts, the point at which Mr. Wallace let out an agonizing scream, absolutely refused to answer any more questions, and demanded to get out, saying that the experimenter could not hold him. The results are shown in Figure 10.9a.

The results so surprised Milgram that he asked members of three different groups (middle-class adults with various occupations, college students, and psychiatrists) to predict what would happen. Their predictions, like Milgram's, were that few research participants would demonstrate much obedience in the experiment. On average, the people Milgram surveyed estimated that the "teacher" would stop at 135 volts. Almost no one surveyed thought anyone would go up to 450 volts. Everyone was wrong (see Figure 10.9b).

The results were astonishing because the machine was a fake. So was Mr. Wallace. He was Milgram's confederate and never received any shocks at all. Also, both of the lots from which you had drawn said "teacher." No matter which one you drew, you would have ended up being the teacher and Mr. Wallace the learner.

The experiment, as you probably have guessed, had nothing at all to do with the effect of punishment on learning. Rather, it was an experiment on obedience. The motivation for the experiment was Milgram's interest in why German soldiers during World War II had obeyed the outrageous genocidal commands of their leaders. Milgram (1963, 1965,

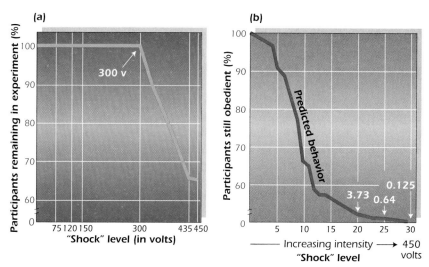

FIGURE 10.9
Milgram's Actual Results, Compared with Predicted Results
(a) To the great surprise of Stanley Milgram, not one research participant stopped administering shocks before the reported level of 300 volts, and an alarming 65% of research participants administered the maximum level of supposed shocks. (b) Compare Milgram's actual results with the predictions made by psychiatrists regarding expected levels of obedience for various reported voltage levels (from Milgram, 1974, p. 30). The psychiatrists estimated that "only a pathological fringe, not exceeding [1 or 2% of the research participants]" would go right up to the end (Milgram, 1974, p. 31).

1974) concluded that people, in general, not just German soldiers, are horrifyingly capable of blind, mindless obedience. Later, Milgram and other researchers found similar results in experiments with women research participants, with participants in other parts of the country, and in locations away from college campuses. In fact, Milgram's findings have been repeated both across age groups and across cultures (Shanab & Yahya, 1977, 1978). Milgram's studies were done before it became standard operating procedure to have a university ethics committee approve research before it was done. Today the studies would not be likely to have been approved, at least in the form they were carried out. At minimum, more would have had to be done to safeguard the mental health of participants who thought they were administering shocks.

The Milgram studies showed us that we may have an appalling ability to tune out the misery of our fellow human beings when responding to the commands of a perceived authority figure. How might we respond to pleas for help from our fellow humans when no authority figure is around?

Although the Milgram research seems to show a negative side of people, people also have a positive side, the side investigated in studies of prosocial behavior.

WHAT PRODUCES PROSOCIAL BEHAVIOR?

Prosocial behavior is any behavior that is approved by society and that benefits individual persons or society as a whole. Of the many kinds of prosocial behavior, this section focuses on how we respond to people who need help. In the Queens section of New York City, in 1964, Kitty Genovese was attacked while returning home from a night job at three o'clock

prosocial behavior • actions that offer some benefit to society in general or to members within society and that are approved by most members of society

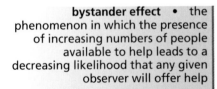

FIGURE 10.10
Seizing the Opportunity to Help
In every condition of Bibb Latané and John Darley's (1970) experiment, helping behavior increased over time. However, the amount of helping behavior decreased dramatically with increases in the number of other people that the research participant thought were participating. More people reported smoke when they thought they were alone than when they thought others were participating in the experiment. (Adapted from Latané and Darley, The Unresponsive Bystander, *copyright © 1970. Used with permission of Prentice-Hall, Inc.)*

in the morning. Just outside her own apartment building, she was stabbed repeatedly over a period of about a half hour by a maniac who eventually killed her. Thirty-eight people living in her apartment complex heard her cries and screams as she was attacked. How many of these neighbors called the police? How many tried to help her in any way whatsoever? Not one. How could people hear someone be attacked over such a long period of time and do absolutely nothing in response? Bibb Latané and John Darley (1968, 1970) tried to answer this question in a series of studies on helping behavior and *bystander intervention,* in which an observer takes steps to help an unknown person or persons in need.

In one of the Latané and Darley experiments, a research participant arrived and was taken to one of a set of small rooms containing intercoms. The research participant was led to believe that between one and five other people were participating in a confidential discussion over the intercom. During the fairly routine opening of the experiment, one of the research participants admitted that he sometimes had terrifyingly serious seizures. After a while, when it was this person's turn to speak again, it became apparent that he was suffering a seizure. He started stuttering, choking, and sounding as though he were in serious distress (Latané & Darley, 1970, p. 96).

As you may have guessed, the apparent seizure victim was not actually having a seizure. In fact, there was only one true research participant. The voices of the other participants were tape-recorded earlier, and the voices were played back over the intercom for each true research participant. The independent variable was the number of people that were believed to be participating in the experiment. The dependent variables were the percentage of participants who helped the apparent seizure victim and the amount of time it took the participants to respond. The results showed clearly that as the number of perceived bystanders increased, the percentages of participants who responded decreased, and their response times became longer (see Figure 10.10).

Kitty Genovese's neighbors were not alone in being unresponsive. They illustrated what has come to be known as the **bystander effect,** in which the presence of other people inhibits helping behavior. The effect occurs in various situations. Each person involved typically feels a **diffusion of responsibility:** The presence of others leads each person to feel less personally responsible for handling a crisis situation. Many other studies

bystander effect • the phenomenon in which the presence of increasing numbers of people available to help leads to a decreasing likelihood that any given observer will offer help

diffusion of responsibility • the phenomenon in which increases in the number of other persons present leads each person to feel less personal responsibility for the events taking place

Why isn't anyone stopping to help this motorist? Would a passing motorist be more likely to stop if this person needed help on a lonely country road?

TABLE 10.1

Factors That May Influence Helping Behavior

Factor	Effect on likelihood of helping behavior		
	Increase	*Probable increase*	*Decrease*
Characteristics of the victim	Similar to bystander (age, gender, etc.)	Somehow related to bystander (e.g., coworker, neighbor)	Bleeding or bloody; recognized member of a stigmatized group (e.g., perceived as less attractive)
Characteristics of the situation	Any situation that increases the likelihood of the bystander being in a good mood	Situation in which the victim and the bystander have an ongoing relationship (e.g., neighbor, coworker)	Larger number of bystanders; greater time pressures on bystander (e.g., being in a hurry)
Characteristics of the bystander	Similar to victim (age, gender, etc.); empathetic; knowledgeable about how to help the victim (e.g., knows CPR or has medical expertise or other relevant knowledge); afraid of appearing unsympathetic by refusing to offer help; in a good mood (having been the recent recipient of the prosocial behavior of others)	Somehow related to victim (e.g., coworker, neighbor); emotional	Responds negatively to characteristics of the victim (e.g., prejudices, negative reactions to transient characteristics such as clothing, grooming, or bleeding); afraid of appearing foolish or incompetent by offering help when unsure of knowing how to help expertly

Note. Preparing to give a speech about the Good Samaritan (a religious figure known for helping strangers) has no effect on helping behavior.

have shown the same results (described in Latané, Nida, & Wilson, 1981). Oddly, the bystander effect appears even when a person's own safety is at stake, such as when the person is in a room being filled with smoke (Latané & Darley, 1968).

Why are people so passive in the face of emergencies, whether the emergencies affect others or even themselves? According to Latané and Darley (1970), we are passive because seeking help is actually more complex than it appears to be. Several factors seem to influence whether people will help (see Table 10.1 for a summary of these factors). According to Latané and Darley, there are at least five steps at which a bystander may decide to do nothing or must decide to do something.

Branching Out

LATANÉ AND DARLEY'S FIVE-STEP MODEL OF BYSTANDER INTERVENTION

According to Latané and Darley, before you take any action to help another person, you must take the following five steps: (a) You need to notice the signs or signals of the emergency. (b) You have to define the situation as an emergency. (c) You have to take responsibility for doing something about the emergency. (d) You have to figure out how to seek or provide help. (e) You must actually carry out your plan for providing or

(CONTINUED)

Following the Mexico City earthquake in 1985, countless volunteers joined professionals in helping others to survive and to recover from the devastation caused by the earthquake. In response to much less dramatic cries for help, people show altruism in hospices, homeless shelters, nursing homes, and other settings.

Branching Out   (CONTINUED)

seeking help. If you fail to complete any one of these steps, you will not take any action to provide helpful intervention.

In some situations, people may do more than help themselves and others through a difficult situation. They even may show **altruism**—selfless sacrifice—to help persons in need. Throughout history, there have been many examples of heroism, in which individuals have decided to make great sacrifices and have even risked their own lives, in order to help others. Recall, for example, the heroism of many rescuers who protected Jews and other persecuted persons during the Nazi reign of terror in Germany (Oliner & Oliner, 1993). Altruism is not considered the norm in individualistic societies, but it certainly offers benefits to society. Evolutionary theorists suggest that altruism also can help the individual who is showing the altruism, in that it makes others more likely to trust and depend on the altruistic individual, thereby giving the altruistic individual a certain degree of power over others he or she might otherwise not have. Of course, people do not always show altruism and prosocial behavior. Some of the time they show antisocial behavior, which is considered next.

ANTISOCIAL BEHAVIOR

In contrast to prosocial behavior, **antisocial behavior** is condemned by society as a whole and is harmful to society or to its members. Although people may disagree as to which particular behaviors and even which kinds of behaviors are antisocial, there are two classes of behavior that people generally agree are harmful to society: prejudice and aggression.

altruism   •   a generous willingness to help another person or persons, even when there is no reward or other observable benefit to the helper; often involves some sacrifice on the part of the helper

antisocial behavior   •   the actions that are harmful to a given society or to its members and that are condemned by the society as a whole

Prejudice

Prejudice is an unfavorable attitude directed toward other groups of people, based on insufficient or incorrect evidence about those groups. Note that prejudice is an attitude toward a group, not toward an individual. Unfortunately, many of our attitudes toward groups are extended to all of the individual members of the groups as well. A negative attitude toward a group, however, is not necessarily a prejudice. For example, if you had ample evidence that a particular group (e.g., a youth gang) was responsible for numerous murders, you would probably not be considered prejudiced for having a negative attitude toward that group. You would be incorrect, however, if you assumed that all members of that group were murderers.

Social Cognition: Social Categorization and Stereotypes

Why do we feel prejudice? Patricia Devine and her colleagues (Devine, Monteith, Zuwerink, & Elliot, 1991) have suggested that prejudice may be viewed as a bad habit, which can be overcome. Another way of explaining prejudice is to view it in terms of how people try to understand other people. Often, we use two cognitive strategies for understanding the people around us: social categorization and stereotypes. Through **social categorization,** we tend to sort people into groups, based on perceived common attributes. We readily categorize people according to their gender, occupation, age, ethnicity, perceived attractiveness, and so on (cf. Neto, Williams, & Widner, 1991). These categories generally have particular defining features (e.g., specific sexual or occupational characteristics).

In addition, we tend to think of prototypes for various categories, based on what we perceive as being typical examples of the categories. When these prototypes are applied to people, the prototypes are considered **stereotypes.** We seem to learn many stereotypes during childhood. For example, cross-cultural studies of children show their increasing knowledge about, and use of, gender stereotypes across the childhood years (e.g., Neto, Williams, & Widner, 1991).

Social categorization and stereotyping are useful in many ways. For example, social categories and stereotypes help us to organize our perceptions of people and provide us with speedy access to a wealth of information (e.g., traits and expected behaviors) about new people whom we meet (Sherman, Judd, & Park, 1989; Srull & Wyer, 1989). More broadly, social categories and stereotypes help us know what to expect from people we do not know well. On the other hand, these same processes of social cognition can lead us to misunderstand and misinterpret the words and actions of people we do not know well.

Social psychologist Claude Steele (1990) has warned that the use of stereotypes can also directly influence the members of particular social categories (e.g., women or African Americans), through stereotype vulnerability. In *stereotype vulnerability,* people's awareness of negative stereotypes about social categories to which they belong actually may lead them to perform poorly, as compared with people who are not aware of negative stereotypes that apply to them. (Recall the effects of self-fulfilling prophecies, mentioned previously.) According to Steele, when the context for performance reminds members of any group regarding the negative stereotypes about their performance (i.e., "People like you do so

prejudice • a negative attitude toward groups of individuals, based on limited or wrong information about those groups

social categorization • the tendency to sort people into groups, according to various characteristics the observer perceives to be common to members of each group

stereotype • a perceived typical example that illustrates the main characteristics of a particular social category, usually based on the assumption that the typical example uniformly represents all examples of the social category

FIGURE 10.11
What Do You See in This Picture?
Groups of six research participants were asked to describe this picture, but only the first research participant in each group actually saw the picture. The first research participant then described the picture to the second research participant, who described the picture to the third research participant, and so on until the sixth participant described the picture to the experimenter. As you might expect, there were distortions in the research participants' descriptions of the picture. In general, these distortions tended to reinforce racial stereotypes. (After Allport & Postman, 1947)

poorly on this type of task"), their performance suffers, but when the context provides no such reminders, their performance is enhanced (see Figure 10.11).

Context cues also can affect the likelihood that we will use stereotypes about other persons. For example (see Eagly, Makhijani, & Klonsky, 1992), when research participants evaluated women versus men leaders, they showed greater gender stereotyping and prejudicial responses toward women leaders in particular contexts: (a) contexts in which the leaders used leadership styles considered more stereotypically masculine (e.g., task oriented and directive, rather than interpersonally oriented and collaborative), or (b) contexts in which women were occupying roles that are male dominated in our society (e.g., athletic coaches, manufacturing supervisors, and business managers). In addition, men were more likely to evaluate women negatively than were other women.

Although social cognition plays a role in the formation of stereotypes, other factors may contribute to their use. For example, motivation and the tendency toward conformity to group norms may also influence the use of stereotypes (Rojahn & Pettigrew, 1992), as shown in the following study.

The Robber's Cave Study

In the summer of 1954, Muzafer Sherif conducted a classic experiment on prejudice at the Robber's Cave State Park in Oklahoma (Sherif, Harvey, White, Hood, & Sherif, 1961/1988). For about a week, two groups of 11-year-old white, middle-class boys participated in typical camp activities (swimming, hiking, etc.). None of the boys had known each other before they went to camp. Each group of boys chose a name for itself, and the boys then printed their groups' names on their caps and on their T-shirts.

After about a week, the boys in each group made a discovery—the existence of the other group of boys. They also discovered that a series of athletic tournaments had been set up that would pit the two groups against each other. During these competitions, conflicts arose and spread well beyond the games. Soon, the members of the two groups had become extremely hostile toward each other. The boys in the opposing groups ransacked each other's cabins, stole from each other, and battled in food fights. Clearly, the investigators had succeeded in creating intergroup prejudice through the competitions.

How could they now reduce or eliminate this prejudice? The investigators created apparent emergencies that had to be resolved through cooperative efforts. In one emergency, the water supply for the camp was lost because of a leak in a pipe. The boys were assigned to intergroup teams to inspect the pipe and to find the leak. In another incident, a truck carrying boys to a campsite got trapped in the mud: Boys from the two teams needed to cooperate in order to get the truck out. By the end of the camping season, the two groups of boys were engaged in a variety of cooperative activities and were playing together peacefully. By forcing people to work together, the prejudices of the members of each group against the other largely had been eliminated.

Branching Out

REDUCING PREJUDICE

What can be done to reduce prejudice? First, we need to recognize how strongly prejudicial attitudes resist being changed. For example, male police officers and police supervisors commonly have prejudicial attitudes against female members of the force (Balkin, 1988; Ott, 1989), despite clear evidence showing women's effectiveness as field patrol officers (described in Balkin, 1988). Some people have suggested that prejudicial treatment against females (51% of the U.S. population) and against minorities will decline when their numbers increase. It turns out, however, that negative prejudicial treatment of a minority group is based more on its relatively lower social status than on its number of members (Ott, 1989).

Another suggestion for reducing prejudice has been the *contact hypothesis,* the view that direct contact between groups will decrease intergroup prejudice (Allport, 1954). However, as shown by the conflicts that still exist in many desegregated neighborhoods and school systems, contact alone does not reduce or eliminate prejudice (N. Miller & Brewer, 1984). The contact also must involve the following four conditions if it is to lessen prejudice: (a) The two interacting groups must be of *equal status;* (b) the contact must involve *personal interactions* between members of the two groups; (c) the groups need to engage in *cooperative activities;* and (d) the surrounding *social norms* must favor reduction of prejudice. An additional way in which to reduce prejudice is to highlight new information that contradicts stereotypes based on limited information (Rojahn & Pettigrew, 1992).

In which of these photos is the aggressor acting impulsively, showing hostile aggression? In which of these photos has the aggressor planned the aggressive act in order to obtain something of value, showing instrumental aggression? What kinds of intervention would be most effective in preventing each kind of aggression?

aggression • a behavior that is intended to cause harm or injury to another person

hostile aggression • a behavior that is intended to cause harm, as a result of an emotional, often impulsive, outburst, caused by pain or distress; the consequences usually lead to little gain for the aggressor and may even lead to losses for the aggressor

instrumental aggression • a behavior that happens to cause harm or injury to another person, as a by-product of trying to get something valued by the aggressor; often is planned, not impulsive

Aggression

Unfortunately, feelings of prejudice sometimes lead to violent actions against persons who are the targets of prejudice. These violent actions (e.g., the many lynchings that took place in the United States from the 1860s through the 1960s) are a form of **aggression,** behavior that is intended to cause harm or injury to another person or persons (R. A. Baron, 1977). There are two main kinds of aggression: hostile aggression and instrumental aggression (R. A. Baron, 1977; Feshbach, 1970). **Hostile aggression** is emotional and is usually impulsive. It is often provoked by feelings of pain or distress. When we engage in hostile aggression, we intend to cause harm to another, regardless of whether we gain through our aggressive actions. For example, if a woman purposely rams her car into the rear of a car that cut her off on the freeway, she is demonstrating hostile aggression. She gains nothing by her actions, and she probably will suffer various unwanted consequences of her actions (e.g., the damage to her own car and the possible financial and legal outcomes resulting from damage to the other car).

In contrast, the purpose of **instrumental aggression** is to get something we value. Often, it is planned, not impulsive. Paid assassins, bank robbers, con artists, and embezzlers show instrumental aggression. The fact that other people are hurt by their actions is merely a by-product of their actions. Their common goal is to get money or something else the aggressors value, and their aggression is merely a means to that end.

The basic physiology underlying aggression seems to be the same for all humans. Researchers have already identified some brain structures (e.g., the hypothalamus and the amygdala) and some hormones (e.g., testosterone) as being involved in aggressive behavior. In addition to these common physiological aspects of aggression, there are many cross-cultural and individual differences in human aggression. Particular differences include the specific circumstances that prompt aggressive impulses and the specific forms in which aggression is expressed. Environmental factors such as pain (Berkowitz, Cochran, & Embree, 1981; Ulrich & Azrin, 1962), discomfort (e.g., high heat; C. A. Anderson, 1987, 1989), or frustration (e.g., Barker, Dembo, & Lewin, 1941; Dollard, Miller, Doob, Mowrer, & Sears, 1939) also contribute to aggression. Another factor that increases the likelihood of aggression is the presence of aggression in the environment.

Violence: Social Learning and Desensitization

Almost all psychologists agree that social learning strongly determines the expression of aggression (Bandura, 1973, 1977b, 1983; R. A. Baron & Richardson, 1992). That is, people learn aggressive behavior by watching aggressive models (refer to Figure 5.4). Therefore, what people learn seems to differ from one context to another because models differ in each context. We know that people show more aggressive behavior in individualistic cultures than in collectivistic cultures (Oatley, 1993). Further, individualistic societies themselves vary in the extent to which they accept and promote aggression (DeAngelis, 1992; Montagu, 1976).

What can we do to prevent aggression, given the importance of social learning in contributing to violent behavior? Clearly, we should pay careful attention to the kinds of role models we provide to one another. For one thing, we should act swiftly to protect children from family violence. In addition, a powerful source of role models is found in almost every American home: television. We know that children play more aggressively immediately after watching violent shows on television (Liebert & Baron, 1972). Similarly, watching violent films seems to increase the aggressiveness of juvenile delinquents, especially among those who are initially the most aggressive (Park et al., 1977). There are significant correlations between the amount of TV violence watched by children and the children's aggression as rated by their peers (Huesmann, Lagerspetz, & Eron, 1984). This finding, because it is correlational, does not tell us for sure what is causing what. For example, more aggressive children may decide to watch more television. However, these correlations appear across four different countries—Australia, Finland, Poland, and the United States—suggesting that the relationship is, if nothing else, persistent across cultures.

The viewing of violent images (e.g., on television and in movies) may also do more to promote violence than just to provide models from which people learn aggressive behavior. Watching violent shows also desensitizes us to the tragic consequences of violence. **Desensitization** occurs when we habituate to a particular stimulus. Without any conscious effort or thought, we gradually become less interested in stimuli that we see often. Gradually, we pay less attention to these violent stimuli, and we show less emotional, physiological, and cognitive responses to violence.

Deindividuation

Another possible cause of aggression is that the aggressor dehumanizes (perceives as not human) the victim of the aggression. What enables some of us to dehumanize others? A possible answer may be understood in terms of **deindividuation,** the loss of a sense of individual identity. Once we feel deindividuated, we seem to be less inhibited from engaging in socially unacceptable behavior (Festinger, Pepitone, & Newcomb, 1952; see Figure 10.12;

FIGURE 10.12
Deindividuation and Aggression
Hypothetically, there is a much greater likelihood that women wearing the mask and nondistinguishing clothing depicted here administered shocks more aggressively than did women who wore their own regular clothing and identifying name tags (Zimbardo, 1970).

desensitization • the gradual habituation to violent stimuli, in which we gradually become less interested in and less responsive to violent stimuli and their tragic consequences

deindividuation • the loss of a sense of individual identity, resulting in fewer controls that prevent the individual from engaging in behavior that violates societal norms and even the individual's personal moral beliefs

Zimbardo, 1970). The aggressive behavior of some mobs is often attributed to the fact that the individuals in the mob become deindividuated.

When social psychologist Philip Zimbardo (1972) conducted a study of deindividuation, he ended up surprising himself as much as he did his fellow scientists. Zimbardo converted the basement of the psychology building at Stanford University into a "jail." Volunteer male research participants were randomly assigned to be either "prisoners" or "guards." As Figure 10.13 shows, Zimbardo led both groups of college students to identify with their new roles, not with their individual identities.

Prisoners almost immediately started acting like prisoners, and guards truly acted like guards. The guards harassed and insulted prisoners and even treated prisoners cruelly, apparently with little or no reason. After a prisoner revolt, which was quickly crushed, the prisoners became depressed. Some even started to experience mental breakdowns. At this point, Zimbardo stopped the experiment. Because the assignment of guards and prisoners was random, the astonishing changes could not be attributed to individual differences.

Several specific methods for reducing aggression have also been proposed, some of which seem to be more successful than others. For example, successful strategies include observing nonaggressive models (e.g., Donnerstein & Donnerstein, 1976), generating responses that are incompatible with aggression (e.g., humorous or sympathetic responses;

FIGURE 10.13

Deindividuation: An Arresting Experiment

Philip Zimbardo used a number of techniques to deindividuate both "prisoners" and "guards." The prisoners wore prison-like uniforms and nylon stocking caps and were referred to by serial numbers instead of by names. Guards also wore uniforms and mirrored sunglasses to hide their facial expressions and they carried clubs. Members of both groups were encouraged to think of themselves in terms of their roles, rather than in terms of their individual identities. Once people are deindividuated, they may act in ways that they would never have thought possible otherwise, whether on the giving or the receiving end of hostile levels of aggression.

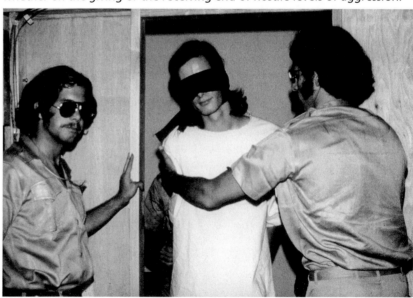

R. A. Baron, 1976), and using cognitive strategies (e.g., simply stopping to think about whether the aggressive action is well advised). Several other strategies for reducing aggression have proven to be utter failures. It turns out that people do not become less aggressive, and they may actually become more aggressive, when they are encouraged to vent their aggressive feelings (Berkowitz & Geen, 1966, 1967; A. H. Buss, 1976; Geen & Quanty, 1977) or when they receive physical punishment for their aggressive actions (Sears, Maccoby, & Levin, 1957; Stevenson-Hinde, Hinde, & Simpson, 1986). It appears that aggressive actions of any kind tend to increase the likelihood of further aggression.

This chapter has described various ways in which the actual, imagined, or implied presence of other persons influences the thoughts, feelings, and behavior of individuals. For instance, the presence of other persons often affects the emotions we feel (e.g., love), as well as our motivation to engage in particular actions (e.g., when obeying the commands of persons in authority). In the following chapter, we focus more specifically on the psychology of motivation and emotion.

The Case of the Rapidly Developing Relationship

After reading chapter 10 of *Pathways to Psychology*, Janet is able to put her finger on what has been bothering her. Her relationship with Tyrone seems to resemble what is referred to in the triangular theory of love as *infatuated love*, especially because the passion between her and Tyrone has developed largely in the absence of intimacy. As she thinks about this, Janet concludes that she and Tyrone have not really had even one serious conversation about themselves. Perhaps he is just quiet, but Janet realizes that she needs something more than passion before she commits herself. Otherwise, Janet thinks, she will end up with a *fatuous love* relationship, which is the last thing she needs. Janet asks Tyrone to wait awhile until they get to know each other better. She suggests they use his request as an opportunity to do just that. The relationship does not work. Once they start talking Janet realizes that she and Tyrone really do not have much in common and that she will not be able to sustain her interest in him over the long term. Janet suggests to a reluctant Tyrone that they see other people as well, and eventually they drift apart.

1. *Social psychologists* try to understand and to explain how the presence of others (actual, imagined, or implied) affects the thoughts, feelings, and behavior of individuals.

What Is Social Cognition?   340

2. *Social cognition* refers to the ways in which we perceive and interpret information about people, whether the information comes from others or from inside ourselves.

3. An experiment in social psychology established the theory of *cognitive dissonance*, which states that when a person's behavior and cognitions do not go together, discomfort results. To ease this discomfort, the person must justify his or her behavior. The experimental results that led to cognitive-dissonance theory have also been explained in other ways, such as by *self-perception theory*, according to which we form our beliefs about ourselves, based on our actions.

4. Attribution theory deals with how we explain the causes of behavior—why we and other people do what we do. In making *attributions*, we look for the cause of the behavior, which can be *personal* or *situational*.

5. Although biases and heuristics help us to make attributions, these mental shortcuts also sometimes lead to mental distortions.

How Do We Form and Change Our Attitudes?   345

6. *Attitudes* are learned (not inborn), stable, relatively lasting evaluations of people, ideas, and things. Attitudes affect our behavior but the links between attitudes and behavior are not always predictable.

7. In studying what influences changes in people's attitudes, psychologists consider characteristics of the recipient of the message, of the message itself, and of the source of the message.

What Are Liking, Loving, and Interpersonal Attraction?   349

8. Social–psychological research asks why we are attracted to some people and not to others. Learning theory answers that we like (or dislike) a person because of the emotional rewards (or punishments) we get in that person's presence. According to *equity theory*, attraction involves a fair balance of give and take. *Cognitive-consistency* theories, such as *balance theory*, focus on a balance both of give and take and of similar likes and dislikes.

9. The *attachment theory of love* suggests there are three main ways in which people relate to those they love: secure, anxious–ambivalent, and avoidant. The *triangular theory of love* posits that love has three components: intimacy, passion, and commitment.

10. According to the love-is-a-story theory of attraction, each of us is drawn to partners who closely match the types of characters in our own personal idealized love stories. Studies show that attraction is based on physical attractiveness, arousal, familiarity, proximity, and similarity.

How Do We Communicate in Our Personal Relationships?   354

11. Successful communication is essential to interpersonal relationships.

12. Men and women appear to communicate differently. Men seem to prefer establishing higher status and preserving their independence; women seem to seek closeness and agreement.

How Do We Interact in Groups?   354

13. Some social psychologists try to understand and explain how groups reach agreement and how individuals perform in a group.

14. In *social facilitation*, the presence of other people improves our performance. In *social interference*, the presence of others hurts our performance.

15. In *social loafing*, individuals show less personal effort as the size of the group increases.

16. Groups often become *polarized*, due both to new information and to shifts toward the group's social *norms*.

17. *Groupthink* occurs when a closely-knit group cares more about agreement than about discussing objective, rational opinions regarding suitable actions. Stress, biased leadership, like-minded group members, and isolation from diverse views make the problems of groupthink worse.

What Are Conformity, Compliance, and Obedience?   358

18. People yield to social pressure by *conforming*, *complying*, and *obeying*.

19. A member of a group may conform only publicly or may also conform privately as well. People who

deviate from the norm often are rejected by the group, but they may lead the way for others to differ from the group as well.

20. Compliance is encouraged through such techniques as *justification, reciprocity, low-balling, foot-in-the-door, door-in-the-face, that's-not-all,* and *hard-to-get.*

21. In Milgram's experiment on obedience to authority figures, most research participants were willing to administer painful shocks to others when following orders to do so. Other research has confirmed Milgram's surprising findings.

What Produces Prosocial Behavior?   365

22. *Prosocial behavior* helps society as a whole or helps its individual members. An example of prosocial behavior is *altruism,* selfless sacrifice to help a fellow human being.

23. In the *bystander effect,* the presence of other people leads each bystander to feel less personal responsibility (through *diffusion of responsibility*) and reduces the likelihood that each bystander will help. Particular characteristics of the victim, the bystander, and the situation may also increase or decrease the likelihood that the bystander will help.

Antisocial Behavior   368

24. *Prejudice* is based on faulty evidence, which in turn often is based on cognitive shortcuts, such as *stereotypes* and *social categorization.* The Robber's Cave study showed how prejudice can be reduced through cooperative activities.

25. *Aggression* is antisocial behavior that harms another person. Aggression may be *hostile* or *instrumental.* People learn aggressive behavior when they see it modeled, such as in the home and in the popular media. The frequent viewing of violence may also lead to *desensitization.* Both physiological and environmental factors also influence aggressive behavior.

26. When *deindividuation* occurs, people lose their sense of individual identity and may behave in ways they would not behave otherwise.

Pathways to Knowledge

Choose the best answer to complete each sentence.

1. Jenny is eating cheesecake and feels a sense of discomfort after just declaring to her friend that she is on a diet. The condition invoked by this situation is referred to as
   (a) justification of effort.
   (b) cognitive dissonance.
   (c) cognitive consistency.
   (d) rationalization.

2. If you were to use the fundamental attribution error to explain why a man cut in front of you in the line at the post office, you would assert that the man
   (a) is a mean, self-centered person.
   (b) is in a hurry to catch his train.
   (c) was previously in line, then had to leave the line to pick up something he forgot.
   (d) is a friend of the postmaster.

3. Johnetta loves going out with Samuel because he often compliments her and praises her for her accomplishments. Based on the preceding description, Johnetta's feelings toward Samuel support the interpersonal attraction theory known as
   (a) equity theory.
   (b) balance theory.
   (c) arousal theory.
   (d) learning (reinforcement) theory.

4. One variable that *is not* typically cited as a factor underlying interpersonal attraction is
   (a) attitudinal similarity.
   (b) physical attraction.
   (c) proximity.
   (d) prejudice in favor of an individual but against the individual's group.

5. Group polarization is an effect whereby
   (a) extreme opinions in a group become more moderate as a result of increased group interaction.
   (b) disagreements among group members lead to polarization of their views.
   (c) the initial positions of group members become more exaggerated as a result of group interaction.
   (d) the group members' main concern is to avoid polarization of their views.

6. Groupthink is *unlikely* to occur when which of the following factors is present?
   (a) There is a high degree of stress in the decision-making process.

(b) There is a strong and impartial leader guiding the decision-making process.

(c) The group comprises mostly like-minded individuals.

(d) The group is ideologically isolated from differing viewpoints.

7. At the request of her husband Billy, Valerie picks up a loaf of bread on her way home from work. Valerie's action shows
   (a) compliance.
   (b) obedience.
   (c) conformity.
   (d) cooperation.

8. The bystander effect occurs when
   (a) the helper is in a good mood.
   (b) the presence of other people inhibits helping behavior.
   (c) the presence of other people facilitates helping behavior.
   (d) helpers feel a close similarity between themselves and the victim.

9. A toddler who forcibly takes away the toy of another toddler is showing
   (a) instrumental aggression.
   (b) hostile aggression.
   (c) displaced aggression.
   (d) secondary aggression.

10. One factor that social psychologists *do not* now consider to be a causal factor in eliciting aggressive behavior is
    (a) exposure to aggressive role models.
    (b) physical discomfort.
    (c) frustration.
    (d) lack of frequent opportunities to show aggression, which would permit the person to "let off steam" and avoid building up aggressive feelings.

Answer each of the following questions by filling in the blank with an appropriate word or phrase.

11. _____ refers to people's efforts to sabotage their own work so as to have an excuse for failure.

12. _____ _____ refers to how we perceive and interpret information about ourselves and other people.

13. Fritz Heider has differentiated _____ and _____ attributions in people's explanatory styles.

14. According to the triangular theory of love, consummate love involves feelings of _____, _____, and _____.

15. The phenomenon of _____ _____ can account for the fact that Tonya always plays her best tennis when the largest groups are present.

16. The phenomenon of _____ _____ can account for the fact that Joseph usually performs much less ably when other people are present, as compared with when he is alone.

17. _____ is demonstrated by selfless sacrifice.

18. When seeking a person's _____, a salesperson might wait to reveal unexpected costs or drawbacks until after obtaining the person's commitment to the deal.

19. _____ is an unfavorable attitude directed toward a group of people, based on insufficient or incorrect evidence.

20. Some ways of reducing _____ include observing prosocial models, encouraging humor or empathy with another person, and stopping to think about the consequences of any actions that are taken.

1. Do you believe that human beings are predisposed to feel prejudice, in one form or another? Why or why not?

2. Design an exercise to help prevent a work group from suffering the ill effects of groupthink.

3. Which of the compliance-seeking strategies is the most likely to be effective in gaining your compliance? Which is the least likely? Why?

The Case of The Quick Temper

R ick has a 3.5 grade-point average and is proud of it. Considering all the extracurricular activities in which he is engaged—the school newspaper, the yearbook, basketball, and a singing group—Rick believes he is doing great. He is not surprised by his excellent scores on the college admissions tests he took.

The one thing that is not going as well as Rick would like is his relationship with his parents. He is used to having things his way but he is willing to compromise. The problem is that when Rick's parents disagree with him he tends to get angry and snap at them. Although later he is willing to find some kind of a compromise, the flare-ups in his anger and the fights that sometimes ensue are chipping away at the good relationship Rick used to enjoy with his parents. He is not sure what to do. His parents have implored him to control himself, but so far, to no avail. They have told him that something has to change.

What can Rick do? Think about this while you read chapter 11. Might Rick find a better pathway by which he can control his anger? Pay special attention to the concept of emotional regulation.

CHAPTER 11
MOTIVATION AND EMOTION

11

What motivates most of us to gain weight or to lose it? What motivates us to explore our environments or to try to achieve success? What emotions do we feel when we accomplish our goals, or when we fail to do so? We address these kinds of questions in this chapter.

Intuitively, the way in which we describe our motivations and our emotions is similar: "I feel like having a hamburger"; "I feel nervous"; "I feel like dancing"; "Dr. Martin Luther King's speeches moved many people to take action." Both motivations and emotions are feelings that cause us to move or to be moved. In fact, the words *motivation* and *emotion* both come from the Latin root *movere,* meaning "to move." Both motivation and emotion seem to come from within us, in response to events or to thoughts. We often feel both as physiological sensations: "I had a gut feeling not to do that"; "When I heard his footsteps behind me again, I panicked—I started shaking, my heart pounded, my throat swelled shut, my palms sweated, and I turned to ice."

HOW DID EARLY PSYCHOLOGISTS EXPLAIN MOTIVATION?

Motivation is an impulse, a desire, or a need that causes us to act. Psychologists study why and how we are motivated to act. More specifically, psychologists ask four different questions (Houston, 1985): (a) What motivates us to *start* acting to go after a particular goal? Why do some people take action, whereas others may never act on their wants and needs? (b) In which *direction* do our actions move us? What attracts us, and what repels us? (c) How *intensively* do we take those actions? (d) Why do some people *persist* for longer periods of time in the things that motivate them, whereas other people often change from one pursuit to another?

Why do people do what they do? Early in the 20th century, psychologists tried to understand motivation in terms of *instinct,* an inherited pattern of behavior which is typical of a particular species of animal (Cofer & Appley, 1964). Much of instinctive behavior is vital to survival both for each individual and for each species as a whole. In fact, naturalist Charles Darwin (1859) promoted instinct theory when he proposed his theory of evolution, in which the survival of each species depends on the ability of the species to adapt to the environment.

Psychologist William James (1890) suggested that humans have both physical instincts (such as sucking and crying) and mental instincts (such as curiosity, fearfulness, and sociability). Other researchers (e.g., McDougall, 1908) added to James's list of instincts (e.g., adding an instinct to dominate others and an instinctive desire to make things). Because the behavior of human animals is so complex, instinct theory eventually became too complicated, with literally thousands of instincts having been proposed (J. W. Atkinson, 1964; Bernard, 1924). As the appeal of instinct theory waned, drive theory became increasingly attractive.

According to *drive theory* (Hull, 1943, 1952; Woodworth, 1918), people have a number of different basic physiological needs: the needs for food, water, sleep, and so on. Taken together, all of these physiological needs are a source of energy, of **drive,** which is a compelling urge to expend energy to reduce these physiological needs. Unfortunately, the assumptions underlying drive theory were weak and evidence piled up against it (White, 1959), so eventually, drive theory also fell out of favor. Other theoretical approaches seemed to be more fruitful in explaining human motivation. For instance, a great deal of research has supported a physiological approach to understanding motivation.

HOW DOES HUMAN PHYSIOLOGY INFLUENCE HUMAN MOTIVATION?

The physiological approach to motivation involves trying to understand the biological bases of motivation in the human body. This approach took off almost by accident. Researcher James Olds misplaced an electrode in a portion of a rat's brain. When the rat's brain was stimulated, the rat acted as if it wanted more stimulation. Olds and his associate Peter Milner (1954) then tested whether the rat was trying to get more stimulation. When electrodes were planted in a particular part of the limbic system of the brain, rats spent more than three quarters of their time pressing a bar to repeat the stimulation. Olds had discovered a pleasure center of the brain. Other researchers showed that cats would do whatever they could to avoid electrical stimulation in a different part of the brain (Delgado, Roberts, & Miller, 1954). Apparently, this other part of the brain caused very unpleasant stimulation. But how can we understand the relationship between the brain and motivation? Three theories for understanding the relationship between motivation and the physiology of the brain are considered here: homeostatic-regulation theory, opponent-process theory, and arousal theory.

Homeostatic-Regulation Theory

Homeostatic regulation is the tendency of the body to maintain a state of equilibrium. In the course of a day, you are subject to several instances of homeostatic regulation that motivate you to wake up, to eat, and to drink. When the body lacks some resource (e.g., sleep, food, liquid), the body tries to get more of that resource. When the body has enough of that resource, it sends signals to stop trying to get that resource. We regulate the needs for food and liquid through homeostatic systems. These systems operate by means of a *negative-feedback loop*, a physiological mechanism whereby the body monitors a particular resource. In such monitoring, the

> **motivation** • an impulse, a desire, or a need that leads to an action
>
> **drive** • a hypothesized composite source of energy, which humans and other animals try to reduce
>
> **homeostatic regulation** • the tendency of the body to maintain a state of equilibrium (balance)

cathy®   **by Cathy Guisewite**

body finds a way to signal the need for an increase in levels of the resource when levels of the resource are low and also finds a way to signal the need for a decrease in levels of the resource when levels are high (see the discussion of hormones in chapter 2). Most people stop eating when they no longer feel hungry, stop drinking when they no longer feel thirsty, or stop sleeping when they no longer feel tired. In the body, negative feedback is gradual, not a switch that goes on or off. For example, suppose that you have had a very active day and arrive at dinner feeling very hungry. At first, you are likely to eat and drink rapidly. However, your rate of eating and drinking will slow down as you finish your meal, because you are receiving feedback indicating that your needs are satisfied (Spitzer & Rodin, 1981). Your body signals to you long before you have finished the meal that you are becoming full.

Homeostatic regulation sounds somewhat like drive theory, but the emphases are different. In drive theory, the focus is on avoiding deficits. Instead, homeostatic-regulation theory more broadly emphasizes the need to maintain equilibrium (balance). Both deficits and surpluses are to be avoided. Next, we consider how the body regulates two motivations: hunger and sexual desire.

Hunger

Although most of us perceive feelings of hunger as coming from our stomachs, these feelings actually originate in an organ much higher in our anatomy: our brains. More specifically, the hypothalamus chiefly regulates hunger. Injury to different parts of the hypothalamus can lead to overeating and obesity (Hetherington & Ranson, 1940; Teitelbaum, 1961) or to undereating and self-starvation (Anand & Brobeck, 1951). How does the hypothalamus know when to signal hunger and when to signal fullness? It appears that our bodies monitor the levels of *lipids* (a form of fat; Hoebel & Teitelbaum, 1966) and of *glucose* (a simple sugar; Anand, Chhina, & Singh, 1962; M. I. Friedman & Stricker, 1976; D. J. Mayer, 1953; Oomara, 1976) in the bloodstream. When the levels of lipids or glucose are too low, the hypothalamus signals us to eat; when the levels are too high, the hypothalamus signals us to stop eating.

Of course, the stomach participates in the regulation of hunger (McHugh & Moran, 1985). In all mammals, the stomach empties at a constant rate; for humans, the rate is slightly over 2 calories per minute. Note that it is the caloric content, rather than the volume of food, that determines how fast the food leaves the stomach. A large bowl of lettuce with no dressing may leave you feeling hungry more quickly than a small piece of cake, because the stomach will empty itself of the lower-calorie lettuce more quickly. As the stomach contracts, we feel more and more hungry. Usually, we start feeling hunger when the stomach is roughly 60% empty and we feel very hungry when the stomach is 90% empty (Sepple & Read, 1989).

Many of us pay a lot of attention to what and how much we eat, in order to control our body weight. Unfortunately, however, statistics on weight loss indicate that more than 90% of weight-losing dieters eventually gain all or almost all of the weight back. There is hope for losing weight, however: The combination of exercise and low-fat, low-calorie dieting may be more effective in achieving weight loss than are dietary restrictions alone (Safer, 1991; Seraganian, 1993).

Dieting often fails because people become more susceptible to binge eating when they are dieting than when they are not dieting (Polivy &

Herman, 1983, 1985). When dieters are subjected to anxiety, depression, or stress, or when they are presented with alcohol or with high-calorie foods, many dieters seem to drop the restraints that have kept them from eating and start to binge. People who are not dieting do not show comparable behavior.

Other factors seem to contribute to obesity as well. Clearly, many of these factors must be environmental, given the fact that rates of obesity have roughly doubled since 1900 (Brownell & Rodin, 1994). One environmental factor is an obvious one, namely, the amount of fat in the diet. The amount of fat that is eaten is highly related to the amount of fat that becomes stored as excess fat in the body (Capaldi & VandenBos, 1991; Drewnowski, 1991). Other environmental factors also matter. For example, people tend to eat more food when presented with a greater variety of foods (Rolls, 1979; Rolls, Rowe, & Rolls, 1982). People also tend to eat more when other people are present than when they are alone (S. L. Berry, Beatty, & Klesges, 1985; deCastro & Brewer, 1992). Further, obese people may be more responsive to these environmental factors than are persons of normal weight (Schachter, 1968, 1971b; Schachter & Gross, 1968; Schachter & Rodin, 1974). Obesity may also be caused by problems in the way the hypothalamus works (Nisbett, 1972). There is further evidence that obese people chronically have higher levels of insulin in their bodies than do nonobese people (Rodin, 1981). The insulin leads them to feel hungrier and thus more responsive to cues that stimulate eating. Diets that urge people to cut consumption of sugar do so in part because the ingestion of sugar leads the body to produce more insulin, which in turn can stimulate hunger.

Stressful situations can lead to overeating. In chapter 2, it was mentioned that the brain secretes endorphins to help it deal with pain. Another effect of endorphins appears to be that they can stimulate eating. One study found that when pigs were administered doses of endorphins, the pigs started to eat more. When given a drug (naloxone) that blocks the effects of endorphins, the pigs ate less (Baldwin, De la Riva, & Ebenezer, 1990). Humans also apparently eat less when they are given naloxone (Mitchell, Laine, Morley, & Levine, 1986).

Anxiety, which often is a result of stressful situations, can lead to overeating (Ganley, 1989). People who are extremely obese (more than double their recommended body weight) are more likely to experience anxiety and depression than are people who are not so obese (Black, Goldstein, & Mason, 1992). Food may provide a source of comfort to people who are very obese and to others as well, much the way other oral activities do from infancy (e.g., thumb-sucking) through adulthood (e.g., smoking). The problem is that the source of comfort later may become a greater source of discomfort as the person becomes upset or even anxious and depressed about his or her overeating.

Unfortunately, fluctuations in weight may be even more damaging to health than is being overweight (Lissner et al., 1991). In other words, you may do yourself more harm by frequently losing and regaining weight than by just leaving your weight alone. To be considered obese, a person must be at least 20% over the normal range for a given height and weight. In the United States, about one in four adults is obese.

Some cross-cultural psychologists have suggested that cultural context may explain some differences in weight. Great individual differences can be observed across both cultures and time. For example, in Samoa, Fiji, Tonga, and other Pacific islands, many males and females weigh much more than the cultural norm for weight in Japan, where very heavy people, such as Sumo wrestlers, clearly stand out in a crowd (W. J. Lonner,

Conceptions of physical beauty vary with time and place. For example, what might be considered an ideal weight in one time period might be considered too high or too low in another time period.

personal communication, December 1993). Cultural differences may go a long way toward explaining weight differences in one culture versus another. As the American taste for fast food and its high fat content catches on in many countries around the world, rates of obesity and the problems that come with obesity have started to increase in other countries in much the same way they have in the United States.

Norms regarding preferred body weight also change across time, as shown by historical collections in art museums. Many time-honored European masterworks, for instance, revere women who have much fuller figures than the slender women who appear in magazines (and other media) in various countries today (Silverstein, Peterson, & Perdue, 1986).

Being overweight is a serious problem for many people but many other people have an opposite problem: being underweight, which may be life-threatening for some. Some people tend to be chronically underweight because they metabolize food very quickly or because they have a kind of hormonal imbalance. In these people, being underweight rarely poses serious health problems.

A minority of underweight people, however, suffer from **anorexia nervosa,** a serious disorder that threatens the health of its sufferers, occasionally ending in death by starvation. People who suffer from anorexia perceive themselves to be fat, so they put themselves on severe weight-loss

anorexia nervosa • an eating disorder in which a person undereats to the point of starvation, based on the extremely distorted belief that she (usually) or he is overweight

The photo on the right shows that this woman was fortunate to have recovered from the life-threatening disorder of anorexia nervosa. Astonishingly, like other anorexics, at the time the photo on the left was taken, this woman was starving herself to death because she perceived herself to be overweight and flabby.

diets (Heilbrun & Witt, 1990). Up to 30% of anorexics die of causes directly tied to the disorder (Szmukler & Russell, 1986). The vast majority (95%) of anorexics are females between 15 and 30 years of age (Gilbert & DeBlassie, 1984). The value that many societies place on slimness seems to help explain why mainly young women suffer from this disorder in the United States and in other countries, such as Denmark and Japan (Nielson, 1990; Suematsu, Ishikawa, Kuboki, & Ito, 1985). Karen Carpenter, who developed a very promising career as a popular singer, died at an early age of heart problems deriving from anorexia.

No one knows exactly what causes anorexia. The roots of anorexia may lie in dysfunctional family relationships (Bruch, 1973), or they may be physiological (Gwirtsman & Germer, 1981). Anorexics may be treated through psychotherapy, drug treatment, and, in severe cases, hospitalization to treat the psychological and physical problems (F. E. Martin, 1985).

More common than anorexia is **bulimia,** in which a person goes on eating binges followed either by vomiting or by purging (e.g., through the use of laxatives). Bulimics also sometimes engage in excessive exercising in order to lose weight. This disorder, like anorexia, is far more common in women than in men, and it primarily occurs during adolescence and young adulthood. Like anorexia, it is very difficult to treat.

Sex

None of us can survive without eating, but a lack of sexual gratification is not life-threatening to us as individuals. As a species, however, sexual

bulimia • a disorder characterized by eating binges followed by episodes of getting rid of the food (e.g., vomiting, taking laxatives)

motivation is as important to survival as is hunger motivation. If no members of the species satisfy their sexual wants, the species will disappear just as certainly as it will from starvation.

The hypothalamus, which plays a role in hunger motivation, also appears to play an important role in sexual motivation. The role is indirect, however. The hypothalamus stimulates the pituitary gland, which in turn releases hormones that influence the production of the sex hormones. There are two main kinds of sexual hormones: *androgens* and *estrogens*. Although both males and females have both androgens and estrogens, males usually have more androgens, and females have more estrogens. Without these hormones, sexual desire disappears, usually only gradually among most humans (Money, Wiedeking, Walker, & Gain, 1976).

Sexual Scripts and Social Norms.   In humans, sexual activity involves at least some degree of cognitive processing. One way to describe the cognitive processes that accompany sexual response is in terms of sexual scripts (Gagnon, 1973; W. H. Simon & Gagnon, 1986). **Sexual scripts** are mental representations of how sequences of sexual events should be enacted. Most of us, whether or not we have ever engaged in sexual intercourse, probably could describe some kind of sexual script, particularly if we have read racy novels, seen romantic TV shows, or watched sexy movies.

Most of us have many possible sexual scripts available. We may decide whether or how to use these scripts, depending on the person we are with, or whether we are with another person at all. The desire for sexual consummation is largely a physiological need but scripts are also socialized through the cultural and societal environment. Some sexual scripts fall outside of societal norms.

Every society attempts to regulate the sexual behavior of its members. For example, all societies impose a taboo against *incest* (sexual contact between particular members of the immediate family). Similarly, most societies attempt to regulate sexual behavior through cultural norms regarding modesty, homosexuality, masturbation, premarital intercourse, marital intercourse, and extramarital intercourse. For example, norms of modesty determine the regions of the male and the female body that should be covered or exposed and that may be decorated or undecorated. Although the specific regions that are to be covered or exposed differ widely from one culture to another, all cultures seem to impose some standards of modesty, at least on one of the sexes, during certain times in the life span.

Homosexuality.   Most cultural norms and sexual scripts are heterosexual, but homosexual scripts are also common. **Homosexuality** is a tendency to direct sexual desire toward another person of the same sex. In women, this tendency is often referred to as *lesbianism*. Technically, however, the term *homosexual* is gender-neutral, so it refers here to both men and women. Although we often speak of homosexuality and heterosexuality as though the two are separate and never overlap, perhaps it is better to consider them as extreme ends of a continuum. At one end are persons who are exclusively homosexual; at the other end are those who are exclusively heterosexual, and many others fall between the two. People who identify themselves as directing their sexual desire to members of both sexes are sometimes referred to as **bisexual**. Researchers have found that about 4% to 10% of men, and a slightly smaller proportion of women, identify themselves as having predominantly homosexual orientations (e.g., see Fay, Turner, Klassen, & Gagnon, 1989; S. M. Rogers &

sexual script • a mental representation regarding how sexual behavior should be carried out during various episodes of sexual interaction

homosexuality • a tendency to direct sexual desire toward another person of the same (*homo-*, same) sex, which probably is based on physiology (nature) but is influenced also by the environment (nurture)

bisexual • a person who directs sexual desire toward members of both sexes

Turner, 1991). At one time, many psychiatrists and psychologists believed that homosexuality was a form of mental illness. However, Evelyn Hooker (1993) conducted extensive research and found *no* inherent association between maladjustment or psychopathology and homosexuality.

What causes homosexuality or bisexuality, or heterosexuality, for that matter? Various explanations exist, some more scientific, some less so (Biery, 1990). Some of the less scientific explanations have included (a) *personal choice*—people simply choose their sexual orientations (this explanation begs the question as to why people choose differing orientations); (b) *arrested development*—homosexuals become fixated in a homosexual phase of psychosexual development (this explanation suggests that all heterosexuals pass through a homosexual phase of development); (c) *social-learning theory*—somehow, homosexuals were rewarded for homosexual leanings and punished for heterosexual leanings (this explanation seems unlikely, given the prejudice against homosexuals in most contemporary societies); and (d) *weak father, strong mother*—homosexuals must have had weak fathers or overly strong mothers. None of these environmental explanations of homosexuality has been supported by research. If nurture cannot satisfactorily account for sexual orientation, can nature? At present, a biological explanation does seem to have gained the most credible research support. For instance, research (J. M. Bailey & Pillard, 1991) has found that if one of a pair of genetically identical male twins is homosexually oriented, then the other is almost three times more likely to have the same orientation as when the twins are fraternal (i.e., not genetically identical). Brain research has also supported a biological basis for homosexuality (LeVay, 1991). Although the biological basis of sexual orientation seems to be well supported by research, other explanations, such as those involving environmental considerations, also may be discovered as a result of further study.

In addition, even if there is a biological basis for homosexuality, other factors may still affect its expression. That is, whether a biological predisposition to homosexuality is actually expressed in homosexual behavior may depend on social learning and other environmental factors. We are unlikely to find a single cause of any given sexual orientation. Rather, it is more likely that a combination of factors leads people one way or another. As Carol Wade and Sarah Cirese (1991) have pointed out, we view homosexuality and sexual orientation according to our culture's prescriptions and prohibitions. To rephrase their thesis, our sexual urges may be inherently biological, but the particular ways in which we are motivated to satisfy those urges seems to be at least partly influenced by our cultural and social environment.

The issue of the origins of homosexuality is far from resolved, however. Daryl J. Bem (1996) has suggested that homosexuality has environmental origins. In particular, his idea is that homosexual behavior results when the child views members of the same sex as more unfamiliar and exotic than members of the opposite sex. The child soon becomes attracted to members of the same sex. In sum, for Bem, what is exotic later becomes erotic.

The homeostatic-regulation theory does a pretty good job of explaining why we seek to satisfy biologically inherited needs such as hunger and thirst. Homeostatic regulation also seems to play a role in our motivation to seek sexual satisfaction. However, this theory alone does not explain why we seek particular expressions of sexual desire (e.g., intercourse with same-sex or opposite-sex consenting adult partners) and not others (e.g., intercourse with other animals or with nonconsenting partners). This theory also fails to address how we *acquire* particular motivations, including the motivation to use psychoactive drugs such as alcohol or nicotine. To explain acquired motivations, a different theory is needed.

Opponent-Process Theory

Richard Solomon (1980; R. L. Solomon & Corbit, 1974) developed opponent-process theory to explain his observations of a pattern of emotional experience when people acquire a motivation, such as the motivation to use psychoactive drugs. According to Solomon, originally, people are at a neutral state, a *baseline*, in which they have not acquired a particular motivation to act (e.g., to smoke a cigarette). In this baseline state, the particular stimulus (e.g., cigarettes) is irrelevant to them. Next, they take a dose of a psychoactive drug (e.g., nicotine absorbed from a puff on a cigarette), experience a "high," and feel a positive emotional state. They feel the high because of the positive effect of the chemical on receptors of the brain. They feel good because of the stimulus. Thus, they have an *acquired motivation* to seek out more of the stimulus. As Solomon discovered, the time course of acquiring a motivation (e.g., the motivation to use psychoactive drugs) tends to follow a pattern (see Figure 11.1). Once people have acquired a motivation, if they then try to stop using the substance and to get rid of the motivation, the pattern changes.

According to Solomon's opponent-process theory, human brains, sooner or later, always seek out emotional neutrality (which is a feeling that is neither positive nor negative). Therefore, when a motivational source moves us to feel emotions, whether positive or negative, we then come under the influence of an opposing motivational force. This opposing force, an **opponent process**, brings us back in the direction of the neutral baseline. As Figure 11.1a shows, our emotional state after smoking a

opponent process • a changing phenomenon that opposes (goes against, in the opposite direction from) an existing force, thereby moving toward a neutral state of balance

FIGURE 11.1
Acquired Motivation
In the beginning of the process of physiological addiction (a), the addictive stimulus elevates you above your neutral baseline level of response. At this point, if you stop using the addictive substance, you fairly quickly return to your neutral baseline level. However, once you become addicted (b), your responses to the substance act only to keep you in a steady state, which serves as your current neutral level of response. If you then abstain from the addictive substance, your responses will cause you to fall below your neutral level of response, and you will experience possibly serious withdrawal.

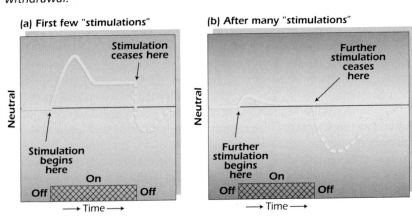

cigarette first rises substantially but then, after many cigarettes over time, starts to fall. It starts to go down when the opponent process begins to oppose the original process. What was pleasurable at first, such as a cigarette, now becomes less so. Thus, we reach a *steady state* of response to the stimulus. The original motivating force stops because the stimulus now only keeps us at a steady state that represents a lower level of pleasure than we previously had been able to achieve. What once was a source of pleasure has now become a new baseline level.

Thus, after using the substance for a long time, the effect of the substance is quite different than it was originally (see Figure 11.1b). Once we *habituate* to the substance, it no longer boosts us above our baseline level. Unfortunately, the opponent process, which was slower to start, is also slower to stop. When the effect of the substance wears off, the effect of the opponent process remains. Therefore, we fairly quickly go into a state of *withdrawal*. We now feel worse than we did before: irritable, cranky, tired, sad, or upset. We may then seek out more of the stimulus in order to relieve the withdrawal symptoms. Ironically, then, what starts off as a habit to reach a high becomes a habit to avoid a low. Fortunately, however, if we decide to ride out the withdrawal, the withdrawal symptoms that took us below our baseline will eventually end and we will return to baseline.

Solomon and his colleagues have applied opponent-process theory to many kinds of acquired motivations, such as motivations to take drugs, to be with a particular person, to eat particular kinds of foods, or even to exercise. In each case, the theory has been remarkably effective in accounting for the data. However, the theory does not satisfactorily address why we would be motivated to take psychoactive drugs in the first place. Nor does it suggest why we would seek to feel more stimulated (i.e., more excited) or less stimulated (i.e., more relaxed) in the first place. Yet another theory is needed to explain these motivations.

Arousal Theory

Suppose that three students of equal intelligence and subject knowledge are about to take an important test. The first student does not care either about the test or about how well she will do on it. The second student wants to do well, but he is not anxious about doing well. He knows that even if he were to do poorly, his life would not be changed permanently for the worse. The third student is extremely nervous about the test, and she believes that her grade on this test will largely determine her future. Which student do you think is most likely to do best on the test?

These three students vary in their levels of **arousal** (alertness, wakefulness, and activation; K. L. Anderson, 1990). Arousal is caused by the activity of the central nervous system, including the brain. The relationship between arousal and efficiency of performance is expressed by the Yerkes–Dodson law, shown in the inverted U-shaped graph in Figure 11.2.

The *Yerkes–Dodson law* (Yerkes & Dodson, 1908) states that people will perform most efficiently when their level of arousal is moderate. According to this law, the student who is both motivated and relaxed will do the best. People generally also feel the best when their level of arousal is moderate (Berlyne, 1967). At low levels of arousal people feel bored, listless, and unmotivated. At high levels of arousal people feel tense or fearful.

The most helpful level of arousal appears also to vary with the task. For relatively simple tasks, the most helpful level of arousal is moderately

arousal • the state of alertness, wakefulness, and activation caused by nervous-system activity

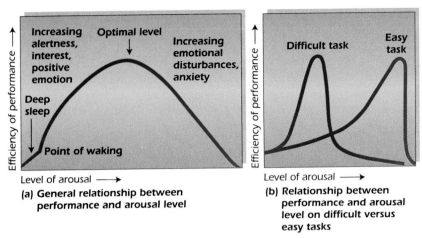

FIGURE 11.2
The Yerkes–Dodson Law
*We feel the strongest motivation when we are moderately aroused—
aroused neither too much nor too little. The linear relationship between
arousal and performance appears to be a hill-shaped curve, resembling an
inverted U. In the hill-shaped curve shown in Graph A, performance is at its
peak when arousal is moderate, and performance levels are lower at both
the low and the high extremes of arousal. Graph B shows that optimally
efficient performance is associated with a higher level of arousal for easy
than for difficult tasks. (After Yerkes & Dodson, 1908)*

high. For difficult tasks, the most helpful level of arousal is moderately
low (Bexton, Heron, & Scott, 1954; Broadhurst, 1957). If you need to
perform a fairly repetitive and boring task, a high level of arousal may
help you get through and may motivate you to be efficient. On the other
hand, if you have to perform a complex task, a low level of arousal
may help you to avoid becoming anxious and thereby may help you to
perform better.

The most helpful levels of arousal also vary across individuals. These
variations may affect how we choose to work. For example, some of us do
our best work when highly aroused, such as when responding to tight
deadlines or to extremely high standards. Others of us work best when
less aroused, such as when we can proceed at a consistent pace, with less
demanding standards. Similarly, different people might seek to raise or
lower the level of arousal in their environments, such as by increasing or
decreasing the amount of visual and auditory stimulation (bright lights,
loud music, etc.). Hence, it appears that arousal theory explains not only
why we may seek drugs that raise or lower our level of arousal, but also
why we may interact with our environment in particular ways.

An illustration of the role of arousal in human emotion can be seen in
a study of arousal and interpersonal attraction (Dutton & Aron, 1974).
The study was conducted in a scenic spot with two bridges in different
places. The first bridge extended over a deep gorge and swayed from side
to side when people walked across it. For most people, walking across this
bridge aroused fear. The second bridge was stable, solid, and near the
ground. Walking across it did not arouse anxiety.

Participants (all males) were assigned to walk across one bridge or the
other, and as they walked across the bridge, they were met by either a
male or a female assistant of the experimenter. The assistant asked each

person to answer a few questions and to write a brief story in response to a picture. After the participants wrote their stories and then finished crossing the bridge, the research assistant gave the men his or her home phone number and remarked that they should feel free to call if they would like further information about the experiment. The experimenters found that those participants who had become aroused by walking across the anxiety-evoking suspension bridge and who were met by a female assistant wrote stories containing relatively high levels of sexual imagery and were more likely than other participants to call the female research assistant at home.

Homeostatic-regulation theory, opponent-process theory, and arousal theory explain some of the physiological bases for motivation. In addition, arousal theory suggests some reasons why different individuals may be motivated to behave differently. Cultural contexts also influence motivation. In earlier chapters (e.g., chapter 10), we explored how we may be motivated to conform to the social norms of our culture. Can all of motivation be understood in terms of our distinctive physiology and cultural context? What else motivates human behavior?

HOW DO PSYCHOLOGICAL NEEDS AND OTHER NEEDS INFLUENCE MOTIVATION?

Murray's Theory of Needs

Psychologist Henry Murray (1938) believed that needs are based in human physiology and that they can be understood in terms of the workings of the brain. He saw a particular set of 20 needs as forming the core of a person's personality. In addition to physiological needs, Murray included such needs as a need for *dominance* (power), for *affiliation* (feeling close to other people), and for *achievement*. A person high in need for affiliation, for example, might be likely to join organizations where he or she could feel a part of a group with other people. A person high in the need for dominance probably would be interested in such organizations only if he or she could lead them or at least have a major say in their activities. He believed that people show marked individual differences in the levels of these needs. Murray also noted that environmental forces press upon people and interact with their needs. Thus, his approach emphasized individual differences to a much greater extent than did many other approaches.

Murray believed that the environment creates forces to which people must respond in order to adapt. How a person copes in the world can be understood largely in terms of the interaction between a person's internal needs and the various pressures of the environment. Some of the needs that Murray proposed have prompted a great deal of research interest. The most widely researched of Murray's proposed needs is the need for achievement, based on an internal standard of excellent performance.

McClelland's Need for Achievement

David McClelland and his colleagues have been particularly interested in the need for achievement (McClelland, 1961; McClelland, Atkinson, Clark, & Lowell, 1953; McClelland & Winter, 1969). According to McClelland (1985), people who are high in the need for achievement (e.g.,

The need for achievement spurs many people to reach academic success.

successful entrepreneurs) seek out moderately challenging tasks, persist at them, and are especially likely to work to gain success in their occupations. Why would people who are high in this need seek out tasks that are moderately challenging? Because these are the tasks in which they are likely both to succeed and to extend themselves. They do not waste time on tasks so challenging that they have little probability of accomplishing these tasks, nor do they bother with tasks so easy that the tasks pose no challenge at all.

Research has shown that our perception of reality strongly affects our motivation to achieve. That is, perceived competence, rather than actual competence, more powerfully predicts how people, especially children, react to demands for achievement (Phillips, 1984). Particularly as girls grow older, they often perceive their competence to be relatively low. Boys, on the other hand, are less likely to show this pattern. The result of this difference between boys and girls can be lower expectations for achievement on the part of girls (Phillips & Zimmerman, 1990). The effect seems to start appearing as early as the kindergarten level (Frey & Ruble, 1987).

The achievement motive may be present in every culture, and it has been the focus of dozens of cross-cultural studies (Maehr & Nicholls, 1980). For example, Chinese parents seem to place great emphasis on their children's achievement, but their focus differs from that of American parents (Ho, 1986). Whereas American children are motivated to achieve primarily for the purpose of being independent, Chinese children are more strongly motivated to achieve to please the family and the community.

Maslow's Need Hierarchy

The needs for affiliation, for power, and for achievement fit well into a hierarchical theory of motivation proposed by Abraham Maslow (1943, 1954, 1970). According to Maslow, our needs form a hierarchy (see Figure 11.3). Once we have satisfied needs at lower levels (e.g., physiological needs and safety needs), we try to satisfy needs at higher levels of the hierarchy (e.g., needs for belongingness and for self-esteem). At the top of the

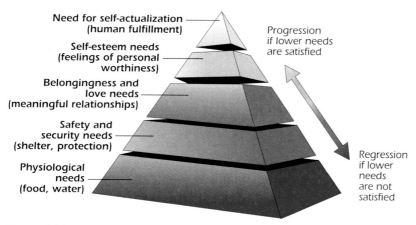

FIGURE 11.3
Maslow's Hierarchy of Needs
According to Abraham Maslow, we must satisfy our more fundamental needs (nearer the base of the hierarchy) before we try to meet the higher level needs (nearer the top of the hierarchy).

hierarchy is our need for self-actualization, in which we try to obtain greater knowledge, artistic beauty, and personal growth, in order to become the best we can be. The following list shows Maslow's hierarchy, in which the lowest levels (and the lowest numbers) are the more basic needs, and the highest levels are the needs that will be pursued only after the more basic needs are met.

1. At the most basic level are the *physiological needs*, such as the needs for food and water. When these needs are not being met, it is very difficult to concentrate on any needs of a higher order. For example, if you are very hungry or thirsty while you are reading these words, you probably are less able to focus on your motivation to learn the information in this textbook than to focus on your desire for food or water.

2. At the second level are *safety and security needs*, the needs for shelter and for protection. We are able to take care of these needs once our basic physiological needs have been met and before we seek to meet higher level needs. For example, if you hear a fire alarm go off near you in your building and you smell smoke, you will be more likely to attend to your need for safety and security than to your need to finish reading this chapter.

3. At the third level of the hierarchy are *belongingness needs*, that is, needs to feel as though other people care about you and that you have a meaningful relationship with and belong to a group of people. For example, suppose that someone you thought was a friend just told you not only that you are not going to go out together this evening, but also that he or she is going with a large group of other people to do something fabulously fun. You are not invited along because you are not welcomed by the group. Chances are that your need for belongingness will now dominate your thoughts and motivations much more than your need to learn this material.

4. On the next level are *self-esteem needs*, that is, needs to feel worthwhile. For example, suppose that you have committed yourself to majoring in psychology, but you are consistently receiving very

low grades on tests in your psychology class. Given the importance of psychology to your conception of yourself, you may find your self-esteem to be plummeting fast. I know I did when, in my freshman introductory psychology class, I received one low grade after another!

5. At the top level of the hierarchy are *self-actualization needs,* which pertain to the fulfillment of human potential. A self-actualized person has reached all or close to all of his or her full potential. Such people are perhaps few and far between, but if you do reach this level, you may be motivated to learn this material just because you enjoy pursuing knowledge for its own sake.

HOW DOES COGNITION INFLUENCE MOTIVATION?

The pursuit of knowledge has led cognitive theorists to try to discover the cognitive processes underlying why people behave as they do. What makes us feel good? What do we find pleasurable? What kinds of stimuli and situations do we seek?

Intrinsic and Extrinsic Motivators

Psychologists frequently describe motivation as being either intrinsic or extrinsic. **Intrinsic motivators** come from within ourselves: We do something because we enjoy doing it. **Extrinsic motivators** come from outside of us: We do something because someone rewards us or threatens us. (Learning theorists refer to extrinsic motivators as reinforcement and punishment.) We act on the basis of intrinsic reasons, extrinsic reasons, or combinations of the two. For example, you might study hard in a given subject because you are really excited about the material and you want to learn it (intrinsic motivation) or you might study hard because you want to get an *A* in the course (extrinsic motivation). If you are lucky, you are able to gain some extrinsic motivators (e.g., earning a living) for doing things you find intrinsically motivating (e.g., feeling competent and able to make a valuable contribution to society).

Society offers many extrinsic rewards, such as money, fame, and power, to ensure that people accomplish tasks that benefit society. The emphasis on extrinsic rewards, however, may actually create problems in motivation. For one thing, people do their most creative work when they are intrinsically motivated (Amabile, 1983, 1985; described also in R. J. Sternberg & Lubart, 1991) because ideas seem to flow most freely when people love what they are doing and view it as fun rather than work. For another thing, the use of extrinsic motivators tends to undermine intrinsic motivation (Condry, 1977; Deci, 1971; D. Greene & Lepper, 1974), even in preschool children (Lepper, Greene, & Nisbett, 1973).

Fortunately, not all extrinsic rewards have a negative effect. Four critical factors seem to determine whether an extrinsic motivator will undermine intrinsic motivation (Cameron & Pierce, 1994; Eisenberger & Cameron, 1996). The first factor is *expectancy*. The extrinsic reward will undermine intrinsic motivation only if the individual expects to receive the reward contingent on performing the tasks. The second factor is the *relevance* of the reward. The reward must be something important to the individual. If you are told that you will receive a spool of thread as a reward

intrinsic motivators • the rewards that come from within the individual, such as the desire to satisfy curiosity

extrinsic motivators • the rewards that come from outside the individual, such as offers of money or threats of punishment

This music student will probably receive extrinsic rewards (e.g., high grades) for practicing on his musical instrument; however, because he has freely chosen to study music, and he has chosen when, where, and how to practice, the undesirable influences of extrinsic motivators will probably be reduced.

for performing a task, and a spool of thread is not of any interest to you, yet you engage in the task anyway, the nominal reward will probably not undermine your intrinsic motivation. Indeed, you may well forget about it (R. Ross, 1975). The third factor is whether the reward is *tangible* (e.g., a certificate, a prize, money, candy, a grade) as a motivating factor. Whereas tangible rewards tend to undermine intrinsic motivation, intangible rewards, such as praise or a smile, do not seem to undermine intrinsic motivation (Deci, 1971, 1972; Swann & Pittman, 1977). The fourth and final factor is whether the reward is *noncontingent*. Tangible rewards are likely to undermine intrinsic motivation when they are noncontingent, and thus are given without regard to whether a task is completed or completed in a high-quality way (Eisenberger & Cameron, 1996).

Consider as an example a teacher who has appreciated the excellent attentiveness of his introductory psychology students and is deciding whether to give a special reward to these students, and if so, how to do it. Most forms of reward probably will not undermine his students' intrinsic motivation, but some will. He informs his students at the beginning of the term that he will pay $10 to every student, just for being in the course. Thus, the rewarded students (a) expect the reward, (b) find it relevant to them because they can spend it, (c) receive a reward that is tangible, and (d) receive the reward noncontingently, whether they complete the course or not and whether or not they do well in the course. The teacher therefore can expect the students' intrinsic motivation to be undermined. Fortunately, the teacher goes bankrupt after a year of implementing this plan and never implements it again.

One of the best ways to remain intrinsically motivated is to adapt what Martin Seligman (1991) refers to as an *optimistic explanatory style*. People with such a style tend to attribute their successes to their own abilities and their failures to the environment. They motivate themselves by telling themselves that they have the ability to overcome the obstacles in their

11.1

HOW TO INTERNALIZE EXTRINSIC MOTIVATION

PUTTING IT TO USE

Almost everyone (e.g., employers, supervisors, parents, and teachers) wishes, at some time, to encourage someone else to be motivated to do something in particular or to act in a particular way that is for their own good. Sometimes, you may need to start out by using some form of extrinsic motivation (e.g., money or praise), and then you can work toward having the person become more intrinsically motivated to do what you want him to. Edward Deci (Deci et al., 1991) and others (e.g., R. Ross, 1975; Swann & Pittman, 1977) have suggested several ways for you to encourage someone to internalize extrinsic motivation and eventually become intrinsically motivated.

1. Help the individual to feel competent and socially related to other persons. Avoid strategies that reduce the person's feelings of competence and of relatedness.

environment. People with a *pessimistic explanatory style*, in contrast, attribute their successes to the environment but their failures to their own lack of ability. They have greater difficulty motivating themselves because they believe that, because they lack the ability to succeed, it is scarcely worth trying.

Some extrinsic motivators are less harmful to intrinsic motivation than are others. Edward Deci and his colleagues (Deci, Vallerand, Pelletier, & Ryan, 1991) have found that extrinsic motivation has differing effects, depending on how much a person can attribute the control of her or his behavior to internal, rather than to external, causes. The harmful effects of extrinsic motivation are greatest when the person attributes the greatest degree of control over his or her behavior to external, rather than to internal, causes. For example, if the person strongly believes that she or he is acting only to obtain rewards or to avoid punishments that are controlled by someone else the harmful effects of extrinsic motivation will be greater than if the person believes his or her actions are controlled by his or her own values.

Curiosity, Self-Determination, and Self-Efficacy

One of the most powerful intrinsic motivators is *curiosity* (the desire to learn or to know). What makes people curious about some things and not others? We tend to be curious about things that are moderately new to us and moderately complicated, compared with what we already know and understand (Berlyne, 1960; Heyduk & Bahrick, 1977). This finding seems to make psychological sense. If something is totally familiar to us (e.g., the words to the U.S. "Pledge of Allegiance") we ignore it; we have nothing to learn from it. At the opposite extreme, if something is wholly new (e.g., technical descriptions of the physics of aircraft-engine designs) we have no basis for understanding it. On the other hand, if we come across

2. Offer the person as much choice as possible in implementing the desired behavior, including choices of materials, of subtasks, of the organization and scheduling of tasks, and so on.

3. Avoid threats of punishment.

4. When using rewards, avoid tangible (touchable) rewards (e.g., money, prizes) that the person feels a strong desire to obtain. Prefer to use intangible rewards, such as smiles or praise, that have less damaging effects on intrinsic motivation.

5. When using rewards, deemphasize the rewards, perhaps offering them as occasional surprises. In any case, do not focus on the rewards as a means of external control.

6. Avoid strategies that emphasize external control, such as competition and deadlines.

7. Acknowledge how the individual feels about carrying out a given task, even if the person's feelings are negative.

8. Use language that shows your awareness and appreciation of the person's independence and competence, rather than using words such as *should, ought,* or *must.*

something that is new but within our ability to understand it we become curious about it and we explore it. For instance, I hope that you find it interesting to investigate (e.g., by reading this psychology textbook) how and why people you know feel, think, and act as they do.

Monkeys confined in boxes learn to solve problems even when the only reinforcement they receive is the chance to look outside the box for a few moments (R. A. Butler, 1953). The longer the monkeys are confined to the boring boxes, the more they will do to have the chance to look outside. Monkeys will also learn a task (e.g., opening latches) just to have something to do (Harlow, Harlow, & Myer, 1950).

Even in everyday activities, we look for ways to be active, to observe and explore, to manipulate aspects of our environments, and to gain mastery over our surroundings (White, 1959). We also try to see ourselves as making things happen. We try to feel control over ourselves and our environments (deCharms, 1968). That is, we actively try to feel self-determination, and we avoid feeling controlled by outside forces. We are often unhappy when we feel controlled, whether it is by another person or even by a substance (as in an addiction). We generally feel unhappy when we believe that our futures are predetermined, or that others are controlling our actions. Rather, we are motivated to be, and to feel, in charge of our own destiny.

According to **self-determination theory** (Deci et al., 1991), humans need to feel *competent* (capable of performing key tasks), *related* (a sense of belonging and being connected to other people), and *autonomous* (independent). The need for relatedness is similar to Murray's need for affiliation and Maslow's needs for belongingness and love. According to self-determination theory, we are all powerfully motivated to meet these three innate needs.

How do our feelings of competence affect the likelihood that we will reach our goals? Albert Bandura (1977a, 1986) has theorized that our **self-efficacy**—our feelings of being competent enough to achieve our goals—powerfully affects whether we can achieve our goals. Your beliefs in your own self-efficacy can come from many different sources: your own direct experiences, how you interpret the experiences of others, what people tell you that you are able to do, and how you assess your own emotional or motivational state. The important thing is that if you feel greater self-efficacy you are more likely to create the outcomes you want. Think about how you view your own competence in various areas of your experience. How efficacious (competent) do you feel? How do your feelings of self-efficacy affect both your motivation and your performance?

---

self-determination theory • a theory suggesting that people need to feel that they can control their own destiny, that they are independent and competent, yet that they are still closely tied to other people

self-efficacy • an individual's belief in her or his own competence to master the environment and to reach personal goals

goal • a future state that an individual wants to reach

plan • a strategy for accomplishing something at some time in the future

---

11.2

PUTTING IT TO USE

GOALS AND PLANS

Years ago, Edward Tolman (1932, 1959) recognized that **goals** can be enormously motivating. Specifically, goals help to motivate high performance in four ways (Locke & Latham, 1985):

1. *Focus attention.* Goals focus your attention on the tasks you need to complete in order to perform well.

2. *Effective use of resources.* Goals help you to pull together the resources you need in order to get where you want to be.

3. *Persistence.* Having goals helps you to continue to try to achieve even when it is hard to do so.

4. *Strategy planning.* You can use your goals as a basis for developing a plan for achieving success. A **plan** is a specific set of strategies for getting where you want to go from where you are (G. A. Miller, Galanter, & Pribram, 1960; Newell & Simon, 1972).

Throughout your life, you must frequently change your goals and your plans, trading off what you ideally want for what you believe you can realistically get. The most effective goals are challenging enough to motivate action while still being reachable.

One way to explain the effects of self-efficacy is to say that self-efficacy relates to *self-fulfilling prophecies* (Rosenthal & Jacobson, 1968). When you believe you can do something, you are more likely to try hard enough to succeed. Each success then leads to greater self-efficacy, which leads to further success. In contrast, people who feel a lower level of self-efficacy may believe that they cannot succeed. As a result, they hardly try. The result is likely to be failure, which leads to the expectation of future failure, which then becomes the basis for more failure. One way in which to enhance your ability to reach your goals is simply to set realistic, highly specific goals and then to make specific plans for meeting your goals.

11.1

FINDING YOUR WAY

Before you read about what psychologists have to say about emotions, think about what you already know and believe about emotions. Look at the photos of New Guinean adults shown in Figure 11.4. For each photo, guess what emotion is being expressed. (We return to these photos again later in this chapter.)

Photo	Emotion
(a)	
(b)	
(c)	
(d)	

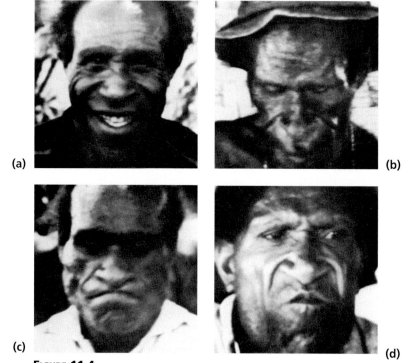

(a)   (b)

(c)   (d)

Figure 11.4
Facial Expressions of Emotion
What emotions are these people expressing?

Many of the theories of motivation work together, rather than in opposition (see Table 11.1). For example, motivation probably has physiological, personality, and cognitive aspects. Almost certainly, these aspects interact. The physiology of the brain and of the endocrine (hormonal)

TABLE 11.1

Three Approaches to Motivational Theory

Approaches to motivation based on physiology, personality, and cognition may be seen as complementary, rather than conflicting, ways of understanding motivation. (Key researchers or theorists are indicated in parentheses following each theory.)

Approaches based on physiology	
Homeostatic-regulation theory (e.g., Keesey et al.)	The systems of the body try to maintain a state of equilibrium, using negative-feedback loops. When a needed resource (e.g., food) is lacking, the body signals to get more of the resource. When the levels of the resource are adequate, the body signals to stop trying to get more of the resource.
Opponent-process theory (Solomon)	The human brain tries to achieve a baseline state of emotional neutrality. When stimuli lead to movements above or below the neutral baseline, opposing forces tend to counteract the upward or downward trend, returning us to the neutral baseline.
Arousal theory (e.g., Yerkes & Dodson)	We perform most effectively when we are motivated by moderate levels of arousal. When arousal is too high, we feel overly anxious and tense, and when arousal is too low, we feel bored and uninterested. At either of the extreme levels of arousal, poor performance is more likely than when arousal is moderate.
Approaches based on personality	
Theory of needs (Murray)	Physiological and psychological needs form the bases for how we interact with our environment. Among the psychological needs, the most widely studied are the needs for affiliation, for power, and for achievement.
Need for achievement (McClelland)	The need for achievement powerfully influences how we interact. People with a high need for achievement seek out tasks that moderately challenge their abilities.
Hierarchy of needs (Maslow)	We try to satisfy needs at successively higher levels once we satisfy needs at relatively lower levels. The sequence of needs is physiological, safety and security, belonging (social support), self-esteem, and self-actualization (fulfilling personal potential to the greatest extent possible).
Approaches based on cognition	
Intrinsic versus extrinsic motivators (Deci et al.; Lepper)	We can be motivated to take action, based on intrinsic forces, such as personal interest, or on extrinsic forces, such as rewards or punishments controlled by other persons. Unfortunately, the use of extrinsic motivators sometimes undermines the effectiveness of intrinsic motivators.
Curiosity (e.g., Berlyne)	We tend to want to explore whatever is moderately new and moderately complicated, as compared with what we already know and understand.
Self-determination (e.g., deCharms; Deci et al.)	We try to find ways to actively explore and manipulate aspects of our surroundings, particularly so that we can gain a sense of mastery over our environments.
Self-efficacy (e.g., Bandura)	We try to feel competent, and we work harder to achieve what we believe we are competent enough to achieve.
Goals and plans (Tolman)	Goals and plans can improve motivation and increase the likelihood of accomplishing particular tasks.

system affects the personality attributes and cognitions we have, just as these personality attributes and cognitions may in turn affect our physiology. Further research may show how to fit together these various approaches to characterize all of human motivation more fully, yet more simply.

WHAT EMOTIONS DO PEOPLE FEEL?

Emotions are psychological feelings, usually accompanied by physiological reactions to stimuli. The stimuli that lead to these responses may come from inside our bodies (e.g., the pain of a stubbed toe), from inside our minds (e.g., the thought that a lover is being overly attentive to someone else), or from our environments (e.g., seeing a poisonous snake within striking distance). The various responses include cognitive (experiential), physiological, and behavioral aspects (J. G. Carlson & Hatfield, 1992). Particular emotional responses may be either preprogrammed (genetic; e.g., feeling frightened while falling) or learned (e.g., feeling afraid of getting a low grade on a psychology examination). Emotions are an integral part of our existence. Indeed, they appear well before language does in the infant.

Emotion and motivation are so closely linked that it is often difficult to distinguish them. For instance, both motivations and emotions are feelings that cause us to move or to be moved; both seem to come from within us, in response to events or to thoughts; and both often involve some accompanying physiological sensations. On the other hand, motivation and emotion differ in some ways, as shown in Table 11.2. Another way to see how motivation and emotion interact is to consider a classic psychological situation: In the **approach–avoidance conflict**, we feel two conflicting

TABLE 11.2

Some Differences Between Motivation and Emotion
Although motivation and emotion have many similarities, they also differ in several ways.

Motivation (motives)	Emotion (feelings)
The prompting stimulus (e.g., hunger) is generally not observable	The prompting stimulus is generally observable
Often seems to be cyclical (e.g., hunger occurs in cycles)	Rarely seems to be cyclical
Energizes, directs, and sustains activity (e.g., hunger prompts the pursuit of food)	May interfere with ongoing activity (e.g., sadness may lead to depression) or may lead to a change in activity (e.g., fear may lead to escape-seeking activities)
Responses are directed outward toward interactions with the external environment	Responses are directed inward (e.g., toward physiological and cognitive activities within the individual)
Generally prompts action and is seen as active	Generally seen as passive

emotion • a psychological feeling, usually accompanied by a physiological reaction

approach–avoidance conflict • the simultaneous presence of two conflicting tendencies: to go toward a stimulus (approach it) and to go away from it (avoid it), based on feeling both positive and negative emotions about the stimulus

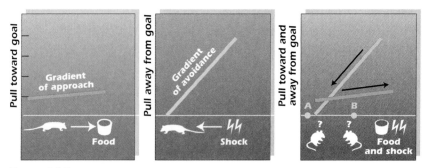

FIGURE 11.5
The Approach–Avoidance Conflict
Motivation and emotion interact in response to a situation that stimulates motivation both to approach something and to avoid it, due to the arousal of both positive and negative emotions toward the object. When the avoidance gradient goes above the approach gradient, the organism pulls away.

FIGURE 11.6
Plutchik's Emotion Wheel
One of the main structural theories of emotion suggests that emotions can be arrayed in a circle (Plutchik, 1980). Emotions closer to each other in the circle are more closely related. Emotions farther away are more distantly related. Emotions opposite each other in the circle are also believed to be emotional opposites.

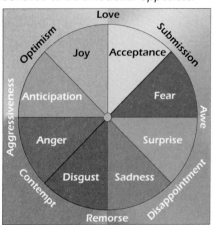

tendencies: (a) We feel positive emotions (e.g., joy) about some aspects of a particular stimulus, so we want to go toward it (i.e., approach it); and (b) we also feel negative emotions (e.g., fear) about some aspects of the stimulus, so we want to go away from it (i.e., avoid it). Two other kinds of conflict are approach–approach conflicts, where both of two options seem desirable (e.g., choosing between two colleges, both of which you would like to attend) and avoidance–avoidance conflicts, where both options seem undesirable (e.g., deciding whether to meet a course distribution requirement by one course that you do not want to take or by another course you also do not want to take).

Suppose, for example, you see someone toward whom you feel strongly attracted. You feel happy just to be near the person. He or she appears to be unattached, so you feel even happier. You feel motivated to approach the person and strike up a conversation. You start walking over. As you get closer, however, your feelings of anxiety start to increase. What if you are rejected? What if the person thinks you are a jerk? As you get closer, you chicken out (see Figure 11.5). The tendency toward avoidance becomes stronger as you approach the person. When the tendency for avoidance becomes greater than the tendency for approach, you are motivated to walk away. Your joy of wanting to be near the person loses out to your feelings of fear and you do nothing. Your motivation to approach the person is intertwined with the emotions you feel as you come closer and closer to making contact. Eventually, though, you may decide the person is worth your taking the risk and so you may approach them despite your fears.

Before we probe various approaches to emotions, it may help to describe briefly the basic kinds of human emotions. Joy, fear, anger, sadness, and disgust are the emotions most often cited as being fundamental to all humans (see Table 11.3). To these emotions, some would add surprise (which is much less commonly identified as a fundamental emotion across cultures), guilt (the private sense of being at fault), and shame (public humiliation; e.g., see Figure 11.6). Refer back to your responses to Finding Your Way 11.1. How do the emotions you observed compare with the basic emotions listed in Table 11.3 and with the emotions depicted in Figure 11.6?

TABLE 11.3

Basic Human Emotions

Although various theorists differ in the emotions they consider to be fundamental, most agree that joy, fear, anger, sadness, and disgust are basic.

Emotion	Findings
Joy. A feeling associated with a sense of well-being, inner harmony, and contentment, often associated with smiling	When people rate their own happiness, the mean rating is about 6 on a 10-point scale (Wesman & Ricks, 1966). Ratings for a given person are remarkably constant from one day to the next, but self-reports of happiness differ across cultures (percentages of self-rated happiness ranged from a low of 34% in South Korea to a high of 52% in Italy; Hastings & Hastings, 1982).
Fear. An unpleasant emotional arousal in response to perceiving a specific, identified danger or threat, focused on a specific situation or object	Fear serves a protective evolutionary function because it motivates people to avoid harmful objects or situations. In contrast, anxiety—an unpleasant emotional arousal in response to a general perception of an unidentified danger or threat, not focused on any particular situation or object of threat—may lead to serious psychological disorders.
Anger. A state of arousal that arises when a person feels frustrated or blocked from reaching a goal, especially if the frustration or injury is believed to have been inflicted intentionally and without justification	About 29% of our overt expression of anger is directed toward people we love, 24% toward people we like, 25% toward acquaintances, and only 8% toward people we actively dislike (Averill, 1980, 1983); only 13% of our expression of anger is directed toward strangers (total = 99%, due to rounding).
Sadness and grief. Whereas *sadness* is a relatively mild feeling of unhappiness, *grief* is sharper, deeper, and usually more long-lasting	This emotion results from an unwanted, involuntary, often permanent, separation; the separation may be from a physical object, situation, or person (e.g., a loved one) or from something intangible, such as a personal belief or skill (e.g., being disabled or made to feel incompetent or powerless).
Disgust. An emotional reaction to being faced by objects or situations that we find extremely unattractive	Disgust serves an adaptive purpose, motivating us to avoid objects or situations that may be harmful (e.g., spoiled meat). When feeling disgust, we psychologically reject something based on its nature, its origin, or its social history (Rozin & Fallon, 1987). What may seem disgusting in one culture (such as piercing of a woman's ears) may not seem disgusting in another.

HOW DO PSYCHOLOGISTS APPROACH TRYING TO UNDERSTAND EMOTIONS?

Just as the approaches to and suggested explanations of motivation are diverse, so, too, are the approaches to understanding human emotions. In reading about evolutionary, psychophysiological, cognitive, and cultural approaches, you may note that many of these approaches offer insights that add to, rather than subtract from, the others.

Emotions in an Evolutionary Perspective

The evolutionary approach to emotions attempts to answer the following question: *Why have emotions developed within the human species as a whole?* Emotions have both a *physiological aspect,* through which we physically react in distinctive ways, and a *cognitive aspect,* through which we interpret how we feel. Both aspects are essential to our survival as a species. From an evolutionary perspective, there are good reasons for

According to many psychologists, the emotions of joy, fear, anger, sadness, and disgust are fundamental to all humans everywhere, although the particular situations that prompt those emotions, and the particular ways in which they are expressed, may differ across cultures.

emotions (Plutchik, 1983). Obviously, the emotions that help to increase the likelihood of reproduction help the replication of the genes associated with such emotions. As humans have gained increasing control over reproduction, emotions may play an increasingly important role. Brief feelings of lust alone usually do not determine when or with whom we will have children. Rather, much more complex and long-lasting emotions typically govern our reproductive choices.

Consider, too, the love parents feel for their children. Obviously, this love brings happiness to both parents and children. The love that bonds parents and children together also serves a purpose for evolutionary survival: It makes it more likely that the parents will ensure the child's safety, health, and survival while the child still depends on the parents.

We also feel other emotions, such as fear and anger (which we enjoy a lot less than love or lust). How do these other emotions enhance our survival as individuals or as a species? For one thing, these emotions prepare us to behave in particular ways in particular situations. For example, anger can prepare us to fight when we have a good chance of defeating a potential attacker. On the other hand, fear can prepare us to run away from a potential attacker who might harm us. Replication of a set of genes depends on the organism that has these genes knowing when to fight a beatable enemy and when to run from an unbeatable one. Appropriate emotional reactions to danger may mean the difference between life and death.

Psychophysiological Approaches to Emotion

Today, psychophysiological approaches to emotion involve cutting-edge technologies, state-of-the-art methodologies, and exciting changes in theories. Surprisingly, psychophysiological approaches are also among the most ancient ones. Ancient Greek and Roman physicians believed that emotional states could be understood in terms of the physiology of the body.

Links Between Our Bodies and Our Emotions

The various theories of emotion to be described will all be discussed in relation to a single scenario. A woman slips on a banana peel and falls down. As a result of her fall, she feels certain physical symptoms (such as pain) and certain emotions (such as anger). But what does she feel when? How do her thought processes and the physiological mechanisms of the brain interact with her emotions? These are the kinds of questions for which the various theories of emotion make different predictions.

The earliest modern theory of emotion was proposed separately by American psychologist William James (1890) and Danish physiologist Carl Lange. Today, the theory that they proposed is termed the *James–Lange theory of emotion.* The James–Lange theory turns common notions about emotion upside down. The commonsense view of emotion is that first we perceive some event in the environment. That event leads us to feel some kind of emotion. As a result of that emotion, psychophysiological changes occur. For example, sadness might lead to crying, or anger might lead us to clench our fists. James and Lange proposed exactly the reverse (Lange & James, 1922). According to James and Lange, we experience bodily changes in reaction to events in the environment. These psychophysiological changes then lead to the feelings we identify as emotions, rather than the other way around (see Figure 11.7).

Ironically, William James's son-in-law, Walter Cannon, became the leading critic of the James–Lange theory (Cannon, 1929). He noted some reasons why the James–Lange theory could not be right. For example, Cannon proposed that different emotions are often associated with the same psychophysiological states within the body. (Today, with more advanced measurement techniques than were available to Cannon, we can recognize better the differences in the psychophysiological states corresponding to various emotions.) In addition, the organs of the body do not provide the kinds of information that people would need to distinguish one emotion from another. Cannon proposed instead that the brain, the thalamus in particular, controls emotional behavior. Bodily reactions alone do not. Philip Bard (1934) later elaborated Cannon's view, so it is sometimes called the Cannon–Bard theory: An environmental event leads to a reaction on the part of the brain, which in turn leads to identification of an emotion (see Figure 11.8).

FIGURE 11.7
James–Lange Theory of Emotion

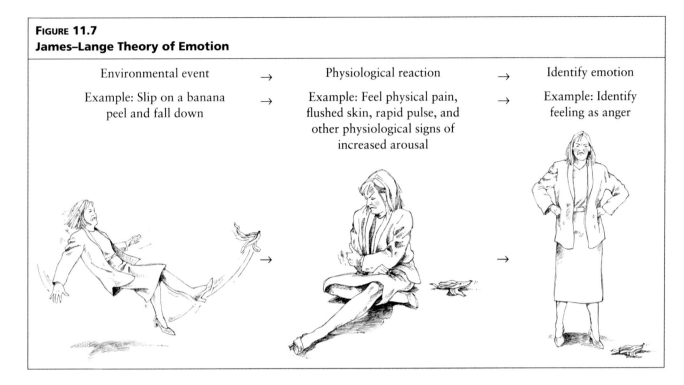

Environmental event → Physiological reaction → Identify emotion

Example: Slip on a banana peel and fall down → Example: Feel physical pain, flushed skin, rapid pulse, and other physiological signs of increased arousal → Example: Identify feeling as anger

FIGURE 11.8
Cannon's Theory of Emotion

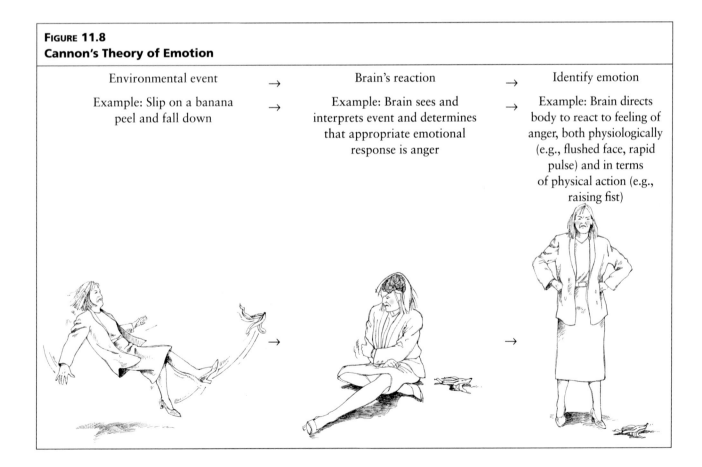

Environmental event → Brain's reaction → Identify emotion

Example: Slip on a banana peel and fall down → Example: Brain sees and interprets event and determines that appropriate emotional response is anger → Example: Brain directs body to react to feeling of anger, both physiologically (e.g., flushed face, rapid pulse) and in terms of physical action (e.g., raising fist)

Psychologists now believe that some aspects of both the James–Lange theory and the Cannon theory are correct. Cannon was correct in recognizing that emotions are largely governed by the brain, especially by several parts of the limbic system (e.g., the hypothalamus and the amygdala; see chapter 2). James and Lange were also correct, however, in noting that physiological changes contribute to people's perceptions of their emotions.

Two Systems for Emotional Responses

As Cannon suspected, in addition to the brain itself, two physiological systems appear to influence our emotional responses: the autonomic nervous system and the endocrine system (see chapter 2). According to Joseph LeDoux (1986; LeDoux, Romanski, & Xagoraris, 1989) and other investigators (Cacioppo & Petty, 1983; Derryberry & Tucker, 1992; Ekman, Levenson, & Friesen, 1983), distinctive patterns of arousal and activity of the autonomic nervous system (see chapter 2) may correspond to different emotions. For instance, when you feel frightened or angry, your autonomic nervous system directs your heart and lungs to speed up their activity, and it directs your digestive system to slow down its activity.

Other researchers (e.g., Henry & Stephens, 1977) have emphasized the role of the endocrine system in emotion. Thus, different emotions may be linked to different relative concentrations of hormones. For example, anger seems to be associated with increased levels of *norepinephrine* (noradrenaline), fear with increased levels of *epinephrine* (adrenaline), and depression with increases in *adrenocorticotropic hormone (ACTH;* see chapter 2). In contrast, joy is marked by decreases in ACTH and other hormones. This endocrine-system approach thereby links moods and emotions with concentrations of hormones. Behavior associated with the particular emotions also is subject to hormonal influences. For example, aggression is associated with increased levels of testosterone (Floody, 1983). Strong correlations do not establish causality, however. We cannot tell whether changes in hormone concentrations cause the emotions, the emotions cause the changes in hormone concentrations, or both depend on other kinds of changes. In many modern theories, then, an environmental stimulus or event leads to the brain's sensing the stimulus or event, thinking about the event and feeling an emotion as a result of the event, and then determining how to react (see Figure 11.9).

Cognitive Approaches to Emotion

Schachter and Singer: Arousal, Cognition, and Emotion

Stanley Schachter and Jerome Singer (1962) developed a **two-component theory of emotion,** which includes a physiological component and a cognitive one. First we experience an environmental stimulus or event, then we sense a feeling of arousal, and then we evaluate the situation and label the arousal as a particular emotion (see Figure 11.10). The first component is *physiological arousal,* which can be caused by any number of things, such as psychoactive drugs or situational stimuli (e.g., a sudden surprise). The second component, which is cognitive, is how the person *labels* that physiological arousal. According to Schachter and Singer, the label determines the emotion we feel. Thus, people who are aroused and

two-component theory of emotion
• a theory asserting that particular emotions have two parts: a feeling of physiological arousal in response to a stimulus, and the cognitive labeling of the physiological arousal as a particular emotion

---

FIGURE 11.9
Contemporary Physiological Theory of Emotion

Environmental event or stimulus	→ Brain senses stimulus event, then brain (limbic system) directs autonomic nervous system and endocrine system to respond appropriately ↕ → Brain thinks about the event (and perhaps also about the physiological reactions) and identifies an emotion	→ Brain determines how to react to the situation
Example: Slip on a banana peel and fall down	→ Example: Brain senses pain, then it immediately (a) directs the autonomic nervous system to increase pulse and breathing rates and (b) directs the endocrine system to release noradrenaline ↕ → Example: Brain cognitively interprets the stimulus event (slipping and falling) and perhaps also the physiological reactions (e.g., flushed skin, heavy breathing) as indicating the emotion of anger	→ Example: Brain figures out how to respond to the situation in terms of taking physical action (e.g., shouting, slapping the floor)

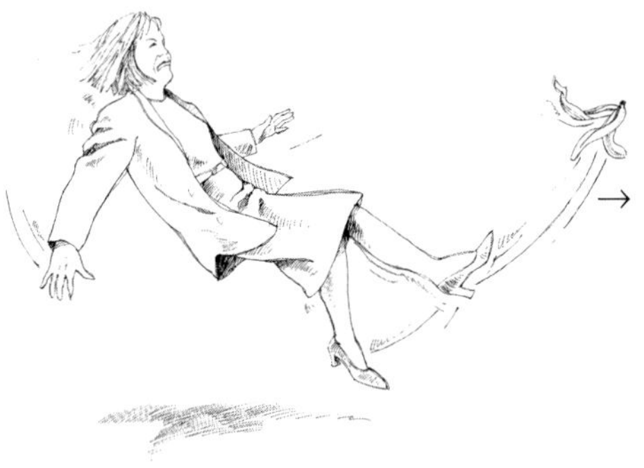

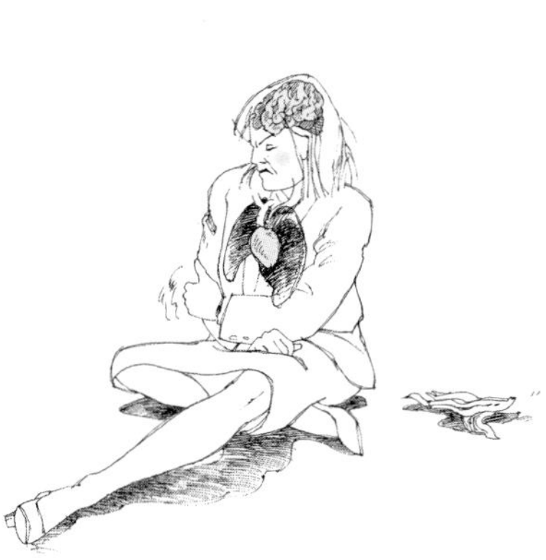

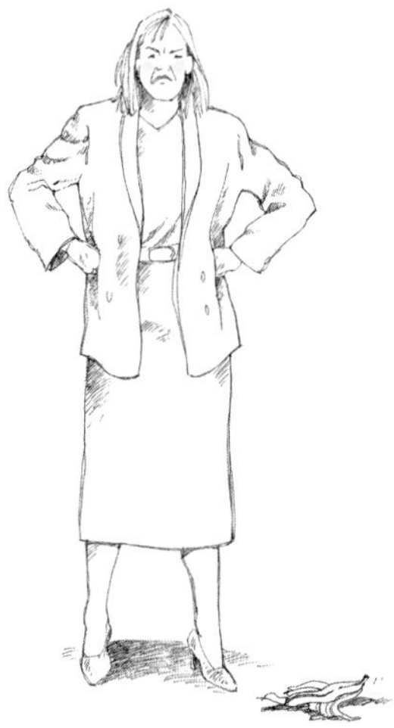

who believe that the appropriate emotional label for the arousal is happiness will feel happy; people who are aroused and who believe that the appropriate emotional label is anger will feel anger. To Schachter and Singer, the arousal is the same in every case. What distinguishes the various emotions is how we label our arousal.

FIGURE 11.10
Schachter and Singer's Theory of Emotion

Stimulus	→	Physiological component	→	Cognitive component
Environmental event or stimulus	→	Sense feeling aroused	→	Evaluate the situation and the feeling of arousal and label the arousal as a particular emotion
Example: Slip on a banana peel and fall down	→	Example: Feel both pain and physiological arousal	→	Evaluate the situation (falling down and feeling pain) and the arousal and label the emotion as anger (or perhaps embarrassment)

Follow-up research has shown that Schachter and Singer were partly wrong (see, e.g., Leventhal & Tomarken, 1986; Marshall & Zimbardo, 1979). For one thing, we can feel physiological differences in the kinds of arousal linked with different emotions. Still, the classic work of Schachter and Singer was important in developing an entire area of psychological theory and research.

Lazarus Versus Zajonc: The Relationship Between Emotions and Cognitions

Decades ago, Magda Arnold (1960, 1970) proposed that what and how we think about a situation partly leads us to feel emotions. Richard Lazarus (1977, 1984; R. S. Lazarus, Kanner, & Folkman, 1980) since has championed and expanded her point of view. According to Lazarus, we appraise a situation in stages: (a) In *primary appraisal*, we determine the possible outcomes of what is about to happen. For example, is the person approaching us about to beg for money, rob us, or start a conversation? (b) In *secondary appraisal*, we have to decide what to do. Given what we decided about the person coming toward us, how should we act? These appraisals continue as events develop. According to Lazarus, each of our appraisals of a situation determines what emotions we feel. Thus, cognition (thoughts regarding appraisals) precedes emotion. First we experience an environmental event or stimulus, then we appraise the situation cognitively, and then we feel an emotion (see Figure 11.11).

In contrast to Lazarus, Robert Zajonc (1980, 1984; Zajonc, Pietromonaco, & Bargh, 1982) has argued that cognition and emotion are basically separate. To Zajonc, emotion is basic and does not require any preceding cognitions. Zajonc and others note that emotions preceded thinking in evolutionary history. Therefore, cognitions do not have to precede emotions. Lower animals do not have to think in order to fear

---

FIGURE 11.11
Arnold and Lazarus's Theory of Emotion

Stimulus	→	Primary appraisal	→	Secondary appraisal
Environmental event or stimulus	→	Appraise the situation, and figure out possible outcomes of the situation	→	Based on the primary appraisal, conduct a secondary appraisal to figure out (a) how to feel emotionally and (b) what to do about the situation
Example: Slip on a banana peel and fall down	→	Example: Answer questions, such as the following, regarding possible outcomes: Have I been seriously injured so that I'll need to seek medical attention? Are other people watching who will think less of me for having tripped?	→	Example: Based on the primary appraisal (e.g., "I haven't been seriously injured, but other people are watching me"), label the emotion as anger or perhaps embarrassment. In addition, figure out what to do about the situation (e.g., shout angrily about the idiot who left the banana peel on the floor)

predators or to attack prey. For that matter, we humans often know how we feel long before we know what we think about a situation.

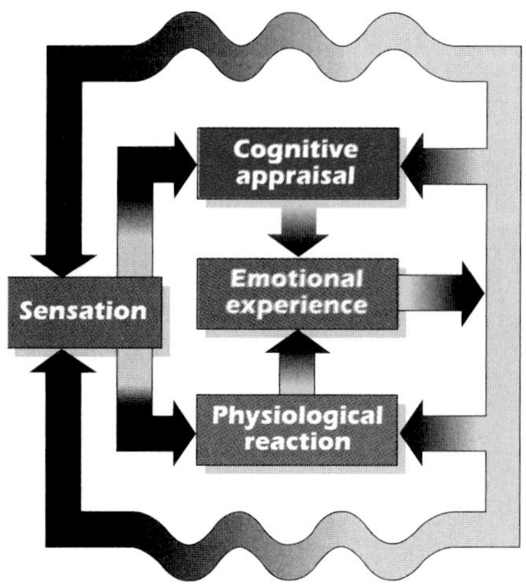

A Synthesis View

Many psychologists believe that we should stop trying to figure out one standard sequence for cognitive appraisal, emotional experience, and physiological arousal. Instead, the sequencing may be viewed as a continuous loop of emotional feedback (Candland, 1977; see Figure 11.12). Although cognitive theories of emotion differ from one another in several ways, all of them agree that emotion and cognition are mutually dependent. Research on *state-dependent memory* supports this mutual dependence. That is, if you learn something while feeling a particular emotion, you are more likely to be able to remember that something when you feel the same emotion again later (Bower, 1981; see also chapter 6). For example, if you study for a test when you are generally feeling happy, then you probably will recall the information from that chapter more easily during the test if you are happy at the time you take the test. But if you study for the test feeling happy and then feel sad at the time of the test, you may find it more difficult to retrieve the information you need at the time of the test.

Cross-Cultural Approaches to Emotion

Physiological and cognitive approaches to emotion narrowly focus on the emotional experiences of each individual. Another approach to the study of emotion takes a broader perspective. Batja Mesquita and Nico Frijda (1992) have conducted an extensive review of the anthropological literature and have a developed a theoretical framework for understanding emotion, based partly on theories by others (such as Lazarus). In their view, when we try to understand emotions, we must consider the following elements: *antecedent events* (events that came before the emotional reaction), *event coding* (interpretation of the event), *appraisal* (evaluation of the event and its possible outcomes), *physiological reaction pattern* (emotion-related changes in the body), *action readiness* (preparedness to respond to the emotion-arousing event), *emotional behavior* (actions following the experience of the emotion), and *regulation* (degree to which the individual tries to make the emotional reaction stronger or weaker). Each of these elements may be influenced by cultural context.

Using an alternative cross-cultural approach, James Russell (1991, 1995) drew two conclusions related to how people categorize emotions. First, not all people sort their emotions according to the basic categories often used by English speakers and other speakers of Indo-European languages. That is, in some cultures, certain emotions of the so-called basic emotions may be omitted from the cultural categories for major emotions; in other cultures, additional emotions may be included in the major cultural categories of emotions. Second, despite these cross-cultural differences, there are many similarities across cultures in the emotions people identify, particularly in regard to emotions associated with particular facial expressions (e.g., Ekman, 1971, 1993; Ekman & Oster, 1979) and vocal expressions (e.g., Bezooijen, Otto, & Heenan, 1983). Also, most cultures do have some label for the basic emotions we identify. Although the range of expression for emotions and the boundaries between various emotions may differ, there are many similarities in how distinctive cultures describe human emotions.

FIGURE 11.12
Emotional Feedback Loop
Our physiological reactions and our cognitive appraisals constantly and reciprocally interact with our perceived emotional experiences.

Various psychophysiological measures have been used to register emotion, including heart rate, respiration rate, blood pressure, and *galvanic skin response (GSR)*, which is affected by sweating. A machine that measures many of these responses at one time is a **polygraph** (*poly-*, many; *-graph*, recording). The polygraph is often called a "lie detector." The idea underlying "lie detection" is to provide an objective measure of whether people are feeling emotional stress. The assumption underlying this idea is that a person who is lying will feel emotional stress and will therefore perspire more, breathe more rapidly, and so on.

Unfortunately, the assumption underlying measurement with a polygraph is not always correct. Polygraphs measure only stress reactions, not the reasons for these reactions. Thus, they will record stress reactions for reasons other than lying, and they will not record as lies statements made by people who feel no stress when telling lies. A common format for polygraph testing is that the polygraph operator asks a series of questions and compares psychophysiological responses to nonthreatening questions ("In what city were you born?") with answers to potentially threatening questions ("Did you cheat on your chemistry exam?"). A more effective format for the use of polygraphs involves questions that assess whether a person possesses information that only a guilty person would know (Bashore & Rapp, 1993).

How accurate are polygraphs? The results of controlled studies are not encouraging. Although professional interpreters of polygraphs have been found to be correct in identifying the guilty parties 76% of the time, these professionals have also labeled as guilty 37% of the innocent subjects they have tested (Kleinmuntz & Szucko, 1984). A review of more than 250 studies of the validity of interpretation of polygraph results shows similar findings (Saxe, Dougherty, & Cross, 1985; see also Ben-Shakhar & Furedy, 1990). Thus, interpreters of results are pretty good at recognizing guilty parties. However, they also identify disturbing numbers of innocent people as being guilty.

In the language of signal-detection theory (see chapter 3), the hit rate is high, but so is the rate of false alarms. Results such as these indicate that polygraph tests, as they are now interpreted, are far from reliable. Because of the high number of false alarms on polygraph tests, results of these tests are no longer admissible as evidence of guilt in criminal prosecutions. How would you feel about taking a polygraph test if you were accused of doing something you did not do?

polygraph • the equipment that records several (*poly-*, many; *-graph*, recording) different physiological responses (e.g., heart rate, respiration rate, blood pressure) at one time; often used for trying to measure emotional reactions

HOW DO PEOPLE EXPRESS EMOTIONS?

Culture and Emotional Expression

Cross-cultural researchers such as Paul Ekman and his colleagues (e.g., Ekman, 1971; Ekman & Oster, 1979) have found great similarity of facial

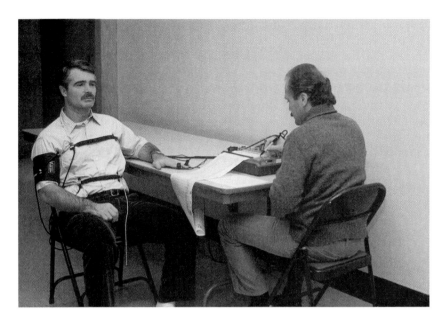

The idea behind "lie detection" is to provide an objective measure of whether people are feeling emotional stress. The assumption underlying this idea is that a person who is lying will feel emotional stress and will therefore perspire more, breathe more rapidly, and so on. Unfortunately, not all people who show signs of stress are lying and not all people who lie show signs of stress. Because of these problems, polygraph results are not generally admissible as evidence during criminal trials.

expressions across cultures. Researchers studied the ability of tribal New Guineans to recognize facial expressions in photographs of Westerners (Ekman & Friesen, 1975).

In the studies by Ekman and his colleagues, both adults and children were quite accurate in recognizing expressions of happiness (Figure 11.4a), sadness (Figure 11.4b), anger (Figure 11.4c), disgust (Figure 11.4d), surprise (not depicted), and fear (not depicted). Americans also were fairly accurate in recognizing New Guinean expressions. The tribe members had almost no previous contact with Westerners, yet their facial expressions and judgments of facial expressions were very similar to those of people in the United States. In all cases, accuracy was greatest for happiness and lowest for fear. This work was confirmed in Brazil, Chile, Argentina, and Japan (Ekman, 1984). Do your own findings agree with the findings by Ekman and his colleagues? Do you find it easy to identify the emotions of the New Guinean adults? How about the faces of infants?

Social Functions of Emotional Expression

Why do many psychologists believe that the expression of emotion seems to be built into our human physiology? Under most circumstances, we benefit from expressing our emotions. The expression of emotion serves at least four different social functions (Izard, 1989): (a) We can communicate our feelings to other people, even when we cannot communicate our thoughts (e.g., even infants, very young children, and speechless adults can express emotion across language groups). (b) We can influence how other people respond to us; for example, mothers respond in different ways, depending on their babies' facial expressions of emotion (Huebner

& Izard, 1988; see also Figure 11.4). (c) We can use emotional expressions to make social interactions easier; for example, a smile can do a lot to "break the ice," sometimes more than words. (d) We can encourage prosocial behavior. For example, our own emotional expressions (e.g., smiles) can affect other people's emotions. When those other people feel positive emotions, they are more likely to behave prosocially (Isen, 1987). In addition, it appears that our facial expressions of emotion may even influence the intensity of our own emotions (e.g., described in Zuckerman, Klorman, Larrance, & Speigel, 1981).

We all know when we experience emotion, but there is considerable disagreement as to how we experience it. For example, Lazarus (1984) believes that cognition is the primary cause of emotion, whereas Zajonc (1984) does not. Mesquita and Frijda (1992) suggest that emotion is part of a complex that closely involves both cognition and behavior, as influenced by a person's cultural context. Whichever theory one accepts, emotion clearly provides an important link between cognition and behavior. Linking back to the beginning of the chapter, we also can see that negative emotions often are what provide us with the motivation to change our behavior and our lives. For example, the sadness experienced over the loss of a close relationship ultimately may motivate us to seek another such relationship. Thus, emotion and motivation work together to enable us to adapt optimally to a rapidly changing environment.

In this chapter, we have considered motivation, emotion, and some of the links between the two. These two constructs are very closely linked to a third one, which in large part determines the kinds of emotions a person experiences. This third construct is personality, which we consider in the next chapter.

The Case of the Quick Temper

While reading chapter 11 of *Pathways to Psychology*, Rick comes to a surprising self-realization. Although he may be intelligent in the traditional sense of cognitive abilities, he lacks an important skill—the ability adequately to regulate his emotions. This realization is a powerful one for Rick, because he has never before questioned his own skills. But the reason Rick has never questioned his skills is because he has always done well on standardized ability tests and in school. He now comes around to the view that there is more to life than what the tests measure or what he needs to succeed in school. Indeed, Rick's lack of ability to regulate his emotions (an aspect of so-called "emotional intelligence") may cost him his good relationship with his parents. What he had before seen as a pesky problem of a quick temper Rick now sees as a more serious problem but one that he can and should conquer. Rick does get hold of his emotions, and both Rick and his parents feel a new sense of communication and closeness.

Summary

How Did Early Psychologists Explain Motivation? 382

1. The study of *motivation* considers questions of motivational direction, initiation, intensity, and persistence.

2. Early explanations of motivation focused on *instincts* (inherited, species-specific typical patterns of behavior) and on *drives* (sources of energy that must be reduced). Both explanations proved unsatisfactory.

How Does Human Physiology Influence Human Motivation? 383

3. Physiological approaches to motivation (homeostatic-regulation, opponent-process, and arousal theories) study how motivation relates to the brain, the autonomic nervous system, and the endocrine system.

4. *Homeostatic regulation* is the tendency of the body to maintain a state of balance. A *negative-feedback loop* tells us when our physiological needs, such as for food or sex, are satisfied.

5. The hypothalamus (located in the brain) is essential to the experience of hunger. The body monitors the levels of lipids and of glucose in the bloodstream, and then it sends signals to start or to stop eating, based on those levels.

6. Sexual motivation is affected by the hypothalamus, which acts through the pituitary gland to produce and release sexual hormones such as androgens and estrogens.

7. Human sexual behavior is controlled partly by *sexual scripts*. A minority of individuals seem to be biologically predisposed toward homosexuality,

although other factors contribute to the expression of sexual orientation.

8. *Opponent-process theory* explains how an addictive drug or habit, started in order to achieve a "high," becomes a habit to avoid a "low." When we feel the effects of a motivational source, we then experience an opposing force—slower to start, slower to stop—which tends to bring us back to baseline.

9. According to the *Yerkes–Dodson law,* people perform most efficiently and creatively when their level of *arousal* is moderate. The ideal level varies both with the task and with the person. High levels are helpful with simple tasks; lower levels are better for complex tasks.

How Do Psychological Needs and Other Needs Influence Motivation?   393

10. Personality theorists take a distinctive approach to motivation. For instance, Murray's theory of needs (e.g., the needs for achievement, power, and affiliation) emphasizes the role of personality in motivation. David McClelland has studied in depth the need for achievement. Maslow described a hierarchy of needs starting with physiological needs, proceeding through needs for security, for belongingness and love, for self-esteem, and finally, for self-actualization.

How Does Cognition Influence Motivation?   396

11. Cognitive approaches to motivation show that people are most creative when *intrinsically motivated; extrinsic motivators* tend to undermine intrinsic ones unless extrinsic motivators can be internalized.

12. We need to satisfy our curiosity and to feel competent and able to achieve our own goals *(self-determination theory* and *self-efficacy theory).* Moderately new and challenging stimuli are more motivating than are either totally familiar and easy ones or wholly new and overwhelming ones.

13. *Goals* that are supported by *plans* are effective motivators.

What Emotions Do People Feel?   403

14. Distinct from but closely linked to motivation is *emotion,* the motivational predisposition to respond experientially, physiologically, and behaviorally to particular internal and external variables. An example of the link between motivation and emotion is the *approach–avoidance conflict,* in which we simultaneously feel conflicting urges both to approach particular stimuli and to avoid them because these stimuli lead to both positive and negative emotions.

15. Major emotions include joy (happiness), fear and anxiety, anger, sadness and grief, and disgust. These emotions can be charted to show relationships among them.

How Do Psychologists Approach Trying to Understand Emotions?   405

16. Emotions serve an evolutionary function. For example, emotions may lead us to fight or to run away when facing an attack, depending on how the danger is perceived and which course of action is more likely to lead to survival.

17. The James–Lange theory claims that bodily changes lead to emotion, rather than the reverse. Cannon and Bard disagreed, claiming that the brain controls emotional reactions.

18. Cognitive theories differ in some ways, but they agree that emotion and cognition are closely linked. According to the Schachter–Singer *two-component theory,* we distinguish one emotion from another based on how we label our physiological arousal. Emotions and cognitions are linked, but we do not yet know which comes first. Lazarus believes that cognition precedes emotion, whereas Zajonc does not.

19. Through cross-cultural studies, emotions may be analyzed in terms of antecedent events, event coding, appraisal, physiological response patterns, action readiness, emotional behavior, and regulation. It appears that although not all people categorize emotions in exactly the same way, there are still many similarities across cultures in the way that people express and identify emotions.

20. We can assess emotional experience through psychophysiological means such as the *polygraph,* although the polygraph is not a reliable way to detect lying.

How Do People Express Emotions?   414

21. The expression of emotion enables us to communicate feelings, influences how others respond to us, makes social interaction easier, and encourages prosocial behavior.

Choose the best answer to complete each sentence.

1. One assumption of the opponent-process theory is that
   (a) motivations are quick to start and quick to stop.
   (b) the brain seeks a balance (equilibrium) between positive and negative emotional states.
   (c) emotions provide an opposing force against thoughts.
   (d) habituation is inevitable with increased arousal.

2. Sexual scripts are
   (a) identical across cultures.
   (b) the same with each potential sexual partner.
   (c) mental representations of characteristic sequences of steps in sexual encounters.
   (d) dependent on the amount of androgen and estrogen in our bodies.

3. According to Maslow's hierarchy of needs, individuals
   (a) may bypass no more than two levels in their quest for self-actualization.
   (b) must satisfy self-esteem needs before achieving belongingness and love needs.
   (c) always end their lives self-actualized.
   (d) must satisfy self-esteem needs before seeking self-actualization.

4. Edward Deci's research has suggested that extrinsic motivators produce the least hindrance to intrinsic motivation when the extrinsic motivators are
   (a) stated up front so that the individual knows what he or she will be receiving.
   (b) tangible and easily identifiable.
   (c) received immediately after the task is accomplished.
   (d) intangible, such as verbal praise or a smile.

5. A central tenet of Bandura's self-efficacy theory is that people's performance on a task will be influenced by
   (a) their beliefs about their ability to perform the task.
   (b) the level of intrinsic motivation involved in performing the task.

   (c) their level of extrinsic motivation.
   (d) the complexity of the task.

6. The James–Lange theory of emotion holds that the experience of fear
   (a) occurs when we subjectively attribute our bodily responses as fearful ones.
   (b) is biochemically produced in the hypothalamus.
   (c) is physiologically similar to the experience of rage.
   (d) causes fearful behavior.

7. According to which theory of emotion will the perception and labeling of our physiological arousal lead us to feel a given emotional response?
   (a) Cannon–Bard theory of emotion
   (b) James–Lange theory of emotion
   (c) Schachter and Singer's two-component theory of emotion
   (d) Lazarus's temporal-sequence theory

Answer each of the following questions by filling in the blank with an appropriate word or phrase.

8. The validity of the _____ relies on the assumption of a high correlation between physiological reactions and specific emotional states.

9. Individuals who identify themselves as having sexual interests in both sexes are referred to as _____.

10. A want or need that causes us to act is called a _____.

11. The _____-_____ _____ holds that the efficiency of performance of a task is an inverted U-shaped function of an individual's arousal level.

12. Negative feelings that a person experiences following the elimination or reduction of a substance to which the person is addicted are called "_____ _____."

13. _____ _____ is the tendency of the body to maintain itself in a state of equilibrium.

14. In his theory of motivation, David McClelland has cited the importance to productive work of an individual's need for _____.

15. If Ralph continued working even if he were no longer paid, we might assume that his work

provided him with a high level of _____ motivation.

Match the following descriptions to the psychological phenomenon (either motivation or emotion) being described:

16. The prompting stimulus is generally observable

17. May interfere with an ongoing activity or even prompt a change in activity; does not energize, direct, or sustain activity

(a) motivation
(b) emotion

18. Responses are directed outward toward interactions with the external environment
19. Rarely seems to be cyclical
20. Generally prompts action and is seen as active

Answers

1. b, 2. c, 3. d, 4. d, 5. a, 6. a, 7. c, 8. polygraph, 9. bisexual, 10. motivation, 11. Yerkes–Dodson law, 12. withdrawal symptoms, 13. Homeostatic regulation, 14. achievement, 15. intrinsic, 16. b, 17. b, 18. a, 19. b, 20. a

1. Compare and contrast the nature of the need for achievement (theorized by McClelland) with the need for self-efficacy (theorized by Bandura).

2. Design a cross-cultural study of motivation. What are some of the confounding factors that will make the design of this study particularly difficult?

3. When advertisers want to motivate you to buy their products or services, they try to tap into basic human motivations. Describe a recent advertisement you have seen or heard. Tell how the advertiser was trying to manipulate your basic motivations to persuade you to buy the advertised product or service.

The Case of The Queasy Math Student

Meera did well in high school math classes, but in her first year of college something snapped. She received a mediocre grade in her college math course and now, as a sophomore, she is doing mediocre work again. As soon as Meera looks at her math textbook, she starts to have a queasy feeling in her stomach. She has trouble motivating herself to do her math homework and when Meera takes math tests she feels defeated before she even starts taking the test.

Meera has talked to her sophomore advisor, who has pointed out to her what she already knows—that based on her high school record and her aptitude-test scores she should be doing much better in math. He suggests that Meera find a tutor and she reluctantly agrees to look for one. She is so discouraged that she doesn't believe a tutor will help. Meera is thinking of dropping the course instead. She realizes that if she drops the course she will pay an enormous price because she needs the course for her premed program. But now Meera is thinking that maybe she does not have the ability to be a doctor if she cannot even get through a sophomore-level math course. She is not sure what to do.

What pathway should Meera follow? Think about this while you read chapter 12. Perhaps the answer is in her own view of herself. Pay special attention to the notion of self-efficacy.

CHAPTER 12
PERSONALITY

CHAPTER OUTLINE

Two key figures in the psychological study of personality are Gordon Allport and Sigmund Freud. When Allport was 22 years old, he managed to arrange a visit with the celebrated psychoanalytic theorist, Sigmund Freud. Ironically, once Allport finally found himself in Freud's presence he did not know what to say, so he mentioned that on the train to Vienna he had observed a young boy with an irrational fear of dirt. The boy had constantly complained to his mother of the dirtiness of the train. Freud then looked at Allport and asked, "Was that little boy you?" Allport considered Freud's response misguided and even silly. For the rest of his life, he followed an approach to personality that was distinctly non-Freudian.

Actually, a psychodynamic theorist might argue as to whether Allport's conclusion was correct because Allport did seem to be greatly concerned with neatness and cleanliness (Faber, 1970). In any case, Allport's reaction to that incident gives us a little insight into his personality.

Personality is an enduring disposition—"all those relatively permanent traits, dispositions, or characteristics within the individual that [give] some measure of consistency to that person's behavior" (Feist, 1990, p. 7). Personality psychologists have come up with several ways to study personality. Some personality psychologists have intensively studied the personalities of individuals over long periods of time. Others have developed and implemented various kinds of tests for measuring the full breadth of personality in many individuals. Still others have studied just a few isolated personality features across individuals.

12.1

Before reading about how personality theorists have described and explained personality, stop for a moment to consider your own personality. Jot down a list of some of your main personality characteristics. If you are having trouble thinking of your main personality characteristics, think about how people you know might describe your personality. List as many of your main personality characteristics as you can identify.

How do you think you came to have these characteristics? Do some of them seem to "run" in your family? Were you born with them? Did your family and early childhood experiences shape your personality? Did your friends, your schools, your community, and your culture shape you? Does your current environment continue to influence who you are or do you pretty much have the same personality characteristics now that you had when you were a young adolescent? Do you make your own decisions regarding your personality (e.g., deciding to become more cheerful, less impulsive, or more easygoing)? Would others see your personality just the way you do and, if not, how much of personality is in the eye of the beholder?

Some psychologists have developed their own theoretical frameworks for understanding personality and for integrating their observations about personality. These various theories can be classified according to a few major different approaches to understanding a particular phenomenon.

This chapter considers some of the principal alternative approaches of personality theory: psychodynamic, humanistic, cognitive–behavioral, and trait, as well as interactionist. Each approach represents a different pathway to the same goal: an understanding of the structure and organization of personality. Within a given approach, the various theories share common elements that tie them into a common view of personality. To evaluate the merits of each approach we use the following set of criteria.

1. *Importance to and influence on the field of psychology.* How have the development of theory and research in the field been affected by this approach at various times?

2. *Testability.* Has the approach given rise to empirically testable propositions, and have these propositions, in fact, been tested?

3. *Comprehensiveness.* To what extent do the theories within the approach give a reasonably complete account of the phenomena they set out to describe or explain?

4. *Parsimoniousness.* How well do the theories in the approach explain the complexity and richness of the world, in terms of a relatively small number of principles?

5. *Usefulness to applications in psychological assessment and psychotherapy techniques.* Can the theory be usefully employed by clinicians and other practitioners?

HOW DO PSYCHODYNAMIC PSYCHOLOGISTS VIEW PERSONALITY?

The Nature of Psychodynamic Theories

When most of us think about personality we think about unchanging characteristics of people. To think of personality as a *dynamic* (changing) *process* requires bold thinking. Psychodynamic theories view these changes as occurring within a complex system of diverse sources of *psychic energy* within each person—the sources of a person's motivation to think, feel, and behave. Of course, psychic energy is only a figure of speech Freudians used to describe a hypothetical construct for explaining human personality; it is not an actual physical form of energy. According to psychoanalytic theory, each energy source pushes the person in a somewhat different direction. As we observe a person's behavior, we are watching the moment-by-moment workings of these multidirectional sources of psychic energy.

Because these sources of psychic energy push the person in many directions, they lead to *internal conflict*. For example, suppose that Mary feels a strong sexual attraction toward her employee, Joe. She also feels a strong wish not to be punished for expressing her sexual urges and she even may feel morally outraged at her own urges.

In psychodynamic theories, *biological drives* (especially sexual ones) and other biological forces play a key role. Psychodynamic theories also emphasize *developmental processes* that underlie personality, particularly emphasizing formative processes that occur during early childhood. The biological and developmental characteristics of psychodynamic theories suggest another of the key features of these theories: *determinism*, which is the idea that our behavior is ruled by forces over which we have little control. Sigmund Freud, who first developed psychodynamic theory, emphasized

personality • the enduring dispositional characteristics of an individual that hold together and explain the person's behavior

determinism somewhat more than did **neo-Freudians,** the psychodynamically oriented theorists who followed Freud.

Psychodynamic theorists also emphasize the role of the **unconscious,** which is an internal structure of the mind that is outside the grasp of our awareness, although they do so in different ways. Freud gave more importance to the unconscious in controlling our behavior than did other psychodynamic theorists. Although each theorist described the unconscious as having some function, the various psychodynamic theorists defined the exact nature and importance of the unconscious differently. For example, Freud considered unconscious sexual desires to be very important in shaping behavior, whereas most of the neo-Freudians did not.

Psychodynamic theorists chiefly have been clinicians. The data on which they have based their theories have tended to come from their *clinical observations* of patients. Clearly, the sample of people observed is not randomly selected: These people are seeking treatment for some kind of psychological problem. If the clinical observer then generalizes from observations of people in the clinical setting to hypotheses about the rest of the population, the possibility of bias is obvious: The personalities and personality development of people in a clinical setting are not necessarily the same as those of other people. A further problem is that clinical settings typically do not lend themselves readily to controlled observation or to rigorous experimentation.

To summarize, the various psychodynamic approaches share a common focus on dynamic processes, sources of changing psychic energy, conflicts, biological adaptation, developmental changes, deterministic and unconscious forces, and clinical observations. Next, we consider how these commonalities appear in a few of the distinct psychodynamic approaches.

Psychoanalysis: The Theory of Sigmund Freud

Sigmund Freud (1856–1939) is considered to be one of the great thinkers of the 20th century. Some psychologists consider his theory to be the most influential in all of psychology. Freud was a Viennese physician who, after living much of his life in Vienna, spent his last days in England as a result of the Nazi occupation of Austria. Although he started off as a neurologist, his interests turned to understanding the relation of the mind to personality, and he is known for his work in developing the psychoanalytic framework.

Organization of the Mind

Freud (1917/1963) believed that the mind exists at two basic levels: conscious and unconscious. In addition to *conscious thought* (of which we are aware) and *unconscious thought* (of which we are unaware), Freud suggested the existence of *preconscious thought* (of which we are not currently aware but which we can bring into awareness more readily than we can bring unconscious thought into awareness). Freud (1933/1964) also believed that the mind can be divided into three basic structures: the id, the ego, and the superego. The id and the superego are largely unconscious and the ego is largely conscious (with some preconscious and unconscious components). One can think of an iceberg, with the conscious part of the mind analogous to the part of the iceberg that is above water. Were one only to see this part of the iceberg, one might conclude that the conscious is all there is to see. But as in an iceberg, most of what is there lies below the surface.

neo-Freudian • a psychodynamically oriented theorist whose views and theories are based on those of Freud

unconscious • the portion of the mind that lies outside our awareness and that we cannot pull into our awareness

At a time when physicists were exploring the laws of thermodynamics, Sigmund Freud (lower left) was developing his psychodynamic theory of personality, which emphasized the dynamic processes underlying personality. Many other influential psychological thinkers were stimulated by his views.

At the most primitive level, the **id** is the unconscious, instinctual source of our impulses, such as sex and aggression. The id is therefore also the source of the wishes and fantasies that arise from these impulses. The id functions by means of **primary-process thought,** which is irrational, instinct-driven, and out of touch with reality. We engage in primary-process thinking as infants and also later in our dreams and in Freudian slips of the tongue (see chapter 4). During primary-process thinking, we accept content and forms of thought that we would reject during other thought processes. For example, during our dreams, we accept many illogical sequences of events and impossible situations.

In his analysis of dreams, Freud also distinguished between the *manifest content* of dreams (the stream of events as we perceive them) and the *latent content* of dreams (the repressed impulses and other unconscious material that give rise to the manifest content). For example, the manifest content of a dream might be to seek refuge from a wild animal. However, the latent content of the dream might be the person's need to seek protection from savage impulses. Freud believed that the primary-process thinking of dreams disguises unacceptable impulses from the id.

Primary-process thinking serves some important functions. It allows for creative ideas that make new and even surprising connections. According to Freudian theory, primary-process thinking offers a way to fulfill some of the wishes that we cannot fulfill in our daily conscious lives. Through our wish fulfillment in dreams, we immediately satisfy the pleasure-seeking impulses of the id. This satisfaction reduces the psychic energy of the id's impulses, thus reducing internal tension and conflict. The psychic energy of the id operates in terms of the **pleasure principle,** focusing on the world as we might like it to be.

The **ego,** in contrast, operates on the basis of the reality principle. Through the **reality principle,** we respond to the real world as we truly

id • a personality structure that is the unconscious, instinctual, and irrational source of primitive impulses

primary-process thought • a form of thought that is unrealistic, irrational, and driven by instincts

pleasure principle • the principle by which the satisfaction of impulses drives all of the functions of the id

ego • a personality structure that is largely conscious and realistic in responding to the events in the world while trying to satisfy the irrational and unconscious urgings of the id and the prohibitions of the superego

reality principle • the principle by which the ego tries to adapt to the real world while still satisfying psychic forces of both the id and the superego

perceive it to be. Thus, the ego is the region of the mind that makes direct contact with reality. The ego mediates between the id and the external world, determining how much we can act on our impulses and how much we must suppress our impulses in order to meet the demands of reality. In other words, the ego tries to find realistic ways in which to satisfy the id's impulses. When we follow the customs of our society because we believe in them we do so because of the operation of the ego. When we follow customs to avoid punishment or to have a good opinion of ourselves, regardless of how we evaluate the customs, we are responding to the superego.

Each person's ego originally develops from the id during infancy. Throughout life, the ego remains in contact with the id, as well as with the external world. The ego relies on **secondary-process thought,** which is basically rational and based on reality. Through secondary-process thought we make sense of the world and we respond to it in a way that will make sense both to ourselves and to others. As you try to make sense of the material in this textbook, you are engaging in secondary-process thought.

Freud's third structure is the **superego,** our internalized representation of the norms and values of our society. The superego emerges later than the id and the ego, largely through our identification with our parents. In fact, to some extent, the superego is an internalized representation of our parents. The superego acts as an internal authority figure, telling us what we can and cannot do. It is based on internalized societal rules.

The superego operates by means of the **idealistic principle,** commanding us to obey our internalized rules for conduct. Whereas the ego is largely rational in its thinking, the superego is not. The superego checks whether we are conforming to our internalized moral authority, not whether we are behaving rationally.

The id, the ego, and the superego are not fixed throughout the life span or even childhood. Rather, they develop. Their developing interactions lead, in part, to stages of psychosexual development.

Stages of Psychosexual Development

Recalling that Freud's theory is *psychodynamic* (i.e., involving active processes of the mind), it makes sense that Freud proposed not only a set of personality structures but also a psychological process through which these structures emerge. Specifically, Freud proposed that each individual's personality develops through a series of psychosexual stages of development. According to Freud, progression through each of these stages is essential to mature personality development.

Unfortunately, however, a person may be unable to progress normally through each of these stages. Occasionally, a person may become *fixated* at one psychosexual stage and unable to progress beyond that stage. In addition, a person sometimes may face a traumatic or otherwise stressful situation (e.g., the birth of a sibling) and may *regress* (develop backwards; the opposite of *progress*) to an earlier stage of development. Table 12.1 identifies the Freudian psychosexual stages of development and notes some of the personality characteristics associated with difficulty in progressing beyond each given stage of development.

The oral stage typically begins during the first 2 years of life, when an infant explores sucking and other oral activity. During this stage, the infant learns that such activity provides not only nourishment, but also pleasure. The anal stage typically occurs between the ages of 2 and 4, during which time the child learns to derive pleasure from urination and especially defecation. The phallic stage typically begins at about 4 years of age and continues until about 6 years of age. Children discover during this

secondary-process thought • a form of thought that is rational and realistic

superego • a personality structure that is unconscious and irrational, based on the rules and prohibitions we have internalized from interactions with our parents

idealistic principle • the principle by which the compulsion to obey an internalized set of rules and prohibitions drives all of the functions of the superego

TABLE 12.1
Freud's Stages of Psychosexual Development

Stages and substages	Characteristics associated with difficulty in progressing out of the given stage
Oral (normally occurs during the first 2 years after birth)	Likely to display many activities centered around the mouth: excessive eating, sometimes followed by dieting and then excessive eating again; excessive drinking; excessive smoking; talking to the point that others wish for ear plugs; and so on.
Oral eroticism	Sucking and eating predominate. Likely to be cheerful, dependent, and needy. Expects to be taken care of by others.
Oral sadism	Biting and chewing predominate. Tends to be cynical and cruel. Always looking to "bite your head off."
Anal (normally occurs during ages 2 to 4)	
Anal-retentive	Excessively neat, clean, meticulous, and obsessive.
Anal-expulsive	Tends to be moody, sarcastic, biting, and often aggressive. Also tends to be decidedly untidy in personal habits and is likely to have a room or an office with books and papers strewn all over it.
Phallic (normally occurs during age 4 to middle childhood)	Tends to be overly preoccupied with him- or herself. Often vain and arrogant and exudes an unrealistic level of self-confidence, as well as of self-absorption.
Latency (middle childhood)	Demonstrates sexual sublimation and repression of sexual desires.
Genital (normal adolescence through adulthood)	Normal adult sexuality, as defined by Freud (i.e., traditional sex roles and heterosexual orientation).

stage that stimulation of the genitals can feel good. This stage also can give rise to *Oedipal conflict*, in which the child starts to feel romantic feelings for the parent of the opposite sex. In particular, boys desire their mothers but fear the powerful wrath of their fathers. The conflict is named for the Greek myth in which Oedipus, who had long been separated from his parents and therefore did not recognize them, killed his father and married his mother. Girls may desire their fathers but worry about the wrath of their mothers (sometimes called the *Electra conflict* after the myth of Electra, who despised her mother for having cheated on and killed her husband, Electra's father).

According to Freud, the Oedipal and Electra conflicts cause great turmoil in children. To resolve these conflicts, children must accept the sexual unattainability of their parents. The feelings they directed toward the opposite-sex parent become *sublimated*, redirected in a more socially acceptable fashion. Freud believed that these feelings go into *latency*, an interim period in which children repress their sexual feelings toward their parents and sublimate their sexual energy into productive fields of endeavor. Eventually, sexual feelings reappear during adolescence, and the feelings that children once felt toward the parents of the opposite sex are now directed toward an agemate of the opposite sex. Ultimately, the child develops a mature relationship with a partner of the opposite sex, thereby entering into the final and mature psychosexual stage, the *genital stage*.

Defense Mechanisms

Failure to progress beyond a given stage of psychosexual development (i.e., fixation) or the return to an earlier stage (i.e., regression) are two of

According to Freud's theory of psychosexual development, the most important crisis of early childhood occurs during the phallic stage of development. During this stage, the child experiences the Oedipal conflict, in which the child starts to feel romantic feelings for the parent of the opposite sex. According to Freud, in the Oedipal conflict, a boy feels sexual desire for his mother but fears the fury of his father. Similarly, Freud presumed that girls would experience an Electra conflict, in which they would desire their fathers but would fear the jealous rage of their mothers.

the ways in which the ego attempts to resolve deep conflicts between the id's strong impulses and the superego's strong prohibitions. Sigmund Freud (1933/1964), along with his daughter Anna Freud (1946), suggested that fixation and regression are just two of several ways in which we respond to conflicts between the id and the superego. According to Sigmund and Anna Freud, people use **defense mechanisms** to protect themselves from unacceptable thoughts and impulses. The goal of these defense mechanisms is to protect the ego from having to deal with information that frightens the ego (e.g., the aggressive impulses of the id) or that causes anxiety for the ego (e.g., the irrationally strict prohibitions of the superego). In addition to fixation and regression, there are eight other main defense mechanisms:

- *Denial.* Occurs when our minds prevent us from consciously acknowledging or giving attention to our sensations and perceptions about unpleasant, unwanted, or threatening situations or events; for example, families of alcoholics may deny perceiving all the obvious signs of alcoholism surrounding them.

- *Repression.* Occurs when we unknowingly block from consciousness any unacceptable or potentially dangerous impulses emanating

defense mechanism • the means by which the ego protects itself from unacceptable thoughts (from the superego) and impulses (from the id)

from the id; for example, an adolescent girl may have repressed her memory of having been sexually molested when she was a child.

- *Projection.* Occurs when we attribute our own unacceptable and possibly dangerous thoughts or impulses to another person; for example, people who are attracted to pornography may become very active in local antipornography associations.

- *Displacement.* Occurs when we redirect an impulse away from the person who prompts the impulse and toward another person who is substantially less threatening than the one toward whom the impulse was originally directed; for example, a young boy who has been harshly punished by his father would like to lash out vengefully against the father, but the boy's ego recognizes that he cannot attack such a threatening figure so, instead, he may become a bully and attack helpless classmates.

- *Sublimation.* Occurs when we transform the psychic energy of unacceptable impulses into acceptable and even admirable behavioral expressions; for example, an artist may rechannel sexual energy into creative products that are valued by the society as a whole.

- *Reaction formation.* Occurs when we transform an unacceptable impulse or thought into its opposite; for example, a son might hate and envy his father because his father has sexual access to his mother, but the son cannot consciously admit to feeling envious, so the son consciously seems to adore his father.

- *Rationalization.* Occurs when we avoid threatening thoughts and explanations of behavior by replacing them with nonthreatening ones; for example, a woman who is married to a compulsive gambler may rationalize (justify) her husband's behavior by attributing it to his desire to win a lot of money because of his great concern for the financial well-being of the family.

- *Identification.* Occurs when we feel intense fear of and intense anger toward another person whom we perceive as powerful; we then seek to identify with the powerful person, fusing our own identity with that of the powerful person; for example, a young girl whose mother frequently is physically abusive may both fear and hate her mother, but instead of expressing these feelings, she identifies with her mother's power, merging her own identity with her mother's.

How did Freud identify these various defense mechanisms? One of the main ways was through the methodology of the case study.

Freud's Case Studies

Freud used a clinical case-study approach for developing his theory. His particular approach was *intensive:* Freud would take a single case and study it in great, analytical detail. His analyses were also *qualitative:* Freud did not try to quantify any aspect of the case studies. Other theorists and researchers have used the case-study approach to gain information that is *extensive* (using many cases) and *quantitative* (measuring amounts of particular variables).

The Neo-Freudians

Freud's work inspired many people to follow his views and many to react against his ideas. Freud's enormous influence prompted many theorists to create their own theories (see, e.g., R. J. Sternberg & Berg, 1992). In general, the neo-Freudians placed more emphasis on the ego and less on the id than did Freud. They also shifted the attention of psychologists more toward conscious processing and away from unconscious processing. The neo-Freudians also deemphasized the role of sexuality and of biology. The shift away from the id, from unconscious processing, and from biological forces signaled a shift away from extreme Freudian determinism. Instead, the neo-Freudians more strongly emphasized the role of the ego in allowing individuals to control their own lives. They also highlighted the role of socialization in the development of the individual's personality. One such neo-Freudian was Alfred Adler.

The Individual Psychology of Alfred Adler

Alfred Adler, one of Freud's earliest students, was also one of the first to break with Freud and to disagree with many of his views. The break, like most of the breakoffs of disciples from Freud, was bitter. Adler did not accept Freud's view that people are victimized by competing forces within themselves. Instead, Adler believed that all psychological phenomena within the individual are unified and consistent among themselves. For example, forces giving rise to the desire for pleasure and to the desire for work need not necessarily oppose each other. Adler also believed that people's vision of the future shapes their actions at least as much as do their experiences in the past. You might then wonder why people sometimes seem to behave inconsistently or unpredictably. To Adler, these apparently inconsistent behaviors can be understood when viewed as being consistently directed toward a single goal: *superiority.*

According to Adler, all of us strive for superiority by attempting to become as competent as possible in whatever we do. This striving for superiority gives meaning and coherence to our actions. Unfortunately, however, some of us feel that we cannot achieve superiority. If we dwell on perceived mistakes and feelings of inferiority, we may come to develop an **inferiority complex**, organizing our lives around these feelings of inferiority. We then may act in ways that try to compensate for these feelings of inferiority, and even may overcompensate. For example, people who seem never to gain enough money or power or fame, no matter how much of any of these things they have, may be overcompensating for feelings of

inferiority complex • a maladaptive personality structure in which we organize our lives around feelings of inferiority, based on perceived mistakes and failings

Is the reason for the success of the Baldwin brothers their constant striving for superiority? According to neo-Freudian Alfred Adler (right), each of us constantly tries to become, and to appear, as competent as possible in all of our actions.

inferiority in the respective domains. Adler also believed in the importance of birth order, suggesting that first-borns are more likely than later-borns to strive toward and reach high levels of achievement.

Adler broke from Freud in his emphasis on striving for superiority. Carl Jung, another early follower of Freud, broke from Freud in another way, especially in his conception of the unconscious.

The Analytical Psychology of Carl Jung

Like Freud, Carl Jung (1875–1961), a Swiss analyst, believed that the mind can be divided into conscious and unconscious parts. However, Jung's view of the unconscious part differed sharply from Freud's view. Jung referred to one layer of the unconscious as the personal unconscious. The **personal unconscious** includes repressed memories and current experiences that are perceived below the level of consciousness. Each person's unique personal unconscious comes solely from his or her own experiences.

Jung referred to a second layer as the **collective unconscious.** This level contains memories and behavioral predispositions that we have inherited from our distant human past. According to Jung, humans have a common collective unconscious because we have the same distant ancestors. Thus, our common ancestral heritage provides each of us with essentially identical shared memories and tendencies.

Across space and time, people tend to interpret experiences in similar ways because of common **archetypes,** which are the inherited tendencies to perceive and act on things in particular ways. Jung found support for the existence of archetypes in the collective unconscious by observing cross-cultural similarities in myths, legends, fairy tales, religions, and even cultural customs.

Carl Jung once was considered the intellectual successor to Freud. When Jung increasingly disagreed with Freud's ideas his relationship with Freud broke off, after which Jung went into a long period of depression. After Jung recovered, he developed his own views of personality, which were clearly distinguished from those of his former mentor.

Fairy tales from around the world include many of the archetypical characters that Jung described. Depicted here is an Indian tale in which the archetypical man and woman are planning a wonderful life together. However, it is a fantasy: The man, Shah Jahan (1629–1658), ordered the building of the Taj Mahal in memory of his beloved deceased wife, Arjumand Banj Bagam, called Muntaz Mahal, or Chosen One of the Palace.

personal unconscious • the part of the unconscious mind that includes the person's distinctive repressed memories and personal experiences

collective unconscious • according to Jungian theory, the part of the unconscious mind that contains memories and behavioral predispositions that all humans share because of our common ancestry

archetype • the inherited tendency to perceive and act in certain ways, common to all

Erik Erikson was trained as a psychoanalyst and was psychoanalyzed by Anna Freud, Sigmund's daughter. Like Anna Freud, Erikson placed much more importance on the role of the ego than did Sigmund Freud or many other neo-Freudians. According to Erik Erikson, our personality continues to develop across the life span, even into old age.

Jung believed that certain archetypes, including the following ones, have evolved in ways that make them particularly important in people's lives: (a) the *persona*—the part of our personality that we show the world, the part that we are willing to share with others; (b) the *shadow*—the part of us that embraces our frightening, hateful, and even evil aspects, which we hide not only from others, but also from ourselves; (c) the *anima*—the feminine side of a man's personality, which shows tenderness, caring, compassion, and warmth toward others, and which is based on emotions; and (d) the *animus*—the masculine side of a woman's personality, the more rational and logical side of the woman. Other archetypes in our collective unconscious include the great mother, the wise old man, the hero, and the villain. What are some traditional stories that you know that include one or more of these archetypes?

The Ego Psychology of Erik Erikson

Neo-Freudian Erik Erikson differed from Freud and from Jung largely by turning attention away from the unconscious mind. Erikson helped shift psychological thinking from emphasizing the role of the unconscious mind (id) to emphasizing the role of the conscious mind (ego). Unlike Freud, Erikson saw the ego as a source of energy in itself, not as dependent on the id for its psychic energy. Also in contrast to Freud, Erikson viewed the ego as much more than a tenuous mediator between the irrational impulsivity of the id and the extreme strictures of the superego. In fact, Erikson considered the ego to be the main source from which we establish our individual identity, synthesizing the effects of our past and the anticipated future. In this way, Erikson (1963, 1968) balanced Freud's emphasis on the past with Adler's emphasis on the future, taking a view of human development that encompassed the entire life span (see chapter 9).

Whereas Erikson, like Freud, is sometimes seen as having an overly "male" orientation in theorizing, Karen Horney is viewed as being among the first psychoanalytic theorists to take women fully into consideration.

The Psychoanalytic Theory of Karen Horney

Although Karen Horney was trained in the psychoanalytic tradition, she later broke with Freud in several key respects. Horney (1937, 1939) believed that Freud's view of personality development was very male oriented and that his concepts of female development were inadequate. She believed that *cultural variables* rather than *biological variables* are the fundamental basis for the development of personality. Horney argued that the psychological differences between men and women are not the result of biology or anatomy. Rather, they result from cultural expectations for each of the two genders.

The essential concept in Horney's theory (1950) is that of basic anxiety in a hostile world. *Basic anxiety* is a feeling of isolation and helplessness in a world conceived as being potentially hostile, due to the competitiveness of modern society. Horney (1937) suggested that we can reduce our basic anxiety by moving toward, against, or away from other people: We move toward other people by showing affection and submissiveness. We move against people by being aggressive, striving for power, prestige, or possessions. We move away from other people by withdrawing from people or simply by avoiding them altogether.

Table 12.2 evaluates psychodynamic research as a whole, using the criteria specified at the outset of this chapter. The evaluation shows an

Karen Horney (left) believed that what women really want are the privileges that the culture gives to men but not to women (Horney, 1939). Her own career was delayed until a German university was willing to admit women to study medicine. These young women (right) meet expectations that differ sharply from Western expectations regarding what women are supposed to do.

TABLE 12.2
Evaluation of the Psychodynamic Paradigm

Criterion	Evaluation
1. Importance to and influence on the field of psychology	This paradigm has spawned, at least indirectly, some research based on theories that developed within the paradigm, as a response to it, or even as a reaction against it. Freud, the first major psychodynamic theorist, is often viewed as the seminal thinker in the psychology of personality. No other psychologist's influence has lasted as long as Freud's. Even today, many clinical psychologists (especially psychiatrists) are loyal adherents to Freudian or neo-Freudian perspectives.
2. Testability of its propositions	On this criterion psychodynamic theories would not rate high, with a relatively small number of experimental investigations. The many case studies tend to be open to various alternative interpretations.
3. Comprehensiveness in accounting for psychological phenomena	The theories are variable regarding the extent to which they give a reasonably complete account of personality phenomena. Freud's theory was comprehensive, as were Adler's and Erikson's, but many other neo-Freudian theories (e.g., Horney) were much less so. All of the psychodynamic theories were generated largely from work with patients who presented adjustment problems, so they may not explain personality in normal persons who have only the usual share of problems.
4. Parsimoniousness of its model of psychological phenomena	In relation to other theories of personality, the psychodynamic theories place in the middle of the range.
5. Usefulness to applications in (a) psychological assessment (b) psychotherapy techniques	(a) The *Thematic Apperception Test*, the *Rorschach Inkblot Test*, and other projective tests have arisen from psychodynamic theory. (b) The extensive influence of psychodynamic theory on psychotherapy is considered in depth in chapter 14.

emphasis on determinism, an emphasis that adherents of an alternative approach, humanism, strongly opposed.

HOW DO HUMANISTIC PSYCHOLOGISTS VIEW PERSONALITY?

Humanists have reacted strongly against the psychodynamic emphasis on determinism and on the importance of the unconscious. Instead, humanists emphasize self-determination and the role of the conscious mind. Humanists share a common view of humans: Unlike other living organisms, we are future oriented and purposeful in our actions. To a large extent, we can create our own lives and shape our own destinies, rather than allowing ourselves to be tossed and turned by inexplicable forces outside our conscious grasp. Although humanists differ widely in their particular beliefs, the core ideas of humanism are well represented in the views of Carl Rogers and of Abraham Maslow (see chapter 11).

Carl Rogers's *person-centered* approach to personality strongly emphasizes the self and each person's perception of self. In fact, Rogers puts the self at the center of his **self theory** of personality. Reality is what the self defines as reality, not some unknowable objective set of things and events outside the self. In other words, to understand a person's reality, one needs to understand not the events that have happened to the person but that person's interpretation of those events. Each person's conception of self begins in infancy and continues to develop throughout the life span. This *self-concept* embraces all the aspects of the self that the person perceives, whether or not these perceptions are accurate or are shared by others. These aspects might include perceived success in love, in school, or at work. In addition, each person has an **ideal self,** those aspects of the self

Carl Rogers (left) and Abraham Maslow (right) were two leading humanistic psychologists.

self theory • a humanistic theory of personality, in which the person's match between the perceived ideal self and real self is considered central to personality

ideal self • all aspects of the self that a person ideally would like to perceive as characterizing the self

that the person would like to have or to show. For example, the person might wish to experience more or deeper love toward his or her significant other than he or she presently experiences.

Rogers strongly influenced psychological thinking by suggesting that greater similarity between the self-concept and the ideal self indicates better psychological adjustment (C. R. Rogers, 1959, 1980). According to Rogers, a key to self-acceptance (a close match between ideal self and self-concept) is feeling **unconditional positive regard** from one or more loved ones. When positive regard (warm feelings of affection and esteem) is conditional, the person may have more difficulty matching the ideal self (which meets the conditions) with the self-concept (which may not meet those conditions).

Like Abraham Maslow, Carl Rogers (1961a, 1980) believed that all people strive toward self-actualization. To Rogers (1978), people have within them the power to make themselves whatever they want to be, if only they choose to use this self-actualizing power. Self-actualizing persons have at least five characteristics:

1. They constantly grow and evolve.

2. They are open to experience, avoid defensiveness, and accept experiences as opportunities for learning.

3. They trust themselves, although they seek guidance from other people. They make their own decisions rather than strictly following what others suggest.

unconditional positive regard • the interpersonal feelings of acceptance, affection, appreciation, or esteem, which are not based on any conditions that the object of regard must meet

TABLE 12.3
Evaluation of the Humanistic Paradigm

Criterion	Evaluation
1. Importance to and influence on the field of psychology	The paradigm has generated even less empirical research than has the psychodynamic paradigm. Still, its messages continue to be relevant: Focus on individuals, on personal choices and opportunities to control fate, and on striving toward self-actualization.
2. Testability of its propositions	Because humanists assert the inseparability of experimenter and experimentee, humanistic theories are, by definition, almost untestable. In addition, humanists' predictions have seldom been operationally defined with sufficient precision to generate experimental tests.
3. Comprehensiveness in accounting for psychological phenomena	Although this paradigm deals with some aspects of human nature, such as the need for self-actualization, or the potentials that lie within us, it leaves a lot unsaid. When compared with the more exhaustive taxonomy of human personality shown in Freud's theory, or in the trait theories, it lacks comprehensiveness.
4. Parsimoniousness of its model of psychological phenomena	These theories are reasonably parsimonious.
5. Usefulness to applications in (a) psychological assessment (b) psychotherapy techniques	(a) Humanists tend to be averse to assessments because tests focus on assigning the client a static set of labels, rather than concentrating on the person's ever-evolving potential for further development. Even the act of giving the test is seen as unduly increasing the apparent distance between therapist and client. (b) Though these theories strongly influenced psychotherapy during the 1960s and early 1970s, they are somewhat less influential today.

4. They have achieved unconditional acceptance from at least some others, which allows them to free themselves from the need to be well liked by all. Given this freedom, they still try to achieve harmonious relationships with other people.

5. They live fully in the present, rather than focusing either on past successes or failures or on future possibilities.

To these characteristics, Maslow might have added that self-actualizers value genuineness in themselves and in others, they enjoy their own company, and they form and follow their own system of beliefs and values, while considering both their own needs and the needs of others.

Rogers believed that evaluations by others, whether positive or negative, lead children to develop conditions of worth, or internalized standards for self-evaluation. Thus, the children internalize the notion that some actions and even feelings will lead to parents' and others' love and approval, whereas other actions and feelings will deprive the children of this love and approval. These conditions of worth ultimately interfere with the individuals' ability to actualize themselves. An implication of this view is that we need to love children unconditionally and not convey to them any conditions on our love for them.

Table 12.3 evaluates the humanistic approach in terms of the five basic criteria being used in this chapter.

HOW DO COGNITIVE–BEHAVIORAL PSYCHOLOGISTS VIEW PERSONALITY?

Cognitive–behavioral approaches to personality try to answer these questions: (a) How do people behave? (b) How do people think? (c) How do behaving and thinking interact to form an enduring, relatively consistent personality?

Early Behavioristic Approaches

Behaviorists try to understand people in terms of the way people act. Behaviorists either downplay or reject the thought processes that other psychologists study, as the behaviorists believe that such processes are irrelevant to psychological study. For example, the behaviorist might seek to explain learning in terms of environmental contingencies, whereas the cognitive psychologist might seek to explain learning in terms of processes that occur "in the head." Behavioral approaches to personality emphasize the explanation of observable behavior in terms of response to environmental events. These explanations usually embrace environmental contingencies (environmental outcomes that depend on—are contingent on—a person's behavior) that lead to various forms of behavior (Skinner, 1974).

We may be able to see how people develop adaptive personalities in response to patterns of reinforcement contingencies in the environment. How do apparently maladjusted personalities develop, though? According to behaviorist B. F. Skinner (1974), people can become maladjusted in several ways. One way is through reinforcement of antisocial behaviors. For instance, a class clown may be reinforced by receiving attention from the teacher and from fellow classmates; a bully may be reinforced by feeling powerful over others and by getting goods and services from the people being bullied. Another way that people can become maladjusted is through punishment of prosocial behaviors, as when an adult punishes a child for truthfully confessing to accidentally breaking a dish.

Behavioral psychologists have emphasized how environmental contingencies influence the development and maintenance of personality. In reaction against the behavioral approach, cognitive psychologists are very much concerned with processes going on in the mind. Cognitive–behavioral psychologists are concerned with the link between mind and behavior. Two such theorists are Julian Rotter and Albert Bandura.

The Social-Learning Theory of Julian Rotter

To Julian Rotter, behavior does not depend solely on external stimuli and reinforcements. Rather, what is important is the meaning of a given external stimulus or reinforcement for each person. Thus, the same sweet candy can be a delightful reward to one person and a nauseatingly sweet food to another. Unlike the behaviorists, Rotter is interested in cognitive aspects of personality, not just behavioral ones. Rotter believes that behavior arises through the interaction between the person and the environment, not just through one or the other (Rotter, 1966, 1990; Rotter & Hochreich, 1975).

By focusing on the individual's perceptions of the environment, Rotter developed a key aspect of his theory: his notion of internal versus external locus of control (Rotter, 1988, 1992). Persons with an **internal locus of control** see a strong causal relationship between what they do and the results of their actions. Internals tend to take personal responsibility for what happens to them. If taken to an extreme, internal persons might even mistakenly blame themselves for events beyond their control. For example, if an extreme internal were laid off during an economic recession in his industry, he likely would feel personally responsible for the layoff and for becoming unemployed.

internal locus of control • a personality orientation based on people's belief that they largely are able to control both what they do and the probable outcomes of what they do

Julian Rotter (left) believes that human behavior is directed toward achieving recognition and status, dominance, independence, protection and dependency, love and affection, and physical comfort. If this drug addict (right) has an external locus of control, she will believe that the problems in her life are caused by forces outside of her control, not by her own actions, such as by her abuse of drugs.

In contrast, people with an **external locus of control** tend to believe that the environment causes the outcomes that follow their own behavior. If taken to an extreme, externals would tend to blame others for the problems they themselves cause. For example, if an extreme external were fired because of her own lack of effort, she might still feel as though other factors (her boss's prejudice, coworkers' conspiracies, etc.) had caused the termination. Thus, internals believe that they have control over their own fate, whereas externals tend to see fate as controlled by luck, by destiny, or by other persons.

Thousands of studies have focused on Rotter's (1966) theory, including cross-cultural ones (Dyal, 1984). For example, cross-cultural researchers have studied both the Indian (Hindu) concept of *karma* and the Chinese concept of *yuan*. Both concepts suggest that people have little or no internal control over their own present destiny, although their moral actions in the present are likely to affect them in future incarnations (Kulkarni & Puhan, 1988; Yang, 1986).

Extreme views in either direction typically involve some distortions of the true causes of events, at least some of the time. Even so, having a more internal locus of control is associated with many positive achievement- and adjustment-related outcomes (see, e.g., Lachman, 1986; Phares, 1988, 1991). The tendency toward an internal locus of control leads a person to feel more able to do whatever must be done. Albert Bandura, another social-learning theorist, is also concerned with people's sense of their ability to do what needs to be done.

The Social-Cognitive Theory of Albert Bandura

To Albert Bandura, a crucial personal variable in personality is our sense of self-efficacy. *Self-efficacy* is the belief that we are competent to do things. This belief seems actually to lead to our being better able to do those things (Bandura, 1986, 1993; Zimmerman & Bandura, 1994; Zimmerman, Bandura, & Martinez-Pons, 1992). If I tell myself I cannot do something, I often will not try very hard to do it, with the result that I will never really learn how to do it well, if at all. As mentioned in the discussion of self-efficacy in chapter 11, if I go ahead and try to do the thing, while constantly telling myself that I will not succeed, my negative expectations may get in the way of what I do. This outcome involves a negative, *self-fulfilling prophecy*, in which the very fact of predicting something about someone can make that thing come true (Rosenthal & Jacobson, 1968).

More broadly, Bandura's theory addresses the *interaction* between how we think and how we act. Bandura's model of **reciprocal determinism** (1986; see also chapter 5) attributes human functioning to a two-way interaction in which personal variables (such as self-efficacy) influence the environment, and the environment, in turn, is influenced by behavior. That is, they reciprocally determine one another (see Figure 12.1). For example, the decision to go to college will be affected by *personal variables*, such as motivation and the ability to succeed in academic work. This decision also will be affected by *environmental events*, such as parental encouragement and the funds to enroll in college. The result is *behavior* (going to college) that in turn will affect the opportunities the student has later in life, such as to pursue occupations that will be unavailable to those who choose not to go to college.

Table 12.4 briefly evaluates the cognitive–behavioral approach in terms of its influence on theory and research and its testability, comprehensiveness,

external locus of control • a personality orientation based on people's belief that the environment surrounding them largely is able to control both what they do and the probable outcomes of what they do

reciprocal determinism • an interaction in which personal variables and environmental variables both influence and are influenced by the behavior of the individual

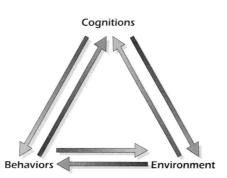

FIGURE 12.1
Albert Bandura and Reciprocal Determinism
Albert Bandura views personality and behavior as affected by, but not completely ruled by, external events over which people have no control. Bandura (1986, 1988) probably places more emphasis on the role of chance in people's lives than do some other theorists. He emphasizes the reciprocal nature of behavior and personal and environmental variables.

TABLE 12.4
Evaluation of the Cognitive–Behavioral Paradigm

Criterion	Evaluation
1. Importance to and influence on the field of psychology	Perhaps because the theories are so testable, they have generated a great deal of research, both by researchers who theorize in this area and by other researchers who choose to test constructs based on these theories.
2. Testability of its propositions	Cognitive–behavioral theories are more testable than psychodynamic or humanistic theories. Theorists have tended to stick closely to their data in their theorizing. Thus, the data base for these theorists tends to be strong.
3. Comprehensiveness in accounting for psychological phenomena	These theories are less comprehensive than some of the competing views of personality. They say a great deal about the aspects of personality and behavior that follow directly from learning, but they do not clearly specify the dimensions on which people differ. By focusing on behavior, they have said somewhat less about the structure of personality than have other theories.
4. Parsimoniousness of its model of psychological phenomena	The theory of Bandura is very parsimonious, primarily because Bandura has adhered so closely to his data, and the theory of Rotter is only slightly less so. In general, these theories rate high on parsimony.
5. Usefulness to applications in (a) psychological assessment (b) psychotherapy techniques	(a) Regarding assessment, Rotter's locus-of-control scale, as well as his scale for measuring interpersonal trust, have been widely used. However, these scales measure narrow bands of personality, not the whole thing. (b) The cognitive–behavioral approach has been highly generative of different methods of psychotherapy (see chapter 14) and has been very influential in health psychology (see chapter 15).

parsimony, and practical applicability. Note that this approach does not clearly specify the exact dimensions along which people differ. Another approach, the trait approach, explicitly attempts to do so.

HOW DO TRAIT THEORISTS VIEW PERSONALITY?

Whereas the theories discussed so far have emphasized various *processes* of personality, trait theories emphasize various *structures* of personality, known as "traits." **Traits** are stable sources of individual differences that characterize what a person is like. The origins of traits are attributed both to nature (hereditary characteristics or predispositions) and to nurture (environmental influences), but the emphasis on one or the other differs across various trait theories. According to some trait theorists, each of us is born with an individually distinctive set of traits—our nature. We may inherit this distinctive set of inborn traits, or at least a predisposition to develop such traits.

For instance, Alexander Thomas and Stella Chess have noticed nine distinctive features of *temperament* (characteristic manners of thinking, acting, or reacting) that first appear in infancy and continue at least through adolescence (A. Thomas & Chess, 1977; A. Thomas, Chess, & Birch, 1970; see Table 12.5). Although Thomas and Chess emphasize the importance of nature in the temperament each person shows during infancy, they also recognize the importance of nurture—each individual's interactions with the surrounding environment. In fact, for Thomas and Chess, the key determinant of personality is the match between an individual's temperament and the individual's environment.

For instance, Lupe, an outgoing, energetic, active, and adaptable child, is delighted that her family's home is attached to her parents' veterinary

trait • a stable characteristic that distinguishes each person

TABLE 12.5
Temperament Characteristics

Characteristic	Question addressed
Activity level	How active are you?
Rhythmicity or regularity of biological cycles	How predictable is your pattern of eating, sleeping, and so on?
Approach/Withdrawal	How outgoing are you?
Adaptability	How easily do you adapt your responses to a new situation?
Threshold of reactivity	How high a level of stimulation is needed to prompt a response in you?
Intensity and energy of reaction	How strongly and energetically do you respond to stimuli?
Quality of dominant mood	In what kind of mood are you most of the time?
Distractibility	How easily are you distracted from pursuing an activity in which you were already interested?
Attention span and persistence despite obstacles	How willing are you to continue to attempt an activity or to solve a problem in the face of obstacles?

After A. Thomas & Chess, 1977; A. Thomas, Chess, & Birch, 1970.

hospital, in which new sights, sounds, and events are constantly appearing and disappearing. Such a stimulating and unpredictable environment is distressing, however, to her older brother Jorge, who is less outgoing, energetic, and adaptable, and who prefers greater predictability and stability. Research indicates that both nature and nurture contribute to the development of our distinctive personality traits (e.g., described in Plomin, 1986, 1989). As adults, however, the effects of our early rearing environments move further into our past, so that the effects of nature may actually increase with age (Plomin, 1989). That is, as the effects of early rearing environments decrease over time, other factors, such as the influence of heredity, contribute relatively more to individual differences among people.

FINDING YOUR WAY

12.2

Has your temperament been relatively stable across your life span? Using Table 12.5, report your own observations of your own temperament now. Next, ask someone (e.g., a parent, grandparent, older sibling, aunt, uncle, or family friend) who has known you since your infancy, or at least before your adolescence, to rate your temperament characteristics, describing your temperament both now and in your early life.

Recall the problems associated with constructive memory of events long past. To reduce the influence of constructive memory, do not tell the person who will answer these questions that you are interested in observing whether personality characteristics are stable across the life span. Emphasize the importance of giving truthful answers. Have the person answer in writing, so that he or she does not tailor his or her answers according to your facial expressions in response. (After the person has answered the questions, you may wish to describe your reason for being interested, but do not do so before the person answers the questions. You may even want this person to review your self-report observations with you after you have both completed these evaluations.)

Some trait theorists hold that personality traits are largely inborn and stable across the life span. Others believe that personality traits develop and change somewhat, although the predisposition to develop particular traits may still be present at birth.

Psychologists often distinguish between two basic kinds of trait theories of personality. According to some theories, all people have essentially the same set of traits, and people differ only in terms of how much they show of each trait. Traits are thus universal. According to other theories, people differ in the set of personality traits they have or at least in the importance of these traits to who they are. Traits, therefore, can be particular to each individual.

Theories Based on Individual Variations of Universal Personality Traits

Some theories emphasizing universal traits try to specify the whole range of personality, suggesting a set of traits that all people possess. This set of traits is believed to characterize fully what people are like. Other theories deal with just a single trait, but in great depth. The following discussion deals with only a few of the many trait theories of personality, those of Raymond Cattell, Hans Eysenck, and the "Big Five" theorists.

The Factor-Analytic Theory of Raymond Cattell

Raymond Cattell studied personality by using *factor analysis,* which identifies the essential variables underlying a wide array of individual differences. These individual differences can be in personality or in any other psychological attribute, such as intelligence or emotions. Cattell basically distinguished two levels of personality traits: surface traits and source traits. **Surface traits** are what we usually observe as characterizing the differences among people, such as whether a person is friendly toward others or unfriendly. To Cattell, however, these surface traits are scientifically less interesting and less important than are the source traits. **Source traits** are the underlying psychological dimensions that generate the surface traits, as described below. Cattell (1979) uncovered 23 source traits (16 main traits; e.g., high vs. low ego strength, submissiveness vs. dominance, social concern vs. unconcern, and naïveté vs. shrewdness plus 7 questionable traits; e.g., conservatism vs. radicalism and group dependency vs. self-sufficiency) by performing factor analysis on numerous surface traits. This method of analysis uncovers sources of individual differences (the source traits) that underlie the observable scores (surface traits).

The Theory of Hans Eysenck

Hans Eysenck's (1952, 1981) theory of personality is as simple as Cattell's is complex. Eysenck argues that personality embraces just three major traits: extroversion, neuroticism, and psychoticism. These elements vary within each individual, along a continuum. The trait of **extroversion** contrasts people who are sociable, lively, and outgoing—*extroverts*—with people who are quiet, reserved, and generally unsociable—*introverts.* People high in **neuroticism** are moody, nervous, irritable, and subject to sudden and seemingly unpredictable mood swings. In contrast, emotionally stable people tend to be less fretful, more uniform in their behavior, and less subject to sudden mood swings. People high in **psychoticism** are solitary, uncaring of others, lacking in feeling and empathy, and insensitive. They are often quite detached from others in their interpersonal relationships.

The "Big Five" Model of Personality

Many personality theorists, including several nontrait theorists, have identified some of the same key personality characteristics in their theories. Arguably, the most widely accepted trait model for the structure of personality is the **"Big Five" theory of personality,** which recognizes the frequent recurrence of five personality traits across studies (especially factor-analytic studies) and even across theorists. The "Big Five" traits were proposed early on by Warren Norman (1963) but have since been championed by many other investigators (e.g., Costa & McCrae, 1992a, 1992b; Digman, 1990; McCrae, 1996; McCrae & John, 1992; Peabody & Goldberg, 1989; Watson, 1989).

surface trait • one of many personality features that characterize differences among people

source trait • one of a relatively few underlying psychological dimensions of personality that generate the numerous surface traits

extroversion • a personality trait characterized by sociability, liveliness, and friendliness

neuroticism • a personality trait characterized by sudden and unpredictable mood swings, nervousness, and irritability

psychoticism • a personality trait characterized by isolation, lack of caring for or about others, lack of feeling and empathy, and insensitivity

"Big Five" theory of personality • a trait theory suggesting that the five key personality traits are neuroticism, extroversion, openness, agreeableness, and conscientiousness

Although different investigators have given the "Big Five" different names, they generally have agreed on the following five characteristics as a useful way to organize and describe individual differences in personality. The descriptions following each of the characteristics depict someone rated high in these traits:

1. *Neuroticism* (see Eysenck's theory). Nervous, emotionally unpredictable, tense, and worried

2. *Extroversion* (see Eysenck's theory). Sociable, outgoing, fun-loving, and interested in interacting with other people

3. *Openness.* Imaginative, intelligent, curious, artistic, and aesthetically sensitive

4. *Agreeableness.* Good-natured, easy to get along with, empathetic toward others, and friendly

5. *Conscientiousness.* Reliable, hard-working, punctual, and concerned about doing things right

12.3

Review the preceding list of five traits, and describe your own personality in terms of the "Big Five" traits. Rate yourself on a scale from 1 to 7 on each of the "Big Five" traits. How would you characterize your strengths and weaknesses based on these ratings?

FINDING YOUR WAY

Although the "Big Five" model of personality enjoys widespread acceptance among many personality psychologists, some objections to the model have been raised. Jack Block (1995), for example, pointed out two major problems with the "Big Five" model: (a) The methods of statistical analysis used to derive the theory have certain limitations (the nature of which goes beyond the scope of this book), and (b) the data from which the factors are derived often consist of nothing more than people's self-reports about their own personalities (see also Hogan, 1996). Although Block has criticized some of the bases for trait models of personality, he does not criticize the fundamental notion underlying universal trait theories: He believes there is a particular set of personality traits, which all individuals possess, to a greater or lesser extent. In fact, Block (1981) has found consistency across the life span for two particular personality traits: *ego control* (a person's ability to control his or her impulsive behavior) and *ego resiliency* (a person's flexibility and responsivity to the demands of the environment).

12.4

What aspects of your personality, if any, are not captured by the "Big Five" traits? How important are these aspects of your personality for influencing what you do?

FINDING YOUR WAY

Not all theorists believe that personality traits are best understood only in terms of traits that are common to all persons. Some theorists, considered next, believe that, to some extent, people not only differ in traits that are shared among them, but can also differ in the traits they possess.

Theories Based on Individual Sets of Distinctive Personality Traits

According to some theories of personality, there is no common set of traits shared by all persons. This type of theory dates back at least to Gordon Allport (discussed at the beginning of the chapter and in chapter 10, regarding prejudice). The critical aspect of Allport's (1937, 1961) theory of personality is that much of personality is characterized by **personal dispositions** (traits that are unique to each individual). Although Allport also mentioned *common traits* (which are the same across individuals), he believed that much of what makes each of us who we are can be found in our personal dispositions rather than in our common traits.

Allport also believed that our various personal dispositions and common traits differ in importance for us. For example, many people possess cardinal traits; a **cardinal trait** is a single trait that dominates an individual's personality and behavior so much that almost everything the person does somehow relates back to this trait (Allport, 1961). For instance, self-effacing compassion may be a cardinal trait of the late humanitarian Mother Teresa, a zany sense of humor may be a cardinal trait of the comic

personal disposition • a trait that is unique to a given individual, according to Allport's theory of personality

cardinal trait • a characteristic that totally dominates the personality and behavior of an individual; many people do not have a cardinal trait

TABLE 12.6
Evaluation of the Trait-Based Paradigm

Criterion	Evaluation
1. Importance to and influence on the field of psychology	This approach has generated quite a bit of empirical research. Only the cognitive–behavioral approach has equaled the trait-based approach in its ability to generate research. On the other hand, trait theories may be said to rely heavily on factor-analytic studies.
2. Testability of its propositions	This paradigm's testability is high: Most of the theories allow for fairly precise predictions, particularly as compared with psychodynamic or humanistic theories.
3. Comprehensiveness in accounting for psychological phenomena	These theories probably fare at least as well as those of any other paradigm in describing the breadth of personality. However, these theories say relatively less than others about the development of personality—how people come to acquire the traits they have.
4. Parsimoniousness of its model of psychological phenomena	The relative parsimony of these approaches depends on the theory being considered. For example, both Eysenck's theory and the "Big Five" are extremely parsimonious, but Cattell's theory is not.
5. Usefulness to applications in (a) psychological assessment (b) psychotherapy techniques	(a) With regard to assessment, many of the trait theories have given rise to personality tests, some of which are widely used. (b) On the other hand, these theories have generated far fewer psychotherapeutic techniques than have the other kinds of theories. Perhaps this is because trait theories tend to focus more on static characteristics and less on dynamic processes.

Robin Williams, and irreverent defiance of convention may be a cardinal trait of the television comedian and producer Roseanne.

Not everyone has a cardinal trait. However, all people do have **central traits,** which are highly important traits in their dispositions; typically, each person has about 5 to 10 of these traits. At the outset of this chapter, you listed your chief personality traits. These traits may be among your central personality traits. If you listed more than a dozen traits, however, some of these traits may be only **secondary traits,** which influence—but are not central to—your behavior. All people are said to have both central traits and secondary traits.

According to some theories of personality, although there is no universal set of personality traits that can be used to predict the behavior of all persons, each individual does have a distinctive set of personality traits, which can be used to predict the person's behavior across various situations. Daryl Bem and Andrea Allen (1974) have questioned this assumption. Instead, these two researchers have suggested that it may be a mistake to try to predict the behavior of all people all of the time, although it may be quite realistic to try to predict the behavior of some people some of the time. In their approach, Bem and Allen found that some people's behavior is consistent for some traits more than for other traits and that some people show greater consistency than do other people.

Table 12.6 briefly evaluates the success of the trait-based approach to understanding personality, based on the various criteria used for each of the personality approaches.

HOW DO INTERACTIONIST PSYCHOLOGISTS VIEW PERSONALITY?

Walter Mischel (1968) criticized trait theories of personality by pointing out that even when people show particular traits on various tests of personality they typically show little consistency of behavior across different situations. That is, their traits do not strongly predict their behavior across situations. For example, a person might be extroverted (outward oriented) when he or she is with close friends, but introverted (inward oriented) when he or she is with strangers. In fact, the correlations between traits and any meaningful kind of behavior are low, around 0.30 (with 1.0 a perfect positive correlation and 0 indicating no relationship). Mischel (1968; Mischel & Peake, 1983) has suggested that personality theorists should concentrate on the relations between situations and behavior, rather than on hypothetically stable traits.

Other researchers (Funder & Ozer, 1983) have tested Mischel's claim that situations more strongly influence behavior than do personality traits. Instead of correlating personality traits across situations, they have correlated situations across behaviors. How well could they predict behavior, based on differences in situations rather than on differences in traits? For example, a child might behave respectfully toward a parent when other people are around, but act disrespectfully when the other people are absent. In such a case, the situation is largely determinative of the child's behavior. The correlation for predicting behavior based on situations was rarely over 0.30, roughly the same as the correlation Mischel found when predicting behavior based on traits. These researchers have argued, therefore, that situations are no better or worse than traits as a basis for predicting behavior.

central trait • a characteristic that stands out in its importance for the personality and behavior of an individual

secondary trait • a personality characteristic that has some influence on behavior but that is not very important to the personality and behavior of the individual

12.1

HOW WELL DOES YOUR PERSONALITY MATCH YOUR POSSIBLE CHOICE OF A CAREER?

Based on your own personality traits, to which kinds of careers would you be better suited? Here are some questions you might want to ask yourself:

1. Would you prefer a career in which you worked mostly alone (e.g., a laboratory researcher or a painter) or would you prefer to work directly with other people most of the time (e.g., a social worker or a teacher)?

2. Would you prefer to compete with others (e.g., a salesperson or a tennis player), to collaborate with others (e.g., a member of a research-and-development team or a dancing ensemble), or to work independently (e.g., a cabinetmaker or a sculptor)?

3. Would you prefer (a) to be responsible for organizing a project and giving orders to others regarding how they should carry out their work (e.g., a manager or a project leader); (b) to be responsible for carrying out specific instructions given to you by others (e.g., a bookkeeper or a baseball player); or (c) to be responsible for organizing and carrying out your own work, given only a deadline and rough guidelines for how to do your work (e.g., a writer or a teacher)?

Because neither situations nor a person's traits seem fully to explain people's actions, many psychologists have come to embrace an approach that considers both: Specifically, the **interactionist approach** emphasizes the interaction between the person and the situation. Actually, Rotter's theory, Bandura's theory, Thomas and Chess's theory, and some other theorists' approaches can be viewed as broadly interactionist. Even Mischel now views personality from an interactionist perspective.

The basic idea is simple: The correlations among traits or between traits and behaviors depend on the kinds of situations the person encounters. For example, to relate extroversion to happiness, the interactionist might suggest that extroverts will be happy if they are involved in frequent interactions with other people. However, extroverts will be unhappy if left to themselves most of the time.

Thus, the interactionist focuses on the interaction between the person and the situation (Bowers, 1973; Endler & Magnusson, 1976), not just on personality traits considered in isolation or on situations alone. In other words, the interactionist approach combines the trait-based approach with the behavioral approach. Interactionists believe we can predict people's behavior only if we consider both their personalities and the kinds of situations in which their behavior arises.

In evaluating each of the major theories of personality, we have considered how each theory may contribute to the development of personality assessments and to the development of psychotherapy techniques. In the next section of this chapter, we consider some of the personality assessments that have emerged from personality theory. In addition, it may be

interactionist approach • a view of personality that emphasizes the interaction between the person and the situation

4. Would you prefer to set your own standards for your performance, or would you prefer to have other persons give you clear and specific guidelines regarding what is expected of you?

5. Would you prefer to work in a job in which there were many deadlines and time pressures (e.g., a daily newspaper reporter, an entertainer, or a firefighter), a job in which there were few or no deadlines or time pressures (e.g., a store clerk or a construction worker), or a job in which there were occasional deadlines and some time pressures, but in which you had some leeway for meeting the job's demands (e.g., a construction supervisor or a store manager)?

6. What are some of the personality characteristics that you would consider important in your coworkers? What are some of the personality characteristics that you would consider to be intolerable in your coworkers?

7. How important is it to you to feel that your work is making an important contribution to individual people's lives? How important is it to you to feel that your work is making an important contribution to society in general?

Compare your answers to the preceding questions with your evaluation of your own personality. What aspects of your personality seem important for the way in which you answered the preceding questions? What other aspects of your personality, not addressed by the preceding questions, are important to your decisions regarding your choice of a career?

useful to think about how an interactionist approach to personality may be applied to the choices we make. For instance, in choosing our careers, we may wish to consider a match between our personality characteristics and the situations in which we potentially may find ourselves (see Putting It to Use 12.1).

HOW DO PSYCHOLOGISTS ASSESS PERSONALITY?

Both the psychodynamic approach to personality and the trait-based approach have led researchers to develop tests designed to measure important aspects of personality. Next, we consider some of the tests designed by psychologists using each approach.

Assessments Based on Psychodynamic Theories: Projective Personality Tests

Many assessment techniques based on the psychodynamic approach have tried to probe the unconscious. These tests are termed **projective personality tests** because they encourage individuals to express, through the test stimuli, their unconscious or preconscious personality characteristics and conflicts. Several projective tests based on psychodynamic theory have been used for assessing personality. The most well-known and widely used

projective personality test • a method of personality assessment based on the psychodynamic approach, which attempts to reach people's unconscious or preconscious personality characteristics and conflicts through their imaginative (primary-process) responses to test items

of these tests are the *Rorschach Inkblot Test* and the *Thematic Appercep-tion Test*. Like most other projective tests, both of these tests are adminis-tered in a one-to-one situation, in which a psychologist interviews and observes the responses of one test-taker at a time.

The *Rorschach Inkblot Test*

In 1921, Hermann Rorschach devised the *Rorschach Inkblot Test*, which is still widely used today. Rorschach developed his test as a way of diag-nosing psychopathology (psychological disorders). Today, however, it is used more commonly for assessing personality across a broad spectrum of individuals. Clinicians who use the test believe that it helps them to ex-plore patients' needs, conflicts, and desires (Exner, 1985; D. Rapaport, Gill, & Schafer, 1968).

The test consists of 10 symmetrical inkblot designs, each printed on a separate card. Five of the blots are in black, white, and shades of gray, and the other five are in color. (For an example of an inkblot similar to those in the Rorschach test, see Figure 12.2.) Rorschach intentionally created each of the inkblots so that they would not look like anything in particular. However, when people look at the inkblots, they tend to see things in them, projecting their personalities into the test stimuli. For example, the perception of movement in a design is sometimes seen as a sign of cogni-tive complexity and intelligence. The examiner carefully records how the examinee describes each blot. Typically, each examinee describes several different things in each of the blots. Although many different scoring sys-tems have been devised for the Rorschach, the most widely used scoring

FIGURE 12.2
Rorschach Inkblot Test
One way of scoring this projective test is to consider the following four factors: location—the place on the blot where the test-taker sees the image; determinants—the examinee's use of three principal characteristics in responding to the blot: form (F), human movement (M), and color (C); content of the descriptions—such subject matter as humans, animals, geography, sex objects or acts, and so on; and popularity—whether the individual gives responses that are unusual or otherwise outside the mainstream of responses. This inkblot is like those on the test, but it is not actually found on the test.

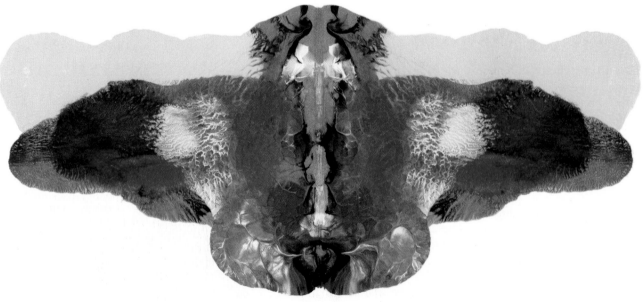

system at present is John Exner's (1974, 1978, 1985; Viglione & Exner, 1983) "Comprehensive System," which considers *the location, determinants, content,* and *popularity* of the responses (see Figure 12.2).

The *Thematic Apperception Test*

Another widely used psychodynamic assessment tool is the *Thematic Apperception Test (TAT;* Morgan & Murray, 1935; Murray, 1943b). In administering the TAT, the examiner presents the test-taker with a series of ambiguous but realistic pictures. (That is, the pictures show realistic drawings of people and objects in situations that could be interpreted in a variety of ways; see Figure 12.3.) Test-takers are expected to project their own personalities into these pictures by describing what has led up to the scene in the picture, what is happening in the picture, and what will happen. For example, a male test-taker's seeing an older man and a younger man in a picture as representing a father and son in conflict might be revealing some of his own feelings of conflict toward his father. *Apperception* refers to this projection of personal information into the stimulus that is perceived.

The TAT may further be scored for different kinds of needs and motivations (see chapter 11), such as achievement motivation (J. W. Atkinson, 1958; McClelland et al., 1953) and power motivation (Veroff, 1957; Winter, 1973). The test has also been used for assessing the use of defense mechanisms. For example, Abigail Stewart (1982; Stewart & Healy, 1985) has used the TAT to find out how different defense mechanisms apply to various psychosexual stages of development. She has classified test-takers as showing characteristics of each of the psychosexual stages, based on four aspects of each story: attitude toward authority, relations with other people, feelings, and orientation to action (Stewart, Sokol, Healy, & Chester, 1986).

Assessing Psychodynamic Tests

Some clinicians (e.g., Spangler, 1992; Stewart, 1982; Stewart & Healy 1989) take projective tests, such as the *Rorschach* and the *TAT,* very seriously. Others (e.g., Mischel, 1986) believe that these tests may lead clinicians to faulty decisions. Mischel (1977, 1986) has argued that clinicians interpret projective tests based on what the clinicians would like to see in the test data, not on what is actually implied by the test data. Mischel also has argued that empirical support for the validity of these tests is quite weak. Some research has supported his view (see, e.g., Chapman & Chapman, 1969; Dawes, 1994). The subjective nature of the scoring for projective tests has led many psychologists to depend on what are termed *objective personality tests.*

Assessments Based on Trait Theories: Objective Tests

The trait-based approach has also led to the development of various personality tests. In order to grasp the wide range of traits expressed in normal and abnormal personalities, psychologists use so-called **objective personality tests,** which are administered to a large number of individuals, using standardized and uniform procedures for scoring. Most objective

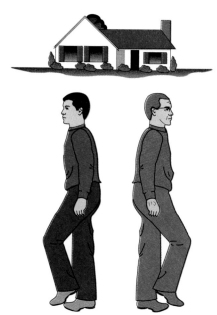

FIGURE 12.3
Thematic Apperception Test (TAT)
Henry Murray (1943b, 1943c) suggested that the examiner must consider six things when scoring the TAT: (a) the hero of the story; (b) the hero's motives, actions, and feelings; (c) the forces in the hero's environment that act on the hero; (d) the outcomes of the story; (e) the types of environmental stimuli that affect the people in the story; and (f) the interests and sentiments that appear in the story.

objective personality test • a method of personality assessment founded on the trait approach, which is standardized and normed based on a large number of individuals, thereby providing scores that allow for easy comparisons across individuals

personality tests are paper-and-pencil tests that psychologists can give to more than one test-taker at one time.

The *Minnesota Multiphasic Personality Inventory*

The most widely used of the objective tests for assessing normal and abnormal personalities is the *Minnesota Multiphasic Personality Inventory* (*MMPI;* Hathaway & McKinley, 1943; the more recent version of the scale is MMPI-2; see also Butcher, Dahlstrom, Graham, Tellegen, & Kaemmer, 1989). The MMPI and the MMPI-2 each consist of 550 statements covering a wide range of topics. Subjects respond to each of the statements as either *true* or *false* (Hathaway & McKinley, 1951, p. 28). For instance, a test-taker might be asked to respond to these statements:

I often feel as if things are not real.	T	F
Someone has it in for me.	T	F

Would you answer true or false to statements such as these? On an actual test, your responses would be compared to the answers of many other people, to come up with a set of scores indicating various characteristics of your personality, as measured at the time of the test.

The MMPI has several strengths: First, the test is objectively scored, which avoids the problems of subjective scoring and interpretation associated with projective tests. Second, the scale has been widely used, so clinicians can use a wealth of data for interpreting and comparing scores. The test also can be used for assessing temporary, situation-related characteristics, as well as for assessing more enduring, stable ones. Third, the test offers several ways for clinicians to assess the believability (validity) of the results. Fourth, the scale covers a wide range of normal and abnormal behaviors and beliefs.

The MMPI also has some drawbacks. The primary drawback is that it is hard to know how to interpret responses to the MMPI. Test-takers may find it hard simply to respond "true" or "false" to items, feeling that such responses are incomplete. People may also try to second-guess the test designers and to answer in ways that will give particular impressions. Also, the MMPI measures only people's impressions of what they are like or of what they do with their time. These responses do not necessarily correspond to what they really are like or to what they actually do. Another criticism has been that both the MMPI and the MMPI-2 (although less so) were standardized using population samples that overrepresented Americans of European ancestry (Butcher & Williams, 1992; Graham, 1990). Hence, the tests may not adequately indicate the normal range of personality characteristics of individuals outside the United States or even of ethnic minorities within the United States (R. L. Greene, 1987; Lonner, 1990). Further and more detailed criticisms are described in Helmes and Reddon (1993).

The MMPI-2 includes so-called validity scales that are supposed to detect test-takers who falsify their answers, whether to look "good" or "bad." However, there is evidence that various kinds of tests to detect honesty in test-taking overlabel people as dishonest (Reike & Guestello, 1990; Camara & Schneider, 1994). A danger of such scales, therefore, is that people may fail to be hired or even may be fired because they are falsely labeled as dishonest. Other kinds of false alarms can arise as well. Cronbach (1990) argued that the MMPI-2 labels too many people as emotionally disturbed. It is therefore especially important to use multiple methods in making diagnoses.

The *Sixteen Personality-Factor Questionnaire*

Many of the drawbacks of the MMPI also apply to other objective tests of personality. Raymond Cattell and his colleagues have devised a test that measures 16 of the personality factors Cattell identified: the *Sixteen Personality-Factor Questionnaire* (16PF; Cattell, 1982; Cattell, Eber, & Tatsuoka, 1970). This paper-and-pencil test asks people whether particular attributes characterize them and whether they do particular things. Separate scores are obtained for each of the 16 personality factors. Based on those simple trait scores, individual scores can be combined, using mathematical formulas, in order to obtain measures of what Cattell considers to be more complex traits, such as anxiety and independence. For example, the measure of anxiety is a combination of scores on six factors. According to Cattell, people who are anxious are easily upset, timid (shy), suspicious, apprehensive (worried), low in personal control, and tense.

Like the MMPI, Cattell's 16PF has been used extensively in other cultures. Cattell firmly believed in the universality of his test. Others, however, have found problems with the cross-cultural use of his test. For instance, many of the items may not be appropriate for other societies even if the items are translated carefully (Brislin, 1986; Lonner, 1990). In addition to the difficulty of translating some words specific to Western culture, the difficulty of ensuring cultural relevance seems to be overwhelming in many cultural contexts.

Evaluation of Personality Tests

The critiques of psychodynamic assessments and of trait-based assessments suggest that the validity of any single test is likely to be limited. When similar results are obtained with multiple kinds of tests, however, we may be more confident in our conclusions. Scientific conclusions must be based on converging sources of information, whether that information is about individuals, groups, or humanity as a whole.

The Roles of Biology and Culture in Personality

Both biology and culture play important roles in personality. Twin studies comparing identical twins raised apart, as well as identical versus fraternal twins, have shown that about half of the individual-differences variation in many personality traits, as well as in intelligence, is inherited (Bouchard, 1997; Bouchard, Lykken, McGue, Segal, & Tellegen, 1990; Loehlin, 1992b; Loehlin, Horn, & Willerman, 1997; Pederson, Plomin, McClearn, & Friberg, 1988; Tellegen, Lykken, Bouchard, Wilcox, & Rich, 1988). However, heritability may differ somewhat as a function of the particular trait, as well as of the population in which it is studied.

Even certain aspects of attitudes, such as religious attitudes, and of behavior, such as watching television in childhood and, in adulthood, divorce, show substantial heritability (Waller, Kojetin, Bouchard, Lykken, & Tellegen, 1990). How could television-watching behavior be heritable, when historically, the overwhelming majority of societies did not even have television? How could divorce be heritable, when today it is not even permitted in many societies? Clearly, it is not the behavior itself that is inherited, but rather the personal predispositions that can lead to that behavior. For example, people who divorce may have a greater predisposition to dissatisfaction or to conflict than do those who do not.

TABLE 12.7
Major Paradigms of Personality Theory

Paradigm	Psychodynamic	Humanistic
Major theorists	Freud, Adler, Jung, Erikson, Horney	Rogers, Maslow
Basis for personality	Conflicting sources of psychic energy	The distinctive human ability to act purposefully and to shape our own destiny by being future oriented
Key features of personality theory	(a) Developmental changes across the life span, with early childhood experiences profoundly influencing adult personality (b) Deterministic view of personality as being largely governed by forces over which the individual has little control (c) Importance of unconscious processes in shaping personality and behavior	*Nondeterministic* view of personality as being subject to the *conscious* control of the individual
Basis for theory development	Case studies of individuals seeking help for psychological problems	Humanistic philosophy, personal experiences, and clinical practice
Key strengths	Importance and influence, comprehensiveness, usefulness to applications	Parsimony
Key weaknesses	Testability	Testability

Interestingly, the variation in traits that is environmental is mostly within rather than between families (Dunn & Plomin, 1990; Harris, 1998; Plomin, 1997). In other words, more important than differences between families in the way children are treated are differences within families in, say, the way earlier- and later-born children are treated or in the friendships they form. We still have much to learn, however, as to just what these differences are.

Culture also is important in personality. On the one hand, the "Big Five" personality traits mentioned earlier (extroversion, agreeableness, conscientiousness, neuroticism, and openness to experience) appear in a number of different cultures, such as the United States, Canada, Finland, Poland, and Germany (Costa & Widiger, 1993; Paunonen, Jackson, Trzebinski, & Fosterline, 1992). On the other hand, the whole notion of a set of personality traits, such as the "Big Five," that reflects an individual outside a context may be a culturally bound notion (see Triandis, 1997). Particular traits, such as self-esteem, that may seem important in a Western society that values the self may seem less important or even self-indulgent in a collectivistic culture that emphasizes the role of the individual as part of a larger group (Markus & Kitayama, 1991). Thus, we need

Cognitive–Behavioral	Trait	Interactionist
Skinner, Rotter, Bandura	Cattel, Eysenck, Allport	Mischel, Bem and Allen
The interactions among thoughts, the environment, and behavior	Stable sources of individual differences that characterize an individual, based on an interaction of nature and nurture	Interaction between the person and the situation
(a) How individuals think about and give meaning to stimuli and events in their environment, as well as to their own behavior (b) People need to feel that they are competent in controlling their environment	(a) *Nomothetic* theorists hold that all people have the same set of traits, but individuals differ in the degree to which they manifest each trait (b) *Idiographic* theorists hold that each individual has a different set of traits that are fundamental to her or his personality	Behavior is determined by interactions between situational factors and personality factors
Experimental findings, as well as the development and use of personality tests	(a) *Nomothetic theories.* Factor analysis or comprehensive assessments of individuals (b) *Idiographic theories.* Comprehensive assessments of individuals, emphasizing individual differences (e.g., through self-reports and naturalistic observations), bolstered by experimental findings	Combination of behavioral observations and psychometric tests
Importance and influence, testability, usefulness to applications	Importance and influence, testability, applications to assessment techniques	Comprehensiveness, accounting for both person and environment
Comprehensiveness	Applications to psychotherapy techniques	Vagueness

to be careful about overgeneralizing both individual personality traits and even the notion of personality traits itself.

Before we conclude this chapter, it may be useful to point to a summary of the major approaches of personality theory, shown in Table 12.7. This chapter has focused on the many aspects of personality as they apply to the normal range of behavior. The following chapter describes many of the ways that personality may be expressed that do not fall within the normal range of behavior.

The Solution to The Case of the Queasy Math Student

After reading chapter 12 of *Pathways to Psychology,* Meera realizes that her problem is not one of ability at all; nor is it one of effort. It is one of *self-efficacy.* Meera lacks confidence in her ability to do the work she needs to do. This lack of self-efficacy is in turn undermining her work.

Instead of tutoring, Meera decides to seek counseling to deal with her problem. She goes to the student counseling center, where she comes to realize that part of her problem is that she feels intimidated by students who are more willing than she to speak up in class and to show what they know. Meera realizes that her withdrawal from the class discussions has led her to withdraw from engaging psychologically with the course, which in turn has undermined her self-efficacy. Meera starts to become more actively involved in the class and finds her sense of self-efficacy improving. Eventually, she ends up with a good grade in the course, good enough for her to continue with her plans to be premed.

Summary

1. *Personality* encompasses those enduring dispositional characteristics of an individual that provide an integrated consistency to the person's behavior.

2. The various approaches to understanding personality can be evaluated in several ways: their importance to and influence on the field of psychology, their testability, their comprehensiveness in accounting for psychological phenomena, their parsimoniousness (simplicity), and their usefulness to applied fields.

How Do Psychodynamic Psychologists View Personality?   425

3. Freud's psychodynamic theory of personality emphasizes dynamic, biologically oriented processes; conflicting sources of psychic energy; and the influence of early development on people's adaptations to their environments.

4. Freud's theory underscored the role of the *unconscious* in the life of the mind. *Neo-Freudians* were more willing to consider conscious influences, as well.

5. Freud described three components of the mind: the *id* (which is largely instinctual and impulsive, and which seeks immediate satisfaction of sexual and aggressive wishes), the *ego* (which is rational and seeks to satisfy the id in ways that adapt effectively to the real world), and the *superego* (which is irrational and seeks to avoid the punishment associated with internalized moral rules). The id operates on the basis of the *pleasure principle,* the ego on the basis of the *reality principle,* and the superego on the basis of the *idealistic principle.*

6. Sigmund and Anna Freud described 10 main *defense mechanisms:* fixation, regression, denial, repression, projection, displacement, sublimation, reaction formation, rationalization, and identification, which they believed people use to protect themselves from unacceptable thoughts and impulses.

7. Freud's theory was largely based on his case studies of individual patients. Freud used dream analysis extensively with his patients, focusing on the latent content of dreams, rather than on their manifest content.

8. Neo-Freudians, such as Adler, Jung, Erikson, and Horney, originally based their theories on Freud's but later differed from Freud and developed their own psychodynamic theories. Most neo-Freudian theories are less deterministic than Freud's theory. The theories take into account the ego and the conscious mind more than did Freud's theory. They also give more consideration to continuing

development of the personality after childhood, as well as to the broader social context within which the individual's personality operates. In particular, Alfred Adler contributed the notion of the *inferiority complex;* Carl Jung, the notion of there being both a *personal unconscious* and a *collective unconscious;* Erik Erikson, the notion that the conscious workings of the ego, rather than the unconscious impulses of the id, dominate personality development across the life span; and Karen Horney, the importance of cultural rather than biological variables in personality, and the idea that basic anxiety leads people to move toward, against, or away from other people.

9. Psychodynamic theories have been criticized because they lack extensive empirical support.

How Do Humanistic Psychologists View Personality? 436

10. Humanistic theorists emphasize individual responsibility and the distinctive value of human experience.

11. Carl Rogers's person-centered approach to personality may be termed *self theory.* Rogers identified the *self-concept* (the aspects of the self that an individual perceives within her- or himself) and the *ideal self* (the aspects of the self that the person wishes to embrace) and emphasized the importance of achieving as close a match as possible between the two.

How Do Cognitive–Behavioral Psychologists View Personality? 438

12. Skinner and other behaviorists tried to explain personality in terms of behavioral responses to environmental contingencies, without considering internal (mental) events.

13. Rotter and Bandura have taken a cognitive–behavioral approach to explaining personality. Rotter has emphasized each person's perceived *internal locus of control* versus *external locus of control.* Bandura has emphasized the interaction of how we think and how we act in a given situation. To Bandura, perceived *self-efficacy* is a key aspect of personality.

14. Cognitive–behavioral theories are easy to test, so they have led to a wealth of empirical research and of clinical and assessment applications.

How Do Trait Theorists View Personality? 442

15. *Traits* are stable sources of individual differences that characterize a person. Both nature and nur-

ture influence these traits, and different theorists give differing emphasis to one or the other.

16. Some personality theories assert that people have essentially the same set of traits and that they differ only in terms of how much of each trait they have. That is, for each trait in the same set of traits, an individual may have more or less of the trait. Other theories state that people differ in terms of which traits they possess; that is, some people do not possess traits that others do.

17. Theories specifying universal traits include those of Raymond Cattell, who used factor analysis to find 23 *source traits;* of Hans Eysenck, who holds that the key personality traits are *extroversion, neuroticism,* and *psychoticism;* and of the *"Big Five" theory of personality,* which includes the traits of neuroticism, extroversion, openness, agreeableness, and conscientiousness.

18. Gordon Allport emphasized the role of *personal dispositions* unique to each individual rather than common traits. Some individuals have *cardinal traits,* which explain almost all the behavior of these individuals. In addition, all people have both *central traits* (highly important characteristics) and *secondary traits* (less important characteristics).

19. Walter Mischel criticized trait theories because they fail to consider situational factors affecting behavior. Others have pointed out that personality factors and situational factors each explain only some of behavioral variation. However, the influence of personality factors on behavior seems higher for some personality characteristics.

How Do Interactionist Psychologists View Personality? 447

20. Many contemporary theorists emphasize an *interactionist approach,* which underscores the interaction between the individual's personality traits and the given situation.

How Do Psychologists Assess Personality? 449

21. *Projective personality tests,* which encourage individuals to project their unconscious characteristics and conflicts in response to open-ended questions, are a product of the psychodynamic tradition.

22. *Objective personality tests* are usually paper-and-pencil tests, which have been standardized and normed for easy comparison of scores across many individuals. Such tests generally emphasize a trait-based approach to personality.

Choose the best answer to complete each sentence.

1. Temperament is best described as an individual's
   (a) personality characteristics that begin in adulthood.
   (b) mood, activity level, and disposition, an aspect of personality.
   (c) tendency to get irritable, frustrated, or angry.
   (d) moods that are dependent on situational factors.

2. The order in which Freud's psychosexual stages of development proceed is
   (a) oral, anal, phallic, latency, genital.
   (b) anal, oral, latency, phallic, genital.
   (c) anal, oral, genital, phallic, latency.
   (d) oral, anal, genital, latency, phallic.

3. Psychodynamic determinism refers to
   (a) behavior that is ruled by unconscious forces over which we have no control.
   (b) behavior that is conscious in origin.
   (c) id impulses that forever will remain unfulfilled.
   (d) the delimiting characteristic of the superego.

4. According to Jung, all archetypes are
   (a) held in the collective unconscious.
   (b) dark and forbidden instinctual urges.
   (c) those parts of the unconscious that are unique to each individual.
   (d) the manifest content of dreams.

5. Carl Rogers's self theory assumes that
   (a) humans are isolated individuals in an indifferent world.
   (b) a person's acceptance of her- or himself leads to a selfish view of the world and to egocentric behavior.
   (c) the self is the focal point from which reality is constructed.
   (d) most people see problems and difficulties only in terms of themselves, rather than by showing unconditional positive regard for others.

6. According to Julian Rotter's social-learning theory, a primary factor that differentiates individuals is in how they
   (a) devote the majority of their psychic energy.
   (b) cope with the numerous unconscious forces that act on their lives.
   (c) show their sociability.
   (d) view their locus of control.

7. The "Big Five" theory of personality includes all the following factors *except*
   (a) altruism.
   (b) neuroticism.
   (c) extroversion.
   (d) conscientiousness.

8. Interactionist approaches to personality assume that
   (a) most people tend to show their characteristic traits across various situations, but some people do not.
   (b) neither the situation nor the person's characteristics alone are the sole influence on behavior.
   (c) individuals show consistent behavioral patterns across situations.
   (d) situations ultimately determine how a given individual will act.

9. According to Erik Erikson, all of the following are core issues that must be confronted during the course of personality development *except*
   (a) guilt versus initiative.
   (b) trust versus mistrust.
   (c) happiness versus sadness.
   (d) identity versus role confusion.

10. In psychosexual development, according to Freud, latency refers to
    (a) the period during which the child explores both male and female sex roles.
    (b) a period when psychosexual development is very rapid and intense.
    (c) a period of dormant and repressed sexual desires.
    (d) the brief period before which the child's sexual orientation becomes solidified.

Answer each of the following questions by filling in the blank with an appropriate word or phrase.

11. Researchers who endorse a _____–_____ theory of personality are concerned with the relationships among people's thoughts, their actions, and their personality characteristics.

12. That part of a dream that deals with events in the dream as we experience them is referred to as the _____ content.

13. Psychodynamic theorists view the mind as organized at two basic levels: the _____ and the _____.

14. Personality attributes that are consistent in an individual are referred to as _____.

15. According to psychodynamic theory, the _____ mediates among the id, the superego, and the external world.

16. The defense mechanism of _____ is characterized by various forbidden thoughts and impulses being attributed to another person rather than to the self.

17. Alfred Adler believed that a primary motivator in our lives is our striving for _____.

18. Karen Horney has proposed that people experience _____ _____, a condition of isolation and helplessness brought about by a competitive world.

19. Psychodynamic assessment sometimes involves the use of _____ _____, which are designed to assess individuals' personality characteristics and conflicts via their responses to ambiguous test questions.

20. According to Eysenck's theory of personality, _____ refers to an individual's tendency to be solitary, lacking in feeling, and insensitive.

21. The _____ _____ _____ _____ is an objective test that is frequently used as a diagnostic tool to assess personality characteristics.

Answers

1. b, 2. a, 3. a, 4. a, 5. c, 6. d, 7. a, 8. b, 9. c, 10. c, 11. cognitive–behavioral, 12. manifest, 13. conscious, unconscious, 14. traits, 15. ego, 16. projection, 17. superiority, 18. basic anxiety, 19. projective tests, 20. psychoticism, 21. *Minnesota Multiphasic Personality Inventory*

Pathways to Understanding

1. Think about the various theories of personality proposed in this chapter. Which theory seems to you to be most reasonable; that is, which theory explains personality most effectively? Describe the strengths and the weaknesses of this theory, as you view them.

2. What steps can you take to ensure that someone you love (hypothetical or real) feels sure of your unconditional positive regard for her or him?

3. What do you consider to be the essential personality characteristics, based on yourself and on the people you know?

The Case of The Ups and Downs

Leah is having a great deal of difficulty understanding her friend Vonda. Ever since she has known her, Vonda has been susceptible to radical mood swings, which Vonda attributes to the ups and downs of life as both a single mom and a full-time college student. When she is up, she is really up and seems to feel like anything is possible for her. Leah loves to spend time with Vonda in her up moods, although she worries that Vonda may go overboard. Sometimes she has, spending lavishly on herself and her kids and obviously beyond her means. When she is in an up mood, Vonda will sometimes go into an exam without cracking open a book to study for the material because she is convinced that she can ace the exam without studying. She never does. In fact, Vonda usually bombs her exams when she is in one of her up moods; or something else goes wrong, such as her receiving a bill that she cannot pay because she has gone overboard in her spending. Soon thereafter, whatever the cause of the upset, Vonda seems to sink into an abyss. She gets very depressed and hardly seems to be able to function at all. She eats little and barely has the energy to take care of her kids or to get through her classes, much less anything else she needs to do. When Vonda is in one of her down moods, Leah tries to cheer her up, but it is far from easy. Eventually, Vonda pulls through and then the cycle just seems to repeat itself. Leah cares a great deal for Vonda but is puzzled about her radical mood swings.

What can Leah do to help Vonda? Think about this while you read chapter 13. What pathway can Leah follow that will help Vonda straighten out her life? Pay special attention to the various mood disorders that are described in the chapter.

CHAPTER 13

ABNORMAL PSYCHOLOGY

13

WHAT IS ABNORMAL BEHAVIOR?

Psychologists have defined abnormal behavior in many ways. To define abnormal behavior adequately, we need to consider several aspects of this concept. **Abnormal behavior** sometimes is viewed as (a) statistically *unusual* (i.e., it deviates from statistically normal, average behavior), (b) *nonadaptive* (i.e., it hampers the individual's ability to function effectively within her or his given environmental context), (c) *labeled as abnormal* by the surrounding society in which the individual is behaving, and (d) characterized by some degree of *perceptual, emotional,* or *cognitive distortion.* For example, someone who feels certain that intelligence agents from Lower Slobovia (a nonexistent country) are out to kill him would be showing abnormal behavior for all four reasons: The fear is (a) statistically unusual because few people share this belief; (b) nonadaptive because the individual is devoting considerable resources to saving himself from the Lower Slobovian agents; (c) labeled as abnormal because other people recognize that Lower Slobovian intelligence agents do not exist; and (d) characterized by a cognitive distortion—the assertion that Lower Slobovian agents exist and are out to kill the individual.

As you might expect, some kinds of abnormal behavior may not show all four aspects of the definition, but most do. In addition, it is important to emphasize that all normal people engage in certain behavior that may be considered abnormal in some respects. What distinguishes normal deviations from serious psychological disorder is the degree to which the behavior is unusual, nonadaptive, identified as abnormal, and indicative of distortion.

13.1

FINDING YOUR WAY

Stop for a moment to think about your own behavior. What is something you do that might be considered statistically unusual or perhaps even labeled as abnormal? For example, do you take unusual risks, such as bungee-jumping or skydiving? Do you do any other things that some people may consider unusual? Although you are aware of some unusual things you do, those things are probably not so unusual that others in your environment are alarmed by them. (For example, you probably do not regularly walk the streets, shouting gibberish or warning that the end of the world is near.)

What is something you do that is nonadaptive for you? For instance, do you sometimes postpone starting a term paper or studying for an exam, even though you know that it will be much harder to do a good job because of your procrastination? Do you occasionally eat or drink things that you know are not good for you? In all likelihood, your nonadaptive behavior does not pose a serious threat to your well-being or to the well-being of people around you. Even some seriously nonadaptive behavior (e.g., engaging in unprotected sexual intercourse with an acquaintance) falls well within the range of normal behavior and is not believed to indicate serious psychological disorder. On the other hand, if you regularly abuse alcohol, cocaine, or other psychoactive substances, or you frequently engage in criminal activity, your nonadaptive behavior may seriously threaten your well-being or that of others, and it indicates some degree of psychological disturbance.

What kinds of perceptual, emotional, or cognitive distortions have you experienced? For example, have you ever emotionally overreacted to a situation, becoming overly defensive in response to what someone else does or says? Have you ever shown any cognitive biases (e.g., the availability heuristic, by which you tend to overweigh evidence that immediately comes to mind, such as in thinking airplanes are more dangerous than automobiles because gruesome media accounts of plane crashes are more readily available than comparable accounts of automobile crashes)? Each of these distortions is shown by psychologically healthy individuals. On the other hand, if you hear voices telling you what to do when you are entirely alone or if you see nonexistent snakes and spiders crawling all over you, you are experiencing distortions that fall outside the range of normal behavior.

No one of the four aspects of abnormal behavior (i.e., being statistically unusual, nonadaptive, labeled as abnormal, or characterized by distortion) in itself would adequately define abnormal behavior. For one thing, whether a particular behavior is statistically unusual or maladaptive varies across differing cultural contexts. Behavior that is quite common and adaptive in one cultural context may be considered highly unusual and maladaptive in another. For example, within some subgroups in American culture, it is customary on Monday evenings in autumn for small groups of people to gather around a small box. The box makes sounds and displays moving photos of athletes prancing around a field and bumping into one another. Although the observers do not talk to one another, from time to time, some or all of the observers burst out with cheers or curses directed toward the box. This behavior toward an inanimate object would seem bizarrely abnormal to those unfamiliar with watching Monday Night Football. For some subgroups of American culture, however, such behavior is not only common but also adaptive in promoting social relationships among the observers. At the same time, those of us who are accustomed to wearing shoes in a Christian place of worship may find it strange to have to take our shoes off before entering a holy Muslim mosque in Jerusalem.

Similarly and even more extremely, American observers might be tempted to label as "crazy" the rituals of African Yoruba or Alaskan Eskimo *shamans* (religious leaders who use magical rituals to bring about therapeutic effects for individuals or for the cultural group as a whole). The Yorubas and the Eskimos, however, clearly consider the behavior of shamans to be highly adaptive and appropriate. They clearly distinguish between shamans and people whose irrational or bizarre behavior is considered abnormal and neither adaptive nor appropriate (Davison & Neale, 1994; Matsumoto, 1994, 1996).

Differences in everyday environmental contexts—the established patterns and norms of the society—clearly influence which kinds of behavior are labeled as abnormal. For example, political dissidents are often labeled as insane in countries governed by totalitarian rule. In Nazi-occupied lands, many heroic individuals who hid persecuted families were considered abnormal by those who became aware of the heroes' behavior.

Even the labels used by mainstream psychiatrists are sometimes subject to question. Once a person has been labeled as mentally ill, even the

abnormal behavior • the ways of thinking or acting that are unusual, that impair the ability to function effectively, that are identified as odd within the surrounding social context, or that involve some degree of distortion in thinking, feeling, or perceiving

person's normal behavior may be viewed as psychologically disturbed. For instance, once people have been hospitalized for mental illness, their behavior may be perceived as disturbed simply because observers of their behavior expect to see signs of psychological disturbance (Rosenhan, 1973; see Figure 13.1). The same behavior that would be perceived as perfectly normal outside a mental hospital may be seen as confirming a diagnosis of abnormality inside the hospital.

Even the last of the four characteristics of abnormal behavior—distortion in perception, emotion, and cognition—may be appropriate and even normal under some circumstances. In fact, Shelley Taylor and Jonathon Brown (1988) argue that some degree of perceptual, emotional, and cognitive distortion is good for our mental health. More specifically, assume that you and I are normal, mentally healthy, well-adjusted people. According to Taylor and Brown, one reason for our mental health is that we seem to misperceive reality, using self-serving biases that overinflate our positive evaluations of ourselves. We also tend to exaggerate our own importance and our ability to control our actions and even our environments. We tint our views of reality and of our future prospects to be far more optimistic than the objective reality would seem to justify. These self-serving distortions seem to enhance our sense of self-esteem, boost our ability to feel happy, and increase our ability to be involved in productive, creative work.

Whatever the characteristics of abnormal behavior, how can such behavior be explained? We consider this question in the next section.

FIGURE 13.1

What Happens When People Are Labeled as Mentally Ill?

In a highly provocative study, David Rosenhan and seven associates pretended to have symptoms of mental illness in order to be admitted as patients in various mental hospitals (Rosenhan, 1973). Once these impostors were admitted (i.e., identified as mentally ill) they stopped showing any symptoms of mental illness and behaved as they normally would. Surprisingly, even the normal behavior of these impostors frequently was taken as evidence of disturbance by members of the hospital staff. Apparently, once people have been labeled as mentally ill, even their normal behavior may be considered to indicate mental illness.

HOW HAVE PEOPLE EXPLAINED ABNORMAL BEHAVIOR?

Varied attempts have been made to understand abnormal behavior. These different pathways to understanding have in common their attempt to explain why some people's thinking, emotions, and behavior deviate from what society considers normal. But they take very different approaches in how they accomplish this end. To many of us today, demonological explanations seem the strangest.

Demonological Explanations

Psychologists seek not only to describe abnormal behavior but also to explain abnormal behavior. Today we try to understand abnormal behavior through rational means and empirical observations. It was not always so. In ancient times, people considered abnormal behavior to be an aspect of *demonology*. They believed that people who showed abnormal behavior were possessed by a supernatural force, often in the form of an evil demon, such as the devil. For example, during the Middle Ages, many Europeans believed that demons caused abnormal behavior. Both women and men who acted oddly often were considered witches and were tortured cruelly in order to rid them of evil spirits. More often than not, they were killed as a result. By the time of the Renaissance, mentally ill Europeans were hospitalized rather than executed. However, their treatment was still far from humane or therapeutic, and many people continued to consider the mentally ill to be witches.

In the past, people saw demons that caused psychological disorders as largely external, subject to extrication via exorcism. Today, we see demons as largely internal, requiring psychological treatment.

Clinical Explanations

Once we rule out demonic explanations of abnormal behavior, other explanations are needed. Modern explanations of abnormal behavior generally have emerged from clinical work. Clinical work involves the treatment of clients (often called "patients" in medical settings, such as clinics or hospitals); *clinicians* are people who treat clients. Clinicians who study abnormal behavior are generally either *psychologists* (who have postgraduate training in clinical psychology, a field of psychology) or *psychiatrists* (who have medical degrees, with specialized training in psychiatry, a field of medicine).

In chapter 12, on personality, we considered psychodynamic, humanistic, behavioral, and cognitive approaches to understanding normal behavior and personality. Here, we briefly review those approaches, considering how they apply specifically to abnormal behavior. In addition, we consider a psychophysiological approach to understanding abnormal behavior, based on how the physiology of the brain (and the endocrine system) affects the functioning of the mind. We also consider a cultural approach, based on the contextualist notion that a person's culture plays a key role in how the person's abnormal behavior may be interpreted and understood. Finally, we suggest an eclectic perspective, which integrates some of the ideas from other approaches.

Psychodynamic Explanations

According to the *psychodynamic perspective,* abnormal behavior results from intrapsychic conflict, that is, conflict within the psyche or mind of the individual. A great deal of this conflict is unconscious, but it nonetheless affects much of what we feel, think, say, and do. For one thing, the ego is constantly battling the id and the superego. The id is governed by the pleasure principle, the ego by the reality principle, and the superego by the idealistic principle, so personality and behavior depend on which psychic force dominates. A person in whom the id dominates will be relatively unrestrained, uninhibited, and perhaps impulsive. A person in whom the ego is stronger will be more restrained, more reality oriented, and more in touch with rational thought. A person dominated by the superego almost will be paralyzed by rules against any behavior that might be considered morally questionable in any way. For example, a person who does pretty much whatever he wants, regardless of societal expectations and the trouble he may land himself in, may be seen as dominated by the id. A person who does what she believes is necessary to achieve school or work success may be seen as dominated by the ego. A person who does whatever he believes his parents require of him, even as an adult, may be seen as dominated by the superego. According to psychodynamic psychologists, powerful intrapsychic conflict among the id, the superego, and the real world may lead to abnormal behavior. For example, a person may become extremely anxious about sexual relations when the desire of the id to have such relations conflicts with simultaneous warnings of a superego. These warnings, developed during childhood, hold such relations to be immoral or sinful. Humanistic psychologists, however, see abnormal behavior quite differently.

Humanistic Explanations

According to the *humanistic approach* to abnormal behavior, psychological problems arise when people do not accept themselves as they are.

People may be overly sensitive to other people's judgments or they may not accept their own nature. The key problem is low self-regard, which leads people to be overly critical of themselves. According to humanists, low self-regard is more likely when people have not received sufficient unconditional positive regard from parents or other significant persons. Low self-regard, according to humanists, is quite common, so that it is "abnormal" not in the sense of being statistically unusual but rather in the sense of being maladaptive to people's adjustment to the environment.

Behavioral Explanations

According to the *behavioral perspective* on abnormal behavior, people show abnormal behavior as a result of classical or operant conditioning, or perhaps social learning. According to this view, psychological disorders arise when a person acquires a set of responses that is involuntary and maladaptive. For example, through classical conditioning, an exaggerated fear of something that normally would not stimulate fear might result if it were accidentally paired, perhaps repeatedly, with a fear-provoking stimulus. In my own case, my being trapped in a self-service elevator as a child led, for many years of my childhood, to my being afraid of self-service elevators. Through operant conditioning, individuals may be reinforced for maladaptive behavior, thereby increasing the likelihood that the behavior will be repeated. Similarly, individuals may be punished for adaptive behavior, thereby decreasing the likelihood that such behavior will occur again. Through social learning, people who observe others (e.g., parents) engaging in abnormal behavior then may engage in such behavior themselves. This perspective is often combined with a cognitive perspective, considered next.

Cognitive Explanations

According to the *cognitive perspective,* abnormal behavior is the result of distorted thinking. The distortions may be in the processes of thinking, the contents of thinking, or both. For example, depressed persons may minimize their own accomplishments or they may believe that no matter what they do, they will fail. People who have an extreme fear of snakes may believe irrationally that all kinds of snakes seriously can harm them. In each case, the person engages in distorted or erroneous thinking. When distorted thoughts are repeated enough to become routine, they may become *automatic thoughts* that lead the individual to feel anxious, depressed, or otherwise disordered much of the time. Psychologists who believe in psychophysiological explanations, considered next, believe that distorted thoughts have a biological basis.

Psychophysiological Explanations

According to the *psychophysiological perspective,* abnormal behavior is due to underlying physiological abnormalities in the nervous system, particularly in the brain, or to abnormalities in the endocrine (hormone) system. Often, these physiological problems involve abnormalities in the structure or tissues of the brain or in neuronal transmission (see chapter 2). For example, brain tumors or injuries may lead to abnormal behavior, such as very high levels of aggression. Similarly, abnormal behavior may result from too much or too little of a transmitter substance or hormone.

But many psychologists believe that biology can provide only a partial explanation of abnormal behavior. Some of these psychologists look to cultural explanations of such behavior.

Cultural Explanations

Whereas physiological psychologists emphasize the importance of biology as a basis for human behavior, cultural psychologists highlight the role of cultural context in explaining human behavior. Cultural psychologists do not claim that all of abnormal behavior arises because of a person's culture. Nonetheless, cultural psychologists do suggest that there are cultural distinctions in what is viewed as abnormal behavior (Matsumoto, 1994, 1996).

What may be viewed as normal behavior within one culture (e.g., Christians who regularly eat beef) may be considered abnormal behavior in another (e.g., Hindus who consider cattle to be sacred). Also, the same basic kind of abnormal behavior may be expressed differently in different cultures. For example, the particular expressions of depression or anxiety may differ across different cultures. Whereas anxious or depressed people in one culture may show many bodily symptoms of anxiety or depression, such as tremors or weight loss, people in another culture may express these disorders in other ways (e.g., by voicing deep fears or extreme feelings of worthlessness; Matsumoto, 1996). Some disorders even seem to be distinctive to a particular culture: *Anorexia nervosa* (a life-threatening eating disorder in which a person starves her- or himself because of a distorted perception that she or he is overweight) is distressingly common in the United States, but it is virtually unknown in many African and Asian countries (Swartz, 1985).

Eclectic Explanations

The preceding explanations of abnormal behavior are based on the view that a single approach can explain the entire range of abnormal human behavior. In my view, no single explanation seems best for explaining all abnormal behavior. Instead, different approaches address different aspects of psychological disorders. Each approach may offer insights not available from other perspectives.

Perhaps psychodynamic psychologists are correct in suggesting that many of the reasons for abnormal behavior lie outside the conscious awareness of the disordered individual. As humanists suggest, some people may be depressed, anxious, or otherwise psychologically troubled because they feel little self-regard and they focus on their failures and their weaknesses more than on their successes and their strengths. Behaviorally oriented theorists may be correct in noting that some people show abnormal behavior in response to unfortunate systems of environmental reinforcement or punishment; other people may develop inappropriate or exaggerated emotional and physiological reactions as a result of classical conditioning. In addition, as cognitive psychologists have suggested, distortions in thinking may contribute to abnormal behavior. Particular physiological disorders or malfunctions also may lead to disordered or maladaptive behavior, and this behavior may be interpreted differently, depending on the cultural context of the disordered individual. Although many psychologists might disagree with some of these approaches to understanding abnormal behavior, most psychologists would accept some of the insights offered by more than one of these approaches.

Many psychologists now believe that the most effective way to explain abnormal behavior considers multiple perspectives. One way of integrating these diverse perspectives may be considered an eclectic approach. From an *eclectic approach,* abnormal behavior probably arises as the result of an interaction of an individual's physiological predisposition, particular environmental events and situations within a given cultural context, distorted thought processes, and inappropriate emotional responses.

HOW DO CLINICIANS DIAGNOSE ABNORMAL BEHAVIOR?

Although clinicians often disagree about how to *explain* abnormal behavior, by the middle of the 20th century, clinicians did begin to reach some formal agreement regarding how to *diagnose* psychological disorders. In 1952, the American Psychiatric Association published its *Diagnostic and Statistical Manual (DSM).* The DSM has been revised several times, and the current (1994) version is known as the *DSM-IV (fourth edition).* The successive revisions of the DSM reflect changes in professionals' views of what constitutes abnormal behavior. Diagnoses can come and go. For example, homosexuality once was viewed as an abnormality, whereas now it is viewed as abnormal only if the individual who is homosexual in orientation feels uncomfortable with this orientation.

The DSM is descriptive and **atheoretical,** not based on any particular theoretical approach to explaining a given disorder. The DSM lists the symptoms necessary for making a diagnosis in each category, without trying to specify the causes of the disorder. Thus, the classification system is based wholly on observable symptoms, making it usable by psychologists and psychiatrists from a wide variety of theoretical orientations. It enables therapists to make diagnoses by specifying not only the various disorders but also by specifying in detail the symptoms of each disorder and how many symptoms and what kinds of symptoms are required to make the diagnosis. No other classification scheme currently available permits equally complete and accurate diagnosis of as wide-ranging a set of syndromes of abnormal behavior as does the DSM.

There are actually five separate dimensions along which individuals are evaluated by DSM-IV. The particular disorders addressed by them will be discussed throughout this chapter. *Axis I* addresses clinical syndromes and contains the major disorders to be discussed, such as schizophrenia and anxiety disorders. *Axis II* addresses personality disorders, such as avoidant and dependent personalities. *Axis III* addresses physical disorders and conditions. Although such disorders can be of the brain, they also can be of any other kind as well, such as asthma, diabetes, heart problems, or physical handicaps. Physical disorders are included because they may interact with or lead to psychological disorders. *Axis IV* addresses the severity of psychosocial stressors in the environment. The diagnostician uses the information from the other axes and from the patient's existing situation and history to determine the level of psychological stress that the patient is experiencing. *Axis V* represents a global assessment of the person's level of functioning. A code of 90 represents minimal danger and a code of 1 represents maximal danger.

The successive editions of the DSM illustrate changes in psychological and psychiatric conceptions of what constitutes a disorder. For example, "multiple personality disorder" came to be viewed as a separate disorder

atheoretical • having no particular theoretical orientation

In his painting, The Scream, *Edvard Munch captured the terror often felt by people with anxiety disorders.*

only relatively recently. Later, its name was changed to "dissociative identity disorder." Today, many psychologists doubt whether it even exists at all, as discussed later in the chapter.

Any diagnostic system, including DSM-IV, is potentially problematic. First, because the system is atheoretical, it gives us no real insight into the causes of the abnormal behavior. A second problem is that DSM-IV does not adequately consider ethnic and cultural differences among patients (S. M. Turner & Hersen, 1985). What one culture considers abnormal behavior another may not. Third, although DSM-IV allows "clinicians to reach the same diagnosis in a remarkably high proportion of cases" (Sartorius, Kaebler, Cooper, Roper et al., 1993b, p. xvi), agreement among clinicians certainly is not perfect. That is, using the DSM-IV, clinicians might not always agree regarding diagnoses. A fourth problem is how to match particular behavior to the descriptive categories. A diagnostician needs to match observed behavior to the symptoms expressed in DSM-IV and then to match those symptoms to a diagnosis.

It is impossible to specify every possible type of behavior, so clinicians must use their own judgment when using any classification system. DSM-IV gives guidelines, but ultimately, the clinician's judgment is key in making the diagnosis. One way that clinicians can improve the effectiveness of their judgment is to use various forms of assessment (see chapter 12). When various sources of information are used, clinicians can integrate and interpret the information, based on their professional expertise. These interpretations eventually may give rise to a diagnosis of a disorder.

Next, we discuss some of the kinds of disorders diagnosed by clinicians. The disorders are described by type under several general classifications, such as anxiety disorders and mood disorders.

WHAT ARE ANXIETY DISORDERS?

Anxiety disorders center on the individual's feelings of **anxiety**—tension, nervousness, distress, or uncomfortable arousal. Psychologists often distinguish between *fear,* which is focused on a specific object or event, and *anxiety,* which is vague and is not directed toward any specific object or event. DSM-IV divides anxiety disorders into five main categories.

1. *Phobias.* A kind of anxiety disorder characterized by an exaggerated, persistent, irrational, and disruptive fear of a particular object, a particular event, or a particular setting, or a fear of a general kind of object, event, or setting

2. *Panic disorder.* A kind of anxiety disorder characterized by brief (usually lasting only a few minutes), abrupt, and unprovoked but recurrent episodes during which a person experiences intense and uncontrollable anxiety

3. *Generalized anxiety disorder.* A kind of anxiety disorder characterized by general, persistent, constant, and often debilitating high levels of anxiety, which are accompanied by psychophysiological symptoms that can last any length of time

4. *Stress disorders,* including *posttraumatic stress disorder.* A stress disorder characterized by the intrusive psychological reenactment of a past traumatic event, such as recurring nightmares or repeated wakeful resurfacing of painful memories of the event while an individual is consciously engaged in unrelated activities; and *acute*

anxiety disorder • a psychological disorder involving the presence of anxiety that is so intense or so frequently present that it causes difficulty or distress for the individual

anxiety • a generalized feeling of dread or apprehension that is not focused on or directed toward any particular object or event

stress disorder, which is a brief mental illness lasting fewer than 4 months that arises in response to a traumatic event and is characterized by perceptual distortions, memory disturbances, or physical or social detachment

5. *Obsessive–compulsive disorder.* A disorder characterized by unwanted, persistent thoughts and irresistible impulses to perform a ritual to relieve those thoughts

These disorders are described in Table 13.1. Roughly 15% of the U.S. population suffer from an anxiety disorder at some time during their lives (Robins, Helzer, Weissman, Orvaschel, Gruenberg, Burke, & Reiger, 1984). All five disorders share several common symptoms that characterize them as anxiety disorders.

TABLE 13.1
Anxiety Disorders

Disorder	Description
Phobia	Persistent, irrational, and disruptive fear of a specific object, activity, or type of situation; a substantially greater fear than seems justified, or a fear that has no basis in reality
Simple phobia	Irrational fear of an object in a situation other than one related to agoraphobia or social phobia
Specific phobia	Extreme fear of being criticized by others, which leads to the avoidance of groups of people
Agoraphobia	Fear of open spaces or of being in public places from which it might be difficult to escape in the event of an anxiety attack; generally involves a fear of losing control or of some terrible, unspecified thing happening outside of the house
*Panic disorder**	Brief (usually lasting only a few minutes), sudden, and unprovoked but recurrent episodes during which a person experiences intense and uncontrollable anxiety and shows psychophysiological symptoms, such as difficulty in breathing, heart palpitations, dizziness, sweating, and trembling; may entail a fear either of losing control of self or of going crazy
Generalized anxiety disorder	General, constant, and often debilitatingly high levels of anxiety that can last any length of time, from a month to years; often described as "free floating" because it cannot be pinned down easily
Stress disorder	An extreme reaction to a highly stressful event or situation
Posttraumatic stress disorder	The psychological reenactment of a traumatic event in the disordered person's past; reexperiencing of the event may take any of several different forms, such as nightmares, powerful memories, or even a perception that the event is occurring again
Acute stress disorder	Acute, brief reactions to stress that directly follow a traumatic event and last fewer than 4 months
Obsessive–compulsive disorder	A disorder involving obsessions and/or compulsions
Obsession	An unwanted, persistent thought, image, or impulse that an individual is unable to suppress; may include obsessive doubts, thoughts, impulses, fears, or images
Compulsion	An irresistible impulse to perform a relatively meaningless act repeatedly and in a stereotypical fashion

*Note. Although agoraphobia and panic disorder are discrete anxiety disorders, the two disorders so commonly occur together that DSM-IV includes a special category for the co-occurrence of the two disorders.

There are four basic kinds of symptoms of anxiety disorders: mood, cognitive, somatic, and motor symptoms. *Mood symptoms* include feelings of tension, apprehension, and sometimes panic. Often, people who experience these symptoms do not know exactly why they are feeling this way. For example, they may have a sense of doom but may not know why. Sometimes, anxious people become depressed, if only because they do not see any way to get rid of the symptoms.

Cognitive symptoms may include spending a lot of time trying to figure out why various mood symptoms are occurring. When unable to identify root causes, the person then may feel frustrated. Often, thinking about the problem actually worsens it, causing the person difficulty in concentrating on other things.

Typical *somatic* (i.e., bodily) *symptoms* include sweating, breathing difficulties, high pulse rate or blood pressure, and muscle tension. These symptoms go along with a high level of arousal of the autonomic nervous system (see chapter 2). These primary symptoms may lead to secondary ones. For example, intensely rapid breathing may lead to feelings of light-headedness or breathlessness. Muscular tension can lead to headaches or muscle spasms. High blood pressure can cause strokes or heart problems. People who suffer from anxiety disorders vary widely in their somatic symptoms. Some people may express their anxiety more in headaches, others in stomachaches, still others in backaches or other bodily symptoms.

Typical *motor symptoms* include restlessness, fidgeting, and various bodily movements that serve no particular purpose (e.g., pacing or finger tapping). People are often unaware of their own motor symptoms. For example, they may pace around a room while others are seated, not realizing that their behavior is unusual.

Virtually everyone experiences symptoms of anxiety some of the time. When does anxiety become an anxiety disorder? What distinguishes the normal anxiety that everyone occasionally experiences from serious psychological problems of anxiety? Generally, three factors must be considered:

1. *Level of anxiety.* It is probably normal to have a slight, occasional reluctance to enter elevators, especially overcrowded rickety-looking ones; it is probably abnormal to use the stairs to get to the 110th floor of a building because of feelings of terror that a well-built elevator will fall to the bottom of the elevator shaft.

2. *Justification for the anxiety.* It is normal to feel somewhat anxious before an important event, such as a final examination, a first date, or an important speech, but it is not normal to feel that same level of anxiety constantly when there are no stressful events on the horizon.

3. *Consequences of the anxiety.* If the anxiety leads to serious negative consequences, such as the loss of a job because of an inability to leave home, the anxiety is more likely to be considered an anxiety disorder.

The particular symptoms diagnosed as disorders vary across cultures. For example, a distinctive anxiety disorder has been observed in Islamic societies, in which the obsessive–compulsive syndrome of *Waswās* has been linked to the Islamic ritual of cleansing and prayer. According to W. Pfeiffer (1982), the syndrome "relates to ritual cleanliness and to the validity of the ritual procedures, which are particularly important in Islam. Thus, the sufferer of *Waswās* finds it hard to terminate the self-cleanings because he is afraid that he is not yet clean enough to carry out his prayers in a lawful manner" (Pfeiffer, 1982, p. 213). Within culturally diverse countries, such as the United States, clinicians often fail to consider variations in symptoms across diverse client populations. For instance, in diagnosing stress-related anxiety disorders, clinicians tend to overemphasize interpersonal sources of stress (e.g., becoming divorced or widowed) and to underemphasize environmental sources of stress (e.g., financial difficulties or low-status and high-pressure jobs; S. M. Turner & Hersen, 1985).

An example of an anxiety disorder is **agoraphobia,** which is an intense fear of open spaces or of being in a public place from which it might be difficult to escape in the event of a panic attack. An example is the case of Mrs. Reiss.

> Mrs. Reiss is a 48-year-old woman who recently was referred to a psychiatric clinic by her general practitioner because of her fears of going out alone. She has had these fears for 6 years, but they have intensified during the past 2 years. As a result, she has not gone out of her house unescorted. Her symptoms first appeared after an argument with her husband. She proceeded to go out to the mailbox and then was overwhelmed with feelings of dizziness and anxiety. She had to struggle back to the house. Her symptoms abated for a few years, but reappeared with greater intensity after she learned that her sister had ovarian cancer. Her symptoms often were worsened by frequent arguments with her husband. She began to feel increasingly apprehensive and fearful upon leaving the front door. If she did leave, she began getting panicky and dizzy after a few minutes on the street. Her heart pounded and she would start perspiring. At this point, she would turn back to her house to alleviate the anxiety. When accompanied by her husband or one of her children, she felt uneasy, but usually was able to enter crowded areas for short periods of time. (After Greenberg, Szmulkler, & Tantam, 1986, pp. 148–149)

Not all anxiety disorders represent phobias, of course. Consider the case of a woman suffering from obsessive–compulsive disorder, which occurs when a person has unwanted, persistent thoughts, images, or impulses that cannot be supressed (obsessions) or irresistible impulses to perform a relatively meaningless act repeatedly and in a stereotypical fashion (compulsion).

> Ruth Langley was 30 years old when she sought help from a therapist after experiencing long-standing fears of contamination. She stated that she became intensely uncomfortable with any dirt on herself or in her immediate environment. After noticing any dirt, she felt compelled to carry out elaborate and time-consuming cleaning procedures. These procedures usually involved thoroughly washing her hands and arms. Moreover, if she found dirt in her apartment, she was compelled to scrub her apartment methodically, in addition to showering in a very regimented manner. Her cleaning rituals have severely restricted her life. She now washes her hands at least four or five times an hour, showers six or seven times a day, and thoroughly cleans her apartment at least twice a day. (After Leon, 1974, pp. 129–130)

Several explanations of anxiety disorders have been suggested. Some of these explanations, which are important to the understanding of anxiety disorders, are shown in Table 13.2. Each explanation offers distinctive insights, and we may better understand particular disorders in particular

agoraphobia • an intense fear of open spaces or of being in a public place from which it might be difficult to escape in the event of a panic attack

TABLE 13.2
Explanations of Anxiety Disorders

Approach	Explanation
Psychodynamic	In general, anxiety arises because of conflicts between the id and superego. When individuals feel impulses from the id that conflict with the superego, they fear the punishment of the superego. Even if they do not act on those impulses, their fears of potential punishment from the superego may cause anxiety. Regarding phobias in particular, Freud suggested that the object of the phobia (e.g., snakes) represents a symbol of some deeper conflict, often involving sexual impulses of some kind.
Humanistic	When people perceive a big difference between their ideal selves (whom they would like to be) and their perceived selves (whom they perceive themselves to be), they feel anxious about their failure to become closer to their ideal selves.
Behavioral	*Classical conditioning:* When a neutral stimulus (e.g., the sight of a dog) is paired with a fear-producing stimulus (e.g., a startlingly loud noise or even a bite), the individual may be classically conditioned to feel fear in the presence of the formerly neutral stimulus. *Operant conditioning:* In obsessive–compulsive anxiety disorder, an individual may temporarily feel less anxiety after engaging in the compulsive behavior and may thus be negatively reinforced (due to reduced anxiety) for the compulsive behavior. *Observational learning:* By observing another person respond fearfully or be seriously harmed in a particular situation, the individual may learn to feel fearful in that situation or in the presence of particular stimuli.
Cognitive	Through *threat-magnifying thoughts,* people may think in ways that exaggerate potential threats and may thereby increase their feelings of anxiety.
Psychophysiological	The levels and activity of neurotransmitters may not be normal, thereby leading to feelings of anxiety. In particular, GABA (gamma-aminobutyric acid), a neurotransmitter substance, acts as a sort of chemical brake on the brain, slowing down the activity of the brain. When the levels of GABA are too low, the activity level of the brain increases, leading to heightened arousal. If people continually feel a heightened level of arousal, they may feel anxious.
Cultural	The cultural context in which people find themselves may influence the development of anxiety disorders. For instance, the anxiety disorder of *koro* (male impotence due to a man's fear that his penis is retracting into his body and that his death is imminent) may be found among some Southeast Asian men, but not among men from other cultures (Matsumoto, 1996).

individuals by using a combination of approaches. For example, anxiety can be treated effectively through a combination of drug therapy with psychotherapy. The prognosis is generally excellent. Another type of disorder is a mood disorder, which is discussed next.

WHAT ARE MOOD DISORDERS?

There are two major **mood disorders** (extreme disturbances in a person's emotional state) listed in DSM-IV: depressive disorders (also termed *unipolar depression* or *clinical depression*) and bipolar disorders.

Depressive Disorders

Depressive disorders involve serious impairment of function as a result of depression, not just feeling temporarily a little down in the dumps. Depression is relatively common. Roughly 10% of men and 20% of women are clinically depressed at some time in their lives (Weissman & Myers,

mood disorder • a psychological disorder involving either periods of extremely sad, low-energy moods or swings between extremely high and extremely low moods

depressive disorders • a mood disorder in which the individual feels so sad and has so little energy that the individual cannot function effectively

1978; Woodruff, Goodwin, & Guze, 1974). A depressed person feels deeply sad and probably feels that life is hopeless. The person probably also experiences a very low level of energy. Even the simplest task, such as getting out of bed or making a meal, may require more effort than the person can call forth. Sometimes, depressed people show slow body movements and even slow speech. They may lose appetite and therefore lose weight. They may have trouble falling asleep, staying asleep, or waking up; they may sleep most of the time or at least may want to sleep much of the time. Depressed people are also at greater risk of suicide than are nondepressed people. (Suicide, which is not actually a specific psychological disorder, but which is clearly abnormal behavior, is discussed later in this chapter.)

The most noticeable symptom of depression relates to mood: Depressed people feel down, discouraged, and hopeless. It may seem to them that nothing is right with their lives. Typical cognitive symptoms of depression are low self-esteem, low motivation, and pessimism. Depressed people often generalize from a single perceived failure or unfortunate event to an overall view that more failures and worse things are yet to come. Table 13.3 describes the various categories of depression, such as *exogenous depression* (chiefly having environmental origins) versus *endogenous depression* (chiefly due to internal, physiological origins), *primary depression* (in which depression is the principal medical disorder) versus *secondary depression* (depression arising from another medical disorder), *involutional depression* (age-related depression), and *postpartum depression* (serious depression following childbirth). Depression usually can be effectively treated through a combination of drug therapy and psychotherapy, and the prospects for recovery generally are excellent.

A large cross-national study involving more than 40,000 subjects in Western and non-Western countries concluded that depressive disorders occur across a broad range of cultures and that more recent generations are at an increased risk of depression, relative to earlier ones (Cross-National Collaborative Group, 1992). The scientists who conducted the study claim that it is the first study to use standard diagnostic criteria across all societies. As other researchers have stated (Kleinman & Good,

TABLE 13.3
Categories of Depression

Disorder	Description
Exogenous versus endogenous depression	
Exogenous depression	Stems primarily from a person's reaction to external, or environmental, factors
Endogenous depression	Primarily induced by internal, or physiological factors, such as low levels of particular neurotransmitters
Primary versus secondary depression	
Primary depression	Depression is the principal medical problem, not another medical disorder
Secondary depression	Another medical disorder has caused the depression
Involutional depression	Associated with advancing age
Postpartum depression	Occurs after childbirth and can last anywhere from a few weeks to a year (the more common "maternity blues" last only 1 or 2 days)

1985; Marsella, Hirschfeld, & Katz, 1987), it is very hard to come up with cross-culturally appropriate uniform diagnostic criteria for disorders.

Related to major depression is *seasonal affective disorder (SAD)*, which is a form of depression that typically occurs during the winter months or the months surrounding them. The fact that this form of depression is relatively more common during the winters in the extreme north, where the sun may shine for just a few hours a day if at all, has suggested a link to available ambient light. Indeed, light therapy has been used to treat this form of depression (Lewy, Sack, Miller, & Itoban, 1987). SAD appears to be linked to irregularities in the body's production of melatonin, which is secreted by the pineal gland and is implicated in the sleeping–waking cycle.

Bipolar Disorders

In addition to depressive disorders, the other main mood disorder is **bipolar disorder**, also termed *manic–depressive disorder*, in which people go through alternating periods of depression (with the same symptoms of depression as just described for depressive disorders) and mania. **Mania** is a mood of boundless joy and highly energetic delight, the opposite polar extreme from depression. The individual is highly excited and often hyperactive. Manic persons may believe that there is no limit to their possible accomplishments and may act accordingly (e.g., trying to climb Mount Everest as an unplanned outing, equipped with a cotton jacket and a pocket knife). Figure 13.2 illustrates the periodic nature of bipolar disorders.

FIGURE 13.2
Stages of a Manic Episode
Case-study research often provides depth of insight not as easily available through laboratory studies, as shown in this longitudinal analysis of nurses' ratings of manic behavior in a patient hospitalized for mania. (After G. Carlson and Goodwin, 1973)

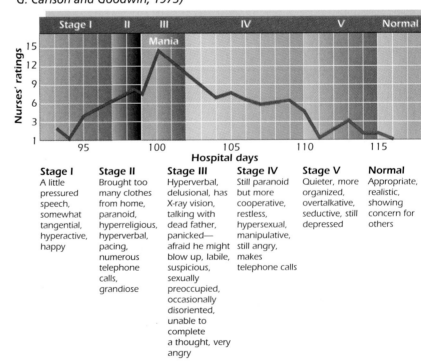

bipolar disorder • a mood disorder in which the individual alternates between periods of depression and of mania

mania • a mood in which the individual feels highly energetic and extremely joyful

During the manic phase, an individual shows an overinflated sense of self-esteem. Manic individuals often have trouble focusing their attention and move quickly from one activity to another. Occasionally, the manic person will suffer from **delusions,** which are false, unfounded beliefs. Manic individuals may spend money wildly, may attempt to start numerous projects they cannot finish, or may engage in a great deal of sexual activity. Consequently, they may end up bankrupt, fired from their jobs, or divorced by their mates. People who are experiencing mania have a greatly reduced need for sleep and tend not to feel tired after very strenuous periods of activity that will have exhausted most other people. Bipolar disorder (which occurs in only about 0.75% to 1% of the population) is much less common than is unipolar depression.

Several explanations of mood disorders have been suggested, as shown in Table 13.4. Different explanations may be more plausible for each type

delusion • a false belief, which contradicts known facts

TABLE 13.4
Explanations of Mood Disorders

Approach	Explanation
Psychodynamic	Depression occurs when we mourn a loss but usually the loss is symbolic, rather than actual, and the loss usually results from an event that occurred during early childhood. Moreover, people feel depressed when they turn their anger inward, against themselves, rather than outward, against others. Turning anger inward not only helps to avoid the actual punishment of the people against whom we might turn but also to minimize punishment from the superego for feeling aggressive impulses.
Humanistic	Victor Frankl (1959) drew largely on his own experience in Nazi concentration camps during World War II. He observed that of those individuals who were not put to death, the greatest difference between those who survived and those who did not seemed to be in the ability to find meaning in their suffering and to relate the experience to their spiritual life. Generalizing from this experience, Frankl suggested that depression results from a lack of purpose in living. Thus, depressed people may improve if they can be helped to find meaning in their lives.
Behavioral	Depressed people have received fewer rewards than nondepressed people and their lack of activity means that they will continue to receive fewer rewards than will nondepressed people.
Cognitive	Building on the notion of learned helplessness, cognitivists would add that depressed people may make cognitive attributions of causality that lead them to believe that they are powerless to make changes in the conditions that are making them unhappy. Depressed people may also engage in distorted thought processes that exaggerate (a) their sense of hopelessness—their inability to change the situation, (b) the negative characteristics of the situation, and (c) the potential likelihood and harmfulness of future outcomes of their situation. Depressed people may also minimize existing and potential future positive characteristics of the situation.
Psychophysiological	*Unipolar disorder:* Low levels of either of two neurotransmitters in the brain—norepinephrine or serotonin—may lead to depression. *Bipolar disorder:* As in unipolar disorder, low levels of norepinephrine may lead to the depressive phase, but in bipolar disorder, brain changes may lead to high levels of norepinephrine, associated with the manic phase of the disorder. Also, because drug therapies are highly effective in treating bipolar disorder, it seems that physiological factors play a role in this disorder. Bipolar disorder also appears to run in families, suggesting possible genetic and physiological aspects of the illness.
Cultural	There are large cultural differences in both rate of depression (Marsella, 1980) and symptoms of depression (Matsumoto, 1996). For instance, depressed Chinese people tend to report somatic symptoms of depression more often than do depressed people from other cultures (Matsumoto, 1996). On the other hand, depressed Americans and Europeans are more likely to report feeling extremely worthless than are depressed Nigerians (Kleinman, 1988). Some cultural psychologists interpret cultural variations as indicating that culture influences the expression, and perhaps even the experience, of depression.

of disorder. For example, behavioral explanations offer interesting insights into depression. However, psychophysiological explanations seem better to explain bipolar disorder. Bipolar disorder is generally treated through a combination of drugs and psychotherapy. The prospects for control of the symptoms of bipolar disorder are quite good although the prospects for an actual cure are not. Generally, people learn to live with the control of the symptoms. This kind of disorder is difficult to live with, but perhaps less so than are dissociative disorders, considered next.

WHAT ARE DISSOCIATIVE DISORDERS?

Dissociative disorders involve a drastic change in a person's awareness of past experiences, present experiences, and personal identity. For some of the dissociative disorders, environmental traumas, such as the stress of war or of abuse in the family, have been more strongly implicated than have hereditary factors. There are three main dissociative disorders: *dissociative amnesia*, *dissociative fugue*, and *dissociative identity disorder* (formerly termed *multiple personality disorder*), as shown in Table 13.5. All of these disorders involve some kind of change in the normally integrative functions of consciousness and identity, which keep the various parts of a person integrated into a single identity. In addition to the three main dissociative disorders, some persons are diagnosed as having *depersonalization disorder*, which involves temporary periods during which such persons experience distortions of their body image, perhaps feeling as if they are detached from their bodies or as if their legs or arms have changed in size.

The most well known of these disorders is dissociative identity disorder. The case of Sybil, which was made into a movie, illustrates interesting aspects of the disorder (Schreiber, 1973), although the validity of the reporting of this case has been questioned. By her adult years, Sybil reportedly had developed 15 distinct identities. Some of the identities were of relatively minor importance, others of more importance. One was a baby, and two were male. From her infancy through her late childhood, Sybil reportedly had been sexually tortured, brutally maltreated, and almost

dissociative disorders •
psychological disorders in which an individual goes through one or more extreme changes in awareness of past and present experiences, personal history, and even personal identity

TABLE 13.5
Dissociative Disorders

Disorder	Description
Dissociative amnesia	An experience of sudden memory loss, usually after a highly stressful life experience; the amnesia usually affects the recollection of all of the events that have taken place during and immediately after the stressful event (see also *acute stress disorder*); it also causes great difficulty in recalling important personal details (e.g., name, place of residence, and identities of family members).
Dissociative fugue	People with this disorder start entirely new lives and experience total amnesia about their past; they move away, assume new identities, take new jobs, and behave as though they were completely different people. Their personalities may even change. As these people begin their new lives, they do not question the fact that their past is lost.
Dissociative identity disorder (formerly called *multiple personality*)	The occurrence of two or more individual identities (personalities) within the same individual, each of which is relatively independent of any others, lives a stable life of its own and from time to time takes full control of the person's behavior.

murdered by her mother, who was schizophrenic. Like Sybil, many of the persons who allegedly develop dissociative personality disorders have experienced shockingly horrible abuse during their early years. For these individuals, the ability to dissociate from abusive experiences actually may have had adaptive elements, given the circumstances.

People occasionally have tried to fake dissociative identity disorder. For example, Kenneth Bianchi, the infamous "Hillside Strangler," pretended to have multiple identities, hoping to be found not guilty of the murder of numerous women by reason of insanity. How did the court know that Bianchi was faking? Among the experts on dissociative disorders brought in as expert witnesses was Martin Orne. Orne cited four reasons why he believed that Bianchi's identities were not real. First, the identity of the supposed murderer, "Steve," changed over time: from being passive at first to becoming abusive and aggressive later. In contrast, true dissociative identities tend to be stable, especially if they have existed over a long period of time. Second, when it was mentioned to Bianchi that true dissociative identity cases tend to have more than just two personalities, a new personality quickly appeared. Thus, Bianchi appeared to create the third personality in order better to simulate the disorder. Third, dissociative identities that exist over a period of time tend to be noticed by other people, but no one appeared to have noticed "Steve," the murderer. Finally, when hypnosis was used to reveal the personality of "Steve," Bianchi showed the characteristics of someone simulating deep hypnosis rather than of someone actually under a hypnotic trance.

There is controversy today over whether dissociative identity disorder really exists (S.D. Miller & Triggiano, 1992; Spanos, 1994). It has been suggested, for example, that some clients may wish to believe they suffer from this disorder or that therapists may implant the idea of this disorder in the clients. Indeed, the diagnosis of dissociative identity disorder skyrocketed as publicity for certain cases highlighted in the media increased. As patients started suing therapists for false diagnoses, the rate of diagnosis started to decrease. At present, therefore, we cannot say for sure whether the disorder is a genuine one or not, but its existence is clearly questionable. Schizophrenia, however, considered next, is believed by virtually all contemporary psychologists to be a genuine disorder.

WHAT IS SCHIZOPHRENIA?

Schizophrenia is actually a set of disorders that encompasses a variety of symptoms. These symptoms include hallucinations—perceptions of sensory stimulation (e.g., sounds and sights) in the absence of any actual corresponding external sensory input from the physical world; delusions—distorted thought processes characterized by erroneous persistent beliefs in the face of strong evidence to the contrary; disturbed thought processes (e.g., a belief that one is a great historical personage, such as Napoleon); disturbed emotional responses—such as *flat affect* (lack of emotional expression), or *inappropriate affect*—(inappropriate emotional expression; e.g., laughing when fear or anger would be appropriate reactions), and odd motor symptoms. Please see Table 13.6 for further important information.

The symptoms of schizophrenia sometimes are characterized as either being *negative* (i.e., not showing a behavior that is normal; subtracting it from the behavioral repertoire or range of behavioral responses) or *positive* (i.e., showing a behavior that is abnormal; adding it to the repertoire). **Negative symptoms** include deficits in behavior, such as blunting of emotions

schizophrenia • a set of psychological disorders involving various perceptual symptoms (e.g., hallucinations), cognitive symptoms (e.g., disturbed thought content or processes), mood symptoms (e.g., lack of appropriate emotional expression), and sometimes even bizarre motor symptoms

negative symptom • a characteristic of a disorder, in which the individual lacks a normal behavior (e.g., not speaking, not showing emotional expression, or not interacting socially)

TABLE 13.6
Symptoms of Schizophrenia

Symptom	Description
Cognitive symptoms	
Hallucinations	Perceptual experiences that have no basis in reality; that is, the person experiencing hallucinations will hear, see, feel, or smell things that are not present.
Delusions	Erroneous beliefs that persist despite strong evidence to the contrary; delusions are of various kinds and they can range from thoughts that are plausible but incorrect to thoughts that are patently ridiculous. A few of the more common delusions follow.
Persecution	The belief that others are spying on the person or are planning to harm the person in some manner. For example, schizophrenics might believe that they are being followed by agents of the CIA. These delusions are the most common ones.
Identity	The deluded person's belief that she or he is somebody else. For example, in *The Three Christs of Ypsilanti,* Milton Rokeach (1964) focused on three patients in a mental hospital in Ypsilanti, Michigan, each of whom believed that he was Jesus Christ.
External causation	The schizophrenics' belief that external forces are making them feel certain things, act in certain ways, or have certain impulses.
Word salad	Rhythmic and rhyming combinations of words are tossed together in ways that make no sense; that is, in addition to having disturbed thought content, the schizophrenic's thought processes are also disturbed.
Cognitive flooding (also termed *stimulus overload*)	The inability to filter out irrelevant internal and external stimuli and thus being forced to attend to a bewildering array of stimuli; the amount of stimulation may become so great that the schizophrenics become unable to cope with the rate of stimulation.
Affective, emotional symptoms	
Flat affect	The patient may stare lifelessly into space, seeming apathetic to the world. Schizophrenics showing flat affect may not answer questions but if they do respond their answers are likely to be given in a toneless voice.
Inappropriate affect	Emotional responses are inappropriate. For example, patients may laugh uncontrollably on hearing that someone close to them is seriously ill or has died or they may become enraged when asked how they are feeling; somewhat less common than flat affect.
Motor symptoms	
Motor disturbances	Schizophrenics (especially those showing flat affect) often show characteristic motor symptoms. In particular, some types of schizophrenics may appear to be in a daze and may not move for weeks, months, or even years. Other types of schizophrenics may exhibit unusually high levels of activity. Unusual facial expressions, repetitive finger and hand movements, and random and purposeless movements are also characteristic.

(affective flattening such that the person shows virtually no strong emotions at all), language deficits (such as reduced ability to form grammatical sentences), apathy, and avoidance of social activity. **Positive symptoms** include delusions, hallucinations, and bizarre behavior, such as the creation of *word salad*, in which a schizophrenic speaker uses strings of words that are only loosely connected, if at all, as in the following passage.

I want to go to bed. I want to go to bed and be in my head. I want to go to bed and be in my bed and in my head and just wear red.

positive symptom • a characteristic of a disorder, in which the individual shows an abnormal behavior (e.g., hallucinations or word salad)

For red is the color that my baby wore and once more, it's true, yes, it is, it's true. Please don't wear red tonight, ohh, ohh, please don't wear red tonight, for red is the color . . .

(A. Bloom, 1993, p. 50).

In order to be classified as schizophrenic, an individual must show (a) impairment in areas such as work, social relations, and self-care; (b) at least two of the cognitive, affective, or motor characteristics described earlier in Table 13.6; and (c) persistence of these symptoms for at least 6 months.

The predicted future of people diagnosed with schizophrenia is not particularly bright. Schizophrenia typically involves a series of *acute* (intense but temporary) episodes with occasional periods of *remission* (relief from symptoms). In many cases, with each successive acute episode of the disorder, the individual becomes less able to function well, even during periods of remission. Most clinicians agree that once people have had a full-fledged episode of schizophrenia, they rarely are rid completely of the disorder. That is, the disease process generally appears to be *chronic* (never going away entirely, either constantly present or showing up again and again). Nonetheless, in most cases, a number of the symptoms can be treated through psychotherapy and drugs (Sartorius, Shapiro, & Jablonsky, 1974). Choice of treatment can depend in part upon the type of schizophrenia that is diagnosed.

Types of Schizophrenia

DSM-IV recognizes five main types of schizophrenia. Of these types, three were recognized more than a century ago.

1. *Disorganized schizophrenia.* Characterized by profound psychological disorganization, hallucinations, and delusions
2. *Catatonic schizophrenia.* Characterized by very long periods of immobility, in which the individuals may stare into space, appearing dazed and completely detached from the rest of the world

Catatonic schizophrenics show waxy flexibility, *assuming odd poses for long periods of time. Although this woman's arm appears to be frozen in place, it can be manipulated into another pose, which she then will continue to hold.*

3. *Paranoid schizophrenia.* Characterized by delusions of persecution or of grandeur

Today, DSM-IV also recognizes two other types of schizophrenia.

4. *Undifferentiated schizophrenia.* A catchall category into which individuals are classified if they do not fit any of the preceding schizophrenic patterns

5. *Residual schizophrenia.* A diagnosis applied to individuals who have had at least one schizophrenic episode and who currently show some mild symptoms, but who do not show the profoundly disturbed behavior that characterizes the other schizophrenias

Table 13.7 categorizes some of the various types of schizophrenia. In addition, DSM-IV includes some other psychotic disorders related to schizophrenia (e.g., delusional disorder, shared psychotic disorder, schizophreniform disorder, and schizoaffective disorder), most of which involve less-severe symptoms or shorter duration of symptoms.

An example of schizophrenia can be seen in the following case.

A 26-year-old woman was referred to a psychiatric hospital after attempting suicide by drug overdose. Her father had been diagnosed as schizophrenic and died when she was 13 years old by committing suicide. She had been hospitalized twice in the past year for various psychotic episodes. For the previous few weeks, she had been convinced that the devil was persecuting her. She would lay awake at night fantasizing that the devil was tapping on her window. She believed that other individuals were talking to her and could read her mind. Many times she felt she was under the devil's control. He would talk through her and had the power to inflict pain. She believed the only way to avoid the devil was to kill herself. Her mother found her on the floor and called the ambulance. At the hospital, she said that she still heard voices talking to her and that they had the power to control her thinking. (After Fottrell, 1983, p.128)

TABLE 13.7
Types of Schizophrenia

Disorder	Description
Disorganized schizophrenia (formerly termed *hebephrenic schizophrenia*)	Characterized by profound psychological disorganization; hallucinations and delusions are common but these symptoms do not seem as fully integrated and as coherently organized as in some of the other kinds of schizophrenia, such as paranoid schizophrenia; often involves incoherent speech.
Catatonic schizophrenia	Characterized by very long periods of immobility in which the individuals may stare into space, appearing dazed and completely detached from the rest of the world.
Paranoid schizophrenia	Characterized by delusions of persecution or of grandeur.
Undifferentiated schizophrenia	A catchall category into which individuals are classified if they do not fit any of the preceding schizophrenic patterns.
Residual schizophrenia	A diagnosis applied to individuals who have had at least one schizophrenic episode and who currently show some mild symptoms but who do not show the profoundly disturbed behavior that characterizes the other schizophrenias.

Demographic Issues in Schizophrenia

Schizophrenia affects 1% to 2% of the U.S. population and is among the most serious of psychological disorders (Robins et al., 1984). Schizophrenia also tends to run in families. Several studies have found that if someone is schizophrenic, chances are good that this person will have other family members who are schizophrenic as well (Gottesman, McGuffin, & Farmer, 1987). For example, among persons with schizophrenia, 44% of identical twins are both schizophrenic, and 12% of fraternal twins are both schizophrenic; moreover, 7% of persons with schizophrenia have schizophrenic siblings, 9% have schizophrenic children, and 3% have schizophrenic grandchildren.

Schizophrenia generally is diagnosed in early adulthood, usually before the age of 45. The incidence of schizophrenia has also been found to vary with socioeconomic status (SES). In particular, persons with lower SES are more likely to be diagnosed as suffering from schizophrenia than are persons with higher SES. The difference is large: Members of the lowest SES group are roughly eight times more likely to be diagnosed with schizophrenia than are members of the middle and upper SES groups (B. S. Dohrenwend & Dohrenwend, 1974; Strauss, Kokes, Ritzler, Harder, & Van Ord, 1978). Many possible explanations (e.g., higher levels of stress associated with lower SES) have been offered regarding this trend (e.g., Hollingshead & Redlich, 1958; Kramer, 1957; Myerson, 1940; R. J. Turner & Wagonfeld, 1967). Also, members of groups that experience discrimination and the stress associated with discrimination are more prone to schizophrenia, regardless of SES (B. P. Dohrenwend et al., 1992).

Several explanations of schizophrenia have been suggested, as shown in Table 13.8. The great differences across SES suggest that environmental factors play a role. The strong familial trends, particularly among identical twins, suggest that inherited biological factors also contribute to the disorder. Thus, an interaction of various factors probably underlies this

Contemporary brain-imaging techniques offer insights into some of the cerebral processes that underlie psychological disorders. For example, these images show the differences in the patterns of activity in a normal brain as compared with the brain of a schizophrenic.

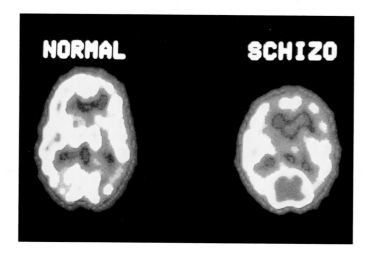

TABLE 13.8
Explanations of Schizophrenia

Approach	Explanation
Psychodynamic	People with schizophrenia return to the earliest (oral) stage of psychological development. In this stage, the ego has not yet adequately differentiated from the id, so the reality principle is not yet operative as a means of checking the id, which operates solely on the pleasure principle.
Humanistic	Humanistic psychologist Thomas Szasz (1961) argued that mental illness is simply a myth—that schizophrenia and other so-called mental illnesses are merely alternative ways of experiencing the world. Humanistic therapist R. D. Laing (1964) has suggested that schizophrenia is not an illness but is merely a label that society applies to behavior it finds problematic. According to Laing, people become schizophrenic when they live in situations that are simply not livable. No matter what they do, nothing seems to work.
Behavioral	People with schizophrenia find their lives and social situations to be so lacking in rewards or even punishments that they begin to ignore the relevant aspects of their environment in favor of irrelevant ones. Their response of paying attention to relevant cues becomes extinguished. Once people are labeled as schizophrenics, their abnormal behavior is more likely to attract the rewarding attention of others and their normal behavior is less likely to do so.
Cognitive	For some reason, people with schizophrenia frequently experience an overload of sensory stimulation or of conflicting thoughts. These bizarre and overwhelming experiences may then cause their other difficulties. For example, when they try to communicate their sensations, perceptions, or thoughts to others, other people cannot understand them. Some suggest that people with schizophrenia lack an adequate filtering mechanism so they cannot screen out irrelevant stimuli and thoughts.
Psychophysiological	As in other disorders, levels of neurotransmitters in the brain may be involved in schizophrenia. Specifically, excessively high levels of dopamine have been linked to schizophrenia (Wong et al., 1986). The effectiveness of various antipsychotic drugs (see chapter 14) also supports the psychophysiological explanation of schizophrenia. Another psychophysiological explanation suggests structural abnormalities in the brain as the cause (Seidman, 1983). In particular, schizophrenia may be linked to deterioration of the brain tissue (Andreasen, Olsen, Dennert, & Smith, 1982).
Cultural	Studies by the World Health Organization have found that auditory hallucinations, delusions of reference, and lack of insight are symptoms that characterize schizophrenia across many cultures (e.g., in Asia, Africa, South and North America, and Europe). On the other hand, other researchers have found cross-cultural variations in the rates of schizophrenia and among patterns of symptoms. Similarly, people with schizophrenia seem to show faster recovery in developing countries in which they are able to return to meaningful work and to rely on an extended kin network (described in Matsumoto, 1996). Some of the cultural universals lend support to psychophysiological explanations, but the numerous cultural variations suggest that cultural context influences the expression and interpretation of schizophrenic symptoms.

disorder. Impulse-control disorders, considered next, also can involve an interaction of various factors.

WHAT ARE IMPULSE-CONTROL DISORDERS?

The DSM-IV designates a special category for "impulse-control disorders not elsewhere classified," all of which involve the failure to resist an impulse to engage in a particular behavior. These disorders and their associated impulses include: (a) *intermittent explosive disorder*—explosive outbursts of emotions; (b) *kleptomania*—stealing; (c) *pyromania*—setting fires; (d) *pathological gambling*—out-of-control betting; and (e) *trichotillomania*—pulling out one's own hair. Relatively little is known regarding the probable origins of these disorders and the disorders are relatively difficult to treat. These disorders are all quite serious, as are most types of personality disorders, considered next.

WHAT ARE PERSONALITY DISORDERS?

Personality disorders are consistent, long-term, extreme personality characteristics that either seriously impair an individual's ability to function well in their environment or cause problems for the individual or for others when the individual is adjusting to normal, everyday situations. The major personality disorders include the following:

- *Paranoid.* Characteristically suspicious of others
- *Narcissistic.* Characteristically have an inflated view of themselves
- *Histrionic.* Characteristically act as though they are on stage
- *Avoidant.* Characteristically seem reluctant to enter into close personal relationships
- *Dependent.* Characteristically lack self-confidence and have difficulty taking personal responsibility for themselves
- *Obsessive–compulsive.* Characteristically show excessive concern with details, rules, and codes of behavior
- *Antisocial.* Characteristically seem superficially charming and apparently sincere, while nevertheless engaging in behavior that harms other individuals

Almost all of us show signs of at least some of these patterns of behavior at least some of the time. For example, what individual occasionally does not find him- or herself excessively concerned with certain types of details in work or personal life? Again, patterns of behavior become abnormal at extreme levels when they are exhibited to an excessive degree so that one's ability to adapt to the demands of everyday life is impeded.

Although it is possible to detect some features of personality disorders during infancy, childhood, or adolescence, these disorders generally are not diagnosed until at least early adulthood. These disorders are difficult to treat and the prognosis is variable. Several other disorders, however, are usually first diagnosed in infancy, childhood, or adolescence.

WHAT DISORDERS ARE USUALLY FIRST DIAGNOSED IN INFANCY, CHILDHOOD, OR ADOLESCENCE?

There are three major **disorders usually first diagnosed in infancy, childhood, or adolescence:** attention-deficit/hyperactivity disorder (ADHD), conduct disorder, and pervasive developmental disorder (PDD).

Children who show *attention-deficit/hyperactivity disorder (ADHD)* have difficulty in focusing attention for reasonable amounts of time; they tend also to be impulsive and disruptive in social settings; they often are unable to sit still and constantly seem to be seeking attention; they are distracted easily by irrelevant stimuli; they have trouble listening to and

personality disorders •
psychological disorders involving exaggerated and maladaptive personality characteristics that persist over a long period of time and that cause problems in the person's adjustment to everyday situations

disorders usually first diagnosed in infancy, childhood, or adolescence •
psychological disorders that are first identified before adulthood

Pervasive developmental disorders in children are trying not only for children, but also for their parents. Fortunately, psychotherapy can help, to some extent, in the treatment of pervasive developmental disorders.

following instructions; and they often talk excessively and are likely to interrupt others. These children are often treated with ritalin or related drugs. Ironically, these drugs serve as stimulants in people who do not show ADHD, despite the fact that they have a calming and focusing effect in individuals with ADHD. The drugs are used widely and have been for a number of years. Concerns exist about their possible long-term side effects, although these side effects are not very well understood. The drugs are prescribed when the benefits are believed to outweigh the costs. Some psychologists are also concerned about the danger of overprescription; for example, prescribing such drugs not because a given child has ADHD, but because the child is bored with school and thus shows misbehavior in the classroom. Responsible practitioners take care not to hand out such prescriptions.

Children who have *conduct disorder* show habitual misbehavior such as stealing, being truant from school, destroying property, fighting (occasionally using weapons in these fights), being cruel both to animals and to other people, and frequently telling lies. Such children tend to get into trouble within the school and sometimes get into legal difficulties as well. Conduct disorders are difficult to treat.

Less common than attention-deficit/hyperactivity disorder and conduct disorder is *pervasive developmental disorder (PDD,* a variant of which is termed *autism* in earlier versions of DSM). PDD is characterized by three main symptoms: (a) These children show minimal to no responsiveness to others and seem oblivious to the world around them, almost as though they were living in another dimension. (b) They show seriously impaired communication, with only minimal language use, nonsensical verbalizations, and even poor nonverbal communication skills. (c) They show a highly restricted range of interest; for instance, they may sit by themselves staring off into space for hours, without a word or a gesture; or they may rock back and forth or ritualistically repeat gestures with their hands. Until recently, it was believed that PDD might be a form of schizophrenia in childhood. It is now believed, however, that PDD and schizophrenia in childhood are different disorders (American Psychiatric Association, 1994). Whereas children with schizophrenia often show a family history of schizophrenia, children with PDD do not. Also, the drugs that reduce or relieve symptoms of schizophrenia are not effective with PDD (see chapter 14). In addition, DSM-IV includes various other disorders in this category of disorders usually first diagnosed in infancy, childhood, or adolescence, such as mental retardation (see chapter 8), learning disorders, motor-skills disorders, feeding and eating disorders, elimination disorders, tic disorders, and communication disorders.

An example of PDD is Jimmy Patterson.

This 5-year-old boy was brought to the inpatient child psychiatric unit at a large city hospital. His parents complained that he was impossible to manage, was not toilet trained, and screamed or gestured whenever he became frustrated or wanted to be noticed. He was allowed a free-play period and an interaction period involving a cooperative task with his mother. He wandered about the playroom and played by himself with a number of toys. His mother then tried to involve him in some cooperative play with wooden blocks. She spoke to Jimmy in a cheerful tone but he seemed not to notice her and moved to an opposite part of the room. Mrs. Patterson made several comments to Jimmy but he remained oblivious to her encouragments. She then tried to begin a jigsaw puzzle with

Jimmy. She led him over to a chair but as soon as he sat down he got up again and continued to wander about the room. His mother then firmly, although not harshly, took Jimmy by the arm and led him over to a chair. Jimmy began to whine and scream and flail his arms about and eventually wiggled out of his mother's grasp. (After G. R. Leon, 1974, p. 9)

WHAT ARE SOME ADDITIONAL PSYCHOLOGICAL DISORDERS?

The DSM-IV also discusses somatoform disorders, sexual disorders, and cognitive-impairment disorders.

Somatoform Disorders

Somatoform disorders center on the person's relationship with his or her own body; they are relatively rare bodily symptoms or complaints of bodily symptoms for which no physiological basis can be found. There are five main kinds of somatoform disorders:

1. The most common somatoform disorder is *pain disorder,* in which people experience pain that cannot be attributed to any physical cause (see also chapter 15).

2. In *conversion disorder,* the sensory or muscular systems are impaired, despite the lack of a known physical cause. The impairment may involve partial or complete paralysis of the arms or legs; seizures; coordination problems; loss or impairment of sensation; insensitivity to pain; inability to see, hear, or speak; or prickly, tingling, or creeping sensations on the skin.

3. In *somatization disorder,* people seek relief from unpleasant chronic physical symptoms for which there is no known physical cause. Of the many symptoms that may arise, some of the most common ones are dizziness, fatigue, nausea, and weakness. Somatization disorder differs from *malingering* (faking symptoms in order to get out of responsibilities) and from *Münchausen syndrome* (in which people fake symptoms in order to keep playing the role of the patient).

4. In *hypochondriasis,* people are preoccupied with the fear that they may have serious illnesses and they overreact to ordinary physical experiences, such as nausea or pain in the abdomen.

5. Persons with *body dysmorphic disorder* are preoccupied with a defect in physical appearance. The defect may be either real or imagined; if it is real, however, it is greatly exaggerated.

Sexual Disorders

Another category of disorders with strong physiological associations is that of sexual disorders. In **sexual disorders,** the individual experiences sexual arousal, thoughts, or behaviors that distress the individual or other persons. The disorder may also cause difficulty for the individual in other aspects of her or his life. DSM-IV specifies the following major types of sexual disorders.

somatoform disorders • psychological disorders in which people experience bodily symptoms for which no physiological basis has been found

sexual disorders • psychological disorders involving problems with sexual arousal, thoughts, or behavior that distresses the individual or other people

1. In *gender-identity disorders*, people feel that their physiological *sex* (either male or female physical identity) differs from their psychological *gender* (either female or male psychological identity with respect to social and societal roles and characteristics).

2. *Paraphilias* are sexual attractions to highly unusual objects. For instance, persons with the following paraphilias are sexually aroused by these unusual objects: *fetishes* (nonhuman objects; e.g., articles of clothing, particularly those of the opposite sex); *pedophilia* (children); *sexual sadism* (the pain of another person); *sexual masochism* (personal experience of pain); *voyeurism* (the secret observation of people who are nude or undressing); and *exhibitionism* (unwanted public display of areas of the body that are perceived as sexually provocative).

3. *Sexual dysfunctions* are disruptions of people's normal sex lives. People with these disorders have difficulty feeling any sexual urge at all, feeling aroused at appropriate times, or having orgasms at appropriate times. They also may feel pain during intercourse. Each of these disorders can be mild to severe and of brief to long duration.

Cognitive-Impairment Disorders

The DSM-IV also includes **cognitive-impairment disorders**, such as *delirium* (a confused, disordered state of mind often involving perceptual distortions); *amnesia* (memory loss); and *dementia*, (a general deterioration in cognitive abilities, especially affecting memory and judgment). Cognitive disorders generally are due to physiological changes in the brain (e.g., Alzheimer's disease, head injury, or *stroke*—sudden changes in the blood supply to the brain; see chapters 2, 4, 6, and 7 for discussion of some aspects of cognitive function and its distortions). In addition, DSM-IV includes eating disorders, sleeping disorders (see chapter 4), *adjustment disorders* (related to extreme difficulties in adjusting to traumas, stressors, and other difficult situations), and substance-related disorders (see chapter 4).

Disorders can lead to many types of problematical behavior. Certainly one of the most problematical types of behaviors is suicide. The desire to commit suicide can follow from a number of disorders, although most commonly it is linked to major depression.

HOW DO PSYCHOLOGISTS VIEW SUICIDE?

To be, or not to be—that is the question:
Whether 'tis nobler in the mind to suffer
The slings and arrows of outrageous fortune,
Or to take arms against a sea of troubles,
And by opposing end them.

(William Shakespeare, *Hamlet, III*, i)

Most of the psychological disorders described in this chapter are rarely life threatening. Depression can be, however, and severe depression often precedes suicide, as in the case of the great American writer, Ernest Hemingway, and of many great figures in history who have suffered from severe depression. William Styron, author of *Sophie's Choice*, is yet another depression sufferer but, unlike Hemingway, Styron to a large extent has been able to overcome his severe depression. Although suicide is not a psychological disorder in itself, it clearly is abnormal behavior. In addition, because of its

cognitive-impairment disorder • a psychological disorder in which normal thought processes become impaired or distorted

Contrary to popular belief, threats of suicide should be taken very seriously. Many people who commit suicide had threatened suicide prior to taking their own lives.

link to depression, it seems appropriate to consider suicide in the context of psychological disorders. Suicide generally is not approved of and frequently is forbidden in society. Even today, several states make it a crime to commit suicide. In this section, we consider first some facts (Douglas, 1967; Gibbs, 1968; Holinger, 1987; National Center for Health Statistics, 1988; Resnik, 1968; Seiden, 1974) and then some myths regarding suicide.

What do we know about suicide? For one thing, suicide occurs in almost all cultures, but it is more common in some cultures than in others. The United States is about average with respect to the other countries of the world. Almost 31,000 suicides are recorded each year in the United States, which makes the U.S. rate of suicide 12.8 per 100,000 people. Many other Western countries have suicide rates of 20 or more per 100,000 people. In fact, Western cultures in general seem to have higher rates of suicide than do non-Western cultures (Carson & Butcher, 1992). In contrast, some cultures (e.g., that of the aborigines of Australia) have no known incidence of suicide whatsoever. Western estimates of suicide are probably much too low because many suicides (e.g., questionable accidents) are not counted as such. Thus, although these statistics would lead us to believe that a suicide occurs in the United States once every 20 minutes, the true frequency is undoubtedly higher.

Age is also a factor in suicide. The rate of suicide rises in old age (particularly among white males), reaching a rate of more than 25 per 100,000 for people between the ages of 75 and 84 years. In addition, although suicide ranks only eighth as a cause of death among adults, in general, it ranks third after accidents and homicides as a cause of death among people between the ages of 15 and 24 years. Among young adults, whites are twice as likely as blacks to kill themselves.

Consider an example of a suicide attempt.

Mr. Wrigley was referred by his general practitioner for an outpatient assessment after suicidal thoughts resulting from depression. Mr. Wrigley recently had been forced to retire as a hospital porter because a series of strokes made lifting heavy equipment impossible. He felt "completely changed" after this incident. He would burst into tears over seemingly trivial events. He had to force himself to eat because he had no appetite, and his sleeping periods became shorter and shorter. His social interactions decreased, and he became more isolated and withdrawn. Mr. Wrigley reported that he made an attempt on his life while having tea with his daughter and wife. He picked up a knife from the table as if to stab himself. He was restrained by his wife, then burst into tears sobbing, "I'm sorry, I'm sorry." (After Greenberg et. al., 1986, pp. 16–17)

Branching Out
MYTHS ABOUT SUICIDE

Many of us wrongly believe numerous myths about suicide (Pokorny, 1968; Shneidman, 1973). Perhaps if you are aware of some of these myths, you may be able to prevent a suicide or at least to help the loved ones left behind to cope with someone's suicide.

Myth 1. People who talk about committing suicide do not actually go ahead and do it. In fact, close to 8 out of 10 of the people who commit suicide have given some warning beforehand that they were about to take their lives. Often, they have given multiple warnings.

Myth 2. All people who commit suicide definitely have decided that they want to die. In fact, many of those who commit suicide are not certain they really want to die. They often take a gamble that someone will save them. Sometimes, for example, people attempting suicide will take pills and then call someone to tell that person of the suicide attempt. If the person is not there, or if that person does not follow through quickly in response to the call, the suicide attempt may succeed.

Myth 3. Suicide occurs more often among people who are wealthy. In fact, suicide is about equally prevalent at all levels of the socioeconomic spectrum.

Myth 4. People who commit suicide are crazy. Although suicide is linked to depression, relatively few of the people who commit suicide are truly out of touch with reality.

Myth 5. People who commit suicide are always depressed beforehand. Although depression is linked to suicide, some people who take their lives show no signs of depression at all. People with terminal physical illnesses, for example, may commit suicide not because they are depressed, but in order to spare loved ones the suffering of having to support them, or because they have made peace with the idea of death and have decided that the time has come.

Myth 6. The risk of suicide ends when a person improves in mood following a major depression or a previous suicidal crisis. In fact, most suicides occur while an individual is still depressed but after the individual starts to show some recovery. Often, people who are severely depressed are unable even to gather the energy to put together the means to commit suicide. Therefore, the improvement may mean that they will feel better and will have the energy to do something about their wish to die.

Myth 7. Suicide is influenced by the cosmos—sun spots, phases of the moon, the position of the planets, and so on. There is no evidence for any of these assertions.

FINDING YOUR WAY

13.2

Suppose that you are volunteering to answer telephones on a suicide hotline. What kinds of strategies would you use to convince a person not to commit suicide? How might you at least convince a person to postpone committing suicide until the person has explored other possibilities for solving her or his problems? What might you actually say to try to prevent someone from committing suicide?

Why do people kill themselves? The two main motivations for suicide appear to be *surcease* (the wish to end the present condition) and *manipulation* (the wish to get other persons to feel or act in particular ways). Those who seek surcease have given up on life. They see death as the only solution to their problems and some take their lives. Slightly more than half of suicides appear to be of this kind. People seeking surcease usually are depressed, hopeless, and relatively certain that they really want their lives to end. The following suicide note, written by author Virginia Woolf to her husband, shows the wish for surcease:

Dearest, I feel certain that I am going mad again: I feel we can't go through another of those terrible times. And I shan't recover this time. I begin to hear voices, and can't concentrate. So I am doing what seems the best thing to do. . . . If anybody could have saved me it would have been you. Everything has gone from me but the certainty of your goodness. I can't go on spoiling your life any longer.

I don't think two people could have been happier than we have been.

In contrast, those who use suicide as a means of manipulation try to maneuver the world according to their desires. They may view suicide as a way to inflict revenge on a lover who has rejected them, to gain the attention of those who have ignored them, to hurt those who have hurt them, or to have the last word in an ongoing argument. Many of those who attempt suicide in this manner are not fully committed to dying but rather are using suicide as a call for attention and help. Indeed, sometimes these people take precautions so that their suicide attempt will not be successful, but these precautions do not always work. Roughly 13% of suicide attempts are of this kind. Unless they receive help, people who attempt manipulative suicide often try committing suicide again and may continue until they succeed in ending their lives.

Psychotherapists need to take suicide threats seriously, both to preserve the lives of their clients and to protect themselves against legal action, whether by someone who unsuccessfully attempts suicide or by kin of someone who succeeds in committing suicide. In general, issues of abnormal behavior raise several legal issues, which are considered next.

WHAT ARE THE LEGAL VIEWS ON ISSUES OF ABNORMAL BEHAVIOR?

Psychologists seek to describe various kinds and aspects of abnormal behavior in order to diagnose the problems of their patients, as well as to understand such behavior. Although these descriptions are imperfect, often permitting ambiguous diagnoses and flawed understandings, they generally serve the purpose for which psychologists intended them. Nonpsychologists, however, may have different requirements, which may lead to different definitions. Abnormal behavior and its definition raise issues of both criminal and civil law.

Criminal Law

In courtrooms and law offices, alternative definitions of abnormal behavior are required, which may differ from the definitions preferred by psychologists. The term *sanity*, for example, is a legal term, not a psychological one, for describing behavior. Some of the most controversial examples of legal descriptions of abnormal behavior have involved criminal behavior. In 1834, a court in Ohio decided that a person could be found not guilty by reason of insanity if the person acted on an "irresistible impulse" that impelled the accused to commit the crime. Thus, the particular category of disorder was not relevant; the ability to resist an impulse was. Later cases upheld the legitimacy of the "not guilty by reason of insanity" defense.

Perhaps the most well-known construction of the insanity defense is the *M'Naghten Rule,* which came as the result of a murder trial in 1834 by a court in England. A Scot, Daniel M'Naghten, tried to assassinate the prime minister of England, and ended up killing the secretary of the prime minister by mistake. M'Naghten was acquitted of the murder charge on the grounds that he had a "mental defect" that prevented him from understanding what he did at the time he committed the act. The *M'Naghten Rule* holds that "to establish a defense on the ground of insanity, it must be clearly proved that, at the time of committing the act, the party accused was laboring under such a defect of reasoning, from disease of the mind, as not to know the nature and quality of the act he [or she] was doing, or if he [or she] did know it, that he [or she] did not know he [or she] was doing what was wrong" (*Stedman's Medical Dictionary,* 1990, p. 1374).

The American Law Institute provided a set of guidelines in 1962 that were intended to reflect the current state of the insanity defense and its legal and psychological implications. These guidelines state that people cannot be held responsible for criminal conduct if, as a consequence of a mental disease or defect, the accused lack the capacity either to recognize the wrongness of their conduct or to act in conformity with the requirements of the law. The guidelines exclude, however, repeated criminal actions or antisocial conduct. In other words, the intent of the guidelines is to cover extraordinary acts, not habitual criminal behavior.

In 1981, John Hinckley Jr. attempted to assassinate President Ronald Reagan in order to impress actress Jodie Foster. Hinckley was found not guilty by reason of insanity. As a result of this case and the outrage that followed the case, a number of states have introduced a new verdict, "guilty but mentally ill." Federal courts have also tightened up guidelines for finding a defendant not guilty by reason of insanity. The Insanity Defense Reform Act, passed by the U.S. Congress in October, 1984, makes it much more difficult for a defendant to escape the punishment of the law, regardless of the defendant's mental state. The topic remains controversial, and some psychiatrists, such as Thomas Szasz (1963; see also Table 13.8), have argued that concepts of mental illness and insanity have no place in the courtroom at all. According to Szasz, acts of violence are as rational and goal directed as any other acts, and perpetrators of such acts should be treated accordingly.

Civil Law

Psychology and the law are also interrelated in noncriminal matters. For example, do the mentally ill have a legal right to treatment? In the case of *Wyatt v. Stickney* (1971), decided in Alabama, the court ruled that the mentally ill do have a legal right to treatment. This ruling has generally held up. However, there is always room for various interpretations of who is mentally ill and really needs treatment. Since the 1980s, federal spending on mental institutions has decreased, so many patients who were formerly in psychiatric hospitals have been released into the streets. There they generally join the ranks of the homeless and can now be seen wandering the streets instead of the halls of mental hospitals.

On the other hand, people suffering from mental illnesses today also are recognized as having a right to refuse treatment unless their behavior is potentially dangerous to themselves or others. In deciding whether to require treatment or confinement, we need to consider not only the rights of the potential patient, but also the rights of people whom they might harm. We must try to find the right balance between the rights of the prospective patient to be free to refuse treatment or hospitalization and the rights of other people to be protected from any harm that the prospective patient might cause. It should be noted, however, that mentally ill people, on average, are no more likely to show aggressive behavior than are people without mental illness. In fact, many psychological disorders, such as depression and some types of schizophrenia, are characterized by reduced social interaction of any kind.

This chapter described some of the main disorders that constitute much of the subject matter of abnormal psychology. Many psychological disorders have not been discussed here. Some disorders are addressed in other chapters (e.g., chapter 4 deals with aspects of substance-abuse disorders), and others are simply outside the scope of an introduction to psychology. Whereas clinical psychologists have reached broad agreement regarding the diagnostic categories (as provided by DSM-IV), there is considerable disagreement regarding the causes of the various syndromes. Psychodynamic, humanistic, behavioral, cognitive, psychophysiological, as well as cultural explanations of these causes may be viewed as either competing or complementary. These approaches also lead to competing or complementary ways to treat these disorders. Their implications for psychotherapy are considered in chapter 14.

The Solution to   The Case of the Ups and Downs

Leah wants to become a psychologist so she looked through her *Pathways to Psychology* book until she found what she was looking for in chapter 13. She suspects that Vonda may be exhibiting symptoms of bipolar mood disorder. Leah realizes that she is no clinical psychologist, but Vonda's up-and-down mood swings seem identical to those she has read about in the description of this disorder.

Leah talks to Vonda and discovers that others in her family show the same sudden and drastic changes in mood. Because Leah has read that bipolar mood disorder tends to run in families, she becomes even more concerned. After much pleading, Leah convinces Vonda at least to see a psychotherapist just to check out this possibility. After several sessions, the psychotherapist in fact diagnoses Vonda as having bipolar mood disorder and puts her on a controlled regimen of lithium therapy combined with psychotherapy. Vonda quickly shows improvement and so does both her life and her children's lives.

Summary

What Is Abnormal Behavior?   462

1. *Abnormal behavior* is statistically unusual, non-adaptive, labeled as abnormal by the surrounding society, and characterized by some degree of perceptual, emotional, or cognitive distortion. Most abnormal behavior can be described in terms of some or all of these characteristics.

How Have People Explained Abnormal Behavior?   465

2. Early explanations of abnormal behavior included witchcraft and spiritual possession by demons.
3. More contemporary explanations of abnormal behavior include psychodynamic, humanistic, behavioral (learning), cognitive, psychophysiological, and cultural perspectives. Eclectic approaches combine aspects of the various explanations.

How Do Clinicians Diagnose Abnormal Behavior?   469

4. Through the development of the *Diagnostic and Statistical Manual, Fourth Edition (DSM-IV)*, clinicians have reached widespread agreement regarding the diagnosis of mental disorders. The DSM-IV classifies psychological disorders according to criteria based on symptoms, rather than in terms of any particular theoretical approach.

What Are Anxiety Disorders?   470

5. *Anxiety disorders* involve the individual's feelings of *anxiety*.
6. DSM-IV divides anxiety disorders into five main categories: (a) phobic disorders, (b) panic disorder, (c) generalized anxiety disorder, (d) stress (post-traumatic or acute) disorders, and (e) obsessive–compulsive disorder.

What Are Mood Disorders? 474

7. DSM-IV lists two major *mood disorders* (extreme disturbances in a person's emotional state): *depressive disorders* (sometimes called "unipolar depression") and *bipolar disorder.* Depression is relatively common and is generally believed to be influenced by situational factors. Bipolar disorder, on the other hand, is much more rare and runs in families, suggesting a possible genetic, biological component. Both disorders, however, probably are influenced by some biological factors and some situational ones.

What Are Dissociative Disorders? 478

8. There are three main *dissociative disorders: dissociative amnesia, dissociative fugue,* and *dissociative identity disorder.* All of these disorders involve some kind of change in the normally integrative functions of consciousness, identity, or motor behavior. This category also includes *depersonalization disorder,* which involves passing episodes during which people experience distortions of their body image.

9. Environmental traumas have been more strongly implicated for dissociative disorders than have hereditary or biological factors.

What Is Schizophrenia? 479

10. *Schizophrenia* is a set of disorders with a variety of symptoms including hallucinations, *delusions,* disturbed thought processes, and disturbed emotional responses, as well as some odd motor symptoms.

11. Types of schizophrenia include disorganized schizophrenia, catatonic schizophrenia, paranoid schizophrenia, undifferentiated schizophrenia, and residual schizophrenia.

12. Of the various explanations for schizophrenia, psychophysiological explanations seem particularly interesting because they may explain familial trends in the development of schizophrenia, as well as the positive outcomes associated with antipsychotic drugs. The specific psychophysiological causes remain unknown, however. In addition, environmental stress (e.g., due to low SES or to societal discrimination) seems to increase the likelihood of being diagnosed as schizophrenic.

What Are Impulse-Control Disorders? 484

13. The following impulse-control disorders not elsewhere classified involve the impulse to engage in a particular behavior: intermittent explosive disorder, kleptomania, pyromania, pathological gambling, and trichotillomania.

What Are Personality Disorders? 485

14. *Personality disorders* are consistent, long-term, extreme personality characteristics that cause the person great unhappiness or that seriously impair the person's ability to adjust to the demands of everyday living or to function well in her or his environment.

15. The major personality disorders are paranoid, narcissistic, histrionic, avoidant, dependent, obsessive–compulsive, and antisocial personality disorders.

What Disorders Are Usually First Diagnosed in Infancy, Childhood, or Adolescence? 485

16. Three major *disorders usually first diagnosed in infancy, childhood, or adolescence* are: attention-deficit/hyperactivity disorder (ADHD), conduct disorder, and pervasive developmental disorder (PDD, autism). In addition, DSM-IV includes several other disorders that commonly appear before adulthood.

What Are Some Additional Psychological Disorders? 487

17. *Somatoform disorders* are relatively rare bodily symptoms or complaints of bodily symptoms for which no physiological basis can be found. There are five main kinds of somatoform disorders: pain disorder, conversion disorder, somatization disorder, hypochondriasis, and body dysmorphic disorder.

18. *Sexual disorders* involve sexual arousal, thoughts, or behaviors that cause the individual or other people emotional distress or difficulty in other aspects of the individuals's life. DSM-IV classifies these disorders into gender-identity disorders, paraphilias, sexual dysfunction, and other sexual disorders.

19. DSM-IV also describes various *cognitive-impairment disorders* (e.g., delirium, amnesia, and dementia), eating disorders, sleeping disorders, adjustment disorders, and substance-related disorders.

How Do Psychologists View Suicide? 488

20. On average, every 20 minutes, at least one person in the United States commits suicide.

21. Many myths surround suicide. Perhaps the most important caution is that any person may decide to commit suicide and that any threats of suicide should be taken seriously.

What Are the Legal Views on Issues of Abnormal Behavior? 492

22. The term *sanity* is a legal term, not a psychological one, for describing behavior. At present, a person's sanity is an important factor in determining prosecution and sentencing for the person's criminal

behavior. Just how sanity should be determined and how it should be considered in making legal judgments still is being evaluated in the courts.

23. Issues of civil law related to abnormal behavior center on an individual's right to obtain or to refuse treatment.

Pathways to Knowledge

Choose the best answer to complete each sentence.

1. According to the various definitions cited, which of the following is *not* a typical characteristic of abnormal behavior?
   (a) labeled abnormal by the society in which the individual lives
   (b) carefully planned
   (c) statistically unusual
   (d) maladaptive to the individual

2. Anxiety disorders may be characterized by both
   (a) psychotic symptoms and somatic symptoms.
   (b) low affect and telegraphic thoughts.
   (c) telegraphic thoughts and somatic symptoms.
   (d) motor symptoms and somatic symptoms.

3. The two main types of mood disorders are
   (a) depressive disorders and generalized anxiety disorders.
   (b) obsessive–compulsive disorders and manic–depressive disorders.
   (c) depressive disorders and bipolar disorders.
   (d) depressive disorders and obsessive–compulsive disorders.

4. An individual cannot remember events during and immediately following a serious airplane crash. The individual probably is suffering from
   (a) dissociative amnesia.
   (b) dissociative fugue.
   (c) dissociative anxiety.
   (d) posttraumatic stress anxiety.

5. A type of schizophrenia characterized by hallucinations, delusions, and disordered thought processes is referred to as
   (a) disorganized.
   (b) residual.
   (c) fragmented.
   (d) dissociative.

6. An individual who is identified as having a histrionic personality disorder shows
   (a) persecutory thoughts.
   (b) exhibitionistic tendencies.

(c) different personalities for different situations.
   (d) exaggerated concern for the well-being of others.

Answer each of the following questions by filling in the blank with an appropriate word or phrase.

7. Depression associated with advanced age is called _____ depression.

8. A(n) _____ is an irresistible desire to perform a certain activity in a specified manner, whereas a(n) _____ refers to the occurrence of unwanted images or impulses one is unable to suppress.

9. A person with _____ _____ is characterized by an extreme fear of being judged or criticized by people, which often leads the individual to become socially isolated.

10. According to DSM-IV, an individual who complains of sudden and inexplicable attacks of fear and anxiety, accompanied by heart palpitations, sweating, and dizziness, will probably be classified as showing _____ _____.

11. Disorders characterized by a drastic change in a person's awareness of past or present experiences and in personal identity are referred to jointly as _____ _____.

12. Some war veterans show _____ _____ _____, which is characterized by recurring and often painful memories and flashbacks of traumatic experiences.

13. An individual who has alternating periods of depressive and of manic symptoms probably is suffering from _____ _____.

14. A depression that appears to be a reaction to external events is termed _____ depression.

15. The category of schizophrenia known as _____ schizophrenia applies to individuals who have previously had at least one schizophrenic episode, but who currently show only mildly disturbed behavior.

16. A desire for sexual contact with children is called _____.

17. A disorder known as _____-_____/_____ disorder is usually first diagnosed in childhood, but may extend into adulthood. Children

with this disorder have difficulty focusing their attention and tend to be impulsive and disruptive.

18. _____-_____ disorder occurs when an individual is uncomfortable with the gender roles linked to his or her sex, and the person identifies instead with the gender roles of the opposite sex.

19. A psychodynamic view is that _____ stems from internalized anger we have toward an actual or symbolically lost loved one.

20. According to DSM-IV, obsessive–compulsive disorder is classified as a(n) _____ _____.

Answers

1. b, 2. d, 3. c, 4. a, 5. a, 6. b, 7. involutional, 8. compulsion, obsession, 9. specific phobia, 10. panic disorder, 11. dissociative disorders, 12. posttraumatic stress disorder, 13. bipolar disorder, 14. exogenous, 15. residual, 16. pedophilia, 17. attention-deficit/hyperactivity, 18. Gender-identity, 19. depression, 20. anxiety disorder

Pathways to Understanding

1. Choose a psychological perspective that you find well-suited to your own beliefs about abnormal behavior. Compare and contrast your preferred perspective with other perspectives, showing why yours makes better sense.

2. Suppose that your English teacher assigns you the task of creating a believable literary character that is schizophrenic. Briefly describe that person as others view the person; then describe how that person sees the world, including other persons.

3. Sometimes, it is tempting to analyze people you know in terms of the disorders they seem to show. What are the risks of assuming this kind of role as an amateur psychologist?

The Case of The Unflagging Self-Helper

Rena loves self-help books. She used a self-help book to try to quit smoking and she nearly did quit. At least she has cut down substantially. Rena has used self-help books to lose weight and has gone through several different diets in this way. On some of these diets she has lost as much as 30 pounds, although now Rena has gained back the weight she has lost and realizes she needs to diet again. Rena is planning to buy a new diet book that just has gone on the market in the hope that she has more luck with this book than she had with the others. She also has used self-help books to try to improve her relationships and has found them useful in guiding how she interacts with men. The last book Rena read suggested a submissive approach and she is, in fact, finding that this approach is working well with her current boyfriend, Sam. At the same time, Rena feels like she is playing a role and is not totally certain that being submissive is worth the costs. On the whole, she sees things as going well for her.

But is everything really going well for Rena? Is she following a pathway that will lead her to success in her life? Think about these issues as you read chapter 14. Pay special attention to the issue of self-help books.

CHAPTER 14
PSYCHOTHERAPY

14

*P*sychotherapy is an intervention by a trained individual that uses the principles of psychology to try to improve the life of the person who receives the intervention. Some of the early providers had questionable training, however.

WHAT WERE SOME EARLY METHODS OF PSYCHOTHERAPEUTIC INTERVENTION?

In ancient times, in Europe, abnormal behavior was viewed as being caused by demons (see chapter 13), so psychotherapeutic "treatment" involved trying to rid the mentally ill person of the supposed demons, often killing or at least torturing the afflicted person in the process. After the end of the Middle Ages, as people became aware that mental illness was not caused by demonic possession, slightly more humane treatments came into being. From about the 1400s through the 1700s, mentally ill persons were housed, and sometimes even treated, in **asylums**—hospitals for mentally ill patients. Many of these asylums resembled overcrowded prisons more than they did mental hospitals. The inmates were treated more like prisoners than patients and were often chained to the walls of the cramped quarters or chained to large iron balls that they had to drag with them wherever they went.

The pathetic treatment of mentally disturbed people appalled Parisian physician Phillipe Pinel (1745–1826). In 1793, Pinel removed the inmates' shackles and, as a result, the inmates became much calmer and more manageable. In the United States, mentally ill people were commonly housed in prisons, along with convicted criminals. Social reformer Dorothea Dix (1802–1887) was instrumental in spurring the development of mental hospitals as separate institutions from prisons, designed for the humane treatment of mentally ill persons.

Any treatment of mental illness should start with a diagnosis. The issue of diagnosis is considered next.

HOW AND WHY DO CLINICIANS DIAGNOSE ABNORMAL BEHAVIOR?

Before a clinician can treat a mentally ill person, the clinician must diagnose the person's problem. As mentioned in chapter 13, the *Diagnostic and Statistical Manual* (*DSM;* now in its fourth edition, DSM-IV) enjoys widespread acceptance as a standard tool for diagnosis (Sartorius, de Girolano, Andrews, German, & Eisenberg, 1993). The DSM-IV is not perfect, however. Also, even if the DSM were flawless, diagnosis and treatment ultimately would depend not on the DSM, but on each individual clinician's judgment, based on his or her clinical experience and professional expertise.

When deciding how to respond to a new client, a clinician must answer three questions: (a) Does the client have a treatable problem? (b) If so, what is the problem? (c) Once the problem is diagnosed, how should the problem be treated? Clinicians use various techniques to answer these questions, some of which were described in chapter 12 (e.g., projective and objective personality tests). No single technique is perfect, so clinicians often use more than one technique. Clinicians then can integrate and interpret a relatively wide variety of information. Once clinicians have

Dorothea Dix was instrumental in encouraging the development of mental hospitals as institutions separate from prisons.

diagnosed particular psychological problems, they can consider how to treat the problems. The particular form of treatment chosen depends on the psychological approach preferred by the individual clinician.

Cross-cultural psychologists have noted that an additional consideration in diagnosis and treatment of psychological disorders should be the cultural context in which the disorders appear (Matsumoto, 1994, 1996). For instance, regarding the diagnosis of schizophrenia, various culture-specific symptoms are observed by people who are members of the Yoruba tribe of Nigeria, such as "an expanded head and goose flesh" (cited in Matsumoto, 1996, p. 237). In diagnosing depressive disorders among the Hopi in the United States, brief episodes of severe depression are more characteristic than are relatively longer periods of depression (Matsumoto, 1996).

It also should be noted that many people who seek the help of psychotherapists do not suffer from any of the psychological disorders described in chapter 13. Many people seek psychotherapy because they feel they need help in handling a particular aspect of their lives, because they wish to enhance their enjoyment of their lives, or because they are facing particularly difficult life circumstances. For instance, Joanie has recognized that her use of alcohol is creating problems in her marriage, so she is looking for some form of psychotherapy to help her to deal both with her alcohol use and to address the problems in her marriage. Paulo, a successful middle-aged salesperson, has started to feel that something is missing from his life, although he is not sure just what he lacks. He goes to a psychotherapist to get help in figuring out both what he wants and how to get what he lacks.

Li's husband of 15 years just died, leaving Li with a 6-month-old, a 2-year-old, and a 4-year-old to raise on her own. While her children are awake, Li is so busy that she does not have time to feel miserable and

asylum • a hospital or other institution for housing and possibly treating mentally ill patients

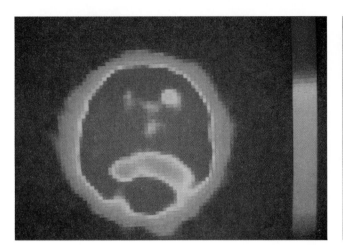 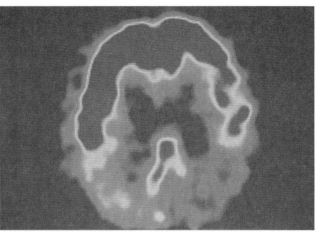

Increasingly, psychologists are able to use various kinds of images of the brain as an aid to diagnosing psychological disorders. Depicted here are PET scans showing a normal brain and the brain of a person diagnosed as having Alzheimer's dementia.

overwhelmed. Once her children are in bed, however, Li feels her life spinning out of her control; every night, she sobs herself to sleep. Li's friend at work keeps telling her that she should see a psychotherapist to help her through this crisis. Different psychotherapists are likely to approach psychotherapy for Li in different ways. Notice that Li's behavior is not abnormal in the sense of its being seriously disordered. Rather it is abnormal because Li is having trouble coping. Psychotherapists help clients deal with problems so that the clients can adjust better to the demands life places upon them. People who seek help should be commended for recognizing that their lives have spun out of full control and for recognizing that they need to gain back control of their lives.

HOW DO DIFFERENT PSYCHOLOGISTS APPROACH PSYCHOTHERAPY?

Each of the many different approaches to psychotherapy has been applied both to serious psychological disorders (such as those described in chapter 13) and to mild psychological problems that arise because of relatively normal difficulties in adjustment or because of the need to cope with difficult situations. Each approach has accompanying advantages and disadvantages. Many of the therapies overlap, but it is still useful to consider the distinctions among the five main approaches: psychodynamic, humanistic, behavioral, cognitive, and biological. In addition, we consider a multicultural approach to psychotherapy. While reading about the distinctive features of these diverse approaches, bear in mind that many practicing psychotherapists use an *eclectic* approach to treatment, drawing on techniques and ideas from more than one of the main approaches to psychotherapy.

Psychodynamic Therapy

Psychodynamic therapies have in common their emphasis on insight as the key to improvement. The basic assumption is that when patients have *insight* into (understanding of) the sources of their problems, their problems will become manageable, and the patients will improve. Psychoanalysis is the main type of psychodynamic therapy.

Psychoanalysis

Psychoanalysts assume that psychological disorders result from unconscious conflicts among the id, the superego, and the demands of the environment. In their view, although people are unaware of these underlying conflicts, the conflicts affect their thoughts, feelings, and especially motivations. The key to helping patients to improve is to help them become conscious of ego-threatening information that has been repressed. Thus, treatment focuses on gradually peeling away layers of protective defenses to discover the underlying causes of psychological problems. For example, if a patient enters psychotherapy in order to conquer anxiety, the anxiety is considered a symptom of unconscious repressed conflicts among feelings, thoughts, and motives. To relieve the anxiety, the therapist must uncover and treat the underlying problem.

How does the therapist actually reveal the unconscious conflicts that underlie an observable disorder? Psychoanalysts use several different techniques (e.g., dream analysis; see chapter 4). The most prominent of these techniques is free association. In **free association,** a person says whatever comes to mind without stopping to check, think about, or edit his or her statements. At first, the patient may find it hard to report all thoughts through free association. With practice, however, the patient usually finds it easier. According to the psychoanalytic view, it is critical not to edit anything out because the most interesting and important details usually are those that the patient does not wish to say aloud. For example, the patient

Visitors to Vienna still can see Sigmund Freud's treatment room, where his neurological patients served as case studies for the development of his psychodynamic theory. On this world-renowned couch, Freud's patients worked through their unconscious conflicts, in response to his psychoanalytic therapy.

free association • a psychodynamic technique in which patients are encouraged to say whatever comes to mind without censoring or otherwise editing their statements

may not want to say that his first free association to *father* is *dictator*. He may think the psychotherapist would not take the association seriously or think that there is something wrong with someone who would generate this kind of association. Typically, to enhance free association the patient is encouraged to relax, for example, by lying down on a couch in a comfortable setting.

Psychoanalysts also may encourage patients to report on their dreams. The psychotherapists then use these dreams as one basis for their analysis. Many psychoanalysts seek to uncover the underlying meanings of these dreams. For example, dreams of finding security in a cave might be interpreted as a desire to return to the safety of the womb. But any dream would have to be interpreted in the full context in which it is offered.

If patients could make free associations and remember dreams that immediately led them to repressed material, psychoanalysis would be over quickly. According to psychoanalytic theory, it does not work that way because of **resistances**, which are attempts, usually unconscious, to block progress. Why would patients try to block progress, especially when they are paying for therapy in order to make progress? Resistances protect patients from dealing with the contents of the unconscious, which are often quite painful. For that reason, patients unconsciously try to resist the therapeutic process. Resistances can take various forms, such as remaining silent, making jokes, or even skipping sessions. Trained psychoanalysts identify and deal with resistances when they arise.

Psychoanalytic therapists remain relatively detached from their patients and have little emotional involvement with them. The therapist seems almost like a shadowy parent figure who tries to help the patient without becoming too involved in the patient's problems. The patient, however, often becomes quite involved with the therapist. Indeed, the patient may start treating the therapist as though the therapist were contributing to the patient's problems. The patient's emotional involvement with the therapist is termed **transference**. The basic notion is that patients shift to the therapist the thoughts and feelings they have had toward others in the past, such as toward their parents. By being detached, therapists actually encourage transference because patients can project onto their therapist whatever conflicts or fantasies arise during therapy. The detached therapist is something like a blank screen onto which patients can project their past relationships. According to Sigmund Freud, such transference helps the patient by bringing out into the open any conflicts that have been suppressed in the past.

All psychoanalysts must themselves first be psychoanalyzed in order to understand better their own conflicts and sources of psychological distress. This understanding is particularly important in order to avoid **countertransference**, in which the therapist projects onto the patient the therapist's own feelings. Therapists who project their own problems onto the patient may fail to help their patients and even may cause harm to their patients.

Offshoots of Psychoanalysis

Psychoanalysis has been important to the historical development of psychotherapy. Among its many contributions, it has generated a variety of offshoots. Many of these offshoots developed from the theories of personality offered by Freud's followers, the neo-Freudians, such as Carl Jung, Erik Erikson, and Karen Horney (described in chapter 12). The various

resistance • a defensive tactic used by patients, usually unconsciously, to keep from becoming aware of unconscious material that affects the progress of therapy

transference • a term used in psychodynamic therapy describing a patient's emotional involvement with the psychotherapist as an authority figure

countertransference • a term used in psychodynamic therapy describing a situation in which the therapist becomes emotionally involved with the patient, projecting the therapist's own feelings onto the patient

forms of neo-Freudian therapy are sometimes termed *ego analysis* because of their common view that the ego is at least as important as the id. In other words, conscious processing is just as important as, and possibly more important than, unconscious processing. People have conscious purposes and goals and, to a large extent, they act to fulfill those goals. According to ego analysts, to understand their patients fully, therapists need to understand not only their patients' early life history, but also their patients' present experiences and future goals and plans.

Psychoanalysis can be a long process, continuing over a period of years, during which the patient and the therapist may meet as often as three to five times per week. Psychoanalysis thus can become very expensive. Psychodynamic therapists, however, have placed increasing emphasis on *time-limited psychotherapy* (Mann, 1973; Strupp, 1981). The idea of such therapy is to apply the principles of psychoanalysis but to effect improvement in a relatively short time.

Humanistic Therapies

Like psychoanalysis and other psychodynamic therapies, humanistic therapies emphasize insight. Beyond this similarity, however, humanistic therapies differ greatly from psychodynamic therapies. For one thing, humanistic therapists refer to the people they treat as "clients," whereas psychodynamic therapists usually refer to them as "patients." This difference in choice of words reflects a deeper difference between the two approaches. Psychodynamic therapy is based on a model of disorder in which an underlying disease process is considered the source of the patient's troubles. In contrast, the humanistic model views each person as an individual with feelings and thoughts that may come into conflict with each other or with society, thereby causing problems in living.

The role of the therapist also differs across models. Psychodynamic therapists believe that only highly skilled psychoanalysts can understand the complexities of the human mind and behavior. Humanistic therapists, on the other hand, believe that clients can be helped to understand their own minds and behavior. Humanistic therapists do not interpret and then provide insights to their patients. Rather, therapists help clients actively gain their own insights.

Another key difference is that, in the psychodynamic view, people are largely ruled by unconscious forces, whereas in the humanistic view, people have free will and are ruled by their own conscious decisions. Psychodynamic therapists often seem to view people as being tossed about by internal forces that the people can scarcely understand, let alone influence. In contrast, humanistic therapists emphasize free will. When people are mentally well, they are aware of and understand their own behavior. People thus can change their behavior at will. Because people are free to make choices, a goal of therapy is to help each client to *feel* completely free in making choices.

All humanistic therapy is centered on the client. Carl Rogers (1961a, 1961b) developed his particular form of **client-centered therapy** (later called "person-centered therapy") on the assumption that clients can be understood only in terms of their own view of reality, which they build for themselves. To client-centered therapists, the actual events that occur in people's lives are less important than the ways in which people interpret those events. Thus, client-centered therapists do not try to impose a theoretical system (such as Freud's) on the client. Instead, they try to

In client-centered therapy, the therapist listens empathically to the client, showing both unconditional positive regard for the client and genuine self-disclosure to the client.

client-centered therapy • a form of humanistic psychotherapy in which the therapeutic interactions center on the client's view of reality

Professor Gallagher and his controversial technique of simultaneously confronting the fear of heights, snakes and the dark.

understand how their clients view the world. Client-centered therapy is also *nondirective*; the therapist is not supposed to guide the course of therapy in any particular direction.

Rogers believed that people are basically good and adaptive, both in what they do and in the goals they set for themselves. When they act otherwise, they need guidance only to see for themselves how to adapt better to their situations. The goal of client-centered therapy is to help people realize their full potential. Rogers believed that there are three keys to successful therapy:

1. *Genuineness,* as shown in the therapist's openness, honesty, self-disclosure, and expression of genuine feelings with the client, as well as with her- or himself.

2. *Unconditional positive regard* toward the client, which encourages the client to feel unconditional positive self-regard.

3. *Accurate empathic understanding* of the client's view of the world.

In client-centered, nondirective therapy, the therapist follows the client's lead; in contrast, in psychodynamic therapy, the therapist has a particular direction in mind regarding how to lead the patient, namely, toward the uncovering of unconscious conflicts. Thus, the course of client-centered therapy is likely to be quite different from that of psychodynamic therapy. Nondirective, client-centered therapists believe that by listening empathically to clients and by helping clients to clarify and explore their own feelings, clients then will feel free to live as they choose.

Some psychotherapists find the humanistic approach to be less scientific, at least in the traditional sense, than they would like.

They also believe that the humanistic approach is more likely to be effective for mild than for severe disorders, and for patients who are more rather than less educated. Some psychotherapists also believe that humanistic therapy represents a paradigm that was more responsive to the way people thought in the 1960s than to the way people think today. But, of course, many psychotherapists continue to believe in and to use humanistic therapy: There is no complete consensus on this or any other form of psychotherapy. Some of the psychotherapists who do not accept a humanistic approach prefer a behavioral approach.

Behavior Therapies

Behavior therapy refers to a collection of techniques, which is based loosely on principles of classical and operant conditioning, as well as on observational learning from models (see chapter 5). Several features characterize behavior therapy. First, whereas psychoanalysis shuns the treatment of symptoms, behavior therapy deliberately focuses only on symptoms. To the behavior therapist, the symptom is the problem. If a person is experiencing anxiety, then the person needs to reduce that anxiety to function effectively. If the person cannot stop counting objects, then it is the counting behavior that needs to be addressed. Behaviorists view themselves as wasting no time looking for underlying causes of the symptoms rooted in the person's past experiences. In short, behavior therapy concentrates on behavior. Behavior therapists do not try to address psychological insights or changes. They focus only on trying to change the maladaptive behavior.

Second, behavior therapy is extremely directive. Although the behavior therapist works with the client, the therapist alone designs a detailed

behavior therapy • various psychotherapeutic techniques based mostly on principles of classical and operant conditioning, as well as some techniques based on observational learning from models

TABLE 14.1

Behavioral Treatments for Psychological Problems

Procedures based on classical conditioning	
Counterconditioning	A particular response to a particular stimulus is replaced by an alternative response to that stimulus. The alternative substitute response is incompatible with the unwanted initial response, such as replacing an initial positive response with a negative one or counterconditioning the patient to feel a negative response instead of a positive one.
Aversion therapy	The therapist seeks to teach the client to experience negative feelings in the presence of a stimulus that is considered inappropriately attractive.
Systematic desensitization	The therapist seeks to help the client learn *not* to experience negative feelings (e.g., anxiety) toward a stimulus that currently prompts a negative response (Wolpe, 1958).
Extinction procedures	A particular maladaptive emotional response to a particular stimulus is weakened and eventually extinguished by presenting the particular stimulus in the absence of whatever stimuli may have prompted the learning of the emotional response.
Flooding	Patients are exposed directly to the stimulus that causes them extreme levels of anxiety so that they realize that nothing horrible happens in the presence of the stimulus. They then can learn to cope with the situation when they face it again in the future.
Implosion therapy	Patients are asked to imagine and, to the extent that they can, relive unpleasant experiences with stimuli that are causing them anxiety. As in systemic desensitization, they only imagine a graduated series of steps; anxiety is extinguished by the absence of any harmful or threatening stimuli in association with the stimulus that provokes the anxiety.
Procedures based on operant conditioning	
Token economy	Patients within institutional or other controlled settings receive *tokens* (tangible objects that have no intrinsic worth) as rewards for showing adaptive behavior. The tokens later can be used in exchange for goods or services that the individuals desire. This technique has been used primarily with children who have PDD (pervasive developmental disorder, including autism), although it has been used with other populations as well.
Behavioral contracting	The therapist and the client draw up a contract and both parties are obliged to live up to it. The contract requires the client to show specific behaviors that are the focus of the therapy, in return for which the therapist will give the client particular things that the client may want, even including permission to terminate the therapy.

treatment plan. Next, the patient follows the therapist's treatment plan and, when the plan has been carried out, the therapy ends. Third, behavior therapy is deliberately short term; the goal is to effect behavioral change quickly. Fourth, behavior therapy often involves the institution of changes in the environment. For example, if the environment currently reinforces maladaptive behavior and punishes adaptive behavior, those contingencies must be changed in order to change the behavior. Finally, behavior therapists take an objective approach, both to the therapy and to the evaluation of the outcomes of the therapy.

Behavior therapy consists of a set of explicit techniques. Basically, these techniques can be categorized roughly as involving classical conditioning, operant conditioning, or observational learning (modeling). Table 14.1 summarizes the treatments involving classical or operant conditioning.

counterconditioning • behavioral techniques based on classical conditioning, emphasizing the substitution of an adaptive response (e.g., relaxation) in place of a maladaptive response (e.g., anxiety) to a particular stimulus

extinction procedures • behavioral techniques based on classical conditioning, in which the goal is to weaken a maladaptive response

modeling • a cognitive and behavioral technique in which people are encouraged to change simply by watching other people successfully cope with challenging problems that affect the observer

Classical conditioning treatments include various **counterconditioning** techniques (e.g., *aversion therapy* or *systematic desensitization*), which replace an unwanted response (e.g., anxiety) to a particular stimulus (e.g., flying) with an alternative response (e.g., physical relaxation) to that stimulus, as well as **extinction procedures,** which include various techniques (e.g., *flooding* or *implosion therapy*) that weaken maladaptive responses. *Operant-conditioning* techniques include the use of a *token economy* or *behavioral contracting.* (Figure 14.1 shows the relative effectiveness of a few behavioral therapies.) In addition, *modeling* may be used as a form of behavioral therapy.

As mentioned in chapter 5, many of the principles of **modeling** come from the work of Albert Bandura (1969). Bandura's basic idea is that people can change simply by watching other people successfully cope with the problems they face. For example, phobic adults have overcome snake phobias by watching other people confront snakes, either in actual live situations or on film (Bandura, Blanchard, & Ritter, 1969). The clients watched as the models moved closer and closer to the snakes; with time, the clients' phobias decreased. Modeling also has been used in various other kinds of therapy. In fact, the therapeutic effects of many kinds of psychotherapy, including therapy groups, may be due, at least partly, to modeling (Braswell & Kendall, 1988). Modeling is partially a cognitive phenomenon.

Some psychotherapists do not accept the behavioral approach. They may believe that it addresses only symptoms, not causes. Thus, they believe,

FIGURE 14.1
Effectiveness of Behavioral Therapies
(a) Aversion therapy, a form of classical conditioning, successfully reduced a patient's response (penile arousal) to an inappropriate stimulus (a fantasy of being tied up; after Marks & Gelder, 1967). (b) A token economy, a form of operant conditioning, successfully increased the wanted behavior (performance of self-help chores) of individuals in an institutional setting. (c) Comparisons of live modeling and participation, symbolic modeling (in which the patient imagines the anxiety-producing stimulus), and systematic desensitization suggest that although all three techniques lead to some behavioral improvement above that of control patients, live modeling and participation is the most effective of these techniques.

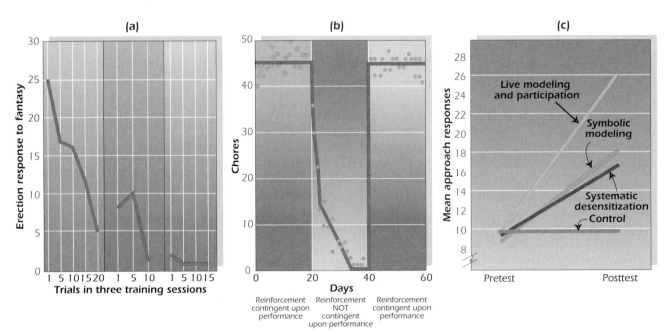

Behavior therapy may involve classical conditioning, operant conditioning, or observational learning (modeling). (a) Through counterconditioning, phobic fliers can learn to respond to airplane flights by feeling relaxed instead of feeling tense and anxious. (b) Observational learning may be helping these children to avoid developing a fear of snakes, but more than observational learning may be needed to help the woman in the background feel less fearful of them.

the underlying disorder is likely to stay with the patient, even if symptoms temporarily vanish. The result will be the same disorder later expressed with different symptoms, or even the same symptoms. Some psychotherapists also criticize this method for not fully addressing people's thought processes. Cognitive approaches to psychotherapy, however, are directed toward thought processes.

Cognitive Approaches to Therapy

Originally, Bandura (1969; Bandura & Walters, 1963) viewed modeling as a behavioral phenomenon. However, as the cognitive revolution proceeded, Bandura started to reformulate the modeling phenomenon in terms of cognitive theory. Indeed, the processes that the observer uses for imitating the model are certainly cognitive ones (Bandura, 1986). In cognitive approaches to therapy, behavioral change is achieved by changing people's thinking. If people can be made to think differently about themselves and their experiences, they can feel and act differently as a result. Albert Ellis's rational-emotive therapy and Aaron Beck's cognitive therapy are both cognitive approaches to psychotherapy.

Rational-Emotive Therapy

When Albert Ellis (1962, 1970, 1973, 1989) formulated **rational-emotive therapy (RET)**, his basic idea was that psychological problems arise because people mentally recite sentences that express incorrect or maladaptive thoughts. In Ellis's view, cognition precedes emotion (see also

rational-emotive therapy (RET) • a form of cognitive therapy based on the notions that (a) incorrect or maladaptive thoughts lead to emotional and other psychological problems, and (b) changes in these thoughts lead to improvements in psychological well-being

chapter 11). Thus, the emotions we feel are caused by the thoughts we have, and we can change our emotions only by changing our thoughts. The goal of Ellis's psychotherapy, therefore, is to change our incorrect and maladaptive thoughts. Ellis's RET and other forms of cognitive therapy have been particularly effective in treating certain anxious patients (Perris & Herlofson, 1993).

Examples of incorrect beliefs that may lead to maladjustment include the following (Ellis, 1970): "You should be loved by everyone for everything you do"; "You need to have perfect self-control at all times"; "You should be thoroughly competent in all respects." To Ellis, the best technique for dealing with incorrect and maladaptive beliefs is to confront the client directly and to dispute the client's beliefs. In other words, the therapist tries to show clients that these false beliefs are leading them to be unhappy and dysfunctional in everyday life. Ellis's goals are similar to those of humanistic therapists: to increase a client's sense of self-worth and to help the client to grow and to make choices by recognizing all of the available options. Beck, considered next, also tries to help clients better use information in choosing from the options available to them.

Beck's Cognitive Therapy

Like Ellis's RET, the cognitive therapy of Aaron Beck (1976, 1986) celebrates the importance of cognition. However, Beck's approach differs from Ellis's in both the cognitive theorizing and the form of the psychotherapy. In Beck's view, people become maladjusted as a result of cognitive distortion. Beck has concentrated particularly on depression, and some findings suggest that the demonstrated effectiveness of cognitive therapy is higher for depressive disorders than for other disorders (Perris & Herlofson, 1993). In treating depression, Beck particularly targets maladaptive schemas (patterns of thinking) that lead us to believe that we are incompetent or worthless.

Some psychotherapists believe that cognitive therapy is incomplete. For example, they may believe that it focuses too much on cognition and not enough on emotion, or they may believe that it works better with more educated or at least more thoughtful clients. Still other therapists believe that it needs to be supplemented with drugs. Therapists who believe in drugs may wish to treat depression and other disorders at least partly through biological therapies.

Biological Therapies

Biological therapies attempt to treat psychological disorders through medical intervention. These therapies differ from those that we have considered up to this point because, in biological therapies, talking (such as in the client–therapist relationship) plays no more of a role than would be the case for any patient–doctor interaction. Biological therapies can be used along with more psychologically oriented therapies, of course, and they often are. When used together, however, psychological therapies tend to play a supportive role rather than a central role in the therapeutic process.

Brief History of Biological Therapies

Biological therapies date back at least to ancient Rome, where particular psychological disorders were viewed as being caused by poisons or other undesirable substances that had entered the body. To rid the body of these

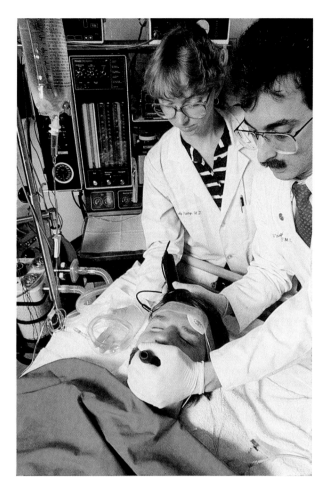

Although electroconvulsive therapy (ECT) is still used by some clinicians, its use is less common and more specific to treatment of severe depression now than it was decades ago. As you can see, even the technical apparatus makes the process seem intimidating. The paddle inserted into the patient's mouth is intended to prevent injury due to the violent contortions associated with the seizures following ECT.

foreign substances, patients were given drugs causing them to vomit or to defecate (Agnew, 1985). Another way of ridding the body of unwanted substances was through selective bleeding. The idea underlying these treatments was to rid the body of whatever substances were causing the mental disturbance. These treatments were used as recently as the 18th century. Another early biological treatment was electrical shock, also used in the 18th and 19th centuries. Apparently, the idea was literally to shock the disorder out of the body and to shock the client into recovery.

In the early 20th century, electrical shock therapy took a form known as **electroconvulsive therapy (ECT)**. ECT has been used for the treatment of severe, long-lasting depression. This form of therapy, still in occasional use today, causes patients to undergo seizures induced by electrical shock. The use of ECT has been controversial for at least two reasons: (a) The loss of memory caused by ECT can be long-lasting, and (b) the procedure destroys neurons of the central nervous system. Also, although the treatment seems to be effective for some patients (Abrams, 1988; Scovern & Kilmann, 1980), it does not work for others (A. I. F. Scott, 1989). Thus, it is almost always a treatment of last resort, particularly for severely depressed patients (Bolwig, 1993). In most cases, depression can be treated with psychotherapy, sometimes combined with antidepressant drugs, making ECT unnecessary.

Another biological treatment proved to be among the most disastrous of the psychiatric profession's attempts to achieve biological cures: *prefrontal lobotomy,* a form of psychosurgery. The basic reason to use **psychosurgery** is to relieve or reduce mental disorders through a procedure

electroconvulsive therapy (ECT) • a form of psychophysiological therapy in which patients undergo electrical shocks, which cause convulsive seizures followed by a period of amnesia and which may relieve severe symptoms of depression

psychosurgery • a procedure intended to relieve psychological problems by probing, slicing, dissecting, or removing some part of the brain

that probes, slices, dissects, or removes some portion of the brain. **Prefrontal lobotomy** involved severing the frontal lobes from the posterior portions of the brain, thereby cutting off all communication between the frontal lobes and the rest of the brain. The operation left many patients *vegetative,* incapable of functioning independently in any meaningful way. Even those operations that were less disastrously tragic could not be considered successful in terms of restoring mental health and normal cognitive function. Unfortunately, between 1935 (when the operation was first introduced) and 1955 (when antipsychotic drugs became the method of choice for treating many of the symptoms of schizophrenia and other disorders), prefrontal lobotomy is estimated to have victimized tens of thousands of patients, primarily in mental institutions (Freeman, 1959). The inventor of the operation even received the Nobel Prize in medicine for his contributions.

Drug Therapies

Since the mid-1950s, the introduction of drug therapies unquestionably has been the major advance in the biological approach to the treatment of mental disorders. There are four main classes of **psychotropic drugs** (i.e., drugs affecting the individual's psychological processes or state of mind): antipsychotic drugs, antidepressant drugs, antianxiety drugs, and lithium.

Antipsychotic Drugs. **Antipsychotic drugs** were a breakthrough in the treatment of psychotic patients. Before the introduction of such drugs, mental hospitals resembled many of our worst stereotypes. They were characterized by wild screaming and even the threat of violence (Carson & Butcher, 1992). Antipsychotic drugs completely changed the atmosphere in many of these wards.

The most commonly used antipsychotic drugs, introduced in the early 1950s, are *phenothiazines*. These antipsychotic drugs relieve the positive symptoms of schizophrenia by blocking receptors for the neurotransmitter dopamine in the schizophrenic brain (see Figure 14.2). Although these drugs successfully treat the positive symptoms of schizophrenia (e.g., hallucinations), they are less successful in treating the negative symptoms (e.g., apathy). The antipsychotic drugs also can have serious side effects, such as dryness of the mouth, tremors, and stiffness of the muscles. At present, there is no clear answer as to how to balance the costs and the benefits of antipsychotic medication. We are far from having magic cure-all pills for treating psychoses.

Antidepressant Drugs. **Antidepressant drugs** traditionally have been of two main kinds: *tricyclics* and *monoamine oxidase (MAO) inhibitors*. Tricyclics are much more frequently used because MAO inhibitors are more toxic, require adherence to a special diet, and generally provide less successful outcomes. However, some people do not respond to tricyclics but do respond to MAO inhibitors, so the MAO inhibitors may be used for these patients.

Both types of antidepressant drugs seem to have roughly the same effect: They increase the concentrations of two neurotransmitters, serotonin and norepinephrine, at particular synapses in the brain (see chapter 2). Concentrations of these neurotransmitters begin to increase almost immediately after patients start taking the drugs. However, the antidepressant effect does not begin immediately. It can take several weeks, and sometimes longer, before the patient starts to feel the effects.

prefrontal lobotomy • an obsolete procedure in which the frontal lobes of the brain are cut off from contact with the rest of the brain, in order to make patients more compliant

psychotropic drug • any of several types of drugs that affect the psychological processes or state of mind of an individual

antipsychotic drug • a drug used for treating psychosis (e.g., schizophrenia)

antidepressant drug • a drug used for treating depression

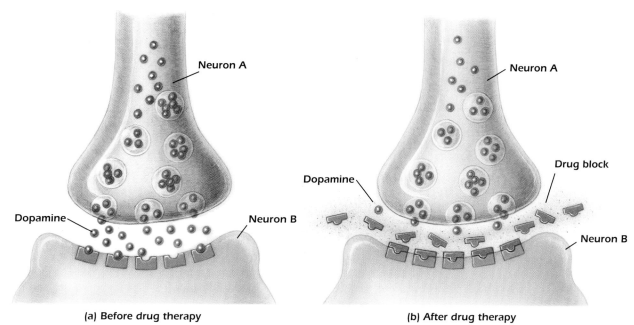

(a) Before drug therapy   (b) After drug therapy

FIGURE 14.2
Antipsychotic Drugs and Dopamine Receptors
Some types of antipsychotic drugs seem to work because they block the ability of the brain to receive the excessive amounts of the neurotransmitter dopamine that lead to some of the positive symptoms of schizophrenia, such as hallucinations and delusions.

A third type of antidepressant drug is a *selective serotonin reuptake inhibitor (SSRI)*. This class of drug has been introduced more recently; it works primarily by inhibiting the reuptake of serotonin. This inhibition of reuptake effectively increases the concentration of the neurotransmitter but it does so less directly than do the other two types of antidepressant drugs. The most well-known of these new drugs is fluoxetine (Prozac). Depressed patients typically start to show improvement after about 3 weeks of taking the drug. The drug seems to work for a wide variety of patients but this drug, too, can have side effects, such as nausea and nervousness (J. O. Cole & Bodkin, 1990; Papp & Gorman, 1990).

From one point of view, drug treatment of depression has been considerably more successful than drug treatment of schizophrenia. Whereas antipsychotic drugs only suppress the symptoms as long as the patient continues to take the drugs, antidepressant drugs seem to cause more lasting change. Patients who stop taking antipsychotic drugs typically return to their earlier psychotic state, whereas patients who stop taking antidepressant drugs often remain symptom free for quite some time, and possibly indefinitely.

When we consider the difference in the long-term effectiveness of antipsychotic versus antidepressant drugs, however, we also must consider the rates of spontaneous recovery. In **spontaneous recovery**, the person's symptoms seem to disappear without any treatment whatsoever. The rate of spontaneous recovery for depression is much higher than that for schizophrenia and other psychoses. Therefore, an unknown proportion of the depressed patients who show improvement through the use of drugs or other psychotherapy might have become better even if they had received no treatment at all.

In addition, researchers and clinicians must consider the effects of **placebos:** Patients may improve simply because they believe that they are

spontaneous recovery • the disappearance of a person's symptoms, which occurs without any treatment whatsoever

placebo • a pill or other substance that the patient believes to have curative or healing properties, but that actually has no such properties; often used as a means of determining whether drug treatments are truly effective or work only because patients believe that they are being helped

being helped, even if the treatment they receive actually has no direct effect whatsoever. To rule out both the effects of spontaneous recovery and the effects of placebos, researchers studying the effects of drugs often use both control groups that take placebos and control groups that simply are put on a waiting list for subsequent treatment (e.g., see Figure 14.3). The control group taking placebos also may be studied using a *double-blind technique* in which both the experimenter administering the treatment and the patient are kept from knowing whether a particular patient is receiving a placebo or an active drug.

Antianxiety Drugs. Clinicians prescribe antianxiety drugs (also called "anxiolytics" or "tranquilizers") to relieve their patients' feelings of tension and anxiety, to increase patients' feelings of well-being, and to combat symptoms of insomnia. The earliest antianxiety drugs, the *barbiturates* (see chapter 4), are rarely used today because they are highly addictive and potentially dangerous. More commonly used are two classes of antianxiety drugs: muscle relaxants and benzodiazepines. The *muscle relaxants* reduce muscular tension and cause feelings of tranquility (calm).

Benzodiazepines also cause muscle relaxation and have an even stronger tranquilizing effect. Two of the most well-known and very widely used drugs are chlordiazepoxide (Librium) and diazepam (Valium). All too often, clinicians have prescribed these drugs without thinking enough about their possible consequences. For example, the use of antianxiety drugs can impair attention and alertness (Schweizer, Rickels, Case, & Greenblatt, 1990) and the tranquilizing effects of these drugs can hinder performance of certain tasks (e.g., listening attentively to a lecture or driving). Thus, the drugs should not be used before or during any activity that requires alertness, intelligent thought, or creativity. The drugs also can be habit forming.

Lithium. In 1949, lithium was found to be effective in treating bipolar (manic–depressive) disorders and it remains the drug of choice for these

FIGURE 14.3
Effectiveness of Antipsychotic Drugs
The rates of unwanted symptomatic behavior are much higher for patients in the placebo-control group than for patients in the treatment group (who received Mellaril, a brand of phenothiazine). In addition, the rate of symptomatic behavior for the treatment group temporarily rose during a brief trial (Observations 41–45) when a placebo was substituted for the drug, and it declined again following reinstitution of the drug treatment. What do you infer from these findings?

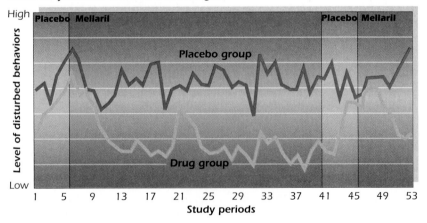

disorders. Lithium is very effective, causing almost immediate relief of symptoms in roughly three fourths of cases. However, it does not relieve depressive symptoms in persons who do not have a bipolar disorder. This finding supports the notion that bipolar disorders differ qualitatively from unipolar depression (M. Baron, Gershon, Rudy, Jonas, & Buchsbaum, 1975). We still do not know why lithium has the effect it does (Manji, Hsiao, Risby et al., 1991). The drug must be used with care because overdoses can lead to convulsions and even to death.

Many psychotherapists are worried that overreliance on drugs will result in temporary rather than long-term benefits. Moreover, the benefits may be in some sense superficial, because the individual treated only with drugs may gain little or no understanding of what his or her problems are or of how to deal with these problems. It is for this reason that drug therapy is usually combined with other forms of therapy for the best results.

No biological approach to psychotherapy possibly can be complete. A complete approach needs to take into account context as well as biology. Multicultural approaches especially take into account the cultural context in which a person lives.

Multicultural Approaches to Psychotherapy

Cross-cultural and multicultural psychologists (e.g., Higginbotham, 1979) have pointed out that many people's responses to treatment depend on the cultural appropriateness of the treatment. For one thing, some psychological disorders more closely match non-Western, culture-specific definitions of abnormal behavior than they match the symptom categories of DSM-IV. People suffering from culture-specific disorders may expect that culture-specific healing practices will be more effective in treating those disorders than will the foregoing five main approaches identified in Western cultures. For instance, the culture-specific disorder of *susto* (an anxiety disorder observed in some Latin American cultures) seems to respond better to treatment by native healers (e.g., *shamans* or *curanderos*) than to Western treatment approaches, such as cognitive–behavioral psychotherapy (Matsumoto, 1996).

Multicultural approaches are also important for the treatment of nonculture-specific psychological disorders. In studies in Seattle and in Los Angeles, Asian Americans and Native Americans were less likely to seek mental-health services than were European Americans and African Americans (S. Sue, 1977). Once in treatment, Americans other than European Americans were much more likely to drop out of treatment (S. Sue, 1977, 1991). According to some research (D. R. Atkinson, Ponce, & Martinez, 1984), the key to effective treatment is not necessarily that the therapist and the client share a common (or even similar) culture and gender, but rather that they share similar worldviews and attitudes toward treatment.

It is not always possible for the therapist and client to share worldviews, but effective therapists can show sensitivity to the cultural perspectives of their clients (Hedstrom, 1994). Psychotherapists who show cultural sensitivity toward their clients are considered more competent and more believable and trustworthy by clients of diverse cultural backgrounds, including Mexican American (D. R. Atkinson, Casa, & Abreu, 1992), African American (D. R. Atkinson, Furlong, & Poston, 1986), and Asian American clients (Gim, Atkinson, & Kim, 1991). How can psychotherapists gain cultural sensitivity? Psychotherapists become increasingly sensitive by working with culturally diverse clients (S. Sue, Akutsu, &

Ideas regarding the optimal form of psychotherapy vary widely from one culture to another.

Higashi, 1985) and by becoming knowledgeable about diverse cultures and lifestyles.

Finally, effective cross-cultural psychotherapists may need to be open to developing their skill in using innovative methods of treating people from diverse cultures, including in their repertoires various culture-specific treatment approaches and techniques (Aldous, 1994). As an example, a Japanese treatment option is *naikan* therapy, in which the patient spends a week meditating from early morning until late evening, focusing on self-analysis and self-improvement, in order to become more fully reintegrated into her or his social network (Murase & Johnson, 1974; Reynolds, 1989). The *naikan* therapist periodically provides brief instructions to the meditator regarding how to direct meditative self-examination for achieving enhanced social integration. Social factors are also important in some alternatives to individual psychotherapy, such as group psychotherapy, considered next.

WHAT ARE SOME ALTERNATIVES TO INDIVIDUAL PSYCHOTHERAPY?

The forms of psychotherapy described in the preceding sections of this chapter largely involve one psychotherapist administering some form of treatment to one client at a time. In some situations, however, various alternatives to one-on-one therapy may be useful. These options include group therapy, couples and family therapy, and self-help. These alternatives to individual psychotherapy also have been widely available among many non-Western societies (Langsley, Hodes, & Grimson, 1993).

Group Therapy

Humanistic therapy, behavior therapy, and cognitive therapy can be administered either individually or in groups. Group therapy may offer some distinct advantages over individual psychotherapy: (a) Group therapy is almost always less expensive than is individual therapy. (b) Groups may offer greater support than does individual therapy because groups usually include several individuals with similar problems. (c) Group therapy offers the potential value of social pressure to change; this pressure may add to (or even replace) the authoritative pressure to change that comes from the

The advantages of receiving psychotherapy in a group setting may include reduced cost, greater social pressure to effect positive changes, and greater diversity of people who may offer a fresh perspective on a troubling situation. The disadvantages of group therapy include the potential for dilution of the treatment and for group dynamics to take precedence over the presenting problem that stimulated the desire to obtain therapy.

When working with children, perhaps as part of family therapy, it may be useful to engage the child in play activities while helping the child to work through psychological difficulties.

therapist. (d) The very dynamic of group interaction may lead to therapeutic change, especially in the cases of people who have problems with interpersonal interactions.

Group therapy also has potential disadvantages: (a) The treatment offered by the therapist may be diluted by the presence of other persons requiring the therapist's attention. (b) Group psychotherapy may shift the focus of the therapy sessions to other issues, such as group interactions, instead of the presenting problems that prompted the members to seek therapy in the first place.

A related form of psychotherapy, which deals with special groups, is couples and family therapy.

Couples and Family Therapy

The goal of couples and family therapy is to treat problems from a *systems perspective*. That is, the therapist treats the problems of the couple or the family unit as a whole system that involves complex internal interactions, instead of treating the separate problems of distinct members of the unit. The identified problem may be centered on the family unit, such as troubled communication among family members. However, the identified problem may also be centered on one member of the unit. The underlying notion in this kind of therapy is that even individual problems often have their roots in the family system. In order to treat the problem, the whole family should be part of the solution. Surprisingly, some apparently individual problems, such as eating disorders, can be treated quite effectively in family therapy, particularly if the disorder is caught early (within 3 years of onset) in a young person (see Langsley et al., 1993).

In cases of marital conflict, couples therapy is more successful than is individual therapy in holding couples together and in bringing them back together (Gurman, Kniskern, & Pinsoff, 1986). Couples therapy tends to be particularly successful for people who have had problems for only a short time before they entered therapy and when the people have not yet initiated action toward divorce. One reason for the greater success of couples therapy is that the therapist can hear the views of both partners. Hearing both points of view enables the therapist to mediate more effectively than does hearing just a single point of view.

In couples therapy, communication and mutual empathy are emphasized. Partners are trained to listen carefully and empathically to each other. They learn to restate what the partner is saying, thereby confirming that they accurately understood the partner's point of view. Partners in unsuccessful relationships often fail to hear even the positive things that each one says about the other (J. M. Gottman, 1979, 1994). Couples also are taught how to make constructive and direct requests of each other, instead of making indirect requests that can be confusing and easily misinterpreted.

Cognitive therapist Aaron Beck (1988) has emphasized the importance of having each partner understand the perspective of the other. He urges partners to clarify the differences in what each partner seeks for the relationship. Each partner may have secret "shoulds"—things that each of us believes that our partner ought to do. Unfortunately, our partner may not believe these things to be important or worth doing. If one or both partners fail to state their "shoulds" clearly, yet both hold these "shoulds" to be essential, problems arise. Beck believes that many problems in a relationship can be attributed to "shoulds" that become *automatic thoughts,* which can rise into consciousness without any effort or intention on the part of the thinker. People can get rid of some of the "shoulds" in their behavior, even without a therapist, by their own self-help.

Self-Help

The preceding discussion has focused on forms of psychotherapy that involve personal interactions between psychotherapists and the clients they serve. Yet another alternative for people seeking psychotherapeutic assistance is self-help. Sometimes, when people seek to help themselves, they join other people who need similar kinds of help, and they help one another. Perhaps the best-known self-help group is Alcoholics Anonymous (AA), which was founded in the mid-1930s. Since the founding of AA, many other related 12-step groups have sprung up, including support groups for persons addicted to other substances, the family members of substance abusers, victims of crimes, persons who have terminal or chronic illnesses, and so on. Essentially, for any problem that may be experienced by more than one person in a geographic region, a support group may be formed, which may offer therapeutic benefit. If a person is fortunate, family members and close friends also may offer a form of therapeutic support.

Another form of self-help may come from reading what other people have to say about coping with many of life's obstacles. Your neighborhood bookstore probably offers many self-help books suggesting how to help yourself resolve almost any problem you could imagine: how to treat addiction (including many books based on AA), how to improve your love life, how to become more assertive, and how to overcome various forms of self-defeating behavior.

Couples therapy is highly effective in helping couples to resolve interpersonal conflict and to enhance communication, particularly if the presenting problems have been of short duration prior to treatment and the couple has not yet started divorce action.

Frequently, when we face psychological and situational difficulties, we can find a great deal of help from our families and friends, who can offer social support, advice, and perhaps direct help. In addition, however, many of us seek help from people in specialized support groups, who may have had to face similar kinds of problems and can therefore provide both empathy and practical ideas for solutions.

Do any of these books actually work? No one knows because no one is monitoring the effectiveness of the various programs. Gerald Rosen (1987) has expressed serious concerns about the value of self-help books. In particular, many such books exaggerate how much help they can offer. Many of the authors of these books appear on television and radio talk shows, where their claims may be even more greatly exaggerated. To the extent that these books and talk shows may lead people away from getting professional help when it is needed, such as for the serious disorders discussed in chapter 13, they may cause more harm than good. At the same time, these self-help resources can be useful for the relatively common, temporary problems of daily living and for occasional spiritual uplift.

In addition to self-help groups and self-help books, folk wisdom sometimes can provide useful guidance for self-help:

> Change your thoughts and you'll change your moods. (a) *Get up and go.* When you most feel like moping, do something—anything. . . . (b) *Make contact with people you care about.* You may not feel like socializing, but others can help to distract you from your depression, give you hugs, listen to you. . . . (c) *Avoid drugs,* including alcohol, which may depress the nervous system and keep you feeling down.
>
> —Linda Tschirart and Mary Ellen Donovan
> (Quoted in Safire & Safir, 1989, p. 92)

The self-help approach highlights an issue that really applies to all forms of psychotherapy. What is the ideal method, if any, and how well do any of these methods work?

14.1

Think about what you do to enable yourself to cope more effectively with the psychologically difficult situations you face. What are some self-help strategies you have used when confronting stressful or psychologically troublesome situations? What advice have you offered to your friends or family members when they have faced psychologically difficult situations?

IS THERE AN OPTIMAL APPROACH TO PSYCHOTHERAPY?

Each kind of psychotherapy makes different assumptions about both the nature of psychological disorders and the best ways in which to treat these disorders. In light of this diversity of approaches, it seems obvious that they cannot all be right. However, the various approaches to psychotherapy may be more complementary than they appear to be.

Consider, for example, the issue of what causes mental disorders. Part of the difference in treatment procedures comes from different views about causation. Psychodynamic theories tend to focus on repressed early childhood experiences as the cause of mental disorders. Humanistic theories consider the primary cause of these disorders to be insufficient feelings of self-worth, insufficient unconditional acceptance by others, or lack of acceptance for all parts of the self. Behavior therapies look to faults in conditioning or in modeling, whereas cognitive theories emphasize maladaptive thoughts, beliefs, or schemas. Biological therapies look to psychophysiological causes of distress, such as abnormal levels of neurotransmitters in the brain.

Does support for one approach necessarily mean that alternative approaches are ruled out? No. For one thing, mental disorders may have causes at different levels of analysis. For example, stressful experiences in early childhood may lead to or even be viewed as inappropriate forms of behavioral conditioning. Inappropriate levels of neurotransmitter substances may lead to maladaptive thoughts. Maladaptive thoughts may lead to low self-esteem. Often, what is cause and what is effect is not clear. Perhaps a combined approach most effectively describes causality by allowing for interactions among causes. For instance, psychophysiological vulnerability and environmental stress may interact with low self-esteem and maladaptive thoughts to cause psychological turmoil.

Differing views of causality lead to differing approaches to treatment. Classical psychodynamic approaches tend to focus on treating the fundamental motivations that give rise to psychological problems. Humanistic approaches and some of the ego-psychology approaches tend to focus on coming to terms with who we are and what we want to do with our lives. Behavioral approaches focus on modifying the stimulus–response mechanisms in the environment. Cognitive approaches tend to focus on altering the troubled person's thought patterns. Biological approaches tend to focus on treating the neurochemical and hormonal imbalances underlying a given psychological disturbance. To understand the nature of psychological processes, we need to combine the various explanations. Similarly, to treat a mental disorder at multiple levels most effectively, we may combine several different therapies into an *eclectic* therapy, a strategy that integrates several approaches (see Figure 14.4).

Ideally, before a clinician chooses an approach to psychotherapy, the clinician should have information regarding the relative effectiveness of each approach. In addition to personal clinical experience, the clinician should have access to information based on empirical research. Ideally, this empirical research would analyze each of the major diagnoses (as shown in chapter 13, based on DSM-IV) in terms of each of the major types of therapies (psychodynamic, humanistic, behavioral, cognitive, and biological). In addition, each investigation would include both placebo control groups and waiting-list control groups. For each type of treatment of each type of diagnosed disorder, the analysis would evaluate each diagnosis in terms of which type of therapy was most effective. In addition, researchers would conduct *meta-analyses*, in which psychologists evaluate and analyze the findings from many studies at a time.

Truly ideal research also would consider other factors that may affect treatment outcomes. For example, the length of treatment dramatically affects outcomes. In one meta-analytic study (Howard, Kopta, Krause, & Orlinsky, 1986), the rate of improvement ranged from 29% to 38% of psychotherapy clients attending between 1 and 3 sessions to 85% of clients attending between 1 and 104 sessions. Clearly, the length of treatment can make a big difference in the observed rate of success. (The average number of psychotherapy sessions for Americans receiving treatment is 14 in a given year; Goleman, 1993.) In addition, an ideal research program might consider the social context of therapy (e.g., individual, family, couple, or group therapy); the type of setting (e.g., inpatient or outpatient); and so on. Although the call for this kind of research first went out decades ago (e.g., Kiesler, 1966; Paul, 1967), this highly complex research has yet to be conducted.

FIGURE 14.4
Psychotherapeutic Approaches of Clinical Psychologists
Out of 415 clinical psychologists surveyed, almost half indicated that they followed an eclectic approach. (After D. Smith, 1982)

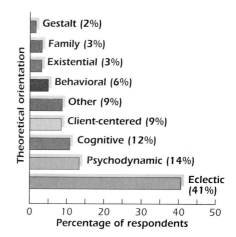

Not all research suggests equal effectiveness of psychotherapies. Many studies have suggested that, on average, behavior therapies and cognitive therapies may be more effective than psychodynamic therapy or no therapy at all (Chambless, 1995; Lambert & Bergin, 1994; A. A. Lazarus, 1990; Weisz, Weiss, Hun, Granger, & Morton, 1995). Moreover, some research suggests that particular therapy techniques may work especially well for particular disorders. For example, fears and phobias seem best to be treated behaviorally by exposing clients to the source of their fears (S. L. Kaplan, Randolph, & Lemli, 1991). But even the behavioral and cognitive techniques have their limitations; for example, they are not particularly effective with personality disorders or schizophrenia (Brody, 1990). Cognitive therapies appear to be particularly effective in treating depression (Robinson, Berman, & Neimeyer, 1990). Thus, there is room for improvement in all techniques.

What do we know about the relative benefits of the various approaches to therapy, based on existing studies? When the researchers' preferences for a particular therapy are ruled out, each type of psychotherapy seems to be just about as effective as the next. However, when the researchers' loyalties are not ruled out, whatever therapy program the researcher prefers seems to fare better in the comparisons across therapy programs. Perhaps, then, the best suggestion to clinicians and their clients is that they should choose the approach, or synthesis of approaches, that seems to work best for them. In addition, a match between the particular therapist and client may be important to successful treatment. For example, some cross-cultural researchers suggest that psychotherapists must consider cultural and other differences when tailoring psychotherapy to individual clients (see, e.g., Axelson, 1993; Ivey, Ivey, & Simek-Morgan, 1993; Pedersen, Draguns, Lonner, & Trimble, in press; D. Sue & Sue, 1990). Such differences may influence the effectiveness of psychotherapy for members of one group or another.

HOW EFFECTIVE IS PSYCHOTHERAPY?

Does psychotherapy work? There has been a great deal of research done in attempts to answer this question. Perhaps the most striking finding is that yes, on average, psychotherapy does work (Lambert & Bergin, 1994; Lipsey & Wilson, 1993; Maling & Howard, 1994; Seligman, 1995).

No one has yet conducted the ideal research that would allow clinicians to choose an optimal approach to psychotherapy, let alone to tailor psychotherapy perfectly to particular client diagnoses. Even so, meta-analytic and other research clearly shows that psychotherapy produces significant improvement in clients, above and beyond any spontaneous recovery that might have occurred (e.g., Andrews, 1993; M. L. Smith & Glass, 1977; Stiles, Shapiro, & Elliott, 1986). In particular, clients who received psychotherapy were, on average, better off than 75% or more of research control participants who did not receive any psychotherapy. Clients who received psychotherapy showed significant improvements in self-esteem and significant reduction in anxiety (greater improvement than about 82% of untreated controls). For people institutionalized for psychotic, alcoholic, or criminal behaviors, those who received psychotherapy showed increases in their level of adjustment greater than only 71% of untreated controls (M. L. Smith & Glass, 1977). However, if you cared deeply about one of the 7 in 10 who responded well to treatment, you probably would be quite pleased with the outcome.

TABLE 14.2

Meta-Analysis of the Course of Psychotherapy

In a meta-analytic study of psychotherapy, the number of patients who rated themselves as improved generally increased in relation to the number of therapy sessions, as did the therapists' ratings of patient improvement (Howard et al., 1986). The specific ratings at each measurement period differed, however, depending on the clinical diagnosis and the source of the rating (patient or therapist).

Total number of sessions	Depressed patients (% rated as improved)		Anxious patients (% rated as improved)		Borderline psychotic patients (% rated as improved)	
	Self-ratings	*Therapists' ratings*	*Self-ratings*	*Therapists' ratings*	*Self-ratings*	*Therapists' ratings*
1–4	44%	31%	36%	5%	21%	0%
5–8	53	46	46	25	33	3
9–13	60	57	54	53	42	11
14–26	69	73	64	87	60	38
27–52	77	86	74	99	75	74
53–104	84	94	82	99	87	95

In addition, length of treatment may be confusing the interpretation of results. For example, see Table 14.2 and Figure 14.5, which show the results of a meta-analytic study by Kenneth Howard and his colleagues (1986). If researchers were to determine the effectiveness of therapy for borderline-psychotic patients in terms of therapist ratings at the conclusion of 8 sessions, the results would be very discouraging, yet if the researchers were to assess therapist ratings for these same patients at the

Figure 14.5

Ratings of Psychotherapy

Although self-ratings and therapist ratings differed, and the degree of improvement differed across different diagnoses, on the whole, the data seem to show that psychotherapy is highly effective for helping people with psychological problems.

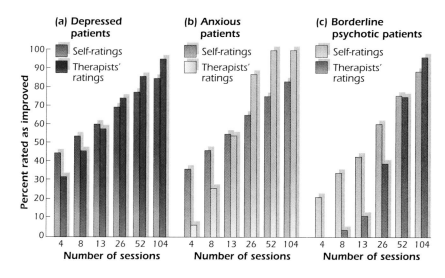

14.1

WHEN AND HOW SHOULD YOU, OR SOMEONE YOU CARE ABOUT, SEEK PSYCHOTHERAPY?

Few of us have serious psychological disorders that require psychological treatment. Serious disorders, by their nature, interfere with the person's ability to carry out normal work and normal interpersonal relationships. All of us occasionally feel anxious but few of us feel so anxious that we are unable to leave the house for weeks at a time. All of us experience occasional distortions of our thoughts, our emotions, and our perceptions but few of us experience such serious distortions that the people around us notice that we cannot stay in touch with reality much of the time. Many of us seem to be a little excessive in our tidiness or our cleanliness but few of us wash our hands hundreds of times each day.

On the other hand, from time to time, each of us faces difficult situations—the loss of a job or of a loved one; conflicts in our interpersonal relationships; serious accidents, injuries, disease, or other health problems; and so on. Sometimes, our family and friends are able to provide us with all the support we need to cope with the difficulties we face. At other times, however, the extent of our need goes beyond the ability of our loved ones to help us. It is at these times that many of us seek professional help from psychotherapists.

Once you make the decision to seek psychotherapy, what kind of psychotherapist should you look for? Following are a few tips:

1. Try to find the particular treatment approach that best suits the problem that leads you to seek psychotherapy. For instance, if you believe that you suffer from bipolar disorder, biological therapies may be one of your best choices. If you seek to get rid of your phobia of flying, behavior therapy may be your best bet. If you are having trouble adapting to a difficult situation, and you want guidance in figuring out your own solution to your problem, you may prefer a talk-oriented therapy such as humanistic or cognitive therapy.

conclusion of 104 sessions, the studies would be highly encouraging. On the other hand, for depressed and anxious clients, therapy results would be much more positive after much shorter durations of therapy.

A study in *Consumer Reports* in 1995, and directed in large part by psychologist Martin Seligman, suggested the efficacy of psychotherapy. In particular, Seligman (1995) reported that patients who received long-term treatment fared substantially better than did those who received only short-term treatment, and that patients who received both medication and psychotherapy did no better than those who received just psychotherapy. No specific type of psychotherapy was, on average, better than any other for any disorder. Psychologists, psychiatrists, and social workers did not differ, on average, in effectiveness, although all were more effective than marriage counselors and family doctors. Patients whose length of therapy or whose choice of therapist was dictated by an insurance company or a managed-care program did worse than did those who had freedom of choice. It is important in evaluating these results to take into account that

2. Make sure that you have faith in the competence and trustworthiness of the therapist and the therapist's approach to treatment.

3. Find a therapist who seems to understand your view of the world, given your distinctive cultural and social experiences.

4. Choose a therapist who seems warm and empathic toward you.

5. After sessions with the psychotherapist, assess whether you feel a greater sense of being able to cope with the difficulties you face. Does the psychotherapist seem to have confidence that you will be able to handle the problems you face?

6. If you are clearly dissatisfied with a therapist and are convinced that the psychotherapist is not right for you, consider stopping treatment with that psychotherapist and replacing the psychotherapist with another one.

7. Consider your finances—does your choice of psychotherapist fit within your budget? In most communities, there are quite a few mental-health agencies that offer various kinds of psychotherapy for modest fees. In addition to publicly funded agencies (e.g., community mental-health agencies), many religious and charitable organizations offer low-cost mental-health services (e.g., Jewish Family Service, Lutheran Social Services); communities with medical schools often offer low-cost (sliding financial scale) psychotherapy; and many communities offer free or low-cost specialized mental-health services (e.g., for veterans and for children). Also, many health insurance plans pay for at least some mental-health services. Do not let finances be your main concern, however. If you get inappropriate free advice at a time when you need help, it could cost you a great deal. Most psychotherapists are willing to work with you regarding payment for services. If you find that a particular psychotherapist is right for you or for someone you love, ask the therapist to help you work out a financial arrangement that is satisfactory. At least some psychotherapists may see it as a matter of ethics to take on some clients who cannot pay the regular hourly rate.

they are based on users' subjective impressions of the effectiveness of therapy rather than on the basis of objective measures of therapeutic outcomes. The response rate for surveys was also very low, which further leaves one at least somewhat skeptical of the validity of the results.

Why does some evidence suggest that many different kinds of psychotherapy are about equally effective for many different people? For one thing, as mentioned previously, research has not yet been conducted that effectively analyzes each type of approach in relation to each type of diagnosis. Also, different therapists may implement each approach in distinctive ways, so that not all psychoanalysts are alike, just as not all behaviorists are alike. This lack of uniformity also makes it difficult to distinguish among the differential effects of the various types of psychotherapy.

Another alternative has been suggested (e.g., Stiles et al.,1986; Torrey, 1986): The various approaches to psychotherapy may have underlying commonalities that go deeper than the superficial differences across therapeutic approaches. For example, cross-cultural research shows that across such

Many communities provide free telephone counseling to people who are facing crises, such as following a rape, spousal abuse, or other violent crime; following sexual molestation; or when contemplating suicide.

diverse psychotherapists as U.S. and European psychiatrists, Native American *shamans*, Latin American *curanderos* (or *curanderas*, in Mexico and elsewhere), and Yoruban *babalawo* (in Nigeria), psychotherapy appears to have five basic components (Torrey, 1986): (a) an emphasis on a shared worldview between client and therapist, including a common language and similar conceptions of causes and effects; (b) distinctive therapist characteristics such as warmth, genuineness, and empathy; (c) client expectations that reflect the culturally relevant beliefs of the client and the therapist; (d) a set of specific techniques used by the therapist (e.g., talking, performing rituals such as systematic desensitization or ceremonial dances, or using biological techniques such as herbs, drugs, or shock therapy); and (e) a process by which the therapist enables or empowers the client to gain increased knowledge, awareness, and mastery, thereby gaining hope. According to E. Torrey, psychotherapists across various cultures perform comparable functions in their respective cultures. Both Western and non-Western therapists use similar techniques; and both get similar results with these techniques.

William Stiles and his colleagues (Stiles et al., 1986) would add to Torrey's list the importance of establishing mutual trust between therapist and client, the therapist's "communication of a new perspective of the [client and the client's] situation" (p. 172), the client's willingness to engage in open and self-disclosing communication, the client's desire to improve, and the client's belief in the effectiveness of the particular psychotherapy being offered. Although we have yet to understand fully the processes by which psychotherapy produces desirable outcomes, it is reassuring to know that such outcomes occur. At the same time, there is a long way to go. For example, psychotherapists more easily and more effectively can treat some kinds of disorders (e.g., mood disorders) than they can other kinds of disorders (e.g., personality disorders). We are far from having all the answers to how best to treat our clients.

It is important to note that not everyone is as positive on the value of psychotherapy as is Seligman (1995). A carefully controlled study, the Fort Bragg Demonstration Project, also set out to test the value of psychotherapy (Bickman, 1996; Bickman et al., 1995). The study involved a unit that served more than 42,000 children and adolescent dependents for more than 5 years, from June, 1990, to September, 1995. This study, unlike Seligman's, evaluated treatment effectiveness rather than relying only on reports of satisfaction from clients. The results suggested that psychotherapy was not particularly useful, and that greater length of time in psychotherapy often did not improve outcomes (see also Dineen, 1998; Hoagwood, 1997). Given positive results of other studies, the results of this study cannot be viewed as conclusive. At the very least, though, they suggest the need to know better under what kinds of circumstances psychotherapy is more or less effective

WHAT ARE SOME KEY ETHICAL ISSUES IN PSYCHOTHERAPY?

In the fall of 1992, advice columnist Ann Landers devoted her entire column to exposing the unethical behavior of a psychiatrist who had held various prestigious positions in psychiatric associations. The disgraced psychiatrist was forced to resign from the American Psychiatric Association after losing a lawsuit brought by former patients of his, who claimed that he had abused them sexually and in other ways. His type of case is not unique, although it is, fortunately, rare. Because psychotherapists are trusted with deeply personal information, when they violate that trust, they can cause enormous harm to their patients. Unfortunately, a few of them do so. Through their unethical behavior, they hurt not only their clients and themselves, but also the entire profession. Of course, unethical behavior is not limited to psychotherapists: It occurs in every profession. (See the Branching Out box that follows regarding an ethical problem arising from a questionable therapeutic technique.)

Branching Out

RECOVERY OF SUPPRESSED MEMORIES: WHAT IS YOUR JUDGMENT?

In May of 1994, a civil court awarded half a million dollars to a man whose adult daughter had accused him of sexually abusing her during her childhood (Berkman, 1994; La Ganga, 1994; Shuit, 1994). The award followed a verdict asserting that the daughter's therapists negligently had reinforced false memories of sexual abuse. The man's 23-year-old daughter had accused him of sexually abusing her after she underwent treatment that her psychotherapists asserted was designed to "recover suppressed memories." When the daughter made those accusations, her father lost his $400,000-a-year job as a vice president of marketing for a major company and her mother divorced him.

In this case, the therapist used questionable therapeutic techniques to elicit the daughter's horrifying recollections. The daughter remains entirely sure of her memories, but many other people, including the jurors in her father's civil case, question their accuracy. Whatever the verdict in cases such as this one, it is clear that both the parent and the child will have suffered greatly. One source (described in Geyelin, 1994) estimates that thousands of parents and their adult children are confronting the heart-wrenching problems posed by trying to determine whether disturbing

(CONTINUED)

Branching Out   (CONTINUED)

memories have arisen from accurate recollection, elicited by techniques that facilitate their recovery, or from inaccurate distortions, introduced by techniques that lead to their creation. Professional organizations of clinical therapists are grappling with the need to guide therapists in the treatment of people who appear to be suffering ill effects from suppressed or repressed memories of painful events.

Perhaps the foremost psychologist in questioning the use of recovered memory in legal proceedings is Elizabeth Loftus (e.g., 1993b). Loftus is particularly concerned about recovered memory in cases of repressed memories of murder (which are very rare) and in cases of childhood sexual abuse (which are less unusual). Childhood sexual abuse appears to be distressingly common (estimates of the proportion of women who have been victimized range from 10% to 50%) and the consequences of allegations of abuse are devastating for both the victim and the accused, as well as their family members and friends. Therefore, determinations regarding the accuracy of recovered memories profoundly affect the lives of many people.

Although many therapists continue to believe in the validity of recovered memories, the evidence available at present suggests that we do not yet have the ability to distinguish true repressed memories from false ones. Until we are better able to be sure of the accuracy of such memories, therapists should continue to help clients to clarify their own feelings and beliefs, to show compassion and empathy for clients who are clearly suffering from some source of inner turmoil, and to help clients to heal and to recover from the pain they are experiencing, whatever its origin.

When you next hear the media discuss a case of recovered memory, how will you judge the accuracy of the memory?

Perhaps even more than many other professionals, psychotherapists are expected to behave ethically toward clients. For example, psychotherapists are expected to refrain from becoming sexually involved with clients. Moreover, psychotherapists are expected to maintain the *confidentiality* (privacy) of communications between themselves and their clients. Only in rare cases may they divulge the contents of these communications. Such cases arise primarily when the therapist determines that clients may be dangerous to themselves or to others. In addition, in some states, psychotherapists must breach confidentiality in a few other situations in which it is believed that greater harm will result if confidentiality is not breached.

Another ethical protection for clients involves *informed consent:* Before clients participate in what are viewed as experimental treatments (e.g., the alleged recovery of repressed childhood memories), they must understand fully what the treatments will involve, including both the experimental nature of the treatments and the likelihood of harmful side effects or consequences. Also, during the experimental treatment, the psychotherapist is expected to preserve the well-being of the participant to the fullest extent possible.

When psychotherapy is implemented appropriately, another benefit appears to be a reduction in overall health-care costs. Thus, when companies provide mental-health counseling for their employees, they obtain not only increases in productivity and decreases in employee absenteeism and turnover, but also savings in the overall cost of health care (Docherty, 1993). Health psychology is the topic of the next, and final, chapter.

The Case of the Unflagging Self-Helper

Rena picks up a copy of *Pathways to Psychology* at the university bookstore and, after reading chapter 14, realizes that she does indeed have a problem. She reads that self-help books are a mixed lot and that many of them do not work. Her realization is that whether she has picked the wrong books or has not followed the advice in those books correctly, none of the books has worked for her. In fact, she is still smoking. Moreover, every time Rena has dieted she has gained back the weight she had lost, so the weight losses have been temporary, at best. And her relationship may be working but Rena realizes that being submissive is just not in her nature, and if the relationship is working by her being submissive, at best, it will work only over the short term. Rena resolves to take a more considered approach to her problems and decides to seek psychotherapy to help with her smoking and weight control. She stops the submissive acts and finds that her relationship with her boyfriend actually improves.

What Were Some Early Methods of Psychotherapeutic Intervention? 500

1. Because early views of mental illness relied on demonological explanations, early treatments centered on trying to expel the demons that caused the illness. Later treatment in *asylums* involved keeping mentally ill persons off the streets, out of sight, with little thought given to humane treatment, let alone to possible *psychotherapy*.

How and Why Do Clinicians Diagnose Abnormal Behavior? 500

2. The DSM system of diagnostic classification has helped clinicians to make appropriate and widely understood diagnoses as a basis for treatment.

How Do Different Psychologists Approach Psychotherapy? 502

3. There are five main approaches to psychotherapy: psychodynamic, humanistic, behavioral, cognitive, and biological approaches. A multicultural approach to psychotherapy is an additional important option. Also, many psychologists use an eclectic approach, which employs aspects of more than one of the main approaches.

4. Psychodynamic therapies emphasize insight into underlying unconscious processes as the key to the therapeutic process. Psychodynamic therapies may be based on Freudian psychoanalysis or on neo-Freudian ego psychology.

5. Humanistic therapies emphasize the therapeutic effects of the therapist's unconditional positive

regard for the client, as exemplified by Rogers's *client-centered therapy.*

6. *Behavior therapies* emphasize techniques based on principles of operant and classical conditioning, as well as observational learning. Classical techniques include *counterconditioning,* such as aversion therapy and systematic desensitization, as well as *extinction procedures,* such as flooding and implosion therapy. Operant techniques include the use of token economies and behavioral contracting. The use of *modeling* may be viewed as a kind of behavioral treatment with an allowance for cognitive processes.

7. Cognitive therapies encourage clients to change their thought contents and processes in order to achieve therapeutic changes in behavior and other desired outcomes. Ellis's *rational-emotive therapy (RET)* and Beck's cognitive therapy are two of the main types of cognitive therapy.

8. Historically, biological treatments of mental illness have included a wide array of treatments, such as *electroconvulsive therapy (ECT)* and *psychosurgery.*

9. The development of effective *psychotropic drugs* has revolutionized biological treatments. Today, the four key classes of psychotropic drugs are *antipsychotics, antidepressants,* antianxiety drugs, and lithium. Although these drugs are certainly not cure-alls, they help many patients to function more effectively and to feel better about how well they function.

What Are Some Alternatives to Individual Psychotherapy?   517

10. Alternatives to individual psychotherapy include group therapy, couples and family therapy, and self-help. Group therapy, couples therapy, and family therapy often address problems specific to interpersonal relationships. They address these problems through the dynamic interplay that occurs during group, couple, or family interactions. In self-help therapies, individuals try to manage their own stressful situations or minor psychological difficulties with the guidance of books, mutual support groups, and other sources of information.

Is There an Optimal Approach to Psychotherapy?   520

11. There is no one single approach to psychotherapy that is ideal for all people in all situations. Rather, the various approaches to psychotherapy may be viewed as complementary alternatives.

12. Each approach to psychotherapy has distinctive advantages and disadvantages, and it may be best to view the approaches as complementary rather than competing. Unfortunately, psychologists have not yet reached the point at which they can prescribe a particular form of therapy for a particular type of psychological problem.

13. The length of treatment and other factors not specific to a particular approach also may play a role in the relative effectiveness of psychotherapy.

How Effective Is Psychotherapy?   522

14. Psychotherapies of various forms have proven to be about equally effective, although under particular circumstances certain kinds of therapy may work. It may be that commonalities across types of therapy explain most of the positive outcomes of psychotherapy. These commonalities include the therapist's trustworthiness, warmth, sincerity, empathy, and communication of a new perspective on the client's situation.

What Are Some Key Ethical Issues in Psychotherapy?   527

15. Because psychotherapists have the potential to influence clients profoundly, they must be especially mindful of ethical considerations, such as the need for confidentiality and for obtaining informed consent for participation in any experimental therapeutic procedures.

Choose the best answer to complete each sentence.

1. In psychodynamic terminology, *countertransference* refers to the process whereby
   (a) thoughts and feelings the patient has toward other individuals are projected onto the therapist.
   (b) the therapist projects her or his own intrapsychic conflicts onto the patient.
   (c) the patient avoids confronting uncomfortable thoughts and feelings by thwarting the progress of therapy.
   (d) the patient's ambivalent feelings toward his or her therapist are projected onto other individuals.

2. Client-centered therapy suggests that all the following factors are keys for successful therapy *except*
   (a) the client's willingness to take constructive criticism from the therapist.
   (b) genuineness on the part of the therapist.
   (c) unconditional positive regard for the client.
   (d) empathetic understanding of the client.

3. Two explicitly directive psychotherapeutic approaches are
   (a) behavior therapy and biological therapy.
   (b) psychodynamic therapy and humanistic therapy.
   (c) humanistic therapy and cross-cultural therapy.
   (d) cross-cultural therapy and biological therapy.

4. A behavioral technique whereby a therapist conditions the client to experience negative feelings in response to a certain undesirable response is termed
   (a) flooding.
   (b) implosion therapy.
   (c) aversion therapy.
   (d) systematic desensitization.

5. If a behavior therapist directly places a patient into an anxiety-provoking situation, in the hope that the anxiety will eventually cease, the therapist is using the technique of
   (a) flooding.
   (b) aversion therapy.
   (c) systematic desensitization.
   (d) maximum sensitization.

6. Biological treatments include all of the following *except*
   (a) antidepressant medication.
   (b) electroconvulsive shock therapy.
   (c) systematic desensitization.
   (d) antipsychotic medication.

Answer each of the following questions by filling in the blank with an appropriate word or phrase.

7. During the 15th and 16th centuries, persons classified as mentally ill were kept in _____, which generally provided harsh treatment in poorly maintained facilities.

8. Cognitive therapy focuses on altering a client's _____ contents and processes, which are viewed as causing the client's psychological distress.

9. In psychoanalysis, the unconscious attempts by the client to sabotage the course of therapy are referred to as _____.

10. MAO inhibitors and tricyclics are examples of _____ drugs.

11. One behavior-therapy technique used to reduce anxiety, _____ _____, teaches the client relaxation techniques and then instructs the client to use those techniques through successively more intense anxiety-provoking situations.

12. In the behavior-therapy technique of _____, an unwanted response to a stimulus is replaced with another, more desirable response.

13. _____ and _____ are examples of extinction procedures whereby unwanted responses are weakened.

14. In _____ therapy, therapists may encourage clients to alter their thought patterns by changing the maladaptive statements they make to themselves in response to stressful situations.

15. Therapists must obtain _____ _____ from clients—that is, an assurance that the clients understand the conditions under which therapy will be conducted.

16. Psychotherapists assure their clients of _____, which means that whatever the client says to the therapist will be kept private.

17. In addition to antidepressant, antianxiety, and antipsychotic drugs, biological psychologists use _____ as a psychotropic drug for treating _____ _____.

Match the following psychotherapeutic approaches to their descriptions of how therapists address the psychological problems of their clients:

18. behavior therapy

(a) treating clients in ways that are appropriate to the clients' worldviews, expectations, and experiences

19. psychodynamic therapy

(b) resolving unconscious conflicts among the id, the superego, and the events that take place in the real world

20. cultural therapy

(c) changing what the client does in response to whatever is happening in the environment

21. humanistic therapy

(d) treating the underlying physiological bases for psychological disorders

22. biological therapy

(e) nondirectively showing the client unconditional positive regard so that the client can fulfill her or his potential

---

Answers

1. b, 2. a, 3. a, 4. c, 5. a, 6. c, 7. asylums, 8. thought, 9. resistance, 10. antidepressant, 11. systematic desensitization, 12. counterconditioning, 13. Flooding, implosion, 14. cognitive, 15. informed consent, 16. confidentiality, 17. lithium, bipolar disorders, 18. c, 19. b, 20. a, 21. e, 22. d

Pathways to Understanding

1. Suppose that you are the editor for psychological self-help books in a large publishing house. Describe the manuscript for a self-help book that you hope to receive or that you plan to have written by one of the authors you know. What psychological problems does the book tackle, and how does it handle them?

2. If you were to have a need for psychotherapy, which method of therapy would you choose? What if you were to decide to become a psychotherapist? Would your choice be the same? Analyze the benefits and drawbacks of the method you would prefer in each role.

3. How could you use the ideas expressed in this chapter to improve your own life?

R*ex hates to lose, which may be why he is one of the top competitors on the university tennis team. When he goes on the court, he gives 100% every time. When he does lose, he feels outraged and determined to conquer his opponent quickly and completely the next time. Often he does.*

Rex's competitiveness comes out in all aspects of his life. He is a fierce competitor in the classroom and likes to demolish his classmates with his superior arguments. Rex also is determined to become president of the university chess club as soon as possible and already he has started jockeying for a position to make sure that there is no question about who will come out on top. There is a lot of competition, and Rex feels stressed out over it, but he is determined to win the presidency nevertheless.

The one area in which Rex perceives himself to be having problems is in his friendships. He is not sure why, but he ends up competing even with his best friends. He feels almost a compulsion to one-up them in whatever accomplishments they may have attained and the result often is that they don't want to be around him. Rex knows that his competitiveness is hurting his friendships but he sees it as in his nature. His whole family is that way and so he figures he is just a chip off the old block.

Does Rex need to do something or should he leave well enough alone? Is there an alternative pathway waiting for him to construct? Think about these issues as you read chapter 15, paying special attention to the issue of Type-A behavior.

15

Rex's experiences with his competitiveness illustrate aspects of the field of **health psychology**, the study of the two-way interaction between the mind and the physical health of the body. For Rex, and for all of us, the interaction of psychological and physiological processes works both ways. In Rex's life, as in any life, there are many pathways individuals can follow. Some of these pathways lead to health and happiness. Others lead to disease and unhappiness. To a large extent, although not to a total extent, we can choose our own pathway.

WHAT DO HEALTH PSYCHOLOGISTS STUDY?

Health psychologists are interested in the psychological aspects of how people stay healthy, prevent illness, become ill, and respond to illness. Health psychologists work in hospitals, in clinics, in private office settings, and in academic settings. Health psychologists work to promote individual and public health. Those interested in public health have as a priority not only individual well-being, but the collective well-being of a community, state, or even country. Specifically, health psychologists often ask the following kinds of questions:

1. *Staying well.* How can people enhance their sense of health and well-being through health-enhancing behavior and lifestyle choices? For example, why do many people have difficulty sticking to an exercise or diet program? What situations might make it easier for people to stick to exercise or diet programs?

2. *Preventing illness or becoming ill.* How do people become vulnerable to illness or injury? How do people prevent illness or injury? How do psychological processes affect people's vulnerability to illness or injury? How do people respond to physical changes that may be symptoms of illness? *Symptoms* are unusual feelings in the body (e.g., a queasy stomach) or observable features of the body (e.g., an itchy rash on the neck) that may indicate some kind of illness or injury. For example, why do many couples still choose not to use condoms during sexual encounters, despite the risk to both partners of contracting acquired immune deficiency syndrome (AIDS) or other diseases and the risk of an unplanned pregnancy for the female? Why do people smoke, drink heavily, or overeat when they know that these behaviors harm them and make them vulnerable to illness?

3. *Responding to illness.* How do people respond to becoming ill? How do they respond to long-term illness? How do people with terminal illnesses cope with their situation? For example, why do some patients with tuberculosis sometimes stop taking their medicine and thereby make their tuberculosis potentially untreatable? Why do some patients with terminal illnesses seem to cope so well with the situations they face?

Health psychologists have observed that people's reactions to illness are usually different when they face an illness that they believe to be **chronic**—occurring repeatedly or constantly present (e.g., migraine headaches or diabetes)—versus one they believe to be **acute**—perhaps intense, but only of short duration on one occasion (e.g., a cold or pneumonia). People suffering from chronic illnesses face a variety of psychological challenges, such as depression and anxiety, which usually are unrelated to the actual physical cause of the illness. Therefore, a part of the mission of health psychology is to help people deal with their psychological reactions to serious illness, particularly if the illness has long-term effects.

The field of health psychology is wide-reaching. Some topics covered within health psychology have already been discussed elsewhere in this book. For example, we discussed sleep and sleep disorders in chapter 4; drug use and drug treatment in chapters 4 and 11; normal, healthy development and functioning of the nervous system in chapters 2 and 9; and hunger and sexual motivation in chapter 11. Other aspects of health psychology have been considered in other chapters as well (e.g., what makes [health-related] messages persuasive was discussed in chapter 10). The present chapter includes only those topics of health psychology that have not been discussed elsewhere.

Health psychologists (as well as other psychologists) can operate at three levels in the prevention of problems. As discussed in chapter 14, *primary prevention* is aimed at preventing problems before they occur. *Secondary prevention* is targeted toward detecting problems early, before they become major problems. Finally, *tertiary prevention* essentially treats problems once they have more fully developed. What it prevents, really, is the continuation of the problem. But many problems can be avoided through lifestyle choices, considered next.

HOW CAN PEOPLE ENHANCE THEIR HEALTH THROUGH LIFESTYLE CHOICES?

One of the primary goals of health psychology is to promote health through the influence of the mind on the body, such as by choosing to engage in health-enhancing behavior. Of course, health psychologists recognize that engaging in health-enhancing behavior does not ensure perfect health. Serious psychological and physiological disorders (e.g., schizophrenia or cancer) can arise despite excellent health practices. Nonetheless, health psychologists assume that people can influence their health through the psychological regulation of their behavior. Researchers sometimes use behavior modification to improve health, as in efforts to stop smoking through this technique (see chapter 14). Research supports this assumption, particularly for health-related behavior that is subject to our conscious control.

SAFE SEXUAL PRACTICES

Why do many adolescents, and even many adults, fail to use measures to avoid sexually transmitted diseases (e.g., AIDS) and unwanted pregnancies? Several reasons have been suggested.

1. *Sheer ignorance.* Many sexually active persons simply underestimate the risk of pregnancy or of sexually transmitted disease.

(CONTINUED)

health psychology • the study of how the mind and the physical health of the body interact

chronic • characteristic of symptoms or illness always present or repeatedly occurring again and again

acute • characteristic of symptoms or illness occurring only for a short time, although probably intense

Would it be a good idea for more moviemakers and TV-show producers to show sexy couples using condoms as they prepare to make love?

Branching Out (CONTINUED)

2. *Moral beliefs that lead to anxiety or guilt about engaging in sexual activity.* For some people, planning for the possibility of sexual intercourse makes them feel too anxious or guilty.

3. *Reluctance to talk about sexual activity or contraception.* Some people feel reluctant to discuss the use of condoms and other forms of protection. It may help for them to bear in mind that it would be far more difficult to discuss various unfortunate outcomes of unprotected sexual intercourse, such as sexually transmitted disease or unwanted pregnancy.

4. *Poor impulse control.* Some people actually may have condoms available, but when the need arises they may fail to use one because they believe that the condom may inhibit their pleasure or the spontaneity of their sexual activity. Poor impulse control can be made worse as a result of using alcohol or other drugs.

5. *Media images.* Most of the lovemaking that appears on television shows or in the movies does not include scenes in which the lovers use condoms as a part of their lovemaking. Hence, these models for romantic and sexual love do not promote the use of safe sexual practices.

6. *Gradient of reinforcement.* The potentially undesirable outcomes of using condoms or other protection (e.g., embarrassment) are immediate, whereas the potentially unwanted outcomes of failing to use such protection (e.g., disease or unwanted pregnancy) are not immediate.

7. *Feeling of invulnerability.* Surprisingly, many adolescents, and even some adults believe that they are somehow protected from contracting sexually transmitted diseases because of their general health, their careful selection of partners, or through some magical protection that they believe will lower their risk of pregnancy or disease.

Which of these reasons seems to you to be the most influential in causing people's failure to protect themselves against unwanted pregnancy or disease? How may health psychologists encourage people to engage in safe sexual practices?

For example, people can significantly reduce their risk of dying at any given age by following seven health-related practices (Belloc & Breslow, 1972; Breslow, 1983). In fact, the risk of death at a given age has been found to decrease almost linearly with the number of the following seven health-related practices that have been implemented: (a) sleeping 7 to 8 hours a day, (b) eating breakfast almost every day, (c) rarely eating between meals, (d) being at a roughly appropriate weight in relation to height, (e) not smoking (see Figure 15.1), (f) drinking alcohol only in moderation or not at all, and (g) exercising or otherwise engaging in rigorous physical activity regularly. Exercise is particularly important.

Of the various types of exercise, by far the most important for overall health and well-being is aerobic exercise. **Aerobic exercise** involves intense

aerobic exercise • activities that are sufficiently intense and long-lasting to stimulate increased heart rate and respiration (breathing)

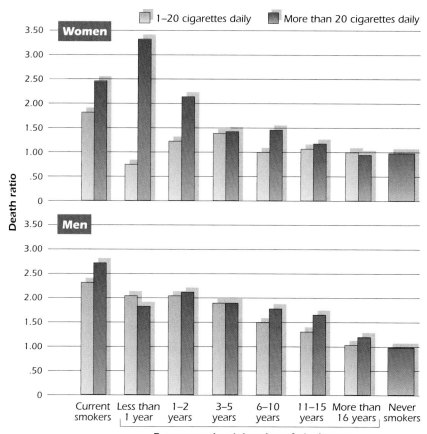

FIGURE 15.1
Death Rates and Smoking
The death rates for former smokers eventually (after about 15 years of not smoking) reach about the same levels as the rates for people who have never smoked.

activities that last more than 20 or 30 minutes and that increase both heart rate and oxygen consumption. These activities enhance *cardiovascular* (heart and blood vessels) and *respiratory* (breathing) fitness (Alpert, Field, Goldstein, & Perry, 1990). Cardiovascular fitness and respiratory fitness particularly help psychological well-being because they increase the amount of oxygen reaching the brain, thereby enhancing cognitive and neurological functions. Aerobic exercises include jogging, speed-walking, running, bicycling, rowing, and swimming. Table 15.1 summarizes the various kinds of exercises and their effects on health.

Many people report that they feel more alert and generally more satisfied with their lives when they exercise aerobically. Immediately during and after exercise, this reaction may be a physiological response to the exercise. In part, the increased *oxygenation* (presence of more oxygen) of the brain may enhance alertness as well as decrease stress. Also, it has been suggested that aerobic exercise triggers the production or release of endorphins. *Endorphins* (a word based on the combination "*endo*genous *morphin*es") are pain-relieving biochemicals that the body produces naturally (e.g., during sexual orgasm or romantic excitation). The presence of endorphins partly may account for the sense of well-being that accompanies aerobic exercise.

TABLE 15.1

Types of Exercise

Various types of exercise offer different kinds of benefits to health, with aerobic exercise leading the list in promoting cardiovascular fitness.

Type	Definition	Effect on health	Examples
Aerobic	High-intensity, long-duration activities that increases both heart rate and oxygen consumption	Valuable to overall health and cardiovascular fitness; increases the amount of oxygen reaching the brain, enhancing cognitive and other neurological functions	Jogging, speed-walking, running, bicycling, rowing, swimming
Anaerobic	Does not require increased consumption of oxygen	Does not increase coronary or respiratory fitness, and may even prove dangerous to persons susceptible to coronary disease	Sprinting and games such as baseball or football, all of which require short and intensive bursts of energy
Isotonic	Requires the contraction of muscles and the movements of joints	Helps to develop muscle mass, but does not improve overall cardiovascular fitness	Weight lifting and some forms of calisthenics
Isometric	Occurs when muscles are contracted against unmoving objects or each other	Increases strength but does not improve overall health	Pushing hard against a wall
Isokinetic	Requires the movement of muscles and joints, but the amount of resistance is adjusted according to the amount of force applied	Enhances muscle strength, but not overall health and cardiovascular fitness	Strength-building machines that involve hydraulic or similar systems

A number of studies have suggested specific psychological benefits of exercise programs, in addition to enhanced health and well-being. For example, regular programs of exercise have been tied to improvements in self-esteem, as well as to reduction of depression (D. Hayes & Ross, 1986; Rodin & Plante, 1989; see Taylor, 1991, for a review). Employee-fitness programs, which have become increasingly common, have even resulted in reduced absenteeism, increased job satisfaction, and reduction in health-care costs (Rodin & Plante, 1989).

15.1

FINDING YOUR WAY

In the past week, how many of the seven health-related practices have you followed? In what aerobic-exercise activities have you participated? How well are you currently promoting your wellness through your lifestyle? What are five steps you can take to improve your health, starting this week?

Also important to psychological health is good nutrition. We eat for two fundamental reasons: to supply raw materials for building new body tissue and to supply energy for the body's internal processes and for its

For people of all ages, exercise is one of the key ways to promote health and well-being. How should you evaluate your exercise program? Focus on how consistently you implement the program, not on how intensely you exercise at a given session or on how formal your program is (e.g., in a scheduled class vs. in a less formal setting).

interactions with our environment. Having an adequate energy supply not only affects the body's basic functioning (e.g., through the activities of the autonomic nervous system, including respiration, circulation, digestion, repairs, etc.) and its ability to interact with the environment (e.g., through the activities of the somatic nervous system), but it also affects the physiological functioning of the central nervous system, the brain and spinal cord. The brain uses up about 20% of available blood sugar and vital neurotransmitters are created from dietary substances (see chapter 2). In short, brains need food.

Although some disagreement exists about how much of particular substances we need, there is broad agreement that a healthful diet (a) is balanced; (b) includes a variety of foods; and (c) contains relatively more complex carbohydrates and fiber and relatively smaller amounts of fats, especially saturated fats and cholesterol. The consensus is that we need a balance of vitamins and minerals, although the exact amounts we need are open to question. The U.S. government has suggested both minimum daily requirements (MDRs) and recommended daily allowances (RDAs) of particular vitamins and minerals, but there is no agreement as to whether the recommended daily allowances are ideal amounts. Table 15.2 summarizes some of the major kinds of food needs people have.

Another important ingredient of health is not smoking. Smoking has been associated with many diseases, including lung cancer, heart disease, emphysema, and hypertension. There are few things one can do that are as effective toward the immediate improvement of one's health as the cessation of smoking.

TABLE 15.2
Calories, the Major Nutrients, and Fiber
In addition to considering calories, people interested in promoting health must consider a balance of major nutrients, as well as fiber.

Nutrient	Function in the body	Psychological symptoms from deficiency or toxicity
Calories	Basic unit of measurement of the energy obtained from food; energy is required by the body for all of its processes	Deficiency may cause apathy and irritability
Carbohydrates Simple carbohydrates	Provide immediate energy but less effective for longer duration	Some correlational studies indicate that a high number of habitually violent people in prisons show abnormally low blood-sugar levels; studies of the effects of simple sugars on cognitive performance and mood show no conclusive results
Complex carbohydrates	Provide excellent stable source of caloric energy	Lack can lead to irritability and apathy; a small proportion of schizophrenics may react to grains with increased psychotic symptoms
Fats (saturated, unsaturated, cholesterol)	An essential source of energy; fats are particularly easy to store in the body, important when food is not constantly available	Can carry either wanted or unwanted substances across the blood–brain barrier to the brain; accumulation of cholesterol and other fats in the blood vessels can lead to stroke
Protein	Used for the construction of new cell material, particularly muscles, hormones, and neurotransmitters	No known direct effects on psychological state or well-being
Fiber	Nonnutritive; cannot be metabolized but aids in the elimination of waste products	No known direct effects on psychological state or well-being

HOW DO PERSONALITY AND STRESS INFLUENCE HEALTH?

The preceding section described some of the ways in which people can influence their own health by engaging in health-promoting behavior and by avoiding behavior that compromises their health. Certainly, people's personalities and life circumstances influence their health-related choices. In what other ways do personality and personal circumstances influence health? For one thing, both factors interact to affect the likelihood that people will fall prey to illness or will experience other problems related to health. The interactions of distinctive individual personalities and specific factors in the environment influence many aspects of health. The word describing these interactions is *stress*. What is stress, and how does it affect our health?

Usually, when we think of stress, we think of feeling mentally distressed and perhaps even physically distressed because of some forms of external pressures, such as time pressure, work pressure, or family pressure. That view of stress is only part of the picture. When researchers investigate stress, they define the term more broadly. **Stress** is a person's response to a situation in which an event or an aspect of the environment causes a person to feel challenged in some way. The causes of stress are termed **stressors.** That is, stressors are changes in the environment that challenge people to cope with the situations they face. Their adaptations to these perceived challenges are **stress responses.** Frequently, the response to stress leads to an increased likelihood of becoming ill (Totman, 1990; Totman, Kiff, Reed, & Craig, 1980), although occasional exposure to stressful situations for brief periods of time may actually enhance the ability to tolerate further stress at a later time (Dienstbier, 1989).

Stressors

Stressors are of several major kinds. One major source of stress includes *major life events* (e.g., starting or graduating from college, marrying or divorcing). The loss of a loved one, whether through the termination of a relationship or death, can cause a great amount of stress. After the death of a spouse, widowed individuals are more likely to experience various kinds of illnesses and are also more likely to die (Stroebe, Stroebe, & Domittner, 1988), presumably in part because of the stress caused by their bereavement. Divorced individuals also are more susceptible to various kinds of diseases, including heart disease and pneumonia, than married individuals (G. Jacobson, 1983). Obviously, some of the effect of bereavement is due to changes in behavior. For example, the bereaved person may be distracted when driving and thus be more likely to be involved in an automobile accident. But evidence suggests that the effect is not purely behavioral. High levels of stress are associated with a lower count of white blood cells and other signs of declining function of the immune system (Laudenslager, 1988). These symptoms are as likely to occur in unhappily married individuals as in people who are unhappy and divorced (Kiecolt-Glaser et al., 1993). Sometimes, less traumatic events play a role in stress as well, such as *everyday hassles* (e.g., getting stuck in traffic, trying to please a difficult boss).

Stressful Life Events

Surprisingly, stressors do not necessarily have to be things we perceive as negative. For example, having a new baby, getting married, and moving to a new home are all stressors because they require the new parent, spouse, or home-dweller to adapt in many ways. Table 15.3 shows the *Social Readjustment Rating Scale (SRRS),* which lists 43 stressors that have been found to affect our health and well-being (Holmes & Rahe, 1967). Most of us would welcome many of these stressors, such as outstanding personal achievement or marriage. Many other stressors are measured only in terms of change, not indicating whether the change was considered positive or negative: change in financial status, living conditions, residence, school, recreation, social activities, the health status of a family member, and so on.

Not all stressors are alike. In the SRRS, Thomas Holmes and Richard Rahe ranked the 43 stressors and assigned different weights to them (described in Holmes & David, 1989). For example, getting married was rated as more stressful (more challenging) than having trouble with a

stress • a person's response to the presence of something in the environment that causes the person to feel challenged in some way

stressor • an event or situation that causes stress

stress response • an adaptation to challenging changes in the environment

TABLE 15.3
Social Readjustment Rating Scale (SRRS)
Thomas Holmes and Richard Rahe (1967) developed a scale for measuring a person's level of stress, based on weightings of life events to which the person has had to adapt. For your own information, in the far-right column, enter the weightings for life events you have experienced within the past year.

Rank (most to least stressful)	Life event	Weighting assigned by Holmes and Rahe	Weighting for events in your life in the past year
1	Death of a spouse	100	
2	Divorce	73	
3	Marital separation	65	
4	Jail term	63	
5	Death of close family member (other than spouse)	63	
6	Personal injury or illness	53	
7	Marriage	50	
8	Fired at work	47	
9	Marital reconciliation	45	
10	Retirement	45	
11	Change in health of family member	44	
12	Pregnancy	40	
13	Sex difficulties	39	
14	Gain of new family member	39	
15	Business readjustment	39	
16	Change in financial state	38	
17	Death of close friend	37	
18	Change to different line of work	36	
19	Change in number of arguments with spouse	35	
20	Mortgage over $10,000 [based on 1967 dollars; would be a higher number today]	31	
21	Foreclosure of mortgage or loan	30	
22	Change in responsibilities at work	29	
23	Son or daughter leaving home	29	
24	Trouble with in-laws	29	
25	Outstanding personal achievement	28	
26	Spouse begins or stops work	26	

(Continued)

TABLE 15.3
Social Readjustment Rating Scale (SRRS) *(Continued)*

Rank (most to least stressful)	Life event	Weighting assigned by Holmes and Rahe	Weighting for events in your life in the past year
27	Begin or end school	26	
28	Change in living condition	25	
29	Revision of personal habits	24	
30	Trouble with boss	23	
31	Change in work hours or conditions	20	
32	Change in residence	20	
33	Change in schools	20	
34	Change in recreation	19	
35	Change in church activities	19	
36	Change in social activities	18	
37	Mortgage or loan less than $10,000 [based on 1967 dollars; would be a higher number today]	17	
38	Change in sleeping habits	16	
39	Change in number of family get-togethers	15	
40	Change in eating habits	15	
41	Vacation	13	
42	Christmas	12	
43	Minor violations of the law	11	
	Total		

boss. These researchers then correlated the stressors with the likelihood of becoming ill. This likelihood was positively correlated with the totals for the weighted values of these stressors. (Recall, however, that correlations suggest only a connection between the two. We cannot determine causality based on correlations alone.)

Since the SRRS was introduced in 1967, the scale has been introduced to other countries, either in its original form or in an adapted form (e.g., Woon, Masuda, Wagner, & Holmes, 1971; Yahiro, Inoue, & Nozawa, 1993). Research on the cross-cultural implementation of the SRRS suggests that the scale does have wide cross-cultural applicability (Lin, Masuda, & Tazuma, 1984), particularly if it is modified appropriately (Woon et al., 1971). Some of the items, some descriptions of the items, and some of the weightings and rankings given to the items may need to be adapted to suit different cultural contexts or different ethnic contexts

According to Thomas Holmes and Richard Rahe, the most stressful life event is the death of a spouse. Do you agree?

FIGURE 15.2
Stressful Life Events
Tragically, on occasion, people fall under moving subway trains and are seriously hurt or killed. The subway-train operators who learn that the train they were operating accidentally killed or maimed someone are much more likely to be on sick leave for a month or more during the year following such a tragic accident. In what other kinds of occupations might you expect workers occasionally to experience highly stressful events?

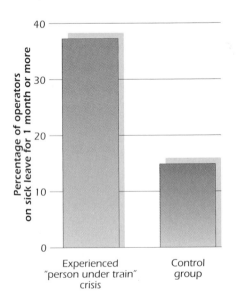

within a richly diverse country such as the United States (Hwang, 1981; Komaroff, Masuda, & Holmes, 1968). It is also important to remember that how stressful an event is may depend on when it occurs in the life cycle. For example, having a baby may have a different effect on a 16-year-old single woman who did not wish to become pregnant versus a 26-year-old married woman who was hoping for the pregnancy.

In some occupations, workers are prone to experiencing highly stressful events (see Figure 15.2). Stressful life events also can be relatively minor or temporary changes, such as being on vacation from work, going away for a weekend, or having a treasured friend or family member visit for a few days. These pleasant changes are stressors because they cause you to adapt in some way: In the middle of the night, in your hotel, or at your campsite you must find your way to the bathroom; while your best friend is visiting, you must cope with new demands on your time and on your physical space. Some of these demands come in the form of everyday hassles. There is no particular number that is indicative of high or intolerable stress. But people often recognize this point in themselves when they feel extremely tense, irritable, susceptible to emotional outbursts, frustrated, or unable to sleep because of inability to stop reflecting upon stressful events.

Everyday Hassles

Not all sources of stress involve major or even minor events in your life. Some stressors are simply *daily hassles*—those routine annoyances or challenges to your ability to cope, such as traffic hassles, disagreements with an acquaintance, getting accustomed to new equipment or appliances, or finding things after you rearrange the items in a cabinet (see, e.g., Figure 15.3). Although no single hassle may be a major source of stress, an accumulation of hassles may very well be a source of stress (e.g., Pearlstone, Russell, & Wells, 1994).

Daily hassles have been associated with reduced immune-system resistance to infection (Brosschot et al., 1994; Farne et al., 1994); with minor

Hassles	
Item	Percentage of times checked
1. Concerns about weight	52.4%
2. Health of a family member	48.1
3. Rising prices of common goods	43.7
4. Home maintenance	42.8
5. Too many things to do	38.6
6. Misplacing or losing things	38.1
7. Yard work or outside home maintenance	38.1
8. Property, investment, or taxes	37.6
9. Crime	37.1
10. Physical appearance	35.9

Uplifts	
Item	Percentage of times checked
1. Relating well with your spouse or lover	76.3%
2. Relating well with friends	74.4
3. Completing a task	73.3
4. Feeling healthy	72.7
5. Getting enough sleep	69.7
6. Eating out	68.4
7. Meeting your responsibilities	68.1
8. Visiting, phoning, or writing someone	67.7
9. Spending time with family	66.7
10. Home (inside) pleasing to you	65.5

FIGURE 15.3
Hassles and Uplifts
This figure shows the 10 most frequently cited daily hassles and the 10 most frequently cited daily uplifts, including the percentages of times people checked off each hassle or uplift.

physical ailments (Kohn, Gurevich, Pickering, & MacDonald, 1994); with negative mood, even lasting through the next day (Caspi, Bolger, & Eckenrode, 1987); and with work-related injuries (Savery & Wooden, 1994). On the other hand, the negative outcomes of daily hassles can be reduced by trying not to think about the hassles (Farne et al., 1994) and by seeking and getting social support (e.g., conversations and fun activities with friends; Flett, Blankstein, Hicken, & Watson, 1995). In contrast, focusing on hassles can lead to stress responses.

Branching Out

STRESSORS AT WORK

For many people, a major source of stress (particularly in terms of everyday hassles) is their work. Several characteristics of a particular job can make the work particularly stressful:

- *Job overload.* Time pressures, such as assembly-line work (where the machine, not the worker, determines the pace) and long workdays (e.g., required overtime or after-hours meetings; Argyle, 1992).

- *Repetitive work.* When the same worker performs the same task again and again, the worker may experience increased levels of stress (Argyle, 1992).

(CONTINUED)

Branching Out (CONTINUED)

- *Lack of control.* Workers who feel that they have no control over most aspects of their work feel high levels of stress, as well as being subject to increased risk of high blood pressure and heart disease (Steptoe & Appels, 1989); for instance, assembly-line workers have very little to say about when and how to carry out the work they do, so they may feel high levels of stress.

- *Danger.* Police officers, firefighters, undersea divers, and coal miners have relatively high levels of stress associated with danger.

- *Job insecurity.* When workers feel unsure of whether they will continue to be employed (e.g., due to economic turmoil or hardships in a given industry) they experience greater levels of stress (Heaney, Israel, & House, 1994).

- *Environmental stress.* Some kinds of workers (e.g., coal miners, steel manufacturers, and rock-concert technicians) suffer from increased stress as a direct result of the environment in which they work (Argyle, 1992). For instance, high levels of dust, industrial pollutants, extreme temperatures, and noise can cause illness or injury, as well as increased stress. Other sources of stress include the need to work at odd hours (e.g., firefighters and shift nurses in hospitals) or to commute frequently or for long periods of time (e.g., suburban dwellers who work in cities).

- *Role conflict.* Most people experience some degree of stressful role conflict at work (e.g., trying to please a client while trying to carry out company policies that the client hates); managers (who must please both their superiors and their subordinates) are often particularly likely to suffer stress as a result of role conflicts (Argyle, 1992).

- *Responsibility for others.* Another reason that managers and supervisors experience high levels of stress is that they must take responsibility for the well-being and the actions of other people (Argyle, 1992); perhaps even more than managers, caregivers (e.g., nurses, social workers, teachers of children with special needs, people who take care of needy adults) suffer from tremendous stress as a result of continually feeling responsible for other people (Maslach & Jackson, 1984; Wilber & Specht, 1994).

Employers can take steps to reduce the amount of stress at work, as well as the impact of work-related stress: (a) Enhance job safety (thereby reducing the danger of the work); (b) reduce the level of noise, dust, and other environmental stressors; (c) enrich the diversity of each worker's job, such as by using automated equipment to reduce the amount of repetitive work and by rotating workers across various tasks; (d) give workers as much autonomy and decision-making authority as is realistic for them to perform their work satisfactorily; (e) provide as much role clarity as possible, so that managers and other workers better understand which of their conflicting roles takes priority in a given situation; and (f) increase the amount of social support provided to caregivers, managers, and workers at all levels, such as by creating opportunities for collaboration and for social interactions—help executives and supervisors to be more supportive of their subordinates. Note, however, that whereas voluntary social interactions seem to reduce stress, obligatory social contacts do not (Bolger & Eckenrode, 1991). The final step is to (g) encourage employees to suggest various ways to minimize stress in the workplace.

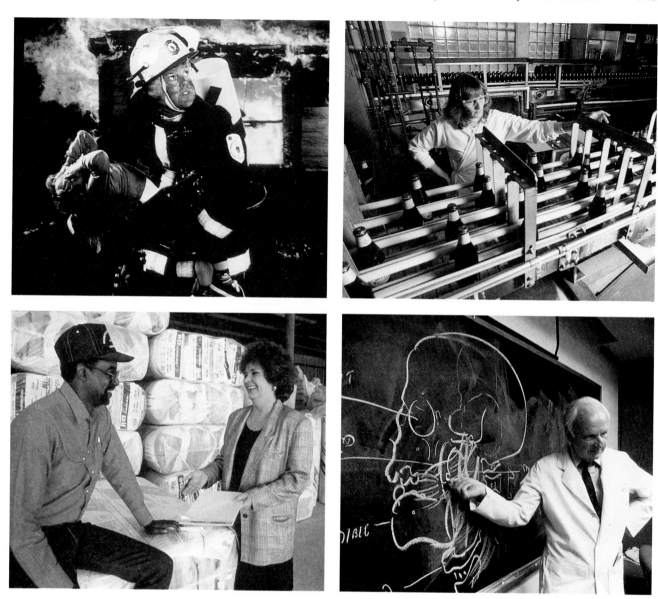

Which of these workers is under the greatest amount of stress? Factors such as overload, repetitive operations, lack of control, physical danger, job insecurity, environmental discomfort, role conflict, and responsibility for other people all contribute to the stress level of a job.

Stress Responses

The discussion thus far has focused on the environment outside the individual. Environmental events alone do not create stress; the individual must perceive the stressor and must respond to the stressor in some way. Often, at least at first, the primary response of the individual is physiological. When we feel challenged (e.g., by the need to adapt), our bodies physiologically prepare us to confront ("fight") or to escape from ("flight") the challenge. This physiological fight-or-flight response may

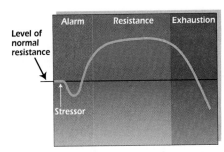

FIGURE 15.4
General Adaptation Syndrome (GAS)

According to Hans Selye, we undergo three phases in responding to stressors: an alarm phase, *in which we shift into high gear, using up our bodily resources at a rapid rate; a* resistance phase, *in which we somewhat shift down from using our resources in such a spendthrift manner; and an* exhaustion phase, *in which our bodily resources are depleted. (After H. Selye, 1974.* Stress without distress. *New York: HarperCollins. Figure 3, p. 39. Copyright © 1974 by M.D.)*

have adaptive evolutionary origins. Constructive coping means that the individual reacts to stress in a way to reduce the stress rather than to do harm to him- or herself.

The physiological fight-or-flight response was discovered by accident. Hans Selye was looking for a new sex hormone when he accidentally happened across a surprising phenomenon: When the body is attacked or is somehow damaged, it seems to respond in the same general way, regardless of the nature of the assault (e.g., shock, extreme temperatures, or fatigue) or the target of the damage (e.g., the whole body or only a particular body part or organ). Selye soon saw the possible implications of this discovery. He then shifted his research to focus on this puzzling physiological response. Selye and other researchers have noted some patterns in our physiological response, which Selye (e.g., 1976) termed the **general adaptation syndrome (GAS)**. There appear to be three phases of response to stress: alarm, resistance, and exhaustion (see Figure 15.4).

Alarm

In the alarm phase, the body immediately is aroused, and the hypothalamus activates the pituitary gland to release a hormone (adrenocorticotropic hormone—ACTH) that triggers the release of hormones from the adrenal glands: corticosteroids, epinephrine (adrenaline), and norepinephrine. These adrenal hormones stimulate the sympathetic nervous system to prompt the heart and lungs to work harder (increasing heart and respiration rate); slow down or stop the activity of the digestive tract, making more blood available to other organs; increase tension in the muscles; increase the production and use of energy (which produces heat); increase perspiration (which helps cool the body); and increase the release of clotting factors into the bloodstream, to minimize blood loss in case of injury (see Figure 15.5). All of these highly adaptive physiological responses go on without our ever having to think about them.

Resistance

The alarm state cannot continue indefinitely. After a short while, the brain and the endocrine (hormonal) system activate the parasympathetic nervous system, thereby applying chemical brakes to slow down how quickly the sympathetic nervous system uses up the body's energy stores. For example, the demands on the heart and lungs decline. Overall, the physiological stress responses decrease in intensity, although they do not return to normal if the perceived stress continues.

Exhaustion

Eventually, even at the reduced rates of use associated with the resistance phase, the body's reserves are exhausted. The body is less able to restore damaged or worn-out tissues, and it is less able to resist *opportunistic infections* (infections that take advantage of weakened resistance to disease; Borysenko & Borysenko, 1982). Normally, when our bodies detect the presence of a threat (e.g., a foreign disease-causing microorganism), we immediately use two lines of natural defense: (a) a specific reaction to a known threat that the body has fought off on previous occasions, and

general adaptation syndrome (GAS) • a general pattern of physiological response to stress, involving three phases: alarm, resistance, and exhaustion

(b) a generalized defensive reaction (e.g., the reaction associated with stress; Maier, Watkins, & Fleshner, 1994).

As an example of your first line of defense, once you have fought off a particular kind of cold or flu virus, your body immediately can recognize and quickly fight off that particular virus if it attacks again. That is, you have been *immunized* (provided with an immune-system defense against a specific disease). Vaccinations also can immunize you against particular diseases by tricking your body into recognizing particular disease-causing microorganisms, so that the body quickly can attack the microorganisms before they have a chance to make you sick.

Your second line of defense is a more general reaction of your immune system to fight off unknown causes of disease. It appears that high levels of stress can weaken your immune system's ability to resist unknown attackers, particularly if the stress continues for an extended period of time (see Figure 15.6). The link between stress and illness has been clearly documented. For instance, stress has been linked to a large number of infectious diseases, including various types of herpes virus infections (e.g., cold sores, chicken pox, mononucleosis, and genital lesions; Jemmott & Locke, 1984; Kiecolt-Glaser & Glaser, 1987; VanderPlate, Aral, & Magder, 1988). Even the anticipation of stress can result in suppressed functioning of the immune system (Kemeny, Cohen, Zegans, & Conant, 1989).

Researchers in the dynamic, cross-disciplinary field of **psychoneuroimmunology** study how our psychological processes, our neural physiology (especially our brains), and our immune systems interact in ways we never previously imagined, let alone understood (e.g., Ader, Felten, & Cohen, 1990, 1991; N. Cohen, Moynihan, Grota, & Ader, 1991). For instance, accumulating evidence suggests that our bodies may be classically conditioned to strengthen or to weaken our natural immune-system defenses against disease (Ader & Cohen, 1991, 1993). Researchers may also choose to study relationships between personality and perceived stress.

FIGURE 15.5
The Body's Response to a Stressful Event
As soon as we face a challenge from the environment, our bodies undergo physiological challenges that alarm and prepare us to react to a potential threat to our well-being.

Although the injection of vaccines can be stressful for all concerned, the widespread use of vaccines has provided immunization to millions of people around the world.

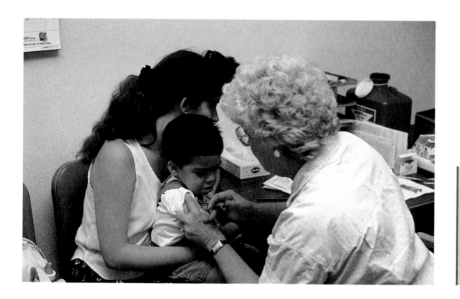

psychoneuroimmunology • a cross-disciplinary field that blends psychology, *neurology* (the study of the brain and nervous system), and *immunology* (the study of the immune system), as well as physiology (e.g., the study of the endocrine system and other biological systems of the body)

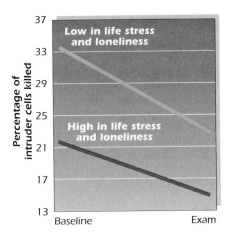

FIGURE 15.6
Stress, Social Isolation, and Immune Defenses

For students who score comparatively high in life stress and in loneliness, the stress of approaching final examination time leads to a notably weakened immune response to attacking intruder cells that may cause infectious disease. (Adapted from Kiecolt-Glaser et al., 1984)

Personality and Perceived Stress

How does personality interact with a person's level of stress? In order for a stressor to lead to a stress response, an individual must perceive the stressor (S. Cohen, Kamarck, & Mermelstein, 1983). That is, it is not the set of events, per se, that results in stress responses such as compromise of the immune system. Rather, stress responses arise from the stress that a person perceives as resulting from these events. For example, if you truly do not notice any need to make any adaptations to having a new roommate or a new job, you may not experience these events as being stressful.

Also, each of us perceives some stressors as being more distressing than are others. For example, suppose that you hate conflict or confrontation of any kind, and you experience situations of conflict or confrontation as being extremely stressful. Someone else might feel little distress in confrontational situations or might even enjoy conflict. If you and this conflict-loving person argue, both of you may experience the physiological alarm phase of the stress response and even the resistance phase. However, because you fret about the confrontation for a while afterward, you may reach the stage of exhaustion. In contrast, the other person may forget all about the conflict moments after it ends, thereby avoiding the exhaustion phase. The notion that perception affects physiology is not new, as shown in the adage regarding mind over matter, "If you don't mind, it doesn't matter."

Each of us also experiences different degrees of internal conflict in response to clashing external demands (work vs. family, spouse vs. friend, etc.). In addition, the very same environment can be experienced as quite different, depending on personality variables. An extrovert who works in a library that serves a remote community of illiterates might be about as distressed as an introvert who leads the recreational activities for a large cruise ship. Each, however, might consider the other's job idyllic. Whether an extrovert or introvert, a person needs to develop mechanisms for appraising stressful situations and then coping with them.

15.2

Think about your own pet peeves or the situations you love to hate. What situations literally might make you sick? Now think about who might consider these peevish situations pleasant. What is it in your personality that makes some situations sickeningly stressful and others quite tolerable?

FINDING YOUR WAY

Appraisal and Coping

Susan Folkman and Richard Lazarus (1988; Folkman, Lazarus, Gruen, & DeLongis, 1986) have proposed a model for the way in which personality factors, stressful circumstances, and health interact. According to Folkman and Lazarus, when we are confronted with a potentially stressful situation, we go through a two-step appraisal process and then a two-dimensional coping process. Both processes interact with our distinctive personalities and with the situation at hand. In **primary appraisal,** we analyze just how much of a stake we have in the outcome of the particular situation. If we have no stake in the outcome, the entire process stops right there.

primary appraisal • the first step in coping with a situation that may be stressful, involving analysis of how much the person will be affected by outcomes of the particular situation

Some health problems attack more than one person at a single blow. For instance, the health of loved ones who care for patients with dementia (e.g., as the result of Alzheimer's disease or multiple strokes) may suffer after providing 24-hour care, 7 days a week to patients who no longer may recognize them.

For example, suppose that I were to tell you of an alarming situation at your college: Some professors have been observed wearing dirty socks! You cannot let this situation continue! Right this instant, you must write a letter to the faculty senate of your college, urging the senate to pass a policy insisting that professors wear clean socks at all times! You must get the letter into the mail immediately!

Did you feel your stress level go up? Probably not. You probably have very little stake in persuading professors to wear clean socks. You may even decide to ignore my urgent plea altogether. Now, compare that level of stress with the level of stress you feel when you think about the final examinations in all of your courses. Unless you are an extraordinarily relaxed student, you probably appraise final exams as being something in which you have a lot at stake. In considering final exams, you would proceed to the next step in the appraisal process: secondary appraisal.

In **secondary appraisal,** we assess what we can do to maximize the likelihood of potentially beneficial outcomes and to minimize the likelihood of potentially harmful outcomes of a given situation. In thinking about final exams, you would try to assess how you could increase the probability that you would score well and decrease the possibility that you would score poorly on any of your exams. The decision to read textbooks and study lecture notes might figure prominently in your secondary appraisal.

Note that both primary and secondary appraisal occur at a cognitive level. At this level, you have not yet cracked a book or jotted a note. Once

secondary appraisal • the process of assessing what can be done about a challenging situation to make it more likely that positive outcomes will result and less likely that harmful outcomes will result

your primary and secondary appraisals are complete, you are ready to begin **coping** with the situation; that is, actually trying to manage the internal and external challenges posed by the situation. According to Folkman and Lazarus, two dimensions of coping serve two different functions: **Problem-focused coping** tackles the problem itself and involves behavioral strategies to resolve the situation. For example, your problem-focused coping strategies might include studying the textbook, attending study sessions, and reviewing your lecture notes. **Emotion-focused coping** involves handling your own emotions in regard to the situation. For example, while studying for the exams, you might try to suppress your anxiety about the exams. Just before taking the exams, you might try some relaxation techniques to reduce your anxiety during the exam.

In situations over which we have more control (e.g., exam grades), problem-focused coping strategies are more likely to lead to more satisfactory outcomes. In situations over which we have less control (e.g., determining what questions your instructor will ask on the exam), emotion-focused coping is more likely to lead to more satisfactory outcomes. The net interaction of primary and secondary appraisal and of problem-focused and emotion-focused coping strategies determines the degree of stress that the individual experiences. According to Folkman and Lazarus, when people feel that their options for coping are inadequate for the situation at hand, they experience greater stress. Low self-esteem also can diminish people's sense of being able to cope with challenging situations (DeLongis, Folkman, & Lazarus, 1988). This perceived inadequacy increases perceived stress, thereby increasing the threat to health and well-being. Social contacts and social support, considered next, however, can reduce stress.

Social Contacts and Social Support

Social isolation is another factor that seems to threaten people's health and well-being (House, Landis, & Umberson, 1988; see Figure 15.6, shown previously. Although obligatory social contacts (e.g., meetings at work or social obligations) do not seem to offer benefits to mental or physical health, voluntary social contacts do (Bolger & Eckenrode, 1991). One reason for the benefits of social contacts may be the opportunities for receiving social support. Social support from various other people is believed to *buffer* against (i.e., reduce the potentially damaging impact of) harmful levels of stress (Schwarzer & Leppin, 1989, 1991). Adequate social support can help people cope with stressors, particularly if such support suits the personality and situational needs of the recipient of the support (I. G. Sarason, Pierce, & Sarason, 1994). The need for social support even may have direct effects on health and well-being: People who have high needs for affiliation, relative to their needs for power and achievement, seem to have stronger immune systems (McClelland, 1987).

Certain kinds of social support also lead to particular health benefits. For instance, friends offer an important source of enjoyable social contacts. Families can also be a resource for pleasant leisure and recreational activities. In addition, friends and families seem to offer distinctive health benefits: People who are married or who have children are also more likely to avoid risky behavior, to take fewer drugs (e.g., alcohol or nicotine [in cigarettes]), and to take other measures to enhance their health (Umberson, 1987). Spouses tend to monitor one another's health and to encourage one another's health-enhancing behavior (Umberson, 1992). On the other hand, for dealing with stress on the job, people seem to be

coping • the processes of managing the internal and external changes presented by a challenging situation

problem-focused coping • adapting to a challenging situation by using strategies to fix the situation and to make it less challenging

emotion-focused coping • adapting to a challenging situation by handling one's own emotions that arise in regard to the situation

helped more by receiving support from their colleagues and supervisors than by receiving support from family members (Argyle, 1992).

15.3

Think about how your social world can help you cope with the aspects of your life that are stressful to you. How can you increase the enjoyable social contacts in your life? Are you experiencing a lot of stress at work or at school? Who are some of the people to whom you can reach out, who can offer you social support for handling the stressful aspects of your life? If you are not close to members of your family, how else might you find encouragement to practice health-enhancing behavior?

Hospitals can foster a lack of sense of control in the patient, and if a sense of control is important for patients' well-being and recovery, what can be done? A number of researchers have sought to figure out what hospitals could do to increase patients' psychological as well as physical well-being. Methods for increasing patients' sense of control are **control-enhancing interventions,** which increase patients' abilities to respond appropriately to illness and eventually to cope effectively with illness. In a classic, trailblazing study by Irving Janis (1958), postoperative recovery was compared in three groups: one group with a low level of fear about an impending operation, a second group with a moderate level of fear, and a third group with a high level of fear. Janis also looked at how well patients in each of the three groups understood and were able to utilize the information given them by the hospital about probable aftereffects of the surgery they received. Janis found that patients in the moderate-fear group had the best postoperative recovery.

Subsequent research has shown that what is most important is the extent to which patients process the information given to them in advance about the effects of the surgery, rather than their level of fear (K. O. Anderson & Masur, 1983; J. E. Johnson, Lauver, & Nail, 1989). Patients who are better prepared regarding what to expect during and after surgery are less emotionally upset after surgery and are also able to leave the hospital more quickly than are uninformed or less informed patients (J. E. Johnson, 1984). Other investigators have extended this work to suggest that patients who are prepared in advance regarding what to expect from a variety of medical procedures may feel a stronger sense of personal control and self-efficacy in mastering their reactions (see Taylor, 1990). This enhanced sense of control and efficacy then results in more positive outcomes.

Research further suggests that it is important to teach patients not only *what* will happen during and after surgery, but also *how* they should respond to what happens. One study showed that if patients are instructed to try to distract themselves from those aspects of surgery that are unpleasant, and to try to concentrate instead on the benefits they will receive from the surgery, the patients will need fewer *analgesics* (pain-relieving drugs) after the surgery (Langer, Janis, & Wolfer, 1975). Other effective control-enhancing interventions include learning both relaxation responses and cognitive–behavioral interventions to overcome anxiety and to adapt to the situation more effectively (Ludwick-Rosenthal & Neufeld, 1988).

control-enhancing interventions • used to increase patients' abilities to respond appropriately to illness, eventually leading to coping effectively with illness

HOW DO PERSONALITY PATTERNS RELATE TO ILLNESS?

Type-A Versus Type-B Behavior Patterns

As this chapter has shown, our psychological makeup affects our choices in health-related behaviors and our responses to potentially stressful situations. How else may our personal psychological characteristics affect our health? In 1974, Meyer Friedman and Ray Rosenman noticed that men who suffered from heart disease seemed to have a particular set of personality characteristics, known as the **Type-A behavior pattern,** which comprises (a) a competitive orientation toward achievement, (b) a sense of urgency about time, and (c) high levels of feelings of anger and hostility. Thus, Type A's tend to work very hard and competitively toward achieving goals, often without feeling much enjoyment in the process; they constantly tend to be racing against the clock; and they tend to feel anger and hostility easily toward other people and other sources of frustration. In contrast to the Type-A behavior pattern is the **Type-B behavior pattern,** characterized by relatively low levels of competitiveness, urgency about time, and hostility. Type-B people tend to be more easygoing, relaxed, and willing to enjoy the process of life as they live it.

A number of studies have found a link between Type-A behavior and coronary heart disease (Booth-Kewley & Friedman, 1987; Friedman et al., 1994; Haynes, Feinleib, & Kannel, 1980). However, some studies have not confirmed the link (e.g., Shekelle et al., 1985). It appears that the three components of Type-A behavior may not contribute equally to the likelihood of having a heart attack. Redford Williams (1986) has argued that the component of anger and hostility is the most deadly one (also described in Taylor, 1990). Other studies have supported this position (e.g., Barefoot, Dahlstrom, & Williams, 1983). Anger and hostility directed against one's self may be quite damaging to health (Dembroski, MacDougall, Williams, Haney, & Blumenthal, 1985; R. Williams, 1986). Also, hostility characterized by suspiciousness, resentment, frequent anger, and antagonism toward others seems to be quite harmful to health (Barefoot, Dodge, Peterson, Dahlstrom, & Williams, 1989; Dembroski & Costa, 1988; R. B. Williams & Barefoot, 1988). Some researchers distinguish between two kinds of hostility that can arise in reaction to stress. *Neurotic hostility* is the kind shown by people who are chronic complainers or who are irritable much of the time. *Antagonistic hostility* is shown by those who seek out conflict and confrontations with others. A further refinement of this body of research suggests that the expression of anger and hostility may have more serious health consequences for men than for women (e.g., Burns, Hutt, & Weidner, 1993; Spicer, Jackson, & Scragg, 1993; L. Wright et al., 1994).

Type-A behavior appears to be somewhat modifiable (M. Friedman et al., 1994; Levenkron & Moore, 1988). A variety of techniques have been used, including relaxation (Roskies, Spevack, Surkis, Cohen, & Gilman, 1978), aerobic exercise, cognitive–behavioral stress management (Blumenthal et al., 1988; Roskies et al., 1986), or some combinations of these techniques (Bruning & Frew, 1987). To a certain extent, you can influence your perceptions by changing your thinking. Some health psychologists focus on changing people's reactions to events so that they feel less distressed in the face of life's challenges. In addition, lifestyle changes might be appropriate interventions. Type-A individuals tend to have very different lifestyles from those of Type-B individuals, and it may be as much the lifestyle as the personality itself that leads to coronary heart disease. For

Type-A behavior pattern • a personality characterized by *high* levels of hostility, as well as by the *pursuit* of competition and time pressure

Type-B behavior pattern • a personality characterized by *low* levels of hostility, as well as by the *avoidance* of competition and time pressure

Two personality patterns seem to influence the likelihood of coronary heart disease: People with a Type-A personality pattern (such as the man on the left) feel a sense of urgency to complete tasks and to achieve success, and they are easily angered when things do not go well. People with a Type-B personality pattern (such as the woman on the right) seem to be able to respond to work pressures without feeling undue urgency, compulsion to achieve success, or high levels of hostility in response to minor frustrations.

example, the Type-A individuals are more likely to place themselves in competitive situations and in situations with great demands on their time.

15.4

Before you read on, stop for a moment to reflect on which pattern describes your own—Type-A or Type-B—behavior. (Clue: If you felt angry at the suggestion to take the time to stop working toward your goal of finishing this chapter as quickly as possible, perhaps you do not need to think too long about which pattern best describes you.) If you are unsure of how you would describe yourself, think about how a family member or a close friend might describe your behavior.

FINDING YOUR WAY

Hardiness and Stress Resistance

The discovery of heart-attack-prone personalities occurred because many health researchers wanted to know how personality attributes may increase people's vulnerability to illness. In contrast, Suzanne Kobasa (1982, 1990; Kobasa, Maddi, Puccetti, & Zola, 1994) has focused on studying a personality trait she calls "hardiness," an aspect of personality that seems to help people resist the health-weakening effects of stress. **Hardiness** includes high internal locus of control, strong commitment to work and to

hardiness • a personality attribute characterized by high internal locus of control, strong commitment to work and other activities, and an outlook that favors challenge and opportunities for personal growth

other activities, and an outlook that views change as a challenge and an opportunity for growth. Compared with other people, people with hardy personalities also tend to find out more information about health in general and about the prevention of illnesses to which they may be vulnerable in particular (Lau, 1988). They also show more health-enhancing behavior, and they believe that they can control their own health (Lau, 1988).

HOW DO OUR MINDS EXPERIENCE PAIN?

Among the most troubling symptoms of illness is pain. **Pain** is the sensory and emotional discomfort associated with actual, imagined, or threatened damage to or irritation of the body (Sanders, 1985). Chapter 3 described the sensory aspects of pain, including the importance of pain as a warning system to alert us that our body tissues are being injured or are recovering from injury. Pain stimuli warn us to avoid further injury or to seek safety and rest to aid in recovery and healing. Here, we discuss the cognitive and emotional aspects of pain, as well as different kinds of pain and various methods for relieving pain.

Many psychologists conceptualize pain in a way very similar to the popular conception of pain: It has both a sensory component (the sensations at the site where the pain starts; e.g., throbbing, aching, or stinging pain) and an affective component (the emotions that go along with the pain; e.g., fear, anger, or sadness). Each of these two components strongly affects the other. Nonetheless, it is possible, at least at some level, to distinguish the contribution of each (Fernandez & Turk, 1992).

Our perceptions of pain also interact with our cognitions regarding pain. Based on our own experiences with and observations of pain, we form our own schemas regarding pain, as well as beliefs regarding our own ability to control pain. The interaction goes both ways: Just as our

FIGURE 15.7
Gate-Control Theory of Pain
According to Ronald Melzack and Patrick Wall, the central nervous system (particularly the brain) acts as a kind of physiological gate, which widens or narrows to allow some pain sensations to enter awareness, but not others.

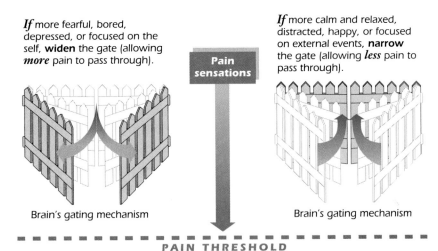

If more fearful, bored, depressed, or focused on the self, **widen** the gate (allowing *more* pain to pass through).

If more calm and relaxed, distracted, happy, or focused on external events, **narrow** the gate (allowing *less* pain to pass through).

Pain sensations

Brain's gating mechanism   Brain's gating mechanism

PAIN THRESHOLD

Awareness/Perception of pain

pain • the sensory and emotional discomfort associated with actual, imagined, or threatened damage to or irritation of tissues of the body

cognitions are affected by our experiences with pain, our cognitions also affect our perception of pain. For example, if we believe that we will be able to overcome pain, we may be more effective in doing so than if we believe that we will be defeated by our sensations of pain (described as "catastrophizing," sometimes as a result of learned helplessness). In fact, self-efficacy beliefs may play an important role in pain control (described in Turk & Rudy, 1992).

One mechanism by which cognition, emotion, and sensation may interact to affect pain perception has been proposed by Ronald Melzack and Patrick Wall (1965, 1982). According to Melzack and Wall's **gate-control theory** of pain, the central nervous system (CNS) serves as a physiological gating mechanism (see Figure 15.7). This gating mechanism can increase or decrease the degree to which pain is perceived, by widening or narrowing the opening of the gate. Through the gating mechanism, cognitions and emotions in the brain can cause the spinal cord to intensify or to inhibit the transmission of pain sensations.

According to this theory, some cognitions and emotions may widen the opening of the gate, lowering our *pain threshold* (the amount of stimulus required to cross the threshold and trigger the awareness of pain), and permitting greater transmission of pain sensations that reach our awareness. Other cognitions and emotions may narrow the passage through the gate, raising our pain threshold and permitting less transmission of pain sensations that reach our awareness. For example, fearful attention to the possibility of pain may widen the gate and lower our pain threshold. However, relaxed attention to other sensations may narrow the gate and raise our pain threshold. Naturally, as the pain reaches the brain, the brain's perception of pain also may affect emotions and cognitions that follow. The distinct patterns of emotion, cognition, and sensation affect the quality, as well as the intensity, of the pain the individual experiences at a given time.

Kinds of Pain

Psychologists (and other clinicians) often distinguish between organic pain and psychogenic pain. **Organic pain** is caused by damage to bodily tissue, such as bruises, cuts, and internal injuries. **Psychogenic pain** is the discomfort that occurs when there appears to be no physical cause of the pain. We need to be careful in labeling pain as "psychogenic" because it is impossible to prove the null hypothesis: Just because the medical profession has been unable to find an organic source of pain does not mean therefore that such pain does not exist or even that there is no organic cause of the pain. Our current tools for diagnosis of the sources of pain are still imprecise (see Turk & Rudy, 1992). A cause may exist that simply has not been found.

In most cases, the experience of pain represents an interaction between physiological and psychological factors. The link between the perception of pain and the presence of a known pathology or injury is not always clear. For instance, in many situations, the experience of pain is delayed for a while after injury or is altogether absent despite serious pathology of the body tissues (Melzack, Wall, & Ty, 1982; see also Fernandez & Turk, 1992).

Whether pain is organic or psychogenic, it can be classified as either acute or chronic. *Acute pain* is the discomfort that a person experiences over a relatively short period of time. Some researchers (e.g., Turk, Meichenbaum, & Genest, 1983) have used a time period of 6 months as

gate-control theory • a possible explanation of pain, suggesting that the central nervous system acts as a physiological barrier through which pain may be allowed to pass under particular circumstances

organic pain • the discomfort caused by observed physical damage to bodily tissue

psychogenic pain • the discomfort for which an observed source of physical damage to bodily tissues has not been found

a cutoff. In other words, the patient who experiences pain for less than 6 months is classified as experiencing acute pain. Pain lasting more than 6 months is referred to as *chronic pain*. It seems, though, that not everyone perceives pain the same way, whether acute or chronic. Personality seems to affect how one perceives pain.

Personality and Pain

Several investigators have tried to discover whether there is a relationship between personality attributes and the experiencing of pain. Such research might sound relatively easy to do. First, you think of a few traits that you believe might be associated with pain perceptions (e.g., irritability or impatience). Next, you test to see whether those traits match up to measurements of people's perceptions of pain.

The problem with this research is the same problem that arises with most correlational studies: Suppose that you find a strong correlation between particular traits and the likelihood of experiencing pain. Which came first, the personality attribute or the experiencing of pain? The existence of a relationship does not indicate the direction or the cause of the relationship. For instance, suppose that high degrees of irritability or impatience are associated with pain. Perhaps a person may be susceptible to experiencing pain because of these particular personality attributes. However, an equally plausible relationship is that the person acquired these personality attributes (e.g., irritability or impatience) as a result of having experienced the pain.

As an example, suppose that we were to find a correlation between scores on tests of anxiety or depression and scores on a scale measuring chronic pain. We scarcely would be surprised if we were to learn that the anxiety or depression was caused by the pain, rather than vice versa. It is also possible that both the personality attribute and the experiencing of pain may depend on a third factor, such as having a painful and life-threatening disease.

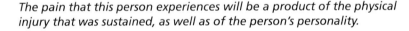

The pain that this person experiences will be a product of the physical injury that was sustained, as well as of the person's personality.

Some research has shown that responses to the *Minnesota Multiphasic Personality Inventory (MMPI;* see chapter 12) can help to identify patients who are particularly susceptible to experiencing pain. Michael Bond (1979) has found that patients who experience either acute or chronic pain tend to score especially high on the hypochondriasis and hysteria scales of the MMPI. People high in hysteria tend to show extreme emotional behavior and also tend to exaggerate the level and seriousness of the symptoms they experience. Chronic-pain patients also tend to score high on depression.

The fact that greater indications of depression are seen in chronic- but not in acute-pain patients suggests that the depression is a result, rather than a cause, of the pain. However, Thomas Rudy, Robert Kerns, and Dennis Turk (1988) have found that the development of depression may be related not just to the experience of pain itself, but also to the conditions associated with pain, such as the reduction in level of activity, a general sense of inability to master the environment, and a diminished sense of personal control. (For some ideas regarding how to control pain, see the following Branching Out box.) Some people have to live with pain or serious illness their whole life, and so they need to develop ways of coping with their health problems.

Branching Out
CONTROL OF PAIN

How can pain be controlled? A wide variety of techniques have been used for controlling pain (Taylor, 1991), many of which are successful, at least for some people some of the time. Following are some of the major methods of pain control:

1. *Pharmacological control.* The administration of drugs (e.g., aspirin, acetaminophen, or ibuprofen, or, for more severe pain, morphine) to reduce pain

2. *Surgical control.* Surgical cuts in the fibers that carry the sensation of pain, intended to prevent or at least to diminish the transmission of pain sensations along the offending nerve fibers; used in treating localized pain, particularly in the limbs

3. *Biofeedback.* Machine-translated feedback given to patients regarding their physiological responses; the feedback translates the body's responses into a form that the patient easily can observe and therefore bring under conscious control; biofeedback methods have been helpful for pain symptoms related to muscle tension (e.g., tension headaches) or to vascular (blood-vessel) disorders (e.g., migraine headaches)

4. *Acupuncture.* A technique originating in Asia that involves the use of needles on particular points on the body; a related Western adaptation of acupuncture is transcutaneous electrical nerve stimulation (TENS)

5. *Hypnosis.* An induced state of deep relaxation, during which patients are given the suggestion that they are not feeling pain (Weisenberg, 1977)

(CONTINUED)

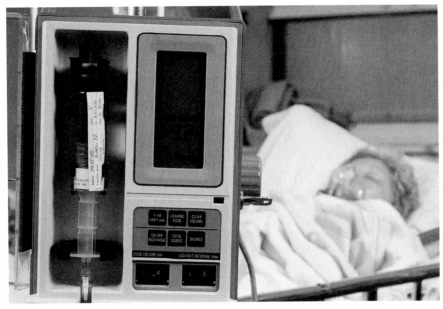
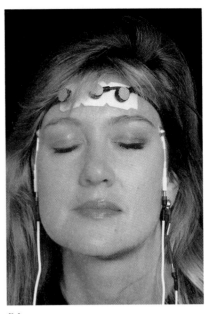

(a)   **(b)**

Two of the techniques used for treating severe pain are (a) self-regulated morphine drip and (b) biofeedback.

Branching Out   (CONTINUED)

6. *Relaxation techniques.* Techniques for relaxing muscles, controlling breathing, and entering a state of low arousal (Davidson & Schwartz, 1976)

7. *Guided imagery.* Used with relaxation techniques as a means to aid relaxation; also may be used as a means of mentally combating the pain or the underlying disease causing the pain

8. *Sensory control through counterirritation.* Involves stimulating or mildly irritating a part of the body that differs from the one experiencing pain; may work as a means of distracting patients from their primary source of pain

9. *Distraction.* Using any means to shift patients' attention away from the pain, to focus on something else

Because so many people experience chronic pain, many pain-treatment centers have arisen around the world. Of those patients who seek treatment in pain clinics, the average amount of time they have endured chronic pain is about 7 years (Turk & Rudy, 1992). Most of these centers use a variety of techniques from among those listed here in helping their patients to cope with pain. Finding the most successful technique becomes particularly important in cases of chronic pain related to serious illness.

HOW DO PEOPLE LIVE WITH SERIOUS, CHRONIC HEALTH PROBLEMS?

We often do not truly value our health until we no longer have it. When we recover from acute illnesses, we sometimes briefly return to cherishing our health, only to forget about it after a little while. People with chronic illnesses do not have this luxury. A widely feared serious chronic illness of our time is acquired immune deficiency syndrome, better known as AIDS.

AIDS: Incidence and Prevention

AIDS is caused by a *retrovirus,* which is a slow-acting virus. The retrovirus, human immunodeficiency virus (HIV), attacks the immune system and especially the helper *T-cells* (specialized, relatively long-living cells that protect the body at the cellular level; G. F. Solomon & Temoshok, 1987). The virus is transmitted by the exchange of bodily fluids that contain the virus, most notably blood and semen.

Tests are now available that can detect whether HIV antibodies are in the body. The presence of these antibodies, which fight the virus as much as possible, indicate whether a person has been infected with HIV. When the antibodies are present, the person is said to be *HIV-positive* (i.e., the HIV retrovirus is in the person's blood).

Being HIV-positive does not mean that the person already has developed AIDS. Individuals differ widely in the time it takes them to develop AIDS from the time they first contract the virus; the latency period can even be as long as 8 to 10 years or longer. Even with full-blown AIDS, it is not the AIDS virus itself that kills people. Rather, death strikes through opportunistic infections that are deadly because the immune system is impaired and cannot fight these infections. Some of the illnesses that eventually kill AIDS patients include rare forms of pneumonia and cancer that do not normally kill people with strong immune systems. Both the rate of diagnosis and the rate of AIDS-related deaths increased for some years and now have started to level off or even decline slightly (see Figure 15.8).

Despite its rapid spread, AIDS can be controlled and, in principle, entirely eliminated through behavioral interventions. Men who engage in sexual relations always should use condoms during sexual intercourse, and both men and women should restrict their number of sexual partners. People who inject themselves with drugs by using needles (whether intravenous drugs, steroids, or other drugs administered via needles) should

Figure 15.8
Trends in Rates of Death From HIV
Different groups show different relative death rates due to the effects of HIV infection.

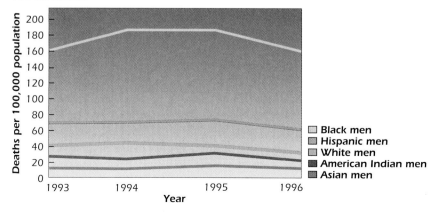

not share needles with other drug users. Prevention is especially important because there is no known cure for AIDS. Moreover, as far as we know, the large majority of people who contract HIV eventually will develop AIDS. Particular drugs seem to postpone the development of the disease. Powerful drug combinations now available may prolong, possibly indefinitely, the development of AIDS. We do not know for sure. Unfortunately, these medications are very expensive and thus available to only a small proportion of individuals who are HIV-positive.

Tests are now available that can detect HIV antibodies in the body, thereby indicating whether a person has been infected. Many people choose to have testing done anonymously via the use of numbered reports (without names) because of the discrimination that has been encountered by people who are HIV-positive, even those who have not shown symptoms of the virus. For example, virtually all life insurance companies now require HIV testing for the issuance of insurance policies, and policies are almost never issued to those who test positive. Moreover, people have lost jobs when they have been identified as HIV-positive. Of course, the most difficult psychological phenomenon associated with HIV infection is the knowledge of the high likelihood that it will become AIDS. AIDS patients need some way to cope with what remains a chronic illness.

Today, triple-drug combination therapies are keeping many people infected with the HIV virus alive for long periods of time. Some people receiving the triple-drug therapies have continued to fight off full-blown AIDS. For others, however, the drugs have stopped working. These drugs typically require complex schedules. For example, some need to be taken with food, some without, and they need to be taken at various times of the day with varying frequencies. It is thus difficult for many people to stay on their drug regimen. Even slight departures from the prescribed regimen quickly can lead to a deterioration of health. New possibilities are beginning to emerge that may simplify the scheduling of drugs. However people may medicate themselves, living with chronic illness is extremely difficult on these people and those around them. Yet, many people are now managing to maintain lives that in many respects are the same as those of people who are not HIV-positive.

Psychological Models for Coping With Chronic Illness

Franklin Shontz (1975) has proposed a stage model of how people react when they realize that they have a serious, chronic, and probably life-threatening disease. The first stage is one of *shock*. People are stunned, bewildered, and often feel detached from the situation: How can this illness be happening to me? The second stage is *encounter*. The person gives way to feelings of despair, loss, grief, and hopelessness. During this stage, people are often unable to function effectively: They do not think well, they have difficulty in planning, and they are ineffective in solving problems. During *retreat,* the third stage, individuals often try to deny the existence of the problem. At the least, they deny the implications of what the illness means for them. Eventually, however, people reach a fourth stage, *adjustment.* During the adjustment stage, they make whatever changes are necessary in order to cope effectively with the reality of the disease.

Shontz's model focuses on the emotional and behavioral aspects of coping. In contrast, Shelley Taylor (e.g., 1983; Taylor & Aspinwall, 1990) has proposed a model highlighting the ways in which people adapt cognitively to serious chronic illness. According to Taylor, patients first try to *find meaning* in the experience of the illness. They may try to figure out what they were doing wrong that led to the illness. Then they start doing right whatever they were doing wrong, or they simply may rethink their own attitudes and priorities in light of their new perspective. Next, patients try to *gain a sense of control* over the illness and over the rest of their lives. They may seek as much information as possible regarding their illness and its treatment. They also may undertake activities that they believe will help either to restore function and well-being or at least to slow down the destructive progress of their illness. Third, patients try to *restore their self-esteem* despite the offense of being struck by such an illness. They may compare their situations with those of others in ways that shed favorable light on their own situations.

Shontz and Taylor focused on processes commonly experienced by people who have chronic illnesses. Other researchers, however, have focused on individual differences in how people cope with chronic illness. Rudolf Moos (1982, 1988; Moos & Schaefer, 1986) has described a *crisis theory* of coping with chronic illness (shown in Figure 15.9). In his theory, Moos attempts to characterize individual differences in people's abilities to cope with serious health problems. According to this model, how well a person copes depends on three sets of factors:

1. *Background and personal factors* (such things as emotional maturity, self-esteem, religious beliefs, and age). For example, men are more likely to respond negatively to diseases that compromise their ability to work; older people will have to live fewer years with a chronic illness than will younger ones, so they may be better able to cope with the prospects.

2. *Illness-related factors* (such things as how disabling, painful, or life-threatening the disease is). Unsurprisingly, the greater the disability, pain, and threat, the more difficulty people have in coping with the illness.

3. *Environmental factors* (such things as social supports, the ability of the person to remain financially sound, and the kinds of conditions in which the person lives). Some factors (e.g., financial difficulties) may diminish the ability to cope, whereas others (e.g., social support) may increase coping ability.

FIGURE 15.9
Three Sets of Factors in Coping
In Rudolf Moos's crisis theory, there are three sets of factors involved in the patient's early phases of adjusting to serious illness. It is the interaction of individual differences and the coping process itself that influences the outcome of the crisis.

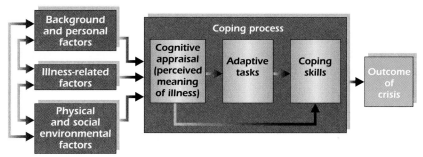

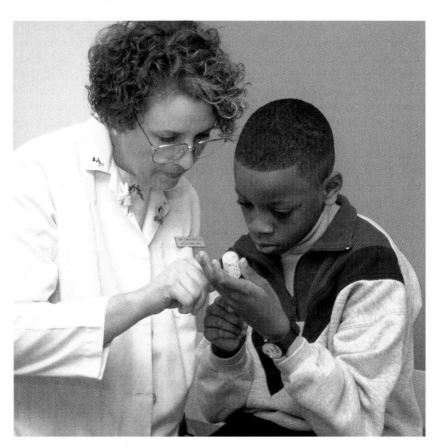

This young diabetic seems to be making the adjustment to his disease. With the help of caring adults, he will probably also manage to find meaning, gain a sense of control, and restore his sense of self-esteem after learning about his illness.

In addition to identifying these three sources of individual differences in coping, Moos has indicated three main components of the coping process: cognitive appraisal, the decision to adapt, and the development of coping skills. *Cognitive appraisal* identifies the meaning and significance of the health problem for the person's life. This cognitive appraisal is similar to the appraisal processes described by Folkman and Lazarus in the perception of stress. Next, as a result of this cognitive appraisal, the person decides how to perform tasks in ways that adapt to the limitations posed by the illness. Once the person has made *decisions regarding how to adapt to the illness,* the person *develops coping skills* for living with the illness. The outcome of the coping process will in turn affect the outcome of the crisis in general—how well the person is able to live with the disabling illness.

Ultimately, the key to coping with serious chronic illness is *adaptation:* The individual will need to make changes and adjustments in order to live happily and effectively. Persons with serious chronic illnesses often must make extraordinary efforts in order to adapt to the environment.

Although most of us do not experience pain or ill health very often, we do confront situations requiring us to adapt in varying ways and to varying degrees. We constantly need to adjust ourselves in order to fit ourselves to our environment. In addition, whether we are healthy or ill, young or old, lucky or not, we can shape our environment. Just as we need to adapt ourselves to fit the environment, we can modify the environment in order to suit ourselves. If there is a key to psychological adjustment, perhaps it is in the balance between adaptation to and shaping of the environment, with the added option of selection. When we find that a particular environment simply cannot be shaped to fit us, and we cannot adapt ourselves to fit it, we can try to find another more suitable environment. It is my hope that you can adapt to, shape, and select your environments, to find what you want in life, reach for it, and ultimately attain it.

The Case of the Type-A Problem

In reading chapter 15 of *Pathways to Psychology*, Rex realizes that he shows many of the classic symptoms of the Type-A personality. He is always in a hurry, tends to be extremely competitive, and easily feels hostility toward those whom he feels are beating him. He would be less concerned about his Type-A behavior were it not for another fact—the link between this kind of behavior and heart attacks. In fact, his father, with a Type-A profile similar to his, is already having heart problems in his early 50s and has been warned by his doctor that if he does not change his lifestyle he runs serious risks. Rex's grandfather died of a heart attack in his early 60s, the first heart attack he had.

Rex realizes that he has to make a decision. If he continues in his current ways he may achieve certain goals he has set for himself but he also may come to a quick demise. If he changes, he risks not meeting his goals. He thinks about the problem-solving cycle and concludes that maybe the solution is to redefine his goals so that he does not have to be so competitive and stressed-out all the time.

Rex decides that winning every contest is not all that important. He figures he can wait to become president of the chess club and that if he never makes it the world will not end. He also realizes that he can afford to lose some tennis games and still maintain his self-esteem. As he reaches these realizations, his tennis game actually improves and he finds for the first time that he is able to be a good friend—not a competitor.

What Do Health Psychologists Study? 536

1. *Health psychology* is the study of the reciprocal interaction between psychological processes and physiological health.
2. We classify illnesses according to their duration: *Acute* illnesses are relatively brief; *chronic* illnesses last for a long time, often across the entire life span.

How Can People Enhance Their Health Through Lifestyle Choices? 537

3. People may enhance their health by making positive lifestyle choices, such as by regularly engaging in *aerobic exercise*, proper diet, and adequate rest, as well as by avoiding harmful drugs.

How Do Personality and Stress Influence Health? 542

4. *Stress* is the situation in which environmental factors cause a person to feel challenged in some way. *Stressors* are situations or events that cause the person to have to adapt to or cope with changes in the situation. These adaptations are *stress responses*.
5. The initial stress response is adaptive in helping the person to prepare to flee from or to fight in the threatening situation. After the initial alarm phase of stress, if the perceived stressor continues to confront the individual, the body shifts down to a resistance phase and finally to an exhaustion phase.
6. Stress has been linked to many diseases, and its direct effects on the immune system now are being explored in the cross-disciplinary field of *psychoneuroimmunology*.
7. Personality influences the perception of stress through the processes of primary and secondary appraisal. In *primary appraisal*, we analyze our stake in the outcome of handling a particular situation. In *secondary appraisal*, we assess what we can do to maximize the probability that helpful outcomes will occur and to minimize the probability that harmful outcomes will occur.
8. In *coping* with stressful situations, we may use *problem-focused coping*, which is directed at solving a problem, and *emotion-focused coping*, which is directed at handling the emotions experienced as a result of the problem.

9. Social contacts and social support play important roles in promoting health and in recovering from illness.

How Do Personality Patterns Relate to Illness? 556

10. Several personality factors influence health, particularly the personality characteristics related to competitiveness, sense of urgency, and anger and hostility. Persons who rate high on these three characteristics have a *Type-A behavior pattern*; persons with a *Type-B behavior pattern* rate low on these characteristics. Of the three characteristics, feelings of anger and hostility seem most clearly threatening to health, particularly in terms of coronary heart disease. Lifestyle differences also may contribute to these effects.
11. The personality trait known as *hardiness* (characterized by internal locus of control, strong commitment to work, and a view of change as being a challenging opportunity for growth) appears to be linked to increased resistance to illness.

How Do Our Minds Experience Pain? 558

12. *Pain* has a sensory component, an affective component, and perhaps also a cognitive component. According to the *gate-control theory* of pain, the CNS acts as a gate that can either raise or lower our threshold for pain.
13. *Organic pain* is caused by damage to bodily tissue. *Psychogenic pain* is the discomfort felt when there appears to be no physical cause of the pain. What may appear to be psychogenic pain, however, may be caused by unidentified organic pathology.
14. Pain may be *acute* (lasting less than 6 months) or *chronic* (lasting 6 months or more).
15. Although several personality traits have been associated with pain, it has proven difficult to determine the direction of causality for these correlations.
16. Methods for controlling pain include pharmacological control (via drugs), surgical control, biofeedback, acupuncture, hypnosis, relaxation techniques, guided imagery, sensory control (e.g., counterirritation), and distraction.

How Do People Live With Serious, Chronic Health Problems? 562

17. AIDS (acquired immune deficiency syndrome) is a fatal illness caused by human immunodeficiency virus (HIV). AIDS is contracted largely through contact with the semen or blood of someone who carries HIV.

18. When people recognize that they have a serious, chronic health problem, they may experience *shock* (stunned detachment), *encounter* (grief and despair), and *retreat* (withdrawal from the problem) before they finally make the needed adjustment. An alternative model describes cognitive adaptations to chronic illness as the needs to *find meaning,* to *gain control,* and to *restore self-esteem.* Factors influencing these reactions include characteristics of the individual (including experiences and background), of the illness, and of the environment. In addition, how well people cope depends on their cognitive appraisal of the illness, their decision to adapt, and their development of coping skills.

19. Three adaptive ways in which to respond to challenging situations are to change the individual (and her or his lifestyle), to change the environment (making it adapt to the individual's different needs and abilities), or to select a different environment.

Pathways to Knowledge

Choose the best answer to complete each sentence.

1. *Health psychology* is the study of
   (a) the mental processes of health professionals.
   (b) mental illness.
   (c) the reciprocal interaction between psychological processes and physiological health.
   (d) mental wellness.

2. *Stress* is
   (a) a reaction to environmental events and stimuli that cause a person to feel challenged in some way.
   (b) a source of physical pain.
   (c) known to be a leading cause of cancer.
   (d) made worse by having too many friends.

3. After the initial alarm phase of stress, if the perceived stressor continues to confront the individual, the body shifts down to a resistance phase and finally to a(n)
   (a) breakdown phase.
   (b) exhaustion phase.
   (c) overworked phase.
   (d) physical wipe-out phase.

4. People who show a Type-A pattern of behavior rate high on the following characteristics:
   (a) competitiveness, sense of urgency, and particularly, anger and hostility.
   (b) bossiness, greed, and particularly, anger and hostility.
   (c) competitiveness, sense of urgency, and particularly, bossiness.
   (d) competitiveness, greed, and particularly, anger and hostility.

5. Psychogenic pain
   (a) appears not to have a physical cause.
   (b) is known not to have a physical cause.
   (c) is caused by damage to bodily tissue.
   (d) is caused by a known organic pathology.

6. Several personality traits have been associated with pain,
   (a) and it is generally easy to determine the direction of causality for these associations.
   (b) most of which have to do with hypochondria and malingering.
   (c) and these traits are generally recognized as being the result of living with pain.
   (d) but it has proven difficult to determine the direction of causality for these associations.

7. Existing methods for controlling pain
   (a) are almost always fully effective for all persons.
   (b) include pharmacological control (via drugs), surgical control, biofeedback, aversion therapy, relaxation techniques, guided imagery, hypnosis, and acupuncture.
   (c) virtually never work for persons who have chronic pain.
   (d) include pharmacological control (via drugs), surgical control, biofeedback, relaxation techniques, distraction, guided imagery, and acupuncture.

8. AIDS is contracted largely
   (a) through sexual relations between monogamous partners who use a condom.
   (b) through contact with the semen or blood of someone who carries HIV.
   (c) through contact with the saliva or nasal fluids of someone who has AIDS.
   (d) by touching, hugging, kissing, or shaking the hand of someone who has AIDS.

Answer each of the following questions by filling in the blank with an appropriate word or phrase.

9. We classify illnesses according to their duration: _____ illnesses are relatively brief; _____ illnesses last for a long time, often across the entire life span.

10. _____ are situations or events that cause a person to have to adapt to or cope with changes in the situation. These adaptations are _____.

11. The effect of stress on the immune system is now being explored in the cross-disciplinary field of _____.

12. In _____ _____ we analyze our stake in the outcome of handling a particular situation.

13. In _____ _____, we assess what we can do to maximize the probability that helpful outcomes will occur and to minimize the probability that harmful outcomes will occur.

14. _____-_____ coping is directed at solving a difficulty with which a person is coping.

15. _____-_____ coping is directed at handling the feelings a person experiences as a result of a problem.

16. When people recognize that they have serious, chronic health problems, they may experience _____ (stunned detachment), _____ (grief and despair), and _____ (withdrawal from the problem) before they finally make the needed _____.

17. AIDS (acquired immune deficiency syndrome) is a fatal illness caused by _____ _____ _____ (HIV).

18. A theoretical model regarding how people cope with chronic illness describes cognitive adaptations to chronic illness in terms of the needs to find _____, to gain _____, and to restore _____.

19. How well people cope depends on their cognitive _____ of their illness, their _____ to adapt, and their development of _____ _____.

20. Three adaptive ways in which to respond to challenging situations are to modify the individual, to modify the environment, or to choose a different _____.

Answers

1. c, 2. a, 3. b, 4. a, 5. a, 6. d, 7. d, 8. b, 9. Acute, chronic, 10. Stressors, stress responses, 11. psychoneuroimmunology, 12. primary appraisal, 13. secondary appraisal, 14. Problem-focused, 15. Emotion-focused, 16. shock, encounter, retreat, adjustment, 17. human immunodeficiency virus, 18. meaning, control, self-esteem, 19. appraisal, decision, coping skills, 20. environment

1. Choose the three pain-control methods you consider to be the most generally effective. Describe three situations in which pain control would be needed and in which one (or two) of the three techniques might be preferable to the other ones. Tell why the chosen method (or methods) would be best.

2. What advice would you give doctors, based on your knowledge of psychology, to help them communicate to patients that the patients have a life-threatening illness?

3. Design a program for enhancing the healthful quality of your lifestyle. Build on successive small steps, rather than to trying to make sweeping changes all at once. What are five small steps you can take this week?

Do you ever wonder whether some groups of people are smarter or more honest than others; or do you wonder whether students who earn better grades work more, on average, than do students who do not earn such high grades? Do you wonder whether, in close relationships, women feel more intimacy toward men, or men toward women? All of these questions can be addressed by using statistics.

Although statistics can help us answer questions, statistics themselves cannot provide definitive answers. The interpretations of statistics, and not the statistics themselves, determine how questions are answered. Statistics provide people with tools: with information to explore issues, to answer questions, to solve problems, and to make decisions. Statistics do not actually explore issues, answer questions, solve problems, or make decisions. People do.

Statistics are useful in psychology and they can be useful to you in your life. To introduce you to statistics, I would like for you to consider this example. Suppose you are interested in aspects of love and how they relate to satisfaction in close relationships. In particular, you decide to explore the three aspects of love in the triangular theory of love (R. J. Sternberg, 1986b, 1988a, 1998b): intimacy (feelings of warmth, closeness, communication, and support), passion (feelings of intense longing and desire), and commitment (desire to remain in the relationship; see chapter 10). You might be interested in the relation of these aspects to each other; or of each of the aspects to overall satisfaction in a close relationship; or of the relative levels of each of these aspects to the love people experience in different close relationships, for example, with lovers, friends, or parents. Statistics can help you explore these interests.

In order to use statistics to evaluate these aspects of love, you first need a scale to measure them. The *Triangular Love Scale,* a version of which is shown in Table A.1, is such a scale (R. J. Sternberg, 1997b, 1998a). If you wish, take it yourself to compare your data with those from a sample of 84 adults whose summary data will be presented later.

Note that this version of the scale has a total of 36 items: 12 items measure intimacy, 12 measure passion, and 12 measure commitment. Each item consists of a statement rated on a 1-to-9 scale, where 1 means that the statement does not characterize the person at all, 5 means that it is moderately characteristic of the person, and 9 means that it is extremely characteristic. Intermediate points represent intermediate levels of feelings. The final score on each of the three subscales is the average of the numbers assigned to each of the statements in that subscale (i.e., the sum of the numbers divided by 12, the number of items).

TABLE A.1

Triangular Love Scale

The blanks represent a person with whom you are in a close relationship. Rate on a 1-to-9 scale the extent to which each statement characterizes your feelings, where 1 = "not at all," 5 = "moderately," and 9 = "extremely." Use intermediate points on the scale to indicate intermediate levels of feelings.

Intimacy

1. I have a warm and comfortable relationship with _____.
2. I experience intimate communication with _____.
3. I strongly desire to promote the well-being of _____.
4. I have a relationship of mutual understanding with _____.
5. I receive considerable emotional support from _____.
6. I am able to count on _____ in times of need.
7. _____ is able to count on me in times of need.
8. I value _____ greatly in my life.
9. I am willing to share myself and my possessions with _____.
10. I experience great happiness with _____.
11. I feel emotionally close to _____.
12. I give considerable emotional support to _____.

Passion

1. I cannot imagine another person making me as happy as _____ does.
2. There is nothing more important to me than my relationship with _____.
3. My relationship with _____ is very romantic.
4. I cannot imagine life without _____.
5. I adore _____.
6. I find myself thinking about _____ frequently during the day.
7. Just seeing _____ is exciting for me.
8. I find _____ very attractive physically.
9. I idealize _____.
10. There is something almost "magical" about my relationship with _____.
11. My relationship with _____ is very "alive."
12. I especially like giving presents to _____.

Commitment

1. I will always feel a strong responsibility for _____.
2. I expect my love for _____ to last for the rest of my life.
3. I cannot imagine ending my relationship with _____.
4. I view my relationship with _____ as permanent.
5. I would stay with _____ through the most difficult times.
6. I view my commitment to _____ as a matter of principle.
7. I am certain of my love for _____.
8. I have decided that I love _____.
9. I am committed to maintaining my relationship with _____.
10. I view my relationship with _____ as, in part, a thought-out decision.
11. I could not let anything get in the way of my commitment to _____.
12. I have confidence in the stability of my relationship with _____.

Scores are obtained by adding scale values for each item in each subscale, and then dividing by 12 (the number of items per subscale), yielding a score for each subscale of between 1 and 9.

DESCRIPTIVE STATISTICS

Descriptive statistics are numbers that summarize quantitative information. They reduce a larger mass of information down to a smaller and more useful base of information.

Measures of Central Tendency

In studying love, you might be interested in typical levels of intimacy, passion, and commitment for different relationships—say, for a lover and for a sibling. There are three ways in which you might find the typical value, or **central tendency,** of a set of data.

The **mean** is the arithmetical average of a series of numbers. To compute the mean, you add up all of the values and divide by the number of values you added.

Another measure of central tendency is the **median,** which is the middle of a set of values. With an odd number of values, the median is the number right in the middle. For example, if you have seven values ranked from lowest to highest, the median will be the fourth (middle) value. With an even number of values, there is no one middle value. For example, if you have eight values ranked from lowest to highest, the median will be the number halfway between (the average of) the fourth and fifth values—again, the middle.

A third measure of central tendency is the **mode,** or most frequent value. Obviously, the mode is useful only when there are at least some repeated values.

Consider, for example, scores of eight people on the intimacy subscale, rounded to the nearest whole number and ranked from lowest to highest: 3, 4, 4, 4, 5, 5, 6, 7. In this set of numbers, the mean is 4.75, or $(3 + 4 + 4 + 4 + 5 + 5 + 6 + 7)/8$; the median is 4.5, or the average of the fourth and fifth values (4 and 5); and the mode is 4, the value that occurs most frequently.

Because the mean fully takes into account the information in each data point, it is generally the preferred measure of central tendency. However, the mean is also sensitive to extremes. If just a few numbers in a set are extreme, the mean will be greatly affected by them. For example, if five people took the passion subscale to indicate their feelings toward their pet gerbils, and their scores were 1, 1, 1, 1, and 8, the mean of 2.4 would reflect a number that is higher than the rating given by four of the five people surveyed.

The median is less sensitive to extremes. In the distribution of passion scores for pet gerbils, the median is 1, better reflecting the distribution than does the mean. However, the median does not take into account all of the information given. For example, the median would have been the same if the fifth score were 2 rather than 8.

The advantage of the mode is that it provides a quick index of central tendency. It is rough, though. Sometimes no number in a set appears more than once, and hence there is no mode. Other times, several numbers appear more than once, so that the distribution is **multimodal** (having more than one mode). The mode takes into account the least amount of information in the set. For these reasons, the mode is the least used of the three measures of central tendency.

---

descriptive statistics • numbers that summarize quantitative information, reducing a larger mass of information to a smaller, more useful base of information

central tendency • the typical value

mean • the arithmetical average of a series of numbers

median • the middle of a set of values

mode • the most frequent value of a set of values

multimodal • having more than one mode

Sometimes it is useful to show obtained values by a **frequency distribution,** which shows numerically the number or proportion of cases at each score level (or interval). In the two cases mentioned in connection with the *Triangular Love Scale,* the frequency distributions would be as follows:

Intimacy subscale		Passion subscale	
Value	*Frequency*	*Value*	*Frequency*
3	1	1	4
4	3	8	1
5	2		
6	1		
7	1		

Frequency distributions also can be represented graphically in various ways. People use graphs to help readers visualize the relations among numbers and to help the readers clarify just what these relations are, as shown in the various line and bar graphs in this textbook.

Measures of Variability

You now know three ways to see the central tendency of a distribution of numbers. Another question you might have concerns the spread of the distribution. How much do scores vary? There are different ways in which you might assess spread, or variability.

A first measure of variability is the **range,** which is the difference between the lowest and the highest values in a distribution. For example, the range of intimacy scores represented earlier is 4 (i.e., 7 – 3). However, the range is a rough measure. For example, consider two distributions of intimacy scores: 3, 4, 5, 6, 7, and 3, 3, 3, 3, 7. Although the range is the same, the variability of scores seems different. Other measures take more information into account.

A second measure of variability is the **standard deviation,** which is, roughly speaking, a measure of the average variation of values around the mean. The advantage of the standard deviation over the range is that the standard deviation takes into account the full information in the distribution of scores. Researchers care about the standard deviation because it indicates how much scores clump together, on the one hand, or are more widely spread, on the other.

To compute the standard deviation, you must:

1. Compute the difference between each value and the mean.
2. Square the difference between each value and the mean (to get rid of negative signs).
3. Sum the squared differences.
4. Take the average of the sum of the squared differences.
5. Take the square root of this average, in order to bring the final value back to the original scale.

Take the two distributions above to see whether their standard deviations are indeed different. The mean of 3, 4, 5, 6, 7 is 5, so the squared

frequency distribution • the number or proportion of cases at each score level or interval

range • the difference between the lowest and highest values in a distribution

standard deviation • a measure related to the average variation of values around the mean

differences of each value from the mean are 4, 1, 0, 1, and 4. The sum of the squared differences is 10, and the average is 2. The square root of 2 is about 1.41, which is the standard deviation. In contrast, the mean of 3, 3, 3, 3, 7 is 3.80. So the squared differences of each value from the mean are .64, .64, .64, .64, and 10.24. The sum of the squared differences is 12.80, and the average, 2.56. The square root of 2.56 is 1.60. Thus, the second distribution has a higher standard deviation, 1.60, than the first distribution, for which the standard deviation is 1.41.

What does a standard deviation tell us? As a measure of variability, it tells us how much scores depart from the mean. At the extreme, if all values were equal to the mean, the standard deviation would be 0. At the opposite extreme, the maximum value of the standard deviation is half the value of the range (for numerical values that are very spread apart).

For typical (but not all) distributions of values, about 68% of the values fall between the mean and plus or minus one standard deviation from that mean; about 95% of the values fall between the mean and plus or minus two standard deviations from that mean. Well over 99% of the values fall between the mean and plus or minus three standard deviations. For example, the mean of the scale for intelligence quotients (IQs) is 100, and the standard deviation is typically 15 (see chapter 8). Thus, roughly two thirds of IQs fall between 85 and 115 (plus or minus one standard deviation from the mean), and about 19 out of 20 IQs fall between 70 and 130 (plus or minus two standard deviations from the mean).

Now that you have read about measures of central tendency and variability, you can appreciate the use of two of these measures, the mean and standard deviation, for the *Triangular Love Scale*. Table A.2 shows means and standard deviations of intimacy, passion, and commitment scores for various relationships computed from a sample of 84 adults. If you took the scale yourself, you can compare your own scores to those of our normative sample.

The Normal Distribution

In the preceding discussion of the percentages of values between the mean and various numbers of standard deviations from the mean, we have been

TABLE A.2
Basic Statistics for the *Triangular Love Scale*

	Intimacy		Passion		Commitment	
	Mean	*SD*	*Mean*	*SD*	*Mean*	*SD*
Mother	6.49	1.74	4.98	1.90	6.83	1.57
Father	5.17	2.10	3.99	1.84	5.82	2.22
Sibling	5.92	1.67	4.51	1.71	6.60	1.67
Lover	7.55	1.49	6.91	1.65	7.06	1.49
Friend	6.78	1.67	4.90	1.71	6.06	1.63

Note: "Friend" refers to best friend of the same sex. "SD" refers to standard deviation. Statistics are based on a sample of 84 adults from southern Connecticut.

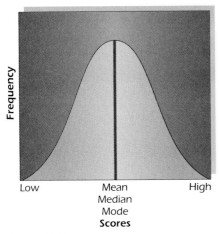

FIGURE A.1
Normal Distribution

As this figure shows, in a normal distribution, the mean, median, and mode are the same.

making an assumption without making that assumption explicit. The assumption is that the distribution of values is a **normal distribution,** that is, a particular distribution in which the preponderance of values is near the center of the distribution, with values falling off rather rapidly as they depart from the center. The shape of the normal distribution is shown in Figure A.1. Notice that the distribution of scores is symmetrical, and that, indeed, the large majority of scores fall close to the center of the distribution.

Many distributions in nature, such as that of height, are roughly normal. In a completely normal distribution, the mean, the median, and the mode are all exactly equal. In skewed (lopsided) distributions, however, these three values are not equal, as shown in Figure A.2.

Types of Scores

Tests and other measures can be scored in different kinds of ways. What are the main kinds of scores that are used in psychological testing and in research, in general?

A standard score is a score that can be used for any distribution at all in order to equate the scores for that distribution to scores for other distributions. *Standard scores,* also called *z-scores,* are defined arbitrarily to have a mean of 0 and a standard deviation of 1. If the distribution of scores is normal, therefore, roughly 68% of the scores will be between −1 and 1, and roughly 95% of scores will be between −2 and 2.

Why bother to have standard scores? The advantage of standard scores is that they render comparable scores that are initially on different scales. For example, suppose two professors who teach the same course to two comparable classes of students differ in the difficulty of the tests they give. Professor A tends to give relatively difficult tests, and the mean score on his tests is 65%. Professor B, on the other hand, tends to give relatively less difficult tests, and the mean score on his tests is 80%. Yet, the

FIGURE A.2
Skewed Distribution

In a skewed distribution, the mean, median, and mode differ. When it is negatively skewed (a), the values of the median and mode are greater than the value of the mean. When a distribution is positively skewed (b), the value of the mean is greater than the other values.

(a) Negatively skewed distribution

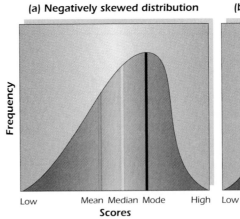

(b) Positively skewed distribution

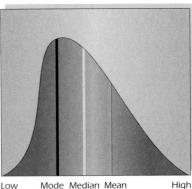

difference in these two means reflects not a difference in achievement, but a difference in the difficulty of the tests the professors give. If we convert scores separately in each class to standard scores, the mean and standard deviation will be the same in the two classes (that is, a mean of 0 and a standard deviation of 1), so that it will be possible to compare achievement in the two classes in a way that corrects for the differential difficulty of the professors' tests.

Standard scores also can be applied to the distributions of love-scale scores described earlier. People who feel more intimacy, passion, or commitment toward a partner will have a higher standard score relative to the mean, and people who feel less intimacy, passion, or commitment will have a lower standard score.

The computation of standard scores is simple. In this computation, you start with a **raw score,** which is simply the score on a given test in whatever units the test is originally scored. The steps for converting a raw score to a standard score are:

1. Subtract the mean raw score from the raw score of interest.
2. Divide the difference by the standard deviation of the distribution of raw scores.

You now can see why standard scores always have a mean of 0 and a standard deviation of 1. Suppose that a given raw score equals the mean. If the raw score equals the mean, when you subtract the mean from that score, you will have the number minus itself, yielding a difference in the numerator (see Step 1 above) of 0. As you know, 0 divided by anything equals 0. Suppose now that you have a score one standard deviation above the mean. When you subtract the mean from that score, the difference will be the value of the standard deviation. When you divide this value (the standard deviation) by the standard deviation (in Step 2 above), you will get a value of 1, because as you know, any value divided by itself equals 1.

Thus, if we take our distribution of intimacy scores of 3, 4, 5, 6, 7, with a mean of 5 and a standard deviation of 1.41, the standard score for a raw score of 6 will be (6 − 5)/1.41, or .71. The standard score for a raw score of 5, which is the mean, will be (5 − 5)/1.41, or 0. The standard score for a raw score of 4 will be (4 − 5)/1.41, or −.71.

Many kinds of scores are variants of standard scores. For example, an IQ of 115, which is one standard deviation above the mean, corresponds to a z-score (standard score) of 1. An IQ of 85 corresponds to a z-score of −1, and so on. The *Scholastic Assessment Test (SAT)* has a mean of 500 and a standard deviation of 100. Therefore, a score of 600 represents a score of one standard deviation above the mean (i.e., a z-score of 1), whereas a score of 400 represents a score of one standard deviation below the mean (i.e., a z-score of −1).

Another convenient kind of score is called the **percentile.** This score refers to the percentage of other individuals in a given distribution whose scores fall below a given individual's score. Thus, on a test, if your score is higher than that of half (50%) of the students who have taken the test (and lower than that of the other half), your percentile will be 50. If your score is higher than everyone else's (and lower than no one else's), your percentile will be 100. In the distribution 3, 4, 5, 6, 7, the score corresponding to the 50th percentile is 5 (the median), because it is higher than half the other scores and lower than half the other scores. The 100th percentile is 7, because it is higher than all the other scores, and lower than none of them.

raw score • the score on a given test in whatever units the test is originally scored

percentile • the percentage of other individuals in a given distribution whose scores fall below a given individual's scores

Correlation and Regression

So, now you know something about central tendency and variability, as well as about the kinds of scores that can contribute to central tendency and variability. You also may be interested in a different question: How are scores on one kind of measure related to scores on another kind of measure? For example, how do people's scores on the intimacy subscale relate to their scores on the passion subscale or to their scores on the commitment subscale? The question here would be whether people who feel more intimacy toward someone also tend to feel more passion or commitment toward that person.

The statistical measure called the **correlation coefficient** addresses the question of the degree of relation between two arrays of values. Basically, correlation expresses the degree of relation between two variables. A correlation of 0 indicates no relation at all between two variables; a correlation of 1 indicates a perfect (positive) relation between the two variables; a correlation of −1 indicates a perfect inverse relation between the two variables. Figure A.3 shows distributions with correlations of 0, 1, and −1.

So, what are the correlations among the various subscales of the *Triangular Love Scale*? For love of a lover, the correlations are very high: .88 between intimacy and passion, .84 between intimacy and commitment, and .85 between passion and commitment. These data suggest that if you feel high (or low) levels of one of these aspects of love toward a lover, you are likely also to feel high (or low) levels of the other two of the aspects toward your lover. However, the correlations vary somewhat with the relationship. For example, the comparable correlations for a sibling are .79, .77, and .76. Incidentally, in close relationships with a lover, the correlations between satisfaction and each of the subscales are .86 for intimacy, .77 for passion, and .75 for commitment.

Now you know that there is a strong relation between intimacy, passion, and commitment in feelings toward a lover, as well as between each of these aspects of love and satisfaction in the relationship with the lover. Can you infer anything about the causal relations from these correlations? For example, might you be able to conclude that intimacy leads to commitment? Unfortunately, you cannot infer anything for sure. Consider three alternative interpretations of the correlation between intimacy and commitment.

One possibility is that intimacy produces commitment. This interpretation makes sense. As you develop more trust, communication, and support in a relationship, you are likely to feel more committed to that relationship. However, there is a second possibility, namely, that commitment leads to intimacy. This interpretation also makes sense. You may feel that until you really commit yourself to a relationship, you do not want to trust your partner with the more intimate secrets of your life or to communicate some of your deepest feelings about things. A third possibility exists as well, namely, that both intimacy and commitment depend on some third factor. In this view, neither causes the other, but rather, both are dependent on some third variable. For example, it may be that intimacy and commitment both depend on a shared sense of values. Without such shared values, it may be difficult to build a relationship based on either intimacy or commitment.

The point is simple: As often is said in statistics, correlation does not imply causation. You cannot infer the direction of causality without further information. Correlation indicates only that there is a relation, not how the relation came to be. You can make a guess about the direction of causal relationship, but to be certain, you would need additional data.

correlation coefficient • a statistical measure that addresses the question of the degree of relation between two arrays of values

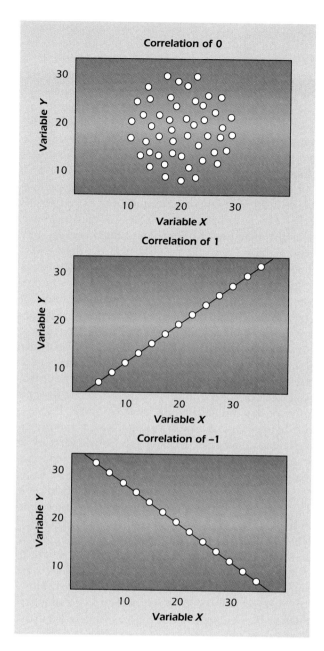

Correlation Coefficient

When two variables show a correlation of 0, increases or decreases in the value of one variable (variable X) bear no relation to increases or decreases in the value of the other variable (variable Y). When variable X and variable Y are positively correlated, increases in X are related to increases in Y, and decreases in X are related to decreases in Y. When variable X and variable Y are negatively (inversely) correlated, increases in X are related to decreases in Y, and decreases in X are related to increases in Y.

In the example of the correlation between intimacy and commitment, you have a problem in addition to direction of causality. How much of a correlation do you need in order to characterize a relationship between two variables as statistically meaningful? In other words, at what level is a correlation strong enough to take the correlation as indicating a true relationship between two variables, rather than a relationship that might have occurred by chance—by a fluke? Fortunately, there are statistics that can tell us when correlations, and other indices, are statistically meaningful. These statistics are called *inferential statistics*.

INFERENTIAL STATISTICS

Inferential statistics are statistics that are used to determine how likely it is that a set of results would be obtained if only chance were at work. When

inferential statistics • statistics that are used to determine how likely it is that results would be obtained if only chance were at work

we speak of the meaningfulness of statistical results, we often use something called a **test of statistical significance.** Such a test tells us the probability of a given result if only chance were at work. A result, therefore, is *statistically significant* when it is unlikely to be due solely to chance factors. It is important for you to realize that a statistical test only can show the probability that one mean or a correlation would be obtained if only chance were at work, or the probability that the difference obtained between one mean and another would be obtained if only chance were operating. You cannot use statistics to estimate the probability that two samples are the same in any respect.

The distinction is an important one. Suppose you have two hypothetical individuals who are identical twins and who always have scored exactly the same on every test they ever have been given. There is no statistical way of estimating the probability that they truly are the same on every test. There always might be some future test that would distinguish them.

Your chances of finding a statistically significant result generally increase as you test more participants because, with greater numbers of participants, random errors tend to average out. Thus, if you tested only one male participant and one female participant for their feelings of intimacy toward their partners, you probably would hesitate to draw any conclusions from this sample about whether there is a difference between men and women in general in their experiencing of intimacy toward their partners. However, if you tested 10,000 men and 10,000 women, you probably would have considerable confidence in your results, so long as your sample was representative of the population of interest.

It is important to distinguish between statistical significance and **practical significance,** which refers to whether a result is of any practical or everyday import. Suppose, for example, that I find that the difference between the men and the women in intimacy feelings is .07 on a 1-to-9 scale. With a large enough sample, the result may reach statistical significance. Is this result of practical significance? Perhaps not. Remember, an inferential statistical test only can tell you the probability of getting a certain result if only chance were at work. It does not tell you how large the difference is, nor whether the difference is great enough really to matter for whatever practical purposes you might wish to use the information. In research, investigators often pay primary attention to statistical significance. However, as a consumer of research, you need to pay attention to practical significance as well, whether the researchers do or not. Ultimately, in psychology, we need to concentrate on results that make a difference to us as we go about living our lives.

test of statistical significance • a test that tells us the probability that a given result would be obtained were only chance at work

practical significance • the characterization of a result as having practical or everyday import

CAREERS IN PSYCHOLOGY

Psychology is a field of study that can be useful in almost any career. Consider just a sampling of how psychology can be practical on a day-to-day basis in a wide variety of careers.

A SMALL SAMPLE OF JOBS IN WHICH PSYCHOLOGY IS USEFUL

Psychology is useful in any job that requires working with others, and that includes just about any job. Here are some examples:

- *Salespeople* can use the techniques of influence and persuasion to try to convince potential customers to buy their products. They also can use psychology to try to figure out what their customers would like in the first place.
- *Managers* can use psychology to develop effective leadership skills. They also can use psychology in understanding their employees and in deciding how and when to allocate work to their employees.
- *Lawyers* can use psychology to infer what appeals are likely to be convincing to a jury or to understand their clients better.
- *Doctors* can use psychology to understand the psychological factors that can lead to, and can accompany, ill health. They also can use psychology to improve their interactions with their patients.
- *Police officers* can use psychology to understand the mind of the perpetrator of a crime whom they are pursuing or to interact more effectively with the general public whom they are dedicated to serve.
- *Food-service workers* can use psychology to serve restaurant patrons better and perhaps thereby obtain better tips.
- *Artists* can use psychology to probe the depths of their own minds and the minds of others and to translate their insights into their own forms of artistic expression.
- *Writers* can use psychology to gain insight into other people and to translate these insights into novels, poems, or feature stories in magazines and newspapers.
- *Teachers* can use psychology to understand their students better and to gain insights about how to teach and motivate their students.
- *Politicians* can use psychology to figure out strategies for getting elected and for giving the best possible service to their constituents.

These examples constitute only a few of the many ways in which psychology can be used in the everyday world of work. Really, almost any job can be done more effectively if the principles of psychology are brought to bear upon the job. In all of these careers, an undergraduate major in psychology, or even a minor in psychology, can be desirable and make a big difference in job performance. In other careers, an undergraduate major and further training are a must.

SPECIALIZED CAREERS IN PSYCHOLOGY

Some jobs require advanced training in psychology or at least a more explicit use of the techniques one learns through psychology. Descriptions of some of these jobs can be found in R. J. Sternberg (1997a), as summarized here. Remember that these jobs constitute only a fraction of the possible jobs open to those who have studied psychology. Remember also that preparation for these jobs is not just a matter of undergraduate or even graduate training. The field of psychology is moving ahead at such a rapid rate that all psychologists must view themselves as embarking on a program of lifelong learning. The problems and techniques you learn about today may be out of date in a matter of a few years or even months. Thus, you constantly need to update yourself throughout your career.

Careers in Clinical and Counseling Psychology: Private Practice

Clinical and counseling psychologists work with clients in order to help them understand psychological problems they may have and, more importantly, to help them correct these problems (see Davis, 1997; Young & Weishaar, 1997). In particular, they can help individuals prevent problems that are about to manifest themselves (called *primary prevention*), help individuals deal with problems before they become serious (called *secondary prevention*), and help individuals deal with problems that already have become serious (called *tertiary prevention*).

Clinical and counseling psychology are similar but certainly not identical. Much of the work in the two areas does overlap, but this overlap is not total. Clinical psychologists are more likely to work with people who have a psychological disturbance and serious mental illnesses typically would be treated by clinical, and not by counseling, psychologists. In most cases, counseling psychologists are likely to work with people who need help in arranging or balancing their lives, perhaps in problems of school, work, or family adjustment but who have no serious mental disorder. Clinical and counseling psychologists also work in different settings. Another difference is in the education they receive. There are separate programs for clinical psychology and counseling psychology. However, even within these two fields, there can be differences in educational background.

Clinical psychologists typically study for either a PhD (doctor of philosophy degree) in the psychology department of a university that has a graduate-level program in clinical psychology or for a PsyD (doctor of psychology degree), either in a psychology department or in a specialized school of professional psychology. The PhD degree typically involves 4 to 6 years of graduate training in psychology plus a 1-year internship, where the PhD candidate gets a chance to practice his or her skills in a supervised situation. Students interested in studying clinical psychology may want to ensure that the program they attend is approved by the American Psychological Association, as such approval certifies that the program meets certain minimal standards deemed to be important by the largest national organization of psychologists in the United States. The PhD degree in any field of psychology requires a combination of graduate course work plus an independent research project leading to a doctoral dissertation—a substantial investigation that may take a year or more to complete. The PsyD degree differs from the PhD in that it typically represents a much greater emphasis on applied, professional training and much less emphasis on research.

Many but not all graduate students receive a master's degree on their way to a doctorate. The master's typically requires 2 years of graduate study, including coursework and possibly a master's thesis, which may be a research study or, in some circumstances, a library-research project. Not all master's students go on to the PhD, and there are various opportunities in psychology for people who have the master's degree but not the doctorate. In some states, individuals with a master's degree may not be able to label themselves as "psychologists," so it is important to check state regulations. In addition, in some states, to be called a "psychologist" one must take an examination to obtain a special license from the state.

Counseling psychologists receive a degree in counseling psychology. Counseling psychology is likely to be found in a Faculty of Education, whereas clinical psychology rarely is. Counseling psychologists are also more likely to get an EdD (doctor of education degree) than are clinical psychologists. Again, students may wish to ensure that they attend an APA-approved program. Training for counseling psychology also typically requires a 1-year internship, as well as course and research work.

Clinical and counseling psychologists may work in a variety of settings, including independent practice, hospitals and medical centers (see B. S. Strauss, 1997), and universities. Counseling psychologists also may work in schools and in industry, as do clinical psychologists on rarer occasions. Many clinical and counseling psychologists divide their time among several office settings.

Some clinical and counseling psychologists have specialties within their fields. One may specialize in depression or mood disorders, another in character disorders, and yet another in the relations between psychological disorders and health (see Brownell & Salovey, 1997, for a discussion of the rapidly growing field of health psychology). Psychologists also may differ in their preferred forms of diagnosis and treatment. For example, some psychologists rely heavily on psychological tests for diagnosis, whereas others never use them at all. Some psychologists prefer psychodynamic therapy based upon the teachings of Freud and his followers, whereas others prefer behaviorally oriented methods, cognitively oriented methods, or a combination of the two. Still other psychologists are eclectic, choosing their preferred therapy techniques as a function of the particular client with whom they are working and the particular problems that present themselves for that client.

The professional landscape for clinical and counseling psychologists has changed over the last few years and is likely to continue to change as the managed-care industry takes increasing control of the administration of health services in the United States. This industry exerts its control through health-maintenance organizations (HMOs) and preferred-provider organizations (PPOs). Individuals become members of such plans either on their own or through their place of work. They then receive care packages that come as the main benefit of membership. Because these plans are for profit, they watch their costs very carefully, which is where they affect the lives of psychologists.

These organizations have an impact on clinical and counseling psychologists in several ways. First, the organizations may limit the number of visits a client is allowed to have with the health-care professional. Clients who once might have been in therapy for many months or even years now may find themselves having to curtail quite severely the number of visits, or to pay for further visits themselves. Second, the organizations may limit the amounts of reimbursements they are willing to pay the psychologists. Psychologists who once might have charged upward of $100 per hour now may find themselves being forced to take as little as half of their previous per hour rate. Third, the organizations may limit the list of providers the individual can go to for care. Psychologists who are not willing to "play the game" of the organizations quickly may find themselves off the approved list, or may find themselves never able to get on the list. Fourth, the organizations typically require large amounts of paperwork and phone calls, which take up time that formerly could have been spent on seeing clients. The phone calls and paperwork may include not only requests for reimbursements but justifications for the care that the psychologist believes the client needs. A psychologist may find a bureaucrat in such an organization, someone who may have little or no relevant training, making a final decision about a client's need for services. Thus, the experience may be not only time-consuming for the psychologist but also potentially humiliating. Finally, there is some pressure on such organizations to select as caregivers people with lesser training who typically will charge less per hour of therapy time.

Despite these facts, many people wish to pursue careers in clinical and counseling psychology, both because the work is so interesting and because the rewards of helping people put their lives in order perhaps are unmatched. Admission to graduate programs in clinical and counseling psychology is very competitive, in many cases, even more competitive than admission to medical school. Those who wish to enter such programs would be well-advised to major in psychology or a related discipline, to take courses in related natural and social sciences, and to obtain the highest grade-point average possible. Research experience and experience in the helping professions (such as serving as a counselor or on a crisis hotline) also can help students gain admission.

In addition to clinical and counseling psychology, another exciting related area is that of community psychology. Community psychologists go beyond the individual to work with problems of mental health and human relationships in community settings (Iscoe, 1997). Although they may work out of an office, their laboratory is the community as a whole. Community psychologists also may teach and may, at times, see individual clients. But typically they work in community centers and organizations, where they reach out to a broad cross-section of the population, especially to people who are underserved or not served at all by traditional mental-health services. Although there are a few graduate programs in community psychology, many community psychologists receive their degrees in clinical or counseling programs with a specialization in community psychology and related fields. There is no formal APA approval mechanism for community-psychology programs, nor for programs to prepare students to work in the many kinds of diverse organizations considered next.

Careers in Psychology Within Diverse Organizations

Many psychologists work not for themselves but rather for established organizations. The range of organizations for which psychologists can work is practically endless. Four of the main kinds of organizations are government (Herrmann, 1997), schools (Poland, 1997), businesses (Tenopyr, 1997), and consulting firms (Beall & Allen, 1997).

Working in Government

Government researchers work for any of the many agencies that constitute local, state, and federal governments. At the national level, for example, the National Science Foundation; the National Institutes of Mental Health; the Departments of the Army, Navy, and Air Force (see Wiskoff, 1997); the Veterans Administration; the Federal Bureau of Investigation; the National Center for Health Statistics; the U.S. Department of Labor; and the U.S. Department of Education are just a few of the many government agencies that employ psychologists.

Government psychologists work in a diverse range of settings and on a diversity of problems. In most settings, the work is largely or totally applied, and the problems are ones that policymakers (from the U.S. Congress on downward) decide are important. Thus, a government psychologist is likely to be told what problems, or at least the range of problems, to work on rather than having total freedom to choose an area of investigation. Although the loss of freedom to choose a problem may be a disadvantage for some, the opportunity to see solutions put into immediate or almost immediate practice can be an advantage that is equaled in few other settings. Government psychologists also are likely to work in teams, many of them interdisciplinary, so that the research approach is likely to be coordinated across a variety of different methodologies and theoretical perspectives. Because of shifts in local, state, and national priorities, psychologists in government may have to abandon projects that are not yet completed as research priorities or funding change. Thus, government psychologists should take their jobs for the love of research and without the burning need to complete every problem on which they start working. They also have to be generalists, because the range of problems can be so wide.

Researchers in government settings typically have master's or doctorate degrees and have well-developed research skills. A background in policy studies also can be quite useful. The researchers typically work in a political environment and so must know or learn how to negotiate the realities of a setting that may be anything but straightforward. Although they often can consult with experts in a variety of fields, statistical skills and research-design skills can be particularly important in these settings.

Working in Schools

School psychologists may have either a master's or a doctorate degree, although there is an increasing tendency for them to pursue the doctorate, either before they have started working in school or once they have started. They typically will have received their advanced training in school psychology in order to prepare for the challenges of their career. Most doctoral programs require some forms of hands-on experience working in schools prior to the awarding of the degree.

The activities pursued by the school psychologist are diverse. Much of the work they do involves casework, dealing with children who are having problems in the school setting. In order to do such casework adequately, they need excellent diagnostic skills and must have acquired a thorough grounding in the use of psychological tests, including tests of intelligence and other cognitive abilities, achievement, and personality. They especially need to be able to diagnose and help design programs for children with various kinds of learning disabilities, attention deficits, mental retardation, and behavioral disorders. They also need to be prepared to help in the design of programs for students with a variety of gifts and talents. Indeed, much of the school psychologist's time may be spent in evaluating children for special-education services, leaving little time for other things that also need to get done.

School psychologists need to understand not only the individual children but the community setting from which they emerge. Often, children's problems start in the home and community, and a psychologist who is not well-aware of the family and community background of a child who is having problems in school probably will be ill-equipped to design any kind of intervention program. Sensitivity to diverse cultural and socioeconomic backgrounds, and to the differences that derive from these backgrounds, is a must for the school psychologist.

School psychologists must work directly with troubled students, with the teachers who have these students in their classrooms, as well as with parents or guardians who may need help in designing an environment at home to cope with these children. Sometimes, of course, these children come from troubled home backgrounds and there may be no parents or guardians easily accessible with whom to work. School psychologists also must be aware of the legal challenges facing schools today, as lawsuits by parents and other groups over what they perceive as inadequate educating of their children constantly loom as a background factor.

Working in Business

Psychologists in business settings often obtain their advanced training in industrial/organizational (I/O) programs. Psychologists in these settings encounter a wide range of problems. Among these problems are designing tools and work environments to maximize productivity (see Nickerson, 1997), devising tests and other assessments to be used for selection and promotion, redesigning jobs in order to increase productivity, deciding on personnel policies for the organization, and helping managers decide how best to take advantage of the human resources available to them.

Sometimes a rough distinction is made between the two branches of I/O psychology, industrial and organizational psychology. Industrial psychology is the more traditional branch of the field, concerned more with devising and validating tests and other forms of assessments for selection and promotion. Industrial psychologists are typically very well-trained in test construction and evaluation and in the psychometric methods that are needed to evaluate test results. They also may be involved in job design and redesign.

Organizational psychology deals more with organizational development, broadly defined. Organizational psychologists may intervene to help work groups that are in conflict with each other, or even to help resolve conflicts that exist within a work group. They also may work with individual managers to help them manage people more effectively, or they may attempt to redesign the way a company works both to improve its productivity and to improve its human-relations aspects. Organizational psychologists are less likely to be involved with the use of tests.

Industrial/organizational psychologists typically have a master's or a doctoral degree. The types of work done by the two groups are somewhat different, and those with a master's degree may end up being supervised by those with a doctoral degree. At the same time, it is not unknown for businesses to harbor suspicions (even if for no good cause) about the practicality of people with a doctorate, so it cannot be said that a doctorate is an advantage in every case.

Employment prospects in this field are excellent, as there seems to be a steady demand for people with industrial/organizational training. Salaries tend to be higher than in some of the other kinds of settings, such as government and schools, so that this specialty has an added financial incentive. For some individuals, I/O psychology can be a route to management, although most people who wish to enter management would seek business-school training and the MBA (master of business administration degree).

Working in a Consulting Organization

Many psychologists find work in a variety of consulting organizations. Such organizations seek contracts with industry and government in order to provide a wide range of services, from research to counseling to marketing. One of the most active specializations of consulting psychologists is in the area of consumer psychology.

Consumer psychologists seek to understand consumer behavior. What motivates people to buy products and services? Why do they stop using products and services that they once enjoyed? What kinds of advertising appeal to people? How can products and services best be packaged so as to have consumer appeal?

Typically, people who work for consulting organizations of any kind have master's- or doctoral-level training and will have specialized in social, I/O, or even consumer psychology. In some kinds of consulting, especially for educational organizations, a background in cognitive psychology can also be useful. There is also a heavy demand for people with excellent methodological and statistical skills, as well as advanced computer skills. These skills are put to use in designing surveys, designing or conducting focus groups, and doing other aspects of product evaluation. Psychologists who work for consulting firms must be highly flexible, as they need to work on a wide diversity of problems, depending on whom their clients are. They also need excellent written- and oral-presentation skills, as a major part of their job is communicating their results to clients. Presentation skills are also important for academic psychologists, who are considered next.

Careers in Academic Psychology

Academic careers generally involve teaching and often research in a college or university setting (Calfee, 1997; Roediger, 1997; Vroom, 1997; Zanna & Darley, 1987). These days, many high schools also offer psychology courses, although in many high schools psychology teachers also teach other subjects, such as history or science. Academic careers give individuals an opportunity to interact and learn from, as well as to teach, students throughout their entire professional careers.

In most universities in the United States, and in some other countries, there is a more or less standardized series of academic ranks, depending upon qualifications and experience. Most academics have a PhD degree, although some may have an alternative doctorate such as an EdD, DBA (doctor of business administration), or PsyD degree. In some colleges and universities, faculty may have just a master's degree (MA or MS), but often the expectation is that the individual will go on to get a doctorate. Initial appointments may be as an instructor, a lecturer, or an assistant professor (in ascending order of advancement). Promotions then can be made to the level of associate professor and finally full professor. Promotion to associate professor can occur anywhere from 3 to 10 years after appointment as an assistant professor. The time to promotion as a full professor is more variable, and some academics are never promoted to full professor. Because of competition, some people may find themselves as part-timers, or in positions that do not lead to the possibility of tenure, which is discussed next.

Most departments offer full-timers the possibility of tenure, which refers to the faculty members being granted a permanent position that they can lose only through gross irresponsibility or negligence or, of course, through resignation or retirement. Tenure decisions typically are made after about 7 years of teaching. Often, faculty members who are not granted tenure are expected to leave the institution and to find themselves an alternative position. The rates at which faculty are granted tenure vary widely from one institution to another. At some institutions, almost everyone who starts with an academic position is tenured; at others, almost no one receives tenure.

Academics can find a primary affiliation with a psychology department, but they also can find an affiliation with a department of education, a business school, or a faculty of child development. Some psychologists teach in medical schools, where their students are future doctors or medical researchers. Academic careers involve a variety of kinds of activities.

Usually, teaching of psychology is a primary responsibility. Teaching may be to undergraduate students, graduate students, or both. In a small department, the academic will need to be a generalist because he or she is likely to teach a wide variety of courses. Sometimes, all of the offerings in a psychology department (or other department) are taught by just a handful of professors. In large departments, faculty can be more specialized and may find themselves teaching more courses in their area of interest. In almost any department, however, faculty will be expected to teach both courses that are in their area of specialization and courses that are needed to meet the teaching needs of the department, whether or not these courses fall exactly in the professors' areas of specialization.

Teaching responsibilities vary widely across colleges and universities. In schools that emphasize teaching responsibilities, a professor may find him- or herself teaching as many as five or more courses per semester. This is considered a heavy teaching load. In other schools that emphasize research, the teaching load is likely to be lighter, perhaps one or two courses per semester. A typical teaching load is probably about two to three courses per semester.

In most colleges and universities, faculty members also are expected to do research. Through their research, they add to the existing knowledge base of the field of psychology. Institutions expect their faculty to publish their work in professionally recognized scholarly journals. Faculty members also occasionally give talks to meetings of professional associations or to other departments. Expectations regarding research differ widely among institutions. Some institutions may be happy to see their faculty publishing even one professional paper per year. Other institutions may expect faculty to publish three, four, or more papers per year. Many institutions expect faculty to obtain research grants or contracts from government organizations that will financially support the research the faculty members do.

Faculty also are expected to do various kinds of service work, including the advising of students, serving on departmental committees, serving on college or university committees, and eventually, taking administrative roles within their department (such as chairman or director of undergraduate studies). Service work also can involve evaluating articles for scholarly journals, evaluating grant proposals, and evaluating candidates for hiring or promotion. Service work can be quite time-consuming but is important for the success and vitality of the field and of the life in any academic department.

In short, academic jobs offer an exciting challenge to individuals who would like to remain in a college or university setting. The academic job market in psychology is better than that in many other fields and psychology students should be encouraged that most people who seek an academic job find one, although it may take a while, may not be their first-choice job, and may even end up being part-time.

Few fields offer a wider diversity of job opportunities than does psychology. The study of psychology can thus be an entrée to almost unlimited career possibilities. Not only is psychology a practical major in terms of getting a job, but it is also practical in terms of financial compensation. Psychologists tend to be fairly well-compensated relative to the total range of jobs available to college graduates. But the rewards of psychology go beyond the practical. There is perhaps no other field of study that can give the rewards of human understanding that psychology gives. In few other fields can one successfully apply the lessons of the classroom to one's everyday life on such a continuing basis.

abnormal behavior the ways of thinking or acting that are unusual, that impair the ability to function effectively, that are identified as odd within the surrounding social context, or that involve some degree of distortion in thinking, feeling, or perceiving

absolute threshold a hypothetical minimum amount of physical energy that an individual can detect for each kind of sensory stimulation; operationally defined as the level at which a stimulus is first detected 50% of the time during many attempts to detect the stimulus

accommodation the process of trying to restore cognitive equilibrium by modifying existing schemas or even creating new ones to fit new information

achievement an accomplishment; an attained level of expertise on performance of a task, or an acquired base of knowledge in a domain or a set of domains

acquisition a phase of learning during which the probability of learning increases

action potential a change in the electrochemical balance inside and outside a neuron; occurs when electrochemical stimulation of the neuron reaches or exceeds the neuron's threshold of excitation

activation–synthesis hypothesis a belief that dreams result from subjective organization and interpretation (synthesis) of neural activity (activation) that takes place during sleep

actor–observer effect the tendency not only to attribute the actions of others to stable internal personal dispositions but also to attribute our own actions to external situational variables

acute characteristic of symptoms or illness occurring only for a short time, although probably intensely

acute toxicity the negative health consequences of a single instance of ingesting a poisonous substance, such as a single overdose of a psychoactive drug

adaptation a temporary physiological response to a sensed change in the environment, which is neither learned nor consciously controlled; the degree of adaptation depends directly on the degree of change in the stimulus, with greater changes producing greater adaptation

addiction a persistent, habitual, or compulsive physiological or at least psychological dependency on one or more psychoactive drugs

additive mixture the mixture of light waves of varying wavelengths, in which each wavelength of light adds to the other wavelengths

adolescence the stage of psychological development between the start of puberty and the time the individual accepts the full responsibilities of being an adult in a given society

aerobic exercise activities that are sufficiently intense and long-lasting to stimulate increased heart rate and respiration (breathing)

aggression a behavior that is intended to cause harm or injury to another person

agnosia severe problems in recognizing and interpreting information sent to the brain from one or more sense organs (*a-*, lack; *gnosis*, knowledge)

agoraphobia an intense fear of open spaces or of being in a public place from which it might be difficult to escape in the event of a panic attack

algorithm the formal path for reaching a solution, which involves one or more successive processes that usually lead to an accurate answer to a question

altruism a generous willingness to help another person or persons, even when there is no reward or other observable benefit to the helper; often involves some sacrifice on the part of the helper

amnesia the loss of partial or total explicit memory

analgesics pain-relieving drugs (e.g., acetaminophen, ibuprofen, and salicylic acid [aspirin])

analysis the process of breaking down a complex whole into smaller elements

anorexia nervosa an eating disorder in which a person undereats to the point of starvation, based on the extremely distorted belief that she (usually) or he is overweight

anterograde amnesia the difficulty in purposefully forming new memories after an injury to memory function without any effect on the ability to retrieve memories stored prior to the injury; one meaning of *antero-* is "before"; people with anterograde amnesia forget new information before they even have a chance to store it

antidepressant drug a drug used for treating depression

antipsychotic drug a drug used for treating psychosis (e.g., schizophrenia)

antisocial behavior the actions that are harmful to a given society or to its members and that are condemned by the society as a whole

anxiety a generalized feeling of dread or apprehension that is not focused on or directed toward any particular object or event

anxiety disorder a psychological disorder involving the presence of anxiety that is so intense or so frequently present that it causes difficulty or distress for the individual

applied research investigations that are intended to lead to clear, immediate, obvious, and practical uses, which may not lead to fundamental understandings of the human mind and behavior

approach–avoidance conflict the simultaneous presence of two conflicting tendencies: to go toward a stimulus (approach it) and to go away from it (avoid it), based on feeling both positive and negative emotions about the stimulus

aptitude a capability for accomplishing something, for attaining a level of expertise on performance of a task or a set of tasks, or for acquiring knowledge in a given domain or set of domains

archetype the inherited tendency to perceive and act in certain ways, common to all

arousal   the state of alertness, wakefulness, and activation caused by nervous-system activity

assimilation   the process of trying to restore cognitive equilibrium by incorporating new information into existing schemas

association areas   the regions of the cerebral lobes that are not part of the sensory or motor cortices but that are believed to connect (associate) the activity of the sensory and motor cortices

associationism   a school of psychology that examines how events or ideas can become associated with one another in the mind

asylum   a hospital or other institution for housing and possibly treating mentally ill patients

atheoretical   having no particular theoretical orientation

attachment   a strong and relatively long-lasting emotional tie between people

attachment theory of love   a view that how we relate to loved ones as adults stems from the way in which we attached to our parents, and particularly our mothers, as infants

attention   the process by which we focus our awareness on some of the information available in consciousness and screen out other information

attitude   a learned, stable, and relatively enduring evaluation (e.g., of a person or an idea); such an evaluation can affect an individual's thoughts, feelings, and behavior

attribution   a mental explanation pointing to the cause or causes of a person's behavior, including the behavior of the person making the attribution

automatic behavior   the conduct that requires no conscious decisions regarding which muscles to move or which actions to take

availability heuristic   a cognitive shortcut in which an individual makes judgments on the basis of how easily he or she can call to mind what are perceived as relevant instances of a given phenomenon

aversive conditioning   the use of punishment as a means of encouraging an individual to try to escape from or to avoid a situation

avoidance learning   the goal of aversive conditioning; an individual learns to stay away from something

avoidant-attachment pattern   a pattern in which a child generally ignores the mother while she is present and in which the child shows minimal distress when the mother leaves; one of three major attachment patterns observed in the strange situation

axon   the long, thin, tubular part of the neuron, which responds to information received by the dendrites and soma of the neuron by either ignoring or transmitting the information through the neuron to the axon's terminal buttons

babbling   a prelinguistic preferential production of only those distinct phonemes characteristic of the language being acquired

balance theory   a cognitive-consistency theory of attraction, suggesting that people who like each other try to maintain a balance (reciprocity) regarding the mutual give and take in the relationship and that they try to maintain similar likes and dislikes

barbiturates   a widely used type of sedative–hypnotic drug; prescribed to reduce anxiety but may lead to grogginess that can impair functioning in situations requiring alertness

basic research   investigations devoted to the study of fundamental underlying relationships and principles, which may not offer any immediate, obvious, or practical value

basilar membrane   one of the membranes separating two of the fluid-filled canals of the inner ear; on this membrane are the hair cells that transduce sound waves

behavior therapy   various psychotherapeutic techniques based mostly on principles of classical and operant conditioning, as well as some techniques based on observational learning from models

behaviorism   a school of psychology that focuses entirely on the association between the environment and emitted behavior

"Big Five" theory of personality   a trait theory suggesting that the five key personality traits are neuroticism, extroversion, openness, agreeableness, and conscientiousness

bilingual   a person who can speak two languages

binocular depth cue   the perceived information about depth, which can be gained only by using two eyes (*bin-*, both; two)

bipolar disorder   a mood disorder in which the individual alternates between periods of depression and of mania

bisexual   a person who directs sexual desire toward members of both sexes

bounded rationality   the recognition that although humans are rational, there are limits to the degree to which they demonstrate rational cognitive processes across situations

brain   the organ of the body that most directly controls thoughts, emotions, motivations, and actions and that responds to information received from elsewhere in the body, such as through sensory receptors

bulimia   a disorder characterized by eating binges followed by episodes of getting rid of the food (e.g., vomiting, taking laxatives)

bystander effect   the phenomenon in which the presence of increasing numbers of people available to help leads to a decreasing likelihood that any given observer will offer help

cardinal trait   a characteristic that totally dominates the personality and behavior of an individual; many people do not have a cardinal trait

case study   intensive investigation of a single individual or set of individuals

central nervous system (CNS)   the part of the nervous system comprising the brain and the spinal cord, including all of the neurons therein

central nervous system (CNS) depressant   a drug that slows the operation of the CNS and is often prescribed in low doses to reduce anxiety and in relatively higher doses to combat insomnia

central nervous system (CNS) stimulant   a drug that arouses and excites the CNS, either by stimulating the heart or by inhibiting the actions of natural compounds that depress brain activity (thereby acting as a "double-negative" on brain stimulation)

central tendency   the typical value

central trait   a characteristic that stands out in its importance for the personality and behavior of an individual

cerebellum   a brain structure that controls bodily coordination, balance, and muscle tone

cerebral cortex   a thin layer of tissue on the surface of the brain, which is responsible for most high-level cognitive processes

chromosomes   rod-shaped bodies that contain innumerable genes; occur in pairs

chronic   characteristic of symptoms or illness always present or repeatedly occurring again and again

chronic toxicity   the negative health consequences of repeated ingestion of one or more poisonous substances, such as opiates and opioids

chunk   a grouping, by which a collection of items is organized into a coherent whole

circadian rhythm   the usual sleeping–waking pattern of physiological changes corresponding roughly to the cycle of darkness and light associated with a single day (*circa-*, around; *-dies*, day [Latin])

classical conditioning   the learning process whereby an originally neutral stimulus becomes associated with a particular physiological or emotional response that the stimulus did not originally produce

client-centered therapy   a form of humanistic psychotherapy in which the therapeutic interactions center on the client's view of reality

cognitive consistency   the reassuring presence of a match between an individual's thoughts (cognition) and that person's behavior

cognitive development   the process by which people's thinking changes across the life span

cognitive dissonance   the discomforting conflict between an individual's thoughts (cognition) and that person's behavior; often as a result of the person's having acted in a way that does not agree with her or his existing beliefs

cognitive-impairment disorder   a psychological disorder in which normal thought processes become impaired or distorted

cognitivism   a school of psychology that underscores the importance of perception, learning, and thought as bases for understanding much of human behavior

collective unconscious   according to Jungian theory, the part of the unconscious mind that contains memories and behavioral predispositions that all humans share because of our common ancestry

collectivism   the tendency to emphasize the interests and well-being of the group over those of each individual

common and uncommon effects   the tendency to infer attributions based on whether the effects of a behavior are ordinary (situational attributions) or are unusual (personal attributions)

compliance   the process in which an individual goes along with a request made by one or more other persons

concept   an idea to which a person may attach various characteristics and with which a person may connect other ideas into a single notion

concrete-operational stage   Piaget's third stage of development (about the period of elementary school), during which the child can mentally manipulate images of concrete objects

conditioned response (CR)   a response that is similar to the UR, but that is elicited from the CS rather than from the US

conditioned stimulus (CS)   an originally neutral stimulus that later will elicit a physiological or emotional response

cone   a relatively short, thick, and less abundant type of photoreceptor, responsible mostly for very clear color vision in bright lighting

confidentiality   an ethical practice in which researchers ensure the privacy of personal information regarding individual research participants

conformity   the process in which an individual shapes her or his behavior to make it consistent with the norms of a group

connotation   an emotional overtone, presupposition, or other nonexplicit meaning of a word

consciousness   the complex phenomenon of actively processing perceptions, thoughts, feelings, wishes, and memories to create a mental reality for adapting to the world

conservation of quantity   the principle that the quantity of something remains the same as long as nothing is removed or added, even if the appearance of the substance changes in form

consolidation   a process by which people integrate new information into existing information stored in long-term memory

constructive memory   the phenomenon by which people build stored memories, based on existing schemas, sensations, experiences, and other stored information

context effects   the influences on perception that come from information in the surrounding environment

contextualist   a psychologist who theorizes about a psychological phenomenon (e.g., intelligence) strictly in terms of the context in which an individual is observed, and who suggests that the phenomenon cannot be understood, let alone measured, outside the real-world context of the individual

contingency   a phenomenon in which one or more stimuli *depend on* the presence of another stimulus

continuous reinforcement   a learning program in which reinforcement always follows a particular operant behavior

control condition   a situation in which some experimental participants are subjected to a carefully prescribed set of circumstances, which are like those of the experimental condition but do not involve the introduction of the independent variable

control-enhancing interventions   used to increase patients' abilities to respond appropriately to illness, eventually leading to coping effectively with illness

controlled experimental design   a plan for conducting research in which the experimenter carefully manipulates or controls independent variables in order to see their effects on dependent variables

cooing   an oral expression that explores the production of all the phones that humans can possibly produce

cooperative principle   the principle of conversation in which it is held that people seek to communicate in ways that make it easy for a listener to understand what a speaker means

coping   the processes of managing the internal and external changes presented by a challenging situation

cornea   the clear, dome-shaped window through which light passes, serving primarily as a curved exterior surface of the eye that gathers and focuses the entering light

corpus callosum   a dense body of nerve fibers that connect the two cerebral hemispheres

correlation   the statistical relationship between two attributes, expressed as a number ranging from −1 (a negative correlation) to 0 (no correlation) to +1 (a positive correlation)

correlation coefficient   a statistical measure that addresses the question of the degree of relation between two arrays of values

correlational design   a plan for conducting research by assessing the degree of association between two (or more) attributes (characteristics of participants, a setting, or a situation)

counterconditioning   behavioral techniques based on classical conditioning, emphasizing the substitution of an adaptive response (e.g., relaxation) in place of a maladaptive response (e.g., anxiety) to a particular stimulus

countertransference   a term used in psychodynamic therapy describing a situation in which the therapist becomes emotionally involved with the patient, projecting the therapist's own feelings onto the patient

creativity   the process of producing something that is both original and valuable

critical period   a time of rapid growth and development, during which particular changes typically occur if they are ever to occur; that is, such changes typically do not occur after the critical period

critical thinking   the conscious direction of mental processes toward representing and processing information, usually in order to find thoughtful solutions to problems, make judgments or decisions, or to reason

cultural psychology   a school of psychology that emphasizes the importance of cultural context in the study of the human mind and behavior

culture-fair   describes the assessment that is equally appropriate for members of all cultures and that comprises items that are equally fair to members of all cultures; probably impossible to attain

culture-relevant   describes the assessment of skills and knowledge that relate to the cultural experiences of the test-takers, by using content and procedures that are appropriate to the cultural context of the test-takers

dark adaptation   the physiological adjustment to decreases in light intensity, during which the rods become more active

data   facts, numbers, and other information

decay   the forgetting of unused stored information due to the passage of time

declarative knowledge   "knowing that"; factual information that a person can state in words

deductive reasoning   a set of processes by which an individual tries to draw a logically certain and specific conclusion from a set of general propositions

defense mechanism   the means by which the ego protects itself from unacceptable thoughts (from the superego) and impulses (from the id)

deindividuation   the loss of a sense of individual identity, resulting in fewer controls that prevent the individual from engaging in behavior that violates societal norms and even the individual's personal moral beliefs

delusion   a false belief, which contradicts known facts

dendrites   the primary parts of the neuron involved in receiving communications from other cells via distinctive receptors on their external membranes

denotation   the strict dictionary definition of a word

dependent variable   an outcome characteristic that varies as a consequence of variation in one or more independent variables

depressive disorders   a mood disorder in which the individual feels so sad and has so little energy that the individual cannot function effectively

descriptive statistics   numbers that summarize quantitative information, reducing a larger mass of information to a smaller, more useful base of information

desensitization   the gradual habituation to violent stimuli, in which we gradually become less interested in and less responsive to violent stimuli and their tragic consequences

detection   the awareness of the presence of a sensory stimulus

development   the changes that are associated with increasing physiological maturity, experience, or an interaction of physiological changes and experiences with the environment

deviation IQs   a means of determining intelligence-test scores, based on deviations from an average score, calculated such that the normative equivalent for the median score is 100; not IQs, strictly speaking, because no quotient is involved

dichotic presentation   a perceptual experience in which each ear receives a different message (*dich-*, in two parts; *-otic*, related to the ears [Greek])

difference threshold   a hypothetical minimum amount of difference that can be detected between two stimuli (see also *just noticeable difference*)

differentiate   to become more highly specialized into distinct parts or types

diffusion of responsibility   the phenomenon in which increases in the number of other persons present leads each person to feel less personal responsibility for the events taking place

discourse   the most comprehensive level of linguistic analysis, which encompasses language use at the level beyond the sentence, such as in conversation, in paragraphs, and so on

disorders usually first diagnosed in infancy, childhood, or adolescence   psychological disorders that are first identified before adulthood

dissociative disorders   psychological disorders in which an individual goes through one or more extreme changes in awareness of past and present experiences, personal history, and even personal identity

distributed learning   the storage of information in memory that occurs over a long period of time rather than all at once

dominant trait   the stronger expression of a genetic trait, which appears in the phenotype of an organism when the genotype comprises two dominant expressions of a trait or a dominant and a recessive expression of a trait

double-blind procedure   an experimental technique whereby neither the experimenters nor the participants know which participants will have received which kind of treatment, or even any treatment at all (e.g., in a control condition)

drive   a hypothesized composite source of energy, which humans and other animals try to reduce

effector   a physiological structure designed to send something, such as motor information, to the parts of the body that act on the environment

ego   a personality structure that is largely conscious and realistic in responding to the events in the world while trying to satisfy the irrational and unconscious urgings of the id and the prohibitions of the superego

egocentric   focused on one's own views without being able to see how others may view a situation

electroconvulsive therapy (ECT)   a form of psychophysiological therapy in which patients undergo electrical shocks, which cause convulsive seizures followed by a period of amnesia and which may relieve severe symptoms of depression

electroencephalogram (EEG)   a recording of the electrical activity of the living brain, as detected by various electrodes (*en-*, in; *cephalo-*, head; *-gram*, record [Greek])

elimination by aspects   a decision-making strategy in which an individual focuses on one attribute of an overabundance of options, forms a minimum criterion for that attribute, and then eliminates all options that do not meet that criterion; the process is repeated until either a single option remains or few enough remain that a more careful selection process may be used

embryo   an individual in the second of the three stages of prenatal development (from about 2 weeks after conception until about the end of the 8th week); the individual undergoes tremendous differentiation and rapid growth and is easily influenced by the maternal environment

emotion a psychological feeling, usually accompanied by a physiological reaction

emotion-focused coping adapting to a challenging situation by handling one's own emotions that arise in regard to the situation

empiricism approach asserting that knowledge is most effectively acquired through experience and observation

encoding the transformation of sensory information into an understandable mental representation that can be stored in memory

encoding specificity the phenomenon by which the retrieval of information depends on the form of representation of the information during encoding

endocrine system a physiological communication network that operates via glands that secrete hormones directly into the bloodstream

episodic memory the memory for particular events that an individual has experienced, as well as for information that is linked to those experiences

equity theory a theory of attraction suggesting that people feel more strongly attracted to those with whom they have more equitable (fair) relationships of giving and taking

experiment an investigation of cause–effect relationships done by controlling or carefully manipulating particular variables to note their effects on other variables

experimental condition a situation in which some experimental participants are exposed to a specific set of circumstances, involving a treatment linked to an independent variable

explicit memory remembering that requires a conscious effort at recollection of information

external locus of control a personality orientation based on people's belief that the environment surrounding them largely is able to control both what they do and the probable outcomes of what they do

extinction a phase of learning when the probability of the CR decreases over time, eventually approaching zero

extinction procedures behavioral techniques based on classical conditioning, in which the goal is to weaken a maladaptive response

extrinsic motivators the rewards that come from outside the individual, such as offers of money or threats of punishment

extroversion a personality trait characterized by sociability, liveliness, and friendliness

feature-detector approach an approach to form perception based on observing the activity of the brain; apparently, specific neurons of the visual cortex respond to specific features detected by photoreceptors

fetus an individual in the third of the three stages of prenatal development (from about the 9th week until birth); a time during which the individual develops enough sophistication to be able to survive outside the mother's uterus

figure a highlighted feature of the perceived environment

formal-operational stage Piaget's fourth stage of development (about the time of adolescence), during which the child becomes able to manipulate abstract ideas and formal relationships

free association a psychodynamic technique in which patients are encouraged to say whatever comes to mind without censoring or otherwise editing their statements

frequency distribution the number or proportion of cases at each score level or interval

functional fixedness a mental set in which an individual fails to see an alternative use for something that previously has been known to have a particular use

functionalism a school of psychology that focuses on active psychological processes, rather than on passive psychological structures or elements

fundamental attribution error the tendency to overemphasize internal causes and personal responsibility and to deemphasize external causes and situational influences when observing the behavior of other people

gate-control theory a possible explanation of pain, suggesting that the central nervous system acts as a physiological barrier through which pain may be allowed to pass under particular circumstances

gender typing the process of acquiring gender-related roles for a given society

gene a basic physiological building block for the hereditary transmission of genetic traits in all life forms

general adaptation syndrome (GAS) a general pattern of physiological response to stress, involving three phases: alarm, resistance, and exhaustion

genotype the genetic makeup for inherited traits, which is not subject to environmental influence (except in cases of genetic mutation)

Gestalt approach an approach to form perception, based on the notion that the whole differs from the sum of its parts

Gestalt psychology (pronounced "gess-TAHLT") a school of psychology holding that psychological phenomena are best understood when viewed as organized, structured wholes, rather than when analyzed into numerous components

gland a group of cells that secretes chemical substances

goal a future state that an individual wants to reach

gradient of reinforcement a phenomenon in which increases in the length of time between an operant and a reinforcer directly decrease the effect of the reinforcement

grammar the study of language in terms of regular patterns that relate to the functions and relationships of words in a sentence, extending as broadly as the level of discourse and as narrowly as the pronunciation and meaning of individual words

ground the features of the perceived environment that are not highlighted, which serve as a background for highlighted features

group a collection of individuals who interact with each other, usually either to accomplish work or to promote interpersonal relationships (or both)

group polarization the tendency to exaggerate the initial views of group members, so that the views become more extreme

groupthink a group process in which group members work so hard to achieve unanimous agreement that they fail to consider realistically the various alternative courses of action available to them

habituation a phenomenon in which a person gradually becomes more familiar with a stimulus and notices it less and less; in *dishabituation,* a once-familiar stimulus changes to become unfamiliar, so the person notices the stimulus once again

hair cell an auditory receptor that transduces sound waves into electrochemical energy

hallucination the perception of sensory stimulation (usually sounds, but sometimes sights, smells, or tactile sensations) in the absence of any actual corresponding sensory input from the physical world

hallucinogenic a type of psychoactive drug that alters consciousness by inducing hallucinations and by affecting the way the drug users perceive both their inner worlds and their external environments

hardiness   a personality attribute characterized by high internal locus of control, strong commitment to work and other activities, and an outlook that favors challenge and opportunities for personal growth

health psychology   the study of how the mind and the physical health of the body interact

heuristics   the informal, speculative, shortcut strategies for solving problems, which sometimes work and sometimes do not

hippocampus   a portion of the limbic system; plays an essential role in the formation of new memories

homeostatic regulation   the tendency of the body to maintain a state of equilibrium (balance)

homosexuality   a tendency to direct sexual desire toward another person of the same (*homo-*, same) sex, which probably is based on physiology (nature) but is influenced also by the environment (nurture)

hormone   a chemical substance secreted by one or more glands; regulates many physiological processes through specific actions on cells, and may affect the way a receptive cell goes about its activities

hostile aggression   a behavior that is intended to cause harm, as a result of an emotional, often impulsive, outburst, caused by pain or distress; the consequences usually lead to little gain for the aggressor and may even lead to losses for the aggressor

humanistic psychology   a school of psychology that emphasizes human potential, as guided by holistic approaches to conscious experiences, rather than analytic approaches to unconscious experience

hypnosis   an altered state of consciousness that usually involves deep relaxation and extreme sensitivity to suggestion and appears to bear some resemblance to sleep

hypothalamus   a brain structure that plays a key role in regulating behavior related to species survival (fighting, feeding, fleeing, and mating)

hypothesis   tentative statement of belief regarding expected outcomes

hypothetical construct   a phenomenon that is believed to exist but that cannot be measured or perceived directly; that is, we cannot directly see, hear, touch, smell, or taste these constructs, however we believe they exist—a hypothetical construct (e.g., memory or intelligence) is *constructed* (built) from *hypotheses* (beliefs)

iconic store   sensory memory for very brief storage of visual images

id   a personality structure that is the unconscious, instinctual, and irrational source of primitive impulses

ideal self   all aspects of the self that a person ideally would like to perceive as characterizing the self

idealistic principle   the principle by which the compulsion to obey an internalized set of rules and prohibitions drives all of the functions of the superego

ill-structured problem   a problem with no clear, obvious, readily available path to solution

illusion   the distorted perception of physical stimuli, sometimes due to altered states of consciousness, to psychological disorder, or to misleading cues in the objects themselves

imaginary audience   an adolescent's unfounded belief that other people are constantly observing, paying attention to, and judging the adolescent

implicit memory   remembering information from prior experience to enhance performance, without being consciously aware of retrieving that information

imprinting   a preprogrammed response in which a newborn animal looks for a particular kind of stimulus and then carries out the response; the specific stimulus that prompts the response is learned

incubation   a period of rest, following a period of intensive effort in problem solving, during which the problem solver puts aside the problem for a while

independent variable   an attribute that is manipulated by the experimenter, while other attributes are held constant (not varied)

individualism   the tendency to emphasize the personal interests and welfare of the individual over those of the group

inductive reasoning   a set of processes by which an individual attempts to reach a probable general conclusion, based on a set of specific facts or observations

inferential statistics   statistics that are used to determine how likely it is that results that are obtained are not due to chance

inferiority complex   a maladaptive personality structure in which we organize our lives around feelings of inferiority, based on perceived mistakes and failings

information processing   the operations by which people mentally manipulate what they learn and know about the world

informed consent   an experimental procedure in which prospective participants are fully informed regarding the general nature of the anticipated treatment procedure and any possible harmful consequences of the treatment

insight   a seemingly sudden understanding of the nature of something, often as a result of taking a novel approach to the object of the insight

insomnia   any of various disturbances of sleep, such as difficulty in falling asleep or in staying asleep

instinct   an inherited, species-specific, stereotyped, and often relatively complex pattern of behavior

instrumental aggression   a behavior that happens to cause harm or injury to another person, as a by-product of trying to get something valued by the aggressor; often is planned, not impulsive

intelligence   comprises the abilities needed to engage in goal-directed adaptive behavior

intelligence quotient (IQ)   broadly, a normative score on an intelligence test, with a mean of 100 and a standard deviation of 15 or 16

interactionist approach   a view of personality that emphasizes the interaction between the person and the situation

interference   a process by which competing information causes people to forget already stored information

internal locus of control   a personality orientation based on people's belief that they largely are able to control both what they do and the probable outcomes of what they do

internalization   the process of absorbing knowledge from a given social environmental context

interneuron   a type of nerve cell that transmits information between sensory and motor neurons

interpersonal development   the process by which people change across the life span in the way they relate to other people

intoxicated   characterized by grogginess, insensibility, or temporary trouble thinking clearly and making reasoned judgments due to the effects of toxins such as alcohol or sedative–hypnotic drugs

intrinsic motivators   the rewards that come from within the individual, such as the desire to satisfy curiosity

introspection   self-examination of inner ideas and experiences

iris   a circular membrane that reflects light beams outward and away from the eye and surrounds the pupil

judgment and decision making   cognitive processes by which an individual may evaluate various options and select the most suitable option from among various alternatives

just noticeable difference (jnd)   a term operationally defined as the point at which an individual can detect the difference between two stimuli at least 50% of the time over a series of attempts to detect the difference

kinesthesis   the sense through which receptors within our muscles and connective tissues inform us about the positions and movements of our skeletal muscles

language   the use of an organized means of combining words in order to communicate

learned helplessness   a learned behavior in which an individual gives up trying to escape from a painful situation after repeatedly failing to escape

learning   any relatively permanent change in the behavior, thoughts, or feelings of an individual that results from experience

lens   a curved interior structure of the eye, which bends light slightly to focus it on the center of the rear surface of the eye

levels-of-processing framework   a view of memory that suggests that the extent to which an experience is remembered is determined by the degree and depth of information processing that takes place

lexicon   the entire set of morphemes in a given language or in a given person's linguistic repertoire

life-span development   the changes that occur within a person over the life span

light adaptation   the physiological adjustment to increases in light intensity, during which the cones become more active

limbic system   a system of brain structures involved in emotion, motivation, and learning

linguistic relativity   a proposition regarding the relationship between thought and language, which asserts that the speakers of different languages have differing cognitive systems, based on the languages they use, and that these different cognitive systems influence the ways in which people speaking the various languages think about the world

linguistic universals   the characteristic patterns of language that apply across all the languages of various cultures

linguistics   the study of language structure and change

lobes   each of the four major regions of the cerebral cortex, comprising the frontal lobe (motor, planning), parietal lobe (somatosensory), temporal lobe (auditory), and occipital lobe (visual)

long-term memory   the storage of practically limitless amount of information for unknown lengths of time

mania   a mood in which the individual feels highly energetic and extremely joyful

massed learning   the storage of information in memory that occurs over a brief period of time

maturation   any relatively permanent change in an individual that occurs strictly as a result of the biological processes of getting older

mean   the arithmetical average of a series of numbers

median   the middle of a set of values

meditation   a set of techniques, used for altering consciousness, to become more contemplative

memory   the process by which past experience and learning can be used in the present

mental age   a means of indicating a person's level of intelligence (generally in reference to a child), based on the individual's performance on tests of intelligence, by indicating the average chronological age of persons who typically perform at the same level of intelligence as the test-taker

mental retardation   a very low level of intelligence, usually reflected by both poor performance on tests of intelligence and poor *adaptive competence* (the degree to which a person functions effectively within a normal situational context)

mental set   a cognitive phenomenon in which an individual is predisposed to use an existing model for representing information, even when the existing model inadequately represents the information in a new situation

metacognition   the process of knowing or thinking about how we use strategies and skills to enhance our thought processes; thinking about how we think

mnemonic devices   the methods or "tricks" for improving memory by combining unrelated bits of information into meaningful verbal information or into visual images (see also *mnemonism*)

mnemonism   the use of special techniques for improving memory skill (see also *mnemonic devices*)

mode   the most frequent value of a set of values

modeling   a cognitive and behavioral technique in which people are encouraged to change simply by watching other people successfully cope with challenging problems that affect the observer

monocular depth cue   the perceived information about depth, which can be gained by using only one eye (*mon-*, one; *-ocular,* related to the eyes)

mood disorder   a psychological disorder involving either periods of extremely sad, low-energy moods, or swings between extremely high and extremely low moods

morpheme   the smallest unit of single or combined sounds denoting meaning within a given language

motivation   an impulse, a desire, or a need that leads to an action

motor   related to moving the muscles

motor neuron   a nerve cell that carries information *away from* the spinal cord and the brain and toward the body parts that are supposed to respond to the information in some way

multimodal   having more than one mode

myelin sheath   a protective, insulating layer of myelin, which coats the axons of some neurons

narcolepsy   a disturbance of the pattern of wakefulness and sleep, in which the narcoleptic periodically experiences an uncontrollable urge to fall asleep and then briefly loses consciousness

narcotic   any drug in a class of drugs derived from opium or synthetically produced to create the numbing, stuporous effects of opium and that lead to drug dependency

natural selection   evolutionary mechanism by which organisms have developed and changed, based on what is commonly called the "survival of the fittest"

naturalistic observation   a research method in which the researcher observes people engaged in the normal activities of their daily lives

nature–nurture controversy   a debate regarding whether our psychological makeup arises from our inherited characteristics (our *nature*) or from our interactions with the environment (our *nurture*)

negative reinforcement   the effect of the removal or cessation (stopping) of an unpleasant stimulus, such as physical or psychological pain or discomfort

negative reinforcer   an unpleasant stimulus event that is removed following an operant response, thereby leading to an increased probability that the operant will be repeated

negative symptom   a characteristic of a disorder, in which the individual lacks a normal behavior (e.g., not speaking, not showing emotional expression, or not interacting socially)

negative transfer   the hindrance of problem solving as a result of prior experience in solving apparently related or similar problems

neodissociative theory   a view of hypnosis asserting that some individuals can separate one part of their conscious minds (which responds to the hypnotist's instructions) from another part (which observes and monitors the events and actions taking place)

neo-Freudian   a psychodynamically oriented theorist whose views and theories are based on those of Freud

neonate   newborn (*neo-*, new; *-nate*, born)

nerve   a bundle of neurons that can be observed as a fiber extending from the central nervous system out to various parts of the body

neuron   a nerve cell, involved in neural communication within the nervous system

neuroticism   a personality trait characterized by sudden and unpredictable mood swings, nervousness, and irritability

neurotransmitter   a chemical messenger, released by the terminal buttons on the axon of a presynaptic neuron, which carries the chemical messages across the synapse to receptor sites on the receiving dendrites or soma of the postsynaptic neuron

norm   a standard of behavior or an expressed attitude, based on the shared trends of the majority in a group

normal distribution   a particular distribution in which the preponderance of values is near the center of the distribution, with values falling off rather rapidly as they depart from the center

normative scores   the set of normative equivalents for a range of raw test scores that represent the normal distribution of scores obtained by giving a test to a huge number of individuals

N-REM sleep   the four stages of sleep that are not characterized by rapid eye movements (REMs) and that are less frequently associated with dreaming

null hypothesis   a proposed expectation of no difference or relation

obedience   the process in which an individual follows the command of an actual or perceived authority figure

object permanence   the cognitive realization that objects may continue to exist even when they are not currently being sensed

objective personality test   a method of personality assessment founded on the trait approach, which is standardized and normed based on a large number of individuals, thereby providing scores that allow for easy comparisons across individuals

olfaction   the sense of smell

operant   a kind of *response* that has some effect on the world

operant conditioning   the process of increasing or decreasing the likelihood that an individual will produce an active behavior (an operant) as a result of interacting with the environment

operational definition   a means for researchers to specify exactly how to test or to measure particular phenomena being studied

opponent process   a changing phenomenon that opposes (goes against, in the opposite direction from) an existing force, thereby moving toward a neutral state of balance

organic pain   the discomfort caused by observed physical damage to bodily tissue

overconfidence   a bias affecting decision making, in which individuals overestimate the probability that their own responses are accurate or even more broadly overvalue their own skills, knowledge, or judgment

overdose   ingestion of a life-threatening or lethal dose of drugs, often associated with the use of psychoactive drugs

overextension error   an overapplication of the meaning of a given word to more things, ideas, and situations than is appropriate for the word; usually made by children or other persons acquiring a language

pain   the sensory and emotional discomfort associated with actual, imagined, or threatened damage to or irritation of tissues of the body

parallel processing   information processing during which multiple operations occur simultaneously

partial-reinforcement schedule   an operant-conditioning program in which a given operant is reinforced at some times but not at other times

percentile   the percentage of other individuals in a given distribution whose scores fall below a given individual's scores

perception   the mental processes that organize and interpret sensory information that has been transmitted to the brain

perceptual constancy   the perception that stimuli remain the same even when immediate sensations of the stimuli change

peripheral nervous system (PNS)   one of the two main parts of the nervous system, comprising the nerve cells that lie outside of the brain and the spinal cord, including the nerves of the face and head

personal attribution   a mental explanation pointing to the cause of behavior as lying within the individual (internal) who performs the behavior (also termed *dispositional attribution*)

personal disposition   a trait that is unique to a given individual, according to Allport's theory of personality

personal unconscious   the part of the unconscious mind that includes the person's distinctive repressed memories and personal experiences

personalism   the tendency to make more personal attributions when the behavior of someone affects us directly but to make more situational attributions when the behavior affects us less directly

personality   the enduring dispositional characteristics of an individual that hold together and explain the person's behavior

personality disorders   psychological disorders involving exaggerated and maladaptive personality characteristics that persist over a long period of time and that cause problems in the person's adjustment to everyday situations

person–environment interaction   the distinctive fit between a given person and his or her environment

phenotype   the expression of an inherited trait, based on the dominant expression of the trait in the genotype and also subject to environmental influence

photoreceptor   a receptor cell that receives and transduces light (*photo-*, light) energy into electrochemical energy

placebo   a pill or other substance that the patient believes to have curative or healing properties, but that actually has no such properties; often used as a means of determining whether drug treatments are truly effective or work only because patients believe that they are being helped

placebo effect   a perceived improvement that occurs simply because people believe that they have received a given treatment, even when they did not actually receive the treatment

placenta   a protective membrane containing a dense network of blood vessels through which the mother's body supplies needed resources (e.g., oxygen, sources of energy, and material resources such as protein and minerals) and removes waste products

plan   a strategy for accomplishing something at some time in the future

pleasure principle   the principle by which the satisfaction of impulses drives all of the functions of the id

polygraph   the equipment that records several (*poly-*, many; *-graph*, recording) different physiological responses (e.g., heart rate, respiration rate, blood pressure) at one time; often used for trying to measure emotional reactions

pons   a brain structure containing nerve cells that pass signals from one part of the brain to another, thereby serving as a kind of bridge

positive reinforcement   the effect of a positive reinforcer (stimulus event) soon after an operant (response)

positive reinforcer   a positive stimulus event that follows an operant and strengthens the associated behavioral response

positive symptom   a characteristic of a disorder, in which the individual shows an abnormal behavior (e.g., hallucinations or word salad)

positive transfer   the facilitation of problem solving as a result of prior experience in solving related or similar problems

posthypnotic suggestion   an instruction received during hypnosis, which the individual is to implement after having wakened, often despite having no recollection of having received the instruction

practical significance   the characterization of a result as having practical or everyday import

practice effect   the outcome of rehearsal, usually involving an improvement in recall or skill

pragmatics   the study of how people use language, emphasizing the contexts in which language is used

pragmatism   a school of psychology that focuses on the usefulness of knowledge

preconscious level   a level of consciousness comprising information that is accessible to, but not continuously available in, awareness

prefrontal lobotomy   an obsolete procedure in which the frontal lobes of the brain are cut off from contact with the rest of the brain, in order to make patients more compliant

prejudice   a negative attitude toward groups of individuals, based on limited or wrong information about those groups

preoperational stage   Piaget's second stage of development (about age 2 years until the age of starting elementary school), during which the child develops language and concepts about physical objects

primary appraisal   the first step in coping with a situation that may be stressful, involving analysis of how much the person will be affected by outcomes of the particular situation

primary-process thought   a form of thought that is unrealistic, irrational, and driven by instincts

primary reinforcer   a stimulus that provides an immediate reinforcement that satisfies the senses

priming   the enhanced access to a particular stimulus or item of information as a result of recent activation of, or exposure to, the same stimulus or a related one

problem-focused coping   adapting to a challenging situation by using strategies to fix the situation and to make it less challenging

problem solving   a set of processes for which the goal is to overcome obstacles obstructing the path to a solution

procedural knowledge   "knowing how"; skills that require a person to follow a set of steps to carry out a task

projective personality test   a method of personality assessment based on the psychodynamic approach, which attempts to reach people's unconscious or preconscious personality characteristics and conflicts through their imaginative (primary-process) responses to test items

prosocial behavior   actions that offer some benefit to society in general or to members within society and that are approved by most members of society

psychoactive drug   a drug (e.g., depressants, stimulants, opiates and opioids, or hallucinogenics) that produces a psychopharmacological effect, thereby affecting behavior, mood, and consciousness

psychobiology   a branch of psychology that seeks to understand behavior through studying anatomy and physiology, especially of the brain

psychodynamic psychology   a school of psychology that emphasizes the importance of (a) conflicting unconscious mental processes and (b) early childhood experiences

psychogenic pain   the discomfort for which an observed source of physical damage to bodily tissues has not been found

psychology   the study of the mind, behavior, and mind–behavior interactions of people and other organisms

psychometric   characterized by psychological measurement (*psycho-*, pertaining to the mind or mental processes; *-metric*, measurement)

psychoneuroimmunology   a cross-disciplinary field that blends psychology, *neurology* (the study of the brain and nervous system), and *immunology* (the study of the immune system), as well as physiology (e.g., the study of the endocrine system and other biological systems of the body)

psychopharmacological   a drug-induced influence on behavior, mood, and consciousness

psychophysics   the systematic study of the relationship between the physical stimulation of a sense organ and the psychological sensations produced by that stimulation

psychosurgery   a procedure intended to relieve psychological problems by probing, slicing, dissecting, or removing some part of the brain

psychotherapy   the use of psychological principles to treat mental disorders or otherwise to improve psychological adjustment and well-being

psychoticism   a personality trait characterized by isolation, lack of caring for or about others, lack of feeling and empathy, and insensitivity

psychotropic drug   any of several types of drugs that affect the psychological processes or state of mind of an individual

puberty   the period of physiological development during which males and females develop primary (i.e., functioning sex organs) and secondary sex characteristics (e.g., body hair and distinctive shape), thereby reaching sexual maturity

punishment the effect of the delivery of a stimulus event that *decreases* the probability of an associated response; results from either presenting an unpleasant stimulus or removing a pleasant one

pupil the hole in the iris (roughly in its center) through which light gains access to the interior of the eye, particularly the retina

quasi-experimental design a plan for conducting research that resembles a controlled experimental design but that does not ensure the random assignment of participants to the treatment and the control groups

questionnaire a set of questions used for conducting a survey

range the difference between the lowest and highest values in a distribution

ratio IQ a means of indicating performance on intelligence tests; expressed as a quotient of mental age divided by chronological age, times 100

rational-emotive therapy (RET) a form of cognitive therapy based on the notions that (a) incorrect or maladaptive thoughts lead to emotional and other psychological problems, and (b) changes in these thoughts lead to improvements in psychological well-being

rationalist person who believes that knowledge is most effectively acquired through reasoning

raw score the score on a given test in whatever units the test is originally scored

reaction range the broad limits within which a particular attribute (e.g., intelligence) may be expressed in various possible ways, given the inherited potential for expression of the attribute in the particular individual

reality principle the principle by which the ego tries to adapt to the real world while still satisfying psychic forces of both the id and the superego

reasoning a set of cognitive processes by which an individual may infer a conclusion from an assortment of evidence or from statements of principles

recall the production of an item from memory

receptor a physiological structure designed to receive something (e.g., a given substance or a particular kind of information), such as sensory information from the sense organs

receptor cell a body cell that is especially suited to detecting and transforming a particular kind of energy that reaches the cell

recessive trait the weaker expression of a genetic trait in a pair of traits, which appears in the phenotype when the genotype comprises two recessive expressions of the trait

reciprocal determinism an interaction in which personal variables and environmental variables both influence and are influenced by the behavior of the individual

recognition the identification of an item as one that was previously stored in memory

reconstructive memory the phenomenon by which people encode, store, and retrieve only the sensations and events they have experienced

reflex an automatic physiological response to an external stimulus, which occurs directly through the spinal cord

rehearsal the repeated reciting of information or the repetition of a procedure

reinforcer a *stimulus* event that increases the probability that the operant associated with it will be repeated

reliability the dependability of a measurement instrument (e.g., a test), indicating that the instrument consistently measures the outcome being measured

REM sleep the distinctive kind of sleep that is characterized by rapid eye movements (REMs) and that is frequently associated with dreaming

representational thought the thinking that involves mental images, such as images of tangible objects

representative sample a subset of a population, carefully chosen to represent the proportionate diversity of the population

repression a Freudian defense mechanism, by which a person keeps troublesome internally generated thoughts and feelings from entering consciousness and thereby causing internal conflicts or other psychological discomfort

research design a way of choosing and interrelating a set of experimental variables and of selecting and assigning participants to experimental and control conditions

resistance a defensive tactic used by patients, usually unconsciously, to keep from becoming aware of unconscious material that affects the progress of therapy

resistant-attachment pattern a pattern in which a child generally shows ambivalence toward the mother while she is present, seeking both to gain and to resist physical contact with her when the mother returns after being gone a short time; one of three attachment patterns observed in the strange situation

reticular activating system a complex network of neurons essential to the regulation of consciousness and to such vital functions as heartbeat and breathing

retina a network of neurons covering most of the rear surface inside the eye, contains the photoreceptors that transduce light energy into electrochemical energy

retrieval the recovery of information from memory for active use or awareness

retrograde amnesia a memory loss that affects the purposeful retrieval of events that occurred before an injury causing memory loss, without any effect on the ability to form new memories; one meaning of *retro-* is "backward"; people with retrograde amnesia forget information stored prior to the injury

rod a long, thin, and abundant type of photoreceptor, responsible mostly for vision in dim lighting

satisficing a decision-making strategy in which an individual chooses the first acceptable alternative that becomes available, without considering all possible alternative options

schedules of reinforcement the patterns by which reinforcements follow operants

schema the cognitive framework for organizing information about a particular concept

schizophrenia a set of psychological disorders involving various perceptual symptoms (e.g., hallucinations), cognitive symptoms (e.g., disturbed thought content or processes), mood symptoms (e.g., lack of appropriate emotional expression), and sometimes even bizarre motor symptoms

secondary appraisal the process of assessing what can be done about a challenging situation to make it more likely that positive outcomes will result and less likely that harmful outcomes will result

secondary-process thought a form of thought that is rational and realistic

secondary reinforcer a stimulus that gains reinforcing value through association with a primary reinforcer

secondary trait a personality characteristic that has some influence on behavior but that is not very important to the personality and behavior of the individual

secure-attachment pattern a pattern in which a child generally shows preferential interest in, but not excessive dependence on, the attention of the mother while she is present and in which the child shows some distress when the mother leaves but can be calmed and reassured by her when she returns; one of three attachment patterns observed in the strange situation

sedative–hypnotics   one of the two primary types of CNS depressants, used to calm anxiety and to relieve insomnia

selective attention   the conscious attempt to perceive some stimuli (e.g., the voice and gestures of a speaker) and to ignore others (e.g., background noises and sights)

self-concept   an individual's beliefs, understandings, and judgments about her- or himself

self-determination theory   a theory suggesting that people need to feel that they can control their own destiny, that they are independent and competent, yet that they are still closely tied to other people

self-efficacy   an individual's belief in her or his own competence to master the environment and to reach personal goals

self-handicapping   the tendency to take actions to undermine our own performance in order to have an excuse in case we fail

self-perception theory   the suggestion that when we are not sure of what we believe, we view our behavior much as an outsider might view our behavior, and then infer our beliefs, based on our actions

self-serving biases   the tendency to be generous to ourselves when interpreting our own actions, pointing to personal causes when we do well and to situational causes when we do poorly

self theory   a humanistic theory of personality, in which the person's match between the perceived ideal self and real self is considered central to personality

semantic memory   the memory for general knowledge of facts that are not linked to particular personal experiences and that organizes internal representations of concepts

semantics   the study of the meanings of words in language

sensation   a message regarding physical stimulation of a sensory receptor

sense   a physical system for receiving a particular kind of physical stimulation and translating that stimulation into an electrochemical message

sensitization   the paradoxical phenomenon in which an intermittent user of a drug actually demonstrates heightened sensitivity to low doses of the drug

sensorimotor stage   Piaget's first stage of development (about the first 2 years after birth), during which the child builds on reflexes and develops the first mental representations of things that are not being sensed at the moment

sensory coding   the physiological form of communication through which sensory receptors convey a range of information about stimuli within the nervous system

sensory memory   the storage of very limited amounts of information for about a fraction of a second

sensory neuron   a nerve cell that receives information from the environment through sensory receptors and then carries that information toward the central nervous system

separation anxiety   the fear of being separated from a primary caregiver, such as a parent

serial processing   information processing in which operations occur sequentially

sexual disorders   psychological disorders involving problems with sexual arousal, thoughts, or behavior that distresses the individual or other persons

sexual script   a mental representation regarding how sexual behavior should be carried out during various episodes of sexual interaction

shape   bring behavior under control by providing a program of reinforcement

short-term memory   the relatively brief memory storage of about seven items

signal detection theory (SDT)   a method of measuring the detection of a sensation, which takes into account the influence of expectations and decision making on detection

simulating paradigm   a research technique for determining the true effects of a psychological treatment (e.g., hypnosis); one group of participants is subjected to the treatment and another group (a control group) does not receive the treatment but is asked to simulate the behavior of persons who do; observers try to distinguish the behavior of the treatment group from that of the control group trying to simulate the treatment group's behavior

situational attribution   a mental explanation pointing to the cause of behavior as lying within the situation (external) in which the individual shows the behavior

skin senses   the means by which we become sensitive to pressure, temperature, and pain stimulation directly on the skin

sleep apnea   a breathing disturbance that occurs during sleep, in which the sleeper repeatedly stops breathing during sleep; a sleep disorder

social categorization   the tendency to sort people into groups, according to various characteristics the observer perceives to be common to members of each group

social cognition   the thoughts and beliefs we have regarding ourselves and other people, based on how we perceive and interpret information that we either observe directly or learn from other people

social desirability bias   the tendency, when trying to infer the dispositions of people, to give undeservedly heavy weight to socially undesirable behavior

social facilitation   the phenomenon in which the presence of other people positively influences the performance of an individual

social interference   the phenomenon in which the presence of other people negatively influences the performance of an individual

social learning   the learning that occurs by observing the behavior of others, as well as by observing any environmental outcomes of the behavior

social loafing   the phenomenon in which each individual member of a group puts forth less effort as the size of the group increases

social psychology   the study of how each person's thoughts, feelings, and behaviors are affected by the presence of others, even if that presence is only implied or imagined

socioemotional development   the process by which people learn about themselves as human beings, as well as the process by which they learn to interact with each other, across the life span; may be viewed as including emotional, personality, interpersonal (social), and moral development

soma   the part of the neuron that performs vital functions for the life of the cell

somatoform disorders   psychological disorders in which people experience bodily symptoms for which no physiological basis has been found

somnambulism   a disorder characterized by sleepwalking

source trait   one of a relatively few underlying psychological dimensions of personality that generate the numerous surface traits

spinal cord   a slender, roughly cylindrical bundle of interconnected neural fibers, which is enclosed within the spinal column and which extends through the center of the back, starting at the brain and ending at the lower end of the small of the back

spontaneous recovery   the disappearance of a person's symptoms, which occurs without any treatment whatsoever

standard deviation   a measure related to the average variation of values around the mean

standardization   the administration of a test in a way that ensures that the conditions for taking the test are the same for all test-takers

statistical significance   characterization of a result as unlikely to be true under the null hypothesis

stereotype   a perceived typical example that illustrates the main characteristics of a particular social category, usually based on the assumption that the typical example uniformly represents all examples of the social category

stimulus discrimination   a response to the observed difference between a new stimulus and the original CS, which makes it less likely that the new stimulus will lead to the CR

stimulus generalization   a response to the observed similarity of a stimulus to the CS, which increases the likelihood that the CR will occur following presentation of the stimulus

storage   the keeping of encoded information in memory

strange situation   an experimental technique for observing attachment in young children

stress   a person's response to the presence of something in the environment that causes the person to feel challenged in some way

stress response   an adaptation to challenging changes in the environment

stressor   an event or situation that causes stress

Stroop effect   the interference experienced in selectively attending to one sensory stimulus (e.g., the color of the ink) while trying to ignore another sensory stimulus (e.g., the word that is printed with the ink of a different color)

structuralism   the first major school of thought in psychology, which focuses on analyzing the components of the mind, such as particular sensations

subconscious level   a level of consciousness that involves less awareness than full conscious awareness and from which information is not easily pulled into the conscious mind

subliminal perception   a form of preconscious processing in which people may have the ability to detect information without being fully aware that they are doing so

subtractive mixture   the remaining combined wavelengths of light that are reflected from an object after other wavelengths of light have been absorbed (subtracted from the reflected light) by the object

successive approximations   a method for shaping behavior by gradually reinforcing operants that are increasingly more similar to the desired behavior

superego   a personality structure that is unconscious and irrational, based on the rules and prohibitions we have internalized from interactions with our parents

surface trait   one of many personality features that characterize differences among people

survey   a method of observing various people's responses to questions regarding their beliefs and opinions

synapse   the area comprising the interneuronal gap, the terminal buttons of one neuron's axon, and the dendrites (or sometimes the soma) of the next neuron

syntax   a level of linguistic analysis, which centers on the patterns by which users of a particular language put words together at the level of the sentence

synthesis   the process of integrating various elements into a more complex whole

taste bud   clusters of taste receptor cells located on the tongue

telegraphic speech   the rudimentary syntactical communications of two or more words, which are characteristic of very early language acquisition, and which seem more like telegrams than like conversation because function morphemes are usually omitted

temperament   a person's distinctive tendency to show a particular mood and a particular intensity and duration of emotions

test   a method for measuring a given ability or attribute in particular individuals at a particular time and in a particular place

test of statistical significance   a test that tells us the probability that a given result would be obtained were only chance at work

thalamus   a brain structure that primarily serves as a relay station for sensory information

theory   a statement of general principles explaining one or more phenomena (events or processes)

theory of multiple intelligences   a theory suggesting that there are eight distinct intelligences that function somewhat independently: linguistic, logical–mathematical, spatial, musical, bodily–kinesthetic, interpersonal, intrapersonal, and naturalist intelligence

thinking   a psychological function that involves the creation and organization of information in the mind

threshold of excitation   the level of electrochemical stimulation at or above which an action potential may be generated, but below which an action potential cannot be generated

tip-of-the-tongue phenomenon   an experience of preconsciousness, in which a person cannot successfully retrieve information known to be stored in memory

tolerance   a consequence of prolonged use of psychoactive drugs, in which the drug user feels decreasing psychopharmacological effects of a given drug at one level of dosage and must take increasing amounts of drugs in order to achieve the same effects, eventually reaching such a high level that further increases will cause overdose

trait   a stable characteristic that distinguishes each person

tranquilizers   one of the sedative–hypnotic drugs used to combat anxiety; considered to be safer than barbiturates, although the potential for drug dependency remains problematic

transduce   the conversion of incoming energy from one form (e.g., mechanical, chemical, electromagnetic) into an electrochemical form of energy for use within the nervous system

transference   a term used in psychodynamic therapy describing a patient's emotional involvement with the psychotherapist as an authority figure

triangular theory of love   a theory suggesting that love has three basic components: intimacy, passion, and commitment

triarchic theory of human intelligence   a theory of intelligence, which asserts that intelligence comprises three aspects (analytical, creative, and practical)

two-component theory of emotion   a theory asserting that particular emotions have two parts: a feeling of physiological arousal in response to a stimulus, and the cognitive labeling of the physiological arousal as a particular emotion

Type-A behavior pattern   a personality characterized by *high* levels of hostility, as well as by the *pursuit* of competition and time pressure

Type-B behavior pattern   a personality characterized by *low* levels of hostility, as well as by the *avoidance* of competition and time pressure

unconditional positive regard   the interpersonal feelings of acceptance, affection, appreciation, or esteem, which are not based on any conditions that the object of regard must meet

unconditioned response (UR)   an automatic physiological or emotional response to a US

unconditioned stimulus (US)   a stimulus that elicits a physiological or emotional response

unconscious   the portion of the mind that lies outside of our awareness and that we cannot pull into our awareness

validity   the extent to which a given form of measurement assesses what it is supposed to measure

verbal comprehension   the ability to comprehend written and spoken (or signed) linguistic input, such as words, sentences, and paragraphs

verbal fluency   the ability to produce written and spoken linguistic output, such as words, sentences, and paragraphs

vestibular system   the sense of balance, governed by receptors in the inner ear, which detect the position and movement of the head, relative to a source of gravity

well-structured problem   a problem with a well-defined path to a solution

withdrawal   the temporary discomfort, which may be extremely unpleasant and sometimes even life-threatening, associated with a reduction or discontinuation of the use of a psychoactive drug, during which the drug user's physiology and mental processes must adjust to an absence of the drug

working memory   an activated portion of long-term memory, as well as a means for moving activated elements into and out of short-term memory

zone of proximal development (ZPD)   a range between the developed abilities that a child clearly shows and the latent capacities that the child might be able to show, given the appropriate environment in which to do so

zygote   an individual in the first of three stages of prenatal development (from the time of conception to implantation and cell differentiation)

Abel, E. L. (1984). *Fetal alcohol syndrome and fetal alcohol effects.* New York: Plenum.

Abrams, R. (1988). *Electroconvulsive treatment: It apparently works, but how and at what risks are not yet clear.* New York: Oxford University Press.

Abramson, L. Y., Metalsky, G. I., & Alloy, L. B. (1989). Hopelessness depression: A theory-based subtype of depression. *Psychological Review, 96*(2), 358–372.

Adams, M. J. (Ed.). (1986). *Odyssey: A curriculum for thinking* (Vols. 1–6). Watertown, MA: Charlesbridge.

Ader, R., & Cohen, N. (1991). The influence of conditioning on immune responses. In R. Ader, D. L. Felten, & N. Cohen (Eds.), *Psychoneuroimmunology* (2nd ed., pp. 611–646). San Diego, CA: Academic Press.

Ader, R., & Cohen, N. (1993). Psychoneuroimmunology: Conditioning and stress. *Annual Review of Psychology, 44,* 53–85.

Ader, R., Felten, D. L., & Cohen, N. (1990). Interactions between the brain and the immune system. *Annual Review of Pharmacology & Toxicology, 30,* 561–602.

Ader, R., Felten, D. L., & Cohen, N. (Eds.). (1991). *Psychoneuroimmunology* (2nd ed.). San Diego, CA: Academic Press.

Adler, J. (1991, July 22). The melting of a mighty myth. *Newsweek,* p. 63.

Adler, T. (1989). Cocaine babies face behavior deficits. *APA Monitor, 20,* 14.

Agnew, J. (1985). Man's purgative passion. *American Journal of Psychotherapy, 39*(2), 236–246.

Ainsworth, M. D. S., Bell, S. M., & Stayton, D. J. (1971). Individual differences in strange-situation behavior in one-year-olds. In H. R. Schaffer (Ed.), *The origins of human social relations.* London: Academic Press.

Ainsworth, M. D. S., Blehar, M., Waters, E., & Wall, S. (1978). *Patterns of attachment.* Hillsdale, NJ: Erlbaum.

Aldous, J. L. (1994). Cross-cultural counseling and cross-cultural meanings: An exploration of Morita psychotherapy. *Canadian Journal of Counselling, 28*(3), 238–249.

Allport, G. W. (1935). Attitudes. In C. M. Murchison (Ed.), *Handbook of social psychology.* Worcester, MA: Clark University Press.

Allport, G. W. (1937). *Personality: A psychological interpretation.* New York: Holt, Rinehart and Winston.

Allport, G. W. (1954). *The nature of prejudice.* Reading, MA: Addison-Wesley.

Allport, G. W. (1961). *Pattern and growth in personality.* New York: Holt, Rinehart and Winston.

Allport, G. W. (1985). The historical background of social psychology. In G. Lindzey & E. Aronson (Eds.), *Handbook of social psychology* (3rd ed., Vol. 1, pp. 1–46). New York: Random House.

Allport, G. W., & Postman, L. J. (1947). *The psychology of rumor.* New York: Henry Holt.

Alpert, B., Field, T., Goldstein, S., & Perry, S. (1990). Aerobics enhances cardiovascular fitness and agility in preschoolers. *Health Psychology, 9,* 48–56.

Amabile, T. M. (1983). *The social psychology of creativity.* New York: Springer-Verlag.

Amabile, T. M. (1985). Motivation and creativity: Effects of motivational orientation on creative writers. *Journal of Personality and Social Psychology, 48,* 393–399.

American Association of University Women Educational Foundation and the Wellesley College Center for Research on Women. (1992). *The AAUW Report: How schools shortchange girls—A study of major findings on girls and education.* Washington, DC: Author.

American Psychiatric Association. (1994). *Diagnostic and statistical manual of mental disorders* (4th ed.). Washington, DC: Author.

Amir, Y., & Sharon, I. (1987). Are social-psychological laws cross-culturally valid? *Journal of Cross-Cultural Psychology, 18,* 383–470.

Amoore, J. E. (1970). *Molecular basis of odor.* Springfield, IL: Thomas.

Amsel, A. (1992). B. F. Skinner and the cognitive revolution. *Journal of Behavior Therapy & Experimental Psychiatry, 23*(2), 67–70.

Anand, B. K., & Brobeck, J. R. (1951). Hypothalamic control of food intake in rats and cats. *Yale Journal of Biology and Medicine, 24,* 123–140.

Anand, B. K., Chhina, G. S., & Singh, B. (1962). Effect of glucose on the activity of hypothalamic "feeding centers." *Science, 138,* 597–598.

Anderson, C. A. (1987). Temperature and aggression: Effects on quarterly, yearly, and city rates of violent and nonviolent crime. *Journal of Personality and Social Psychology, 52,* 1161–1173.

Anderson, C. A. (1989). Temperature and aggression: Ubiquitous effects of heat on occurrence of human violence. *Psychological Bulletin, 106*(1), 74–96.

Anderson, J. R., & Bower, G. H. (1973). *Human associative memory.* New York: Wiley.

Anderson, K. L. (1990). Arousal and the inverted-U hypothesis: A critique of Neiss's "Reconceptualizing arousal." *Psychological Bulletin, 107,* 96–100.

Anderson, K. O., & Masur, F. T., III. (1983). Psychological preparation for invasive medical and dental procedures. *Journal of Behavioral Medicine, 6,* 1–40.

Andersson, B. E. (1989). Effects of public daycare: A longitudinal study. *Child Development, 60,* 857–866.

Andreasen, N. C., Olsen, S. A., Dennert, J. W., & Smith, M. R. (1982). Ventricular enlargement in schizophrenia: Definition and prevalence. *American Journal of Psychiatry, 139,* 292–296.

Andrews, G. (1993). The benefits of psychotherapy. In N. Sartorius, G. de Girolano, G. Andrews, G. A. German, & L. Eisenberg (Eds.), *Treatment of mental disorders: A review of effectiveness.* Geneva, Switzerland, and Washington, DC: World Health Organization and American Psychiatric Press.

Andrich, D., & Styles, I. (1994). Psychometric evidence of intellectual growth spurts in early adolescence. *Journal of Early Adolescence, 14,* 328–344.

Antrobus, J. (1978). Dreaming for cognition. In A. Arkin, J. Antrobus, & S. Ellman (Eds.), *The mind in sleep: Psychology and psychophysiology* (pp. 569–581). Hillsdale, NJ: Erlbaum.

Antrobus, J. (1991). Dreaming: Cognitive processes during cortical activation and high afferent thresholds. *Psychological Review, 98,* 91–121.

Argyle, M. (1992). *The social psychology of everyday life.* New York: Routledge.

Aristotle. (1987). *The works of Aristotle* (Vol. 1). Chicago, IL: Encyclopaedia Britannica.(Original work ca. 335 B.C.)

Arkes, H. R., Bohem, L. E., & Xu, G. (1991). The determinants of judged validity. *Journal of Experimental Social Psychology, 27,* 576–605.

Arnold, M. B. (1960). *Emotion and personality* (Vols. 1–2). New York: Columbia University Press.

Arnold, M. B. (1970). Perennial problems in the field of emotion. In M. B. Arnold (Ed.), *Feelings and emotions* (pp. 169–185). New York: Academic Press.

Asch, S. E. (1951). Effects of group pressure upon the modification and distortion of judgments. In H. Guetzkow (Ed.), *Groups, leadership, and men.* Pittsburgh: Carnegie.

Asch, S. E. (1952). *Social psychology.* New York: Prentice-Hall.

Asch, S. E. (1955). Opinions and social pressure. *Scientific American, 193,* 31–35.

Asch, S. E. (1956). Studies of independence and conformity: A minority of one against a unanimous majority. *Psychological Monographs, 70,* 416.

Atkinson, D. R., Casa, A., & Abreu, J. (1992). Mexican American acculturation, counselor ethnicity and cultural sensitivity, and perceived counselor competence. *American Psychologist, 39,* 515–520.

Atkinson, D. R., Furlong, M. J., & Poston, W. C. (1986). Afro-American preferences for counselor characteristics. *Journal of Counseling Psychology, 33,* 326–330.

Atkinson, D. R., Ponce, F. Q., & Martinez, F. M. (1984). Effects of ethnic, sex, and attitude similarity on counselor credibility. *Journal of Counseling Psychology, 31,* 588–590.

Atkinson, J. W. (Ed.). (1958). *Motives in fantasy, action, and society.* Princeton, NJ: Van Nostrand.

Atkinson, J. W. (1964). *Introduction to motivation.* New York: Van Nostrand.

Atkinson, R. C., & Shiffrin, R. M. (1968). Human memory: A proposed system and its control processes. In K. W. Spence & J. T. Spence (Eds.), *The psychology of learning and motivation: Advances in research and theory* (Vol. 2). New York: Academic Press.

Atkinson, R. C., & Shiffrin, R. M. (1971). The control of short-term memory. *Scientific American, 225,* 82–90.

Averill, J. R. (1980). A constructivist view of emotion. In R. Plutchik & H. Kellerman (Eds.), *Emotion: Theory, research, and experience: Vol. 1 Theories of emotion* (pp. 305–339). New York: Academic Press.

Averill, J. R. (1983). Studies on anger and aggression: Implications for theories of emotions. *American Psychologist, 38,* 1145–1160.

Axelson, J. A. (1993). *Counseling and development in a multicultural society* (2nd ed.). Pacific Grove, CA: Brooks/Cole.

Axline, V. (1964). *Dibs: In search of self.* New York: Ballantine.

Baddeley, A. D. (1966). Short-term memory for word sequences as function of acoustic, semantic, and formal similarity. *Quarterly Journal of Experimental Psychology, 18,* 362–365.

Baddeley, A. D. (1989). The psychology of remembering and forgetting. In T. Butler (Ed.), *Memory: History, culture and the mind.* London: Basil Blackwell.

Baddeley, A. D. (1990a). *Human memory.* Hove, England: Erlbaum.

Baddeley, A. D. (1990b). *Human memory: Theory and practice.* Needham Heights, MA: Allyn & Bacon.

Baddeley, A. D. (1993). *Your memory: A user's guide.* London: Prion, Multimedia Books.

Bahrick, H. P., Bahrick, P. O., & Wittlinger, R. P. (1975). Fifty years of memory for names and faces: A cross-sectional approach. *Journal of Experimental Psychology: General, 104,* 54–75.

Bahrick, H. P., & Phelps, E. (1987). Retention of Spanish vocabulary over eight years. *Journal of Experimental Psychology: Learning Memory and Cognition, 13,* 344–349.

Bailey, J. M., & Pillard, R. C. (1991). A genetic study of male sexual orientation. *Archives of General Psychiatry, 48*(12), 1089–1096.

Baillargeon, R., & DeVos, J. (1991). Object permanence in young infants: Further evidence. *Child Development, 62,* 1227–1246.

Baldwin, B. A., De la Riva, C., & Ebenezer, I. S. (1990). Effects of intracerebroventricular injection of dynorphin, leumorphin, and a neoendorphin on operant feeding in pigs. *Physiology and Behavior, 48,* 821–824.

Bales, R. F. (1950). Interaction process analysis: A method for the study of small groups. Reading, MA: Addison-Wesley.

Bales, R. F. (1970). *Personality and interpersonal behavior.* New York: Holt, Rinehart and Winston.

Balkin, J. (1988). Why policemen don't like policewomen. *Journal of Police Science and Administration, 16*(1), 29–38.

Bandura, A. (1965). Influence of models' reinforcement contingencies on the acquisition of imitative responses. *Journal of Personality and Social Psychology, 1,* 589–595.

Bandura, A. (1969). *Principles of behavior modification.* New York: Holt, Rinehart and Winston.

Bandura, A. (1973). *Aggression: A social learning analysis.* Englewood Cliffs, NJ: Prentice-Hall.

Bandura, A. (1977a). Self-efficacy: Toward a unifying theory of behavioral change. *Psychological Review, 84,* 181–215.

Bandura, A. (1977b). *Social learning theory.* Englewood Cliffs, NJ: Prentice-Hall.

Bandura, A. (1983). Psychological mechanisms of aggression. In R. G. Geen & E. I. Donnerstein (Eds.), *Aggression: Theoretical and empirical reviews: Vol. I. Theoretical and methodological issues* (pp. 1–40). New York: Academic Press.

Bandura, A. (1986). *Social foundations of thought and action: A social cognitive theory.* Englewood Cliffs, NJ: Prentice-Hall.

Bandura, A. (1988). Self-efficacy conception of anxiety. *Anxiety Research, 1*(2), 77–98.

Bandura, A. (1993). Perceived self-efficacy in cognitive development and functioning. Annual meeting of the American Educational Research Association, San Francisco, California. *Educational Psychologist, 28*(2), 117–148.

Bandura, A. (1996). *Self-efficacy: The exercise of control.* New York: Freeman.

Bandura, A., Blanchard, E. B., & Ritter, B. (1969). Relative efficacy of desensitization and modelling approaches for inducing behavioral, affective, and attitudinal changes. *Journal of Personality and Social Psychology, 13,* 173–199.

Bandura, A., Ross, D., & Ross, S. A. (1963). Imitation of film-mediated aggressive models. *Journal of Abnormal and Social Psychology, 66,* 3–11.

Bandura, A., & Walters, R. H. (1963). *Social learning and personality development.* New York: Ronald Press.

Banks, M. S., & Salapatek, P. (1983). Infant visual perception. In M. M. Haith & J. J. Campos (Eds.), *Handbook of child psychology: Infancy and developmental psychobiology* (4th ed., Vol. 2). New York: Wiley.

Barber, T. X. (1964a). Hypnotic "colorblindness," "blindness," and "deafness." *Diseases of the Nervous System, 25,* 529–537.

Barber, T. X. (1964b). Toward a theory of "hypnotic" behavior: Positive visual and auditory hallucinations. *Psychological Record, 14,* 197–210.

Bard, P. (1934). On emotional experience after decortication with some remarks on theoretical views. *Psychological Review, 41,* 309–329.

Barefoot, J. C., Dahlstrom, W. G., & Williams, R. B. (1983). Hostility, CHD incidence and total mortality: A 25-year follow-up study of 255 physicians. *Psychosomatic Medicine, 45,* 559–563.

Berry, D. S., & McArthur, L. Z. (1986). Perceiving character in faces: The impact of age-related craniofacial changes on social perception. *Psychological Bulletin, 100*(1), 3–18.

Berry, J. W., Poortinga, Y. H., Segall, M. H., & Dasen, P. R. (1992). *Cross-cultural psychology.* New York: Cambridge University Press.

Berry, S. L., Beatty, W. W., & Klesges, R. C. (1985). Sensory and social influences on ice cream consumption by males and females in a laboratory setting. *Appetite, 6,* 41–45.

Berscheid, E., & Walster, E. (1974). A little bit about love. In T. Huston (Ed.), *Foundations of interpersonal attraction.* New York: Academic Press.

Bexton, W. H., Heron, W., & Scott, T. H. (1954). Effects of decreased variation in the sensory environment. *Canadian Journal of Psychology, 8,* 70–76.

Bezooijen, R. V., Otto, S. A., & Heenan, T. A. (1983). Recognition of vocal expressions of emotion: A three-nation study to identify universal characteristics. *Journal of Cross-Cultural Psychology, 14,* 387–406.

Bialystok, E., & Hakuta, K. (1994*). In other words: The science and psychology of second-language acquisition.* New York: Basic Books.

Bickman, L. (1996). A continuum of care: More is not always better. *American Psychologist, 51.*

Bickman, L., Guthrie, P. R., Foster, E. M., Lambert, E. W., Summerfelt, W. T., Breda, C. S., & Heflinger, C. A. (1995). *Evaluating managed mental health services: The Fort Bragg Experiment.* New York: Plenum.

Biederman, I. (1987). Recognition-by-components: A theory of human image understanding. *Psychological Review, 94,* 115–147.

Biery, R. E. (1990). *Understanding homosexuality: The pride and the prejudice.* Austin, TX: Edward-William.

Binet, A., & Simon, T. (1916). *The development of intelligence in children* (E. S. Kite, Trans.). Baltimore: Williams & Wilkins.

Black, D. W., Goldstein, R. B., & Mason, E. E. (1992). Prevalence of mental disorder in 88 morbidly obese bariatric clinic patients. *American Journal of Psychiatry, 149,* 227–234.

Block, J. (1981). Some enduring and consequential structures of personality. In A. I. Rabin, J. Arnoff, A. M. Barclay, & R. A. Zucker (Eds.), *Further explorations in personality.* New York: Wiley.

Block, J. (1995). A contrarian view of the five-factor approach to personality description. *Psychological Bulletin, 117*(2), 187–215.

Block, M. A. (1970). Alcohol: Man and science. *New York State Journal of Medicine, 70*(21), 2732–2740.

Bloom, A. (1993). Silver water. In A. Bloom, *Come to me* (pp. 87–98), New York: HarperCollins.

Bloom, B. S. (1964). *Stability and change in human characteristics.* New York: Wiley.

Blumenthal, J. A., Emery, C. F., Walsh, M. A., Cox, D. R., Kuhn, C. M., Williams, R. B., & Williams, R. S. (1988). Exercise training in healthy Type A middle-aged men: Effects to behavioral and cardiovascular responses. *Psychosomatic Medicine, 50,* 418–433.

Bolger, N., & Eckenrode, J. (1991). Social relationships, personality, and anxiety during a major stressful event. *Journal of Personality & Social Psychology, 61*(3), 440–449.

Bolwig, T. G. (1993). Biological treatments other than drugs (electroconvulsive therapy, brain surgery, insulin therapy, and photo therapy). In N. Sartorius, G. de Girolano, G. Andrews, G. A. German, & L. Eisenberg (Eds.), *Treatment of mental disorders: A review of effectiveness.* Geneva, Switzerland, and Washington, DC: World Health Organization and American Psychiatric Press.

Bond, M. H. (Ed.). (1988). *The cross-cultural challenge to social psychology.* Newbury Park, CA: Sage.

Bond, M. R. (1979). *Pain: Its nature, analysis and treatment.* New York: Longman.

Bongiovanni, A. (1977). *A review of research on the effects of punishment in the schools.* Paper presented at the Conference on Child Abuse, Children's Hospital National Medical Center, Washington, DC.

Booth-Kewley, S., & Friedman, H. S. (1987). Psychological predictors of heart disease: A quantitative review. *Psychological Bulletin, 101,* 343–362.

Borbely, A. (1986). *Secrets of sleep.* New York: Basic Books.

Bornstein, M. H., & Bruner, J. S. (Eds.). (1989). *Interaction on human development: Crosscurrents in contemporary psychology services.* Hillsdale, NJ: Erlbaum.

Bornstein, M. H., & Krasgenor, N. A. (Eds.). (1989). *Stability and continuity in mental development: Behavioral and biological perspectives.* Hillsdale, NJ: Erlbaum.

Bornstein, M. H., & Sigman, M. D. (1986). Continuity in mental development from infancy. *Child Development, 57,* 251–274.

Borysenko, M., & Borysenko, J. (1982). Stress, behavior, and immunity: Animal models and mediating mechanisms. *General Hospital Psychiatry, 4,* 59–67.

Bothwell, R. K., Brigham, J. C., & Malpass, R. S. (1989). Cross-racial identification. *Personality & Social Psychology Bulletin, 15*(1), 19–25.

Bouchard, T. J. (1997). IQ similarity in twins reared apart: Findings and responses to critics. In R. J. Sternberg & E. L. Grigorenko (Eds.), *Intelligence, heredity, and environment* (pp. 126–160). New York: Cambridge University Press.

Bouchard, T. J., Lykken, D. T., McGue, M., Segal, N. L., & Tellegen, A. (1990). Sources of human psychological differences: The Minnesota study of twins reared apart. *Science, 205,* 223–228.

Bouchard, T. J., & McGue, M. (1981). Familial studies of intelligence: A review. *Science, 212,* 1055–1059.

Bower, G. H. (1981, February). Mood and memory. *American Psychologist, 36*(2), 129–148.

Bower, G. H. (1983). Affect and cognition. *Philosophical Transaction: Royal Society of London* (Series B), *302,* 387–402.

Bower, G. H., Karlin, M. B., & Dueck, A. (1975). Comprehension and memory for pictures. *Memory and Cognition, 3,* 216–220.

Bowers, K. S. (1973). Situationism in psychology: An analysis and critique. *Psychological Review, 80,* 307–336.

Bowers, K. S. (1976). *Hypnosis for the seriously curious.* New York: Norton.

Brand, C. (1996). *The g factor: General intelligence and its implications.* Chichester, England: Wiley.

Bransford, J. D., & Johnson, M. K. (1972). Contextual prerequisites for understanding: Some investigations of comprehension and recall. *Journal of Verbal Learning and Verbal Behavior, 11,* 717–726.

Braswell, L., & Kendall, P. C. (1988). Cognitive–behavioral methods with children. In K. S. Dobson (Ed.), *Handbook of cognitive–behavioral therapies.* New York: Guilford Press.

Brazelton, T. B. (1983). Precursors for the development of emotions in early infancy. In R. Plutchik & H. Kellerman (Eds.), *Emotion: Theory, research, and experience* (Vol. 2). New York: Academic Press.

Brehm, J. (1966). *A theory of psychological reactance.* New York: Academic Press.

Brehm, S. S., & Brehm, J. W. (1981). *Psychological reactance: A theory of freedom and control.* New York: Academic Press.

Brehm, S. S., & Kassin, S. M. (1990). *Social psychology.* Boston: Houghton Mifflin.

Breslow, L. (1983). The potential of health promotion. In D. Mechanic (Ed.), *Handbook of health, health care, and the health professions.* New York: Free Press.

Brewer, J. B., Zhao, Z., Desmond, J. E., Glover, G. H., & Gabrieli, J. D. E. (1998). Making memories: Brain activity that predicts how well visual experience will be remembered. *Science, 281,* 1185–1187.

Brigham, J. C., & Malpass, R. S. (1985). The role of experience and contact in the recognition of faces of own- and other-race persons. *Journal of Social Issues, 41*(3), 139–155.

Brislin, R. W. (1986). The wording and translation of research instruments. In W. J. Lonner & J. W. Berry (Eds.), *Field methods in cross-cultural research.* Newbury Park, CA: Sage.

Broadhurst, P. L. (1957). Emotionality and the Yerkes–Dodson law. *Journal of Experimental Psychology, 54,* 345–352.

Brody, N. (1990). Behavior therapy versus placebo: Comment on Bowers and Clum's meta-analysis. *Psychological Bulletin, 107,* 106–109.

Brosschot, J. F., Benschop, R. J., Godaert, G. L. R., Olff, M., et al. (1994). Influence of life stress on immunological reactivity to mild psychological stress. *Psychosomatic Medicine, 56*(3), 216–224.

Brown, J. A. (1958). Some tests of the decay theory of immediate memory. *Quarterly Journal of Experimental Psychology, 10,* 12–21.

Brown, R. (1965). *Social psychology.* New York: Free Press.

Brown, R. (1973). *A first language: The early stages.* Cambridge, MA: Harvard University Press.

Brown, R., & McNeill, D. (1966). The "tip of the tongue" phenomenon. *Journal of Verbal Learning and Verbal Behavior, 5,* 325–337.

Brownell, K. D., & Rodin, J. (1994). The dieting maelstrom: Is it possible and advisable to lose weight? *American Psychologist, 49,* 781–791.

Brownell, K. D., & Salovey, P. (1997). Health psychology: Where psychology, biology, and social factors intersect. In R. J. Sternberg (Ed.), *Career paths in psychology* (pp. 269–286). Washington, DC: American Psychological Association.

Bruch, H. (1973). *Eating disorders: Obesity, anorexia nervosa, and the person within.* New York: Basic Books.

Bruning, N. S., & Frew, D. R. (1987). Effects of exercise, relaxation, and management skills training on physiological stress indicators: A field experiment. *Journal of Applied Psychology, 72*(4), 515–521.

Burger, J. M. (1986). Increasing compliance by improving the deal: The that's-not-all technique. *Journal of Personality and Social Psychology, 51,* 277–283.

Burleson, B. R., & Denton, W. H. (1992). A new look at similarity and attraction in marriage: Similarities in social-cognitive and communication skills as predictors of attraction and satisfaction. *Communication Monographs, 59*(3), 268–287.

Burns, J. W., Hutt, J., & Weidner, G. (1993). Effects of demand and decision latitude on cardiovascular reactivity among coronary-prone women and men. *Behavioral Medicine, 19*(3), 122–128.

Burnstein, E., & Vinokur, A. (1973). Testing two classes of theories about group-induced shifts in individual choice. *Journal of Experimental Social Psychology, 9,* 123–137.

Burnstein, E., & Vinokur, A. (1977). Persuasive arguments and social comparison as determinates of attitude polarization. *Journal of Experimental Social Psychology, 13,* 315–332.

Buss, A. H. (1976). Aggression pays. In J. L. Singer (Ed.), *The control of aggression and violence: Cognitive and physiological factors.* New York: Academic Press.

Buss, D. M., & Schmitt, D. P. (1993). Sexual strategies theory: A contextual evolutionary analysis of human mating. *Psychological Review, 100,* 204–232.

Butcher, J. N., Dahlstrom, W. G., Graham, J. R., Tellegen, A., & Kaemmer, B. (1989). *Minnesota Multiphasic Personality Inventory (MMPI-2): Manual for administration and scoring.* Minneapolis, MN: University of Minnesota Press.

Butcher, J. N., & Williams, C. L. (1992). *Essentials of MMPI-2 and MMPI-A interpretation.* Minneapolis, MN: University of Minnesota Press.

Butler, J., & Rovee-Collier, C. (1989). Contextual gating of memory retrieval. *Developmental Psychobiology, 22,* 533–552.

Butler, R. A. (1953). Discrimination learning by rhesus monkeys to visual exploration motivation. *Journal of Comparative and Physiological Psychology, 46,* 95–98.

Byrne, R. (1995). *The thinking ape: Evolutionary origins of intelligence.* Oxford: Oxford University Press.

Byrnes, J. P. (1988). Formal operations: A systematic reformulation. *Developmental Review, 8,* 66–87.

Cacioppo, J. T., & Petty, R. E. (1979). Effects of message repetition and position on cognitive responses, recall, and persuasion. *Journal of Personality and Social Psychology, 37,* 97–109.

Cacioppo, J. T., & Petty, R. E. (1980). Persuasiveness of commercials is affected by exposure frequency and communicator cogency: A theoretical and empirical analysis. In J. H. Leigh & C. R. Martin (Eds.), *Current issues and research in advertising.* Ann Arbor: University of Michigan Press.

Cacioppo, J. T., & Petty, R. E. (1983). *Social psychophysiology: A sourcebook.* New York: Guilford Press.

Calfee, R. (1997). Learning about learning: Psychologists in schools of education. In R. J. Sternberg (Ed.), *Career paths in psychology* (pp. 31–47). Washington, DC: American Psychological Association.

Camara, W. J., & Schneider, D. L. (1994). Integrity tests. *American Psychologist, 49,* 112–119.

Cameron, J., & Pierce, W. D. (1994). Reinforcement, reward and intrinsic motivation: A meta-analysis. *Review of Educational Research, 64,* 363–423.

Campbell, D. T. (1960). Blind variation and selective retention in creative thought and other knowledge processes. *Psychological Review, 67,* 380–400.

Candland, D. K. (1977). The persistent problems of emotion. In D. K. Candland, J. P. Fell, E. Keen, A. I. Leshner, R. Plutchik, & R. M. Tarpy (Eds.), *Emotion* (pp. 1–84). Monterey, CA: Brooks/Cole.

Cannon, W. B. (1929). *Bodily changes in pain, hunger, fear, and rage, on account of recent researches into the function of emotional excitement* (2nd ed.). New York: Appleton.

Cantor, J., & Engle, R. W. (1993). Working memory capacity as long-term memory activation: An individual differences approach. *Journal of Experimental Psychology: Learning, Memory, and Cognition, 19*(5), 1101–1114.

Capaldi, E., & VandenBos, G. (1991). Taste, food exposure, and eating behavior. *Hospital and Community Psychiatry, 42,* 787–789.

Carlson, G., & Goodwin, F. K. (1973). The stages of mania: A longitudinal analysis of the manic episode. *Archives of General Psychiatry, 28*(2), 221–228.

Carlson, J. G., & Hatfield, E. (1992). *Psychology of emotion.* New York: Harcourt Brace Jovanovich.

Carraher, T. N., Carraher, D., & Schliemann, A. D. (1985). Mathematics in the streets and in the schools. *British Journal of Developmental Psychology, 3,* 21–29.

Carroll, D. W. (1986). *Psychology of language.* Monterey, CA: Brooks/Cole.

Carroll, J. B. (1993). *Human cognitive abilities: A survey of factor-analytic studies.* New York: Cambridge University Press.

Carson, R. C., & Butcher, J. N. (1992). *Abnormal psychology and modern life* (9th ed.). New York: HarperCollins.

Caspi, A., Bolger, N., & Eckenrode, J. (1987). Linking person and context in the daily stress process. *Journal of Personality & Social Psychology, 52*(1), 184–195.

Cattell, R. B. (1971). *Abilities and their structure, growth and action.* Boston: Houghton Mifflin.

Cattell, R. B. (1979). *Personality and learning theory.* New York: Springer.

Cattell, R. B. (1982). *The inheritance of personality and ability: Research methods and findings.* New York: Academic Press.

Cattell, R. B., Eber, H. W., & Tatsuoka, M. M. (1970). *Handbook for the Sixteen Personality Factor Questionnaire.* Champaign, IL: Institute for Personality and Ability Testing.

Ceci, S. J. (1990). *On intelligence . . . more or less.* Englewood Cliffs, NJ: Prentice-Hall.

Ceci, S. J. (1991). How much does schooling influence general intelligence and its cognitive components? A reassessment of the evidence. *Developmental Psychology, 27*(5), 703–722.

Ceci, S. J. (1996). *On intelligence . . . more or less* (Expanded ed.). Cambridge, MA: Harvard University Press.

Ceci, S. J., Bronfenbrenner, U., & Baker, J. G. (1988). Prospective remembering, temporal calibration, and context. In M. M. Grunberg, P. Morris, & U. R. Sykes (Eds.), *Practical aspects of memory: Current research and issues.* New York: Wiley.

Ceci, S. J., & Bruck, M. (1993). Suggestibility of the child witness: A historical review and synthesis. *Psychological Bulletin, 113,* 403–439.

Ceci, S. J., & Bruck, M. (1995). *Jeopardy in the courtroom.* Washington, DC: APA Books.

Ceci, S. J., Nightingale, N. N., & Baker, J. G. (1992). In D. K. Detterman (Ed.), *Current topics in human intelligence: Vol. 2. Is mind modular or unitary?* (pp. 61–82). Norwood, NJ: Ablex.

Ceci, S. J., & Roazzi, A. (1994). The effects of context on cognition: Postcards from Brazil. In R. J. Sternberg & R. K. Wagner (Eds.), *Mind in context: Interactionist perspectives on human intelligence.* New York: Cambridge University Press.

Cerella, J. (1985). Information processing rates in the elderly. *Psychological Bulletin, 98,* 67–83.

Chaiken, S., & Eagly, A. (1983). Communication modality as a determinant of persuasion: The role of communicator salience. *Journal of Personality and Social Psychology, 45,* 241–256.

Chambless, D. L. (1995). Training in and dissemination of empirically validated psychological treatments: Report and recommendations. *The Clinical Psychologist, 48,* 3–24.

Chapman, L. J., & Chapman, J. P. (1969). Illusory correlation as an obstacle to the use of valid psychodiagnostic signs. *Journal of Abnormal Psychology, 74,* 271–280.

Chase, W. G., & Simon, H. A. (1973). The mind's eye in chess. In W. G. Chase (Ed.), *Visual information processing* (pp. 215–281). New York: Academic Press.

Chasnoff, I. J., Griffith, D. R., MacGregor, S., Dirkes, K., & Burns, K. (1989). Temporal patterns of cocaine use in pregnancy. *Journal of the American Medical Association, 261,* 1741–1744.

Cherry, E. C. (1953). Some experiments on the recognition of speech with one and two ears. *Journal of the Acoustical Society of America, 25,* 975–979.

Chi, M. T. H., Glaser, R., & Farr, M. (Eds.). (1988). *The nature of expertise.* Hillsdale, NJ: Erlbaum.

Chi, M. T. H., & Koeske, R. D. (1983). Network representations of a child's dinosaur knowledge. *Developmental Psychology, 19,* 29–39.

Chomsky, N. (1957). *Syntactic structures.* The Hague, The Netherlands: Mouton.

Chomsky, N. (1959). [Review of the book *Verbal behavior*]. *Language, 35,* 26–58.

Chorney, M. J., Chorney, K., Seese, N., Owen, M. J., Daniels, J., McGuffin, P., Thompson, L. A., Detterman, D. K., Benbow, C., Lubinski, D., Eley, T., & Plomin, R. (1998). A quantitative trait locus associated with cognitive ability in children. *Psychological Science, 9,* 159–166.

Cialdini, R. B. (1988). *Influence: Science and practice* (2nd ed.). Glenview, IL: Scott, Foresman/Little, Brown.

Cialdini, R. B., Cacioppo, J. R., Bassett, R., & Miller, J. A. (1978). Low-ball procedure for producing compliance: Commitment and cost. *Journal of Personality and Social Psychology, 36,* 463–476.

Cialdini, R. B., Vincent, J. E., Lewis, S. K., Catalan, J., Wheeler, D., & Darby, B. L. (1975). Reciprocal concessions procedure for inducing compliance: The door-in-the-face technique. *Journal of Personality and Social Psychology, 31,* 206–215.

Ciompi, L., & Eisert, M. (1969). Mortality and causes of death in alcoholics. *Social Psychiatry, 4*(4), 159–168.

Clark, H. H., & Chase, W. G. (1972). On the process of comparing sentences against pictures. *Cognitive Psychology, 3,* 472–517.

Clark, H. H., & Clark, E. V. (1977). *Psychology and language: An introduction to psycholinguistics.* New York: Harcourt Brace Jovanovich.

Clarke-Stewart, K. A. (1989). Infant day care: Maligned or malignant? *American Psychologist, 44,* 266–273.

Clore, G. L., & Byrne, D. (1974). A reinforcement-affect model of attraction. In T. L. Huston (Ed.), *Foundations of interpersonal attraction* (pp. 143–170). New York: Academic Press.

Cofer, C. N., & Appley, M. H. (1964). *Motivation: Theory and research.* New York: Wiley.

Cohen, J. (1981). Can human irrationality be experimentally demonstrated? *Behavioral and Brain Sciences, 4,* 317–331.

Cohen, N., Moynihan, J. A., Grota, L. J., & Ader, R. (1991). Behavioral and immunological evidence of reciprocal signaling between the immune system and the central nervous system. In R. C. A. Frederickson, J. L. McGaugh, & D. L. Felten (Eds.), *Peripheral signaling of the brain: Role in neural-immune interactions and learning and memory: Vol. 6. Neuronal control of bodily function: Basic and clinical aspects* (pp. 37–54). Lewiston, NY: Hogrefe & Huber.

Cohen, S., Kamarck, T., & Mermelstein, R. (1983). A global measure of perceived stress. *Journal of Health & Social Behavior, 24*(4), 385–396.

Cole, J. O., & Bodkin, J. A. (1990). Antidepressant drug side effects. *Journal of Clinical Psychiatry, 51,* 21–26.

Cole, M., Gay, J., Glick, J., & Sharp, D. W. (1971). *The cultural context of learning and thinking.* New York: Basic Books.

Collier, G. (1994). *Social origins of mental ability.* New York: Wiley.

Condry, J. (1977). Enemies of exploration: Self-initiated versus other-initiated learning. *Journal of Personality and Social Psychology, 18,* 105–115.

Conrad, R. (1964). Acoustic confusions in immediate memory. *British Journal of Psychology, 55,* 75–84.

Cooper, J., Zanna, M. P., & Taves, P. A. (1978). Arousal as a necessary condition for attitude change following induced compliance. *Journal of Personality and Social Psychology, 36,* 1101–1106.

Cooper, V. M. (1994, May 3). Need a job? Find a problem you can solve. *Christian Science Monitor, 76,* p. 36.

Corcoran, E. (1993, February 21). Computers, cultures and solving problems. *Washington Post, 116,* p. H6.

Corina, D. P., Poizner, H., Bellugi, U., Feinberg, T., et al. (1992). Dissociation between linguistic and nonlinguistic gestural systems: A case for compositionality. *Brain & Language, 43*(3), 414–447.

Corina, D. P., Vaid, J., Bellugi, U. (1992). The linguistic basis of left hemisphere specialization. *Science 255*(5049), 1258–1260.

Cosmides, L. (1989). The logic of social exchange: Has natural selection shaped how humans reason? Studies with the Wason selection task. *Cognition, 31,* 187–276.

Costa, P. T., & McCrae, R. R. (1992a). Four ways five factors are basic. *Personality & Individual Differences, 13*(6), 653–665.

Costa, P. T., & McCrae, R. R. (1992b). "Four ways five factors are not basic": Reply. *Personality & Individual Differences, 13*(8), 861–865.

Costa, P. T., & Widiger, T. A. (Eds.). (1993). *Personality disorders and the five-factor model of personality.* Washington, DC: American Psychological Association.

Craik, F. I. M., & Lockhart, R. S. (1972). Levels of processing: A framework for memory research. *Journal of Verbal Learning and Verbal Behavior, 11,* 671–684.

Crick, F., & Mitchison, G. (1983). The function of dream sleep. *Nature, 304,* 111–114.

Cronbach, L. J. (1990). *Essentials of psychological testing* (5th ed.). New York: Harper & Row.

Cross-National Collaborative Group. (1992). The changing rate of major depression. *Journal of the American Medical Association, 268*(21), 3098–3105.

Crowder, R. G. (1976). *Principles of learning and memory.* Hillsdale, NJ: Erlbaum.

Csikszentmihalyi, M. (1988). Society, culture, and person: A systems view of creativity. In R. J. Sternberg (Ed.), *The nature of creativity* (pp. 325–339). New York: Cambridge University Press.

Csikszentmihalyi, M. (1996). *Creativity.* New York: HarperCollins.

Cummins, J. (1976). The influence of bilingualism on cognitive growth: A synthesis of research findings and explanatory hypothesis. *Working Papers on Bilingualism, 9,* 1–43.

Damon, W., & Hart, D. (1982). The development of self-understanding from childhood to adolescence. *Child Development, 53,* 841–864.

Daneman, M., & Carpenter, P. A. (1980). Individual differences in working memory and reading. *Journal of Verbal Learning and Verbal Behavior, 19,* 450–466.

Daneman, M., & Tardif, T. (1987). Working memory and reading skill re-examined. In M. Coltheart (Ed.), *Attention and performance: Vol. 12. The psychology of reading* (pp. 491–508). Hove, England: Erlbaum.

Darwin, C. (1859). *Origin of species.* London: John Murray.

Davidson, R. J., & Schwartz, G. E. (1976). Psychobiology of relaxation and related states: A multiprocess theory. In D. Mostofsky (Ed.), *Behavior modification and control of physiologic activity.* Englewood Cliffs, NJ: Prentice-Hall.

Davis, K. L. (1997). Emphasizing strengths: Counseling psychologists. In R. J. Sternberg (Ed.), *Career paths in psychology* (pp. 93–115). Washington, DC: American Psychological Association.

Davison, G. C., & Neale, J. M. (1994). *Abnormal psychology* (6th ed.). New York: Wiley.

Dawes, R. M. (1994). *House of cards.* New York: Free Press.

Dawkins, R. (1989). *The selfish gene* (new ed.). New York: Oxford University Press.

DeAngelis, T. (1992, May). Senate seeks answers to rising tide of violence. *APA Monitor,* p. 11.

DeCasper, A. J., & Fifer, W. P. (1980). Of human bonding: Newborns prefer their mothers' voices. *Science, 208,* 1174–1176.

DeCasper, A. J., & Spence, M. J. (1986). Prenatal maternal speech influences newborns' perception of speech sounds. *Infant Behavior and Development, 9,* 133–150.

deCastro, J. M., & Brewer, E. M. (1992). The amount eaten in meals by humans is a power function of the number of people present. *Physiology and Behavior, 51,* 121–125.

deCharms, R. (1968). *Personal causation: The internal affective determinants of behavior.* New York: Academic Press.

Deci, E. L. (1971). Effects of externally mediated rewards on intrinsic motivation. *Journal of Personality and Social Psychology, 18,* 105–115.

Deci, E. L. (1972). Intrinsic motivation, extrinsic reinforcement, and inequity. *Journal of Personality and Social Psychology, 22,* 113–120.

Deci, E. L., Vallerand, R. J., Pelletier, L. G., & Ryan, R. M. (1991). Motivation and education: The self-determination perspective. *Educational Psychologist, 26*(3–4), 325–346.

De Jong, W. (1979). An examination of self-perception mediation of the foot-in-the-door effect. *Journal of Personality and Social Psychology, 37,* 2221–2239.

Delgado, J. M. R., Roberts, W. W., & Miller, N. E. (1954). Learning motivated by electrical stimulation of the brain. *American Journal of Physiology, 179,* 587–593.

DeLongis, A., Folkman, S., & Lazarus, R. S. (1988). The impact of daily stress on health and mood: Psychological and social resources as mediators. *Journal of Personality and Social Psychology, 54*(3), 486–495.

Dembroski, T. M, & Costa, P. T. (1988). Assessment of coronary-prone behavior: A current overview. *Annals of Behavioral Medicine, 10,* 60–63.

Dembroski, T. M., MacDougall, J. M., Williams, R. B., Haney, T. L., & Blumenthal, J. A. (1985). Components of Type A, hostility, and anger in relationship to angiographic findings. *Psychosomatic Medicine, 47,* 219–233.

Dement, W. C. (1976). *Some must watch while some must sleep.* New York: Norton.

Dement, W. C., & Kleitman, N. (1957). The relation of eye movements during sleep to dream activity: An objective method for the study of dreaming. *Journal of Experimental Psychology, 55,* 543–553.

Denny, N. W. (1980). Task demands and problem-solving strategies in middle-aged and older adults. *Journal of Gerontology, 35,* 559–564.

Derryberry, D., & Tucker, D. M. (1992). Neural mechanisms of emotion. *Journal of Consulting and Clinical Psychology, 60,* 329–338.

Detterman, D. K., & Sternberg, R. J. (Eds.). (1982). *How and how much can intelligence be increased?* Norwood, NJ: Ablex.

Devine, P. G., Monteith, M. J., Zuwerink, J. R., & Elliot, A. J. (1991). Prejudice with and without compunction. *Journal of Personality and Social Psychology, 60*(6), 817–830.

Dienstbier, R. A. (1989). Arousal and physiological toughness: Implications for mental and physical health. *Psychological Review, 96*(1), 84–100.

Digman, J. M. (1990). Personality structure: Emergence of the five-factor model. *Annual Review of Psychology, 41,* 417–440.

Dineen, T. (1998). Psychotherapy: The snake oil of the 90s? *Skeptic, 6*(3), 54–63.

Dion, K. K., Berscheid, E., & Walster, E. (1972). What is beautiful is good. *Journal of Personality and Social Psychology, 24,* 285–290.

Dittes, J. E., & Kelley, H. H. (1956). Effects of different conditions of acceptance upon conformity to group norms. *Journal of Abnormal and Social Psychology, 53,* 100–107.

Dixon, R. A., & Baltes, P. B. (1986). Toward life-span research on the functions and pragmatics of intelligence. In R. J. Sternberg & R. K. Wagner (Eds.), *Practical intelligence: Nature and origins of competence in the everyday world* (pp. 203–235). New York: Cambridge University Press.

Docherty, J. (1993, May 23). Pay for mental health care—and save. *New York Times,* Sect. 3, p. 13.

Dohrenwend, B. P., Levav, I., Schwartz, S., Naveh, G., Link, B. G., Skodol, A. G., & Stueve, A. (1992). Socioeconomic status and psychiatric disorders: The causation-selection issue. *Science, 255,* 946–952.

Dohrenwend, B. S., & Dohrenwend, B. P. (1974). *Stressful life events.* New York: Wiley.

Dolan, M. (1995, February 11). When the mind's eye blinks. *Los Angeles Times, 114,* pp. A1, A24, A25.

Dollard, J., Miller, N., Doob, L., Mowrer, O. H., & Sears, R. R. (1939). *Frustration and aggression.* New Haven, CT: Institute of Human Relations, Yale University Press.

Donnerstein, E., & Donnerstein, M. (1976). Research in the control of interracial aggression. In R. G. Geen & E. C. O'Neal (Eds.),

Perspectives on aggression (pp. 133–168). New York: Academic Press.

Douglas, J. D. (1967). *The social meanings of suicide*. Princeton, NJ: Princeton University Press.

Drewnowski, A. (1991). Obesity and eating disorders: Cognitive aspects of food preference and food aversion. *Bulletin of the Psychonomic Society, 29*, 261–264.

Duke, L. (1992, December 16). Poll of Latinos counters perceptions on language, immigration. *Washington Post, 116*, p. A4.

Duncker, K. (1945). On problem-solving. *Psychological Monographs, 58*(5, Whole No. 270).

Dunn, J., & Plomin, R. (1990). *Separate lives: Why siblings are so different*. New York: Basic Books.

Durlach, N. I., & Colburn, H. S. (1978). Binaural phenomenon. In E. C. Carterette & M. P. Friedman (Eds.), *Handbook of perception* (Vol. 4). New York: Academic Press.

Dutton, D. G., & Aron, A. P. (1974). Some evidence for heightened sexual attraction under conditions of high anxiety. *Journal of Personality and Social Psychology, 30*, 510–517.

Dyal, J. A. (1984). Cross-cultural research with the locus of control concept. In H. Lefcourt (Ed.), *Research with the locus of control construct: Vol. 3. Extensions and limitations*. San Diego, CA: Academic Press.

Eagly, A. H., & Chaiken, S. (1975). An attribution analysis of communicator attractiveness. *Journal of Personality and Social Psychology, 32*, 136–144.

Eagly, A. H., Makhijani, M. G., & Klonsky, B. G. (1992). Gender and the evaluation of leaders: A meta-analysis. *Psychological Bulletin, 111*(1), 3–22.

Early, P. C. (1989). Social loafing and collectivism: A comparison of the United States and the People's Republic of China. *Administrative Science Quarterly, 34*, 565–581.

Ebbinghaus, H. E. (1964). *Memory: A contribution to experimental psychology*. New York: Dover. (Original work published 1885)

Edgerton, R. (1967). *The cloak of competence*. Berkeley, CA: University of California Press.

Edmonston, W. E., Jr. (1981). *Hypnosis and relaxation*. New York: Wiley.

Egeth, H. E. (1993). What do we not know about eyewitness identification? *American Psychologist, 48*(5), 577–580.

Eisenberger, R., & Cameron, J. (1996). Detrimental effects of reward: Reality or myth? *American Psychologist, 51*, 1153–1166.

Ekman, P. (1971). Universals and cultural differences in the facial expression of emotion. In J. Cole (Ed.), *Nebraska Symposium on Motivation* (Vol. 19, pp. 207–284). Lincoln, NE: University of Nebraska Press.

Ekman, P. (1984). Expression and the nature of emotion. In P. Ekman & K. Scherer (Eds.), *Approaches to emotion* (pp. 319–343). Hillsdale, NJ: Erlbaum.

Ekman, P. (1993). Facial expression and emotion. *American Psychologist, 48*, 384–392.

Ekman, P., & Friesen, W. V. (1975). *Unmasking the face*. Englewood Cliffs, NJ: Prentice-Hall.

Ekman, P., Levenson, R. W., & Friesen, W. V. (1983). Autonomic nervous system activity distinguishes among emotions. *Science, 221*, 1208–1210.

Ekman, P., & Oster, H. (1979). Facial expression of emotion. *Annual Review of Psychology, 30*, 527–554.

Elkind, D. (1967). Egocentrism in adolescence. *Child Development, 38*, 1025–1034.

Elkind, D. (1981). Recent research in cognitive and language development. In L. T. Benjamin, Jr. (Ed.), *The G. Stanley Hall lecture series* (Vol. 1). Washington, DC: American Psychological Association.

Elkind, D. (1985). Egocentrism redux. *Developmental Review, 5*, 218–226.

Ellis, A. (1962). *Reason and emotion in psychotherapy*. Secaucus, NJ: Lyle Stuart.

Ellis, A. (1970). *Reason and emotion in psychotherapy*. New York: Lyle Stuart.

Ellis, A. (1973). Rational-emotive therapy. In R. J. Corsini (Ed.), *Current psychotherapies*. Itasca, IL: Peacock.

Ellis, A. (1989). The history of cognition in psychotherapy. In A. Freeman, K. M. Simon, L. E. Beutler, & H. Arkowitz (Eds.), *Comprehensive handbook of cognitive therapy* (pp. 5–19). New York: Plenum.

Endler, N. S., & Magnusson, D. (1976). Toward an interactional psychology of personality. *Psychological Bulletin, 83*, 956–974.

Engle, R. W. (1994). Individual differences in memory and their implications for learning. In R. J. Sternberg (Ed.), *Encyclopedia of intelligence*. New York: Macmillan.

Engle, R. W., Cantor, J., & Carullo, J. J. (1992). Individual differences in working memory and comprehension: A test of four hypotheses. *Journal of Experimental Psychology: Learning, Memory, and Cognition, 18*(5), 972–992.

Engle, R. W., Carullo, J. J., & Collins, K. W. (1992). Individual differences in working memory for comprehension and following directions. *Journal of Educational Research, 84*(5), 253–262.

Engle, R. W., & Oransky, N. (1999). Multi-store versus dynamic models of temporary storage in memory. In R. J. Sternberg (Ed.), *The nature of cognition* (pp. 515–555). Cambridge, MA: MIT Press.

Ericsson, K. A., Chase, W. G., & Faloon, S. (1980). Acquisition of a memory skill. *Science, 208*, 1181–1182.

Erikson, E. H. (1963). *Childhood and society* (2nd ed.). New York: Norton.

Erikson, E. H. (1968). *Identity, youth, and crisis*. New York: Norton.

Exner, J. E. (1974). *The Rorschach: A comprehensive system* (Vol. 1). New York: Wiley.

Exner, J. E. (1978). *The Rorschach: A comprehensive system* (Vol. 2). *Current research and advanced interpretation*. New York: Wiley.

Exner, J. E. (1985). *The Rorschach: A comprehensive system* (2nd ed., Vol. 1). New York: Wiley.

Eysenck, H. J. (1952). *The scientific study of personality*. London: Routledge & Kegan Paul.

Eysenck, H. J. (Ed.). (1981). *A model for personality*. New York: Springer.

Eysenck, H. J. (1984). Intelligence versus behaviour. *The Behavioral and Brain Sciences, 7*(12), 290–291.

Eysenck, H. J., & Kamin, L. (1981). *The intelligence controversy: H. J. Eysenck vs. Leon Kamin*. New York: Wiley.

Faber, M. D. (1970). Allport's visit with Freud. *The Psychoanalytic Review, 57*, 60–64.

Fagan, J. F., III, & Montie, J. E. (1988). Behavioral assessment of cognitive well-being in the infant. In J. Kavanagh (Ed.), *Understanding mental retardation: Research accomplishments and new frontiers*. Baltimore: Brookes.

Falco, M. (1992). *The making of a drug-free America: Programs that work*. New York: Times Books.

Fantz, R. L. (1958). Pattern vision in young infants. *Psychological Record, 8*, 43–47.

Fantz, R. L. (1961). The origin of form perception. *Scientific American, 204*, 66–72.

Farah, M. J. (1988). The neuropsychology of mental imagery: Converging evidence from brain-damaged and normal subjects. In J. Stiles-Davis, M. Kritchevsky, & U. Bellugi (Eds.), *Spatial cognition: Brain bases and development* (pp. 33–56). Hillsdale, NJ: Erlbaum.

Farne, M. A., Boni, P., Corallo, A., Gnugnoli, D., et al. (1994). Personality variables as moderators between hassles and objective indications of distress (S-IgA). *Stress Medicine, 10*(1), 15–20.

Fay, R. E., Turner, C. F., Klassen, A. D., & Gagnon, J. H. (1989). Prevalence and patterns of same-gender sexual contact among men. *Science, 1989, 243,* 338–348.

Fazio, R. H., Zanna, M. P., & Cooper, J. (1977). Dissonance and self-perception: An integrative view of each theory's proper domain of application. *Journal of Experimental Social Psychology, 13,* 464–479.

Feingold, A. (1992). Good-looking people are not what we think. *Psychological Bulletin, 111,* 304–341.

Feist, J. (1990). *Theories of personality* (3rd ed.). Fort Worth, TX: Holt, Rinehart and Winston.

Fernandez, E., & Turk, D. C. (1992). Sensory and affective components of pain: Separation and synthesis. *Psychological Bulletin, 112*(2), 205–217.

Feshbach, S. (1970). Aggression. In P. H. Mussen (Ed.), *Carmichael's manual of child psychology.* New York: Wiley.

Festinger, L., & Carlsmith, J. M. (1959). Cognitive consequences of forced compliance. *Journal of Abnormal and Social Psychology, 58,* 203–210.

Festinger, L., Pepitone, A., & Newcomb, T. (1952). Some consequences of de-individuation in a group. *Journal of Abnormal and Social Psychology, 47,* 382–389.

Festinger, L., Schachter, S., & Back, K. (1950). *Social pressures in informal groups: A study of human factors in housing.* New York: Harper & Brothers.

Feuerstein, R. (1980). *Instrumental enrichment: An intervention program for cognitive modifiability.* Baltimore: University Park Press.

Feynman, R. (1985). *Surely you're joking, Mr. Feynman.* New York: Norton.

Field, T. (1978). Interaction behaviors of primary versus secondary caregiver fathers. *Developmental Psychology, 14,* 183–184.

Field, T. (1990). *Infant daycare has positive effects on grade school behavior and performance.* Unpublished manuscript, University of Miami, Coral Gables, Florida.

Finnegan, L. P. (1982). Outcome of children born to women dependent upon narcotics. In B. Stimmel (Ed.), *The effects of maternal alcohol and drug abuse on the newborn.* New York: Haworth Press.

Fiore, E. (1989). *Encounters: A psychologist reveals case studies of abductions by extraterrestrials.* New York: Doubleday.

Fischhoff, B., Slovic, P., & Lichtenstein, S. (1977). Knowing with certainty: The appropriateness of extreme confidence. *Journal of Experimental Psychology: Human Perception and Performance, 3,* 552–564.

Flavell, J. H., & Wellman, H. M. (1977). Metamemory. In R. V. Kail, Jr., & J. W. Hagen (Eds.), *Perspectives on the development of memory and cognition* (pp. 3–33). Hillsdale, NJ: Erlbaum.

Flett, G. L., Blankstein, K. R., Hicken, D. J., & Watson, M. S. (1995). Social support and help-seeking in daily hassles versus major life events stress. *Journal of Applied Social Psychology, 25*(1), 49–58.

Floody, O. R. (1983). Hormones and aggression in female mammals. In B. B. Svare (Ed.), *Hormones and aggressive behavior* (pp. 39–89). New York: Plenum.

Flynn, J. R. (1987). Massive IQ gains in 14 nations: What IQ tests really measure. *Psychological Bulletin, 101,* 171–191.

Fogel, A. (1992). Movement and communication in human infancy: The social dynamics of development. *Human Movement Science, 11*(4), 387–423.

Folkman, S., & Lazarus, R. S. (1988). *Manual for the ways of coping questionnaire.* Palo Alto, CA: Consulting Psychologists Press.

Folkman, S., Lazarus, R. S., Gruen, R. J., & DeLongis, A. (1986). Appraisal, coping, health status, and psychological symptoms. *Journal of Personality and Social Psychology, 50*(3), 571–579.

Ford, C. S., & Beach, F. A. (1951). *Patterns of sexual behavior.* New York: Harper & Row.

Fottrell, E. (1983). *Case histories in psychiatry.* New York: Churchill Livingston.

Foulkes, D. (1985). *Dreaming: A cognitive-psychological analysis.* Hillsdale, NJ: Erlbaum.

Frankl, V. (1959). *From death camp to existentialism.* Boston: Beacon.

Franks, J. J., & Bransford, J. D. (1971). Abstraction of visual patterns. *Journal of Experimental Psychology, 90*(1), 65–74.

Frazier, T. M., David, G. H., Goldstein, H., & Goldberg, I. D. (1961). Cigarette smoking and prematurity. *American Journal of Obstetrics and Gynecology, 81,* 988–996.

Freedman, J. L., & Fraser, S. C. (1966). Compliance without pressure. *Journal of Personality and Social Psychology, 4,* 195–202.

Freeman, W. (1959). Psychosurgery. In S. Arieti (Ed.), *American handbook of psychiatry* (Vol. 2, pp. 1521–1540). New York: Basic Books.

Frensch, P. A., & Sternberg, R. J. (1989). Expertise and intelligent thinking: When is it worse to know better? In R. J. Sternberg (Ed.), *Advances in the psychology of human intelligence.* Hillsdale, NJ: Erlbaum.

Freud, A. (1946). *The ego and the mechanisms of defense.* New York: International Universities Press.

Freud, S. (1954). *Interpretation of dreams.* London: Allen & Unwin. (Original work published 1900)

Freud, S. (1963). Introductory lectures on psychoanalysis. In *Standard edition of the complete psychological works of Sigmund Freud* (Vols. 15 & 16). London: Hogarth. (Original work published 1917)

Freud, S. (1964). New introductory lectures. In *Standard edition of the complete psychological works of Sigmund Freud* (Vol. 21). London: Hogarth. (Original work published 1933)

Frey, K. S., & Ruble, D. N. (1987). What children say about classroom performance: Sex and grade differences in perceived competence. *Child Development, 58,* 1066–1078.

Friedman, M., & Rosenman, R. H. (1974). *Type A behavior and your heart.* New York: Knopf.

Friedman, M., Thoresen, C. E., Gill, J. J., Ulmer, D., et al. (1994). Alteration of Type A behavior and its effect on cardiac recurrences in post myocardial infarction patients: Summary results of the recurrent coronary prevention project. In A. Steptoe & J. Wardle (Eds.), *Psychosocial processes and health: A reader* (pp. 478–506). Cambridge, England: Cambridge University Press.

Friedman, M. I., & Stricker, E. M. (1976). The physiological psychology of hunger: A physiological perspective. *Psychological Review, 83,* 409–431.

Friedrich-Cofer, L., & Huston, A. C. (1986). Television violence and aggression: The debate continues. *Psychological Bulletin, 100*(3), 364–371.

Funder, D. C., & Ozer, D. J. (1983). Behavior as a function of the situation. *Journal of Personality & Social Psychology, 44*(1), 107–112.

Gabrenya, W. K., Latané, B., & Wang, Y. E. (1983). Social loafing in cross-cultural perspective: Chinese in Taiwan. *Journal of Cross-Cultural Psychology, 14,* 368–384.

Gabrenya, W. K., Wang, Y. E., & Latané, B. (1985). Social loafing on an optimizing task: Cross-cultural differences among Chinese and Americans. *Journal of Cross-Cultural Psychology, 16,* 223–242.

Gagnon, J. H. (1973). Scripts and the coordination of sexual conduct. In J. K. Cole & R. Riensteiber (Eds.), *Nebraska Symposium on Motivation* (Vol. 21, pp. 27–59). Lincoln, NE: University of Nebraska Press.

Galton, F. (1883). *Inquiry into human faculty and its development.* London: Macmillan.

Ganley, R. (1989). Emotion and eating in obesity: A review of the literature. *International Journal of Eating Disorders, 8,* 343–361.

Garcia, J. (1981). Tilting at the paper mills of academe. *American Psychologist, 36*(2), 149–158.

Garcia, J., & Koelling, R. A. (1966). The relation of cue to consequence in avoidance learning. *Psychonomic Science, 4,* 123–124.

Gardner, H. (1983). *Frames of mind: The theory of multiple intelligences.* New York: Basic Books.

Gardner, H. (1993a). *Creating minds: An anatomy of creativity seen through the lives of Freud, Einstein, Picasso, Stravinsky, Eliot, Graham, and Gandhi.* New York: HarperCollins.

Gardner, H. (1993b). *Multiple intelligences: The theory in practice.* New York: Basic Books.

Gardner, H. (1993c). Seven creators of the modern era. In J. Brockman (Ed.), *Creativity,* 28–47. New York: Simon and Schuster.

Gardner, H. (1995). *Leading minds.* New York: Basic Books.

Gardner, H. (1999). Are there additional intelligences? The case for naturalist, spiritual, and existential intelligences. In J. Kane (Ed.), *Education, information, and transformation.* Englewood Cliffs, NJ: Prentice-Hall.

Gardner, M. (1978). *Aha! Insight.* New York: Freeman.

Gardner, R. A., & Gardner, B. T. (1969). Teaching sign language to a chimpanzee. *Science, 165,* 664–672.

Gazzaniga, M. S. (1970). *The bisected brain.* New York: Appleton-Century-Crofts.

Gazzaniga, M. S. (1985). *The social brain: Discovering the networks of the mind.* New York: Basic Books.

Geen, R. G., & Quanty, M. B. (1977). The catharsis of aggression: An evaluation of a hypothesis. In L. Berkowitz (Ed.), *Advances in experimental social psychology* (Vol. 10). New York: Academic Press.

Geiselman, R. E., Fisher, R. P., MacKinnon, P. P., & Holland, H. L. (1985). Eyewitness memory enhancement in the police interview: Cognitive retrieval mnemonics versus hypnosis. *Journal of Applied Psychology, 70,* 401–412.

Gelles, R. J., & Straus, M. A. (1988). Intimate violence. New York: Simon & Schuster.

Gelman, R., & Baillargeon, R. (1983). A review of some Piagetian concepts. In P. H. Mussen (Series Ed.), J. Flavell & E. Markman (Vol. Eds.), *Handbook of child psychology: Cognitive development* (4th ed., Vol. 3, pp. 167–230). New York: Wiley.

Gelman, S., Bullock, M., & Meck, E. (1980). Preschoolers' understanding of simple object transformations. *Child Development, 51,* 691–699.

Gerstein, D. R., & Harwood, H. J. (Eds.). (1990). *Treating drug problems: A study of the evolution, effectiveness, and financing of public and private drug treatment systems.* Washington, DC: National Academy of Science Institute of Medicine, National Academy Press.

Geyelin, M. (1994, May 15). Lawsuits over false memories face hurdles. *Wall Street Journal,* p. 10(N).

Gibbs, J. C. (Ed.). (1968). *Suicide.* New York: Harper & Row.

Gibbs, J. C., Arnold, K. D., Ahlborn, H. H., & Cheesman, F. L. (1984). Facilitation of sociomoral reasoning in delinquents. *Journal of Consulting and Clinical Psychology, 52,* 37–45.

Gibson, J. J. (1950). *The perception of the visual world.* Boston: Houghton-Mifflin.

Gick, M. L., & Holyoak, K. J. (1980). Analogical problem solving. *Cognitive Psychology, 12,* 306–355.

Gick, M. L., & Holyoak, K. J. (1983). Schema induction and analogical transfer. *Cognitive Psychology, 15,* 1–38.

Gilbert, E., & DeBlassie, R. (1984). Anorexia nervosa: Adolescent starvation by choice. *Adolescence, 19,* 840–846.

Gill, M. M. (1972). Hypnosis as an altered and regressed state. *International Journal of Clinical and Experimental Hypnosis, 20,* 224–337.

Gilligan, C. (1982). *In a different voice: Psychological theory and women's development.* Cambridge, MA: Harvard University Press.

Gilligan, C., & Attanucci, J. (1988). Two moral orientations: Gender differences and similarities. *Merrill-Palmer Quarterly, 34,* 223–237.

Gilly, M. C. (1988). Sex roles in advertising: A comparison of television advertisements in Australia, Mexico, and the United States. *Journal of Marketing, 52*(2), 75–85.

Gim, R. H., Atkinson, D. R., & Kim, S. J. (1991). Asian-American acculturation, counselor ethnicity and cultural sensitivity, and ratings of counselors. *Journal of Counseling Psychology, 38,* 57–62.

Gladwin, T. (1970). *East is a big bird.* Cambridge, MA: Belknap.

Glenberg, A. M. (1977). Influences of retrieval processes on the spacing effect in free recall. *Journal of Experimental Psychology: Human Learning & Memory, 3*(3), 282–294.

Glenberg, A. M. (1979). Component-levels theory of the effects of spacing of repetitions on recall and recognition. *Memory & Cognition, 7*(2), 95–112.

Glucksberg, S., & Danks, J. H. (1975). *Experimental psycholinguistics.* Hillsdale, NJ: Erlbaum.

Glueck, B. C., & Stroebel, C. F. (1975). Biofeedback and meditation in the treatment of psychiatric illness. *Comprehensive Psychiatry, 16,* 302–321.

Goddard, H. H. (1917). Mental tests and immigrants. *Journal of Delinquency, 2,* 243–277.

Godden, D. R., & Baddeley, A. D. (1975). Context-dependent memory in two natural environments: On land and underwater. *British Journal of Psychology, 66,* 325–331.

Golbus, M. S. (1980). Teratology for the obstetrician: Current status. *American Journal of Obstetrics and Gynecology, 55,* 269.

Goleman, D. (1987, November 24). Teen-age risk-taking: Rise in deaths prompts new research effort: Experts seek ways to head off the peril. *New York Times,* p. 13(N).

Goleman, D. (1993, April 18). When a long therapy goes a little way. *New York Times,* Sect. 4, p. 6.

Goleman, D. (1995). *Emotional intelligence.* New York: Bantam.

Gottesman, I. I., McGuffin, P., & Farmer, A. E. (1987). Clinical genetics as clues to the "real" genetics of schizophrenia. *Schizophrenia Bulletin, 13,* 23–47.

Gottfried, A. E., & Gottfried, A. W. (Eds.). (1988). *Maternal employment and children's development.* New York: Plenum.

Gottman, J. M. (1979). *Marital interaction.* New York: Academic Press.

Gottman, J. M. (1994). *Why marriages succeed or fail.* New York: Simon & Schuster.

Gottman, J. M., Notarius, C., Gonso, J., & Markman, H. J. (1976). *A couple's guide to communication.* Champaign, IL: Research Press.

Graf, P., & Schacter, D. L. (1985). Implicit and explicit memory for new associations in normal and amnesic subjects. *Journal of Experimental Psychology: Learning, Memory, and Cognition, 11,* 501–518.

Graham, J. R. (1990). *MMPI-2: Assessing personality and psychopathology.* New York: Oxford University Press.

Gray, A. L., Bowers, K. S., & Fenz, W. D. (1970). Heart rate in anticipation of and during a negative visual hallucination. *International Journal of Clinical and Experimental Hypnosis, 18,* 41–51.

Green, D. M., & Swets, J. A. (1966). *Signal detection theory and psychophysics* (Reprint). New York: Krieger.

Greenberg, M., Szmukler, G., & Tantam, D. (1986). *Making sense of psychiatric cases.* New York: Oxford University Press.

Greene, D., & Lepper, M. R. (1974). Effects of extrinsic rewards on children's subsequent intrinsic interest. *Child Development, 45,* 1141–1145.

Greene, R. L. (1987). Ethnicity and MMPI performance: A review. *Journal of Consulting and Clinical Psychology, 55,* 497–512.

Greenfield, P. M. (1994). Independence and interdependence as developmental scripts: Implications for theory, research, and practice. In P. M. Greenfield & R. R. Cocking (Eds.), *Cross-cultural roots of minority child development* (pp. 1–37). Hillsdale, NJ: Erlbaum.

Greenfield, P. M. (1997). You can't take it with you: Why ability assessments don't cross cultures. *American Psychologist, 52,* 1115–1124.

Greenfield, P. M., & Cocking, R. R. (Eds.). (1994). *Cross-cultural roots of minority child development.* Hillsdale, NJ: Erlbaum.

Greenwald, A. G., Klinger, M. R., & Schuh, E. S. (1995). Activation by marginally perceptible ("subliminal") stimuli: Dissociation of unconscious from conscious cognition. *Journal of Experimental Psychology: General, 125*(1), 22–42.

Greenwald, A. G., Spangenberg, E. R., Pratkanis, A. R., & Eskenazi, J. (1991). Double-blind tests of subliminal self-help audiotapes. *Psychological Science, 2*(2), 119–122.

Gregory, R. L. (1987). Recovery from blindness. In R. L. Gregory, *The Oxford companion to the mind* (pp. 94–96). New York: Oxford University Press.

Grice, H. P. (1967). William James Lectures, Harvard University, published in part as "Logic and conversation." In P. Cole & J. L. Morgan (Eds.), *Syntax and semantics: Speech acts* (Vol. 3, pp. 41–58). New York: Seminar Press.

Griffith, D. R., Azuma, S. D. & Chasnoff, I. J. (1994). Three-year outcome of children exposed prenatally to drugs. Special Section: Cocaine babies. *Journal of the American Academy of Child and Adolescent Psychiatry, 33,* 20–27.

Griffith, R. M., Miyago, M., & Tago, A. (1958). The universality of typical dreams: Japanese vs. Americans. *American Anthropologist, 60,* 1173–1179.

Grolier's international encyclopedia. (1992). Danbury, CT: Grolier.

Gruber, H. E. (1981). *Darwin on man: A psychological study of scientific creativity* (2nd ed.). Chicago: University of Chicago Press. (Original work published 1974)

Gruber, H. E. (1995). Insight and affect in the history of science. In R. J. Sternberg & J. E. Davidson (Eds.), *The nature of insight* (pp. 398–431). Cambridge, MA: MIT Press.

Guilford, J. P. (1950). Creativity. *American Psychologist, 5,* 444–454.

Gurman, A. S., Kniskern, D. P., & Pinsoff, W. M. (1986). Research on the process and outcome of marital and family therapy. In S. L. Garfield & A. E. Bergin (Eds.), *Handbook of psychotherapy and behavior change* (3rd ed.). New York: Wiley.

Gustavson, C. R., & Garcia, J. (1974). Aversive conditioning: Pulling a gag on the wily coyote. *Psychology Today, 8*(3), 68–72.

Gustavson, C. R., & Nicolaus, L. K. (1987). Taste aversion conditioning in wolves, coyotes, and other canids: Retrospect and prospect. In H. Frank (Ed.), *Man and wolf: Advances, issues, and problems in captive wolf research: Vol. 4. Perspectives in vertebrate science* (pp. 169–203). Dordrecht, Netherlands: Junk, Publishers.

Gwirtsman, H. E., & Germer, R. H. (1981). Abnormalities of dexamethasone suppression test and urinary MHPG in anorexia nervosa. *American Journal of Psychiatry, 138,* 650–653.

Haglund, M. M., Ojemann, G. A., Lettich, E., Bellugi, U., et al. (1993). Dissociation of cortical and single unit activity in spoken and signed languages. *Brain & Language, 44*(1), 19–27.

Haier, R. J., Siegel, B., Tang, C., Abel, L., & Buchsbaum, M. S. (1992). Intelligence and changes in regional cerebral glucose metabolic rate following learning. *Intelligence, 16*(3–4), 415–426.

Haith, M. M. (1979). Visual cognition in early infancy. In R. B. Kearsley & I. E. Sigel (Eds.), *Infants at risk: Assessment of cognitive functioning.* Hillsdale, NJ: Erlbaum.

Hakuta, K. (1986). *Mirror of language.* New York: Basic Books.

Halpern, D. F. (1997). Sex differences in intelligence: Implications for education. *American Psychologist, 52,* 1091–1102.

Harkins, S. G. (1987). Social loafing and social facilitation. *Journal of Experimental Social Psychology, 23,* 1–18.

Harkins, S. G., & Szymanski, K. (1987). Social loafing and social facilitation: New wine in old bottles. In C. Hendrick (Ed.), *Review of personality and social psychology: Group processes and intergroup relations* (Vol. 9, pp. 167–188). Beverly Hills, CA: Sage.

Harlow, H. F. (1949). The formation of learning sets. *Psychological Review, 56,* 51–65.

Harlow, H. F., Harlow, M. K., & Meyer, D. R. (1950). Learning motivated by a manipulation drive. *Journal of Experimental Psychology, 40,* 228–234.

Harris, J. R. (1998). *The nurture assumption.* New York: Free Press.

Harter, S. (1990). Causes, correlates, and the functional role of global self-worth: A life-span perspective. In R. J. Sternberg & J. Kolligian, Jr., (Eds.), *Competence considered* (pp. 67–97). New Haven, CT: Yale University Press.

Hastings, E. H., & Hastings, P. K. (Eds.). (1982). *Index on international public opinion, 1980–81.* Westport, CT: Greenwood Press.

Hatfield, E., & Rapson, R. L. (1992). Similarity and attraction in close relationships. *Communication Monographs, 59*(2), 209–212.

Hatfield, E., & Walster, G. W. (1978). *A new look at love.* Reading, MA: Addison-Wesley.

Hathaway, S. R., & McKinley, J. C. (1943). *Manual for the Minnesota Multiphasic Personality Inventory.* New York: Psychological Corporation.

Hathaway, S. R., & McKinley, J. C. (1951). *The Minnesota Multiphasic Personality Inventory* (Rev. ed.). New York: Psychological Corporation.

Havighurst, R. J. (1967). *Development tasks and education.* New York: David McKay.

Hayes, C. (1951). *The ape in our house.* New York: Harper & Row.

Hayes, D., & Ross, C. E. (1986). Body and mind: The effect of exercise, overweight, and physical health on psychological well-being. *Journal of Health and Social Behavior, 27,* 387–400.

Haynes, S. G., Feinleib, M., & Kannel, W. B. (1980). The relationship of psychosocial factors to coronary heart disease in the Framingham Study: III. Eight-year incidence of coronary heart disease. *American Journal of Epidemiology, 111,* 37–58.

Hazan, C., & Shaver, P. R. (1987). Romantic love conceptualized as an attachment process. *Journal of Personality and Social Psychology, 52,* 511–524.

Hazan, C., & Shaver, P. R. (1994). Attachment as an organizational framework for research or close relationship. *Psychological Inquiry, 5,* 1–22.

Heaney, C. A., Israel, B. A., & House, J. S. (1994). Chronic job insecurity among automobile workers: Effects on job satisfaction and health. *Social Science & Medicine, 38*(10), 1431–1437.

Heath, S. B. (1983). *Ways with words.* New York: Cambridge University Press.

Heath, S. B., & McLaughlin, M. W. (1993). *Identity and inner-city youth.* New York: Teachers College Press.

Hedstrom, L. J. (1994). Morita and Naikan therapies: American applications. *Psychotherapy, 31*(1), 154–160.

Heider, F. (1958). *The psychology of interpersonal relations.* New York: Wiley.

Heilbrun, A. B., & Witt, N. (1990). Distorted body image as a risk factor in anorexia nervosa: Replication and clarification. *Psychological Reports, 66,* 407–416.

Helmes, E., & Reddon, J. R. (1993). A perspective on developments in assessing psychopathology: A critical review of the MMPI and MMPI-2. *Psychological Bulletin, 113*(3), 453–471.

Helmholtz, H. E. L. von. (1896). *Vorträge und Reden.* Braunschweig: Vieweg und Sohn.

Helmholtz, H. E. L. von. (1930). The sensations of tone (A. J. Ellis, Trans.). New York: Longmans, Green. (Original work published 1863)

Helmholtz, H. E. L. von. (1962). *Treatise on physiological optics* (3rd ed., J. P. C. Southall, Ed. and Trans.). New York: Dover. (Original work published 1909)

Hennessey, B. A., & Amabile, T. M. (1988). The conditions of creativity. In R. J. Sternberg (Ed.), *The nature of creativity* (pp. 11–38). New York: Cambridge University Press.

Henry, J. P., & Stephens, P. M. (1977). *Stress, health, and the social environment: A sociobiologic approach to medicine.* New York: Springer-Verlag.

Hering, E. (1964). *Outlines of a theory of the light sense* (L. M. Hurvich & D. Jameson, Trans.). Cambridge, MA: Harvard University Press. (Original work published 1878)

Herity, B., Moriarty, M., Daly, L., Dunn, J., & Bourke, G. J. (1982). The role of tobacco and alcohol in the aetiology of lung and larynx cancer. *British Journal of Cancer, 46,* 961–964.

Herrmann, D. (1997). Rewards of public service: Research psychologists in the government. In R. J. Sternberg (Ed.), *Career paths in psychology* (pp. 151–163). Washington, DC: American Psychological Association.

Herrnstein, R., & Murray, C. (1994). *The bell curve.* New York: Free Press.

Hetherington, A. W., & Ranson, S. W. (1940). Hypothalamic lesions and adiposity in the rat. *Anatomical Record, 78,* 149–172.

Heuch, I., Kvale, G., Jacobsen, B. K., & Bjelke, E. (1983). Use of alcohol, tobacco and coffee, and risk of pancreatic cancer. *British Journal of Cancer, 48,* 637–643.

Heyduk, R. G., & Bahrick, L. E. (1977). Complexity, response competition, and preference implications for affective consequences of repeated exposure. *Motivation and Emotion, 1,* 249–259.

Higginbotham, H. N. (1979). Culture and mental health services. In A. J. Marsella, G. De Vos, & F. L. K. Hsu (Eds.), *Perspectives on cross-cultural psychology* (pp. 307–332). New York: Academic Press.

Hilgard, E. R. (1965). *Hypnotic susceptibility.* New York: Harcourt, Brace & World.

Hilgard, E. R. (1977). *Divided consciousness: Multiple controls in human thought and action.* New York: Wiley.

Hilts, P. J. (1995). *Memory's ghost: The strange tale of Mr. M and the nature of memory.* New York: Simon & Schuster.

Hintzman, D. L. (1978). *The psychology of learning and memory.* San Francisco: Freeman.

Ho, D. Y. F. (1986). Chinese patterns of socialization. In M. H. Bond (Ed.), *The psychology of the Chinese people.* Hong Kong: Oxford University Press.

Hoagwood, K. (1997). Interpreting nullity: The Fort Bragg Experiment—a comparative success or failure? *American Psychology, 52,* 548.

Hobson, J. A. (1989). *Sleep.* New York: Scientific American Library.

Hoebel, B. G., & Teitelbaum, G. (1966). Weight regulation in normal and hypothalamic hyperphagic rats. *Journal of Comparative and Physiological Psychology, 61,* 189–193.

Hoffman, L. W. (1989). Effects of maternal employment in the two-parent family. *American Psychologist, 44,* 283–292.

Hogan, R. (1996). A socioanalytic perspective on the five-factor model. In J. S. Wiggins (Ed.), *The five-factor model of personality: Theoretical perspectives* (pp. 163–179). New York: Guilford Press.

Holder, M. D., Bermudez-Rattoni, F., & Garcia, J. (1988). Taste-potentiated noise-illness associations. *Behavioral Neuroscience, 102*(3), 363–370.

Holder, M. D., Yirmiya, R., Garcia, J., & Raizer, J. (1989). Conditioned taste aversions are not readily disrupted by external excitation. *Behavioral Neuroscience, 103*(3), 605–611.

Holinger, P. C. (1987). *Violent deaths in the United States.* New York: Guilford Press.

Hollingshead, A. B., & Redlich, F. C. (1958). *Social class and mental illness.* New York: Wiley.

Hollis, K. L. (1990). The role of Pavlovian conditioning in territorial aggression and reproduction. In D. A. Dewsbury (Ed.), *Contemporary issues in comparative psychology* (pp. 197–219). Sunderland, MA: Sinauer Associates.

Hollis, K. L., Cadieux, E. L., & Colbert, M. M. (1989). The biological function of Pavlovian conditioning: A mechanism for mating success in the blue gourami (Trichogaster trichopterus). *Journal of Comparative Psychology, 103*(2), 115–121.

Hollis, K. L., Martin, K. A., Cadieux, E. L., & Colbert, M. M. (1984). The biological function of Pavlovian conditioning: Learned inhibition of aggressive behavior in territorial fish. [Special issue: Ecological and developmental contexts in the study of learning.] *Learning & Motivation, 15*(4), 459–478.

Hollis, K. L., ten Cate, C., & Bateson, P. (1991). Stimulus representation: A subprocess of imprinting and conditioning. *Journal of Comparative Psychology, 105*(4), 307–317.

Holmes, T. H., & David, E. M. (Eds.). (1989). *Life change, life events, and illness: Selected papers.* New York: Praeger.

Holmes, T. H., & Rahe, R. (1967). The social readjustment rating scale. *Journal of Psychosomatic Research, 11,* 213–218.

Holyoak, K. J. (1984). Analogical thinking and human intelligence. In R. J. Sternberg (Ed.), *Advances in the psychology of human intelligence* (Vol. 2, pp. 199–230). Hillsdale, NJ: Erlbaum.

Honsberger, R. W., & Wilson, A. F. (1973). Transcendental meditation in treating asthma. *Respiratory Therapy: The Journal of Inhalation Technology, 3,* 79–80.

Hooker, E. (1993). Reflections of a 40-year exploration: A scientific view on homosexuality. *American Psychologist, 48*(4), 450–453.

Horn, J. R. (1994). Theory of fluid and crystallized intelligence. In R. J. Sternberg (Ed.), *Encyclopedia of human intelligence* (Vol. 1, pp. 443–451). New York: Macmillan.

Horney, K. (1937). *The neurotic personality of our time.* New York: Norton.

Horney, K. (1939). *New ways in psychoanalysis.* New York: Norton.

Horney, K. (1950). *Neurosis and human growth: The struggle toward self-realization.* New York: Norton.

House, J. S., Landis, K. R., & Umberson, D. (1988). Social relationships and health. *Science, 241*(4865), 540–545.

Houston, J. P. (1985). *Motivation.* New York: Macmillan.

Hovland, C. I., & Weiss, W. (1951). The influences of source credibility on communication effectiveness. *Public Opinion Quarterly, 15,* 635–650.

Howard, K. I., Kopta, S. M., Krause, M. S., & Orlinsky, D. E. (1986). The dose-effect relationship in psychotherapy. *American Psychologist, 41*(2), 159–164.

Hubel, D. H., & Wiesel, T. N. (1963). Receptive fields of cells in the striate cortex of very young, visually inexperienced kittens. *Journal of Neurophysiology, 26,* 994–1002.

Hubel, D. H., & Wiesel, T. N. (1968). Receptive fields and functional architecture of the monkey striate cortex. *Journal of Physiology, 195,* 215–243.

Hubel, D. H., & Wiesel, T. N. (1979). Brain mechanisms of vision. *Scientific American, 241,* 150–162.

Huebner, R. R., & Izard, C. E. (1988). Mothers' responses to infants' facial expressions of sadness, anger, and physical distress. *Motivation and Emotion, 12,* 185–196.

Huesmann, L. R., Lagerspetz, K., & Eron, L. D. (1984). Intervening variable in the TV violence-aggression relation: Evidence from two countries. *Developmental Psychology, 20,* 746–775.

Hull, C. L. (1943). *Principles of behavior.* New York: Appleton-Century-Crofts.

Hull, C. L. (1952). *A behavior system: An introduction to behavior theory concerning the individual organism.* New Haven, CT: Yale University Press.

Hunt, E. B. (1978). Mechanics of verbal ability. *Psychological Review, 85,* 109–130.

Hunt, M. M. (1959). *A natural history of love.* New York: Knopf.

Hurvich, L., & Jameson, D. (1957). An opponent-process theory of color vision. *Psychological Review, 64,* 384–404.

Huston, A. C. (1983). Sex-typing. In E. M. Hetherington (Ed.) & P. H. Mussen (Series Ed.), *Handbook of child psychology* (4th ed., Vol. 4, pp. 387–467). New York: Wiley.

Huston, A. C. (1985). The development of sex-typing: Themes from recent research. *Developmental Review, 5,* 1–17.

Hwang, K. K. (1981). Perception of life events: The application of nonmetric multidimensional scaling. *Acta Psychologica Taiwanica, 22,* 22–32.

Inhelder, B., & Piaget, J. (1958). *The growth of logical thinking from childhood to adolescence.* New York: Basic Books.

Insko, C. A. (1965). Verbal reinforcement of attitude. *Journal of Personality and Social Psychology, 21,* 621–623.

Intelligence and its measurement: A symposium. (1921). *Journal of Educational Psychology, 12,* 123–147, 195–216, 271–275.

Iscoe, I. (1997). Reaching out: Community psychologists. In R. J. Sternberg (Ed.), *Career paths in psychology* (pp. 117–132). Washington, DC: American Psychological Association.

Isen, A. M. (1987). Passive affect, cognitive processes, and social behavior. In L. Berkowitz (Ed.), *Advances in experimental social psychology* (Vol. 20, pp. 203–253). New York: Academic Press.

Ivey, A. E., Ivey, M. B., & Simek–Morgan, L. (1993). *Counseling and psychotherapy: A multicultural perspective.* Boston: Allyn & Bacon.

Izard, C. E. (1989). The structure and functions of emotions: Implications for cognition, motivation, and personality. In I. S. Cohen (Ed.), *The G. Stanley Hall lecture series* (Vol. 9, pp. 39–73). Washington, DC: American Psychological Association.

Izard, C. E., Kagan, J., & Zajonc, R. B. (1984). *Emotions, cognition, and behavior.* New York: Cambridge University Press.

Jackson, N. E. (1984). Intellectual giftedness: A theory worth doing well. *The Behavioral and Brain Sciences, 7*(12), 294–295.

Jacobson, G. (1983). *The multiple crises of marital separation and divorce.* New York: Grune & Stratton.

Jacobson, J. L., Jacobson, S. W., & Humphrey, H. E. (1990). Effects of exposure to PCBs and related compounds on growth and activity in children. *Neurotoxicology & Teratology, 12,* 319–326.

Jacobson, J. L., Jacobson, S. W., Padgett, R. J., Brunitt, G. A., & Billings, R. L. (1992). Effects of prenatal PCB exposure on cognitive processing efficiency and sustained attention. *Developmental Psychology, 28,* 297–306.

James, W. (1890). *Psychology.* New York: Holt.

Janis, I. L. (1958). *Psychological stress.* New York: Wiley.

Janis, I. L. (1972). *Victims of groupthink.* Boston: Houghton Mifflin.

Jemmott, J. B., III, & Locke, S. E. (1984). Psychosocial factors, immunologic mediation, and human susceptibility to infectious diseases: How much do we know? *Psychological Bulletin, 95,* 78–108.

Jensen, A. R. (1998). *The g factor.* Greenwich, CT: Praeger.

Jerison, H. J. (1982). The evolution of biological intelligence. In R. J. Sternberg (Ed.), *Handbook of human intelligence* (pp. 723–791). New York: Cambridge University Press.

Johnson, J. E. (1984). Psychological interventions and coping with surgery. In A. Baum, S. E. Taylor, & J. E. Singer (Eds.), *Handbook of psychology and health* (Vol. 4, pp. 167–188). Hillsdale, NJ: Erlbaum.

Johnson, J. E., Lauver, D. R., & Nail, L. M. (1989). Process of coping with radiation therapy. *Journal of Consulting and Clinical Psychology, 57,* 358–364.

Johnson, K. (1994, July 2). Corporate conscience: Insurer gives retreat a social mission. *New York Times, 143,* pp. 21, 24.

Johnson-Laird, P. N. (1999). Formal rules versus mental models of reasoning. In R. J. Sternberg (Ed.), *The nature of cognition* (pp. 587–624). Cambridge, MA: MIT Press.

Jones, E. E., & Davis, K. E. (1965). From acts to dispositions: The attribution process in person perception. In L. Berkowitz (Ed.), *Advances in experimental social psychology* (Vol. 2). New York: Academic Press.

Jones, E. E., & Nisbett, R. (1971). *The actor and the observer: Divergent perceptions of the causes of behavior.* Morristown, NJ: General Learning Press.

Kandel, E. R., & Schwartz, J. H. (1982). Molecular biology of learning: Modulation of transmitter release. *Science, 218*(4571), 433–442.

Kaplan, C. A., & Davidson, J. E. (1989). *Incubation effects in problem solving.* Manuscript submitted for publication.

Kaplan, S. L., Randolph, S. W., & Lemli, J. M. (1991). *Treatment outcomes in the reduction of fear: A meta-analysis.* Paper presented at the annual meeting of the American Psychological Association, San Francisco.

Katz, D., & Stotland, E. (1959). A preliminary statement to a theory of attitude structure and change. In S. Koch (Ed.), *Psychology: A study of a science* (Vol. 3, pp. 423–475). New York: McGraw-Hill.

Kay, P. (1975). Synchronic variability and diachronic changes in basic color terms. *Language in Society, 4,* 257–270.

Keller, M., Eckensberger, L. H., & von Rosen, K. (1989). A critical note on the conception of preconventional morality: The case of stage 2 in Kohlberg's theory. *International Journal of Behavioral Development, 12*(1), 57–69.

Kellogg, W. N., & Kellogg, L. A. (1933). *The ape and the child.* New York: McGraw-Hill.

Kelman, H. C. (1982). Ethical issues in different social science methods. In T. L. Beauchamp, R. R. Faden, R. J. Wallace, & L. Walters (Eds.), *Ethical issues in social science research.* Baltimore: Johns Hopkins University Press.

Kemeny, M. E., Cohen, R., Zegans, L. S., & Conant, M. A. (1989). Psychological and immunological predictors of genital herpes recurrence. *Psychosomatic Medicine, 51,* 195–208.

Kenrick, D. T., & Keefe, R. C. (1992). Age preferences in mates reflect sex differences in human reproductive strategies. *Behavioral and Brain Sciences, 15,* 75–133.

Kenrick, D. T., & Trost, M. R. (1993). The evolutionary perspective. In A. E. Beall & R. J. Sternberg (Eds.), *Perspectives on the psychology of gender.* New York: Guilford Press.

Keppel, G., & Underwood, B. J. (1962). Proactive inhibition in short-term retention of single items. *Journal of Verbal Learning and Verbal Behavior, 1,* 153–161.

Kiecolt-Glaser, J. K., et al. (1984). Psychosocial modifiers of immunocompetence in medical students. *Psychosomatic Medicine, 46*(1), 7–14.

Kiecolt-Glaser, J. K., & Glaser, R. (1987). Psychosocial influences on herpes virus latency. In E. Kurstak, Z. J. Lipowski, & P. V. Morozov (Eds.), *Viruses, immunity, and mental disorders* (pp. 403–412). New York: Plenum.

Kiecolt-Glaser, J. K., Malarkey, W. B., Chee, M., & Newton, T., et al. (1993). Negative behavior during marital conflict is associated with immunological down-regulation. *Psychosomatic Medicine, 55,* 395–409.

Kiesler, D. J. (1966). Some myths of psychotherapy research and the search for a paradigm. *Psychological Bulletin, 65,* 110–136.

Kihlstrom, J. F. (1984). Conscious, subconscious, unconscious: A cognitive view. In K. S. Bowers & D. Meichenbaum (Eds.), *The unconscious: Reconsidered.* New York: Wiley.

Kihlstrom, J. F. (1985). Hypnosis. *Annual Review of Psychology, 36,* 385–418.

King, G. R., & Logue, A. W. (1987). Choice in a self-control paradigm with human subjects: Effects of changeover delay duration. *Learning & Motivation, 18*(4), 421–438.

Kitchener, K. S., & Brenner, H. G. (1990). Wisdom and reflective judgment: Knowing in the face of uncertainty. In R. J. Sternberg (Ed.), *Wisdom* (pp. 212–229). New York: Cambridge University Press.

Kleinman, A. (1988). *Rethinking psychiatry: From cultural category to personal experience*. New York: Free Press.

Kleinman, A., & Good, B. (1985). *Culture and depression*. Berkeley, CA: University of California Press.

Kleinmuntz, B., & Szucko, J. J. (1984). A field study of the fallibility of polygraphic lie detection. *Nature, 308*, 449–450.

Kleitman, N. (1963). *Sleep and wakefulness* (2nd ed.). Chicago: University of Chicago Press.

Knox, V. J., Crutchfield, L., & Hilgard, E. R. (1975). The nature of task interference in hypnotic dissociation: An investigation of hypnotic behavior. *International Journal of Clinical and Experimental Hypnosis, 23*, 305–323.

Kobasa, S. C. O. (1982). The hardy personality: Toward a social psychology of stress and health. In G. S. Sanders & J. Suls (Eds.), *Social psychology of health and illness*. Hillsdale, NJ: Erlbaum.

Kobasa, S. C. O. (1990). Stress-resistant personality. In R. E. Ornstein & C. Swencionis (Eds.), *The healing brain: A scientific reader* (pp. 219–230). New York: Guilford Press.

Kobasa, S. C. O., Maddi, S. R., Puccetti, M. C., & Zola, M. A. (1994). Effectiveness of hardiness, exercise, and social support as resources against illness. In A. Steptoe & J. Wardle (Eds.), *Psychosocial processes and health: A reader* (pp. 247–260). Cambridge, England: Cambridge University Press.

Kohlberg, L. (1963). The development of children's orientations toward a moral order: Pt. 1. Sequence in the development of moral thought. *Vita Humana, 6*, 11–33.

Kohlberg, L. (1983). *The psychology of moral development*. New York: Harper & Row.

Kohlberg, L. (1984). The psychology of moral development: The nature and validity of moral stages. In *Essays on moral development* (Vol. 2). New York: Harper & Row.

Köhler, W. (1927). *The mentality of apes*. New York: Harcourt Brace.

Kohn, P. M., Gurevich, M., Pickering, D. I., & MacDonald, J. E. (1994). Alexithymia, reactivity, and the adverse impact of hassles-based stress. *Personality & Individual Differences, 16*(6), 805–812.

Kolb, B., & Whishaw, I. Q. (1990). *Fundamentals of human neuropsychology* (3rd ed.). New York: Freeman.

Komaroff, A. L., Masuda, M., & Holmes, T. H. (1968). The Social Readjustment Rating Scale: A comparative study of Negro, Mexican, and white Americans. *Journal of Psychosomatic Research, 12*(2), 121–128.

Kosslyn, S. M. (1975). Information representation in visual images. *Cognitive Psychology, 7*(3), 341–370.

Kosslyn, S. M. (1988). Aspects of a cognitive neuroscience of mental imagery. *Science, 240*, 1621–1626.

Kramer, M. A. (1957). A discussion of the concepts of incidence and prevalence as related to epidemiologic studies of mental disorders. *American Journal of Public Health, 47*, 826–840.

Kulkarni, S. S., & Puhan, B. N. (1988). Psychological assessment: Its present and future trends. In J. Pandey (Ed.), *Psychology in India: The state of the art: Vol. 1. Personality and mental processes*. New Delhi: Sage.

Kurtines, W., & Greif, E. B. (1974). The development of moral thought: Review and evaluation of Kohlberg's approach. *Psychological Bulletin, 81*, 453–470.

Lachman, M. E. (1986). Locus of control in aging research: A case for multi-dimensional and domain-specific assessment. *Psychology and Aging, 1*, 34–40.

LaFraniere, S. (1992, August 27). Identifying "Ivan": Does memory mislead? *Washington Post, 115*, p. A29.

La Ganga, M. L. (1994, May 14). Father wins in "false memory" case. *Los Angeles Times*, p. A1.

Laing, R. D. (1964). Is schizophrenia a disease? *International Journal of Social Psychiatry, 10*, 184–193.

Lambert, M. J., & Bergin, A. E. (1994). The effectiveness of psychotherapy. In A. E. Bergin & S. L. Garfield (Eds.), *Handbook of psychotherapy and behavior change* (4th ed.). New York: Wiley.

Lange, R. C., & James, W. (1922). *The emotions*. Baltimore: Williams & Wilkins.

Langer, E. J., Blank, A., & Chanowitz, B. (1978). The mindlessness of ostensibly thoughtful action. *Journal of Personality and Social Psychology, 36*, 635–642.

Langer, E. J., Janis, I. L., & Wolfer, J. A. (1975). Reduction of psychological stress in surgical patients. *Journal of Experimental Social Psychology, 11*, 155–165.

Langlois, J. H., Ritter, J. M., Casey, R. J., & Savin, D. B. (1995). Infant attractiveness predicts maternal behaviors and attitudes. *Developmental Psychology, 31*, 164–172.

Langsley, D. G., Hodes, M., & Grimson, W. R. (1993). In N. Sartorius, G. de Girolano, G. Andrews, G. A. German, & L. Eisenberg (Eds.), *Treatment of mental disorders: A review of effectiveness*. Geneva, Switzerland, and Washington, DC: World Health Organization and American Psychiatric Press.

Larkin, J. H., McDermott, J., Simon, D. P., & Simon, H. A. (1980). Expert and novice performance in solving physics problems. *Science, 208*, 1335–1342.

Latané, B. (1981). The psychology of social impact. *American Psychologist, 36*, 343–356.

Latané, B., & Darley, J. M. (1968). Group inhibition of bystander intervention. *Journal of Personality and Social Psychology, 10*, 215–221.

Latané, B., & Darley, J. M. (1970). *The unresponsive bystander: Why doesn't he help?* New York: Appleton-Century-Crofts.

Latané, B., Nida, S. A., & Wilson, D. W. (1981). The effects of a group size on helping behavior. In J. P. Rushton & R. M. Sorrentino (Eds.), *Altruism and helping behavior: Social, personality, and developmental perspectives*. Hillsdale, NJ: Erlbaum.

Latané, B., Williams, K., & Harkins, S. (1979). Many hands make light the work: The causes and consequences of social loafing. *Journal of Personality and Social Psychology, 37*, 822–832.

Lau, R. R. (1988). Beliefs about control and health behavior. In D. S. Gochman (Ed.), *Health behavior* (pp. 43–63). New York: Plenum.

Laudenslager, M. L. (1988). The psychobiology of loss: Lessons from humans and nonhuman primates. *Journal of Social Issues, 44*, 19–36.

Lazar, I., & Darlington, R. (1982). Lasting effects of early education: A report from the consortium for longitudinal studies. *Monographs of the Society for Research in Child Development, 47*(2–3, Serial No. 195).

Lazarus, A. A. (1990). If this be research . . . *American Psychologist, 58*, 670–671.

Lazarus, R. S. (1977). A cognitive analysis of biofeedback control. In G. E. Schwartz & J. Beatty (Eds.), *Biofeedback: Theory and research* (pp. 69–71). New York: Academic Press.

Lazarus, R. S. (1984). On the primacy of cognition. *American Psychologist, 39*, 124–129.

Lazarus, R. S., Kanner, A., & Folkman, F. (1980). Emotions: A cognitive-phenomenological analysis. In R. Plutchik & H. Kellerman (Eds.), *Emotion: Theory, research and experience: Vol. 1. Theories of emotion*. New York: Academic Press.

Lederer, R. (1991). *The miracle of language*. New York: Pocket Books.

LeDoux, J. E. (1986). The neurobiology of emotion. In J. E. LeDoux & W. Hirst (Eds.), *Mind and brain: Dialogues in cognitive neuroscience* (pp. 301–354). Cambridge, England: Cambridge University Press.

LeDoux, J. E., Romanski, L., & Xagoraris, A. (1989). Indelibility of subcortical emotional memories. *Journal of Cognitive Neuroscience, 1,* 238–243.

Leicht, K. L., & Overton, R. (1987). Encoding variability and spacing repetitions. *American Journal of Psychology, 100*(1), 61–68.

Leon, G. R. (1974). *Case histories about deviant behavior: A social learning analysis.* Boston: Holbrook Press.

Lepper, M. R., Greene, D., & Nisbett, R. E. (1973). Undermining children's intrinsic interest with extrinsic rewards: A test of the "overjustification" hypothesis. *Journal of Personality and Social Psychology, 28,* 129–137.

Lester, B. M., Corwin, M. J., Sepkoski, C., Seifer, R., et al. (1991). Neurobehavioral syndromes in cocaine-exposed newborn infants. *Child Development, 62,* 694–705.

LeVay, S. (1991). A difference in hypothalamic structure between heterosexual and homosexual men. *Science, 253,* 1034–1037.

Levenkron, J. C., & Moore, L. G. (1988). The Type A behavior pattern: Issues for intervention research. *Annals of Behavioral Medicine, 10,* 78–83.

Leventhal, H., & Tomarken, A. J. (1986). Emotion: Today's problems. *Annual Review of Psychology, 37,* 565–610.

Levine, B. (1993, January 20). How to tell a "woopie" from a "fizzbo." *Los Angeles Times, 112,* pp. E1, E6.

Levy, J., Trevarthen, C., & Sperry, R. W. (1972). Perception of bilateral chimeric figures following hemispheric deconnexion. *Brain, 95,* 61–78.

Lewis, M., & Brooks-Gunn, J. (1981). Visual attention at three months as a predictor of cognitive functioning at two years of age. *Intelligence, 5,* 131–140.

Lewy, A., Sack, L., Miller, S., & Itoban, T. M. (1987). Anti-depressant and circadian-phase shifting effects of light. *Science, 235,* 352–367.

Liebert, R. M., & Baron, R. A. (1972). Some immediate effects of televised violence on children's behavior. *Developmental Psychology, 6,* 469–475.

Lin, K-M., Masuda, M., & Tazuma, L. (1984). Problems of eastern refugees and immigrants: IV. Adaptational problems of Vietnamese refugees. *Psychiatric Journal of the University of Ottawa, 9*(2), 79–84.

Linscheid, T. R., Hartel, F., & Cooley, N. (1993). Are aversive procedures durable? A five-year follow-up of three individuals treated with contingent electric shock. [Special issue: Aversives: II.] *Child and Adolescent Mental Health Care, 3*(2), 67–76.

Lipsey, M. W., & Wilson, D. B. (1993). The efficacy of psychological, educational, and behavioral treatment: Confirmation from meta-analysis. *American Psychologist, 48,* 1181–1209.

Lissner, L., Odell, P. M., D'Agostino, R. B., Stokes, J., Kreger, B. E., Belanger, A J., & Brownell, K. D. (1991). Variability of body weight and health outcomes in the Framingham population. *New England Journal of Medicine, 324,* 1839–1844.

Locke, E. A., & Latham, G. P. (1985). The application of goal setting to sports. *Journal of Sport Psychology, 7,* 205–222.

Loehlin, J. C. (1992a). *Genes and environment in personality development.* Newbury Park, CA: Sage.

Loehlin, J. C. (1992b). Using EQs for a simple analysis of the Colorado Adoption Project data on height and intelligence. *Behavior Genetics, 22,* 234–245.

Loehlin, J. C., Horn, J. M., & Willerman, L. (1997). Heredity, environment, and IQ in the Texas Adoption Project. In R. J. Sternberg & E. L. Grigorenko (Eds.), *Intelligence, heredity, and environment* (pp. 105–125). New York: Cambridge University Press.

Loehlin, J. C., Lindzey, G., & Spuhler, J. N. (1975). *Race differences in intelligence.* New York: Freeman.

Loehlin, J. C., Vandenberg, S. G., & Osborne, R. T. (1973). Blood-group genes and Negro–white ability difference. *Behavioral Genetics, 3,* 267–270.

Loewenstein, G., & Furstenberg, F. F. (1991). Is teenage sexual behavior rational? *Journal of Applied Social Psychology, 21*(12), 957–986.

Loftus, E. F. (1975). Leading questions and the eyewitness report. *Cognitive Psychology, 7,* 560–572.

Loftus, E. F. (1977). Shifting human color memory. *Memory and Cognition, 5,* 696–699.

Loftus, E. F. (1993a). Psychologists in the eyewitness world. *American Psychologist, 48*(5), 550–552.

Loftus, E. F. (1993b). The reality of repressed memories. *American Psychologist, 48*(5), 518–537.

Loftus, E. F., & Doyle, J. M. (1992). *Eyewitness testimony: Civil and criminal* (2nd ed.). Charlottesville, VA: Michie Co.

Loftus, E. F., & Ketcham, K. (1991). *Witness for the defense: The accused, the eyewitness, and the expert who puts memory on trial.* New York: St. Martin's Press.

Loftus, E. F., Miller, D. G., & Burns, H. J. (1978). Semantic integration of verbal information into a visual memory. *Journal of Experimental Psychology: Human Learning and Memory, 4,* 19–31.

Loftus, E. F., Miller, D. G., & Burns, H. J. (1987). Semantic integration of verbal information into a visual memory. In L. W. Wrightsman, C. E. Willis, & S. M. Kassin (Eds.), *On the witness stand: Vol. W. Controversies in the courtroom.* Newbury Park, CA: Sage.

Logue, A. W., King, G. R., Chavarro, A., & Volpe, J. S. (1990). Matching and maximizing in a self-control paradigm using human subjects. *Learning & Motivation, 21*(3), 340–368.

Lonner, W. J. (1989). The introductory psychology text: Beyond Ekman, Whorf, and biased IQ tests. In D. M. Keats, D. Munro, & L. Mann (Eds.), *Heterogeneity in cross-cultural psychology.* Amsterdam: Swets & Zeitlinger.

Lonner, W. J. (1990). An overview of cross-cultural testing and assessment. In R. W. Brislin (Ed.), *Applied cross-cultural psychology.* Newbury Park, CA: Sage.

Lonner, W. J., & Berry, J. W. (1986). Sampling and surveying. In W. J. Lonner & J. W. Berry (Eds.), *Field methods in cross-cultural research: Vol. 8. Cross-cultural research and methodology series.* Beverly Hills, CA: Sage.

Lorenz, K. (1937). The companion in the bird's world. *Auk, 54,* 245–273.

Lorenz, K. (1950). The comparative method in studying innate behavior patterns. *Symposium for the Society for Experimental Biology, 4,* 221–268.

Lovaas, O. I. (1968). Learning theory approach to the treatment of childhood schizophrenia. In *California Mental Health Research Symposium: No. 2. Behavior theory and therapy.* Sacramento, CA: California Department of Mental Hygiene.

Lovaas, O. I. (1977). *The autistic child.* New York: Wiley.

Ludwick-Rosenthal, R., & Neufeld, R. W. J. (1988). Stress management during noxious medical procedures: An evaluative review of outcome studies. *Psychological Bulletin, 104,* 326–342.

Lumsdaine, A. A., & Janis, I. L. (1953). Resistance to "counterpropaganda" produced by one-sided and two-sided "propaganda" presentation. *Public Opinion Quarterly, 17,* 311–318.

Luria, A. R. (1968). *The mind of a mnemonist.* New York: Basic Books.

Lykken, D. T. (1998). *A tremor in the blood.* New York: Plenum.

Ma, H. K. (1988). The Chinese perspectives on moral judgment development. *International Journal of Psychology, 23*(2), 201–227.

MacFarlane, A. (1975). Olfaction in the development of social preferences in the human neonate. *Ciba Foundation Symposium, 33,* 103–117.

Maehr, M., & Nicholls, J. (1980). Culture and achievement motivation: A second look. In N. Warren (Ed.), *Studies in cross-cultural psychology* (Vol. 2). London: Academic Press.

Maier, S. F., Watkins, L. R., & Fleshner, M. (1994). Psychoneuroimmunology: The interface between behavior, brain, and immunity. *American Psychologist, 49*(12), 1004–1017.

Main, M., Kaplan, N., & Cassidy, J. (1985). Security in infancy, childhood, and adulthood: A move to the level of representation. In I. Bretherton & E. Waters (Eds.), *Growing points of attachment theory and research: Monographs of the Society for Research in Child Development, 50* (Nos. 1–2), 67–104.

Maling, M. S., & Howard, K. I. (1994). From research to practice to research to . . . In P. F. Talley, H. H. Strupp, and S. F. Butler (Eds.), *Psychotherapy research and practice: Bridging the gap.* New York: Basic Books.

Mandler, J. M. (1990). A new perspective on cognitive development in infancy. *American Scientist, 78,* 236–243.

Manji, H. K., Hsiao, J. K., Risby, E. D., et al. (1991). The mechanisms of action of lithium: I. Effects on serotonergic and noradrenergic systems in normal subjects. *Archives of General Psychiatry, 48,* 505–512.

Mann, J. (1973). *Time-dated psychotherapy.* Cambridge, MA: Harvard University Press.

Mantyla, T. (1986). Optimizing cue effectiveness: Recall of 500 and 600 incidentally learned words. *Journal of Experimental Psychology: Learning, Memory, and Cognition, 12,* 66–71.

Maqsud, M., & Rouhani, S. (1990). Self-concept and moral reasoning among Batswana adolescents. *Journal of Social Psychology, 130*(6), 829–830.

Marcel, A. J. (1983). Conscious and unconscious perception: An approach to the relations between phenomenal experience and perceptual processes. *Cognitive Psychology, 15,* 238–300.

Marcia, J. E. (1966). Development and validation of ego identity status. *Journal of Personality and Social Psychology, 3*(5), 551–558.

Marcia, J. E. (1980). Identity in adolescence. In J. Adelson (Ed.), *Handbook of adolescent psychology* (pp. 159–187). New York: Wiley.

Marks, I. M., & Gelder, M. G. (1967). Transvestism and fetishism: Clinical and psychological changes during faradic aversion. *British Journal of Psychiatry, 113,* 711–729.

Markus, H. R., & Kitayama, S. (1991). Culture and the self: Implications for cognition, emotion, and motivation. *Psychological Review, 98*(2), 224–253.

Marsella, A. J. (1980). Depressive experience and disorder across cultures. In H. C. Triandis & J. Draguns (Eds.), *Handbook of cross-cultural psychology: Vol. 6. Psychopathology* (pp. 237–289). Boston: Allyn & Bacon.

Marsella, A. J., Hirschfeld, R. M. A., & Katz, M. M. (1987). *The measurement of depression.* New York: Guilford Press.

Marshall, G. D., & Zimbardo, P. G. (1979). Affective consequences of inadequately explained arousal. *Journal of Personality and Social Psychology, 37,* 970–985.

Martin, F. E. (1985). The treatment and outcome of anorexia nervosa in adolescents: A prospective study and five-year follow-up. *Journal of Psychiatric Research, 19,* 509–514.

Martin, J. A. (1981). A longitudinal study of the consequences of early mother–infant interaction: A microanalytic approach. *Monographs of the Society for Research in Child Development, 46*(203, Serial No. 190).

Martin, L. (1986). Eskimo words for snow: A case study in the genesis and decay of an anthropological example. *American Psychologist, 88,* 418–423.

Martindale, C. (1981). *Cognition and consciousness.* Homewood, IL: Dorsey Press.

Maslach, C., & Jackson, S. E. (1984). Burnout in organizational settings. *Applied Social Psychology Annual, 5,* 133–153.

Maslow, A. H. (1943). A theory of human motivation. *Psychological Review, 50,* 370–396.

Maslow, A. H. (1954). *Motivation and personality.* New York: Harper & Row.

Maslow, A. H. (1970). *Motivation and personality* (2nd ed.). New York: Harper & Row.

Masters, W. H., & Johnson, V. E. (1966). *Human sexual response.* Boston: Little, Brown.

Matarazzo, J. D. (1992). Biological and physiological correlates of intelligence. *Intelligence, 16*(3, 4), 257–258.

Matsumoto, D. (1994). *People: Psychology from a cross-cultural perspective.* Belmont, CA: Brooks/Cole.

Matsumoto, D. (1996). *Culture and psychology.* Belmont, CA: Brooks/Cole.

Mayer, D. J. (1953). Glucostatic mechanism of regulation of food intake. *New England Journal of Medicine, 249,* 13–16.

Mayer, G. R., Butterworth, T., Nafpaktitis, M., & Sulzer-Azaroff, B. (1983). Preventing school vandalism and improving discipline: A three-year study. *Journal of Applied Behavior Analysis, 16*(4), 355–369.

Mayer, J. D., & Gehr, G. (1996). Emotional intelligence and the identification of emotion. *Intelligence, 22,* 89–114.

Mayer, J. D., & Salovey, P. (1993). The intelligence of emotional intelligence. *Intelligence, 197,* 433–442.

Mayer, J. D., & Salovey, P. (1995). Emotional intelligence and the construction and regulation of feelings. *Applied and Preventive Psychology, 4,* 197–208.

McArthur, L. Z., & Berry, D. S. (1987). Cross-cultural agreement in perceptions of babyfaced adults. *Journal of Cross-Cultural Psychology, 18*(2), 165–192.

McCarley, R. W., & Hobson, J. A. (1981). REM sleep dreams and the activation-synthesis hypothesis. *American Journal of Psychiatry, 138,* 904–912.

McClelland, D. C. (1961). *The achieving society.* Princeton, NJ: Van Nostrand.

McClelland, D. C. (1985). *Human motivation.* New York: Scott, Foresman.

McClelland, D. C. (1987). *Human motivation.* Cambridge, England: Cambridge University Press.

McClelland, D. C., Atkinson, J. W., Clark, R. A., & Lowell, E. L. (1953). *The achievement motive.* New York: Appleton-Century-Crofts.

McClelland, D. C., & Winter, D. G. (1969). *Motivating economic achievement.* New York: Free Press.

McCrae, R. R. (1996). The social consequences of experiential openness. *Psychological Bulletin, 120,* 323–337.

McCrae, R. R., & John, O. (1992). An introduction to the five-factor model and its applications. *Journal of Personality, 60,* 175–215.

McDougall, W. (1908). *An introduction to social psychology.* London: Methuen.

McGarry-Roberts, P. A., Stelmack, R. M., & Campbell, K. B. (1992). Intelligence, reaction time, and event-related potentials. *Intelligence, 16*(3–4), 289–313.

McHugh, P. R., & Moran, T. H. (1985). The stomach: A conception of its dynamic role in satiety. In J. M. Sprague & A. N. Epstein (Eds.), *Progress in psychobiology and physiological psychology* (Vol. 11, pp. 197–232). Orlando, FL: Academic Press.

McKenna, J., Treadway, M., & McCloskey, M. E. (1992). Expert psychological testimony on eyewitness reliability: Selling psychology before its time. In P. Suedfeld & P. E. Tetlock (Eds.), *Psychology and social policy* (pp. 283–293). New York: Hemisphere.

Meeker, W. B., & Barber, T. X. (1971). Toward an explanation of stage hypnosis. *Journal of Abnormal Psychology, 77,* 61–70.

Meier, R. P. (1991). Language acquisition by deaf children. *American Scientist, 79,* 60–76.

Meltzoff, A. N. (1988a). Imitation of televised models by infants. *Child Development, 59*(5), 1221–1229.

Meltzoff, A. N. (1988b). Infant imitation and memory: Nine-month-olds in immediate and deferred tests. *Child Development, 59*(1), 217–225.

Melzack, R., & Wall, P. D. (1965). Pain mechanisms: A new theory. *Science, 150,* 971–979.

Melzack, R., & Wall, P. D. (1982). *The challenge of pain.* New York: Basic Books.

Melzack, R., Wall, P. D., & Ty, T. C. (1982). Acute pain in an emergency clinic: Latency of onset and descriptor patterns related to different injuries. *Pain, 14*(1), 33–43.

Merriam-Webster's collegiate dictionary (10th ed.) (1993). Springfield, MA: Merriam-Webster.

Mesquita, B., & Frijda, N. H. (1992). Cultural variations in emotions: A review. *Psychological Bulletin, 112*(3), 179–204.

Metcalfe, J. (1986). Feeling of knowing in memory and problem solving. *Journal of Experimental Psychology: Learning, Memory, and Cognition, 12*(2), 288–294.

Metcalfe, J., & Wiebe, D. (1987). Intuition in insight and noninsight problem solving. *Memory & Cognition, 15*(3), 238–246.

Milgram, S. (1963). Behavioral study of obedience. *Journal of Abnormal and Social Psychology, 67,* 371–378.

Milgram, S. (1965). Some conditions of obedience and disobedience to authority. *Human Relations, 18,* 57–76.

Milgram, S. (1974). *Obedience to authority: An experimental view.* New York: Harper & Row.

Miller, G. A. (1956). The magical number seven, plus or minus two: Some limits on our capacity for processing information. *Psychological Review, 63,* 81–97.

Miller, G. A. (1990). *The science of words.* New York: Scientific American Library.

Miller, G. A., Galanter, E. H., & Pribram, K. H. (1960). *Plans and the structure of behavior.* New York: Holt, Rinehart and Winston.

Miller, N., & Brewer, M. B. (Eds.). (1984). *Groups in contact: The psychology of desegregation.* New York: Academic Press.

Miller, S. D., & Triggiano, P. J. (1992). The psychophysiological investigation of multiple personality disorder: Review and update. *American Journal of Clinical Hypnosis, 35,* 47–61.

Milner, B., Corkin, S., & Teuber, H. L. (1968). Further analysis of the hippocampal amnesic syndrome: 14-year follow-up study of H. M. *Neuropsychologia, 6,* 215–234.

Mischel, W. (1968). *Personality and assessment.* New York: Wiley.

Mischel, W. (1977). On the future of personality measurement. *American Psychologist, 32,* 246–254.

Mischel, W. (1986). *Introduction to personality* (4th ed.). New York: Holt, Rinehart and Winston.

Mischel, W., & Peake, P. K. (1983). Some facets of consistency: Replies to Epstein, Funder, and Bem. *Psychological Review, 90,* 394–402.

Mishkin, M., & Petri, H. L. (1984). Memories and habits: Some implications for the analysis of learning and retention. In L. R. Squire & N. Butters (Eds.), *Neurophysiology of memory* (pp. 287–296). New York: Guilford Press.

Mitchell, J. E., Laine, D. E., Morley, J. E., & Levine, A. S. (1986). Naloxone but not CCK-8 may attenuate binge-eating behavior in patients with bulimia syndrome. *Biological Psychiatry, 21,* 1399–1406.

Moghaddam, F. M., Taylor, D. M., & Wright, S. C. (1993). *Social psychology in cross-cultural perspective.* New York: Freeman.

Money, J., Wiedeking, C., Walker, P. A., & Gain, D. (1976). Combined antiandrogenic and counseling program for treatment of 46 XY and 47 XYY sex offenders. *Hormones, Behavior, and Psychopathology, 66,* 105–109.

Montagu, A. (1976). *The nature of human aggression.* New York: Oxford University Press.

Moos, R. H. (1982). Coping with acute health crises. In T. Millon, C. Green, & R. Meagher (Eds.), *Handbook of clinical health psychology.* New York: Plenum.

Moos, R. H. (1988). Life stressors and coping resources influence health and well-being. *Psychological Assessment, 4,* 133–158.

Moos, R. H., & Schaefer, J. A. (1986). Life transitions and crises: A conceptual overview. In R. H. Moos (Ed.), *Coping with life crises: An integrated approach.* New York: Plenum.

Morgan, C. D., & Murray, H. A. (1935). A method for investigating fantasy: The Thematic Apperception Test. *Archives of Neurology and Psychiatry, 34,* 289–306.

Morton, T. U. (1978). Intimacy and reciprocity of exchange: A comparison of spouses and strangers. *Journal of Personality and Social Psychology, 36,* 72–81.

Moscovici, S., & Zavolloni, M. (1969). The group as a polarizer of attitudes. *Journal of Personality and Social Psychology, 12,* 125–135.

Murase, T., & Johnson, F. (1974). Naikan, Morita, and Western psychotherapy: A comparison. *Archives of General Psychiatry, 31*(1), 121–128.

Murray, H. A. (1938). *Explorations in personality.* New York: Oxford University Press.

Murray, H. A. (1943a). *Explorations in personality.* New York: Oxford University Press. (Original work published 1938)

Murray, H. A. (1943b). *Thematic Apperception Test.* Cambridge, MA: Harvard University Press.

Murray, H. A. (1943c). *The Thematic Apperception Test: Manual.* Cambridge, MA: Harvard University Press.

Murstein, B. I. (1986). *Paths to marriage.* Beverly Hills, CA: Sage.

Murstein, B. I., & Brust, R. G. (1985). Humor and interpersonal attraction. *Journal of Personality Assessment, 49*(6), 637–640.

Myers, D. G., & Lamm, H. (1976). The group polarization phenomenon. *Psychological Bulletin, 83,* 602–627.

Myerson, A. (1940). [Review of *Mental disorders in urban areas: An ecological study of schizophrenia and other psychoses.*] *American Journal of Psychiatry, 96,* 995–997.

Nash, M. (1987). What, if anything, is regressed about hypnotic age regression? A review of the empirical literature. *Psychological Bulletin, 102*(1), 42–52.

National Center for Health Statistics. (1988). Advance report of final mortality statistics, 1986. *NCHS Monthly Vital Statistics Report, 37*(Suppl. 6).

Neisser, U. (1982). Snapshots or benchmarks? In U. Neisser (Ed.), *Memory observed: Remembering in natural contexts.* San Francisco: Freeman.

Neisser, U. (Ed.). (1998). *The rising curve.* Washington, DC: American Psychological Association.

Nelson, C. (1990). *Gender and the social studies: Training preservice secondary social studies teachers.* Doctoral dissertation, University of Minnesota.

Neto, F., Williams, J. E., & Widner, S. C. (1991). Portuguese children's knowledge of sex stereotypes: Effects of age, gender, and socioeconomic status. *Journal of Cross-Cultural Psychology, 22*(3), 376–388.

Newcomb, T. M. (1943). *Personality and social change.* New York: Dryden.

Newell, A., & Simon, H. A. (1972). *Human problem solving.* Englewood Cliffs, NJ: Prentice-Hall.

Newman, L. S., & Baumeister, R. F. (1994, August). *"Who would wish for the trauma?" Explaining UFO abductions.* Paper presented at the meeting of the American Psychological Association, Los Angeles, CA.

Newport, E. L. (1990). Maturational constraints on language learning. *Cognitive Science, 14,* 11–28.

Nickerson, R. S. (1997). Designing for human use: Human-factors psychologists. In R. J. Sternberg (Ed.), *Career paths in psychology* (pp. 213–243). Washington, DC: American Psychological Association.

Nickerson, R. S., & Adams, M. J. (1979). Long-term memory for a common object. *Cognitive Psychology, 11,* 287–307.

Nicolaus, L. K., Cassell, J. F., Carlson, R. B., & Gustavson, C. R. (1983). Taste-aversion conditioning of crows to control predation on eggs. *Science, 220*(4593).

Nicolaus, L. K., Farmer, P. V., Gustavson, C. R., & Gustavson, J. C. (1989). The potential of estrogen-based conditioned aversion in controlling depredation: A step closer to the "magic bullet." *Applied Animal Behaviour Science, 23*(1–2), 1–14.

Nicolaus, L. K., & Nellis, D. W. (1987). The first evaluation of the use of conditioned taste aversion to control predation by mongooses upon eggs. *Applied Animal Behaviour Science, 17*(3–4), 329–346.

Nielson, S. (1990). Epidemiology of anorexia nervosa in Denmark from 1983–1987: A nationwide register study of psychiatric admission. *Acta Psychiatricia Scandinavica, 81,* 507–514.

Niemczynski, A., Czyzowska, D., Pourkos, M., & Mirski, A. (1988). The Cracow study with Kohlberg's moral judgment interview: Data pertaining to the assumption of cross-cultural validity. *Polish Psychological Bulletin, 19*(1), 43–53.

Nisan, M., & Kohlberg, L. (1982). Universality and variation in moral judgment: A longitudinal and cross-sectional study in Turkey. *Child Development, 53,* 865–876.

Nisbett, R. E. (1972). Hunger, obesity, and the ventromedial hypothalamus. *Psychological Review, 79,* 433–453.

Nisbett, R. E. (1995). Race, IQ, and scientism. In S. Fraser (Ed.), *The bell curve wars: Race, intelligence and the future of America* (pp. 36–57). New York: Basic Books.

Nisbett, R. E., Caputo, C., Legant, P., & Maracek, J. (1973). Behavior as seen by the actor and as seen by the observer. *Journal of Personality and Social Psychology, 27,* 154–164.

Noel, J. G., Forsyth, D. R., & Kelley, K. N. (1987). Improving the performance of failing students by overcoming their self-serving attributional biases. *Basic & Applied Social Psychology, 8*(1–2), 151–162.

Norman, W. T. (1963). Toward an adequate taxonomy of personality attributes: Replicated factor structure in peer nomination personality ratings. *Journal of Abnormal and Social Psychology, 66,* 574–583.

Notarius, C. I. (1996). *Marriage: Will I be happy or will I be sad?* Pacific Grove, CA: Brooks/Cole Publishing.

Notarius, C. I., & Markman, H. (1993). *We can work it out.* New York: Putnam.

Nuñes, T. (1994). Street intelligence. In R. J. Sternberg (Ed.), *Encyclopedia of human intelligence* (Vol. 2, pp. 1045–1049). New York: Macmillan.

Oatley, K. (1993). Those to whom evil is done. In R. S. Wyer & T. K Srull (Eds.), *Perspectives on anger and emotion: Advances in social cognition* (Vol. 6, pp. 159–165). Hillsdale, NJ: Erlbaum.

Ogbu, J. U. (1982). Origins of human competence: A cultural-ecological perspective. *Annual Progress in Child Psychiatry & Child Development,* 113–140.

Ogbu, J. U. (1986). The consequences of the American caste system. In U. Neisser (Ed.), *The school achievement of minority children.* Hillsdale, NJ: Erlbaum.

Ogbu, J. U. (1988). Cultural diversity and human development in black children and poverty: A developmental perspective. In D. T. Slaughter (Ed.), *New directions in child development* (Vol. 42). San Francisco: Jossey-Bass.

Olds, J., & Milner, P. (1954). Positive reinforcement produced by electrical stimulation of septal area and other regions of the rat brain. *Journal of Comparative and Physiological Psychology, 47,* 419–427.

Oliner, S., & Oliner, P. (1993). The roots of human attachments. In Arthur Dobrin (Ed.), *Being good and doing right: Readings in moral development* (pp. 121–139). Lanham, MD: University Press of America.

Oomara, Y. (1976). Significance of glucose insulin and free fatty acid on the hypothalamic feeding and satiety neurons. In D. Novin, W. Wyrwicka, & G. Bray (Eds.), *Hunger: Basic mechanisms and clinical implications.* New York: Raven Press.

Orne, M. T. (1959). Hypnosis: Artifact and essence. *Journal of Abnormal Psychology, 58,* 277–299.

Ornstein, R. (1977). *The psychology of consciousness* (2nd ed.). New York: Harcourt Brace Jovanovich.

Ornstein, R. (1986). *The psychology of consciousness* (2nd rev. ed.). New York: Pelican Books.

Ott, E. M. (1989). Effects of male-female ratio at work: Policewomen and male nurses. *Psychology of Women Quarterly, 13*(1), 41–57.

Overton, W. F. (1990). *Reasoning, necessity, and logic: Developmental perspectives.* Hillsdale, NJ: Erlbaum.

Paivio, A. (1971). *Imagery and verbal processes.* New York: Holt, Rinehart and Winston.

Papini, M. R., & Bitterman, M. E. (1990). The role of contingency in classical conditioning. *Psychological Review, 97*(3), 396–403.

Papp, L., & Gorman, J. M. (1990). Suicidal preoccupation during fluoxetine treatment. *American Journal of Psychiatry, 147,* 1380.

Park, R. D., Berkowitz, L., Leyens, J. P., West, S. G., & Sebastian, R. J. (1977). Some effects of violent and nonviolent movies on the behavior of juvenile delinquents. In L. Berkowitz (Ed.), *Advances in experimental social psychology* (Vol. 10). New York: Academic Press.

Park, R. D., & Walters, R. H. (1967). Some factors influencing the efficacy of punishment training for inducing response inhibition. *Monographs of the Society for Research in Child Development, 32*(1, Whole No. 109).

Paul, G. L. (1967). Strategy of outcome research in psychotherapy. *Journal of Consulting Psychology, 31,* 109–118.

Paunonen, S. P., Jackson, D. N., Trzebinski, J., & Fosterline, G. (1992). Personality structure across cultures: A multimethod evaluation. *Journal of Personality and Social Psychology, 62,* 447–456.

Pavlov, I. P. (1928). *Lectures on conditioned reflexes: The higher nervous activity of animals* (Vol. 1, H. Gantt, Trans.). London: Lawrence & Wishart.

Pavlov, I. P. (1955). *Selected works.* Moscow: Foreign Languages Publishing House.

Payne, J. (1976). Task complexity and contingent processing in decision making: An information search and protocol analysis. *Organizational Behavior and Human Performance, 16,* 366–387.

Peabody, D., & Goldberg, L. R. (1989). Some determinants of factor structures from personality-trait descriptors. *Journal of Personality and Social Psychology, 57*(3), 552–567.

Pearlstone, A., Russell, R. J. H., & Wells, P. A. (1994). A re-examination of the stress/illness relationship: How useful is the concept of stress? *Personality & Individual Differences, 17*(4), 577–580.

Pedersen, P. B., Draguns, J. G., Lonner, W. J., & Trimble, J. E. (Eds.). (in press). *Counseling across cultures* (4th ed.). Newbury Park, CA: Sage.

Pederson, N. L., Plomin, R., McClearn, G. E., & Friberg, L. (1988). Neuroticism, extraversion, and related traits in adult twins reared apart and reared together. *Journal of Personality and Social Psychology, 55,* 950–957.

Pelchat, M. L., & Rozin, P. (1982). The special role of nausea in the acquisition of food dislikes by humans. *Appetite, 3*(4), 341–351.

Perkins, D. N. (1995). Insight in mind and genes. In R. J. Sternberg & J. E. Davidson (Eds.), *The nature of insight* (pp. 495–533). Cambridge, MA: MIT Press.

Perkins, D. N., & Grotzer, T. A. (1997). Teaching intelligence. *American Psychologist, 52*, 1125–1133.

Perris, C., & Herlofson, J. (1993). Cognitive therapy. In N. Sartorius, G. de Girolano, G. Andrews, G. A. German, & L. Eisenberg (Eds.), *Treatment of mental disorders: A review of effectiveness.* Geneva, Switzerland, and Washington, DC: World Health Organization and American Psychiatric Press.

Peterson, L. R., & Peterson, M. J. (1959). Short-term retention of individual verbal items. *Journal of Experimental Psychology, 58*, 193–198.

Petty, R. E., & Cacioppo, J. T. (1981). *Attitudes and persuasion: Classic and contemporary approaches.* Dubuque, IA: William C. Brown.

Pfaffman, C. (1974). Specificity of the sweet receptors of the squirrel monkey. *Chemical Senses and Flavor, 1*, 61–67.

Pfeiffer, W. M. (1982). Culture-bound syndromes. In I. Al-Issa (Ed.), *Culture and psychopathology.* Baltimore: University Park Press.

Phares, E. J. (1988). *Introduction to personality* (2nd ed.). Glenview, IL: Scott, Foresman.

Phares, E. J. (1991). *Introduction to personality* (3rd ed.). New York: HarperCollins.

Phillips, D. A. (1984). The illusion of incompetence among academically competent children. *Child Development, 55*, 2000–2016.

Phillips, D. A., & Zimmerman, M. (1990). The developmental course of perceived competence and incompetence among competent children. In R. J. Sternberg & J. Kolligian, Jr. (Eds.), *Competence considered* (pp. 41–77). New Haven, CT: Yale University Press.

Piaget, J. (1969). *The child's conception of physical causality.* Totowa, NJ: Littlefield, Adams.

Piaget, J. (1972). *The psychology of intelligence.* Totowa, NJ: Littlefield, Adams.

Pinker, S. (1994). *The language instinct.* New York: William Morrow.

Plomin, R. C. (1986). *Development, genetics, and psychology.* Hillsdale, NJ: Erlbaum.

Plomin, R. C. (1989). Environment and games: Determinants of behavior. *American Psychologist, 44*, 105–111.

Plomin, R. C. (1997). Identifying genes for cognitive abilities and disabilities. In R. J. Sternberg & E. L. Grigorenko (Eds.), *Intelligence, heredity, and environment* (pp. 89–104). New York: Cambridge University Press.

Plomin, R. C., & McClearn, G. E. (Eds.). (1993). *Nature, nurture, and psychology.* Washington DC: APA Books.

Plutchik, R. (1980). *Emotion: A psychoevolutionary analysis.* New York: Harper & Row.

Plutchik, R. (1983). Emotions in early development: A psychoevolutionary approach. In R. Plutchik & H. Kellerman (Eds.), *Emotion: Theory, research, and experience* (Vol. 2). New York: Academic Press.

Poe, E. A. (1979). The tell-tale heart. In *Tales of Edgar Allan Poe* (p. 179). Franklin Center, PA: Franklin Library. (Original work published 1843)

Poincaré, H. (1913). *The foundations of science.* New York: Science Press.

Poizner, H., Bellugi, U., & Klima, E. S. (1990). Biological foundations of language: Clues from sign language. *Annual Review of Neuroscience, 13*, 282–307.

Poizner, H., Kaplan, E., Bellugi, U., & Padden, C. A. (1984). Visual-spatial processing in deaf brain-damaged signers. *Brain & Cognition, 3*(3), 281–306.

Pokorny, A. D. (1968). Myths about suicide. In H. Resnik (Ed.), *Suicidal behaviors.* Boston: Little, Brown.

Poland, S. F. (1997). Pathways to change and development: The life of a school psychologist. In R. J. Sternberg (Ed.), *Career paths in psychology* (pp. 165–184). Washington, DC: American Psychological Association.

Polivy, J., & Herman, C. P. (1983). *Breaking the diet habit.* New York: Basic Books.

Polivy, J., & Herman, C. P. (1985). Dieting and binging. *American Psychologist, 40*, 193–201.

Poon, L. W. (1987). *Myths and truisms: Beyond extant analyses of speed of behavior and age.* Address to the Eastern Psychological Association Convention.

Posner, M., & Keele, S. W. (1968). On the genesis of abstract ideas. *Journal of Experimental Psychology, 77*(3, Pt. 1), 353–363.

Pratkanis, A. R., Eskenazi, J., & Greenwald, A. G. (1994). What you expect is what you believe (but not necessarily what you get): A test of the effectiveness of subliminal self-help audiotapes. *Basic & Applied Social Psychology, 15*(3), 251–276.

Premack, D. (1971). Language in chimpanzees? *Science, 172*, 808–822.

Pullum, G. K. (1991). *The Great Eskimo vocabulary hoax and other irreverent essays on the study of language.* Chicago: University of Chicago Press.

Ramey, C. T. (1994). Abecedarian project. In R. J. Sternberg (Ed.), *Encyclopedia of human intelligence* (Vol. 1, pp. 1–3). New York: Macmillan.

Rapaport, A. (1960). *Fights, games, and debates.* Ann Arbor, MI: University of Michigan Press.

Rapaport, D., Gill, M. M., & Schafer, R. (1968). *Diagnostic psychological testing.* New York: International Universities Press.

Reed, T. E. (1993). Effect of enriched (complex) environment on nerve conduction velocity: New data and review of implications for the speed of information-processing. *Intelligence, 17*(4), 533–540.

Reed, T. E., & Jensen, A. R. (1992). Conduction velocity in a brain nerve pathway of normal adults correlates with intelligence level. *Intelligence, 16*(3–4), 259–272.

Regan, D. T. (1971). Effects of a favor and liking on compliance. *Journal of Experimental Social Psychology, 7*, 627–639.

Reike, M. L., & Guestello, S. J. (1990). Unresolved issues on honesty and integrity testing. *American Psychologist, 50*, 458–459.

Reitman, J. S. (1974). Without surreptitious rehearsal, information in short-term memory decays. *Journal of Verbal Learning and Verbal Behavior, 13*, 365–377.

Renzulli, J. S. (1986). The three ring conception of giftedness: A developmental model for creative productivity. In R. J. Sternberg & J. E. Davidson (Eds.), *Conceptions of giftedness* (pp. 53–92). New York: Cambridge University Press.

Rescorla, R. A. (1967). Pavlovian conditioning and its proper control procedures. *Psychological Review, 74*, 71–80.

Resnik, H. L. P. (Ed.). (1968). *Suicidal behaviors.* Boston: Little, Brown.

Rest, J. R. (1979). *Development in judging moral issues.* Minneapolis: University of Minnesota Press.

Rest, J. R. (1983). Moral development. In P. H. Mussen (Ed.), *Handbook of child psychology* (4th ed., Vol. 3, pp. 556–629). New York: Wiley.

Restak, R. (1984). *The brain.* New York: Bantam.

Reynolds, D. K. (1989). On being natural: Two Japanese approaches to healing. In A. A. Sheikh & K. S. Sheikh (Eds.), *Eastern and Western approaches to healing: Ancient wisdom and modern knowledge* (Wiley series on health psychology/behavioral medicine) (pp. 180–194). New York: Wiley.

Ringelmann, M. (1913). Recherches sur les moteurs animés: Travail de l'homme. *Annales de l'Institut National Agronomique, 2s série, tom XII*, 1–40.

Roark, A. C. (1992, August 18). It's dope, so chill; for the young, slang's "mad" new words are straight off the streets of Los Angeles. *Los Angeles Times, 111*, pp. E1, E7.

Robins, L. N., Helzer, J. E., Weissman, M. M., Orvaschel, H., Gruenberg, E., Burke, J. D., & Regier, D. (1984). Lifetime prevalence of specific psychiatric disorders in three sites. *Archives of General Psychiatry, 41*, 949–958.

Robinson, L. A., Berman, J. S., & Neimeyer, R. A. (1990). Psychotherapy for the treatment of depression: A comprehensive review of controlled outcomes research. *Psychological Bulletin, 100*, 30–49.

Rodin, J. (1981). Current status of the internal–external hypotheses for obesity: What went wrong? *American Psychologist, 36*, 361–372.

Rodin, J., & Plante, T. (1989). The psychological effects of exercise. In R. S. Williams & A. Wellece (Eds.), *Biological effects of physical activity* (pp. 127–137). Champaign, IL: Human Kinetics.

Rodriguez, M., Mischel, W., & Shoda, Y. (1989). Cognitive person variables in the delay of gratification of older children at risk. *Journal of Personality & Social Psychology, 57*(2), 358–367.

Roediger, H. L., III. (1980). Memory metaphors in cognitive psychology. *Memory and Cognition, 8*(3), 231–246.

Roediger, H. L., III. (1997). Teaching, research, and more: Psychologists in an academic career. In R. J. Sternberg (Ed.), *Career paths in psychology* (pp. 7–29). Washington, DC: American Psychological Association.

Rogers, C. R. (1959). A theory of therapy, personality, and interpersonal relationships, as developed in the client-centered framework. In S. Koch (Ed.), *Psychology: A study of a science* (Vol. 3). New York: McGraw-Hill.

Rogers, C. R. (1961a). *On becoming a person: A client's view of psychotherapy.* Boston: Houghton Mifflin.

Rogers, C. R. (1961b). *On becoming a person: A therapist's view of psychotherapy.* Boston: Houghton Mifflin.

Rogers, C. R. (1978). The formative tendency. *Journal of Humanistic Psychology, 18*(1), 23–26.

Rogers, C. R. (1980). *A way of being.* Boston: Houghton Mifflin.

Rogers, S. M., & Turner, C. F. (1991). Male–male sexual contact in the U.S.A.: Findings from five sample surveys, 1970–1990. *Journal of Sex Research, 28*(4), 491–519.

Rojahn, K., & Pettigrew, T. F. (1992). Memory for schema-relevant information: A meta-analytic resolution. *British Journal of Social Psychology, 31*(2), 81–109.

Rokeach, M. (1964). *The three Christs of Ypsilanti.* New York: Columbia University Press.

Rolls, B. J. (1979). How variety and palatability can stimulate appetite. *Nutrition Bulletin, 5*, 78–86.

Rolls, B. J., Rowe, E. T., & Rolls, E. T. (1982). How sensory properties of food affect human feeding behavior. *Physiology and Behavior, 29*, 409–417.

Rosch, E. (1973). On the internal structure of perceptual and semantic categories. In T. E. Moore (Ed.), *Cognitive development and the acquisition of language.* New York: Academic Press.

Rosen, G. M. (1987). Self-help treatment books and the commercialization of psychotherapy. *American Psychologist, 42*(1), 46–51.

Rosenhan, D. L. (1973). On being sane in insane places. *Science, 179*, 250–258.

Rosenthal, R., & Jacobson, L. (1968). *Pygmalion in the classroom: Teacher expectation and pupils' intellectual development.* New York: Holt, Rinehart and Winston.

Roskies, E., Seraganian, R., Hanley, J. A., Collu, R., Martin, N., & Smilga, C. (1986). The Montreal Type A intervention project: Major findings. *Health Psychology, 5*, 45–69.

Roskies, E., Spevack, M., Surkis, A., Cohen, C., & Gilman, S. (1978). Changing the coronary-prone (Type A) behavior pattern in a nonclinical population. *Journal of Behavioral Medicine, 1*, 201–216.

Ross, L. (1977). The intuitive psychologist and his shortcomings: Distortions in the attribution process. In L. Berkowitz (Ed.), *Advances in experimental social psychology* (Vol. 10). New York: Academic Press.

Ross, R. (1975). Salience of reward and intrinsic motivation. *Journal of Personality and Social Psychology, 32*, 245–254.

Rotter, J. B. (1966). Generalized expectancies for internal versus external control of reinforcement. *Psychological Monographs, 80*(1, Whole No. 609).

Rotter, J. B. (1988). Internal versus external control of reinforcement: A case history of a variable. American Psychological Association: Distinguished Scientific Contributions Award Address (1988, Atlanta, Georgia). *American Psychologist, 45*(4), 489–493.

Rotter, J. B. (1990). Internal versus external control of reinforcement: A case history of a variable. *American Psychologist, 45*, 489–493.

Rotter, J. B. (1992). "Cognates of personal control: Locus of control, self-efficacy, and explanatory style": Comment. *Applied & Preventive Psychology, 1*(2), 127–129.

Rotter, J. B., & Hochreich, D. J. (1975). *Personality.* Glenview, IL: Scott, Foresman.

Rouhana, N. N., & Bar-Tal, D. (1998). Psychological dynamics of intractable ethnonational conflicts: The Israeli–Palestinian case. *American Psychologist, 53*, 761–770.

Rovee-Collier, C., Borza, M. A., Adler, S. A., & Boller, K. (1993). Infants' eyewitness testimony: Effects of postevent information on a prior memory representation. *Memory & Cognition, 21*(2), 267–279.

Rozin, P., & Fallon, A. (1987). A perspective on disgust. *Psychological Review, 94*, 23–41.

Ruch, J. C. (1975). Self-hypnosis: The result of heterohypnosis or vice versa? *International Journal of Clinical and Experimental Hypnosis, 23*, 282–304.

Rudy, T. E., Kerns, R. D., & Turk, D. C. (1988). Chronic pain and depression: Toward a cognitive-behavioral mediation model. *Pain, 35*, 129–140.

Russell, J. A. (1991). Culture and categorization of emotions. *Psychological Bulletin, 110*(3), 426–450.

Russell, J. A. (1995). Is there universal recognition of emotion from facial expression? A review of the cross-cultural studies. *Psychological Bulletin, 115*(1), 102–141.

Russell, M. J. (1976). Human olfactory communication. *Nature, 260*, 520–522.

Russell, W. R., & Nathan, P. W. (1946). Traumatic amnesia. *Brain, 69*, 280–300.

Sacks, O. (1990). *Seeing voices: A journey into the world of the deaf.* New York: HarperPerennial.

Sacks, O. (1995). *An anthropologist on Mars: Seven paradoxical tales.* New York: Knopf.

Sadker, M., & Sadker, D. (1984). *Year three: Final report, promoting effectiveness in classroom instruction.* Washington, DC: National Institute of Education.

Safer, D. J. (1991). Diet, behavior modification, and exercise: A review of obesity treatments from a long-term perspective. *Southern Medical Journal, 84*, 1470–1474.

Safire, W., & Safir, L. (Eds.). (1989). *Words of wisdom: More good advice.* New York: Fireside, Simon & Schuster.

Salovey, P., & Mayer, J. D. (1990). Emotional intelligence. *Imagination, Cognition, and Personality, 9*, 185–244.

Salthouse, T. A. (1996). Constraints on theories of cognitive aging. *Psychonomic Bulletin and Review, 3*, 287–299.

Salthouse, T. A., & Somberg, B. L. (1982). Skilled performance: Effects of adult age and experience on elementary processes. *Journal of Experimental Psychology: General, 111*(2), 176–207.

Sanders, S. H. (1985). Chronic pain: Conceptualization and epidemiology. *Annals of Behavioral Medicine, 7*(3), 3–5.

Sarason, I. G., Pierce, G. R., & Sarason, B. R. (1994). General and specific perceptions of social support. In W. R. Avison & I. H. Gotlib (Eds.), *Stress and mental health: Contemporary issues and prospects for the future* (Plenum series on stress and coping) (pp. 151–177). New York: Plenum.

Sarason, S. B., & Doris, J. (1979). *Educational handicap, public policy, and social history.* New York: Free Press.

Sartorius, N., de Girolano, G., Andrews, G., German, G. A., & Eisenberg, L. (Eds.). (1993). *Treatment of mental disorders: A review of effectiveness.* Geneva, Switzerland, and Washington, DC: World Health Organization and American Psychiatric Press.

Sartorius, N., Kaelber, C., Cooper, J. E., Roper, M. T., et al. (1993). Progress toward achieving a common language in psychiatry: Results from the field trial of the clinical guidelines accompanying the WHO classification of mental and behavioral disorders in ICD-10. *Archives of General Psychiatry, 50*(2), 115–124.

Sartorius, N., Shapiro, R., & Jablonsky, A. (1974). The international pilot study of schizophrenia. *Schizophrenia Bulletin, 2,* 21–35.

Savage-Rumbaugh, S., McDonald, K., Sevcik, R. A., Hopkins, W. D., & Rubert, E. (1986). Spontaneous symbol acquisition and communicative use by pygmy chimpanzees (Pan paniscus). *Journal of Experimental Psychology: General, 112,* 211–235.

Savery, L. K., & Wooden, M. (1994). The relative influence of life events and hassles on work-related injuries: Some Australian evidence. *Human Relations, 47*(3), 283–305.

Saxe, L., Dougherty, D., & Cross, T. (1985). The validity of polygraph testing: Scientific analysis and public controversy. *American Psychologist, 40,* 355–366.

Scarr, S. (1997). Behavior genetic and socialization theories of intelligence: Truce and reconciliation. In R. J. Sternberg & E. L. Grigorenko (Eds.), *Intelligence, heredity, and environment.* New York: Cambridge University Press.

Schachter, S. (1968). Obesity and eating. *Science, 161,* 751–756.

Schachter, S. (1971a). *Emotion, obesity, and crime.* New York: Academic Press.

Schachter, S. (1971b). Some extraordinary facts about obese humans and rats. *American Psychologist, 26,* 129–144.

Schachter, S., & Gross, L. (1968). Manipulated time and eating behavior. *Journal of Personality and Social Psychology, 10,* 98–106.

Schachter, S., & Rodin, J. (1974). *Obese humans and rats.* Hillsdale, NJ: Erlbaum.

Schachter, S., & Singer, J. (1962). Cognitive, social, and physiological determinants of emotional state. *Psychological Review, 69,* 379–399.

Schacter, D. L. (1989a). Memory. In M. I. Posner (Ed.), *Foundations of cognitive science* (pp. 683–725). Cambridge, MA: MIT Press.

Schacter, D. L. (1989b). On the relation between memory and consciousness: Dissociable interactions and conscious experience. In H. L. Roediger & F. I. M. Craik (Eds.), *Varieties of memory and consciousness: Essays in honor of Endel Tulving.* Hillsdale, NJ: Erlbaum.

Schaffer, H. R. (1977). *Mothering.* Cambridge, MA: Harvard University Press.

Schaie, K. W. (1989). Perceptual speed in adulthood: Cross-sectional and longitudinal studies. *Psychology and Aging, 4,* 443–453.

Scharfe, E., & Bartholomew, K. (1994). Reliability and stability of adult attachment patterns. *Personal Relationships, 1,* 23–43.

Schliemann, A. D., & Magalhües, V. P. (1990). *Proportional reasoning: From shops, to kitchens, laboratories, and, hopefully, schools.* Proceedings of the Fourteenth International Conference for the Psychology of Mathematics Education, Oaxtepec, Mexico.

Schreiber, F. R. (1973). *Sybil.* New York: Warner Paperback.

Schwarzer, R., & Leppin, A. (1989). Social support and health: A meta-analysis. *Psychology & Health, 3*(1), 1–15.

Schwarzer, R., & Leppin, A. (1991). Social support and health: A theoretical and empirical overview. *Journal of Social & Personal Relationships, 8*(1), 99–127.

Schweizer, E., Rickels, K., Case, G., & Greenblatt, D. J. (1990). Long-term therapeutic use of benzodiazepines: II. Effects of gradual taper. *Archives of General Psychiatry, 47*(10), 908–915.

Scott, A. I. F. (1989). Which depressed patients will respond to electroconvulsive therapy? The search for biological predictors of recovery. *British Journal of Psychiatry, 154,* 8–17.

Scott, J. (1991, August 26). Judging the risk of infection: The AIDS epidemic is making patients fearful of being infected by health-care workers. But some say the odds are far less that one will be hit by lightning. *Los Angeles Times,* p. A1.

Scovern, A. W., & Kilmann, P. R. (1980). Status of electroconvulsive therapy: Review of the outcome literature. *Psychological Bulletin, 87,* 260–303.

Scoville, W. B., & Milner, B. (1957). Loss of recent memory after bilateral hippocampal lesions. *Journal of Neurology, Neurosurgery, and Psychiatry, 20,* 11–19.

Sears, R. R., Maccoby, E., & Levin, H. (1957). *Patterns of child rearing.* Evanston, IL: Row, Peterson.

Segall, M. H., Campbell, D. T., & Herskovits, M. J. (1966). *The influence of culture on visual perception.* New York: Bobbs-Merrill.

Seiden, R. H. (1974). Suicide: Preventable death. *Public Affairs Report, 15*(4), 1–5.

Seidman, L. J. (1983). Schizophrenia and brain dysfunction: An integration of recent neurodiagnostic findings. *Psychological Bulletin, 94,* 195–238.

Selfridge, O. G. (1959). Pandemonium: A paradigm for learning. In D. V. Blake & A. M. Uttley (Eds.), *Proceedings of the Symposium on the Mechanization of Thought Processes* (pp. 511–529). London: Her Majesty's Stationery Office.

Seligman, M. E. P. (1975). *Helplessness.* San Francisco: Freeman.

Seligman, M. E. P. (1989). Research in clinical psychology: Why is there so much depression today? In Ira S. Cohen (Ed.), *The G. Stanley Hall lecture series* (Vol. 9, pp. 79–96). Washington, DC: American Psychological Association.

Seligman, M. E. P. (1991). *Learned optimism.* New York: Norton.

Seligman, M. E. P. (1995). The effectiveness of psychotherapy: The consumer reports study. *American Psychologist, 50,* 965–983.

Seligman, M. E. P., & Maier, S. F. (1967). Failure to escape traumatic shock. *Journal of Experimental Psychology, 74,* 1–9.

Selman, R. (1981). The child as friendship philosopher. In J. M. Gottman (Ed.), *The development of children's friendships.* Cambridge, England: Cambridge University Press.

Selye, H. (1974). *Stress without distress.* Philadelphia: Lippincott.

Selye, H. (1976). *The stress of life* (Rev. ed.). New York: McGraw-Hill.

Sepple, C. P., & Read, N. W. (1989). Gastrointestinal correlates of the development of hunger in man. *Appetite, 13,* 183–191.

Seraganian, P. (Ed.). (1993). *Exercise psychology: The influence of physical exercise on psychological processes.* New York: Wiley.

Seymour, R. B., & Smith, D. E. (1987). *Guide to psychoactive drugs: An up-to-the-minute reference to mind-altering substances.* New York: Harrington Park Press.

Shanab, M. E., & Yahya, K. A. (1977). A behavioral study of obedience in children. *Journal of Personality and Social Psychology, 35,* 530–536.

Shanab, M. E., & Yahya, K. A. (1978). A cross-cultural study of obedience. *Bulletin of the Psychonomic Society, 11,* 267–269.

Shapiro, D. H., & Giber, D. (1978). Meditation and psychotherapeutic effects: Self-regulation strategy and altered states of consciousness. *Archives of General Psychiatry, 35,* 294–302.

Shapiro, P., & Penrod, S. (1986). Meta-analysis of facial identification studies. *Psychological Bulletin, 100*(2), 139–156.

Shaver, P. R. (1994, August). *Attachment and care giving in adult romantic relationships*. Paper presented at the annual meeting of the American Psychological Association, Los Angeles.

Shekelle, R. B., Hulley, S. B., Neaton, J. D., Billings, J. H., Borhani, N. O., Gerace, T. A., Jacobs, D. R., Lasser, N. L., Mittelmark, M. B., & Stamler, J. (1985). The MRFIT behavior pattern study: II. Type A behavior and incidence of coronary heart disease. *American Journal of Epidemiology, 122*, 559–570.

Shepard, R. N. (1990). *Mindsights*. New York: W. H. Freeman.

Sheppard, J. A., & Arkin, R. M. (1989). Self-handicapping: The moderating role of public self–consciousness and task importance. *Personality and Social Psychology Bulletin, 15*, 252–265.

Sherif, M., Harvey, L. J., White, B. J., Hood, W. R., & Sherif, C. W. (1988). *The Robber's Cave experiment: Intergroup conflict and cooperation*. Middletown, CT: Wesleyan University Press. (Original work published 1961)

Sherman, S. J., Judd, C. M., & Park, B. (1989). Social cognition. *Annual Review of Psychology, 40*, 281–326.

Shibazaki, M. (1983). Development of hemispheric function in hiragana, kanji and figure processing for normal children and mentally retarded children. *Japanese Journal of Special Education, 21*(3), 1–9.

Shimada, J., & Otsuka, A. (1981). Functional hemispheric differences in kanji processing in Japanese. *Japanese Psychological Review, 24*(4), 472–489.

Shimamura, A. P., & Squire, L. R. (1986). Korsakoff's syndrome: A study of the relation between anterograde amnesia and remote memory impairment. *Behavioral Neuroscience, 100(2)*, 165–170.

Shneidman, E. S. (1973). Suicide. In *Encyclopedia Britannica*. Chicago: Encyclopedia Britannica.

Shontz, F. C. (1975). *The psychological aspects of physical illness and disability*. New York: Macmillan.

Shuit, D. P. (1994, May 22). Verdict heats up memory debate. *Los Angeles Times*, p. A3.

Sibitani, A. (1980). The Japanese brain. *Science, 80*, 22–26.

Siegel, E. F. (1979). Control of phantom limb pain by hypnosis. *American Journal of Clinical Hypnosis, 21*(4), 285–286.

Siegler, R. S. (1986). *Children's thinking*. Englewood Cliffs, NJ: Prentice-Hall.

Siegler, R. S. (1991). *Children's thinking* (2nd ed.). Englewood Cliffs, NJ: Prentice-Hall.

Silverstein, B., Peterson, B., & Perdue, L. (1986). Some correlates of the thin standard of bodily attractiveness in women. *International Journal of Eating Disorders, 5*, 145–155.

Simon, H. A. (1957). *Administrative behavior* (2nd ed.). Totowa, NJ: Littlefield, Adams.

Simon, H. A. (1976). Identifying basic abilities underlying intelligent performance of complex tasks. In L. B. Resnick (Ed.), *The nature of intelligence* (pp. 65–98). Hillsdale, NJ: Erlbaum.

Simon, W. H., & Gagnon, J. H. (1986). Sexual scripts: Permanence and change. *Archives of Sexual Behavior, 15*(2), 97–120.

Simonton, D. K. (1988). *Scientific genius*. New York: Cambridge University Press.

Simonton, D. K. (1994). *Greatness: Who makes history and why*. New York: Guilford Press.

Simonton, D. K. (1995). Foresight in insight: A Darwinian answer. In R. J. Sternberg & J. E. Davidson (Eds.), *The nature of insight* (pp. 495–534). Cambridge, MA: MIT Press.

Simonton, D. K. (1998). Donald Campbell's model of creative process: Creativity as blind variation and selective retention. *Journal of Creative Behavior, 52*, 153–158.

Siskin, B., Staller, J., & Rorvik, D. (1989). *What are the chances? Risks, odds, and likelihood in everyday life*. New York: Penguin.

Skinner, B. F. (1974). *About behaviorism*. New York: Knopf.

Skinner, B. F. (1986). Why I am not a cognitive psychologist. In T. J. Knapp & L. C. Robertson (Eds.), *Approaches to cognition: Contrasts and controversies* (pp. 79–90). Hillsdale, NJ: Erlbaum.

Skinner, B. F. (1988). The phylogeny and ontogeny of behavior. In A. C. Catania & S. Harnad (Eds.), *The selection of behavior: The operant behaviorism of B. F. Skinner: Comments and consequences* (pp. 382–461). New York: Cambridge University Press.

Smith, D. (1982). Trends in counseling and psychotherapy. *American Psychologist, 37*, 802–809.

Smith, M. L., & Glass, G. V. (1977). Meta-analysis of psychotherapy outcome studies. *American Psychologist* (November), 752–760.

Smith, P. B., & Bond, M. H. (1994). *Social psychology across cultures: Analysis and perspectives*. Boston: Allyn & Bacon.

Smith, P. B., & Öngel, Ö. (1994). Who are we and where are we going? JCCP approaches its hundredth issue. *Journal of Cross-Cultural Psychology, 25*(1), 25–54.

Snarey, J. R., Reimer, J., & Kohlberg, L. (1985a). Development of social-moral reasoning among kibbutz adolescents: A longitudinal cross-cultural study. *Developmental Psychology, 21*, 3–17.

Snarey, J. R., Reimer, J., & Kohlberg, L. (1985b). The kibbutz as a model for moral education: A longitudinal cross-cultural study. *Journal of Applied Developmental Psychology, 6*, 151–172.

Snow, C. E. (1977). The development of conversation between mothers and babies. *Journal of Child Language, 4*, 1–22.

Solomon, G. F., & Temoshok, L. (1987). A psychoneuroimmunologic perspective on AIDS research: Questions, preliminary findings, and suggestions. *Journal of Applied Social Psychology, 17*, 286–308.

Solomon, R. L. (1980). The opponent-process theory of motivation: The costs of pleasure and the benefits of pain. *American Psychologist, 35*, 681–712.

Solomon, R. L., & Corbit, J. D. (1974). An opponent-process theory of motivation: I. Temporal dynamics of affect. *Psychological Review, 81*, 119–145.

Spangler, W. (1992). Validity of questionnaire and TAT measures of need for achievement: Two meta-analyses. *Psychological Bulletin, 112*, 140–154.

Spanos, N. P. (1992). Compliance and reinterpretation in hypnotic responding. *Contemporary Hypnosis, 9*(1), 7–15.

Spanos, N. P. (1994). Multiple identity enactments and multiple personality disorder: A socio-cognitive perspective. *Psychological Bulletin, 116*, 143–165.

Spanos, N. P., DuBreuil, S. C., & Gabora, N. J. (1991). Four month follow-up of skill training induced enhancements in hypnotizability. *Contemporary Hypnosis, 8*, 25–32.

Spearman, C. (1927). *The abilities of man*. New York: Macmillan.

Specter, M. (1989, May 7). Seeing risk everywhere: In epidemic of fear, major threats ignored. *Washington Post*, pp. A1, A20.

Spelke, E. (1976). Infant's intermodal perception of events. *Cognitive Psychology, 8*, 553–560.

Sperling, G. (1960). The information available in brief visual presentations. *Psychological Monographs: General and Applied, 74*, 1–28.

Sperry, R. W. (1964). The great cerebral commissure. *Scientific American, 210*(1), 42–52.

Spicer, J., Jackson, R., & Scragg, R. (1993). The effects of anger management and social contact on risk of myocardial infarction in Type As and Type Bs. *Psychology and Health, 8*(4), 243–255.

Spitzer, L., & Rodin, J. (1981). Human eating behavior: A critical review of studies in normal weight and overweight individuals. *Appetite, 2*, 293–329.

Springer, S. P., & Deutsch, G. (1985). *Left brain, right brain*. New York: Freeman.

Squier, L. H., & Domhoff, C. W. (1997). The presentation of dreaming in introductory psychology textbooks: A critical examination with suggestions for textbook authors and course

Barefoot, J. C., Dodge, K. A., Peterson, B. L., Dahlstrom, W. G., & Williams, R. B. (1989). The Cook–Medley hostility scale: Item content and ability to predict survival. *Psychosomatic Medicine, 51,* 46–57.

Barker, R. G., Dembo, T., & Lewin, K. (1941). Frustration and regression: An experiment with young children. *University of Iowa Studies in Child Welfare, 18*(1).

Baron, J. (1988). *Thinking and deciding.* New York: Cambridge University Press.

Baron, M., Gershon, E. S., Rudy, V., Jonas, W. Z., & Buchsbaum, M. (1975). Lithium carbonate response in depression. *Archives of General Psychiatry, 32,* 1107–1111.

Baron, R. A. (1976). The reduction of human aggression: A field study of the influence of incompatible reactions. *Journal of Applied Social Psychology, 6,* 260–274.

Baron, R. A. (1977). *Human aggression.* New York: Plenum.

Baron, R. A., & Byrne, D. (1991). *Social psychology: Understanding human interaction* (6th ed.). Boston: Allyn & Bacon.

Baron, R. A., & Richardson, D. R. (1992). *Human aggression* (2nd ed.). New York: Plenum.

Baron, R. S. (1986). Distraction-conflict theory: Progress and problems. In L. Berkowitz (Ed.), *Advances in experimental social psychology.* Orlando, FL: Academic Press.

Barr, H. M., Streissguth, A. P., Darby, B. L., & Sampson, P. D. (1990). Prenatal exposure to alcohol, caffeine, tobacco, and aspirin: Effects on fine and gross motor performance in 4-year-old children. *Developmental Psychology, 26,* 339–348.

Barrett, P. T., & Eysenck, H. J. (1992). Brain evoked potentials and intelligence: The Hendrickson paradigm. *Intelligence, 16*(3–4), 361–381.

Barron, F. (1988). Putting creativity to work. In R. J. Sternberg (Ed.), *The nature of creativity* (pp. 76–98). New York: Cambridge University Press.

Bartlett, F. C. (1932). *Remembering: A study in experimental and social psychology.* Cambridge, England: Cambridge University Press.

Bartoshuk, L. M. (1991). Sensory factors in eating behavior. Thirty-first annual meeting of the Psychonomic Society: Symposium on experimental approaches to eating and its disorders (1990, New Orleans, Louisiana). *Bulletin of the Psychonomic Society, 29*(3), 250–255.

Bartoshuk, L. M., Duffy, V. B., & Miller, I. J. (1994). PTC/PROP taste: Anatomy, psychophysics, and sex effects. Kirin International Symposium: On bitter taste (1993, Tokyo, Japan), *Physiology & Behavior, 56*(6), 1165–1171.

Bashore, T. R., Osman, A., & Hefley, E. F. (1989). Mental slowing in elderly persons: A cognitive psychophysiological analysis. *Psychology and Aging, 4,* 235–244.

Bashore, T. R., & Rapp, P. E. (1993). Are there alternatives to traditional polygraph procedures? *Psychological Bulletin, 113*(1), 3–22.

Basow, S. A. (1986). *Gender stereotypes: Traditions and alternatives* (2nd ed.). Belmont, CA: Brooks/Cole.

Baumrind, D. (1985). Research using intentional deception: Ethical issues revisited. *American Psychologist, 40,* 165–174.

Baumrind, D. (1986). Sex differences in moral reasoning: Response to Walker's (1984) conclusion that there are none. *Child Development, 57,* 511–521.

Bayley, N. (1993). *The Bayley Scales of Mental and Motor Development* (Revised). New York: Psychological Corporation.

Bayley, N. (1968). Behavioral correlates of mental growth: Birth to thirty-six years. *American Psychologist, 23,* 1–17.

Beall, A. E., & Allen, T. W. (1997). Why we buy what we buy: Consulting in consumer psychology. In R. J. Sternberg (Ed.), *Career paths in psychology* (pp. 197–211). Washington, DC: American Psychological Association.

Beall, A. E., & Sternberg, R. J. (Eds.). (1993). *Perspectives on the psychology of gender.* New York: Guilford Press.

Beck, A. T. (1976). *Cognitive therapy and the emotional disorders.* New York: International Universities Press.

Beck, A. T. (1986). Cognitive therapy: A sign of retrogression of progress. *The Behavior Therapist, 9,* 2–3.

Beck, A. T. (1988). Cognitive approaches to panic disorder: Theory and therapy. In S. Rachman & J. D. Maser (Eds.), *Panic: Psychological perspectives.* Hillsdale, NJ: Erlbaum.

Bekerian, D. A. (1993). In search of the typical eyewitness. *American Psychologist, 48*(5), 574–576.

Bellack, A. S., Hersen, M., & Kazdin, A. E. (Eds.). (1990). *International handbook of behavior modification and therapy* (2nd ed.). New York: Plenum.

Belloc, N. D., & Breslow, L. (1972). Relationship of physical health status and family practices. *Preventive Medicine, 1,* 409–421.

Bellugi, U., Poizner, H., & Klima, E. S. (1989). Language, modality and the brain. *Trends in Neuroscience, 12*(10), 380–388.

Belsky, J. (1990). Parental and nonparental child care and children's socioemotional development: A decade in review. *Journal of Marriage and the Family, 52,* 885–903.

Bem, D. J. (1967). Self-perception: An alternative interpretation of cognitive dissonance phenomena. *Psychological Review, 74,* 183–200.

Bem, D. J. (1972). Self perception theory. In L. Berkowitz (Ed.), *Advances in experimental social psychology* (Vol. 6). New York: Academic Press.

Bem, D. J. (1996). Exotic becomes erotic: A developmental theory of sexual orientation. *Psychological Review, 81,* 506–520.

Bem, D. J., & Allen, A. (1974). On predicting some of the people some of the time: The search for cross-situational consistencies in behavior. *Psychological Review, 81,* 506–520.

Bem, S. L. (1981). Gender schema theory: A cognitive account of sex typing. *Psychological Review, 88,* 354–364.

Benbow, C. P., & Stanley, J. C. (1980). Sex differences in mathematical ability: Fact or artifact? *Science, 210,* 1262–1264.

Ben-Shakhar, G., & Furedy, J. J. (1990). *Theories and applications in the detection of deception: A psychophysiological and international perspective.* New York: Springer-Verlag.

Benson, H. (1977). Systemic hypertension and the relaxation response. *New England Journal of Medicine, 296,* 1152–1156.

Berger, K. S. (1980). *The developing person.* New York: Worth.

Berglas, S., & Jones, E. E. (1978). Drug choice as a self-handicapping strategy in response to noncontingent success. *Journal of Personality and Social Psychology, 36,* 405–417.

Berkman, L. (1994, May 22). "I really was hurt by the verdict." (Holly Ramona says jury's decision will undermine her attempt to recover damages from her father, Gary Ramona, who she alleges molested her.) *Los Angeles Times,* p. A3.

Berkowitz, L., Cochran, S., & Embree, M. (1981). Physical pain and the goal of aversively stimulated aggression. *Journal of Personality and Social Psychology, 40,* 687–700.

Berkowitz, L., & Geen, R. G. (1966). Film violence and the cue properties of variable targets. *Journal of Personality and Social Psychology, 3,* 525–530.

Berkowitz, L., & Geen, R. G. (1967). Stimulus qualities of the target of aggression: A further study. *Journal of Personality and Social Psychology, 5,* 364–368.

Berlin, B., & Kay, P. (1969). *Basic color terms: Their universality and evolution.* Los Angeles: University of California Press.

Berlyne, D. E. (1960). *Conflict, arousal, and curiosity.* New York: McGraw-Hill.

Berlyne, D. E. (1967). Arousal reinforcement. In D. Levine (Ed.), *Nebraska Symposium on Motivation* (pp. 1–110). Lincoln, NE: University of Nebraska Press.

Bernard, L. L. (1924). *Instinct.* New York: Holt, Rinehart and Winston.

instructors. *Dreaming: Journal of the Association for the Study of Dreams, 8(3),* 149–168.

Squire, L. R. (1986). Mechanisms of memory. *Science, 232,* 1612–1619.

Squire, L. R. (1987). *Memory and the brain.* New York: Oxford University Press.

Sroufe, L. A. (1979). Socioemotional development. In J. D. Osofsky (Ed.), *Handbook of infant development.* New York: Wiley.

Srull, T. K., & Wyer, R. S., Jr. (1989). Person memory and judgment. *Psychology Review, 96(1),* 58–83.

Standing, L., Conezio, J., & Haber, R. N. (1970). Perception and memory for pictures: Single-trial learning of 2500 visual stimuli. *Psychonomic Science, 19,* 73–74.

Stedman's medical dictionary (25th ed.). (1990). Baltimore: Williams & Wilkins.

Steele, C. (1990, May). A conversation with Claude Steele. *APS Observer,* pp. 11–17.

Steptoe, A., & Appels, A. (Eds.). (1989). *Stress, personal control and health.* Chichester, England: Wiley.

Stern, D. (1977). *The first relationship: Mother and infant.* Cambridge, MA: Harvard University Press.

Stern, W. (1912). *Psychologische Methoden der Intelligenz-Prüfung.* Leipzig, Germany: Barth.

Sternberg, R. J. (1985a). *Beyond IQ: A triarchic theory of human intelligence.* New York: Cambridge University Press.

Sternberg, R. J. (1985b). Implicit theories of intelligence, creativity, and wisdom. *Journal of Personality and Social Psychology, 49,* 607–627.

Sternberg, R. J. (1986a). *Intelligence applied: Understanding and increasing your intellectual skills.* San Diego, CA: Harcourt Brace Jovanovich.

Sternberg, R. J. (1986b). A triangular theory of love. *Psychological Review, 93,* 119–135.

Sternberg, R. J. (1987). Teaching intelligence: The application of cognitive psychology to the improvement of intellectual skills. In J. B. Baron & R. J. Sternberg (Eds.), *Teaching thinking skills: Theory and practice* (pp. 182–218). New York: W. H. Freeman.

Sternberg, R. J. (1988a). Triangulating love. In R. J. Sternberg & M. L. Barnes (Eds.), *The psychology of love* (pp. 119–138). New Haven, CT: Yale University Press.

Sternberg, R. J. (1988b). *The triarchic mind.* New York: Viking.

Sternberg, R. J. (Ed.). (1990). *Wisdom: Its nature, origins, and development.* New York: Cambridge University Press.

Sternberg, R. J. (1994). Love is a story. *The General Psychologist, 30(1),* 1–11.

Sternberg, R. J. (1995). For whom the bell curve tolls: A review of *The bell curve. Psychological Science, 6,* 257–261.

Sternberg, R. J. (1996). Love stories. *Personal Relationships, 3,* 1359–1379.

Sternberg, R. J. (Ed.). (1997a). *Career paths in psychology.* Washington, DC: American Psychological Association.

Sternberg, R. J. (1997b). Construct validation of a triangular love scale. *European Journal of Social Psychology, 27,* 313–335.

Sternberg, R. J. (1997c). *Successful intelligence.* New York: Plume.

Sternberg, R. J. (1998a). *Cupid's arrow.* New York: Cambridge University Press.

Sternberg, R. J. (1998b). *Love is a story.* New York: Oxford University Press.

Sternberg, R. J. (Ed.). (1999). *Handbook of creativity.* New York: Cambridge University Press.

Sternberg, R. J., & Berg, C. A. (1992). Adults' conceptions of intelligence across the adult life span. *Psychology and Aging, 7(2),* 221–231.

Sternberg, R. J., & Davidson, J. E. (Eds.). (1986). *Conceptions of giftedness.* New York: Cambridge University Press.

Sternberg, R. J., & Davidson, J. E. (Eds.). (1995). *The nature of insight.* Cambridge, MA: MIT Press.

Sternberg, R. J., Ferrari, M., Clinkenbeard, P. R., & Grigorenko, E. L. (1996). Identification, instruction, and assessment of gifted children: A construct validation of a triarchic model. *Gifted Child Quarterly, 40,* 129–137.

Sternberg, R. J., & Grigorenko, E. L. (1997a). The cognitive costs of physical and mental ill health: Applying the psychology of the developed world to the problems of the developing world. *Eye on Psi Chi, 2,* 20–27.

Sternberg, R. J., & Grigorenko, E. L. (Eds.). (1997b). *Intelligence, heredity, and environment.* New York: Cambridge University Press.

Sternberg, R. J., Grigorenko, E. L., Ferrari, M., & Clinkenbeard, P. (1999). Triarchic analysis of an aptitude-treatment interaction. *European Journal of Psychological Assessment, 15,* 1–11.

Sternberg, R. J., & Hojjat, M. (Eds.). (1997). *Satisfaction in close relationships.* New York: Guildford Press.

Sternberg, R. J., & Lubart, T. I. (1991). An investment theory of creativity and its development. *Human Development, 34,* 1–31.

Sternberg, R. J., & Lubart, T. I. (1995). *Defying the crowd.* New York: Free Press.

Sternberg, R. J., & Lubart, T. I. (1996). Investing in creativity. *American Psychologist, 51,* 677–688.

Sternberg, R. J., Okagaki, L., & Jackson, A. (1990). Practical intelligence for success in school. *Educational Leadership, 48,* 35–39.

Sternberg, R. J., & Ruzgis, P. (Eds.). (1994). *Personality and intelligence.* New York: Cambridge University Press.

Sternberg, R. J., Torff, B., & Grigorenko, E. L. (1998). Teaching for successful intelligence raises school achievement. *Phi Delta Kappan, 79,* 667–669.

Sternberg, R. J., & Wagner, R. K. (Eds.). (1994). *Mind in context: Interactionist perspectives on human intelligence.* New York: Cambridge University Press.

Sternberg, R. J., Wagner, R. K., Williams, W. M., & Horvath, J. A. (1995). Testing common sense. *American Psychologist, 50,* 912–927.

Sternberg, S. (1966). High-speed memory scanning in human memory. *Science, 153,* 652–654.

Sternberg, S. (1969). Memory-scanning: Mental processes revealed by reaction-time experiments. *American Scientist, 4,* 421–457.

Stevenson-Hinde, J., Hinde, R. A., & Simpson, A. E. (1986). Behavior at home and friendly or hostile behavior in preschool. In D. Olweus, J. Block, & M. Radke-Yarrow (Eds.), *Development of antisocial and prosocial behavior: Research, theorism, and issues.* Orlando, FL: Academic Press.

Stewart, A. J. (1982). The course of individual adaptation to life changes. *Journal of Personality and Social Psychology, 42,* 1100–1113.

Stewart, A. J., & Healy, J. M., Jr. (1985). Personality and adaptation to change. In R. Hogan & W. H. Jones (Eds.), *Perspectives in personality* (Vol. 1, pp. 117–144). Greenwich, CT: JAI Press.

Stewart, A. J., & Healy, J. M. (1989). Linking individual development and social changes. *American Psychologist, 44(1),* 30–42.

Stewart, A. J., Sokol, M., Healy, J. M., & Chester, N. L. (1986). Longitudinal studies of psychological consequences of life changes in children and adults. *Journal of Personality and Social Psychology, 50,* 143–151.

Stiles, W. B., Shapiro, D. A., & Elliott, R. (1986). Are all psychotherapies equivalent? *American Psychologist, 41(2),* 165–180.

Strauss, B. S. (1997). Treating, teaching, and training: Clinical psychologists in hospitals. In R. J. Sternberg (Ed.), *Career paths in psychology* (pp. 133–147). Washington, DC: American Psychological Association.

Strauss, J. S., Kokes, F. R., Ritzler, B. A., Harder, D. W., & Van Ord, A. (1978). Patterns of disorder in first admission psychiatric patients. *Journal of Nervous and Mental Disease, 166,* 611–623.

Streissguth, A. P., Martin, D. C., Barr, H. M., Sandman, B. M., Kirchner, G. L., & Darby, B. L. (1984). Intrauterine alcohol and nicotine exposure. Attention and reaction time in 4-year-old children. *Developmental Psychology, 20,* 533–541.

Streissguth, A. P., Sampson, P. D., & Barr, H. M. (1989). Neurobehavioral dose-response effects of prenatal alcohol exposure in humans from infancy to adulthood. Conference of the Behavioral Teratology Society, the National Institute on Drug Abuse, and the New York Academy of Sciences: Prenatal abuse of licit and illicit drugs (1988, Bethesda, Maryland). *Annals of the New York Academy of Sciences, 562,* 145–158.

Stroebe, W., Stroebe, M., & Domittner, G. (1988). Individual and situational differences in recovery from bereavement: A risk group identified. *Journal of Social Issues, 44,* 143–158.

Stroop, J. (1935). Studies of interference in serial verbal reactions. *Journal of Experimental Psychology, 18,* 624–643.

Strupp, H. H. (1981). Toward a refinement of time-limited dynamic psychotherapy. In S. H. Budman (Ed.), *Forms of brief therapy.* New York: Guilford Press.

Sue, D., & Sue, D. (1990). *Counseling the culturally different* (2nd ed.). New York: Wiley.

Sue, S. (1977). Community mental health services to minority groups: Some optimism, some pessimism. *American Psychologist, 32,* 616–624.

Sue, S. (1991, August). *Ethnicity and mental health: Research and policy issues.* Invited address presented at the annual meeting of the American Psychological Association, San Francisco.

Sue, S., Akutsu, P. D., & Higashi, C. (1985). Training issues in conducting therapy with ethnic-minority-group clients. In P. Pedersen (Ed.), *Handbook of cross-cultural counseling and therapy.* New York: Greenwood Press.

Suematsu, H., Ishikawa, H., Kuboki, T., & Ito, T. (1985). Statistical studies on anorexia nervosa in Japan: Detailed clinical data on 1,011 patients. *Psychotherapy and Psychosomatics, 43,* 96–103.

Sulzer-Azaroff, B., & Mayer, G. R. (1991). *Behavior analysis for lasting change.* Fort Worth, TX: Holt, Rinehart and Winston.

Swann, W. B., Jr., & Pittman, T. S. (1977). Initiating play activity in children: The moderating influence of verbal cue on intrinsic motivation. *Child Development, 48,* 1125–1132.

Swartz, L. (1985). Anorexia nervosa as a culture-bound syndrome. *Social Science and Medicine, 20,* 725–730.

Swets, J. A., Tanner, W. P., Jr., & Birdsall, T. G. (1961). Decision processes in perception. *Psychological Review, 68,* 301–340.

Szasz, T. S. (1961). *The myth of mental illness.* New York: Harper & Row.

Szasz, T. S. (1963). *Law, liberty, and psychiatry.* New York: Macmillan.

Szmukler, G. I., & Russell, G. F. M. (1986). Outcome and prognosis of anorexia nervosa. In K. D. Brownell & J. P. Foreyt (Eds.), *Handbook of eating disorders.* New York: Basic Books.

Tanford, S., & Penrod, S. (1984). Social influence model: A formal integration of research on majority and minority influence processes. *Psychological Bulletin, 95,* 189–225.

Tannen, D. (1986). *That's not what I meant! How conversational style makes or breaks relationships.* New York: Ballantine.

Tannen, D. (1990). *You just don't understand: Women and men in conversation.* New York: Ballantine.

Taylor, S. E. (1983). Adjustment to threatening events: A theory of cognitive adaptation. *American Psychologist, 38,* 1161–1173.

Taylor, S. E. (1990). Health psychology: The science and the field. *American Psychologist, 45*(1), 40–50.

Taylor, S. E. (1991). *Health psychology* (2nd ed.). New York: McGraw-Hill.

Taylor, S. E., & Aspinwall, L. G. (1990). Psychological aspects of chronic illness. In G. R. Van den Bos & P. T. Costa, Jr. (Eds.), *Psychological aspects of serious illness.* Washington, DC: American Psychological Association.

Taylor, S. E., & Brown, J. D. (1988). Illusion and well-being: A social psychological perspective on mental health. *Psychological Bulletin, 103*(2), 193–210.

Teitelbaum, P. (1961). Disturbances in feeding and drinking behavior after hypothalamic lesions. In M. R. Jones (Ed.), *Nebraska Symposium on Motivation.* Lincoln, NE: University of Nebraska Press.

Tellegen, A., Lykken, D. T., Bouchard, T. J., Jr., Wilcox, K. J., & Rich, S. (1988). Personality similarity in twins reared apart and together. *Journal of Personality and Social Psychology, 54,* 1031–1039.

Tenopyr, M. L. (1997). Improving the workplace: Industrial/organizational psychology as a career. In R. J. Sternberg (Ed.), *Career paths in psychology* (pp. 185–196). Washington, DC: American Psychological Association.

Terman, L. M. (1925). *Genetic studies of genius: Mental and physical traits of a thousand gifted children* (Vol. 1). Stanford, CA: Stanford University Press.

Terman, L. M., & Merrill, M. A. (1937). *Measuring intelligence.* Boston: Houghton Mifflin.

Terman, L. M., & Merrill, M. A. (1973). *Stanford-Binet Intelligence Scale: Manual for the third revision.* Boston: Houghton Mifflin.

Terman, L. M., & Oden, M. H. (1959). *Genetic studies of genius: The gifted group at midlife* (Vol. 4). Stanford, CA: Stanford University Press.

Terrace, H. S. (1979). *Nim.* New York: Knopf.

Thomas, A., & Chess, S. (1977). *Temperament and development.* New York: Brunner/Mazel.

Thomas, A., Chess, S., & Birch, H. G. (1970). The origin of personality. *Scientific American, 223*(2).

Thomas, V. J., & Rose, F. D. (1991). Ethnic differences in the experience of pain. *Social Science and Medicine, 32,* 1063–1066.

Thompson, S. K. (1975). Gender labels and early sex role development. *Child Development, 46,* 339–347.

Thorndike, E. L. (1898). Animal intelligence: An experimental study of the associative processes in animals. *Psychological Monographs, 2* (Whole No. 8).

Thorndike, E. L. (1911). *Animal intelligence: Experimental studies.* New York: Macmillan.

Thurstone, L. L. (1938). *Primary mental abilities.* Chicago: University of Chicago Press.

Tinbergen, N. (1951). *The study of instinct.* Oxford, England: Clarendon.

Tolman, E. C. (1932). *Purposive behavior in animals and men.* New York: Appleton-Century-Crofts.

Tolman, E. C. (1959). Principles of purposive behavior. In S. Koch (Ed.), *Psychology: A study of science* (Vol. 2, pp. 92–157). New York: McGraw-Hill.

Torrance, E. P. (1974). *The Torrance tests of creative thinking: Technical-norms manual.* Bensenville, IL: Scholastic Testing Services.

Torrance, E. P. (1984). *Torrance tests of creative thinking: Streamlined (revised) manual, Figural A and B.* Bensenville, IL: Scholastic Testing Services.

Torrance, E. P. (1988). The nature of creativity as manifest in its testing. In R. J. Sternberg (Ed.), *The nature of creativity* (pp. 43–75). New York: Cambridge University Press.

Torrey, E. F. (1986). *Witchdoctors and psychiatrists: The common roots of psychotherapy and its future.* New York: Harper & Row.

Totman, R. (1990). *Mind, stress, and health.* London: Souvenir Press.

Totman, R., Kiff, J., Reed, S. E., Craig, J. W. (1980). Predicting experimental colds in volunteers from different measures of recent life stress. *Journal of Psychosomatic Research, 24*(3–4), 155–163.

Townsend, J. T. (1971). A note on the identifiability of parallel and serial processes. *Perception and Psychophysics, 10,* 161–163.

Treisman, A. (1960). Contextual cues in selective listening. *Quarterly Journal of Experimental Psychology, 12,* 242–248.

Triandis, H. C. (1990). Cross-cultural studies of individualism and collectivism. In J. Berman (Ed.), *Nebraska Symposium on Motivation, 1989* (pp. 41–133). Lincoln, NE: University of Nebraska Press.

Triandis, H. C. (1994). Culture and social behavior. In W. J. Lonner & R. S. Malpass (Eds.), *Psychology and culture.* Boston: Allyn & Bacon.

Triandis, H. C. (1997). Cross-cultural perspectives on personality. In R. Hogan, J. Johnson, & S. Broggs (Eds.), *Handbook of personality psychology* (pp. 439–464). San Diego, CA: Academic Press.

Triandis, H. C., McCusker, C., Betancourt, H., Iwao, S., et al. (1993). An eticemic analysis of individualism and collectivism. *Journal of Cross-Cultural Psychology, 24*(3), 366–383.

Triandis, H. C., McCusker, C., & Hui, C. H. (1990). Multimethod probes of individualism and collectivism. *Journal of Personality and Social Psychology, 59,* 1006–1020.

Tripathi, A. N. (1979). Memory for meaning and grammatical structure: An experiment on retention of a story. *Psychological Studies, 24*(2), 136–145.

Triplett, N. (1898). The dynamogenic factors in pacemaking and competition. *American Journal of Psychology, 9,* 507–533.

Trivers, R. L. (1971). The evolution of reciprocal altruism. *Quarterly Review of Biology, 46,* 35–57.

Tsunoda, T. (1979). Differences in the mechanism of emotion in Japanese and Westerner. *Psychotherapy and Psychosomatics, 31*(1–4), 367–372.

Tulving, E. (1972). Episodic and semantic memory. In E. Tulving & W. Donaldson (Eds.), *Organization of memory.* New York: Academic Press.

Tulving, E., & Thomson, D. M. (1973). Encoding specificity and retrieval processes in episodic memory. *Psychological Review, 80,* 352–373.

Turk, D. C., Meichenbaum, D., & Genest, M. (1983). *Pain and behavioral medicine: A cognitive behavioral perspective.* New York: Guilford Press.

Turk, D. C., & Rudy, T. E. (1992). Cognitive factors and persistent pain: A glimpse into Pandora's box. *Cognitive Therapy and Research, 16*(2), 99–122.

Turner, J. C. (1987). *Rediscovering the social group: A self-categorization theory.* Oxford, England: Basil Blackwell.

Turner, R. J., & Wagonfeld, M. O. (1967). Occupational mobility and schizophrenia: An assessment of the social causation and the social selection hypothesis. *American Sociological Review, 32,* 104–113.

Turner, S. M., & Hersen, M. (1985). The interviewing process. In M. Hersen & S. M. Turner (Eds.), *Diagnostic interviewing* (pp. 12–13). New York: Plenum.

Tversky, A. (1972a). Choice by elimination. *Journal of Mathematical Psychology, 9*(4), 341–367.

Tversky, A. (1972b). Elimination by aspects: A theory of choice. *Psychological Review, 79,* 281–299.

Tversky, A., & Kahneman, D. (1973). Availability: A heuristic for judging frequency and probability. *Cognitive Psychology, 5,* 207–232.

Ulrich, R., & Azrin, N. H. (1962). Reflexive fighting in response to aversive stimulation. *Journal of the Experimental Analysis of Behavior, 5,* 511–520.

Umberson, D. (1987). Family status and health behaviors: Social control as a dimension of social integration. *Journal of Health and Social Behavior, 28,* 306–319.

Umberson, D. (1992). Gender, marital status, and the social control of health behavior. *Social Science & Medicine, 34*(8), 907–917.

United States Department of Labor, Bureau of Labor Statistics (1992). *Statistical Abstract of the United States* (112th ed.). Washington, DC: U.S. Department of Commerce.

United States Department of Labor, Bureau of Labor Statistics (1994). *Statistical Abstract of the United States* (114th ed.). Washington, DC: U.S. Department of Commerce.

VanderPlate, C., Aral, S. O., & Magder, L. (1988). The relationship among genital herpes simplex virus, stress, and social support. *Health Psychology, 7,* 159–168.

Vernon, P. A., & Mori, M. (1992). Intelligence, reaction times, and peripheral nerve conduction velocity. *Intelligence, 16*(3, 4), 273–288.

Veroff, J. (1957). Development and validation of a projective measure of power motivation. *Journal of Abnormal and Social Psychology, 54,* 1–8.

Viglione, D. J., & Exner, J. E. (1983). Current research in the comprehensive Rorschach system. In J. N. Butcher & C. D. Spielberger (Eds.), *Advances in personality assessment* (Vol. 2, pp. 13–40). Hillsdale, NJ: Erlbaum.

Vissing, Y. M., Straus, M. A., Gelles, R. J., & Harrop, J. W. (1991). Verbal aggression by parents and psychosocial problems of children. *Child Abuse & Neglect, 15*(3), 223–238.

Vokey, J. R., & Read, J. D. (1985). Subliminal messages: Between the devil and the media. *American Psychologist, 40,* 1231–1239.

Vroom, V. H. (1997). Teaching the managers of tomorrow: Psychologists in business schools. In R. J. Sternberg (Ed.), *Career paths in psychology* (pp. 49–68). Washington, DC: American Psychological Association.

Vygotsky, L. S. (1962). *Thought and language.* Cambridge, MA: MIT Press. (Original work published 1934)

Vygotsky, L. S. (1978). *Mind in society: The development of higher psychological processes.* Cambridge, MA: Harvard University Press.

Wade, C., & Cirese, S. (1991). *Human sexuality* (2nd ed.). New York: Harcourt Brace Jovanovich.

Wagner, D. A. (1978). Memories of Morocco: The influence of age, schooling, and environment on memory. *Cognitive Psychology, 10,* 1–28.

Wagner, D. A., Schacter, D. L., Rotte, M., Koutstaal, W., Maril, A., Dale, A. M., Rosen, B. R., & Buckner, R. L. (1998). Building memories: Remembering and forgetting of verbal experiences as predicted by brain activity. *Science, 281,* 1188–1191.

Walker, L. J. (1989). A longitudinal study of moral reasoning. *Child Development, 60,* 157–166.

Wallace, R. K., & Benson, H. (1972). The physiology of meditation. *Scientific American,* 84–90.

Waller, N. G., Kojetin, B. A., Bouchard, T. J., Lykken, D. T., & Tellegen, A. (1990). Genetic and environmental influences on religious interests, attitudes, and values: A study of twins reared apart and together. *Psychological Science, 1,* 138–142.

Walster, E., Aronson, E., Abrahams, D., & Rottman, L. (1966). The importance of physical attractiveness in dating behavior. *Journal of Personality and Social Psychology, 4,* 508–516.

Walster, E., & Berscheid, E. (1974). A little bit about love: A minor essay on a major topic. In T. L. Huston (Ed.), *Foundations of interpersonal attraction.* New York: Academic Press.

Walster, E., Walster, G. W., & Berscheid, E. (1978). *Equity: Theory and research.* Boston: Allyn & Bacon.

Walters, G. C., & Grusec, J. F. (1977). *Punishment.* San Francisco: Freeman.

Warrington, E. (1982). The double dissociation of short- and long-term memory deficits. In L. S. Cermak (Ed.), *Human memory and amnesia.* Hillsdale, NJ: Erlbaum.

Warrington, E., & Shallice, T. (1972). Neuropsychological evidence of visual storage in short-term memory tasks. *Quarterly Journal of Experimental Psychology, 24*(1), 30–40.

Wason, P. C., & Johnson-Laird, P. N. (1972). *Psychology of reasoning: Structure and content.* London: B. T. Batsford.

Watson, D. (1989). Strangers' ratings of the five robust personality factors: Evidence of a surprising convergence with self-report. *Journal of Personality & Social Psychology, 57*(1), 120–128.

Wechsler, D. (1974). *The measurement and appraisal of adult intelligence*. Baltimore: Williams & Wilkins.

Weisberg, R. W. (1995). Prolegomena to theories of insight in problem solving: A taxonomy of problems. In R. J. Sternberg & J. E. Davidson (Eds.), *The nature of insight* (pp. 157–196). Cambridge, MA: MIT Press.

Weisenberg, M. (1977). Pain and pain control. *Psychological Bulletin, 84*, 1008–1044.

Weiss, R. S. (1975). *Marital separation*. New York: Basic Books.

Weissman, M. M., & Myers, J. K. (1978). Affective disorders in a United States urban community: The use of research diagnostic criteria in an epidemiologic survey. *Archives of General Psychiatry, 35*, 1304–1311.

Weisz, J. R., Weiss, B., Hun, S. S., Granger, D. A., & Morton, T. (1995). Effects of psychotherapy with children and adolescents revisited: A meta-analysis of treatment outcome studies. *Psychological Bulletin, 117*, 450–468.

Wells, G. L. (1993). What do we know about eyewitness identification? *American Psychologist, 48*(5), 553–571.

Werner, E. E. (1972). Infants around the world. *Journal of Cross-Cultural Psychology, 3*(2), 111–134.

Wertheimer, M. (1959). *Productive thinking* (rev. ed.). New York: Harper & Row. (Original work published 1945)

Wesman, A. E., & Ricks, D. F. (1966). *Mood and personality*. New York: Holt, Rinehart and Winston.

Wever, R. A. (1979). *The circadian system of man*. Heidelberg, West Germany: Springer-Verlag.

White, R. W. (1959). Motivation reconsidered: The concept of competence. *Psychological Review, 66*, 297–33.

Whitehouse, W. G., Dinges, D. F., Orne, E. C., & Orne, M. T. (1988). Hypnotic hypermnesia: Enhanced memory accessibility or report bias? *Journal of Abnormal Psychology, 97*(3), 289–295.

Whitley, B. E., Jr., & Frieze, I. H. (1985). Children's causal attributions for success and failure in achievement settings: A meta-analysis. *Journal of Educational Psychology, 77*, 608–616.

Wickelgren, I. (1998). A new route to treating schizophrenia? *Science, 281*, 1264–1265.

Wilber, K. H., & Specht, C. V. (1994). Prevalence and predictors of burnout among adult day care providers. *Journal of Applied Gerontology, 13*(3), 282–298.

Williams, G. C. (1966). *Adaptation and natural selection*. Princeton, NJ: Princeton University Press.

Williams, R. B. (1986). An untrusting heart. In M. G. Walraven & H. E. Fitzgerald (Eds.), *Annuals editions: Human development 86/87*. Guilford, CT: Dushkin.

Williams, R. B., Jr., & Barefoot, J. C. (1988). Coronary-prone behavior: The emerging role of the hostility complex. In B. K. Houston & C. R. Snyder (Eds.), *Type A behavior pattern: Current trends and future directions* (pp. 189–211). New York: Wiley.

Winter, D. G. (1973). *The power motive*. New York: Free Press.

Wiskoff, M. F. (1997). Defense of the nation: Military psychologists. In R. J. Sternberg (Ed.), *Career paths in psychology* (pp. 245–268). Washington, DC: American Psychological Association.

Wolpe, J. (1958). *Psychotherapy by reciprocal inhibition*. Stanford, CA: Stanford University Press.

Wong, D. F., Wagner, H. N., Tune, L. E., Dannals, R. F., Pearlson, G. D., Links, J. M., Tamminga, C. A., Broussolle, E. P., Ravert, H. T., Wilson, A. A., Toury, J. K. T., Malat, J., Williams, J. A., O'Tuma, L. A., Snyder, S. H., Kuhar, M. J., & Gjedde, A. (1986). Positron emission tomography reveals elevated Dz dopamine receptors in drug-naive schizophrenics. *Science, 234*, 1558–1563.

Woodruff, R. A., Goodwin, D. W., & Guze, S. B. (1974). *Psychiatric diagnosis*. New York: Oxford University Press.

Woodworth, R. S. (1918). *Dynamic psychology*. New York: Columbia University Press.

Woolfolk, R. L., Carr-Kaffashan, K., McNulty, T. F., & Lehrer, P. M. (1976). Meditation training as a treatment for insomnia. *Behavior Therapy, 7*, 359–365.

Woon, T., Masuda, M., Wagner, N. N., & Holmes, T. H. (1971). The Social Readjustment Rating Scale: A cross-cultural study of Malaysians and Americans. *Journal of Cross-Cultural Psychology, 2*, 373–386.

Wright, L., Abbanato, K. R., Lancaster, C., Bourke, M. L., et al. (1994). Gender-related subcomponent differences in high Type A subjects. *Journal of Clinical Psychology, 50*(5), 677–680.

Wright, R. (1994). *The moral animal*. New York: Vintage.

Wright, R. H. (1977). Odor and molecular vibration: Neural coding of olfactory information. *Journal of Theoretical Biology, 64*, 473–502.

Wright, R. H. (1982). *The sense of smell*. Boca Raton, FL: CRC Press.

Yahiro, K., Inoue, M., & Nozawa, Y. (1993). An examination on the Social Readjustment Rating Scale (Holmes et al.) by Japanese subjects. *Japanese Journal of Health Psychology, 6*(1), 18–32.

Yang, K. (1986). Chinese personality and its change. In M. H. Bond (Ed.), *The psychology of the Chinese people*. Hong Kong: Oxford University Press.

Yerkes, R. M., & Dodson, J. B. (1908). The relation of strength of stimulus to rapidity of habit formation. *Journal of Comparative Neurology and Psychology, 18*, 459–482.

Young, J., & Weishaar, M. E. (1997). Psychologists in private practice. In R. J. Sternberg (Ed.), *Career paths in psychology* (pp. 71–91). Washington, DC: American Psychological Association.

Yuille, J. C. (1993). We must study forensic eyewitnesses to know about them. *American Psychologist, 48*(5), 572–573.

Yussen, S. R. (1977). Characteristics of moral dilemmas written by adolescents. *Developmental Psychology, 13*, 162–163.

Yussen, S. R. (1984). A triarchic reaction to a triarchic theory of intelligence. *The Behavioral and Brain Sciences, 7*(12), 303.

Zaidel, E. (1983). A response to Gazzaniga: Language in the right hemisphere, convergent perspectives. *American Psychologist, 38*(5), 542–546.

Zajonc, R. B. (1965). Social facilitation. *Science, 149*, 269–274.

Zajonc, R. B. (1968). Attitudinal effects of mere exposure. *Journal of Personality and Social Psychology Monograph Supplement, 9*(2), 1–27.

Zajonc, R. B. (1980). Compliance. In P. B. Paulus (Ed.), *Psychology of group influence* (pp. 35–60). Hillsdale, NJ: Erlbaum.

Zajonc, R. B. (1984). On the primacy affect. *American Psychologist, 39*, 117–129.

Zajonc, R. B., & Markus, G. B. (1979). Birth order and intellectual development. *Psychological Review, 82*, 74–88.

Zajonc, R. B., & Mullally, P. R. (1997). Birth order: Reconciling conflicting effects. *American Psychologist, 52*, 685–699.

Zajonc, R. B., Pietromonaco, P., & Bargh, J. (1982). Independence and interaction of affect and cognition. In M. S. Clark & S. T. Fiske (Eds.), *Affect and cognition* (pp. 211–227). Hillsdale, NJ: LEA.

Zamansky, H. S., & Bartis, S. P. (1985). The dissociation of an experience: The hidden observer observed. *Journal of Abnormal Psychology, 94*, 243–248.

Zanna, M. P., & Darley, J. M. (Eds.). (1987). *The compleat academic: A practical guide for the beginning social scientist*. New York: McGraw-Hill.

Zaragoza, M. S., McCloskey, M., & Jamis, M. (1987). Misleading postevent information and recall of the original event: Further evidence against the memory impairment hypothesis. *Journal of Experimental Psychology: Learning, Memory, and Cognition, 13*(1), 36–44.

Zeidner, M. (1990). Perceptions of ethnic group modal intelligence scores: Reflections of cultural stereotypes or intelligence test scores? *Journal of Cross-Cultural Psychology, 21*, 214–231.

Zigler, E., & Berman, W. (1983). Discerning the future of early childhood intervention. *American Psychologist, 38,* 894–906.

Zimbardo, P. G. (1970). The human choice: Individuation, reason, and order versus deindividuation, impulse, and chaos. In W. J. Arnold & D. Levine (Eds.), *Nebraska symposium on motivation, 1969.* Lincoln, NE: University of Nebraska Press.

Zimbardo, P. G. (1972, April). Psychology of imprisonment. *Transition/Society,* 4–8.

Zimmerman, B. J., & Bandura, A. (1994). Impact on self-regulatory influences on writing course attainment. *American Educational Research Journal, 31*(4), 845–862.

Zimmerman, B. J., Bandura, A., & Martinez-Pons, M. (1992). Self-motivation for academic attainment: The role of self-efficacy beliefs and personal goal setting. *American Educational Research Journal, 29*(3), 663–676.

Zola-Morgan, S. M., & Squire, L. R. (1990). The primate hippocampal formation: Evidence for a time-limited role in memory storage. *Science, 250,* 228–290.

Zuckerman, M., Klorman, R., Larrance, D. T., & Speigel, N. H. (1981). Facial, autonomic, and subjective components of emotion: The facial feedback hypothesis versus the externalizer-internalizer distinction. *Journal of Personality and Social Psychology, 41,* 929–944.

ILLUSTRATION CREDITS

Chapter 3
Figure 3.1, "Snellen Vision Chart." Copyright © The Optical Society of America; Figure 3.15, "Gestalt Principles of Perception" from Roger Shepard, *Mind Sights*, 1990. Copyright © 1990 by W. H. Freeman & Co. All rights reserved; Figure 3.19, "Shape Constancy." Based on J. J. Gibson, *The Perception of the Visual World*, 1950.

Chapter 6
Finding Your Way 6.1, "War of the Ghost" from Bartlett, *Remembering: A Study in Experimental and Social Psychology*, 1932. Published by Cambridge University Press. All rights reserved by the publisher; Figure 6.6, "What's Wrong With This Picture?" Drawings of U.S. cent from R. S. Nickerson and M. J. Adams, "Long-Term Memory for a Common Object" in *Cognitive Psychology*, Vol. 11, pp. 287–307.

Chapter 8
Table 8.1, "Gardner's Eight Intelligences" from Howard Gardner, "Seven Intelligences" in *Multiple Intelligences*, 1993. Published by Basic Books, Inc. All rights reserved.

Chapter 9
Figure 9.1, "Familiar Versus Unfamiliar" from Mandler, "A New Perspective in Cognitive Development in Infancy" in *American Scientist*, Vol. 78, pp. 236–243; Table 9.2, "Kohlberg's Theory of the Development of Moral Reasoning." Adapted from L. Kohlberg, *The Psychology of Moral Development*. Copyright © 1983 by Harper & Row.

Chapter 10
Figure 10.6, "Line Length and the Norm" from Solomon Asch, "Line Length and Group Influence," 1956. All rights reserved by the author; Figure 10.7, "Social Status and Conformity" from R. A. Lippe, *Introduction to Social Psychology*, p. 536. Wadsworth Publishing; Figure 10.9, "Milgram's Results on Voltage Levels" based on Stanley Milgram, *Obedience to Authority*, 1974. Published by HarperCollins. All rights reserved by the publisher; Figure 10.11, "What Do You

See in This Picture?" Adapted from Brehm and Kassin, *Social Psychology*, 1990, p. 180. Published by Houghton Mifflin Co. All rights reserved by the publisher.

Chapter 11
Figure 11.1, "Acquired Motivation," based on Solomon and Corbit, "An Opponent-Process Theory of Motivation: I. Temporal Dynamics of Affect" in *Psychological Review*, Vol. 81, 1974, pp. 119–145. Copyright © 1974 by the Psychological Review. No portion of this text may be reproduced without permission of the American Psychological Association; Table 11.2, "Some Differences Between Motivation and Emotion." Adapted from J. G. Carlson and E. Hatfield, *Psychology of Emotion*, 1992, p. 30. Copyright © 1992 by Harcourt Brace; Figure 11.6, "Plutchik's Emotion Wheel." Based on Plutchik, "A Language for the Emotions" in *Psychology Today* magazine. Copyright © 1980 by Sussex Publishers, Inc. All rights reserved.

Chapter 14
Figure 14.1c, "Effectiveness of Various Therapies," from *Journal of Personality and Social Psychology*, Vol. 13, pp. 173–199. Copyright © 1969 by the American Psychological Association. No portion of this text may be reprinted without permission of the American Psychological Association; Figure 14.3, "Effectiveness of Antipsychotic Drugs" from "Effectiveness of Antipsychotic Drugs Versus Placebo" from *Schizophrenia: Pharmacotherapy and Psychotherapy*, 1972.

Chapter 15
Figure 15.2, "Stressful Life Events" from Kagan and Segal, 1995, 8th Edition, p. 440. Copyright © 1995 by Harcourt Brace & Company, Inc.; Figure 15.4, "General Adaptation Syndrome (GAS)." From H. Selye, *Stress Without Distress*, 1974, p. 39. Copyright © 1974 HarperCollins Publishers, Inc. All rights reserved; Figure 15.8, "Trends in Rates of Death From HIV Infection Among Men 24–44 Years Old, by Sex and Race/Ethnicity, USA, 1993–1996. Centers for Disease Control Prevention.

Chapter 1
p. 6, top left, © Larry Mulvehill/Rainbow; p. 6, top right, © Elena Rooraid/PhotoEdit; p. 6, bottom left, © Bob Daemmrich/Stock Boston; p. 6, bottom right, © H. Gans/The Image Works; p. 7, top left, © Kathleen Olson; p. 7, top right, © Matthew McVay/Tony Stone Images; p. 7, bottom left, © Bob Strong/The Image Works; p. 7, bottom right, © Bill Bachmann/The Image Works; p. 8, David Hiser/Tony Stone Images; p. 10, © Robert E. Daemmrich/Tony Stone Images; p. 11, © Jonathan Selig/Photo 20-20; p. 16, © Jeff Greenberg/PhotoEdit; p. 23, © 1987 Lawrence Migdale; p. 24, © Tom McCarthy/PhotoEdit; p. 30, © Nubar Alexanian/Stock Boston; p. 33, Vatican Museum and Galleries/Scala/SuperStock; p. 34, Culver Pictures; p. 37, Courtesy of Wellesley College Archives, photo by Partridge; p. 38, The Granger Collection, New York; p. 39, left, Carl Rogers Memorial Library; p. 39, right, University of Akron, Psychology Archives.

Chapter 2
p. 51, left, © Michael Tweedie/Photo Researchers; p. 51, right, © Michael W. F. Tweedie/Bruce Coleman, Inc.; p. 54, CNRI/SPL/Photo Researchers; p. 62, © D. W. Fawcett/Komuro/Science Source/Photo Researchers; p. 76, © H. Christoph/Black Star; p. 77, top, CNRI/SPL/Photo Researchers; p. 77, middle top, Ohio Nuclear Corporation/SPL/Photo Researchers; p. 77, middle bottom, CNRI/SPL/Photo Researchers; p. 77, bottom, © Spencer Grant/Stock Boston; p. 79, THE FAR SIDE, © 1986, FARWORKS, INC. Distributed by Universal Press Syndicate. Reprinted with permission. All rights reserved; p. 80, © Biophoto Associates/Science Source/Photo Researchers; p. 81, © John Coletti/Stock Boston.

Chapter 3
p. 101, © Fritz Goro, Life Magazine © Time Warner; p. 112, The Granger Collection; p. 113, National Gallery, London/E. T. Archive, London/SuperStock; p. 118, left, © Norm Snyder 1995; p. 118, right, © Norm Snyder 1985.

Chapter 4
p. 134, © Phillipe Plailly/SPL/Photo Researchers; p. 137, left, Michel Siffre, © National Geographic Society; p. 137, right, Michel Siffre, © National Geographic Society Image Collection; p. 137, © 1994 Joe Dator/The Cartoon Bank, Inc.; p. 142, The Granger Collection, New York; p. 146, © Esbin-Anderson/The Image Works; p. 148, © Mark Reinstein/Liaison Agency.

Chapter 5
p. 162, left, © Nina Leen/Life Magazine; p. 162, right, William Lishman and Associates; p. 164, Bettmann Archive;

p. 169, © Jonathon Nourok/PhotoEdit; p. 170, left, © Stuart R. Ellins, Ph.D.; p. 170, right, © Stuart R. Ellins, Ph.D.; p. 175, © 1994 Joe Dator/The Cartoon Bank, Inc.; p. 185, top, Dr. Albert Bandura; p. 185, bottom left, Dr. Albert Bandura; p. 185, bottom right, Dr. Albert Bandura.

Chapter 6
p. 194, Reproduced with the permission of the SOUTH WALES ECHO, U.K.; p. 195, © 1988 Joseph Nettis/Stock Boston; p. 200, © Michael Newman/PhotoEdit; p. 204, © Bob Daemmrich/Stock Boston; p. 205, © Bob Daemmrich/The Image Works; p. 206, Seth Poppel Yearbook Archives; p. 209, left, © Jerry Berndt/Stock Boston; p. 209, right, © Peter Southwick/Stock Boston; p. 213, © Lawrence Migdale; p. 217, © Dr. Carolyn Rovee-Collier; p. 218, left, © Charles Feil/Stock Boston; p. 218, right, © Bonnie Kamin; p. 218, bottom, Drawing by W. Miller, © 1986 The New Yorker Magazine, Inc.; p. 220, © Michael Newman/PhotoEdit; p. 223, left, © Bob Daemmrich/The Image Works; p. 223, right, © Don Couch.

Chapter 7
p. 230, © Stephen Ferry, Liaison Agency; p. 232, © Bill Stanton/Rainbow; p. 234, left, © SuperStock; p. 234, middle, © SuperStock; p. 234, right, © SuperStock; p. 239, © Russell Schleipman/Offshoot; p. 242, © Jeff Greenberg/The Image Works; p. 245, © Dorothy Littell Greco/Stock Boston; p. 247, left, © David Young-Wolff/PhotoEdit; p. 247, right, © Tony Savino/The Image Works; p. 249, © Bill Aron/PhotoEdit; p. 252, © Glenn Bernhardt; p. 257, © Sylvain Grandadam/Tony Stone Images; p. 259, © Tony Freeman/PhotoEdit.

Chapter 8
p. 269, top left, UPI/Corbis; p. 269, top right, The Bettmann Archive; p. 269, bottom left, UPI/Corbis–Bettmann; p. 269, bottom right, © Ulf Anaerson/Gamma Liaison; p. 279, Dr. Michael Cole; p. 280, © 1996 Sidney Harris; p. 282, The Granger Collection; p. 283, © George Holton/Photo Researchers; p. 285, © Topham/The Image Works; p. 287, © Rob Crandall/Stock Boston; p. 290, top, T. K. Wanstal/The Image Works; p. 294, left, © Dan McCoy/Rainbow; p. 294, middle, AP/Wide World Photos; p. 294, right, © William Greenblatt/Liaison Agency; p. 290, bottom, Drawing by W. Miller; © 1992 The New Yorker Magazine, Inc.

Chapter 9
p. 305, top left, © Network Pro/The Image Works; p. 305, top right, © Steven Rubin/The Image Works; p. 305, bottom left, © Jim Corwin/Stock Boston; p. 305, bottom right, © Tony Freeman/PhotoEdit; p. 306, © Robert Daemmrich/Tony Stone Images; p. 307, left, (left) © Bill Anderson/

Monkmeyer; p. 307, right, © G. L. Vygodskaya; p. 309, top left, © Lennart Nilsson, A CHILD IS BORN, Dell Publishing Company; p. 309, top right, © Lennart Nilsson, A CHILD IS BORN, Dell Publishing Company; p. 309, bottom left, © Lennart Nilsson, A CHILD IS BORN, Dell Publishing Company; p. 309, bottom right, © Bob Daemmrich/The Image Works; p. 311, © Richard Pasley/Stock Boston; p. 312, left, © Myrleen Ferguson Cate/PhotoEdit; p. 312, right, © Myrleen Ferguson Cate/PhotoEdit; p. 313, left, © Michael Newman/PhotoEdit; p. 313, right, © Tom McCarthy/PhotoEdit; p. 314, left, © Goodman/Monkmeyer; p. 314, right, © Goodman/Monkmeyer; p. 315, © Laura Dwight/PhotoEdit; p. 319, © 1995 by Bill Keane, Inc. Distributed by King Features Syndicate, Inc. All rights reserved. Reprinted with special permission of King Features Syndicate; p. 322, top left, © Tony Freeman/PhotoEdit; p. 322, top right, © Tony Freeman/PhotoEdit; p. 322, bottom left, © Tony Freeman/PhotoEdit; p. 324, John F. Kennedy Library; p. 331, © Jerry Bauer.

Chapter 10

p. 341, top left, © Herb Snitzer/Stock Boston; p. 341, top right, © Hazel Hankin/Stock Boston; p. 341, bottom left, © Dan McCoy/Rainbow; p. 341, bottom right, © Cary Wolinsky/Stock Boston; p. 346, © Tom McCarthy/Rainbow; p. 352, left, © Bill Bachmann/The Image Works; p. 352, right, © Michael Newman/PhotoEdit; p. 355, left, © J. Berndt/Stock Boston; p. 355, right, © J. Berndt/Stock Boston; p. 356, © Spencer Grant/PhotoEdit; p. 359, top left, © Eastcott/The Image Works; p. 359, top right, © Bob Daemmrich/Stock Boston; p. 359, bottom, © John Chiasson/Gamma Liaison; p. 360, top, Dr. Solomon Asch; p. 360, bottom, © Anthony Gutierrez/Liaison Agency; p. 363, Copyright © 1965 by Stanley Milgram, from the film OBEDIENCE, distributed by the Pennsylvania State University, Audio Visuals Service; p. 366, © Charlie Westerman/Gamma Liaison; p. 368, Corbis/Nik Wheeler; p. 372, top, © Frank Siteman/Stock Boston; p. 372, bottom, © Cathlyn Melloan/Tony Stone Images; p. 373, P.G. Zimbardo, Inc.; p. 374, P.G. Zimbardo, Inc.

Chapter 11

p. 383, CATHY © Cathy Guisewite. Reprinted with permission of UNIVERSAL PRESS SYNDICATE. All rights reserved; p. 386, Scala/Art Resource, NY; p. 387, left, © William Thompson/The Picture Cube; p. 387, right, © William Thompson/The Picture Cube; p. 394, © Myrleen Ferguson/PhotoEdit; p. 397, © 1990 Lawrence Migdale; p. 399, © Nubar Alexanian/Stock Boston; p. 401, top left, Copyright Paul Ekman, 1972; p. 401, top right, Copyright Paul Ekman, 1972; p. 401, bottom left, Copyright Paul Ekman, 1972; p. 401, bottom right, Copyright Paul Ekman, 1972; p. 406, top left, © Nita Winter/The Image Works;

p. 406, top middle, © Ed Lettau/SuperStock; p. 406, top right, © SuperStock; p. 406, bottom left, © Mark Greenlar/The Image Works; p. 406, bottom right, © Lawrence Migdale/Stock Boston; p. 415, © M. Siluk/The Image Works.

Chapter 12

p. 427, The Bettmann Archive; p. 430, Christie's Image/SuperStock; p. 432, left, © Ron Davis/Shooting Star; p. 432, middle, Joan Jedell/Shooting Star; p. 432, right, UPI/Bettmann Newsphotos; p. 433, bottom, © Christina Dameyer/Photo 20-20; p. 433, top, The Bettmann Archive; p. 434, UPI/Bettmann; p. 435, left, The Bettmann Archive; p. 435, right, © Michele Burgess/Stock Boston; p. 436, left, Corbis/Roger Ressmeyer; p. 436, right, Archives of the History of American Psychology—The University of Akron; p. 439, left, Courtesy of Dr. Julian B. Rotter; p. 439, right, © Dan McCoy/Rainbow; p. 441, Dr. Albert Bandura.

Chapter 13

p. 464, © PhotoEdit; p. 465, The Granger Collection, New York; p. 470, National Gallery, Oslo, Norway/Bridgeman Art Library/London/SuperStock; p. 481, © Grunnitus/Monkmeyer; p. 483, © NIH/Science Source/Photo Researchers; p. 486, © Ellen Senisi/The Image Works; p. 490, © Michael Newman/PhotoEdit.

Chapter 14

p. 501, © Stock Montage; p. 502 all, © Dan McCoy/Rainbow; p. 503, AP/Wide World Photos; p. 505, © Jerry Howard/Stock Boston; p. 509, left, © Richard Howard/Offshoot Stock; p. 509, right, © Lionel Delevingne/Stock Boston; p. 511, © Will and Deni McIntyre/Photo Researchers; p. 516, © Martin Rogers/Stock Boston; p. 517, © Michael Newman/PhotoEdit; p. 518, © David Young-Wolff/PhotoEdit; p. 519, top, © Bob Daemmrich/Stock Boston; p. 519, bottom, © Bob Daemmrich/Stock Boston; p. 526, © Mary Kate Denny/PhotoEdit.

Chapter 15

p. 539, © Esbin-Anderson/The Image Works; p. 542, Reuters/Bettmann; p. 544, © David Young-Wolff/PhotoEdit; p. 550, top left, © Dan and Will McCoy/Rainbow; p. 550, top right, © Andre Abecassis/Photo 20-20; p. 550, bottom left, © Bob Daemmrich/Stock Boston; p. 550, top right, © Richard Pasley/Stock Boston; p. 552, © Tony Freeman/PhotoEdit; p. 554, © Glen Korengold/Stock Boston; p. 557, left, © Gary A. Conner/PhotoEdit; p. 557, right, © John Coletti/Stock Boston; p. 561, © Michael Dwyer/Stock Boston; p. 563, left, © Michael English/Medical Images, Inc.; p. 563, right, © William McCoy/Rainbow; p. 567, © Ken Glaser/Southern Stock/PNI.

NAME INDEX